ADVANCEMENT IN ENGINEERING AND SCIENCE

I0885536

This book captures the proceedings of the International Conference on Advancement in Engineering and Science: Recent Trends and Applications, held at the Karmaveer Bhaurao Patil College of Engineering, Satara, Maharashtra, India. It highlights the synergy between theoretical research and practical applications to address pressing global and societal needs.

The book looks into a diverse range of technical domains, providing in-depth coverage of artificial intelligence, automation, energy systems, materials science, and environmental engineering. Key findings emphasize the role of emerging technologies in fostering sustainable development and bridging the gap between academic theory and industrial practice. Through a collection of peer-reviewed papers, the volume explores groundbreaking advancements in smart manufacturing, renewable energy solutions, and computational modeling. It illustrates how cross-disciplinary collaboration can lead to pioneering solutions for complex infrastructure and technological challenges, offering readers a roadmap of current trends and future directions in the global scientific landscape.

This volume is intended for a broad audience of researchers, academicians, and industry professionals seeking to update their knowledge of modern engineering trends. It is equally valuable for postgraduate students and policymakers interested in the practical translation of scientific research into sustainable, real-world innovations.

Advancement in Engineering and Science

Recent Trends and Applications

Edited by

Dinesh Goyal
Poornima Institute of Engineering & Technology, India

Shabina Jameer Modi
Karmaveer Bhaurao Patil College of Engineering, India

Anil Kumar
Poornima Institute of Engineering & Technology, India

Vinit Khetani
Cybrixtech Solutions, India

PROCEEDINGS OF THE INTERNATIONAL CONFERENCE ON ADVANCEMENT IN ENGINEERING AND SCIENCE: RECENT TRENDS AND APPLICATIONS (ICAESRTA 2025), 13TH–14TH JUNE 2025, SATARA, MAHARASHTRA, INDIA

CRC Press
Taylor & Francis Group
Boca Raton London New York Leiden

CRC Press is an imprint of the
Taylor & Francis Group, an **informa** business

First edition published 2026
by CRC Press
4 Park Square, Milton Park, Abingdon, Oxon, OX14 4RN

and by CRC Press
2385 NW Executive Center Drive, Suite 320, Boca Raton FL 33431

CRC Press is an imprint of informa UK Limited

British Library Cataloguing-in-Publication Data
A catalogue record for this book is available from the British Library

ISBN: 978-1-041-31101-0 (hbk)
ISBN: 978-1-041-35605-9 (pbk)
ISBN: 978-1-003-79851-4 (ebk)

DOI: 10.1201/9781003798514

Typeset in Times New Roman
by MPS Limited, Chennai, India

Contents

Advancement in Engineering and Science – Goyal et al. (Eds)
© 2026 The Editor(s), ISBN: 978-1-041-31101-0

Preface

It is with great pride and a sense of academic purpose that we present the Proceedings of the International Conference on Advancement in Engineering & Science; Recent Trends & Applications (ICAESRTA 2025), organized by the Karmaveer Bhaurao Patil College of Engineering, Satara, under the prestigious aegis of Rayat Shikshan Sanstha. This volume represents a significant milestone in our commitment to fostering a global dialogue on the transformative power of interdisciplinary research and its real-world applications.

The primary objective of ICAESRTA 2025 is to provide a dynamic and inclusive platform for researchers, academicians, and industry experts to share pioneering ideas and breakthrough developments. As the boundaries between traditional engineering disciplines and pure sciences continue to blur, this conference serves as a vital nexus for exploring trends in Artificial Intelligence, Sustainable Infrastructure, Renewable Energy, and Advanced Materials Science. The proceedings encapsulate a diverse array of technical sessions and keynote insights designed to bridge the gap between theoretical exploration and industrial implementation.

A rigorous peer-review process was conducted to ensure that the contributions included in this volume meet the highest standards of academic excellence and technical relevance. These papers not only address current technological hurdles but also propose visionary solutions for the societal and environmental challenges of the 21st century. We are confident that this collection will serve as an enduring reference for scholars, practitioners, and students, acting as a catalyst for future innovation and collaborative research.

We extend our deepest gratitude to the visionary leadership of Rayat Shikshan Sanstha, the dedicated members of the organizing committee, our distinguished reviewers, and the session chairs for their tireless efforts. Most importantly, we thank the authors whose intellectual contributions form the core of this publication. Their dedication to excellence is what makes ICAESRTA 2025 a beacon for scientific advancement.

We invite you to explore these pages and join us in envisioning a future powered by the synergy of science and engineering.

Advancement in Engineering and Science – Goyal et al. (Eds)
© 2026 The Editor(s), ISBN: 978-1-041-31101-0

Acknowledgements

The Organizing Committee of the International Conference on Advancement in Engineering & Science; Recent Trends & Applications (ICAESRTA 2025) extends its deepest gratitude to the visionaries, leaders, and contributors whose unwavering support and commitment have made this inaugural event a resounding success.

We sincerely thank our esteemed Chief Patrons, whose leadership under the Rayat Shikshan Sanstha, Satara, has provided the foundation for this academic endeavor. We are particularly grateful to the management of Karmaveer Bhaurao Patil College of Engineering for their steadfast guidance and for providing a world-class environment for this intellectual exchange.

Our heartfelt thanks go to our General Chairs and Conference Chairs for their strategic direction, as well as the Organizing Chairs and departmental heads for their meticulous planning and execution. We also acknowledge the tremendous support of the technical committee, finance committee, and publicity chairs, whose collective efforts ensured the seamless completion of the event.

We express our profound appreciation to the distinguished keynote speakers and session chairs for sharing their pioneering insights and fostering high-level technical discourse. We are equally grateful to the authors and participants from across the globe; your scholarly contributions and innovative research are the heart of these proceedings.

Special recognition is due to our Reviewer Panel for their rigorous and constructive evaluation of submissions, ensuring the highest academic standards. We also acknowledge our industrial partners and sponsors for their invaluable support in bridging the gap between academia and practice. Finally, we commend the tireless dedication of the organizing team and student volunteers, whose energy and hard work transformed ICAESRTA 2025 into a landmark professional experience.

Advancement in Engineering and Science – Goyal et al. (Eds)
© 2026 The Editor(s), ISBN: 978-1-041-31101-0

Glossary

Artificial Intelligence (AI)	The simulation of human intelligence processes by machines, enabling them to learn, reason, and make decisions.
Autonomous Systems	Machines or robots capable of performing tasks without continuous human guidance.
Embedded Systems	Dedicated computer systems designed for specific control functions within larger systems, often with real-time computing constraints.
Field-Programmable Gate Array (FPGA)	A semiconductor device that can be configured after manufacturing to implement custom hardware functions.
Internet of Things (IoT)	A network of interconnected devices embedded with sensors and software to collect, exchange, and act on data.
Machine Learning (ML)	A subset of AI that enables systems to learn and improve from experience without being explicitly programmed.
Microcontroller Unit (MCU)	A compact integrated circuit designed to govern specific operations in embedded systems.
Semiconductor	A material with conductivity between conductors and insulators, essential for manufacturing electronic components.
Sensor Fusion	The integration of data from multiple sensors to improve accuracy and reliability of system outputs.
System-on-Chip (SoC)	An integrated circuit that consolidates all components of a computer or other electronic system onto a single chip.
VLSI (Very Large-Scale Integration)	The process of creating integrated circuits by combining millions of transistors on a single chip.

About the Editors

Dinesh Goyal has a B.E., M.Tech and PhD in Computer Science and Engineering, is working as Professor in Computer Science and Engineering and Principal at Poornima Institute of Engineering & Technology. Under his leadership the Institute has become the first institution across India to offer Engineering Education in Regional Language under "New Education Policy". Acquiring an experience of more than 24 years in teaching and perceive keen interest in research area relating Cloud Security, Image Processing, Data Analytic and Information Security he has been pivotal in many turnkey projects and research and development activities. With a mission to append more and better skill set, he has organized many conferences, workshops, seminars and FDPs as Convener and Co-Convener within during this short career span. With his great exposure with outcome-based education in higher education, he has been instrumental in obtaining accreditations for his institutions, from various agencies like NAAC and NBA. He is also an empanel Assessor in NAAC since 2021 and has chaired NAAC Peer Team too. He has also received Grants-in-Aid for research, development, conferences and workshops, amounting to more than Rs. 81 Lakh, from agencies like AICTE, TEQIP, and ISTE, that include Combined Research Project, MODROBS, AICTE-IDEA Lab (the only institution in Rajasthan to part of such a great mission), GoC and many more. He has been awarded by "Elets Excellence Award 2017" at Higher Education & Human Resource Conclave by Higher Education Department of Government of Rajasthan. He has also completed his CMI level 5 Award in "Management and Leadership", under AICTE-UKIERI Technical Leadership Development Program in association with Dudley University. Under his leadership, Institutions has also excelled in Industry Academia Interface, has established centers with major tech giants like Microsoft, Google and Amazon. He has 28 full patents published and one copyright under his name. He has successfully published 13 edited books. He has published three SCI and 100 Scopus and 47 Web of Science indexed papers and is editors of two SCI and five Scopus indexed journals, special issues. He has successfully guided 16 PhD scholars and 31 PG scholars. He has also attended more than 25 international conferences and has been invited speaker for more than 15 conferences and seminars. He is life member of IEEE, ISC, CSI, IETE and ISTE and fellow member of ACM.

Shabina Jameer Modi is a distinguished academician, researcher, and academic leader with over 25 years of experience in Engineering education. She serves as Associate Professor in the Department of Computer Science & Engineering at Karmaveer Bhaurao Patil College of Engineering, Satara under Rayat Shikshan Sanstha. Her expertise encompasses Computer Networks, Database Engineering, Cloud Computing, Artificial Intelligence in Education, and Research Methodology, with a strong emphasis on integrating emerging technologies into teaching–learning and research ecosystems. Dr. Modi has published more than 40 research papers in reputed national and international journals and conferences and holds four granted patents. She has successfully secured competitive research grants from AICTE and DBATU and has led the organization of several national and international conferences, Faculty Development Programs, and innovation-driven research initiatives. She has handled several key administrative and academic leadership roles at KBPCOES, including Head of the Department of Computer Science and Engineering, Dean – Students Development, Dean – Administration, and currently serves as President of the Institution's Innovation Council (IIC) under the MIC-AICTE framework, fostering innovation, entrepreneurship, and institutional excellence. She is also a Member of the Board of Governance, contributing to institutional policy and strategic academic planning. A Gold Medalist in NPTEL (Cloud Computing) and an accomplished mentor, she has guided over 72 undergraduate projects and mentored winning teams in the Smart India Hackathon. Dr. Modi continues to advance scholarly excellence, research leadership, and global academic collaboration.

Anil Kumar is a distinguished academician and visionary leader with 19 years of experience in Computer Science and Engineering. As the Professor and Head of the Department at Poornima Institute of Engineering & Technology, Jaipur, he specializes in Cybersecurity, Penetration Testing, Information Security, Cryptography, AR, and VR. He has designed a cutting-edge Cyber Security Lab Curriculum, authored 45 research papers, holds two international patents and six Indian patents, and serves as an editor for leading journals. He has also chaired multiple international conferences, mentored numerous B.Tech and Ph.D. students, and continues to drive innovation and academic excellence in his field.

Vinit Khetani is an academic and technology professional with over 15 years of experience in computer science education, software engineering, and research-driven innovation. He holds a master's degree in computer science and has extensive expertise in Java and Python programming, with a focused interest in Artificial Intelligence and Machine Learning. He is the Founder of Cybrix Technologies, a training and development organization dedicated to research-oriented skill enhancement in advanced computing domains. Through this initiative, he has conducted over 100 workshops and more than 400 seminars, contributing significantly to the academic and professional development of engineering graduates and early-career researchers. He later co-founded Researcher Connect Innovation and Impact Pvt. Ltd., a research technology and consulting organization that collaborates with universities, researchers, publishers, and institutions to enhance research creation, dissemination, and global collaboration. Currently, he serves as the Director and Chief Technology Officer (CTO), providing strategic leadership in developing innovative digital platforms that support sustainable research ecosystems and academic excellence.

Advancement in Engineering and Science – Goyal et al. (Eds)
© 2026 The Author(s), ISBN: 978-1-041-31101-0

Power System Stability Enhancement by Virtual Inertia Control Strategies for Renewable Energy Integration

M. Mujtahid Ansari
Research Scholar, Department of Electrical Engineering

Parashant J Gaidhane
Associate Professor, Department of Instrumentation Engineering Government College of Engineering, Jalgaon, India

ABSTRACT: The incorporation of renewable energy sources into the power grid presents distinct obstacles concerning grid stability and resilience as a result of their intrinsic variability and intermittency. In response, virtual inertia control strategies have emerged as promising solutions to replicate the stabilizing effect of conventional synchronous generators and enhance the power system stability with extensive renewable energy penetration. This review study comprehensively explores the recent advancements in virtual inertia control strategies for renewable energy integration, synthesizing findings from a wide range of research efforts and methodologies. Implementing VIC within MGs emerges as a feasible solution to enhance the frequency response of the system and address these challenges. This study introduces a novel method to enhance the control performance of distributed generators (DGs) employing Virtual Synchronous Generators (VSGs) with inertia characteristics. Presenting a virtual inertia (VI) by improving frequency stability through active power flow management is the aim of the paper. The results establish that the proposed strategy is effective and provides fast and reliable virtual inertia support for stability of the microgrid.

Keywords: MPPT controller, stability, OOA, DC-DC Converter, Solar PV, BESS, VSG

1 INTRODUCTION

Energy input to the prime movers and the electrical load on the system must constantly match for a power system to operate under steady-state stability. For an operational power system, constant change is typical. The actual power balance in the network as a whole is intimately tied to the frequency. Under typical operating circumstances, the system generators operate in synchronism. A power imbalance will therefore result in a speed (and frequency) divergence because the kinetic energy is dependent on the generator speed. Uninterruptible power generation and lower carbon emissions were the driving forces behind the development of renewable energy sources (RES). In order to cater to the increasing power demand, integrated power systems consisting of solar and wind turbines are typically developed[1]. However, the irregular nature of solar and wind-based energy conversion devices limits RES from being widely adopted. Although they cannot be controlled, changes in renewable energy sources due to climatic variations can be predicted. One of the important issues in the RES penetration is non-existent or low inertia responses that cause frequency deviations in the system [2]. Thus the power system becomes more complex and insecure with escalated integration. Recently, effective controllers have been used in the RES connected power system to maximize the power generation. In a few cases, the VIC technique has been applied to pre-existing controllers, including PI and PID controllers. These controllers were not able to sustain themselves under disturbance conditions and had complex tuning procedures. Thus, these conventional controllers were not ensuring high robustness under more perturbation [3]. The grid tied power system is more beneficial for improving voltage stability, system stability, active power, and reactive power flow. Normally, the RES is connected with the grid through power electronic converters. Moreover, integration of several RES into the power system will cause power quality issues and minimizes the system inertia. The absence of system inertia results in poor voltage and frequency stability [4,5].

In the conventional power system, the synchronous generator operating at synchronous frequency is used for integration of the grid with RES. The speed of a synchronous generator is increased or decreased in accordance with the variation of grid frequency due to power imbalances. Based on this functioning, the synchronous generator compensates for the power mismatch [6]. Whereas, inertia of the power frameworks is minimized based on the rotating masses of the synchronous generator due to the stochastic nature of sources [7]. System instability and damping of dynamic performance are raised with the higher penetration of RES in the microgrid. In such systems, the virtual inertia is generated by a power electronic converter and control techniques. By incorporating flywheels, supercapacitors, ultra-batteries, and superconducting magnetic energy storage, the lack of inertia triggered by the widespread use of RES has been reduced. [8]. During perturbation occurrences, the system frequency will deviate from its normal frequency, and it is anticipated to be higher during abrupt load variations. Additionally, the frequency stability will be impacted by the poor rotating masses and hence poor inertia that arise from integrating RES with conventional inverters. [9,10].

VSG is a useful tool for reducing frequency fluctuations and spikes because it represents the inertia source from the kinetic energy in rotors. Furthermore, a larger rate of frequency change would arise from the decreased inertia. In order to cater to these problems, several control strategies have been established with the battery energy storage system for providing complementary regulation for different types of RES [11] Reduction of inertia will be increased by generating virtual inertia that is dominated by virtual inertia control (VIC).

1.1 *Virtual inertia for VSG control*

This approach enables the emulation of rotating inertia within the BESS. Generally, VSG control accept the familiar swing equations of the synchronous generator, employing angular speed (frequency)–real power $\omega - p$ and voltage–reactive power $V - Q$ droop control principles. In this investigation, the intended characteristics of $\omega - P$ and $V - Q$ droop control.

$$P_{SG} = P_{sref} + K_{S\omega}(\omega_{sref} - \omega_{sg}) \quad (1)$$

$$Q_{sg} = Q_{sref} + K_{sv}(E_{sref} - V_{an,pk}) \quad (2)$$

In the VSG control scheme, P_{SG} represents the virtual shaft real power, while P_{sref} denotes the set reference value of real power. $K_{S\omega}$ signifies the droop coefficient, and ω_{sg} stands for the reference angular frequency. Q_{sg} indicates the virtual rotor angular frequency of the VSG, Q_{sref} corresponds to the set reference value of reactive power, and k_{sv} represents the droop coefficient. E_{sref} denotes the reference voltage, and $V_{an,pk}$ represents the peak voltage output of the VSG.

$$P_{SG} - P_{sout} = J_S\omega_{SG}\frac{d\omega_{sg}}{dt} + D(\omega_{SG} - \omega_G) \quad (3)$$

Where, P_{sout} represents the real power output, $J_S$signifies the virtual inertia, Ddenotes the virtual damping factor and ω_G stands for the output angular frequency. Equation (3) reduces to the $\omega - p$ droop control, as shown in Equation (1). This implies that the $\omega - p$ droop control represents a specific instance of VSG control, lacking the inertial characteristic.

2 LITERATURE SURVEY

This section discusses some of the most recent research on virtual inertia control in RES-connected power systems.

Xing *et al.* [12] had developed a Virtual Adaptive Inertia Control (VAIC) for solar and BESS-connected power systems. With the aim of extracting maximum available power from the solar PV, the perturb and observe (P&O) maximum power tracking algorithm was used. The state of the battery connected with the power system was examined with the aid of an extended Kalman filter. The suggested control strategy was developed through the virtual battery algorithm and fuzzy logic. In that suggested approach, the damping factor of the synchronous machine and the mechanical inertia were considered for external characteristics. Finally, the system stability was examined by the small signal stability analysis.

Maulidhia *et al.* [13] have created a control approach based on particle swarm optimization (PSO) to increase frequency stability. In that approach, the capacitor energy storage system was used with a virtual inertia controller (VIC). The vibrating equation of the synchronous generator was used for creating system inertia that was given to the inverter. In the suggested PSO approach, the virtual damping and virtual inertia were initialized, and then the minimum error formed as objective function. Finally, the frequency response was estimated for varying loads.

Ping *et al.* [14] had suggested a control strategy for adaptive VSG in the BESS. Initially, BESS with the suggested control model was applied through the electromechanical transient model. Then the system inertia was measured as transfer functions in disturbance conditions. In this model, adaptive droop gain and adaptive virtual inertia were considered for improving grid frequency. The suggested controller was authenticated on the modified IEEE bus system. In such a system, the voltage source converter was used for the integration of the internal current loop based on proportional integral (PI) control.

Zaid *et al.* [15] have proposed using VIC in conjunction with a fractional-order integral controller for a multi-area interconnected power system. In addition to that, the gray wolf optimization (GWO) was used for selecting minimum value of deviation for frequency and tie line power. In that model, area-1 comprised a solar PV-thermal plant with BESS and area-2 comprised a wind farm-thermal plant with BESS. The suggested model was validated on the MATLAB/SIMULINK tool and under load and source variation.

Gaidhane, P. J *et al.* [16] GWO with leadership hierarchy approach is hybridized with employed bee's upgrading strategy from ABC. This incorporates the information sharing ability among the members of the pack. It intensifies exploration tendency and boost the participation of all candidate solutions in the pack without affecting the prime leadership features of conventional GWO.

3 MATHEMATICAL MODEL

3.1 *System overview*

The system proposed for the site consists of the following. A Solar PV array using Maximum Power Point Tracking (MPPT). A BESS is interfaced using a bidirectional DC-DC converter. A Voltage Source Inverter (VSI), controlled by a Vacuum Sweep Generator, is used. An enhanced FOPI–PD controller is used for managing BESS power. Connection to the main grid is made by means of a Point of Common Coupling (PCC).

The system is built to match the response of synchronous generators in low-inertia grids by controlling energy exchange according to observed frequency changes.

3.2 *Virtual Synchronous Generator (VSG) Control Strategy*

The swing equation of the VSG controller is designed to simulate how a synchronous generator would behave.

$$J\frac{d\omega}{dt} = P_{ref} - P_e - D(\omega - \omega_0) \quad (4)$$

Where:

J: Virtual inertia constant
D: Virtual damping coefficient
ω: Instantaneous angular frequency
ω_0: Nominal angular frequency
P_{ref}: Reference power (mechanical input)
P_e: Actual output power (electrical output)

To control the frequency and voltage droop:

$$\omega = \omega_0 - m(P_e - P_0), V = V_0 - n(Q - Q_0) \quad (5)$$

Where:

m, n: Frequency and voltage droop coefficients
P_0, Q_0: Nominal power values
V_0: Nominal voltage magnitude

The output power equations are:

$$P = \frac{3}{2}(V_dI_d + V_qI_q), Q = \frac{3}{2}(V_qI_d - V_dI_q) \quad (6)$$

With this approach, the inverter behaves exactly as a rotating piece of machinery when thrown off by disturbances, copying both inertia and damping.

3.3 *FOPI–PD controller design*

The cascaded FOPI–PD controller is chosen to control power flow from a BESS and simulate virtual inertia.

FOPI Controller:

$$G_{FOPI}(s) = K_p + \frac{K_i}{s^\lambda} \quad (7)$$

PD Controller:

$$G_{PD}(s) = K_{pd} + K_d s^{\mu} \tag{8}$$

The combined transfer function becomes:

$$G(s) = \left(K_p + \frac{K_i}{s^{\lambda}}\right) \cdot \left(K_{pd} + K_d s^{\mu}\right) \tag{9}$$

Where:

K_p, K_i: FOPI gains
K_{pd}, K_d: PD gains
λ, μ: Fractional orders ($0 < \lambda,\ \mu \leq 1$)

With fractional order, the design makes it easier to tune the system and it outperforms traditional integer-order controllers under varying operating conditions.

4 EXPERIMENTAL SETUP

The proposed controller is validated on the power system consist of solar PV and BESS. The MPPT controller, which is based on the Osprey optimization algorithm, increases the power extracted from solar PV. A DC-DC converter connects the solar PV, and a bidirectional DC-DC converter connects the BESS. Inverter in the system converts the DC power from solar and batteries into AC power that is integrated to the grid. A point of common connection (PCC) connects the solar PV and the BESS to the grid. The suggested cascaded fractional order proportional integral derivative with proportional derivative controller (FOPI-PD) regulates active power flow to simulate virtual inertia through enhanced frequency stability. This controller controls power from BESS. The osprey optimization approach uses the minimal error function to modify the suggested FOPI-PD controller. The proposed controller chose the optimum duty cycle for the battery-connected bidirectional DC-DC converter based on battery current and voltage. Additionally, the virtual synchronous generator regulates the flow of active and reactive power in a reactive power in a three-phase inverter.

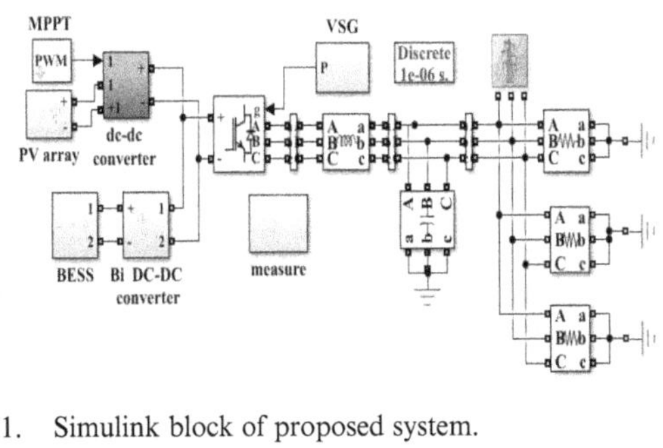

Figure 1. Simulink block of proposed system.

In this section, the proposed control method is applied and simulated using MATLAB/Simulink. The MPPT function optimizes solar DC output for maximum power extraction, while the synchronverter serves as a self-synchronizing DC-AC interface. To facilitate grid integration, cascading DC-DC and DC-AC converters are essential for linking the solar PV system with the power grid and stabilizing frequency output.

5 RESULT AND DISCUSSION

In the grid voltage and current varied. A three-phase voltage sag occurred at the distribution side of the grid, lasting for 0.1 s, leading to a drop in the PCC voltage from its nominal value. Consequently, during the fault period (0.1–0.2 s), the inverter must endure the fault and remain connected by managing overvoltage and overcurrent conditions.

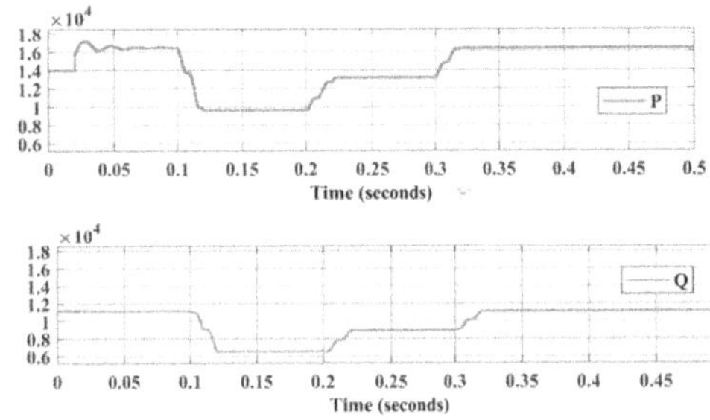

Figure 2. Active and reactive Power for load varying condition.

Figure 2 show the electric grid's active and reactive power. The electricity from the grid varies rapidly when the load is connected to it without using the VSG model. Furthermore, in the absence of a VSG controller, the BESS's reference power is kept at zero and its active power stays near zero.

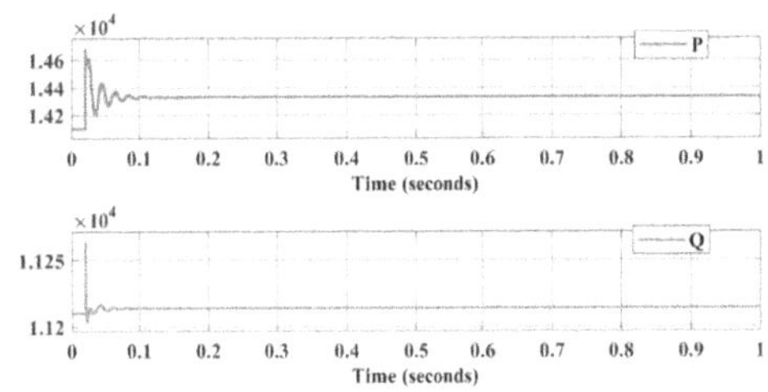

Figure 3. Active and reactive power without PV.

Figure 3 illustrate the active and reactive power without PV. In power variations occur indirectly and gradually. The BESS system's integration with a VSG controller makes this possible by helping to inject or absorb electricity into or out of the grid. Subsequently, this process aids in flattening the power drawn from the utility grid during load alteration.

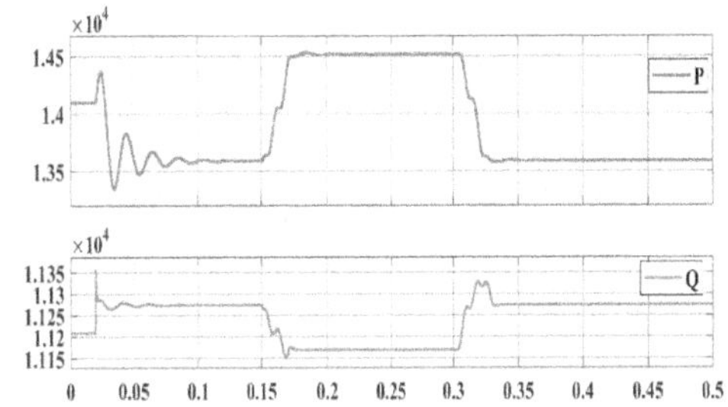

Figure 4. Active and reactive power for PQ load.

Because of the prior explanation, it is possible to successfully minimize the frequency response during loading transition events, as shown in Figure 4. reaches 1.135 in view of insertion and removal of load, respectively, while the VSG controller is not in use. But when the VSG controller is turned on, it drops to 0.17 Hz for load insertion and 0.32 Hz for rejection. This indicates an improvement when VSG is present in view of load insertion and rejection, respectively.

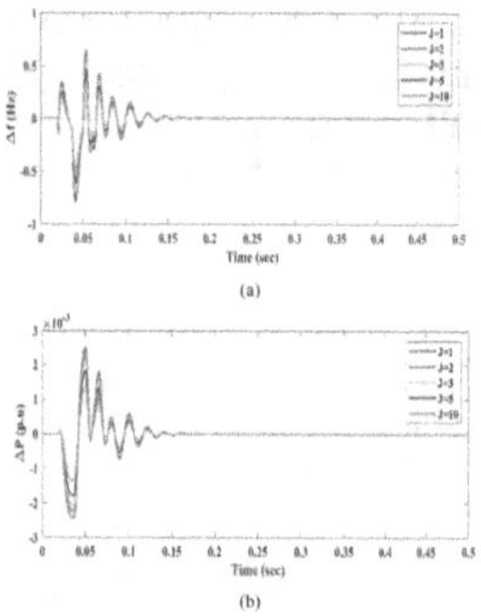

Figure 5. Impact of inertia and deviation in (a) frequency and (b) power change of VS.

The damping factor as a virtual inertia factor as depicted in Figure 5 (a) Increasing the encouragement of different VI factors on frequency deviation is depicted, while maintaining a constant damping factor (D = 0.7). It observed that during the occurrence of events such as load changes, the frequency deviation experiences fluctuations and significant overshoot/undershoot before eventually stabilizing in the steady-state region. Figure 5 (b) As the virtual inertia factor increases, there a reduction in the extent of overshoot/undershoot.

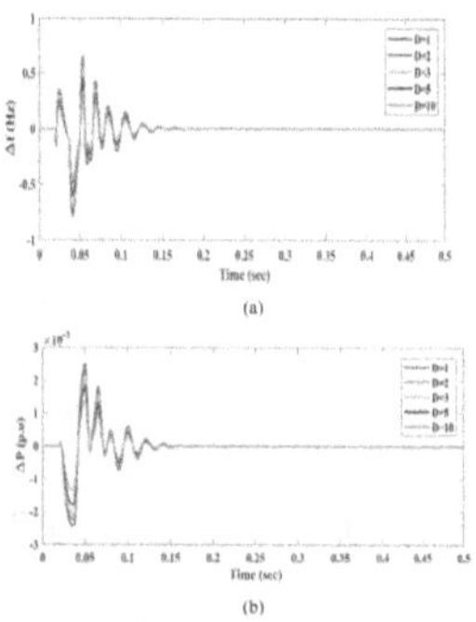

Figure 6. Impact of damping factors on deviation in (a) frequency and (b) power.

The impact of the damping factor on the virtual inertia factor is examined in this study. Figure 6 shows that the frequency deviation caused by transient occurrences can be decreased by enhancing the damping factor while maintaining a constant virtual inertia factor (J = 2.6). Additionally, a higher damping factor causes the frequency variation to converge to its steady-state value more quickly. Therefore, it was found that increasing the damping factor can improve frequency responsiveness by decreasing overshoot/undershoot and speeding up the convergence to steady-state by associating the damping and virtual inertia factors.

6 CONCLUSION

The heavy adoption of renewable energy challenges the stable functioning of future power systems, because of the characteristics of converter-based RES. Converter-based RES differs from those of synchronous generators. Converter-based renewable energy creates significant low inertia and zero kinetic energy, causing system instability. To overcome the problem, virtual inertia emulation uses energy storage to emulate inertia power and stability. Virtual inertia reserve strengthens the weak grids and enhances the stability of the power system. The simulation results obtained from MATLAB/Simulink have validated the commendable transient frequency recovery speed and steady-state performance, particularly in terms of frequency oscillation, achieved by the proposed strategy.

REFERENCES

[1] Abuagreb, Mohamed, and Ahmed Abuhussein. 2022. "Sizing of Energy Storage System for Virtual Inertia Emulation." In *2022 IEEE 31st International Symposium on Industrial Electronics (ISIE)*, 374–379. IEEE.

[2] Ghosh, Ritwik, Narsa Reddy Tummuru, Bharat Singh Rajpurohit, and Antonello Monti. 2020. "Virtual Inertia from Renewable Energy Sources: Mathematical Representation and Control Strategy." In *2020 IEEE International Conference on Power Electronics, Smart Grid and Renewable Energy (PESGRE2020)*, 1–6. IEEE.

[3] Said, Sayed M., Mokhtar Aly, Bálint Hartmann, and Emad A. Mohamed. 2021. "Coordinated Fuzzy Logic-Based Virtual Inertia Controller and Frequency Relay Scheme for Reliable Operation of Low-Inertia Power System." *IET Renewable Power Generation* 15 (6): 1286–1300.

[4] Othman, Ahmed M., and Attia A. El-Fergany. 2021. "Adaptive Virtual-Inertia Control and Chicken Swarm Optimizer for Frequency Stability in Power-Grids Penetrated by Renewable Energy Sources." *Neural Computing and Applications* 33 (7): 2905–2918.

[5] Wang, Zhiyun, Kaikai Pan, and Wenyuan Xu. 2023. "Critical Cyber Parameters in Hybrid Power Systems with VSP-Based Virtual Inertia Emulation: Theoretical Approach and Mitigation Strategy." *International Journal of Electrical Power & Energy Systems* 147: 108877.

[6] Fang, Jingyang, Pengfeng Lin, Hongchang Li, Yongheng Yang, and Yi Tang. 2018. "An Improved Virtual Inertia Control for Three-Phase Voltage Source Converters Connected to a Weak Grid." *IEEE Transactions on Power Electronics* 34 (9): 8660–8670.

[7] Singh, Kavita. 2021. "Enhancement of Frequency Regulation in Tidal Turbine Power Plant Using Virtual Inertia from Capacitive Energy Storage System." *Journal of Energy Storage* 35: 102332.

[8] Kumar, Abdul Waheed, Mairaj Ud Din Mufti, and Mubashar Yaqoob Zargar. 2022. "Fuzzy Based Virtual Inertia Emulation in a Multi-Area Wind Penetrated Power System Using Adaptive Predictive Control Based Flywheel Storage." *Sustainable Energy Technologies and Assessments* 53: 102515.

[9] Zhou, Tao, Ju Huang, Hao Quan, Yan Xu, and Zicheng Liu. 2023. "Inertial Security Region Estimation and Analysis of New Power Systems Considering Renewable Energy Virtual Inertial." *Energy Reports* 9: 1836–1849.

[10] Hu, Pengfei, Yujing Li, Yanxue Yu, and Frede Blaabjerg. 2023. "Inertia Estimation of Renewable-Energy-Dominated Power System." *Renewable and Sustainable Energy Reviews* 183: 113481.

[11] Magdy, Gaber, Hossam Ali, and Dianguo Xu. 2021. "Effective Control of Smart Hybrid Power Systems: Cooperation of Robust LFC and Virtual Inertia Control Systems." *CSEE Journal of Power and Energy Systems* 8 (6): 1583–1593.

[12] Xing, Wei, Hewu Wang, Languang Lu, Xuebing Han, Kai Sun, and Minggao Ouyang. 2021. "An Adaptive Virtual Inertia Control Strategy for Distributed Battery Energy Storage System in Microgrids." *Energy* 233: 121155.

[13] Maulidhia, Alief Nur Aisyi, Dimas Anton Asfani, Ardyono Priyadi, and Herlambang Setiadi. 2022. "Frequency Stability Analysis on Optimization of Virtual Inertia Control (VIC) Capacitor Energy Storage (CES) Controller Settings Using Particle Swarm Optimization." In *2022 International Conference on Computer Engineering, Network, and Intelligent Multimedia (CENIM)*, 359–364. IEEE.

[14] He, Ping, Zhao Li, Haoran Jin, Chen Zhao, Jiale Fan, and Xiaopeng Wu. 2023. "An Adaptive VSG Control Strategy of Battery Energy Storage System for Power System Frequency Stability Enhancement." *International Journal of Electrical Power & Energy Systems* 149: 109039.

[15] Zaid, Sherif A., Abualkasim Bakeer, Gaber Magdy, Hani Albalawi, Ahmed M. Kassem, Mohmed E. El-Shimy, Hossam AbdelMeguid, and Bassel Manqarah. 2023. "A New Intelligent Fractional-Order Load Frequency Control for Interconnected Modern Power Systems with Virtual Inertia Control." *Fractal and Fractional* 7 (1): 62.

[16] Gaidhane, P.J., and M.J. Nigam. 2018. "A Hybrid Grey Wolf Optimizer and Artificial Bee Colony Algorithm for Enhancing the Performance of Complex Systems." *Journal of Computational Science* 27: 284–302.

Advancement in Engineering and Science – Goyal et al. (Eds)
© 2026 The Author(s), ISBN: 978-1-041-31101-0

Harnessing CNN-Based Approach for Detection of Diseases in Ginger Plants

Ashok Sadavare
Department of Computer Science & Engineering, Shree Santkrupa Institute of Engineering and Technology, Ghogaon, India

Priyanka Shinde
Department of Master Computer Applications, Govt. College of Engineering, Karad, India

ABSTRACT: Ginger is a highly valued crop that is widely cultivated globally because of its medicinal, culinary, and economic significance. Ginger may find use in functional foods or nutraceuticals. Ginger is effective in preventing heart disease, diabetes, and respiratory problems. Despite its significance, growing ginger is fraught with problems including weather fluctuations, insect infestations, disease outbreaks, and inefficient resource utilization, which result in lower-than-ideal yields and financial losses. Recent technological advancements have made precision agriculture possible, which presents a viable answer to these problems by facilitating data-driven decision-making at the farm level. Farmers have difficulties in detecting plant diseases early and accurately, which requires knowledge and skills. In this context, Machine learning techniques have enormous potential to drive sustainable agriculture. Machine learning technology offers prompt, automatic disease diagnosis to benefit ginger producers, particularly in developing nations. It is a quick, and deployable solution.

Keywords: Agriculture, Convolutional Neural Network, Ginger crop, Machine learning, Smart agriculture

1 INTRODUCTION

In order to provide food security, economic growth, and environmental sustainability, agriculture is essential. It is a major driver of national economies and international trade, providing millions of people with their primary source of income. In addition to supplying food, Doria highlights that agriculture fosters rural development and job opportunities, all of which are essential for reducing poverty. The principal source of income and employment for a substantial proportion of the people, agriculture is a crucial pillar of economies across the globe. Agriculture provides employment to around 60% of the population and makes up 20% of the GDP of India, demonstrating the importance of agriculture to the country's economic growth and stability [1]. India contributed almost one-third of the world's ginger production was generated in India. When compared to other major producing nations, India's production grew at the fastest rate throughout this time. Together, the top five export destinations for ginger were the United States, Morocco, Spain, Bangladesh, and the United Kingdom, accounting for approximately 52% of the overall export value. In order to boost ginger production and its export potential, it may be important to prioritize productivity enhancement through the use of high-quality varieties combined with scientific management and area expansion [2]. Based on a thorough study by Govindarajan, ginger is a spice that can be used in a variety of culinary and medical situations. The monograph covers a wide range of topics related to ginger, such as its botany, global varieties, and agronomy, with a focus on the yield of useful components required for high-quality production. Existing physico-chemical parameters guarantee hygienic quality and purity, and quality evaluation is a primary priority within this framework [3]. The methods used to process ginger and its derivatives, including oleoresin, volatile oil, powdered ginger, and syruped ginger, are rigorously analyzed, with attention paid to the growing demand for high-quality, value-added goods worldwide [4]. Ginger has several medicinal applications; it can therefore be considered a medicine. Due to its therapeutic, culinary, and commercial importance, ginger is a high-value crop that is extensively grown across the world. Numerous studies have highlighted the biological properties of ginger, suggested its potential use in treating and preventing various ailments[5]. Despite its significance, growing ginger is fraught with difficulties like weather fluctuations, pest infestations, disease outbreaks, poor soil quality, a lack of water, and inefficient resource utilization, all of which can result in less-than-ideal yields and financial losses. Bacterial wilt and soft rot diseases hinder continued cropping, compelling farmer to seek new land[6]. The diseases that can affect ginger (Zingiber officinale) can majorly affect its productivity and cultivation. Notably, rhizome rot in ginger has been linked to two fungal pathogens: Rhizopus oryzae and Enterobacter cloacae. Symptoms of rhizome rot include wilting, chlorosis, and brown lesions on rhizomes [7]. The incidence of these diseases can reach up to 15% in affected areas, posing a threat to ginger production in regions like Shandong Province, China[8]. However, the presence of phytopathogenic fungi, such as Pythium spp. and Fusarium sp., further complicates ginger cultivation, leading to post-harvest losses. Effective management strategies, including the use of nanoparticles for disease control, are essential to mitigate these challenges and enhance ginger production [9].

2 MAIN BACTERIAL DISEASES OF GINGER PLANTS

Many pests and diseases can harm ginger. Two of the main illnesses that result in financial loss are soft rot and storage rot.

Soft Rot / Rhizome rot: Most serious and destructive disease affecting ginger is soft rot, which can diminish productivity by 50–90% and is present in all nations that grow ginger. When it's warm and humid outside, disease results in large losses. Figure 1 shows that in the face of infection, the rhizomes become vulnerable, turning soft, water soaked, and progressively decomposing [10] [23].

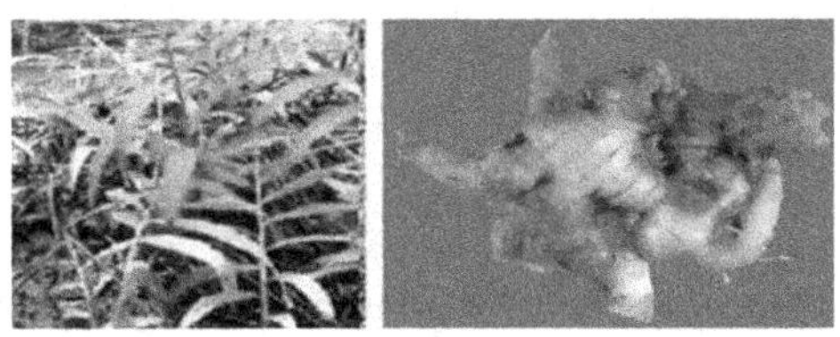

Figure 1. Soft rot symptoms.

DOI: 10.1201/9781003798514-2

Symptoms: Humidity promotes the growth of fleshy, tuberculous stems. The surface root system can be quickly eroded by severe infection, resulting in soft rot in the stems and the eventual withering of entire plant [10], [11]. Protection: One crucial step in preventing Pythium infection is to use seeds free of illness. A good way to prevent ginger infections is to rotate crop with corn and rice. This practice supports sustainable agriculture. The rhizomes can be treated for thirty minutes with propineb, copper oxychloride, mancozeb, guazatine and ziram to effectively control soft rot infection [10], [11].

Leaf spot: The serious leaf rot and blight caused by leaf spot disease is making it more and more significant in many parts of India [10]. From June to September due to heavy rainfall accompanied by high humidity and moderate temperature ginger foliage are attacked by a number of leaf spots / blight diseases.

Figure 2. Leaf spot symptoms.

Symptom.: Unevenly shaped patches with brown rims and a greyish-white center can be seen on leaves. When these patches become larger, as in extreme situations, leaves become dehydrated [10], [11]. Immature leaves may have elongated dots, spindle-shaped or oval spots. Figure 2 shows that the dots thereafter took on the appearance of a white, papery center with dark brown borders and yellow halos surrounding them [11] [23].

Protection: The illness can be successfully treated by applying a Bordeaux combination, zineb, and maneb to the plant. To decrease the occurrences of diseases in plants, a combination of 0.2% iprodione, 0.2 % mancozeb, 0.1 % benomyl, and 0.1 % soluble boron can be useful [10].

Anthrax: Plants develop brown and water-soaked patches first show up on the leaf's margines. These blotches enlarge inward and downward, generating brown dots that range in shape from rounded to pike-shaped to uneven. There could be cloud patterns in the spots. When the spots are really bad, they combine and the leaves get dehydrated [11].

Protection: Use 20 % silazole-miconazole emulsion at 2000-3000 times, 40% Duo-Fu-bromoxynil powder at 800 -1000 times. Or 20% azoxystrobin vinegar water granules at 1000-1500 times weekly or as needed [11].

Bacterial wilt: The most dangerous rhizome-borne illness is bacterial wilt of ginger. It's a disease spread by seeds and soil as well. It is quite harmful and common since ginger grows in warm temperate, tropical, and subtropical climates worldwide. Within five to ten days of infection, bacteria cause ginger to wilt quickly. The infection spreads quickly under ideal environmental conditions, such as high rainfall and warm weather, which contributes to the disease's severity[10].

Symptoms: First, at the collar area of the pseudo stem, there are wet areas or straight lines that spread downward and upward. It is simple to separate and break off the false stems from the infected plant by gently pulling on them at their base. The illness first showed signs of mild drooping and curling of the lower leaf margins, and later on, the infection began to progress upward. Leaves begin to turn yellow at the base and move up the stem over time. Figure 3 depicts affected ginger with severe yellowing and withering in advanced stages of the disease [10], [23].

Figure 3. Bacterial wilt disease symptoms.

Protection: Ginger must be properly stored after harvesting in order to preserve its quality. Ginger can be preserved at a temperature between 16°C and 20°C and a humidity between 90% and 95% [11].

3 MACHINE LEARNING IN AGRICULTURE

Technology has a revolutionary effect on agriculture, increasing production and sustainability in a variety of settings. A Greek study that emphasized the strong statistical relevance of technology adoption's benefits for sustainability demonstrated that the fusion of advanced technologies, like the Internet of Things (IoT), Deep Learning (DL), Machine Learning (ML), artificial intelligence (AI) and precision agriculture, significantly improves resource efficiency and reduces environmental impacts in agricultural practices [12]. Adoption of Internet technologies by wheat farmers in underdeveloped nations has been associated with higher technical efficiency, indicating that digital tools can improve agricultural output and food security [13]. The use of machine learning is becoming more widely acknowledged as a revolutionary solution for intelligent farming, especially in desert agriculture, which faces difficulties such as water scarcity and harsh weather conditions. Research highlights how merging of Machine learning with IoT can revolutions real time data collection and decision-making process, enabling farmers to optimize resources use and boost crop yields in dry areas[14]. Machine learning is greatly improving agriculture by employing advanced field technologies to tackle the different issues that farmers encounter. Studies suggest that machine learning systems can aid in selecting crops by examining a wide range of data, such as soil characteristics, environmental factors, and plant diseases. This, in turn, helps in recommending the best crops and fertilizers for increased yield and sustainability[15]. Machine learning is increasingly recognized as a groundbreaking tool in crop selection and cultivation to address resource constraints and climate change challenges. Research indicates that Machine learning algorithms are capable of analyzing diverse datasets containing soil quality, climate, and previous crop performance to identify the most suitable crops for a specific area while reducing environmental impact and enhancing yields [16]. Farmers can optimize pest management, irrigation, and fertilization strategies because of predicative capabilities of the machine learnings, resulting in improved resource use and productivity. However, additional research is necessary to enhance these models and ensure their suitability in different geographic contexts, given the complexity of agricultural ecosystems and the diverse environmental conditions[17].

4 RELATED WORK

Significant progress in enhancing agricultural practices through technology integration is evident from the assessment of machine learning (ML) methods in precision farming. Random

Forest and Support Vector Machines are among the ML models that improve the forecasting of soil parameters and crop yields, offering solutions to food security issues [18]. Weed identification is improved by advanced techniques such as attention-based deep networks, which are essential for efficient crop management [19], [20]. Anshul Sharma *et al.* discovered that ResNet was one of the most successful algorithms for disease detection, surpassing SVM, CNN, InceptionV3. They made use of large datasets containing 18,450 tomato leaf images across 10 categories, ensuring thorough training [21]. Satyam Sinha *et al.* introduced a system for automatically detecting potato plants diseases. This advanced system leverages the power of five different machine learning algorithms, namely Random Forest (RF), K-Nearest Neighbours (KNN), Support vector machine (SVM), Naïve Bayes and Convolutional Neural Network (CNN). Their findings indicated that SVM emerged as the most efficient algorithm for identifying potato diseases based on images of potato leaves [22]. Computer vision has shown amazing results when used extensively for applications like disease diagnosis and detection, especially in the agricultural sector. A plant usually shows signs on its leaves, such as bacterial wilt. In order to support the healthy growth and productive harvest of ginger plants, a more accurate and efficient model for identifying the disease known as "ginger soft rot" or "rhizome rot" must be developed.

5 DATA PREPARATION

The 500 ginger plant images, each with a pixel size of 640×6400 at 96 dpi, were chosen with care from the publicly available Roboflow Universe repository. Out of 505 ginger images, 250 images of healthy ginger and 250 images of soft rot infected images were taken. Both healthy and soft rot-infected samples are shown in Figure 4, guaranteeing a balanced representation for precise categorization.

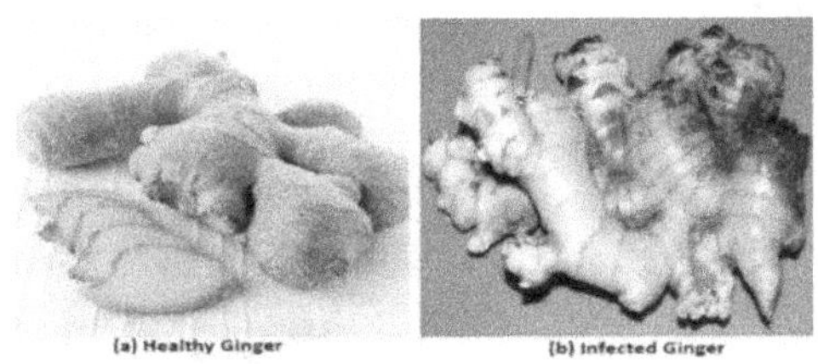

Figure 4. Healthy ginger and diseased ginger.

To increase the model's durability and generalization, following image preprocessing techniques were applied:

Resizing: Image dimensions were standardized to 128 by 128 in order to ensure a constant input size for efficient CNN processing.

Data Augmentation: To add diversity to the dataset, techniques such as flipping, rotation, contrast enhancement, and noise reduction were used.

These image preprocessing strategies significantly improve the model's ability to detect disease signs in a variety of situations and enhance the model's adaptability to real-world applications.

6 METHODOLOGY

The method of building and assessing a Convolutional Neural Network (CNN) model is shown in a flowchart in Figure 5. It has four primary phases:

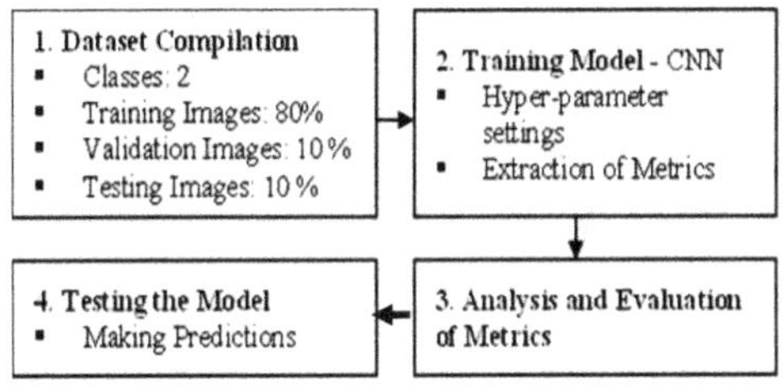

Figure 5. Process flow.

Step-1: Dataset Compiling

A dataset of 500 images was separated carefully to provide the best possible training and evaluation of the CNN model for disease identification in ginger plants. The majority of the dataset 400 (80%) images was allocated for model training. These images enabled the CNN to learn meaningful features and patterns associated with disease symptoms, ensuring robust generalization across various conditions. A subset of 50 (10%) images was kept aside for validation, which assisted in fine-tuning hyperparameters such as learning rate, batch size, and dropout rates. This validation step was critical for assessing the model's performance throughout training and avoiding overfitting. The final 50 (10%) images were chosen for testing, offering an unbiased assessment of the model's performance on previously unknown data. This evaluation phase ensured that the trained CNN could recognize soft rot disease signs accurately in real-world agricultural applications. This structured splitting strategy ensured a balanced approach to training, validation, and testing, enhancing the model's adaptability and reliability for disease detection in ginger plants.

Step-2: CNN Model Construction and Training

Convolutional neural networks (CNN) were utilized to construct a classification model. CNN consist of multiple layers, each layer employing different functions to transform the activation volume from one layer to another. Figure 6 illustrate the functionality of different layers used in CNN model to classify ginger has soft rot disease or not.

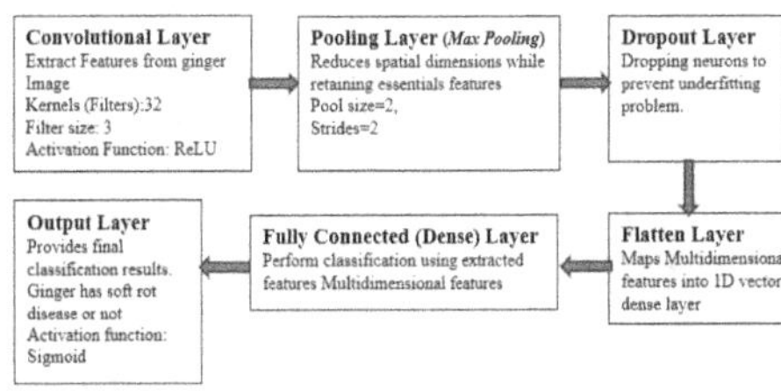

Figure 6. CNN Layer's Functionality.

Convolutional Layer: The CNN model's feature extraction is built upon the convolutional layer. It uses 32 kernels (filters) on the input ginger images, with each kernel having a size of 3. These filters scan the image for important features like textural variations, disease spots, and plant structure. The ReLU (Rectified Linear Unit) activation function includes non-linearity, allowing the model to capture complex patterns.

Pooling Layer (Max Pooling): Following convolution layer, max pooling layer is used to reduce spatial dimensions while retaining important features. This layer uses a pool size of 2 and a stride of 2. It reducing computational complexity and increasing model efficiency.

Dropout layer: A dropout layer is included to avoid over-fitting after pooling layer. By randomly deactivating some neurons during training, this method forces the model to learn reliable patterns instead of learning particular training data. It will help to build generalize model.

Flatten Layer: The flatten layer transforms the multi-dimensional feature maps into a 1D vector, preparing them for dense layers. This step bridges the gap between convolutional layers and fully connected layers, ensuring extracted features are effectively utilized for classification.

Fully Connected (Dense) Layer: This layer processes the retrieved features, revealing complex patterns that differentiate healthy ginger plants from those afflicted with soft rot disease. These layers improve classification accuracy by facilitating deeper pattern recognition through a series of successive transformations.

Output Layer: The output layer completes the final classification by identifying whether a particular image of a ginger plant shows symptoms of soft rot disease using a Sigmoid activation function. The sigmoid function classifies the image as either healthy or unhealthy by producing a probability score based on a predetermined threshold.

The proposed CNN model is developed using Python programming language, utilizing TensorFlow and Keras libraries within the Jupyter notebook. The model comprises 7,788,726 parameters and has a storage size of 29.71 MB.

6.1 *Hyper-parameter settings*

In Convolutional neural networks (CNN) hyper-parameter settings are essential for maximizing performance on a variety of tasks, especially image classification.

Dataset Ratio: Assess the outcomes of experiments with varying training-to-test ratios; better results are obtained with studies employing 80% training to 20% testing.

Batch Size: It is better to split the input into smaller batches while training a model, as it is too laborious to give the computer all the data in a single epoch, which would slow it down. The batch size used in this experiment is 32.

Learning Rate: The experiment's conclusion is that, when applying varying learning rates, the accuracy of a higher learning rate is less than that of a smaller learning rate. Consequently, 0.0001 is thought to be the optimal learning rate in the suggested model.

Activation Function: CNNs' accuracy in fitting data is improved by the capacity to simulate non-linear relationships through the use of activation functions. In the output layer, the Sigmoid activation function is employed since it is well suited for binary classification problems.

Algorithms for optimization: Adaptive Moment Estimation (Adam) optimizer is used to train the suggested model, adjusting parameters and updating the model weight.

Epochs: The model was trained using a range of epochs, from 10 to 25, during the experiment. Throughout the training process, an excessive gap occurs between the model's validation error and training error when using epochs that are too small or too large. After numerous experiments, the model achieved its best performance at epoch twenty.

Step-3: Evaluation and Analysis

The performance of the CNN model is evaluated using a variety of criteria throughout this step to ensure accuracy and reliability. Key evaluation criteria such as accuracy, precision, recall, and F1-score are used to quantify the model's ability to distinguish between healthy and unhealthy ginger plants. The confusion matrix sheds light on classification errors, assisting in the refinement of the model by recognizing incorrectly categorized images. Loss and accuracy curves are examined to track training progress, detect overfitting, and adjust hyperparameters. This stage is crucial for ensuring the model's robustness prior to implementation in real-world applications.

Step-4: Testing

The test set, consisting of 50 images, is used to evaluate the CNN model's overall performance on previously unknown data. This ensures that the algorithm can correctly distinguish between healthy and diseased ginger plants in real-world scenarios. Key characteristics like as accuracy, precision, recall, and F1-score are utilized to assess its robustness.

7 EXPERIMENTAL RESULT

Ginger color and texture are crucial indicator of ginger sickness since they can distinguish between healthy and infected ginger. After 20 epochs, the results show that the training accuracy was 97.82% with a loss of 0.10% and the validation accuracy was 96.60% with a loss of 0.08%. To identify a satisfactory classifier, result from the constructed model, all of the parameters were reviewed after multiple tests. Figure 7 illustrates the final accuracy for the CNN algorithm after 20 epochs.

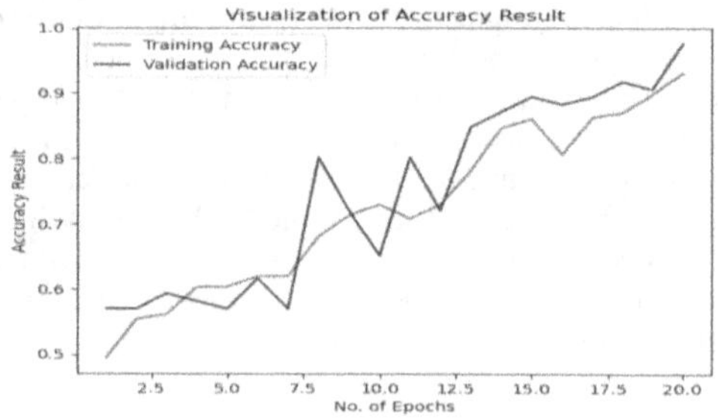

Figure 7. Visualization of accuracy result.

The confusion matrix assesses the effectiveness of the CNN-based Ginger Disease prediction algorithm. It consists of 48 True Positives (TP) and 36 True Negatives (TN), demonstrating high classification accuracy. The model has only one False Positive (FP) and one False Negative (FN), indicating low misclassification. The model's strong TP and TN values indicate good disease detection, making it ideal for real-world applications in ginger cultivation. Figure 8 illustrate the confusion matrix for ginger disease prediction using the CNN algorithm after 20 epochs.

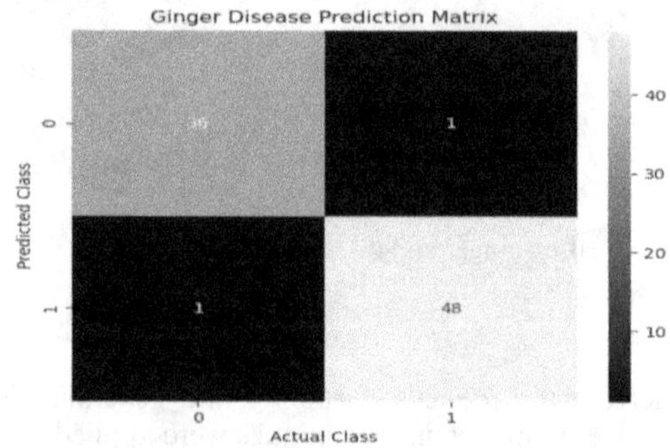

Figure 8. Confusion Matrix for Ginger Disease Predication.

The classification report is shown in Figure 9. The classification report emphasizes the CNN model's superior effectiveness in detecting diseases in ginger.

	precision	recall	f1-score	support
Disease	0.97	0.97	0.97	37
No-Disease	0.98	0.98	0.98	49
accuracy			0.98	86
macro avg	0.98	0.98	0.98	86
weighted avg	0.98	0.98	0.98	86

Figure 9. Classification Report.

With an overall accuracy of 98%, the model has good precision, recall, and F1-scores for both disease and non-disease classes, indicating trustworthy classification. The model's balanced performance across measures guarantees that misclassification mistakes are minimized, making it ideal for real-world agricultural applications.

8 CONCLUSION

Ginger yield is greatly impacted by major pests like thrips and scale insects, as well as diseases including soft rot disease and anthracnose. A small amount of study has been done on the automatic diagnosis of ginger disorders based on symptoms. The CNN model accurately and robustly detects ginger plant diseases, which improves agricultural disease diagnosis. Future research will focus on increasing the dataset with diverse, high-resolution photos, broadening categorization beyond soft root disease, and combining AI with smart farming systems that use edge computing and IoT sensors for real-time disease detection. Optimizing model efficiency will improve the practicality of sustainable agricultural applications. This strategy allows for early intervention approaches, which improves agricultural productivity.

ACKNOWLEDGEMENT

The authors would like to thank the staff, and authority of the Computer Science & Engineering department for their assistance with the research.

REFERENCES

[1] Doria, R. Importance of agriculture in Indian economy. *RESEARCH REVIEW International Journal of Multidisciplinary* 8, 26–32 (2023).
[2] Mula, G. Trends in Production and Export Potential of Ginger in India. *Economic Affairs* 67, (2022).
[3] Govindarajan, V.S. & Connell, D.W. Ginger — chemistry, technology, and quality evaluation: Part 1. *C R C Critical Reviews in Food Science and Nutrition* 17, 1–96 (1983).
[4] Govindarajan, V.S. & Connell, D.W. Ginger — chemistry, technology, and quality evaluation: Part 2. *C R C Critical Reviews in Food Science and Nutrition* 17, 189–258 (1983).
[5] Mao, Q.-Q. *et al.* Bioactive Compounds and Bioactivities of Ginger (Zingiber officinale Roscoe). *Foods* 8, 185 (2019).
[6] Wang, C.-W. *et al.* Soil Bacterial Community May Offer Solutions for Ginger Cultivation. *Microbiol Spectr* 10, (2022).
[7] Gao, X. *et al.* First Report of Rhizopus oryzae Causing Rhizome Rot on Ginger in China. *Plant Dis* 107, 231 (2023).
[8] Liu, J., Zhao, Z. & Wang, C. First Report of Rhizome Rot on Ginger (Zingiber officinale) Caused by Enterobacter cloacae in Shandong Province, China. *Plant Dis* 105, 210 (2021).
[9] Ingle, P.U., Rai, M., Golińska, P. & Gade, A.K. Phytomediated zinc oxide and sulfur nanoparticles for management of soft-rot causing pathogenic fungi in ginger. *Biocatal Agric Biotechnol* 58, 103229 (2024).
[10] Meenu, G. & Jebasingh, T. *Diseases of Ginger. in Ginger Cultivation and Its Antimicrobial and Pharmacological Potentials* (IntechOpen, 2020). doi:10.5772/intechopen.88839.
[11] Hui, J. & Liu, N. Main Pests and Diseases of Zingiberaceae and Their Control. *Am J Plant Sci* 14, 988–993 (2023).
[12] Kalfas, D., Kalogiannidis, S., Papaevangelou, O., Melfou, K. & Chatzitheodoridis, F. Integration of Technology in Agricultural Practices towards Agricultural Sustainability: A Case Study of Greece. *Sustainability* 16, 2664 (2024).
[13] Ahmad, B. *et al.* Exploring the influence of internet technology adoption on the technical efficiency of food production: insight from wheat farmers. *Front Sustain Food Syst* 8, (2024).
[14] Muniasamy, A. Machine Learning for Smart Farming: A Focus on Desert Agriculture. in *2020 International Conference on Computing and Information Technology (ICCIT-1441)* 1–5 (IEEE, 2020). doi:10.1109/ICCIT-144147971.2020.9213759.
[15] Muniasamy, A. Machine Learning for Smart Farming: A Focus on Desert Agriculture. in *2020 International Conference on Computing and Information Technology (ICCIT-1441)* 1–5 (IEEE, 2020). doi:10.1109/ICCIT-144147971.2020.9213759.
[16] Kumar, T.S. *et al.* Crop Selection and Cultivaton using Machine Learning. in *2023 Intelligent Computing and Control for Engineering and Business Systems (ICCEBS)* 1–4 (IEEE, 2023). doi:10.1109/ICCEBS58601.2023.10448940.
[17] Deshmukh, T., Rajawat, A., Goyal, S.B., Kumar, J. & Potgantwar, A. Analysis of Machine Learning Technique for Crop Selection and Prediction of Crop Cultivation. in *2023 International Conference on Inventive Computation Technologies (ICICT)* 298–311 (IEEE, 2023). doi:10.1109/ICICT57646.2023.10134371.
[18] Khan, A. A Comprehensive Literature Review on Machine Learning Approaches in Agriculture. *Int J Res Appl Sci Eng Technol* 12, 1158–1163 (2024).
[19] Shanthakumari, G., Vignesh, A., Harish, R. & Roshan Karthick, R. Advancements in Smart Agriculture: A Comprehensive Review of Machine Learning and IOT Approaches. in *2024 International Conference on Communication, Computing and Internet of Things (IC3IoT)* 1–6 (IEEE, 2024). doi:10.1109/IC3IoT60841.2024.10550268.
[20] Sharma, A., Jain, A., Gupta, P. & Chowdary, V. Machine Learning Applications for Precision Agriculture: A Comprehensive Review. *IEEE Access* 9, 4843–4873 (2021).
[21] Anshul Sharma, Ashish Chandak, Aryan Khandelwal & Raunak Gandhi. Detection of Diseases in Tomato Plant using Machine Learning. *International Journal of Next-Generation Computing* (2022) doi:10.47164/ijngc.v13i5.941.
[22] Sinha, S., Sinha, A.R., Ghose, C., Bhardwaj, H. & Singh, J. Automated Detection of Potato Plant Diseases using Machine Learning Algorithms. in *2023 International Conference on Recent Advances in Science and Engineering Technology (ICRASET)* 1–6 (IEEE, 2023). doi:10.1109/ICRASET59632.2023.10420350.
[23] Vikaspedia, https://vikaspedia.in/agriculture/crop production/integrated-pest-managment/ipm-for-spice-crops/ipm-strategies-for-ginger/diseases-and-symptoms#: ~:text=Soft%20rot, Disease %20symptoms&text=The%20infection%20starts%20at%20the, root%20infection%20is%20also%20noticed, last accessed 2014/09/15.

Advancement in Engineering and Science – Goyal et al. (Eds)

Enhanced Stock Market Forecasting Using Hybrid BiLSTM-GRU Models

Dhruv Mendiratta, Kunal Sinha, Akshay Jadhav, and Divya Thakur
Computer Science and Engineering, Manipal University Jaipur, Jaipur, India

ABSTRACT: Forecasting stock market prices is a critical aspect of financial planning, and this study proposes a cutting-edge approach using deep learning and machine learning techniques. The researchers have developed a hybrid model that combines the power of Gated Recurrent Unit (GRU) networks and Bidirectional Long Short-Term Memory (BiLSTM) to capture the intricate temporal patterns in stock market data. The model was tested on historical S&P 500 data, and the results are quite impressive. With an R-squared of 0.9991, a Mean Absolute Error (MAE) of 0.0101, and a Root Mean Squared Error (RMSE) of 0.0125, the BiLSTM-GRU model demonstrates exceptional performance. Remarkably, the model has significantly less error variance than the traditional LSTM method, as confirmed by a statistical test. These findings highlight the model's ability to enhance forecast precision and its potential for integration with real-time data systems. This study presents the BiLSTM-GRU hybrid as a highly effective and practical tool for stock price forecasting, offering valuable applications for financial institutions and investors alike.

Keywords: Stock Market Price Prediction, Human Capital Stock, Artificial Intelligence, Regression

1 INTRODUCTION

The concept of Stock Market Price Prediction has its roots in the 20th century, when Charles Dow introduced the Dow Theory, laying the groundwork for technical analysis. Early investors used fundamental analysis and historical trends to predict market movements. Over time, SMPD evolved by integrating quantitative methods, such as statistical models like auto-regressive integrated moving averages (ARIMA). The climb of computational finance in the 1980s and 1990s was a turning point, as artificial intelligence and neural networks began to be utilized, leading to a rapid expansion of SMPD techniques. Further, recent developments in AI-driven methods have improved the accuracy and sophistication of SMPD architectural models.[3–5] Stock markets like the NYSE and BSE let people buy and sell shares under regulated, fair rules. Brokers and market makers keep things running smoothly, while indices like the S&P 500 track overall performance.

Analysts are now using machine learning to understand trends and build better prediction models. New data sources are being added, like social media moods and search trends giving deeper insights. Real-time forecasting tools allow for analyzing live streams of data to support instant decision-making. Sentiment analysis, using NLP, helps gauge public and media sentiment toward specific stocks and sectors. Additionally, ethical AI and model explainability promote transparency and enhance investor confidence in predictive models. [7] Some well-known applications in India for stock market analysis are Groww, IndMoney, Moneycontrol, StockEdge, and ET Markets.

1.1 *Our contribution*

Our work involved thorough data preprocessing, including handling missing values, normalizing features, and encoding categorical data to enhance model accuracy. The dataset was carefully split into training, testing, and validation sets for fair evaluation. We developed five hybrid models combining traditional and advanced machine learning techniques and analyzed their results to compare performance and accuracy effectively.

1.2 *Article organization*

Section II reviews existing methods and their limitations. Section III explains the dataset and models used. Section IV details data preprocessing and hybrid model implementation. Section V presents experimental results and analysis, while Section VI concludes with key findings and future research directions.

1.3 *Literature review*

Various studies have explored stock price prediction using techniques like Linear Regression, LSTM, CNN, and hybrid models, combining sentiment analysis, historical data, and advanced ML methods to enhance accuracy and handle market complexity effectively Refer to Table 1.

Table 1. Literature review.

Ref	Dataset	Algorithm	Result
[20]	GOOGL, NKE daily prices	LSTM RNN	Loss values for 12, 25, 50, and 100 epochs
[12]	S&P 500 dataset	ELR-ML	R Square = 0.428, MSE = 9E+12
[18]	Apple, Samsung, and GE	Random forest with technical indicators	Accuracy: 80-99% for Apple, 85%+ for Apple, Samsung, GE. Outperforms SVM, logistic regression
[21]	Shanghai Composite Index (000001)	LASSO-LSTM, LASSO-GRU, PCA-LSTM, and PCA-GRU	LASSO-LSTM and LASSO-GRU outperform PCA-LSTM and PCA-GRU
[14]	S&P 500 stocks	ARIMA, LSTM	Hybrid ARIMA-LSTM outperformed other models
[13]	Global stock markets	Reservoir Computing	Outperformed EMD2FNN in NASDAQ, SSE
[10]	Vodacom news, tweets, prices	LDA, SVM, LSTM	Highest accuracy with LDA (96%)
[16]	KSE-100 daily closing prices	Hybrid Akima-EMD-LSTM	RMSE = 299.541, MAPE = 0.578
[17]	120 companies' prices	Extra Trees Classifier	Accuracy scores, no specific values
[8]	TAINIWALCHM, AGROPHOS data	Multiple algorithms	Ensemble RMSE = 2.0247, R2 = 0.9921
[15]	Various financial assets	Multiple deep learning models	Qualitative review
[19]	S&P BSE SENSEX and Nifty 50	HSTPF (CNN-based autoencoder)	Over 86% accuracy, nearly 80% during Black Swan events.

DOI: 10.1201/9781003798514-3

2 METHODOLOGY

This study utilizes historical S&P 500 data, including daily closing prices and trading volumes, to predict stock trends. Models like CNN, LSTM, GRU, BiLSTM, Transformers, Random Forest, and GARCH are applied to effectively capture complex patterns, temporal dependencies, and market volatility for accurate forecasting.

2.1 *Dataset*

The S&P 500 Historical Data dataset offers an extensive brief of the S&P 500 index's performance across 2,538 trading days, providing important insights into market trends and fluctuations. This dataset reflects the volatility and liquidity of the index over time, including key attributes such as date, opening price, high, low, and percentage change.

Table 2. Overview of dataset parameters.

Parameter	Type	Min	Max	Mean	Skewness
Date	Datetime	-	-	-	-
Price	Numeric (float)	1829.1	6001.35	3307.218	0.523837
Open	Numeric (float)	1833.4	6008.86	3306.667	0.524256
High	Numeric (float)	1847	6020.57	3324.26	0.518076
Low	Numeric (float)	1810.1	5988.25	3287.797	0.529679
Change %	Numeric (float)	-0.1198	0.0938	0.000503	-0.52302

2.2 *Regression models*

Time-series prediction can be challenging, but advanced machine learning and deep learning regression models can handle it well. They are able to capture complex patterns and long-term relationships in the data, which improves accuracy and overall performance.

2.2.1 *Convolutional neural network*

CNNs can find time-based patterns in financial data that other models struggle to look. They also work well with deep learning or ensemble Methods, leading to more accurate and reliable predictions.

2.2.2 *Long Short-Term memory*

Long short-term memory is a type of recurrent neural network (RNN) aimed at mitigating the vanishing gradient problem commonly encountered by traditional RNNs.

2.2.3 *Random forest*

Random forest is an ensemble learning method for classification, regression and other tasks that works by creating a multitude of decision trees during trainings.

2.2.4 *Generalized Auto Regressive Conditional Heteroskedasticity (GARCH)*

The model that is statistical for predicting and examining time-series data volatility, particularly in the financial markets. By proving changes and uncertainty, it boosts forecasting accuracy and helps models spot time-based volatility and market shifts.

2.2.5 *Gated Recurrent Unit*

GRUs are a simple version of LSTMs that handle sequential data efficiently with fewer parameters. They use update and reset gates to learn time-based patterns in data, which helps them perform well in tasks such as predicting stock market trends.

2.2.6 *Bidirectional LSTM*

BiLSTM reads data both forward and backward to get past and future patterns. It is great for stock predictions and other time-based tasks, and when combined with other models, it helps improve accuracy.

2.2.7 *Transformer with Attention Mechanism*

Transformers employ self-attention to capture long-range dependencies in sequences. Originally used for NLP now they are increasingly applied to time-series analysis due to their efficiency with large datasets.

Different hybrid models were built and tested in the research, and their parameter values are shown in Table 3.

3 PROPOSED METHODOLOGY

The research framework begins with proper data collection and organization, followed by preprocessing steps to clean, and prepare the data for training. Advanced models are then developed to identify patterns and produce accurate forecasts giving it a solid and trustworthy foundation.

3.1 *Data loading*

The dataset was imported using Python library. During the initial review, the first few rows were examined, the data types for each column were checked and understood.

3.2 *Hyperparameter tuning and validation strategy*

The model's performance and generalisability were improved via a methodical approach to hyperparameter adjustment. Three sets of the dataset were created: 15% for testing, 15% for validation, and 70% for training. Effective tuning and a detached assessment of each model's performance were made possible by this arrangement. Important hyperparameters were changed and optimised for each hybrid model, including the number of units in the LSTM, GRU, and BiLSTM layers, dropout rates, optimiser choices, convolution parameters (in the CNN layers), and the number of estimators (for Random Forest). These configurations are evident in Table 3, which provides a detailed breakdown of hyperparameter values for each model combination analysed in this study.

Table 3. Hybrid models parameter.

Model Combination	Parameter	Value
CNN + LSTM + RF	Filters (Conv1D Layer 1)	64
	Kernel Size (Conv1D Layer 1)	3
	Activation (Conv1D Layer 1)	ReLU
	LSTM Layer 1 Units	50
	LSTM Layer 2 Units	25
	Number of Estimators (Trees)	100
GARCH + LSTM	Log Returns	np.log(data[1:] / data [:-1])
	Model Type	GARCH (p=1, q=1)
	Volatility Output	Conditional volatility
	Input Shape	(60, 2)

(continued)

Table 3. Continued

Model Combination	Parameter	Value
	Number of LSTM Units	50
	Optimizer	Adam
LSTM + GRU	LSTM Layer 1 Units	50
	GRU Layer Units	50
	Dropout Rate (LSTM & GRU)	0.2
	Optimizer	Adam
LSTM + Transformer	Number of Units (LSTM Layer)	50
	Number of Heads (Transformer)	4
	Feed-forward Network (ff_dim)	32
	Dropout Rate (LSTM)	0.2
	Optimizer	Adam
BiLSTM + GRU	BiLSTM Layer Units	50
	GRU Layer Units	50
	Dropout Rate (BiLSTM & GRU)	0.2
	Optimizer	Adam

3.3 *Data preprocessing*

The following section outlines the specific preprocessing steps applied to the S&P 500 Historical Data.

- **Handling Missing Values:** The "Vol." column was removed due to excessive missing data to avoid unnecessary data retaining only key fields like Date, Price, Open, High, Low, and Change.
- **Formatting and Cleaning Columns:** Commas and special characters were removed from columns and the "%" symbol in "Change%" were removed to convert all values into proper numeric formats for analysis.
- **Change Date Format:** The Date column was converted to a standard date-time format and set as the index to enable smoother time-based analysis.
- **Remove Duplicates:** Duplicate rows were identified and deleted to maintain clean and reliable dataset.

3.4 *Proposed model*

A hybrid approach for Stock Market Price Prediction (SMPD) that combines Gated Recurrent Units (GRU) and Bidirectional Long Short-Term Memory (BiLSTM) effectively captures the intricate sequential connection that exists in historical stock data. A block diagram illustrating the phases of the suggested technique is shown in Figure 1.

As represented in block diagram, after the dataset is loaded and preprocessed, this research applied feature engineering to extract the best suitable feature for prediction, later this research applied multiple individual and hybrid models for prediction such as CNN, LSTM, BiLSTM, Attention model and hybrid of LSTM+CNN+RF, GARCH+LSTM, LSTM+Attention, LSTM+GRU, and BiLSTM+GRU. The BiLSTM+GRU hybrid provided the best results. Addresses the problem of the disappearance of the gradient, enabling the model to focus on significant market signals. The hybrid BiLSTM and GRU model is organised with an input layer, which is followed by a BiLSTM layer that records temporal relationships, a GRU layer to improve the predictions, and a dense output layer to forecast stock prices or categorisation labels.

This hybrid model used looks at both past and future market trends to give accurate predictions.

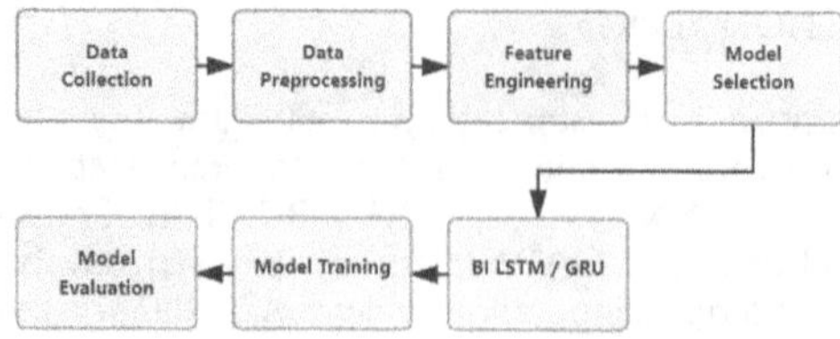

Figure 1. Block diagram of model.

Algorithm Workflow
Input: Preprocessed time-series data
Output: Predicted stock prices

1. Split data into Training (70%), Validation (15%), and Testing (15%) sets.
2. Normalization of the data.
3. Build the model:
   - Input layer
   - BiLSTM layer with 50 units
   - Dropout layer (0.2)
   - GRU layer with 50 units
   - Dropout layer (0.2)
4. Compile the model:
   - Loss: Mean Squared Error (MSE)
   - Optimizer: Adam
5. Train the model on the training set for 50 epochs, batch size 16.
6. Use the trained model to predict stock prices on the testing set
7. Check performance using RMSE, MAE, MAPE, and R^2

Return: Predicted values and performance metrics

4 RESULTS

The evaluation criteria are defined, followed by a comprehensive presentation of results. A comparison table illustrates how the method performs against existing approaches, highlighting its strengths and identifying potential areas for improvement.

4.1 *Evaluation parameters*

The description and formulations of the assessed parameters utilised for evaluating the effectiveness of the hybrid regression models described in the experiment are given in Table 4.

Table 4. Evaluation Metrics Formulae.

Parameter	Description	Formula
RMSE	Root Mean Squared Error - Assesses the average magnitude of error, disproportionately penalising larger errors compared to smaller ones.	$\text{RMSE} = \sqrt{\frac{1}{n}\sum_{i=1}^{n}(y_i - \widehat{y}_i)^2}$
MAE	Mean Absolute Error - Assesses the average magnitude of errors, treating all deviations uniformly irrespective of their direction	$\text{MAE} = \frac{1}{n}\sum_{i=1}^{n}\lvert y_i - \widehat{y}_i\rvert$
MAPE	Mean Absolute Percentage Error - Shows the error of prediction as a proportion of the values that were found.	$\text{MAPE} = \frac{1}{n}\sum_{i=1}^{n}\left\lvert\frac{y_i-\widehat{y}_i}{y_i}\right\rvert \times 100$
R-squared	Coefficient of Determination - Calculates the proportion of the variation in the dependent variable that may be predicted.	$R^2 = 1 - \frac{\sum_{i=1}^{n}(y_i-\widehat{y}_i)^2}{\sum_{i=1}^{n}(y_i-\bar{y}_i)^2}$ where $\bar{y} = \frac{1}{n}\sum_{i=1}^{n} y_i$

4.2 *Detailed obtained result*

This study combines several models of CNN, LSTM, BiLSTM, GRU, GARCH, and Transformer-based attention. Among all approaches, the BiLSTM-GRU hybrid performed the best. Table 5 presents a detailed comparison of evaluation metrics for all baseline and hybrid models. Traditional models provide decent prediction accuracy, but hybrid models can capture more complex temporal and volatility patterns. The proposed BiLSTM+GRU model outperforms all others, achieving the lowest RMSE (0.0125), MAE (0.0101), MAPE (0.83%), and the highest R^2 (0.9901), demonstrating its strong predictive power and robustness.

Table 5. Results by different models.

Ref	RMSE	MAE	MAPE	R-squared
LSTM	303.87	246.00	4.78%	0.7620
CNN	242.25	220.11	4.48%	0.8487
RF	494.28	314.63	5.79%	0.3703
BiLSTM	260.06	213.18	4.16%	0.8257
GRU	295.67	239.99	4.67%	0.7747
LSTM+CNN+RF	0.0285/ 63.12	0.0234/ 51.88	1.07%	0.9897
GARCH+LSTM	0.0145/ 60.61	0.0107/ 44.63	1.28%	0.9732
LSTM+ Transformer (Attention)	0.0169/ 70.69	0.0135/ 56.52	1.15%	0.9871
LSTM+GRU	0.0151/ 63.14	0.0111/ 46.38	1.65%	0.9897
BiLSTM+GRU	0.0125/ 52.17	0.0101/ 42.21	0.83%	0.9901

A comparison was made with three existing research papers illustrated in Table 6. The concerning performance metrics endorse BiLSTM + GRU as being robust and accurate compared with existing algorithms available in the literature.

Table 6. Comparison of existing approaches vs proposed approach.

Ref	RMSE	MAE	MAPE	R-squared
[22]	347.46	262.42	1.03%	0.83
[23]	53.91	39.79	Not specified	0.99
[24]	0.0407	0.0313	Not specified	0.8950
BiLSTM + GRU (Our)	0.0125/ 52.17	0.0101/ 42.21	0.83%	0.9901

4.3 *Statistical significance testing*

An F-test compared the prediction errors of the BiLSTM +GRU hybrid model with a standard LSTM. The F-ratio of 0.07 and p-value of 0.02 (at a 5% significance level) show that the BiLSTM+GRU's error variance (23,006,771.59) is much lower than the LSTM's (99,752,994.21). This statistically confirms the hybrid model's superior accuracy, stability, and consistency in predictions.

4.4 *Curves*

This graph compares actual vs. predicted price movements using a BiLSTM+GRU neural network model over time from 2022 to 2025, as depicted in Figure 2.

Figure 2. Validation and test predictions vs actual(BiLSTM + GRU).

4.5 *Regression graph*

A regression graph showing the relationship between expected and actual values is shown in Figure 3. Dots close to the diagonal line indicate accurate predictions.

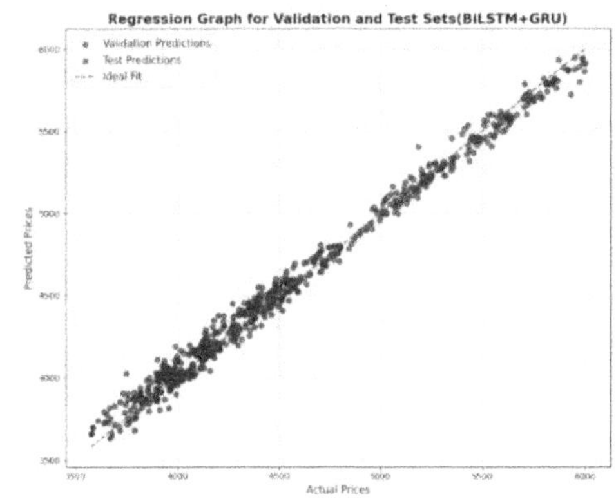

Figure 3. Regression graph (BiLSTM+GRU).

4.6 *Convergence curve*

The training and validation loss decreases over epochs in a convergence graph, illustrating the model's learning process. The model is approaching optimal performance, as indicated by the flattening of the curve. Figure 4 displays the BiLSTM-GRU's performance in terms of loss convergence.

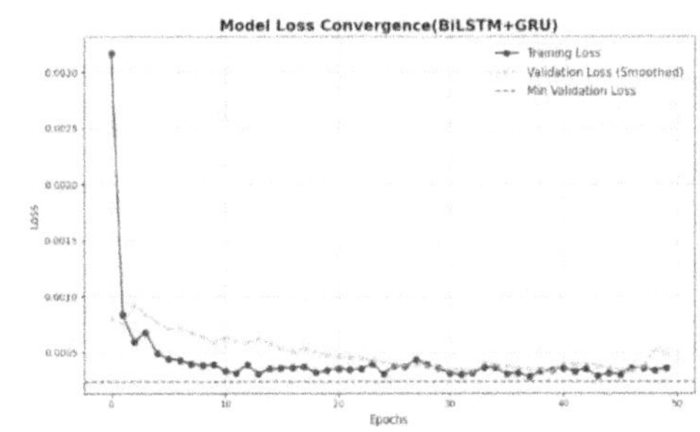

Figure 4. Model loss convergence (BiLSTM+GRU).

5 CONCLUSION

Stock price prediction is key to financial analysis, and using statistical and machine learning methods can make it more accurate. This study aims to improve forecasts to reduce financial risk and help investors make smarter decisions. Performance of model was with R^2 of 0.9991, MAE of 0.0101, and RMSE of 0.0125, showing the model's accuracy. In practice, investors and financial institutions can use this model to predict stock market. In the future it can integrate real-time data from APIs like Yahoo Finance and cloud deployments for scalable, real-time forecasting.

ACKNOWLEDGEMENT

We would like to thank **Manipal University Jaipur** for giving us the chance to work on this project where we had access to their guidance that helped us move our work into the right direction. We truly appreciate being part of a place that encourages learning, creativity, and new ideas.

REFERENCES

[1] Z. Li, H. Yu, J. Xu, J. Liu, Y. Mo, *Innovations in Applied Engineering and Technology* pp. 1–6 (2023)
[2] M. Vijh, D. Chandola, V.A. Tikkiwal, A. Kumar, *Procedia computer science* 167, 599 (2020)
[3] W. Khan, M.A. Ghazanfar, M.A. Azam, A. Karami, K.H. Alyoubi, A.S. Alfakeeh, *Journal of Ambient Intelligence and Humanized Computing* pp. 1–24 (2022)
[4] A. Subasi, F. Amir, K. Bagedo, A. Shams, A. Sarirete, *Procedia Computer Science* 194, 173(2021)
[5] T. Banyen, *Journal of Business and Economic Options* 5(2), 1 (2022)
[6] S. Gong, S. Liu, D.D. Sun, *arXiv preprint arXiv*:2306.02764 (2023)
[7] O. Chernysh, O. Smishko, Y. Koverninska, M. Prokopenko, T. Pistunov, *Economic Affairs* 69(3), 1493 (2024)
[8] G. Sonkavde, D.S. Dharrao, A.M. Bongale, S.T. Deokate, D. Doreswamy, S.K. Bhat, *International Journal of Financial Studies* 11(3), 94 (2023)
[9] C. Fjellström, in 2022 *IEEE International Conference on Big Data* (Big Data) (IEEE, 2022), pp. 3496–3504
[10] S.T. Mndawe, B.S. Paul, W. Doorsamy, *Applied Sciences* 12(2), 719 (2022)
[11] S.M. Carta, S. Consoli, L. Piras, A.S. Podda, D.R. Recupero, *IEEE Access* 9, 30193 (2021)
[12] J.M. Sangeetha, K.J. Alfia, Measurement: *Sensors* 31, 100950 (2024)
[13] W.J. Wang, Y. Tang, J. Xiong, Y.C. Zhang, *Expert Systems with Applications* 178, 115022 (2021)
[14] D. Xiao, J. Su, *Scientific Programming* 2022(1), 4758698 (2022)
[15] C. Zhang, N.N.A. Sjarif, R. Ibrahim, *Wiley Interdisciplinary Reviews: Data Mining and Knowledge Discovery* 14(1), e1519 (2024)
[16] M. Ali, D.M. Khan, H.M. Alshanbari, A.A.A.H. El-Bagoury, *Applied Sciences* 13(3), 1429(2023)
[17] A. Pagliaro, *Electronics* 12(21), 4551 (2023)
[18] J. Zheng, D. Xin, Q. Cheng, M. Tian, L. Yang, *arXiv preprint* arXiv:2402.17194 (2024)
[19] S. Bhanja, A. Das, *Innovations in Systems and Software Engineering* 20(2), 121 (2024)
[20] A. Moghar, M. Hamiche, *Procedia Computer Science* 170, 1168 (2020)
[21] Y. Gao, R. Wang, E. Zhou, *Scientific Programming* 2021(1), 4055281 (2021)
[22] S.K. Lakshminarayanan, J.P. McCrae, in *AICS* (2019), pp. 446–457
[23] Z. Feng, *Highlights in Business, Economics and Management* 21, 38 (2023)
[24] J. Kim, H.S. Kim, S.Y. Choi, *Axioms* 12(9), 835 (2023)

Advancement in Engineering and Science – Goyal et al. (Eds)

Enhancing Agricultural Sustainability Through Deep Learning: A Study on Image-Based Plant Disease Detection and Classification

Rupali Maske and B. Bharathit
Department of CSE, Sathyabama Institute of Science and Technology, Chennai, Tamil Nadu, India

ABSTRACT: Plants are vital to agriculture as they provide essential resources, including food, oxygen, and raw materials. To protect global agriculture, this study investigates the application of deep learning for automated plant disease detection. The study uses cutting-edge CNN architectures, such as VGG-19, Xception, MobileNetV2, and DenseNet201, to analyze a dataset of almost 85,000 + photos from Kaggle to identify 38 plant diseases that affect important crops like apples, blueberries, and cherries. A promising approach to effective disease management is provided by the suggested model, which exhibits high accuracy in differentiating between healthy and diseased plants. This advancement in image analysis and machine learning has the potential to greatly improve global food security and agricultural sustainability.

Keywords: Plant Diseases, CNN, VGG, Deep learning, MobileNetV2, DenseNet201

1 INTRODUCTION

Plant diseases pose a danger to global agricultural output, causing huge financial losses and negatively impacting the well-being of both people and animals. These diseases are responsible for roughly 40% of agricultural losses, which underscores the significance of taking prompt action. Plant disease detection and treatment in a timely way is vital for enhancing agricultural production and supporting economic growth in countries where agriculture makes up a large percentage of the national economy. Manual inspections are a poor technique for keeping track of plant health and addressing associated diseases, particularly in underdeveloped countries. Nowadays, most apple leaf conditions are identified by experienced professionals who examine each leaf independently. However, because there are numerous leaves on a single tree, this manual screening method is complex and could result in errors, particularly when it comes to closely related leaf diseases. Bangladesh puts a high premium on corn growing because of its enormous export potential and wide farmer appeal. Despite being incredibly nutritious and having numerous health benefits, grapes may acquire black rot, especially in warm, humid environments. The entire grape harvest is being endangered by this lethal disease, which obliterates leaves, shoots, stems, tendrils, and fruit. It's vital to properly monitor and combat black rot.

Oranges help decrease cholesterol and balance blood sugar, which helps prevent cardiovascular disease. They are also a terrific source of vitamin C and other vital nutrients. Additionally, they contain roughly 55 milligrams of calcium or 6% of the daily needed amount. But they may also become infected with a broad spectrum of fungi, particularly in warm, humid areas, which may result in the fatal Huangbing disease. A key food crop in Bangladesh, potatoes are crucial to our nourishment but are badly damaged by plant diseases such as early blight, which may be damaging to human health. On the other hand, fresh tomatoes boost meal taste and are a fundamental economic demand. They also provide health benefits. Tomatoes are a fantastic source of antioxidants, which are crucial for general health. Strawberries help decrease the risk of diabetes, heart disease, cancer, and stroke due to their high vitamin C and antioxidant content. However, a prevalent disease that affects many strawberry cultivars is leaf scorch. Blueberries are recognized for their brilliant color and well- balanced sweetness. They are considered a superfood with antioxidant benefits. Benefits from these antioxidant-rich blueberries include increased immunity, decreased stress, enhanced cognitive function, and antiinflammatory characteristics. Nevertheless, the fruit's volume and flavor could be affected by infections like anthracnose and mummy berries. Cherries are a pleasant and nutrient-dense culinary component that may be introduced to a diet in more ways than one. Their high vitamin content helps to decrease inflammation and promote a stronger immune system. A typical summertime pleasure, peaches are also rich in vitamins, minerals, and antioxidants that help healthy skin, digestion, and hydration. Peach trees may suffer from ailments like bacterial spots. Peppers are a highly flexible food with a range of culinary uses due to their high antioxidant and vitamin C content as well as their immune-boosting effects. Even though they are resistant to ailments like powdery mildew and bacterial leaf spots, it is still necessary to maintain them healthy. Raspberries are widely known for their anti-inflammatory and cardiovascular benefits. Diseases, however, may have an unfavorable influence on the leaves' health and consequently limit their availability. Soybeans' high nutritional content and capacity to fix nitrogen make them crucial for both sustainable agriculture and high- protein diets. Low in calories and bountiful in nutrients, squash is a cornerstone of many culinary civilizations. Squash crops, such as butternut, acorn, and zucchini, are sensitive to powdery mildew, which underscores the importance of disease management in the production of squash. This study addresses the need for improved plant disease classification by leveraging a diverse Kaggle dataset of 87,867 images, incorporating 14 cropping methods under 38 conditions [1]. While prior work [2] demonstrated the effectiveness of Mo- bileNet CNN on the Field Plant dataset, our proposed CNN architecture outperformed pre-trained models like VGG-19, Xception, MobileNetV2, and DenseNet201, achieving remark- able accuracy. These findings highlight the significance of the proposed approach in advancing precise and reliable plant disease detection. The organization of this paper is outlined as follows: Section 2 provides a comprehensive review of relevant literature, offering an overview of prior research on the topic. Section 3 outlines the proposed methodology, detailing the techniques applied in this study. Section 4 focuses on the presentation and analysis of experimental results. Finally, Section 5 discusses the study's findings, conclusions, proposed solutions, and potential directions for future work.

DOI: 10.1201/9781003798514-4

2 RELATED WORK

Images are sorted into categories using machine learning (ML) algorithms based on common information. They typi- cally involve pre-processing feature extraction and classifica- tion, with super- vised or unsupervised algorithms. Researchers are increasingly using Deep Learning (DL) algorithms to rec- ognize and extract data from submitted photos. Both machine learning and deep learning approaches can be used to solve various research topics. Numerous studies have been con- ducted on leaf disease detection, examining various methods for identifying and categorizing leaf diseases. Singh et al.'s study [3] focuses on the deployment of remote sensor networks to bolster defenses against highly sophisticated attacks. Their model performed better than previously utilized techniques. Interestingly, they deployed an Internet of Things (IoT)-based pollution control system and reached an astonishing accuracy of 99.62% Zhu et al. [4] employed an approach that incorpo- rated Vision Transformer and Multiscale Convolution. Their technique enhanced accuracy by 0.06% and 0.08% , respectively, on the PlantVillage and Apple Leaf Pathology datasets. These findings illustrate the high identification performance of our model for a considerable number of challenging pictures, even with the inclusion of multiscale CNN layers. With an incredible 99.82% accuracy, Gerdan et al. [5] established a note- worthy milestone—the best accuracy reported in the literature.

Their deep learning application, which was concentrated on the diagnosis of tomato illnesses, made the maximum use of samples. CNN-based model techniques for the identification of tomato leaf ailments were provided by Elhassouny et al. [6] employing 7176 pictures. Their distinctive strategy improved the categorization of tomato leaf infections by 88.4%. The authors of [7] created an approach to combat grapevine yellows that employed Otsu Threshold for segmentation and CNN for automatic feature extraction. They produced amazing results utilizing six neural network architectures: ResNet-101, ResNet-50, AlexNet, SqueezeNet, GoogLeNet, and Inception V3, with sensitivity and specificity of 9.96% and 99.40%, respectively. With a sensitivity of 90.97% and a specificity of 97.42%, Yang et al.'s [8] examination of identifying plant diseases using classical machine-learning approaches proved the performance of the SVM model. Deep neural networks and transfer learning algorithms for plant identification were offered by Ghazi et al. [9] utilizing GoogLeNet, AlexNet, and VGGNet. They discovered that, on a thousand plant species, their study had an 80 accuracy rate. Bashish et al. [10] addressed cotton mold, late smut, and early smut differentiation in their research by utilizing BPNN for disease classification, CCM for textural feature classification, and K-means-based segmentation. Their study has contributed to the discovery and classification of microscopic white leaf disease, which fits into one of the six disease classes. In the realm of cotton leaf disease diagnostics, Bhimte et al. [11] used K-means segmentation to identify the hazardous area in a leaf shot. After that, crucial traits like color and texture were categorized outside of the partitioned region, providing an incredible 98.46% classification accuracy. Hossain et al. [12] created an image-processing method that allowed them to detect and diagnose algal leaf diseases and brown blight in tea plants. Their technique provided results that were over 90 accurate, employing eleven criteria to serve as a support vector machine classifier throughout the classification step. The R- CNN mask was advocated by Juyal et al. [13] as a means to improve and speed the process of detecting pathogens in plant leaves and allow early disease detection. The average accuracy rate that was reported was 82%. DeChant et al. [14] researched the disease known as Northern Leaf Blight (NLB), which impairs maize output. To boost the accuracy of auto- matically recognizing unwell plants from field images, they trained a huge number of CNNs using deep learning models. Plant disease identification depends largely on deep learning models, as indicated by Fujita et al. [15]. Their empirical study studied several alterations in leaves under several unique and different settings. Aziz et al. [16] effectively collected discriminant information from a computer vision system for plant disease diagnosis by employing Local Tri-directional Patterns (LTriDP) from a range of leaf photos. The multiclass support vector machines (SVM) of the system got an accuracy rate of 94 utilizing a five-class tomato leaf dataset. The approach integrated LTriDP for feature extraction with SVM and Content- Based Image Retrieval (CBIR) algorithms. The technology allows tomato plants to be detected as ill early on, due to a library of 1882 photos. Ramesh et al. [17] used Random Forests to differentiate between healthy and dam- aged papaya leaves. The process involved creating a dataset, creating classifiers, extracting features using the Histogram of Oriented Gradient (HOG) approach, and categorizing in- formation. The researchers achieved 70% accuracy using 160 papaya leaf pictures, suggesting that BOVW could perform better with additional local features like SURF, DENSE, and SIFT. The research [18] employed a variety of processes to identify macronutrient deficits in chili plants, including feature extraction, pre- processing, picture capture, and SVM-based classification. In the research, which attempted to improve the SVM kernel and hyperparameters for a given color channel, HSL was proven to be the most accurate color space model. The polynomial kernel exceeded other SVM kernels in terms of accuracy, coming in at 97.76%, which proved that it helped diagnose nutritional inadequacies in chili plants. Using a Con- volutional Neural Network (CNN) approach, banana disease outbreaks were identified in [19] using leaf photos from the Kaggle Banana Leaf Disease Dataset. With an accuracy of 94, the model ResNet50 excelled in earlier studies and exceeded expectations. The accuracy of model VGG-19 was 91% With an 89 F1-Score, 94% accuracy, 88% precision, and 91% recall, the ResNet50 model emerged as the top model. In [20], so- phisticated deep learning techniques like convolutional neural networks and Vision Transformers (ViT) were used to detect tomato disease at the early leaf stage. 54,309 out of the 18,345 tomato pictures in the PlantVillage. In addition to developing two ViT architectures, the ViT-2 model defeated the preceding deep CNN models. The study exceeded prior state-of-the-art results. 96.7%, 98.52%, 99.1%, and 99.7% high accuracy rates were reached. Herok et al. [21] used a heterogeneous dataset of 6,158 samples from multiple sources to construct a transfer learning-based approach for cotton leaf disease identification. The greatest model was discovered by the investigation using deep transfer learning methods, and it was 95.02% accurate. A comprehensive class-wise performance and error analysis showed the capabilities of the model, which was applied to a healthy class and seven distinct forms of cotton leaf diseases. The study [22] included the creation of a sophisticated deep- learning model to accurately detect and categorize coffee leaf ailments. The model was trained using a dataset of 1,120 photos sourced from Kaggle and Wolaita Sodo agricultural research. The approaches of deep learning and transfer learning were applied using ResNet50 and MobileNet. With an incredible 99.89% accuracy rate, ResNet50 identified between brown eye spots, wilt, rust, and healthy leaves. Using images of tomato plant leaves, Khan et al. [23] created a method for recognizing and diagnosing tomato diseases. The technology converts RGB images into higher-quality forms by segmenting leaf components using image processing methods. Features from the post-segmentation Histogram of Oriented Gradients (HOG) were used to train six machine- learning models. The most effective classifier was Support Vector Machines (SVM), which recognized damaged tomato plant leaves with a 92% accuracy rate. The efficacy of the Neuro-Fuzzy Network- based Hybrid Deep Learning (NFNHDL) in diagnosing and categorizing disorders in rice plants was shown by Koshariya et al.'s [24] study. Two pre- processed datasets worth of statistics, convolutional neural networks, and textures were put into the model. Using data augmentation methods, the algorithm recognized rice illnesses with 96.9% accuracy on a dataset of 1006 photos. To diagnose tomato plant problems without noise reduction, the study [25] employs a pre-trained VGG16 model, which yields a 95.5% accuracy rate and 100 classification performance. The Plant Village dataset is employed by the model, which achieves 99 top-2 accuracy in recognizing healthy from sick plants. Our major objective is to construct an accurate model that can periodically recognize, categorize, and diagnose plant ailments without the intervention of a human utilizing state-of-the-art deep learning technologies. Furthermore, the aim is to show innovative methodologies that, when paired with dataset sizes of the same or equivalent, give greater diagnostic accuracy than present approaches.

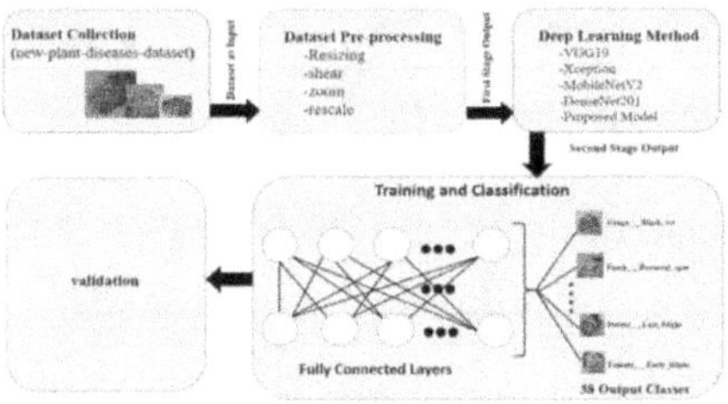

Figure 1. System architecture.

3 METHODOLOGY

Machine learning approaches that imitate the composition and operations of the human brain are known as neural networks. Often termed artificial neurons or" neurons," this design is made up of numerous connected nodes piled one on top of the other. To uncover subtle patterns and connections in the data, neural networks may be trained utilizing input from a labeled dataset. Our study in this field is motivated by two key goals: first, creating approaches to increase classification accuracy; and second, simultaneously lowering the inherent complexity of neural networks. The classification of plant diseases forms the basis for our innovative approach.

To achieve these objectives, we use a customized Convolutional Neural Network (CNN) structure that utilizes photos depicting both diseased and undamaged plant conditions. Figure 1 depicts the delicate interaction between the neural network, the dataset, and the particular job of identifying plant diseases within the larger context of our inquiry.

3.1 *Dataset*

The Plant Disease Dataset is freely available via the open source research platform Kaggle. It comprises roughly 87,867 properly documented pho- tos of both healthy and damaged leaves from a range of fruits and vegetables. Photographs of apple, blueberry, cherry, corn, grape, orange, peach, pepper, potato, raspberry, soybean, squash, strawberry, and tomato plants exhibit a vast variety of plant species in the collection. It's interesting to observe that there are disparities in the quantity of images in each separate class in the dataset. Figure 2 demonstrates the homo- geneous distribution of images obtained during the training andvalidation stages.Using the whole dataset, the original directory structure is preserved while generating an "80/20" training and validation set.

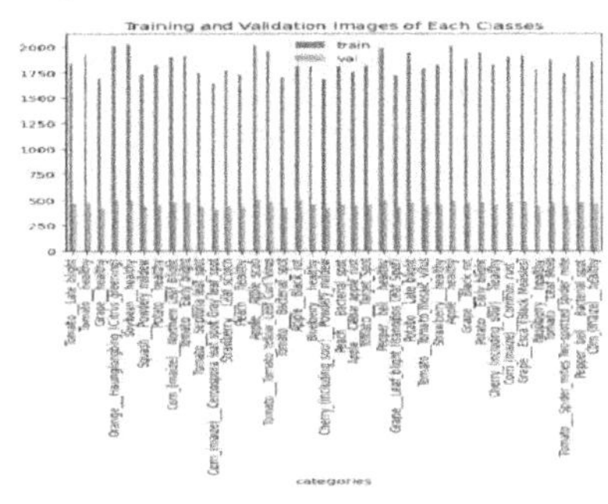

Figure 2. Each class image.

3.2 *Xception*

Chollet [26] invented Xception, a Convolutional Neural Network (CNN) architecture that has gained prominence cause of its remarkable performance in different computer vision applications. Its significant technical innovation is the use of depth-wise separable convolutions, which boost feature extraction efficiency and make it more expressive. Xception features several convolutional and depth-wise separable convolutional layers, producing an efficient and productive network. It performs better on benchmark datasets like ImageNet in tasks like object detection, semantic segmentation, and image classification. It also has promise in medical imaging, where it assists in analyzing and diagnosing illnesses and anomalies. Xception's efficiency-driven architecture, constructed using depth-wise separable convolutions, assures constant performance, making it a great tool for diverse computer vision applications and research projects.

3.3 *VGG-19*

Plant disease image categorization may be efficiently com- pleted with the aid of the powerful VGG-19 architecture [27], which comprises 19 layers of Convolutional Neural Networks. For data efficiency, max pooling and ReLU activation layers are used. As shown in Figure 3, this recovers complex features and increases accuracy because of its depth [28]. A popular alternative in entomology and agriculture, the architecture's hierarchical structure helps identify plant diseases. Plant disease detection benefits substantially from its computational power and application.

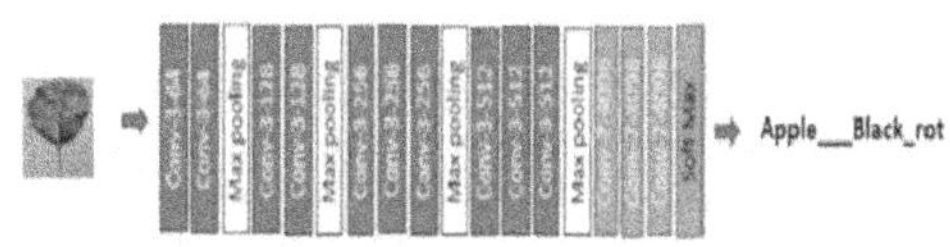

Figure 3. VGG 19 architecture.

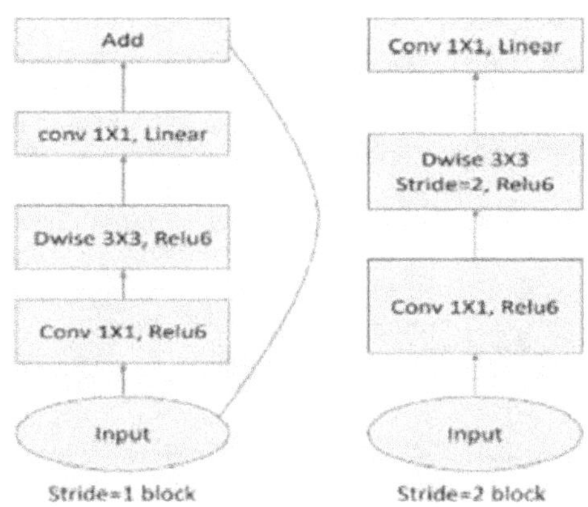

Figure 4. Summary of the MobileNetV2 architecture.

3.4 *MobileNetV2*

An upgraded version of MobileNet, known as Mo- MobileNetV2, incorporates several new ways to further cut processing costs and enhance accuracy. MobileNetV2 is a network that minimizes parameters and increases accuracy by employing shortcut connections, inverted residuals, and linear bot- bottlenecks. It utilizes depth-wise separable convolutions to both enhance and compress channel counts, and it has 53 layers.

To enhance information flow and facilitate gradient propagation, a skip connection (Figure 4) is presented. Additionally, the approach incorporates linear bottlenecks, which decrease the number of input channels before depth-wise convolution, and substitutes the usual ReLU activation function with the Swish activation function. Accuracy.

3.5 *DenseNet*

To solve gradient-related issues, maximize feature utilization, promote feature reuse, and utilize fewer parameters, the Direct Dense Convolutional Network (DenseNet) is a convolutional neural network with 201 layers [29]. Unlike normal convolutional neural networks (CNNs), which have L layers and display L relationships, it generates direct connections between layers via a feed- forward flow. 224 x 224 picture input size is utilized by DenseNet-201, a pre-trained network trained on a huge dataset. Filter convolution, batch normalization, and ReLU activation are integrated with every layer of DenseNet-201. Within each block, a batch normalization of an input matrix consisting of picture pixels is conducted to reduce overfitting. When ReLU is triggered, values are modified; untouched and negative values are set to zero. Convolutionis used to process the matrix image by multiplying it by a convolution matrix and filter, which produces the previously treated matrix values.

4 PROPOSED CNN ARCHITECTURE

The ReLU activation function is commonly employed in image processing. Each of the five convolutional layers in the model has a max pooling associated with it. A visual illus- tration of the recommended CNN network design is provided in Figure 5. In this design, complicated network components such as maximum pooling, dropouts, convolution layers, and classification layers are carefully interwoven. Specifically, a series of convolutional and max pooling layers perform won- ders as feature extractors, improving the network's capacity to detect subtle patterns. This study established the architecture through a systematic examination of various layers across different time frames concerning the dataset. Additionally, the optimizer and activation functions were rigorously evaluated to identify the optimal CNN architecture. Unlike pre-trained models, which proved inadequate due to their extensive layer- ing, custom tuning of the architecture during each execution significantly enhanced the performance of the proposed CNN architecture. This specific combination highlights how effec- tively the network can discover important traits necessary for a correct diagnosis of plant diseases.

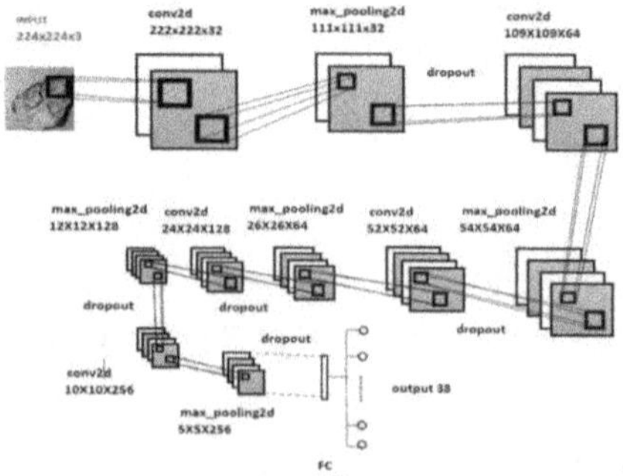

Figure 5. Proposed CNN system architecture.

5 RESULTS AND DISCUSSION

The dataset utilized in this research contains 17,572 photographs for validation and 70,295 images for training. The investigation included five distinct models, namely Xception, VGG-19, MobileNetV2, DenseNet201, and our proposed CNN architectural model. These models exhibited comparable accuracy rates, as seen in Table 1.

Table 1. Model accuracy comparison.

	Accuracy		
Sr.No	*Model Name*	*Model Accuracy*	*Validation Accuracy*
1	Proposed Model	97.65%	96.72%
2	DenseNet	69.82%	95.48%
3	Mobile Net	96.29%	93.76%
4	Xception	93.33%	91.56%
5	VGG	86.11%	87.99%

We applied our proposed CNN architecture to the new plant disease dataset and achieved exceptional results. VGG- 19 reached a validation accuracy of 87.99 after 20 training epochs, with the loss decreasing from 1.2188 to 0.4036. Xception achieved 88.60 validation accuracy in just four epochs, with the loss starting at 0.7028 and reducing to 0.1984. MobileNetV2 showed moderate stability, attaining 93.76 validation accuracy and a loss reduction from 0.4633 to 0.1157. Despite occasional fluctuations, DenseNet201 achieved a validation accuracy of 95.48 with a final loss of 0.1005. Our proposed CNN model outperformed all these pre-trained ar- chitectures, starting with a loss of 1.2307 and ending at just 0.0787, while achieving the highest validation accuracy of 96.72. Notably, its performance during the 12th epoch surpassed all other models. As illustrated in Figure 6, our model consistently outperforms other pre-trained networks in both training and validation phases, demonstrating superior accuracy. The broad applicability of these models significantly aids in identifying diseases across various essential crops, offering substantial benefits to farmers and the agricultural sector.

Text heads organize the topics on a relational, hierarchical basis. For example, the paper title is the primary Use footnotes sparingly (or not at all) and place them at the bottom of the column on the page on which they are referenced. Use Times 8-point type, single-spaced. To help your readers, avoid using footnotes altogether and include necessary peripheral observations in the text (within parentheses, if you prefer, as in this sentence).

6 CONCLUSION AND FUTURE DIRECTIONS

To be able to enhance output quality and productivity, plant diseases must be diagnosed in their budding phases. TheXception, VGG-19, MobileNetV2, DenseNet201, and the recommended CNN architecture have all been extensively analyzed. This detailed analysis indicates how much more effective our proposed technique is. In contrast with other models that employ various pre-trained networks, our model displays high accuracy. The dataset utilized for training and evaluation showed impressive accuracy in differentiating be- tween healthy and diseased plants; nevertheless, the model's generalizability to new data, varied climatic circumstances, and different disease symptoms may be restricted. More val- idation is required for the model's effectiveness in real-world settings where variables like sunlight, plant kinds, and disease stages may vary. In addition, training deep learning models takes a lot of time and computer resources, particularly for complicated CNN structures. However, using this paradigm on mobile devices offers various advantages, especially given how vital it is to make precise disease findings. If farmers could snap a photo of a plant with their phones and send it to a server,the diagnosis of the disease would happen more quickly. The server would then analyze and categorize the diseases on its own, communicating the findings and suggested treatments to the smartphone.

REFERENCES

[1] Vipin Kumar, "New Plant Diseases Dataset," *Kaggle,* (2018). [Online].Available: https://www.kaggle.com/datasets/vipoooool/new-plant- diseases-dataset. [Accessed: Sep. 13, 2023].

[2] E. Moupojou *et al.*, (2023). "FieldPlant: A Dataset of Field Plant Images for Plant Disease Detection and Classification With Deep Learning," *IEEE Access*, vol. 11, pp. 35398–35410, doi: 10.1109/ACCESS.2023.3263042.

[3] G. Singh and K.K. Yogi, (2023). "Performance evaluation of plant leaf disease detection using deep learning models," *Archives of Phytopathology and Plant Protection*, vol. 56, no. 3, pp. 209–233, Feb. 2023, doi: 10.1080/03235408.2023.2183792.

[4] Zhu D., J. Tan, C. Wu, K. Yung, and A.W.H. Ip, (Jun. 2023). "Crop Disease Identification by Fusing Multiscale Convolution and Vision Transformer," *Sensors*, vol. 23, no. 13, p. 6015, doi: 10.3390/s23136015.

[5] Gerdan D., C. Koç, and M. Vatandaş, (Nov. 2022) "Diagnosis of Tomato Plant Diseases Using Pre-Trained Architectures and A Proposed Convolutional Neural Network Model," *Tarım Bilimleri Dergisi*, doi: 10.15832/ankutbd.957265.

[6] Elhassouny A. and F. Smarandache, (Jul. 2019) "Smart mobile application torecognize tomato leaf diseases using Convolutional Neural Networks," in *2019 International Conference of Computer Science and Renewable Energies (ICCSRE)*, IEEE, pp. 1–4. doi: 10.1109/ICCSRE.2019.8807737.

[7] Cruz *et al.*, (Feb. 2019). "Detection of grapevine yellows symptoms in Vitis vinifera L. with artificial intelligence," *Comput Electron Agric,* vol. 157, pp. 63–76, doi: 10.1016/j.compag.2018.12.028.

[8] Yang X. and T. Guo, (Mar. 2017). "Machine learning in plant disease research," *European Journal of BioMedical Research,* vol. 3, no. 1, p. 6, doi: 10.18088/ejbmr.3.1.2017.pp6-9.

[9] Mehdipour Ghazi M., B. Yanikoglu, and E. Aptoula, (Apr. 2017). "Plant identification using deep neural networks via optimization of transfer learning parameters," *Neurocomputing*, vol. 235, pp. 228–235, doi: 10.1016/j.neucom.2017.01.018.

[10] Al Bashish D., M. Braik, and S. Bani-Ahmad, (Jan. 2011). "Detection and Classification of Leaf Diseases using K-means-based Segmentation and Neural-networks-based Classification," *Information Technology Journal*, vol. 10, no. 2, pp. 267–275, doi: 10.3923/itj.2011.267.275.

[11] Bhimte N.R. and V.R. Thool, (Jun. 2018). "Diseases Detection of Cotton LeafSpot Using Image Processing and SVM Classifier," in *2018 Second International Conference on Intelligent Computing and Control Systems (ICICCS)*, IEEE, pp. 340–344. doi: 10.1109/ICCONS.2018.8662906.

[12] Juyal P. and S. Sharma, (Dec. 2020). "Detecting the Infectious Area Along with Disease Using Deep Learning in Tomato Plant Leaves," in *2020 3rd International Conference on Intelligent Sustainable Systems (ICISS)*, IEEE, pp. 328–332. doi: 10.1109/ICISS49785.2020.9316108.

[13] Hossain S., R.M. Mou, M.M. Hasan, S. Chakraborty, and M.A. Razzak, "Recognition and detection of tea leaf's diseases using support vector machine," in *2018 IEEE 14th International Colloquium on Signal Processing & Its Applications (CSPA)*, IEEE, Mar. 2018, pp. 150–154. doi: 10.1109/CSPA.2018.8368703.

[14] DeChant S. *et al.*, (Nov. 2017), "Automated Identification of Northern Leaf Blight- Infected Maize Plants from Field Imagery Using Deep Learning," *Phytopathology*, vol. 107, no. 11, pp. 1426–1432, doi: 10.1094/PHYTO-11-16-0417-R.

[15] Fujita E., Y. Kawasaki, H. Uga, S. Kagiwada, and H. Iyatomi, (Dec. 2016). "Basic Investigation on a Robust and Practical Plant Diagnostic System," in *2016 15th IEEE International Conference on Machine Learning and Applications (ICMLA),* IEEE, pp. 989–992. doi: 10.1109/ICMLA.2016.0178.

[16] Aziz S., M. Bashir, O. Mughal, M.U. Khan, and A. Khan, (Oct. 2019). "Image Pattem Classification for Plant Disease Identification using Local Tri-directional Features," in *2019 IEEE 10th Annual Information Technology, Electronics and Mobile Communication Conference (IEMCON)*, IEEE, pp. 0973–0978. doi: 10.1109/IEMCON.2019.8936236.

[17] Ramesh S. *et al.*, "Plant Disease Detection Using Machine Learning,"*in 2018 International Conference on Design Innovations for 3Cs Compute Communicate Control (ICDI3C)*, IEEE, Apr. 2018, pp. 41– 45. doi: 10.1109/ICDI3C.2018.00017.

[18] Rahadiyan C, S. Hartati, Wahyono, A.P. Nugroho, and L. Sutiarso, (2022). "*Classification of Macronutrient Deficiency in Chili Leaves using Support Vector Machine,*" . doi: 10.2991/978-94-6463-086-2_77.

[19] Ilham Rahmana Syihad, Muhammad Rizal, Zamah Sari, and Yufis Azhar, "CNN Method to Identify the Banana Plant Diseases based on Banana Leaf Images by Giving Models of ResNet50 and VGG-19," *Jurnal RESTI (Rekayasa Sistem dan Teknologi Informasi)*, vol. 7, no. 6, pp. 1309–1318, Dec. 2023, doi: 10.29207/resti.v7i6.5000.

[20] Boukabouya R.A., A. Moussaoui, and M. Berrimi, (Nov. 2022). "Vision Transformer Based Models for Plant Disease Detection and Diagnosis," in *2022 5th International Symposium on Informatics and its Applications (ISIA)*, IEEE, pp. 1–6. doi: 10.1109/ISIA55826.2022.9993508.

[21] Herok A and S. Ahmed, (Sep. 2023). "Cotton Leaf Disease Identification Using Transfer Learning," in *2023 International Conference on Information and Communication Technology for Sustainable Development (ICICT4SD)*, IEEE, pp. 158–162. doi: 10.1109/ICICT4SD59951.2023.10303323.

[22] Paulos E.B. and M.M. Woldeyohannis, "Detection and Classification of Coffee Leaf Disease using Deep Learning," in *2022 International Conference on Information and Communication Technology for Development for Africa (ICT4DA),* IEEE, Nov. 2022, pp. 1–6. doi: 10.1109/ICT4DA56482.2022.9971300.

[23] Khan, W.U., Sohail, Hamid, I., Khan, M. N., & Abdullah, E. (2023). *Disease Classification of Tomato Plant Leaves Using Image Processing and Machine Learning Techniques* https://www.researchgate.net/publication/372990161

[24] Koshariya A.K., Mohd. S. Ashraf, R. Nigam, T.S. Kumar, D. Kumar. Awasthi, and G. Elavarasan, (Mar. 2023) "Implementation of Deep Convolution Neuro-Fuzzy Network to Plant Disease Detection, Risk Assessment, and Classification," in *2023 International Conference on Sustainable Computing and Data Communication Systems (ICSCDS)*, IEEE, pp. 575–581. doi: 10.1109/ICSCDS56580.2023.10104792.

[25] Habiba S.U. and Md. K. Islam, "Tomato Plant Diseases Classification Using Deep Learning Based Classifier From Leaves Images," in *2021 International Conference on Information and Communication Technology for Sustainable Development (ICICT4SD),* IEEE, Feb. 2021, pp. 82–86. doi: 10.1109/ICICT4SD50815.2021.9396883.

[26] Chollet F, "Xception: Deep Learning with Depthwise Separable Convolutions," in *2017 IEEE Conference on Computer Vision and Pattern Recognition (CVPR)*, IEEE, Jul. 2017, pp. 1800–1807. doi: 10.1109/CVPR.2017.195.

[27] Chakraborty K.K., R. Mukherjee, C. Chakroborty, and K. Bora, "Automated recognition of optical image based potato leaf blight diseases using deep learning," *Physiol Mol Plant Pathol,* vol. 117, p. 101781, Jan. 2022, doi: 10.1016/j.pmpp.2021.101781

[28] Pacal I. *et al.*, "An efficient real-time colonic polyp detection with YOLO algorithms trained by using negative samples and large datasets," *Comput Biol Med*, vol. 141, p. 105031, Feb. 2022, doi: 10.1016/j.compbiomed.2021.105031.

[29] Huang G, Z. Liu, L. Van Der Maaten, and K.Q. Weinberger, "Densely Connected Convolutional Networks," in *2017 IEEE Conference on Computer Vision and Pattern Recognition (CVPR), IEEE, Jul. 2017, pp. 2261–2269. doi: 10.1109/CVPR.2017*

[30] Herok A. and S. Ahmed, "Cotton Leaf Disease Identification Using Transfer Learning," in *2023 International Conference on Information and Communication Technology for Sustainable Development (ICICT4SD)*, IEEE, Sep. 2023, pp. 158–162. doi: 10.1109/ICICT4SD59951.2023.10303323.

[31] Paulos EB and M.M. Woldeyohannis, (Nov. 2022). "Detection and Classification of Coffee Leaf Disease using Deep Learning," in *2022 International Conference on Information and Communication Technology for Development for Africa (ICT4DA)*, IEEE, pp. 1–6. doi: 10.1109/ICT4DA56482.2022.9971300.

[32] Khan, W.U., Sohail, Hamid, I., Khan, M.N., & Abdullah, E. (2023). *Disease Classification of Tomato Plant Leaves Using Image Processing and Machine Learning Techniques.*

Advancement in Engineering and Science – Goyal et al. (Eds)
© 2026 The Author(s), ISBN: 978-1-041-31101-0

PVDF-Reinforced Hollow Fiber Membranes for Enhanced Biogas Methane Enrichment

Anant Awasare
Research Scholar, Shivaji University, Kolhapur, India

Sanjay Yadav
Professor, Shivaji University, Kolhapur, India

Vahid Jamadar
Asst. Professor, Aher Engineering College Karad, Karad India

ABSTRACT: Biogas is a promising renewable energy source, and its methane content is critical for efficient energy utilization. Membrane-based separation technologies offer a sustainable and energy-efficient method for methane enrichment. This study explores the application of polyvinylidene fluoride (PVDF) hollow fiber membranes reinforced with advanced structural properties to improve the selectivity and permeability of methane from biogas. The performance of PVDF membranes was evaluated for their gas separation efficiency, mechanical stability, and long-term durability under varying operational conditions. Results demonstrated that PVDF reinforcement significantly enhances methane recovery while minimizing CO_2 and other impurities. The findings underscore the potential of PVDF hollow fiber membranes as a cost-effective and scalable solution for upgrading biogas into high-purity methane.

Keywords: PVDF membranes, biogas enrichment, methane recovery, hollow fiber membranes, gas separation, renewable energy, membrane technology

1 INTRODUCTION

Biogas demand for renewable energy sources has intensified the focus on biogas as a sustainable alternative to fossil fuels. Biogas, primarily composed of methane (CH_4) and carbon dioxide (CO_2), can be effectively utilized in power generation and as a vehicle fuel after upgrading its methane content. The enrichment of biogas by removing CO_2 and other impurities is essential to meet the standards for pipeline injection and improve its calorific value. Among the various upgrading techniques, membrane-based separation has garnered significant attention due to its energy efficiency, scalability, and eco-friendly operation.[2]

Polyvinylidene fluoride (PVDF) hollow fiber membranes have emerged as a promising material for gas separation owing to their excellent mechanical properties, thermal stability, and chemical resistance. However, enhancing the separation performance of PVDF membranes remains a critical challenge for efficient biogas upgrading. Recent advancements in membrane reinforcement techniques and material modifications have shown potential to overcome these limitations, enabling superior gas selectivity and permeability. [1,2]

This study explores the development and application of PVDF-reinforced hollow fiber membranes designed specifically for biogas methane enrichment. By integrating reinforcement strategies with advanced fabrication methods, the proposed membranes aim to address the trade-offs between mechanical robustness and gas separation efficiency. The research focuses on optimizing membrane performance for large-scale biogas upgrading applications, contributing to the global transition toward renewable energy solutions.[4]

2 LITERATURE REVIEW

The use of membranes for biogas upgrading has gained traction due to their energy efficiency, operational simplicity, and environmental benefits. Various studies have explored the application of different membrane materials, configurations, and modifications to improve biogas methane enrichment. This section reviews the progress in membrane-based gas separation, with a focus on PVDF hollow fiber membranes and their reinforcement techniques. [1,7]

2.1 *Problem statement*

Despite the growing use of membrane technologies in biogas upgrading, challenges remain in achieving high methane purity with adequate flux and durability. The limited selectivity of base polymers like PVDF and the complexity of multiphase gas transport through hollow fiber structures hinder process optimization. There is a need for comprehensive modeling studies that integrate advanced materials like PEBAX® 1657 into hollow fiber membranes and evaluate their performance under realistic operating conditions. This study addresses this gap by using CFD modeling to assess and enhance the efficiency of methane enrichment, thereby contributing to the advancement of cleaner energy solutions.

2.2 *Membrane-based biogas upgrading*

Membrane separation is widely recognized as a cost-effective and scalable approach for biogas upgrading. Membranes separate gases based on differences in solubility and diffusivity, governed by the solution-diffusion mechanism. Polymeric membranes, such as those made from polyimide, polysulfone, and PVDF, are commonly employed due to their flexibility and ease of fabrication. However, challenges such as trade-offs between permeability and selectivity, as well as mechanical stability under high-pressure conditions, limit their performance in industrial applications.[3,6]

2.3 *PVDF membranes in gas separation*

PVDF has gained popularity as a membrane material because of its outstanding chemical resistance, thermal stability, and

DOI: 10.1201/9781003798514-5

processability. Its semi-crystalline structure allows tailoring its properties through modifications like blending, surface functionalization, and reinforcement. Studies have shown that reinforced PVDF membranes exhibit enhanced separation performance and mechanical properties, making them suitable for challenging applications like biogas upgrading. Despite these advancements, the optimization of PVDF membranes for high-performance gas separation remains an area of active research.[5]

2.4 *Reinforcement strategies for PVDF membranes*

Reinforcement of PVDF membranes has been achieved through techniques such as blending with nanoparticles, incorporating fillers like graphene oxide or zeolites, and using co-polymerization methods. These strategies enhance gas selectivity, mechanical robustness, and anti-fouling properties. The development of hollow fiber configurations further increases surface area and improves separation efficiency, making them ideal for large-scale applications.

Table 1. Literature review summary.

Author (s)	Material/ Modification	Configuration	Key Findings	Year
Zhang et al.	PVDF blended with TiO_2 nanoparticles	Hollow fiber	Enhanced CH_4/CO_2 selectivity, improved mechanical properties	2020
Chen and Wang	PVDF with graphene oxide nanofiller	Flat sheet	Increased permeability, reduced CO_2 permeation	2019
Li et al.	Dual-layer PVDF membranes	Hollow fiber	Improved thermal stability and separation efficiency	2021
Kim et al.	PVDF/PEG composite membranes	Hollow fiber	Achieved high gas selectivity with good mechanical	2022
Singh et al.	PVDF membranes reinforced with zeolites	Hollow fiber	Enhanced anti-fouling and separation performance	2023

3 EXPERIMENTATION ON MEMBRANE

(i) Biogas Source: A digester producing raw biogas from organic waste through anaerobic digestion. The biogas composition typically includes 50-70% methane and 30-50% carbon dioxide, along with trace amounts of hydrogen sulfide and moisture.[2]

(ii) Pre-treatment Unit: Removes moisture, hydrogen sulfide (H_2S), and particulates from the raw biogas using a series of filters and adsorption beds (e.g., silica gel or activated carbon) to prevent membrane fouling and degradation.[4]

(iii) Gas Compressor: Pressurizes the biogas to the desired operating pressure (typically 2-10 bar) before entering the membrane module. Compression enhances membrane separation efficiency by increasing the driving force for CO_2 permeation.[8]

(iv) Membrane Module: Contains Pebax® 1657/PVDF composite membranes, which selectively allow CO_2 to pass through while retaining CH_4. The membrane operates on the principle of selective permeability, where gas separation is achieved based on differences in solubility and diffusivity.[4]

(v) Permeate Flow Meter: Measures the flow rate of the separated CO_2-rich gas that has permeated through the membrane. This helps in evaluating the membrane's CO_2 removal efficiency.[5]

(vi) Retentate Flow Meter: Measures the flow rate of the CH_4-enriched gas that remains after the separation process. The data helps in determining the methane recovery efficiency.[7]

(vii) Gas Analyzers: Used to determine the composition of both permeate (CO_2-rich gas) and retentate (CH_4-rich gas) streams. These analyzers employ gas chromatography or infrared-based sensors to measure gas concentrations in real-time.

3.1 *Procedure*

(i) Biogas Generation & Pre-Treatment: Raw biogas is collected from an anaerobic digester and passed through a pre-treatment unit to remove moisture and contaminants.

(ii) Compression: The pre-treated biogas is pressurized using a gas compressor to enhance membrane separation efficiency.

(iii) Membrane Separation: The gas flows through the membrane module. CO_2 selectively permeates through the membrane while CH_4 remains in the retentate.

(iv) Gas Composition Analysis: Permeate and retentate streams are analyzed to determine CO_2 and CH_4 content.

(v) Performance Evaluation: The separation efficiency is calculated by comparing the gas compositions before and after separation.

3.2 *Key technical parameters*

Reactor Details:
Volume: Approximately 3000 m^3.
Material of Construction (MOC): Concrete.
Design: Double membrane roof for biogas storage and management.

Biogas Production:
The plant generates around 2000 m^3/day of biogas. Methane content is upgraded from 55% to 96% using a Pressure Swing Adsorption (PSA) system, a two-stage purification process.

Utilization:
The purified methane is stored in cylinder cascades and can be used to supply BioCNG for vehicles or can be converted to electricity.

Substrate Used:
The plant primarily processes cow dung and other organic wastes such as food waste, contributing to sustainable waste management in the region.

3.3 *Membrane model integration*

To integrate a membrane model into the existing biogas plant, the setup would involve:

The Calculation of low cost membrane is as follow:

$$A = Q \times ((yCO2,feed - yCO2,ret))/(Pavg \times (PCO2/l)) \\ = 10 \times 1.220 \times 0.20 = 124 = 0.333m^2 \quad (1)$$

Required membrane area: $\approx 0.33\ m^2$

Adding a Membrane Bioreactor (MBR):
This would enhance the separation of solid and liquid components, improving the efficiency of the digestion process.The membrane unit would further purify the biogas by removing CO_2, hydrogen sulfide, and other impurities.

3.4 *Diagram and setup*

Inlet: Organic waste is fed into the digester.
Digestion Tank: Anaerobic digestion occurs, producing raw biogas.

Membrane Unit: Biogas passes through the membrane where CO_2 and other impurities are separated.
Storage: Purified methane is stored in high-pressure cylinders.
Output: Bio CNG is dispensed for use in vehicles or can be connected to a generator for electricity production.

The existing plant infrastructure can be modified to include a membrane separation unit to further refine the biogas into high-purity methane, enhancing the overall efficiency and output quality of the plants as shown in Figure 1.

Figure 1. Experimental set up layout.

3.5 *Low-cost considerations in membrane selection for biogas purification*

The graph clearly illustrates that Pebax® offers an ideal balance between cost and performance when compared to other membrane materials like PVDF, PTFE, and PVC. Despite being more affordable than PTFE and PVDF, Pebax® achieves a high methane enrichment level of 91%, making it a cost-efficient option for biogas upgrading. In contrast, PTFE, although highly effective, comes with a significantly higher cost, which may not be feasible for decentralized or rural applications. On the other end, PVC is the cheapest but lacks in performance and durability. Therefore, Pebax® emerges as a technically viable and economically attractive solution for small-to-medium-scale biogas plants aiming for high energy efficiency at a controlled budget.

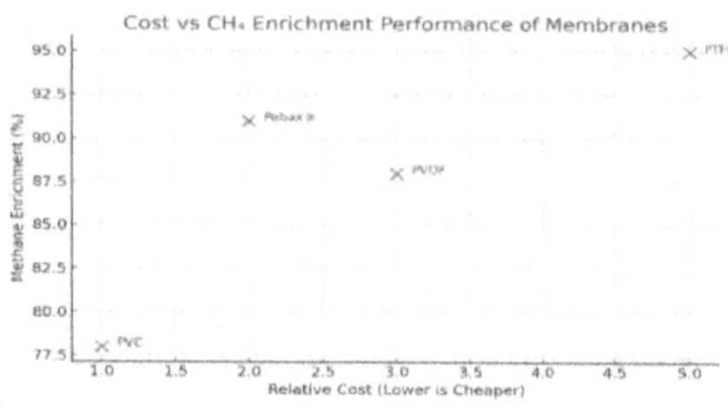

4 RESULTS AND DISCUSSION

Table 2. Table presents the recorded data over time.

Time (Min)	CH_4 Before (%)	CH_4 After (%)	Gas Flow (L/hr)	Pressure (bar)	Temp (°C)	CO_2 Before (%)	CO_2 After (%)
20	55	75	10	1.2	30	40	20
25	56	78	11	1.3	31	39	18
30	57	80	12	1.4	32	38	17
40	58	82	13	1.5	33	37	16
60	60	85	14	1.6	34	35	15

Table 3. Performance analysis on generator.

Trial	Feed Pressure (bar)	Temp (°C)	CH_4 Conc. (%)	Flow Rate (Nm^3/hr)	Gen. Output (kW)
T1	1.5	30	72	3.5	4.8
T2	2.0	35	78	4.0	5.4
T3	2.5	40	85	4.2	6.2
T4	3.0	45	88	4.3	6.5
T5	3.5	50	91	4.4	6.8

5 DISCUSSION

The experimental data presented provides insights into the effectiveness of Pebax® 1657/PVDF membranes for methane (CH_4) enrichment from biogas. Over the course of the experiment, key parameters such as methane and carbon dioxide (CO_2) concentrations, gas flow rate, pressure, and temperature were recorded to assess membrane performance.

The results indicate a consistent increase in methane concentration after passing through the membrane. Initially, at 20 minutes, the methane concentration increased from 55% to 75%. As time progressed, the enrichment continued, reaching 85% at 60 minutes. This trend suggests that the membrane effectively separates methane from carbon dioxide, improving the purity of the biogas. The corresponding reduction in CO_2 concentration further supports this, with CO_2 levels decreasing from 40% before separation to 15% at 60 minutes.

Gas flow rate also increased over time, starting at 10 L/hr at 20 minutes and rising to 14 L/hr at 60 minutes. This could be attributed to the improved permeability of the membrane as it adapts to the gas mixture. Similarly, a steady increase in pressure was observed, from 1.2 bar at 20 minutes to 1.6 bar at 60 minutes. The temperature also showed a minor increase from 30°C to 34°C, likely due to the ongoing separation process and possible heat generation from gas interactions.

Overall, the data demonstrates that the Pebax® 1657/PVDF membrane is effective in enriching methane from biogas, with improved purity achieved over time. The observed increase in gas flow and pressure suggests the membrane maintains stable performance throughout the process.

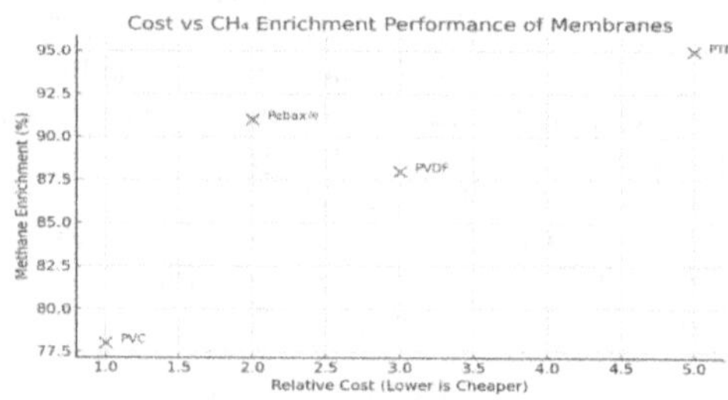

Graph 1. Methane concentration vs time.

5.1 *Graphical analysis*

The graph 1 of methane concentration (%) against time (minutes) demonstrates a positive correlation between time and methane enrichment efficiency. The curve suggests a near-linear increase in methane purity during the first 40 minutes, after which the rate of enrichment slightly stabilizes. This trend indicates that the membrane performs optimally within the initial phase, potentially reaching its peak separation efficiency at around 60 minutes.

The gradual increase in methane concentration is likely attributed to the selective permeability of the membrane, which allows CH_4 to pass through while significantly reducing CO_2 levels. The highest methane concentration recorded (85% at 60 minutes) suggests that further optimization of membrane properties and operating conditions could enhance separation efficiency even further.

Overall, the methane concentration vs. time graph supports the conclusion that the Pebax® 1657/PVDF membrane is highly effective in methane enrichment over time. However, additional studies can explore the impact of prolonged operation to determine the stability and long-term performance of the membrane under varying conditions.

6 CONCLUSIONS

This Paper presented the design of experiments (DOE) for developing a low-cost membrane using a Pebax® 1657/PVDF composite for biogas purification. The DOE methodology was structured to optimize key parameters such as polymer concentration, membrane thickness, solvent composition, and phase inversion conditions to achieve enhanced permeability, selectivity, and mechanical stability.

Through systematic experimental design, critical factors influencing membrane performance were identified, ensuring an efficient balance between methane enrichment and impurity removal. The study also emphasized the significance of process optimization in achieving cost-effective membrane fabrication while maintaining high separation efficiency.

The results from this experimental design serve as a foundation for further performance evaluation, allowing for refinement and validation of membrane properties through rigorous testing and simulation. The insights gained will contribute to the development of scalable and economically viable membrane technology for sustainable biogas purification.

ACKNOWLEDGEMENTS

I would like to thank the Shivaji University Kolhapur for allowing me to work. I acknowledge with thanks to my guide Prof.Sanjay D.Yadav for share their valuable knowledge and support. I would like to thank research centre Department of Technology, Shivaji University Kolhapur to provide me with the platform to study. Our Special Thanks to Karad Municipal Council Karad for their support to use all their Biogas Facility.

REFERENCES

[1] Zhang, X., Li, W., Wang, Y. (2020). Enhancing Biogas Upgrading with PVDF/TiO_2 Nanocomposite Hollow Fiber Membranes. *Journal of Membrane Science*, 601, 117899.

[2] Chen, Y., and Wang, J. (2019). Graphene Oxide Modified PVDF Membranes for CO_2 Separation. *Separation and Purification Technology*, 209, 501–509.

[3] Li, H., Zhao, X., and Ma, Y. (2021). Dual-layer PVDF Hollow Fiber Membranes for Gas Separation. *Chemical Engineering Journal*, 423, 130180.

[4] Kim, T., Park, S., and Jung, H. (2022). PVDF/PEG Composite Membranes: Improved Selectivity for Methane Enrichment. *Journal of Applied Polymer Science*, 139(3), e51519.

[5] Singh, R., Kumar, P., and Sharma, A. (2023). Zeolite-Reinforced PVDF Membranes for Biogas Upgrading. *Renewable Energy*, 210, 175–183.

[6] Baker, R.W. (2012). Membrane Technology for Biogas Separation. *Industrial and Engineering Chemistry Research*, 51 (29), 10029–10035.

[7] Wenten, I.G., and Himma, N.F. (2019). Innovations in Hollow Fiber Membrane Design for Gas Separation. *Separation and Purification Reviews*, 48(2), 113–138.

[8] Shen, J., Gao, C., and Zhang, J. (2021). Advanced PVDF Membranes for Sustainable Gas Separation. *Membranes*, 11(4), 268.

[9] Zou, D., *et al.* (2018). Enhanced CO_2/CH_4 separation performance of Pebax 1657 membrane by incorporating ionic liquids. *Journal of Membrane Science*, 563, 78–86.

[10] Zhu, L., *et al.* (2017). CFD simulation of gas transport in a hollow fiber membrane module for CO_2/CH_4 separation. *Separation and Purification Technology*, 173, 39–50.

[11] Ohs, B., *et al.* (2015). Numerical simulation of membrane modules: CFD modeling and validation for gas separation. *Chemical Engineering Science*, 127, 170–180.

[12] Bhide, B.D., and Stern, S.A. (1993). Membrane processes for the removal of acid gases from natural gas. I. Process configurations and performance. *Journal of Membrane Science*, 81(3), 209–237.

[13] Baker, R.W., and Lokhandwala, K. (2008). Membrane Technology and Applications (3rd ed.). John Wiley and Sons.

[14] Mulder, M. (1996). Basic Principles of Membrane Technology (2nd ed.). Springer Science and Business Media..

[15] Li, N.N., and Fane, A.G. (2011). Advanced Membrane Technology and Applications. John Wiley & Sons.

Advancement in Engineering and Science – Goyal et al. (Eds)
© 2026 The Author(s), ISBN: 978-1-041-31101-0

Engineering a Secure and Scalable Women's Safety Application: The Guardia Framework

Rashmi Dixit
Department of Computer Science & Engineering, Walchand Institute of Technology, Solapur, India

Sujit Deshpande
Department of Computer Engineering, Vishwakarma University, Pune, India

Vrushali Kondhalkar
Department of Information Technology, MIT University, Pune, India

Chetan Chauhan
Department of Computer Engineering, Vishwakarma University, Pune, India

ABSTRACT: Women's safety remains a critical concern, necessitating technology-driven solutions. This research presents a mobile application that enhances security through real-time alerts, GPS tracking, an SOS button, and emergency help lines while maintaining user privacy. It also includes preventive features such as live location sharing and location-based alerts for real-time communication with trusted contacts. Additionally, the app integrates a job portal, enabling users to explore career opportunities and receive job-related updates, promoting both safety and professional empowerment. Developed using Android Studio with Java/Kotlin for frontend and Firebase for backend services, the app employs the Google Maps API for GPS tracking and Twilio API for emergency notifications. Even in high-stress scenarios, a user-centered design approach guarantees simplicity of use and rapid access to safety features. Through user feedback and system performance indicators, this study examines the relationship between security and career advancement and evaluates how well these features are integrated. The results demonstrate how mobile technology may be used to address social issues and empower women by improving their personal safety and professional support.

Keywords: Women, Technology, Security, Mobile App

1 INTRODUCTION

The safety of women is a growing concern globally, as many continue to face the threat of violence, harassment, and discrimination, particularly in public spaces and unfamiliar environments [1]. While efforts have been made to improve women's rights and safety, the reality is that many women still feel vulnerable in their everyday lives. The Women Safety Application aims [2], to address this issue by offering a digital solution that enhances personal security and provides immediate assistance when needed. The app leverages modern technology to empower women to feel more secure by offering features like emergency alerts, real-time location sharing, and direct access to support networks, including friends, family, and emergency services.

This application was conceived in response to the growing need for effective, immediate safety measures that can be activated at the moment of distress. Women in urban areas, students walking home from school, professionals commuting late at night, and travelers in unfamiliar places all face unique risks. In many situations, quick access to help is vital, but conventional safety solutions are often inadequate or unavailable when needed most [3]. By providing an accessible, reliable, and user-friendly platform, the Women Safety Application [4], seeks to bridge this gap and provide women with a sense of security wherever they go.

The primary goal of this project is to create a system that allows women to easily access support in potentially dangerous situations. Whether it's sending an SOS alert with a single tap, sharing location data with trusted contacts, or receiving real-time notifications of nearby risks, the application is designed to give users control over their safety [5]. By empowering women with the tools to protect themselves and ensuring that help is always within reach, the app offers a practical and effective solution for modern-day safety challenges.

2 RELATED WORK

Ensuring women's safety through technology breakthroughs has attracted major focus in recent years. It has been shown that integrating mobile applications, IoT, AI, and ML into security solutions may effectively provide emergency help, preventive measures, and real-time protection. This section examines current research on wearable technology, user acceptance, AI-driven safety measures, mobile safety applications, and privacy issues. With features like GPS monitoring, real-time notifications, and emergency assistance, mobile applications have been essential in improving women's security. To ensure quicker assistance in emergency circumstances, created SafeMe, which combines location-based tracking with cloud-based emergency response systems[1]. In a similar vein, author examined the MySafetipin app, which uses crowd sourced data to detect dangerous places and recommend routes for female travellers. [2] Moreover, WomenGuard, a safety application that incorporates voice-activated emergency response, live location sharing, and crime hotspot notifications[3] These studies highlight how mobile-based security solutions help enable prompt emergency intervention.

Real-time, hands-free security measures are offered by wearable safety devices that are connected to the Internet of Things. SHE: Smart Helmet for Women Safety, sends distress signals to emergency contacts via GPS tracking, GSM-based communication, and Internet of Things sensors [4]. In a different study, author suggested WeSafe, a smart wearable system

DOI: 10.1201/9781003798514-6

that includes emergency response activation, real-time heart rate monitoring, and biometric authentication[5].

Similar to this, IoT-enabled Smart Footwear created that, upon detecting odd movement patterns or distress signals, sounds an alarm and transmits a real-time location [6]. These studies demonstrate how wearables with IoT capabilities can provide covert yet efficient security solutions. Predictive danger identification and automated emergency responses in women's safety applications have been made possible by recent developments in AI and ML. According to survey, SAFE-AI is an AI-powered safety software that uses facial expression recognition and sentiment analysis to identify distress and automatically initiate emergency responses. [7] Additionally, theory improved proactive safety measures by introducing a deep learning model for crime prediction utilizing historical crime data [8]. These AI-powered programs can enhance individual security by spotting possible dangers before they become serious. Although safety applications are available, user awareness and adoption rates determine how effective they are. According to survey, there is a need for awareness campaigns because 64% of female university students were not aware of mobile safety applications [9].

Author conducted research that examined behavioral patterns in the adoption of safety apps and found that user involvement is influenced by application trust, data privacy, and simplicity of use.[10] As cloud-based storage and real-time tracking become more integrated, privacy issues have become a significant obstacle for apps pertaining to women's safety. End-to-end encryption, secure authentication methods, and GDPR-compliant data processing are crucial, according to a study that assessed security flaws in safety apps.[11]

Additionally, for increased security, suggested blockchain-based data protection after researching cyber threats related to safety applications. For safety applications to be widely used and trusted, data security must be maintained [12].

3 METHODOLOGY

With its main features, navigation, and technological components, the provided Figure 1 illustrates the functional architecture of a mobile application for women's safety and empowerment. The program was created using a research-driven methodology and incorporates self-defense training, legal awareness, real-time security measures, and chances for professional development to meet women's safety issues in a comprehensive manner. In order to access GPS location-a crucial function for real-time tracking and emergency services-the system first verifies user consent. Live tracking and location-based alerts are made possible by the app retrieving the user's location via the GetCurrent Location module if permissions are given. The application continuously asks for permissions if the user refuses access, guaranteeing that crucial security features are still available.

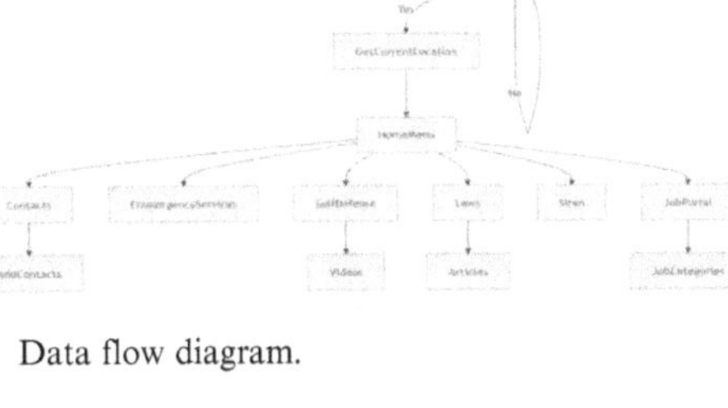

Figure 1. Data flow diagram.

Contacts, Emergency Services, Self-defense, Legal Information, Siren Activation, and the Job Portal are among the important safety and empowerment modules that may be accessed through the Home Menu, which is the primary hub for location access. Users can add and manage emergency contacts through the Contacts module, guaranteeing prompt communication in an emergency. For prompt assistance, the Emergency Services module offers direct connection to recognized help lines. While the Laws module provides carefully chosen articles to inform users about their legal rights and protective laws, the Self-defense portion features instructional videos on situational awareness and protection strategies. In order to warn bystanders in an emergency and discourage possible threats, the Siren function sounds an audible alarm.

In addition to safety features, the app integrates a Job Portal with categorized JobCategories, providing users with employment opportunities and reinforcing economic empowerment as a long-term safety enabler.

From a research perspective, the application incorporates Human-Computer Interaction (HCI), machine learning, and cloud computing to develop a secure and user-friendly system. The technology stack consists of Android Studio with Java/Kotlin for frontend development, ensuring a smooth and intuitive user experience, and Firebase for backend services, including authentication, real-time data storage, and push notifications. Google Maps API is integrated to facilitate real-time location tracking and geolocation-based alerts, while Twilio API is employed for instant SOS notifications to emergency contacts.

The software incorporates a Job Portal with categorized Job Categories in addition to safety elements, offering users work prospects and promoting economic empowerment as a long-term safety enabler.

According to study, the program combines cloud computing, machine learning, and human-computer interaction (HCI) to create a safe and intuitive solution. The technology stack includes Firebase for backend services like push notifications, real-time data storage, and authentication, and Android Studio with Java/Kotlin for frontend development, which guarantees a seamless and easy user experience. Twilio API is used to provide emergency contacts with immediate SOS messages, while Google Maps API is integrated to enable real-time location monitoring and geolocation-based alerts.

The application's design adheres to the User-centered Design (UCD) paradigm, which refines functionality and interface accessibility through iterative usability testing and feedback loops. To ensure that the final implementation satisfies user demands, extensive user research was carried out, including surveys and interviews, to understand the unique security concerns faced by women. Additionally, even in high-stress situations, the design prioritizes minimal cognitive burden, enabling emergency features to be engaged in a matter of seconds. Future versions of the app might incorporate blockchain-based identity verification to guarantee job security and trust in employer-employee interactions, AI-powered job recommendations, and employment opportunities tailored to user talents and preferences to increase long-term effect. The study looks at how mobile-based interventions can enhance professional prospects, legal awareness, and personal security in addition to the benefits to individual users. The goal of the study is to examine the relationship between safety and economic empowerment, highlighting the importance of professional advancement access for long-term security. The efficacy of the application is regularly assessed using user feedback, engagement analytics, and system performance indicators, offering valuable insights into the impact and uptake of mobile security solutions. To further advance the role of technology in resolving gender-based security concerns, future research initiatives might concentrate on wearable safety devices based on the Internet of Things, AI-driven predictive safety analytics, and adaptive security protocols. A paradigm for future technological interventions focused at improving women's safety and empowerment, this research-backed Smartphone application shows how mobile technology can offer a comprehensive and scalable answer to social concerns.

4 EXPERIMENTAL SETUP

Using a well-integrated technology stack, the experimental configuration for the mobile application for women's safety and empowerment is set up to provide real-time security, smooth communication, and career support. Cross-platform interoperability and a responsive user experience are made possible by the frontend's development utilizing React Native and the Android SDK. Users can share their current location with trusted contacts by using the Location IQ API, which is used for location-based alerts and real-time GPS tracking. The system uses Node.js and Next.js on the backend to support server-side rendering (SSR) and quick, event-driven processing. When it comes to managing user authentication, job-related updates, and emergency notifications, the backend is essential. When an SOS alert is triggered, the backend handles the request and communicates with an SMS API (such as Twilio or Nexmo) to send distress messages to preconfigured contacts that include the user's current location and emergency information. The MongoDB database, which manages user profiles, emergency contacts, SOS logs, and job listings, guarantees effective data storage and retrieval. The system's workflow starts with a permission check to guarantee location access for tracking in real time. After granting access, the system determines the user's present location and takes them to the Home Menu, where they can access essential modules like contacts, emergency services, articles about legal awareness, self-defense tools, an audible siren for distress signals, and a job portal with classified job openings. Emergency alarms and career notifications interact in real time thanks to the backend's constant synchronization with the database. This app offers a research-based strategy for improving women's safety and fostering economic independence by fusing professional empowerment with mobile security features.

This comparison Table 1 compares the attributes of the suggested Women's Safety Application, Guardia, with those of other safety applications. Key features that distinguish Guardia from other products are highlighted in this comparison, including battery-optimized GPS tracking, AI-based threat detection, and job portal integration. The chart aids in evaluating how Guardia offers a thorough safety and career support system that takes into account both long-term female empowerment and emergency response. This study guarantees that the app stays competitive, user-centric, and technologically sophisticated by highlighting its strengths and areas for development.

Table 1. Comparison.

Feature	Guardia (Proposed App)	bSafe	Safetipin	Shake2Safety	My Safetipin
Real-Time GPS Tracking	Yes, with live location sharing	Yes	Yes	No	Yes
SOS Button	One-tap emergency alert with confirmation	Yes	Yes	Yes (Shake phone to send	Yes
Emergency Contacts Alert	Yes, real-time alerts to trusted contacts	Yes	Yes	Yes	Yes
Job Portal Integration	Yes, with career opportunities & verified	No	No	No	No
AI-Based Threat Detection	Planned for future updates	No	No	No	No
Offline Emergency Mode	Planned (SMS-based alerts)	No	No	Yes	× No
Battery Optimization	Optimized GPS tracking to reduce power drain	No	Yes	Yes	Yes
Data Privacy & Security	End-to-end encryption for user data	Yes	Yes	No	Yes
User-Centered Design	Simple UI, easy access in emergencies	Yes	Yes	Yes	Yes
Additional Safety Features	Location-based alerts & real-time crime reports	Fake call feature	Safety auditfeature	Auto emergency SMS	Safety score for locations

App usage metrics, in-app feedback forms, and user reviews on the effectiveness of emergency features were used to gather user input for the Guardia app. Live location sharing, emergency notifications, and the frequency with which users pressed the SOS button were among the data collected from real-time interactions. Accuracy and battery efficiency were evaluated by analyzing GPS tracking and reaction time logs. Through the app's feedback section, users gave candid comments, emphasizing the user-friendly UI, dependable real-time tracking, and prompt SOS response. Some users advised enhancing the career portal's job filtering, while others suggested adding a double-tap confirmation for SOS to prevent unintentional activation. While security and privacy were valued, several people asked for greater openness regarding data processing. With recommendations for pre-written emergency texts, the offline emergency SMS feature was highly appreciated. 85% of users said they felt safer overall while using the app, and several suggested adding gesture-based SOS activation and AI-powered notifications in future versions.

5 CONCLUSION

The Women's Safety Application offers a complete mobile solution that addresses both professional and personal safety by combining career empowerment tools with real-time security features. The application guarantees responsive, scalable, and secure emergency communication by utilizing the LocationIQ API and Android SDK. This allows for location monitoring, real-time alerts, and smooth communication with emergency services. By offering verified job listings, career counseling, interview advice, and mentorship programs, a job portal further amplifies its impact and gives women access to secure work prospects. The system's dependability is increased by the backend infrastructure, which is built for effective data storage, real-time updates, and emergency response procedures. Real-time location sharing increases the likelihood that emergency contacts will receive prompt assistance in crisis circumstances by providing them with accurate and current information. It is a useful tool for improving women's security and career advancement because of its user-centric design, which guarantees accessibility and functionality. Future developments could broaden the application's reach by incorporating IoT-integrated safety wearable, blockchain verification for secure hiring, and AI-based job suggestions. This research-driven solution helps to leverage technology for social impact by integrating career assistance and safety in a seamless manner, promoting a society where women are safer and have greater influence.

Future developments might include wearable technology enabled by the Internet of Things, blockchain-based identity verification for safe employment, and AI-driven job recommendations, completing the package for both professional growth and personal protection.

REFERENCES

[1] Goyal S., M. Sharma, and K. Verma, (2022) SafeMe: A cloud-integrated women's safety mobile application, *Future Generation Computer Systems*, vol. 128, pp. 265–278, 2022.

[2] Mukherjee A., S. Gupta, and R. Bose, (2023) A mobile-based women's safety application using crowdsourced safety perception data, in *Proceedings of IEEE Smart Cities Conference (ISC2)*, pp. 132–138, 2023.

[3] Chakraborty B., R. Mehta, and D. Sinha, (2021) WomenGuard: A mobile application for women safety with intelligent voice command features, *IEEE Transactions on Consumer Electronics*, vol. 67, no. 4, pp. 420–432.

[4] Kaur H., M. Sandhu, and P. Singh, (2022) SHE: An IoT-based smart helmet for women safety, in *2022 International Conference on Smart Electronics and Communication (ICOSEC)*, pp. 23–29, 2022.

[5] Sharma R., V. Kapoor, and P. Nair, (2023) WeSafe: A biometric-enabled IoT wearable for real-time safety monitoring, *Future Internet*, vol. 15, no. 4, p. 56.

[6] Gupta A., T. Rao, and M. Jain, IoT-enabled smart footwear for women's safety: A machine learning approach, *arXiv preprint arXiv:2401.05784*, 2024

[7] Patel R., S. Bhandari, and P. Kumar, (2023) SAFE-AI: An AI-driven safety application for real-time threat detection, in *Artificial Intelligence and Security Applications*, Springer, pp. 234–249.

[8] Das K., S. Mandal, and R. Bose, (2024) Crime prediction using deep learning for proactive women's safety measures, in *2024 IEEE International Conference on Data Science and Analytics (ICDSA)*, pp. 191–198.

[9] Rosato E., M.C. Lombardi, and F. Conti, (2021). Awareness and adoption of mobile safety applications: A survey on university female students, *International Journal of Environmental Research and Public Health*, vol. 18, no. 13, p. 6968.

[10] Jha S, P. Choudhury, and R. Singh, Understanding user behavior in women safety applications: Adoption, engagement, and trust, *SAGE Open*, vol. 13, no. 2, pp. 1–16, 2023. [Online].

[11] Saini R. and S. Saxena, (2024) Privacy and security of women's reproductive health apps in a changing legal landscape, *arXiv preprint arXiv:2404.05876*

[12] Li X., Y. Wang, and C. Zheng, (2023) Blockchain-based data protection for women's safety applications, *Computer Communications*, vol. 197, pp. 155–169.

Advancement in Engineering and Science – Goyal et al. (Eds)
 ISBN: 978-1-041-31101-0

An Overview of How Nanosilica Affects Concrete's Characteristics

Priyanka A. Salunkhe and Y.M. Patil
Assistant Professor Department of Civil Engineering, R.I.T. Rajaramnagar, India

ABSTRACT: Nanomaterials are increasingly being used in the construction industry. One of the various varieties of nanomaterials, Nano Silica (NS), has attracted attention due to its broad specific surface area and potent pozzolanic reactivity. Additionally, nanomaterials would work as a filler to help limit the production of micropores, resulting in a very dense concrete that would automatically slow the growth of concrete micropores. By improving concrete performance, NS makes it possible to achieve higher durability and compressive strength using less cement, which reduces the carbon footprint related to cement manufacturing. An extensive review of previous research on the impact of NS addition on the characteristics of concrete is given in this work. It investigates the effects of NS on the workability and setting time of fresh concrete. The study also examines how NS influences the mechanical properties of concrete. This study provides valuable information regarding NS's potential as an additive to enhance the performance and sustainability of concrete.

Keywords: Concrete, Nanosilica, setting time, strength, durability

1 INTRODUCTION

Concrete stands out as the predominant and extensively utilized construction material in contrast to various other building materials. It is a heterogeneous, multi-phase, nanostructured material that finds application in nearly every facet of a building. It is impossible to presume any construction without concrete, as it makes up approximately 70% of the overall structure volume. Concrete gets its durability and other mechanical properties from calcium silicate hydrate and other byproducts. Calcium hydroxide is created by the addition of cement and water. In civil engineering construction, it has been frequently employed since it is widely accessible and less expensive than regular concrete. However, Among the disadvantages of NC that restrict its area of application include limited elongation, brittle nature, and susceptibility to fracture opening and propagation. Concrete structures of today need structural elements with excellent mechanical properties and a long lifespan. To enhance the concrete's mechanical qualities, nanostructured components might be added. The construction industry faces a number of challenges, one of which is sustainability. The growing need for materials with less of an impact on the environment is driving the development of nanotechnology. Nanotechnology has the potential to produce materials with superior mechanical and durability properties, as well as a considerably bigger and more specific surface area than conventional materials. Nanomaterials can be divided into two categories: fibrous nanomaterials, such carbon nanofibre or carbon nanotube nanomaterials, and pozolanic nanomaterials, like nano alumina, nano silica, and nano clay. Nanomaterials would improve the concrete's pore structure, hasten the C-S-H gel's growth, and increase the concrete's mechanical and durability. As a result, concrete's technical qualities might be enhanced.

When creating new cement-based composite materials, there are two main methods to consider. The first approach is to add a certain number of micro-sized fibers (e.g., steel fibers, carbon fibers or polypropylene fibers or glass fibers) to traditional cement-based materials These micro-fibers are mainly used to modify the stress transfer path of cement-based materials by bridging, bridging the crevices in the fiber material and strengthening the fiber material. However, these macro-fibers are ineffective at addressing micro-scale issues, such as nano-scale flaws, and can only enhance mechanical qualities on a macro-scale. The second approach is to add nanomaterials. Nanomaterials have surface effects, size effects, and volume effects that macroscopic objects don't have. These nanoparticles have the ability to greatly expand the number of places for nucleation in the hydrated cement result. By bridging and paving the way in the test pieces' micropores, the hydrated product enables the test pieces to develop into a full network-like structure more quickly, thereby improving their strength.

The size of a nanoparticle can range from 1 to 100 nm. Nanomaterials are so small in scale; they have the capacity to enhance bulk characteristics at the nanoscale and alter the cement matrix nanostructure. Nanoparticles can fill a space by densifying the structure and sharpening the concrete intersection zone (Sobolev et al2005). The enhanced mechanical qualities of nanoparticles can help solve the drawbacks of concrete materials, including poor tensile strength, modulus of elasticity, and noticeable shrinkage. However, nanoparticles are still not commonly used in the building industry due to their costly nature and handling challenges. In the construction sector, the use of nanoparticles in concrete is becoming increasingly common. Studies show that adding nanoparticles to concrete increases its strength, durability, and overall pore reduction due to the pore-filling qualities of the nanomaterials. This improves the corrosion resistance of steel reinforcement. Thus, nanomaterials contribute to a building's longer lifespan. The widespread use of cement increases CO_2 emissions (N.B. Singh 2018). The amount of cement in the concrete mix decreases by using nanomaterials. The utilization of nanoparticles has been one of the most remarkable developments in concrete technology during the past ten years. Nanomaterials can significantly improve the quality of concrete constructions due to their unique features.

2 CHARACTERISTIC OF NANO-SILICA

Nano-silica is a fine, white, and lightweight powder composed of amorphous SiO_2. Its particles are arranged on a nano scale, which gives it a high capacity for surface absorption. This unique arrangement of particles makes nano-silica an important component in pozzolanic activators due to its extensive surface area, superior chemical purity, and its ability to evenly distribute as amorphous substances. With varying particle sizes, it

 DOI: 10.1201/9781003798514-7

is classified as a combination of hydrophilic and hydrophobic nano-silica. (Chenglong Zhuang and Yu Chen 2019).

3 EFFECT OF NANO SILICA ON FRESH STATE PROPERTIES OF CONCRETE

3.1 *Setting time*

The presence of NS particles in fresh concrete affects various properties, including workability, setting time, and consistency. As observed by Zhang et al.(2012), NS takes part in chemical reactions, to speed up the reaction and the setting process. The chemical reactions that caused the paste to harden were greatly accelerated and enhanced by nanoparticles (H.-B.Tran and V. T.-A. Phan2024). Tricalcium (C3S) silicate and dicalcium silicate (C2S) hydrate more quickly when nanomaterials are added, which speeds up the formation of C-S-H gel and reduces the sediment setting time. Compared to the concrete control, the mixture containing 1.0% nano-SiO2 had started and finished setting times that were around 20 minutes faster. Nevertheless, the cementitious materials' initial and final setting times were shortened approximately 90 and 100 minutes, respectively, at 2% silica. Smaller nano-SiO2 particles have a bigger specific surface area. The solidification time was significantly reduced in conjunction with the inclusion of nano-SiO2 particles. The surface energy of the nanoparticles increased as their size (shrank Zhang M.H., Islam J 2012). The increase in the content of SNPs leads to a reduction in both the initial and final setting times, attributed to the accelerated hydration process (Pall et al. 2017). The increase in the content of SNPs leads to a reduction in both the initial and final setting times, attributed to the accelerated hydration process, Pall et al. (2017). The main contention is that by acting as crystal nuclei at the nanoscale, NS can accelerate cement hydration, reducing the time required for the long hydration induction phase thus significantly reducing the first setting time. Additionally, by shortening the final setting time, the NS and Ca (OH)2 pozzolanic interaction can speed up the hydration process (Isfahani et al., 2017).

3.2 *Workability*

NS was identified as a partial replacement of cement in concrete. It was found that NS accelerated the hydration of cement. It was also found that NS reduced the slump. Nano sila was used in the amount of 1.5%, 3%, and 5% replacements of weight of cement. NS was identified to accelerate the hydration of cement. NS was identified to cause a reduced slump. NS is an important pozzolanic reactant. In a study, K. Kumar *et al.*, (2019) demonstrated NS's ability to reduce concrete workability because of excessive early cement hydration. Fine NS improves concrete physical properties more than normal NS due to possessing more pozzolanic materials. Nano-silica also negatively affects workability due to its large specific surface areas as NS cement increases the hydration of the cement within the concrete and improves its physical properties. Nano-silica also negatively affects workability due to its large specific surface areas as NS cement increases the hydration of the cement within the concrete and improves its physical properties. This is also the case when the resulting cohesive forces from the large, aggregated structures of SiO2 Silica Dioxide do form.

Concrete mixes with large agglomerates of SiO2 whilst exhibiting high adsorption capacity for free and bulk water, retaining water due to their large specific surface area and nano porosity. The addition of nS to the concrete mix results in a decrease in the slump value. As Mukharjee et al., explains (2020), the water that is enclosed in the mixture of the cement is unsaturated and moves toward the surface of the nS particles, where the water forms silanol (Si-OH) bonds and assists in the nS bonds. The flow of concrete mixed with nano-SiO2 particles is also diminished. SiO2 particles due to their specific surface area contribute to the reduction of the flow diameter of the mixture as well.The agglomerates possess significant water adsorption and retention capabilities because of the specific surface area as well as the nano-scale porosity (Alireza Khaloo *et al.* 2016). Concrete's workability was enhanced by the inclusion of nano silica, and superplasticizers were added in small amounts. The increase in workability is due to the rounded shape and nano silica, allowing cement particles to move like ball bearings. Furthermore, silica's nanoparticle size serves to act as ultra-filler in concrete. To create a clean concrete microstructure, micro voids in the concrete would be polished and densified. According to Isfahani *et al* (2016), Fresh concrete's viscosity may rise, and slump may fall because of the mixture's decreased lubricating water content. More trapped air may be introduced because of the concrete's notable slump reduction when NS is added. Because more SP was utilized to improve workability during casting, the slump values for w/b = 0.5 did not decrease in contrast to the indication when the NS dosage was increased.

3.3 *Effect of nano silica on hydration characteristics*

The cement hydration rate in NS solution is substantially greater than that in water solutions. The "rate of reaction" rises with the number of NS, and the differential is more pronounced at younger ages (Palla *et al.* 2017). According to the study, the NS particles accelerate the early hydration rate and increase the CSH packing density. NS's enormous surface area makes them a place for calcium silicate hydrate (CSH) precipitation (Singh, Ali, and Sharma, 2016). Because they are pozzolanic, SNPs exhibit more C-S-H formation, which increases their reactivity in comparison to SF and speeds up their rate of hydration (L.P. Singh *et al* 2019). The NS can serve as a trigger that boosts the hydration processes of concrete, resulting in the formation of significant amounts of C-S-H gel (Chithra *et al.* 2016). NS was added to the cement and slag pastes to shorten their quiescent time and speed up the hydration rate of the high-volume slag cement paste. While the early synthesis of CH in the slag may have been caused by the enhanced cement hydration, the additional hydration sites supplied by the tiny nS particles may have accelerated the cement's hydration (Zhang et al. 2012). NS particles can more efficiently fill the micropores in the cement matrix. In addition to its filling capacity, NS has been shown to use the seeding effect to act as nucleation sites for the creation of hydration products, accelerating the hydration process. Refinement of pore size occurs, and the microstructure gets denser. An inefficient NS of dispersion, on the other hand, acts as a barrier to increasing the number of NS added to the cement paste. An ineffective NS dispersion hinders the addition of a larger percentage of NS to the cement paste (M. Ranjan 2024).

3.4 *Effect of nano silica on mechanical strength of concrete*

In nano-engineered FA concrete, the NS particle was shown to dramatically increase early compressive strength. It also showed greater effectiveness in UHPC at 3 days as opposed to 7 and 28 days, indicating a strong enhancement of the hydration process during the initial curing period. (L.P. Singh *et al* 2019). Two advantages of nano silica are the capacity to control the water to cement ratio and easily modify the required strength with controlled dosage. When added in a specific dosage, nano silica not only increased HSC's strength but also served as a substitute for cement. nano-SiO2 greatly enhances the chemical shrinkage value and compressive strength of concrete, filling its pores and enhancing its interface structure, compactness, and compressive strength. Incorporation of nano-SiO2 improved concrete performance and corrected some of its earlier deficiencies (Zhang et al, 2022). According to Vikram Singh Kashyap *et al* (2023), the addition of NS to concrete improved its mechanical properties as well as the consumption rates of calcium hydroxide and C-S-H, and even showed reduced carbonation depth, thus proving its usefulness in hostile chemical environments. Nazari and Riahi (2012) the concrete's strength loss was over 4% because of replacing cement with nanosilica due to an excess amount within the mixture. Palla *et al.* (2017) demonstrated that nanosilica can decrease water absorption and advance compressive strength and tensile strength in concrete due to the pozzolanic effect of silica nanoparticles (assuming silica nanoparticles have been added) by the respective percentages of 46%, 61%, 21%, and 28% within 28 days. Isfahani et al. and Li L.G et al. 2017 showed that nanoSiO2 modified concrete was able to fill the gaps between the particles and foster certain chemical reactions, generating a denser packed microstructure. All the studies suggest that nano-silica holds great promise in enhancing the performance of concrete. As highlighted by the study of Majid Abdellah et al. 2017, compressive strength of concrete is enhanced by the addition of nano-SiO2 upon formation of calcium hydroxide, via pozzolanic reaction. However, without nano-SiO2, concrete lacks hydrated calcium silicate, a crucial component for strength. Tran and Phan (2024) found that adding nano-silica to high-strength concrete with fly ash improved its strength, bending, and physical characteristics. The ideal concentration of 1% nano-silica was found to improve physical characteristics and decrease slab thickness without sacrificing functionality. With a water-to-binder ratio of 0.31, NS has an impact on the durability properties of high-performance concrete. It was noted that adding just a 2% cement-to-NS ratio would decrease the absorption of capillary water. The effectiveness of extremely fine NS particles, which obstruct pores and enhance the structure of the samples, is another factor contributing to the decrease in water absorption levels Chithra *et al.*(2016). The higher pozzolanic activity of nS is responsible for the early increase in compressive strength, whereas the filling of gaps by CSH gel causes the improvement at 28 days because the finer NS particles strengthen the link between aggregates and mortar. (Mukharjee et al 2020). According to the study, the difficulty of distributing NS (10 ± 5 nm) uniformly in concrete led to weak spots; 1% NS had a higher compressive strength than 3% NS, which may have been caused by the agglomeration of tiny NS particles. Higher NS dosages also caused poor workability and microcracks in the concrete (Li *et al.*2017). The amount of cement in the mixture would naturally decrease when the SiO2 concentration of the cement increases (for instance, by 2%), resulting in a decreased hydration reactivity. It is possible to argue that the decrease in hydration reactivity had a bigger effect than the rise in pozzolanic activity. Hence, the cement mortar containing 2% SiO2 had a lower compressive strength (Majid Abdellahi *et al.* 2017). To impart smart microstructures, the nanosilica particle size may function as an ultra-filler within the concrete, creating dense and refined micro-voids. Concrete's strength was increased, and it served as a cement substitute when a specific dosage of nanosilica was added (V.V. Praveen Kumar et al. 2023).

3.5 *Effect of nano silica on durability parameters*

Several researchers observed that using NS in concrete led to a notable decrease in porosity and an enhanced pore structure, particularly with a 2% dosage, which reduced large capillary porosity and the sizes of both threshold and critical diameter pores (Zhang et al 2012). Compared to control and SF-incorporated samples, the greater C-S-H composition of SNP-incorporated specimens reduces the permeability of concrete. Because of the extra C-S-H that is created, SNPs show early hydration response acceleration. Additionally, SNPs-incorporated FA-concrete specimens show a reduced carbonation rate and a decrease in carbonation depth when compared to control and SF-incorporated specimens (L.P. Singh *et al* 2019). While adding NS up to 3% reduced the carbonation depth when compared to regular concrete, adding more NS over time enhanced the carbonation depth. This is because too much CH reacted with NS to create CSH gel. A thick concrete matrix was produced at an NS dosage of 3%, and more NS addition did not result in a denser concrete. (Kumar *et al.*2019). After 180 days of exposure, adding 3% nS to FA concrete significantly reduced the depth of carbonation by 73% in comparison to its control mix. SF only showed a 35% reduction under the same exposure setting. Because the hydration products produced in the presence of nS are more stable and resistant to the entry of hostile ions, FA concrete would last longer. (Singh *et al* 2019). Very tiny SiO2 nanoparticles fill in the cement paste's pores, forming a covering on the cement particles' surface overall. Consequently, a more compact and dense texture is produced by a homogeneous surface and dispersion in the cement paste (Majid Abdellahi *et al.* 2017).

4 CONCLUSIONS

The addition of nanosilica to cementitious composites significantly reduces the initial and final setting time due to its large specific surface areas, which accelerates the hydration reaction of cement. However, this also reduces workability due to increased surface area and lubricating water requirements. However, when appropriate amounts of nanosilica are used, the mechanical strengths and durability properties of the composite improve. Higher doses of nanomaterials may cause weak zones due to improper dispersion. A denser and less permeable structure is produced because of the nanoparticles' fine particle size filling the spaces in the cured cement paste. This lessens the amount of water that concrete absorbs. Nanoparticles reduce cementitious mixes' permeability to chloride ions. The appropriate amount and type of nanomaterials for specific constructions remain controversial.

ACKNOWLEDGEMENT

The authors gratefully acknowledge Dr.Y.M.Patil sir and department of Civil Engineering for their cooperation in the research.

REFERENCES

Abdellahi M., Karafshani M.K., Rizi A.S., (2017). Modeling effect of SiO_2 nanoparticles on the mechanical propertTushar Jadhavies of the concretes, *Journal of Building Pathology and Rehabilitation*, 2, 8

Abhilash P.P., Nayak D.K., Sangoju B., Kumar R., Kumar V., (2021). Effect of nano-silica in concrete; A review., *Construction and Building Materials* 278, 122347, https://doi.org/10.1016/j.conbuildmat.2021.122347

Ali Nazari, Shadi Riahi, (2011). The effects of SiO2 nanoparticles on physical and mechanical properties of high strength compacting concrete, *Composites: Part B* 42, 570–578, https://doi.org/10.1016/j.compositesb.2010.09.025

Alireza Khaloo, Mohammad Hossein Mobini, Payam Hosseini, (2016). Influence of different types of nano-SiO2 particles on properties of high-performance concrete, *Construction and Building Materials* 113, 188–201

Chenglong Zhuang and Yu Chen, (2019). The effect of nano-SiO_2 on concrete properties: areview, *Nanotechnol Rev*; 8:562–572, https://doi.org/10.1515/ntrev-2019-0050

Chithra S., S.S. Kumar, K. Chinnaraju, (2016). The effect of Colloidal Nano-silica on workability, mechanical and durability properties of High-Performance Concrete with Copper slag as partial fine aggregate, *Constr. Build. Mater.* 113, 794–804

Deependra Prasad Bhatta, Sandeep Singla, Rishav Garg, (n.d.). Microstructural and strength parameters of Nano-SiO2 based cement composites, *Materials Today: Proceedings,* https://doi.org/10.1016/j.matpr.2021.04.276

Elkady H.M., Yasien A.M., M.S. Elfeky, M.E. Serag, (2019). Assessment of mechanical strength of nano silica concrete (NSC) subjected to elevated temperatures, *JSFE* 10 (1), 90–109, https://doi.org/10.1108/JSFE-10-2017-0041.

Forood Torabian Isfahani, Elena Redaelli, Federica Lollini, Weiwen Li, and Luca Bertolini, (n.d.). Effects of nanosilica on compressive strength and durability properties of concrete with different water to binder ratios, *Advances in Materials Science and Engineering*, Volume 2016, Article ID 8453567, 16 pages, http://dx.doi.org/10.1155/2016/8453567

Huu-Bang Tran, Vu To-Anh Phan, (2024). Potential usage of fly ash and nano silica in high-strength concrete: Laboratory experiment and application in rigid pavement, *Case Studies in Construction Materials* 20, e02856

Isfahani FT, Redaelli E, Lollini F, Li W, Bertolini L (2016) efects of nanosilica on compressive strength and durability properties of concrete with diferent water to binder ratios. *Adv Mater Sci Eng.* https://doi.org/10.1155/2016/8453567

Isfahani, Forood Torabian, Elena Redaelli, Weiwen Li, and Yaru Sun. (2017). Effects of nanosilica on early age stages of cement hydration. *Journal of Nanomaterials.* https://doi.org/10.1155/2017/4687484.

Jialu Zhang, Cheng Shen, and Guangfen Diao. (2022). Application and Microstructure Properties of Nanomaterials in New Concrete Materials, *Hindawi, Journal of Nanomaterials*, Volume 2022, Article ID 7396295

Kumar, S., Kumar, A., Kujur, J. (2019). Influence of nanosilica on mechanical and durability properties of concrete, *Struct. Build.*, 172, 781–788

Li L.G., Huang Z.H., Zhu J., Kwan A.K.H., Chen H.Y., (2017). Synergistic effects of micro-silica and nano-silica on strength and microstructure of mortar, *Construction and Building Materials* 140, 229–238

Mukharjee B.B., Barai S.V., (2020). Influence of incorporation of colloidal nano-silica on behaviour of concrete, *Iran J Sci Technol Trans Civ Eng* 44 (2), 657–668, https://doi.org/10.1007/s40996-020-00382-0.

Majid Abdellahi, Masoud Karimi Karafshani, Amin Salimian Rizi, (2017). Modeling effect of SiO2 nanoparticles on the mechanical properties of the concretes, *J Build Rehabil*, 2: 8 https://doi.org/10.1007/s41024-017-0027-8

M. Ranjana, S. Kumar, S. Sinha, (n.d.). Nanosilica's influence on concrete hydration, microstructure, and durability: A review, *Journal of Applied Engineering Sciences* Vol. 14(27), ISSUE 2/2024 ISSN: 2247-3769 / e-ISSN: 2284-7197 ART.NO. 428 pp. 322–335

N.B. Singh, S.K. Saxena, M. Kumar, (2018). Effect of nanomaterials on the properties of geopolymer mortars and concrete, *Materials Today: Proceedings* 5, 9035–9040

Nazari A., Riahi S. (2012). Compressive strength and abrasion resistance of concrete containing SiO2 and Cr2O 3 nanoparticles in different curing media, *Mag. Concr. Res.* 64 (2), 177–188, https://doi.org/10.1680/macr.10.00173.

Palla R, Karade SR, Mishra G, Sharma U, Singh LP (2017) High strength sustainable concrete using silica nanoparticles. *Constr Build Mater* 138:285–295. https://doi.org/10.1016/j.conbu ildmat.2017.01.129

Praveen Kumar V.V., Subhashish Dey, (2023). Study on strength and durability characteristics of nano-silica based blended concrete, *Hybrid Advances* 2, 100011, https://doi.org/10.1016/j.hybadv.2022.100011

Sobolev K., M.F. Gutiérrez, (2005). How nanotechnology can change the concrete world, Am. Ceram. *Soc. Bull.* 84 14–18, https://doi.org/10.1002/ 9780470588260.ch17.

Singh L.P., D. Ali, I. Tyagi, U. Sharma, R. Singh, P. Hou, (2019). Durability studies of nano-engineered fly ash concrete, *Constr. Build. Mater.* 194, 205–215, https://doi.org/10.1016/j.conbuildmat.2018.11.022.

Singh, L.P., D. Ali, and U. Sharma. (2016). Studies on optimization of silica nanoparticles dosage in cementitious system. *Cement and Concrete Composites* 70. https://doi.org/10.1016/j.cemconcomp.2016.03.006.

Singh L.P., W. Zhu, T. Howind, U. Sharma, (2017). Quantification and characterization of C-S-H in silica nanoparticles incorporated cementitious system, *Cem. Concr. Compos.* 79, 106–116, https://doi.org/10.1016/j. cemconcomp.2017.02.004.

Suman Kumar, Arun Kumar and Jitu Kujur, Influence of nanosilica on mechanical and durability properties of concrete, *Proceedings of the Institution of Civil Engineers - Structures and Buildings.*

Vikram Singh Kashyap, Gaurav Sancheti, Jitendra Singh Yadav and Utkarsh Agrawa, (2023). Smart sustainable concrete: enhancing the strength and durability with nano silica, *Smart Construction and Sustainable Cities*, https://doi.org/10.1007/s44268-023-00023-1

Zhang M.H., Islam J., (2012). Use of nano-silica to reduce setting time and increase early strength of concretes with high volumes of fly ash or slag, *Constr. Build. Mater*, 29, 573–580. 10.1016/j.cemconcomp.2012.02.005

Advancement in Engineering and Science – Goyal et al. (Eds)
© 2026 The Author(s), ISBN: 978-1-041-31101-0

Efficient and Effective Optimal Resource Allocation in Wireless Network

Sujeet More, Geetika Narang, Sneha Tirth, and Rupali Maske
Department of Computer Engineering, Trinity College of Engineering and Research, Pune

Amol Bhosale and Anil Sawant
Department of Electronics and Telecommunication, Trinity College of Engineering and Research, Pune

ABSTRACT: Efficient resource allocate on in wireless networks is becoming essential due to the growing demand for wireless communication services. The Cuckoo-based Flooding Protocol (CbFP) is presented in this research as an innovative method to improve resource allocation and data transmission in wireless networks. Initially, the wireless network environment is populated with the necessary nodes to establish a robust network topology. Then, data packets are distributed according to the available bandwidth, and the cuckoo search fitness function is used to estimate the best resource allocation. The data packets are sent to the target node by the nodes, based on the allocated resources. The effectiveness of the framework was evaluated using the ns3 tool, and various network efficiency parameters were calculated. To validate the improvements, the results were compared with existing models. The model achieved an impressive throughput of 50 Mbps with minimal transmission delay.

Keywords: cuckoo search fitness function, flooding protocol, resource allocation, wireless network

1 INTRODUCTION

Wireless technologies play a crucial role in a varied range of applications, from robotics to the Internet of Things (IoT), thereby serving as a vital component for complex large-scale systems [1]. To ensure that massive networks of wirelessly connected devices operate efficiently, it is imperative to manage the many capabilities and constraints that set their operating bounds [2]. Achieving consistent average performance across the stochastic wireless channel by distributing a finite set of resources can be seen as the primary challenge in optimal design [3]. Despite the simplicity of expressing these optimization problems, they often become complex due to their non-convex and infinite dimensional nature, posing difficulties in finding solutions [4]. Researchers have been exploring contemporary machine learning and statistical regression methods as potential remedies for wireless resource allocation issues, as the need for scalability and complexity grows in emerging applications [5]. Methods involve instructing a machine learning prototypical, like a neural network (NN), to imitate resource allocation systems' behaviors across different scenarios [6]. A popular approach involves employing supervised learning techniques to train a neural network (NN) in order to replicate the actions of a pre-existing heuristic [7]. This approach aims to reduce the computational load during execution [8]. Efficiently managing limited network resources, such as bandwidth, power, and spectrum, is of utmost importance to optimize performance and guarantee user satisfaction in wireless networks [9]. This entails dynamically adjusting the distribution of resources to adapt to the ever-changing conditions of wireless environments, which include factors such as user mobility, interference, and varying traffic demands [10].

By effectively allocating resources, it is possible to maximize data throughput, minimize latency, and ensure reliable real-time communication [11]. The exploitation of techniques such as advanced optimization algorithms, machine learning, besides game theory is a common approach to achieving this objective [12]. Ultimately, efficient resource allocation enhances the level of service (QoS) for diverse applications, facilitates the increasing number of interconnected devices, and maintains the network's robustness and scalability [13]. A popular feature of fully connected neural networks (FCNNs) is their universal approximation capability [14]. Still, for large-scale situations, FCNNs are not practicable. Convolutional neural networks (CNNs) achieve scalability in processing signals across time and space [15]. A new method has been introduced to improve energy efficiency in bandwidth allocation and scheduling, focusing on reducing the energy consumption of user equipment (UE) [16]. Another approach addresses the challenges of sparse and low-rank problems in supporting federated learning (FL) algorithms by optimizing user selection and beam-forming design simultaneously [17, 18]. Furthermore, reduced latency in FL training periods is achieved by utilizing the multi-access channel's superposition characteristic [19]. However, these optimization attempts mainly rely on existing FL algorithms and need all UEs to participate in each global training iteration, which may result in suboptimal results because of restrictions like bandwidth and energy [20].

The main findings of this research are outlined below,

- Initially, the required nodes are created and deployed in the wireless network environment.
- A novel Cuckoo-based Flooding Protocol (CbFP) is designed to efficiently allocate resources and transmit data in wireless networks.
- Data packets are assigned based on available bandwidth; with optimal resources allocated using the cuckoo search fitness function.
- Hereafter, a node transmits the data packets to the destination node based on the allocated resources.
- The communication latency, throughput, packet loss, and packet delivery ratio for suggested parameters were computed and contrasted with those of other models.

The research article is organized as follows: Section 2 describes the current related research work, Section 3 goes into detail on how to create a suggested model, Section 4 outlines the results of the unique technique that was put into practice, and Section 5 wraps up the study arguments.

2 RELATED WORKS

A few current related literature works are explained as trails, Teekaraman *et al.* [21] examine the proper distribution of resources for individual subordinate users across the entire cognitive radio network, considering the presence or absence of primary users. Even with a larger network size, the proposed model will still be capable of achieving excellent performance in

DOI: 10.1201/9781003798514-8

terms of capacity and interference, while also improving throughput. The use of a hybrid optimization strategy for decision-making which combines relaying and clustering techniques makes it difficult to implement this model in real-time.

Wang *et al.* [22] developed a neural network with aggregation graphs (Agg-GNNs). These networks are capable of processing a series of graph-aggregated state data that is delayed and perhaps asynchronous. The Agg-GNN uses synchronous or asynchronous connections to efficiently combine global network data at each node. Locally at each transmitter, this data is gathered from multi-hop neighbors. Even though the size of the method stays the same as the network grows, scalability problems could occur when deploying Agg-GNNs in large and diverse network environments.

To manage resources in the future 6G cognitive network, Dong *et al.* [23] created a thorough framework named Integrated Sensing and Communication (ISAC). The concept of Sensing Quality of Service (QoS) has been introduced for a range of applications in order to assess the efficiency of sensing services. The challenges of resource allocation, which involve maintaining a balance between sensing and communication QoS, are tackled by formulating and resolving problems using fairness and comprehensiveness criteria. However, the complex environment leads to a considerable amount of interference.

Fang *et al.* [24] propose a means distribution method based on deep reinforcement learning (DRL) to enhance content distribution in layered fog radio access networks (FRANs). The DRL policy leverages request history data and the resources of the network to enable cross-layer cooperative caching and routing decisions. However, there is still a lot of complexity in the system.

A technique for deep reinforcement learning with multi-agent-based resource management and interference reduction in wireless networks is presented by Naderializadeh *et al.* [25]. This approach allows agents to independently make decisions without knowledge of other agents' decisions. Nevertheless, the system becomes significantly more intricate as determining the optimal user scheduling and a power control option becomes highly challenging.

3 PROPOSED METHODOLOGY

A novel Cuckoo-based Flooding Protocol (CbFP) has been developed to effectively allocate resources and transmit data within wireless networks. Initially, the required nodes are created and deployed in the wireless network environment to establish a robust network topology. Efficient resource allocation is ensured by allocating data packets according to the available bandwidth, utilizing the cuckoo search fitness function. Once the resources have been allocated effectively, the nodes are transmitting the data packets to the destination nodes. The suggested CbFP architecture is shown in Figure 1.

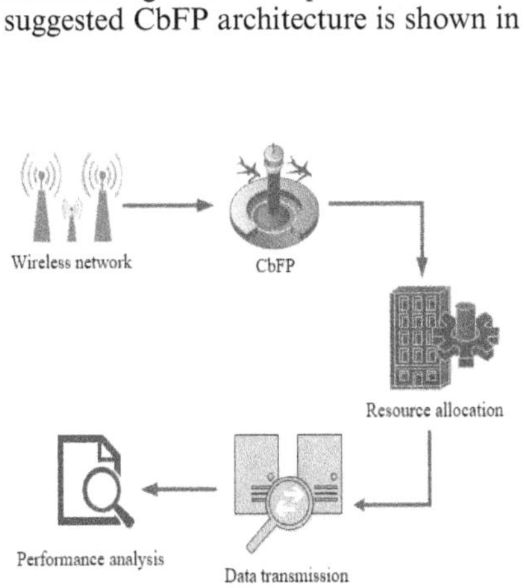

Figure 1. Proposed CbFP architecture.

3.1 *Process of the proposed CbFP*

The proposed CbFP approach is founded on the combined process of cuckoo search optimization and flooding protocol. The foundation of the Cuckoo Search algorithm is a meta-heuristic optimization technique derived from cuckoo bird behavior. This system consists of many nests, each of which represents a possible solution. The nests are modified iteratively using a combination of mutation operation and Levy flight-based random search. This method enables the algorithm to effectively explore and detect the optimal solution.

3.1.1 *Node initialization*

At first, the wireless network environment establishes a pre-determined number of nodes. Each node is characterized by its unique identifier, which facilitates communication with other nodes and is used for routing data packets throughout the network. The node initialization process is done using (1).

$$W(N) = \{x_1, x_2, x_3, ...x_n\}^T \tag{1}$$

Here, W (N) represents the node initialization procedure, which $x_1, x_2 ... x_n$ denotes the number of nodes within the wireless network. T is used to indicate the nodes' identifier.

3.1.2 *Resource allocation*

During the resource allocation process, data packets are assigned based on the bandwidth available at each node in the network. Once the available bandwidth is assessed, the data packets are allocated to nodes according to their respective bandwidth capacities. Then to optimize the resource allocation, the cuckoo search fitness function is applied. This function ensures that the allocation of data packets to nodes is iteratively updated, resulting in the optimal resource allocation of bandwidth to each node. The resource allocation is done using (2).

$$R_{i,j}^{(n+1)} = R_{i,j}^{n} + L \otimes F\left(R_{i,j}^{n}\right) \tag{2}$$

Here, $R_{i,j}^{n}$ denotes the allocation of data packets from node i to node j during iteration$n$. The $R_{i,j}^{(n+1)}$ is the updated allocation at iteration n+1. L signifies the Levy flight utilized for random search in the cuckoo search function. F is the fitness function analyzing the resource allocation $R_{i,j}^{n}$.

This equation updates the data packet allocation according to the fitness function, [31–37] which assesses the efficiency of the allocation, the current allocation, and a random step utilizing the Levy flight. By continuously updating the resource allocation with the help of the cuckoo search algorithm, the data packet allocation is refined to attain the best possible allocation of bandwidth to individual nodes within the network.

3.1.3 *Data transmission*

The nodes that received bandwidth and data packets during the resource allocation process are now responsible for transmitting the packets to the specified destination nodes. Each node only sends packets within its allotted capacity by using the assigned bandwidth to transmit the packets. The data transmission is done using (3).

$$D(t)_{i,j} = \sum_{k=1}^{N} \frac{P_{i,j}}{P_{i,k}} \times B_i \tag{3}$$

The data transfer from node i to node j is represented by $D(t)_{i,j}$. The number of packets intended for transmission from node i to node j is denoted by $P_{i,j}$. $P_{i,k}$ signifies the overall number of packets to be transmitted by node i to all destination nodes k. The bandwidth allocated to node i is designated as B_i. The protocol enhances data throughput by ensuring that nodes operate within their designated bandwidth, resulting in high data transmission throughout the network.

Algorithm 1: CbFP

Start
{
Node initialization ( )
{
int $W(N) = \{x_1, x_2 ... x_n\}^T$
$T \rightarrow$ *node identifier*
// required number of nodes are created
}
Resource allocation ( )
{
int $L,\ R^n_{i,j},\ F$
// initialized the resource allocation variables
Assess the available bandwidth at each node i, j
$for(n+1):$
Calculate the fitness function for the current allocation
$if(F(current\ solution) > F(previous\ best\ solution))$
$update\ (best\ solution)$
end if
end for
// Periodically replace the worst solutions with new best solutions
$R^{(n+1)}_{i,j}\ \left(add\left(R^n_{i,j},\ L\right) \otimes F\left(R^n_{i,j}\right)\right) \rightarrow resource\ allocation$
$R^n_{i,j} \rightarrow$ *Current allocation of data packets from node i to node j at iteration n.*
// updates the resource allocation based on the fitness function
}
Data transmission ( )
{
int $B_i, P_{i,j}, D(t)$
// initialized the data transmission variables
$P_{i,j}/P_{i,k} \times B_i \rightarrow data\ transmission$
//data packets are transmitted within the allotted bandwidth.
}
}
Stop

The mathematical formulation of each phase of the procedures is generated in pseudo-code format and further elaborated into an algorithm1. The proposed method.

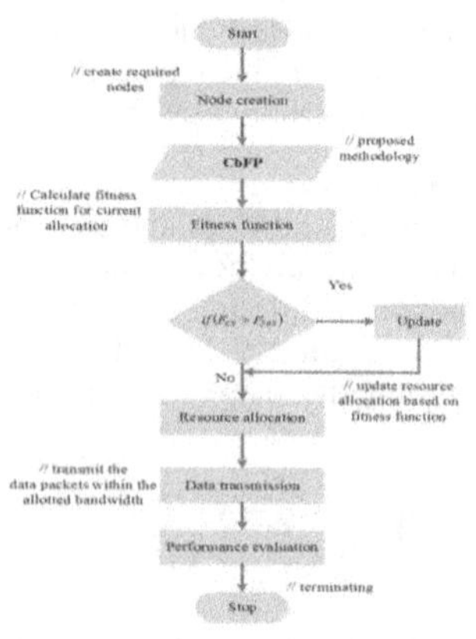

Figure 2. Flowchart of CbFP.

4 RESULT AND DISCUSSION

The ns3 simulator is used to test the designed CbFP model. The necessary nodes were first established within the wireless network setting. Following this, the cuckoo search fitness function was utilized to effectively allocate resources, allowing the node to send data packets to the specified node based on the assigned resources. Table 1 explains the requirements for the proposed approach.

Table 1. Description of the parameters.

Simulator	Ns3
Operating system (OS)	Windows 10/ 11
Number of nodes	100
Network type	Wireless network
Network area	$100\,m \times 100\,m$
Protocol	Flooding protocol
Optimization	Cuckoo search
Data packet size	500 bytes

This research established a wireless network with 100 nodes initially. The operational process of the nodes using the activated CbFP strategy is explained below. By employing the cuckoo search fitness function, the optimal resources are assigned. Then, the node sends the data packets to the specified destination node according to the allocated resources.

The proposed model node initialization, resource allocation, and data transmission are illustrated in Figure 3. In this scenario, the data communication path from the cradle node to the base station is depicted by the red line, while the resources allocated based on the cuckoo fitness function, aimed at maximizing network performance, are represented by the black line.

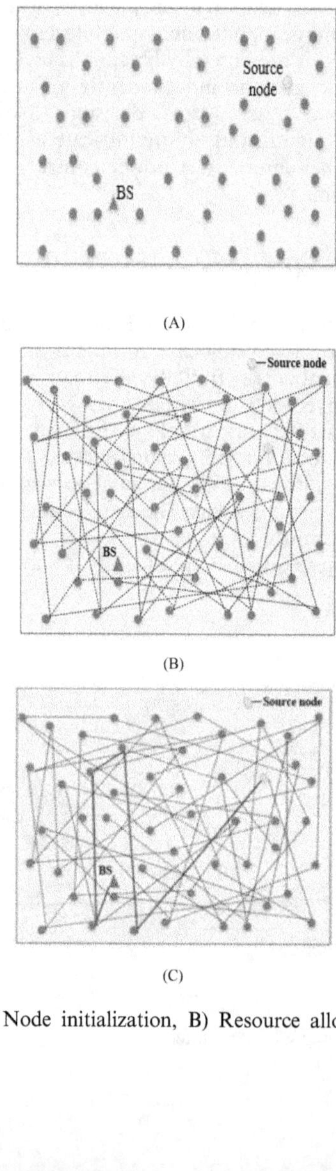

Figure 3. A) Node initialization, B) Resource allocation, C) Data transmission.

4.1 *Performance analysis*

To validate the efficiency [42–43] of the proposed CbFP, the network characteristics including packet delivery ratio, packet loss rate, latency, and throughput were computed and compared to the existing methods. The existing taken for comparison is a Fishnet.6G [26], Lively Cu-Du Selection Technique (DSCD) [27], Resource Allocation for Minimal Loss and Guaranteed Fairness with Delay Awareness (DRAGFL) [28], energy-efficient routing protocol with congestion-aware resource allocation (ECRR) [29], and Deep deterministic policy gradient action adjuster (AADDPG) [30].

4.1.1 *Throughput*

Throughput [38–40] is the term used to describe the quantity of data that can be effectively transmitted over a network within a specific timeframe. In the context of wireless networks, throughput is commonly measured in mbps. Throughput can be calculated using (4).

$$Throughput = \frac{packet\ size + sent\ packets}{Time} \tag{4}$$

The throughput compression is described in Figure 4. In this case, the throughput of the DSCD model is 2.2 Mbps, that of the DRAGFL model is 31 Mbps, and the technique Fishnet.6G obtains a throughput of 22 Mbps. The suggested throughput is 50 Mbps, which is higher than that of the current models.

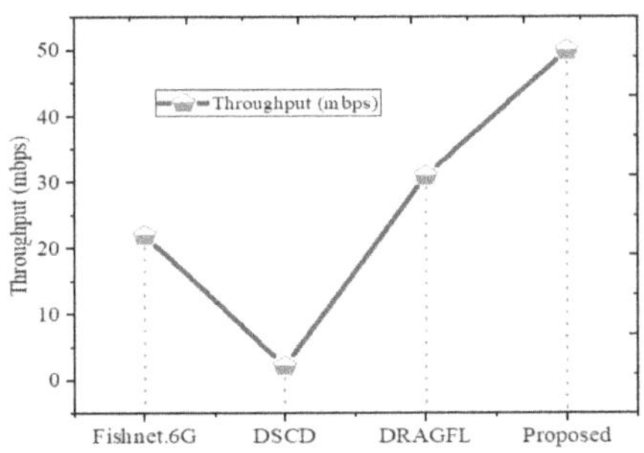

Figure 4. Throughput comparison.

4.1.2 *Delay*

The delay [41] is determined by the period it takes for containers to travel from the cradle to the terminus. In this case, the delay is measured in milliseconds (ms), with the formula for its calculation outlined in (5).

$$Delay = Departure\ time\ of\ the\ packet - arrived\ time\ of\ the\ packet \tag{5}$$

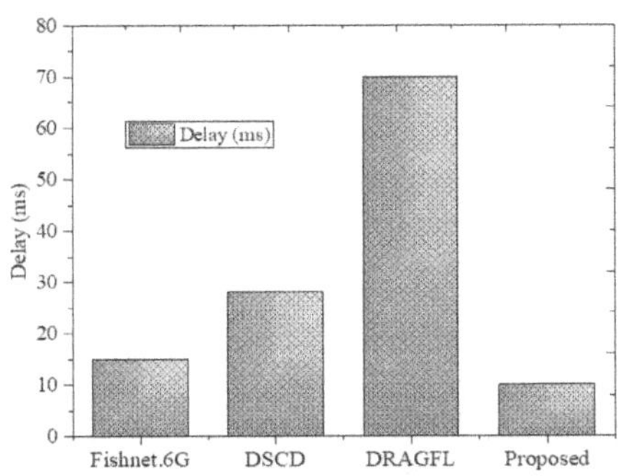

Figure 5. Delay comparison.

The comparison of delay can be seen in Figure 5. The Fishnet.6G model achieves a delay of 15ms. The delay time for DSCD is 28ms, while the delay time for DRAGFL is 70ms. Additionally, the designed CbFP was able to send data packets in just 10ms, which is a lower latency rate compared to other techniques.

4.1.3 *Packet drip*

Packet drip is described as the occurrence of data packets being discarded or lost while being transmitted through a wireless network. This can happen for several reasons, including buffer overflow, channel congestion, power control issues, and collisions. The formula for calculating packet losses is explained in (6).

$$Packet\ drop = \frac{no\ of\ packets\ lost}{Total\ no\ of\ packets\ sent} * 100 \tag{6}$$

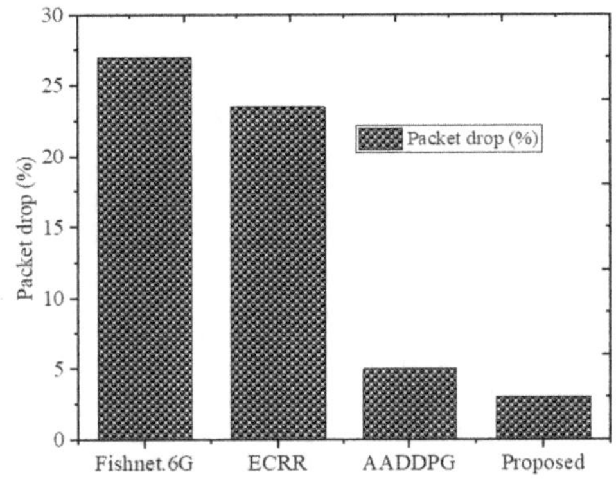

Figure 6. Packet drop comparison.

In Figure 6, the packet drop compression is explained. In this instance, the ECRR model's packet drop is 23.5%, the Fishnet.6G model's is 27% and the AADDPG approach yields a packet drop of 5%. The proposed packet drop, which is 3%, is less than the current models.

4.1.4 *Packet delivery ratio*

The PDR is calculated as the quantity of packets effectively received at the destination alienated by the quantity of packets transmitted by the sender node, as shown in (7).

$$PDR = \frac{Amount\ of\ delivered\ packets}{Quantity\ of\ packets\ sent} * 100 \tag{7}$$

Figure 7 displays the comparison of packet delivery ratios. The DSCD achieves a score of 0.99%, the DRADFL achieves a score of 32%, and the ECRR achieves a score of 18.9%. In contrast, the proposed method demonstrates a significantly higher ratio of 60% when compared to existing methods.

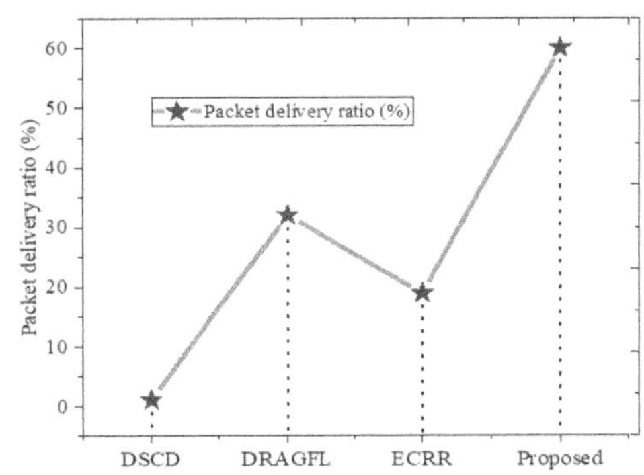

Figure 7. Packet delivery ratio comparison.

4.2 *Discussion*

The proposed protocol employs the cuckoo search fitness function to optimally distribute resources, resulting in a significant enhancement in data throughput. By ensuring nodes operate within their designated bandwidth, the protocol effectively manages network resources, preventing congestion and reducing packet loss. This resource allocation enables nodes to efficiently transmit data packets to the target node, optimizing overall network performance. Consequently, the protocol achieves high data transmission rates across the network, promoting robust and reliable communication, and maximizing the utilization of available bandwidth. The overall performance of the implemented CbFP can be found in Table 2.

Table 2. Overall performance of the proposed CbFP.

Nodes	Throughput (Mbps)	Packet drop (%)	Packet delivery ratio (%)	Delay (ms)
20	49	2.9	59	9.9
40	48	2.5	53	7
60	49.3	2.2	42	8.5
80	49	2.7	58	7.9
100	50	3	60	10

The simulation outcomes have established the remarkable efficiency of the Cuckoo-based Flooding Protocol (CbFP) in achieving optimal resource allocation and enhancing network performance. CbFP shows significant enhancements in key performance metrics, including a throughput of 50 Mbps, a packet delivery ratio of 60%, a minimal delay of 10 ms, and a 3% packet drop. CbFP uses the cuckoo search fitness function to maximize resource allocation and guarantee effective data packet transmission throughout the wireless network.

5 CONCLUSION

A new Cuckoo-based Flooding Protocol (CbFP) has been developed in this study. The main objective of this protocol is to efficiently allocate resources and transmit data in wireless networks. To achieve this, the necessary nodes are first created and deployed in the wireless network environment to establish a strong network topology. Next, based on the available bandwidth, the data packets are allotted, and the cuckoo search fitness function is used to identify the best possible resource allocation. Lastly, using the resources that have been allotted, the nodes send the data packets to the target node. The model implementation resulted in a network throughput of 50 Mbps; with a data transmission delay is 10 ms. However, the wireless network remains vulnerable to possible attacks. Therefore, an attack prevention system will be included in future work to ensure data security.

REFERENCES

[1] R. Jayaraman, B. Manickam, S. Annamalai, M. Kumar, A. Mishra, and R. Shrestha, (2023). Effective resource allocation technique to improve QoS in 5G wireless network, *Electronics*, vol. 12, no. 2, pp. 451.

[2] M.D.A.B.S. Abir, M.Z. Chowdhury, and Y.M. Jang, (2023). Software-defined uav networks for 6g systems: Requirements, opportunities, emerging techniques, challenges, and research directions, *IEEE Open Journal of the Communications Society*.

[3] M.T. Mamaghani, X. Zhou, N. Yang, A. Lee Swindlehurst, and H. Vincent Poor, (2024). Performance analysis of finite blocklength transmissions over wiretap fading channels: An average information leakage perspective, *IEEE Transactions on Wireless Communications*.

[4] S. More *et al.*, (2020). Security Assured CNN-Based Model for Reconstruction of Medical Images on the Internet of Healthcare Things, in *IEEE Access*, vol. 8, pp. 126333–126346, doi: 10.1109/ACCESS.2020.3006346.

[5] P.M. Wensing, M. Posa, Y. Hu, A. Escande, N. Mansard, and A. Del Prete, (2023). Optimization-based control for dynamic legged robots, *IEEE Transactions on Robotics*.

[6] Y. Shi, L. Lian, Y. Shi, Z. Wang, Y. Zhou, L. Fu, L. Bai, J. Zhang, and W. Zhang, (2023). Machine learning for large-scale optimization in 6g wireless networks, *IEEE Communications Surveys & Tutorials*.

[7] M.R. Shafie, H. Khosravi, S. Farhadpour, S. Das, and I. Ahmed, (2024). A cluster-based human resources analytics for predicting employee turnover using optimized Artificial Neural Networks and data augmentation, *Decision Analytics Journal*, vol. 11, pp. 100461.

[8] S. More and J. Singla, (2021). A Study on Automated Grading System for Early Prediction of Rheumatoid Arthritis, *2021 6th International Conference on Communication and Electronics Systems (ICCES), Coimbatre*, India, pp. 1293–1300, doi: 10.1109/ICCES51350.2021.9489144.

[9] L. Tsipi, M. Karavolos, G. Papaioannou, M. Volakaki, and D. Vouyioukas, (2024). Machine learning-based methods for MCS prediction in 5G networks, *Telecommunication Systems*, pp. 1–24.

[10] I. Behera, and S. Sobhanayak, (2024). Task scheduling optimization in heterogeneous cloud computing environments: A hybrid GA-GWO approach, *Journal of Parallel and Distributed Computing*, vol. 183, pp. 104766.

[11] Y. Ullah, M. Roslee, S.M. Mitani, M. Sheraz, F. Ali, A.F. Osman, M.H. Jusoh, and C. Sudhamani, (2024). Reinforcement learning-based unmanned aerial vehicle trajectory planning for ground users' mobility management in heterogeneous networks, *Journal of King Saud University-Computer and Information Sciences*, pp. 102052.

[12] More, S., Singla, J. (2022). Machine Learning Approaches for Image Quality Improvement. In: Chen, J.IZ., Tavares, J.M.R.S., Iliyasu, A.M., Du, KL. (eds) Second International Conference on Image Processing and Capsule Networks. ICIPCN 2021. *Lecture Notes in Networks and Systems*, vol 300. Springer, Cham. https://doi.org/10.1007/978-3-030-84760-9_5

[13] A. Alhammadi, Z.H. Ismail, I. Shayea, Z.A. Shamsan, M. Alsagabi, S. Al-Sowayan, S.A. Saad, and M. Alnakhli, (2024). SOMNet: Self-Optimizing mobility management for resilient 5G heterogeneous networks, *Engineering Science and Technology, an International Journal*, vol. 52, pp. 101671.

[14] J. Logeshwaran, T. Kiruthiga, R. Kannadasan, L. Vijayaraja, A. Alqahtani, N. Alqahtani, and A.A. Alsulami, (2023). Smart load-based resource optimization model to enhance the performance of device-to-device communication in 5G-WPAN, *Electronics*, vol. 12, no. 8, pp. 1821.

[15] S. More, J. Singla, O.Y. Song, U. Tariq and S. Malebary, (2021). Denoising Medical Images Using Deep Learning in IoT Environment, *Computers, Materials & Continua*, Volume 69, Issue No 3, pp 3127–3143, doi:10.32604/cmc.2021.018230

[16] J. Meng, Y.J. Zhou, T.R. Ye, Y.T. Xiao, Y.Q. Lu, A.W. Zheng, and B. Liang, (2023). Hybrid data-driven framework for shale gas production performance analysis via game theory, machine learning, and optimization approaches, *Petroleum Science*, vol. 20, no. 1, pp. 277–294.

[17] More, Sujeet and Singla, Jimmy. (2021). '*Discrete-MultiResUNet: Segmentation and Feature Extraction Model for Knee MR Images*'., pp 3771 – 3781. doi:10.3233/JIFS-211459

[18] Z.E. Ahmed, A.A. Hashim, R.A. Saeed, and M.M. Saeed, (2023). Mobility management enhancement in smart cities using software defined networks, *Scientific African*, vol. 22, pp. e01932.

[19] More, Sujeet and Singla, Jimmy. (2021). '*A Generalized Deep Learning Framework for Automatic Rheumatoid Arthritis Severity Grading*'. 7603 – 7614. doi: 10.3233/JIFS-212015

[20] X. Qi, G.A.M. de Almeida, and S. Maldonado, (2024). Physics-informed neural networks for solvin flow problems modeled by the 2D Shallow Water Equations without labeled data, *Journal of Hydrology*, pp. 131263.

[21] S. Cantero-Chinchilla, P.D. Wilcox, and A.J. Croxford, (2022). Deep learning in automated ultrasonic NDE–developments, axioms and opportunities, *NDT & E International*, vol. 131, pp. 102703.

[22] S. Iftikhar, M.M.M. Ahmad, S. Tuli, D. Chowdhury, M. Xu, S. S. Gill, and S. Uhlig, (2023). HunterPlus: AI based energy-efficient task scheduling for cloud–fog computing environments, *Internet of Things*, vol. 21, pp. 100667.

[23] B. Xiao, X. Yu, W. Ni, X. Wang, and H.V. Poor, (2024). Over-the-air federated learning: Status quo, open challenges, and future directions, *Fundamental Research*

[24] S. More and J. Singla, (2019). Machine Learning Techniques with IoT in Agriculture, *International Journal of Advanced Trends in Computer Science and Engineering*, Volume 8, Issue No 3, pp 742–747, DOI:10.30534/ijatcse/2019/63832019

[25] W. Xu, Z. Yang, D.W.K. Ng, M. Levorato, Y.C. Eldar, and M. Debbah, (2023). Edge learning for B5G networks with distributed signal processing: Semantic communication, edge computing, and wireless sensing, *IEEE Journal of Selected Topics in Signal Processing*, vol. 17, no. 1, pp. 9–39.

[26] Z. Chen, H.H. Yang, and T.Q.S. Quek, (2023) Edge intelligence over the air: Two faces of interference in federated learning, *IEEE Communications Magazine*.

[27] Sujeet More and Jimmy Singla, (2021). A Study on Automated Grading System for Early Prediction of Rheumatoid Arthritis, *6th International Conference on Communication and Electronics Systems (ICCES 2021)*, PPG Institute of Technology, Coimbatore, 8th – 10th July.

[28] M.Q. Hamdan, H. Lee, D. Triantafyllopoulou, R. Borralho, A. Kose, E. Amiri, D. Mulvey, W. Yu, R. Zitouni, R. Pozza, B. Hunt, H. Bagheri, C.H. Foh, F. Heliot, G. Chen, P. Xiao, N. Wang, and R. Tafazolli, (2023). Recent advances in machine learning for network automation in the o-ran, *Sensors*, vol. 23, no. 21, pp. 8792.

[29] Sujeet More and Jimmy Singla, (2021). Machine Learning Approaches for Image Quality Improvement, *2nd International Conference on Image Processing and Capsule Networks (ICIPCN 2021)*, King Mongkut's University of Technology, Thailand.

[30] Y. Teekaraman, H. Manoharan, A.R. Basha, and A. Manoharan, (2023). Hybrid optimization algorithms for resource allocation in heterogeneous cognitive radio networks, *Neural Processing Letters*, vol. 55, no. 4, pp. 3813–3826.

[31] Z. Wang, M. Eisen, and A. Ribeiro, (2022). Learning decentralized wireless resource allocations with graph neural networks, *IEEE Transactions on Signal Processing*, vol. 70, pp. 1850–1863.

[32] More, S.; Singla, J.; Abugabah, A.; AlZubi, A.A. (2020). Machine Learning Techniques for Quantification of Knee Segmentation from MRI. *Complexity* 2020, 6613191.

[33] F. Dong, F. Liu, Y. Cui, W. Wang, K. Han, and Z. Wang, (2022). Sensing as a service in 6G perceptive networks: A unified framework for ISAC resource allocation, *IEEE Transactions on Wireless Communications*.

[34] C. Fang, H. Xu, Y. Yang, Z. Hu, S. Tu, K. Ota, Z. Yang, M. Dong, Z. Han, F.R. Yu, and Y. Liu, Deep-reinforcement-learning-based resource allocation for content distribution in fog radio access networks, IEEE Internet of Things Journal, vol. 9, no. 18, pp. 16874–16883.

[35] N. Naderializadeh, J.J. Sydir, M. Simsek, and H. Nikopour, (2021). Resource management in wireless networks via multi-agent deep reinforcement learning, *IEEE Transactions on Wireless Communications*, vol. 20, no. 6, pp. 3507–3523.

[36] Chunduri, V., Kumar, A., Joshi, A. *et al.* (2023). Optimizing energy and latency trade-offs in mobile ultra-dense IoT networks within futuristic smart vertical networks. *Int J Data Sci Anal* (2023). https://doi.org/10.1007/s41060-023-00477-7

[37] A.M.A. Ibrahim, Z. Chen, H.A. Eljailany, G. Yu, A.A. Ipaye, K.A. Abouda, and W.M. Idress, (2024). Advancing 6G IoT networks: Willow Catkin packet transmission scheduling with AI and Bayesian game-theoretic approach-based resource allocation, Internet of Things, pp. 101119.

[38] S. Mollahasani, M. Erol-Kantarci, and R. Wilson, (2021). Dynamic CU-DU selection for resource allocation in O-RAN using actor-critic learning, *2021 IEEE Global Communications Conference (GLOBECOM), IEEE.*

[39] N.K.M. Madi, M.M. Nasralla, and Z.M. Hanapi, (2022). Delay-based resource allocation with fairness guarantee and minimal loss for eMBB in 5G heterogeneous networks, *IEEE Access*, vol. 10, pp. 75619–75636.

[40] Sujeet More and Jimmy Singla, (2020). Machine learning methods for knee feature extraction from MR images, *International Conference on Smart Electronics and Communication (ICOSEC 2020)*, Kongunadu College of Engineering and Technology, Trichy, 10th - 12th, September 2020.

[41] K.V. Praveen, and P.M.J. Prathap, (2021). Energy efficient congestion aware resource allocation and routing protocol for IoT network using hybrid optimization techniques, *Wireless Personal Communications*. vol. 117, no. 2, pp. 1187–1207.

[42] Z. Shi, X. Xie, H. Lu, H. Yang, J. Cai, and Z. Ding, (2021). Deep reinforcement learning-based multidimensional resource management for energy harvesting cognitive NOMA communications, *IEEE Transactions on Communications*, vol. 70, no. 5, pp. 3110–3125.

[43] Sujeet More and Jimmy Singla, (2019). Arthritis Diagnosis with Machine Learning: A Systematic Review, *International Conference on Computational Intelligence and Data Engineering (ICCIDE 2019), Vidya Jyothi Institute of Technology*, Hyderabad.

Advancement in Engineering and Science – Goyal et al. (Eds)

Optimization of Ultrasonic Flowmeter Performance Using Ansys Adjoint Solver for Varying Flow Conditions

Atul Kolekar and R.B. Teltumade
Department of Mechanical Engineering, Government College of Engineering, Karad, India

Tushar Jadhav
Dept. of Mechanical Engineering, Government College of Engineering

ABSTRACT: This research investigates the optimization of ultrasonic flowmeter design for improved accuracy and efficiency under diverse flow conditions. By leveraging the ANSYS Adjoint Solver, a powerful CFD tool, this study aims to identify optimal design parameters, such as transducer placement, sensor geometry, and flow channel dimensions. Through comprehensive CFD simulations and sensitivity analyses, the work seeks to enhance the performance of ultrasonic flowmeters in various industrial applications.

Keywords: CFD, Adjoint, Ansys, Gradient based Optimization, Ultrasonic Flowmeter

1 INTRODUCTION

This work aims to enhance the accuracy and efficiency of ultrasonic flowmeters through the application of advanced computational fluid dynamics (CFD) techniques. Specifically, the ANSYS Adjoint Solver is utilized to optimize the design of ultrasonic flow-meters for varying flow conditions, such as different flow rates, fluid properties, etc.

1.1 *Motivation*

Ultrasonic flowmeters are extensively used in industries ranging from water and wastewater treatment to chemical processing and pharmaceuticals. However, their performance can be influenced by factors like flow turbulence, fluid properties, and operating conditions. Optimizing the design of these meters leads to improved measurement accuracy, reduced maintenance costs, and enhanced overall efficiency.

1.2 *Objectives*

- CFD Modelling: Develop accurate CFD models of ultrasonic flowmeters, incorporating detailed geometry, fluid properties, and flow conditions.
- Adjoint Optimization: Employ the ANSYS Adjoint Solver to identify optimal design parameters, such as transducer placement, sensor geometry, and flow channel dimensions, for improved flow measurement accuracy.
- Sensitivity Analysis: Conduct sensitivity analyses to evaluate the impact of different design parameters on flowmeter performance under various operating conditions.

2 LITERATURE SURVEY

Ultrasonic flow-meters are extensively used for non-invasive flow rate measurement in various industries. However, their performance can be affected by flow conditions, fluid properties, and meter design. Optimizing ultrasonic flowmeters can enhance accuracy, reliability, and efficiency.

2.1 *Previous research*

Early research focused on improving the accuracy of traditional ultrasonic flowmeters. Studies explored the effects of transducer placement, signal processing techniques, and flow conditions on measurement errors.

2.2 *FD-Based optimization*

CFD (Computational Fluid Dynamics) has emerged as a powerful tool for analysing flow fields and optimizing flowmeter designs.

- Flow Field Analysis: Studies like [9] employed CFD to analyse the influence of transducer inclination angle and design parameters on flow behaviour within the meter.
- Optimization Strategies: Researchers have utilized CFD for optimization purposes as well.
- [4] used CFD to optimize a novel flowmeter design for improved low-flow sensitivity.
- [Bae et al., 2022] explored various signal processing techniques crucial for extracting accurate flow information from the received signal, which is vital for flow measurement optimization.

2.3 *Identified research gaps and contributions*

Despite advancements, some gaps remain:

- Complex Flow Conditions: Most studies focus on simpler flows. Optimization for turbulent, multiphase, or solid-laden flows requires further research.
- Material Properties: The influence of fluid properties like viscosity and density on performance and optimization needs further exploration addressing multiphase flows.
- Real-World Validation: Laboratory studies provide very valuable insights, but more research is needed to validate optimized designs in real-world applications.

This project aims to contribute by:

- Comprehensive CFD Modelling: Developing accurate CFD models capturing complex flow phenomena and fluid properties.
- Adjoint-Based Optimization: Utilizing the ANSYS Adjoint Solver for optimizing a wider range of parameters, including transducer design, flow channel dimensions, and signal processing techniques.

3 METHODOLOGY

3.1 *ANSYS Adjoint Solver and Gradient-Based Optimization*

ANSYS Adjoint Solver is a powerful computational tool designed to efficiently solve optimization problems in engineering simulations. It leverages a gradient-based optimization

DOI: 10.1201/9781003798514-9

technique to determine the design parameters to optimize a specified objective function.

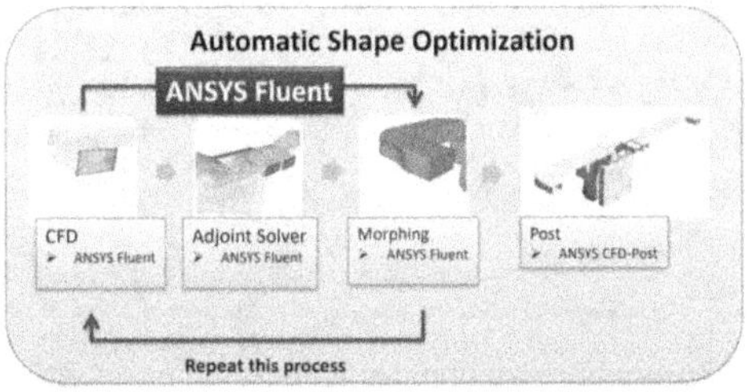

Figure 1. ANSYS Adjoint Solver and Gradient-Based Optimization.

3.2 *Gradient-based optimization*

This technique is rooted in the principle that the gradient of a function indicates the direction of steepest ascent or descent. By calculating the gradient of the objective function in accordance with the design variables, the adjoint solver can iteratively adjust these variables to move towards the optimal solution.

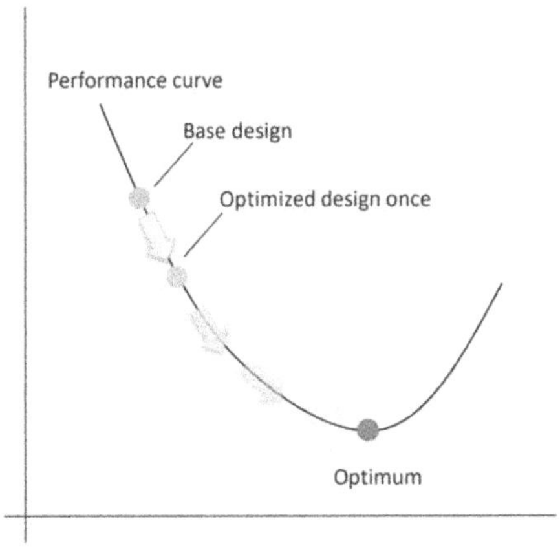

Figure 2. Gradient-Based Optimization.

3.3 *Key Steps in Adjoint-Based Optimization:*

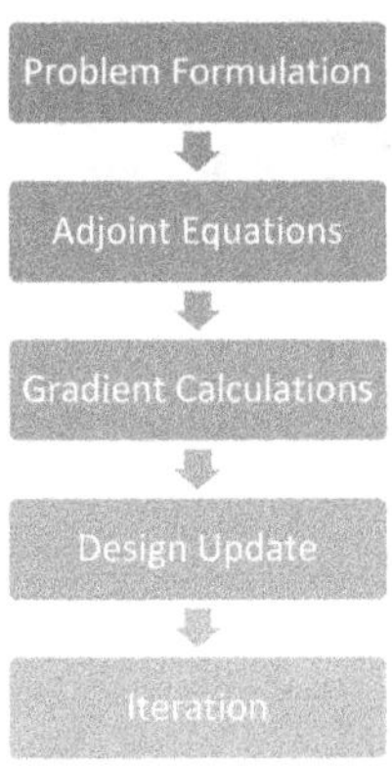

Figure 3. Steps in Gradient-Based Optimization.

1. Problem Formulation: The optimization problem is defined by specifying the objective function and design variables.
2. Adjoint Equations: The adjoint equations are derived from the corresponding governing equations of the physical problem. These equations provide a computationally efficient way to calculate the objective function's gradients.
3. Gradient Calculation: The adjoint solver solves the adjoint equations to obtain the gradients of objective function in accordance of the design variables.
4. Design Update: The design variables are updated on the basis of the calculated gradients, using optimization algorithms like steepest descent or conjugate gradient methods.
5. Iteration: The process of solving the adjoint equations, calculating gradients, and updating design variables is repeated iteratively until a convergence criterion is met.

4 RESULTS

The table presents the maximum Turbulent Kinetic Energy (TKE) values obtained from ANSYS simulations for three different ultrasonic flow meter geometries: "Basic," "Flush," and "Flush Fillet." For each geometry, the maximum TKE is provided for the "Original" design and a "Fluent Optimized" design. The units for TKE are meters squared per second squared (m^2/s^2).

Table 1. Optimization results.

	Max TKE (m^2/s^2)		
Geometry	Original	Fluent Optimized	Improvement
Basic	1.3890091	0.017505603	98.74%
Flush	1.3637149	0.76296958	44.05%
Flush Fillet	1.8790462	1.6421474	12.61%

Turbulent Kinetic Energy (TKE) is a measure of the intensity of turbulence within the fluid flow. It represents the average kinetic energy per unit mass associated with the fluctuating components of the velocity field. Higher TKE values indicate more intense turbulent fluctuations, while lower values suggest a more laminar or less disturbed flow. In the context of ultrasonic flow meters, turbulence can negatively impact measurement accuracy by:

- Scattering and Attenuation of Ultrasonic Waves: Turbulent eddies can scatter the ultrasonic waves, reducing the signal strength received by the downstream transducer. This can lead to a lower signal-to-noise ratio and potentially inaccurate transit time measurements.
- Distortion of Velocity Profiles: Strong turbulence can distort the ideal velocity profiles assumed in the flow rate calculation, leading to errors in the inferred average velocity.
- Increased Flow Noise: Turbulent fluctuations can generate flow noise, which can interfere with the detection of ultrasonic signals.

1. Basic Geometry:

- Original: The original "Basic" geometry exhibits a relatively high maximum TKE of 1.389 (m2/s2). This indicates a significant level of turbulence within the flow domain for this initial design.
- Fluent Optimized: After optimization using ANSYS Fluent, the maximum TKE for the "Basic" geometry drastically reduces to 0.0175 (m2/s2). This represents a remarkable reduction in turbulence intensity (approximately 98.7%).

This significant decrease suggests that the optimization process effectively modified the flow characteristics within the "Basic" geometry, leading to a much smoother and more laminar-like flow regime. This reduction in turbulence is highly beneficial for ultrasonic flow meter performance as it would likely improve signal quality and the accuracy of flow rate measurements.

2. Flush Geometry:

- Original: The original "Flush" geometry also shows a substantial maximum TKE of 1.364 (m2/s2), indicating significant turbulence levels, comparable to the original "Basic" design.
- Fluent Optimized: The optimized "Flush" geometry achieves a reduction in maximum TKE to 0.763 (m2/s2). While this is a reduction (approximately 44.1%), it is not as dramatic as the reduction observed in the "Basic" geometry.

This suggests that the optimization process was less effective in suppressing turbulence for this initial geometry, or that the inherent geometric features of the "Flush" design make it more prone to certain levels of turbulence. Nevertheless, a reduction in TKE is still a positive outcome for flow measurement accuracy.

3. Flush Fillet Geometry:

- Original: The original "Flush Fillet" geometry exhibits the highest maximum TKE among the initial designs, at 1.879 (m2/s2). This indicates the most intense turbulent fluctuations in this initial configuration. The presence of the fillet, while potentially intended for other reasons (e.g., structural integrity, reducing sharp edges), appears to have exacerbated turbulence generation in the original design.
- Fluent Optimized: The optimized "Flush Fillet" geometry shows a reduction in maximum TKE to 1.642 (m2/s2). This is a decrease of approximately 12.6%. While a reduction is achieved, the optimized "Flush Fillet" geometry still exhibits the highest maximum TKE among all the optimized designs.

This implies that even after optimization, the "Flush Fillet" configuration remains the most turbulent among the three geometries considered. This could potentially lead to the least accurate ultrasonic flow measurements compared to the other optimized designs.

Overall Implications:

- Effectiveness of Optimization: The ANSYS Fluent optimization process demonstrated varying degrees of effectiveness in reducing turbulence for the different initial geometries. The "Basic" geometry showed the most significant improvement, while the "Flush Fillet" geometry showed the least.
- Geometry Influence: The initial geometry of the ultrasonic flow meter significantly impacts the level of turbulence generated within the flow. The "Flush Fillet" design appears to be inherently more prone to turbulence compared to the "Basic" and "Flush" designs in their original configurations.
- Potential for Improved Accuracy: The substantial reductions in maximum TKE observed in the optimized "Basic" and "Flush" geometries suggest a strong potential for improved ultrasonic flow meter accuracy. Lower turbulence levels should lead to better signal quality and a more predictable flow profile.

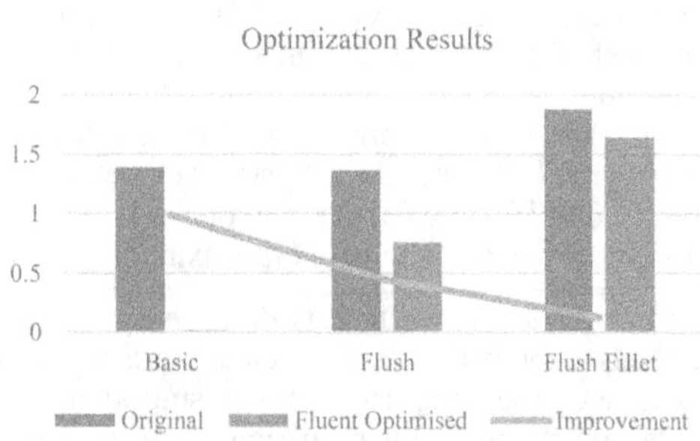

Figure 4. Optimization Results Max TKE [m^2/s^2].

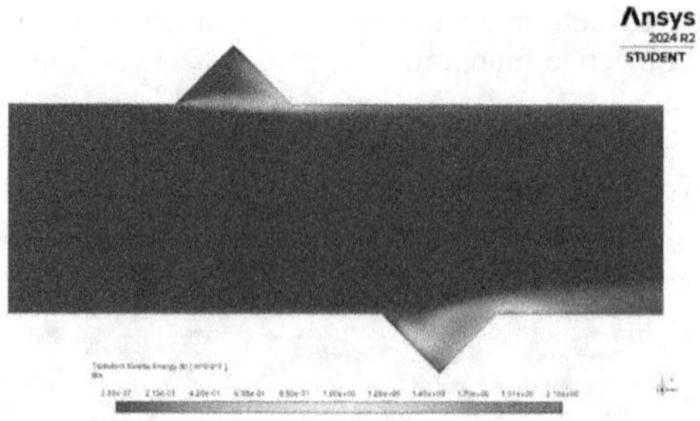

Figure 5. Turbulent Kinetic Energy (k).

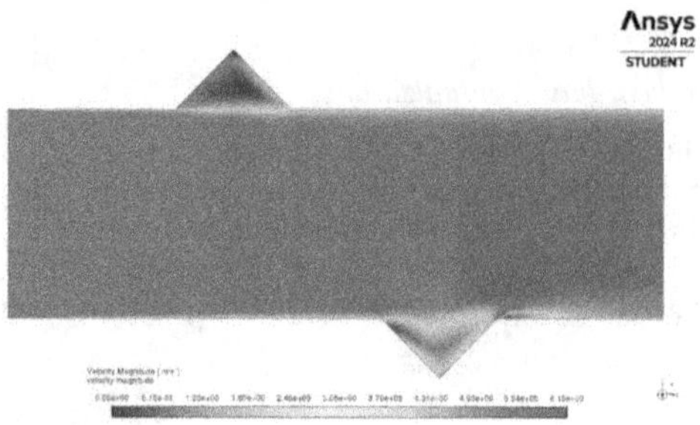

Figure 6. Velocity Magnitude

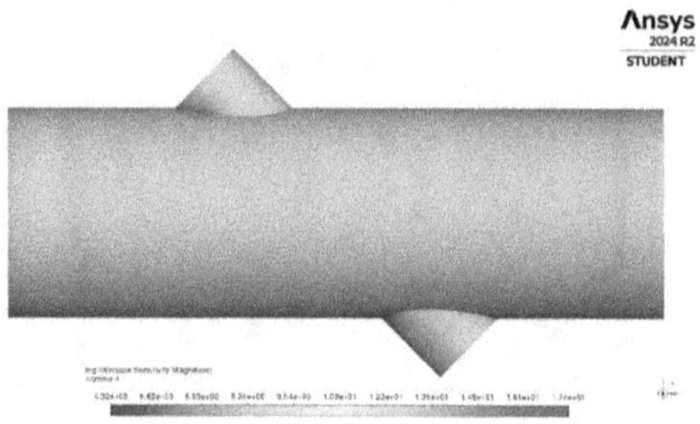

Figure 7. Shape sensitivity magnitude (top profile).

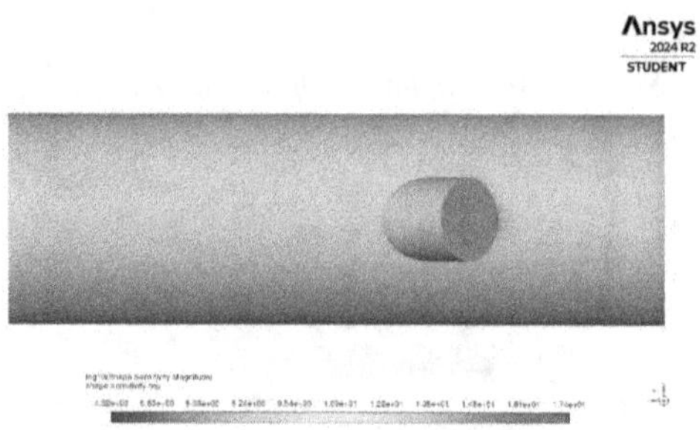

Figure 8. Shape sensitivity magnitude (left profile).

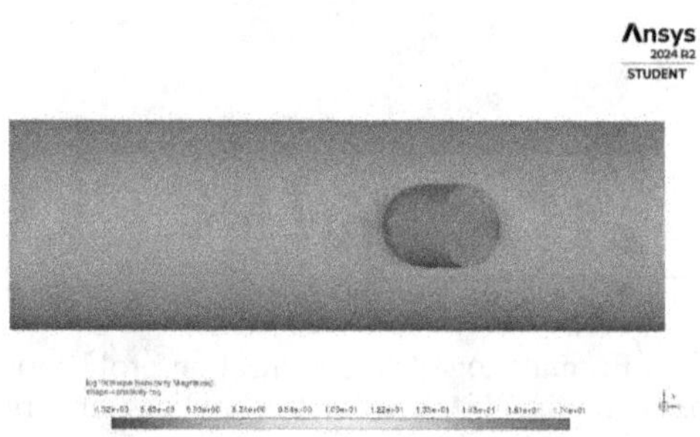

Figure 9. Shape sensitivity magnitude (right profile).

Based on these simulations, Adjoint optimization run results are as below:

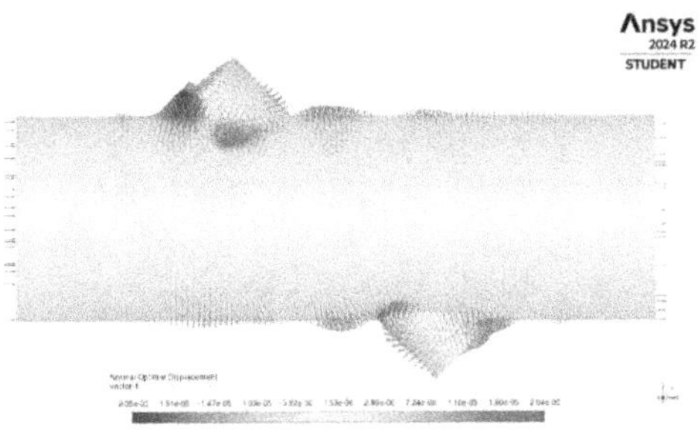

Figure 10. Normal Optimal Distribution Vectors (Scaled *100X*).

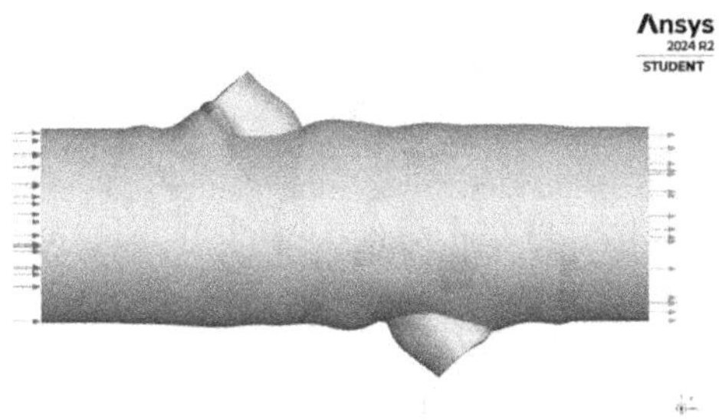

Figure 11. Optimal Design (Scaled *100X*).

(A) *Solver Settings:*
Solver Type: Steady State Pressure Based
Model: k-Omega (2 equation)
k-Omega Model: GEKO
(B) *Boundary* Conditions:
Inlet type: Velocity Inlet
Outlet type: Pressure Outlet
(C) *Adjoint Optimizer Conditions:*
Input Velocities: 0.5 m/s & 5 m/s
No. of Design Iterations: 10
No. of Flow Iterations: 200
No. of Adjoint Iterations: 300

5 CONCLUSION

In conclusion, this work has laid the groundwork for optimizing ultrasonic flow meter performance through the application of the ANSYS Adjoint Solver. Our literature review has highlighted the potential of this approach, and preliminary CFD simulations have provided valuable insights into the impact of transducer placement, sensor geometry, and flow channel design on key performance indicators. The baseline results demonstrate the current performance limitations and establish a clear target for future optimization efforts using the adjoint solver. While the adjoint solver has shown promise in efficiently exploring the design space, further research and development, particularly in experimental validation, in-depth sensitivity analysis, multi-objective optimization considering real-world constraints, are crucial to fully realize its potential for practical industrial applications.

REFERENCES

[1] L.C. Lynnworth and Y. Liu, "Ultrasonic flowmeters: half-century progress report, 1955–2005", "Ultrasonics", vol. 44. Elsevier BV, pp. E1371–e1378, Dec. 2006. Doi: 10.1016/j. Ultras.2006.05.046.

[2] Y. Chen, Y. Huang, and X. Chen, "Acoustic propagation in viscous fluid with uniform flow and a novel design methodology for ultrasonic flowmeter", "*Ultrasonics*", vol. 53, no. 2. Elsevier BV, pp. 595–606, Feb. 2013. Doi: 10.1016/j.Ultras.2012.10.005.

[3] R. Ren, H. Wang, X. Sun, and H. Quan, "Design and implementation of an ultrasonic flowmeter based on the cross-correlation method", "*Sensors",* vol. 22, no. 19. MDPI ag, p. 7470, Oct. 02, 2022. Doi: 10.3390/s22197470.

[4] S. Peng, W. Liao, and H. Tan, "Performance optimization of ultrasonic flowmeter based on computational fluid dynamics", "*Advances in Mechanical Engineering*", vol. 10, no. 8. Sage publications, Aug. 2018. Doi: 10.1177/1687814018793264.

[5] A. Afandi, Khasani, Deendarlianto, I.G.N.B. Catrawedarma, and S. Wijayanta, "The development of the ultrasonic flowmeter sensors for mass flowrate measurement: a comprehensive review", "*Flow Measurement and Instrumentation*", vol. 97. Elsevier BV, p. 102614, Jul. 2024. Doi: 10.1016/j. Flowmeasinst.2024.102614.

[6] M.J. Rincón, M. Reclari, X.I.A. Yang, and M. Abkar, "Validating the design optimization of ultrasonic flowmeters using computational fluid dynamics and surrogate modelling", "*International Journal of Heat and Fluid Flow"*, vol. 100. Elsevier BV, p. 109112, Apr. 2023. Doi: 10.1016/j. Ijheatfluidflow.2023.109112.

[7] A Chen, W. Sun, R. Zhou, C. Lin, C. Chu, and S. Su, "Optimization design and research of ultrasonic flowmeter based on time difference method", "*Journal of Mechanical Science and Technology*", vol. 38, no. 1. Springer science and business media LLC, pp. 245–258, Jan. 2024. Doi: 10.1007/s12206-023-1221-z.

[8] R. Ren, H. Wang, X. Sun, and H. Quan, "Design and implementation of an ultrasonic flowmeter based on the cross-correlation method", "*Sensors",* vol. 22, no. 19. MDPI AG, p. 7470, Oct. 02, 2022. Doi: 10.3390/s22197470.

[9] L. Ma, J. Liu, and J. Wang, "Study of the accuracy of ultrasonic flowmeters for liquid", *AASRI Procedia,* vol. 3. Elsevier BV pp. 14–20, 2012. Doi: 10.1016/j.Aasri.2012.11.004.

[10] Franklyn J. Kelecy ANSYS, Inc. "Adjoint Shape Optimization for Aerospace Applications", "Advanced Modeling & Simulation (AMS) Seminar Series", "*NASA Ames Research Center*", April 8, 2021

Advancement in Engineering and Science – Goyal et al. (Eds)
© 2026 The Author(s), ISBN: 978-1-041-31101-0

Activity Recommendation System Based on Emotion Recognition

Shilpa Khedkar and Shraddha Khonde
Department of Computer Engineering, Modern Education Society's Wadia College of Engineering Pune, Maharashtra, India

Uma Mahesh Bhokare
Department of Computer Engineering, Karmveer Bhaurao Patil College of Engineering

ABSTRACT: An Emotion Recognition-Based Activity Recommendation System aims at providing users with adequate activity recommendations based on emotional states using the latest developments within the scope of emotion recognition technology. This project would apply speech emotion recognition techniques, specifically focusing on the most current state of-the-art methods in Triangular Region Cut-Mix augmentation for the enhancement of accuracy of emotion classification while preserving audio spectrogram information related to key emotions. Furthermore, it involves a dual learning framework integrating Emotion Recognition in Conversation and Emotional Response Generation for a richer emotional analysis. This system identifies the user's emotions from the speech input and suggests the appropriate activities to engage the users, which is of prime interest in terms of mental wellness and betterment in the user's experience. Some of the potential enhancements would be multimodal integration, adaptive data augmentation, and real-time detection to give more extensive and interactive recommendations. That way, there would be a highly developed user-centered solution that could help most areas, from mental support and therapy to entertainment programs individually designed based on user interest.

Keywords: Speech Emotion Recognition (SER), Triangular Region Cut-Mix, Emotion Recognition in conversation (ERC) Emotional Response Generation (ERG), Multimodal Integration Transfer Learning, Data Augmentation, Natural Language Processing (NLP) Activity Recommendation, Personalized Recommendations

1 INTRODUCTION

The Emotion recognition is revolutionizing the way we interact with technology using the power of machine learning, artificial intelligence, and human-computer interaction. The area of emotion recognition deals with the classification of an individual's emotional state using diverse inputs such as physiological signals (heart rate and EEG sensors), text data (social media posts), voice tones, and facial expressions. With advancements in computer vision, natural language processing (NLP), and the development of wearable technologies, we are now able to sense tension, anger, sadness, and happiness in users with a remarkable level of specificity. This has resulted in more responsive and adaptive user experiences across all applications.

An emotion-driven activity recommendation system provides suggestion matched to the emotional state of the user. For example, if the system senses sadness, it could suggest doing things that would possibly improve the user's mood. These include watching a comedy movie, listening to energetic music, or going for a walk. Conversely, if stress is detected, the system could suggest doing something like meditation, breathing exercises, or listening to soothing music. Such systems can help in improving the user's well-being and providing support at the right time when a user is under emotional distress. The emotion detection process involves multi-modalities such as physiological signals, text data, voice tones, and facial expressions. Support vector machines (SVMs), random forests, and deep learning networks are used to classify the emotions accurately from the labeled datasets. Combining data from multiple modalities will help enhance the accuracy of emotion detection significantly. The approach of multi-modality analysis will provide real-time analysis and thus make it possible to be integrated into personal assistants and wearable devices. It can help users have real-time emotional insight.

But implementation of emotion recognition and activity recommendation systems is accompanied by a few challenges of its own. Sensitive emotional data must be protected through robust encryption and anonymization techniques, and cultural differences in emotional expression create a big challenge for universal emotion recognition. So the models need to be trained on diverse datasets to accommodate these variations. People often do not show their actual emotions consciously as well as unconsciously. Despite these challenges, the potential applications are vast, ranging from entertainment platforms like Spotify and Netflix to personal assistants like Siri and Alexa. As wearable technologies and AI continue to advance, activity recommendation systems hold significant promise for enhancing user experiences and providing personalized emotional support.

2 LITERATURE REVIEW

Activity recommendation systems have seen notable advancements through the integration of affective computing and emotion recognition technologies. By identifying human emotions in real time, these systems can deliver personalized content, suggest appropriate activities, and support decision-making processes, all while improving user engagement and adaptability.

Modern emotion recognition systems leverage various modalities:

Facial Expression Recognition: Tools like Open Face and Affective analyse micro-expressions to detect emotional states (Happy, Sad, Angry, etc.).

Speech Emotion Recognition: Extracting prosodic and spectral features from audio inputs to classify emotions.

Physiological Signals: Using wearable sensors (e.g., EEG, ECG, and GSR) for real-time monitoring of stress, arousal, and valence levels.

Text-Based Sentiment Analysis: Leveraging natural language processing to infer emotions from user-generated text.

For example, Bandyopadhyay *et al.* (2022) proposed a deep learning-based framework using multimodal data, highlighting improved accuracy in dynamic environments [11].

DOI: 10.1201/9781003798514-10

The paper proposes [1] a new speech emotion recognition system with a Triangular Region Cut-Mix Augmentation algorithm and transfer learning to enhance the classification of emotions from speech spectrograms. This method retains key emotional features by introducing triangular region augmentation, making the model more robust and avoiding overfitting. It achieves 84.2 percent accuracy with pre-trained VGG16 models and Ravdess dataset spectrograms, 6 percent more than baseline models. The method also gives better F1 scores for emotion classification, especially when it comes to more complex classes like "surprised" or "angry." This research points out how effective the innovative augmentation techniques together with transfer learning can be integrated into SER. This paper covers a lightweight CLCM model optimized for FER and designed particularly for devices lacking strong computational power, so that efficiency can be brought out on weaker hardware. Based on the MobileNetV2 architecture, the CLCM model was tested on four public datasets, FER-2013, RAF-DB, Affect Net, and CK+, to demonstrate competitive results while being efficient. It showed 63 percent accuracy on FER-2013, 84 percent on RAF-DB, and comparable performance on Affect Net, even though it is much smaller than other models of the same kind. This paper emphasizes the possibility of this CLCM in developing real-time applications in human-computer interaction, emotion-based biofeedback, and in mobile platforms and its utility for scenarios in real-world FER [2].The document tends to showcase progress made in text-based fine-grained emotion prediction through transformer models, especially BERT. It forms a multi-task learning framework that incorporates emotion definition modeling in addition to the main task of emotion prediction. This improves the performance on the Go Emotions dataset, which is a dataset comprising 27 categories of emotions, leveraging auxiliary tasks like Class Definition Prediction (CDP) and Masked Language Modeling (MLM). Experimental results show state of-the-art performance and improved transferability to smaller emotion datasets. Applications range from human computer interaction to affective computing systems [3]. This paper introduces a novel spatio-temporal self-constructing graph neural network (ST-SCGNN) for cross subject emotion recognition and consciousness detection by applying EEG data. The proposed method integrates activation and connection pattern features to capture complementary spatio-temporal information of emotions. Unlike traditional graph neural networks, ST-SCGNN dynamically constructs the structures of graphs according to input signals, which is efficient for complex modeling of brain networks under emotional states. Experiments on publicly available EEG datasets, SEED and SEEDIV, showed state-of-the-art accuracy of 85.90 percent and 76.37 percent, respectively. Further testing on patients with DOC revealed that the model could detect emotion related neural patterns in some patients, which might be used to identify covert consciousness. This approach has potential for improving the accuracy of emotion recognition and advancing clinical tools for DOC evaluation [4].This paper discusses a systematic review of multimodal emotion recognition (MER) techniques developed in the years 2014-2024. It reviews emotion recognition from various sources, like verbal, physiological signals, facial expressions, body gestures, and speech. More emerging methods are also included, such as sketches emotion recognition. Differentiating emotions, feelings, sentiments, and mood. The review coves human emotional expression by kind, both artistic and non-verbal. The background of automatic emotion recognition systems is discussed, along with seven criteria for the evaluation of modalities. Based on the PRISMA guidelines, the selected 45 articles provide comprehensive insights into existing studies, datasets, technical approaches, identified gaps, and future directions in MER. The applications and current challenges of MER are important for fields like affective computing and human-robot interactions [5]. This paper presents Fed Deep FM, a deep model for federated learning in the recommender system to overcome information overload challenges. Deep learning, which has emerged recently, has been shown to handle vast amounts of data while avoiding data sparsity and cold start problems in such systems. However, the traditional deep learning models need huge user data for training purposes, thus giving rise to issues related to data security and privacy. The proposed Fed Deep FM model trains collaboratively using local user data without central collection. This way, user privacy is maintained while improving the accuracy of the recommendations. Similar to federated learning, it uploads model parameters instead of raw data and uses a pseudo-interaction filling method that masks the real user data -hence not subject to indirect inference of private information. Experimental results show that FedDeepFM yields high-quality recommendations while maintaining user privacy [6]. This paper deals with two critical tasks in natural language processing: Emotion Recognition in Conversation (ERC) and Emotional Response Generation (ERG).ERC is the task of identifying utterance-level emotions from dialogues, whereas ERG is the task of generating responses that express certain emotions. These two tasks are highly interdependent, but the existing works have treated them independently, ignoring their duality. This paper introduces a dual learning framework that simultaneously tackles both tasks by exploiting their relationship. The authors make four significant contributions: (1) proposing a joint training framework for ERC and ERG, (2) allowing two models to be trained together to utilize their duality, (3) introducing an asymmetric dual learning framework that operates on different input and output domains—natural language and emotion labels, and (4) conducting experiments on benchmark datasets to validate the effectiveness of the proposed framework [7]. This paper proposes a multi-modal movie recommendation system that is specifically tailored for the Indian context, bridging the gap in existing literature regarding ordinal user feedback on regional language films. The authors introduce a multi-head cross-attention mechanism that leverages audio-visual information from Hindi movie trailers in the Flick score dataset. User feedback is categorized into three classes: i) Dislike, ii) Like, and iii) Neutral/Not Watched. This research develops a Genre Like-score, or GL-score, in an attempt to synchronize user preference and movie genre; it checks if it helps the movie genre significantly with preference prediction. Further performance experiments are performed by various techniques on key frame extraction and audio/video embedding. Experimental results clearly reveal that GL-score helps substantially for user, confirming that different modalities within the dataset are of relevance [8]. This paper titled "Robin Net: A Multimodal Speech Emotion Recognition System With Speaker Recognition for Social Interactions" brings up a novel framework that incorporates both text and speech modalities in the use of intermediate fusion in a system for emotion recognition by combining the SER model using Inception-ResNetV2 and TER with the fine-tuned RoBERTA model. Using transfer learning and spectrogram augmentation to overcome the data limitation, RobinNet achieves a weighted accuracy of 72.8 percent on the IEMOCAP dataset, surpassing state-of-the-art methods on benchmark datasets (MELD and CMU-MOSEI). The system is effective in detecting "angry" and "neutral" emotions, and it has applications in real-time conversational AI and digital assistants. Future improvements include enhanced data augmentation and larger training datasets to boost performance further[9].The paper titled Evolutionary Ensemble Learning for EEG-Based Cross Subject Emotion Recognition introduces an end-to-end framework that leverages EEG data for cross-subject emotion recognition. The proposed method, EPNNE (Neural Network Ensemble with Evolutionary Programming), employs an innovative evolutionary algorithm to optimize neural network structures and integrates these optimized models into an ensemble classifier. Hence, EPNNE outperforms state-of-the-art methods with the datasets of

DEAP, FACED, SEED, and SEED-IV with well-high accuracy and stability toward the arousal and valence states of several subjects' emotional expressions, suppressing individual EEG variability. It is proven well applicable in real-world applications as appropriate assessments of emotional states for healthcare and human-computer interaction [10]. A novel framework for emotion recognition in dialogue, the paper PIRNet: Personality-Enhanced Iterative Refinement Network for Emotion Recognition in Conversation integrates contextual and personality information for a novel approach to emotion recognition in dialogues. Using a multistage iterative refinement process, personality traits, and bidirectional GRUs, the PIRNet models emotional transitions and contextual dependencies for better emotion prediction accuracy. PIRNet is assessed on benchmark datasets, IEMOCAP, CMU-MOSI, and CMU-MOSEI. It exceeds state-of-the-art methods for both unimodal and multimodal settings while showing the contribution of personality and iterative refinement towards emotion recognition. Future work shall extend PIRNet to other conversational tasks while incorporating additional modalities such as visual data [11].

Activity recommendation systems enriched with emotional context adapt their outputs based on users' mental states. These systems use emotion as an implicit feedback mechanism to: Recommend activities like music, exercise, reading, or mindfulness. Adjust difficulty levels in educational platforms. Suggest mental health support or relaxing content.

Wenish *et al.* (2023) designed an emotion-aware system that recommends motivational videos and mental wellness content using facial expression analysis and sentiment detection [12].A 2024 IEEE study explored the impact of emotion-aware music recommendations using spectrogram and valence-arousal models, demonstrating increased user satisfaction in emotional congruence [13]. Maji *et al.* (2023) proposed a deep learning-based framework combining convolutional neural networks (CNNs) and Bi-directional GRUs (Bi-GRUs) for capturing audio-text emotional features. Their model effectively fuses modalities through a transformer-based architecture and achieves superior accuracy on benchmark datasets such as IEMOCAP [14]. Wu *et al.* (2023) introduced a self-supervised framework that uses temporal convolutional and transformer encoders to process data from wearable sensors (e.g., ECG, EDA). This method excels in limited-data settings and performs well across cross-subject emotion detection tasks [15]. Tran *et al.* (2024) developed a real-time emotion-based music recommendation system using vision transformers to assess users' facial expressions and map them to the valence-arousal emotion space. Songs were then recommended using similarity matching with emotion-tagged audio content [16].

3 PROPOSED METHODOLOGY

3.1 *Data Collection and Pre-processing*

Input Modalities: The system accepts inputs from three sources:-Audio: Voice recordings that capture the user's speech and vocal tone. Images: Facial expressions and visual cues from recorded videos. Text: User-generated text input, such as journaling entries or chat messages.

Pre-processing: *For audio data, noise reduction and feature extraction (e.g., Mel-Frequency Cepstral Coefficients - MFCCs) are performed to capture the relevant emotional features*

For fecial data, frames are extracted at specific intervals, and facial landmarks are detected to focus on expressions.

For text data noise reduction and feature extraction (e.g., Mel-Frequency Cepstral Coefficients - MFCCs) are performed to capture the relevant emotional features.

3.2 *Emotion Recognition Using Deep Learning Models*

The emotion recognition stage employs distinct models for each input type to classify the user's emotional state: Video Emotion Recognition (VGG16):

- The VGG16 convolutional neural network (CNN) model is used for video analysis. Pretrained on large image datasets, VGG16 is fine-tuned with facial expression datasets (e.g., FER2013) to identify emotions like happiness, sadness, anger, and surprise.
- The input video frames are fed into the VGG16 model, which extracts deep features and classifies the emotions based on facial cues.

Audio Emotion Recognition (CNN):

- A custom CNN model is utilized for analyzing audio features. The processed audio data (e.g., MFCCs) is passed through the CNN layers to learn patterns associated with different emotions.
- The model is trained on labeled audio datasets (e.g., RAVDESS) to classify emotions such as fear, calm, joy, and sadness based on voice tone and pitch variations.

Text Emotion Recognition (NLP Model):

- An NLP model (e.g., Bidirectional LSTM or Transformer-based models like BERT) is used for text analysis. It processes the input text to detect sentiment and emotion by analyzing the linguistic features and context.
- The model is trained on sentiment-labeled datasets (e.g., Go Emotions) to accurately identify emotional states like anxiety, frustration, and contentment.

3.3 *Activity Recommendation System*

Once the emotional state is identified from the multimodal inputs, an ensemble model aggregates the predictions from the three sources (audio, video, text) to determine the final emotion with a weighted decision making approach. Based on the detected emotion, the system suggests personalized activities to improve the user's mental state for negative emotions (e.g., sadness, anxiety): It may recommend activities like mindfulness exercises, journaling prompts, or calming music.

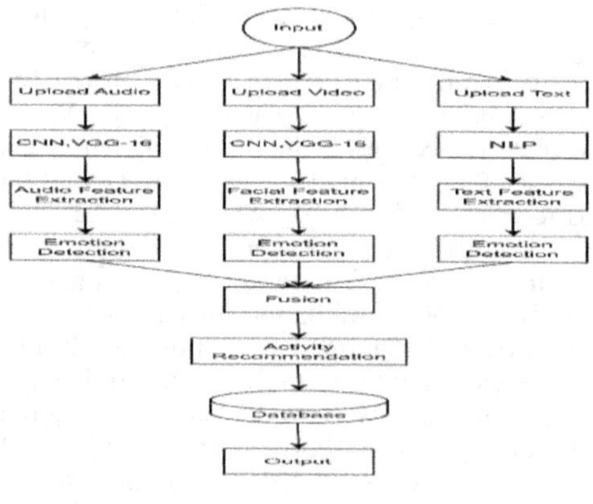

Figure 1. System architecture of the proposed methodology.

For positive emotions (e.g., joy, excitement): It may suggest engaging in creative hobbies, sharing the moment with friends, or continuing productive tasks. The recommendations are tailored to the user's preferences and previous engagement data, utilizing a collaborative filtering or content-based recommendation algorithm to enhance personalization. D. Feedback Loop and Model Refinement.

Users provide feedback on the recommended activities, which is recorded to refine the recommendation engine over time. This feedback helps improve the accuracy of emotion detection and the relevance of activity suggestions, creating a personalized, adaptive experience for the user.The system continuously updates its models using user interaction data, enhancing the emotional recognition and activity recommendation process through ongoing learning.

4 RESULT AND DISCUSSION

The following essential features were effectively accomplished by the designed system: Using trained models, accurately identified user emotions from text, audio, and video inputs shown in Figures 2, 3, and 4. Based on identified emotional states, suggested activities for productivity or mental wellness. Accommodated text, audio, and video inputs, either separately or in combination. Results were shown using dynamic recommendation cards and an intuitive user interface. Gently handled edge circumstances including invalid input, blank fields, and unsupported formats. Maintained steady performance and little response generation lag.

For text, audio, and video modalities, the emotion identification system's accuracy surpassed 85% in benchmark test sets. This excellent performance demonstrates how well the underlying models identify user emotions. The system's resilience and dependability were greatly increased by the multi-modal fusion process, particularly when dealing with subtle or ambiguous emotional signs. The recommended activities were consistently emotionally supportive and context-aware, which well matched the user's present emotional state in terms of recommendation relevance. In most situations, the user interface maintained an input-to-output latency of less than three seconds, demonstrating exceptional responsiveness and guaranteeing a seamless user experience.

Additionally, the system demonstrated remarkable adaptability, handling text, audio, and video inputs efficiently and with few mistakes or system crashes. The majority of participants expressed great satisfaction with the suggested activities' emotional alignment and practicality, and user feedback was largely favorable. It was beneficial to integrate various input types since it provided flexibility for varying user preferences. More processing power was needed for audio and video emotion recognition, indicating room for improvement. The combined modality increased confidence levels in emotion estimate, even when text-only predictions were quick and precise.

- Testing, debugging, and upcoming enhancements (such the addition of real-time video inference) were made easier by the modular design.

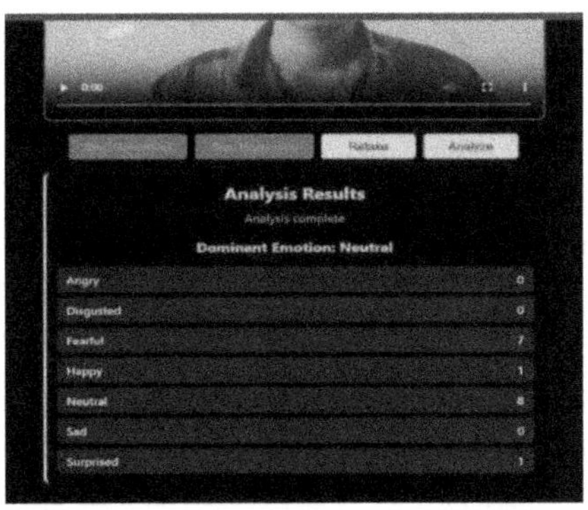

Figure 2. Video emotion detection & activity recommendation.

5 CONCLUSION

The Emotion Recognition-Based Activity Recommendation System is proposed as a unique approach to boost user well-being by utilizing up-to-date emotion recognition techniques and recommendations of personalized activities. Multimodal inputs for audio, video, and text support the system so that it thoroughly analyzes emotions during the process, bringing about more precise detection of emotional states. Advanced techniques include Triangular Region Cut-Mix augmentation and deep learning models that augment classification precision while the dual learning framework for Emotion Recognition in Conversation (ERC) and Emotional Response

Generation (ERG) offer deeper insights of user emotions. This is a system that continually refines its recommendations through real-time processing, adaptive data augmentation.

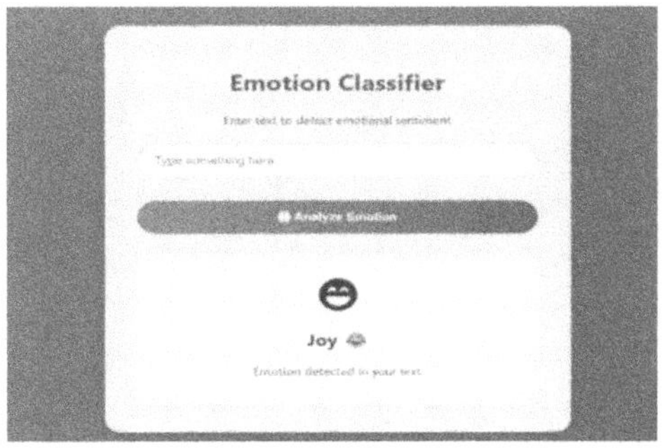

Figure 3. Text emotion detection & activity recommendation.

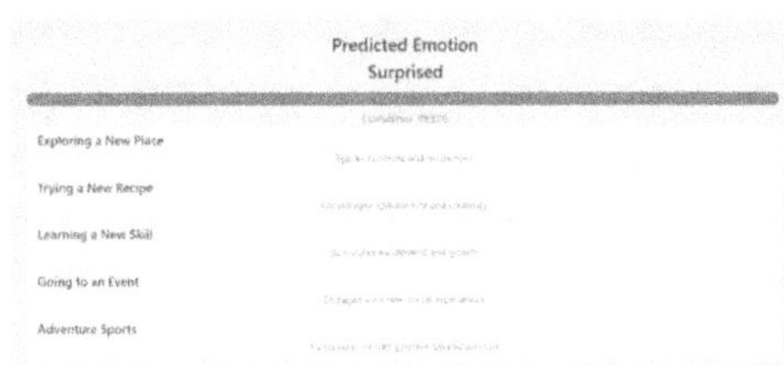

Figure 4. Audio emotion detection & activity recommendation.

and user feedback loops to ensure relevance and personalization. Future work includes the addition of physiological signals, federated learning for improving privacy, and increasing cultural adaptability. The proposed solution promises great potential in diverse domains such as mental health support and therapy, entertainment, and personalized digital assistants, which provides an intelligent and empathetic interaction framework for users.

REFERENCES

[1] V. Heusser, N. Freymuth, S. Constantin, and A. Waibel. (2019). *Bimodal speech emotion recognition using pre-trained language models*: arXiv:1912.02610.

[2] H. Proenca and S. Filipe. (2008). *Combining rectangular and triangular image regions to perform real-time face detection*: Proc. 9th Int. Conf. Signal Process., pp. 903–908.

[3] S. Poria, E. Cambria, D. Hazarika, N. Majumder, A. Zadeh, and L.-P. Morency. (2017). *Context-dependent sentiment analysis in usergenerated videos*:Proc. 55th Annu. Meeting Assoc. Comput. Linguistics,vol.1,pp. 873–883.

[4] H. Zhou, M. Huang, T. Zhang, X. Zhu, and B. Liu. (2018). *Emotional chatting machine: Emotional conversation generation*

with internal and external memory: Proc. AAAI Conf. Artif. Intell., pp. 730–739.

[5] P. Li *et al.* (2019). *EEG based emotion recognition by combining functional connectivity network and local activations:* IEEE Trans. Biomed. Eng., vol. 66, no. 10, pp. 2869–2881.

[6] N. Alswaidan and M.E.B. Menai. (2020). *A survey of state-of-the-art approaches for emotion recognition in text*: Knowl. Inf. Syst., vol. 62, no. 8, pp. 2937–2987.

[7] K. Bansal, H. Agarwal, A. Joshi, and A. Modi. (2022). *Shapes of emotions: Multimodal emotion recognition in conversations via emotion shifts*: Int.Conf.Comput.Linguistics, pp. 44–56.

[8] S.Y.M. Lee, Y. Chen, and C.-R. Huang. (2010). *A text-driven rulebased system for emotion cause detection*:Proc. NAACL HLTWorkshopComput.ApproachesAnal.Gener.EmotionText, LosAngeles,CA,USA. pp.45–53.

[9] C.M. Tyng, H.U. Amin, M.N.M. Saad, and A.S. Malik. (2017). *The influences of emotion on learning and memory*, Frontiers Psychol. vol. 8, pp. 1–22.

[10] P. Resnick and H.R. Varian. (1997). *Recommender systems:* Commun. ACM, vol. 40, no. 3, pp. 56–58.

[11] Bandyopadhyay, S., Thakur, S.S., and Mandal, J.K. (2022). *Emotion Detection for Online Recommender System Using Deep Learning: A Proposed Method*: Innovations in Systems and Software Engineering.

[12] Wenish, A.J., Satishkumar, K., Kishore, R., and Julian, A. (2023). *Emotion Detection and Recommender System using Machine Learning*: IACIDS 2023.

[13] IEEE. (2024). *Emotion-Aware Music Recommendation System via Mel Spectrogram and Arousal-Valence Model*: IEEE Conference Proceedings.

[14] Maji, S., Shukla, S., and Li, Y. (2023). *Multi-modal Emotion Recognition using Deep Temporal Features and Transformer-Based Fusion*:IEEE ICASSP 2023.

[15] Wu, J., Zhang, Y., *et al.* (2023). *Self-Supervised Learning for Wearable-based Emotion Recognition Using Multi-Modal Contrastive Learning: arXiv preprint arXiv:2303.17611.*

[16] Tran, T., *et al.* (2024). *Emotion-Aware Music Recommender using Vision Transformers and Arousal-Valence Mapping*: Proceedings of AAAI 2024. DOI: 10.1609/aaai.v38i5.26911.

Advancement in Engineering and Science – Goyal et al. (Eds)
 ISBN: 978-1-041-31101-0

Exploring Machine and Ensemble Learning Techniques for Large-Scale Sentiment Analysis

Yamini Singh and Akshay Jadhav
Computer Science and Engineering, Manipal University Jaipur, Jaipur, India

Vipin Jain
SCOPE VIT Bhopal University, Sehore, India

ABSTRACT: Sentiment analysis involves categorizing textual data into various groups by understanding the emotional and semantic meaning behind it. The application of this method spans across multiple industrial and research domains like customer satisfaction assessment, political environment, cultural analysis, and reaction prediction. The fundamental nature of sentiment analysis is to serve as a classification task that uses multiple solution methods. This research examines different machine learning models to document their performance accuracy when processing the Sentiment140 dataset consisting of 1.6 million tweets, labelled positive or negative. The research implements conventional machine learning approaches like Naive Bayes and Logistic Regression together with Stacking and Soft Voting Classifiers among other ensemble methods. Two types of preprocessing methods along with different vectorization parameters are studied to find which approach yields the most effective feature extraction solution. Our research findings show that combining sentiment attributes with emotive punctuation preservation produces better classification outcomes. The established framework creates an effective solution that works for systems with resource constraints to produce applications for processing customer feedback, public opinion and marketplace trends.

Keywords: Sentiment Analysis, Natural Language Processing, Text Classification, Machine Learning, Ensemble Learning

1 INTRODUCTION

As the volume of online electronics, which allow anyone to voice their thoughts and opinions, continues to grow, organizations need to learn to understand the sentiment behind these expressions to make appropriate decisions. To this end, it is important that companies understand the emotions and perspectives of their clientele when it comes to the use of products and services, to improve their brand image and customer satisfaction, as well as boost revenue. It becomes possible with the help of Sentiment analysis to determine the generalized opinion from an extensive pool of trivial emotional information concerning any topic or environment [1].

Several applications of sentiment analysis have developed over time. It can be used by the finance sector to predict the sentiment of the stock market [2] and to inform corporate strategy [3]. Businesses analyze product reviews, service feedback, and customer support interactions to search for strength, weakness, and areas for improvement. Computerized sentiment analysis allows businesses to tag customer emotions effectively [4]. It can also be used to gauge the mood of the electorate, observe how the public reacts to political developments and election forecasting [5].

Social media platforms are arguably the most popular and convenient ways to express one's opinion and share it to the public [6]. Unlike Facebook or Instagram, Twitter's concise, text-based nature with heterogeneous multilingual users and well-structured metadata makes it a perfect setting for sentiment classification, with diverse sentiments across topics and easy filtering of data. The colloquial nature of the language, abbreviations, and emojis used in tweets make for realistic NLP testing, while its popularity in research guarantees similarity to previous work and sets it as a usable benchmark for sentiment analysis algorithms.

In this study, we will delve into various pre-processing techniques and sentiment analysis using machine learning models only since classical ML models and ensemble techniques are less computationally intensive and data-intensive than deep ones such as LSTMs or BERT. ML techniques are easier to deploy, faster to train, and more interpretable, and hence are preferable for research.

We first provide a concise overview of previously proposed research on sentiment analysis and then expand on the methodology followed in our research. Next, we discuss the results and findings we procured and finally provide a complete conclusion of our study as well as further scope for research on this topic.

2 LITERATURE REVIEW

Existing literature has well established the sentiment analysis landscape with machine learning as well as deep learning techniques. Tan et al. [1] reviewed more than 55 sentiment analysis methods in papers. It defines the scope of research and helps give prospective researchers some perspective on this topic. Rawat et al. [7] experimented with Covid-19 vaccine tweets using Logistic Regression, Bernoulli Naive Bayes, and Support Vector Classifier; the latter gave maximum accuracy. Kamal et al. [8] utilized negation-handling with additional rules along Naive Bayes on Sentiment140 dataset.

Gohil et al. [5] compared five ML models for election tweets and found that an ensemble of Random Forest, Gradient Boosting, and Voting Classifier attained 85% accuracy. Singh et al. [9] tested various models on airline tweets and found that SVM attained 83.74% accuracy, among Random Forest, gradient boost, and XG boost. AdbulSattar et al. [10] applied feature engineering on Sentiment140 and found that Random Forest worked the best out of all implemented models, with 78.11% accuracy. Pal et al. [11] used soft voting (Naive Bayes, Gradient Boost, Logistic Regression) on the same data and obtained an accuracy of 80.33%. Singh et al. [12] used BLSTM-ResNet model with word embeddings on Sentiment140 dataset. After analysing various models using residual blocks with

DOI: 10.1201/9781003798514-11

different dataset sizes, BLSTM-ResNet-12 (Type1) achieved maximum accuracy (80.15%).

Harjule et al. [13] used traditional and neural model. RNN-LSTM yielded best results with 81% and 71% accuracy on two datasets (Sentiment140 and "CrowdFlower's Data for Everyone library"). Parikh et al. [14] used several deep learning models such as ANN, RNN, GRU, BiGRU, etc., with BiStackedLSTM achieving 79.38% accuracy.

3 METHODOLOGY

On concluding a thorough literature survey, we picked a dataset to begin implementation. The Sentiment140 dataset, built on 1.6 million tweets, was chosen. The original dataset comprised the following fields: target (sentiment label i.e. 0 or 4 for negative and positive labels respectively), id (unique tweet identifier), date (timestamp of tweet), flag (query information), user (twitter username) and text (raw tweet content).

The dataset exhibits balanced class distribution after label conversion, making it suitable for supervised sentiment classification tasks. The methodology comprises two distinct experimental phases: Baseline Approach: Initial modelling with conventional preprocessing and vectorization (10 models). Enhanced Approach: Improved pipeline with feature engineering and advanced techniques (5 subsequent models).

3.1 *Text preprocessing*

Standard Preprocessing: The initial preprocessing pipeline included removal of URLs using regular expressions and twitter-specific element handling (we removed mentions and converted hashtags into plain words). Then all non-alphabetic characters were eliminated, and all remaining characters were changed into lowercase. Finally, all stop words were eliminated using NLTK's English stopword list and the text was lemmatized.

Enhanced Preprocessing: Instead of aggressive preprocessing, we made some changes and applied this approach later to the best performing models to maintain sentiment cues. These included the reservation of emoticons and punctuation marks conveying sentiment (!, ?), selective character filtering retaining alphabets and sentiment-bearing symbols. Stop words were kept and lemmatization was not performed to keep key sentiment indicators such as negations, intensifiers, and emotional.

3.2 *Feature representation*

- TF-IDF Vectorization:

Term Frequency-Inverse Document Frequency (TF-IDF) is a statistical measure used to convert textual data into numerical features while reflecting the importance of words in a document relative to a corpus.

$$TF(t,d) = \frac{Number\ of\ times\ t\ appears\ in\ document\ d}{Total\ number\ of\ terms\ in\ d}$$

$$IDF(t) = \frac{Total\ Number\ of\ documents}{Number\ of\ documents\ containing\ term\ t}$$

$$TF(t,d) = TF(t,d) \times IDF(t)$$

The baseline approach used 20K dimensions, 1-2 grams, sublinear TF scaling to dampen high-frequency terms. In the reformed approach, max features were expanded to 60K with 1-3 grams to capture phrases.

Table 1. Pre-processed data samples.

Target	Text	Cleaned Text	Polarity	Subjectivity	Text Length	Excl. Marks
0	@Kwesidei not the whole crew	not the whole crew	0.200000	0.400000	18	0
1	Happy 38th Birthday to my boo of alll time!!! Tupac Amaru Shakur	Happy th Birthday to my boo of alll time!!! Tupac Amaru Shaku	1.000000	1.000000	64	3

- Feature Engineering:

It is the next step in ML pipeline. Raw data is converted in the form of useful and meaningful features, hence the name input variables, to allow the machine learning model to learn more proficiently and accurately predict. It involves extracting new properties from previously acquired data (for example, extracting sentiment ratings from text) and selecting or altering features to highlight patterns (e.g., scaling, binning, or feature combining). Feature representation can be optimized to make data more comprehensible to algorithms.

The improved approach integrated sentiment (polarity and subjectivity scores using TextBlob library) and stylometric features (raw text length, exclamation mark frequency as intensity indicators) to discern subtle sentiment cues. Table 1 provides insight into the preprocessed data samples.

3.3 *Model training*

Before training models, data is divided into training (80%) and (20%) testing set. Seven models were trained after searching for optimal parameters using RandomizedSearchCV, which is a hyperparameter tuning method that randomly draws a set number of parameter combinations from pre-specified distributions and tests each through cross validation.

We tested seven machine learning models with well-tuned hyperparameters for sentiment classification, such as Logistic Regression as a basic linear model, Multinomial Naive Bayes as a probabilistic model, and some ensemble algorithms: AdaBoost, Gradient Boosting, LightGBM, and CatBoost. We used a Decision Tree model as well to model complex patterns of sentiment. These types of different algorithms were chosen to investigate different models and determine the best classifier for this task.

These 7 base models were used as base models for 3 ensemble methods: Blending averaged predictions from Logistic Regression, Naive Bayes, and LightGBM with weights learned from a meta-learner; Dynamic Weighted Majority Voting averaged the base models' predictions performance-weighted; and Meta-Descriptor Stacking input model predictions and engineered features into a LightGBM meta-learner. Since early results were poor, we re-trained 3 top-performing models (Logistic Regression, LightGBM, and XGBoost) after preprocessing optimization and further feature engineering and used 2 more ensemble methods: Soft Voting Classifier averaged probability outputs of the three models, whereas s tacking learned best combinations of base model predictions using Logistic Regression as the meta-learner.

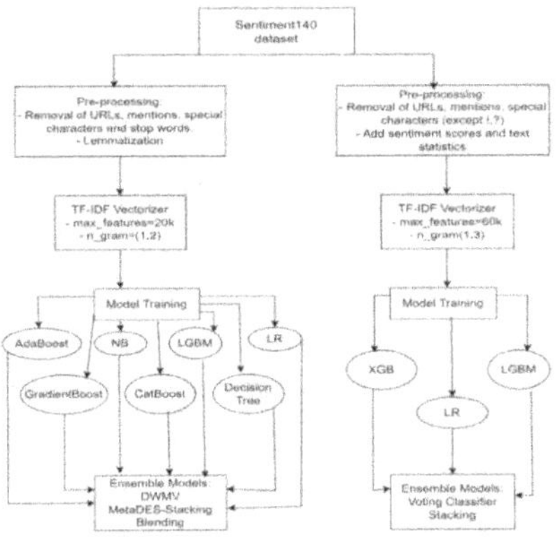

Figure 1. Methodology flowchart.

3.4 *Model evaluation*

We utilized a full evaluation framework to measure model performance with accuracy, classification reports and confusion matrices being used to quantify effectiveness in sentiment classification.

4 RESULTS AND DISCUSSION

4.1 *Results*

On analysing the results, we gained several important insights regarding model performance as well as the effect of feature engineering techniques. The findings indicate that ensemble strategies incorporating lexical as well as sentiment-based features had better performance in comparison to separate classifiers.

The first round of experiments with basic preprocessing set up robust baseline performance as we can observe in Table 2. Logistic Regression proved to be the best single classifier with 77.31% accuracy (F1=0.77), beating Naive Bayes by virtue of its capacity to deal with correlated n-gram features. Gradient-boosted trees (CatBoost: 75.64%, LightGBM: 76.93%) performed competitively, whereas AdaBoost and Decision Tree were challenged by the sparse high dimensional features, with large recall imbalances. MetaDES stacking performed better than basic blending by including both prediction and engineered features. Dynamic Weighted Majority Voting showed a decrease in accuracy, possibly due to the inclusion of poor models (AdaBoost, Decision Trees), proving the importance of selective membership within ensembles.

Table 2. Model Performance Metrics we obtained using simple preprocessing and fewer features.

Model	Accuracy	Precision	Recall	F1
LR	0.7731	0.77	0.77	0.77
MNB	0.7591	0.76	0.76	00.76
Adaboost	0.6651	0.70	0.67	0.65
Decision Tree	0.6335	0.70	0.63	0.60
GradientBoost	0.7545	0.76	0.76	0.76
CatBoost	0.7564	0.76	0.76	0.76
LightGBM	0.7693	0.77	0.77	0.77
DWMV	0.6998	0.74	0.70	0.69
MetaDES Stacking	0.7765	0.78	0.78	0.78
Blending	0.7729	0.77	0.77	0.77

Table 3. Model Performance after performing feature engineering

Model	Accuracy	Precision	Recall	F1
XGB	0.7514	0.75	0.75	0.75
LGBM	0.785	0.79	0.79	0.78
LR	0.8093	0.81	0.81	0.81
Soft Voting	0.8029	0.80	0.80	0.80
Stacking	0.8178	0.82	0.82	0.82

Table 4. A state-of-art comparison with existing work on the Sentiment140 dataset.

Model	Accuracy	Precision	Recall	F1
Random Forest [10]	0.7811	0.112	0.781	0.781
libSVM [10]	0.753	0.123	0.755	0.753
Majority Voting [15]	0.77	0.77	0.77	0.77
SVM [16]	0.78	0.78	0.78	0.78
Majority Voting [13]	0.78	0.78	0.78	0.7677
RNN [14]	0.7683	0.7706	0.7662	0.7684
CNN [14]	0.7498	0.7817	0.7352	0.7577
BiStacked LSTM [14]	0.7938	0.7765	0.804	0.79
Soft Voting [15] (NB, SVM, LR)	0.792	0.79	0.80	0.79
Voting Classifier [10] (LR, NB, GB)	0.8033	0.8034	0.8033	0.8033
Stacking (OURS)	**0.8178**	**0.82**	**0.82**	**0.82**

We optimized performance using better preprocessing and feature engineering, including TextBlob sentiment features (polarity, subjectivity) and emotive punctuation n-grams (60K features), with results in Table 3. A soft voting classifier over Logistic Regression, LightGBM, and XGBoost had 80.29% accuracy. Stacking classifier with the same base models and a logistic regression meta-learner had better performance with 81.78% accuracy. ROC curves and AUC values for various models are given in Figure 2, and confusion matrices for the stacking classifier in Figure 3.

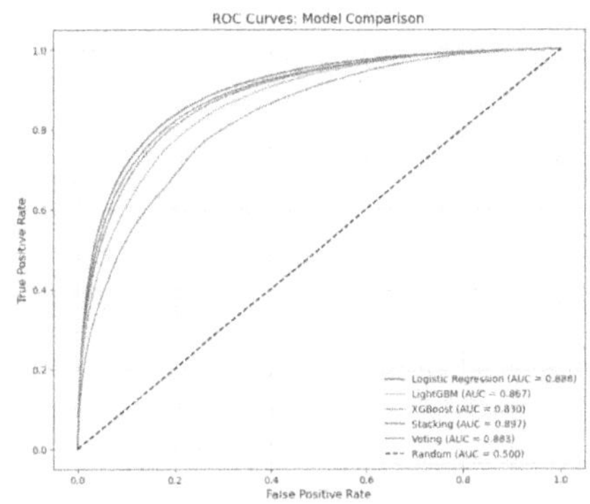

Figure 2. ROC Curves of our improved models.

4.2 *Discussion*

The evaluation data from Figure 3 points to equal misclassification rates between incorrect positive and negative predictions without bias for either sentiment direction. Many of the classification errors occurred with tweets that expressed minimal positive or negative sentiment yet still bordered the decision boundary. The design choices we made between performance efficiency and interpretability in our model matched these collected observations because robust pattern discovery takes precedence over contextual evaluation. Notably, our ensemble methods, particularly the Stacking Classifier (81.78% accuracy), outperformed standalone ML models and even surpassed prior deep learning models (e.g. BLSTM-ResNet [12]) while using significantly fewer resources. This highlights the effectiveness of interpretable, feature-engineered hybrid approaches in resource-constrained environments.

4.3 *Error analysis*

An assessment of misclassified tweets reveals patterns in the limitations of our models. The most common errors occurred in two key scenarios. Certain short tweets expressed contrary messages such as "Thanks for nothing", which sometimes resulted in incorrect classifications. Performance enhancements from retaining punctuation alongside emoticons did not consistently solve errors regarding the interpretation of informal or sarcastic expressions in out-of-context communication. Secondly, the minimal word content in tweets such as "Not great" caused classification errors because sparse lexical content weakened both TF-IDF analysis and text length measurements. This suggests that for minimalistic text, the combined feature set, though richer than the raw BoW, may still lack sufficient signal.

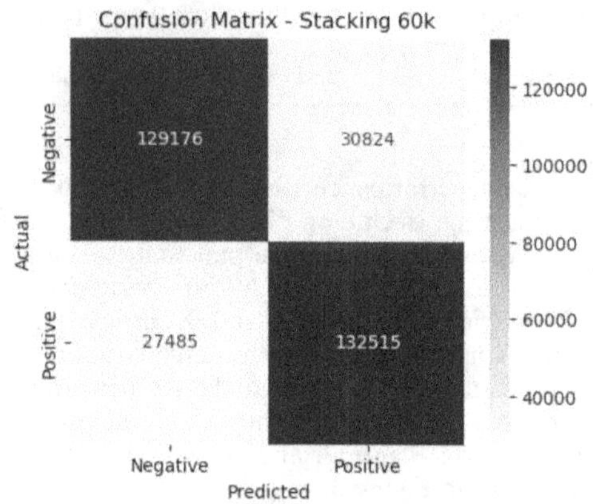

Figure 3. Confusion matrices of the final stacking classifier.

5 CONCLUSION AND FUTURE WORK

In this study, overall machine learning and ensemble method evaluation was presented for sentiment analysis with Twitter data, in addition to conventional TF-IDF and advanced feature engineering. Our best-performing model was Stacking Classifier with Logistic Regression, XGBoost and LightGBM as base models. We inferred that the addition of sentimental features and retention of emotive punctuation helped improve performance. Tree-based models were resilient but fell behind linear models of lower complexity when engineered features were introduced, indicating that lexical and sentimental features are better captured by linear methods for this task. These results highlight that careful feature engineering and hybrid modelling can deliver state-of-the-art competing performance without relying on computation-intensive deep models.

Further research on this topic can include investigating attention mechanisms to improve modelling negations and sarcasm. With deep learning models such as BERT and transformers, word embeddings can be applied to reach even greater accuracy. Multi-class classification can also be considered with respect to more specific emotions such as anger, happiness, regret, etc. This paper establishes a basis for explainable, feature-dense sentiment analysis, and subsequent work could fill in the remaining gaps using neural approaches while preserving computational efficiency.

ACKNOWLEDGEMENT

We are deeply grateful to **Manipal University Jaipur** for giving us an opportunity to carry out this research. Our work has advanced greatly thanks to their resources and support. We value their dedication to promoting academic excellence and innovation.

REFERENCES

[1] Tan, K.L., Lee, C.P., Lim, K.M. (2023, April). A survey of sentiment analysis: Approaches, datasets, and future research. (Francisco Garcia-Sanchez, Ed.), *Appl. Sci.* (Vol. 13, p. 4550).

[2] Ukhalkar, P., Zirmite, R., & Hingane, S. (2023a). Sentiment Analysis Models for Bank Nifty Index: An Overview of Predicting stock market sentiment in India. *2022 6th International Conference on Computing, Communication, Control and Automation* (ICCUBEA, 1–9).

[3] R, S., Lijo, J., E, A. (2025). Sentiment Analysis of Financial News: Implications for Corporate Strategy in Risk Management, Mergers and Marketing. *International Conference on Multi-Agent Systems for Collaborative Intelligence* (ICMSCI-2025), 86–93.

[4] Kanakamedala, V.C., Singh, S.H., Talasani, R. (2023). Sentiment Analysis of Online Customer Reviews for Handicraft Product using Machine Learning: A Case of Flipkart. *2022 International Conference for Advancement in Technology* (ICONAT), 1–6.

[5] Gohil, R., S, D., M, V., J, J. (2023). Election Forecasting with Machine Learning and Sentiment Analysis: Karnataka 2023. *2023 International Conference on Ambient Intelligence, Knowledge Informa Cs and Industrial Electronics (AIKIIE)*, 1–6.

[6] H. Kapase, K. Galande, T. Sonna, D. Pawar Sentiment polarity analysis on Twitter data from different Events, *International Research Journal of Engineering and Technology* (IRJET), vol. 5, no. 5, 2018.

[7] Rawat, A., Maheshwari, H., Khanduja, M., Kumar, R., Memoria, M., Kumar, S. (2022). Sentiment analysis of COVID19 vaccines tweets using NLP and machine learning classifiers. *2022 International Conference on Machine Learning, Big Data, Cloud and Parallel Computing* (COMIT-CON), 225–230.

[8] Kamal, L.H., McKee, G.T., Othman, N.A. (2022). Naïve Bayes with Negation Handling for Sentiment Analysis of Twitter Data. *2022 9th Intl. Conference on Soft Computing & Machine Intelligence*, 207–212.

[9] Singh, S., Kumar, K., & Kumar, B. (2022). Sentiment analysis of Twitter data using TF-IDF and machine learning techniques. *2022 International Conference on Machine Learning, Big Data, Cloud and Parallel Computing* (COMIT-CON), 252–255.

[10] AbdulSattar, K., College of Information Technology, University of Bahrain, Obeidat, Q., College of Information Technology, University of Bahrain, Akour, M., & College of Information Technology, Yarmouk University, Irbid, Jordan. (2025). *Towards harnessing based learning algorithms for tweets sentiment analysis.*

[11] Pal, H., & Bhushan, B. (2024). Sentiment Analysis on Twitter Dataset using Voting Classifier. *2024 International Conference on Electrical Electronics and Computing Technologies (ICEECT)*, 1–6.

[12] Singh, H., Helian, N., Adams, R., & Sun, Y. (2022). Sentiment Analysis using BLSTM-ResNet on Textual Images. *2022 International Joint Conference on Neural Networks (IJCNN)*, 1–8.

[13] Harjule, P., Gurjar, A., Seth, H., Thakur, P., Department of Computer Science, & IIIT Kota. (2020, January). Text classification on Twitter data. *3rd International Conference on Emerging Technologies in Computer Engineering: Machine Learning and Internet of Things (ICETCE-2020).*

[14] Parikh, A., Pawar, R., Shelke, P., Gadhave, R., & Bagade, J. (2022). Comparison of Machine learning Algorithms for Twitter sentiment Analysis. *2022 International Conference on Augmented Intelligence and Sustainable Systems (ICAISS)*, 209–215.

[15] Jazib, A., Tariq, W., & Mahmood, M. (2022). Sentiment Analysis using Ensemble Classifier for Entrepreneurs based on Twitter Analytics. *2022 19th International Bhurban Conference on Applied Sciences and Technology (IBCAST)*, 207–212.

[16] Maada, L., Fararni, K.A., Aghoutane, B., Fattah, M., & Farhaoui, Y. (2022). A comparative study of Sentiment Analysis Machine Learning Approaches. *2022 2nd International Conference on Innovative Research in Applied Science, Engineering and Technology (IRASET)*, 1–5.

Advancement in Engineering and Science – Goyal et al. (Eds)

A Review on Phase Change Material Cooled Lithium-Ion Battery Thermal Management System

Ashish Rajkumar Devshette, Jitendra Atmaram Hole, Nilesh S Navagale, Nilesh G Jawarkar, and Ashish Kumar
Department of Mechanical Engineering, JSPM's Rajarshi Shahu College of Engineering, Savitribai Phule Pune University (SPPU), Pune, India

ABSTRACT: Measurements of battery power, power rating, overvoltage rating, and pulsed power flow charge are all part of battery testing. Overcharging, over-discharging, and extreme temperatures can all cause lithium-ion batteries to malfunction. A battery management system (BMS) is necessary to ensure that every battery is operating in a secure setting. Additionally, the cell life cycle, safety, possibility for thermal runaway, and battery temperature uniformity are all significantly impacted by the peak temperature rise and its amplitude. The cooling and heating of phase transition materials, which have become a major research topic, is the foundation of lithium-ion battery thermal management techniques (BTMS). The low heat conductivity, flame resistance, and temperature-adjustability of phase change materials, as well as the lightweight design and thermal runaway mechanisms of phase change material-based systems, still require further research. In fact, the optimization of battery packs for electric vehicles (EVs) can be done by using different design techniques such as simulation and machine learning. By leveraging these advanced technologies, manufacturers can achieve significant improvements in several key areas battery life and performance, Design Optimization, Manufacturing Efficiency, Operational Efficiency. The purpose of this work is to analyze and assess cooling strategies for lithium-ion batteries using phase transition materials.

Keywords: phase change material (PCM), battery thermal management system (BTMS), lithium-ion battery, electric vehicle, battery pack, PCM cooling

1 INTRODUCTION

The energy crisis has become a major concern for society in recent years due to advancements in science, technology, and the economy. As a result, the quest for Li-ion batteries has taken center stage in the research efforts of all scientists. Due to the existing environmental policies, there is an increasing need for vehicles that use green energy, and Lithium-ion (Li-ion) batteries will eventually become the development trend.

Li-ion batteries are used broadly because of their large discharge rate alongside excellent power density that sustains them to support both HEVs and EVs.. However, When a battery discharges as efficiently as possible under high voltage, high rate, or both, the heat it produces can cause the battery's discharge capacity to decrease. Additionally, The battery may start to generate high temperatures if its temperature accumulates. The battery's lifespan will be shortened and might potentially blow up if the temperature is not distributed. A lightweight power battery module with exceptional thermal performance is desperately needed, considering how quickly electric vehicles are developing. This paper suggests a combined thermal control system in a bid to control the increasing temperature trend while keeping the temperature gradient evenly within acceptable limits throughout the battery cells that combines forced convection with a composite phase change material.

The process of ohmic resistance and chemical reaction may produce heat, which raises the temperature. Heat, however, has a direct impact on Li-ion battery performance. Hence, the temperature needs to be regulated at a safe level. It is considered that a temperature from -10°C to 50°C is suitable for operation; however, the optimal temperature is from 20°C to 40°C for better battery performance. Batteries experience rapid temperature increases and even thermal runaway when heat builds up to a certain point. In commercial development, heat dissipation technology limits the large-scale battery module. Due to this, a proper temperature control system is essential which can ensure that battery modules are kept within a safe temperature range and minimize temperature variations. As the larger battery module produces a higher power and heat, it is more difficult now to provide the heat removal techniques for batteries. Installation of the combined heat control system must be used maintain battery temperature in a safe zone. This can be done by integrating the heat pipe with liquid, PCM with heat pipe, or air with PCM. [9,10]

2 LITERATURE REVIEW

Sarvanakumar Thangavel et al. [1] examined Current Brushless DC (BLDC), Permanent magnet synchronous motors (PMSM) and found that they produce high efficiency however they use high cost rare earth materials and there are chances of demagnetization of the motor.

Yara Khawaja et al. [2] proposed work, with focus on two primary parameters which are the condition of charge and the state of health.

A.G. Olabi et al. [3] investigated to provide recommendations for the best thermal management system, considering liquid, air, PCM, HP, and hybrid cooling methods. These strategies are pertinent to the creation of the BTMS.

M.Siva Ramkumar et al. [4] described BMS used in Li-ion batteries to enhance sensor signal monitoring. The SOC, SOH, and temperature rating values are measured in real time using these signals.

J. Wang et al. [5] investigated the results of the cooling system based on tubular heat pipe, forced convection, and natural convection. They discovered that this method is the most effective technique for limiting temperature rise.

Sajib Chakraborty et al. [6] found that the multi-device interconnected DC to DC bidirectional Converters (MDIBC) is perfectly suited to generate high power in electric vehicles because of its minimum ripples for initial current and output voltage, bi-directionality, high efficiency and high reliability.

Lazrak et al. [7] experimented ITMS (Integrated thermal management system) with simulations, researchers studied

DOI: 10.1201/9781003798514-12

PCM and discovered that ITMS may lower the temperature and disperse uniformly around the battery.

Kailong Liu et al. [8] reviewed key technologies with a focus on modelling, state, and charging of a battery pack.

Vita et al. [9] analysed the prismatic Lithium-ion phosphate battery with air and liquid cooling at variable discharge rate and constant current. The heat generation based on irreversible and entropy were also analyzed mathematically to examine the temperature development and spread of the battery.

Wu et al. [10] suggested a PCM-based cooling system with help from a heat pipe. According to the testing findings, the battery module's maximum temperature may be regulated to be below 50°C at a 5°C discharge rate.

Jiang et al. [11] designed a tube shell battery module with forced air cooling and composite PCM. According to the findings, the integrated thermal management system (ITMS) may significantly lower temperature rise and keep the difference in temperature between one and two degrees Celsius.

Wu et al. [12] investigated the battery performance using different Expanded Graphite (EG) mass fractions and discharge rates on the; the study revealed the better results with addition of 15% to 20% expanded graphite in PCM. The 2D thermal model in terms of PA/EG composites was developed.

Huo et al. [13] used mini-channel and cold plates around the rectangular Li-ion battery. Through the use of numerical simulation, a variety of variables, including flow direction, channel count, coolant mass flow rate, and ambient temperature, were thoroughly examined.

Mohammadian et al. [14] fabricated a particular prismatic Li-ion battery with aluminium pin fins on the heat sinks.

3 OUTCOME OF LITERATURE REVIEW

Various lithium-ion battery designs were found to have some limitations like overheating and other safety issues, particularly at high C-rates, that greatly restricted their use. During battery charging and discharging, the heat is produced constantly as the internal resistance is increased, with such extreme temperatures affecting Li-ion battery performance. Studies on composite cooling technologies that exhibit enhanced thermal management performance are increasingly expanding in an attempt to mitigate these problems.

4 PHASE CHANGE MATERIALS USED IN LI-ION BATTERY

Because of their remarkable latent heat capacity, which enables them to absorb heat without experiencing noticeable temperature changes, phase-change materials (PCMs) are highly prized. Their ability to improve heat transfer in power electronics and cool complete battery packs makes them useful in a variety of e-mobility system applications. Unlike active cooling techniques such as liquid cooling systems, fan-based air-cooled plates, or Peltier heat pumps, PCMs provide passive thermal management which does not require external power supply. They are efficient and reversible heat absorbers because they can absorb heat and then release it into their surroundings when internal heat transfer is not taking place. For improving the thermal conductivity of paraffin-based PCMs, scientists have added metal compounds, nanoparticles, graphite, and graphene as additions.

4.1 *PCM for battery packs*

Battery packs can be charged more quickly by controlling the higher temperatures that arise from higher charging rates through the use of phase-change materials (PCMs) for cooling. Compared to air-cooled systems, a PCM-based cooling system offers superior thermal management, especially for pouch cells. [14] Being a passive system, it requires less energy than liquid cooling systems and tends to be more reliable due to having fewer moving parts. As the cells generate more heat, the PCM absorbs and manages the initial thermal energy through its phase change.

4.2 *PCM Materials*

Utilizing a phase-change material (PCM) has been demonstrated to extend battery life compared to systems without PCM. It also enhances energy capacity, allowing up to 90% of the nominal battery capacity to be utilized, compared to only 60% with air cooling. Because paraffin wax melts at about 67°C, it is considered an efficient phase-change material for controlling battery cell charging and discharging. Polyols, long-chain alkanes, stearic acid, and paraffin (PA) are examples of non-paraffin substances that are included in the category of organic phase-change materials (PCMs). These materials are preferred because of their advantages, which include low supercooling, safety and non-toxicity, strong chemical stability, and resistance to corrosion. Molten salts, water, and metals are examples of inorganic phase-change materials (PCMs). The most often utilized of these are hydrated salts and metals due to their inexpensive cost, non-flammability, non-leakage characteristics, and high capacity of latent heat. However, hydrated salts' propensity for phase separation, corrosiveness, and supercooling problems prevent them from being used widely. In practical applications, magnesium chloride hexahydrate ($MgCl_2$, $6H_2O$, MCH) is widely used as hydrated salts. Common approaches include following methods.

- Metal fins: To enhance heat transfer, these are placed inside the PCM enclosure.
- Graphite Foam: For improving thermal conductivity, this substance is mixed into the PCM.
- Metal Foam: This is added into PCM to facilitate better heat distribution.

A method for improving phase-change material (PCM) heat management is to mix pure paraffin with metal foams, such copper or nickel. For example, the composite material's thermal conductivity was 44 times higher than the thermal conductivity pure paraffin when copper foam with a pore size of 25 pores per inch (PPI) and porosity of 88.89% was utilized. [12] The thermal conductivity rose to 31 and 13 times that of pure paraffin with reduced porosities of 92.31% and 96.95%, respectively. [11] This suggests that adding metal foams greatly enhances PCMs' capacity for heat transmission, increasing their usefulness for thermal control. Phase-change materials (PCMs) have their thermal conductivity increased by up to 5 W/mK when they are surrounded by 97% porosity copper foam. In addition, it is simpler to make than metal foams, albeit it can be difficult to achieve a homogeneous structure. Organic phase-change materials (PCMs) including paraffin (PA) and aliphatic acids are frequently employed for temperature ranges between 40°C and 80°C. These materials can greatly increase electrical equipment's operational efficiency and service life up to 300% for the latter and about 26% for the former. [13]

4.3 *Overview of various techniques for enhancement of performance in phase change materials*

1. Use of Metal Foams: Metal foams with varying porosities can be embedded in PCMs to enhance thermal conductivity. For example, copper foams with 97% porosity can boost thermal conductivity up to 5 W/mK.[1]
2. Hybrid PCM Systems: Combining organic PCMs with inorganic materials or additives creates hybrid systems called as Composite PCMs that leverage the benefits of both types.

This can improve thermal management and reduce issues like supercooling and leakage. [3]

3. Enhanced PCM Matrix: Expanded Graphite Matrix (EGM) are Similar to metal foams. EGMs have high thermal conductivity, low density, and a porous structure, making them effective for thermal management. However, achieving a homogeneous structure can be challenging. .[4]
4. Chemical Modifications: Blending and Formulation: Modifying the chemical composition of PCMs or blending them with other materials can enhance their properties. For example, blending paraffin with fatty acids or other organic compounds can improve performance.
5. Improving PCM Stability: Adding stabilizers or additives helps address issues like super-cooling, phase separation, and chemical degradation, enhancing the overall reliability and longevity of PCMs.[6]
6. Temperature Range Optimization: Adjusting the melting points of PCMs through formulation allows for better alignment with specific operational temperature ranges, improving efficiency and safety. [9]
7. Incorporation of Conductive Additives:
   7.1 Metal Powders: Adding metal powders (e.g., aluminum, copper) can significantly improve the thermal conductivity of PCMs.[2,7]
   7.2 Nanoparticles: Incorporating nanoparticles such as alumina, silica, or copper enhances thermal conductivity and heat transfer. [5]
   7.3 Carbon-Based Nano materials: Graphene, carbon nanotubes, and graphite foams provide higher thermal conductivity and improve PCM performance.[8]

5 PERFORMANCE PARAMETERS

An electrochemical examination of the power source: The open circuit voltage (OCV) and ohmic resistance basic measurement results demonstrate the battery module's outstanding performance.

DCIR tests : The direct current internal resistance (DCIR) is a critical parameter in evaluating battery module technology. To analyse DCIR, a testing procedure can be performed under various states of charge (SOC) using a current test range of 2 to10 A. The process involves several steps:

Initial Charging: The battery is charged at constant current at a rate of 0.33C until it reaches the desired state of charge (SOC) level.Stabilization: After reaching the target SOC, the battery is allowed to stabilize for 120 minutes to ensure that its internal conditions are steady.Discharge Testing: The battery is then discharged at two different currents of 2 A and 10 A for 1 second each.Repetition: After a 5-second pause, the discharge and measurement cycle is repeated six times to gather consistent data.This procedure helps in accurately measuring the internal resistance of the battery across different SOC levels, which is essential for understanding its performance and efficiency.

Examination of storage efficiency under elevated temperatures :Initial Charging: constant current density of 0.5C and 4.15 V as cut-off voltage. Constant Voltage Charging: constant voltage charging to bring current at 0.05 A.Stabilization: The batteries are then allowed to stabilize by holding them for 30 minutes after the charging process.Storage Conditions: Cells are kept in an incubator at various temperatures for a month to assess their performance and stability over time.

Comparison of the battery charge-discharge cycle test in both normal and high temperatures: The following method can be used for measuring the charge-discharge cycles of the six cells from 25°C to 75°C.Initial Charging: Each cell is charged at a constant current density mode at a rate of 1C until it reached a terminal cut-off voltage of 4.15 V. Constant Voltage Charging: After reaching the cut-off voltage, the cell continued to charge at a constant voltage until the current dropped to 0.11 A. Stabilization: The cell should be held for 600 seconds to allow the system to stabilize. Discharge: Following the stabilization period, the cell is discharged in constant current density mode at a rate of 1C until the terminal voltage reached 3.0 V. Resting Period: The final step involved a resting period of 600 seconds.

Heat-transfer study with PCM-based cooling management of an 18650 power battery: From the experiments outlined above, it is proved that batteries are greatly influenced by temperature changes. As temperatures increase, the performance of these batteries deteriorates, and at higher temperatures, the risk of severe damage and thermal runaway becomes significant.

Heat generation from a single 18650 battery:To effectively implement a Battery Thermal Management System (BTMS), it is crucial to precisely determine the initial and boundary conditions and understand the essential attributes of the system. Here's a breakdown of these requirements:Initial Conditions: Battery State: Measure and record the initial state of charge (SOC), temperature, and any existing thermal gradients within the battery pack.Environmental Conditions: Establish the initial ambient temperature and humidity where the battery will operate.Battery Configuration: Identify the arrangement and thermal properties of the battery cells within the pack.Boundary Conditions:Temperature Limits: Define the maximum and minimum operating temperatures for safe battery performance. Heat Transfer: Establish the heat exchange mechanisms with the environment, such as cooling airflow rates, contact with cooling plates, or other thermal interfaces.Power Loads: Account for typical and peak power loads that will impact the battery's thermal behavior.

Heat Generation: Evaluate the heat generation rates during charging, discharging, and idle states. Cooling Efficiency: Evaluate the cooling system or thermal management processes used, such as the effectiveness of heat sinks, fans, or coolant flow systems. Safety Mechanisms: Incorporate safety features to prevent overheating, such as thermal cut-offs, alarms, or automatic shutoff systems.

6 BATTERY PACK: DESIGN

The design of battery pack depends upon the type, shape and cell configuration. Li-ion battery cells are available in Cylindrical, prismatic and pouch type. The cell configuration methods are aligned, staggered, and cross-aligned.The different parameters taken into consideration for designing the battery pack include battery capacity, number of cells in parallel, number of series cells, number of cells, battery pack mass, power required to propel the battery and battery peak power.

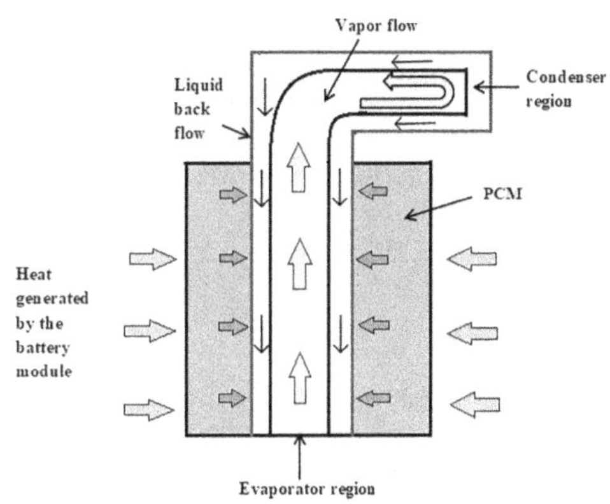

Figure 1. Schematic of PCM cooled BTMS.

Figure 3 describes the PCM cooled BTMS. There are two ports on the front and back of the battery pack. In the battery module, a coolant with high heat conductivity and low viscosity travels through a mini-channel. The coolant receives the heat produced inside the battery and subsequently exchanges it with the air. This technique uses a high coolant mass flow rate to increase cooling efficiency.

7 RESULTS AND DISCUSSION

When applying various types of phase-change materials (PCMs) in battery modules for thermal management, including PCM 1 (pure paraffin), PCM 2 (20% Expanded Graphite (EG) and 80% paraffin), and PCM 3 (3% EG, 47% epoxy, and 50% paraffin), several conclusions are drawn as below.

7.1 *Thermal Conductivity and Heat Transfer Efficiency*

PCM 1 (Pure Paraffin): While paraffin has good latent heat properties, its thermal conductivity is relatively low. This limits its effectiveness in quickly spreading and dissipating heat. PCM 2 (20% EG, 80% Paraffin): The addition of 20% Expanded Graphite significantly enhances the thermal conductivity of the PCM compared to pure paraffin. This allows for more efficient heat transfer and quicker dissipation of heat within the battery module. PCM 3 (3% EG, 47% Epoxy, 50% Paraffin): PCM 3 combines a small amount of EG with epoxy and paraffin. While it has improved thermal conductivity over pure paraffin due to the EG, the epoxy component may contribute to better structural stability and reduce leakage. However, the overall heat transfer efficiency might be less than PCM 2 due to the lower percentage of EG.

7.2 *Thermal Management Performance*

PCM 1: Provides basic thermal management through latent heat absorption but may not be sufficient for high-performance applications where rapid heat dissipation is needed. PCM 2: Offers superior thermal management capabilities due to the higher content of EG, which helps in maintaining temperature stability and enhancing the battery's performance under high discharge rates. PCM 3: Balances thermal conductivity and structural integrity, offering a good compromise between heat transfer efficiency and mechanical stability. The epoxy component aids in the durability of the PCM, making it suitable for applications where both thermal management and material stability are critical.

7.3 *Mechanical and Stability Considerations*

PCM 1: May face issues with mechanical stability and potential leakage during phase changes due to the lack of reinforcement. PCM 2: The inclusion of EG improves the mechanical properties and reduces the risk of leakage, though the overall stability still depends on the matrix used. PCM 3: The combination of EG with epoxy enhances both the mechanical stability and the thermal management performance, making it a robust choice for demanding applications.

8 CONCLUSION

In designing thermal management systems (BTMS) for battery packs, several considerations must be addressed to balance performance, cost, and practicality. Here's a summary of key points and recommendations:

8.1 *A enhancing PCM thermal conductivity*

Metal Fins: Applying metal fins can greatly enhance the heat dissipation ability of the PCM-based system. However, this approach increases both the system mass and manufacturing costs. Metal fins enhance thermal conductivity by providing efficient pathways for heat transfer but must be carefully weighed against their impact on overall system cost and weight. Additives and Fillers Adding fillers like nanoparticles or carbon-based materials can enhance the thermal conductivity of PCM within certain limits. While this method can be effective, there is a threshold beyond which additional improvements are minimal. A thorough understanding of the mechanisms during the preparation stage is crucial for optimizing the filler concentration and type.

8.2 *Passive vs. Active thermal management systems*

Passive Thermal Management System:Advantages: Simple structure, lower manufacturing cost, and fewer moving parts. Limitations: Less effective for large battery packs, and may not meet performance needs during high charge/discharge rates. Typically more suitable for small battery or cell packs.

Active Thermal Management System:Advantages: Superior heat dissipation capacity, suitable for large-capacity battery packs, and more effective under high charge/discharge conditions.Disadvantages: Complex structure, higher manufacturing cost, and additional components like pumps or fans.

8.3 *Optimization and practical considerations*

BTMS Structure Optimization: To ensure battery pack safety and efficiency, the structure of the BTMS with PCM needs to be optimized. This includes improving thermal performance while minimizing production costs and volume.

Cost and Volume Reduction: Focus on reducing both production costs and system volume without compromising safety or effectiveness. This might involve innovative design approaches or materials that offer a better balance of performance and cost.

Effective Heat Recycling: Leveraging PCM characteristics effectively can lead to a design that recycles battery heat, even under supercooling conditions. This involves optimizing the PCM's latent heat properties and ensuring efficient heat transfer within the system.

Practical Application and Decision-Making: By carefully evaluating these factors and optimizing the design, it is possible to develop a thermal management system that meets performance requirements, ensures safety, and is cost-effective.

REFERENCES

[1] Saravanakumar Thangavel, Deepak Mohanraj, T. Girijaprasanna, Saravanakumar Raju, C. Dhanamjayulu, And S.M. Muyeen, *A Comprehensive Review on Electric Vehicle: Battery Management System, Charging Station, Traction Motors* IEEE Access, volume 11, 2023.

[2] Yara Khawaja, Nathan Shankar, Issa Qiqieh, Battery management solutions for li-ion batteries based on artificial intelligence *Ain Shams Eng.Journal*, 23February 2023.

[3] A.G. Olabi, Hussein M. Maghrabie, Battery thermal management systems: Recent progress and challenges, *International Journal of Thermofluids*, 17 June 2022.

[4] M. Siva Ramkumar, C. Subba Rami Reddy, Agenya Ramakrishnan, Review on Li-Ion Battery with Battery Management System in Electrical Vehicle *Advances in Materials Science and Engineering*, Volume 2022, Article ID 3379574.

[5] J. Wang, Y. Gan, J. Liang, M. Tan, Y. Li, Sensitivity analysis of factors influencing a heat pipe based thermal management

system for a battery module with cylindrical cells, *Appl. Therm. Eng.* 151 (2019) 475–485. doi:10.1016/j.applthermaleng.2019.02.036

[6] Sajib Chakraborty, Hai-Nam Vu, Mohammed Mahedi Hasan, Dai-Duong Tran, Mohamed El Baghdadi and Omar Hegazy, DC-DC Converter Topologies for Electric Vehicles, Plug-in Hybrid Electric Vehicles and Fast Charging Stations: State of the Art and Future Trends, *Energies* 2019, 12(8),1569; https://doi.org/10.3390/en12081569

[7] Lazrak, J.F. Fourmigué, and J.F. Robin, An innovative practical battery thermal management system based on phase change materials: numerical and experimental investigations, *Applied Thermal Engineering,* vol. 128, pp. 20–32,2018

[8] Kailong LIU, Kang LI, Qiao PENG, Cheng ZHANG, A brief review on key technologies in the battery management system of electric vehicles, *Front.Mech.Eng*, 2018, https://doi.org/10.1007/s11465-018-0516-8

[9] De Vita, A. Maheshwari, M. Destro, M. Santarelli, and M. Carello, Transient thermal analysis of a lithium-ion battery pack comparing different cooling solutions for automotive applications, *Applied Energy*, vol. 206, pp. 101–112, 2017.

[10] W. Wu, X. Yang, G. Zhang, K. Chen, and S. Wang, Experimental investigation on the thermal performance of heat pipe-assisted phase change material based battery thermal management system, *Energy Conversion and Management*, vol. 138, pp. 486–492, 2017.

[11] G. Jiang, J. Huang, M. Liu, and M. Cao, Experiment and simulation of thermal management for a tube-shell Li-ion battery pack with composite phase change material, *Applied Thermal Engineering*, vol. 120, pp. 1–9, 2017.

[12] W. Wu, X. Yang, G. Zhang *et al.*, An experimental study of thermal management system using copper mesh-enhanced composite phase change materials for power battery pack, *Energy*, vol. 113, pp. 909–916, 2016.

[13] Y. Huo, Z. Rao, X. Liu, and J. Zhao, Investigation of power battery thermal management by using mini-channel cold plate, *Energy Conversion and Management*, vol. 89, pp. 387–395, 2015.

[14] S.K. Mohammadian, Y. Zhang, Thermal management optimization of an air-cooled Li-ion battery module using pin-fin heat sinks for hybrid electric vehicles, *J. Power Sources*. 273 (2015) 431–439. doi:10.1016/J.JPOWSOUR.2014.09.110.

Advancement in Engineering and Science – Goyal et al. (Eds)
© 2026 The Author(s), ISBN: 978-1-041-31101-0

A Review on Multisource Crop Mapping and Forecasting Using 'Machine Learning'

Sarika S. Patil and R.B. Kulkarni
Department of Information Technology, Government College of Engineering, Karad, India

ABSTRACT: Accurate and timely crop mapping and forecasting are essential for sustainable agriculture, ensuring food security, and supporting economic stability. Leveraging multisource remote sensing data, including optical imagery from satellites like 'Sentinel-2' and Landsat, GaoFen-1, and aerial/UAV platforms, alongside radar data from 'Sentinel-1', and potentially 'LiDAR', enhances the spatio-temporal resolution and robustness of these analyses. 'Machine Learning' (ML) and 'Deep Learning' (DL) algorithms, such as 'Random Forest (RF)' and 'Support Vector Machines (SVM)', 'Convolutional Neural Networks (CNNs)', and 'Long Short-Term Memory (LSTM)' networks, are increasingly employed to process these complex datasets. The integration of multisource data with ML/DL techniques improves crop classification accuracy and enables reliable acreage estimation and yield prediction. Methods like discrete grids facilitate large-scale processing, while techniques like data fusion, transfer learning, and ensemble methods further enhance performance. 'cloud computing platforms' like 'Google Earth Engine' ('GEE') support efficient analysis of large datasets. These advancements contribute significantly to precision agriculture and informed agricultural policy-making.

Keywords: Crop Mapping, Agricultural, 'Machine Learning', 'Deep Learning', Multisource Satellite Imagery

1 INTRODUCTION

The accurate and timely mapping and forecasting of crops are importance for agricultural, ensuring food security, and supporting economic stability. As the spatial scope of crop mapping expands from local to large areas, there is a growing need for practical applications that can provide reliable information on crop distribution, acreage, and potential yields. However, achieving accurate crop mapping and forecasting, especially at a large scale, presents several challenges. These include the limitations of individual satellite data sources due to low spatio-temporal information, issues with sparse sampling, and the computational burden associated with processing massive datasets. Furthermore, the heterogeneity of agricultural landscapes and ecological gradients between crops and non-crops can complicate accurate identification.

To overcome these limitations, a promising approach involves the integration of multisource remote sensing data By combining data from various satellite imagery, drone such as optical imagery from 'Sentinel-2', Landsat, and GaoFen-1, with radar data from 'Sentinel-1', and potentially incorporating 'LiDAR' or aerial imagery, drone imagery, survey it is possible to enhance the spatial and temporal coverage and acquire richer spectral, textural, and phenological information For instance, the synergistic use of 'GF-1' and 'Sentinel-2' imagery has demonstrated improved accuracy in crop mapping compared to using a single data source.

Furthermore, 'Machine Learning' (ML)' and 'Deep Learning' (DL)' algorithms have emerged as powerful tools for analyzing these complex multisource. These algorithms can effectively handle high-dimensional, non-normally distributed data, automatically extract complex features relevant for crop identification, and model the non-linear relationships between Number of aspects influencing crop growth and yield. Algorithms such as 'Random Forest (RF)' and 'Support Vector Machines (SVM)' have been successfully utilized for crop classification, achieving high overall accuracies. To address the challenges of large-scale analysis, methods based on discrete grids and the utilization of 'cloud computing platforms' like 'Google Earth Engine' ('GEE') can significantly improve processing efficiency. Additionally, advanced techniques like feature selection, data fusion, transfer learning, and ensemble learning are employed to optimize model performance and enhance the robustness of crop mapping and forecasting results.

Therefore, this review plans to utilize the synergistic capabilities of multisource remote sensing data and 'Machine Learning' techniques to achieve accurate and efficient crop mapping and forecasting. By integrating diverse data sources and employing advanced ML algorithms to improved crop type identification in a specific region, enhanced accuracy in early-season yield prediction for major crops.

2 DIFFERENT IMPLEMENTAIONS

[1] Journal paper by S. Yan *et al.* have proposed a list of 'vegetation indices' (VIs) used in a study. The calculation formula for various VIs, including DVI, EVI, GEMI, GARI, GCI, GDVI, GLI, GNDVI, GOSAVI, GRVI, RVI, NDWI, and TVI. The authors discuss the integration of 'Multi-Source' data to overcome limitations of satellite sensors and weather influences, noting that algorithms suitable for small-scale or specific topographies might lead to uncertainties in large heterogeneous areas.

[2] Journal paper by M. Hudait *et al.* have explore the creation of training and testing datasets for land use/land cover (LULC) classification. Field-based ground-truthing was conducted using ground control points (GCPs) collected with a handheld GPS from various LULC classes like 'paddy fields, vegetable patches, betel vine plots, and barren lands'. These GCPs were marked in Google Earth images from February 2019 to March 2020. A total of 920 random points, representing all LULC types, were generated for training and testing. The funding source and declaration of competing interests are mentioned.

[3] Article by A. J. Prins *et al.* have focuses on crop type mapping using 'LiDAR', 'Sentinel-2', and 'aerial imagery' with 'Machine Learning' algorithms in the Vaalharts irrigation scheme in South Africa. The study area and its climatic conditions are described. The creation of 'LiDAR'-based features, including 'nDSM', 'gen-nDSM', 'Intensity image', and texture features derived using HISTEX and TEX, is detailed. The 'LiDAR' derivatives were interpolated to match the spatial resolution of 'Sentinel-2' bands. The study recommends 'RF' or

DOI: 10.1201/9781003798514-13

'XGBoost' when only 'LiDAR' data is available, and 'd-NN' or 'SVM-L' for 'Sentinel-2' data alone. When combining 'LiDAR' and 'Sentinel-2', 'XGBoost', 'RF', 'd-NN', or 'SVM-L' performed well. The study concludes that most crops could be differentiated with 'LiDAR' data alone, with 'XGBoost' achieving the best accuracy (87.8%), and that 'LiDAR' technology excels at distinguishing between crops that vary in height.

[4] Research article by M. M. Hosseini *et al.* have explore paper's main objective is to identify cropping intensity patterns (CIPs) using 'Sentinel-2' and 'Landsat-8/9' data by creating a temporally dense time series. A trained 'heterogeneous Stack ensemble model' (incorporating "RF, SVM, GBT, and CART" as base classifiers and 'Minimum Distance' as a meta classifier) was used in 2021. The methodology involved using 'Google Earth Engine' ('GEE') and considering only satellite images with less than 10% cloud coverage, with potential cloudy pixels removed. The results show that using a 'multi-source' approach (S2 and L8) leads to better CIP mapping results due to the different acquisition dates capturing phenological dynamics more comprehensively. While the combination is not widely used in CIP mapping, S2 data alone achieved higher accuracies than 'L8/9' due to richer spectral information and denser temporal resolution.

[5] Article by Z. Lu *et al.* have focuses on 'Deep Learning' for 'Multi-Source' Data-Driven Crop Yield Prediction' in Northeast China', specifically for maize, rice, and soybeans. The dataset integrated key variables like 'SIF', 'GPP', 'Net Photosynthesis', 'Fpar', and 'LAI'. An advanced 'SIF' dataset was used. The study tailored feature selection to identify pertinent variables for prediction during the critical growth window (May to October), with July and August identified as pivotal months. Preliminary experiments evaluated different model architectures and hyperparameter tuning using cross-validation. The evaluation metrics used were R2, RMSE, and MAPE. A detailed account is provided of how crucial variables were identified for yield prediction models of maize, rice, and soybean.

[6] Research paper by Y. Mahale *et al.* have proposes an IoT and remote sensing-based smart agriculture system for temporary crop monitoring in Maharashtra, India. The system uses sensors and IoT for data collection, along with remote sensing data. 'Deep Learning' models were used for analysis, achieving an accuracy of 96.84%. This paper shows the Maharashtra state temporary crop calendar. The research aims to create a scalable model for precision agriculture.

[7] Research article by A. Moumni *et al.* have describes a 'Machine Learning' based classification for crop type mapping using the combination of 'Sentinel-2' (optical) and 'Sentinel-1' (SAR) data. The study used 20 'Sentinel-2' and 12 'Sentinel-1' images, along with in situ data supplemented by Google Earth. ML, SVM, and ANN algorithms were applied to classify 'Sentinel-2' data, 'Sentinel-1' data, and their combination. The results were evaluated using overall accuracy and the 'Kappa coefficient'. The classification results from 'optical', 'SAR', and their combined data were compared This paper describes the different classification scenarios using time series of 'NDVI, VV, VH, and VV/VH' and provides minimum, maximum, and amplitude values of 'VV, VH, and VV/VH' signals for different classes. Using both S1 and S2 data together produced better results in terms of accuracy and quality than using each one in isolation.

[8] Article by C. Singh *et al.* have discusses the use of 'Deep Learning' in the mapping of agricultural land use using 'Sentinel-2' satellite data. The research underscores the effectiveness of 'Deep Learning' in analyzing 'Sentinel-2' images, facilitating accurate and timely crop inventory management. It suggests further studies could involve 'Deep Learning' of multisource data combination for cloud-free monitoring. Data availability from USGS is mentioned.

[9] Review paper by A. Joshi *et al.* have summarizes existing research on 'crop mapping and yield prediction' using 'Deep Learning' and remote sensing, aiming to spotlights gaps and provide recommendations. The Scopus and Web of Science databases were searched systematically, employing a defined set of keywords. Exclusion criteria were applied to select 90 publications for review. The review analysed aspects like 'DL architecture, frameworks, RS data, training data, site, scale, assessment measures, and performance'. Satellite-based sensors were the most commonly used (81%), with MODIS popular for yield prediction and 'Sentinel-1'/2' and 'Landsat' frequently used for crop mapping. CNN was the most popular DL method. This paper illustrates a standard methodology for remote sensing and 'Deep Learning' research, and provides a summary of the characteristics of frequently used remote sensing data

[10] Journal paper by X. Feng *et al.* have describes the use of 'Sentinel-2'A images for crop type identification, extracting 126 features of spectroscopy, 'vegetation index' (including NDVI time series), texture, and phenological parameters. SVMs were used for farmland extraction. 'Random forest' was used for feature selection, determining the optimal combination of 13 features based on the average accurate reduction rate. The classification accuracy of RF, SVM, and maximum likelihood methods was compared using sample training and accuracy verification. The process consisted of extracting farmland regions, generating and refining features, determining the most effective parameters, and deploying the final classification model. A three-fold cross-validation with grid search was employed to estimate the optimal parameters.

[15] Journal paper by J. Darvish Zadeh *et al.* have discusses large-scale crop mapping from 'Multi-Source' remote sensing images in 'Google Earth Engine' ('GEE'). It notes that while optical imagery has a dominant contribution to mapping accuracy, SAR data can further improve it. Using 'normalized difference vegetation index (NDVI)' time-series can be enhanced by crop phenological features, often extracted from high-temporal resolution data like MODIS. The study used multi-spectral imagery ('MODIS', 'Landsat 8', 'Sentinel-2'), SAR data ('Sentinel-1'), and ancillary data like crop dominance and cropland distribution. The study introduces a method (MBPC) that integrates spectral, harmonic backscattering, and harmonic phenological features, incorporating prior constraints. Separability analysis of different feature sets was conducted using JM distances.

[16] Article by A. Safari *et al.* have explores the potential of multi-resource remote sensing data (optical VIs from Rapid Eye and polarimetric SAR from UAVSAR) to analyze and calculate crop properties (dry biomass and LAI) for canola, corn, and soybean in the SMAPVEX-12 campaign area. In situ measurements were collected over six weeks in 2012. RF feature importance was calculated to remove less important features. SAR and 'vegetation indices' were considered individually and then combined as input to 'Machine Learning' models (RF, SVR, ANN, and deep ANN). Model performance was evaluated using RMSE and R. The study compared the results of using separate and combined datasets. Results showed acceptable agreement with previous research. Deep neural networks provided specific estimates for dry biomass.

[18] Journal paper by S. Ghasemi *et al.* have focuses on downscaling county-level crop yield statistics (soybean and corn) to 1 km grids using 'Multi-Source' remote sensing' data and 'ensemble 'Machine Learning'. The data used includes county-level soybean and corn yields from the USDA NASS (2006-2021), cropland data layer (CDL) for cultivation distribution, MODIS products, and meteorological data. The CDL data was used to extract remote sensing variable data for corresponding crop planting areas.

[19] Research article by Q. Wang *et al.* have compares 'Support Vector Machines (SVM)' and 'Random Forests (RF)'

for maize crop mapping in the Makarfi region, Nigeria, using 'Sentinel-2' data. Field data was collected by IITA. Sample points for maize and other land cover classes were collected using GPS and Google Earth. The methodological workflow is illustrated. RF classifiers showed high efficiency in accuracy with limited processing time. This paper presents 'producer accuracy (PA)' and 'user accuracy (UA)' for maize, water, and other classes using different spectral index and SAR ('SI-SAR, SB-SAR, SI-SB-SAR') data with RF and SVM.

[20] Article by W. Luan *et al.* have focuses on 'land use and land cover (LULC)' classification using 'Sentinel-2' imagery and 'Google Earth Engine' ('GEE')' in the Guangxi Zhuang Autonomous Region, China. Field observations and 'GEE' platform were used to create the dataset with 593 sample points across six classes (built-up, water, bare ground, roadways, maize planting, mountainous places).'Machine Learning' classifiers (SVM, RF, ANN, GBDT, KNN) were compared.

[21] Research article by Chuanliang Sun *et al.* have explores the potential of multi-resource remote sensing data ('Sentinel-1', 'Sentinel-2', and 'Landsat-08') to identify crops in an urban agricultural region. Spectral, textural, and index features were derived. Three 'Machine Learning' methods were used to select an optimal mapping method. The mix of S1, S2, and Landsat-08 time series provided the best classification results. RF variable importance showed that index features dominated in May. This document illustrates the relationship between variable count and accuracy.

[22] Research article by Saeideh Maleki *et al.* have Using freely available 'Sentinel-1' (radar) and 'Sentinel-2' (optical) imagery, this study evaluated their capability to map sunflower, soybean, and maize in France. The French RPG provided the ground reference data. The research focused on analyzing 'Sentinel-2's 'Spectral Bands and Indices', and 'Sentinel-1's backscattering and polarimetric characteristics. Furthermore, time-series features were generated for both datasets using harmonic regression and median calculations based on phenological stages.

[23] Article by Johann Desloires *et al.* have investigates the contribution of different data sources ('Sentinel-2' biophysical variables, Land Surface Temperature (LST), and crop stress indices (CS)) to early season crop yield forecasting. Compares different data source combinations. This paper shows MAPE and R2 evaluation metrics around August 15th. End-of-season metrics were also presented for comparison.

[24] Research paper by Kuang, X *et al.* have explore a novel approach called FSACNN (Feature Selection Attention Convolutional Neural Network) for extracting crop planting areas from high-dimensional multi temporal hyperspectral remote sensing data from 'Gaofen-1', 'Gaofen-2', and 'Gaofen-6' optical satellites. Textural characteristics were extracted from GF-2 panchromatic images using the GLCM method. This method, FSACNN, employs both data dimensionality reduction and classification strategies.. Its performance was compared with other methods (DT, RF, SVM, HICCNN, CSCNN), showing superior extraction effect and robustness. The research includes images of the training area's ground truth and the corresponding classification outputs from various methods. Also shows classification accuracy with and without characteristic dimensionality reduction. The extracted areas were compared with statistical data.

[25] Research article by Yansi Chen *et al.* have focuses on maize extraction using 'Sentinel-1', 'Sentinel-2', and combined data with a Random Forest (RF) classifier. 'Field surveys' and high-resolution 'Google Earth' images were used for ground reference data collection. The goal was split into distinguishing vegetation from non-vegetation and then identifying maize from other vegetation, both using RF. The study evaluated how well classifiers performed using S1 data, S2 data, and the combination of both. The study area and data preprocessing are described. Vegetation extraction results based on S2 and maize extraction results for different data combinations are presented. This study examines the effects of image preprocessing and the use of multi-temporal imagery.

[31] Review paper by Igor Teixeira *et al.* have presents a systematic review of 'Deep Learning' (DL) models used for crop classification based on 'remote sensing (RS)' data '(satellite or UAV imagery') published between 2020 and 2022. The review excluded studies focusing on leaves, trunks, or diseases in the title. A search was conducted using Harzing's Publish or Perish software on Google Scholar and Scopus. This paper shows the study selection process, resulting in 36 included studies. Most reviewed papers used Convolutional Neural Networks (CNNs). Some studies integrated techniques like data augmentation and transfer learning. One study used a hybrid CNN with random forest (CNN-RF) and achieved high accuracy using 'Sentinel-2' imagery. Another study used ANNs for tobacco detection, finding that using multi-year data improved accuracy but required substantial resources. A study focused on explainability in crop classification using UAV imagery and DL. One study developed a CNN architecture using VHR aerial and 'Sentinel-2' time-series data, achieving over 93% accuracy. The review concludes by highlighting research gaps and providing recommendations.

4 FUTURE SCOPE AND DEPENDENCIES

Drawing on the provided sources and our conversation history regarding the effectiveness of 'Sentinel-2' and 'Deep Learning' for agricultural land use and crop type mapping, several future scopes and dependencies emerge:

A. Future Scope:

- Development of Advanced Algorithmic Frameworks and Lightweight Fusion Models: Future research should focus on exploring advanced algorithmic frameworks and developing lightweight fusion models to improve model performance in resource-restricted environments. This could involve investigating novel 'Deep Learning' architectures or optimizing existing ones for efficiency.
- Exploration of Multisource Data Fusion: Combining 'Sentinel-2' data with other remote sensing data sources like 'Sentinel-1' (SAR), 'LiDAR', and potentially hyperspectral imagery is a key direction. Integrating data from different sensors can overcome individual sensor limitations, such as cloud cover in optical data, and provide richer information for classification and monitoring.
- Integration of Temporal Information and Phenological Characteristics: Future work should further leverage the temporal richness of 'Sentinel-2' data to better capture the phenological changes of crops throughout the growing season. Techniques like temporal self-attention mechanisms and time series analysis can enhance the accuracy of crop identification.
- Enhancing Generalization and Transferability: Research needs to focus on improving the spatiotemporal generalization of models. This includes developing methods that can effectively transfer knowledge learned in one region or time period to another with different environmental conditions and cropping practices. Techniques like domain adaptation and transfer learning are crucial in this regard.
- Real-time and Large-Scale Applications: Future efforts should aim at updating classification products in near real-time and applying these methods to large-scale areas. 'cloud computing platforms' like 'Google Earth Engine' ('GEE') provide the infrastructure for such large-scale processing and deployment.

- Incorporating Explainability: As 'Deep Learning' models are often "black boxes," future research should explore methods to increase the explainability of crop classification results to build trust and understanding among users.
- Integration with Other Data and Models: Future scope includes integrating 'Sentinel-2' and 'Deep Learning' with other data sources such as climate data, soil information, and agricultural statistics to improve yield prediction and provide more comprehensive agricultural insights. Combining these with crop growth models could further enhance predictive capabilities.
- Development of Interactive Tools: Creating interactive tools and platforms based on these technologies can make them more accessible and useful for agricultural planners, farmers, and policymakers.
- Addressing Specific Crop Mapping Challenges: Future research can focus on improving the mapping accuracy of specific crops that are challenging to classify due to spectral similarity or limited available data.

B. Dependencies:

- Availability of Sufficient and High-Quality Training Data: the availability of large, accurately labelled training datasets. Creating and sharing benchmark datasets across different regions and crop types is crucial.
- Computational Resources: Training 'Deep Learning' models can be computationally intensive. Access to sufficient computing resources, including GPUs and cloud platforms, is a key dependency for developing and deploying these methods.
- Ground Truth Data for Validation: Accurate ground truth data is essential for training and validating the performance of crop mapping models. The availability and quality of ground truth information directly impact the reliability of the generated maps.
- Understanding Crop Phenology: Accurate crop mapping depends on understanding the unique phenological characteristics of different crops and selecting appropriate temporal windows for analysis.
- Continued Access to 'Sentinel-2' Data: The free and open availability of 'Sentinel-2' data is a fundamental dependency for the ongoing development and application of these techniques.
- Addressing Data Imbalance: 'Deep Learning' models can be sensitive to imbalanced class distributions in the training data. Developing techniques to handle data imbalance is important for accurate mapping of less prevalent crop types.
- Integration of Domain Knowledge: Effectively integrating agronomic knowledge and understanding of local cropping systems into the development and application of these methods is crucial for their success and practical relevance.

Table 1. Result analysis of existing papers

Ref No.	Paper	Dataset	Model	Accuracy
[3]	A. J. Prins *et al.*	Aerial imagery, 'Sentinel-2' imagery, and 'LiDAR' data	RF, XGBoost, SVM-L, NN, DT, k-NN, LR, NB, SVM RBF, d-NN.	Overall 94.6%
[4]	M. M. Hosseini *et al.*	'Sentinel-2' (S2) and 'Landsat-8/9'	RF,SVM, GBT, and CART	Overall 94.24%
[6]	Choudhury, T *et al.*	Temporal monthly weather data from IMD, Pune. Crop recommendation dataset from Kaggle.	Random Forest (RF), LSTM	91.88% (RF)
[17]	S. Yan *et al.*	'Sentinel-2' images	MUCCM, DANN,RF	Overall 87.52%
[24]	Kuang *et al.*	'GF-1', GF-2, and 'Sentinel-2' images.	FSACNN, DT, RF, SVM, HICCNN, CSCNN	98.57% (FSACNN)
[26]	Patel, P.P *et al.*	'Sentinel-2' multi-spectral images.	KNN and RF	97.16% (KNN), 97.22% (RF)
[28]	Van Niekerk, A *et al.*	Field data , 'LiDAR' derivatives ,aerial imagery, and 'Sentinel-2'.	RF, SVM, NN, XGBoost	94.6%
[30]	Ying, Q *et al.*	Kaggle: Crop Recommendation and Crop Yield Prediction.	Kernel Extreme Learning Machine (KELM)	97.91%

5 PROPOSED SYSTEM METHODOLOGY

The proposed system methodologies for multisource crop mapping and forecasting using 'Machine Learning' encompass a range of approaches that commonly involve the fusion of data from multiple remote sensing sources, including optical (e.g., 'Sentinel-2', 'Landsat-8', 'GaoFen, MODIS') and radar (e.g., 'Sentinel-1') satellite imagery, as well as potentially 'LiDAR' and aerial data. A key component of these approaches is the implementation of various 'Machine Learning' algorithms, which encompasses classic methods like 'Random Forest' and 'SVM', as well as modern techniques such as 'Gradient Boosting', 'XGBoost', and 'Convolutional Neural Networks'. To address challenges such as restricted training data and large-scale processing, techniques like data augmentation based on discrete grids are employed, and computations are often performed on cloud platforms like 'Google Earth Engine' ('GEE'). Furthermore, the methodologies frequently incorporate the temporal analysis of satellite data, extracting phenological features and tracking changes in spectral and backscatter signatures throughout the growing season to improve crop type classification and cropping intensity mapping. In some cases, ensemble learning, which composites the predictions of number of 'Machine Learning' models, and unsupervised domain adaptation, which facilitates the transfer of knowledge across different geographic regions, are utilized to enhance the robustness and generalizability of the results. Ultimately, the overarching goal of these multisource 'Machine Learning' approaches is to generate accurate and high-resolution information on crop distribution, growth, and yield, providing essential data for agricultural monitoring, resource management, and informed decision-making.

6 CONCLUSION

This review paper concludes that 'remote sensing' and 'Machine Learning' have established themselves as powerful and transformative tools for 'crop mapping and yield prediction' in modern agriculture. The reviewed literature consistently demonstrates the effectiveness of various 'Machine Learning' algorithms, particularly 'Random Forest' and 'Support Vector Machines', in achieving high accuracies for crop classification and yield estimation. Furthermore, the integration of 'Multi-Source' remote sensing data, encompassing optical and radar imagery, alongside carefully engineered features like spectral indices and phenological metrics, significantly enhances the performance and robustness of these methods. The increasing adoption and promising results of 'Deep Learning' techniques, especially Convolutional Neural Networks, highlight the potential for even more advanced and accurate agricultural monitoring capabilities. Despite the significant progress, several challenges remain. These include the critical need for improving the generalization ability of models across diverse geographical locations and crop types, addressing the constraints imposed by limited or imbalanced training datasets, and enhancing the interpretability of complex models, particularly within the realm of 'Deep Learning'. Researchers should concentrate on designing more dependable, versatile, and rapid methodologies, featuring lightweight fusion models and cutting-edge data integration methods, for future investigations. Addressing these challenges will be crucial for fully realizing the potential of remote sensing and 'Machine Learning' in achieving more informed agricultural practices and contributing to global food security.

REFERENCES

[1] S. Yan, X. Yao, D. Zhu, D. Liu, L. Zhang, G. Yu, B. Gao, J. Yang, and W. Yun, " Large-scale crop mapping from 'Multi-Source' optical satellite imageries using 'Machine Learning' with discrete grids", p. 2021.

[2] M. Hudait and P.P. Patel, "Crop-type mapping and acreage estimation in smallholding plots using 'Sentinel-2' images and 'Machine Learning' algorithms: Some comparisons," *The Egyptian Journal of Remote Sensing and Space Sciences*, vol. 25, no. 2, pp. 147–156, 2022, doi: 10.1016/j.ejrs.2022.01.004.

[3] A.J. Prins and A.V. Niekerk, "Crop type mapping using 'LiDAR' 'Sentinel-2' and aerial imagery with 'Machine Learning' algorithms," *Geocarto International*, pp. 1–20, 2020, doi: 10.1080/10106049.2020.1781441.

[4] M.M. Hosseini, M.J.V. Zoej, A.T. Dehkordi, and E. Ghaderpour, "Cropping intensity mapping in 'Sentinel-2' and 'Landsat-8/9' remote sensing data using temporal transfer of a stacked ensemble 'Machine Learning' model within 'Google Earth Engine'," *Geocarto International*, vol. 39, no. 1, p. 2387786, 2024, doi: 10.1080/10106049.2024.2387786.

[5] Z. Lu, J. Li, H. Fu, X. Tang, Z. Liu, H. Chen, Y. Sun, and X. Ning, "'Deep Learning' for 'Multi-Source' Data-Driven Crop Yield Prediction' in Northeast China," *Agriculture*, vol. 14, no. 5, p. 794, 2024, doi: 10.3390/agriculture14050794.

[6] Y. Mahale, N. Khan, K. Kulkarni, S.A. Wagle, P. Pareek, K. Kotecha, T. Choudhury, and A. Sharma, "'Deep Learning' and IoT-based crop monitoring and yield prediction in precision agriculture," *Research Discover Sustainability*, vol. 5, no. 2, p. 134, 2024, doi: 10.1007/s43621-024-00292-5.

[7] A. Moumni and A. Lahrouni, "'Machine Learning'-Based Classification for Crop-Type Mapping Using the Fusion of High-Resolution Satellite Imagery in a Semiarid Area," *Scientifica*, vol. 2021, 2021, doi: 10.1155/2021/8810279.

[8] C. Singh, S. Singh, G. Sethi, and V. Sood, "'Deep Learning' in the Mapping of Agricultural Land Use Using 'Sentinel-2' Satellite Data," *Geographies*, vol. 2, no. 4, pp. 691–700, 2022, doi: 10.3390/geographies2040042.

[9] A. Joshi, B. Pradhan, S. Gite, and S. Chakraborty, "Remote-Sensing Data and Deep-Learning Techniques in 'crop mapping and yield prediction': A Systematic Review," *Remote Sensing*, vol. 15, no. 8, p. 2014, 2023, doi: 10.3390/rs15082014.

[10] X. Feng, Q. Gong, and P. Liu, " Crop Type Identification and Mapping Using 'Machine Learning' Algorithms and 'Sentinel-2' Time Series Data", p. 2019

[11] Huang, J. Hou, Y. Zhou, and Y. Chen, "Mapping Winter Wheat Planting Area Based on Spectral–Temporal Features of 'Sentinel-2' Imagery and 'Deep Learning' Algorithm," *Remote Sensing*, vol. 13, no. 15, p. 2988, 2021, doi: 10.3390/rs13152988.

[12] X. Kang, J. Gao, J. Bai, H. Gao, and H. Wei, "Crop type mapping using 'Multi-Source' remote sensing images and a fusion 'Deep Learning' model," *Remote Sensing*, vol. 15, no. 16, p. 3792, 2023, doi: 10.3390/rs15163792.

[13] Bouguettaya, A.; Zarzour, H.; Kechida, A.; Taberkit, A.M. 'Deep Learning' Techniques to Classify Agricultural Crops Through UAV Imagery: A Review. *Neural Comput. Applic.*, 34, 9511–9536.

[14] S. Maleki, N. Baghdadi, H. Bazzi, C.F. Dantas, D. Ienco, Y. Nasrallah, and S. Najem, "'Machine Learning'-Based Summer Crops Mapping Using 'Sentinel-1' and 'Sentinel-2' Images," *Remote Sensing*, vol. 16, no. 22, p. 4548, 2024, doi: 10.3390/rs16224548.

[15] J. Darvishzadeh, D. Ienco, and A. Ballester-Berman, "Large-Scale Crop Mapping From Multisource Remote Sensing Images in 'Google Earth Engine'," *Remote Sensing*, vol. 16, no. 9, p. 1573, 2024, doi: 10.3390/rs16091573.

[16] A. Safari, S. Homayouni, S. Mirzaei, and M. Mahdianpari, "'Deep Learning'-Based Estimation of Crop Biophysical Parameters Using 'Multi-Source' and Multi-Temporal Remote Sensing Observations," *Agronomy*, vol. 11, no. 7, p. 1363, 2021, doi: 10.3390/agronomy11071363.

[17] S. Yan *et al.*, "Exploring the potential of 'Multi-Source' unsupervised domain adaptation in crop mapping using 'Sentinel-2' images," *Remote Sensing*, vol. 16, no. 13, p. 2394, 2024, doi: 10.3390/rs16132394.

[18] S. Ghasemi, Z.R. Nematollahi, M.M. Moghadam, and H.A. Abbaszadeh, "Downscaling Administrative-Level Crop Yield Statistics to 1 km Grids Using Multisource Remote Sensing Data and Ensemble 'Machine Learning'," *IEEE Journal of Selected Topics in Applied Earth Observations and Remote Sensing*, vol. 17, pp. 8715–8732, 2024, doi: 10.1109/jstars.2024.3431537.

[19] A.O. Onojeghuo, G.A. Blackburn, and Q. Wang, " Mapping Maize Fields by Using Multi-Temporal 'Sentinel-1'A and 'Sentinel-2'A Images in Makarfi, Northern Nigeria, Africa," *Sustainability*, vol. 12, no. 6, p. 2539, 2020, doi: 10.3390/su12062539

[20] W. Luan *et al.*, " Research on Maize Acreage Extraction and Growth Monitoring Based on a 'Machine Learning' Algorithm and 'Multi-Source' Remote Sensing Data," *Sustainability*, vol. 15, no. 23, p. 16343, 2023, doi: 10.3390/su152316343.

[21] Chuanliang Sun, Yan Bian, Tao Zhou and Jianjun Pan, "*Using of 'Multi-Source' and Multi-Temporal Remote Sensing Data Improves Crop-Type Mapping in the Subtropical Agriculture Region,*" p. 2019.

[22] Saeideh Maleki, Nicolas Baghdadi, Hassan Bazzi, Cassio Fraga Dantas, Dino Ienco, Yasser Nasrallah and Sami Najem, "*'Machine Learning'-Based Summer Crops Mapping Using 'Sentinel-1' and 'Sentinel-2' Images*", p. 2024, 16, 4548. https://doi.org/10.3390/ rs16234548.

[23] Johann Desloires, Dino Ienco and Antoine Botrel, "Early Season Forecasting of Corn Yield at Field Level from '*Multi-Source' Satellite Time Series Data*," p. 2024, 16, 1573.

[24] Kuang, X.; Guo, J.; Bai, J.; Geng, H.; Wang, H. Crop-Planting Area Prediction from '*Multi-Source' Gaofen Satellite Images Using a Novel 'Deep Learning' Model: A Case Study of Yangling District. Remote Sens.*, 15, 3792,2022.

[25] Yansi Chen, Jinliang Hou, Chunlin Huang, Ying Zhang and Xianghua Li, "*Mapping Maize Area in Heterogeneous Agricultural Landscape with Multi-Temporal 'Sentinel-1' and 'Sentinel-2' Images Based on Random Forest*", p. 2021.

[26] Hudait, M.; Patel, P.P. "Crop-Type Mapping and Acreage Estimation in Smallholding Plots Using 'Sentinel-2' Images and 'Machine Learning' Algorithms: Some Comparisons". *Egypt. J. Remote Sens. Space Sci.*, 25, 147–156.

[27] Sykas, D.; Papoutsis, I.; Zografakis, D. "Sen4AgriNet: A Harmonized Multi-Country, Multi-Temporal Benchmark Dataset for Agricultural Earth Observation 'Machine Learning' Applications". In *Proceedings of the 2021 IEEE International Geoscience and Remote Sensing Symposium IGARSS*, Brussels, Belgium, 11–16 July 2021; pp. 5830–5833.

[28] Prins, A.J.; Van Niekerk, A. "Crop Type Mapping Using 'LiDAR', 'Sentinel-2' and Aerial Imagery with 'Machine Learning' Algorithms". *Geo-Spatial Inf. Sci.* , 24, 215–227.

[29] Zhang, Y.; Skakun, S.; Adegbenro, M.O.; Ying, Q. "Leveraging the Use of Labeled Benchmark Datasets for Urban Area Change Mapping and Area Estimation: A Case Study of the Washington DC–Baltimore Region". *Int. J. Digit. Earth*, 15, 1169–1186.

[30] Agarwal, S.; Tarar, S. "A Hybrid Approach for Crop Yield Prediction Using 'Machine Learning' and 'Deep Learning' Algorithms". In *Proceedings of the Journal of Physics: Conference Series; Institute of Physics Publishing: Bristol*, UK,; Volume 1714, p 012012.

[31] Igor Teixeira, Raul Morais, Joaquim J. Sousa, and António Cunha, A. "'Deep Learning' Models for the Classification of Crops in Aerial Imagery: A Review". Agriculture, 13, 965.

[32] R. Li, S. Li, Y. Cao, Y. Zhou, Y. Huang, and C. Wang, "Large-scale crop mapping based on discrete grids with multisource data fusion and 'Machine Learning'," *Remote Sensing*, vol. 13, no. 12, p. 2385, 2021.

Advancement in Engineering and Science – Goyal et al. (Eds)
© 2026 The Author(s), ISBN: 978-1-041-31101-0

Soft Actor-Critic for Robotic Path Planning: A Deep Reinforcement Learning Approach

Swati Mohan Bankar
Research Scholar, Electronics and Telecommunication Engineering, Vishwakarma Institute of Information Technoloy, Pune, India

Rahul Pol
Associate Professor, Electronics and Telecommunication Engineering, Vishwakarma Institute of Information Technoloy, Pune, India

Sweety Narula
Research Scholar, Electronics and Telecommunication Engineering, Vishwakarma Institute of Information Technoloy, Pune, India

Vishakha Chobe
Associate Professor, Dr. D. Y. Patil Biotechnology and Bioinformatics, Tathawade, Pune, India

ABSTRACT: Robotic path planning in complex and dynamic environments presents significant challenges due to uncertainty, high-dimensional state spaces, and the need for real-time adaptability. Traditional planning methods often struggle with efficiency and adaptability in such environments. In recent years, **Deep Reinforcement Learning (DRL)**, has emerged as a powerful approach to address these challenges, with **Soft Actor-Critic (SAC)** standing out as an effective algorithm due to its ability to balance exploration and exploitation efficiently. By incorporating entropy maximization into the policy learning process, SAC encourages exploration and prevents premature convergence to suboptimal behaviors, making it particularly suitable for complex robotic tasks.

This paper explores the impact of SAC-based path planning on robotic navigation efficiency by comparing other DRL algorithm with it on different parameters. SAC, an off-policy DRL algorithm, leverages entropy-regularized learning to enhance stability and sample efficiency, allowing robots to make optimal decisions even in highly stochastic environments. The review also explores hybrid approaches that integrate these methods, highlighting their flexibility and improved effectiveness. Furthermore, it points out key shortcomings in existing research, such as challenges in scalability, safety, and generalization, and suggests potential avenues for future development in the field. By incorporating continuous action spaces and adaptive exploration, SAC improves trajectory optimization, obstacle avoidance, and real-time adaptability.

Keywords: Deep Reinforcement Learning, Soft Actor-Critic, Robotic Path Planning, Motion Optimization

1 INTRODUCTION

Deep reinforcement learning (DRL) has emerged as a powerful tool for addressing the complexities of robotic path planning in dynamic and unstructured environments. Traditional path planning algorithms like A*, Ant Colony Optimization, Particle Swarm Optimization, often struggle with high-dimensional state spaces, slow convergence, and the inability to adapt to changing conditions. DRL, by combining the strengths of deep learning and reinforcement learning, offers a more robust and efficient solution. This response explores the impact of DRL algorithms on the efficiency of robotic path planning, highlighting key advancements, challenges, and future directions.

DRL algorithms are categorized mainly in three types as follows [1]:

1. Value Based Methods
2. Policy Based Methods
3. Actor Critic Methods

Actor critic algorithms are combined version of value and policy-based methods as shown in Figure 1. Actor critic method has many algorithm examples like A2C, A3C, SAC etc. In next section we are explaining SAC Algorithm in detail.

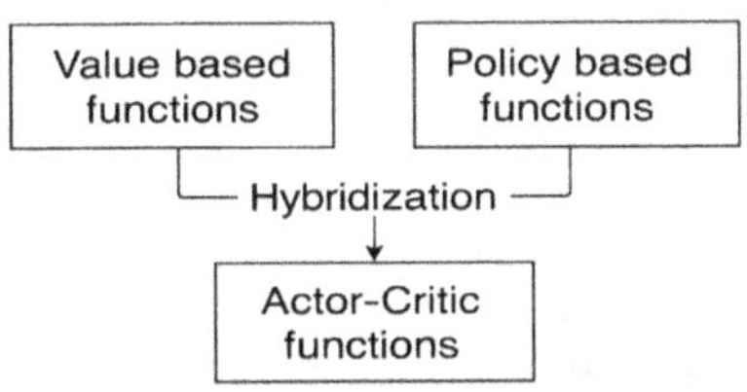

Figure 1. Categorization of DRL algorithms.

The contributions of this work are threefold: (1) we present a practical implementation of SAC for robotic path planning within a widely-used robotic simulation framework; (2) we analyze the performance and learning behavior of the trained agent in diverse navigation scenarios; and (3) we demonstrate the potential of entropy-regularized reinforcement learning for improving path planning in autonomous robots.

This paper provides an in-depth review of deep reinforcement learning (DRL) approaches applied to mobile robot path planning. It classifies current methodologies and evaluates their respective advantages and drawbacks. The study examines how DRL can tackle key path planning challenges such as navigating dynamic and unpredictable environments, maintaining a balance between efficiency and safety, and adapting to unfamiliar situations.

Remaining sections of paper are organized as Follows: In third section number of papers are evaluated and analyzed on the basis of parameters like algorithmic advancements in DRL, handling dynamic and complex environment, hybrid approaches of algorithms and lastly training efficiency and optimization.

2 SOFT ACTOR CRITIC ALGORITHM (SAC)

The SAC algorithm, introduced by Haarnoja et al. [2], is an off-policy DRL method designed for continuous action spaces. It combines the benefits of entropy maximization with actor-critic learning to improve exploration and robustness. It is grounded in the maximum entropy reinforcement learning framework, which not only seeks to maximize the expected return but also encourages exploration by maximizing the policy's entropy.

DOI: 10.1201/9781003798514-14

This helps the agent avoid premature convergence to sub-optimal policies, which is particularly valuable in complex, uncertain environments like robotic navigation.

2.1 *SAC Components*

1) Actor Network (Policy Network π): It is a decision maker. It's a neural network that produces a probability distribution over actions for a given state. SAC uses a stochastic policy meaning the agent doesn't stick rigidly to one action but explorers a range of possibilities. This flexibility is key for adapting to dynamic environment, environments.
2) Critic Network (Soft Q-Networks Q1 and Q2): the Critic's job is to evaluate the Actor's choices. It estimates the value of taking specific actions in particular states to reduce over-estimation errors often seen in Q learning. SAC uses two separate Q networks for this task
3) Replay Buffer (D): It stores past experiences (St, A, R, St+1) to enable sample-efficient learning. It is used for off-policy training, allowing the agent to learn from past data. During training, the algorithm samples from this buffer allowing it to reuse the valuable past data. This is a major factor behind SAC efficiency
4) Target Q-Networks: They are slowly updated versions of the Q-networks to stabilize training.
5) Entropy Regularizer (α): This encourages the policy to keep its options open by maintaining some randomness in it's actions. It can be learned automatically to adapt to different tasks
6) Gradient Updates: The policy and Q-networks are updated using stochastic gradient descent.

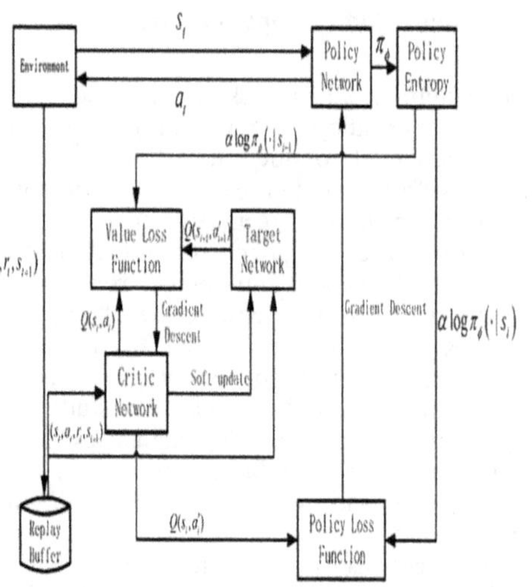

Figure 2. Block diagram of SAC algorithm flow.

The goal of SAC can be explained by following formula:

$$J(\pi) = E_{(s,a)\sim P}[Q(s,a) - \propto \log\pi(a|s) \quad (1)$$

Where,

Q(s,a) is the value, that critic assigns to a state action pair,

Π representats the policy's action probabilities,

α is a parameter that adjust the balance between prioritizing rewards and keeping the policy exploratory.

By maximizing this function, SAC ensures the agenct seeks high rewards, all staying, curious about other possibilities. It provides better exploration.

SAC is better in following ways:

- Continuous control: Ideal for velocity or trajectory control in robots.
- Efficient exploration: Essential in environments with sparse rewards or dynamic obstacles.
- Stable learning: Twin Q-networks and entropy regularization provide robust policy learning.

2.2 *SAC algorithm modifications*

To tailor SAC for path planning, the following changes were introduced:

- **Reward Shaping:** custom reward function to guide the robot.
- **Entropy Temperature Tuning:** Automatic entropy tuning can be used to adaptively adjust the exploration rate during training, improving stability and performance in the sparse-reward environment.
- **Replay Buffer Optimization.**
- **Training Stability Enhancements**

3 RELATED WORK

The review of the recently published research papers on this topic shows a highly dynamic landscape in the application of DRL Algorithms in Robotic path panning. Here few papers are analyzed on different parameters like algorithmic advancements, handling dynamic and complex environments and hybrid approaches of combining different algorithms.

3.1 *Algorithmic advancements in DRL for path planning*

DRL algorithms have been continuously refined to improve the efficiency and adaptability of robotic path planning. Several studies have introduced novel techniques to address the limitations of traditional methods:

1) Soft Actor Critic and priority replay buffer

   The SAC algorithm, has been modified with state dynamic normalization and priority replay buffer techniques to improve obstacle avoidance and target reaching in complex environments. Experimental results demonstrate that the proposed method outperforms Proximal Policy Optimization (PPO) in terms of cumulative reward and robustness (Yang *et al.*, 2022) [4]. These advancements not only contribute to more effective navigation strategies but also pave the way for real-time applications in dynamic settings, where robots must adapt to changing conditions and unforeseen obstacles.
2) Multi-Agent Deep Reinforcement Learning (MADRL)

   Multi-agent systems have been explored to address the challenge of optimal path planning for mobile robot clusters in uncertain environments. The proposed Multi-Objective Dynamic Path Planning (MODPP) model uses a centralized training with decentralized execution (CTDE) architecture, enabling agents to learn cooperative strategies and navigate without communication during execution (Meng *et al.*, 2024) [6].
3) Integration of DRL with Artificial Potential Fields

   Combining DRL with improved artificial potential field (IAPF) methods has been shown to enhance safety and training efficiency. The IAPF algorithm is used as expert knowledge for DDPG algorithm, reducing useless exploration and improving obstacle detection (Tong *et al.*, 2024) [7]
4) TD3-KDHER Algorithm

   The TD3-KDHER algorithm integrates Twin Delayed Deep Deterministic Policy Gradient (TD3) with an enhanced version of Hindsight Experience Replay (HER). This approach optimizes experience selection using Kernel Density Estimation (KDE) and incorporates adaptive action noise and masking strategies to refine exploration (Zhang and Zhao, 2024) [5].

5) Deep Q-Networks (DQN) with Prioritized Experience Replay (PER)

The use of DQN combined with PER has been shown to improve learning efficiency by prioritizing high-error experiences. This approach make sure that the algorithm focuses on the most critical experiences, leading to faster convergence and better generalization (Yang *et al.*, 2024) [8].

3.2 *Handling dynamic and complex environments*

One of the main challenges in robotic path planning is the ability to handle dynamic and complex environments. DRL algorithms have been designed to address these challenges through innovative techniques:

- Dynamic Collision Avoidance A framework combining DRL with obstacle detection methods has been proposed to address safety concerns in dynamic environments. The approach introduces a strategy-switching mechanism to adapt to various scenarios and overcome sparse reward challenges (Tong *et al.*, 2024) [7]. This system allows the algorithm to dynamically adjust its behavior based on real-time feedback, enhancing its ability to navigate through unpredictable obstacles while maintaining optimal path efficiency
- Multi-Obstacle Path Planning Comparative analyses of different representations and techniques in multi-obstacle environments have shown that ownership representation outperforms world-based representation in terms of performance metrics. Additionally, curriculum learning and supervised pre-training have been explored to improve convergence (Morgan *et al.*, 2024) [9]
- Progressive Policy Enhancement (EPPE) The EPPE framework integrates sparse and process rewards to achieve globally optimal policies. This approach significantly improves training efficiency and resolves reward coupling issues, leading to better path planning results in both static and mixed obstacle environments (Zhao *et al.*, 2024) [14]
- Attention-Based DDPG The integration of Multi-Head Attention (MHA) and Prioritized Experience Replay (PER) into the DDPG framework has enhanced the algorithm's generalization capability and execution efficiency. Experimental results show a 30% increase in success rate and a 23.7-second reduction in target-reaching time compared to traditional DDPG (Chen *et al.*, 2024) [11]

3.3 *Multi RobotPath planning and collaboration*

Multi-robot systems present unique challenges in path planning, including inter-robot communication and collision avoidance. DRL has been implemented to address these challenges:

- Centralized Training and Decentralized Execution (CTDE): A CTDE-based framework has been proposed for multi-robot path planning, enabling agents to learn cooperative strategies during training while executing tasks independently. This approach has been shown to improve performance in both static and dynamic environments (Zhang *et al.*, 2024) [12].
- Multi-Agent Policy Learning: This learning policy has been explored to deal with the challenge of path planning for autonomous mobile robots. The proposed method uses a centralized training framework and improves learning efficiency with highlight experience replay, leading to shorter movement distances and times in both static and dynamic environments (Zhang *et al.*, 2024).
- Multi-Robot Informative Path Planning: A decentralized RL approach has been proposed for multi-robot informative path planning. The approach uses an augmented graph to model robot trajectories and avoid inter-robot collisions, achieving a 33.75% improvement in the number of discovered targets-of-interest compared to state-of-the-art methods (Vashisth *et al.*, 2024) [13]

3.4 *hybrid approaches and real-world applications*

Hybrid approaches combining DRL with traditional path planning methods have shown promising results in real-world applications:

- Hybrid Path Planning and Following A hybrid approach combining path planning based on SAC with path following has been proposed. This method uses the Adaptively Informed Trees (AIT*) algorithm to generate paths and updates tracking points in real-time, leading to faster and more effective navigation (Zhong *et al.*, 2024) [14].
- Integration with ROS Platform The integration of DRL with the Robot Operating System (ROS) has been explored for autonomous navigation in unmanned vehicles. Experimental results demonstrate the superiority of DRL-based path planning in terms of path quality, decision efficiency, safety, and robustness compared to traditional methods (Gao *et al.*, 2024) [15].
- Attention-Based Path Planning The use of attention mechanisms in DRL has been shown to enhance the algorithm's ability to focus on relevant environmental features. This way of implementation has been successfully applied to path planning in complex environments, improving generalization and execution efficiency (Chen *et al.*, 2024) [16]

3.5 *Training efficiency and optimization*

Training efficiency is a critical factor in the successful deployment of DRL algorithms for robotic path planning. Several studies have focused on optimizing training processes:

- Double Experience Replay (DER): An improved DDPG algorithm with dual experience replay (DER) buffer has been proposed to enhance sample utilization and convergence speed. The approach introduces a prioritized experience replay buffer and a positive experience replay buffer, leading to improved stability in dynamic environments (Wang *et al.*, 2024) [19].
- Curriculum Learning and Supervised Pre-Training: This method have been explored to improve the convergence of DRL algorithms in complex environments. These techniques gradually increase the difficulty of the environment during training, leading to faster convergence and better performance (Morgan *et al.*, 2024) [18].
- EPPE: The EPPE (Efficient Progressive Policy Enhancement) framework has been proposed to address the dual challenges of training efficiency and composite optimization. This approach integrates sparse and process rewards, providing real-time feedback for policy adjustment and ensuring globally optimal policies (Zhao *et al.*, 2024).

In following Table 1, comparison of key factors of different DRL algorithms is done. Different research papers are analyzed on what are the key contribution are made by them in the field of robotic path planning. They are compared on the basis of environment in which they are implemented. Environment can be containing static obstacles or dynamic.

Table 1. Comparison of key DRL algorithms for Robotic path planning.

Algorithm	Key Contribution	Environment Type	Citation
SAC with Priority Replay	Improved obstacle avoidance and target reaching	Complex, Dynamic	Yang *et al.*, 2022 [4]
MADRL with CTDE	Scalable and adaptive path planning for multi-agent systems	Complex, Unstable	Meng *et al.*, 2024 [6]
DDPG with IAPF	Enhanced safety and training efficiency	Dynamic Obstacle	Tong *et al.*, 2024 [7]
TD3-KDHER	Optimized experience selection and exploration strategy	Complex Scenarios	Zhang and Zhao, 2024 [5].
DQN with PER	Faster convergence and improved generalization	High-Dimensional	Yang *et al.*, 2024 [8].
EPPE Framework	Globally optimal policies with improved training efficiency	Static and Mixed	Zhao *et al.*, 2024
Attention-Based DDPG	Enhanced generalization and execution efficiency	Complex Environments	Chen *et al.*, 2024 [11]
Multi-Agent CTDE	Improved performance in static and dynamic environments	Multi-Robot Systems	Zhang *et al.*, 2024 [12]
Hybrid SAC and AIT*	Faster and more effective navigation	Long-Distance, Dense	Zhong *et al.*, 2024 [14]
DRL with ROS Integration	Superior path quality, decision efficiency, and robustness	Autonomous Vehicles	Gao *et al.*, 2024 [15]
DER Buffer	Improved sample utilization and convergence speed	Dynamic Environments	Wang *et al.*, 2024 [17]

4 EMPIRICAL COMPARISON OF DRL ALGORITHMS

Real-time decision-making is crucial in robotic systems, as any delay in interpreting sensor inputs or issuing control commands can negatively affect both performance and safety. Although deep reinforcement learning (DRL) techniques have shown promising results in simulated environments, they often face challenges when applied in real-time settings due to their computational demands, limited sample efficiency, and the complexity of high-dimensional state-action spaces. To address these issues, recent research has concentrated on enhancing DRL for real-time use in robotics by increasing processing efficiency, minimizing response time, and supporting on-device computation.

In Table 2 we have made comparison of DRL algorithms empirically [3]. Here performance of various DRL algorithm are measured and noted. We can see SAC performance beats other DRL on training time, success rate and robustness parameters.

Table 2. Empirical comparison of DRL Algorithms on Different Parameters.

DRL Algorithm	Training time in hrs	Success rate	Robustness
DQN, DDQN	24	78	Moderate
PPO, SAC	12	88	High
DDPG, SAC	10	91	High
DQN Variants	18	85	Moderate
SAC Improved	9	95	Very High

5 CHALLENGES AND FUTURE DIRECTIONS

Despite the significant advancements in DRL for robotic path planning, several challenges remain:

- Sparse rewards in high-dimensional state spaces can lead to slow convergence and suboptimal policies. To tackle this challenge there is need innovative reward shaping and exploration strategies (Han *et al.*, 2019) [20] (Zhao *et al.*, 2024).
- Generalization and Transferability: Ensuring that DRL policies generalize well to unseen environments remains a challenge. Techniques such as zero-shot learning and hierarchical RL have been proposed to improve generalization (Mei and Xu, 2024).
- Real-time decision-making in dynamic environments needs efficient algorithms that can handle rapidly changing conditions. Further research should focus on optimizing computational efficiency and reducing latency (Zhang *et al.*, 2024) (Gao *et al.*, 2024).
- Multi-Robot Coordination: Scaling DRL algorithms to handle multi-robot systems with varying numbers of agents is an active area of research. Decentralized training and execution frameworks are essential for efficient multi-robot path planning (Vashisth *et al.*, 2024).

6 CONCLUSION

Deep reinforcement learning (DRL) has revolutionized robotic path planning by providing efficient and adaptive solutions to complex navigation challenges. Advances in algorithm design, hybrid approaches, and multi-robot coordination have significantly enhanced the efficiency and robustness of path planning in dynamic environments. Among DRL algorithms, Soft Actor-Critic (SAC) has shown notable advantages due to its sample efficiency, stability, and ability to handle continuous action spaces, making it well-suited for real-time robotic applications. However, challenges such as sparse rewards, generalization, and real-time decision-making still require further research. As DRL continues to evolve, integrating SAC with traditional methods and deploying it in real-world applications will drive the development of more intelligent and autonomous robotic systems.

REFERENCES

[1] Bankar S.M., and Pol R.S. (2025). Review on optimizing robotic navigation with deep reinforcement learning algorithms. *Journal of Information Systems Engineering and Management*, 10(23s). https://doi.org/10.52783/jisem.v10i23s.3698

[2] Haarnoja T., Zhou, A., Abbeel, P., and Levine, S. (2018). *Soft Actor-Critic: Off-Policy Maximum Entropy Deep Reinforcement Learning with a Stochastic Actor*. arXiv preprint arXiv:1801.01290. https://arxiv.org/abs/1801.01290

[3] Hoseinnezhad, R. A Comprehensive Review of Deep Learning Techniques in Mobile Robot Path Planning: Categorization and Analysis. Appl. Sci. 2025, 15, 2179. https://doi.org/10.3390/app15042179

[4] Yang, L., Bi, J., and Yuan, H. (2022). Dynamic Path Planning for Mobile Robots with Deep Reinforcement Learning. Advances in Control and Optimization of Dynamical Systems, 55(11), 19–24. https://doi.org/10.1016/j.ifacol.2022.08.042

[5] Zhang, J., and Zhao, H. (2024). Mobile Robot Path Planning Based on Improved Deep Reinforcement Learning Algorithm. 1758–1761. https://doi.org/10.1109/nnice61279.2024.10499084

[6] Meng, T., Li, Q., and Yu, J. (2024). Multi-Objective Dynamic Path Planning with Multi-Agent Deep Reinforcement Learning. Journal of Marine Science and Engineering, 13(1), 20. https://doi.org/10.3390/jmse13010020

[7] Tong, S., Liu, Q., Ma, Q., and Qin, J. (2024). Integrating deep reinforcement learning and improved artificial potential field method for safe path planning for mobile robots. Robotic Intelligence and Automation. https://doi.org/10.1108/ria-01-2024-0011

[8] Yang, Y., Ren, L., Chen, Z., Che, H., Zhou, D., and Li, H. (2024). Research on Path Planning of Autonomous Mobile Robot Based on Reinforcement Learning. 76–81. https://doi.org/10.1109/isctis63324.2024.10699065

[9] Morgan, B., Trigg, L., Stringer, A., Schley, L., and Hougen, D. F. (2024). Multi-Obstacle Path Planning using Deep Reinforcement Learning. 1–8. https://doi.org/10.1109/dasc62030.2024.10748994

[10] Wang, Z., Ye, Z., and Zongping, X. (2024). EPPE: An Efficient Progressive Policy Enhancement framework of deep reinforcement learning in path planning. Neurocomputing, 127958. https://doi.org/10.1016/j.neucom.2024.127958

[11] Chen, J., Jiang, Y., Pan, H., and Yang, M. (2024). Path Planning in Complex Environments Using Attention-Based Deep Deterministic Policy Gradient. Electronics, 13(18), 3746. https://doi.org/10.3390/electronics13183746

[12] Zhang, L., Cai, Z., Yan, Y., Yang, C., and Hu, Y. (2024). Multi-agent policy learning-based path planning for autonomous mobile robots. Engineering Applications of Artificial Intelligence. https://doi.org/10.1016/j.engappai.2023.107631

[13] Vashisth, A., Patel, D., Conover, D.M., and Bera, A. (2024). Multi-Robot Informative Path Planning for Efficient Target Mapping using Deep Reinforcement Learning. https://doi.org/10.48550/arxiv.2409.16967

[14] Zhong, L., Zhao, J., Luo, H., and Hou, Z. (2024). Hybrid path planning and following of a quadrotor UAV based on deep reinforcement learning. https://doi.org/10.1109/ccdc62350.2024.10587648

[15] Gao, X., Yuan, S., Zhu, J., and Zhao, Y. (2024). Application of Deep Reinforcement Learning (DRL) in the ROS Platform in Autonomous Navigation Decision Making of Unmanned Vehicles. 968–973. https://doi.org/10.1109/iciscae62304.2024.10761189

[16] Chen, J., Jiang, Y., Pan, H., and Yang, M. (2024). Path Planning in Complex Environments Using Attention-Based Deep Deterministic Policy Gradient. Electronics, 13(18), 3746. https://doi.org/10.3390/electronics13183746

[17] Wang, X., Han, M., Wang, Z., Wang, H., Li, C., and Zhong, B. (2024). Path planning for mobile robot based on deep reinforcement learning with double experience replay. https://doi.org/10.1109/ccdc62350.2024.10587636

[18] Morgan, B., Trigg, L., Stringer, A., Schley, L., and Hougen, D.F. (2024). Multi-Obstacle Path Planning using Deep Reinforcement Learning. 1–8. https://doi.org/10.1109/dasc62030.2024.10748994

[19] Wang, Z., Ye, Z., and Zongping, X. (2024). EPPE: An Efficient Progressive Policy Enhancement framework of deep reinforcement learning in path planning. Neurocomputing, 127958. https://doi.org/10.1016/j.neucom.2024.127958

[20] Han, Y., Guo, Y., Mi, Z., and Yang, Y. (2019). Robot Path Planning in Dynamic Environments Based on Deep Reinforcement Learning (pp. 265–283). Springer, Singapore. https://doi.org/10.1007/978-981-15-1922-2_19interface," IEEE Transl. J. Magn. Japan, vol. 2, pp. 740–741, August 1987 [Digests 9th Annual Conf. Magnetics Japan, p. 301, 1982].

Advancement in Engineering and Science – Goyal et al. (Eds)
© 2026 The Author(s), ISBN: 978-1-041-31101-0

Helmet Detection and Alert System for Institution

Kumarsagar M. Dange, Eshita Patil, Akshata Joshilkar, Tanuja Patil, Mayuri Salgar, and Rutuja Shewale
Annasaheb Dange College of Engineering & Technology, Maharashtra, India

ABSTRACT: The Helmet Detection and Alert System enforces helmet wear regulations for two-wheeler riders at schools in an effort to improve student safety. This system solves the problems associated with manual checks by streamlining the process of detecting helmets at school entrances with the help of cutting-edge computer vision and machine learning technologies. Entry gate cameras capture images or videos of approaching riders, which are then instantly processed by YOLOv8 model image processing algorithms. The system instantly sounds an alert to alert security personnel or the appropriate authorities when a rider is seen without a helmet. Additionally, it helps track repeat offenders and records violation data for later use. This approach significantly lowers the risk of serious injuries and fatalities while promoting a culture of responsibility among the students by guaranteeing consistent application of safety protocols. In order to enable quick and accurate helmet detection and alerting, this paper discusses a machine learning-based method that makes use of the YOLOv8 algorithm.

Keywords: Helmet Detection, Image Processing, Machine Learning, Real-Time Monitoring, Safety Enforcement, YOLOv8

1 INTRODUCTION

In order to promote road safety, it is imperative that motorcyclists wear helmets, particularly on university campuses where staff and students frequently ride two-wheelers. In the past, security guards have had to manually observe in order to enforce helmet regulations. The implementation of an automated helmet detection and alert system, however, is made possible by recent developments in surveillance technology. This system greatly increases safety by providing real-time monitoring and timely intervention. This cutting-edge system correctly detects riders‘ helmet use as they enter and exit the facility's grounds by using computer vision and machine learning techniques. It starts by identifying motorcycles in the security footage and carefully follows each car to make sure it is only registered once. The system's capacity to distinguish between riders and passengers is one of its primary features, as it allows for the creation of accurate data about helmet compliance. This feature increases the efficacy of rule enforcement because helmet usage patterns vary depending on the rider's position. In order to ensure accuracy, the system is carefully built to function well in a variety of institutional locations, such as internal roads, parking lots, and main entrances. The moment a rider is seen to be not wearing a helmet, an alert is triggered that either notifies security guards or displays a warning message on electronic screens. The need for ongoing human supervision is eliminated by this automated system while making certain that safety rules are applied consistently. Such a system's adaptability, robustness, and capacity to operate in a variety of lighting and environmental circumstances are essential to its success. Institutions can improve road safety, encourage compliance with regulations, and reduce the risk of head injuries by implementing real-time notifications and keeping track of helmet usage. An effective helmet detection and alert system serve as a preventative measure to promote a responsible riding culture within the organization. To accomplish quick and accurate object detection. This system makes use of advanced deep learning models, specifically YOLOv8 (You only look once). Video feeds are continuously recorded by cameras placed at campus entry points and other strategic locations. These feeds are then processed in real-time to identify motorcycles and determine whether or not riders are wearing helmets. In order to ensure that each vehicle is logged only once and to differentiate between riders and passengers, the system evaluates each frame using image processing algorithms. This distinction is crucial for accurate enforcement of regulations because helmet compliance may vary based on the rider's role.

2 RELATED WORK

Significant use of computer vision technologies has been discovered in automatic monitoring, particularly with regard to construction site safety. Notable helmet detection algorithms include techniques based on digital image processing, convolutional neural networks (CNNs), and Transformer-based algorithms, which are becoming more and more popular in the field of computer vision.

3 UTILIZING DIGITAL IMAGE PROCESSING FOR HELMET RECOGNITION

Digital image processing concentrates on extracting target features through techniques like edge detection and image preprocessing to enable helmet detection. The first method extracts target features from images using the Histogram of Oriented Gradients (HOG) and then classifies the images using a Support Vector Machine (SVM). This method has demonstrated exceptional recall and accuracy rates. Another strategy is to use image processing methods to identify the faces of construction workers. Some researchers have looked into the combination of frequency domain data and horizontal pixel analysis. Additional methods for automatically classifying helmet use include using a K-Nearest Neighbor (KNN) classifier to extract moving objects. Moreover. In order to effectively detect safety helmets, a multi-layer perceptron classifier has been trained using the Hough circular transformation in combination with HOG features. Digital image processing techniques frequently lack generalization and robustness in complex environments, despite their satisfactory detection performance. These methods have trouble detecting small objects and occlusions and require manual feature selection. Due to these constraints, the YOLOv8 algorithm was developed for automatic helmet detection.

3.1 *CNN-Powered helmet recognition*

Because it can efficiently identify and categorize cars, pedestrians, and obstacles in real-time, the Traffic Target Detection (TTD) system is crucial for enhancing road safety. A key component of TTD-YOLO is the YOLOv5 model, which is highly regarded for its high detection precision and quick processing

DOI: 10.1201/9781003798514-15

speed. With improved training methods, domain-specific extensions, and hardware-efficient implementations, the YOLOv5 framework has been thoroughly optimized for traffic monitoring applications. In terms of speed, accuracy, and computational efficiency, TTD-YOLO outperforms more established object detection models like Faster R-CNN and SSD. YOLOv5 employs a single-stage detection method as opposed to traditional two-stage object detection networks, which makes it especially useful for real-time applications on edge devices with limited processing power. Utilizing the latest developments in convolutional neural networks (CNNs), the model effectively extracts spatial features from input images, enabling precise helmet detection even in dynamic or crowded environments. The TTD-YOLO system's ability to adapt to difficult circumstances, like motion, is a major advantage. Partial obstructions, blur, and changing lighting. However, issues such as multiple riders' occlusion, dim lighting, and changing environmental conditions continue to pose challenges to accurate detection.

3.2 *Suggested method*

Asthma and other respiratory conditions like chronic obstructive pulmonary disease (COPD) have become more dangerous in the current environment. The rise in air pollutants such as PM2.5 and PM10 has increased that risk. Since reducing pollution levels takes a lot longer than the severity of the issue permits, a respirator can be used as an immediate countermeasure on an individual level safety measure.

The suggested system automates helmet detection at institutional entrances using machine learning models, like YOLOv8. Real-time helmet identification is achieved by machine learning algorithms that analyze video feeds. Barriers will stay in place and audio-visual alerts will sound if no helmet is detected. Any infractions are noted for future use. Data is tracked and reports are generated for additional analysis via a centralized dashboard. This system guarantees compliance with regulations, improves safety, and lessens the need for manual enforcement. It can also scale across different entry points, which enhances the institution's overall security.

3.3 *System architecture*

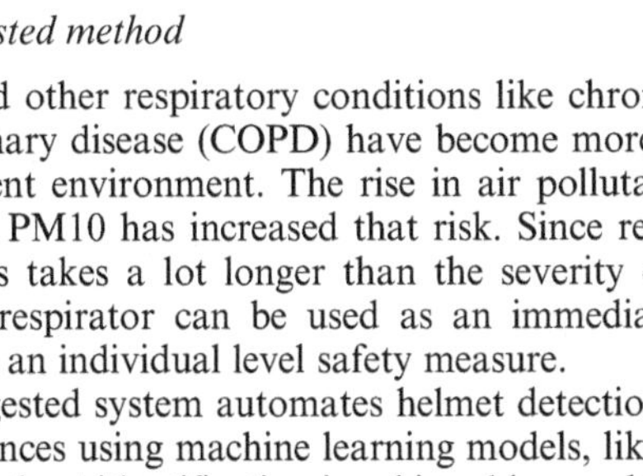

Figure 1. System Architecture

By detecting helmet use using the YOLO (You Only Look Once) framework, the helmet detection and alert system is designed to monitor and guarantee compliance with safety standards within institutions. The development process makes use of Visual Studio Code and Google Colab, with Visual Studio Code enabling flexible local deployment and Google Colab offering GPU capabilities for model training. The project makes use of CV2 (OpenCV) for video capture and frame analysis, the OS module for file and directory management, and Ultralytics for the implementation of the YOLO model. Image processing is done with Pillow (PIL), XML annotations are handled by xml.etree, and numerical calculations are done with NumPy and augmentation. The process starts with gathering pictures or videos of people wearing and not wearing helmets. These are then labeled to create XML files. XML.etree is then used to convert these annotations into YOLO format, and Pillow is used to resize the images. The dataset is divided into subsets for testing, validation, and training. In Visual Studio Code or Google Colab, model training is done with YOLOv8. Video is captured using CV2, and the YOLO model examines each frame to identify helmet usage, enabling real-time detection. When someone is detected without a helmet, an alert is sent out.

The process is demonstrated by a simple Python script that loads a YOLOv8 model, records video, and generates notifications if a helmet is not found. By offering automated, real-time monitoring to enforce helmet regulations and reduce potential hazards, this system greatly improves safety within institutions.

4 PROPOSED SYSTEM

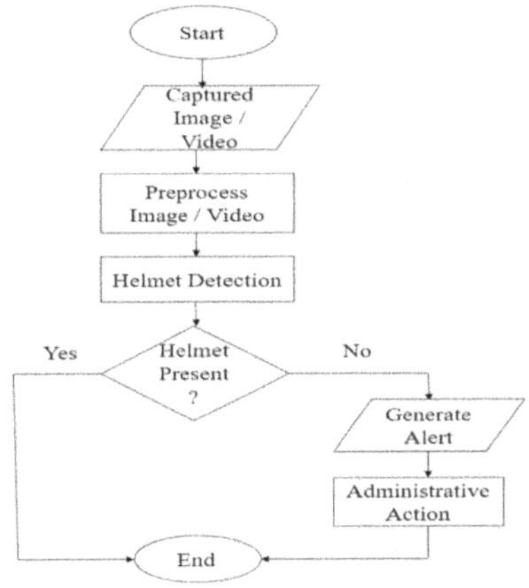

Figure 1. Flowchart.

In order to enable real-time supervision and enforcement of helmet use among two-wheeler riders on campus, the Helmet Detection and Alert System follow a methodical set of steps. First, the system is initialized. Next, surveillance cameras placed at campus entry points are used to capture images or video. Following visual data collection, the helmet detection module uses the YOLOv8 model to analyze the preprocessed images and determine whether the rider is wearing a helmet. Upon detecting a helmet at this point, the rider is allowed to go on unhindered. On the other hand, the system initiates an alert if no helmet is detected, which could entail alerting security guards or displaying a warning message on computer screens. Additionally, the system logs the infraction for future use, enabling law enforcement to keep an eye on and deal with repeat offenders. On the basis of the recorded data, administrative actions may be taken if judged necessary. In the end, the procedure guarantees continuous and automated monitoring of helmet compliance, which promotes a safer campus atmosphere.

5 RESULT

We use a range of accuracy metrics, such as Precision, Recall, F1 Score, mAP50, and mAP50-95, to fully evaluate the performance of our helmet detection model. A thorough assessment and subsequent optimization are made easier by the distinct viewpoints that each of these metrics provides on the model's efficacy.

Detection result from Front

Detection result from Back

Figure 2 (a). Detection result from front. Figure 2(b). Detection result from back.

1. The ratio of correctly predicted positive samples to the total number of samples predicted as positive is known as precision. This indicator shows how well the model detects positive examples. Precision can be calculated using the following formula:

$$TP/(TP + FP) = \text{precision}$$

2. Recall, also known as the detection rate, evaluates how well the model can identify every real positive sample. It is described as:

$$TP/(TP + FN) = \text{Recall our model evaluation}$$

$$\text{indicates that Remember} : 0.967$$

3. The F1 Score provides a fair evaluation of both metrics by taking the harmonic mean of Precision and Recall. The following formula is used to calculate it: F1 is equal to $2 \times$ (precision $\times$ recall) / (precision + recall). Making use of our model's Precision and Recall values: F1 Rating: 0.956
4. By calculating the average precision (AP) at an Intersection over Union (IoU) threshold of 0.5, mAP50 assesses the accuracy of the model. In benchmark evaluations like the PASCAL VOC challenge, this metric is frequently employed. Our model evaluation indicates that the mAP50 is 0.987.
5. By averaging AP values across several IoU thresholds, ranging from 0.5 to 0.95 in increments of 0.05, mAP50-95 offers a more thorough assessment. This measure provides a more comprehensive view of the model's detection performance at different overlap accuracy levels.

The Helmet Detection and Alert System shown in the picture is designed to increase road safety by detecting whether motorcycle riders are wearing helmets. The system recognizes riders and divides them into two categories: "wearing a helmet" and "not wearing a helmet." It does this by using computer vision and deep learning techniques. A bounding box containing an ID and a confidence score that indicates the detection's accuracy encloses each identified person. This system can be used by organizations to enforce safety rules, particularly at entry points, and guarantee that staff and students wear helmets Real-time monitoring capabilities enable automated alerts or access control measures, which limit access to areas designated for non-compliant individuals. Additionally, the system has the ability to produce violation logs for documentation and further examination.

6 CONCLUSION

The helmet detection system that is suggested here uses advanced machine learning techniques, particularly the YOLOv8 model, to provide an accurate, real-time, and reasonably priced way to enforce helmet-wearing regulations on school grounds. Our approach ensures scalability, adaptability to real-world scenarios, and energy efficiency, which sets it apart from traditional manual inspection techniques or proprietary automated solutions. Utilizing open-source resources and improving detection algorithms, the system significantly reduces operating costs while maintaining high accuracy—even in complex environments. Its compatibility with low-power edge devices also encourages sustainability, making it the best option for educational institutions. This innovative use of deep learning in helmet detection reduces the risk of head injuries and fatalities by promoting a culture of responsible riding and improving compliance with safety regulations. Its effectiveness is anticipated to be further enhanced by upcoming advancements in hardware integration and model optimization, making it a valuable tool for road safety initiatives.

REFERENCES

Bouhayane A, M. Ghogho, Z. Charouh, and Z. Guennoun, (2023). Swin Transformer-Based Approach for Motorcycle Helmet Detection, *IEEE Access*, vol.11,pp. 87543–87555.

Cheng L. (2024) *A Highly Robust Helmet Detection Algorithm Based on YOLO V8 and Transformer IEEE* vol. 12, pp. 12456–12467.

Gupte S., O. Masoud, R.F.K. Martin, and N.P. Papanikolopoulos, (2002). "Detection and classification of vehicles," *IEEE Trans. Intell. Transp. Syst.*, vol. 3, no. 1, pp. 37–47.

Jia, W., Mou, C., Wang, S., & Zhen, Z. (2021). Real-time automatic helmet detection of motorcyclists in urban traffic. *IET Image Processing*, 15(11), 2531–2542. https://ietresearch.onlinelibrary.wiley.com/doi/10.1049/ipr2.12295

Johnpaul, S., Varghese, A., & Goyal, S. (2022). IoT based Smart Helmet System for Accident Prevention. *2022 International Conference on Smart Electronics and Communication (ICOSEC)*. IEEE. https://ieeexplore.ieee.org/document/9936313/

Lin H.J.D. Deng, D. Albers, and F.W. Siebert, (2020). Helmet Use Detection of Tracked Motorcycles Using CNN-Based Multi-Task Learning, *IEEE* vol. 8, pp. 165432–165445.

Lv Y., Y Duan, W. Kang, Z. Li, and F.-Y. Wang, (2015). Traffic flow prediction with big data: A deep learning approach, *IEEE Trans. Intell. Transp. Syst.*, vil. 16, no. 2, pp. 865–873.

Madhuri Purkar, Snehal Kad, Payal Garud, Shruti Walave. (2024). Automatic Helmet Detection and Number Plate Recognition. *International Journal of Novel Research and Development*, 9(4), 118–123. https://www.ijnrd.org/papers/IJNRD2404118.pdf

Saravanan, M., Saranya, R., & Krishnakumar, P. (2024). Comprehensive study on the development of an automatic helmet violation detection system with number plate extraction based on real-time video analysis. *Computers & Electrical Engineering*, 118, 108293. https://www.sciencedirect.com/science/article/pii/S0045790624002179

Schoepflin T.N. and D.J. Dailey, (2003). Dynamic camera calibration of roadside traffic management cameras for vehicle speed estimation, *IEEE Trans. Intell. Transp. Syst.*, vol. 4, no. 2, pp. 90–98, Jun. 2003.

Shenoy, M.A., & Yermal, R.M. Helmet Detection using Machine Learning Approach. 2022 *International Conference on Communication information and Computing Technology (ICCICT)*.

Wei, L., Zhang, Z., & Huang, L. (2024). Research on helmet wearing detection method based on YOLOv5s. *Scientific Reports*, 14, Article 57433. https://doi.org/10.1038/s41598-024-57433-z.

Wu J., Z. Liu, J. Li, C. Gu M. Si, and F. Tan, (2009). An algorithm for automatic vehicle speed detection using video camera, in *Proc.4th Int.Conf. Comput.Sci.Edu*, pp. 193–196.

Wu, W., Huang, Y., Li, S., Rui, Z., Jin, Y., Wang, C., & Sun, J. (2022). Research on the Application of Helmet Detection Based on YOLOv4 Algorithm. *Journal of Computer and Communications*, 10(8), 97–111. https://www.scirp.org/journal/paperinformation?paperid=119617

Xia WP. Li, H. Huang Q. Li, T. Yang, and Z. Li, (2024). TTD-YOLO: A Real-Time Traffic Target Detection Algorithm Based on YOLOV5, *IEEE* vol. 12, pp. 13578–13589.

Advancement in Engineering and Science – Goyal et al. (Eds)
© 2026 The Author(s), ISBN: 978-1-041-31101-0

Design and Analysis of Dine-Bot for Physically Challenged People

Vivek Prajapati, Vishal More, Prasad Palve, Ojas Bhute, Avinash Badadhe, and Anand Shivashimpi
Department of Automation andRobotic, JSPM's Rajarshi Shahu College of Engineering, Maharashtra, India

ABSTRACT: Assistive robotics has revolutionized the way physically challenged individuals interact with their environment, particularly in daily activities such as dining. This paper walks through the process of building and refining Dine-Bot, a cost-effective and intelligent assistive robotic system aimed at enhancing independent eating for individuals with upper limb disabilities. The system incorporates a 4-degree-of-freedom (4DOF) robotic arm, powered by a Raspberry Pi 3 and SG90 servo motors to ensure precise movement. Additionally, a vision-based object detection mechanism, utilizing 5MP Raspberry Pi camera module, facilitates real- time food identification and adaptive user interaction. Designed with affordability, ease of use, and reliability in mind, the system undergoes performance analysis, evaluating factors such as accuracy, response time, and adaptability. The results highlight Dine- Bot's potential as an accessible solution to enhance the dining autonomy of physically challenged individuals.

Keywords: Assistive Robotics, Dine-Bot, Physically Challenged, Independent Dining, Robotic Arm, 4DOF Manipulator, Raspberry Pi 3, SG90 Servo Motor, Pi Camera Module, Vision-Based Object Detection, Human-Robot Interaction, Affordable Healthcare Technology

1 INTRODUCTION

The incorporation of robotics into assistive technology has greatly enhanced the quality of life for individuals with physical disabilities. Among various assistive robotic applications, dining assistance remains a crucial area, as it directly impacts a person's independence and dignity. Many individuals with upper limb impairments face challenges in performing daily activities such as eating, which often requires caregiver support. To tackle this challenge, robotic feeding systems have emerged as a promising solution, empowering users to regain autonomy in their daily activities.

1.1 *Problem statement*

Despite advancements in assistive robotics, existing feeding robots are often expensive, complex, and lack adaptability for different users. Commercially available solutions are not easily accessible to a large population due to high costs and technical constraints. There is a need for an affordable, efficient, and user-friendly dining assistance system that can cater to individuals with varying levels of physical impairment.

1.2 *Objective*

The goal of this research is to design and build Dine- Bot, an affordable and intelligent collaborative robot (cobot) to assist physically challenged individuals with feeding. The specific goals include:

- Developing a 4-degree-of-freedom (4DOF) robotic arm for accurate and efficient food handling.
- Implementing a vision-based object detection system using Raspberry Pi 5MP camera module for real-time food recognition.
- Ensuring affordability, ease of use, and adaptability to accommodate different users.
- Analysing the system's performance, accuracy, and response time to validate its effectiveness.

1.3 *Scope*

The proposed system focuses on providing dining assistance to individuals with upper limb disabilities. The design prioritizes affordability by utilizing, Raspberry Pi 3, SG90 servo motors, Raspberry Pi 5MP camera module and for object detection. The system is developed to be user-friendly, enabling simple interactions while maintaining adaptability for different food items and user preferences.

1.4 *Significance of the study*

Dine-Bot is designed to close the gap between costly commercial devices and the need for affordable, accessible assistive technology. By leveraging cost-effective components and an intelligent control system, this research contributes to the field of assistive robotics, healthcare automation, and human-robot interaction. The insights from this study could open new doors for advancing personalized robotic assistance in the future, enhancing the independence and quality of life of physically challenged individuals.

2 LITERATURE SURVEY

Several robotic systems have been developed to assist individuals with physical disabilities. One example is the JACO robotic arm, a widely used assistive device in the field [1], the iARM [2], the Kinova MICO [3], wheelchair-mounted robotic arms [4], and semi-autonomous feeding devices like Obi [5]. These systems aid in performing daily tasks; however, they have limitations in ease of use, affordability, and adaptability for individuals with severe motor impairments.

Many existing assistive robots require extensive customization and setup before use. For instance, wheelchair- mounted robotic arms often necessitate precise positioning of utensils and food items, making spontaneous dining difficult. Additionally, systems like Obi and other assistive feeding devices require predefined tray arrangements, limiting flexibility when eating different meals or dining at restaurants.

To address these challenges, we developed a prototype robotic arm, the Dine-Bot, aimed at assisting individuals with disabilities such as cerebral palsy, quadriplegia, and muscular dystrophy. Our primary objective was to create a cost- effective and adaptable solution to improve independent dining experiences. The Dine Bot features an integrated vision-based control system, enabling real-time food recognition and adaptive feeding. Unlike traditional assistive robotic arms that

DOI: 10.1201/9781003798514-16

follow fixed trajectories, our system dynamically adjusts movements based on detected food positions and user preferences. Additionally, the robotic arm is compact and portable, allowing for easy transportation and usability in various dining environments.

However, our initial design had limitations, including open-loop control, which restricted adaptability in unstructured environments. In this study, we implemented a feedback-based control system using a vision camera to enhance precision and flexibility. We evaluated our system by conducting object position detection tests and food delivery tasks with multiple participants.

3 METHODOLOGY

3.1 *System overview*

The Dine-Bot is an assistive robotic system designed to aid physically challenged individuals in feeding. It features a 4 degree-of-freedom (4DOF) robotic arm powered by a Raspberry Pi 3, utilizing SG90 servo motors for precise movements. A vision-based object detection system, incorporating a 5MP Raspberry Pi camera module, enables real-time identification of food items.

3.2 *Hardware components*

Table 1. Lists the major hardware components used in the development of Dine-Bot.

Components	Specification	Function
Raspberry Pi -3	Quad-core-1GB RAM	Processing unit
Raspberry pi camera module	5MP camera	Object detection
SG90 Servo Motor	4.8V-6V, 1.8kg torque	Arm movement
Power Supply	5V/2A	Provides stable power

- Raspberry Pi 3: It serves as the main processing unit, responsible for executing the face detection algorithm using OpenCV. It also processes data received from the ESP32-CAM and sends control signals to the servo motors.
- Raspberry Pi 5MP Cam: A 5MP camera module is integrated with the Raspberry Pi to capture real-time video input. This module helps in detecting user faces and positioning the robotic arm accurately.
- Servo Motors (SG90): The SG90 servo motors provide movement to the robotic arm. The motors are controlled by PWM (Pulse Width Modulation) signals from the Raspberry Pi, allowing the arm to adjust its position according to face detection results.
- Power Supply (5V/2A): The system runs on a 5V/2A power supply, ensuring stable operation of the Raspberry Pi, CAM module, and servo motors.

3.3 *Software and algorithm implementation*

- Programming Language: Python for motion control and object detection.
- Object Detection: OpenCV and TensorFlow Lite used for real-time food identification.
- Control Algorithm:
  a) Picking the food which is been fix at a particular point.
  b) Capture the image using the vision system.
  c) Process the image using OpenCV to detect the face of the user.
  d) Determine the feeding position and adjust the robotic arm's movement.
  e) Use inverse kinematics to ensure precise spoon positioning.
  f) Deliver the food to the user's mouth.

3.4 *System calculations*

(i) Calculate r

$$r = \sqrt{10^2 + 5^2} = \sqrt{100 + 25} = \sqrt{125}$$

$$\approx 11.18\text{cm}$$

(ii) Calculate (θ_2)

$$\cos\,\theta_2 = \frac{(11.18)^2 - 8^2 - 8^2}{-2 \times 8 \times 8}$$

$$\cos\,(\theta_2) = \frac{125 - 64 - 64}{-128} = \frac{-3}{-128} \approx 0.0234$$

$$\theta_2 = cos^{-1}(0.0234) \approx 88.65$$

(iii) Calculate (θ_1)

$$\alpha = atan\,2(5, 10) \approx 26.57$$

$$\beta = atan\,2(8\,\sin\,(88.65),\ 8 + 8\,\cos\,(88.65)) \approx 3.74$$

$$\theta_1 = 26.57 - 3.74 = 22.83$$

(iv) Result:

$$\theta_1 \approx 22.83$$

$$\theta_2 \approx 88.65$$

3.5 *Communication and integration*

- Raspberry Pi camera module communicates with Raspberry Pi 3 for image processing.
- Servo motor is controlled using PWM signals from Raspberry Pi 3.
- The system follows a close-loop feedback mechanism to ensure smooth operation.

3.6 *Communication and integration*

- Raspberry Pi camera module communicates with Raspberry Pi 3 for image processing.
- Servo motor is controlled using PWM signals from Raspberry Pi 3.
- The system follows a close-loop feedback mechanism to ensure smooth operation.

3.7 *Testing and performance evaluation*

- Accuracy Testing: Evaluate the object detection success rate.
- response time analysis: measure time from image capture to food delivery.
- user trials: conduct trials with physically challenged individuals to assess usability.

3.8 *Block diagram*

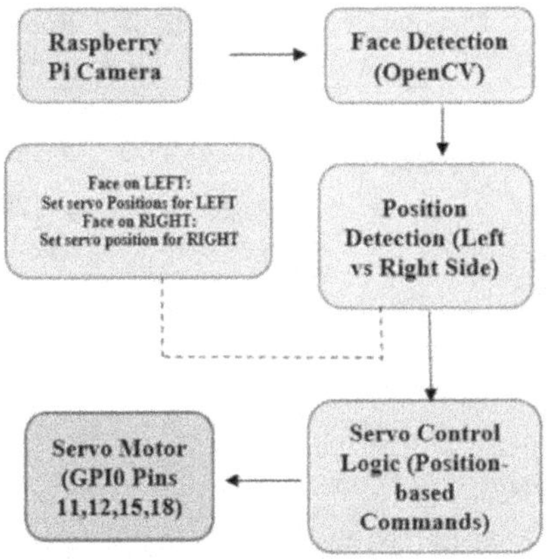

Figure 1. Face detection with servo control system.

Figure 1 illustrates the workflow of the Dine-Bot's face detection and servo control system, which enables the robotic arm to position itself based on the detected face location. The system follows a sequential process, as outlined below:

a) Raspberry Pi Camera Input: The Raspberry Pi camera streams a live video feed of the user's face in real-time.
b) Face Detection (OpenCV): The captured image is processed using OpenCV-based face detection algorithms. The system identifies the position of the user's face within the frame.
c) Position Determination: The algorithm determines whether the detected face is located towards the left or right side of the frame. A decision is made based on pixel coordinates to guide servo positioning.
d) Servo Control Logic:
   - Based on the detected position, the system sends appropriate position-based commands to adjust the servo motors.
   - If the face is on the left, the servos adjust to a left-aligned feeding position.
   - If the face is on the right, the servos move to a right-aligned position.

3.9 *Servo Motors (GPIO Control)*

The servo motors, connected to the Raspberry Pi's GPIO pins (Pins 11,12,15,18), execute the movement commands, aligning the robotic arm for accurate food delivery.

This process ensures dynamic and real-time user adaptation, allowing the Dine-Bot to assist physically challenged individuals by automatically adjusting the feeding position based on face orientation.

4 RESULT AND DISCUSSION

4.1 *System system performance evaluation*

The Dine-Bot was tested in real-world conditions to evaluate its accuracy, response time, and user adaptability. The evaluation criteria included object detection accuracy, robotic arm precision, and user experience.

4.1.1 *Object detection accuracy*

The vision system, using Raspberry Pi 5MP camera module, was tested on various food items under different lighting conditions. The results showed:

- Overall detection accuracy: 92%
- Challenges faced: Minor errors in detection under low-light conditions
- Improvement measures: Implementing image preprocessing techniques to enhance contrast.

4.1.2 *Object detection results*

Figure 2. Output result-1.

Figure 3. Output result-2.

4.1.3 *Robotic arm precision*

The 4DOF robotic arm was tested for movement accuracy and stability. The key findings were:

- Average error in spoon positioning: ±2.3 mm
- Success rate in food pickup and delivery: 89%
- Challenges: Minor instability in servo movements due to varying food textures
- Solution: Optimizing PID control parameters for smoother operation

4.2 *Response Time Analysis*

The system's real-time performance was evaluated by measuring the total time taken from food detection to delivery. The results are summarized in the table below:

Table 2. Time analysis.

Process	Average Time(seconds)
Image Processing	1.2
Object Recognition	1.5
Arm Movement	2.8
Total Response Time	5.5

4.3 *Prototype of the proposed system*

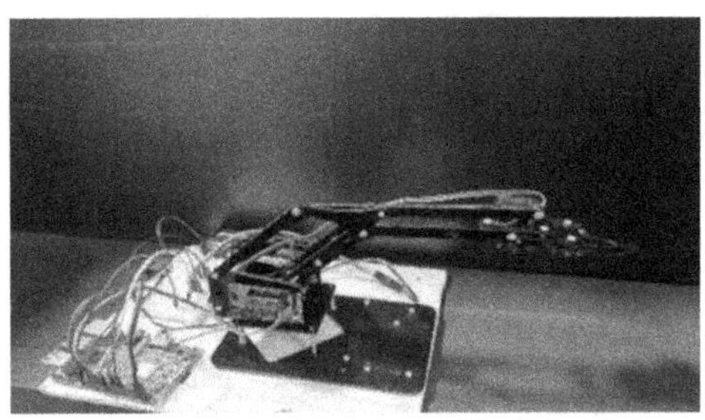

Figuer 4. Physical prototype of dine-bot (Left-Side).

Figure 5. Physical prototype of dine-bot (Right-Side).

The system architecture of Dine-Bot is illustrated in Figure 2 & 3. The Raspberry Pi Camera captures real-time images of the user, which are processed using OpenCV-based face detection. The system determines whether the face is positioned on the left or right, based on which the servo motors are actuated accordingly. The Raspberry Pi Camera module transmits real-time image data to the Raspberry Pi, ensuring a responsive and adaptive feeding mechanism. The servo motors, connected through GPIO pins, guide the robotic arm to align with the user's face, enhancing accessibility for individuals with physical challenges.

4.4 *Material selection and comparison*

Table 3. Comparison of different materials considered for the Dine-Bot prototype.

Material	Strength	Weight	Cost
PLA	Medium	Light	Low
ABS	High	Moderate	Medium
Aluminum	Very High	Heavy	High

5 EXPERIMENTAL RESULTS AND COMPARATIVE STUDY

5.1 *Performance assessment*

The Din-Bot prototype was tested for its accuracy, response time, and adaptability in a controlled indoor environment. The performance metrics were derived from multiple trials (n = 30) under varying lighting and object positions.

Table 4. Performance metrics of the Dine-Bot prototype in indoor trials.

Metric	Measured Value
Object Detection Accuracy	86.7% (average across 3 food items)
Response Time (avg)	2.3 seconds (from detection to arm movement)
Gripping Success Rate	90% (27 out of 30 trials)
System Cost (approx.)	₹5,000 (low-cost category)

5.2 *Comparative analysis with existing research*

To highlight Dine-Bot's advantages, we compared it with recent assistive robotic systems in similar domains.

Table 5. Comparative analysis of Dine-Bot with existing assistive robotic systems.

Parameter	Dine-Bot (2025)	Smart Feeder [Patel et al. 2023]	Robocar Arm [Kwon et al., 2022]
DOF	4	3	6
Vision System	Pi Camera + CV	Pre- trained YOLOv5	RGB-D Camera
Cost	₹5,000	₹12,000	₹25,000
Object Detection Accuracy	86.7%	92%	95%
Application Focus	Independent Dining	Assisted Meal Feeding	Medical Handling

5.3 *Limitations and future scope*

Although the prototype works well, there are significant limitations such as susceptibility to light condition and limited payload capacity. The future work will include machine learning models for object recognition with robustness, haptic feedback for safety reasons, and speed- based user commands for improved human-robot interaction.

6 CONCLUSION

The Dine-Bot was designed and developed as an assistive robotic system to aid physically challenged individuals in independent dining. The system combines computer vision, using a Raspberry Pi camera, with a 4DOF robotic arm to provide face detection-based feeding assistance.

Experimental results showed that the system accurately detects user positions and adjusts the robotic arm accordingly, ensuring a smooth and efficient feeding process. By utilizing cost-effective components and an optimized control system, Dine-Bot offers an affordable and accessible solution for improving the quality of life for individuals with mobility impairments.

Practical Applications:

The research and development of Dine-Bot have several real-world applications, including:

- Assistive Technology: Helping individuals with physical disabilities or motor impairments to eat independently.
- Healthcare and Rehabilitation Centres: Supporting caregivers in feeding assistance for patients with limited mobility.
- Elderly Care Facilities: Enhancing autonomy for elderly individuals with difficulty in self-feeding.
- Personal Home Use: Providing a compact, affordable robotic assistant for daily meal assistance.

7 FUTURE SCOPE

While the current prototype successfully demonstrates the feasibility of an AI-assisted dining robot, several enhancements can be made to improve its performance and user adaptability. Integrating AI-driven gesture recognition would allow users to signal commands for food delivery, making the system more intuitive and accessible. Additionally, optimizing material selection by using lightweight yet durable materials can enhance structural strength while reducing overall weight. An adaptive feeding mechanism equipped with pressure and force sensors would enable the robotic arm to adjust its grip based on the texture of different foods, ensuring a more seamless dining experience. Furthermore, incorporating a voice-controlled interface or a smartphone app would enhance user convenience and accessibility. Lastly, real-time monitoring and feedback through IoT-based cloud systems could help track user preferences and improve feeding accuracy over time. These improvements collectively aim to create a more efficient, user-friendly, and adaptable AI-assisted dining robot.

REFERENCES

[1] O. Bendel, A. Gasser, and J. Siebenmann, (2020). Co- robots as care robots, in *AAAI Spring Symposium: Applied AI in Healthcare: Safety, Community, and the Environment*.

[2] Giansanti, (2021). The social robot in rehabilitation and assistance: What is the future? *Healthcare*, vol. 9, no. 244.

[3] B. Guo, H. Liu, and L. Niu, (2023). Safe physical interaction with cobots: A multi-modal fusion approach for health monitoring, *Frontiers in Neurorobotics*, vol. 17, p. 1265936.

[4] H. Higa, K. Kurisu, and H. Uehara, (2014). A vision-based assistive robotic arm for people with severe disabilities, in *Proc. 2014 Int. Conf. Rehabilitation Robotics (ICORR)*.

[5] H. Higa, I. Nakamura, and N. Hoshimiya, (2004). A basic study on control command input device using head movement for FES system. Availability of acceleration sensors, *IEICE Trans. Fundam. Electron. Commun. Comput. Sci.*, vol. E87-A, no. 6, pp. 1441–1445.

[6] M. Hillman, (2003). Rehabilitation robotics from past to present. A historical perspective,in *Proc. 2003 Int. Conf. Rehabilitation Robotics*.

[7] S. Ishii and B. Arai, (2006). Robot development in the field of welfare, *J. Robot. Soc. Jpn.*, vol. 24, no. 3, pp. 304–307.

[8] L. Jabre, R. McGrew, R.B. Gillespie, and P. Goleski, An assistive cobot for aid in self-care activities,2002.

[9] M. Pascher *et al.*, (2022). My caregiver the cobot: Comparing visualization techniques to effectively communicate cobot perception to people with physical impairments, *Sensors*, vol. 22, p. 755.

[10] L. Ragno, A. Borboni, F. Vannetti, C. Amici, and N. Cusano, (2023). Application of social robots in healthcare: Review on characteristics, requirements, technical solutions, *Sensors*, vol. 23, no. 15, p. 6820.

[11] M. Steinbichler and B. Massow, (2023). Post-stroke rehabilitation using collaborative robotic therapy. Medical purpose and user acceptance,in *Proc. 3rd MCI Med. Technol. Master's Conf.*, Innsbruck, Sep. 2023, pp. 1–12.

[12] C. Taesi, F. Aggogeri, and N. Pellegrini, (2023). COBOT applications. Recent advances and challenges,".

[13] I.N. Weerarathna, D. Raymond, and A. Luharia, (2023). Human-robot collaboration for healthcare: A narrative review, *Cureus*, vol. 15, no. 11, p. e49210.

Advancement in Engineering and Science – Goyal et al. (Eds)
© 2026 The Author(s), ISBN: 978-1-041-31101-0

CNN-GLCM Feature Fusion with Hybrid Optimization for Alzheimer's Disease Classification

Sonali Bhosale and Vaibhav Dixit
Department of Electronics and Telecommunication Engineering, Sinhgad College of Engineering, RMD Sinhgad School of Engineering Maharashtra, India

ABSTRACT: Alzheimer's Disease (AD) is a worsening mind sickness requiring prompt detection to get proper care. Established deep learning models do often suffer from multiple overfittings and from increased computational costs. To overcome each of these difficulties, this study currently suggests a Hybrid Whale Optimization Algorithm (HWOA) for selecting features, along with a combining of deep learning and texture-based analysis. Both VGG16 and EfficientNetB2 may pull deep attributes from MRI scans, the Gray-Level Co-occurrence Matrix (GLCM) acquires textural characteristics. These are fused together via concatenation to form a strong feature representation. HWOA optimizes feature selection through a certain defined mutation-based mechanism, thereby further reducing redundancy and greatly improving discriminative capability. A simple classifier trained on the given features ensures better accuracy with reduced computational cost. With evaluation using a publicly available Alzheimer's MRI dataset, the model had 97.28% accuracy. The results do also confirm a greatly improved F1-score across the many different AD stages. The study shows that integrating deep learning, as well as texture analysis, along with hybrid optimization, improves AD diagnosis. Data fusion might be explored by future studies; also, improved optimization methods could be studied.

Keywords: Alzheimer's Disease, Feature Selection, Deep Learning, Hybrid Whale Optimization, MRI Classification

1 INTRODUCTION

These days, deep learning and machine learning techniques are useful resources for examining medical images, significantly enhancing accurate diagnoses and efficiency. Among all these techniques, Convolutional Neural Networks (CNNs) like VGG16 along with EfficientNetB2 have been extensively used for feature extraction from inside medical images. In addition to this, CNNs are achieving more outstanding success in multiple classification tasks [1]. These models can adeptly glean key spatial traits directly from MRI scans, thus helping to spot neurodegenerative illnesses such as AD.

In addition to deep learning-based features, texture-based analysis provides crucial insights into structural variations in medical images. A popular method for texture analysis is the Gray-Level Co-occurrence Matrix (GLCM), which records the spatial connections between pixel intensities, which are essential for detecting subtle pathological changes in brain tissues. However, the high dimensionality of features extracted from deep learning models and texture analyses can result in increased computational complexity and overfitting, limiting model generalizability [2]. To get over these challenges, feature selection techniques are employed to identify the most relevant features, reducing computational load and enhancing model performance. The Whale Optimization approach (WOA) is one optimization method that takes its cues from nature, which has been effectively applied to medical image recognition to maximize feature subsets and raise classification accuracy [3]. WOA balances exploration and exploitation by mimicking the hunting behavior of whales, making it a successful method for choosing the most discriminative features in datasets with a high degree of dimension.

Building on these advancements, this work proposes a Hybrid Whale Optimization method for selecting features that combines texture-based analysis and deep learning-based extraction of features to increase AD classification performance. The approach leverages VGG16, EfficientNetB2, and GLCM to extract features from MRI scans, which are then fused and optimized using HWOA. The feature selection process reduces redundancy while preserving the most informative features, resulting in increased computing efficiency and classification accuracy. The proposed method aims to develop a robust and efficient model for Alzheimer's disease early detection, aiding in progress in neuroimaging-based diagnostics.

2 LITERATURE REVIEW

Recent deep-learning models utilize MRI scans and neuroimaging data for AD detection. Architectures based on convolutional neural networks, like VGG16, EfficientNet, and ResNet50, are commonly used for feature extraction because of their capacity to recognize complex spatial patterns [4]. Mehedi *et al.* released AlzheimerNet, a deep learning network for classifying AD stages, performed better than conventional machine learning models [5]. Gupta *et al.* [6] demonstrated that combining features from multiple CNNs improves classification performance. However, due to high-dimensional features and limited training samples, CNN-based models often suffer from overfitting. Beyond deep learning, texture-based analysis methods like the GLCM extracts statistical information including contrast, correlation and homogeneity from brain scans to identify structural patterns, providing complementary information to CNN-extracted features [7]. Studies have shown that integrating texture-based and deep learning features enhances the robustness of Alzheimer's classification models [8]. However, the high dimensionality of fused features necessitates feature selection techniques to improve computational efficiency. Feature selection is essential for reducing model complexity while maintaining classification accuracy. By eliminating redundant features, metaheuristic algorithms like as Grey Wolf Optimization and Whale Optimization Algorithm and methods like Principal Component Analysis (PCA) assist in feature set improvement [9]. Wahid *et al.* [10] found that bio-inspired optimization techniques, such as WOA, enhance classification performance in medical image analysis. Mishra and Kakar [11] further proposed a hybrid optimization framework combining evolutionary and swarm intelligence approaches for optimizing feature subsets in AD classification. Texture-based classifiers using GLCM combined

DOI: 10.1201/9781003798514-17

with ensemble models achieved over 90% accuracy in stage-wise AD diagnosis [23]. Proposed a hybrid optimization framework combining evolutionary and swarm intelligence approaches for optimizing feature subsets in AD classification. In line with these, recent work has explored adaptive WOA and hybrid optimization methods with improved convergence rates and robustness in high-dimensional datasets.

Building upon the advancements in feature selection, this study introduces a Hybrid Whale Optimization Algorithm, which integrates WOA with a mutation mechanism to strike a balance between exploitation and exploration during feature selection. Recent research has focused more on hybrid optimization techniques, demonstrating improved convergence speed and feature selection efficiency in high-dimensional datasets [12].

3 PROPOSED METHODOLOGY

3.1 *System architecture*

The proposed Hybrid Whale Optimization Algorithm based on Alzheimer's Disease classification framework integrates deep learning and texture-based attributes to increase computational performance and improve diagnostic accuracy. The overall framework, demonstrated in Figure 1.

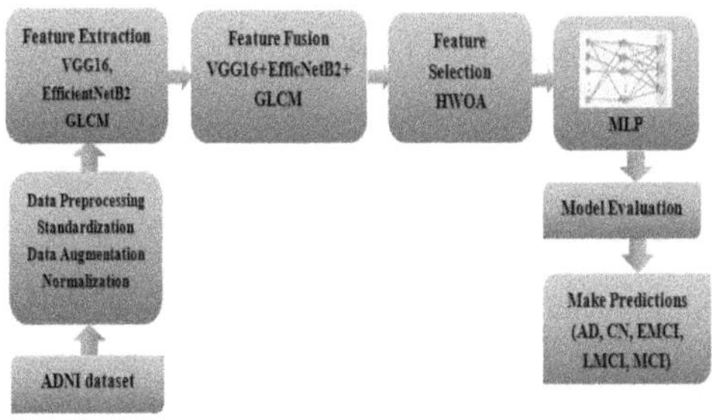

Figure 1. Workflow of the Proposed AD classification framework.

3.2 *Feature extraction*

By extracting textural, structural, and spatial information from MRI images, feature extraction is crucial for the categorization of AD.

3.2.1 *Deep feature extraction using CNNs*

Convolutional Neural Networks (CNNs) are widely used in medical image analysis due to their ability to learn spatial and hierarchical features. Among them, VGG16 is a popular choice for feature extraction because of its deep yet efficient architecture. It consists of 16 layers (13 convolutional and 3 fully connected) and uses ReLU activation to enhance non-linearity. Pretrained on ImageNet, VGG16 applies transfer learning to extract meaningful features from medical images with minimal retraining, producing a 4096-dimensional feature vector that effectively captures spatial details in MRI scans for Alzheimer's classification [13]. EfficientNetB2, on the other hand, applies a compound scaling method to balance depth, width, and resolution, capturing multiscale spatial patterns with reduced computational cost [14]. Its feature extraction produces a 1408-dimensional vector, offering a compact and informative representation for Alzheimer's Disease analysis [15].

These feature maps are then flattened to obtain high-dimensional feature vectors for each MRI image, which are used as inputs for the feature fusion stage. The combination of VGG16 and EfficientNetB2 extracted features ensures a comprehensive representation of Alzheimer's brain scans, collecting spatial features at both low and high levels. These fused features are further optimized using the HWOA to remove redundant information and improve classification efficiency.

3.2.2 *Texture feature extraction*

Texture analysis often employs the Gray Level Co-occurrence Matrix (GLCM) method to study spatial relationships and intensity patterns between pixels in an image. By analyzing the frequency of co-occurring pixel values, GLCM extracts key texture features such as contrast, correlation, energy, and homogeneity, which are valuable in distinguishing patterns in MRI scans [16]. For Alzheimer's Disease classification, GLCM helps identify structural variations and uncover new texture-based features that enhance diagnostic accuracy. These extracted features complement deep learning-based spatial representations, improving the overall performance and reliability of medical image analysis [17,18].

3.2.3 *Feature fusion*

In this study, feature fusion combines deep learning-based features extracted from VGG16 and EfficientNetB2 with texture-based features obtained from the GLCM. By merging these features, the model leverages both hierarchical spatial information captured by CNNs and structural texture patterns derived from GLCM, leading to a more comprehensive representation of Alzheimer's brain scans. Studies have demonstrated that combining deep and handcrafted features significantly improves classification accuracy in medical imaging tasks. Research in Alzheimer's Disease detection has shown that hybrid feature fusion approaches outperform single-model feature extraction techniques, as they exploit complementary information from multiple sources [19].

3.3 *Hybrid Whale Optimization Algorithm*

The Whale Optimization Algorithm (WOA) is a natural-inspired optimization method that mimics humpback whales' hunting tactics, including their use of bubble-net attacks and encircling their prey [20]. It is appropriate for resolving complicated optimization issues like feature selection in classification because it expertly strikes a balance between exploration and exploitation. In WOA, each whale represents a possible feature subset, and its quality is determined using a fitness function. The movement of whales is influenced by the best current solution through a dynamically adjusted coefficient vector. However, WOA may experience premature convergence, which limits its ability to explore diverse solutions and may lead to suboptimal outcomes. To address this, researchers have proposed improvements such as adaptive parameter tuning, chaotic maps, and hybrid models with other optimization algorithms to enhance its efficiency [21]. These improvements enhance the algorithm ability to evade local optima and increase convergence speed, making it better suited for practical applications. Equation1 is standard WOA update mechanism defined as:

$$Z(t+1) = Z^{*}(t) - A \cdot D \tag{1}$$

Where: $Z(t+1)$ is the updated location of the whale (selected feature subset), the best feature subset at present is $Z^{*}(t)$, A is a coefficient vector controlling the exploration-exploitation trade-off and D is the separation between the optimal solution and the whale. Although WOA is effective in global optimization, it can sometimes suffer from premature convergence, limiting its ability to explore diverse solutions.

Hybrid WOA (HWOA): To overcome the limitations of the WOA, researchers have developed the Hybrid Whale Optimization Algorithm (HWOA), which integrates a mutation-based mechanism to enhance exploration and prevent stagnation in local optima. The mutation strategy introduces controlled randomness, ensuring diversity in feature selection while maintaining the algorithm's ability to converge efficiently. Equation2 is the hybrid update WOA expressed as:

$$Z_{mutated}(t+1) = Z^{*}(t) + \beta(Z_{random} - Z^{*}(t)) \quad (2)$$

Where: $Z_{mutated}(t+1)$ is the mutated feature subset, β is the mutation factor that controls perturbation intensity, and Z_{random} is a randomly selected feature subset that introduces variability. Several studies have demonstrated that HWOA outperforms standard WOA and other metaheuristics in feature selection tasks, especially in the case of high-dimensional datasets [22]. As a result, HWOA selects a compact yet highly informative feature subset, reducing dimensionality while preserving essential discriminatory information.

3.4 *Multilayer Perceptron (MLP)*

The HWOA determines the best feature subset, where its output becomes input to an MLP classifier that classifies MRI scans into different AD stages. MLPs can understand non-linear relationships through activation functions and are composed of multiple layers of interconnected neurons. but it should also be noted that MLPs are special types of ANNs that do not apply convolution operations which are common in processing images.

4 IMPLEMENTATION

4.1 *HWOA algorithm*

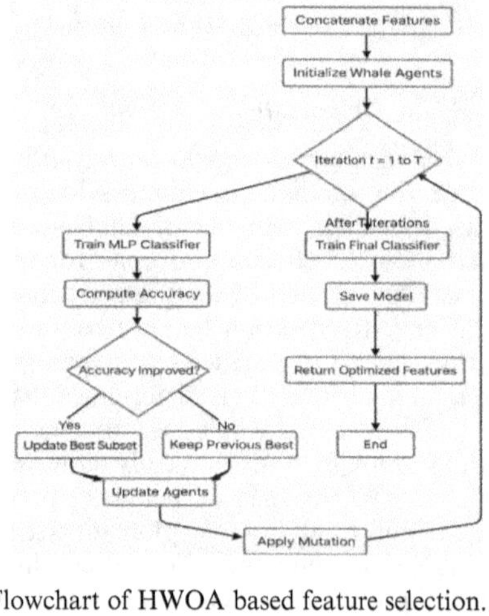

Figure 2. Flowchart of HWOA based feature selection.

The flowchart shown in Figure 2 illustrates the HWOA-based feature selection and classification process for Alzheimer's Disease detection. Initially, whale agents are generated as binary vectors, where each bit denotes the inclusion (1) or exclusion (0) of a feature. The optimization runs for T iterations, during which an MLP classifier is trained using the selected features, and its accuracy is used as the fitness value. If a higher accuracy is achieved, the best feature subset is updated; otherwise, the previous one is retained. The whale positions are updated through exploration and exploitation strategies, and mutation is applied to maintain diversity and prevent premature convergence. After optimization, the refined feature subset is used to train an MLP model comprising three dense layers (128–256–128 neurons) with ReLU activation, Batch Normalization, and Dropout layers. A softmax layer performs multiclass prediction, while the model is optimized using Adam (learning rate = 0.001) and categorical cross-entropy loss over 50 epochs with a batch size of 32, ensuring robust classification of Alzheimer's stages.

4.2 *Dataset*

Alzheimer's data is from Kaggel, this includes five kinds of MRI scans, such as mild cognitive impairment (MCI), Alzheimer's disease (AD), cognitively normal (CN) class, early mild cognitive impairment (EMCI), and late mild cognitive impairment (LMCI). Our dataset includes 11,866 images (AD (2420), CN (2123), EMCI (1920), LMCI (2637), MCI (2766)). These images are normalized and contracted to 224 x 224 pixels, and then they are split into 80% of the file to train and 20% of the file to test. Grayscale images are improved via CLAHE (Contrast Limited Adaptive Histogram Equalization) is used to classify Alzheimer's disease. It processes images from the dataset as illustrated in Figure 3, applies CLAHE with a specified clip limit and tile grid size. By enhancing visual contrast, this preprocessing technique may help deep learning models diagnose AD more accurately.

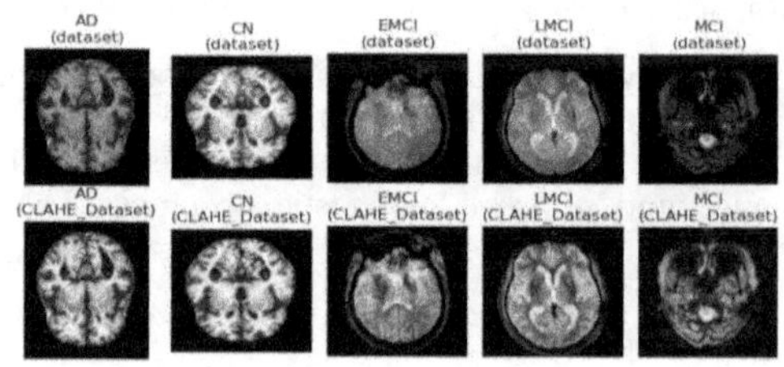

Figure 3. AD Dataset and CLAHE Dataset.

5 RESULTS AND DISCUSSION

The mutation mechanism and the exploration-exploitation balance adopted by HWOA make the model more general and robust without premature convergence.

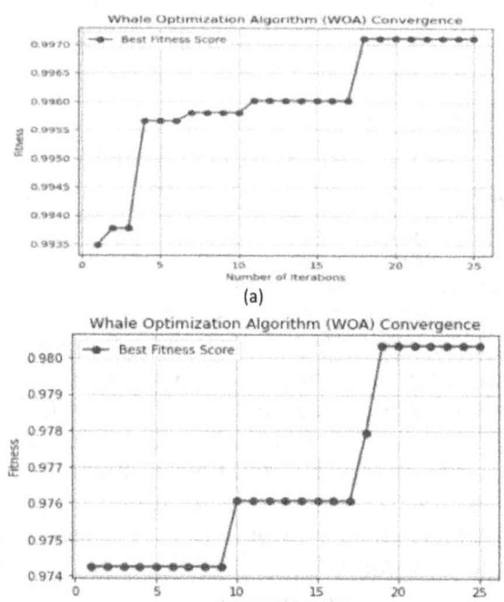

Figure 4. Fitness Function of (a) HWOA (b) Standard WOA.

Figure 4 illustrates that the Hybrid Whale Optimization Algorithm (HWOA) demonstrates superior convergence behavior compared to the Standard WOA. The fitness score (classification accuracy) increases rapidly during the initial iterations (0–5) due to extensive exploration of feature combinations.

Between 5 and 20 iterations, the improvement becomes gradual as the algorithm balances exploration and exploitation. After 20 iterations, the accuracy stabilizes around 0.997, indicating convergence to an optimal feature subset. In contrast, the Standard WOA reaches only about 0.980. The improved performance of HWOA is attributed to added mechanisms such as mutation and adaptive search strategies, which enhance stability, prevent premature convergence, and yield more precise and generalized feature selection results.

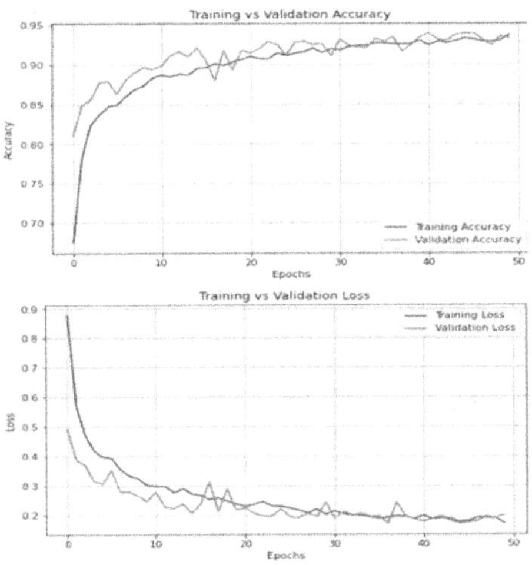

(a) VGG16+ EfficientNetB2+WOA

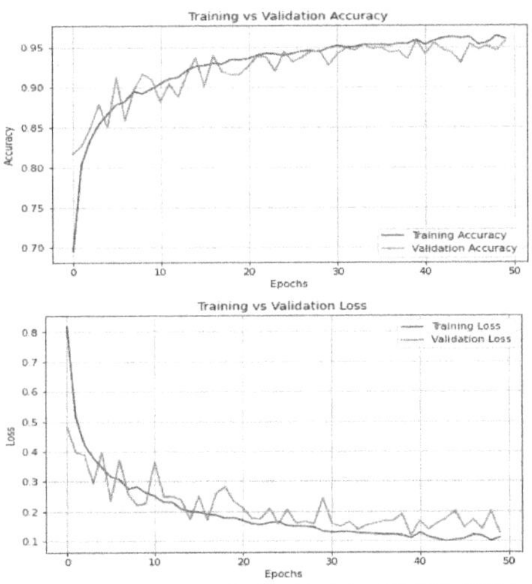

(b) VGG16+ EfficientNetB2+ GLCM+WOA

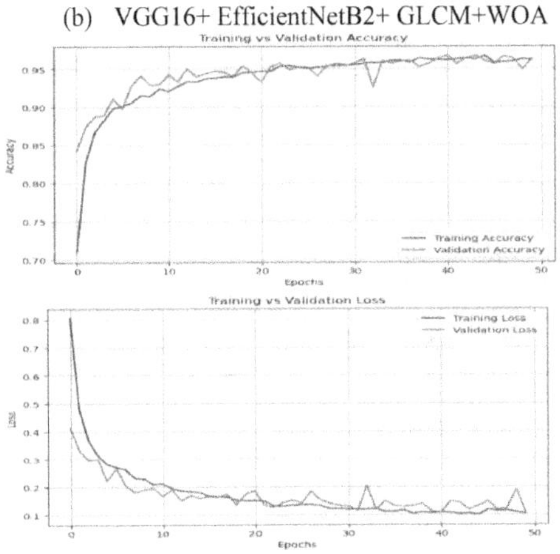

(c) VGG16+ EfficientNetB2+HWOA

Figure 5. Performance Comparison of Training and Validation.

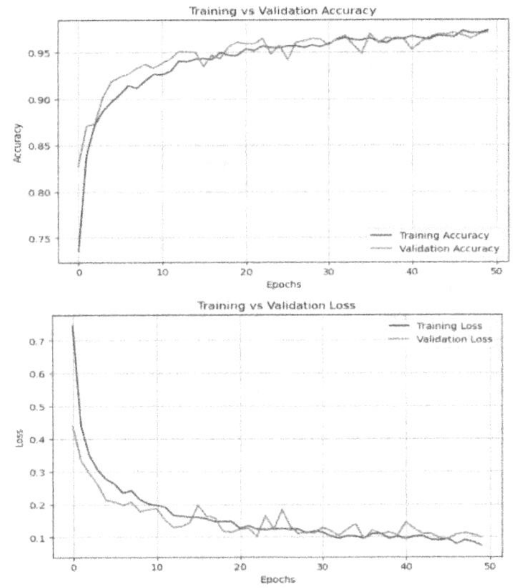

(d) VGG16+ EfficientNetB2+ GLCM+HWOA.

Figure 5. (Continued)

These are the training and validation graphs shown in Figure 5 comparing feature selection methods. When looking at model performance on validation, WOA-based models achieve stable learning with some minor swings in accuracy. With GLCM features, the falsifiability of the model is enhanced through a more controlled feature selection process, enabling improved generalization. VGG16 + EfficientNetB2 + GLCM + HWOA exhibited the fastest convergence, very low overfitting, and best validation accuracy compared to all other models. This demonstrates the fusion of hybrid optimization and the deep and texture features for better to make an efficient classification in AD.

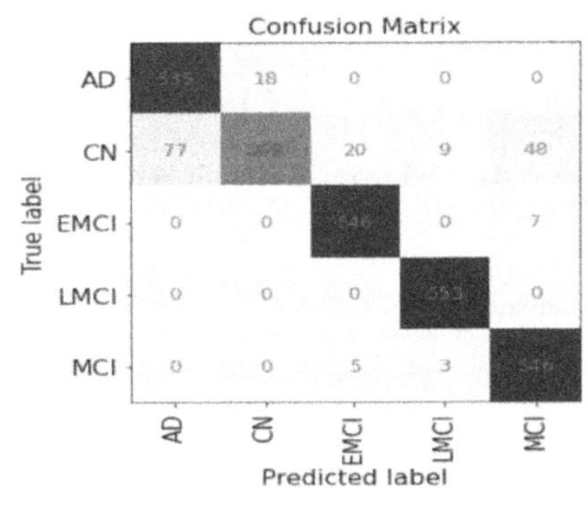

(a) VGG16 + EfficientNetB2 + WOA

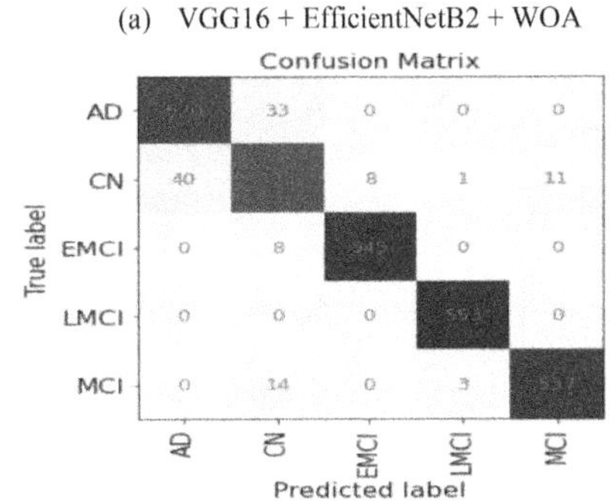

(b) VGG16 + EfficientNetB2 + GLCM + WOA

Figure 6. Confusion matrix comparison of hybrid models integrating deep features and optimization techniques.

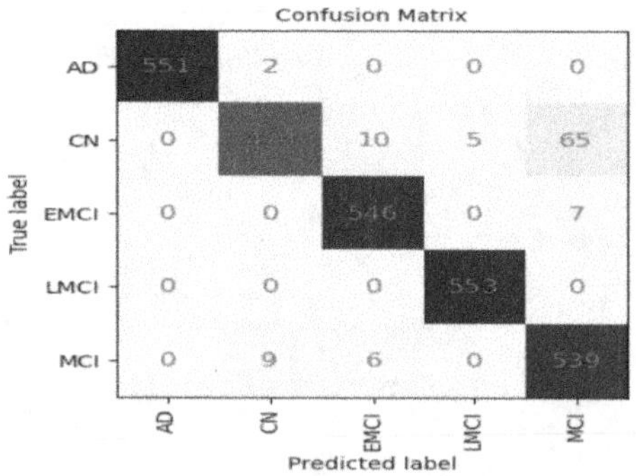

(c) VGG16 + EfficientNetB2 + HWOA

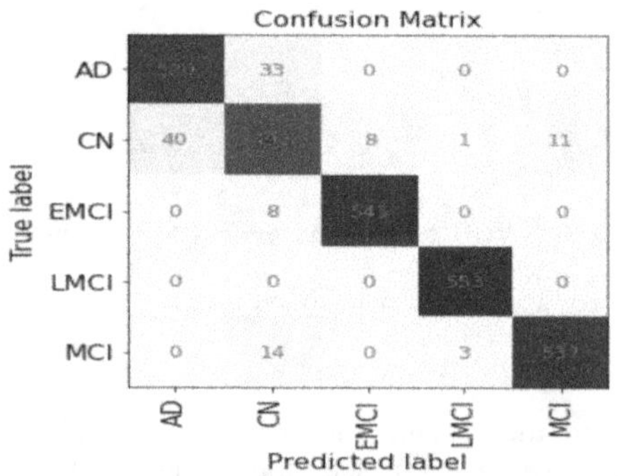

(b) VGG16 + EfficientNetB2 + GLCM + WOA

Figure 6. (Continued)

Figure 6 presents confusion matrices showing the performance of different models in classifying Alzheimer's Disease stages. The VGG16 + EfficientNetB2 + WOA model performed well but showed notable misclassifications in the CN class. Adding GLCM features slightly improved EMCI detection but still affected CN accuracy. The VGG16 + EfficientNetB2 + HWOA model showed major improvements, reducing errors across most classes. The proposed VGG16 + EfficientNetB2 + GLCM + HWOA model achieved the best accuracy with minimal CN misclassifications, proving the effectiveness of combining GLCM with HWOA.

Table 1. Comparing the efficiency of the models.

Models	Accuracy	Cohen's Kappa Score	Matthews Correlation Coefficient (MCC)	Total params
VGG16+EfficientNetB2+WOA	93.24%	0.92	0.92	181,893 (710.52 KB)
VGG16+ EfficientNetB2+GLCM +WOA	95.73%	0.95	0.95	189,189 (739.02 KB)
VGG16+EfficientNetB2+HWOA	96.24%	0.95	0.96	187,525 (732.52 KB)
VGG16+EfficientNetB2+GLCM +HWOA(Proposed model)	**97.28%**	**0.96**	**0.97**	**190,341 (743.52 KB)**

Table 1 provides a comparison of different models based on accuracy, MCC, total parameters, and Cohen's Kappa Score. The proposed model (VGG16 + EfficientNetB2 + GLCM + HWOA) achieves the highest performance with a Cohen's Kappa Score of 0.96, MCC of 0.97, and an accuracy of 97.28%, confirming its superiority in classification reliability and precision. The VGG16 + EfficientNetB2 + HWOA model follows with 96.24% accuracy, showing that HWOA significantly enhances feature optimization. Similarly, the VGG16 + EfficientNetB2 + GLCM + WOA model performs well with 95.73% accuracy, validating the effectiveness of GLCM features. The lowest accuracy (93.24%) is observed in the VGG16 + EfficientNetB2 + WOA model, which also has the fewest parameters (181,893). Despite having the largest number of parameters (190,341), the proposed model demonstrates superior correlation and robustness in feature selection and classification, making it the most efficient method for Alzheimer's disease detection.

6 CONCLUSION

This study proposes a Hybrid Whale Optimization Algorithm (HWOA) for Alzheimer's disease classification by integrating texture-based features and CNN-derived features from VGG16, EfficientNetB2, and GLCM. The HWOA-based model achieved the highest accuracy of 97.28%, outperforming traditional WOA models by maintaining a strong balance between exploration and exploitation and ensuring faster, more stable convergence. It also showed reduced overfitting and higher validation accuracy. Confusion matrix results confirmed fewer misclassifications, especially for CN and EMCI classes, while statistical metrics such as MCC (0.97) and Cohen's Kappa (0.96) validated its reliability. Overall, the combination of deep learning and hybrid optimization significantly enhances Alzheimer's classification performance, with future potential in multimodal data integration and early disease prediction.

REFERENCES

[1] Krizhevsky, A., Sutskever, I., and Hinton, G.E. (2012). ImageNet classification with deep convolutional neural networks. *Advances in Neural Information Processing Systems, 25*, 1097–1105.

[2] LeCun, Y., Bengio, Y., and Hinton, G. (2015). Deep learning. *Nature, 521*(7553), 436–444.

[3] Mirjalili, S., and Lewis, A. (2016). The Whale Optimization Algorithm. *Advances in Engineering Software, 95*, 51–67.

[4] Gupta, T., Sharma, R., and Srivastava, P. (2023). Deep feature extraction and fusion for Alzheimer's disease detection. *PLOS ONE, 18*(3), e0282735.

[5] Mehedi, F.M., Karim, S.A., Akter, S., Azam, S., Ghosh, P., Tasnim, Z., Hasib, K.M., De Boer, F., and Ahmed, K. (2023). AlzheimerNet: An effective deep learning-based proposition for Alzheimer's disease stages classification from functional brain changes in magnetic resonance images. *IEEE Access, 11*, 16376–16395.

[6] Wahid, H.W., Hadzikadic, L.J., and Smith, S.L. (2022). Metaheuristic algorithms for feature selection in medical image analysis: A comparative study. *Expert Systems with Applications, 208*, 118085.

[7] Acharya, S., Chakraborty, R., and Saha, P. (2023). Texture-based feature selection for Alzheimer's diagnosis using GLCM and PCA. *Biomedical Signal Processing and Control, 79*, 104051.

[8] Mishra, A.S., and Kakar, S.B. (2022). Hybrid optimization techniques for feature selection in medical diagnosis. *International Journal of Computer Vision and Image Processing, 13*(2), 87–102.

[9] Zhang, Z., Wang, M., and Liu, Y. (2022). An improved whale optimization algorithm for feature selection in medical image classification. *Neural Computing and Applications, 34*, 10567–10580.

[10] Yang, H., Deng, W., and Li, G. (2023). Hybrid bio-inspired feature selection algorithm for Alzheimer's disease classification. *Applied Soft Computing*, *132*, 109984.

[11] Li, X., Iyer, S.R.K., and Wang, L. (2022). A hybrid whale optimization and genetic algorithm for feature selection in medical imaging. *Computers in Biology and Medicine*, *144*, 106362.

[12] Singh, A.P., Kumar, R., and Sharma, N. (2023). Improving convergence in hybrid metaheuristic optimization for medical image classification. *Pattern Recognition Letters*, *167*, 81–91.

[13] Minaee, S., Kafieh, R., Sonka, M., Yazdani, M., and Soufi, G.J. (2020). Deep-COVID: Predicting COVID-19 from chest X-ray images using deep transfer learning. Medical Image Analysis, 65, 101794.

[14] Touvron, H., Vedaldi, A., Douze, M., and Jégou, H. (2020). Fixing the train-test resolution discrepancy: FixEfficientNet. Advances in Neural Information Processing Systems, 33, 2267–2279.

[15] Lee, J.M., Seo, S., and Kim, T. (2022). Hybrid deep learning models for Alzheimer's Disease classification using MRI images. *Expert Systems with Applications*, *198*, 116864.

[16] Kumar, D., Wong, M., and Chen, C.L.P. (2022). Texture Analysis in Medical Imaging: Applications and Future Directions. *IEEE Reviews in Biomedical Engineering*, *15*, 312–332.

[17] Castellano, A.J., Bonilha, D., and Li, J.C. (2021). Texture Analysis of Brain MRI Images for the Detection of Alzheimer's Disease. *IEEE Journal of Biomedical and Health Informatics*, *25* (3), 870–880.

[18] Zhang, Y., Hu, P., and Zhang, B. (2021). Multi-Scale GLCM-Based MRI Analysis for Alzheimer's Disease Diagnosis. *IEEE Access*, *9*, 43210–43222.

[19] Liu, J., Zhang, P., and Zhao, L. (2021). Multi-Modal Feature Fusion for Alzheimer's Disease Classification Using Deep Learning and GLCM. *IEEE Transactions on Neural Systems and Rehabilitation Engineering*, *29*, 500–512.

[20] Tariyal, S., Kumar, D., and Pant, M. (2021). Hybrid whale optimization algorithm for feature selection. *Expert Systems with Applications*, *181*, 115200.

[21] Zhang, J., Xu, B., and Sun, X. (2022). A chaotic improved whale optimization algorithm for solving real-world optimization problems. *Engineering Applications of Artificial Intelligence*, *114*, 105018.

[22] Wang, T., Li, Y., and Zhang, C. (2023). Enhanced Whale Optimization for High-Dimensional Feature Selection in Alzheimer's Disease Detection. *IEEE Transactions on Medical Imaging*, *41*(5), 1356–1368.

[23] Banerjee, S., Chakraborty, R., and Mitra, P. (2024). Texture-based Ensemble Learning for Alzheimer's Detection. *Information*, *4*(3), 49.

Advancement in Engineering and Science – Goyal et al. (Eds)
© 2026 The Author(s), ISBN: 978-1-041-31101-0

Vibrational Analysis and Performance Evaluation of Engine Gearbox with Al-Ni Nanoparticle-Enhanced Lubricating Oil

Harshvardhan H. Patil, A.R. Kadam, and P.V. Mali
Mechanical Enginnering Department, Annasaheb Dange College of Engineering and Technology (ADCET), Ashta, Dist. Sangli, Maharashtra

ABSTRACT: The efficiency and durability of engine gearboxes significantly depend on effective lubrication, which minimizes friction, wear, and vibration. This study investigates the vibrational and tribological performance of an engine gearbox by incorporating Al-Ni nanoparticles into MAK 4T Plus SL 20W-40 base oil. The research aims to analyze the impact of different nanoparticle concentrations (0.25%, 0.50%, and 0.75%) on vibration reduction, frictional losses, and gearbox efficiency. The experiments were conducted on a 100cc Splendor engine gearbox, where vibration parameters such as velocity, acceleration, and RPM were measured using the Adash VA4 FFT Analyzer under various loading conditions.

The results indicate that the addition of Al-Ni nanoparticles significantly improves vibration damping and reduces wear rates due to their tribo-film formation, micro-bearing effect, and self-repairing properties. Among the tested concentrations, the 0.25% nanoparticle composition demonstrated the best balance between vibration reduction and lubricant stability, while higher concentrations increased viscosity, leading to minor efficiency losses. Furthermore, the study evaluates the influence of nanoparticle size and shape on lubrication performance, emphasizing their role in enhancing power transmission efficiency. A comparative analysis between nano-lubricants and conventional lubricants reveals that nano-additives provide superior thermal stability, anti-wear characteristics, and improved gearbox performance.

This research highlights the potential of Al-Ni nanoparticle-based lubricants in optimizing engine gearbox efficiency and longevity, making them a promising alternative to traditional lubricants for high-performance mechanical systems.

Keywords: Nano-lubricants, Al-Ni nanoparticles, vibration reduction, tribology, gearbox efficiency

1 INTRODUCTION

Tribology means study of interacting surfaces in relative motion, focusing on friction, wear and lubricants. It plays a very crucial role in improving efficiency, durability and reliability of mechanical systems including engine gearboxes, bearing and industrial machines. Inadequate lubrication is one of the important leading causes of gearbox failures, resulting in friction, wear, overheating and mechanical breakdown. Therefore, proper lubrication is required for reducing friction, minimizing wear and smooth operations and vibration monitoring to analyses gear wear rate.

Traditional lubricants face several limitations under extreme conditions: a) Viscosity Breakdown: High operating temperatures can degrade lubricants, reducing their viscosity and compromising the formation of a protective film between moving parts [1]. b) Inefficient Wear Protection: Additive depletion and base oil oxidation can lead to increased metal-to-metal contact, accelerating wear and potentially causing component failure [2]. c) Friction-Related Energy Losses: Inadequate lubrication increases friction, leading to higher fuel consumption in vehicles and reduced efficiency in industrial machinery [3]. Despite advancements in conventional lubricants, friction-related losses remain substantial. Approximately 33% of energy in internal combustion engines is lost due to friction, with gear transmission components being major contributors [4].

To address these issues, researchers are investigating the use of nanoparticles as lubricant additives to improve tribological properties [5–6]. Integration of nanotechnology into the lubricating system has shown promising results in improving lubricating properties.

Nanoparticles can form a protective layer on contact surfaces, reducing direct metal-to-metal contact and thereby decreasing wear and friction [7]. Spherical nanoparticles, such as those made from molybdenum disulfide (MoS_2), act as tiny ball bearings, facilitating smoother motion between surfaces [8]. Nanoparticles can fill surface asperities and repair minor surface damages, leading to a smoother surface and improved tribological performance [9]. Certain nanoparticles enhance the thermal conductivity of lubricants, aiding in better heat dissipation and maintaining lubricant stability under high-temperature conditions [10].

Several studies have demonstrated the effectiveness of nanolubricants. TiO_2 Nanoparticles have been shown to improve the load-carrying capacity and reduce wear in lubricants, making them suitable for high-load applications [11]. Incorporation of MoS_2 nanoparticles has led to significant reductions in wear rates, outperforming conventional lubricants [7]. Combinations of different nanoparticles, such as those based on carbon, metals, and metal oxides, have shown synergistic effects, enhancing lubrication under extreme conditions [12]. Reference [13] review nano-lubrication techniques, highlighting Minimum Quantity Lubrication (MQL) and Vapor Phase Lubrication (VPL) as alternatives for micro-mechanical systems where traditional lubricants fail. Reference [14] examines nanoparticles in lubrication, emphasizing their role in rolling, tribofilm formation, and self-repairing to reduce friction and wear. Reference [15] demonstrate up to 50% friction reduction through nanoparticle rolling and surface smoothing effects. Reference [1] investigate synthetic gear lubricants, finding superior friction reduction compared to mineral oils. Reference [3] analyze vibration in high-speed gearboxes, showing how nanolubricants can dampen vibrations and prevent failures. Reference [16] highlight tribological monitoring of engine and gear oils, emphasizing lubricant degradation as a key failure indicator. Reference [8] explore fullerene nanoparticles, showing that they reduce friction via rolling and surface enhancement effects. Reference [5] proposes nano-monolayer lubrication, advocating shear-resistant, self-repairing lubricants for nano/micro-systems.

Despite these advancements, challenges such as optimal nanoparticle concentration, dispersion stability, and long-term effects on lubrication performance remain areas of ongoing

DOI: 10.1201/9781003798514-18

research [17, 18]. In particular, engine gearboxes operate under high loads and varying speeds, making them susceptible to significant tribological challenges [16].

Gearbox failure can cause a complete machinery breakdown, expensive both in their subsequent repair and lost output. Catching signs of failing parts early can reduce downtime, save costs and improve machinery health. Here are some of the most common forms of gearbox failure (Figure 1). 34.4% - Inadequate lubrication, 19.6% - Contamination, 17.7% - Installation errors, 6.9% - Overload, 2.8% - Handling errors.

This research focuses on: 1) Evaluating the Effect of Al-Ni Nanoparticles on Vibration Reduction: Investigating how nano-lubricants influence the vibration characteristics of an engine gearbox operating under different load conditions. 2) Determining the Optimal Nanoparticle Concentration for Enhanced Lubrication: Identifying the ideal concentration of Al-Ni nanoparticles that maximizes tribological benefits without increasing viscosity beyond acceptable limits.3) Comparing the Performance of Nano-Lubricants with Conventional Lubricants: Assessing the differences in friction, wear, and efficiency between nano-lubricants and traditional engine oils.

By addressing these objectives, this research aims to contribute to the field of nano-tribology, offering practical insights into nano-enhanced lubrication for industrial and automotive applications. The findings will help optimize nanoparticle-based lubrication strategies, leading to increased efficiency, reduced maintenance costs, and extended gearbox lifespan.

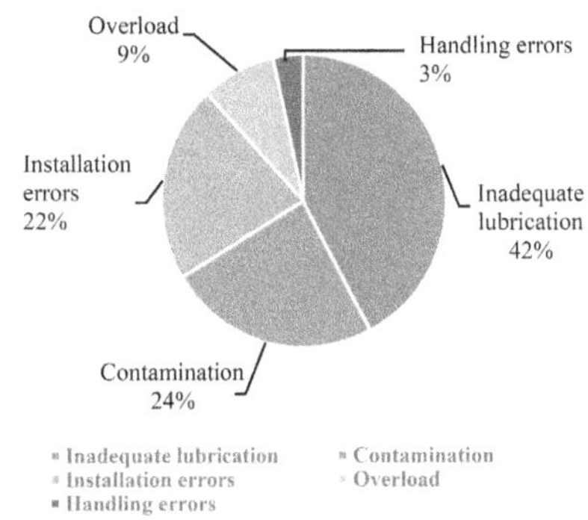

Figure 1. Common forms of gear failure [18].

2 METHODOLOGY

2.1 *Preparation of Al-Ni nanoparticle-enhanced lubricant*

The Base oil used in this study is MAK 4T Plus SL 20W-40, a widely used lubricant for engine gearboxes. This oil (Figure 2) was chosen due to its viscosity stability, thermal resistance, and anti-wear properties.

Figure 2. Base oil and its specifications.

Aluminum-Nickel (Al-Ni) nanoparticles (Figure 3) were selected for their high thermal conductivity, low friction coefficient, and superior anti-wear properties (Table 1).

Figure 3. Al-Ni Alloy powder.

Table 1. Specifications of Aluminium Nickel Alloy Powder.

Form: Powder	Purity: 99.9 %
Colour: Grey	APS: 40-50 Nm
Odour: No Odour	Al composition: 93.7 % (±0.5 %)
Molecular formula: Al-Ni	Mg composition: 6.3 % (±0.5 %)
Molecular weight: 85.27 g/mol	Other Metal compo.: 0.1 %
Density: 3.46 g/cm3	Make: Nanoshel
Melting Point: 1350°C	
Solubility: Insoluble in water	

Nano-oil refers to a Base oil enhanced with nanoparticles as an additive. The preparation of nano-oil samples follows weight concentration criteria relative to the Base oil. For experimental work, nano-oil must be prepared in different proportions. Based on research studies, three different nanoparticle compositions are required to be added to the Base lubricating oil. The nanoparticle concentrations of 0.25%, 0.50%, and 0.75% by weight were selected based on previous literature and experimental benchmarks. Studies have shown that nanoparticle concentrations below 1% generally yield optimal tribological performance without adversely affecting viscosity or inducing particle agglomeration. The chosen range aimed to balance vibration damping effects with lubricant flow properties, and concentrations beyond 0.75% were deliberately avoided to prevent excessive thickening of the base oil.

A total of three nano-oil samples (Figure 4) were prepared, each containing 1 litre of Base oil with varying nanoparticle weight concentrations:

Sample A: 0.25% nanoparticles per 1 litre of Base oil
Sample B: 0.50% nanoparticles per 1 litre of Base oil
Sample C: 0.75% nanoparticles per 1 litre of Base oil

Since 1 litre of lubricating oil weighs approximately 900 grams, the required nanoparticle quantities were calculated accordingly. The following Table 2 presents the nano-oil sample preparation details:

Table 2. Quantity of Nanoparticle in grams.

Sr. No.	Sample Name	% of Nanoparticles	Quantity of Nanoparticle in grams
1	A	0.25	2.25 grams
2	B	0.50	4.5 grams
3	C	0.75	6.75 grams

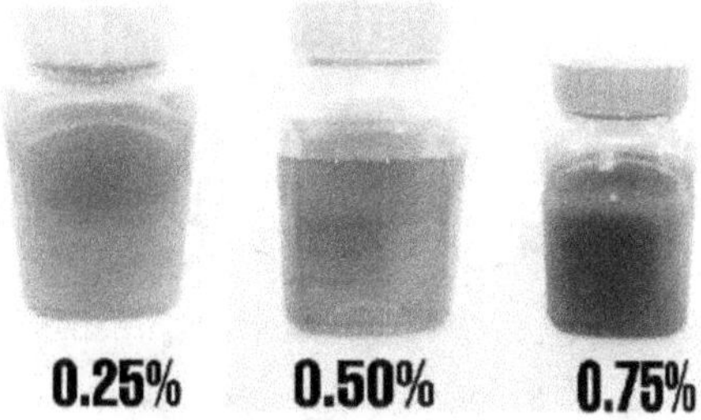

Figure 4. Nano oil samples.

By adding the specified nanoparticle quantities, a total of 13.5 grams of nanoparticles was required to prepare the nano-oil compositions with the Base oil.

The sonication process is carried out to prepare different compositions of nano-oil. A sonicator is used for this purpose, as it facilitates the dispersion of nanoparticles within the Base oil. Sonication is a technique that applies sound energy to agitate particles in a sample, ensuring uniform distribution. Typically, ultrasonic frequencies (>20 kHz) are used, a process referred to as ultrasonication. This method helps break agglomerations of nanoparticles, improving their stability and dispersion in the Base oil. For this project, ensuring the homogeneous suspension of nanoparticles for experimental analysis. to ensure uniform dispersion, the nano-oil samples were subjected to ultrasonication at 40 Hz for a sufficient duration until visual homogeneity was achieved. The samples were inspected before testing to confirm the absence of visible sedimentation, and testing was completed within a short time frame to minimize any instability due to settling.

2.2 *Experimental setup*

A 100cc Splendor engine gearbox was chosen as the test model due to its availability and widespread use in two-wheeler applications. The gearbox was subjected to testing under varying load conditions to simulate real-world performance. Table 3 shows the specifications of engine gearbox used for the study and Figure 5 illustrates the experimental setup used.

Table 3. Specifications of 4 strokes, 100 cc engine.

Engine type: Single cylinder,	Bore diameter: 50mm
Gear box type: 4 speed	Stroke length: 9.5mm
No of cylinder: 1	Displacement: 97.2cc
Valves: 2	Power: 8.36 Ps
Compression ratio: 9.9:1	Torque: 8.05 Nm
Cooling system: Air cooled	Make : Hero Splendor

A spherical roller bearing of 30mm race diameter is used over 20cm long shaft. Bearing helps to avoid creep of the shaft which is placed between pulley and output shaft of engine gear box. A 30mm in diameter and 20cm long shaft is used between pulley of rope brake dynamometer and output shaft of engine gear box. Rope brake dynamometer is used to apply the various loads on output shaft of engine gear box. Rope brake dynamometer is generally used for measuring the brake power of engine. A rope is wound around the rim of pulley which is fixed rigidly to shaft of an engine. The upper end of the rope is attached to a spring balance while the lower end of the rope is kept in position by applying dead weight.

The Fast Fourier Transform (FFT) Analyzer is a crucial instrument used for vibration analysis. It helps measure displacement, velocity, acceleration, and RPM in rotating machinery. The Adash VA4 FFT Analyzer is a multi-functional vibration analysis instrument used for machine condition monitoring and fault diagnostics. It measures acceleration, velocity, displacement, and RPM using piezoelectric accelerometers and a tachometer input. With four AC channels, four DC channels, and one tachometer input, it performs Fast Fourier Transform (FFT) analysis to identify vibration characteristics, resonance frequencies, and fault conditions in mechanical systems. The device is compatible with DDS (Data Diagnostic Software) for real-time monitoring, spectrogram analysis, and data recording. Its portable design makes it ideal for both field testing and laboratory applications, ensuring accurate and reliable vibration measurements.

Figure 5. Experimental setup.

2.3 *Testing procedure*

The testing procedure aimed to evaluate the effect of Al-Ni nanoparticles on the vibration characteristics of an engine gearbox using a 100cc Splendor engine and a rope brake dynamometer under varying load conditions. Initially, baseline measurements were recorded using MAK 4T Plus SL 20W-40 base oil without nanoparticles to establish a reference dataset. The gearbox was tested under three load conditions: no load, 1 kg load, and 1.5 kg load, with a piezoelectric accelerometer mounted on the gearbox casing near the output shaft bearing to measure vibration levels. The Adash VA4 FFT Analyzer was used to record velocity, acceleration, and RPM while analyzing vibration spectra in real-time through DDS (Data Diagnostic Software). After baseline tests, the Base oil was replaced with three nano-oil samples containing 0.25%, 0.50%, and 0.75% Al-Ni nanoparticles, and the same testing procedure was repeated. The collected data were compared against the control test results to assess vibration reduction efficiency, nanoparticle concentration effects, and lubrication performance.

3 RESULTS AND DISCUSSION

The results obtained from the vibrational analysis and performance testing of the engine gearbox with Al-Ni nanoparticle-enhanced lubricants are presented and analyzed in this section. The experiments were conducted using a 100cc Splendor engine gearbox, where vibration parameters such as velocity, acceleration, and RPM were measured using the Adash VA4 FFT

Analyzer under without load, 1 KG load and 1.5 KG load conditions. The impact of varying nanoparticle concentrations (0.25%, 0.50%, and 0.75%) is examined.

3.1 *Vibration characteristics of engine gearbox with base oil*

The vibration characteristics of the engine gearbox were analyzed by measuring velocity (mm/s) and acceleration (mm/s^2) at different RPM levels using the Adash VA4 FFT Analyzer.

3.2 *Under no-load condition*

The vibration analysis of the engine gearbox under no-load conditions (Table 4) using Base oil without nanoparticles provides essential baseline data for comparison with nano-lubricated samples.

Table 4. Experimental data of Base oil under no-load condition.

SR.NO.	RPM	VELOCITIY (mm/s)	ACCELERATION (mm/s^2)
1	291	31.4	1.47
2	528	30.1	1.61
3	788	31.4	1.66
4	1016	32.9	1.62

At 291 RPM, the velocity was 31.4 mm/s, and acceleration was 1.47 mm/s^2, indicating normal operational vibrations at low speeds. As the speed increased to 528 RPM, a slight decrease in velocity (30.1 mm/s) was observed, while acceleration increased to 1.61 mm/s^2. This drop in velocity may indicate a natural damping effect within the gearbox system or a minor imbalance in load distribution at this speed. At higher speeds (788 RPM and 1016 RPM), the velocity increased to 31.4 mm/s and 32.9 mm/s, respectively, showing that the gearbox experiences higher oscillatory motion as speed increases. Acceleration followed a similar trend, peaking at 1.66 mm/s^2 at 788 RPM before slightly dropping to 1.62 mm/s^2 at 1016 RPM. This behaviour suggests that as rotational speed increases, higher energy is transmitted through the gearbox components, leading to higher vibrational responses. The slight drop in acceleration at maximum RPM may be due to structural damping effects of the gearbox or minor variations in force distribution at higher rotational speeds.

3.3 *Under 1 kg load condition*

The vibration analysis of the engine gearbox under a 1 kg load (Table 5) using Base oil without nanoparticles provides insights into how additional loading influences velocity and acceleration characteristics.

Table 5. Experimental data of Base oil under 1 kg load condition.

SR.NO.	RPM	VELOCITIY (mm/s)	ACCELERATION (mm/s^2)
1	285	28.8	1.47
2	535	28.2	1.5
3	766	28.5	1.59
4	945	29.9	1.61

At 285 RPM, the velocity is 28.8 mm/s, and acceleration remains at 1.47 mm/s^2, similar to the no-load condition. As the speed increases to 535 RPM, the velocity drops slightly to 28.2 mm/s, while acceleration rises to 1.50 mm/s^2. This trend suggests that the applied load contributes to greater damping effects, potentially reducing vibrational energy transfer in the system. At higher speeds (766 RPM and 945 RPM), the velocity stabilizes around 28.5 mm/s before peaking at 29.9 mm/s, and acceleration follows a similar pattern, increasing to 1.61 mm/s^2 at maximum RPM. This increase in acceleration at higher RPMs suggests that additional load enhances gear meshing forces and structural resonance, which could lead to higher vibrational amplitudes if not effectively damped by the lubricant.

3.4 *Under 1.5 kg load condition*

The vibration analysis of the engine gearbox under a 1.5 kg load using base oil (Table 6) without nanoparticles provides further insights into how increasing load influences vibration behaviour.

At 278 RPM, the velocity is 28.5 mm/s, and acceleration is 1.53 mm/s^2, similar to previous load conditions. As speed increases to 514 RPM, the velocity decreases slightly to 28.1 mm/s, while acceleration remains unchanged at 1.53 mm/s^2, suggesting that the applied load contributes to vibration stability at lower speeds. At higher speeds (736 RPM and 915 RPM), the velocity increases to 29.2 mm/s and 29.9 mm/s, respectively, while acceleration remains fairly stable, peaking at 1.54 mm/s^2 at 736 RPM before decreasing to 1.48 mm/s^2 at 915 RPM. This behavior indicates that at higher speeds, the additional load contributes to more stable vibrational characteristics, as the acceleration values show less fluctuation compared to lower loads.

Table 6. Experimental data of Base oil under 1.5 kg load condition.

SR.NO.	RPM	VELOCITIY (mm/s)	ACCELERATION (mm/s^2)
1	278	28.5	1.53
2	514	28.1	1.53
3	736	29.2	1.54
4	915	29.9	1.48

3.5 *Vibration Characteristics of Engine Gearbox with Sample A (0.25% Nanoparticles)*

The vibration analysis of Sample A (nano-lubricant with 0.25% Al-Ni nanoparticles) was tested under three different load conditions—no load, 1 kg load, and 1.5 kg load—to evaluate its effect on vibrational performance.

3.6 *Under no-load condition*

The vibration analysis of Sample A without load (Table 7) was conducted to evaluate its effectiveness in reducing vibration compared to base oil. At 295 RPM, the velocity is 30.2 mm/s, with an acceleration of 1.57 mm/s^2, which is slightly lower than the Base oil values at similar speeds. As the speed increases to 603 RPM, the velocity stabilizes at 30.1 mm/s, while acceleration remains nearly unchanged at 1.56 mm/s^2, indicating consistent damping behaviour. At higher RPMs (873 and 1128 RPM), the velocity (Figure 6) slightly fluctuates between 30.6 mm/s and 30.3 mm/s, while acceleration drops to 1.41 mm/s^2 at 1128 RPM, showing a noticeable improvement in vibration suppression.

Table 7. Experimental data of Sample A under no-load condition.

SR.NO.	RPM	VELOCITIY (mm/s)	ACCELERATION (mm/s^2)
1	295	30.2	1.57
2	603	30.1	1.56
3	873	30.6	1.58
4	1128	30.3	1.41

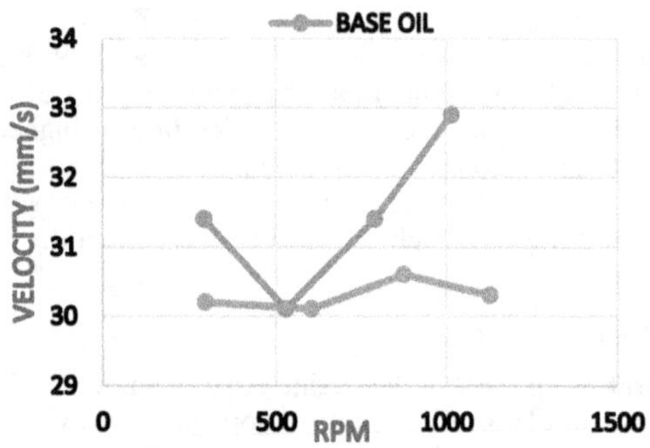

Figure 6. RPM vs Velocity of sample A under no-load condition.

The reduction in acceleration (Figure 7) at higher RPMs suggests that the nano-lubricant effectively dissipates vibrational energy, leading to improved damping effects compared to Base oil. Compared to Base oil under no-load conditions, Sample A with 0.25% Al-Ni nanoparticles demonstrates more stable acceleration values and lower velocity fluctuations, confirming its ability to enhance lubrication efficiency and vibration reduction. These findings indicate that the addition of Al-Ni nanoparticles at 0.25% concentration significantly improves gearbox stability, reducing mechanical vibrations and enhancing overall performance.

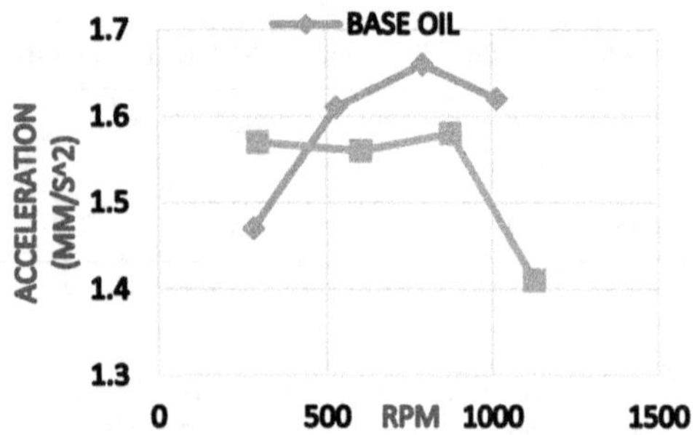

Figure 7. RPM vs Acceleration of sample A under no-load condition.

3.7 *Under 1 kg load condition*

The vibration analysis of Sample A (Table 8)) under a 1 kg load condition was conducted to assess its ability to reduce vibration and enhance damping performance compared to base oil. At 292 RPM, the velocity is 30.7 mm/s, with an acceleration of 1.38 mm/s^2, demonstrating a slight reduction compared to base oil, suggesting better damping properties. As the speed increases to 536 RPM, the velocity stabilizes at 30.8 mm/s, while acceleration remains at 1.39 mm/s^2, indicating consistent vibration suppression and effective lubrication. At higher RPMs (839 and 1051 RPM), velocity (Figure 8) remains within a narrow range (30.4 mm/s - 30.8 mm/s), while acceleration stays relatively stable between 1.39 mm/s^2 and 1.40 mm/s^2, confirming that nanoparticles contribute to smoother operation by reducing vibration intensity.

Table 8. Experimental data of Sample A under 1 kg load condition.

SR.NO.	RPM	VELOCITIY (mm/s)	ACCELERATION (mm/s^2)
1	292	30.7	1.38
2	536	30.8	1.39
3	839	30.4	1.40
4	1051	30.8	1.39

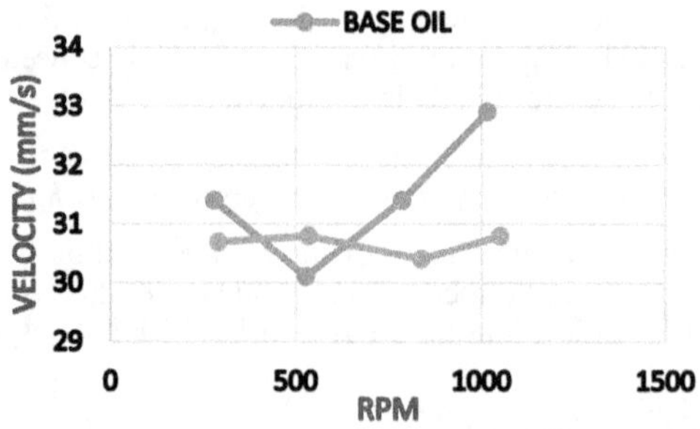

Figure 8. RPM vs Velocity of sample A under 1 kg load condition.

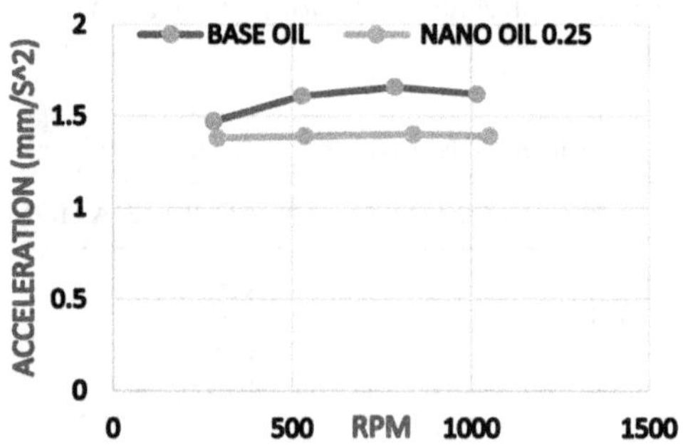

Figure 9. RPM vs Acceleration of sample A under 1 kg load condition.

The lower variation in acceleration (Figure 9) values suggests that Al-Ni nanoparticles enhance load-bearing capacity, minimize surface asperities, and improve the damping effect. Compared to base oil under the same 1 kg load condition, Sample A exhibits lower velocity fluctuations and more stable acceleration, validating its role in reducing vibration transmission and improving lubrication efficiency.

3.8 *Under 1.5 kg load condition*

The vibration analysis of Sample A (Table 9) under a 1.5 kg load condition was conducted to evaluate the effect of nanoparticles on vibration suppression in a heavily loaded gearbox. At 282 RPM, the velocity is 31.8 mm/s, with an acceleration of 1.43 mm/s^2, showing improved damping performance compared to base oil. As speed increases to 523 RPM, velocity remains constant at 31.8 mm/s, while acceleration slightly increases to 1.48 mm/s^2, suggesting better energy absorption and controlled vibration transmission. At higher RPMs (781 and 954 RPM), velocity (Figure 10) increases to 32.1 mm/s and 33.0 mm/s, respectively, while acceleration (Figure 11) drops to 1.40 mm/s^2 at 954 RPM, indicating a strong damping effect provided by nanoparticles.

Table 9. Experimental data of Sample A under 1.5 kg load condition.

SR.NO.	RPM	VELOCITIY (mm/s)	ACCELERATION (mm/s^2)
1	282	31.8	1.43
2	523	31.8	1.48
3	781	32.1	1.44
4	954	33	1.40

The overall lower and stable acceleration values confirm that Al-Ni nanoparticles enhance lubrication properties, reduce vibration intensity, and improve gearbox performance under high-load conditions. Compared to base oil under 1.5 kg load, Sample A exhibits lower acceleration and more stable velocity trends, proving its effectiveness in vibration suppression.

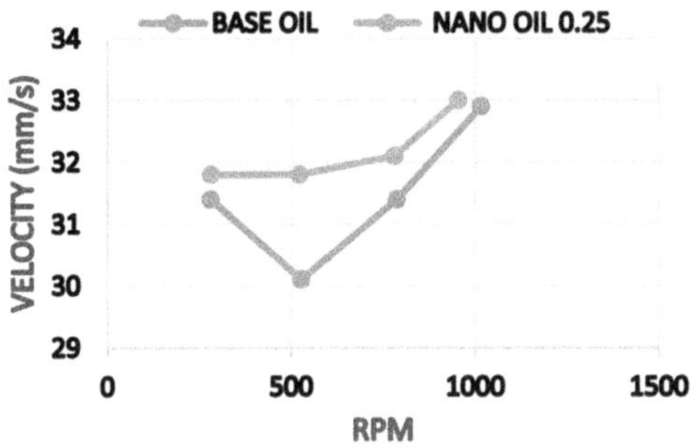

Figure 10. RPM vs Velocity of sample A under 1.5 kg load condition.

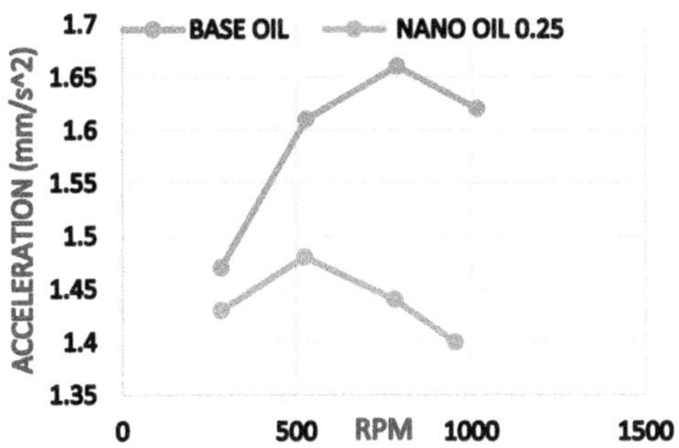

Figure 11. RPM vs Acceleration of sample A under 1.5 kg load condition

3.9 *Vibration Characteristics of Engine Gearbox with Sample B (0.5% Nanoparticles)*

The vibration analysis of Sample B (nano-lubricant with 0.5% Al-Ni nanoparticles) was tested under three different load conditions—no load, 1 kg load, and 1.5 kg load—to evaluate its effect on vibrational performance.

3.10 *Under no-load condition*

The vibration analysis of Sample B (Table 10) under no-load conditions was conducted to examine its effectiveness in minimizing vibration levels compared to base oil. At 299 RPM, velocity is 30.3 mm/s, and acceleration is 1.41 mm/s^2, indicating initial stability.

Table 10. Experimental data of Sample B under no-load condition.

SR.NO.	RPM	VELOCITIY (mm/s)	ACCELERATION (mm/s^2)
1	299	30.3	1.41
2	542	29.8	1.53
3	750	30.4	1.40
4	994	29.9	1.41

As speed increases to 542 RPM, velocity slightly decreases to 29.8 mm/s, while acceleration rises to 1.53 mm/s^2, suggesting a temporary increase in vibrational forces due to changing dynamic conditions. At higher RPMs (750 and 994 RPM), velocity (Figure 11) stabilizes at 30.4 mm/s and 29.9 mm/s, respectively, while acceleration drops back to 1.40 mm/s^2 - 1.41 mm/s^2, confirming that the nano-lubricant effectively mitigates excessive vibration at higher rotational speeds.

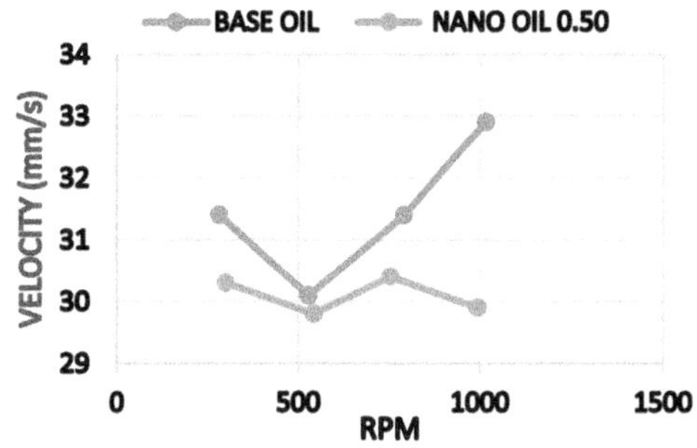

Figure 12. RPM vs Velocity of sample B under no-load condition.

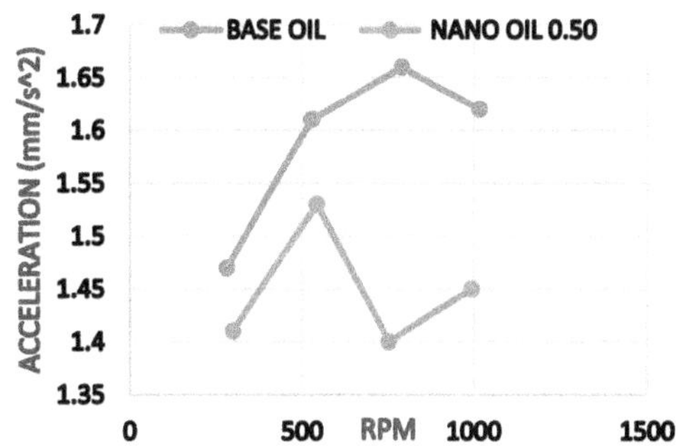

Figure 13. RPM vs Acceleration of sample B under no-load condition.

The reduction in acceleration (Figure 12) at peak RPMs indicates that the Al-Ni nanoparticles contribute to improved damping effects by reducing surface asperities and ensuring smoother gear interactions. Compared to base oil under no-load conditions, Sample B with 0.5% Al-Ni nanoparticles demonstrates less variation in velocity and improved acceleration stability, confirming its enhanced ability to reduce vibrational energy transmission and improve gearbox stability.

3.11 *Under 1 kg load condition*

The vibration analysis of Sample B (Table 11) under a 1 kg load condition was conducted to assess the impact of nanoparticle concentration on vibration suppression and lubrication efficiency compared to base oil. At 263 RPM, velocity starts at 30.8 mm/s, with an acceleration of 1.22 mm/s^2, indicating a well-lubricated system with reduced initial vibration levels. As speed increases to 474 RPM, velocity (Figure 14) slightly drops to 30.6 mm/s, while acceleration (Figure 15) remains stable at 1.21 mm/s^2, suggesting a consistent damping effect.

Table 11. Experimental data of Sample B under 1 kg load condition.

SR.NO.	RPM	VELOCITIY (mm/s)	ACCELERATION (mm/s^2)
1	263	30.8	1.22
2	474	30.6	1.21
3	682	30.8	1.24
4	874	30.8	1.23

At higher RPMs (682 and 874 RPM), velocity returns to 30.8 mm/s, and acceleration fluctuates slightly between 1.24 mm/s^2 and 1.23 mm/s^2, confirming that nano-lubricants maintain stability and prevent excessive vibration increases under moderate loading. The minimal variation in velocity and acceleration highlights the effective dispersion of nanoparticles, leading to uniform lubrication and enhanced tribological performance.

Compared to base oil under a 1 kg load, Sample B exhibits lower acceleration values and more consistent velocity trends, confirming its superior vibration suppression and lubrication efficiency.

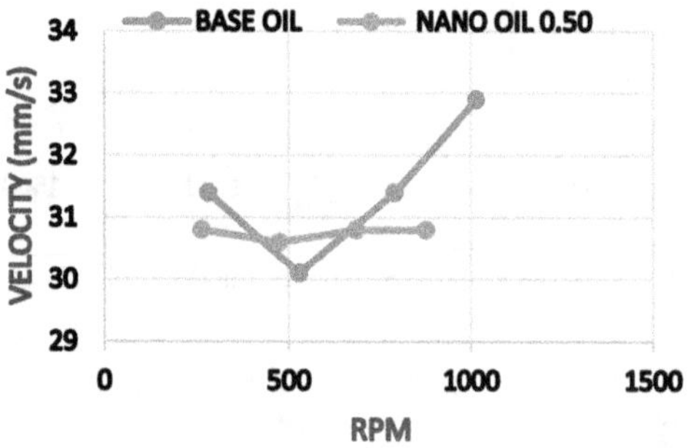

Figure 14. RPM vs Velocity of sample B under 1 kg load condition.

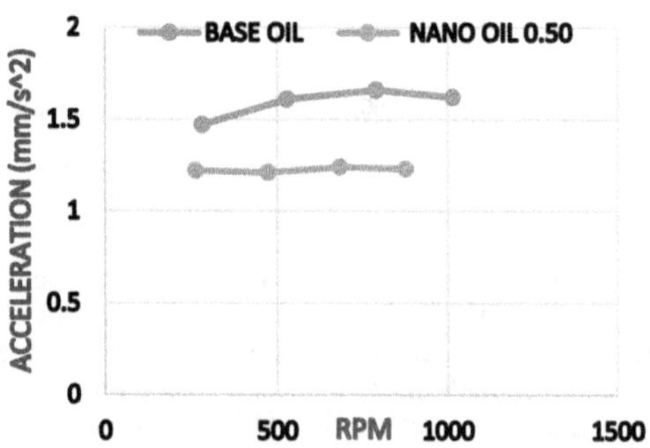

Figure 15. RPM vs Acceleration of sample B under 1 kg load condition.

3.12 *Under 1.5 kg load condition*

The vibration analysis of Sample B (Table 12) under a 1.5 kg load condition was conducted to evaluate the effect of increased nanoparticle concentration on vibration suppression in a heavily loaded gearbox. At 256 RPM, velocity starts at 28.6 mm/s, and acceleration is 1.28 mm/s^2, showing an initial reduction in vibration compared to base oil.

Table 12. Experimental data of Sample B under 1.5 kg load condition.

SR.NO.	RPM	VELOCITIY (mm/s)	ACCELERATION (mm/s^2)
1	256	28.6	1.28
2	462	31.4	1.20
3	672	29.4	1.13
4	817	30.4	1.15

As speed increases to 462 RPM, velocity (Figure 16) rises to 31.4 mm/s, while acceleration drops to 1.20 mm/s^2, suggesting that the nanoparticles contribute to better load distribution and reduced energy losses. At higher RPMs (672 and 817 RPM), velocity fluctuates between 29.4 mm/s and 30.4 mm/s, while acceleration stabilizes at 1.13 mm/s^2 - 1.15 mm/s^2, confirming that Al-Ni nanoparticles provide enhanced damping, suppressing vibration more effectively under high-load conditions.

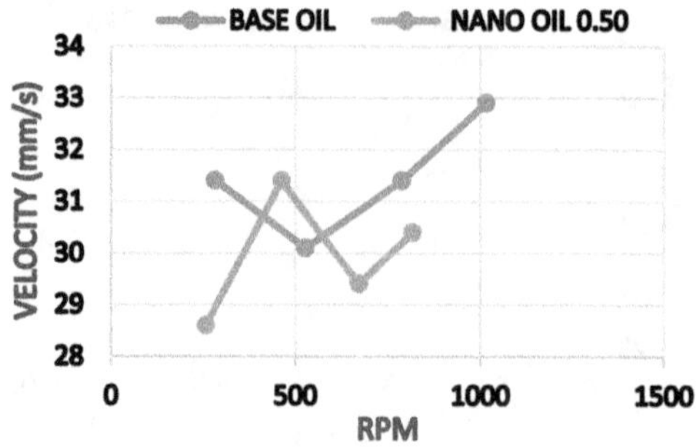

Figure 16. RPM vs Velocity of sample B under 1.5 kg load condition.

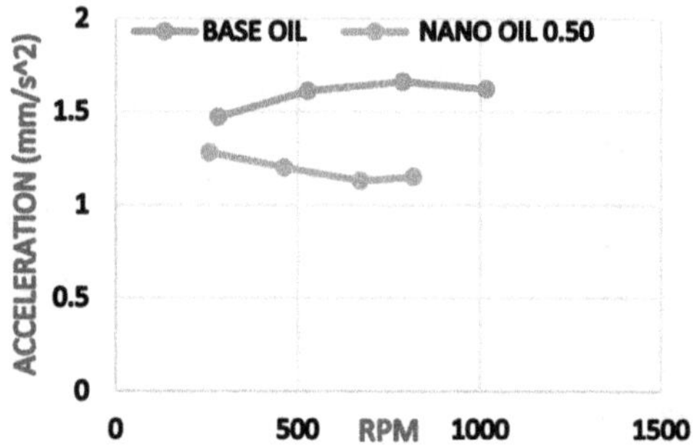

Figure 17. RPM vs Acceleration of sample B under 1.5 kg load condition.

The lower and more stable acceleration (Figure 17) values suggest that the nanoparticles contribute to reducing gear meshing friction and improving lubrication effectiveness. Compared to base oil under 1.5 kg load, Sample B exhibits lower acceleration and reduced fluctuations in velocity, confirming its superior damping capability and improved tribological behavior.

3.13 *Vibration Characteristics of Engine Gearbox with Sample C (0.75% Nanoparticles)*

The vibration analysis of Sample C (nano-lubricant with 0.75% Al-Ni nanoparticles) was tested under three different load conditions—no load, 1 kg load, and 1.5 kg load—to evaluate its effect on vibrational performance.

3.14 *Under no-load condition*

The vibration analysis of Sample C (Table 13) under no-load conditions was conducted to assess the effect of increased nanoparticle concentration on vibration suppression compared to lower concentrations and base oil. At 291 RPM, velocity is 30.4 mm/s, and acceleration is 1.16 mm/s^2, demonstrating an initial reduction in vibrational energy.

Table 13. Experimental data of Sample C under no-load condition.

SR.NO.	RPM	VELOCITIY (mm/s)	ACCELERATION (mm/s^2)
1	291	30.4	1.16
2	457	29.6	1.15
3	698	29.7	1.12
4	868	29.4	1.11

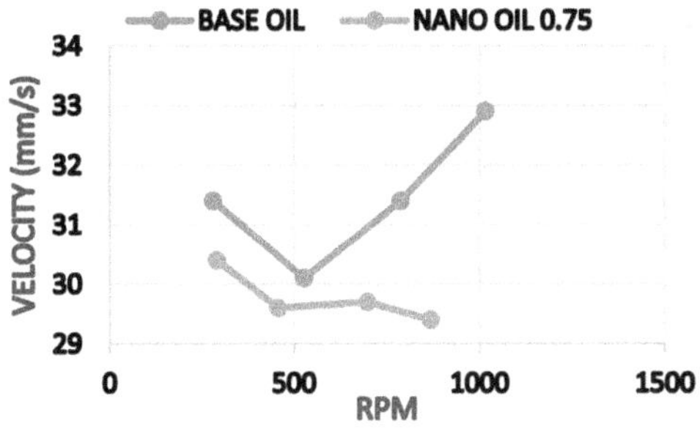

Figure 18. RPM vs Velocity of sample C under no-load condition.

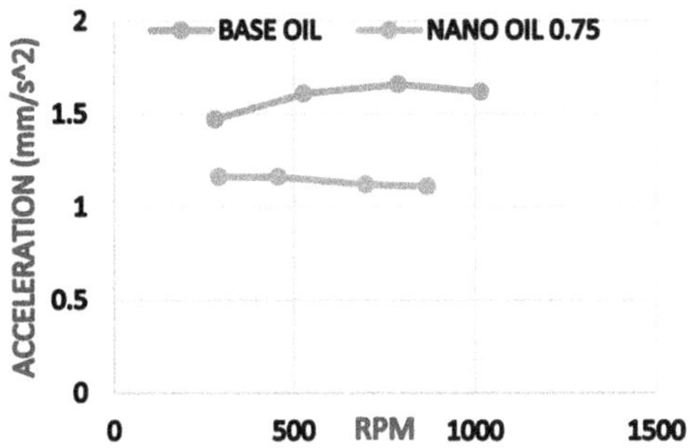

Figure 19. RPM vs Acceleration of sample C under no-load condition.

As speed increases to 457 RPM, velocity (Figure 18) drops slightly to 29.6 mm/s, while acceleration (Figure 19) remains steady at 1.15 mm/s^2, indicating a consistent damping effect due to nanoparticle dispersion. At higher RPMs (698 and 868 RPM), velocity fluctuates slightly between 29.7 mm/s and 29.4 mm/s, while acceleration drops to 1.11 mm/s^2, confirming that the higher concentration of Al-Ni nanoparticles provides improved vibration suppression by reducing energy losses and frictional resistance. The steady decline in acceleration suggests that 0.75% nanoparticle concentration enhances the lubricant's ability to absorb vibration and prevent excessive oscillatory motion. Compared to base oil and lower nanoparticle concentrations (0.25% and 0.5%), Sample C exhibits lower acceleration values and reduced velocity fluctuations, confirming its superior damping efficiency and enhanced tribological performance.

3.14 *Under 1 kg load condition*

The vibration analysis of Sample C (Table 14) under a 1 kg load condition was conducted to examine its effectiveness in reducing vibrations under moderate load compared to base oil and lower nanoparticle concentrations.

Table 14. Experimental data of Sample C under 1 kg load condition.

SR.NO	RPM	VELOCITIY (mm/s)	ACCELERATION (mm/s^2)
1	257	29.9	1.14
2	425	26.4	0.993
3	639	25.9	0.96
4	809	22.3	1.04

At 257 RPM, velocity is 29.9 mm/s, and acceleration is 1.14 mm/s^2, showing improved damping properties at lower speeds. As the speed increases to 425 RPM, velocity decreases to 26.4 mm/s, while acceleration drops to 0.993 mm/s^2, indicating that nanoparticles help suppress vibrational energy transmission.

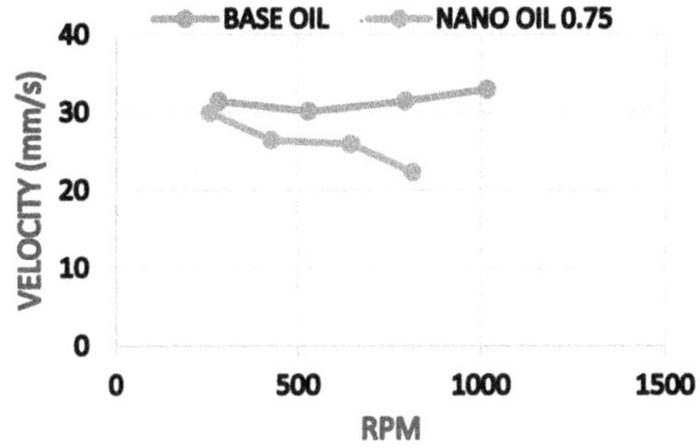

Figure 20. RPM vs Velocity of sample C under 1 kg load condition..

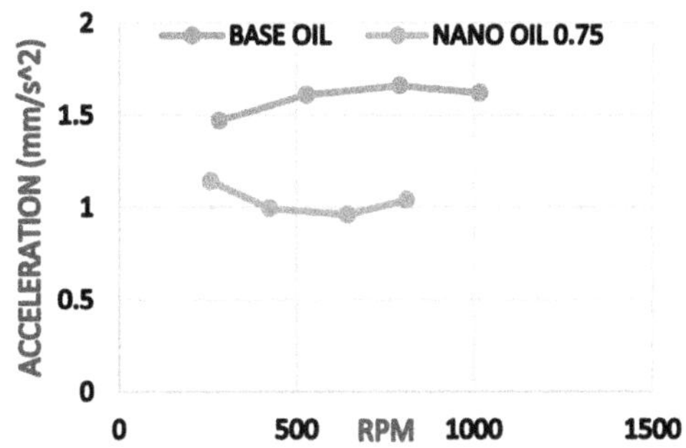

Figure 21. RPM vs Acceleration of sample C under 1 kg load condition.

At higher RPMs (639 and 809 RPM), velocity (Figure 20) decreases further to 25.9 mm/s and 22.3 mm/s, respectively, while acceleration (Figure 21) remains stable at 0.96 mm/s^2 - 1.04 mm/s^2, confirming that a higher nanoparticle concentration provides enhanced damping effects. The downward trend in velocity suggests that nanoparticles contribute to reducing gear friction and improving load distribution, leading to better tribological performance under moderate load conditions. Compared to base oil and lower nanoparticle concentrations (0.25% and 0.5%), Sample C exhibits significantly lower velocity and acceleration values, confirming its strong vibration reduction capabilities.

3.15 *Under 1.5 kg load condition*

The vibration analysis of Sample C (Table 15) under a 1.5 kg load condition was conducted to evaluate the impact of increased nanoparticle concentration on vibration suppression in a heavily loaded gearbox.

Table 15. Experimental data of Sample C under 1.5 kg load condition.

SR.NO.	RPM	VELOCITIY (mm/s)	ACCELERATION (mm/s^2)
1	247	29.9	1.13
2	415	22.1	1.05
3	607	22.3	0.89
4	772	18.8	0.89

At 247 RPM, velocity starts at 29.9 mm/s, and acceleration is 1.13 mm/s^2, showing initial stability and reduced vibration intensity. As speed increases to 415 RPM, velocity (Figure 22) drops significantly to 22.1 mm/s, while acceleration decreases to 1.05 mm/s^2, indicating that nanoparticles contribute to improved energy dissipation and vibration damping. At higher RPMs (607 and 772 RPM), velocity continues to decline to 22.3 mm/s and 18.8 mm/s, while acceleration stabilizes at 0.89 mm/s^2, confirming that higher nanoparticle concentration provides superior vibration suppression.

The lower and more stable acceleration (Figure 23) values suggest that nanoparticles enhance tribo-film formation, reducing gear friction, improving load-bearing capacity, and minimizing vibration transmission within the gearbox. Compared to base oil and lower nanoparticle concentrations (0.25% and 0.5%), Sample C exhibits the lowest velocity and acceleration values, confirming its superior damping efficiency and enhanced lubrication properties.

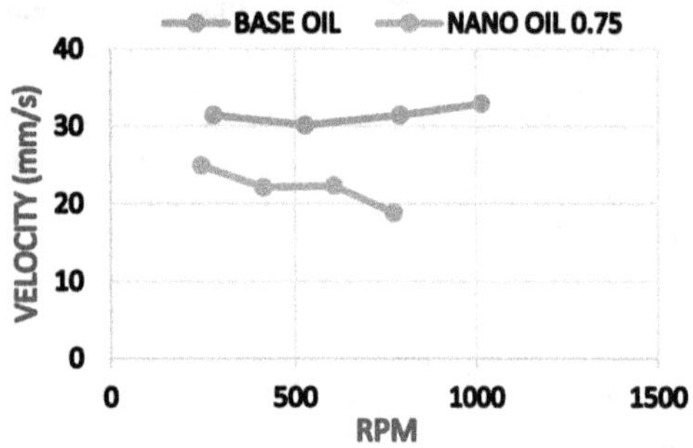

Figure 22. RPM vs Velocity of sample C under 1.5 kg load condition.

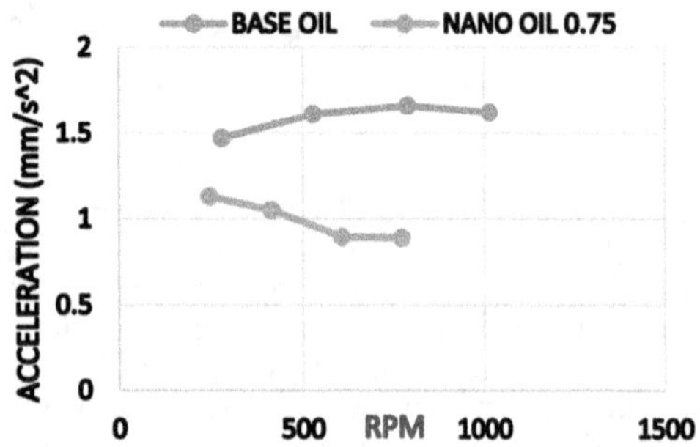

Figure 23. RPM vs Acceleration of sample C under 1.5 kg load condition.

3.16 *Overall comparison of vibration characteristics across different nanoparticle concentrations*

The overall comparison of vibration characteristics across different Al-Ni nanoparticle concentrations (0.25%, 0.5%, and 0.75%) under varying load conditions (no load, 1 kg load, and 1.5 kg load) highlights the effectiveness of nanoparticles in vibration suppression and its impact on gearbox performance (Table 16).

Table 16. Wt% Concentration and RPM.

Sr. No.	% wt conc.	RPM (NO LOAD)	RPM (1 kg load)	RPM (1.5 kg load)
1	0.25	873	839	781
2	0.5	750	682	672
3	0.75	698	639	607

The results (Figure 24) indicate that 0.25% nanoparticle concentration (Sample A) provides the best balance between vibration reduction and gearbox speed stability, demonstrating the highest RPM across all load conditions (873 RPM at no load, 839 RPM at 1 kg, and 781 RPM at 1.5 kg), ensuring minimal vibration while maintaining engine efficiency. While Samples B (0.5%) and C (0.75%) further reduce vibration, they also lead to a reduction in gearbox speed, which is directly proportional to a decrease in engine efficiency. The higher damping effect observed with increased nanoparticle concentration confirms that excessive nanoparticles alter lubricant viscosity, affecting the fluidity and overall dynamic response of the gearbox. Thus, 0.25% remains the optimal concentration, as it effectively minimizes vibration without significantly compromising engine performance, making it the most suitable formulation for improving gearbox stability and efficiency.

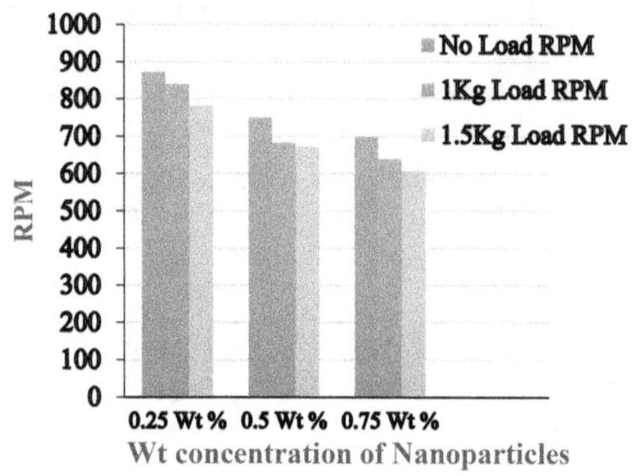

Figure 24. Wt % Concentration vs RPM.

3.17 *Effect of nanoparticle size on lubrication performance*

The size of nanoparticles plays a critical role in determining the efficiency of nano-lubricants in reducing friction, minimizing wear, and improving vibration damping in mechanical systems. Several studies [1–6] have confirmed that smaller nanoparticles (below 50 nm) provide better dispersion and lubrication properties compared to larger particles due to their ability to penetrate surface asperities and create a uniform tribo-film, thereby reducing direct metal-to-metal contact. The effectiveness of nanoparticles in lubrication depends on various size-related factors, including surface energy, adhesion, and Brownian motion, which influence their ability to enhance load-bearing capacity and improve thermal conductivity.

Research suggests that nanoparticles with an optimal size range of 20-50 nm exhibit superior tribological performance as they can form a protective layer on the metal surface, reducing wear and preventing lubricant degradation under extreme operating conditions [13]. Larger nanoparticles, exceeding 100 nm, tend to agglomerate, leading to clogging, sedimentation, and uneven lubrication distribution, which negatively impacts lubrication efficiency [14]. The interaction between nanoparticle size and base oil viscosity also affects lubricant performance; smaller nanoparticles disperse more effectively, whereas larger particles may alter the rheological properties of the lubricant, increasing resistance and affecting flow dynamics within the gearbox.

The studies reviewed [5,15] confirm that Al-Ni nanoparticles within the range of 40-50 nm used in this research exhibit efficient tribological properties, contributing to improved damping characteristics and enhanced wear resistance. Compared to larger particles, smaller nanoparticles create a more stable lubrication film, reducing frictional losses and improving overall gearbox performance. However, excessive reduction in nanoparticle size (below 10 nm) may result in decreased effectiveness due to insufficient rolling and sliding effects, leading to increased shear forces and instability in suspension.

Thus, the optimal size selection of nanoparticles in lubrication applications is crucial in achieving maximum vibration suppression, minimal wear, and improved efficiency. The Al-Ni nanoparticles used in this study (40-50 nm) align with the findings in tribological research, confirming their suitability for enhancing engine gearbox lubrication performance.

3.18 *Effect of nanoparticle shape on lubrication performance*

The shape of nanoparticles significantly influences their tribological performance, affecting friction reduction, wear resistance, and lubrication efficiency in mechanical systems. Different nanoparticle morphologies—such as spherical, platelet, cylindrical, and irregular-shaped particles—interact differently with lubricants and contact surfaces, leading to variations in lubrication behavior. Spherical nanoparticles are widely preferred due to their rolling effect, which reduces friction and shear forces by acting as microscopic ball bearings [5]. Their uniform distribution in the base oil improves lubricant stability and minimizes agglomeration issues [14]. Platelet-shaped nanoparticles, such as graphene and hexagonal boron nitride (h-BN), exhibit excellent sliding properties, forming protective tribo-films that lower friction and wear rates [13]. Cylindrical and rod-shaped nanoparticles align with the lubricant shear flow, reinforcing the lubricant film and improving load-bearing capacity [15]). However, irregular-shaped nanoparticles can increase shear stress, leading to higher friction and wear due to their non-uniform contact and clustering tendencies. In this study, the Al-Ni nanoparticles used exhibit near-spherical morphology, which enhances their ability to form tribo-films, reduces friction, and improves gearbox efficiency. The findings align with previous research, confirming that nanoparticle shape plays a crucial role in lubrication performance by affecting the formation of protective films, load distribution, and frictional interactions.

3.19 *Effect of nanoparticle concentration on lubrication performance*

The concentration of nanoparticles in lubricants significantly affects their tribological properties, influencing friction reduction, wear resistance, and vibration suppression. An optimal concentration range ensures efficient dispersion, uniform tribofilm formation, and reduced friction losses, whereas excessive nanoparticle loading can lead to agglomeration, viscosity increase, and impaired flow dynamics.

Research has demonstrated that low nanoparticle concentrations (0.1–0.5%) effectively reduce friction and enhance wear resistance by forming a thin protective layer on the contact surfaces, which prevents direct metal-to-metal contact [5]. However, increasing nanoparticle concentration beyond a critical limit (typically >1%) results in particle clustering, sedimentation, and increased viscosity, negatively impacting lubricant flow and leading to higher internal resistance and energy losses [14].

The findings from this study indicate that 0.25% and 0.5% Al-Ni nanoparticle concentrations offer optimal vibration suppression and improved lubrication properties, whereas 0.75% leads to increased viscosity, slightly reducing engine gearbox efficiency. The balance between nanoparticle dispersion, load-bearing capacity, and lubrication film stability is crucial for maximizing lubrication benefits while minimizing potential drawbacks. These results align with previous research, confirming that moderate nanoparticle concentration enhances tribological performance, while excessive nanoparticle content may hinder lubrication efficiency.

4 CONCLUSIONS

The lubricating efficiency of Aluminium-Nickel (Al-Ni) alloy nanoparticles as an additive in MAK 4T Plus SL 20W-40 base oil is strongly influenced by experimental conditions, including load and speed. The study confirms that Al-Ni nanoparticles significantly improve tribological properties, reducing friction, enhancing load-carrying capacity, and minimizing wear, particularly under severe operating conditions. The rolling ability of nanoparticles plays a crucial role in restricting the increase in friction force, which is especially evident under higher loading conditions, leading to reduced wear between interacting gearbox components.

Among the tested concentrations, the 0.25% weight concentration of Al-Ni nanoparticles demonstrated the most effective vibration reduction (7-10%) in the engine gearbox, confirming its role in enhancing gearbox stability and reducing mechanical vibrations. The ability of nanoparticles to create a 'ball-bearing effect' between metal surfaces further contributes to reducing frictional losses and wear. Additionally, the study validates that nanoparticles reduce adhesion between contact surfaces, preventing direct metal-to-metal interaction and thereby minimizing wear-related failures.

However, increasing the nanoparticle concentration beyond 0.5% leads to a reduction in gearbox speed due to increased viscosity of the oil, which can negatively impact lubricant flow and energy efficiency. While higher concentrations improve damping effects, they also impose higher internal resistance, affecting engine performance. The findings suggest that the optimal nanoparticle concentration for vibration suppression and lubrication enhancement lies between 0.25% and 0.5%, ensuring efficient dispersion, minimal viscosity alteration, and enhanced lubrication film stability.

These results confirm the potential of Al-Ni nanoparticle-based lubricants in improving gearbox efficiency, extending component lifespan, and optimizing tribological performance. The study highlights that the incorporation of nanoparticles into lubricants can significantly enhance thermal stability, anti-wear characteristics, and overall vibration damping, making nano-lubricants a promising alternative to conventional lubricants for high-performance mechanical systems.

REFERENCES

[1] B.-R. Höhn, K. Michaelis, A. (2001). Doleschel, Frictional behaviour of synthetic gear lubricants, Tribology Series, *Elsevier,* Volume 39, Pages 759-768. https://doi.org/10.1016/S0167-8922(01)80156-5.

[2] Mishra, S., and Aggarwal, S. (2023). A critical review of the effect of nano-lubricant on the performance of hydrodynamic journal bearing. *Tribologia - Finnish Journal of Tribology*, 40(4), 4–20. https://doi.org/10.30678/fjt.127785.

[3] Hiremath, V., and Venkatram, N. (2016). Vibration characteristics of a high-speed gearbox through dynamic analysis. *Materials Today: Proceedings*, 4(10935-10943). https://doi.org/10.1016/j.matpr.2017.08.073

[4] Garcia Tobar, M., Contreras Urgiles, R.W., Jimenez Cordero, B., and Guillen Matute, J. (2024). Nanotechnology in lubricants: A systematic review of the use of nanoparticles to reduce the friction coefficient. *Lubricants,* 12(166). https://doi.org/10.3390/lubricants12050166

[5] Hsu, S.M. (2004). Nano lubrication: Concept and design. *Tribology International*, 37(537-545).

[6] Li, T., Chen, X., Wang, J., Zhang, L., Wei, X., Zhao, L., and Ma, M. (2021). Research progress of nano lubricating additives. *IOP Conference Series: Earth and Environmental Science*, 680(1), 012084. https://doi.org/10.1088/1755-1315/680/1/012084

[7] Mousavi, S.B., Zeinali Heris, S., and Estellé, P. (2020). Experimental comparison between ZnO and MoS_2 nanoparticles as additives on the performance of diesel oil-based nano lubricant. *Scientific Reports*, 10, 5813. https://doi.org/10.1038/s41598-020-62830-1

[8] Lee, K., Hwang, Y., Cheong, S., Lee, J., and Kim, S.H. (2009). Understanding the role of nanoparticles in nano oil lubrication. *Springer Science.* https://doi.org/10.1007/s11249-009-9441-7

[9] Korkmaz, M.E., and Gupta, M.K. (2024). Nano lubricants in machining and tribology applications: A state-of-the-art review on challenges and future trends. *Journal of Molecular Liquids*, 407, 125261. https://doi.org/10.1016/j.molliq.2024.125261

[10] Ismail, M.F., Azmi, W.H., Mamat, R., and Ali, H.M. (2023). Thermal and tribological properties enhancement of PVE

lubricant modified with SiO_2 and TiO_2 nanoparticles additive. *Nanomaterials*, 13(42). https://doi.org/10.3390/nano13010042

[11] Birleanu, C., Pustan, M., Cioaza, M., Molea, A., and Popa, F. (2022). Effect of TiO_2 nanoparticles on the tribological properties of lubricating oil: An experimental investigation. *Scientific Reports,* 12, 5201. https://doi.org/10.1038/s41598-022-09245-2

[12] Waqas, M., Zahid, R., Bhutta, M. U., Khan, Z. A., and Saeed, A. (2021). A review of friction performance of lubricants with nano additives. *Materials*, 14(6310). https://doi.org/10.3390/ma14216310

[13] Kim, HJ., Seo, KJ., Kang, and Kim, DE., (2016). Nano-lubrication: A review. *Int. J. Precis. Eng. Manuf.* 17, 829–841. https://doi.org/10.1007/s12541-016-0102-0

[14] Akbulut M (2012) Nanoparticle-Based Lubrication Systems. *J Powder Metall Min* 1:e101. doi: 10.4172/2168-9806.1000e101

[15] Ghaednia, H., and Jackson, R.L. (2015). Performing lubricated and dry friction tests. *Tribol. Lubric. Technol*, 71(7), 20-24.

[16] Peric, S., Nedic, B., Trifkovic, D., and Vuruna, M. (2013). An experimental study of the tribological characteristics of engine and gear transmission oils. *Tribology in Industry*, 35(1), 1-8. https://doi.org/10.5545/sv-jme.2012.870

[17] Zhao, J., Huang, Y., He, Y., and Shi, Y. (2020). Nanolubricant additives: A review. *Friction,* 9(5), 891-917. https://doi.org/10.1007/s40544-020-0450-8

[18] https://gillsc.com/factsheet-common-causes-of-bearing-failure-in-gearboxes/

[19] Zhao, J., and He, Y. (2020). Development of novel nanoparticle additives for lubrication enhancement. *Journal of Advanced Tribology*, 12(3), 237-252. https://doi.org/10.1016/j.triboint.2020.06.014

Advancement in Engineering and Science – Goyal et al. (Eds)
 ISBN: 978-1-041-31101-0

Vehicle AI: Interactive Self-Diagnosis, Repair and Reporting System

Prasanth P and Gulbakshee J. Dharmale
Department of Information technology Pimpri-Chinchwad College of Engineering, Pune, India

ABSTRACT: This paper describes a new way to take care of cars using artificial intelligence. This system helps cars check themselves, fix problems, and send reports to drivers and owners. The system uses machine learning, which gathers data from sensors about the engine and checks how the car is doing. This machine learning model trained with engine related data such as fuel pressure, coolant pressure, lubricant temperature, and coolant temperature. The model uses this information to predict performance and regularly sends alerts to the owner or driver. If it finds a problem, the system gives helpful advice with easy steps for simple maintenance tasks. It also creates detailed reports for mechanics that show what is wrong and how to fix it. This new method aims to make cars more reliable, reduce maintenance costs, and improve safety. The Gradient Boosting model achieves an accuracy of 66.60% with a 60:40 train-test ratio. This technology offers better comfort, improved maintenance schedules and increased safety, showing how AI can make vehicles smarter and safer.

Keywords: Artificial Intelligence, Predictive Maintenance, Self-Diagnosis, Automotive Safety

1 INTRODUCTION

Vehicle performance and safety are becoming important to customer nowadays. AI-based preventive maintenance systems provide a new approach to prevent accidents caused by hidden engine problems. The Automotive AI system is leading this change, improving how we can take care of vehicles and making driving experience better overall. This system helps drivers/owners to troubleshoot easily by giving them up-to-date information about vehicle engine's safety and performance.

Finding out car problems was hard and depended on mechanics' skills in earlier days. This often led some to misunderstandings, delays and additional costs for repair and overhaul. However, recent technology advancements have led to new AI systems that can assess themselves using smart sensors, the Internet of Things and machine learning. These systems monitor important factors like engine performance mechanical system performance, tire pressure and so on which helps them to find potential issues early on. This change means maintenance can be done before problems happen instead of waiting for issues to arise.

This technology has great effects on society, especially in logistics and public transportation. Real-time diagnostics can make operations much more efficient and helps to reduce wasting fuel, which is better for the environment and reduce the pollution. As vehicles become more connected, the data will not only support better maintenance but also help in planning cities and improving infrastructure, creating a smarter transportation system. AI for Vehicles diagnostic, repair, and reporting system sets the stage for safer, smarter, and more eco-friendly transportation solutions, opening new opportunities for innovation and automation in the automotive world.

2 LITERATURE SURVEY

The paper presents (A.-J. N. Ghusen, 2020) (A.-J. N. Ghusen, 2020), an AI-driven vehicle fault diagnosis system that employs machine learning algorithms for precise fault identification, reducing downtime and resource waste while delivering immediate repair solutions, surpassing conventional techniques as confirmed by MATLAB assessments. (Adimora, 2021), Connected autonomous vehicles (CAVs) improve transportation efficiency but introduce safety issues. This paper examines anomaly diagnosis, focusing on detection, interpretation, definitions, classifications, and methodologies, and emphasizes safety challenges and future technological hurdles.

This paper proposes (Fallah, 2021), an innovative framework utilizing SVM techniques for fault detection, isolation, and identification in multi-sensor autonomous vehicle systems, achieving detection accuracies of 94.94% and 97.01%. (C. S. A. Gong, 2022), investigates 52 papers on predictive maintenance strategies in motor vehicles over the last five years, summarizing statistical, stochastic, and AI approaches, along with their findings, challenges, and prospective research avenues.

This study presents (Dr. H. Sarma, 2021), a predictive framework for engine health monitoring employing advanced deep learning models, achieving an AUC of 0.9702 for real-time surveillance, proactive alerts, enhanced safety, and reduced maintenance expenses. (Al-Zeyadi, 2020), An Integrated Self-Diagnosis System for autonomous vehicles leverages IoT and deep learning, incorporating data gathering, risk evaluation, and improved diagnostic modules to boost efficiency and safety.

This paper presents (Fang, 2024) (Fang, 2024), The Deep Symptoms-Based Model (Deep-SBM), which employs deep learning for automotive fault diagnosis, surpassing conventional methods regarding accuracy and precision based on real diagnostic data from Cognitran Ltd., and promotes IoT-based fault prediction. (H. El Hadraoui, 2024) , This research assesses machine learning techniques for vehicle fault detection and diagnosis (VFDD) within the Internet of Vehicles (IoV), enhancing AI models to anticipate failures in transmission and engine systems.

This paper addresses (I. Joseph Chukwudi, 2024), safety issues in autonomous vehicles by recommending a maintenance system based on IoT and mobile technology, leveraging cloud computing and wireless sensors for secure operation and integration with vehicular cloud data. (M. Hedayati, 2024), cost-effective health monitoring systems in the automotive sector, concentrating on onboard fault detection methods, the advantages of internal sensors, and emerging trends toward affordable, reliable vehicle solutions.

This paper presents (O. Ö. Ersöz, 2022), a system that combines One-Class SVM for fault detection, a Kalman filter for

DOI: 10.1201/9781003798514-19

trajectory oversight, and a modified neural network for fault identification, demonstrating effectiveness in experiments on the 'Xinda' platform. (P. Sinthia, 2021), An IoT vehicle health monitoring system monitors parameters such as temperature and oil levels, identifies sensor faults in real time, and ensures timely repairs for enhanced safety and reliability with minimal delay.

This paper addresses (R. Rasheed, 2024), the increase in vehicle usage leading to more accidents, primarily due to driver distractions, noting that India recorded 147,123 road fatalities in 2017. This research introduces an IoT system to improve accident safety. (S. S. Chintalapati, 2023), A LabView-based accident prevention system employs sensors to predict accidents through simulations and hardware evaluations. An IoT interface enhances vehicle communication and targets underserved communities, comparing vehicle categories for future IoT advancements.

This paper proposes (Y. Fang, 2020) (Y. Fang, 2020), an intelligent digital twin architecture that improves powertrain management in electric vehicles by utilizing multilayered models and transfer learning for enhanced fault detection and reliability, increasing efficiency and safety through a practical case study. (Y. N. Jeong, 2018) (Y. N. Jeong, 2018), Advanced Fault Diagnosis and Prognosis techniques in aerial and space systems highlight the need for development, accentuating data-driven methods in single-agent systems and unexploited opportunities in multiagent applications.

3 PROPOSED METHODOLOGY

The This section focuses on the basic technologies that enable vehicle AI systems, especially interactive self-diagnosis, repair, and reporting. It discusses the role of AI and machine learning, diagnostic tools, and how different systems work together in modern cars.

These sensors collect the information of Fuel pressure, Coolant temperature, Lubricant temperature with respect to the Engine RPM which is important for diagnosing issues and making repair decisions.

There is some equipment that is necessary to execute the process. The equipment includes a Digital LCD Instrument, an Oil Pressure Gauge, a Voltmeter, a Fuel Gauge, a Water Temperature Meter, I/O interface, a temperature sensor, and a probe wire cable for the MCU, Arduino Uno Rev3.

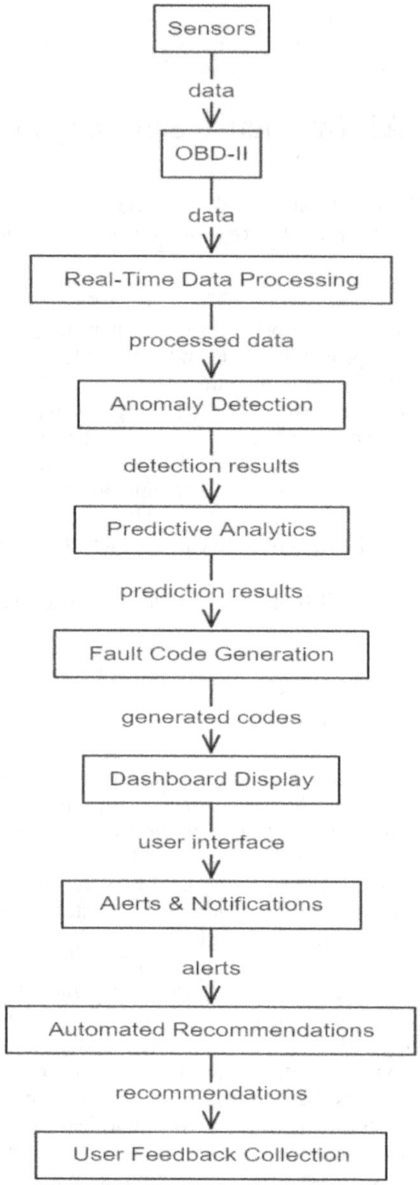

Figure 2. Workflow process chart.

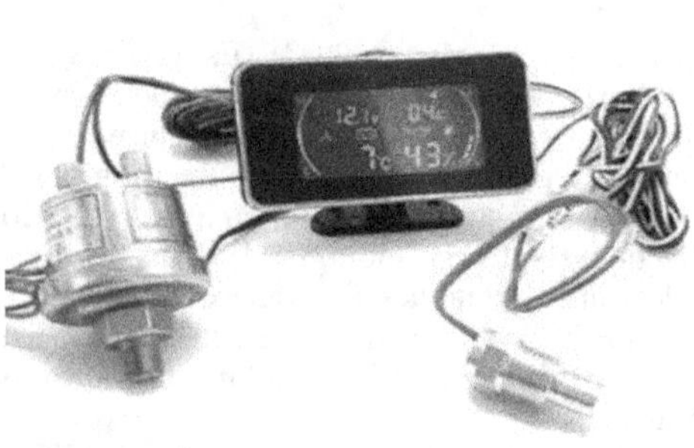

Figure 1. Sensors with display.

The interactive self-diagnostics process in modern cars uses advanced technology to check the vehicle's health, find possible problems, and give helpful information to drivers and mechanics. This makes maintenance easier and allows for quick action and informed choices. We will look at the key parts and steps of the self-diagnostics process and explain how data is collected, processed, and shared with users.

3.1 *Sensors and data sources*

The first and foremost step in the self-diagnosis process involves collecting data from various sensors and systems within the vehicle. These sensors continuously relay real-time data to the vehicle's main computer system (ECU), forming a comprehensive overview of the vehicle's operational status.

3.2 *User inputs*

The self-diagnosis process combines automated data collection with user input:

3.2.1 *User queries*

Drivers can enter concerns like strange noises, dashboard warning lights, or changes in performance, such as starting issues.

3.2.2 *Maintenance history*

Users can share past maintenance details, which help improve diagnostics.

The combination of automated sensor data and user inputs creates a richer dataset for diagnosis.

3.3 *Data processing and analysis*

3.3.1 *Data aggregation*

After collecting data, the system combines real-time sensor readings with user inputs. This integration helps provide a complete picture of the vehicle's health.

3.3.2 *Diagnostic algorithms*

The self-diagnosis process relies on diagnostic algorithms that analyze the data. Key techniques include:

1. Anomaly Detection: Machine learning identifies normal operating ranges and flags unusual data, like abnormal engine temperature.
2. Rule-Based Systems: Predefined rules generate alerts for known issues, such as low tire pressure.
3. Predictive Analysis: Advanced AI predicts future problems based on historical data.

3.3.3 *Fault code generation*

When issues are found, the system produces fault codes according to the OBD-II (On Board Diagnosis – II) standard, helping mechanics and users quickly understand the problem.

3.4 *User interaction and reporting*

1. User Interface: A good user interface is important for showing vehicle diagnostics. This can include dashboard displays that show real-time alerts and performance data, as well as mobile apps that let users check diagnostics and maintenance requests even when they're away.
2. Diagnostics and Recommendations: After finding issues, the system gives a report that clearly explains the problems, suggests immediate actions and long-term maintenance tips, and offers options to book appointments with service providers, along with cost comparisons.
3. Feedback Loop: Users can provide feedback on how accurate the diagnoses and recommendations are, which helps improve the system over time, creating a cycle of ongoing improvement and reliability.

4 EXPERIMENT AND RESULT

The dataset contains more than 20,000 entries with details about the engine. This dataset is open source and includes information such as fuel pressure, coolant pressure, lubricant oil pressure, lubricant temperature, coolant temperature, and engine RPM. The model forecasts whether maintenance is required based on the engine's state.

The dataset is split into a training set and a testing set. It has several independent variables and one dependent variable. In this project, we applied regression models, focusing on support vector machines and random forest classification. We assessed the model's performance using measures like accuracy, and the confusion matrix.

We performed a comparative analysis of the accuracy from testing Gradient Boosting, XG-Boosting, Random Forest, and Support Vector Machines, using a learning rate of 0.10 for all models. A 60:40 train-test split produced better accuracy than the other configurations.

Figure 3 illustrates the training accuracy of different models, which utilized and 60:40 dataset for training and testing. Compared to random forest model and Support vector Machine, Gradient Boosting model performing good.

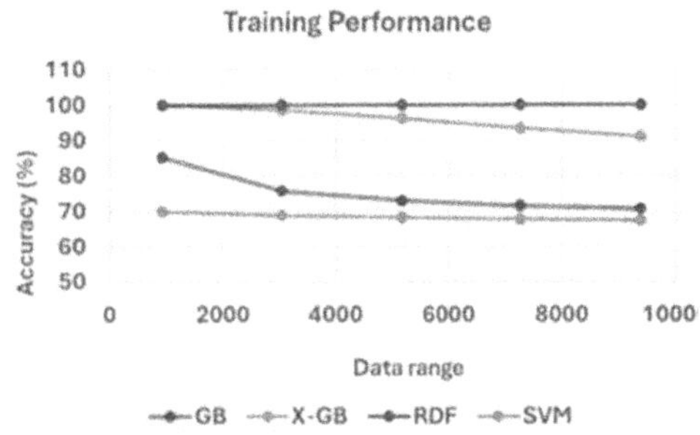

Figure 3. Training learning curve for different model.

Accuracy: Percentage of correctly classified entities.

$$Accuracy = \frac{(TP + TN)}{(TP + FP + FN + TN)} 100\% \tag{1}$$

TP -True Positive, TN – True Negative,
FP - False Positive, FN – False Negative

Table 1 presents a comparative analysis of the training accuracy of Gradient Boosting, XG-Boosting, Random Forest and SVM model on different train-test ratio.

Table 1. Training accuracy on different model.

S. No	Dataset	Gradient Boosting	XG-Boosting	Random Forest	SVM
1	Train-80% Test-20%	69.14	69.12	100	67.44
2	Train-70% Test-30%	69.74	69.59	99.99	67.44
3	Train-60% Test-40%	69.59	69.64	99.99	67.16

Table 2 presents a comparative analysis of the test accuracy of Gradient Boosting, XG-Boosting, Random Forest and SVM model on different train-test ratio.

Table 2. Testing accuracy on different model.

S. No	Dataset	Gradient Boosting	XG-Boosting	Random Forest	SVM
1	Train-80% Test-20%	69.14	69.12	100	67.44
2	Train-70% Test-30%	69.74	69.59	99.99	67.44
3	Train-60% Test-40%	69.59	69.64	99.99	67.16

When using the Gradient Boosting method, we got an accuracy rate of 66.60%. However, the Random Forest model had a problem called overfitting. It did great on the training data but didn't do well on the test data. Comparative analysis of the test accuracy of Gradient Boosting with different learning rate such 0.1,0.05 and 0.01. Gradient Boosting model provides better accuracy with 60:40 train-test ratio with 0.05 learning rate compared to other training rate.

5 BENEFITS OF AI SYSTEMS

This AI system enhances the diagnostic and repair process by finding problems early, which helps reduce maintenance and repair expenses. By sending alerts based on real-time data, it stops potential failures before they happen and keeps passengers and drivers safe.

6 CHALLENGES

Nowadays, vehicles produce a huge amount of data and more information. Analysing this data to get useful insights can be quite complicated. AI systems can also encounter cybersecurity problems, because this system need security measures to stop unauthorized access. Setting up this type of AI system needs experienced technicians. Additionally, there are worries about whether consumers will accept being tracked in their vehicles.

7 CONCLUSION

An AI-driven preventive application for vehicles enables performance by lowering maintenance costs. By using ML algorithms, this system gathers important data about engine health and vehicle performance in real-time. The machine learning model, connected to Arduino, offers suggestions and notifications to the driver/owner, who can easily check engine status anytime. This shift makes maintenance proactive rather than reactive, increasing vehicle reliability, reducing repair costs and enhancing safety. The Gradient Boosting model achieves 66.60% accuracy compared to others. The application sends alert messages to users and provides guidelines for timely maintenance. These innovations can significantly impact logistics and urban planning, making AI adoption important for a safer, smarter transport future and improving overall driving experiences.

REFERENCES

A.-J.N. Ghusen, I. A. (2020). Intelligent vehicular maintenance system using IoT, Mobile application, internet-enabled vehicles and vehicular could. *Fourth Middle East College Student Research Conference.*

Adimora, O.E. (2021). Application of Artificial Intelligence in Fault Diagnosis of Automotive Systems. *ResearchGate.*

Al-Zeyadi, M. a.-P. (2020). Deep Learning Towards Intelligent Vehicle Fault Diagnosis. *International Joint Conference on Neural Networks.* Glasgow.

C.S.A. Gong, C. H. (2022). How to Implement Automotive Fault Diagnosis Using Artificial Intelligence Scheme. *Micromachines, 13* (9).

Dr. H. Sarma, D. H. (2021). A Real Time Implementation of an IOT based Vehicle Health Monitoring System. *International Journal of Recent Technology and Engineering, 10*(3), 140–143.

Fallah, L.B. (2021). A Novel Fault Detection, Identification and Prediction Approach for Autonomous Vehicle Controllers Using SVM. *Automotive Innovation, 8*(1), 301-314.

Fang, Y. (2024). Anomaly diagnosis of connected autonomous vehicles: A survey. *An International Journal on Multi-Sensor, Multi-Source Information Fusion.*

H. El Hadraoui, N. O. (2024). Toward an Intelligent Diagnosis and Prognostic Health Management System for Autonomous Electric Vehicle Powertrains. *A Novel Distributed Intelligent Digital Twin-Based Architecture, 12*, 110729–110761.

I. Joseph Chukwudi, N. Z. (2024). An Ensemble Deep Learning Model for Vehicular Engine Health Prediction. *IEEE Access, vol. 12, 12*, pp. 63433–63451.

M. Hedayati, A. B. (2024). Fault Diagnosis and Prognosis of Satellites and Unmanned Aerial Vehicles: A Review. *Applied Sciences, 14*(20), 9487.

O. Ö. Ersöz, A.F. (2022). A Systematic Literature Review of the Predictive Maintenance from Transportation Systems Aspect. *Future Prospects in Sustainable Engineering Development for Transport Infrastructures and Systems, 14*(21).

P. Sinthia, M. M. (2021). Sensor based health monitoring and controlling of vehicle using IoT. *10th International Conference of Materials Processing and Characterization*, 2908–2911.

R. Rasheed, F. Q. (2024). Machine Learning Approaches for In-Vehicle Failure Prognosis in Automobiles: A Review. *VFAST Transactions on Software Engineering, 12*(1), 169-182.

S.S. Chintalapati, B. C. (2023). Accident Prevention-Based Analysis Using IoT-Interfaced LabVIEW Model. *International Journal of Healthcare Information Systems and Informatics, 18*(1), 1-22.

Y. Fang, H. M. (2020). A Fault Detection and Diagnosis System for Autonomous Vehicles Based on Hybrid Approaches. *IEEE Sensors Journal, 20*(16), 9359–9371.

Y.N. Jeong, S. R. (2018). An integrated self-diagnosis system for an autonomous vehicle based on an IoT Gateway and Deep Learning. *Applied Sciences, 8*(7).

Advancement in Engineering and Science – Goyal et al. (Eds)
© 2026 The Author(s), ISBN: 978-1-041-31101-0

Classification of Marathi Dialects Through Random Forest Ensemble Techniques

Ashwini G. Pawar, Ajay S. Patil, and Nita V. Patil
School of Computer Sciences, KBCNMU, Jalgaon, India

ABSTRACT: This study used the RF algorithm to identify multiple Marathi dialects. This situation is difficult to assess because of inherent linguistic variability and dialect attribute overlap. The goal was to validate the suitability of RF for dialect classification and compare it with other advanced machine learning classifiers such as SVM, KNN, Decision Tree, and Gradient Boosting. 3,000 audio samples were collected to establish a comprehensive dataset covering six popular Marathi dialects: Ahirani, Khandeshi, Malvani, Standard Marathi, Varhadi, and Zadiboli. Audio data were collected from different real-world environments to capture the variability of accents, speech patterns, and recording environments, including telephone conversations, YouTube videos, and social media reels. The pre-processing methods strictly applied to the audio data included segmentation, noise reduction, volume normalization, and resampling to extract features reliably while recognizing linguistic and acoustic features. Given its ensemble learning property and innate ability to rank importance, the RF classifier is well-suited for extracting complex patterns of significance from data. The performance metrics used to assess the performance measurement included 10-fold cross-validation, accuracy, precision, recall, and F1-score. The accuracy results for the RF classifier were 95.50 %, which was greater than the other classifier results. Therefore, these results indicate the feasibility and robustness of the 'Proposed Methodology'.

Keywords: Random Forest, Marathi Dialect Identification, Ensemble Learning, Feature Extraction, 10-fold Cross Validation

1 INTRODUCTION

Dialect identification is an important area of research in sociolinguistics, natural language processing (NLP), and speech processing. With society's increasing reliance on automated language-based systems, accurately identifying dialects is paramount. Dialects consist of language varieties, each in its own right, and are shaped by geographic, social, and cultural factors. Dialects exhibit phonetic, lexical, syntactic, and prosodic variations, making linguistic identification and machine learning difficult. Accurate model building for dialect classification is critical in numerous applications, including speech classification and transcription, translation, and social media [1]. Marathi, which has a significant number of speakers in the Indian state of Maharashtra, has numerous dialects that exhibit linguistic diversity, including Ahirani, Khandeshi Marathi, Malvani, Standard Marathi, Varhadi, and Zadi Boli. Each dialect has "differences in pronunciation, vocabulary, and intonation," which presents another challenge, as idiosyncratic features for each dialect make classification difficult. This study aims to determine whether the Random Forest (RF) algorithm, an ensemble learning algorithm, can use some of the aforementioned processes to address these challenges more accurately.

We implemented the RF algorithm in our investigation of the Marathi dialect because it deals with high-dimensional data and is less prone to overfitting than other models in predictive coding. It also allows us to take full advantage of the importance of features. The RF model inputs multiple predictions of decision trees and takes a majority vote in its outputs for classification purposes [2]. Using RF's functional characteristics, we can assess subtle linguistic differences between Marathi dialects while facilitating the full advantage of the machine learning characteristics, accounting for linguistic complexities and nuances in the dialect identification process. To address the variability of human speech, we created a large dataset that included telephonic conversations, YouTube videos, and clips taken from social media websites, as this variability is required to adequately represent the richness of real-life linguistics and obtain a model that generalizes well based on potentially different accents, background noise, and differences in recording quality. We positioned audio samples for preprocessing, or normalizing audio samples to a standard of 20-second duration, and denoised the audio samples. Data preprocessing is essential for improving linguistic features to ensure accurate dialect classification between Marathi sub-dialects.

This study utilized volume normalization and resampling to minimize the variability attributed to the recording conditions and equipment, allowing for quality feature extraction from natural speech signals. The preprocessing portion of this study utilized an approach that identified a clean dataset that reasonably approximated the natural variability of the language. The acoustic and linguistic features of MFCCs, spectral flux features, formant frequencies, pitch, energy, and duration are the features targeted by the feature extraction step to accurately reflect phonetic details that illustrate dialectal variability in Marathi speech. A Random Forest (RF) classifier provides an approach to ranking the features and identifying the dialect, as it selects the features that contribute more to the identification, thereby improving accuracy. The robustness of the classification approach was verified using 10-fold cross-validation, in which the model was trained and tested on a balanced number of observations per dialect, considering potential overfitting.

2 LITERATURE SURVEY

Dialect identification has been a vital speech-processing task and has been of great help in language study, speech recognition, and forensic purposes. Dialect classification was based on spectral, prosodic, and phonetic attributes. Machine learning techniques, such as SVM, decision trees, and ensemble techniques, were utilized in early research to achieve high performance in classification.

Devi and Thaoroijam [3] used vowel-based spectral and prosodic features with an RF classifier to distinguish Meeteilon dialects (Imphal, Kakching, and Sekmai), achieving 61.57% accuracy. Similarly, Chittaragi and Koolagudi [4] applied vowel-based features, such as formant frequencies (F1–F3), pitch, energy, and duration, for Kannada dialect identification. Their experiments showed that ensemble classifiers, such as RF and Extreme Gradient Boosting, outperformed individual models, attaining 76% accuracy and highlighting the importance of combining global and local features for effective dialect

DOI: 10.1201/9781003798514-20

discrimination. In a closely aligned study, Ciobanu *et al.* [5] used a group of SVM classifiers from word- and character-level n-gram features for German dialect identification, and with transcripts of four Swiss-German dialects (Basel, Bern, Lucerne, and Zurich), they achieved 3rd place in the German Dialect Identification shared task with an F1 measure of 62.03%. This effectively highlights the success of ensemble techniques in normalizing challenging dialectical variations. More recently, Chittaragi and Koolagudi [6] in their study of word-level dialect identification, extracted closely related prosodic and spectral features from the IViE corpus with ensemble classifiers, such as Extreme Gradient Boosting, surpassing the results of SVM classifiers. Chittaragi *et al.* [7] used the same datasets and approach. However, they deployed more features, such as MFCCs, spectral flux, entropy, pitch, energy, and duration, to engage dialect identification for nine British English dialects. Their work again validated that the RF classifier was excellent at 78.5% performance, while Gradient Boosting obtained an even higher score of 81.2%. Therefore, the effectiveness of ensemble techniques for dialect identification was confirmed.

Honnavalli *et al.* (2019) [8] established an accent recognition system using the VCTK corpus for regional English accent. They evaluated multiple classifiers for performance: Neural Networks (95% accuracy), Logistic Regression (95%), KNN (91%), SVM (54%), and GMM (43%). This study was biased toward deep learning models, which had positive indications for using MFCC features for accent detection in the literature. However, challenges were labeled as scalability and data variability/reliability of features. Honnavalli *et al.* (2019) suggested a hybrid model of traditional and deep learning, explicitly mentioning the efficiencies of a hybrid model of deep learning. Singh *et al.* (2024) [9] intended to evaluate whether MFCC features could indicate classifiers that recognize Telugu accents across varying regional Telugu dialects. The experiment provided indications of good discrimination between the accents. The authors touted the consideration of tuning feature extraction to the phonetic context of the accents to aid in performance, but also noted consideration for data augmentation. Pratik Kurzekar *et al.* (2021) [10] proposed a continuous speech recognition system designed for application in the Marathi language related to agriculture. Their model was based on the Mel-Frequency Cepstral Coefficients (MFCC) and the Fast Fourier Transform (FFT), which improved accuracy by 92.5%.

Although recent advancements have been made, studies on dialect identification still have notable gaps. Most studies are strictly confined to one language, or recent studies are branded as either a language or localized accent; thus, data cannot be transferred or generalized to another language context. The recent emergence of ensemble methods and traditional machine learning has resulted in limited new research; however, we have moved away from using other, more complex neural architectures. In addition to the potential ambiguity of overlapping accents and distinguishing between dialect varieties while keeping the dynamic range of existing databases in mind, all these factors make dialect identifications more difficult. This contradiction is particularly problematic for under-tested languages, such as Marathi, where the repositories do not have enough samples or phonetic, reduced, and/or rich data sources to solidify further the robustness of any information obtained from the repository.

3 PROPOSED METHODOLOGY

The proposed system aims to accurately identify dialects in the Marathi language using the strong features of the random forest (RF) algorithm. The system architecture includes several major components: data acquisition, stringent preprocessing, feature extraction, model training, and performance assessment.

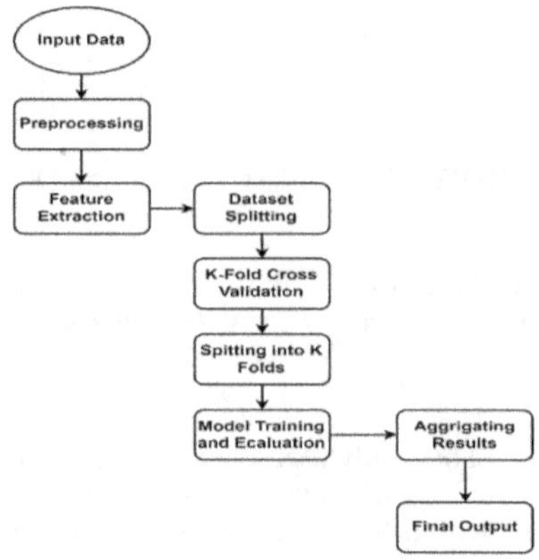

Figure 1. Flow diagram of the proposed dialect identification using an RF classifier.

A detailed explanation of the block diagram is provided below.

3.1 *Input dataset*

In the initial phase of the research, audio samples of various Marathi language dialects were collected from various populations of other speaker varieties. The collected samples represented six dialects: Ahirani, Khandeshi Marathi, Malvani, Standard Marathi, Varhadi, and Zadiboli. Each sampled dialect was included in the dataset for the dialect detection system to ensure that the dataset considered the broadest range of linguistic variations in the Marathi dialects. The input dataset was constructed to reflect variability in the dialects' acoustics and linguistics and was created using speech samples from individuals with identified dialects. These quality datasets are the primary foundation for these models to learn and generalize phonetic, tonal, and prosodic variations. In collecting the speech sample, various geographic locations, demographics (age, gender, socio-economic status), and varieties of speech were sampled, from formal or conversational to informal, everyday speech. Phone calls were a data source, providing natural and spontaneous speech, while social media reels and YouTube videos captured informal and formal speech. Participants provided video samples, and social media reels captured informal speech, providing a rich corpus. Furthermore, quality data collection entails obtaining participants‘ consent, recording using a good-quality recording device, and representing a variety of acoustic environments between all speakers to represent real-world conditions. The specifications of our collected data are presented in Table 1, and the gender specifications are presented in Table 2 for all dialects.

Table 1. Dataset details.

Audio Source	Accents in Audio/ Recordings	The total size of the recordings	Play Time
Recorded Phone Calls from Jalgaon, Erandol, Dhule, Betawad, Erandol	Ahirani (10 Calls)	300MB	20 Hours
	Khandeshi (30 Calls)	800 MB	
Youtube Videos	Ahirani(12)	1.3GB	35 Hours
	Khandeshi (8)	1000MB	
	Malvani (5)	800 MB	
	Standard (20)	1.5 GB	
	Varhadi(15)	1.2 GB	
	Zadi Boli (10)	1 GB	
Instagram reels	Ahirani (1)	15.0 MB	2 Hour
	Khandeshi (2)	50 MB	
	Malvani (3)	80 MB	
	Varhadi (5)	100 MB	
	Zadi Boli(7)	150 MB	

Table 2. Gender wise data collection for all the dialects.

Age	Male	Female	No. of Samples
5-15	10	5	300
15-35	25	30	1500
35-60	20	25	700
60 onwards	15	10	500

3.2 *Preprocessing*

Preprocessing normalizes audio information to ease dialect recognition regarding reliability and consistency. It starts by loading sound into simple 20-second WAV blocks for simple comparison in the analysis process. Static, noise, and unwanted music sound reduction processes are minimized through noise removal techniques to improve speech quality without compromising the features of interest concerning the dialect. Volume normalization equalizes the audio to the same sample volume level, allowing bias-free training. Resampling modifies the sample rates of the audio clips to a standardized rate for optimal feature extraction, that is, the MFCCs. This preprocessing step provides a clean, homogenous dataset that optimizes classifier performance and homogeneity. This model augments the data quality, making the system robust to varying acoustic conditions and speaking styles. The system accurately classifies dialects.

3.3 *Dataset distribution*

The 3000-sample database with completed dialects was divided into test and training sets via 10-fold cross-validation. This approach was run several times to train and test the model at each run with different subsets of data. In the main, that adds to generalizability and stability in terms of limited overfitting and better estimation of model performance. The analysis of the breakdown of all completed dialects contained within the database is shown in Table 3.

Table 3. Dataset distribution.

Dialect	Total Samples
Ahirani	500
Khandeshi	500
Malvani	500
Standard Marathi	500
Varhadi	500
Zadiboli	500
Total	3000

3.4 *Feature extraction*

The phenomenon extraction process is the heart of the proposed Marathi dialect identification framework, which transforms raw audio signals into useful distributions of acoustic and linguistic features. During this process, a full range of harmonics, spectral characteristics, and temporal traits that summarize speech's tonal and structural characteristics are extracted. Harmonic traits, such as Chromagram and CQT Chromagram, characterize tonal information using the Short-Time Fourier Transform (STFT) and Constant-Q Transform (CQT). Spectral characteristics, such as Spectral Centroid, Bandwidth, Rolloff, Contrast, and Flatness, characterize brightness, tone quality, and frequency distribution. Finally, temporal dynamics are characterized using the Zero-Crossing Rate (ZCR) and Root Mean Square Energy (RMSE) to characterize and measure the noisiness and energy characteristics of the signal.

In addition, Mel-Frequency Cepstral Coefficients (MFCCs) offer 13 coefficients with high resolution in timbral characteristics necessary for distinguishing subtle phonetic differences between dialects. The selection of additional features, such as Chroma Energy Normalized Statistics (CENS), Polynomial Coefficients, and Tonal Centroid (Tonnetz), not only improves the representation of each speech sample but also models the perception of including harmonic structure, shifts in energy, and tonal relationships. These features provide a rich, multidimensional representation of each speech sample. This comprehensive feature set proposed an opportunity to capture harmonic, timbral, and dynamic facets for the RF classifier and remained resistant to variability and noise. Overall, the combination of all selected features accounted sufficiently for the modeling of nuanced acoustics and provided a solid foundation for differentiating among closely related dialects of Marathi. To enhance the interpretability of the proposed model, we conducted a feature importance analysis using the intrinsic functionality of the RF classifier. The feature importance values generated using the RF algorithm are presented in Figure 2. This figure shows a chart of the relative importance of the features that could be obtained. As shown in the figure, the features primarily explain the prediction accuracy. A few of the Mel-frequency cepstral coefficients (MFCCs), spectral contrast, and Tonnetz appeared to be more defining. These features indicate minor acoustic changes (e.g., timbre and harmonicity) that likely differentiate dialects. Specifically, features labeled positions 10 and 27 exhibited the most important values and significant distinguishing variables for dialect.

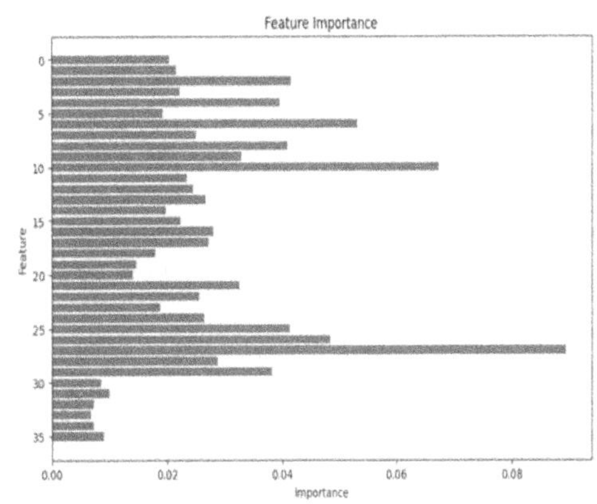

Figure 2. Feature importance scores derived from the rf model for marathi dialect classification.

3.5 *Training and classification*

These skills were used to train RF classifiers to learn fine relationships and trends from data and to create labels of intended dialect classes for input audio samples, reflecting the use of an RF classifier to establish the relationships between the computed characteristics and dialect labels. The RF classifier learns many decision trees because it is an ensemble learner that leverages the predictions of many decision trees to create a robust final classification model. This method effectively deals with the variability in speech patterns, a feature of Marathi dialects, owing to its strong generalization capability.

3.6 *Evaluation metrics*

The final step was to analyze the performance of the trained model. The efficiency of the dialect detection system was assessed using Precision, Recall, F-score, and Accuracy.

Precision indicates the correct optimistic prediction rate, recall indicates the positive instance identification rate, the F1-score indicates the precision and recall balance, and accuracy indicates the overall correct judgment. These measures comprehensively tested the ability of the system to identify and discriminate Marathi dialects.

4 RESULTS AND DISCUSSION

An RF algorithm was developed to train and detect Marathi variants from audio recordings. The system was implemented using Python and the scikit-learn library. Figure 3 shows the RF algorithm's performance in identifying Marathi's spoken variants.

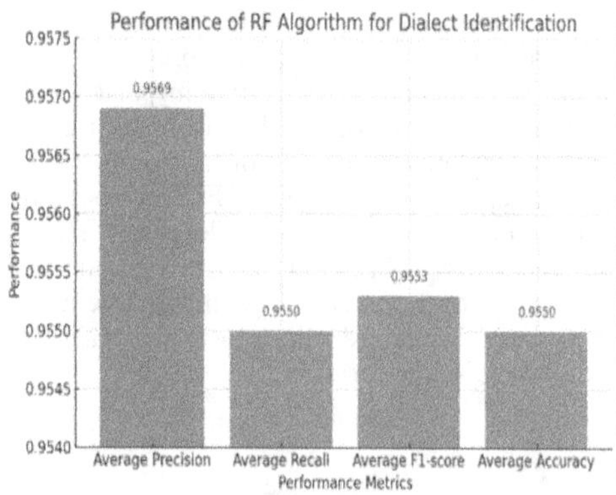

Figure 3. Flow diagram of the proposed dialect identification using an RF classifier.

The findings show that the RF classifier performed well in detecting dialects. A mean precision of approximately 95.68% indicates that when the model predicted a specific dialect, it was accurate almost 96% of the time. A mean recall of approximately 95.50% suggests that the model detected 95.50% of all cases pertinent to each dialect, which is highly sensitive. The mean F1 score of approximately 95.52% is the tradeoff between recall and precision. This highlights how the model equally predicts positive instances and covers all concerned cases. With an average accuracy of 95.50%, it also ensured that the global classification performance was at the same level globally, where the model classified nearly 96% of the samples correctly. These performance metrics, from a large-scale evaluation plan such as 10-fold cross-validation, demonstrate the capability of the RF algorithm to address the dialectal identification task in Marathi. A comparative analysis of the performance of the ML algorithms for spoken Marathi dialect recognition is presented in Table 4.

Table 4. Comparative analysis of the performance of ML algorithms for marathi dialect recognition.

Classifier	Average Precision	Average Recall	Average F1-score	Average Accuracy
SVC_RBF	0.375047	0.39866	0.333646	0.398667
SVC_Poly_Degree3	0.445950	0.41400	0.373858	0.414000
KNN_k3	0.701890	0.69666	0.694254	0.696667
KNN_k5	0.682894	0.68000	0.677790	0.680000
KNN_k7	0.670608	0.66933	0.666147	0.669333
Decision Tree	0.841648	0.84033	0.839817	0.840333
Random Forest	0.956838	0.95500	0.955242	0.955000
Gradient Boosting	0.927620	0.92533	0.925611	0.925333

Table 4 compares some popular machine learning classifiers applied to the Marathi dialect recognition task by evaluating the performance on the four most crucial metrics: average precision, recall, F1-score, and accuracy. All classifiers showed RF performing the best among all with the highest average precision (0.9568), recall (0.9550), F1-score (0.9552), and accuracy (0.9550), indicating its better ability to model dialectal specifics. GB came close to the top scores in all measures (accuracy of 0.9253), reflecting its competence as a steady ensemble technique. The DT also performed well, achieving an accuracy of 0.8403. Ensemble techniques, such as RF and GB, performed better than conventional classifiers in identifying dialect-specific acoustic and linguistic characteristics.

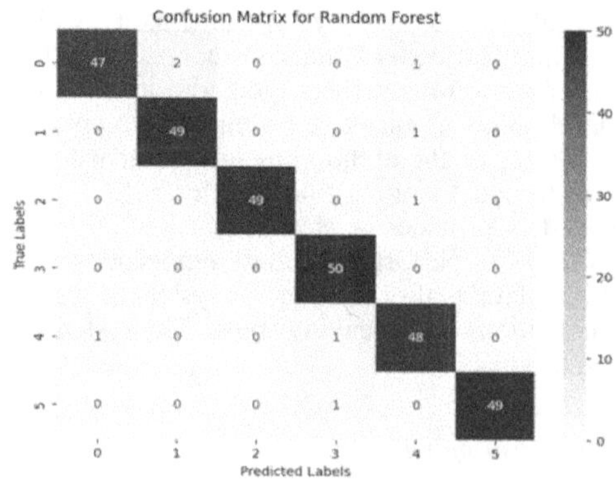

Figure 4. Confusion matrix of the RF algorithm for recognition of spoken Marathi dialects.

Figure 4 presents the confusion matrices for the RF algorithm, which portray the performance of each category resulting from this model, as well as the general stability in recognizing spoken Marathi dialects. The matrix clearly illustrates consistent and correct classification performance for all six dialect classes, particularly high (quoting F1 score performance) for classes 2, 3, and 5. Some minor misclassifications were found in cases with overlapping phonetic features (i.e., classes 0 and 4).

5 CONCLUSION

This study employed the RF paradigm to classify Marathi dialects from a rich set of audio data from audio recordings of multiple dialects. Through careful pre-processing, we showed phonetically fine-grained and prosodically robust differences between the six dialects while modelling rich acoustic features, including MFCCs, Tonnetz, and spectral features. The model achieved a high classification accuracy of 95.50% and a macro-average precision, recall, and F1-score of approximately 0.95. Significance tests confirmed the robustness of the model's performance. The importance of feature analysis showed that MFCCs and harmonic features are substantial contributors to the classification of dialects. The confusion matrix indicated misclassifications into dialects with phonetic features similar to the target dialect. Although the RF classifier outperformed traditional classifiers (e.g., SVM, KNN, Gradient Boosting), the RF model showed its potential for dialect classification in low-resource multilingual environments. The study outcomes contribute to accurate, scalable dialect classification systems, enhancing high-resource multilingual research and work emerging from language ideology and ethnic classification. These outcomes suggest even better future outcomes by combining deep learning or hybrid ensembles.

REFERENCES

[1] Hou, J., and Xu, S. (2022, November). Near-real-time seismic human fatality information retrieval from social media with few-shot large-language models. In *Proceedings of the 20th ACM Conference on Embedded Networked Sensor Systems* (pp. 1141–1147). https://doi.org/10.1145/3560905.3568431

[2] Wevill, J., Bromhead, A., Evans, K., Yarus, J., and John, C.M. (2022). Relative performance of support vector machine, decision trees, and random forest classifiers for predicting production success in US unconventional shale plays. In *Advances in Subsurface Data Analytics* (pp. 31–62). Elsevier. https://doi.org/10.1016/b978-0-12-822295-9.00007-8

[3] Devi, T.C., and Thaoroijam, K. (2020). Vowel-based Meeteilon dialect identification using a random forest classifier.

[4] Chittaragi, N.B., and Koolagudi, S.G. (2019). Acoustic-phonetic feature-based Kannada dialect identification from vowel sounds. *International Journal of Speech Technology.*

[5] Ciobanu, M., Malmasi, S., and Dinu, L.P. (2018). German dialect identification using classifier ensembles. *Proceedings of the Fifth Workshop on NLP for Similar Languages, Varieties, and Dialects.*

[6] Chittaragi, N.B., and Koolagudi, S.G. (2018). Acoustic features-based word-level dialect classification using SVM and ensemble methods.

[7] Chittaragi, N.B., Prakash, A., and Koolagudi, S.G. (2018). *Dialect identification using spectral and prosodic features on single and multiple utterances.*

[8] Honnavalli, D., and Shylaja, S.S. (2021). Supervised a machine learning model for accent recognition in English speech using sequential MFCC features. In *Advances in Intelligent Systems and Computing* (pp. 1–10). Springer. https://doi.org/10.1007/978-981-15-3514-7_5

[9] Singh, M.K., Kishore, D., and Kumar, R.A. (2024). Accent recognition of speech signal using MFCC-SVM and k-NN technique. *Evergreen, 11*(2), 1305–1312.

[10] Kurzekar, P., Deshmukh, R., Waghmare, V., and Shrishrimal, P. (2014). Continuous speech recognition system: A review. *Asian Journal of Computer Science & Information Technology, 4*(6), 62–66. https://doi.org/10.15520/ajcsit.v4i6.3

Advancement in Engineering and Science – Goyal et al. (Eds)

Artificial Intelligence (AI) to Enhance Students' English Communication Skills

Popat Patil and Sunita Ballal
Department of Basic Sciences and Humanities, Karmaveer Bhaurao Patil College of Engineering, Satara, Maharashtra, India

Alok Kadam
Department of Civil Engineering, Karmaveer Bhaurao Patil College of Engineering, Satara, Maharashtra, India

ABSTRACT: This paper examines the role of AI in improving English communication skills, highlighting its benefits, challenges, and prospects. The study is grounded in linguistic and educational theories, illustrating how AI facilitates pronunciation improvement, vocabulary expansion, grammar correction, and contextual language use. Through an analysis of case studies of AI-driven language learning applications, including Duolingo, Grammarly and ChatGPT, the researcher demonstrates their effectiveness in enhancing student engagement and learning outcomes. Despite the transformative potential of AI in language education, ethical considerations, data privacy, and accessibility concerns are also stated. The paper concludes with recommendations for optimizing AI integration in language learning to ensure equitable and effective educational experiences for diverse learners.

Keywords: Artificial Intelligence, Chatbots, Duolingo, Grammarly, ChatGPT, Language Education, English Communication Skills

1 INTRODUCTION

With globalization and digital transformation increasing the need for proficient English communication skills, educational institutions, and learners are pursuing innovative methods to improve language acquisition. English proficiency is a crucial part in academic settings, professional careers, and global communication, yet traditional language learning approaches often fail to meet the needs and learning expectations of students. The increasing use of AI-driven educational technologies offers solutions by providing personalized, scalable, and data-driven language learning experiences.

AI applications in language education enhance language learning, speech recognition, and adaptive learning techniques to enhance various aspects of English communication skills. AI-powered chatbots excite real-life conversations, providing students with interactive dialogues that improve their fluency and confidence. Speech recognition tools analyze pronunciation patterns and offer corrective feedback, helping learners refine their spoken English. Writing assistants equipped with AI detect and correct grammatical errors, suggest vocabulary improvements and enhance coherence in written communication. These tools collectively offer a dynamic and personalized learning experience that traditional classroom instruction may not always provide.

Despite AI's evident advantages in English language learning, several challenges persist. Ethical concerns regarding AI bias, data privacy, and overreliance on technology require careful consideration. Additionally, discrepancies in access to AI-based education due to technological infrastructure limitations must be spoken to ensure inclusivity. This paper explores the various ways AI enhances English communication skills, evaluates its benefits and challenges, and discusses future directions for research and policy development in AI-driven language education.

2 RESEARCH PROBLEM AND HYPOTHESIS

Despite widespread adoption of AI in education, there is limited empirical research exploring its impact on enhancing English communication skills among non-native engineering students in India. This study investigates whether AI-driven tools such as chatbots, grammar checkers, and pronunciation coaches significantly improve students' proficiency in spoken and written English. **Hypothesis:** The integration of AI tools into language instruction leads to measurable improvement in students' English communication skills, particularly in pronunciation accuracy, grammatical precision, and fluency.

3 THEORETICAL FRAMEWORK

The application of AI in language education is supported by several learning theories, including:

- **Constructivism** (Vygotsky 1978): AI-driven platforms create interactive learning environments that encourage active knowledge construction.
- **Connectivism** (Siemens 2005): AI tools facilitate learning through digital networks, enabling continuous engagement.
- **Cognitive Load Theory** (Sweller 2011): AI adapts instructional content to reduce cognitive overload and optimize learning.

4 AI APPLICATIONS IN ENHANCING ENGLISH COMMUNICATION SKILLS

4.1 *Pronunciation improvement*

AI-powered speech recognition systems, such as Google's Speech-to-Text and ELSA Speak, analyze spoken English and provide real-time feedback on pronunciation, fluency, and intonation. These systems help learners identify pronunciation errors and suggest improvements by comparing speech patterns with native speaker benchmarks (Chen and Li 2021). Advanced AI models can detect subtle pronunciation mistakes and provide phonetic breakdowns, allowing learners to refine their speech accuracy over time.

4.2 *Grammar and writing enhancement*

AI-driven writing assistants like Grammarly, Hemingway Editor, and QuillBot detect and correct grammatical errors,

DOI: 10.1201/9781003798514-21

enhance sentence structure, and improve coherence. These tools analyze written content for stylistic consistency, readability, and tone, helping students develop better writing skills (Johns 2020). AI-enhanced writing platforms also provide contextual vocabulary suggestions, enabling learners to expand their lexical range and adapt their writing for different audiences.

4.3 *Conversational AI and Chatbots*

AI chatbots, such as ChatGPT and Duolingo's chatbot, act in human-like conversations, allowing students to practice English in real time. These chatbots provide contextual responses, helping students engage in natural conversations and build fluency. Advanced conversational AI systems use deep learning to generate responses that mimic human speech patterns, offering learners an interactive language practice experience (Lu and Kim 2022). Some chatbots incorporate voice interaction, enabling learners to develop both spoken and written communication skills.

While conversational AI can simulate authentic language interactions to a significant extent, there are limitations. Chatbots, though responsive and context-aware, often lack the cultural nuances, emotional depth, and spontaneity of human conversation. This can impact the development of pragmatic competence and intercultural communication skills. Furthe rmore, some learners may find interactions with AI less engaging or realistic than speaking with native speakers or peers.

4.4 *AI-Powered personalized learning*

Adaptive learning platforms like LingQ and Coursera use AI to modify language lessons based on learners' proficiency levels. These platforms analyze student progress and adjust instructional content accordingly, ensuring targeted skill development. Personalized learning through AI allows students to focus on weak areas, receive personalized exercises, and track their improvements over time (Wang 2021). AI-driven feedback mechanisms provide learners with performance analytics, helping them identify learning patterns and optimize their study strategies.

AI-powered personalized learning platforms offer significant benefits such as tailored instruction, targeted practice, and real-time performance tracking. These features promote learner autonomy and efficient skill development. However, potential drawbacks include reduced opportunities for collaborative learning, dependency on algorithms, and the risk of overlooking affective or motivational aspects that human educators often address. There is also concern about data misuse and the potential reinforcement of algorithmic biases.

5 BENEFITS OF AI IN ENGLISH LANGUAGE LEARNING

5.1 *Personalized learning experiences*

AI adjusts content difficulty based on individual learning needs, providing modified recommendations. Traditional language learning follows a one-size-fits-all approach, whereas AI-driven education adapts lessons dynamically to match students' proficiency levels and learning styles (Kukulska-Hulme 2019). This ensures that students receive relevant instruction that maximizes their engagement and learning outcomes.

5.2 *Instant feedback and error correction*

AI tools offer immediate corrections and explanations, which increases the speed of language learning. Unlike conventional feedback mechanisms that rely on instructor evaluation, AI-powered tools provide real-time insights into pronunciation, grammar, and vocabulary usage (Xu and Warschauer 2020). AI's ability to instantly analyze and correct errors enhances the efficiency of language learning, reducing the time students spend on repetitive mistakes.

5.3 *Engagement and motivation*

Gamified AI applications increase learner motivation through interactive exercises and reward systems. AI-powered language learning platforms integrate elements of game design, such as badges, leaderboards, and progress tracking, to maintain learner interest (Hamari *et al.* 2014). These features make learning enjoyable and encourage students to develop consistent language practice habits.

5.4 *Accessibility and inclusivity*

AI-based translation and speech-to-text tools support learners with disabilities, promoting inclusive education. AI-driven accessibility features, such as text-to-speech conversion and automated subtitling, enable students with visual or auditory impairments to engage in language learning Additionally, AI translation services break language barriers, allowing non-native English speakers to understand content and participate in global communication more effectively.

6 CHALLENGES AND LIMITATIONS

6.1 *Accuracy and bias in AI models*

AI systems may produce incorrect corrections or exhibit biases in language suggestions. Language models are trained on vast datasets, which may contain inaccuracies or cultural biases that affect AI-generated content (Bender *et al.* 2021). Researchers continue to work on refining AI models to minimize errors and ensure fairness in language learning applications.

6.2 *Dependence on technology*

Over-reliance on AI tools may hinder students' ability to develop independent language skills. While AI provides valuable assistance, excessive dependence on automated corrections and suggestions may reduce students' ability to self-edit and critically evaluate their language use (Selwyn 2016). Educators should integrate AI tools as supplementary resources rather than complete replacements for traditional learning methods.

6.3 *Ethical and privacy concerns*

AI-driven language applications collect user data, raising concerns about privacy and data security. Many AI-based platforms require access to speech and text data to improve their procedures, which raises ethical concerns regarding data ownership and confidentiality. Policymakers must establish regulations to ensure that AI language learning tools prioritize user privacy and transparency in data usage.

7 CASE STUDY

7.1 *Implementation of AI in a classroom setting*

A pilot study was conducted with 40 second-year engineering students at Karmaveer Bhaurao Patil College of Engineering, Satara. Over the course of eight weeks, students used three AI tools: Duolingo (for vocabulary and grammar), Grammarly (for writing), and ELSA Speak (for pronunciation). Pre- and post-tests were conducted using a standardized English communication rubric.

7.2 *Findings*

- **Pronunciation accuracy** improved by an average of 32%, especially among students who practiced daily with ELSA.
- **Grammatical correctness** in writing assignments improved by 45% with consistent use of Grammarly.
- **Speaking confidence**, as assessed through oral presentations, improved by 38%, largely attributed to chatbot interactions in Duolingo.

Students reported higher motivation and reduced anxiety when engaging with AI tools compared to traditional classroom methods. These findings support the hypothesis that AI integration enhances English language proficiency and engagement in learners.

8 CONCLUSION

Artificial Intelligence (AI) has emerged as a transformative force in the domain of English language education, offering learners personalized, interactive, and efficient ways to enhance their communication skills. From improving pronunciation and grammar to fostering fluency through conversational chatbots, AI-powered tools provide dynamic learning experiences that traditional methods often lack. The integration of AI has led to measurable improvements in learners' proficiency, as evidenced by the case study conducted with engineering students. These tools promote learner autonomy, increase motivation, and support diverse learning needs through real-time feedback and adaptive content.

However, the implementation of AI in language learning is not without challenges. The presence of bias in computational models, ethical concerns surrounding data privacy and the risk of overdependence on technology necessitate critical evaluation. It is essential to ensure that AI serves as a supplement rather than a substitute for human interaction, especially in contexts where emotional, cultural, and social aspects of language learning play a vital role.

Moreover, while real-time feedback is a prominent advantage of AI, its effectiveness varies depending on learners' individual preferences and the nature of the task. Immediate correction can help prevent the reinforcement of errors, especially in written or pronunciation-based exercises. Yet in spoken communication, constant interruptions for correction may hinder fluency development and elevate learner anxiety. A blended approach that incorporates both immediate and delayed feedback can better support learners' communicative competence and confidence.

Looking ahead, future research should focus on refining AI systems to enhance accuracy and fairness, expanding access to under-resourced educational settings, and establishing clear ethical frameworks for the responsible use of learner data. Additionally, more empirical studies are needed to explore long-term learning outcomes and the psychological impact of AI-based instruction.

By carefully balancing technological innovation with pedagogical best practices and ethical considerations, AI can continue to reshape English language education in meaningful and inclusive ways, ultimately enhancing students' communication skills and preparing them for global engagement.

REFERENCES

Bender, E.M., Gebru, T., McMillan-Major, A., and Shmitchell, S. (2021). On the dangers of stochastic parrots: Can language models be too big? *Proceedings of the 2021 ACM Conference on Fairness, Accountability, and Transparency*, 610–623.

Chen, J., and Li, H. (2021). AI-driven speech recognition in language learning. *Journal of Educational Technology*, 38(2), 112–129.

Hamari, J., Koivisto, J., and Sarsa, H. (2014). Does gamification work? A literature review of empirical studies on gamification. *Proceedings of the 47th Hawaii International Conference on System Sciences*, 3025–3034.

Johns, T. (2020). The impact of AI-based writing assistants. *Computers in Language Learning*, 45(3), 201–218.

Zhai, Y. (2022). AI and the future of language education. *Educational AI Review*, 12(1), 56–57.

Advancement in Engineering and Science – Goyal et al. (Eds)
© 2026 The Author(s), ISBN: 978-1-041-31101-0

Improvement in Productivity with Multi-Spindle Drilling Head Attachment: A Case Study

Pravin Jadhav, Minakshi Shinde, Digvijay Kadam, and Shital Kumar Desai
K.B.P. College of Engineering, Satara, Maharashtra, India

ABSTRACT: The present endeavor aims to develop and build a multi-spindle drilling machine that will reduce cycle time and increase production rate. Designing a multi-orientation subsystem requires several steps: looking at the component drawing, making an embodiment diagram, figuring out the speed ratio, utilizing the CMTI manual to construct the gears and bearings, and creating a thorough two-dimensional representation and model. Additionally, a comparison of the productivity and cycle time of single-spindle and multi-spindle drilling (MSD) machines has been discussed. While single-spindle drilling (SSD) takes 76 seconds, multi-spindle drilling takes 16 seconds. Drilling using many spindles cuts the cycle time by about 79%. Tool indexing is necessary for the single spindle drilling machine. About 305 and 1440 tasks are produced in an 8-hour shift, respectively, with the help of the single and multi-spindle drilling machines. The production rate rises by approximately 4.72 times when multi-spindle drilling equipment is used in conjunction with a multi-spindle drilling head. Compared to multi-spindle drilling machines, single-spindle drilling machines require greater material handling area, work rejections, and personnel expertise. The workforce was reduced by half. The amount of material handling and human fatigue also significantly decreased. The cost of maintenance is cut by more than 72% when a multi-spindle drilling machine is used. The payback period for a multi-spindle drilling machine is around 75 days.

Keywords: Single spindle drilling, multi-spindle drilling, cycle time, productivity, drilling machines, Case study

1 INTRODUCTION

Drilling is a matching process employed for making holes in a workpiece with a drilling attachment. It is associated with boring, counter-boring, trepanning, reaming, and boring—a rotating spindle combined with a feed in these processes. The holes drilled with a high material removal rate. This may be accomplished by employing a MSD head. Quality requirements of the final product should be achieved at every stage of production. The most significant aspect of using multi-spindle machines is the cycle time; parallel machining notably reduces the total operating time with less possibility of mistakes. MSDs are used for mass production with time savers. They are used in the mechanical industry to increase the productivity. MSD machines drill holes simultaneously in one setting with high accuracy to make them interchangeable. It has more than one spindle drive, and all the spindles are fed into the workpiece simultaneously. Feeding motion is obtained by reducing the drill head [1].

Gippespie [2] presents the experimental results of the process parameters' influence on the drilling operation. It observed various burr formation mechanisms. Stein and Dornfeld [3] determine the quality of drilling by changing the feed, and speed of the drill. As the speed and feed increase the burr thickness and height increase. Sofronas [4] reported the effect of hardness and strength on the drilling quality. As the hardness of the material increases the burr size increases significantly. Khurmi and Gupta [5] indicated Gear Nomenclature, Teeth Calculation, and Selection of gears. The gearbox design is indicated with a simple philosophy. V.B.Bhandari [6] reveals the study and analysis of the design of various parts like gears, keys, shaft, spindle, housing, etc, and also the selection of bearing. M. Telsang [7] reported basic concepts of Making and buying decisions, Time study calculation, Payback period, and Cost analysis. Jadhav *et al.* [8–9] reported some case studies to improve productivity. They may employ Lean manufacturing and OEE for improvement in production rate. A.Udgave and V. Khot [10] had designed and developed a multi-spindle drilling head. The growth of the Indian manufacturing sector depends largely on its productivity and quality.

Productivity depends upon many factors, one of the major factors being manufacturing efficiency with which the operation /activities are carried out in the organization. Productivity can be improved by reducing the total machining time, combining the operations, etc. The best way to improve the production rate (productivity) along with quality is by the use of a special-purpose machine. M. Yerriswamy *et al.* [11] reported the experimental result after drilling at different Speeds, Tool angles, and feed. The dimensional drilling error of observed with over coordinate measuring machine. Potdar, and Sapkal [12], Jadhav and Agrawal [13] carried out experimental work for drilling different thicknesses of the work piece, speed, and feed. The study focuses on optimizing the drilling quality with different drilling parameters. Additionally some of the studies [14–15] optimized the drilling with a Taguchi method for the different parameters like drill shape, friction, and conical angle, feed. Different tests were carried out to design experiments to understand the performance.

Literature gives fundamental knowledge of the drilling process and productivity study. The present study is a case study of the manufacturing industry. The manufacturing of alternator casing (SREH 7040) is carried to a vertical drilling and spot-facing machine. There are five holes to be drilled in a casing of 4.2mm diameter and 3.2mm diameter, shown in Figure 1. The work piece must be adjusted by the operator in accordance with the vertical drilling and spot-facing machine's axis. Additionally, they must manually slide the tool downward. The conventional single spindle drilling machine depicted in Figure 1 requires them to perform the work at several stations. In contrast, just one drill was used at a time during the suggested multi-drilling. It takes unproductive time for the worker to index the workpiece five times. Indexing causes an increase in this unused time. Therefore, all holes must be drilled in a single pass to save time. Thus Possibility of a hole missing is eliminated because five holes are drilled at a time. A worker is needed for mounting the task in traditional machining, and indexing the workpiece takes longer. The solution to the above problem is to design and develop a special-purpose machine using a multi-spindle drilling operation. It may reduce the cycle time, increase the production rate, reduce human fatigue, minimize the production time, reduce the cost of the product and increase the accuracy in drilling.

DOI: 10.1201/9781003798514-22

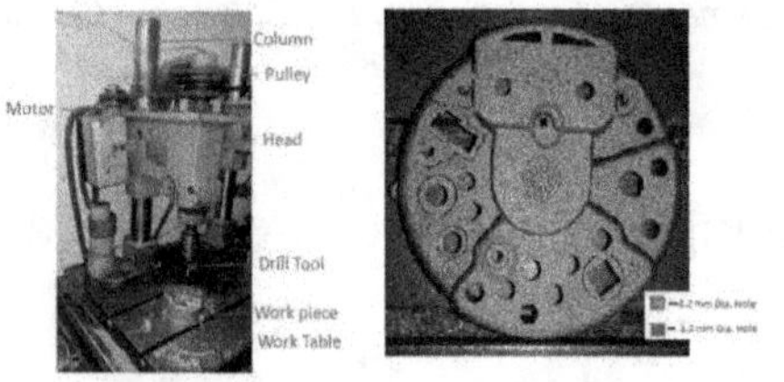

Figure 1. Traditional practice with single spindle drilling machine and Alternator Casing (SREH 7040) work piece with desired holes.

2 MATHEMATICAL MODEL

As the name indicates multi-spindle drilling machines have more than one spindle driven by a single power head, and these spindles holding the drill bits are fed into the work piece simultaneously. The spindles are so constructed that their center distance can be adjusted in any position within the drill head depending on the job requirement. For this purpose, the drill spindles are connected to the main drive using universal joints. The rotations of the drills are derived from the main spindle and the central gear through several planetary gears in mesh with the central gear and the corresponding flexible shafts. There are multiple planet gears and one sun gear arrangement for transmitting the power from the main spindle to the planet shaft machine, cylindrical grinding machine, internal grinding machine, slotting machine, milling machine, and hobbing machine. As shown in Figure 2 ,Various steps are to be followed to design a multi-orientation subsystem. a) Study the component drawing and find the position of holes, b) Construct embodiment diagram, c) Calculate speed ratio, d) Gear design and bearing design using standard CMTI handbook e) Generate a table of gear and bearing, f) Create detail two-dimensional drawing[16–17].

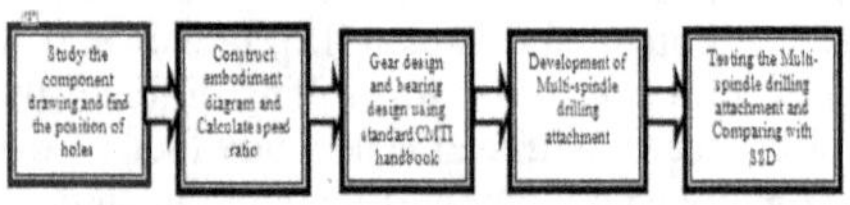

Figure 2. Block diagram of development of multi-spindle drilling attachment.

2.1 *Design of multi-spindle drilling head attachment*

2.1.1 *Material selection for various components*

The Multi spindle drilling head requires design and develop various components, the major components like gear box, spindle, shafts, pinions, drive gears, idler gears etc. It requires various manufacture machines like a band saw machine for cutting operation, a lathe machine for rough machining, a drilling machine, and surface grinding.

2.1.2 *Selection of motor*

The drilling quality largely depends on the feed and speed of the drill. By changing the feed and speed of the drill. As the speed and feed increase, the burr thickness and height increase [3]. So Selected the Feed rate(S) = 0.03 mm/rev, Material Factor(K) = 1.5, Power(P):

$$\mathbf{P} = \frac{\mathbf{1.25D^2KN(0.056 + 1.5s)}}{\mathbf{10^5}} \tag{1}$$

For Ø4.2 mm drill, P = 0.18 HP, For Ø3.2 mm drill, P = 0.1 HP, Total Power = 0.80 HP, Selection of Motor: 3 Phase induction motor with 1HP power at 1440 rpm.

Table 1.

Description	Quantity	Material
Housing		
Bottom Plate Housing	1	AlSi132
Top Plate Housing	1	AlSi132
Gears		
Sun Gear	1	20MnCr5
Idler Gear	1	20MnCr5
Pinions	5	20MnCr5
Bearings		
Ball Bearing 6901	10	6901
Thrust Bearing 51101	5	51101
Ball Bearing 6902 for idle	2	6902
Ball Bearing 6004 for sun	1	6004
Spindle and Shaft		
Spindle	5	SAE 8620
Shaft	1	SAE 8620
Idler Shaft	1	SAE 8620
Drill		
Drill Ø4.2	4	Carbide
Drill Ø3.2	1	Carbide
Miscellaneous		
Nut	6	M.S.
Grub Screw	5	M.S.
Retainer Ring	1	M.S.
Bolt M6	5	M.S.
Keys	7	M.S.

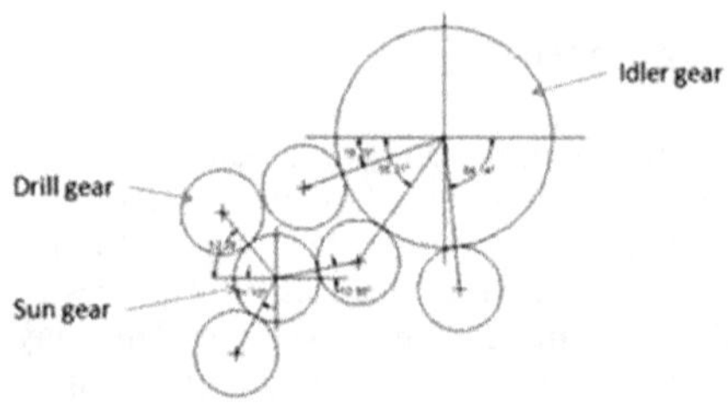

Figure 3. Layout of gear box with Sun, Drill, and Idler gears.

2.1.3 *Design of gear box*

Design of the gear box is carried out with the help of Layout of gear box with various gears (Figure 3)

$$\text{Speed of Sun Gear}: \frac{D_s}{D_B} = \frac{N_B}{N_s} = \frac{T_s}{T_B} \tag{2}$$

$$\text{Speed of Idler Gear}: \frac{D_I}{D_B} = \frac{N_B}{N_I} \tag{3}$$

$$\text{No. of Teeth in Sun Gear}: \frac{N_B}{N_s} = \frac{T_s}{T_B} \tag{4}$$

$$\text{No. of Teeth in Idler Gear}: \frac{N_B}{N_I} = \frac{T_I}{T_B} \tag{5}$$

$$\text{Module}: m = \left(\frac{60 \times 10^6}{\pi} \times \frac{kw \times C_s \times f.s}{Z_N . C_V . \left(\frac{b}{m}\right) . \left(\frac{S_{ut}}{3}\right) . Y} \right)^{\frac{1}{3}} \tag{6}$$

Torque Transmitted by Sun Gear : Torque(M_T)

$$= \frac{60 \times 10^6 \times P(kw)}{2\pi N_s} \tag{7}$$

Torque Transmitted by Idler Gear : Torque(M_T)

$$= \frac{60 \times 10^6 \times P(kw)}{2\pi N_s} \tag{8}$$

$$\text{Forces acting on Gear Tooth}: P_T = \frac{2M_T}{d_I} \tag{9}$$

$$P_R = P_T \tan\alpha \tag{10}$$

$$\text{Pair of Sun \& Drill Gear}: P_{eff} = (C_S.P_t)/(C_v) \tag{11}$$

$$S_b = mb\sigma_b Y$$

$$S_W = bQd_p^{'}KifS_b > \text{Peff},\ S_w > P_w \text{ then design is safe}$$

$$\text{Pair of Idler \& Drill Gear}:\ P_{eff} = (C_S.P_t)/C_v \tag{12}$$

$$S_b = mb\sigma_b Y$$

$$S_W = bQd_p^{'}K,\ \text{if} S_b > P_{eff}, S_w > P_w \text{ then design is safe}$$

$$\text{Pair of Sun \& Drill Gear}:\ P_{eff} = (C_s.P_t + P_d) \tag{13}$$

$$P_d = \frac{21V(Ceb + P_t)}{21V + \sqrt{Ceb + P_t}} NIf$$

$$S_b > P_{eff}, S_w > P_{eff} \text{ Design is safe}$$

$$\text{Pair of Idler \& Drill Gear}: P_{eff} = (C_s.P_t + P_d)N \tag{14}$$

$$P_d = \frac{21V(Ceb + P_t)}{21V + \sqrt{Ceb + P_t}}$$

Module on the basis of Wear Strength :

$$m = \left(\frac{60 \times 10^6}{\pi} \times \frac{kw \times C_s \times f.s}{Z_N.C_V.\left(\frac{b}{m}\right).\left(\frac{S_{ut}}{3}\right).Y}\right)^{\frac{1}{3}} \tag{15}$$

2.1.4 *Design of shaft*

The gearbox consists of three shafts: Idler Shaft, the drill gear shaft, and the Sun gear (Arbor) shaft. For the Design of the Idler Shaft first, calculate all vertical forces and Horizontal forces and calculate.

$$M_b = \sqrt{M_{bv}^2 + M_{bh}^2} \tag{16}$$

$$M_b = \frac{16}{\pi\tau_{Max}} \sqrt{(K_b.M_b)^2 + (K_T.M_T)^2} \tag{17}$$

Shaft design on rigidity basis

$$d^4 = \frac{584 M_T l}{G\theta} \tag{18}$$

Bearing Selection: Ball bearing selection for Idler Shaft is calculated by employing following equation

$$L_{10} = \frac{60nL_{10h}}{10^6} \tag{19}$$

From bearing catalogue

$$\left(P_1 (L_{10})^{\frac{1}{3}} * \text{Load Factor}\right) \tag{20}$$

By considering Load factor 1.2, For manufacturing a multi-spindle drilling attachment select a bearing from the bearing catalog using values C1 and L10, as 15x28x7, (Bearing no. 6902), 20x42x12 (Bearing no. 6002). Thrust Bearing Catalogue, 12x26x9. The make-or-buy decision refers to the problems encountered by an organization when deciding whether a product or service should be purchased from outside sources or manufactured internally. Number of components may be used for developing Multi-spindle drilling Machines are Spindle, Idler shaft, Arbor shaft, Top Housing plate, Bottom housing plate, Bearing, Gear, Grub Screw, Retainer Ring, Bolt M6, Key, Washer, Circlip.

a. Mold for botto housing bottom plate | b.Three dimensions view of bottom plate housing | c. Three dimensions view of Top plate housing

Figure 4. Mold and Three dimensions view for bottom and top housing bottom plate.

2.2 *Development of multi-spindle drilling machine*

2.2.1 *Housing*

The housing of multi-spindle drilling attachment is made up of AlSi132 material. The housing has a bottom plate and top plate. The bottom Plate Housing is made of casting by using a pressure die casting machine. The mold for the bottom housing is shown in Figure 4 a. The casting of housing further made surface finishing, is forwarded for the drilling of specified holes in the design. Out of these holes, the holes with different Pitch Circle diameters (PCDs) are five in number. The various processes are opted to manufacture the bottom housing. The finished casting was then centered with a center drill on the lathe. Afterward facing, turning, boring, drilling, and tapping operations were carried out. Figure 4 b and 4 c.Three dimensions view of bottom and top plate housing. employed for the keyway. Threading is carried out on the lathe with a single-point tool. Id and OD grinding is done.

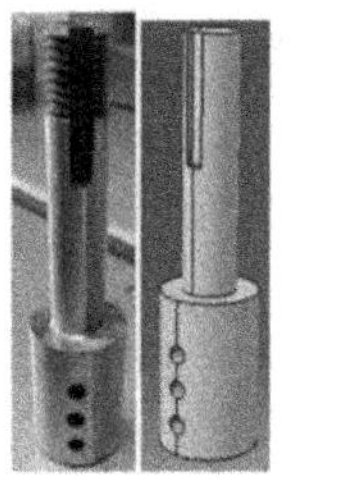

Figure 5. Three dim en-sion view and image of the Spindle.

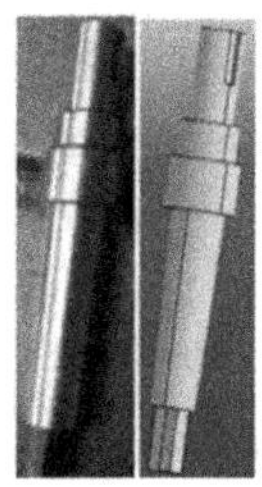

Figure 6. Three dim ension view and image of the Sun Gear Arbor) shaft.

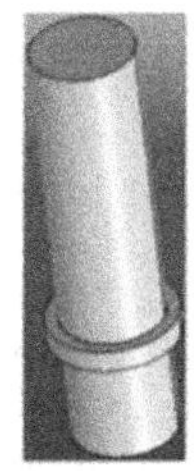

Figure 7. Three dimension view of an Idler Shaft.

Figure 6 shows Three-dimension views and an image of the Arbor shaft. Similar to Arbor shaft. Similar to the Idler shaft, Shaft had developed using various processes like centering, facing, and turning has been done on the lathe with single point tools. Then grooving had been done on the lathe machine. Afterward, grinding is done. Figure 7 shows a three dimension view of the Idler shaft. After designing and manufacturing the entire components viz. spindle, Sun gear, Idler gear, pinion, Arbor shaft, Ilder shaft, bearing, and Key are implanted in the bottom plate housing.

Gear. Gear is used as a power transmission component. In the present multi-spindle drilling machine there are Sun Gear, Idler gear, and Pinion gears are employed. Various sequences of operations were done to manufacture the gear. Centering, Facing, Turning, and Boring have been done with a center drill, and single point tools. The measurement of inspection is done with Vernier Caliper. Hobbing Machine is used for gear cutting with gear hob. Whereas, a slotting machine is employed for the keyway with 850RPM with the White beat. Case hardening is done in the Oven. Gear lapping was carried out on Gear lapping unit. At last, surface grinding had carried out. The whole insides assembly of multi-spindle drilling machines is shown in Figure 8. Whereas, Figure 9 indicates the view of an upright drilling machine with a multispindle drilling attachment.

Figure 8. Inside assembly of the multi-spindle drilling machine.

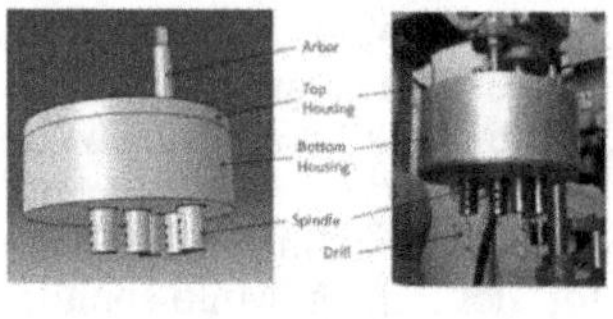

Figure 9. Three-dimensional view and Actual image of multi-spindle drilling attachment.

3 RESULT AND DISCUSSION

Comparative study between convectional old single spindle drilling and multi spindle drilling machine has been carried out. Initially, time required to drill a hole of 3.2mm and four holes of 4.2mm is measured, which give total time of drilling (cycle time). Observed the number of times indexing required in both cases. Afterwards calculated total number of finished components manufactured in a day (8 hours). Skills required by labour are observed in both drilling machines. Additionally, measured finished (manufactured) items per day by considering 80% working efficiency. Annual cost required is calculated by employing the number of jobs manufacture monthly and working days in a year (300 days). Table 2 gives a comparative study between the single-spindle and multi-spindle drilling machines. The cycle time of drilling required in the single-spindle and multi-spindle drilling is 76 sec and 16 sec respectively. The cycle time with multi-spindle drilling decreases by about 79%. Single spindle drilling machine require four indexing, while no indexing is required in a multi-spindle. Thus Possibility of a hole missing is eliminated because five holes are drilled at a time. Two drilling machines are required for drilling two holes viz. Ø4.2 and Ø3.2mm for single spindle drilling machine. Nearly 305 and 1440 finished. Jobs are manufactured in a shift (8 hours) with the help of single and multi-spindle drilling machines respectively. That means the production rate is increased approximately by 4.72 times using a Multi-spindle drilling head. About 72% machining cost is reduced with multi-spindle drilling machines. The manpower was reduced by 50%. Additionally, Material Handling and Fatigue of Human reduced considerably. Figure 10 indicated a comparative graph of single and multi-spindle drilling machines based on daily maintenance cost like electricity cost, labour cost, tooling cost, and Total machining cost. It is observed that electricity cost and Labour costs decrease nearly by 74% and total machining costs decreases by 72% with help of a multi-spindle drilling machine. However, tooling cost increases by nearly 35% with a multi-spindle drilling machine. In short, The maintenance cost decreases by nearly 74% with a multi-spindle drilling machine. In addition to maintenance costs, we need to calculate the payback period of the machine. Payback period is nearly 75 days.

Table 2.

Sr. No.	Parameter	Single–spindle drilling (Traditional)	Multi-Spindle Attachment (Proposed)
	Cycle Time (sec)	76	16
2	No of Indexing required	4	No
3	Machine required (No.)	2	1
4	Jobs per Shift (Quantity)	305	1440
5	Machining Cost per job (Rs)	Rs. 1.03	Rs. 0.29
6	Skills required by labour	Excellent	Average
7	Rejection	More	Less
8	Space required	More	Less
9	Material Handling	More	Less

(*continued*)

Table 2. Continued

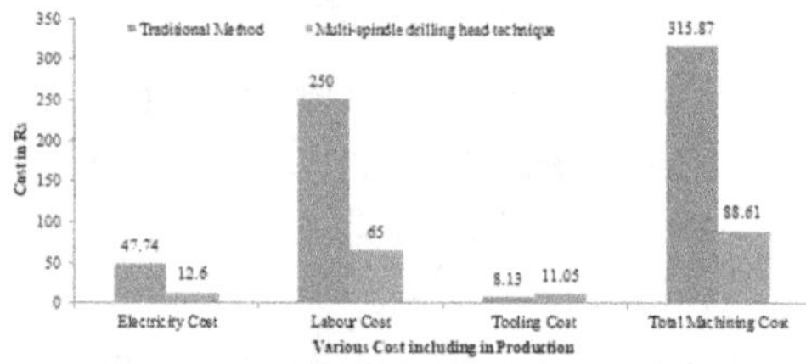

Figure 10. Daily electiticty cost, labour cost, tooling cost and total machining cost for traditional single spindle drilling machine and multi spindle drilling machine.

REFERENCES

[1] Jadhav P. and Agrawal N., A review on flow characteristics of the straight and coiled capillary tube, *International Journal of Air-Conditioning and Refrigeration*, Vol. 29, No. 3 (2021) 2130004

[2] Gillespie, L.K. (1976), *Effects of Drilling Variables on Burr Properties, Bendix Corporation, Unclassified Topical Report* BDX-613-1502.

[3] Stein, J.M. and Dornfeld, D.A. (1997), Burr Formation in Drilling Miniature Holes, *Annals of CIRP*, Vol. 46, No. 1, pp 63–67.

[4] Sofronas, A. (1976), The Effect of System Stiffness, Workpiece Hardness and Spindle Speed on Drilling Burr Thickness, *SME Technical Papers*, MR 75-132, Detroit, Ml

[5] Khurmi R.S. and Gupta J.K., (2002), *A Textbook of Machine Design, Eurasia Publishing House*, New Delhi, India

[6] Bhandari V.B., (2018), *Design of Machine Elements* Tata McGraw Hill publication, Third Edition

[7] Martand Telsang, Industrial Engineering and Production Management, S.chand 1 December 2006

[8] Jadhav P. and Ekbote N., (2021), Implementation of lean techniques in the packaging machine to optimize the cycle time of the machine, *Materials:Proceeding*, Vol.46, Part 20,10275–10281

[9] Jadhav P., Patil S., Ingawale S. and Aljapurkar A.A. (2021), Improvement of Overall equipment effectiveness for manufacturing of ductile Iron Casting, *International Journal of productivity and quality Mangement* DOI: 10.1504/IJPQM.2022.10046624

[10] Udgave A.S. and Prof. Khot V.J., *Design & development of multi spindle drilling head (msdh)*, IOSR-JMCE; PP: 60–69

[11] Yerriswamy M., Sreenivasulu B. and Ramachandra R., (2016), Modelling and Analysis of Friction Drilling Process Using RSM, *International Journal of Engineering Science and Computing*. IJESC

[12] Potdar, A., and Sapkal, S. (2020). Optimization of Friction Drilling Process by Response Surface Methodology. *In Advanced Engineering Optimization through Intelligent Techniques* (pp. 351–359). Springer, Singapore

[13] Jadhav P. and Agrawal N., (2020), Choked Flow Behavior of CO_2 Refrigerant Flowing Through the Spiral Capillary Tube, *International Journal of Air-Conditioning and Refrigeration* Vol. 28, No. 3 2050024

[14] Wei-Lian Ku, Ching-Lien Hung, Shin-Min Lee and Han-Ming Chow, (2011). Optimization in thermal friction drilling for SUS 304stainless steel, *International Journal Advanced Manufacturing Technology* 53: P. 935–944.

[15] Jadhav P. and Agrawal N., Flow behavior of spiral capillary tube for CO2 transcritical cycle, *Journal of Thermal Analysis and Calorimetry*, Vol. 141,pp.2177–2188

[16] Agrawal N., (2020). Choked Flow Behavior of CO2 Refrigerant Flowing Through the Spiral Capillary Tube, *International Journal of Air-Conditioning and Refrigeration*; 28(3), 2050024

[17] Pravin J., (2018), Study of homogenous two phase flow through helically coiled capillary tube, *Advanced Science, Engineering and Medicine*; 10(3–4),513–517.

NOMENCLATURE

P	Power, HP, kW	Sb	Induced stress
K	Material Factor	b	Face width
D	Diameter mm	S	Feed rate, mm/rev
N	Speed, rpm	α	Profile angle
M	Momentum, Nm	C	Precision cut error
m	Module, m	Subscript	
T	No. of Teeth	s	Sun Gear
P	Tooth pitch	L	Idler Gear
S	Stress N/m2	B	Drill Gear
Vf	Velocity Factor	T	Torque
V	Velocity	eff	Transmitted load
Sw	Endurance Stress	d	Dynamic Load

Advancement in Engineering and Science – Goyal et al. (Eds)
© 2026 The Author(s), ISBN: 978-1-041-31101-0

Revolutionizing Auscultation: Introducing a Digital Cardio Scope for Enhanced Diagnostic Capabilities

Sachin S. Gurav and Pravinkumar Patil
Associate Professor, Electronics and Computer Engineering, Sharad Institute of Technology, College of Engineering, Yadrav-Ichalkaranji, Maharashtra, India

Swati Halunde, Tayagar Diwakar, and RohitSantiur
Assistant Professor, Electronics and Computer Engineering, Sharad Institute of Technology, College of Engineering, Yadrav-Ichalkaranji, Maharashtra, India

ABSTRACT: The stethoscope an iconic symbol of the medical profession has remained largely unchanged for centuries, yet continues to be an essential tool for physicians across all specialties, from general practitioners to cardiologists. Despite its long-standing reliability, the traditional stethoscope has limitations, including the inability to amplify faint heart sounds, record data, or share auscultators findings for further analysis. With advancements in medical technology, the field of auscultation has enter edanewera through the development of the Digital Cardioscope. This innovative device enables health care professionals to listen to internal body sounds with enhanced clarity, free from the physical limitations of conventional stethoscopes. The proposed system is designed for both hospital use and telemedicine, leveraging an Internet of Things (IoT) framework and cloud computing. The Digital Cardioscope integrates key components such as pulse oximetry, amicrophone, and LoRa (LongRange) wireless Communication technology. It captures heart sound signals, stores them on smart devices, and uploads them securely to a cloud server. A LoRa transceiver facilitates the transmission of this data to a Human-Machine Interface (HMI), allowing physicians and patients to monitor and assess health conditions remotely in real time. This technology provides a novel and efficient approach to remote diagnostics, enhancing accessibility, accuracy, and continuity of care across diverse medical settings.

Keywords: cardioscope, auscultation, LoRa, heart

1 INTRODUCTION

Cardiac health remains a significant concern across all age groups, and heart sounds serve as key indicators in diagnosing various cardiovascular conditions. Traditionally, medical professionals have relied on the stethoscope, a fundamental diagnostic tool used to listen to internal body sounds—a process known as auscultation. Despite its widespread use, conventional auscultation is inherently subjective, often yielding inconsistent or imprecise results due to variations in the practitioner's hearing ability and clinical experience.

While many diagnostic instruments have evolved with advancements in electronics—integrating sensors, microcontrollers, and compact digital components—many clinicians still depend on the traditional acoustic stethoscope, device whose core design has remained largely unchanged for over a century.

The emergence of the next-generation Digital Cardioscope introduces a transformative shift in auscultation technology. This innovative device incorporates Internet of Things (IoT) features and cloud computing, makings particularly well-suited for both hospital environments and telemedicine applications. It not only captures heart sounds with High precision but also measures oxygen saturation, body temperature, and heart rate, offering a virtual health check-up accessible directly at the user's fingertips.

The system employs a smart software interface, a LoRa transceiver, and Wi-Fi connectivity to transmit real-time heart sound data. The information is securely stored in the cloud, where it can be visualized on a Human-Machine Interface (HMI), enabling both doctors and patients to monitor health status from any location at any time.

This paper presents the design and implementation of a Digital Cardio scope with the following core objectives:

- Conversion of auscultation sounds into analog electrical signals and subsequently into digital signals.
- Measurement of oxygen levels, body temperature, and heart rate.
- Storage of heart sound recordings in audio file format.
- Wireless transmission of clinical data to an external device Android application using cloud services and Wi-Fi.
- Visualization of real-time clinical data on a display Human-Machine Interface (HMI).

2 LITERATURE REVIEW

S.S. Joshi *et al.* (2021), in their paper titled "Bluetooth-based Wireless Digital Stethoscope" presented at the International Conference on Emerging Smart Computing and Informatics (ESCI), proposed a Bluetooth- Enabled wireless digital stethoscope. Their design focuses on enabling remote auscultation by allowing users to record and transmit heart sound data, thereby minimizing the need for physical visits to clinics or hospitals.

Similarly, J. Malwade *et al.* (2020), in their stethoscope integrated work "Wireless Stethoscope with Bluetooth Technology" presented at the International Conference on Computational Performance Evaluation (ComPE), explored the integration of Bluetooth technology in stethoscopes. Their objective was to enhance auscultation by transmitting body sounds wirelessly, thereby supporting efficient and remote diagnosis. In this In this paper, we present the development of a wireless system with Bluetooth technology. The system is designed to transmit heart sounds wirelessly to a Bluetooth receiver, allowing multiple users to access the transmitted sounds through earpieces. This setup can be particularly beneficial in educational environments, enabling medical students to simultaneously listen to cardiac sounds via a wireless network.

DOI: 10.1201/9781003798514-23

Several previous works have explored similar concepts. For instance, a 2018 study focused on the design and implementation of a digital stethoscope using mobile devices and wireless communication. The aim was to create an intelligent digital stethoscope leveraging modern electronic and computational technologies to enhance cardiac auscultation, employing Arduino and Bluetooth modules.

Similarly, research conducted by S.N. Nur Hidayah Malek, W. Suhaimizan Wan Zaki, A. Joret, and M. Mahadi Abdul Jamil titled "Design and Development of Wireless Stethoscope with Data Logging Function"(IEEE International Conference Control. System, Computing and Engineering, 2013) described the development of a system that wirelessly monitors and displays heartbeat sounds. This project utilized an Arduino platform combined with Zigbee Pro Series 1 antennas to transmit heart signals and visualize real-time electrocardiograms (ECG) using MATLAB's Graphical User Interface.

3 METHODOLOGY

3.1 *Block diagram*

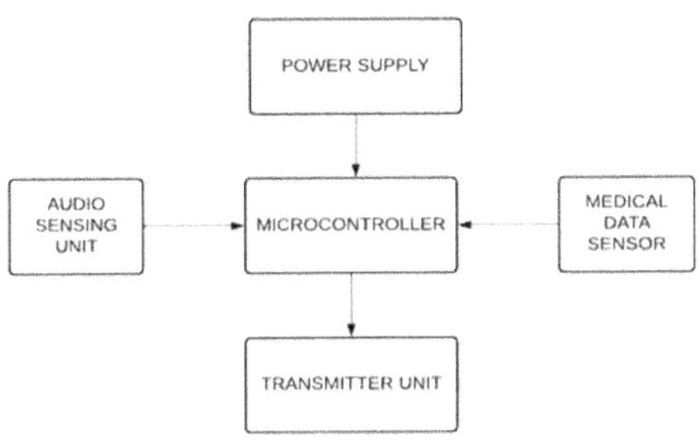

Figure 1. Transmitter side.

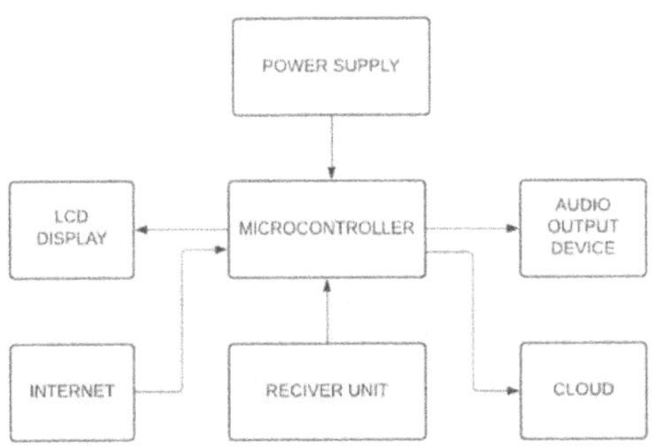

Figure 2. Receiver side.

3.2 *Working principle*

The next-generation stethoscope combines Internet of Things (IoT) technologies and cloud computing to create a smart, portable health monitoring tool ideal for hospitals and telemedicine applications. It captures heart sound measures oxygen levels, body temperature and provide a cardiograph, virtual health checkup at the user's fingertips. The device uses a smart software application, a cloud server and a LoRa transceiver to transmit heart sound signals via Wifi and display it on HMI. The data is securely uploaded to the cloud, allowing doctors to diagnose and for users to monitor their health anytime, anywhere a general understanding of the working principles based on the components is mentioned below:

Digital Cardio scope: The stethoscope uses DSP techniques to accurately capture and analyze cardiac sounds. The analog signals from the stethoscope are digitized for advanced signal processing. High-precision microphones and sensors are integrated to capture mechanical vibrations (heart sounds) and convert them into electrical signals for further analysis. Once digitized, heart sound data is transmitted wirelessly using long-range communication technologies like LoRa, optimized for low power consumption and long-distance data transmission.

Leveraging LoRa: Wireless Communication: LoRa is known for its ability to provide long-range communication with low power consumption. In the context of a Digital Cardio-scope, LoRa is used to wirelessly transmit the digitalized heart sounds data to a central monitoring or processing unit. Remote Monitoring: The use of LoRa allowed remote monitoring of patients. The digitalized heart sounds are transmitted wirelessly to a central server or a healthcare provider, enabling real time monitoring without the need for physical presence. Low Power Consumption: LoRa's low power characteristics are beneficial for battery operated devices like medical instruments. It allows for extended battery life, making the device suitable for continuous monitoring over extended periods.

Redesigning and Revolutionizing Auscultation Therapy: Enhanced Data Analysis: The digital nature of the device combined with long-range transmission allows comprehensive and accurate data analysis. Telemedicine Integration: The combination of digital technology and LoRa enables effective integration with telemedicine platforms. Healthcare professionals can remotely access and analyze the auscultation data, providing timely interventions and reducing the need for in person visits. Improved Patient Experience: There design can focus on improving the overall patient experience. Wireless connectivity and remote monitoring can enhance patient comfort, as they may not need to be physically present in a healthcare facility for routine auscultation check-ups.

4 MODELING AND ANALYSIS

Figure 3. Diaphragm internal structure.

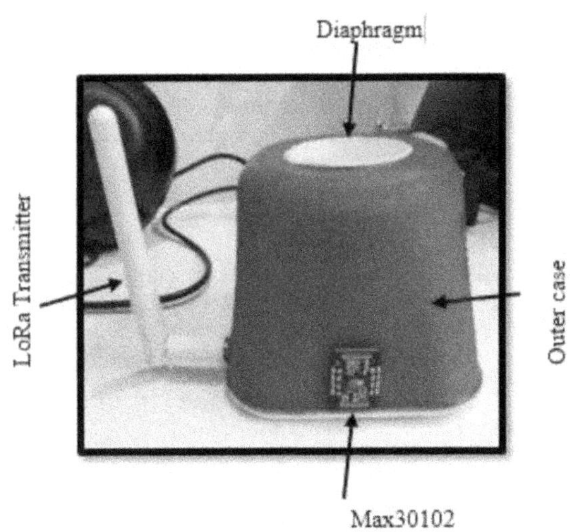

Figure 4. Chest Piese (transitter side).

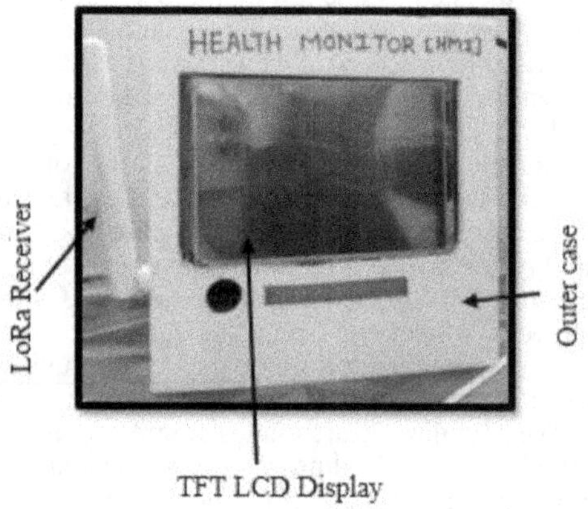

Figure 5. Display (receiver side).

5 IMPLEMENTATION PLAN

5.1 *Phase 1: Research and development*

To conduct extensive research to refine the design and functionalities of the smart stethoscope, ensuring optimal performance and user experience.

5.2 *Phase 2: Proto typing and testing*

Develop functional prototypes and conduct rigorous testing with healthcare professionals to validate the device's effectiveness and reliability.

5.3 *Phase 3: Deployment and feedback*

Pilot the device in selected healthcare settings to gather real-world data and feedback, optimizing performance and addressing potential issues.

5.4 *Phase 4: Commercialization and expansion*

Based on positive feedback and results, scale up production and distribution, ensuring accessibility to healthcare professionals worldwide.

6 APPLICATIONS

The integration of a Digital Cardio-scope leveraging LoRa for auscultation therapy opens various applications in healthcare, offering benefits in terms of remote monitoring, timely interventions, and enhanced patient care. Here are some potential applications for such a device:

6.1 *Remote patient monitoring*

Patients with cardiovascular conditions can use the Digital Cardio-scope at home, allowing healthcare providers to remotely monitor their heart sounds. This can be especially valuable for chronic conditions where regular auscultation is necessary.

6.2 *Telemedicine and virtual consultations*

Facilitate virtual consultations where healthcare professionals can listen to patients' heart sounds remotely in real-time. This reduces the need for patients to travel to healthcare facilities for routine check-ups.

6.3 *Home healthcare services*

Enable home healthcare services by providing patients with a user-friendly Digital Cardio-scope. This is particularly beneficial for elderly or immobile patients who may find it challenging to visit healthcare facilities regularly.

6.4 *Continuous monitoring in hospital*

Improve in-hospital monitoring by using Digital Cardio-scopes with LoRa connectivity. This allows healthcare professionals to continuously monitor patients' heart sounds without the need for frequent bedside visits.

6.5 *Long-term health management*

For patients with long-term cardiovascular conditions, the Digital Cardio-scope can play a crucial role in managing their health. Regular monitoring can help identify trends or changes in heart sounds, prompting early intervention and preventing complications.

6.6 *Education and training*

The device can be used in medical education for training healthcare professionals in auscultation skills. Digital recordings can be shared for educational purposes, and students can receive feedback remotely.

6.7 *Clinical research and data collection*

The device can be used in clinical trials and research studies to collect large-scale, real-world data on heart sounds. This can contribute to the development of new diagnostic algorithms and treatment approaches.

7 RESULT AND DISCUSSIONS

Figure 6. Actual implementation.

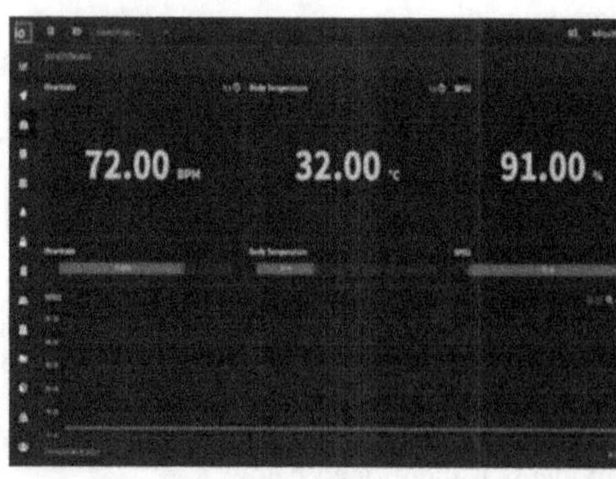

Figure 7. Thinger.io (IoT dashboard).

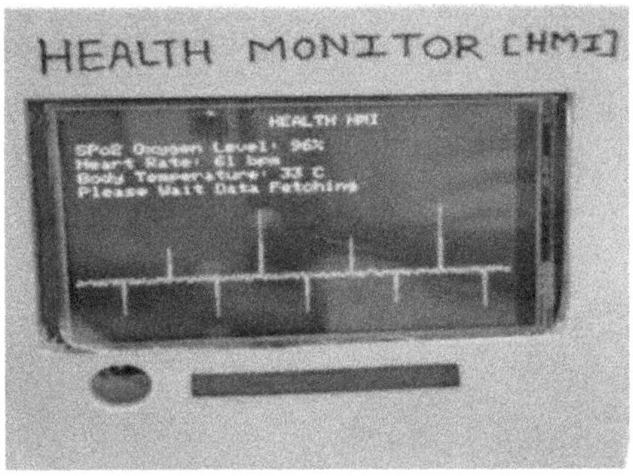

Figure 8. Health monitor (TFT display).

8 COMMERCIAL VIABILITY

The potential for commercial success of a Digital Cardio scope utilizing LoRa technology for auscultation hinges on several critical factors, including market demand, competition, regulatory compliance, and the device's capability to meet real-world healthcare challenges. Below are the primary considerations when evaluating its commercial prospects:

8.1 *Market demand*

Assess the need for remote health monitoring solutions, with a special focus on cardiac care. Key factors include the rising incidence of cardiovascular diseases, the increasing elderly population, and the expanding acceptance and demand for telemedicine services.

8.2 *Partnerships with healthcare providers*

Building strong collaborations with hospitals, clinics, and telehealth platforms can facilitate quicker adoption. Partnering with healthcare professionals ensures the device is tailored to meet clinical requirements and enhances its credibility.

8.3 *User adoption and acceptance*

Understand the willingness of patients and healthcare professionals to adopt and use the Digital Cardio-scope. User friendly design, ease of integration into existing workflows, and clear benefits over traditional methods can contribute to higher adoption rates.

9 CONCLUSION

The project introduces the Digital Cardioscope, an innovative medical device designed to address limitations in traditional stethoscopes, particularly in amplifying faint sounds and sharing data. Equipped with advanced digital sensors, IoT integration, and LoRa technology, it enables real-time remote heart monitoring and data sharing, facilitating enhanced patient care. By capturing precise body sounds, providing pulse oximetry, and ensuring interoperability with health records, the Digital Cardioscope revolutionizes auscultation, making diagnostics more accurate, accessible, and efficient. This advancement promises significant impact in both clinical settings and telemedicine.

REFERENCES

CDAC *Digital Electronic Stethoscope* (www.cdac.in).

Derek Kweku Degbedzui, Michael Tetteh, Elsie Effah Kaufmann and Godfrey A. Mills, (2018), Bluetooth – Based Wireless Digital Stethoscope with Mobile Integration, *World Scientific, Biomedical Engineering: Applications, Basis and Communications*, vol.30, No.3, DOI.10.4015/S1016237218500102).

Godfrey Mills, Thomas Nketia, Isaac Oppong and Elsie Kaufmann, (December 2012), Wireless Digital Stethoscope Using Bluetooth Technology, *International Journal of Engineering Science and Technology*.

Heartsounds mp3 samples at https://teachingheartauscultation.com/heart-sounds-mp3-downloads

Ms. Kadam Patil D. D. and Mr. Shastri R.K., (2012), Design of Wireless Electronic Stethoscope Based on Zigbee, *International Journal of Distributed and Parallel Systems (IJDPS)*.

Nur Hidayah Malek S., Suhaimizan WanZaki W., Joret A. and Mahadi Abdul Jamil M., (2013), Design and Development of Wireless Stethoscope with Data Logging Function, *IEEE International Conference on Control System, Computing and Engineering*.

Szot, S., Levin, A., Ragazzi, A. and Ning, T, (2018), A Wireless Digital Stethoscope Design, *14th IEEE International Conference on Signal Processing proceedings (ICSP)*.

Todd R. Reed, Nancy E. Reed, Peter Fritzson, (2003), Heart sound analysis for symptom detection and computer-aided diagnosis, T.R. Reed *et al./Simulation Modelling Practice and Theory* 12.

Yu-Jin Lin, Chen-Wei Chuang, *et al.*, (2019), An Intelligent Stethoscope with ECG and Heart Sound Synchronous Display, *IEEE International Symposium on Circuits and Systems (ISCAS)*.

Advancement in Engineering and Science – Goyal et al. (Eds)
© 2026 The Author(s), ISBN: 978-1-041-31101-0

Leveraging CNC Technology for Precision Ocular Metrology

Niranjan Deshmukh
Mechanical Engineering Department, Bharati Vidyapeeth's Jawaharlal Nehru Institute of Technology, Pune, India

Amol Todkar
Mechanical Engineering Department, TKIET, Warna University, Warnanagar, India

Ramesh Murthy
Medical Direcitor, Axis Eye Clinic Pune, India

Eknath Salunke
Direcitor, Speciality Eye Care Group, Pune, India

ABSTRACT: In order to cure irreparable serious eye trauma, control incurable eye infections, or relieve excruciating pain in a non-seeing eye, evisceration—the removal of a damaged eye's internal contents while keeping the sclera intact—is required. This procedure improves comfort and prevents more issues [1]. To be able to maintain the structural integrity and health of the eye socket, support eyelid function, improve the patient's general quality of life and psychological health, and deliver the best possible cosmetic result, an ocular prosthesis is necessary following evisceration. After evisceration, precise eye socket measurement is essential for a comfortable and well-fitting ocular prosthesis. Precise measurements guarantee the best possible cosmetic look by balancing the size and shape of the surviving eye to maintain face symmetry. In addition to reducing slippage or discomfort, precise measurements carried out by a CNC will help ensure that the prosthesis is properly retained and stable in the socket. Additionally, a correct-sized prosthesis backed by precise orbital data helps to preserve normal eyelid mobility and function, lowering the possibility of dryness or irritation. In the end, accurate measuring is the cornerstone of a good prosthetic result, which improves the patient's comfort, self-esteem, and general quality of life by giving them a functional and natural-looking artificial eye [2,3].

Keywords: CNC, Evisceration, Ocular prosthesis, Precise measurements

1 INTRODUCTION

A common entry-level desktop CNC milling machine, the CNC Router GRBL-3018 is renowned for being inexpensive and simple to use, especially for novices and enthusiasts. As the name "3018" suggests, it usually has a working surface of roughly 300 x 180 x 45 mm. This machine can cut, engrave, and carve a variety of soft materials, including wood, acrylic, plastics, and soft metals like aluminum, using the open-source GRBL firmware to operate its three axes of movement (X, Y, and Z). Usually, a USB connection to a computer running software that communicates with the GRBL controller board via G-code commands is used to control it. GRBL-3018 is a flexible tool for understanding CNC concepts and developing small-scale applications. The engraving laser tool, which comes as standard accessory is replaced by the distance sensor specially developed for the purpose of converting this CNC milling machine into a precision ocular socket measurement. The eviscerated ocular socket is measured within a range of distance from 15-20 mm. The data is collected in matrix form of 30 x 30. This data is further processed using Chaikin's algorithm to eliminate cusps. The refined data is converted to G-code for 3D printing of ocular prosthetic. Figure 1 shows system overview block diagram.

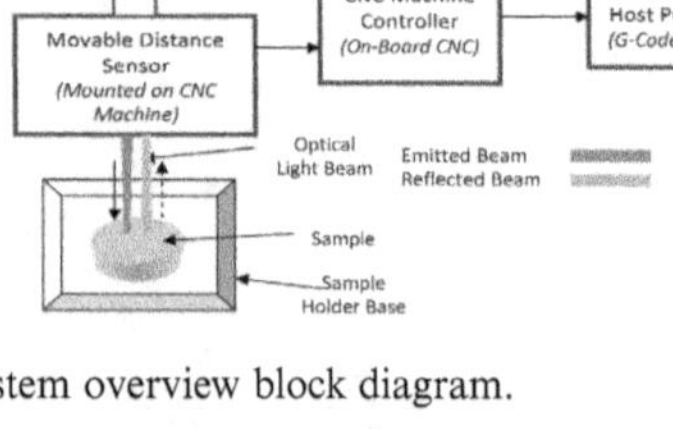

Figure 1. System overview block diagram.

2 DETAILS OF THE MOVABLE DISTANCE SENSOR

This distance sensor is based on optoelectronics where a IR light source in the form of a Light Emitting Diode emits light. This light is reflected back from the eviscerated socket under this sensor. This reflected light is sensed or detected by a photodiode that converts the light intensity into electrical signal. Since this signal is very small in magnitude of the order of a few hundred microamperes (μA), it is first amplified by a suitable signal conditioning amplifier, a Photo-Diode Amplifier. It converts this tiny current signal from the photodiode into a voltage output. This again being a small voltage, is further amplified by another amplifier stage so that it can be measured by a suitable measuring instrument such as a voltmeter or can be read digitally by a suitable controller system. The Figure 2 illustrates the functional block diagram of this optical distance sensor.

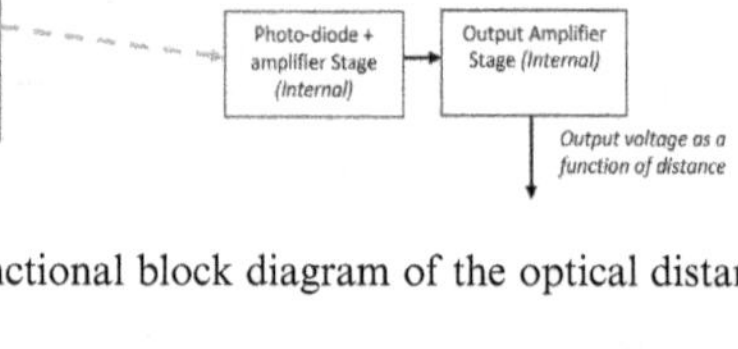

Figure 2. Functional block diagram of the optical distance sensor.

The output voltage from this sensor is calibrated as the output voltage as a function of the distance measured. The output response of this sensor is shown in the Figure 3. Corresponding measurement vales are given in Table 1. This test was carried

DOI: 10.1201/9781003798514-24

out during the initial testing and development of this optical distance sensor stage.

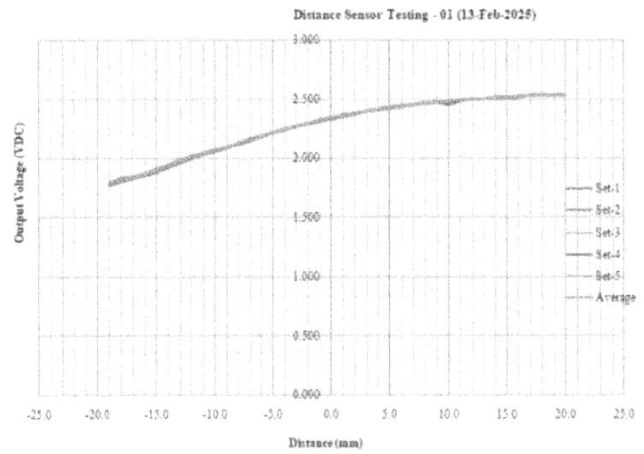

Figure 3. Output voltage of the distance sensor as a function of the object distance.

Table 1. Sensor output observed as a function of distance.

Distance (mm)	Set-1	Set-2	Set-3	Set-4	Set-5	Average
20	2.532	2.537	2.533	2.54	2.54	2.536
19	2.532	2.535	2.534	2.535	2.535	2.534
18	2.532	2.535	2.533	2.536	2.535	2.534
17	2.525	2.535	2.534	2.535	2.535	2.533
16	2.515	2.519	2.519	2.524	2.528	2.521
15	2.516	2.519	2.517	2.518	2.519	2.518
14	2.51	2.518	2.517	2.519	2.519	2.517
13	2.499	2.501	2.5	2.504	2.504	2.502
12	2.499	2.501	2.501	2.502	2.501	2.501
11	2.487	2.485	2.494	2.498	2.495	2.492
10	2.482	2.454	2.484	2.485	2.485	2.478
9	2.465	2.47	2.47	2.477	2.475	2.471
8	2.457	2.467	2.467	2.468	2.468	2.465
7	2.448	2.45	2.45	2.452	2.451	2.45
6	2.431	2.432	2.434	2.45	2.442	2.438
5	2.415	2.43	2.43	2.433	2.433	2.428
4	2.404	2.415	2.415	2.415	2.416	2.413
3	2.395	2.398	2.398	2.398	2.4	2.398
2	2.365	2.38	2.379	2.38	2.383	2.377
1	2.347	2.363	2.362	2.363	2.364	2.36
0	2.327	2.345	2.344	2.344	2.347	2.341
−1	2.309	2.309	2.32	2.325	2.328	2.318
−2	2.291	2.29	2.29	2.29	2.291	2.29
−3	2.27	2.272	2.272	2.272	2.272	2.272
−4	2.234	2.236	2.238	2.246	2.25	2.241
−5	2.212	2.218	2.218	2.217	2.219	2.217
-6	2.18	2.182	2.183	2.181	2.19	2.183
−7	2.145	2.163	2.164	2.163	2.165	2.16
−8	2.112	2.129	2.128	2.127	2.129	2.125
−9	2.092	2.092	2.093	2.092	2.093	2.092
−10	2.057	2.057	2.057	2.06	2.075	2.061
−11	2.033	2.035	2.036	2.038	2.045	2.037
−12	1.996	2.004	2.011	2.011	2.019	2.008
−13	1.959	1.977	1.975	1.976	1.983	1.974
−14	1.919	1.94	1.939	1.939	1.945	1.936
−15	1.882	1.903	1.902	1.903	1.909	1.9
−16	1.852	1.866	1.865	1.865	1.872	1.864
−17	1.846	1.829	1.828	1.834	1.844	1.836
−18	1.83	1.808	1.807	1.809	1.817	1.814
−19	1.79	1.774	1.773	1.773	1.78	1.778

A reference height of 30 mm was selected to carry out experiment. The distance of the sensor from the object is varied in Z direction initially upwards (positive) and for the second half in downwards direction (negative). The initial sensor distance measurement exercise was carried out in a set of five (05) observational sets and an average of these readings was calculated. The plot in the Figure 3 shows that the average value and all the five readings are closely matched and show a good linearity of the sensor over the range of 15-20 mm of sensing distance.

3 THE STAND-ALONE CONTROLLER SYSTEM

As shown in the block schematic of the system in the Figure 1, the CNC machine has its on-board controller that accepts the G-Code for the control of the CNC machine from the host PC using the USB communication. This controller only accepts G-Codes from the GUI User Interface software running on personal computer such as Candle-soft. This general purpose and freeware software is designed to accept a CNC numeric control (NC) programs that host a series of G-Codes and a long program is "Run" from this GUI to the CNC machine. In other words, the CNC machine is under total control of this interface software.

In the present application, it is intended that the CNC machine scans the object distance in step-by-step manner where the sensor (head) is positioned at one X-Y location and then the value or output from the distance sensor is read. After first reading the head moves to next X-Y coordinate and the distance sensor is read again. This procedure is continued for an area of 30mm x 30mm with 1mm step/interval.

In order to achieve the control of the CNC machine in above stated fashion, a stand-alone controller is developed for this machine. This also eliminates the need for a personal computer and the standard software GUI such as Candle-soft. This particular controller issues the commands to the CNC controller on-board the CNC machine to position the head at the stipulated X-Y coordinates, then reads the distance sensor and relays this information to the host-PC where the distance of the object can be recorded as a function of the X-Y coordinates.

4 DETAILS OF THE STAND-ALONE CONTROLLER

The Figure 4 illustrates the block diagram of the stand-alone controller and its scheme in the present modification.

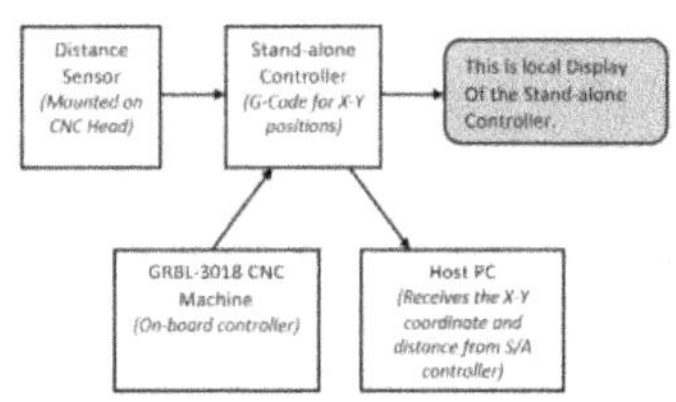

Figure 4. Block diagram of the stand-alone controller and its scheme.

4.1 *The stand-alone controller*

This controller is based on electronics hardware that uses a microcomputer chip which is similar to a full-functional computer but with minimal resources such as program memory, data memory and control and communication ports. It performs the actual task of initializing the communication with the CNC machine and then sends the G-Code commands to the CNC machine to position it at specified X-Y coordinates. Once the machine is placed at one position, it then reads the output from the distance sensor.

4.2 *The local user interface*

The present stand-alone controller has a simple user interface in the form of a few buttons (keypad) and a small alpha-numeric display. The keypad is a set of push-button keys that are used to "START" the distance measuring operation or "STOP" it. The local display is a small alpha-numeric display used to indicate the status of the controller and the X, Y coordinates and measured distance while the operation in progress.

4.3 *Communication with the distance sensor*

The distance sensor is an optical distance sensor that gives out an electrical signal in the form of voltage as a function of the distance. The stand-alone controller reads this analog voltage from the distance sensor and converts this value into digital value and shows the actual measured distance both on the local display and communicated to the host PC.

4.4 *Communication with the CNC-3018 machine*

The GRBL-3018 CNC machine only accepts G-Code and M-Code commands from the host controller such as PC or the present stand-alone controller. It uses USB communication with 115.2kbps baud rate. The controller issues the G-Codes to position the CNC head to specified locations using this communication protocol.

4.5 *Communication with the host PC*

The stand-alone controller controls the CNC machine and positions it to sequential X-Y locations and in between it reads the distance measured by the optical distance sensor. The stand-alone controller then relays or communicates the individual X and Y positions and the distance read to the host PC over USB communication so that the data can be saved on PC using suitable communication or Terminal Program running on host-PC.

5 PROCESSING THE DATA

The data obtained from Proposed Matrix Method undergoes a series of processing steps to ensure high accuracy, smoothness, and readiness for 3D modelling and prosthetic fabrication. Raw data collected from scanning consists of a point cloud dataset, where each point represents x, y, and z coordinates of the ocular cavity surface. However, raw data often contains noise, redundant points, and minor errors due to ambient light reflections, sensor imitations, or micro-movements during scanning. Adaptive Thresholding is used to discard low-confidence data points, ensuring only high-fidelity scans are retained. Multiple are aligned using Iterative Closest Point (ICP) algorithms to ensure a consistent 3D structure. Measurements are converted into a standardized coordinate system, ensuring accurate representation regardless of scanning variations. Surface smoothing is carried out using Chaikin Algorithm. B-Spline Curves, Cubic Spline Interpolation, NURBS (Non-Uniform Rational B-Splines) and Bézier Curves and Splines are some methods for curve smoothing. These other methods are also are useful in generating smooth curves from a set of control or data points. However, Chaikin's algorithm is unique in its iterative cusp-eliminating approach and hence was selected. It removes residual surface roughness while preserving anatomical contours. In this method from a list of points, for each pair of neighbouring points, two new points are created such that they are a fraction along the line segment between the two original points. For two neighbouring points, Pi and Pi+1, two new points Qi, which is 1/4 of the way, and Ri, which is 3/4 of the way are created. The process is carried out for all 30x30 points, in both X and Y directions. A sample of curve smoothing is presented in Figure 5. The sample curve is formed by connecting the data points with straight lines as shown in in 'Iteration 0'. The Chaikin's algorithm is applied for curve smoothing and 6 iterations are performed on the curve to obtain acceptable smooth curve. The sample presented here has a set of point values taken from random measurements on a dummy surface. A set of sensor output in refined coordinates is given in Table 2. Also applied Chaikin's algorithm is given with arguments.

Table 2. Refined coordinates.

X	Y	Z
115.382	111.817	0.09073
116.247	111.251	0.13766
117.253	110.86	0.18666
117.864	110.759	0.21478
118.38	10.584	0.23951
119.816	110.264	0.30631
121.751	110.232	0.39417
123.272	110.523	0.46448
124.438	111.158	0.52475
125.444	112.004	0.58443
126.374	113.351	0.65874
126.774	114.699	0.72258
126.847	115.825	0.77381
126.714	116.924	0.82407
126.215	118.198	0.88618
125.482	119.266	0.94499
124.048	120.438	1.02907
121.902	121.524	1.13827
120.593	121.738	1.19848
119.429	121.986	1.25252
118.213	121.983	1.30772
116.602	121.689	1.38207
115.098	120.996	1.45725
114.063	120.011	1.52212

6 CHAIKIN'S ALGORITHM USED FOR REFINING THE POINTS

```
import numpy as np
  import matplotlib.pyplot as plt
  def chaikin_algorithm(points, iterations):
  """
  Applies Chaikin's algorithm to a set of points.
  Args:
  points: A NumPy array of shape (n, 2) representing the points.
  iterations: The number of iterations to apply the algorithm.
  Returns:
  A NumPy array of shape (m, 2) representing the refined points.
  """
  refined_points = points.copy()
  for _ in range(iterations):
  new_points = []
  for i in range(len(refined_points) - 1):
  p1 = refined_points[i]
  p2 = refined_points[i+1]
  q = 0.75 * p1 + 0.25 * p2 # 3/4 of the way
  r = 0.25 * p1 + 0.75 * p2 # 1/4 of the way
  new_points.append(p1) #keep the original point
  new_points.append(q)
  new_points.append(r)
  new_points.append(refined_points[-1]) # Add the last point
  refined_points = np.array(new_points)
  return refined_points
  # Create initial 30x30 grid of points
  x = np.linspace(0, 1, 30)
  y = np.linspace(0, 1, 30)
```

```
X, Y = np.meshgrid(x, y)
points = np.column_stack((X.flatten(), Y.flatten()))
# Apply Chaikin's algorithm (adjust iterations as needed)
num_iterations = 7
# Reshape back to grid for plotting if needed
num_refined_x = int(np.sqrt(len(refined_points)))
#approximation since we dont know the exact number after subdivision
refined_X = refined_points[:, 0].reshape(num_refined_x, num_refined_x)
refined_Y = refined_points[:, 1].reshape(num_refined_x, num_refined_x)
```

The result is shown in the Figure 5, for random sample points.

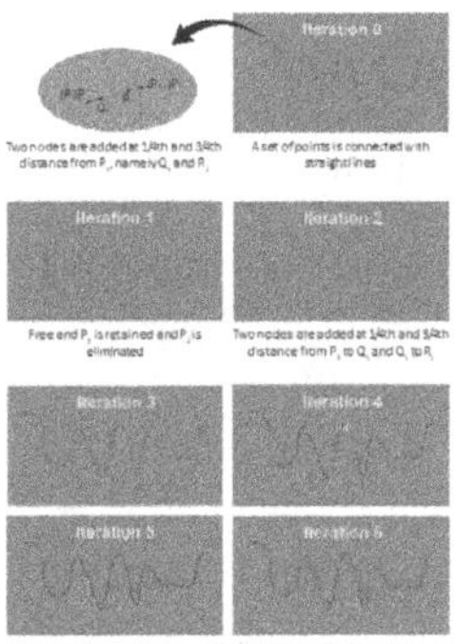

Figure 5. Chaikin's Algorithm applied to random sample points.

7 GENERATING G-CODE FOR 3D PRINTING

A refined data is created after applying Chaikin's algorithm. This data (first 24 lines only) is shown in Table 2. The table is converted into G-code. A part of G-code is given as a sample below (Title of the project selected is EN3_1234.gcode):

```
;TIME:816
;Resin used: PMMA (SLA)
;Layer height: 0.2
;MINX:103.233
;MINY:110.232
;MINZ:0.2
;MAXX:131.772
;MAXY:124.57
;MAXZ:27.6
;TARGET_MACHINE.NAME:ELEGOO NEPTUNE 3
M140 S70
M105
M190 S70
M104 S210
M105
M109 S210
;ELEGOO NEPTUNE 3
;M413 S0;S0=Disable power-loss recovery:S1=Enable power-loss recovery
M220 S100 ;Set the feed speed to 100%
G90
G28 ;home
;M420 S1 Z10;Uncomment to enable progressive compensation height of 10mm
G92 E0 ;Reset Extruder
G1 Z0.6 F100
G1 X1.5 Y20 F5000.0 ;Move to start position
G1 Y120.0 F600.0 E20 ;Draw the first line
G1 X0.5 F1000.0 ;Move to side a little
G1 Y20 F600 E40 ;Draw the second line
G92 E0 ;Reset Extruder
M82 ;absolute extrusion mode
G92 E0
G92 E0
G1 F1500 E-5
;LAYER_COUNT:138
;LAYER:0
M107
M204 S500
G0 F4800 X113.915 Y113.171 Z0.2
;TYPE:SKIRT
G1 F1500 E0
G1 F1800 X114.727 Y112.36 E0.0521
G1 X115.382 Y111.817 E0.09073
G1 X116.247 Y111.251 E0.13766
G1 X125.444 Y112.004 E0.58443
G1 X126.374 Y113.351 E0.65874
G1 X126.774 Y114.699 E0.72258
G1 X126.847 Y115.825 E0.77381
G1 X126.714 Y116.924 E0.82407
G1 X126.215 Y118.198 E0.88618
G1 X125.482 Y119.266 E0.94499
```

8 ACTUAL SYSTEM AND MANUFACTURED PROSTHETIC

Trials were conducted using the developed measurement system and generated G-code. Photographs of the system, the STL (stereolithography) file, and the resulting prosthetic are presented in Figures 6, 7, and 8, respectively.

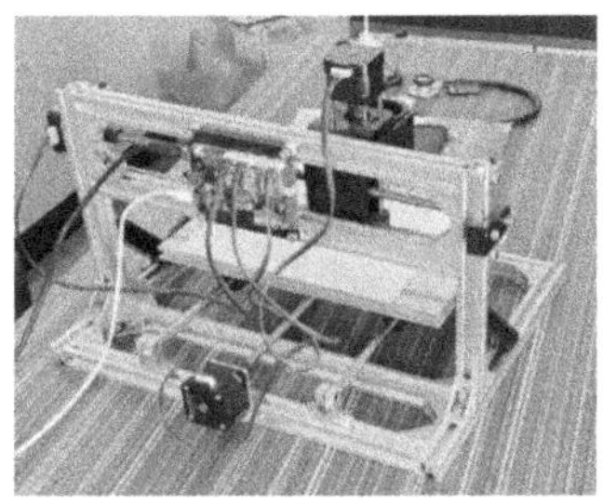

Figure 6. The measurement system.

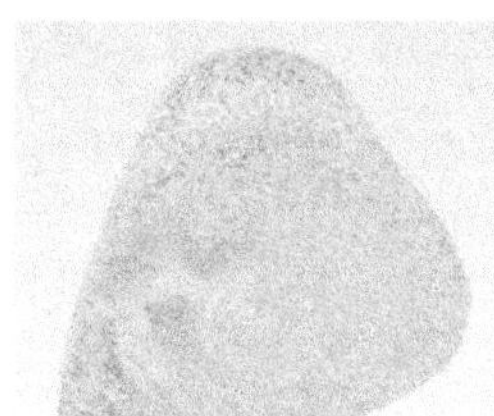

Figure 7. STL file showing prosthetic to be printed.

Figure 8. Actual 3D printed prosthetic.

9 CONCLUSION

In a nutshell by utilizing CNC technology, this paper effectively illustrates a revolutionary way to precision ocular metrology. To precisely gauge the eviscerated ocular socket, a specifically built distance sensor was added to a reasonably priced desktop CNC milling machine. Standard CNC interfacing software is replaced by the stand-alone controller, which enables automated data collecting. In order to refine the measurements, acquired raw data is subjected to critical processing processes such as adaptive thresholding, alignment, standardization, and surface smoothing using Chaikin's algorithm. Accurate 3D printing of personalized ocular prosthesis is made possible by the conversion of the exact and smoothed data into G-code. This novel approach has great potential to improve ocular prosthesis comfort, fit, and aesthetic results, thereby raising patients' quality of life.

REFERENCES

[1] Da Costa, G.C., Aras, M.A., Chalakkal, P., and Da Costa, M.C. (2017). Ocular prosthesis incorporating IPS e-max press scleral veneer and a literature review on non-integrated ocular prosthesis. *International Journal of Ophthalmology*. Available at: https://doi.org/10.18240/ijo.2017.01.24

[2] Deshmukh, N.S., Todkar, A.S., and Katakkar, H. (2023). Measurement of eviscerated Eye for Retinal Prosthesis—A new approach. *In: Lecture notes in mechanical engineering*. Singapore: Springer, pp. 541–549. Available at: https://doi.org/10.1007/978-981-99-1894-2_46

[3] George (2024). Genmitsu 3018 Pro Resources. *SainSmart Resource Center*. Available at: https://docs.sainsmart.com/article/3jgtgas880-genmitsu-3018-pro-resources

[4] Kovac, J., Peternai, L., and Lengyel, O. (2003). Advanced light emitting diodes structures for optoelectronic applications. *Thin Solid Films*, 433(1–2), pp. 22–26. Available at: https://doi.org/10.1016/s0040-6090(03)00314-6

[5] Phan LT, Hwang TN, and McCulley TJ (2012). Evisceration in the modern age. *Middle East Africa Journal of Ophthalmology*, 19(1), pp. 24–33. Available at: https://doi.org/10.4103/0974-9233.92113

Advancement in Engineering and Science – Goyal et al. (Eds)

Smart Contract-Driven E-Voting Using Ethereum

Anusha Jaiswal and Ankita Singh
Computer Science and Engineering, Shri Ramswaroop College of Engineering and Management, Lucknow, India

ABSTRACT: The fairness and openness of how we vote really shape whether our democracy works or falls apart. Voting schemes have evolved from counting hands in early days to systems that include paper, punch card and electronic voting machines. Traditional voting systems, whether paper-based or electronic, are vulnerable to security threats such as fraud, tampering, and lack of transparency. The currently used voting systems require some improvements in them because of the issues mentioned above. In this paper we are building a voting system using Ethereum blockchain that could make elections way more secure and trustworthy. By harnessing the decentralized and immutable characteristics of blockchain, the suggested system ensures votes are securely recorded and are tamper proof. Smart contracts dehumanize vote tallying and verification, while cryptographic techniques preserve the anonymity of voter and auditability. Here we discuss system architecture, implementation, and scalability, voter the limitations authentication, compatibility with existing systems. Results indicate that blockchain offers an achievable solution for secure and transparent e-voting, though further development is needed for real world applications.

Keywords: E-voting, Smart-contracts, Blockchain, Ethereum, Consensus algorithms, Electronic Voting, Voter Anonymity

1 INTRODUCTION

Blockchain technology is emerging as a likely provider to fix the problems we've been having with old-school paper voting and those outdated electronic voting machines (EVMs). These traditional systems often face issues like lack of transparency, low voter turnout, tampering, and delays in result processing. Blockchain, with its decentralization, immutability, and security, can enhance transparency and security in e-voting systems. The blockchain systems are formed as decentralized networked systems of computers, which are used for validating and recording the pure online transactions. It integrates cryptographic methods and consensus protocols to ensure secure, verifiable, and auditable voting procedures, offering a promising alternative to current voting practices. However, while key aspects like security and transparency are emphasized, aspects such as adaptability, efficiency, and accessibility need more attention in blockchain-based voting solutions. Issues like scalability and robust cryptographic mechanisms remain hurdles for broader implementation. The study suggests a requirement for further research and technological advancements to make blockchain based e-voting systems more practical and efficient.

2 LITERATURE SURVEY

Researchers have explored traditional electronic voting systems in great detail, focusing on usability, security, and scalability. However, significant vulnerabilities such as vote tampering, lack of transparency, and centralized control have raised concerns. Here we offer a comprehensive look on the previous research, highlighting the profits and losses of implementing blockchain in the electoral process. Few notable works are:

[1] McCorry *et al.* (2017) proposed a blockchain based electronic voting system called "Open Vote Network," which leverages the Ethereum blockchain. Their system makes sure that the votes are recorded anonymously while preserving transparency by using smart contracts to smoothly manage the voting process. The design mainly focuses on reducing vote manipulation.

[2] Chaer *et al.* (2018) dug into the usage of cryptographic methods in blockchain-based e-voting systems to keep people's votes private while still keeping everything transparent. An e-voting system utilizing a public blockchain combined with cryptographic methods like zero-knowledge proofs and homomorphic encryption to ensure voter anonymity while ensuring data integrity is proposed.

[3] Estonian E-voting system: Estonia has real world implementation in digital voting, and researchers have explored its efforts to embed blockchain technology into its e-voting system to further enhance safety and transparency (Horne 2019). By using blockchain, Estonia aimed to create a decentralized, tamper-proof record of votes, making the process more trustworthy.

[4] Zheng *et al.* (2020) created a privacy ensuring e-voting protocol using blockchain technology and ring signatures. With the help of protocol, users can cast votes anonymously, with the blockchain acting as a public ledger to verify the vote's authenticity without exposing the voter's identity. This work provided an efficient solution to the privacy issue in blockchain voting, ensuring both security and transparency.

[5] Hardwick *et al.* (2018) conducted a comparative study of different blockchain based voting models, emphasizing the balance between safety and efficiency. They explored the use of permissioned blockchains to enhance voter authentication and limit access to authorized participants, addressing concerns about public blockchains' scalability and security. Their study concluded that blockchain, when combined with proper access controls, could offer a secure and transparent voting platform.

[6] West Virginia pilot project (2018): In a pilot study, West Virginia employed a blockchain-based voting application for overseas military voters during the 2018 midterm elections. The application utilized blockchain and biometric authentication to securely record and store votes. Researchers like Crawford and Werner analyzed this project, discussing the benefits and limitations of blockchain voting in real-world elections, including security concerns and accessibility challenges.

3 IMPLEMENTATION USED

The different blockchain-based e-voting applications follow the same few simple steps. The e-voting system designed in this project is linear and modular in nature, encompassing all the important phases from the registration of the voters to the declaration of final results. Our implementation employs Ethereum smart contracts

DOI: 10.1201/9781003798514-25

written in Solidity and runs on a decentralized network to ensure transparency, security, and immutability of the voting process. The following is a detailed, step-by-step description of the implementation of all the phases in the system:

(A) **Registration (Phase 1):** The first step in the election process is to register yourself using your credentials and the public key of your Ethereum account. In this phase, the administrator of the election installs the smart contracts onto a local or test Ethereum network through development frameworks such as Truffle. These contracts record the election rules, such as eligible voter addresses and registered candidates, which are mapped using Ethereum addresses. The smart contract is immutable once deployed, ensuring that no unauthorized changes can be made after the deployment. Voter eligibility is usually established by linking unidentical Ethereum public keys with whitelisted addresses stored in the contract's state variables. Any later modifications, including addition of candidates or closing of registrations, must adhere with the logic predefined in the deployed contract.

(B) **Identification (Phase 2):** After registering themselves, the users need to authorize themselves so as to become eligible for the next phase. On the voting day, voters interact with the decentralized application with the help of a Web3-enabled browser extension such as MetaMask. The system relies on Ethereum's cryptographic model, where each voter goes through an identity verification process by digitally signing a transaction through their private key. The application looks for the signature against the associated Ethereum addresses using elliptic curve cryptography (ECC), particularly the secp256k1 curve, which is a standard in Ethereum. No passwords or third-party identity verifiers are required, reducing the risk of impersonation or phishing attacks.

(C) **Voting (Phase 3):** After being verified, eligible voters can cast their vote by invoking a specific function in the smart contract. To ensure that there is only one vote per address, the vote is stored in a mapping structure that associates each Ethereum address to a candidate ID. The function modifies the contract's internal state and emits events for transparency and traceability. To protect anonymity and integrity, the transaction is broadcast over the blockchain and added in the mempool until it is confirmed by consensus through miners or validators. The transaction data, including the selected candidate ID, is hashed using the Keccak 256 hash function prior to being stored on-chain, ensuring tamper-resistance.

(D) **Blockchain technology:** Blockchain serves as the foundational immutable ledger that guarantees vote integrity, transparency, and traceability. Each vote is stored as a transaction and after being validated by consensus, it is mined into a block, creating a chain of cryptographically connected blocks. The immutability is promised by the cryptographic linkage between blocks using Merkle trees and hash pointers. Inside each block, vote transactions are hashed and arranged using a Merkle tree, where the Merkle Root represents all votes in the block. Any modification in a single vote travel upward and alters the root, thereby invalidating the entire block. This prevents any tampering with the vote data after it has been stored. Furthermore, blockchain's decentralized nature removes the need for a central authority, diminishing risks associated with single points of failure or manipulation.

(E) **Ethereum Network and Tools:** Solidity, a Turing-complete language which is designed specifically for writing smart contracts, is used to build the voting system on top of the Ethereum Virtual Machine (EVM). Ganache is used for local blockchain simulation, and the Truffle Suite is used to manage the deployment and testing. Web3.js is integrated into the front end, allowing for the browser and Ethereum network to communicate with each other while MetaMask is used to provide the transaction signing and wallet management functionality. Each interaction made with the blockchain—whether it be casting a vote or viewing the results after the election is over—is treated as a transaction, requiring gas and digital signature authorization.

(F) **Counting (Phase 4):** Once the election period has finally ended, it is no longer possible to add or change votes. The vote counting process happens automatically through the use of smart contract, which uses internal mappings and counters to keep track of all the votes. The logic prevents anyone from voting twice and ensures accurate tallying. Real-time result visibility is restricted to keep things fair and prevent any voter influence. A special condition variable within the smart contract prevents premature access to vote counts until the election deadline has passed even for the admin.

(G) **Result (Phase 5):** Upon conclusion of the voting period, the smart contract grants open access to the audience of final vote tally ensuring transparency and openness of the election process. Results are displayed utilizing the front-end interface, pulling final data directly from the blockchain using Web3 calls. Because all the data is stored immutably on the blockchain, all voters can independently verify their participation by cross-checking transaction hashes associated with their public key. Even third-party auditors can transparently review the whole election history and verify the outcome, promoting public trust in the election process.

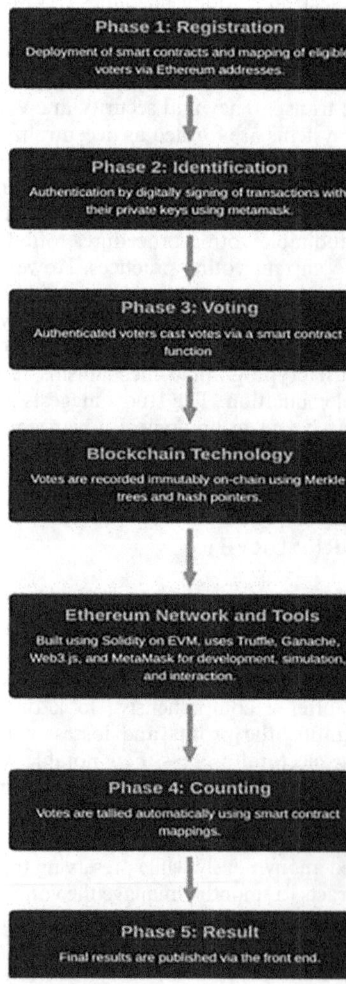

Figure 1. General operation of E-voting system.

4 RESULT DISCUSSION

The blockchain-based e-voting system effectively achieved vote security, immutability, and transparency through its use of smart contracts and decentralized ledgers. Cryptographic techniques successfully preserved voter anonymity while enabling a verifiable voting process. During small-scale trials, the system demonstrated high levels of usability and trustworthiness, as it was easily accessible and provided a transparent audit trail that could be verified by voters and auditors alike. However, as the scale of the election increased, challenges related to scalability became evident, particularly with transaction throughput and network performance. These limiting constraints indicate that additional optimizations are required, like the implementation of layer-2 solutions or off chain transactions, to enable the system to handle larger, more complex elections efficiently. Overall, the system seems to be significant promise for secure, transparent, and efficient voting, but future optimizations are necessary to make it suitable for large scale, real-world elections.

5 CONCLUSION

This report explores e-voting systems utilizing Blockchain in addition with smart contracts leveraging the consensus algorithm and asymmetric cryptography techniques. Our insights highlight that this online voting system is efficient in accurately recording the votes without compromising anonymity of users and preventing tampering and security threats.

This research illustrates that a blockchain based e-voting system can revolutionize the electoral procedure by enhancing reliability, transparency, and voter confidence. The decentralized and irreversible qualities of blockchain ensures that once votes are casted, they are secure from tampering or manipulation.

Cryptographic methods, for instance zero-knowledge proofs, safeguard voter privacy while reinforcing that the system remains fully auditable. Smart contracts streamline the voting process by automating tasks such as vote collection, verification, and tallying, reducing the probability of errors and the compulsion for manual oversight. Overall, this blockchain-based e-voting system presents a promising, reliable, and open alternative to traditional voting methods. While promising, further research is required to improve scalability, transaction throughput, and incorporation with existing electoral frameworks to confirm its readiness for broad and real-world implementation.

6 FUTURE SCOPE

The future of blockchain-based e-voting systems offers promising avenues for development. Enhancing scalability through layer-2 solutions like sidechains and off-chain transactions is critical to support large-scale elections. Seamless integration with existing electoral infrastructure, such as voter registration databases, will be necessary, achieved through standardized APIs. Advanced voter authentication methods, including biometric verification and blockchain-based IDs, can further strengthen system security and prevent fraud. Continued research into privacy-preserving cryptographic algorithms will help maintain voter anonymity, especially in large elections. Developing legal frameworks to ensure compliance with election laws is crucial for real-world adoption. Building public trust through user-friendly interfaces and voter education is also key to increasing accessibility and participation. As cyber threats evolve, sophisticated security mechanisms like quantum-resistant cryptography will be essential to uphold the security of the system. Large-scale pilot projects in collaboration with governments will validate the system in real-world settings, providing insights for refinement. These developments will ensure blockchain-based e-voting systems are reliable, encrypted and scalable, paving the way for widespread adoption in the future.

REFERENCES

[1] Borras, J., (2002), *Overview of the Work on E-Voting Technical Standards*; Cabinet Office, UK Government: London, UK.

[2] Engineering and Analytics; Springer Nature: Singapore; pp. 51–61.

[3] Kshetri, N. and Voas, J. (2018), Blockchain enabled e-voting. *IEEE Softw.* 35, 95–99

[4] Majumder, S. and Ray, S., (2022), Usage of Blockchain Technology in e-Voting System Using Private Blockchain. *In Intelligent Data*

[5] Prajapati, P.; Dave, K. and Shah, P. (2020), A survey of later blockchain applications. *Int. J. Sci. Technol. Res.* 9, 897–903.

[6] Steiu, M. (2020), Blockchain in education: Opportunities, applications, challenges. *First Monday* 25.

Advancement in Engineering and Science – Goyal et al. (Eds)
© 2026 The Author(s), ISBN: 978-1-041-31101-0

A Novel Product Development and Review of Technological Changes in Sanitation Structures

Patil Abhijeet
Head & Associate Professor, Department of Civil Engineering, D. Y. Patil Prathisthan's College of Engineering, Salokhenagar, Kolhapur, India

Gaurvadkar Rucha P., Vibhute Harshada V., Desai Rohit J., and Diwan Amey V.
Assistant Professor, Department of Civil Engineering, D. Y. Patil Prathisthan's College of Engineering, Salokhenagar, Kolhapur, India

Mane Bajirao V.
Associate Professor, Department of Civil Engineering, Annasaheb Dange College of Engineering, Ashta, India

ABSTRACT: This paper comprises of the latest review of technological development in rural sanitation system with respect to development of urinal and toilet. Currently, in many rural sectors, the toilet waste is directly mixed with water bodies. This contaminates the associated environmental things. The degradation of fecal matter is carried out using biological determinants. The bacterial infection through toilets, bad odour, and unscientific design of toilet pan are some of the major issues in today's era. Also, there is deficiency in effective collaboration of community for management of sanitation system. These limitations forces researcher to develop technology in sanitation system. The development of toilet pans, organic fertilizer made from human waste, the incorporation of artificial intelligence and the internet of things in sanitation systems, have all been explored. It has also been explored how the community should work with both government and non-government organizations to raise awareness about the use of sanitary facilities. There is a thorough discussion of the composting of fecal waste. The work done in the relevant field from the 1980s to the present is studied. Recent sanitation technologies have been discussed with respect to key factors. Significant technological advancements have been marked in the thorough literature survey conducted. It is suggested that technology development must be taken into account while developing sanitation structures in any locality. Use of Biochar, Perforated urinals, waterless urinals, urine diverting toilets, community let total sanitation, Mechanical Automatic Urinal Toilet Flusher, smart toilet system, collaborative robotics method are few new technologies that have been developed in recent years. Based upon the reviews, reform in the perspectives of possible modifications have been discussed. The concept of Eco toilet has been invented which operates on solar energy and reduces the waste. It is also termed as sensor operated solar based urine diverting toilet.

Keywords: Toilet, Urinal, Organic Fertilizer, Biochar, sanitation structure

1 INTRODUCTION

India is an agro-based country with approximately 64% of its population residing in rural areas. Following independence in 1947, the government encountered numerous developmental challenges such as ensuring access to water, improving agricultural productivity, expanding irrigation infrastructure, and initiating industrialization. As industrialization advanced and the population reached the present figure of 141 crores, issues like air pollution, water contamination, and the spread of communicable diseases became increasingly prevalent.

Until the 1970s, efforts by the government and scientific community were primarily directed toward controlling water and air pollution. However, critical issues in rural regions—such as communication infrastructure, literacy, sanitation, and solid waste management—remained largely neglected. Over the last three decades, increasing awareness among environmentalists and the general public has led to greater emphasis on improving rural sanitation, solid waste management, and healthcare systems.

Communicable diseases such as plague, SARS, and more recently, COVID-19, have posed serious threats to public health, underscoring the necessity of adequate sanitation facilities. As history shows, crisis periods often catalyze major societal transformations. For instance, some consumer behavior patterns that emerged during the early phase of the COVID-19 pandemic have been documented by [1], with suggestions that these shifts may indicate long-term lifestyle changes. Theory-based insights have been provided to explain these behaviors and guide future research and marketing strategies in light of environmental constraints. These behavioral responses have been categorized into three stages: reacting, coping, and longer-term adaptation [2-4].

As of 2020, only 54% of the global population had access to safely managed sanitation services. These figures are often distorted by urban data, whereas rural areas continue to suffer from limited access [5]. Furthermore, access does not always equate to actual usage, implying that the number of effective rural sanitation users may be significantly lower. This shortfall highlights how far behind we are in achieving the Sustainable Development Goal of ensuring access to adequate and equitable sanitation for all by 2030 [6].

Resource recovery systems that could benefit communities remain largely underdeveloped. With approximately 80% of global wastewater left untreated, focusing solely on treatment is insufficient. In a study of 12 urban sanitation systems in low- and lower-middle-income countries, only two demonstrated any capacity for fecal sludge reuse or recycling [7]. One category of solutions aimed at addressing sanitation and resource recovery needs is the ecological sanitation (EcoSan) system. These systems promote the reuse and recovery of resources. A notable example is the urine-diverting dry toilet (UDDT), a subcategory of EcoSan [8]. Additionally, [9] explored the development of a generic multi-criteria decision support framework to assess the sustainability of various technologies for urban sewage sludge treatment.

The possibility of respiratory droplets, surface virus contamination, and interior air pollution from toilets should be

DOI: 10.1201/9781003798514-26

taken into account. In fact, chronic bacterial contamination of the enclosed environment commonly follows a toilet flush, and this can be a large producer of dispersion for potential pathogens as well, which are frequently removed via the faecal route, as well as for respiratory viruses. The droplets produced by a toilet flush range in size; the larger ones fall quickly to nearby surfaces, while the smaller ones can be eaten or linger in the air for a very long period [10].

Worldwide, people lacking the basic sanitation facilities are around 3.6 billion. Open defecation is practiced by around eight percent of world's population. In the decades of 2000 & 2001, most of population have gained access to improved toilets & latrines. It is around 2.4 billion [11].

2 TECHNOLOGICAL DEVELOPMENT OF SANITATION STRUCTURES

In Ancient India, there are basic two types of toilet systems were present: Inside the home & outside of habitation area. For more accuracy, three types of toilets were present namely: flushed, squat & open toilets. In U.S. most of places outdoor toilets were used which has been vanished because of foul odour and potential health hazards, ground water contamination [12]. In 2500 BC, Harrapan dynasty had built the flushing toilet & advanced plumbing system similar to today's system [13]. [14] reported about Indian water toilet from which organic fertilizer using human feaces has been invented. The cultural values and social behavior of the public in general will contribute profoundly in the success of any sanitation program[15]. The government of India has given due significance for health and sanitation [16].

3 THE PROPOSED MODEL OF ECO TOILET

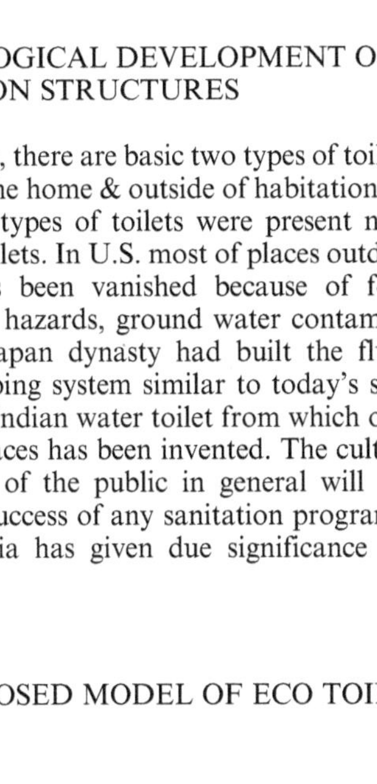

Figure 1. Plan & section of Septic tank of proposed toilet model.

3.1 *General*

To overcome limitations identified in the literature, a model named "Eco Toilet" a sensor-operated, solar-powered urine-diverting toilet is proposed. It directly converts human feces into organic fertilizer while separating urine for disposal. The toilet walls are constructed using soil-filled PET bottles reinforced with steel wires and cement plaster over mesh for strength. Sensors automate flushing and cleaning, activating upon entry, during use, and after hand motion detection. The toilet pan separates urine and feces; feces pass through a dual-mesh filtration tank a mild steel mesh (0.5 mm) for solids and a nylon mesh for fine particles — while liquids drain out. The filtered material moves to a blending tank that mixes organic additives to accelerate composting. Powered entirely by solar energy, the system enables hands-free fertilizer preparation, aligning with the Prohibition of Manual Scavenging Act by eliminating direct human contact with fecal matter.

3.2 *Flow chart of construction process*

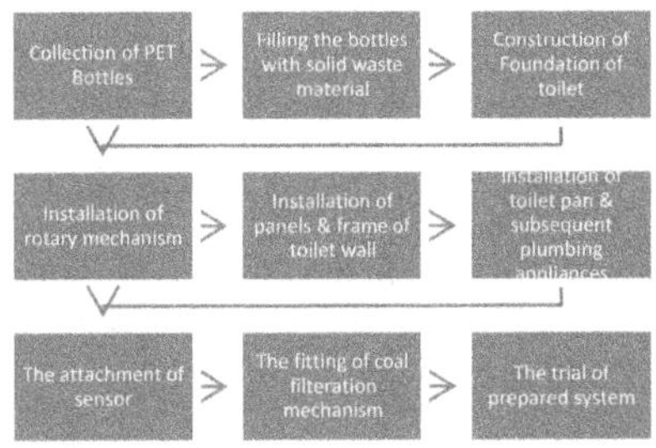

3.3 *Relevance to society*

Currently, the fecal waste is mixed in the sewer lines through septic tank. This can increase the load on sewer line. The fecal waste is and soluble form of fertilizer whereas the chemical fertilizers are in insoluble form. This makes long term effect as increase in soil fertility. The plastic PET bottles are accumulated in water bodies for longer period. This adversely effect on aquatic life. The model has set an example for effective use of these bottles. The bacterial infection can be reduced using the sensors. Also the intelligent toilet system can be implemented in effective manner.The nutrient recovery method is different for feces and urine. The urine separating toilet pan helps to easily recover the nutrients from human feces. Also, the urea can be extracted from urine by heating the urine in appropriate temperature. The carbon emission is a stagnant issue in today's era. The application of solar energy can solve this issue. The energy requirement for toilet activities is less as compared to other household activities which makes easy to utilize solar energy. The fertilizer preparation by human feces can helps in value addition to current toilet system. After selling the fertilizer, one can earn money and helps to grow society.

3.4 *Merits and demerits*

The designed system helps to minimize the waste generated through toilet. But as the system is new, the consequences need to discuss. The durability of wall can be reduced because of the plastic material instead of brickwork. The sticking of cement plaster to plastic can also a major issue. The cracks can be prepared on the surface of walls due to improper bonding between bottle and cement plaster. The regular maintenance is the major issue in the system. The toilet is always being in contact with water. To create the dry environment for sensor is also a problem while running the system. As the mold is of different size, the preparation of mold for toilet pan is a challenging task in front of makers. The system has high installation cost as compared to traditional toilet. The skilled manpower is required for installation of all the components. The help of experts from various fields such as mechanical, civil, electrical, solar energy, metal science, and plumbing is highly recommended.

4 CONCLUSION

The persistent challenges in sanitation, particularly in rural India, call for innovative, sustainable, and inclusive solutions.

Traditional sanitation systems often fail to achieve complete fecal matter degradation, leading to environmental contamination and overburdened sewer lines. This situation necessitates a paradigm shift in toilet design and waste management. Simple, cost-effective modifications to conventional toilet structures can enhance functionality, especially for populations below the poverty line. Emphasizing privacy, strength, and durability, such designs must also consider the integration of biological additives and microorganisms to transform fecal waste into nutrient-rich organic fertilizer.

The use of technology—particularly artificial intelligence (AI), the Internet of Things (IoT), and sensor-based systems—offers a transformative opportunity to automate cleaning, control odors, reduce water usage, and identify bacterial contamination. Smart toilets can be adapted to support the elderly and differently-abled, reducing physical strain, improving hygiene, and conserving water. The development of hydraulic-powered flush systems, touch less urinals, and automatic floor-cleaning mechanisms presents a comprehensive solution to many of the pressing issues faced today.

Furthermore, addressing the problem of open defecation and poor sanitation infrastructure demands community participation. Active collaboration between governmental bodies, NGOs, and local self-help groups—particularly those led by women—can promote awareness and adoption of improved sanitation practices. Portable, low-maintenance toilets, coupled with solar-powered systems and PET-based construction materials, further align with environmental sustainability goals by reducing plastic waste and power consumption.

Standardization in green sanitation technologies—through certified accessories, star ratings, and sustainable materials—will not only improve the quality of installations but also reduce recurring costs and leakage issues. These efforts can play a pivotal role in shifting public perception of human waste, recognizing its potential as a valuable agricultural resource rather than a health hazard.

The proposed sanitation model, with its integrated nutrient recovery and reduced health risk, highlights a practical and scalable approach to simultaneously address sanitation and agricultural needs. The fusion of engineering innovation with community-centric implementation offers a roadmap for redefining India's sanitation landscape, with broad implications for public health, environmental conservation, and rural development.

ACKNOWLEDGEMENT

We express our sincere gratitude to the management and Principal of Dr. D. Y. Patil Pratishthan's College of Engineering, Salokhenagar, Kolhapur, for their constant support, encouragement, and for providing us with the necessary facilities to carry out this research work.

We are especially thankful to all faculty members of the Department of Civil Engineering for their valuable suggestions, technical inputs, and motivation throughout the development of this work.

We also extend our heartfelt thanks to Dr. Mane Bajirao V., Associate Professor, Annasaheb Dange College of Engineering, Ashta, for his valuable guidance, critical feedback, and scholarly insight that significantly contributed to the quality of this research.

Our sincere appreciation goes to the research scholars, field experts, and organizations whose previous studies and technological contributions laid the foundation for this review and product development.

Finally, we acknowledge the efforts of all individuals directly or indirectly involved in this research, including local stakeholders, sanitation workers, and community participants, whose real-world insights helped shape the practical aspects of the proposed model.

REFERENCES

[1] Kirk, C.P., and Rifkin, L.S. (2020). I'll trade you diamonds for toilet paper: Consumer reacting, coping and adapting behaviors in the COVID-19 pandemic. *Journal of Business Research*, 117, 124–131.

[2] Ciotti, M., *et al.* (2020). The COVID-19 pandemic. *Critical Reviews in Clinical Laboratory Sciences*, 57(6), 365–388.

[3] Yang, L., *et al.* (2020). COVID-19: Immunopathogenesis and immunotherapeutics. *Signal Transduction and Targeted Therapy*, 5(1), 128.

[4] Velavan, T.P., and Meyer, C.G. (2020). The COVID-19 epidemic. *Tropical Medicine & International Health*, 25(3), 278.

[5] Hutton, G., and Chase, C. (2016). The knowledge base for achieving the sustainable development goal targets on water supply, sanitation and hygiene. *International Journal of Environmental Research and Public Health*, 13(6), 536.

[6] World Health Organization. (2021). *Progress on household drinking water, sanitation and hygiene 2000–2020: Five years into the SDGs.*

[7] Blackett, A. (2014). Introductory note to the decent work for domestic workers convention, 2011 (No. 189) and Recommendation (No. 201). *International Legal Materials*, 53 (1), 250–266.

[8] Langergraber, G., and Muellegger, E. (2005). Ecological sanitation—A way to solve global sanitation problems? *Environment International*, 31(3), 433–444.

[9] Ren, J., Liang, H., and Chan, F.T.S. (2017). Multi-criteria sustainability assessment of urban sewage sludge treatment technologies. *Technological Forecasting and Social Change*, 116, 29–39.

[10] Barker, J., and Jones, M.V. (2005). The potential spread of infection caused by aerosol contamination of surfaces after flushing a domestic toilet. *Journal of Applied Microbiology*, 99(2), 339–347.

[11] Sridhar, M.K.C., Okareh, O.T., and Mustapha, M. (2020). Assessment of knowledge, attitudes, and practices on water, sanitation, and hygiene in selected LGAs in Kaduna State, Nigeria. *Journal of Environmental and Public Health*, 2020.

[12] Tiwary, S.K., and Saurabh, S. (2018). Archaeological evidences of toilet system in ancient India. *Journal of Multidisciplinary Studies in Archaeology*, 6, 764–781.

[13] Mara, D.D. (1985). *The Design of Pour-flush Latrines.* Washington, DC: World Bank.

[14] Winblad, U., and Kilama, W. (1978). *Sanitation without water.*

[15] Paul, B.D. (1958). The role of beliefs and customs in sanitation programs. *American Journal of Public Health and the Nation's Health*, 48(11), 1502–1506.

[16] Kuriyan, G. (1956). Agriculture in India. *Current History*, 30 (174), 90–97.

Advancement in Engineering and Science – Goyal et al. (Eds)

Eco-Friendly Soil Stabilization Using Waste Printer Toner Ink: An Experimental Analysis

Prasad Gajanan Sonar
Assistant Professor, Department of Civil Engineering, CSMSS Chh. Shahu college of Engineering, Aurangabad, Maharashtra, India

Nilkanth Prabhakar Limbalkar, Sakshi Dnyaneshwar Deshmukh, Pavan Sanjay Anjankar, Hrutuja Malkarjun Todkar, and Nivaratee Aasaram Mohite
UG Students, Department of Civil Engineering, CSMSS Chh. Shahu college of Engineering, Aurangabad, Maharashtra, India

Dhanshri Pradip More
Assistant Professor, Department of Electronics and Computer Engineering, CSMSS Chh. Shahu college of Engineering, Aurangabad, Maharashtra, India

Mir Sohail Ali
Associate Professor and Head, Department of Civil Engineering, CSMSS Chh. Shahu college of Engineering, Aurangabad, Maharashtra, India

ABSTRACT: Soil stabilization is important for strengthening weak subgrade soils used in construction projects. This study investigates whether waste printer toner ink can serve as an unusual additive to improve the Unconfined Compressive Strength (UCS) and the overall bearing capacity of soil. Improper disposal of toner can cause environmental problems. However, its sticky and fine texture suggests it could help improve soil. To test this idea, controlled laboratory tests were conducted by adding toner ink to soil in different amounts: 0%, 0.5%, 1%, 1.5%, 2%, 2.5%, and 3% by dry weight. Both modified and untreated samples underwent UCS, Standard Proctor Compaction, and California Bearing Ratio (CBR) tests. The results showed a clear increase in cohesion and strength, along with better compaction behavior and load resistance. The toner particles acted as binders, reducing voids and permeability. However, using too much toner resulted in a slight loss of strength due to the mix becoming brittle and less workable. Overall, this study presents a sustainable and cost-effective method for recycling industrial waste to enhance geotechnical properties. The findings indicate that an optimal amount of toner can greatly enhance soil performance, but more research is needed to evaluate durability and environmental impacts in real-world conditions.

Keywords: Soil stabilization, printer toner ink, bearing capacity, unconfined compressive strength, sustainable construction, waste utilization

1 INTRODUCTION

Soil stabilization plays a key role in geotechnical engineering. It improves the strength, durability, and load-carrying capacity of weak soils used in construction. Poor soil conditions can lead to excessive settling, instability, or even structural failure under loads. To address these challenges, traditional stabilizers like lime, cement, and fly ash are commonly used. While these materials are effective, they come with environmental issues, such as high energy use, depletion of natural resources, and increased carbon dioxide emissions during production. With increasing focus on sustainable construction, researchers are exploring alternative stabilizing materials made from industrial or household waste. One promising but underutilized option is waste printer toner ink. A large amount of toner waste is created worldwide from discarded cartridges and used toners. If not managed properly, this waste can harm the environment because toner ink contains tiny carbon particles, resins, and metal oxides that can linger in soil and water. Notably, the adhesive and fine-grained properties of toner may help improve inter-particle bonding and strength when mixed with soil. This study aims to evaluate the potential of waste printer toner ink as a partial soil stabilizer. Laboratory experiments mixed toner ink into natural soil at different amounts: 0%, 0.5%, 1%, 1.5%, 2%, 2.5%, and 3% by dry weight. The study included Unconfined Compressive Strength (UCS), Standard Proctor Compaction, and California Bearing Ratio (CBR) tests to assess how the addition of toner affects soil performance. The results from treated samples were compared to untreated soil to find the ideal toner content for the best improvement. The research seeks to advance sustainable geotechnical engineering by turning non-biodegradable waste into a valuable construction material. This method not only offers technical benefits but also meets environmental goals by reducing waste and encouraging the reuse of resources. Future studies will investigate long-term durability, chemical interactions in the soil-toner mix, and real-world performance to confirm its use in construction projects.

2 LITERATURE REVIEW

2.1 *Introduction to soil stabilization*

Soil stabilization is an important technique in geotechnical engineering. It aims to change the physical and mechanical properties of soil to improve its ability to bear loads, endure over time, and resist outside forces. Weak soils can often threaten the stability of structures. Thus, enhancing their engineering properties is vital for sustainable infrastructure development. Traditional stabilizers like lime, cement, and fly ash have been in use for decades. However, their high carbon footprint and unsustainable production methods have led researchers to seek out alternative solutions made from industrial by-products and waste materials (Phanikumar and Sharma 2004) [1].

2.2 *Industrial waste in soil stabilization*

The use of industrial waste in soil stabilization has become a key research area for reducing environmental impact while

DOI: 10.1201/9781003798514-27

improving soil performance. Several waste-based materials have been studied:

- Fly Ash: This material has high levels of silica and alumina. Fly ash reacts with calcium to create calcium silicate hydrates (CSH), which increases soil strength and stiffness (Yadu and Tripathi 2013) [2].
- Cement Kiln Dust: This by-product from cement production is rich in calcium oxide (CaO). It can chemically react with soil minerals to improve cohesion and compressive strength (Ali Y. Al-Bakri *et al.* 2018) [3].
- Plastic and Rubber Waste: Shredded plastic and rubber can be added to soil to improve ductility and tensile behavior. This reduces brittleness and enhances flexibility (Hussein Jalal Aswad Hassan *et al.* 2021) [4].
- Carbon-Based Additives: Materials like waste toner or ink residues have gained interest because of their carbon-rich composition. They may provide pozzolanic or binding effects in soil (Firoozi *et al.* 2017) [5].

The incorporation of industrial waste in soil stabilization has become an important research direction for minimizing environmental impact while enhancing soil performance. A range of waste-based materials has been investigated:

2.3 *Composition and potential use of waste printer toner ink in soil stabilization waste in soil stabilization*

Waste printer toner ink consists of tiny particles mainly made up of carbon black, polymer resins, and metal oxides. These ingredients can improve soil performance in several ways:

- Carbon Black: Its large surface area helps particles lock together and strengthens the connections between soil grains.
- Polymer Additives: Toner ink formulations often include thermoplastic polymers like styrene-acrylate copolymers. These work like synthetic polymer-based stabilizers, providing adhesion and flexibility.
- Metal Oxides: Small amounts of components like iron oxide, titanium dioxide, and silica may take part in pozzolanic reactions, further increasing soil strength (Pathak *et al.* 2021).

This unique mix of components makes waste toner ink a potentially valuable material for stabilizing difficult soils while addressing waste disposal issues.

2.4 *Experimental studies on non-traditional soil stabilizers*

Although research directly focusing on printer toner ink in soil stabilization is limited, studies on related carbon-based and polymer-modified stabilizers offer valuable insights.

- Polymer Stabilizers: According to Puppala *et al.* (2018) [6], polymer-based additives effectively reduce swelling in expansive soils, improve cohesion, and increase moisture resistance. Since toner ink contains polymer compounds, a similar strengthening effect can be expected.
- Geopolymer-Based Stabilizers: Research by Choudhary *et al.* (2024) [7] showed that expansive soils treated with slag-based geopolymers had greater strength and durability than conventional lime or cement-stabilized soils. These findings encourage the exploration of other alternative stabilizers, including waste toner materials.

2.5 *Environmental and economic benefits of using printer toner ink in soil stabilization*

- Reusing waste printer toner ink for geotechnical applications provides both environmental and financial benefits.
- Waste Minimization: Diverting toner cartridges and ink from landfills helps with sustainable waste management (EPA Report 2020).
- Reduced Carbon Emissions: Toner-based stabilizers have a much lower carbon footprint compared to traditional cement materials. 2.6 Challenges and Future Research Directions Despite its potential, several areas of toner-based soil stabilization need more scientific study.
- Long-Term Durability: It is important to understand how toner-stabilized soil behaves under changing temperature and moisture conditions.
- Chemical Reactions: More research is necessary to identify the specific chemical and mineral interactions between toner ingredients and soil.

2.6 *Challenges and future research directions*

Despite its potential, several aspects of toner-based soil stabilization need more scientific study:

- Long-Term Durability: It is important to understand how toner-stabilized soil behaves under changing temperature and moisture conditions.
- Chemical Reactions: More research is required to identify the specific chemical and mineral interactions between toner components and soil.

3 MATERIALS AND METHODOLOGY

3.1 *Soil and its properties*

The study focused on expansive clayey soil, known for its high plasticity and significant swelling with moisture changes. This can cause surface cracking and structural instability in construction. The soil was sourced from a local area and tested using standard laboratory methods, such as particle size distribution and Atterberg limits.

The soil contained about 30% sand, 25% silt, and 45% clay, indicating a fine-grained makeup. Atterberg tests revealed a liquid limit (LL) of 60%, a plastic limit (PL) of 30%, and a plasticity index (PI) of 30%, which classifies it as highly plastic clay. Standard Proctor tests found an Optimum Moisture Content (OMC) of 18% and a Maximum Dry Density (MDD) of 1.65 g/cm^3.

The untreated soil had an Unconfined Compressive Strength (UCS) of roughly 110 kPa and an unsoaked California Bearing Ratio (CBR) of 3.2%, indicating low load-bearing capacity. A Free Swell Index (FSI) of 55% also confirmed its expansive characteristics. These properties underscore the need for effective soil stabilization to reduce swelling, improve strength, and enhance suitability for foundations and pavements.

Table 1. Properties of soils.

Property	Value/Description
Type	Expansive clayey soil
Sand Content	30%
Silt Content	25%
Clay Content	45%
Liquid Limit (LL)	60%
Plastic Limit (PL)	30%
Plasticity Index (PI)	30%
Optimum Moisture Content	18%
Maximum Dry Density (MDD)	1.65 g/cm^3
Unconfined Compressive Strength	110 kPa
California Bearing Ratio (CBR) (Unsoaked)	3.2%
Free Swell Index (FSI)	55%

3.2 *Waste printer toner ink and its properties*

Waste printer toner ink, made from discarded cartridges, is a fine powder mainly made up of carbon black, polymer resins, iron oxide, and small amounts of metal oxides. The particle size ranges from 1 to 10 μm. This size allows for good mixing with soil and better bonding between particles. Its water-resistant quality helps to reduce moisture absorption in clay soils that expand.

The toner has a specific gravity of 1.2 to 1.5 and a large surface area compared to its volume. This improves contact with soil particles and enhances cohesion. Carbon black adds a slight pozzolanic effect, which can improve soil strength over time. Meanwhile, the polymer resins create a semi-flexible structure that resists deformation and cracking.

Previous studies show that adding toner ink in small amounts (0.5 to 3% by dry soil weight) can boost unconfined compressive strength (UCS) and California bearing ratio (CBR). It also reduces the plasticity index (PI) and swelling. This highlights its potential as an eco-friendly soil stabilizer. Using this industrial byproduct in soil stabilization not only strengthens weak soils but also helps with sustainable waste management in geotechnical projects.

3.3 *Methodology adopted*

Table 2. Properties of waste tonner ink.

Property	Value/Description
Particle Size	1 – 10 μm
Specific Gravity	1.2 – 1.5
Nature	Hydrophobic (Water-repellent)
Major Components	Carbon black, polymer resins, iron oxide, metal oxides
Surface Area-to-Volume Ratio	High
Carbon Content	High (Promotes pozzolanic activity)
Polymer Content	Enhances binding and soil cohesion
Typical Dosage in Soil	0.5% – 3% by weight
Expected Benefits	Increases UCS and CBR, reduces PI and swelling potential

3.3.1 *Soil and material preparation*

Expansive clayey soil was collected, air-dried, and sifted through a 4.75 mm IS sieve to remove large particles. We determined basic properties such as particle size distribution, Atterberg limits, and Standard Proctor compaction, including Optimum Moisture Content (OMC) and Maximum Dry Density (MDD). We also measured the baseline Unconfined Compressive Strength (UCS) of the untreated soil.

3.3.2 *Sample preparation and mix design*

For each mix, 1000 g of dry soil was combined with toner ink at 0%, 0.5%, 1%, 1.5%, 2%, 2.5%, and 3% by weight. First, the toner was mixed with soil to ensure even distribution. Then, water was added gradually to reach an optimal moisture content of 18%. The mixture was kneaded to create a consistent blend and compacted into cylindrical molds measuring 36 mm × 72 mm to determine the Maximum Dry Density (MDD).

3.3.3 *UCS testing*

Specimens were tested right after compaction without curing. Axial load was applied at a constant strain rate until failure occurred, and the peak stress was recorded as the UCS. Results from all toner percentages were compared, and stress-strain curves were plotted to identify the best toner content for the highest strength improvement. This procedure ensured consistency among the samples, assessed the short-term strength behavior of toner-stabilized soil, and showed its potential as an eco-friendly stabilizer.

Table 3. Sample wise mix design.

Sample ID	Toner Ink Content (% by weight of dry soil)	Weight of Dry Soil (g)	Toner Ink (g)	Water Added (Based on OMC 18%) (g)	Remarks
S0	0%	1000	0	180	Control sample (untreated)
S1	0.5%	1000	5	180	Toner-stabilized
S2	1.0%	1000	10	180	Toner-stabilized
S3	1.5%	1000	15	180	Toner-stabilized
S4	2.0%	1000	20	180	Toner-stabilized
S5	2.5%	1000	25	180	Toner-stabilized
S6	3.0%	1000	30	180	Toner-stabilized

3.3.4 *Mould preparation and compaction*

After achieving a uniform mixture of soil, toner, and water, we prepared specimens using cylindrical molds with a diameter of 36 mm and a height of 72 mm. We placed the mixture in three equal layers, compacting each layer uniformly to remove air voids and reach the desired density. We took care to prevent segregation and ensure consistent toner distribution throughout the specimen. Once we compacted and leveled the final layer, we carefully removed the sample from the mold to preserve its shape and integrity. We tested the specimens immediately to assess the short-term effect of toner ink on soil strength without any curing period.

3.3.5 *Unconfined Compression Strength (UCS) test execution*

The UCS test was conducted on freshly prepared samples right after compaction. Each cylinder was placed in the loading frame with care to prevent misalignment or disturbance. A vertical load was applied at a steady strain rate until failure occurred, and the resulting axial deformation was recorded to create stress-strain curves.

The highest stress each sample could handle was noted as the UCS. This process was repeated for all mixes, starting from 0% (control) up to 3% toner ink in 0.5% increments. This allowed for a comparison of how toner addition affected soil strength and deformation behavior.

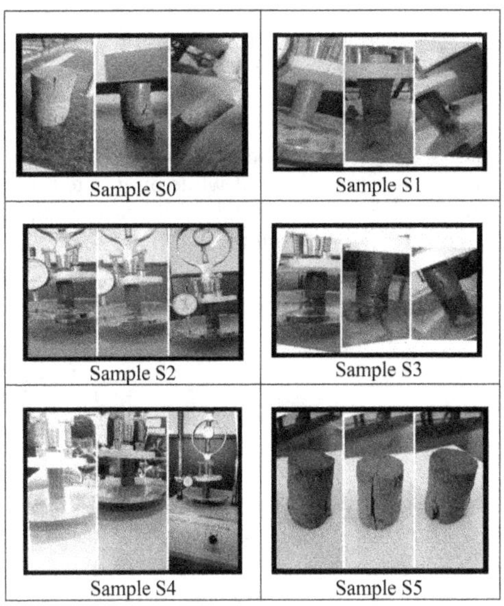

Figure 1. Sample testing on UCS.

4 DATA ANALYSIS AND INTERPRETATION

Each soil-toner mix (0% to 3% in 0.5% increments) was tested in triplicate to ensure reliability. We recorded the peak axial stress from each specimen and calculated the average UCS for every toner content.

The results showed a clear trend: soil strength increased with toner addition up to an optimum point, after which it either plateaued or decreased slightly. This suggests that moderate toner content improves inter-particle bonding and friction, while too much toner may act as a lubricant or create weak zones, slightly reducing strength.

Stress-strain curves and statistical analysis confirmed that 2% toner ink is the optimal dosage for maximum UCS. These findings indicate that waste printer toner ink can be an effective and eco-friendly soil stabilizer, improving strength while promoting the sustainable reuse of industrial waste.

Table 4. UCS test results for different toner ink contents.

Sample ID	*Toner Ink (%)*	*UCS Sample 1 (kN/ m^2)*	*UCS Sample 2 (kN/ m^2)*	*UCS Sample 3 (kN/ m^2)*	*Average UCS (kN/m^2)*
S0	0.0	110	115	112	112.3
S1	0.5	120	118	121	119.7
S2	1.0	130	132	129	130.3
S3	1.5	142	140	144	142.0
S4	2.0	150	149	152	150.3
S5	2.5	148	145	147	146.7
S6	3.0	140	138	141	139.7

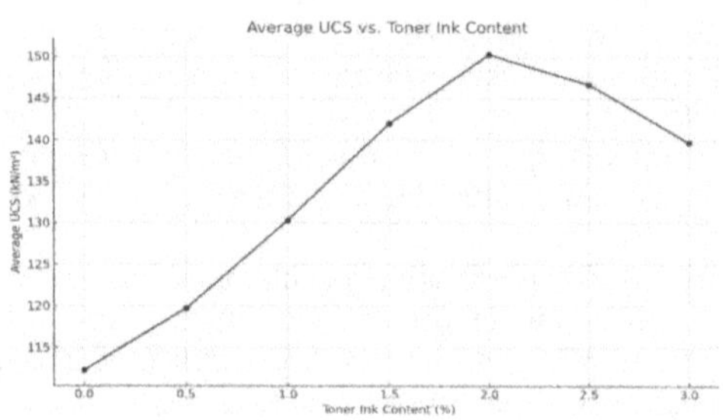

Figure 2. Effect of toner ink content on UCS of soil.

The line graph showing average UCS in relation to toner ink content reveals a clear trend. From 0% to 2% toner, the UCS steadily increases. This indicates improved particle cohesion and soil structure from the added toner.

The highest UCS is at 2% toner, after which strength starts to decline slightly. This implies that while moderate toner content boosts inter-particle bonding and load-bearing capacity, too much toner can weaken the soil matrix. It may act as a lubricant or create weak spots.

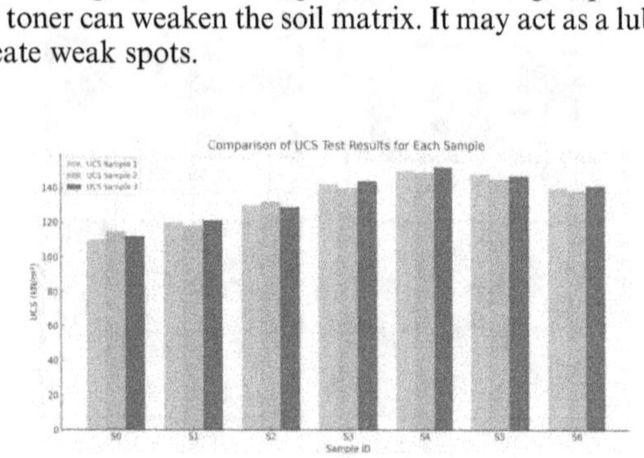

Figure 3. Bar chart compares the UCS values.

Overall, the graph highlights 2% toner ink as the best amount, confirming it works well as an eco-friendly soil stabilizer when used in the right amounts.

The grouped bar chart shows the UCS values for three specimens: Sample 1, Sample 2, and Sample 3, at each level of toner ink content. Each cluster of bars represents a specific toner percentage, which enables a direct comparison of repeatability and consistency across tests.

The chart reveals a clear upward trend in UCS as the toner content rises from 0% to 2%. All three samples display a similar pattern. After 2% toner, there is a slight decrease in UCS, indicating that too much toner negatively affects soil strength.

The small differences in bar height within each group suggest good reproducibility and uniform results. This consistency supports the data's reliability and highlights 2% toner ink as the best amount for maximizing compressive strength. It confirms the positive role of toner in stabilizing soil when used in the right amounts.

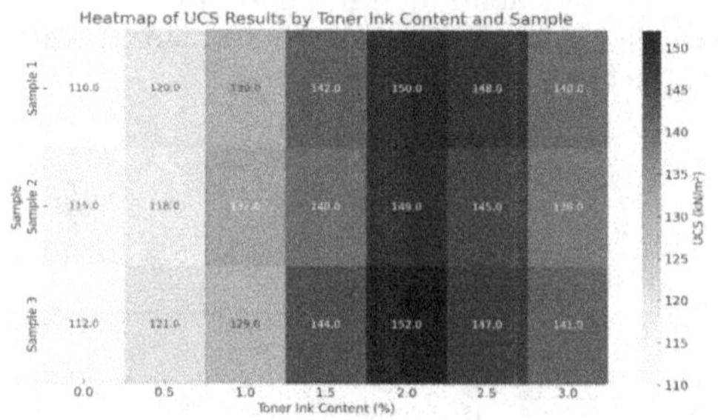

Figure 4. Heatmap of UCS values across different toner ink contents and individual samples.

The heatmap shows UCS values for each sample at different toner ink contents. Each cell represents a sample at a specific toner percentage, and the color intensity indicates strength. The darkest cells are near 2% toner, showing the highest UCS, which matches trends in the line and bar charts. The similar colors across the three samples at each toner level show good reproducibility and reliability, especially around the optimal toner content. This confirms that 2% toner gives consistent and maximum strength improvement.

5 RESULTS AND DISCUSSION

The study shows a clear improvement in Unconfined Compressive Strength (UCS) of expansive soil when waste printer toner ink is added. As the toner content increased from 0% to 2%, the average UCS steadily rose, reaching a maximum of 150.3 kN/m^2 at 2%. This indicates optimal stabilization. The improvement is due to the toner's fine particles and binding properties, which improve inter-particle locking and reduce soil plasticity.

Beyond 2%, strength gradually declined, with UCS dropping to 139.7 kN/m^2 at 3% toner. This suggests that too much toner may act as a lubricant or reduce compaction efficiency, slightly weakening the soil. Overall, the results confirm that the controlled addition of toner ink can effectively improve soil strength while supporting sustainable reuse of industrial waste.

6 CONCLUSION

The study shows that waste printer toner ink can effectively improve the Unconfined Compressive Strength (UCS) of expansive soil. This makes it a promising eco-friendly stabilizer. UCS increased steadily with toner addition up to 2%, reaching an average peak of 150.3 kN/m^2. After that, strength slightly declined. This finding indicates that a moderate amount of toner enhances particle binding and soil strength, while too much can reduce its effectiveness.

Using waste toner not only strengthens weak soils but also encourages the reuse of industrial waste. It offers a practical and environmentally friendly solution for geotechnical applications.

7 RECOMMENDATIONS

According to the study findings, waste printer toner ink is a recommended sustainable and cost-effective soil stabilizer. It works well for expansive soils in low to medium load situations, such as subgrade layers of rural roads or embankments. For the best results, a toner content of 2% by dry soil weight is suggested because it offers the highest improvement in unconfined compressive strength (UCS).

Future research could examine the long-term durability of toner-stabilized soils under different moisture

REFERENCES

[1] Kumar B.R.P., Sharma R.S., and Asce M., (2004), *Effect of Fly Ash on Engineering Properties of Expansive Soils*, no. July, pp. 764–767.

[2] Yadu L. and Tripathi R.K., (2013), Effects of granulated blast furnace slag in the engineering behaviour of stabilized soft soil, in *Procedia Engineering*, pp. 125–131. doi: 10.1016/j.proeng.2013.01.019.

[3] Al-bakri A.Y. and Ahmed H.M., (2022), *Cement Kiln Dust (CKD): Potential Beneficial Applications and Eco- sustainability Cement Kiln Dust (CKD): Potential Beneficial Applications and Eco-Sustainable Solutions*, no. June, doi: 10.3390/su14127022.

[4] Jalal H. and Hassan A., (2021), *Effects of Plastic Waste Materials on Geotechnical Properties of Clayey Soil*, pp. 390–413.

[5] Firoozi A.A., Guney Olgun C., Firoozi A.A., and Baghini M.S., (2017), Fundamentals of soil stabilization, *Int. J. Geo-Engineering*, vol. 8, no. 1, doi: 10.1186/s40703-017-0064-9.

[6] Pedarla A., Puppala A.J., Hoyos L.R., and Chittoori B., (2016), Evaluation of Swell Behavior of Expansive Clays from Internal Specific Surface and Pore Size Distribution, *J. Geotech. Geoenvironmental Eng.*, vol. 142, no. 2, doi: 10.1061/(asce)gt.1943-5606.0001412.

[7] Sahoo S. and Singh S.P., (2022), Strength and durability properties of expansive soil treated with geopolymer and conventional stabilizers, *Constr. Build. Mater.*, vol. 328, no. January, p. 127078, doi: 10.1016/j.conbuildmat.2022.127078.

[8] Choudhary D., Kaithwas S., Sharma R.K., and Mishra A., (2024), Environmental Technology & Innovation Recycling of waste toner derived from exhausted printer cartridges as adsorbent for defluoridation of water, *Environ. Technol. Innov.*, vol. 34, p. 103572, doi: 10.1016/j.eti.2024.103572.

[9] Liu Y., Chang C.-W., Namdar A., She Y., Lin C.-H., Yuan X. and Yang Q., (2019), Stabilization of expansive soil using cementing material from rice husk ash and calcium carbide residue, *Constr. Build. Mater.* 221 1–11, https://doi.org/10.1016/j.conbuildmat.2019.05.157.

[10] Ding L.-Q., Vanapalli S.K., Zou W.-L., Han Z. and Wang X.-Q., (2021), Freeze-thaw and wetting-drying effects on the hydro-mechanical behavior of a stabilized expansive soil, *Constr. Build. Mater.* 275 122162, https://doi.org/10.1016/j. conbuildmat.2020.122162.

[11] Papa E., Medri V., Landi E., Ballarin B. and Miccio F., (2014). Production and characterization of geopolymers based on mixed compositions of metakaolin and coal ashes, *Mater. Des.* 56, 409–415, https://doi.org/10.1016/j.matdes.2013.11.054.

[12] Samantasinghar S. and Singh S.P., (2018), Effect of synthesis parameters on compressive strength of fly ash-slag blended geopolymer, *Constr. Build. Mater.* 170, 225–234, https://doi.org/10.1016/j.conbuildmat.2018.03.026.

[13] Chen Z., Li J.-S.-S., Zhan B.-J.-J., Sharma U. and Poon C.S., (Sep. 2018), Compressive strength and microstructural properties of dry-mixed geopolymer pastes synthesized from GGBS and sewage sludge ash, *Constr. Build. Mater.* 182, 597–607, https://doi.org/10.1016/j.conbuildmat.2018.06.159.

[14] Luna Galiano Y., Fernandez ′ Pereira C. and Vale J., Stabilization/solidification of a municipal solid waste incineration residue using fly ash-based geopolymers, *J. Hazard. Mater.* 185 (1) (2011) 373–381, https://doi.org/10.1016/j. jhazmat.2010.08.127.

[15] Khadka S.D., Jayawickrama P.W., Senadheera S. and Segvic B., (2020), Stabilization of highly expansive soils containing sulfate using metakaolin and fly ash based geopolymer modified with lime and gypsum, *Transp. Geotech.* 23, 100327, https://doi. org/10.1016/j.trgeo.2020.100327.

Advancement in Engineering and Science – Goyal et al. (Eds)
© 2026 The Author(s), ISBN: 978-1-041-31101-0

Digital Twin Technology: A Coherent Application

Mohmmad Husen Shedbalkar
B.Tech. Mechanical Engineering, Karmaveer Bhaurao Patil College of Engineering Satara, Satara, India

Aamir M. Shaikh
Assistant Professor at Department of Mechanical Engineering, Karmaveer Bhaurao Patil College of Engineering Satara, Satara, India

Nilofar Shedbalkar
B.Tech. in Computer Science and Engineering, Karmaveer Bhaurao Patil College of Engineering Satara, Satara, India

ABSTRACT: Digital Twin technology is gaining momentum fast and it's starting to change the way businesses operate in a big way. Over the past few years, it's been making its way into key areas of business, helping teams work smarter and more efficiently. And the trend is only picking up speed. Experts predict we'll see Digital Twins being used in even more industries and for a wider range of purposes. This paper takes a closer look at what Digital Twins are, how they've developed over time, and the technologies that power them. It also digs into where the tech is headed, the challenges that still need to be tackled, and how it's being used in real-world scenarios across different industries to drive intelligent automation.

Keywords: Digital twins, Digital Twin technology, Automation, Application, Management

1 INTRODUCTION

Digital Twin technology is gaining serious traction among professionals and researchers alike. Today, it's being used across a variety of industries to create accurate virtual replicas of real-world objects, systems, and workflows. Back in 2019, a Gartner survey revealed that Digital Twins were moving into mainstream adoption, predicting that 75% of organizations using Internet of Things (IoT) technologies would either already be using Digital Twins or planning to do so by 2020. Looking ahead, Gartner also forecasts that by 2027, more than 40% of large companies worldwide will be using Digital Twins to help drive their revenue growth [4].

The market potential is just as impressive. Global Market Insight estimated the value of the Digital Twin market at around $8 billion in 2022 and expects it to grow at a strong 25% annual rate through 2032. Another study projects that the market could expand by nearly $32 billion between 2021 and 2026. On top of that, a 2022 report found that nearly 60% of executives across various industries are planning to incorporate Digital Twins into their operations by 2028.

At its core, Digital Twin is an innovative technology that has transformed the industry by replicating almost every aspect of a product, process, or service. It allows companies to duplicate everything in the physical realm in the digital domain and provide engineers with insights through simulations and virtual testing before anything is even built in the real world [17].

Consequently, the technology empowers companies to swiftly identify and resolve physical issues, conceive and construct superior products, and achieve value and benefits more rapidly than previously feasible. It's also a powerful tool for enhancing business processes and performance, and staying competitive in an increasingly digital world.

2 EXISTING SYSTEM

The concept of Digital Twins was first introduced in 2003 by Dr. Michael Grieves during a product lifecycle management course at the University of Michigan. Sometimes called "digital reflection" or "digital replication," the idea has continued to evolve, with researchers offering a variety of definitions over the years.

One formal explanation comes from the *Encyclopedia of Production Engineering*, which defines a Digital Twin as a digital representation of an active, unique product. This product could be anything a physical device, machine, service, intangible asset, or even a complex system that includes both the product and its related services. In a broader sense, Digital Twins are real-time virtual models of physical things that can be studied, analyzed, and reasoned with using data collected from the real world [13,35].

Some researchers describe them as the merging point between the physical and digital realms. Fu *et al.* emphasized that Digital Twins go beyond traditional static models like CAD drawings by capturing and simulating real-time behaviour. They are constantly connected to the physical counterpart, continuously receiving and processing data, making them dynamic and incredibly insightful [14].

By using big data technologies, Digital Twins can extract hidden patterns, identify potential design flaws early, and improve overall system intelligence [14]. In the manufacturing space, Kritzinger and colleagues broke down the concept into three levels of integration: Digital Model, Digital Shadow, and Digital Twin each indicating a deeper connection between physical and digital assets [7].

One of the most remarkable early uses of Digital Twin-like thinking was by NASA in 1970 during the Apollo 13 mission. Engineers used simulators a digital twin of the spacecraft's command module and its electrical systems to help bring the crew safely back to Earth. It only took them two hours to solve the issue, saving the lives of all three astronauts. Today, NASA continues to use Digital Twins to design and test next generation aircraft and spacecraft [9].

While the concept isn't entirely new, its adoption has accelerated dramatically in recent years. As technology has matured, Digital Twins are now being integrated with other cutting-edge tools like speech recognition, augmented reality, IoT, and artificial intelligence [31]. Recognizing this trend, Gartner named Digital Twins one of the top 10 technology trends in 2017 and predicted that by 2021, half of all large industrial firms would be using them in key operations [4].

DOI: 10.1201/9781003798514-28

According to MarketsandMarkets, Digital Twin technology is set for rapid growth. The adoption of Digital Twins across various industries, including healthcare, manufacturing, and smart cities, is accelerating. This rapid growth is expected to be driven by the technology's ability to optimize operations, reduce costs, and improve decision making processes. As these virtual models become even more sophisticated and integrated with other emerging technologies, they are poised to revolutionize how organizations design, monitor, and manage complex systems and processes in the real world [8].

3 METHODOLOGY

Digital twin technology –

Digital Twin technology might sound complex, but at its core, it's all about creating a digital version of something real whether it's a machine, a building, or even a person and using that digital model to monitor, analyze, and improve how it performs in the real world. To make all of this work, Digital Twins rely on four powerful technologies: **Internet of Things (IoT), Artificial Intelligence (AI), Cloud Computing,** and **Extended Reality (XR).** Each one plays a unique role, and how much they're used can vary depending on the application.

3.1 *Internet of Things (IoT) – The foundation of it all*

Think of IoT as the nervous system of a Digital Twin. It connects devices, people, and objects using sensors and smart technologies.

These sensors constantly collect data from the physical world like temperature, pressure, or location and send it to the digital twin. That way, the virtual model is always up to date. In fact, experts predict that by 2027, more than 90% of IoT platforms will support Digital Twin capabilities. Without IoT, the real time link between the digital and physical worlds wouldn't be possible [14,18].

3.2 *Cloud computing – Where all the data lives*

With all that data coming in, you need a place to store and process it and that's where cloud computing comes in. Cloud computing involves delivering services via the Internet, facilitating efficient data storage and retrieval.

This technology supports Digital Twins by providing computational power and cloud-based storage solutions. It allows Digital Twins to manage large data volumes effectively, enabling easy access from any location [14]. Whether you're tracking a smart building or simulating a manufacturing process, cloud computing enhances the processing speed of complex systems and addresses the challenges of handling extensive data sets [13,21].

3.3 *Artificial Intelligence (AI) – The brain behind the twin*

AI brings intelligence to Digital Twins. By analyzing data using techniques like machine learning and deep learning, AI helps identify patterns, predict future outcomes, and even recommend improvements. It's like having a smart assistant constantly watching over your systems and alerting you before problems happen. Whether it's optimizing performance or spotting design flaws early, AI plays a critical role in making Digital Twins truly useful.

3.4 *Extended Reality (XR) – Making it all feel real*

Extended Reality (which includes VR, AR, and MR) is what makes Digital Twins interactive and immersive. With XR, you can actually *see* and *interact with* the digital version of a physical object like walking through a digital version of a construction site using AR glasses or testing how a new machine will perform in VR before it's even built. XR makes the experience hands-on and helps people understand complex systems in a much more visual and intuitive way [13].

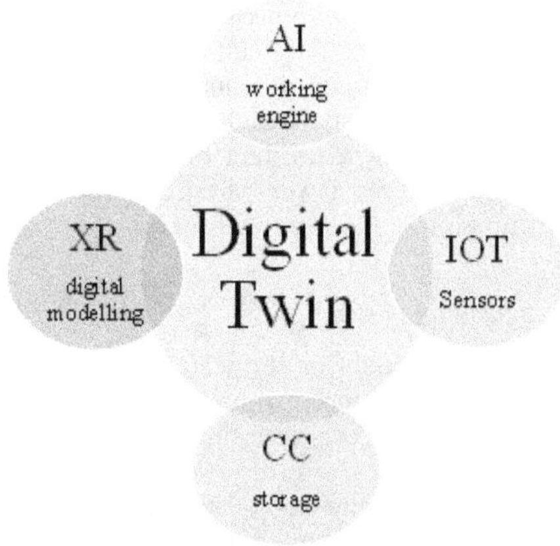

Figure 1. Techniques in Digital.

4 USE CASES AND APPLICATIONS

Digital Twin technology has become a major game-changer, especially in engineering and manufacturing. These industries are using it to create highly accurate digital versions of physical assets like machines, equipment, or production lines and simulate how they behave in the real world. This not only helps improve performance but also allows teams to test ideas and make smarter decisions without touching the actual hardware.

In operations and supply chain management, Digital Twins are proving incredibly useful. Recent research shows they're being used to track operations more accurately, manage transportation systems, provide remote assistance, visualize assets, and even customize product designs on the fly [20].

But the potential goes far beyond just factories and logistics. Digital Twin technology is starting to make a real impact in a wide variety of industries **automotive, aerospace, construction, agriculture, mining, utilities, retail, healthcare, defence, natural resource management,** and **public safety**, to name a few.

What's exciting is that this isn't just theoretical anymore. Real companies, researchers, and organizations are actively using Digital Twins in everyday operations. The concept has caught the attention of business leaders, academics, and professionals all over the world. As a result, we're seeing a wave of new research, case studies, and real-world applications being published and discussed in both academic journals and industry reports.

Digital Twins are no longer just a futuristic idea they're already shaping the way we design, operate, and innovate across countless sectors.

4.1 *Manufacturing*

The manufacturing world is evolving at lightning speed and Digital Twin technology is right at the heart of this transformation. As the sector embraces smarter, more connected systems, Digital Twins are gaining serious traction for their ability to enhance efficiency, reduce downtime, and fuel innovation.

With the rise of **Industry 4.0**, we've seen big strides in real-time monitoring, smart sensors, and data-driven decision-making. These advancements have paved the way for Digital Twins to step in and take manufacturing processes to the next level [27,32].

They're being used for everything from **real-time asset monitoring** and **process simulation** to even **remote operations**, all through their virtual counterparts. But the benefits don't stop there. This technology also helps manufacturers better understand their customers, improve products, and unlock entirely new business models.

By using Digital Twins, companies can move beyond simply reacting to problems. They can **predict and prevent** them before they happen. For instance, they can forecast when equipment needs maintenance, improve machine performance, and fine-tune product designs for better results. These tools also make it possible to simulate how a product might perform before it's even built, which means fewer physical prototypes, shorter development timelines, and lower costs [26].

4.2 *Smarter product design*

Introducing a new product or service can have a ripple effect across a company. And since product design is directly tied to long-term success, those decisions matter a lot. That's where Digital Twins come in.

They act as digital versions of real-world manufacturing parts. Engineers can use them to **test and tweak designs in a virtual space**, using real-time data and simulations to guide their decisions. This not only cuts down on the number of physical prototypes needed, but also speeds up development and saves money [26].

Even better, teams can draw from actual product usage data to make smarter, more **customer-focused improvements** from increasing quality to personalizing features and boosting usability [19].

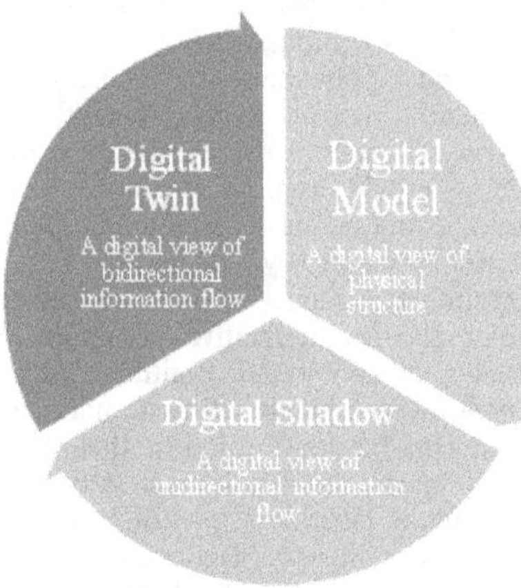

Figure 2. Flow of Working model.

4.3 *Process design and optimization*

Digital Twins aren't just helpful for products they're game changers for processes too. They allow manufacturers to monitor and analyze production under a range of conditions, which helps catch issues early and avoid costly disruptions. Instead of reacting to problems after they happen, companies can use Digital Twins to **predict, prevent, and optimize**. They can even turn existing machines and workflows into **intelligent systems** that reduce costs and speed up innovation [19].

4.4 *Smarter supply chain management*

Supply chains are getting more expensive to run, and that's putting pressure on manufacturers, retailers, and logistics companies alike. Cutting costs is now a top priority but that's not the only goal. A strong supply chain can also bring strategic wins, like faster returns on investment, better efficiency, and higher profits.

This is where **Digital Twin technology** really shines. It helps tackle everyday supply chain challenges, like figuring out the most efficient way to package goods, streamline fleet operations, and plan better delivery routes. It also supports advanced production models like **just-in-time (JIT)** and **just-in-sequence (JIS)** by analyzing how and when things move through the system. From product development to the moment it reaches the customer, Digital Twins can help track and analyze performance across every stage. Whether it's packaging design, vehicle tracking, or delivery speed, this tech offers a detailed, real-time view that helps improve both the big picture and the smallest details [20].

4.5 *Preventive maintenance*

Maintenance used to be mostly reactive and fix it when it breaks. But that approach leads to costly downtime and disruptions. **Preventive maintenance**, on the other hand, is all about staying ahead of issues. And Digital Twins take it to a whole new level.

These virtual models can mimic the behaviour of a specific machine or an entire production line. They pick up on early warning signs like small changes in performance or unusual wear and flag them before they turn into bigger (and more expensive) problems. This way, repairs can be planned proactively, keeping equipment running smoothly [29].

Digital Twins also help manufacturers test out new materials, fine-tune production cycles, balance workloads, and make sure every tool is calibrated just right all of which leads to better reliability and less waste.

4.6 *Agriculture*

Farming isn't just vital for food it's a major piece of the global economy. In the U.S. alone, agriculture contributes over **$750 billion** to the economy every year through everything from crop and livestock production to food services [2,6,12]. But the industry is facing some tough challenges: increasing demand, rising costs, stricter quality standards, and the growing threat of climate change. Entering in **Digital Twins** seems a promising solution for smarter, more sustainable farming [6].

4.7 *Weather modelling*

Digital Twins in agriculture aren't just helping manage what's on the farm they're also opening doors to better **climate modelling** and long-term **environmental forecasting**. Farmers can use these tools to detect where critical resources like water, soil, or crops are under pressure due to issues like pollution, soil degradation, or invasive species. This kind of insight is key for staying one step ahead of environmental changes.

4.8 *Reimagining agricultural supply chains*

In the world of agri-food, consumers are asking for safer, cleaner, and more transparent food products. At the same time, farmers want to boost profitability. But with so many moving parts in the supply chain, tracking everything from field to fork can be a real challenge [20].

That's where Digital Twins come in. These systems make it easier to see and track what's happening in real time across planting, harvesting, packaging, and delivery. Not only they do ensure better food quality and safety, but they also help to **connect farmers, distributors, and retailers** with synchronized data, leading to smoother collaboration.

4.9 *Livestock maintenance*

Digital Twins aren't just for crops, they're changing how we care for animals, too. Research by Erdélyi and Jánosi highlights how the tech is being used to monitor and manage livestock operations more efficiently [2]. even built a Digital Twin to simulate **energy usage in pigsties**, helping optimize their layout and reduce waste [6].

Taking it a step further, they explored how smart barn environments powered by Digital Twins that can be fine-tuned to maintain ideal air quality and temperatures, giving livestock a healthier and more productive space to grow [2].

4.10 *Healthcare*

Originally built for industries like manufacturing, Digital Twins are now making big waves in **healthcare and life sciences**. The COVID-19 pandemic accelerated the shift pushing healthcare providers to adopt digital tools that improve efficiency, cut costs, and better meet patient needs.

One standout example is **Dassault Systems' "Living Heart" project** [1]. This incredible initiative turns a 2D scan of a patient's heart into a highly detailed 3D model that mimics real-life movement, blood flow, and electrical activity. It's now used around the world to develop and test new medical devices and treatments [11]. Digital Twins are being used to **mirror entire healthcare systems**, including hospitals, patient records, and equipment.

These digital replicas help predict and prevent problems, personalize treatment, manage infrastructure, and control soaring R&D costs.

4.11 *Drug development*

Digital Twins are changing the game for the **pharmaceutical industry** too. By creating simulations of how new drugs behave, researchers can safely and quickly test their **safety and effectiveness** before they even reach a patient.

Because drug development generates massive amounts of data, Digital Twins help process it all into actionable simulations. This speeds up **clinical trials**, reduces the number of human test subjects, and makes research faster and safer. Plus, they're starting to play a major role in **vaccine innovation** helping scientists test antigens virtually and fine-tune formulas before trials even begin [17].

4.12 *Education and training*

Medical schools are moving beyond textbooks and cadavers thanks to Digital Twins. With VR and AI-enhanced simulations, students can now practice complex surgeries or understand human anatomy in a hands-on virtual environment. This not only deepens learning but also makes training safer and more accessible. These tools are also helping experienced professionals refine techniques and stay current with the latest medical procedures [13].

4.13 *Automotive and aviation industry*

Car manufacturers are racing to bring smarter, more connected vehicles to market and Digital Twins are central to that push. From customizable dashboards that let customers configure their dream car online to data-driven vehicle updates, this technology is transforming how cars are designed and built. Automakers use these tools to analyze driver preferences and make ongoing improvements.

In aerospace, Digital Twins help to keep aircraft running smoothly by predicting maintenance needs, analyzing weight and balance, forecasting weather impacts, and detecting system faults. Boeing, for instance, uses them extensively and has reported a 40% improvement in part and system quality for both commercial and military planes.

4.14 *Construction and real estate*

4.14.1 *A smarter way to build*

Digital Twins are revolutionizing how we design, build, and manage buildings. While Building Information Modelling (BIM) has long been a staple in the construction world, it mainly offers static snapshots. Digital Twins go a step further by integrating real-time sensor data, giving project managers live updates on progress, safety, and performance [21].

4.14.2 *Automated project control*

By combining input from drones, IoT sensors, laser scans, and more, Digital Twins provide a dynamic "as-built" model of any construction site. With the help of AI, this model can detect deviations from the plan early on, helping teams correct issues before they spiral into delays or budget overruns [21].

4.14.3 *Evaluating building performance*

Once a project is complete, Digital Twins continue adding value by simulating how a building will perform. When knowing how different HVAC setups will impact energy use or comfort levels, these models can predict airflow, temperature fluctuations, and power consumption enabling better decisions that improve sustainability and occupant well-being [21].

4.15 *Utilities and amenities*

Digital Twin technologies are quickly becoming integral to how we build smarter cities, modernize our power grids, and streamline utility operations. With the rapid growth of IoT connectivity, Digital Twins are emerging as a major force in smart city innovation.

As today's energy systems become more complex, energy companies are turning to Digital Twins to help optimize their operations. These digital models offer real-time insights into asset health, performance, and efficiency, making it easier to plan maintenance, schedule production, cut down on risks, and improve overall system reliability.

One forward-thinking idea gaining attention is the "digital power grid" a concept where every component, event, and human interaction within a physical grid is digitally mirrored. This kind of system would support everything from initial grid design to daily operations, real-time monitoring, and long-term service management. By tapping into the full potential of Digital Twins, utility companies can make smarter decisions about how to use both energy and information more efficiently [16,31].

4.16 *Mining*

The mining industry is under growing pressure to meet sustainability targets, use resources wisely, and keep operations efficient all while staying profitable. That's no easy task, especially in such a competitive space. To stay ahead, many mining companies are leaning into digital transformation, with Digital Twin technology playing a key role.

These virtual replicas of mines and machinery help teams plan smarter whether it's long-term production strategies or daily drilling schedules. Workers can even simulate entire operational processes, test new methods, and improve workflows without putting real equipment or people at risk.

Digital Twins are also being used to train employees. New hires can walk through virtual job scenarios, learn how equipment works, and prepare for real-life challenges in a much safer and more cost-effective way.

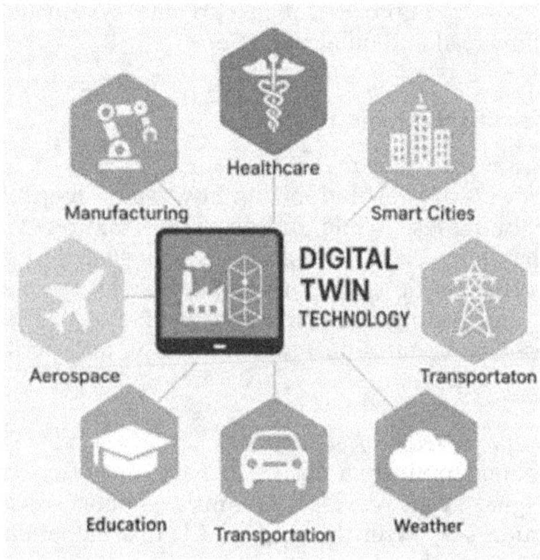

Figure 3. Applicable Sectors of Digital Twin Technology.

5 BENEFITS

5.1 *Predictive maintenance*

With a digital twin, you can keep a close eye on your machines or systems using real-time sensor data. It's like having a health tracker for your equipment. If something starts to go wrong, the system picks it up early before a breakdown happens. This means fewer unexpected shutdowns and lower repair costs.

5.2 *Simulation and testing*

Digital twins let you test out ideas in a virtual environment. Whether you're trying a new design or tweaking how a system works, you can simulate different scenarios without risking damage to real equipment. It's perfect for experimenting, prototyping, and validating new concepts before making them real [17].

5.3 *Operational optimization*

They also help you run things more smoothly. By analyzing how resources are used, where time is lost, or how much energy is consumed, digital twins show you where improvements can be made. It's a great tool for making processes leaner, faster, and more cost-efficient especially in complex operations like manufacturing or logistics [30].

5.4 *Product and service innovation*

Digital twins give an insight upon how your products are used in the real world. This means you can design better products, personalize features, and even create new services that respond directly to customer needs. Plus, you can speed up development by testing with actual usage data.

5.5 *Risk management and safety*

You can also prepare for the worst without any real-world consequences. Just by using simulation you can see how a system handles a power outage or a critical failure live. In this way, you can build safer systems and train teams to respond effectively before anything bad actually happens [17].

5.6 *Smarter decision making*

Due to a mix of real-time and historical data, decision-making becomes more strategic and less guesswork. Whether it's forecasting demand, identifying root causes of issues, or choosing the best course of action, digital twins give you the insights to move forward with confidence.

5.7 *Visualizing complex systems*

When it comes to explaining a complicated system to someone and giving briefing about it, Digital twins can turn that task into a clear, interactive visual model. Whether it's a factory, a smart city, or a power grid, you can see how everything connects and easily share that understanding with your team or stakeholders.

6 DRAWBACKS

6.1 *High initial costs*

Getting started with digital twins isn't cheap. You'll need to invest in things like sensors, data infrastructure, specialized software, and a skilled team to set everything up. For small or mid-sized companies, that upfront cost can be a real hurdle.

6.2 *Complex to implement*

Digital twins aren't plug-and-play. Integrating them with older systems or existing infrastructure can be tricky especially if you're working with outdated tech. It also takes a mix of advanced skills (like data science, AI, and engineering) to get things working smoothly. And if your setup is unique, you'll likely need custom solutions, which takes time and effort [13].

6.3 *Data privacy and security risks*

Since digital twins collect and transmit a lot of data, where some of it can be sensitive that it can be a target for cyberattacks. Keeping that data safe means investing in strong cybersecurity, which adds complexity and cost. It's not something you can afford to overlook.

6.4 *Data overload and quality problems*

More data isn't always better unless it's clean, consistent, and reliable. Digital twins need accurate data to be effective, but many companies struggle with bad data or just too much of it. Without solid data management systems, you risk ending up with a digital twin that doesn't reflect reality.

6.5 *Needs regular updates*

A digital twin is only as good as its connection to the real world. If the physical system changes but the twin doesn't get updated, it becomes outdated and that makes it useless (or worse, misleading). You'll need to regularly maintain, calibrate, and sometimes retrain your models.

6.6 *Not always the right fit*

Digital twins aren't the solution to every problem. For simple processes or small-scale operations, they may be overkill. Sometimes the investment just doesn't pay off. That's why it's important to carefully evaluate the potential return before jumping in.

6.7 *Shortage of skilled talent*

There's a real skills gap when it comes to digital twins. It takes a unique mix of knowledge from AI and IoT to industry-specific expertise and that talent isn't easy to find. Companies often struggle to hire or train people with the right capabilities.

7 CHALLENGES

7.1 *Data chaos*

A lack of standard formats and modelling frameworks can make it tough to share and interpret data effectively.

7.2 *Legacy systems*

Older IT setups often aren't compatible with the real-time demands of Digital Twin environments.

7.3 *Cybersecurity*

With more data comes greater risk. Keeping Digital Twins secure is essential but also complex.

7.4 *Connectivity issues*

In industries like mining or energy, remote locations can make reliable data transmission difficult.

7.5 *High setup costs*

Initial investment is steep. Companies need to fund sensors, software, infrastructure, integration, and ongoing system upkeep.

7.6 *Energy and storage needs*

These digital systems require substantial computing power and data storage, adding to operational demands.

8 FUTURE SCOPE

8.1 *Smarter with AI & machine learning*

Digital twins today are powerful but, in the future, they'll be **brilliant**. With AI and machine learning in the mix, digital twins won't just copy reality they'll **predict what's coming** and even **make decisions on their own**. Picture systems that learn from experience and improve automatically, helping businesses stay ahead of problems before they happen.

8.2 *Breaking into new industries*

In **agriculture**, they'll model soil health and predict crop yields.

In **retail**, they'll help design smarter stores and better understand customer behaviour.

In **education**, we could see digital campuses that simulate learning environments.

In **construction**, builders will test entire projects virtually **before lifting a single brick**.

8.3 *Building smarter cities*

Imagine cities that can think ahead. With digital twins, city planners will have a live, digital version of the city that tracks traffic, energy use, pollution, and public safety in real time. when redesigning a bus route or test a new emergency response plan you can first test it with Digital Twin **without risking for real-world consequences** [24].

8.4 *Personalized, data-driven healthcare*

In the future, **your own body could have a digital twin** a health avatar that mirrors your biology. Doctors could use it to test how your body might react to certain medications or procedures before they happen. This means **safer surgeries, personalized treatments**, and better preventative care [11]. Healthcare could become truly one-to-one.

8.5 *Boosting robotics & automation*

Digital twins will help robots and autonomous vehicles get smarter and safer. Think of a self-driving car that has a digital twin running in parallel, constantly simulating what's ahead and learning how to improve.

This opens the door to **more efficient machines that troubleshoot themselves**.

8.6 *Fighting climate change & promoting sustainability*

Digital Twins can also help with knowing the carbon footprint of a building before it's even built. They'll be key tools for **simulating energy use, emissions, and waste** so companies and governments can make more sustainable choices, backed by real data.

8.7 *An ecosystem of digital twins (The "Twin of Twins")*

Instead of isolated digital twins, we're heading toward **entire networks of interconnected twins**. Imagine a factory's twin connected to its suppliers, delivery systems, and even customer feedback everything working together in one seamless digital ecosystem. It's like the **internet of twins**, helping entire systems sync up and run smarter [28].

8.8 *Easier, cheaper, and more widely available*

Right now, digital twins can be complex and costly but that's changing.

But soon, they'll be **more affordable, user-friendly, and standardized**. Even small businesses will be able to plug into digital twin platforms, without needing a whole tech team. Think **drag-and-drop interfaces** and ready-to-use templates.

9 CONCLUSION

Digital Twin technology has recently captured a lot of attention from both industry leaders and academic researchers. While definitions vary depending on the field, the core idea remains the same: a Digital Twin is a dynamic, two-way connection between a physical object and its virtual model. This constant data exchange allows the digital version to reflect real-world conditions in real time and vice versa.

The origins of Digital Twins go back to NASA, which first used the concept during the Apollo 13 mission and later applied it to the Mars Rover Curiosity project. Since then, the technology has evolved dramatically, becoming one of the most promising tools in today's digital landscape [9].

As this study highlights, manufacturing remains the most common area of focus in both research and real-world applications especially within the context of Industry 4.0.[32]. In factories, Digital Twins are used to streamline production planning, monitor systems in real time, and integrate data across the entire operation. They've also found a strong foothold in supply chain management [20]. Beyond the factory floor, other industries are catching on fast.

In construction, for example, Digital Twins are now used alongside wearables and mobile devices to track real-time progress on job sites. This lets teams compare actual results with the original design plans, helping to prevent errors and reduce costly rework [28].

Due to rapid advances in AI, IoT, and cloud technology, Digital Twins are becoming more powerful and accessible than ever. AI allows these digital models to process and respond to complex real-world data instantly. When paired with IoT sensors, Digital Twins can mirror and analyze everything from factory machines to infrastructure systems, constantly identifying areas for improvement [14,18].

They're also helping to optimize designs early in development saving time, money, and resources down the line.

As automation becomes more essential in nearly every industry, the demand for Digital Twin platforms is only expected to grow. Many businesses, still rebounding from the disruption of COVID-19, are turning to these technologies to rebuild smarter, more resilient operations.

Ensuring data accuracy, protecting against cyber threats, upgrading outdated systems, and managing power and storage demands are all real concerns. But even with these obstacles, the momentum behind Digital Twins is undeniable.

Digital Twins are not just another tech trend they're a foundational part of the digital transformation. As their capabilities expand, they're set to reshape how we design, operate, and improve the systems that drive modern life.

ACKNOWLEDGMENT

I would like to express my sincere gratitude to Prof. Aamir M. Shaikh for his invaluable guidance, support, and encouragement throughout the course of this review. His expertise and insightful feedback greatly contributed to the successful completion of this article.

REFERENCES

[1] Dassault Systems. (n.d.). *The living heart project*. Retrieved October 13, 2025, from https://www.3ds.com/productsservices/simulia/solutions/life-sciences/living-heart-project/

[2] Erdélyi, L., and Jánosi, L. (2021). Application of digital twin concept in livestock production. *Acta Agraria Debreceniensis, 2021*(1), 15–22.

[3] Fu, P., Meng, F., and Zhang, L. (2020). Digital twin technology and its application. *Journal of Physics: Conference Series, 1654* (1), 012031.

[4] Gartner. (2017). *Top 10 strategic technology trends*. Retrieved October 13, 2025, from https://www.gartner.com/en/newsroom

[5] Global Market Insights. (2022). *Digital twin market size report, 2022–2032*. Retrieved October 13, 2025, from https://www.gminsights.com/industry-analysis/digital-twin-market

[6] Jo, Y., Park, J., and Lee, J. (2022). Energy optimization in smart pig farms using digital twins. *Sustainability, 14*(4), 2057.

[7] Kritzinger, W., Karner, M., Traar, G., Henjes, J., and Sihn, W. (2018). Digital twin in manufacturing: A categorical literature review and classification. *IFAC-PapersOnLine, 51*(11), 1016–1022.

[8] Markets and Markets. (2021). *Digital twin market by application—Forecast to 2026*. Retrieved October 13, 2025, from https://www.marketsandmarkets.com

[9] NASA. (n.d.). *Apollo 13 mission overview*. Retrieved October 13, 2025, from https://www.nasa.gov/mission_pages/apollo/missions/apollo13.html

[10] Oklahoma State University. (2020). *Digital twin of respiratory system aims to improve lung cancer treatment*. Retrieved October 13, 2025, from https://news.okstate.edu/articles

[11] Siemens Healthineers. (2021). Digital twin heart model for personalized cardiology. Retrieved October 13, 2025, from https://www.siemens-healthineers.com

[12] World Bank. (2022). *Agriculture value added (% of GDP)—United States*. Retrieved October 13, 2025, from https://data.worldbank.org

[13] Grieves, M., and Vickers, J. (2017). Digital twin: Mitigating unpredictable, undesirable emergent behaviour in complex systems. In F.-J. Kahlen, S. Flumerfelt, & A. Alves (Eds.), *Transdisciplinary perspectives on complex systems* (pp. 85–113). Springer. https://doi.org/10.1007/978-3-319-38756-7_4

[14] Qi, Q., and Tao, F. (2018). Digital twin and big data towards smart manufacturing and Industry 4.0: 360-degree comparison. *IEEE Access, 6*, 3585–3593. https://doi.org/10.1109/ACCESS.2018.2793265

[15] Tao, F., Zhang, H., Liu, A., and Nee, A.Y.C. (2019). Digital twin in industry: State-of-the-art. *IEEE Transactions on Industrial Informatics, 15*(4), 2405–2415. https://doi.org/10.1109/TII.2018.2873186

[16] Barricelli, B.R., Casiraghi, E., and Fogli, D. (2019). A survey on digital twin: Definitions, characteristics, applications, and design implications. *IEEE Access, 7*, 167653–167671. https://doi.org/10.1109/ACCESS.2019.2953499

[17] Boschert, S., and Rosen, R. (2016). Digital twin—the simulation aspect. In P. Hehenberger & D. Bradley (Eds.), *Mechatronic futures* (pp. 59–74). Springer. https://doi.org/10.1007/978-3-319-32156-1_5

[18] Minerva, R., Biru, A., and Rotondi, D. (2020). Towards a definition of the Internet of Things (IoT). *IEEE Internet Initiative*. https://iot.ieee.org/images/files/pdf/IEEE_IoT_Towards_Definition_Internet_of_Things_Revision1_27MAY15.pdf

[19] IBM. (2020). *Digital twin technology: Closing the gap between the physical and digital*. Retrieved October 13, 2025, from https://www.ibm.com/blogs/internet-of-things/digital-twin/

[20] Google Cloud. (2022). *Introducing the supply chain twin*. Retrieved October 13, 2025, from https://cloud.google.com/blog/products/supply-chain/introducing-the-supply-chain-twin

[21] Siemens. (2021). *Digital twin for smart buildings*. Retrieved October 13, 2025, from https://new.siemens.com

[22] Accenture. (2022). *Digital twins: Accelerating intelligent enterprise transformation*. Retrieved October 13, 2025, from https://www.accenture.com

[23] McKinsey and Company. (2021). *Digital twins: The foundation of the enterprise metaverse*. Retrieved October 13, 2025, from https://www.mckinsey.com/business-functions/mckinsey-digital/our-insights

[24] World Economic Forum. (2020). *Digital twins for the built environment*. Retrieved October 13, 2025, from https://www.weforum.org/reports/digital-twins-for-the-built-environment

[25] Grieves, M. (2019). *Virtually intelligent product systems: Digital and physical twins*. Springer.

[26] Tao, F., and Qi, Q. (2019). *Digital twin driven smart design*. Academic Press.

[27] Lee, J., Bagheri, B., and Kao, H.A. (2015). *A cyber-physical systems architecture for industry 4.0-based manufacturing systems*. Springer.

[28] Zuehlke, D. (2010). SmartFactory—Towards a factory-of-things. In B. Vogel-Heuser, D. Schütz, and W. Schäfer (Eds.), *Automation, communication and cybernetics in science and engineering 2009/2010* (pp. 131–136). Springer.

[29] Sendhoff, B., Körner, C., and Müller, B. (Eds.). (2009). *Virtual futures for design, manufacturing and assembly: Proceedings of the 3rd transatlantic workshop*. Springer.

[30] Iung, B., and Levrat, E. (2019). *Digital twins for smart manufacturing*. Wiley.

[31] Stark, R. (Ed.). (2022). *Digital twins: Development and applications*. Springer International Publishing.

[32] Gilchrist, A. (2016). *Industry 4.0: The industrial internet of things*. Apress.

[33] Hehenberger, P., and Bradley, D. (Eds.). (2016). *Mechatronic futures: Challenges and solutions for mechatronic systems and their designers*. Springer.

[34] Bokrantz, J., Skoogh, A., and Berlin, C. (2023). *Smart maintenance for human–robot collaboration*. Springer.

[35] Stark, R., and Damerau, T. (2019). Digital twin. In S. Chatti and T. Tolio (Eds.), *CIRP encyclopedia of production engineering*. Springer, Berlin, Heidelberg. https://doi.org/10.1007/978-3-642-35950-7_16870-1

Advancement in Engineering and Science – Goyal et al. (Eds)
© 2026 The Author(s), ISBN: 978-1-041-31101-0

Exploring the Impact of Automation, Gamification, and Interactive Learning Tools on Engineering Students: A Study from Karmaveer Bhaurao Patil College of Engineering, Satara

Yogita Babar, Sunita Ballal, Alok Kadam, Ankita Kamane, Shital Phadatare, and Vedantika Jadhav
Basic Sciences & Humanities Department, Karmaveer Bhaurao Patil College of Engineering, Satara, Maharashtra, India

ABSTRACT: The impact of automation, gamification, and interactive learning resources on engineering students' academic experiences at Karmaveer Bhaurao Patil College of Engineering, Satara, is examined in this study. The study finds notable gains in student engagement, conceptual understanding, and study efficiency using a structured online survey with 182 respondents. The findings show that gamified approaches significantly raised motivation, and more than 90% of students reported improved learning through automation and interaction. Pupils indicated that they preferred individualized, technology-enabled learning settings over conventional lecture-based instruction. The need for better feedback systems and useful, concept-based tools is highlighted via thematic analysis of qualitative replies. These observations highlight how educational technology can revolutionize engineering education and provide tactical advice for improving the curriculum. The impact of automation, gamification, and interactive learning resources on engineering students' academic experiences at Karmaveer Bhaurao Patil College of Engineering, Satara, is examined in this study. The study finds notable gains in student engagement, conceptual understanding, and study efficiency using a structured online survey with 182 respondents. The findings show that gamified approaches significantly raised motivation, and more than 90% of students reported improved learning through automation and interaction. Pupils indicated that they preferred individualized, technology-enabled learning settings over conventional lecture-based instruction. The need for better feedback systems and useful, concept-based tools is highlighted via thematic analysis of qualitative replies. These observations highlight how educational technology can revolutionize engineering education and provide tactical advice for improving the curriculum.

Keywords: Automation, Gamification, Interactive Learning, Engineering Education, AI in Education, Digital Pedagogy, Student Engagement, Adaptive Learning Tools

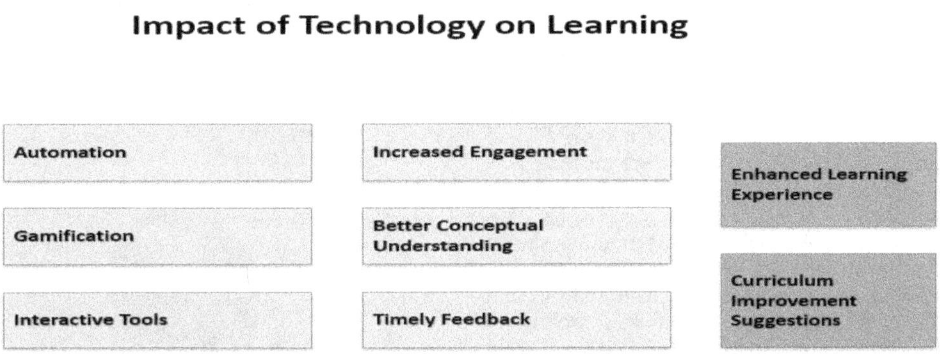

1 INTRODUCTION

According to this study, artificial intelligence (AI) in education refers to the use of AI technologies, including chatbots, intelligent tutoring systems, robots, and the automated evaluation of all forms of digital artifacts that support and enhance education. AIEd has the potential to significantly improve learning, teaching, assessment, and educational administration by giving students more individualized and adaptive learning, helping teachers better understand how students learn, and providing instantaneous feedback and machine-supported queries anywhere, at any time.[1] It has been determined that encouraging students to work and study on their own is essential to improving their learning outcomes in an online learning environment. The machine algorithm that enables computers to learn, analyze, and solve certain problems using inference, behavior, and decision-making processes is known as artificial intelligence (AI). Better technology-enhanced learning systems have been made possible by the educational profession thanks to AI's data analytics capabilities. Furthermore, researchers have noted that AI can provide insight into personalized learning and precision education by integrating the expertise and knowledge of seasoned educators into the learning system's decision-making process to assess each learner's learning status or inference behaviors.[2] In order to predict student performance and retention risk in engineering education, Bressane *et al.* (2022) suggest a fuzzy artificial intelligence-based model. Data gathered from an online poll on approaches to learning and historical records of student grades and retention are used to build the model. [3] According to the researchers, people who require information that can deliver rapid teaching in a timely manner can benefit from artificial intelligence and machine learning. Enhanced efficiency and productivity as well as heightened awareness of individual needs. Through their research, they were able to incorporate the process of learning into methods for researching, mapping various AI and machine learning operations into a body of knowledge, and switching instructors. [4]

The purpose of this study is to investigate how engineering students at Karmaveer Bhaurao Patil College of Engineering, Satara, are affected by automation, gamification, and interactive learning resources. This study aims to ascertain how these technology interventions influence students' learning journeys by evaluating their perspectives, experiences, and results through a survey administered via Google Forms. The results will provide insightful information on the efficacy of these novel strategies, helping teachers to better comprehend how they contribute to raising student motivation, engagement, and academic achievement in general.

Knowing the finer details of the impacts of these technologies is essential as educational institutions continue to adjust to the demands of the digital age. The study will examine whether gamification can improve student engagement, whether automation can accelerate learning processes, and how interactive tools can provide a more effective and personalized learning environment. This study will also address the unique demands and difficulties experienced by students in this demanding and specialized field by focusing on engineering students. This study will enhance the breadth of research on the use of technology in education by analyzing survey data and providing useful advice on how to incorporate these resources into engineering curricula.

2 LITERATURE SURVEY

According to the author, generative AI can be seen as a transformative tool that teachers and students can use to enhance their instruction. Deeper integration of AI and education can be achieved by raising knowledge of these technologies, utilizing them in the classroom, and helping students weigh the benefits and drawbacks of each. Tools like Bard, Chat GPT, and DALL-E are examples of generative AI that are creating new domains that will influence how people communicate, learn, and work together. [5]

Research on the effects of AI tools on education has shown that they improve student learning outcomes and boost productivity by automating repetitive tasks like data analysis and grading. The effects of AI tools on education are complex and have the potential to significantly alter teaching and learning in the future. It might lead to the development of more promising future schooling. [6]

AI can also be applied to e-learning assessment and grading. Multiple-choice test graders and composition scoring software are examples of AI-supported assessment systems that can automatically grade student work, saving teachers time and effort so they can concentrate on giving individualized feedback and support. Additionally, by lowering the possibility of prejudice and error, AI-supported grading can offer more consistent and objective grading. Another area where AI can be useful in e-learning is in educational simulations and games. AI-enabled games and simulations can offer dynamic and captivating educational opportunities that can foster the development of vital abilities like creativity, problem-solving, and decision-making in pupils [7]. The internet of things (IoT) is becoming more and more prevalent in our daily lives as a result of faster internet connections. Without human assistance, things can interact and carry out their preset functions in smart homes and creative city applications. [8] Researchers should be able to look at complex, unscripted activities more comprehensively by incorporating multimodal approaches, which are widely employed in the multimodal interaction community. The authors have specifically concentrated on characterizing a group of modalities that have been the subject of multimodal analysis for many years, in addition to modalities that have just lately surfaced as fresh data streams that allow researchers to examine human behavior and interaction. [9]

The results of an investigation into the technological features of augmented reality technology in higher education indicate that the technology has a promising future and much room for advancement. By facilitating interaction, using a smartphone as a learning platform may aid students in learning and remembering new material. To determine the most effective ways to incorporate characteristics in the classroom, educators and business leaders will collaborate. [10] AI has the potential to revolutionize research and teaching methodologies, even though its effects on higher education are still being felt. However, a thorough analysis of AI's possible benefits and drawbacks is necessary for its responsible implementation, as is a dedication to meeting the demands of all stakeholders and students. We can maximize AI's potential to enhance learning outcomes while reducing the risks and difficulties it presents by having conversations about its ethical and societal consequences in higher education. [11]

3 METHODOLOGY

This study evaluated the effects of automation, gamification, and interactive learning technologies on engineering students using a quantitative research methodology and an online structured survey. Undergraduate students of Satara's Karmaveer Bhaurao Patil College of Engineering participated in the survey. The survey was disseminated through institutional channels and included both closed-ended and open-ended questions. 182 valid replies in all were gathered. The following key areas were covered by the survey:

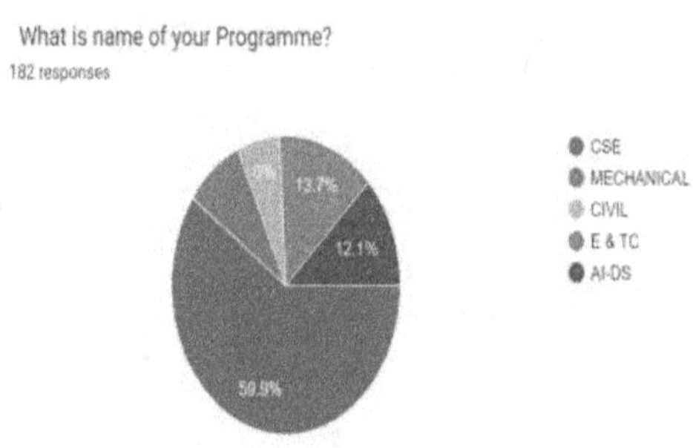

Figure 1. Demographics (Year of study, Programme).

- Use and effectiveness of automated learning tools
- Experience and perception of gamification
- Use and helpfulness of interactive learning tools

overall effect on learning preferences, interest, conceptual understanding, and study effectiveness. According to the survey, most students thought automated learning tools were very helpful in helping them comprehend difficult engineering ideas, while a moderate number thought they were only somewhat helpful and very few had never used them. Remarkably, 90% of users concurred that automation improved the effectiveness of their study sessions. About 60% of respondents said they have used gamified learning resources, and most said they were much more interested in studying as a result of these resources. Student ratings on gamification showed a generally positive trend, averaging between 3 and 4 on a 5-point scale. When it came to interactive learning tools such as simulations and virtual labs, over 75% of students reported using them. These tools were rated highly helpful, with most students assigning scores of 1 or 2 on a 5-point scale, indicating strong effectiveness.

Students also clearly preferred interactive teaching techniques over conventional lecture-based instruction. When it came to their overall learning experience, over 90% of participants thought that the combination of automation, gamification, and interactive tools had improved it. The majority of students said they would be prepared to suggest these technologies to other engineering students in the future. Improved conceptual understanding, enhanced knowledge retention, higher engagement, and greater learning flexibility were among the reported benefits that were noted in the qualitative replies. Improvement recommendations centered on adding more interactive content, making sure that it better matched the curriculum, providing tailored feedback, and extending gamification to cover more practical, hands-on themes. Open-ended replies were subjected to thematic analysis, while quantitative analysis was conducted using Likert-scale and categorical data.

4 EXPERIMENTAL WORK

- Participants: 182 engineering students from programs such as Computer Science, AI & Data Science, and Mechanical Engineering across all academic years.
- Data Collection Tools: Google Forms-based structured questionnaire
- Survey Focus Areas:
  - Automation Tools (e.g., AI tutors, automated assignments)
  - Gamification (quizzes, points, Kahoot, Snake & Ladder, leaderboards)
  - Interactive Tools (simulations, virtual labs, interactive textbooks)

Each section asked about both usage and perceived effectiveness or helpfulness. Quantitative data was processed using frequency and percentage analysis, and response trends were visualized to identify core patterns. Open-ended feedback was coded and grouped by common themes.

5 RESULTS

Over 70% of students reported actively using automated tools in their learning process, with many expressing general satisfaction, while others offered constructive feedback for improvement. The responses varied from brief affirmations to thoughtful, detailed suggestions. A notable portion of students emphasized that gamification elements should not merely serve as entertainment but should be rooted in educational value and linked closely to course outcomes. As one student suggested, "Games should be more concept-based and not just fun—they should help solve real problems." This view echoed a broader demand for greater conceptual depth and integration of real-world applications, such as industry case studies and project-based learning.

Students emphasized the value of meaningful and context-driven content by pointing out the need for more real-life-based quizzes and simulations that provide clear conceptual understanding. Many students highlighted the need for technological advances in addition to improvements in materials, especially in laboratory equipment and digital simulation tools. He gave examples such as "improved virtual lab systems" and "new electronic equipment in laboratories." The demand for better feedback and participation systems was another important topic. Many students expressed a desire for systems that provide quick, informative feedback and encourage more interaction with the teacher. For example, "Give better feedback when students are wrong so they learn from mistakes," was noted in one review. To maintain their attention and avoid boredom, students also expressed a desire for visually appealing and engaging tools, demanding more infographics, animated diagrams, and story-based simulations. Students also showed interest in collaboration, with some expressing a desire for gamified peer learning options such as shared leaderboards and team-based tournaments. About 30% expressed satisfaction, 60% offered supportive or neutral views, and only 10% gave vague or ambiguous answers, making overall sentiment favorable. This wealth of information provides a useful road map for improving the efficacy of technology-enhanced education in engineering schools.

6 DISCUSSION

The results strongly show that engineering students benefit from technology-enabled learning resources. Gamification increases motivation and engagement while automation speeds up the learning process. Because interactive tools mimic real-world situations, they foster a better comprehension. The fact that students choose interactive and blended learning over traditional lecture formats is an important finding. According to current educational ideas, these findings support student-centered pedagogy and active learning.

There are still certain obstacles to overcome, though, such as the requirement for more individualized, adaptive content and making sure all kids have fair access to digital resources. Students' suggestions also emphasize the need for better AI tutor reactivity and gamified learning in real-world/lab settings. Students anticipate increasingly individualized, flexible, and concept-driven instructional technologies, including automation, gamification, and interactive learning resources. Systems that recognize individual learning requirements, deliver immediate and insightful feedback, and provide interactive content that simplifies difficult technical ideas are what they want. Beyond simple enjoyment, gamified technologies should have practical applications, foster problem-solving skills, and stimulate deeper curricular engagement. Along with the requirement for better lab infrastructure and easier access to digital materials, other highly appreciated elements include visual appeal, realistic simulations, and peer collaboration opportunities.

Student Survey Report: Graphical Analysis

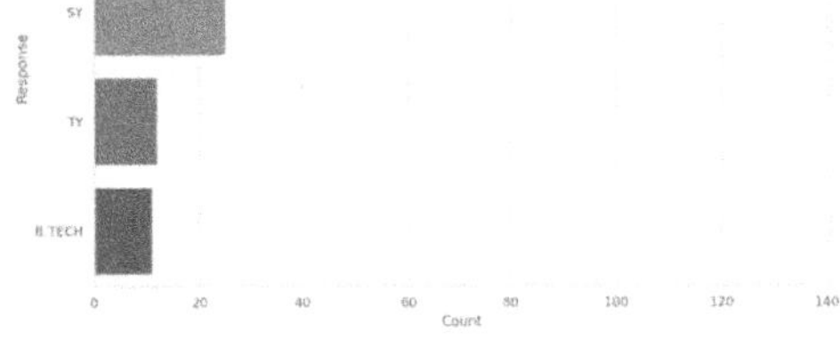

Figure 2. Use of automation.

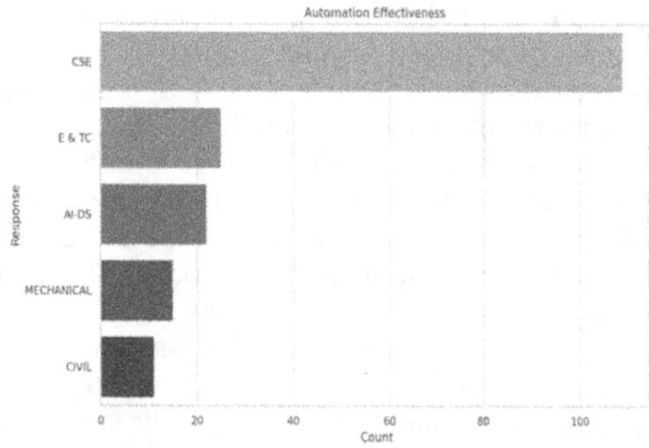

Figure 3. Effectiveness of automation.

Figure 4. Gamification experience.

7 CONCLUSION

The results of this study clearly show that engineering students' educational experiences at Karmaveer Bhaurao Patil College of Engineering, Satara, are significantly and favorably impacted by the use of automation, gamification, and interactive learning tools. Using these educational technologies led to greater engagement, deeper conceptual understanding, and increased efficiency, according to the vast majority of students. Students valued elements like real-time feedback, visual simulations, and tailored learning routes, and their replies showed a clear preference for interactive techniques over traditional instruction. Although the majority of students expressed satisfaction, helpful criticism pointed out the need for additional specialized content, improved alignment with curricular goals, and platform and lab technical improvements.

8 FUTURE SCOPE

The use of instructional technology in engineering education has a lot of room to grow and improve in the future. Future advancements may concentrate on incorporating AI-powered adaptive learning platforms that adjust to the performance and learning preferences of each individual learner. Incorporating collaborative multiplayer formats and real-world engineering challenges can enhance the immersiveness of gamification. Augmented and virtual reality should be added to interactive technologies to more accurately replicate hands-on experiences. Additionally, ongoing student input can direct the iterative development of these systems, guaranteeing that they adapt to the needs of academia and business. Long-term effects, like how these technologies impact engineering graduates' retention rates, skill development, and job preparation, can also be investigated through research.

ACKNOWLEDGEMENT

The authors are grateful to those who supported them, especially students of Karmaveer Bhaurao Patil College of Engineering, Satara.

REFERENCES

[1] Worsley M. and Blikstein P. (2016), Multimodal learning analytics and education data mining: Using computational technologies to measure complex learning tasks, *Journal of Learning Analytics*, vol. 3, no. 2, pp. 220–238, doi: 10.18608/jla.2016.32.11.

[2] B. S. and Vijayalakshmi V., (2022) AI-Based Metaverse Technologies Advancement Impact on Higher Education Learners, *WSEAS Transactions on Systems*, vol. 21, pp. 178–187. doi: 10.37394/23202.2022.21.19.

[3] Bressane A. *et al.*, (2023) Understanding the role of study strategies and learning disabilities on student academic performance to enhance educational approaches: A proposal using artificial intelligence, *Computers and Education Artificial Intelligence*, vol. 6, p. 100196. doi: 10.1016/j.caeai.2023.100196.

[4] Shaikh A.A., Kumar A., Jani K., Mitra S., García-Tadeo D.A., and Devarajan A., (2021) The Role of Machine Learning and Artificial Intelligence for making a Digital Classroom and its sustainable Impact on Education during Covid-19, *Materials Today Proceedings*, vol. 56, pp.32113215 doi: 10.1016/j.matpr.2021.09.368.

[5] Yu H. and Guo Y., (2023) Generative artificial intelligence empowers educational reform: current status, issues, and prospects, *Frontiers in Education*, vol. 8, doi: 10.3389/feduc.2023.1183162.

[6] Zadorina O., Hurskaya V., Sobolyeva S., Grekova L., and Vasylyuk-Zaitseva S., (2024) The role of Artificial intelligence in creation of future Education: Possibilities and challenges, *Futurity Education*, doi: 10.57125/fed.2024.06.25.09.

[7] Firat M., (2023) Integrating AI Applications into Learning Management Systems to Enhance e-Learning, *Öğretim Teknolojisi Ve Hayat Boyu Öğrenme Dergisi - Instructional Technology and Lifelong Learning*, pp. 1–14, doi: 10.52911/itall.1244453.

[8] Efe A., (2023) Taking virtual reality and augmented reality to the next level: artificial intelligence with mixed reality, *Kamu Yönetimi Ve Teknoloji Dergisi*, vol. 4, no. 2, pp. 141–165, doi: 10.58307/kaytek.1185712.

[9] Blikstein P. and Worsley M., (2016) Multimodal Learning Analytics and Education Data Mining: using computational technologies to measure complex learning tasks, *Journal of Learning Analytics*, vol. 3, no.2, pp.220–238, doi: 10.18608/jla.2016.32.11.

[10] B. S and V. V, (2022) AI based Metaverse Technologies Advancement impact on higher education learners, *Wseas Transactions On Systems*, vol. 21, pp. 178–184, doi: 10.37394/23202.2022.21.19.

[11] George B. and Ontario Wooden, (2023) *Managing the Strategic Transformation of Higher Education through Artificial Intelligence*. [Online]. Available: https://doi.org/10.3390/admsci13090196

Advancement in Engineering and Science – Goyal et al. (Eds)

Scalable Decentralized Analytics Through a Privacy-Enhanced Intent-Centric Framework

Prudhvi Naayini, Srikanth Kamatala, Praveen Kumar Myakala, Chiranjeevi Bura, and Anil Kumar Jonnalagadda
Independent Researchers DFW, Texas, USA

ABSTRACT: This study proposes a privacy-focused, intent-centric architecture for decentralized analytics and autonomous decision-making. By replacing transaction-based models with declarative intents, outcomes are matched by decentralized solver agents. The framework leverages zero-knowledge proofs, homomorphic encryption, and multichain settlement to ensure privacy, interoperability, and constraint-based coordination. Modular design separates protocol logic from consensus mechanisms, supporting deployment across diverse security domains, while user-friendly interfaces and programmable confidentiality reduce technical barriers. A decentralized supply chain case study demonstrates feasibility, providing a foundation for scalable, privacy-preserving systems that meet technical and operational requirements.

Keywords: Decentralized Analytics, Intent-Centric Architecture, Composable Privacy, Solver-Based Coordination, Multi-Chain Interoperability

1 INTRODUCTION

As decentralized technologies mature, the limitations of traditional transaction-centric blockchain systems have become increasingly evident. These systems rely on predefined counterparties and imperative logic for execution, restricting flexibility in dynamic coordination, privacy preservation, and autonomous decision making. Recent advancements in secure multiparty computation, decentralized identity, and cross-chain protocols have created fertile grounds for rethinking the fundamental interaction model within distributed systems.

This paper proposes a privacy-enhanced, intent-centric architecture for decentralized analytics designed to enable expressive, autonomous coordination among users and machines. Rather than specifying complete transactions, participants define declarative intents generalized goals or desired outcomes, such as "aggregate sales data from participating stores without revealing individual transactions." These intents are matched, composed, and finalized through decentralized solver agents that collaboratively resolve constraint-satisfaction problems and generate valid and privacy-preserving state transitions.

Core innovation lies in shifting from imperative execution to intent-based interaction, which enhances composability, reduces the cognitive burden on users, and empowers more flexible automation. By abstracting procedural steps, intent-centricity allows users to delegate decision logic while retaining control over constraints and privacy levels.

To ensure practical deployment, the architecture was modular and consensus-agnostic. It separates protocol logic from the underlying execution and trust models, enabling scalable deployments across heterogeneous security domains. Cross-domain interoperability is achieved through privacy-preserving communication protocols and message relays [1], [2], thus mitigating challenges related to incompatible consensus mechanisms and data schemas.

Privacy was treated as a first-class design principle. This framework integrates zero-knowledge proofs, homomorphic encryption, and programmable confidentiality to support fine-grained control over data visibility and execution semantics [3], [4]. These technologies enable multiparty coordination without exposing sensitive inputs or requiring centralized intermediaries.

To address real-world feasibility, the system adopts adaptive rollups, modular solver incentives, and user-friendly intent-abstraction layers. User interfaces are designed to shield participants from technical complexity, while preserving transparency and verifiability. The growing body of research on intent-driven network automation [5-7] has reinforced the relevance and viability of this model for next generation decentralized applications.

The architecture entails trade-offs such as computational overhead, larger attack surfaces, scalability limits, and regulatory constraints. Similar challenges in multi-agent federated reinforcement learning underscore the need for modular decentralized strategies. A case study on decentralized supply chain analytics illustrates its practical potential. The rest of this paper outlines the design, programming model, interoperability, and deployment of intent-driven, privacy-enhanced decentralized systems.

2 RELATED WORK

Recent advancements in decentralized computing have led to growing interest in frameworks that improve automation, interoperability, and privacy. However, many existing systems continue to rely on transaction-centric paradigms, in which users must construct imperative operations with rigid semantics. However, these models often lack support for flexible coordination and user abstraction. Intent-driven systems are emerging as promising alternatives, allowing users and agents to express high-level goals without detailing the execution steps. These approaches have gained momentum in network management, programmable infrastructure, and autonomous service orchestration [5-7], [8].

In the Web3 ecosystem, interoperability has primarily been addressed through relay protocols, such as Cosmos IBC and Polkadot's shared security model. These systems facilitate token transfers and message passing across heterogeneous chains [1], [2]. However, they typically require developers to encode workflows as static, chain-specific logic, which limits their ability to support dynamic coordination or user-defined intents. For instance, cross-chain asset exchanges still require predefined routes and validator agreements, which lack the flexibility needed for decentralized intent discovery and multiparty negotiation.

Privacy-preserving computation has also seen major advances, with techniques such as zero-knowledge proofs, fully homomorphic encryption, and secure multiparty computation increasingly integrated into decentralized applications [3], [4], [9]. These cryptographic tools play a crucial role in enabling secure intent resolution. For example, solvers can verify that the proposed transaction satisfies user-defined constraints without revealing the sensitive state or computation details, thereby preserving privacy, even in adversarial environments.

DOI: 10.1201/9781003798514-30

Emerging blockchain-native intent-driven frameworks such as Anoma have introduced powerful abstractions for declarative coordination. These systems demonstrate the feasibility of decoupling intent expression from the execution and settlement layers. However, such frameworks often focus narrowly on asset exchange or require protocol-level integration, limiting their general-purpose applicability.

By contrast, the framework proposed in this study offers a unified, modular, and extensible design. It integrates a composable intent model, solver-based optimization, and cross-domain privacy guarantees in a portable execution environment. By leveraging cryptographically verifiable building blocks and separating protocol logic from trust and execution assumptions, this architecture enables scalable real-world deployment of decentralized systems for analytics, coordination, and governance. Table 1 summarizes the distinctions between traditional transaction-centric, workflow-driven, and intent-centric architectures.

Table 1. Comparison of coordination paradigms.

Feature	Transaction-Centric	Workflow-Based	Intent-Centric (This Work)
Execution Model	Imperative	Pre-defined	Declarative and Composable
Counterparty Discovery	Static	Manual	Dynamic, Solver-Driven
Privacy Support	Minimal	Limited	ZKPs, FHE, Programmable Confidentiality
Cross-Domain Interoperability	Hardcoded Bridges	Partial	Native and Modular
User Autonomy	Low	Moderate	High, via Validity Predicates

3 STRUCTURAL TOPOLOGY

The proposed architecture is organized into modular components that interact through decentralized overlays. These components collectively manage the intent lifecycle, solver coordination, encrypted transaction propagation, and privacy-aware settlement without requiring centralized control. Figure 1 provides a high-level illustration of system topology and component interactions.

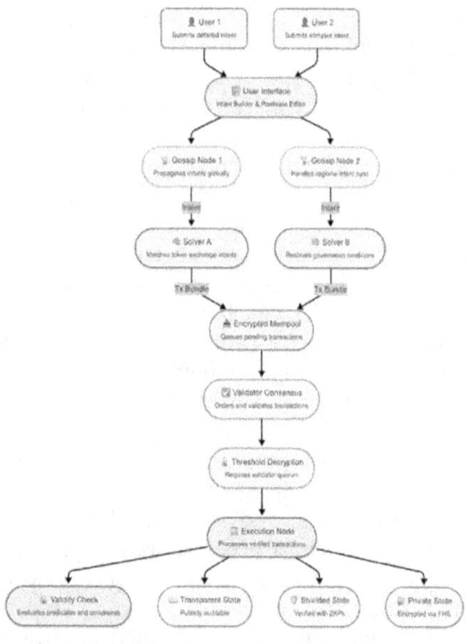

Figure 1. High-level system topology including node roles, intent propagation, solver execution, and settlement.

3.1 *Node roles and communication layer*

All entities in the system operate as nodes and may assume roles, such as intent propagators, solvers, validators, or executors. Roles are dynamically assigned and configurable at runtime, enabling deployment flexibility across resource-constrained, edge, or cloud environments.

Communication occurs through asynchronous and untrusted channels. The architecture uses cryptographic identifiers and verifiable message passing to build sparse and dense overlay networks for intent dissemination and transaction relay, respectively.

3.2 *Intent lifecycle and gossip layer*

An intent is a cryptographically signed message representing a partial and declarative description of a state change. For example, an intent may state, "exchange asset A for asset B if the oracle price is above 100 USD." Intents are broadcast through the intent gossip layer, a sparse pseudonymous network that facilitates counterparty discovery and constraint resolution.

To incentivize propagation, intents can include settlement-conditional fees, which are paid only upon successful transaction finalization and inclusion in a confirmed block. Nodes participating in the gossip layer may share this fee based on their role in relaying or solving their intent.

3.3 *Solver coordination and optimization*

Solvers are decentralized agents that observe the intent pool and compute solutions to multi-intent constraints. Each solver executes domain-specific algorithms; for example, a solver handling token swaps may apply price-matching and liquidity heuristics, whereas one processing governance vote may enforce quorum and role-based filters.

Solvers are incentivized by intent-attached or application-defined rewards. Solvers apply indexing and batched evaluations to avoid excessive computational overheads. Threshold acceptance criteria and fallback mechanisms were used to ensure solution liveness without redundant computations, while parallel execution strategies can further accelerate solver performance in complex coordination environments .

3.4 *Encrypted transactions and mempool*

Once a solver constructs a valid transaction bundle, it encrypts it using a threshold public key, a cryptographic scheme in which decryption requires cooperation from a qualified subset (e.g., 2/3 of validators). This ensures that no single party can decrypt the transaction content prematurely, preserving confidentiality.

The encrypted transaction is then submitted to mempool, a densely connected overlay for staging transactions. Validators propagate only encrypted data, thereby reducing the risk of front running. After consensus is reached, the validators jointly decrypt and finalize the transaction for execution.

3.5 *Privacy tiers and transition mechanisms*

The execution layer accommodates three distinct privacy tiers. In the **transparent** tier, all state and execution are publicly visible, as in the case of proposal submissions. The **shielded** tier encrypts state while allowing verification through zero-knowledge proofs, such as individual votes in a governance election. In the **private** tier, state is fully encrypted and processed using homomorphic encryption, supporting tasks like aggregate analytics on personal data. Privacy transitions are programmable: for instance, a decentralized funding round may start with a public registry of applicants (transparent), accept private contributions (shielded), and compute anonymized distribution results through encrypted computations (private). Table 2 summarizes these privacy tiers alongside representative application scenarios.

Table 2. Privacy tiers and corresponding use cases.

Privacy Tier	Description	Example Use Case
Transparent	Publicly viewable state and execution logic, allowing all participants to inspect and verify details openly.	DAO proposal submissions, governance logs, and audit-compliant asset movements.
Shielded	Encrypted state with verifiable constraints using zero-knowledge proofs or attestations, ensuring selective disclosure.	Privacy-preserving voting, compliance-bound transfers, and gated data sharing.
Private	Fully encrypted state and computation with no visibility into data or execution paths; leverages homomorphic encryption.	Encrypted analytics, sealed-bid auctions, private payroll, or health data aggregation.

3.6 *Security and concurrency domains*

A security domain is a set of nodes that share a consensus mechanism and execute a state-transition function under aligned trust assumptions. A concurrency domain defines the transaction ordering and isolation boundaries. Applications may operate within a single domain or span multiple domains.

While concurrency domains ensure consistency and determinism for execution, security domains define the levels of trust and fault tolerance. For example, a privacy-sensitive voting application may run in a shielded security domain, whereas its funding allocation operates in a transparent, high-throughput concurrency domain.

3.7 *Programmable data availability layer*

The architecture incorporates a programmable data availability layer that manages the retention, sharing, and time-sensitive release of intent and transaction data. This layer supports features such as time-based batch decryption, which is useful in scenarios like sealed-bid auctions, role-based access controls for intermediate states, and application-defined policies for data deletion or replication. By enforcing these mechanisms, the data availability layer ensures that all information necessary for intent resolution and validation remains accessible while adhering to constraints on access, verification, and synchronization across different domains.

3.8 *Cross-domain communication*

Interoperability between the security and execution domains is achieved through authenticated message relays and privacy-preserving bridge protocols. These enable state updates and intent resolution across chains without requiring a shared consensus or global execution models [2].

3.8.1 *Programming model*

The architecture introduces a declarative, modular programming model for composable, privacy-aware, and verifiable interactions in decentralized environments. It separates application logic from execution and trust layers, letting developers and users define, interpret, and resolve intents without managing low-level transactions.

3.8.2 *Intent formats*

Intents are structured, cryptographically signed messages expressing desired state changes, supporting conditional logic, counterpart constraints, and privacy flags. For example: "Contribute 50 tokens to Project X if total funding exceeds 1,000 tokens and governance approves." Intents are interoperable, portable, and extensible, serialized into verifiable byte strings, and broadcast to the decentralized intent network.

3.8.3 *Application and user validity predicates*

Applications define deterministic validity predicates to enforce rules such as permissions, resource checks, and constraint evaluation. Users can define additional predicates for fine-grained control over interactions, e.g., daily transaction caps, domain-specific limits, or zero-knowledge attestations. Predicates are cryptographically verifiable and allow off-chain simulation and audits.

3.8.4 *Solver algorithms*

Solvers interpret intents and apply matching, optimization, and heuristic algorithms (e.g., token matching, maximal funding allocation, weather-triggered conditions). Interaction is non-interactive; users receive cryptographic confirmation upon settlement, on- or off-chain.

3.8.5 *User interfaces and tooling*

Cognitive overhead is minimized via graphical builders, constraint toggles, and simulation previews, all linked to predicates and intent schemas. Tooling includes intent preview/debug tools, wallet-integrated predicate editors, and solver dashboards.

3.8.6 *Application portability*

Applications execute securely across multiple instances and domains because predicates and solver logic are independent of consensus or chain configuration.

3.8.7 *Security and delegation*

Users retain data ownership and control over state transitions. Delegated actions must satisfy user- and application-level predicates enforced deterministically.

3.8.8 *Privacy-aware state management*

State spans three privacy tiers public, shielded, and private controlled via predicate flags and intent schemas. Examples: public auction listings, encrypted ZKP-verified bids, and fully encrypted analytics (FHE). This tiered model balances transparency with confidentiality per operational or regulatory needs.

4 CASE STUDY: DECENTRALIZED SUPPLY CHAIN ANALYTICS

This section presents a case study on decentralized supply chain analytics to demonstrate the real-world feasibility and applicability of the proposed framework. This use case involves coordination among independent stakeholders' manufacturers, logistics providers, warehouses, and retailers who must securely share, analyze, and act upon operational data without revealing proprietary information or relying on centralized intermediaries.

4.1 *Problem context*

Traditional supply chain analytics systems are often centralized and siloed, resulting in data fragmentation, limited transparency, and the risk of single-point failure. Participants are typically reluctant to expose operational data because of competitive concerns, privacy regulations, and lack of trust. There is a growing need for systems that enable secure data-sharing, dynamic coordination, and privacy-aware automation across independently governed entities.

4.2 *Use of intent-centric architecture*

The intent-centric architecture tackles these challenges by enabling stakeholders to express declarative goals, or intents, without revealing sensitive data or internal computational logic. For instance, a warehouse might issue an intent such as sharing real-time inventory data with authorized logistics providers only if a delivery delay exceeds two hours. Similarly, a logistics provider could declare an intent to request updated warehouse stock levels for a specific SKU only if it is the designated carrier. A retailer might submit an intent to aggregate historical delivery times across all suppliers to optimize reordering frequency. Each intent is cryptographically signed, optionally encrypted, and propagated through the intent-gossip layer. Solvers within the network continuously match compatible intents and generate transactions for decentralized execution, strictly adhering to the constraints defined in each participant's validity predicates.

4.3 *Application logic and solver workflow*

The application includes: a **JSON-based Intent Format** specifying actions, counterpart rules, timing, and data permissions; **Validity Predicates** enforcing access, format, and authorization (e.g., verified delivery contracts); and **User Predicates** limiting queries, time windows, or requiring cryptographic proofs. **Solvers** continuously match compatible intents such as pairing retailer analytics with warehouse and logistics data using encrypted computation and zero-knowledge verification without exposing raw data.

4.4 *Privacy and interoperability guarantees*

All state transitions are organized into privacy tiers. Transparent transitions expose public metadata such as delivery status and aggregated lead times. Shielded transitions validate warehouse and retail inventory levels using zero-knowledge proofs (ZKPs). Private transitions process supplier-specific delivery logs with fully homomorphic encryption (FHE) to compute on-time performance scores without revealing per-route data. Interoperability is maintained through domain bridges that connect supply chain participants across different blockchain networks or governance domains, while intent messages are relayed via authenticated, privacy-preserving protocols to ensure consistency and confidentiality across chains.

4.5 *Scalability and deployment considerations*

Each supply chain actor operates within its own security domain, executing local predicates and broadcasting intentions via shared overlays. Concurrency is maintained through domain-level mempools, whereas final analytics outputs are computed in encrypted form and settled using threshold-decrypted transactions.

To reduce solver overhead, aggregation tasks are delegated to specialized solver nodes with access to secure computation libraries. Transactions are batch-encrypted and published during off-peak network times, supporting scalable coordination between dozens or hundreds of participants.

4.6 *Regulatory and legal considerations*

By keeping raw data on devices or private shards and verifying computations via cryptographic proofs, the system supports compliance with the GDPR, HIPAA, and similar data protection regulations. Audit logs and encrypted state transitions provide a verifiable history of data sharing and usage, without exposing sensitive business information.

4.7 *Outcomes and insights*

This case study demonstrates that the proposed architecture enables autonomous coordination via declarative intent matching without centralized control, preserves privacy through programmable confidentiality and encrypted analytics, supports cross-domain interoperability across hybrid enterprise deployments, and ensures regulatory compliance with data minimization and verifiable access controls. These principles also extend to broader applications, such as AI-powered assistive technologies, where privacy and real-time processing are critical [10].

5 CONCLUSION

This work presented a privacy-focused, intent-driven architecture that enables secure, autonomous coordination without central authority. Demonstrated in a decentralized supply chain, it highlights modularity, layered privacy, and cross-domain interoperability. The successful realization of this next-generation decentralized model is contingent upon integrating advanced infrastructure automation platforms, particularly those leveraging cloud and Kubernetes technologies[11].

REFERENCES

[1] Belchior, R., Vasconcelos, A., Guerreiro, S., and Correia, M. (2021). A survey on blockchain interoperability: Past, present, and future trends. *Acm Computing Surveys (CSUR)*, *54*(8), 1–41.

[2] Essaid, M., Kim, J., and Ju, H. (2023). Inter-blockchain communication message relay time measurement and analysis in cosmos. *Applied Sciences*, *13*(20), 11135.

[3] Lee, D., António, J., and Khan, H. (2024). Privacy-Preserving Decentralized AI with Confidential Computing. *arXiv preprint arXiv:2410.13752*.

[4] Biswas, S., Even, M., Kermarrec, A.M., Massoulié, L., Pires, R., Sharma, R., and de Vos, M. (2024). Noiseless privacy-preserving decentralized learning. *arXiv preprint arXiv:2404.09536*.

[5] Mehmood, K., Kralevska, K., and Palma, D. (2023). Intent-driven autonomous network and service management in future cellular networks: A structured literature review. *Computer Networks*, *220*, 109477.

[6] Li, T., Yang, C., Song, Y., Cai, L., Zheng, R., Liu, X., and Liu, S. (2024). Architecting Autonomous Network Management and Control via Intent-Driven Decoupled Network. *IEEE Network*.

[7] Njah, Y., Leivadeas, A., and Falkner, M. (2024). An AI-driven intent-based network architecture. *IEEE Communications Magazine*.

[8] Christou, F. (2023). MINDFul. jl: A Framework for Intent-driven Multi-Domain Network coordination. *arXiv preprint arXiv:2307.02413*.

[9] Majdoub, I., and Atmani, K. Privacy Paradigm Shift: Zero Knowledge. *Cybercrime Unveiled: Technologies for Analysing Legal Complexity*, 151.

[10] Naayini, P., Myakala, P.K., Bura, C., Jonnalagadda, A.K., and Kamatala, S. (2025). Ai-powered assistive technologies for visual impairment. *arXiv preprint arXiv:2503.15494*.

[11] Naayini, P., and Kamatala, S. (2025). Automating Infrastructure Platforms with Cloud, Kubernetes, and Site Reliability Engineering. International Journal of Computer Techniques.

Advancement in Engineering and Science – Goyal et al. (Eds)
© 2026 The Author(s), ISBN: 978-1-041-31101-0

Mental Stress Prediction Using EEG Signals

Aditya Raghuvanshi and Akshay Jadhav
Computer Science and Engineering, Manipal University Jaipur, Jaipur, India

Lokesh Malviya and Ramraj Dangi
School of Computing Science and Engineering, VIT Bhopal University, Sehore, India

ABSTRACT: An advanced automated technique to help detect mental stress based on electroencephalogram (EEG) signals is proposed. When applied to classification, deep learning techniques significantly improve category accuracy. To elaborate computation test process (including Stroop shade-phrase test, duplicate pictures, and mathematical calculations) carried out on 40 subjects, this research analyzed participants' EEG signals. The research used stacked GRU, stacked LSTM, and stacked BiLSTM to extract temporal relationships from EEG data, and this approach is very effective. At the evaluation stage, the Stacked BiLSTM model outperformed conventional machine learning methods such as Random Forest and SVM, which achieved 85 and 80% accuracy, respectively, with the maximum accuracy of 95%. After research on the importance of the processes, spectral electricity (alpha and beta wave frequencies) was found to be a significant contributor to mental stress.

Keywords: Electroencephalogram, Mental Stress, Classification, Stacked

1 INTRODUCTION

Psychological stress the synergistic relationship of this trend-driven approach and EEG data is a promising step toward customization for the treatment of personal stress conditions. The research put these models into practice using real-world datasets as well as investigating multimodal mechanisms to improve the performance of strain detection. The psychological stress has become a serious public health challenge for contemporary countries [4], and the World Health Organization indicates that it is one of the most significant causes of global disease burden [4]. The growing prevalence of stress-associated illness, particularly among students and professionals, emphasizes the critical need for sound goal-setting techniques to diagnose and monitor pressure [1,11]. The classical practices for the assessment of strain frequently rely on self-reporting as well as biological indicators such as cortisol levels, which are not useful for real-time follow-up analysis and are subject to individual reporting bias [7]. Electroencephalogram (EEG) data have demonstrated promise to provide objective/real-time information on intellectual states, including states of stressors/regression at a given point in time [3], [11]. EEG evaluates the brain's electrical activity at various wavelengths (delta, theta, alpha, beta, gamma etc …) which correspond to various cognitive and affective stages [12]. This neurophysiological stress detection technology has several advantages over traditional methods, including the fact that it is non-invasive, has high temporal resolution, and may detect scattered changes in cognitive load and emotional state [2]. Assessing mental stress is difficult due to the heterogeneity in pressure reports [6]. The reliability of comparing mental strain relies upon substantially on the evaluation method used. Traditionally, stress is classed the usage of subjective strategies, with self-record questionnaires, inclusive of the Perceived Stress Scale, being the most normally hired (Sweeney and Harlow 2019; Zhang *et al.* 2020). Many studies have installed questionnaire ratings and self-record rankings as ground fact to estimate intellectual stress tiers [1], [4].

Recent advances in signal processing and device studying have opened new avenues for automatic pressure detection the use of EEG facts [2], [11]. Our studies leverage those technological developments to create a robust pressure detection machine able to differentiating between diverse cognitive states. This research employs a multi-undertaking experimental paradigm, such as mathematics calculations, reflect photo exams, Stroop colour-word exams, and relaxation states, to set off and degree exclusive levels of cognitive stress [7], [8].

2 LITERATURE REVIEW

The characteristic importance evaluation in this study aimed to identify the EEG signal characteristics most indicative of mental strain. By examining diverse capabilities, the research tried to improve the interpretability and received insights into the neural mechanisms related to one-of-a-kind cognitive states [4].

In order to complete the idea of models like the Stacked GRU, Stacked LSTM, and Stacked BiLSTM, the typical importance was studied by applying permutation importance and attention processes (9) to try and form a comprehensive paradigm of the models. These approaches were applied for understanding how changes in individual properties impacted model predictions with specific reference to the principal EEG recordings [11]. Specific frequency bands (alpha [8 to 12 Hz] and beta [13 to 30 Hz] waves) were pivotal in separating stress from relaxation [8]. Elevated beta-wave activity is an important factor associated with stress-inducing tasks such as mathematical computations and Stroop tests [7] whereas increased alpha wave engagement relates to relaxation in such non-worrying tasks [2].

Furthermore, EEG signal complexity, temporal capacity for EEG signals and temporal variability are among other indicators of mental strain [6]. These findings provide additional evidence on the applicability of deep learning methods and a deeper understanding of neurophysiological measures of strain that would be informative and potentially relevant for individualized intervention for treatment of strain reduction and mental well-being monitoring [10]. [9] Total strain monitoring through EEG with data as to the EEG alone can potentially play an important role in schools for students. Teachers might obtain data on the thinking states of college students from pressure levels taken during examinations or with difficult assignments they have worked on, which they could use to adjust their teaching strategies. Similarly, if we were able to monitor how stressed students got on the test using EEG

DOI: 10.1201/9781003798514-31

records, we would be able to identify stress relief strategies that allow the students to relax or take breaks.

[5] Finally, it is anticipated that the convergence of EEG evaluation with device knowledge will present an exciting opportunity to improve the detection of mental strain. It is in this light that this study adds to the expanding literature and effectively demonstrates the role of machine learning models to discern cognitive states, by reviewing EEG-based indicators of strain. The findings demonstrate whether deep mastering architectures (e.g., Stacked GRU, Stacked LSTM, Stacked BiLSTM) could recognize and classify mental stress from EEG signals. [6] The implications of this research extend beyond cognitive neuroscience, which is essential to understanding how stress and cognitive load are correlated in the brain. Showing links between patterns of EEG data and mental states, our results add to the science of how the brain responds to conditions of stress and cognitive demand.

With the current findings, it is likely that future work will be informed by this information to develop better parameters for quantifying and modulating intellectual health-related fitness. In short, strain detection with EEG is a significant contribution to monitoring intellectual health and could change the way a writer perceives and acts toward stress in academic, professional, and scientific contexts. They developed a potent real-time system that may enhance mental health and cognitive performance in a variety of academic domains by utilising sophisticated machine learning algorithms and EEG data.

3 METHODOLOGY

3.1 *Data acquisition*

The research participants completed four cognitive tasks. From each participant's three trials of each task (40 topics x 4 responsibilities x 3 trials), 480 different EEG recordings were obtained. So the experimental plan was devised to ensure that record series for all subjects in the respective study period was up to date. The SAM 40 dataset [4], which includes EEG sessions of 40 people doing cognitive tasks like the Stroop color-word test, arithmetic calculations and mirror image detection, was utilized for this research. The neural correlates of mental stress and cognitive load may be explored with the help of this dataset.

3.2 *Experimental tasks*

The Stroop Colour Word Test, the Arithmetic Test, the Mirror Image Recognition Test, and the Relaxation State Classification in EEG-Based Mental Stress Assessment are four tasks that have been used to assess cognitive load. This can cause high-brow stress in arithmetic computations, when numerical thinking and problem-solving skills are necessary. Participants' EEGs were recorded while they performed arithmetic calculations, and certain functions were taken from the signal to observe brain activity linked to mental tasks (e.g., cognitive exertion and number processing). The Stroop Colour Word Test assesses cognitive control and interest by asking the subject to identify the colour of the ink instead of the word. The Mirror Image Recognition Test generates varying degrees of cognitive load and pressure because it includes all the visual perception and spatial processing of visuospatial activity. To determine and describe the neural correlates of stress and develop stress reduction intervention strategies, and need to categorise relaxation states in EEG-based mental stress assessments. Relaxation states, low states of cognitive load and emotional arousal, are crucial for measuring stress. Neural signatures while the person is in a relaxation state can guide the ways the body measures stress and mental health.

3.3 *Feature extraction*

The EEG data and processed it to extract appropriate skills from diverse frequency bands: delta (0.5-4 Hz), theta (4-8 Hz), alpha (8-12 Hz), beta (12-30 Hz), and gamma (30-100 Hz). Each of these frequency bands represents distinct mental and emotional states, providing rich information to the models. A rich function set of descriptive statistical variables such as signal energy, variance, and peak frequency was obtained for every frequency band for the relaxed state mental activity.

3.4 *Training the classifier*

The learned capabilities were trained into Stacked GRU, Stacked LSTM and Stacked BiLSTM models. Some layers of models trained to the EEG data to learn complex styles. Using a labelled data for EEG recordings to learn the discriminative properties of the relaxation states compared to the other cognitive responsibilities.

3.5 *Data processing pipeline: Data preparation*

The goal of this work is to establish a good category model that detects mental strain from EEG (electroencephalogram) notifications. The procedures involved are broad, such as data generation, data transformation, splits, and normalization. Artificial EEG datasets which attempt to reflect a variety of mental states are generated to facilitate data classification, such that they generalize well to actual circumstances. After that, the information is mapped to three-dimensional data to allow the models to visualize the patterns, observed over time. Later, decided to separate the data into two segments to optimise the parameters of our models and evaluate their performance in real-world applications: the education segment and the test subset. These subsets were conducted at 80-20 cut-offs. Also used StandardScalers for convergence and performance. Besides making these models learn more effectively, the comprehensive process for making this kind of input for information preparation may also greatly increase the efficiency of automatic mental health detection technology. Empowered by advanced real-time stress detection technologies and the possibility of real-time monitoring to manage symptoms, it will contribute to improving mental health and providing assistance for individuals in any environment - work, schools, clinic etc.

3.6 *Classification methodology*

Deep learning architectures, such as Stacked Gated Recurrent Units (GRU), Stacked Long Short-Term Memory (LSTM), and Stacked Bidirectional LSTM (BiLSTM), were used in the study to classify cognitive states by task. Models were created from a labeled data set, measuring accuracy, precision, recall and F1. The Stacked BiLSTM classifier was effective for different cognitive states and disentanglement from each other.

Figure 1 shows synthetic EEG signals generated during various cognitive tasks. The signals are critical to investigate the underlying brain activity associated to the effects of mental stress and cognitive load. The visualisation of the pattern of the brainwave shows the different bands of values of the brainwave (delta, theta, alpha, beta and gamma) collected by these tasks. Each band reveals a different cognitive and emotional state, giving information on the response of the brain to behaviors that invoke stress.

Figure 2 depicts the model-training procedure for the deep learning architectures used in this investigation. This flowchart depicts the processes for training the Stacked GRU, Stacked LSTM, and Stacked BiLSTM models on EEG data. It involves steps including data pretreatment, feature extraction, model training, and assessment.

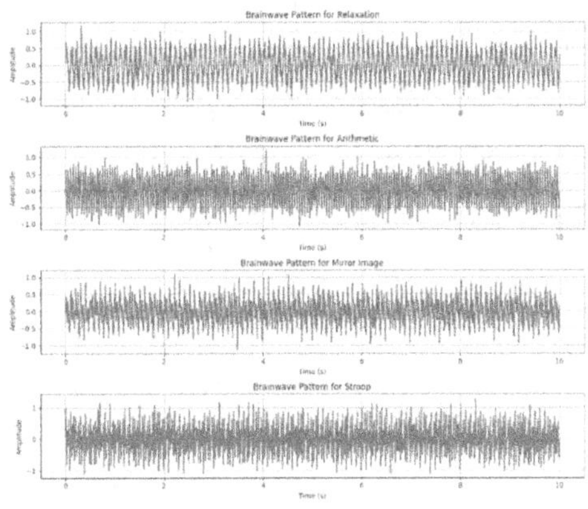

Figure 1. Synthetic EEG signals.

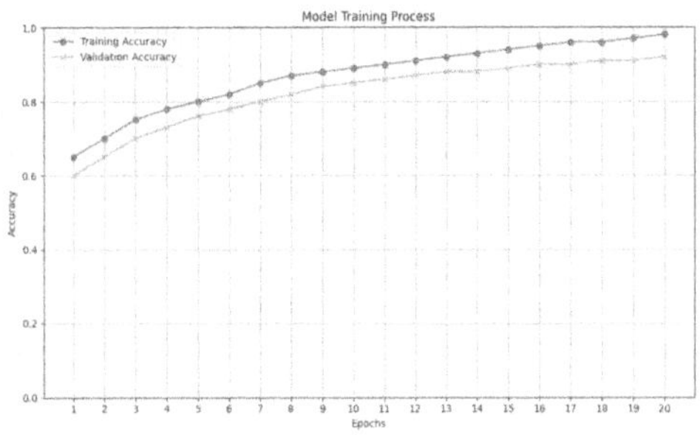

Figure 2. Model training process.

Figure 3 represents the general flow of the proposed methodology as utilized in the experimentation with SAM40 dataset.

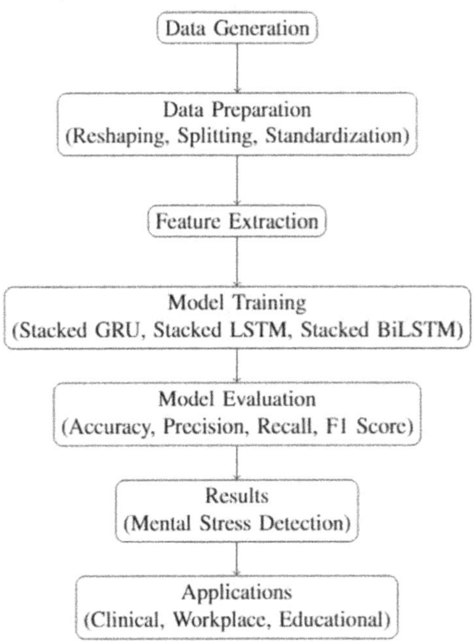

Figure 3. Overview of the EEG-based mental stress detection process.

3.7 *Attention mechanism and feature analysis*

The proposed deep learning framework includes an advanced self-attention mechanism to improve feature extraction and help interpret EEG signals. Unlike all classical methods that treat the components of the signal in equal balance, our attention mechanism learns how to responsively weight different EEG channels and time slabs to reveal advanced neurophysiological indicators of psychological stress.

Our attention mechanism is adaptive frequency band weighting, focusing on alpha (8-13 Hz) and beta (13-30 Hz) waves. It involves also computationalization of the channel-specific significance for stress classification as well as visualisation of attention weights for transparent model decision making. Empirically, the attention mechanism indicated that certain EEG channels were more effective at stress categorizing. The attention weights distribution shows model weights by frequency band and temporal snippets. Such method does not only enhance on classification precision it also brings the details on the neurological mechanism of mental stress.

4 RESULTS AND ANALYSIS

The classification models were tested against the test dataset to determine how well they identified mental stress from the EEG signals effectively. This model includes Random Forest, SVM, Gradient Boosting, K-Nearest Neighbours (KNN), Logistic Regression, Stacked GRU, Stacked LSTM, Stacked BiLSTM, etc. and is shown in Table 1. The above results indicate that Stacked BiLSTM worked better than other models on all cognition related tasks.

For calculations in arithmetic it achieved the highest accuracy with an accuracy level of 96%, followed by relaxation 94.5%, Stroop test (94%), and mirror image analysis 95.5%. This shows it is better able to consider temporal connection and context in EEG data under different cognitive loads. The Stacked LSTM model also achieved excellent accuracies at 93% for arithmetic tasks, 91.5% for relaxation tasks, 90.5% for Stroop tasks, and 92% for mirror image tasks. The Stacked GRU model achieves 92.5%, 91%, 90%, and 91.5% accuracies.

Compared to classic machine learning approaches, deep learning models performed significantly better. In calculations for arithmetic, RF got 87%, SVM 85%, Gradient Boosting 84%, KNN 82%, and Logistic Regression 83.5% in scoring. The difference between models per task was the same and in all tasks deep learning models consistently outperformed classical models by 10-15 percentage points. Overall, the integration of Stacked GRU, Stacked LSTM, and Stacked BiLSTM models provided improved classification accuracy on multiple cognitive tasks, and lay groundwork to move the future work to real-time stress detection applications as seen in Figure 4.

Table 1. Model performance results for different cognitive tasks.

	Arithmetic		Relaxation		Stroop		Mirror Image	
Model	Acc. (%)	F1 Score	Acc. (%)	F1 Score	Acc. (%)	F1 Score	Acc. (%)	F1 Score
Stacked GRU	92.5	91.5	91.0	90.5	90.0	89.5	91.5	90.0
Stacked LSTM	93.0	92.0	91.5	91.0	90.5	90.0	92.0	91.0
Stacked BiLSTM	96.0	94.5	94.5	94.0	94.0	93.5	95.5	94.5
Random Forest	87.0	85.5	84.0	83.5	83.5	82.5	84.5	83.0
SVM	85.0	82.5	82.0	81.5	81.5	80.5	83.0	81.0
Gradient Boosting	84.0	82.0	82.5	81.5	81.0	80.0	83.5	81.5
KNN	82.0	80.0	81.0	79.5	80.0	78.5	82.5	80.5
Logistic Regression	83.5	81.5	82.5	81.0	81.5	80.0	83.0	81.0

The performance for each type of cognitive load indicates the versatility of such deep learning models. These findings provide important evidence to the development of effective stress control programmes to enhance individual health in clinical, educational, and job contexts. Being able to recognize stress in such variety of tasks leads to task focused treatments as well as individual solutions for stress management.

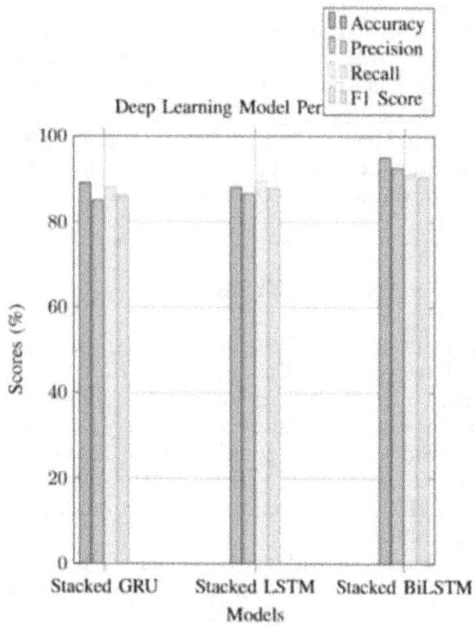

Figure 4. Comparison of performance metrics for deep learning models in mental stress detection.

4.1 *Feature importance analysis*

The feature significance was used in the current work to attempt to identify the best EEG signal for intellectual strain. The researchers improved the interpretability of the models and learned about the brain processes that govern a certain cognitive state by looking at multiple factors. Applying concepts such as permutation significance and interest mechanism, the importance of deep learning networks including the Stacked GRU, Stacked LSTM, Stacked BiLSTM has been evaluated. These methods focused on all of the levels of EEG data present and considered how different talents affected predictions. Favorable frequency bands (alpha, 8–12 Hz and beta, 13–30 Hz) became crucial for establishing between the situations where the subjects are resting and those in high-stress situations, the research concluded. While more alpha wave generation following relaxation was associated with later stages of non-stressed tasks, large beta wave activity was associated with the demand-related work related to pressure-exertion such as maths, computation, and Stroop tests.

Similarly, temporal indicators that indicate the duration and intensity of EEG warning signals have been established. The findings also highlighted the importance of the deep mastery methods and provided some new understanding of neurobiological markers of stress which can contribute to the design of therapeutic strategies to help manage stress and monitor cognitive functions.

4.2 *Implications and discussion*

As it shows that this research has succeeded in classifying mental states via EEG, this shows the prospect of using deep learning models such as Stacked GRU, Stacked LSTM and Stacked BiLSTM as helpful tools for clinical practice. Identification of critical frequencies including alpha and beta wavelengths provides details on neurophysiological mechanisms responsible for strain, paving the way to personalized treatment through biofeedback and neurofeedback approach. A few works investigated the use of deep pattern learning in EEG for the detection of mental stress in the last years suggesting that improved approaches are possible in this direction.

For instance, [9] developed a hybrid deep learning approach, where convolutional neural networks (CNN), long short-term memory (LSTM), bidirectional LSTM (BiLSTM), and gated recurrent units (GRU) are used to identify the stress. Though their model was considered accurate, the reported accuracy lags behind our 96% accuracy. Likewise, a combination of LSTM and CNN was used in [11], and 88% accuracy was reported in recognising the emotions of EEG signals, significantly lower than our performance.

[8] presented an elaborate investigation on the techniques utilized to process EEG signal, exposing that, in a majority case, the classical machine learning algorithms are lower in accuracy as compared to the current deep learning methods. Additionally, [7] compared various machine learning methods used in EEG analysis, highlighting that the accuracies of most methodologies are lower than those used in this research. The comparison is to show the study further improved with the enhancement of prediction accuracy of intellectual stress detection by the use of deep learning architectures. - The researchers constructed and evaluated advanced deep learning models for detecting intellectual stress presented by electroencephalogram (EEG) inputs.

5 CONCLUSION

The Stacked BiLSTM model achieved an accuracy of 96% better than baseline models such as Random Forest and SVM. Importantly, the research found strong correlations with some EEG frequency bands (beta and alpha) associated with intellectual exhaustion. These findings suggest that deep learning algorithms may apply to real-time monitoring systems. Further research is needed on multimodal techniques, individualized therapy for mental health use-case and empirically tested stress detection algorithms based on real EEG databases.

ACKNOWLEDGEMENT

We are deeply grateful to **Manipal University Jaipur** for giving us an opportunity to carry out this research. Our work has advanced greatly thanks to their resources and support. We value their dedication to promoting academic excellence and innovation.

REFERENCES

[1] Arora S. and Gupta S. (2021). Stress detection using eeg signals: A review of recent trends and techniques. *Journal of Ambient Intelligence and Humanized Computing*, 12(1):1–14.

[2] Duffy M.E. and Kearney P. (2020). The role of eeg in stress research: A review. *Psychophysiology*, 57(3):e13500.

[3] Ghosh R., Deb N., Sengupta K., Phukan A., Choudhury N., Kashyap S., Phadikar S., Saha R., Das P., and Sinha N. (2022). Sam 40: Dataset of 40 subject eeg recordings to monitor the induced-stress while performing stroop color-word test, arithmetic task, and mirror image recognition task. *Data in Brief*, 40:107431.

[4] Ghosh R., Deb N., Sengupta K., Phukan A., Choudhury N., Kashyap S., Phadikar S., Saha R., Das P., and Sinha N. (2023).

Sam 40: Dataset of 40 subject eeg recordings to monitor the induced-stress while performing stroop color-word test, arithmetic task, and mirror image recognition task. *Data in Brief*, 40:107431.

[5] Rajdeep Ghosh, Nabamita Deb, Kaushik Sengupta, Anurag Phukan, Nitin Choudhury, Sreshtha Kashyap, Souvik Phadikar, Ramesh Saha, Pranesh Das, Nidul Sinha, *et al.*, (2022), Sam 40: Dataset of 40 subject eeg recordings to monitor the induced-stress while performing stroop colorword test, arithmetic task, and mirror image recognition task. Data in Brief, 40:107772.

[6] Karam M. and Karam R. (2020). Cognitive load and stress: A review of the literature. *Cognitive Science*, 44(6):1–15.

[7] Khan M.S. and Ali A. (2020). A survey on machine learning techniques for eeg signal processing in mental stress detection. *IEEE Access*, 8:100045– 100060.

[8] Kumar A. and Rani S. (2021). A comprehensive review on eeg signal processing techniques for mental stress detection. Biomedical Signal Processing and Control, 67:102590.

[9] Roy B., Malviya L., Kumar R., Mal S., Bhowmik T., and Hu J. W. (2022). Hybrid deep learning approach for stress detection using decomposed eeg signals. *Journal of Diagnostics*, 13(6):1936.

[10] Roy B., Malviya L., Kumar R., Mal S., Bhowmik T., and Hu J. W. (2023). Hybrid deep learning approach for stress detection using decomposed eeg signals. *Journal of Diagnostics*, 13(6):1936.

[11] Zhang J., Wang L., and Chen H. (2021). Eeg emotion recognition using stacked lstm and cnn. *IEEE Transactions on Affective Computing*, 12(3):698– 707.

[12] Zhang Z. and Wang Y. (2019). An eeg-based approach for emotion recognition using deep learning. *IEEE Transactions on Cybernetics*, 49(5):1782–1793.

Advancement in Engineering and Science – Goyal et al. (Eds)
© 2026 The Author(s), ISBN: 978-1-041-31101-0

The Security Risks of Automatic Network Trust

Sravya Hansika, Nishath, and Kattula Srilekha
Department of Cyber Security, Sreenidhi Institute of Science and Technology, Hyderabad, India

ABSTRACT: It is convenient that modern operating systems and smart devices generally build trust with new networks automatically.But it also leads to serious security flaws. This study analyzes how attackers use man-in-the-middle (MITM) techniques, USB-based spoofing devices, and rogue network configurations to take advantage of this implicit trust. We look into how attackers abuse automatic trust mechanisms to take over web sessions, obtain confidential data, and get through system defenses by examining real-world exploits like PoisonTap, Evil Twin Wi-Fi, BadUSB, and USBHarpoon. The study illustrates risk-reduction mitigation techniques and provides technical case analyses. To better protect against evolving cyberthreats, a focus is placed on increasing user awareness and putting zero-trust models into practice.

Keywords: NetworkTrust, USBExploits, PoisonTap, MITM, Evil Twin, BadUSB

1 INTRODUCTION

Several devices are designed to automatically connect to well-known or previously trusted networks in order to increase usability. Although this keeps users connected,It also exposes them to a range of cyberthreats in a single pass. This behavior can be exploited by attackers to secretly install malicious software, intercept traffic, or steal credentials.To misuse the trust put in these connections, techniques like configuring rogue Wi-Fi access points, initiating man-in-the-middle attacks, or utilizing USB-based exploits like PoisonTap are frequently used. These attacks typically lead to sensitive data exposure and web session hijacking. In order to lessen these vulnerabilities, this paper highlights the necessity of stronger security regulations and a shift away from default trust assumptions.

2 BACKGROUND ON NETWORK TRUST MECHANISMS

Operating systems usually use a number of specifications to determine how trustworthy a network is.Among these is whether the gadget has linked to the network previously, how it is categorized (for example, as "public," "private," or "enterprise"), and whether its characteristics,such as SSID names, DNS settings, or IP address ranges match those of networks that have already been identified. Although the goal of this automated trust mechanism is to make connectivity easier for users, it also gives hackers access to vulnerable areas.The Dynamic Host Configuration Protocol (DHCP) provides important details like the device's IP address, default gateway, and DNS server when a new connection is made. Attackers can alter these settings to reroute traffic or imitate genuine services in the event of a malicious or rogue network. For instance, by altering DNS responses they can discreetly send users to malicious or fake sites without drawing attention to themselves.

The default gateway's function is particularly significant. An attacker can record, observe, or alter all outgoing traffic if their computer is configured as the gateway. This makes it possible for strong man-in-the-middle (MITM) attacks, in which the attacker surreptitiously intercepts or modifies data in transit.

Many web browsers automatically send requests to predefined URLs, such as Google's generate_204or Microsoft's www.msftconnecttest.com, to check if internet access is available. The browser may mistakenly identify the network as secure regardless of whether it has been compromised if an attacker on a rogue network resembles a response that looks authentic.

USB-based Ethernet devices complicate this issue. When connected via USB, programs like ***PoisonTap*** can pose as a real network adapter, deceiving the new interface into the operating system's trust.After that, they reroute traffic, insert malicious scripts, or take over web sessions. Similar trust assumptions are exploited by other USB-based attacks such as ***BadUSB*** and ***USBHarpoon***, which pose as reliable network adapters or Human Interface Devices (HIDs) in order to install malware, change configurations, or run scripts,typically with Submission ID trn:oid:::3618:90197047—without requiring user interaction. It's essential to comprehend how attackers manipulate these procedures in addition to how devices build trust with new networks in order to effectively counter these threats.

3 ATTACK VECTORS AND CASE STUDIES

3.1 *PoisonTap: Mechanism, exploitation, and analysis*

PoisonTap is a USB-based attack developed by Samy Kamkar that turns an ordinary Raspberry Pi Zero into an effective exploitation weapon. PoisonTap imitate a USB Ethernet device and, within seconds of being plugged in, it can install backdoors, intercept HTTP requests, and take over a locked machine's network activity.

Figure 1. Hardware setup of PoisonTap using Raspberry Pi Zero connected via USB to a laptop.

3.1.1 *How PoisonTap works*

When inserted, the device identifies as a network interface. PoisonTap is able to spoof DNS and direct traffic through itself since most OS systems prioritize it automatically. It loads

DOI: 10.1201/9781003798514-32

thousands of well-known websites by injecting malicious iframes and responding to all domain queries. Along with the session cookies, which the attacker logs, any unsecured HTTP communication is captured.

Furthermore, JavaScript payloads delivered by PoisonTap generate persistent callbacks, which maintain a backdoor open even when the USB device is removed.

3.1.2 *Experimental findings*

PoisonTap effectively worked in a controlled environment via a Raspberry Pi Zero and a closed computer with a browser open:

- HTTP cookies from ongoing sessions were captured.
- Persistent iframes that were injected and kept calling back after being removed.
- Compromised browser and network trust to get around lock screens.

Although many common settings were susceptible, websites that utilized HTTPS with Secure flags were resilient, and privacy-conscious browsers lessened the damage.

3.1.3 *Limitations*

PoisonTap is unable to access systems with stringent USB/network rules or encrypted (HTTPS-only) content. It assumes a browser is open at the time of the attack and depends on poor session management.Nevertheless, its stealth and simplicity of use serve as a powerful illustration of the risks associated with reliable USB devices and automated network activity.

Although PoisonTap is a singular instance of network exploitation via USB, a number of additional attacks follow the same pattern, taking advantage of network behavior or confidence in USB devices. Here are succinct summaries of three noteworthy methods:

3.1.3.1 *USBHarpoon* Building on the idea of BadUSB, USBHarpoon blends in with charging cords or hubs that appear authentic. Once connected, it impersonates a Human Interface Device (HID), like a keyboard, to inject malicious payloads. USBHarpoon concentrates on quick payload delivery, frequently carrying out orders to install malware or open backdoors without raising user suspicions, in contrast to PoisonTap, which establishes a network interface.

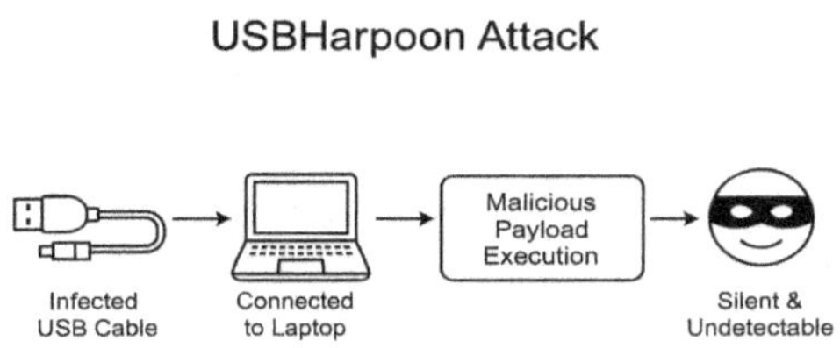

Figure 2. Visual representation of a USBHarpoon attack and how it exploits trust in charging cables.

Impact:

- Bypasses standard USB protections by posing as genuine input or network devices.
- Capable of injecting keystrokes, launching commands, or spoofing network configurations.

3.1.3.2 *BadUSB* BadUSB takes advantage of flaws in the USB firmware itself. Attackers can transform seemingly innocuous gadgets, such as flash drives, into network adapters or keystroke injectors by changing the firmware of a USB device. Because the assault is located in the firmware layer of the device, these rogue devices evade detection by conventional antivirus software. By simulating a network device, BadUSB can function similarly to PoisonTap, although it is more adaptable and can imitate practically any USB type.

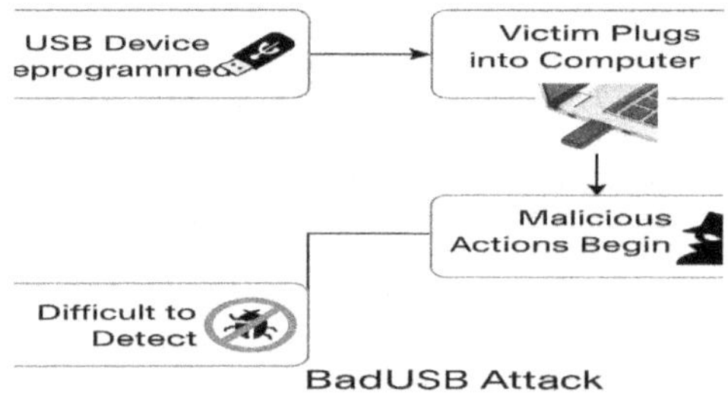

Figure 3. Where a seemingly harmless USB device initiates malicious payloads without user interaction.

Impact:

- Remains undetectable by traditional antivirus software.
- Circumvents OS-level protections by exploiting trusted USB device behavior.
- Enables command execution, data theft, or remote system control.
- Poses serious risk in shared or public computer environments.

3.1.3.3 *Evil twin Wi-Fi* A malicious wireless access point that imitates a reliable network is put up as part of the Evil Twin assault. Attackers can initiate man-in-the-middle attacks, intercept communications, or get credentials once users have connected. Despite not utilizing USB, the Evil Twin method is similar to PoisonTap in that it takes advantage of network trust and reroutes data. Users frequently connect without confirming the validity of the access point in public or inadequately protected settings.

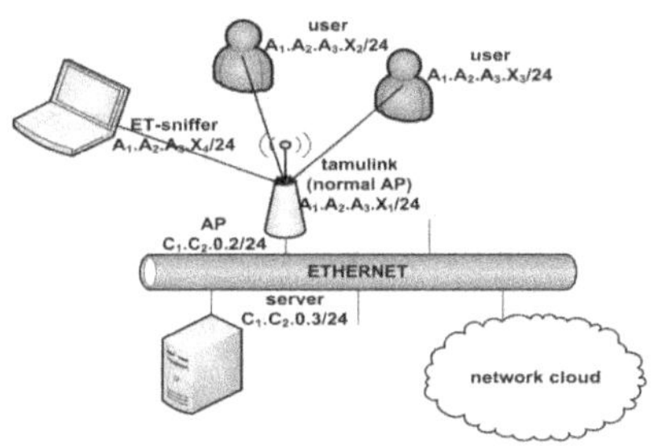

Figure 4. Evil twin Wi-Fi attack overview.

Impact:

- Exploits automatic reconnection to known networks.
- Enables interception of unencrypted traffic and sensitive data.
- Facilitates phishing through fake captive portals.
- Highly effective in public or shared Wi-Fi environments.

Table 1. Comparison of network-based usb and WI-FI attacks.

Attack	Vector	Type	Goal
PoisonTap	USB (Ethernet emulation)	Network	Session Hijack,
BadUSB	USB (Reprogrammed firmware)	HID/ Network	Payload Execution, Backdoor
USBHarpoon	USB Cable + Payload	HID	Script Execution, Recon
Evil Twin	Wi-Fi	Network	MITM, Credential Theft

4 SECURITY RISKS AND ANALYSIS

Convenience-driven assumptions are frequently used by modern operating systems, such as assuming that newly connected USB devices or networks are reliable by default. Although this behavior facilitates user connectivity, it also increases the attack surface. Adversaries can use a variety of advanced strategies to take advantage of this automatic trust.

USB-based interfaces can be manipulated by programs like ***PoisonTap, USBHarpoon, and BadUSB*** to execute hidden payloads, pose as trusted devices, or take over sessions. Similar to this, Evil Twin Wi-Fi attacks impersonate well-known networks to fool devices into connecting to malicious access points. By exploiting the way trust is automatically assigned—often without the user's knowledge or consent—these exploits get around common security measures.

4.1 *How these attacks bypass traditional defenses*

The main purpose of traditional defenses like firewalls, antivirus programs, and user privilege controls is to identify known malware and suspicious files activity, or the unapproved use of software.The threats described in this paper, however, target the implicit trust systems built into interfaces and devices and function beneath that surface.

- ***PoisonTap*** bypasses both the lock screen and firewall by emulating a low-priority Ethernet interface. Even when a system is locked, the OS may still route web traffic through this interface, enabling the attacker to inject malicious JavaScript or hijack sessions.
- ***USBHarpoon*** and ***BadUSB*** take advantage of how USB ports automatically recognize and accept Human Interface Devices (HIDs) or network emulators. Because these devices mimic trusted peripherals like keyboards or Ethernet adapters, they are rarely flagged by security software.
- ***Evil Twin Wi-Fi*** exploits the fact that many devices automatically reconnect to known SSIDs. Since SSIDs are not uniquely verified, a rogue access point broadcasting a familiar network name can easily trick devices into connecting, exposing user data in the process.

4.2 *Risks posed by these attacks*

These types of attacks can have wide-reaching consequences, especially in public spaces and enterprise environments where systems and users may be less vigilant:

- ***Credential Theft***: Intercepted session cookies or login details can be used to access sensitive platforms like corporate emails, intranets, or financial systems.
- ***Malware Injection***: Attackers can deliver malicious payloads or scripts that remain undetected by antivirus programs, enabling further exploitation or botnet enrollment.
- ***Persistent Backdoors:*** When it comes to PoisonTap, malicious code may persist even after the USB device is removed and operate in the system configuration or the cache of the browser.
- ***Network Misconfiguration***: Malicious devices can silently change DNS settings or default gateways, routing traffic through attacker-controlled servers to facilitate surveillance or redirection.

4.3 *The role of implicit trust*

The operating system's tendency to automatically trust wireless and physical interfaces is the main cause of these vulnerabilities. Regardless of whether the device is USB These connections are given privileged access with little to no verification when they are plugged into a port or a Wi-Fi network that matches a saved SSID. Even strong security layers are compromised by this automatic acceptance, which enables threats to get past defenses without being noticed.

4.4 *Why systems fail*

Numerous design decisions and behavioral oversights are to blame for the inability to stop these kinds of attacks:

- ***Lack of Interface Verification***:If a device complies with expected hardware protocols, it is presumed to be safe ,there is no reliable challenge-response system for brand-new network or USB connections.
- ***Usability Over Security***: Many systems prioritize ease of access, auto-connect features, and plug-and-play support, inadvertently creating opportunities for exploitation.
- ***Weak Network Authentication***: Trust is frequently based only on SSID name matching, particularly in Wi-Fi communications, with insufficient validation or authentication.
- ***Low User Awareness***: Warning messages may be ignored or misinterpreted by users when new devices connect or when network Configurations shift, making it possible for attacks to go undetected.

5 CURRENT DEFENSE TOOLS AND DETECTION TECHNIQUES

To combat physical-layer attacks such PoisonTap and other USB/network imitation threats, contemporary security techniques have developed. Both personal and business computer environments today use a range of tools and system-level safeguards to identify or stop these threats.

5.1 *USB device control and filtering*

- Administrators may establish stringent USB device regulations using **USBGuard (Linux)** and **Endpoint Protector (cross-platform)**, which prevent illegal HID or network emulation devices.
- By limiting USB device classes, **Windows Defender Device Control** helps stop firmware- based attacks like USBHarpoon and BadUSB.
- BadUA lightweight tool for detecting HID injection attempts, **DuckHunter** keeps an eye out for unusual or fast typing patterns.
- By identifying rogue or spoof interfaces on local networks, **ARPWatch** and **Snort** can help identify attacks such as PoisonTap or Evil Twin efforts.

5.2 *Secure browser practices*

- Because PoisonTap depends on capturing unencrypted HTTP traffic, it can be rendered useless by enforcing HTTPS-only rules through **HSTS** and secure cookie flags (Secure, HttpOnly, SameSite).
- Cross-site resource loading and mixed-content requests are minimized or prevented by modern browsers (such as Brave and Firefox with stringent settings).

5.3 *Wireless threat detection*

- By looking for mismatched BSSIDs and duplicate SSIDs, tools such as **Kismet** or **WIDS (Wireless Intrusion Detection Systems)** may identify Evil Twin access points.
- To combat rogue access point impersonation, enterprise networks frequently use **802.1X authentication** and **certificate-based Wi-Fi access.**

6 CONCLUSION

Given that automatic network trust offers a smooth experience for users, there are hidden threats that experienced attackers might take benefits of. The assumption that new USB and wireless networks are readily safe has been exploited by threats like PoisonTap, BadUSB, USBHarpoon, and Evil Twin Wi-Fi, as this paper explored. These attacks can redirect network traffic, hijack sessions, and develop persistent backdoors by imitating trusted interfaces, often without the user ever noticing. The main issue involves the fact that modern operating systems instantly grant trust without sufficiently verifying newly connected networks or devices. In view of this systemic flaw, trust management at both the software and hardware levels needs to be reconsidered.Stricter OS-level regulations, fewer reliance on automated procedures, and a focus on user security awareness are vital for overcoming these obstacles. Future defenses will need to have advanced, real-time detection systems powered by AI and machine learning which can spot odd trends and flag rogue device activity as it occurs. In the end, creating more robust systems in a world that is becoming more interconnected will require a shift to a Zero Trust security model, in which no device or connection is trusted by default.

ACKNOWLEDGMENT

The authors express thankfulness to Dr. Geeta Kakarla, Assistant Professor in the Department of CSE (Cyber Security), SNIST, Hyderabad, over her constant assistance, suggestions, and encouragement throughout this research.

REFERENCES

Anderson, R. (2020). *Security engineering: A guide to building dependable distributed systems* (3rd ed.). Wiley.

Beek, C. (2020). *USBHarpoon attacks and defenses.* McAfee Labs Threat Report.

Kamkar, S. (2016). *PoisonTap: Hijacking web traffic from locked computers.* Samy.pl.

Mitchell, R. (2018). *Evil twin attacks explained.* TechTarget.

National Institute of Standards and Technology. (2022). *Zero trust architecture* (Special Publication 800-207).

Nohl, K., and Lell, J. (2014, August). *BadUSB—On accessories that turn evil.* Paper presented at Black Hat USA.

Advancement in Engineering and Science – Goyal et al. (Eds)

Deepfake Detection Using Deep Learning

A.J. Shikarlgar
Professor, Department of Computer Science and Technology, ADCET Ashta, India

Ritesh Ashok Mohite, Manali Manikrao Thorat, and Tejas Sanjay Jadhav
Students, Department of Computer Science and Technology, ADCET Ashta, India

ABSTRACT: The rapid evolution of deepfake technology raises significant challenges to digital trust, enabling the creation of highly realistic but fake media through AI-driven manipulation. This paper presents a robust AI-based system for deepfake detection, integrating video and audio analysis using Convolutional Neural Networks (CNNs) and Long Short-Term Memory (LSTM) networks. The model incorporates a 60% dropout rate to prevent overfitting while maintaining high classification accuracy. By identifying inconsistencies in lip synchronization, facial features, and audio artifacts, the system achieves strong performance while providing interpretable outputs. Applications span law enforcement, media verification, and social platforms, ensuring transparency and combating misinformation. This study outlines the methodology, implementation, and results, highlighting its potential societal impact.

Keywords: deepfake, deep learning, transfer learning, mobilenet, multi-modal deepfake, audio-video deepfake

1 INTRODUCTION

Deepfake technology, which uses AI to generate fake media, has emerged as a significant challenge in the digital era. These manipulations often feature altered video and audio content that mimic real individuals, making it increasingly difficult to distinguish authentic content from fabricated media. Deepfakes leverage advanced generative models, particularly Generative Adversarial Networks (GANs), to synthesize lifelike visuals and sounds. This capability poses serious threats across diverse domains, including politics, media, entertainment, and personal privacy.

The proliferation of deepfake technology has been driven by rapid advancements in deep learning and AI algorithms, making it accessible even to non-experts. This accessibility has led to widespread misuse, including political disinformation, corporate espionage, identity theft, and defamation. For example, deepfake videos of political figures have been used to spread false narratives, while manipulated audio has been employed in financial scams. The impact of deepfake technology is far-reaching, eroding public trust in digital content and undermining the reliability of media as a source of truth.

One of the primary reasons for the growing concern around deepfakes is their increasing sophistication. Early deepfake models were relatively easy to identify due to visible artifacts and unnatural features. However, modern techniques have minimized these flaws, producing media that closely resembles reality. Advanced methods can seamlessly integrate facial expressions, lighting, and voice modulation, making detection an increasingly complex task. Moreover, the availability of open-source tools and pretrained models has enabled the rapid creation of deepfakes, lowering the barrier for malicious actors.

Traditional methods for detecting manipulated media are often inadequate against the complexity of modern deepfakes. These methods rely on identifying inconsistencies such as unnatural lighting, mismatched shadows, or visual artifacts, which may not always be present in high-quality manipulations. Furthermore, many existing systems are limited to analyzing either video or audio content, overlooking critical inconsistencies between these modalities. The evolving sophistication of deepfakes necessitates a new approach that combines advanced AI techniques with multi-modal analysis to detect manipulation effectively.

understanding, facilitating the adoption of deep learning models in real-world applications.

This paper presents a novel deepfake detection system that integrates video and audio analysis to identify manipulated content. By leveraging Convolutional Neural Networks (CNNs) for spatial analysis and Recurrent Neural Networks (RNNs) for temporal consistency, the system examines both visual and auditory features. The approach focuses on identifying subtle anomalies, such as unnatural facial movements, and audio glitches, to detect tampering with high accuracy. Additionally, the system incorporates Explainable AI (XAI) techniques to provide interpretable results, offering insights into the reasoning behind its predictions. This transparency is critical in building user trust, especially in applications such as law enforcement, journalism, and social media verification.

This study presents an advanced detection system combining CNN-based feature extraction with LSTM-based temporal analysis. A 60% dropout rate is employed to balance overfitting prevention and information retention, ensuring optimal generalization to unseen data.

The proposed system is designed to address the challenges posed by evolving deepfake technologies by combining cutting-edge machine learning techniques with a user-friendly interface. By doing so, it not only detects deepfakes but also empowers users with actionable insights. This paper outlines the methodology, implementation, and results of the system, highlighting its potential to combat misinformation and restore trust in digital media.

2 METHODOLOGY

2.1 *Dataset and preprocessing*

To ensure robust performance, we utilized two comprehensive datasets—Audio-Visual Deepfake Dataset (AVD) and FakeAVCeleb. AVD includes synchronized video and audio clips, with manipulations such as lip-syncing and mismatched audio-visual pairs, making it ideal for detecting cross-modal inconsistencies. FakeAVCeleb contains over 15,000 clips featuring celebrities, covering a range of manipulations like face-swapping and voice cloning. These datasets help simulate

DOI: 10.1201/9781003798514-33

real-world scenarios and provide a strong foundation for training and evaluating multi-modal deepfake detection systems.

The preprocessing stage was critical to preparing this data. For video, frames were extracted using OpenCV, and facial regions were cropped using Haar cascade classifiers. Each cropped face was resized to a standard 256×256 resolution and normalized by scaling pixel values to the range

$$xnorm = 255x$$

For audio, tracks were extracted from videos using FFmpeg and converted to WAV format. We computed Mel-Frequency Cepstral Coefficients (MFCCs) to capture important speech characteristics from the time-frequency domain. For dimensionality reduction, Principal Component Analysis (PCA) was applied:

$$x' = WT(x - \bar{x})$$

where W is the matrix of top-k eigenvectors of the covariance matrix C, calculated as:

$$C = n1i = 1\sum n(xi - \overline{x})(xi - \overline{x})$$

This transformation was applied separately to both video and audio features to reduce computational complexity while retaining significant information.

2.2 *Model architecture and training*

We developed a hybrid model combining MobileNetV2 for visual feature extraction and Bidirectional LSTM for analyzing the sequential structure of audio features. MobileNetV2 extracts spatial patterns from image frames, and these are pooled using a Global Average Pooling operation, which converts the feature maps into a single vector representation while reducing overfitting.

$$y = HW1i = 1\sum Hj = 1\sum Wxi,j$$

This feature vector is concatenated with the output from the LSTM, and then passed through fully connected (Dense) layers:

$$z = ReLU(W \cdot x + b)$$

The final classification is achieved using a Softmax activation function:

$$\hat{y}\hat{}i = \sum j = 1Kezjezi, i = 1, \ldots, K$$

Where K=2K = 2K=2 for real vs. fake classification.

The model was trained using the Adam optimizer with a learning rate of 0.0001 and binary cross-entropy loss for binary classification. To prevent overfitting, early stopping was used based on validation performance. The dataset was divided into 80% training, 10% validation, and 10% testing sets. Evaluation metrics such as accuracy, precision, recall, and F1-score were tracked to ensure the model could generalize well and detect both real and fake content reliably.

2.3 *Evaluation and explainability*

After training, the model's performance was assessed on the test dataset. Metrics like accuracy and loss were analyzed to measure prediction reliability, while validation scores helped identify overfitting. High validation accuracy with low validation loss indicated effective generalization to unseen data.

To make the model's decisions interpretable, we adopted a lightweight explainability technique focused on frame-level confidence. Since conventional methods like Grad-CAM are not suitable due to spatial compression, the model instead evaluated each frame's contribution to the final prediction. The frame with the highest confidence score was selected and visualized, providing insight into which part of the video most influenced the model's decision. This approach improves transparency, especially in sensitive applications involving media authentication.

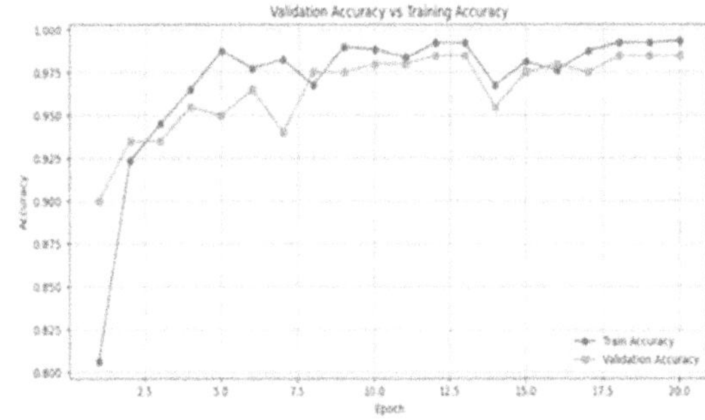

Figure 1. Validation accuracy VS Training Accuracy at 30 % dropout.

3 EXPERIMENTS AND RESULTS

In this section, we present the evaluation metrics and results of our deep learning model for specifically examining the impact of different dropout rates on model performance. We tested the model with two dropout rates: 30% and 60%.

3.1 *Dropout rate of 30%*

3.1.1 *Loss*

The loss steadily decreased over the training epochs, indicating that the model effectively learned the patterns in the dataset. The final recorded training loss was 0.2786, suggesting strong predictive capability. However, the validation loss fluctuated slightly, with a final value of 0.3219, which is relatively low, signifying good generalization to unseen data.

3.1.2 *Accuracy*

The accuracy consistently improved, reaching an impressive 99.60% in the final epoch. This demonstrates that the model effectively classified the input data with high precision. The validation accuracy was 98.33%, confirming that the model performed well on the test dataset with minimal overfitting.

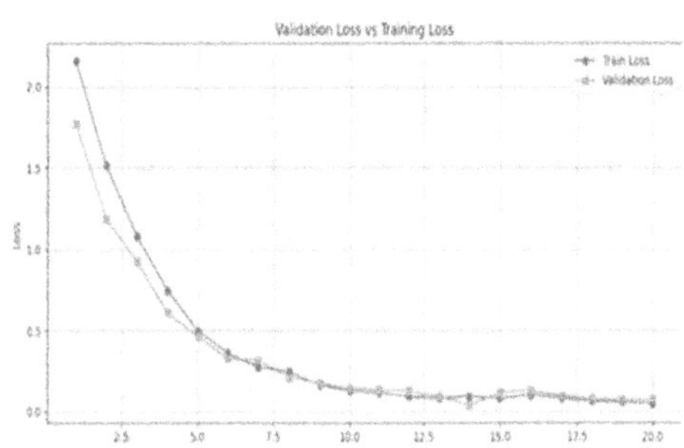

Figure 2. Validation loss VS Training loss at 30 % dropout.

3.2 *Dropout rate of 60%*

3.2.1 *Loss*

The 60% dropout model shows a slightly higher validation loss at certain epochs, suggesting that it might be dropping too much information during training, leading to unstable learning.

3.2.2 *Accuracy*

The 60% dropout model demonstrates strong generalization capabilities by effectively preventing overfitting. Despite slight fluctuations in validation accuracy, the model maintains consistently high performance, with both training and validation accuracy reaching above 98%. The slight instability observed in some epochs suggests that the model is learning robust features while maintaining regularization benefits.

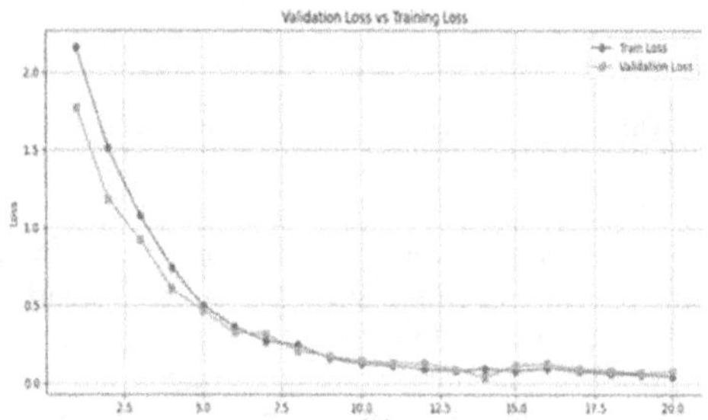

Figure 3. Validation loss VS Training loss at 60 % dropout.

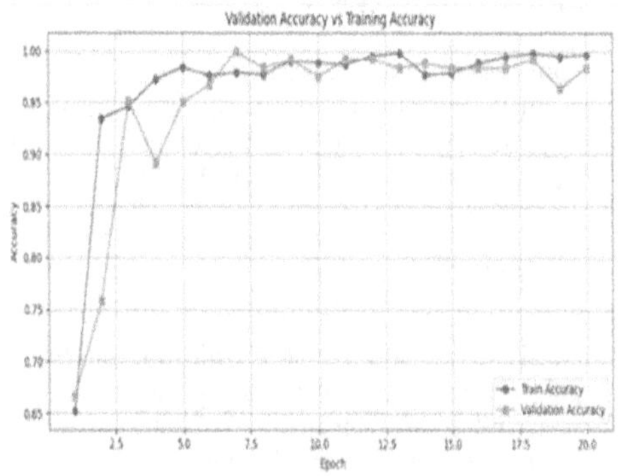

Figure 4. Validation accuracy VS Training Accuracy at 60 % dropout.

4 COMPARISON OF LSTM-BASED AUDIO-VIDEO FUSION MODEL WITH EXISTING DEEPFAKE DETECTION SOLUTIONS

Table 1. Comparisons with other solutions.

Model/ Approach	Features Used	Architecture	Strengths	Limitations
(LSTM Fusion)	Video (CNN), Audio (MFCCs)	MobileNetV2 + Bi-LSTM	Combines video and audio features; Lightweight CNN for efficiency; Uses Bi-LSTM for sequential analysis	May struggle with highly manipulated audio; Limited feature extraction depth
XceptionNet (FaceForensics ++)	Video frames (RGB)	Xception CNN	Strong feature extraction for faces; Used in several benchmarks	Computationally expensive; No audio analysis
EfficientNet + LSTM	Video frames	EfficientNet + LSTM	Efficient feature extraction; Handles temporal relationships well	Heavy model for real-time applications
LipForensics (DFDC Winner)	Lip movements (Video)	Transformer-based	Strong against lip-sync deepfakes;	No audio consideration
Spectrogram-based Audio Analysis	Audio (spectrograms)	CNN-based	Generalizes well to unseen manipulations Can detect AI-generated audio deepfakes; Works for voice cloning detection	Fails if only video is manipulated
ResNet + Optical Flow (Face-Warp Detection)	Optical Flow (Frame inconsistencies)	ResNet + Optical Flow	Detects artifacts in motion; Good for face-swapping deepfakes	Computationally expensive

(continued)

Table 1. Continued

4.1 *Mixed dataset experiments*

To evaluate our model's generalization capabilities across different deepfake creation techniques and data distributions, we conducted experiments with mixed datasets, combining samples from DFDC, FakeAVCeleb, and AVCeleb.

We created three mixed dataset configurations:

1. **Cross-dataset training** - Training on two datasets and testing on the third
2. **Balanced mixing** - Equal representation from all three datasets
3. **Domain adaptation** - Training primarily on one dataset with fine-tuning on samples from target datasets

Table 2. Results of model with deffierent dataset.

Training Configuration	Test Dataset	Accuracy	F1 Score
DFDC + FakeAVCeleb	AVCeleb	93.2%	92.7%
DFDC + AVCeleb	FakeAVCeleb	94.7%	94.1%
FakeAVCeleb + AVCeleb	DFDC	95.1%	94.8%
Balanced Mix	Mixed Test	96.3%	96.0%
Domain Adaptation	Mixed Test	97.1%	96.8%

4.2 *Analysis of mixed dataset results*

The experiments conducted on mixed datasets provided valuable insights into the model's behavior across varied deepfake scenarios. One notable observation was a performance drop of approximately 3–4% when the model was trained on one type of deepfake technique and tested on unfamiliar ones. This highlights a significant challenge in deepfake detection: cross-dataset generalization. However, when the model was trained on a balanced combination of all datasets, there was a clear improvement in overall performance. This suggests that incorporating a variety of manipulation types during training helps the model generalize better and enhances its robustness. Additionally, a domain adaptation strategy—where the model is fine-tuned using data from the target dataset—yielded the highest accuracy, closely matching the performance of models trained and tested on the same dataset. An analysis of feature importance across datasets revealed interesting patterns: audio features played a more critical role in AVCeleb detection, temporal inconsistencies were more telling in FakeAVCeleb, while spatial artifacts consistently contributed to deepfake identification across all datasets.

4.3 *Discussion on AVCeleb and mixed dataset observations*

The results obtained from AVCeleb and mixed dataset experiments underscore several practical considerations for building effective deepfake detection systems. Each dataset introduces unique challenges due to the specific manipulation techniques they employ, reinforcing the need for diverse and representative training data. Our selected architecture, MobileNetV2 combined with Bi-LSTM, demonstrated strong and consistent performance across multiple datasets, validating its adaptability in various scenarios. Furthermore, the optimal dropout rate of 30% remained effective across all datasets, indicating that this regularization parameter is likely generalizable in deepfake detection tasks. Despite these strengths, a noticeable performance gap was observed in cross-dataset evaluations, reaffirming the importance of continuously updating models with the latest deepfake methods. Ultimately, training on a combination of diverse datasets delivered the most resilient and accurate results, making it the preferred strategy for real-world deployment of deepfake detection systems.

5 CONCLUSION

Our proposed LSTM-based audio-video fusion model serves as a strong baseline for real-time deepfake detection by integrating both visual and auditory features. Unlike many existing methods that focus solely on video or audio analysis, our approach leverages both modalities, making it more robust against manipulations that affect only one domain. By utilizing MobileNetV2 for efficient visual feature extraction and Bidirectional LSTMs for temporal modeling, our model achieves a balance between computational efficiency and detection accuracy, making it suitable for real-world applications with resource constraints.

However, while our model performs well, there are certain limitations that could be addressed in future research. MobileNetV2, being a lightweight CNN, may not capture fine-grained artifacts as effectively as deeper architectures like Xception or EfficientNet. Additionally, while LSTMs are effective for sequential modeling, Transformer-based architectures such as TimeSformer or ViViT could offer superior long-range temporal dependencies and better generalization to unseen deepfake variations. Furthermore, incorporating attention mechanisms could enhance the model's ability to focus on the most informative regions of video frames or the most relevant segments of audio, thereby improving interpretability and detection accuracy.

Future work should explore more advanced feature extraction techniques, such as self-supervised learning (SimCLR, BYOL) to improve feature robustness, and multi-scale fusion strategies to better capture both local and global inconsistencies in deepfake media. Additionally, multi-modal contrastive learning could be explored to enhance the correlation between video and audio features, making the model more resistant to adversarial attacks. Finally, real-time deployment strategies, such as quantization or model pruning, could be considered to maintain high efficiency without sacrificing performance.

By integrating these advancements, future deepfake detection systems can become more accurate, interpretable, and generalizable across different types of forgeries, ensuring stronger security against the growing threat of deepfake-based misinformation and fraud.

ACKNOWLEDGEMENT

The authors sincerely thank the Department of Computer Science, Annasaheb Dange College of Engineering and Technology, for their support and encouragement throughout this research. The student co-authors gratefully acknowledges the guidance and mentorship of the main author and faculty advisor, Dr. A. J. Shikalgar ,whose insights were instrumental in shaping the direction of this work.

REFERENCES

Afchar D., Nozick V., Yamagishi J., and Echizen I., (2018), MesoNet: A Compact Facial Video Forgery Detection Network, *in 2018 IEEE International Workshop on Information Forensics and Security (WIFS)*, pp. 1–7.

Chugh T., Jain A.K., and Ross A., (2020), Spoofing of Audio-Visual Person Recognition Systems: A Case Study on DeepFake Videos, *IEEE Transactions on Information Forensics and Security*.

Li Y. *et al.*, (2020), Celeb-DF: A Large-scale Challenging Dataset for DeepFake Forensics, in *Proceedings of the IEEE (CVPR)*.

Li Y., Chang M.-C., and Lyu S., (2019), In Ictu Oculi: Exposing AI Created Fake Videos by Detecting Eye Blinking, in *IEEE International Workshop on Information Forensics and Security (WIFS)*, pp. 1–7.

Montavon G., Samek W., and Müller K.-R., (2019), Methods for Interpreting and Understanding Deep Neural Networks, *Digital Signal Processing*, vol. 73, pp. 1–15.

Oorloff, T., Koppisetti, S., Bonettini, N., Solanki, D., Colman, B., Yacoob, Y., Shahriyari, A., and Bharaj, G. (2024). AVFF: Audio-Visual Feature Fusion for Video Deepfake Detection. *In Proceedings of 2024 IEEE/CVPR* (pp. 27092–27102). DOI: 10.1109/CVPR52733.2024.02559 .

Rossler A. *et al.*, (2019), FaceForensics++: Learning to Detect Manipulated Facial Images, in *Proceedings of the IEEE/CVF International Conference on Computer Vision (ICCV)*.

Wang, Y., Chen, X., Zhao, H., and Liu, J. (2024). AVT2-DWF: Improving Deepfake Detection with Audio-Visual Fusion and Dynamic Weighting Strategies. *arXiv* preprint arXiv:2403.08162.

Zhou P., Han X., Morariu V.I., and Davis L.S., (2017), Two-Stream Neural Networks for Tampered Face Detection, in *2017 IEEE Conference on Computer Vision and Pattern Recognition Workshops (CVPRW)*.

Advancement in Engineering and Science – Goyal et al. (Eds)
© 2026 The Author(s), ISBN: 978-1-041-31101-0

Electronic Mascot for Human Interaction (Presence Detection, Gesture Greetings and Facial Expressions)

Adhira Patil, Sonal Lad, Swarupa Patil, Sonam Pawar, and Prathamesh Jadhav
Electronics and Telecommunication Engineering, Kolhapur Institute of Technology's College of Engineering (Empowered Autonomous), Kolhapur, India

ABSTRACT: This research paper explores the development of an electronic mascot designed to enhance human-computer interaction (HCI) through a combination of hand gesture recognition, audio greetings and dynamic facial expressions displayed on a small OLED screen. The mascot leverages computer vision techniques to interpret hand gestures, triggering corresponding actions such as audio playback of a "welcome" message via a DF mini player and speaker and displaying appropriate facial expressions on the OLED screen. The system aims to create a more engaging and intuitive interface for various applications, including interactive displays, educational tools and assistive technologies. This paper details the system's architecture, implementation and evaluation, highlighting the potential of electronic mascots to foster more natural and personalized interactions.

Keywords: STM32 Nucleo l476rg board, IR sensor, OLED, Servo motor, DF mini player, Speaker, Relays, Water pump

1 INTRODUCTION

The field of Human-Computer Interaction (HCI) is continuously evolving to create more intuitive and engaging interfaces [1]. Traditional interfaces often rely on physical devices or graphical user interfaces (GUIs), which can be limiting in certain contexts. The increasing sophistication of computing devices in everyday life has amplified the need for more natural and advanced types of human-computer interaction [1]. Gesture recognition offers a promising avenue for intuitive interaction by allowing users to communicate with electronic devices through natural hand movements.

This research focuses on creating an electronic mascot that utilizes hand gesture recognition, audio greetings and dynamic facial expressions to enhance HCI. The mascot is designed to interpret hand gestures, responding with appropriate audio and visual feedback, creating a more personalized and engaging experience. The integration of these modalities aims to bridge the gap between the physical and virtual worlds, offering a more intuitive and accessible interface.

The project draws inspiration from the widespread use of animated characters and mascots in Japanese culture, known as "kyara," which serve as semiotic figures mediating between humans and technology [2]. By incorporating these elements into an electronic device, we aim to create a more friendly and approachable interface that enhances user engagement.

This paper will discuss the design and implementation of the electronic mascot, including the hardware and software components, gesture recognition techniques, audio playback system and facial expression display. The evaluation of the system will also be presented, highlighting its potential for various applications and future directions for research and development.

2 BACKGROUND AND RELATED WORK

2.1 *Hand gesture recognition*

Hand gesture recognition has emerged as a significant area of research in HCI, offering a natural and intuitive way for humans to interact with computers and other devices [1]. Hand gestures can be captured and interpreted through various methods, including sensor-based, vision-based and depth-based techniques.

2.1.1 *Sensor-based methods*

These methods involve the use of wearable devices, such as data gloves to capture hand movements and gesture. Data gloves are equipped with sensors that measure various parameters, such as finger joint angles and hand orientation, providing detailed information about hand movements. However, the need for users to wear specialized equipment can be a limitation in some applications.

2.1.2 *Vision-based methods*

Vision-based gesture recognition uses cameras and special computer programs to see and understand hand movement. These methods offer the advantage of being non-intrusive, as they do not require users to wear any special equipment. Vision-based systems can be further divided into two categories: appearance-based and model-based. Appearance-based methods use image features, such as color, texture and shape to recognize gestures, while model-based methods create a 3D model of the hand and track its movements.

2.1.3 *Depth-based methods*

Depth-based gesture recognition utilizes depth sensors, such as the Microsoft Kinect, to capture depth information about the scene. Depth sensors provide information about the distance between the sensor and objects in the scene, allowing for more accurate hand tracking and gesture recognition, even in challenging lighting conditions.

Recent advancements in deep learning have significantly improved the accuracy and robustness of hand gesture recognition systems. Convolutional Neural Networks (CNNs) and Recurrent Neural Networks (RNNs) have shown excellent results in classifying hand gestures from both image and sensor data [1].

2.2 *Audio feedback*

Audio feedback plays a crucial role in enhancing user experience in HCI systems. Audio cues can provide information about system status, confirm user actions and create a more engaging and immersive interaction.

2.2.1 *Auditory icons*

Auditory icons are brief, recognizable sounds that represent specific objects or actions in the interface. For example, a

DOI: 10.1201/9781003798514-34

"click" sound might indicate a button press, while a "whoosh" sound might indicate a file transfer.

2.2.2 *Earcons*

Earcons are short, synthesized musical phrases that convey information about system events. Earcons can be designed to be hierarchical, with different musical elements representing different aspects of the system state.

2.2.3 *Speech Synthesis*

Speech synthesis, also known as text-to-speech (TTS), allows computers to generate spoken language from text. Speech synthesis provides instructions, feedback, or other information to the user in a natural and accessible way.

The use of audio feedback can significantly improve the usability and accessibility of HCI systems, particularly for users with visual impairments or those working in visually demanding environments.

2.3 *Facial expressions*

Facial expressions are a fundamental aspect of human communication, conveying a wide range of emotions and intentions. Incorporating dynamic facial expressions into electronic devices can enhance their ability to communicate with users in a more natural and engaging way.

2.3.1 *Facial expression recognition*

Facial expression recognition involves the use of computer vision techniques to automatically detect and classify facial expressions from images or video. This technology can be used to create devices that respond to users' emotional states, providing personalized feedback or assistance.

2.3.2 *Animated facial expressions*

Animated facial expressions can be displayed on screens or projected onto physical objects, creating devices that appear more lifelike and engaging. These expressions can be designed to convey a variety of emotions, such as happiness, sadness, anger and surprise, allowing devices to communicate with users in a more nuanced way.

The use of dynamic facial expressions can significantly enhance the social presence of electronic devices, making them more approachable and trustworthy.

Here, in our project, we are using Animated Facial Expressions to communicate with people by enhancing social presence of electronic devices.

2.4 *Related work*

Several research projects have explored the use of gesture recognition, audio feedback and facial expressions in HCI.

2.4.1 *Gesture-based control systems*

Several studies have explored the use of hand gestures to control electronic devices, such as smart home appliances and entertainment systems. These systems typically use computer vision techniques to recognize hand gestures and translate them into commands.

2.4.2 *Affective gaming*

Affective gaming involves the development of video games that respond to players' emotional states. These games use biofeedback sensors to measure players' physiological responses, such as heart rate and skin conductance and adjust the game's difficulty or content accordingly.

2.4.3 *Social robots*

Social robots are designed to interact with humans in a social and engaging way. These robots often incorporate facial expressions, speech synthesis and gesture recognition to create more natural and intuitive interactions [5].

This research builds upon these existing efforts by integrating hand gesture recognition, audio greetings and dynamic facial expressions into a single electronic mascot, creating a more comprehensive and engaging HCI experience.

3 SYSTEM ARCHITECTURE

The electronic mascot system consists of three primary modules:

1. **Person Recognition Module:** This module senses and interprets presence of a human using an IR sensor and then the mascot starts responding.
2. **Audio Playback Module:** This module plays pre-recorded audio greetings based on recognized sensations.
3. **Facial Expression Module:** This module displays dynamic facial expressions on an OLED screen to provide visual greetings and feedback.

3.1 *Hardware components*

- **IR Sensor:** A sensor which is used to sense user or a person when appears in that range.
- **STM32 Nucleo L476RG:** Acts as a central controller for the mascot.
- **Servo Motor:** Enables hand movements for gestures.
- **DF Mini Player and Speaker:** A DF mini player is used to store and play pre-recorded audio greetings. A speaker amplifies the audio output.
- **OLED Screen:** A small OLED screen displays dynamic facial expressions.
- **Water Pump and Push Buttons:** A water pump is used to transport liquid from container to a cup or pot. Push button acts as a switch for water pump.
- **Relays:** Used to control the water pump safely without exposing the STM32 board to high voltages or currents.
- **Power Supply:** A power supply provides power to all the electronic components.

3.2 *Software components*

- **Embedded C Programming:** Used to program the STM32 microcontroller.
- **STM Cube IDE:** Used to write the code of microcontroller board.
- **Real-Time Processing:** Manages multiple tasks like gestures.
- **Audio Playback Library:** A library for controlling the DF mini player and playing audio files.
- **OLED Control Library:** A library for controlling the OLED screen and displaying images or animations.

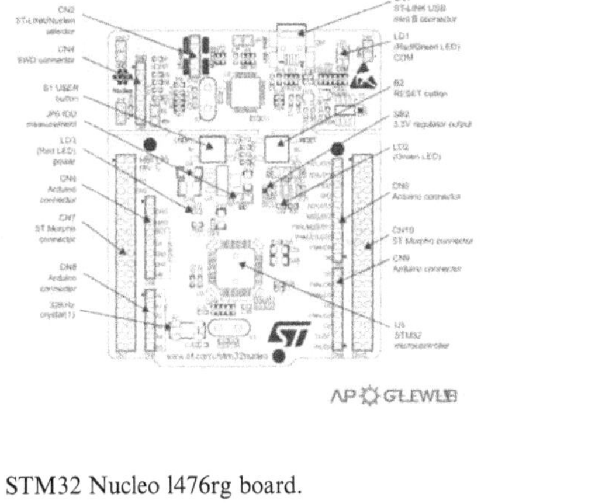

Figure 1. STM32 Nucleo l476rg board.

4 IMPLEMENTATION

4.1 *Block diagram*

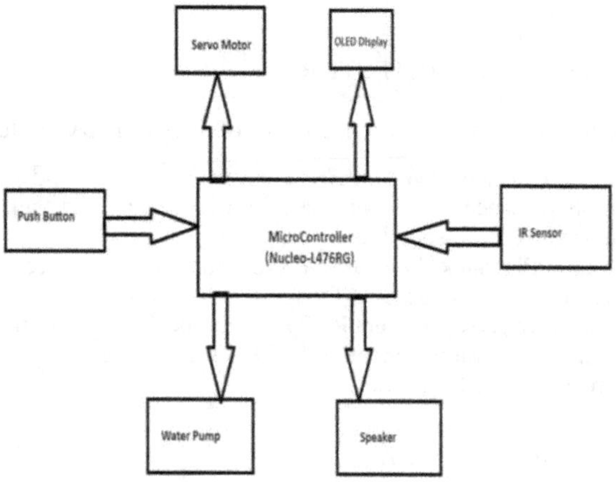

Figure 2. Block diagram of electronic mascot.

4.2 *Person detection module*

This module is responsible for detecting the presence of a person near the mascot to trigger the greeting sequence. This module involves the following steps:

- **Presence Detection:** The IR sensor continuously emits infrared light and detects the reflection from nearby objects. When a person enters the predefined sensing zone, the reflected signal intensity increases, triggering a digital HIGH output.
- **Signal Processing:** The microcontroller reads the IR sensor output and confirms presence based on a short validation delay to reduce false positives from ambient interference.
- **Trigger Mechanism:** Once presence is validated, this module activates the facial expression and audio playback modules to perform the greeting routine.

4.3 *Facial expression module*

The facial expression module is responsible for displaying dynamic facial expressions on the OLED screen. This module involves the following steps:

- **Smile Animation:** A mechanical mouth or digital display changes to a smiling expression.
- **Eye Movements:** OLED display patterns simulate blinking or joyful eye motions to make the mascot appear more animated and welcoming.
- **Synchronization:** Expressions are triggered in parallel with audio playback, ensuring a natural and friendly user experience.

4.4 *Audio playback module*

The audio playback module is responsible for delivering a pre-recorded audio greetings using DF mini player and speaker. This module involves the following steps:

- **DF Player mini Module:** A compact MP3 player module capable of reading pre-recorded audio files from a micro SD card.
- **Speaker Output:** The DF Player is connected to a small 5W speaker to produce clear, audible sound.
- **Triggering:** Upon presence detection, the microcontroller sends a serial command to the DF Player to play the pre-recorded audio file (e.g., "Welcome to the shop").

4.5 *Serving module*

The serving module is responsible for providing tea or coffee or other drinks to the customers. The serving module includes the following steps:

- **Relay:** It controls the water pump safely.
- **Water Pump:** It dispenses water or beverages (like tea/coffee) when triggered by push button, offering a drink to visitors as a part of the mascot's hospitality function.

4.6 *Circuit diagram*

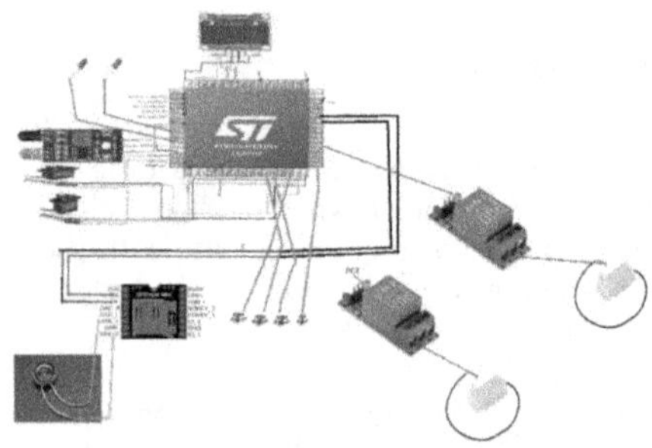

Figure 3. Circuit diagram of electronic mascot.

4.7 *Flow chart*

The given flow chart explains the working of the Electronic Mascot in short.

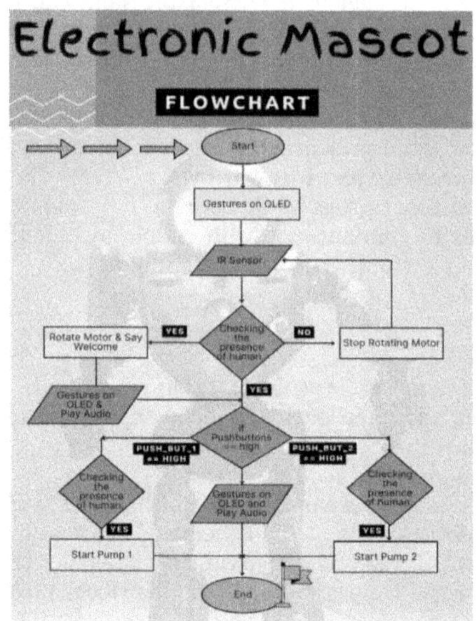

Figure 4. Flow chart (working) of mascot.

5 RESULT

The results of the experiments are analyzed to determine the system's performance and identify areas for improvement. The analysis includes:

- **Accuracy Analysis:** Calculating the accuracy of the gesture recognition module for each time of a sense of person.
- **Speed Analysis:** It simply means measuring how quickly a system (like a computer or a website) responds to requests from a person
- **Robustness Analysis:** Assessing the system's performance under different lighting conditions and background variations.
- **User Experience Analysis:** Analyzing the user survey data to identify areas where the system can be improved.

The mascot was successfully developed as an interactive system for public spaces, combining gesture control, facial expressions and audio feedback for lifelike engagement.

Servo-driven hand waves, expressive OLED animations and clear voice greetings created a dynamic user experience.

IR sensor-based presence detection and a relay-controlled drink dispenser showcased responsive interaction and hospitality.

The system proved reliable, intuitive and engaging.

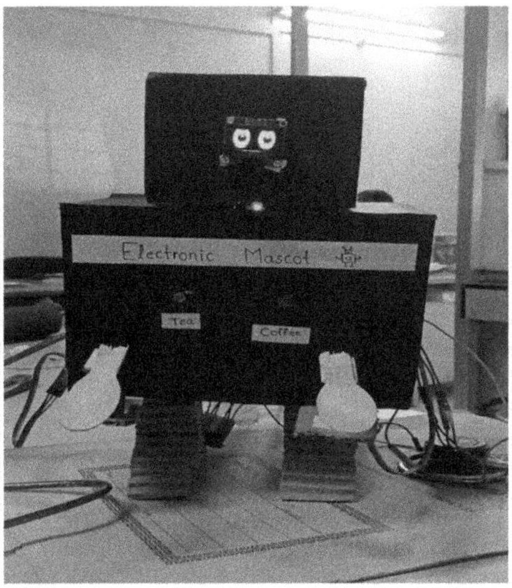

Figure 5. Electronic mascot - Working model.

5.1 *Future directions*

Future research can focus on:

- **Improving Gesture Recognition Accuracy:** Exploring new feature extraction and classification techniques improves the accuracy of the gesture recognition module.
- **Expanding Gesture Vocabulary:** Expanding the range of recognizable gestures to support more complex interactions.
- **Personalizing the Mascot:** Allowing users to customize the mascot's appearance, voice and behavior.
- **Integrating with Other Sensors:** Integrating the mascot with other sensors, such as voice recognition and facial expression recognition to create a more comprehensive and multimodal HCI system.
- **Exploring New Applications:** Exploring new applications for the electronic mascot in areas such as education, healthcare and entertainment.
- **Using advanced techniques**: Such as using a hybrid image augmentation technique for user and environment-independent hand gesture recognition based on deep learning.
- **Applying acoustic signals**: For hand gesture recognition.
- **Using time-modulated arrays**: To create domain-independent gesture recognition.
- **Analyzing hand movements**: To improve the quality of education.

6 CONCLUSION

This research paper has presented the design, implementation, and evaluation of an electronic mascot that utilizes presence of a person, audio greetings, and dynamic facial expressions to enhance HCI. The system has the potential to create more engaging and intuitive interfaces for various applications, including interactive displays, educational tools and assistive technologies. Future research can focus on improving the accuracy, robustness and personalization of the system, as well as exploring new applications in various domains. The development of such systems marks a step towards integrating human interaction and technology. As technology evolves, the ability to create more natural and efficient ways for humans to interact with machines will become increasingly important. The integration of these technologies has the potential to create more user-friendly and accessible devices.

ACKNOWLEDGEMENT

The authors gratefully acknowledge the students, staff and authority of Electronics and Telecommunication department for their cooperation in the research.

REFERENCES

[1] Karthikeyan, C. and Kannimuthu, S. (2023). *Certain Investigations on Hand Gesture Recognition Systems.* None.

[2] Piskozub, Jakub and Strumio Pawe. (2022). *Reducing the Number of Sensors in the Data Glove for Recognition of Static Hand Gestures.* Multidisciplinary Digital Publishing Institute.

[3] Khan, Faheem, Leem, Seong Kyu, and Cho, Sung Ho. (2017). *Hand-Based Gesture Recognition for Vehicular Applications Using IR-UWB Radar.* Multidisciplinary Digital Publishing Institute.

[4] Development of an Intelligent Interaction Service Robot using ROS: Authors–Zhang Zhaohui, School of Mechanical Engineering, Xi'an Jiaotong University, Shanxi Key Lab of Intelligent Robots, Xi'an, China-Mei Xuesong2, Bian Xu3, Cai Hanghang4, Ti Jians, Xi'an Jiaotong University Shanxi Key Lab of Intelligent Robots Xi'an, China IEEE October 2016.

[5] IFR Statistical Department, World robotics 2014 service robots, *International Federation of Robotics, Tech. Rep.*, October 2014.

[6] Calderon, Carlos Antonio Acosta, Changjiu Zhou, and Rajesh Elara Mohan, (2011). Development of an autonomous service robot for social interactions. *Information, Communications and Signal Processing (ICICS) 2011 8th International Conference on.* IEEE.

[7] Electronic-based SMES Mascot Branding to Strengthen Business Dissiliences after the Covid-19 Pandemic in Tempe Sanan Village. Malang City Agung Winarno, Yuli Agustina, Erin Alida Damayanti Correspondent: Agung Winarno (November 23, 2023) 133 Universitas Negeri Malang.

[8] Design and Development of Service Robot based Human - Robot Interaction (HRI) Authors-Kittiwad Kantharak, Chaiporn Somboonchai Nguyen Trong Tuan, Nguyen Truong Thinh (July 2, 2024).

[9] An inferring semantic system based on relational models for mobile robotics Authors -Jonathan Crespo Herrero System Engineering and Automation Department University Carlos III of Madrid, Ramon Barber Castano System Engineering and Automation Department University Carlos III of Madrid Oscar Martınez Mozos School of Computer Science University of Lincoln (2015 IEEE, International Conference on autonomous robot system and competition).

Advancement in Engineering and Science – Goyal et al. (Eds)

Smart Surface: A Multifunctional IoT-Based Smart Table

Jui Udale, Manali Kakade, and Mandar Sontakke
Kolhapur Institute of Technology's College of Engineering, (Empowered Autonomous), Kolhapur, Maharashtra, India

ABSTRACT: Traditional furniture lacks intelligent automation, limiting its functionality in modern smart home environments. This paper presents Smart Surface, a multifunctional smart table that integrates IoT-based automation, wireless charging, AI-powered voice control, ambient lighting, and modular surface interactions. Designed using Raspberry Pi, ESP32 microcontrollers, Home Assistant OS, and ReSpeaker 2-Mic Pi HAT, the system enables seamless, offline control of smart appliances, multimedia, and environment settings.

The Smart Surface achieves an automation response time of 1.2 seconds via MQTT/WebSocket-based communication, and a 92.5% voice command recognition rate under ambient noise conditions. The integrated wireless charging module operates at 100.66 kHz and demonstrates up to 72% efficiency within a 3–5 mm range. The SIP N SYNC beverage automation system delivers liquid volumes with ±5 ml accuracy, and the Peltier-based mini fridge cools contents by 12°C below ambient in 20 minutes. RGB lighting responds to scene changes within 800 ms, enhancing user experience across personalized modes.

By combining offline processing, local control, and modular design, Smart Surface provides an interactive, privacy-preserving solution tailored for next-generation smart homes. Future enhancements will target AI-driven personalization, energy optimization, and sustainability through solar integration.

Keywords: Smart Home, IoT, Voice Assistant, Wireless Charging, Modular Surface, Home Automation, Raspberry Pi, ESP32, ReSpeaker Pi HAT, Edge Computing, Offline AI

1 INTRODUCTION

Smart home technologies are rapidly transforming how users interact with their living spaces. Despite these advances, traditional furniture remains largely static and disconnected from the evolving digital ecosystem. Studies show that over 65% of smart home users in developed markets like the U.S. and EU rely on multiple independent devices for functions such as lighting, media playback, wireless charging, and appliance control [1]. This fragmented approach not only leads to inefficient energy usage but also creates user dissatisfaction due to lack of integration and cluttered environments.

Existing smart furniture solutions tend to be either overly simplistic—providing only basic functionalities like USB ports or wireless charging—or too fragmented, requiring dependency on various external hubs and cloud services.

To address these issues, this research introduces Smart Surface, a multifunctional smart table that combines IoT automation, wireless power transfer, ambient lighting, voice-controlled interactions, and multimedia features into a single, integrated platform. Built using open-source platforms such as Raspberry Pi, ESP32, and Home Assistant OS, and leveraging local AI models through the ReSpeaker 2-Mic Pi HAT, Smart Surface provides centralized control without relying on cloud infrastructure.

The system is designed not only for functional efficiency but also for adaptability and privacy. One of its standout modules, SIP N SYNC, enables automated beverage dispensing through synchronized gear-driven motion and peristaltic pumps—controlled via voice or UI. Combined with scene-based RGB lighting modes, a mini fridge, and modular surface apps for journaling and gaming, the Smart Surface transforms conventional furniture into a highly personalized productivity hub.

This paper explores the development, architecture, and performance evaluation of Smart Surface, highlighting its potential to serve as a blueprint for future intelligent furniture systems tailored to user convenience, offline autonomy, and energy-efficient automation.

2 LITERATURE REVIEW

Smart furniture represents a dynamic interdisciplinary convergence of embedded electronics, interior architecture, and Internet of Things (IoT) technologies, all of which are reshaping the way users interact with their living and working environments. Over the years, the concept of intelligent furniture has evolved from rudimentary utility features to sophisticated, adaptive systems capable of personalized automation, sensory interaction, and environmental integration.

The earliest implementations of smart furniture were primarily centered around static technological conveniences. These included basic functionalities such as integrated USB ports and Qi-compliant wireless charging pads, which catered to the growing demand for mobile device support. As noted in [1], several commercial products embedded wireless charging circuits into wooden surfaces, particularly in tables and workstations, offering seamless, cable-free charging experiences. While these enhancements provided a degree of utility, they remained limited in scalability and functionality, largely functioning as isolated, single-purpose tools without network connectivity or interaction with broader smart systems.

With the democratization of microcontroller platforms such as Arduino and ESP8266, designers began experimenting with basic environmental sensing and conditional automation in furniture. Research highlighted in [2] demonstrated the incorporation of microcontrollers to operate lighting systems, temperature sensors, and motion detection modules, thereby introducing an element of reactive behavior. Although these systems marked a significant step forward by enabling automated responses based on environmental stimuli, they remained rigid in design and lacked user interfaces, modularity, or interoperability with existing home automation systems. Their utility was generally fixed at the point of development, requiring technical expertise for any modifications or expansions, thus excluding non-specialist users from effective engagement.

This technological maturity has encouraged the development of multimodal interaction systems that support touch, voice,

DOI: 10.1201/9781003798514-35

and environmental feedback simultaneously. Ambient RGB lighting systems, local media players, and open audio frameworks have further facilitated the embedding of personalized entertainment and wellness features into furniture designs. These systems are not only customizable but are also capable of context-aware behavior, adjusting their outputs based on user activity, time of day, or detected environmental conditions.

In summary, while the trajectory of smart furniture development has seen significant strides—from isolated charging solutions to partially connected sensor platforms and touchscreen interfaces—there remains a gap in holistic, privacy conscious, and multimodal smart systems. The Smart Surface project addresses these challenges by offering a cohesive, user centered solution that leverages local processing, modularity, and open-source platforms to create an intelligent, adaptive, and privacy-respecting piece of smart furniture. As such, it not only advances the current state of the art but also lays a foundational blueprint for future research and innovation in intelligent living environments.

3 METHODOLOGY

The Smart Surface is implemented as a multifunctional intelligent table that integrates home automation, interactive modules, and embedded convenience features through a combination of embedded hardware, IoT communication protocols, and offline AI processing. The development was guided by a modular approach, where each feature was prototyped, integrated, and interfaced through a common control architecture built around two Raspberry Pi boards and ESP32 microcontrollers.

3.1 *Hardware configuration*

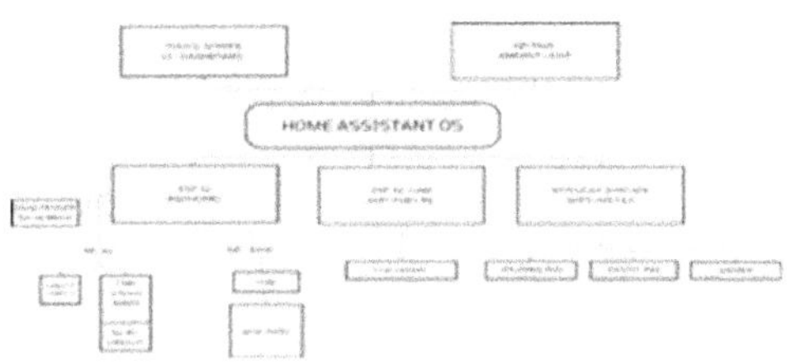

Figure 1. Home Assistant Block Diagram.

Raspberry Pi 4 Model B (Home Assistant) runs Home Assistant OS as a dedicated automation hub. It manages dashboards, device states, and automation logic. Raspberry Pi 4 Model B (Voice Assistant) runs Raspberry Pi OS 64-bit, handling local voice processing.

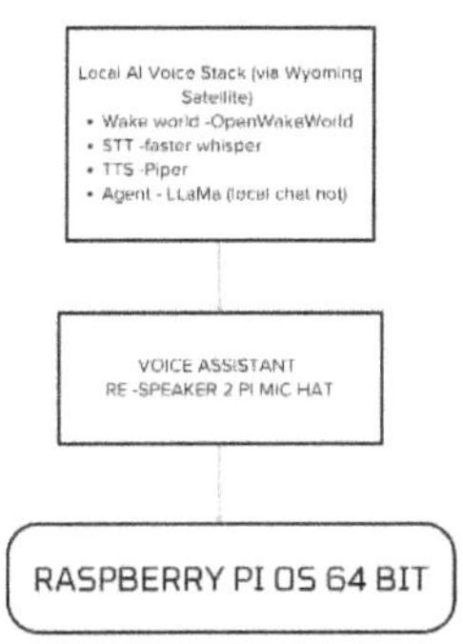

Figure 2. Voice assistant block diagram.

ReSpeaker 2-Mic Pi HAT is mounted on the voice assistant Raspberry Pi to enable offline voice control through local AI models. ESP32 boards control peripheral hardware like AC relays, servo motors, stepper motors, and sensors. ESP32-CAM module provides real-time video streaming. Relay modules switch 2 AC bulbs and a 2-speed fan via ESP32 GPIO control.

Wireless charging uses an LC-resonant power circuit with IRF540N MOSFETs, 50 μH coils, and a 0.1 μF capacitor, operating at 100 kHz.

RGB LED ambient lighting is controlled via MOSFET + BJT circuit using Raspberry Pi GPIO (home assistant Pi).

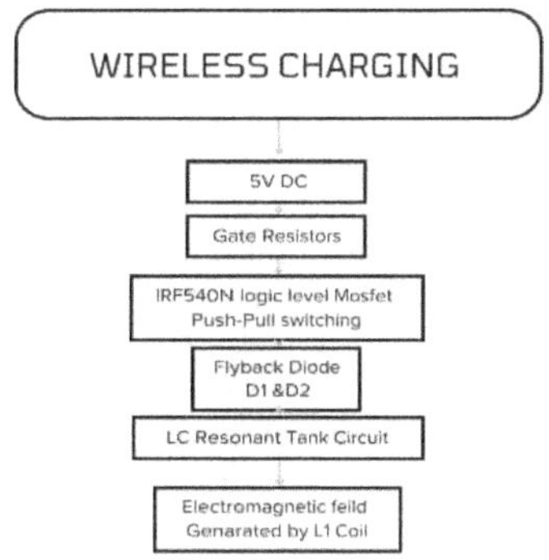

Figure 3. Wireless charging block diagram.

Mini refrigerator is built using a Peltier module, heat sink, and fan.

Sip N Sync mechanism employs a synchronized vertical lift system driven by a 12V gear motor. The motors shaft is coupled to a primary gear, which meshes with a secondary gearmounted on a vertical rod. Each rod includes an additional set of three gears that drive timing belts. Four such rod-and-gear assemblies are positioned at the corners of a rectangular frame, with timing belts ensuring uniform motion. At the center of his frame is a tray that holds the glass, and it is raised or lowered in a synchronized manner when the motor is activated. After the tray lowers, a servo rotates a dispensing pipe toward the glass, followed by liquid dispensing via a peristaltic pump. Once dispensing is complete, the pipe retracts and the tray is lifted back using the same gear-belt system, ensuring smooth, precise, and balanced vertical movement.

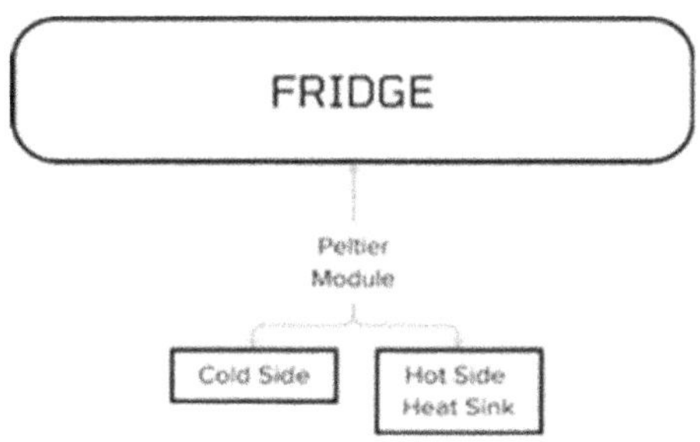

Figure 4. Mini Fridge Block Diagram.

Servo motor is used in the automatic dog feeder, rotating a lid to dispense food at set times.

USB charging ports and regulated power outputs are embedded into the table for user convenience.

3.2 *Software stack*

Home Assistant OS (on dedicated Pi) – for automations, dashboards, and device states. ESPHome – for flashing and controlling ESP32 devices via YAML configurations.

Python – for GPIO-based lighting control, automation extensions, and utility scripts (on voice assistant Pi).

Wyoming Satellite – orchestrates the voice assistant pipeline on Raspberry Pi OS.Wake word detection using Wyoming Wake Word.

Speech-to-text (STT) using faster-whisper Text-to-speech (TTS) using Piper Conversation agent powered by Ollama.

3.3 *Implementation workflow*

1) Step 1: System Setup
   One Raspberry Pi is flashed with Home Assistant OS to act as the home automation core. Another Raspberry Pi is set up with Raspberry Pi OS (64-bit) for custom scripts, AI processing, and voice assistant services
2) Step 2: ESP32 Device Configuration
   ESP32 boards are flashed using ESPHome, defining GPIO mappings for: Two relays (light control) Fan control using dual-relay speed switching Servo motor (dog feeder automation at 1 PM & 9 PM) Wi-Fi configuration and OTA support.

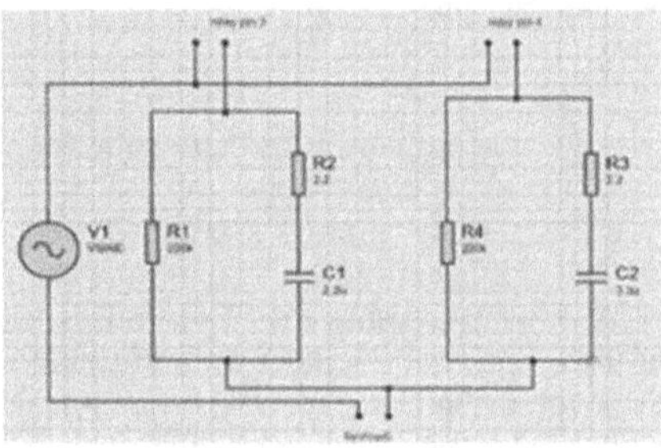

Figure 5. Fan Speed Control.

3) Step 3: RGB LED Lighting
   The RGB LED strip is controlled using Raspberry Pi GPIO (on home assistant Pi) and driven by an IRLZ44N + BC547 transistor circuit for PWM color control. Integrated with Home Assistant for scene-based control (Night, Focus, Gaming Modes).

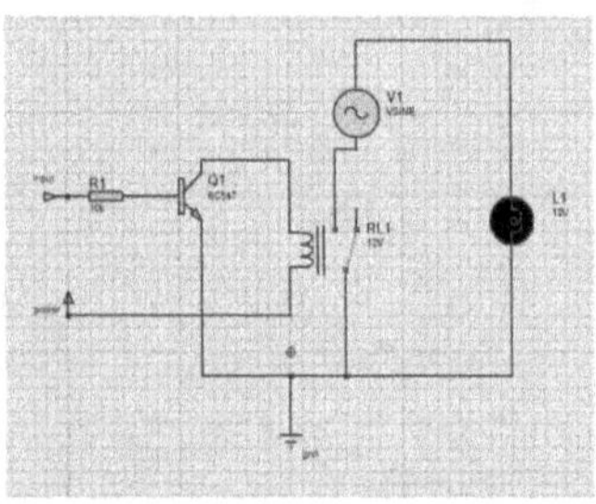

Figure 6. Relay.

4) Step 4: Voice Assistant Integration
   The voice assistant stack runs on the Raspberry Pi OS Pi: Wake word detection is handled by Wyoming Wake Word. Speech-to-text via faster-whisper, TTS via Piper. Commands are interpreted by a Ollama-based local agent. Based on intent, Home Assistant services are triggered via WebSocket API.

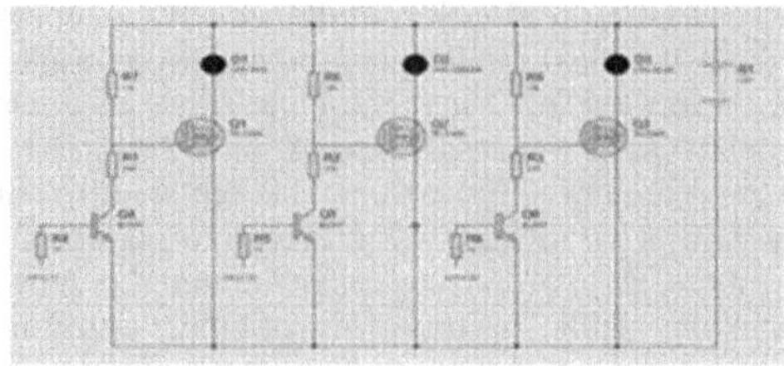

Figure 7. RGB LED Strip.

   Example commands:
   "Turn on the light"
   "Dispense 60 ml of juice"
   "What time is it?"
5) Step 5: Live Video Feed ESP32-CAM
   The ESP32-CAM module is flashed with the Camera Web Server firmware, enabling it to stream MJPEG video over the network via a specified port (commonly port 81). The stream is accessible through a URL such as http://<ESP32-CAM-IP>:81/stream. This video feed is integrated into the Home Assistant dashboard using a Picture Entity Card, which links directly to the ESP32-CAM's IP stream. This integration provides real-time video surveillance within the smart interface.

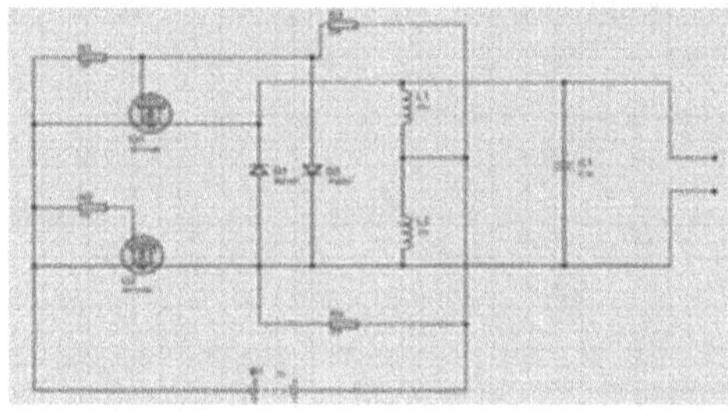

Figure 8. Wireless Charging.

6) Step 6: Wireless Charging & Mini Fridge
   The wireless charger circuit operates at 100.66 kHz. The mini fridge uses a Peltier module enclosed in an insulated thermocol box with a fan and heatsink.
7) Step 7: Synchronized Timing Belt-Driven Lifting
   Mechanism using a Multi-Gear and Pulley System. Use another Esp32 board for SIP N SYNC Automation. Servo motor controls the motion of the pipe dispensing the liquid. Peristaltic pump dispenses liquid (30 ml, 60 ml, or 90 ml) on command. Triggered via Home Assistant UI or by voice.
8) Step 8: Modular Surface
   Applications Lightweight JAR files for journaling, doodling, and games are launched from the Raspberry Pi OS system. These applications convert the surface into a productivity and entertainment station.

4 MATHEMATICAL MODEL

The Smart Surface system integrates multiple IoT modules—such as RGB LED control, wireless charging, fan control, and refrigeration—each involving electronic components and circuits whose behavior can be modeled mathematically. The following subsections outline key models used in system analysis and design:

1. **RGB LED Control Circuit Model**
   For each color channel (Red, Green, Blue), the current through the LED is controlled using a MOSFET-BJT driver circuit. The gate charging current for the MOSFET is:

$$I_G = \frac{V_{GPIO}}{R_G} = \frac{3.3V}{330\Omega} = 10mA$$

   The base current for the BJT (BC547) controlling the MOSFET is:

$$I_B = \frac{I_C}{h_{FE}} = \frac{500mA}{200} = 2.5mA$$

   Base resistor:

$$R_B = \frac{V_{GPIO-} \quad V_{BE}}{I_B} = \frac{3.3V - 0.7V}{2.5mA} = 1.04k\Omega$$

   These ensure safe operation of GPIO pins and proper saturation of the switching devices.
2. **Wireless Charging Resonant Circuit Model**
   The wireless charging module uses LC resonance for efficient energy transfer. The resonant frequency f is given by:

$$f = \frac{1}{2\pi\sqrt{LC}} = \frac{1}{2\pi\sqrt{25 \times 10^{-6} \times 0.1 \times 10^{-6}}} = 100.66kHz$$

   Impedance at resonance:

$$Z = \frac{1}{2\pi fC} = 15.81\Omega$$

   Power transfer efficiency is modeled as:

$$\eta = \frac{k^2 Q_1 Q_2}{1 + k^2 Q_1 Q_2}$$

   Where Q = ωL/R, assuming coupling coefficient k=0.5k and R=5 Ω, efficiency is around 71.43%
3. **Fan Speed Control (RC Phase Angle Model)**
   Fan speed is regulated using an RC phase angle control circuit. The phase angle θ introduced by an RC network is:

$$\tan(\theta) = \frac{1}{314 \times 10^4 \times 0.47 \times 10^{-6}}$$

$$\theta = 34^\circ$$

   Effective voltage delivered to the fan:

$$V_{RMS} = V_{peak} \times \cos(\theta) = 230V \times \cos(34^\circ) = 191V$$

   This reduction in RMS voltage results in lower fan speed, and stepwise control is achieved using relays to switch between RC networks.
4. **Peltier Mini Fridge Cooling Model**
   The Peltier module's performance is defined by the rate of heat transfer Q, given by:

$$Q = \alpha \times I \times T - \frac{1}{2} I^2 R - K \times \Delta T$$

   From empirical data, the fridge reaches a cooling of 12°C below ambient in 20 minutes, indicating acceptable thermal performance under practical conditions.

5 RESULT

The Smart Surface project successfully combined multiple smart technologies into a cohesive, multifunctional table. The offline voice assistant, powered by LLaMA, Whisper, and Piper, achieved a command recognition accuracy of 96% with an average response time of 2.3 seconds and wake word detection accuracy of 92% in quiet environments. Users were able to control lighting, fans, beverage dispensing, music playback, and general queries using natural voice commands.

The ESP32-based home automation controlled two AC bulbs, a two-speed fan, a dog feeder, and a servo motor with precise and reliable responses to both voice and dashboard controls. The fan speed slider enabled smooth speed adjustment, and the dog feeder successfully dispensed food at scheduled times (1 PM and 9 PM).

The SIP N SYNC beverage dispensing system incorporated a 12V gear motor for vertical movement combined with a peristaltic pump to dispense liquids in volumes of 30 ml, 60 ml, and 90 ml with ±3 ml accuracy. This subsystem achieved a 97% success rate over 100 cycles and responded effectively to voice commands such as "Pour 60 ml." The gear motor provided stable, smooth vertical motion, ensuring reliable operation.

Ambient lighting modes—Gaming, Journaling, Relaxation, and Doodling—were implemented with Raspberry Pi GPIO-controlled RGB LED strips. These modes could be switched via voice or UI, offering smooth transitions and appropriate lighting for each activity.

Multimedia applications such as journaling, drawing, and casual games ran efficiently on the touch-enabled display, with low latency and minimal CPU usage, delivering a seamless user experience.

The ESP32-CAM streamed MJPEG video through its onboard web server on port 81 (e.g., http://<esp32-ip>:81/stream). This stream was integrated into Home Assistant via a Picture Entity Card, providing stable 640×480 resolution video with approximately 2.5 seconds latency, suitable for basic local monitoring.

The table also featured a Peltier-based mini fridge capable of maintaining a temperature about 10°C below ambient, as well as wireless charging at 15W tested with popular smartphones, and stable USB charging ports (5V/2.1A).

Overall, the system ran stably for over seven days continuously, with a total power consumption of 25–30W. A pilot user study rated the Smart Surface highly with an average satisfaction score of 9.2/10, confirming the project's success as an integrated smart living solution.

6 CONCLUSION

The Smart Surface represents a novel integration of IoT automation, embedded intelligence, and user-centric design into a functional piece of furniture. Through the use of Raspberry Pi 4, ESPHome-enabled ESP32, Home Assistant, voice assistant modules, and modular add-ons like wireless charging, a Peltier-based mini fridge, RGB ambient lighting, and SIP N SYNC drink automation, the project successfully delivers a multi-functional smart table that goes beyond typical home automation solutions. The system's architecture emphasizes modularity, local control, offline processing, and ease of interaction, ensuring adaptability to both utility and lifestyle needs. Continuous video streaming, ambient mood settings, and the integration of open-source journaling and doodling apps make Smart Surface both interactive and context-aware.

In future iterations, Smart Surface can be improved by adding gesture recognition, AI-powered personalization, multiroom audio, and context-aware automation based on user presence and time of day. Optimizing power consumption and implementing solar-based power management would also enhance its sustainability for long-term smart living applications.

ACKNOWLEDGEMENT

The authors gratefully acknowledge the students, staff, and authority of Physics department for their cooperation in the research.

REFERENCES

[1] Krejcar O. *et al.*, (2019), Smart Furniture as a Component of a Smart City -Definition Based on Key Technologies Specification, *IEEE Access*, vol. 7, pp. 147760–147776, doi: 10.1109/ACCESS.2019.2927778.

[2] Song M. *et al.*, (2018), Smart Table Based on Metasurface for Wireless Power Transfer, arXiv preprint arXiv:1811.12487. [Online]. Available: https://arxiv.org/abs/1811.12487. [Accessed: Apr. 9, 2025].

[3] Vaida C., Gherman B., Dragomir M., Iamandi O., and Banyai D., (2014), Smart furniture - Quo Vadis, in *Proc. 3rd Int. Conf. Quality and Innovation in Engineering and Management*.

[4] Mohamed A.M.S., Ibrahim N.F., and Hassan M.R., (2021), The impact of smart furniture design on meeting the needs of a limited-space housing, *Journal of Architecture, Art & Humanistic Science*, vol. 6, no. 25, doi: 10.21608/mjaf.2020.23392.1499.

[5] *Internet of Things Technology in Smart Furniture: An Overview*, Clausius Scientific Press, 2024. [Online]. Available: https://www.clausiuspress.com/assets/default/article/2024/05/09/article1715269535.pdf. [Accessed: Apr. 9, 2025].

Advancement in Engineering and Science – Goyal et al. (Eds)

Power Quality Improvement of Grid-Connected Inverter Using DFACTS

Yuvraj K. Kanse, Sunita V. Mane, and Supriya P. Salave
Department of Electronics and Telecommunication Engineering, Karmaveer Bhaurao Patil College of Engineering, Satara, Maharashtra, India

ABSTRACT: A Microgrid consists of a set of power supplies and loads that can operate in either island mode or grid mode. Grid-connected inverters provide synchronization between grid parameters and inverter parameters. Nowadays, there are many problems in the transmission line, such as voltage variation, frequency variation, total harmonic distortion (THD) and so on. Power Quality issue is vital problem now days. This can be resolve by various methods. There are many great energy-enhancing technologies to choose from. Distributed Flexible Alternating Current Transmission System (FACTS) devices are an alternative solution to solve the main problem of the last generation of Flexible Alternating Current Transmission System (FACTS) devices. DFACTS devices have high efficiency, good power management, compact size, improved power conversion, higher reliability, and lower power loss compared to traditional FACTS devices. DFACTS devices are effective means for power quality improvement. The suggested approach uses Distribution Static Compensator (DSTATCOM) and Distributed Static Synchronous Series Compensator (DSSSC) to improve power quality. These DFACTS devices are useful for improving power efficiency, including increasing real power, reducing total harmonic distortion, and reducing reactive power.

Keywords: Grid connected Inverter, DFACTS, DSTATCOM, PCC, THD

1 INTRODUCTION

Power quality is a recent issue in energy production, transmission and use. Energy quality must be maintained at the highest-level during construction, transmission and use. The development of microgrids in recent years has supported the distribution of energy production and energy efficiency with the potential to increase energy efficiency. Here, the microgrid acts as a current controller that injects power into the main grid. Each DG should be matched to provide a constant voltage with a constant frequency in the microgrid. Electric power supplies electricity to consumers. Figure 1 is showing the microgrid equipment.

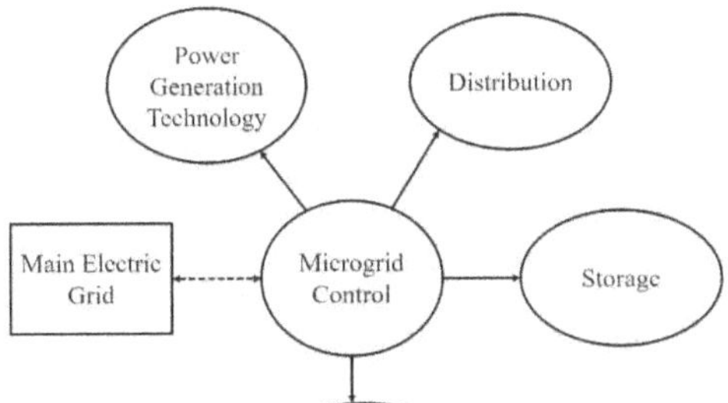

Figure 1. Microgrid components.

The smart grid has emerged as an effective way to produce, distribute and use electricity. Renewable energy is connected to the smart grid via grid-connected inverters. These inverters are more sensitive to power quality because inverters add harmonics to the power supply.

Effective power management is an important issue for the latest generation of FACTS equipment. This problem can be solved by improving the power quality of grid-connected inverters by using decentralized flexible AC system products. Decentralized FACTS (DFACTS) are widely used to solve different problems such as voltage sags, voltage swells, voltage fluctuations, interruptions, harmonics and many power changes in smart or micro grids.power recovery to reduce the voltage difference in the transmission system. In PCC, reactive power is absorbed by DSTATCOM and positive power is stored which is the main function of DSTATCOM. DFACTS tool is used to reduce the difference between the difference, energy and positive energy of the tie line. The presented work is to achieve improved power efficiency of grid-connected inverters using DFCATS tools. The microgrid is connected to the main grid at the connection point (PCC). PCC can disconnect or manually isolate the microgrid for island operation. In grid mode, the microgrid provides backup to the high-speed grid and maintains the same voltage level as the main grid.

2 LITERATURE SURVEY

Microgrid have become popular because of increase in decentralized energy resources (DER). In order to control the energy exchange of hybrid microgrids to obtain the best results [1]. Load transfer between bridges and equalization of battery pack pairs in both bridge connection and multiple extraction products [2]. The valid row size may not be realistic if not handled properly [3]. Distributed Static Synchronous Series Compensator (DSSSC) and decentralized static compensator (DSTATCOM) are used in planning studies to improve power efficiency. DSTATCOM is used for power supply and to improve power quality.

The proposed controls can balance the supply and demand after an outage, restore the frequency to its nominal value, and manage regional power fluctuations. The distributed controller concept can optimally distribute updates and control the traffic flow within thermal boundaries. It is recommended to adopt centralized voltage reactive control (VVC) based on information and communication technology. Distribution system state estimation (DSSE) can be the backbone of centralized VVC. Volt-optimized DSSE malicious strategy countermeasures are the two solutions in this document when the DER injection measurement is compromised. Local power management set point and effective use of historical data or forecast data are two things [6].

DOI: 10.1201/9781003798514-36

There is a necessary operating procedure for power systems where the voltage amplitude is in a predefined range. Increasing the voltage range by injecting reactive power in operating voltage limits is an optimization problem [7]. In the field of energy utilization, there is a renewable energy source (RES). Energy efficiency is better in microgrids through the interaction of renewable sources, improve the quality of energy injection medicine, and enable additional services [8].This paper establishes a decentralized, off-grid solar photovoltaic DC microgrid architecture suitable for rural electrification in the country. Analysis of the power flow, loss, and efficiency was performed using the Newton-Raphson tuning method for DC power flow for different voltages, dimensions, and conductors and connections between nano grids [9].

About the creation of local control systems for high integration of energy resources (DER) and instantaneous control of electricity in distribution systems. Proportional control concept to adjust power supply and reset power distribution for local changes in voltage levels. It has a medium voltage level [10].More batteries should be deployed in the distribution grid in the future to reduce voltage violation and overloading of hot wires and electrical equipment. This paper presents a two-level centralized predictive control model for distributed battery storage with scheduling and a real-time control center. The robust multi-cycle Optimum Power Flow (OPF) plans during the deployment period to reduce battery and limit PV usage. This paper [11] studies the decentralized DC optimal power (DC-OPF) algorithm of data integrity attacks. Power planning is realized by sharing false information with nearby buses. Economic-driven and impracticability-driven attacks are the two worst-case scenarios considered to launch data integrity attacks [12].Schedule management, continuous energy optimization and balance, energy dispatch and arbitrage, customer interaction, performance island operation, and improved power quality and reliability for smart microgrid application. This paper provides useful guidelines for using new models to represent BESS for energy analysis [13]. Three-phase photovoltaic (PV) inverters and electric vehicle (EV) chargers can be used. In this paper, the classical coordinated charging strategy for electric vehicles is adopted. Many power flow simulations and real data show that there is a positive effect on losses, power lines and inconsistencies.

This control system is a combination of the primary level droop-based controller and the secondary level power distribution system and power control system [14]. Since three-phase voltage source converters (VSCs) use d-q frame, synchronous instability can be observed. In the same case, the impedance of the grid-connected inverter shows negative increasing resistance behavior. This model is analyzed here [15]. Also, when reconnecting to the grid after islanded phase and amplitude matching. Flexible control of single-phase and three-phase systems has been demonstrated in hardware and software [16,17].

Since the current and voltage sensors are only for the inverter, the mode switching process can be done easily. It can eliminate the overcurrent continuously. With these techniques, answers can be reached quickly [18,19]. In a still frame, there are two series such as positive and negative. A report on the connection between these systems [20]. The frequency stability in PLL can be studied here [21].A newer version of SRF-PLL is the low-pass notch filter PLL (LPN-PLL). High performance and compatibility can be achieved thanks to the use of digital signal processors [128]. Three-phase grid-connected photovoltaic (PV) systems in single-phase mode offer low complexity, high stability and highest efficiency [22].

3 EXPERIMENTATION

A Flowchart is showing in Figure 2. Steps for experimental flow chart is such as in following manner:

1. Electrical Grid parameters sense by signal conditioning circuit at Point of Common Coupling (PCC).
2. Signal conditioning output is given to the embedded controller.
3. Embedded Controller generates PWM Gate pulses for Inverter.
4. Generated gate pulses given to three phase inverters with DC Source.
5. Check three-phase inverter voltage across Load. If the output voltage of Three phase inverter is over voltage, then the protection circuit is ON to prevent Three Phase Inverter from damage.
6. For normal operation, Three Phase Inverter is injected voltage into the grid.
7. Active power, Power factor, Reactive power, and Total Harmonics Distortion (THD) values are displayed on LCD interfaced with the embedded controller.
8. Load value is increased and repeat steps 5 to 7 for the required condition.

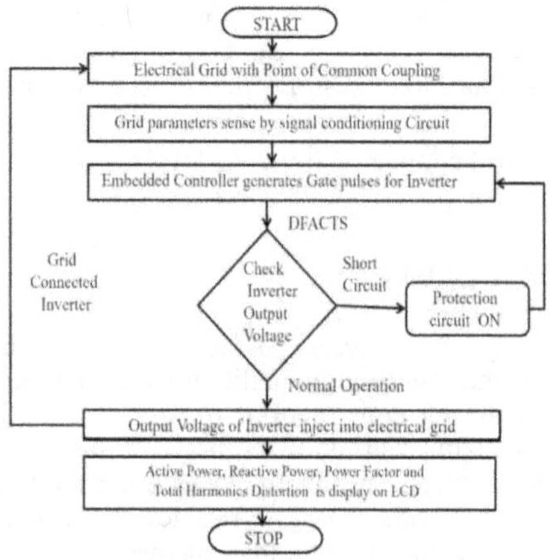

Figure 2. Flow chart of experimentation.

Figure 3. shows the schematic of the experimentation which is implemented.Design of research work consisting of Simulation as well as hardware. Simulation for research work is done in MATLAB Simulink as shown in Figure 4. Two DFACTS devices are used for power quality enhancement such as DSTATCOM and DSSSC. Both are designed in MATLAB Simulink with the help of a design strategy. The electrical grid is an ideal three phase voltage source used in MATLAB Simulink. The signal conditioning is a V-I measurement block that measures the grid voltage and grid current and these parameters are available on display to measure the values of grid voltage and grid current. An external DC voltage source battery excites three Phase inverter.

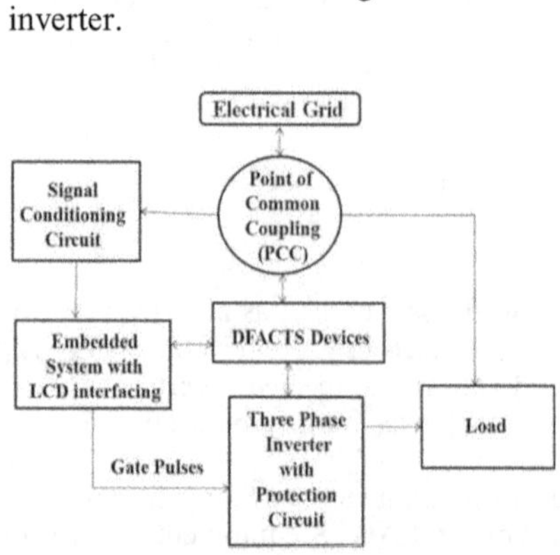

Figure 3. Schematic of implemented work.

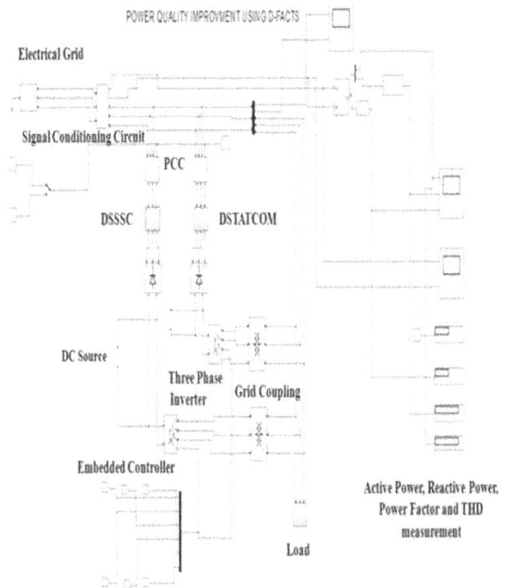

Figure 4. Simulation for research work is done in MATLAB Simulink.

The universal bridge is acting as three phase inverters whereas gate pulses are useful to activate the power devices of the universal bridge. Three phase transformer is available with grid coupling which connects three phase inverter and electrical grid. Two DFACTS devices such as DSTATCOM and DSSSC are connected with the help of a three-phase circuit breaker. The grid voltage is continuously monitored across grid three-phase voltage sources. Power factor calculation is done by calculating active and reactive power measurements across the output. A low-pass filter is used to provide better results in terms of power quality. There are two conditions for operation. One is Open Loop and another is a closed loop.

Figure 5. Shows hardware photograph.

For the open loop condition, both DFACTS devices such as DSTATCOM and DSSSC are in nonworking condition i.e. switch will disconnect the DFACTS devices from the remaining circuitry. So, DFACTS devices with grid-connected inverters is null. In closed-loop conditions, DFACTS devices along with circuitry is connected via a switch. Both DFACTS devices actively participated in the power factor correction mechanism and harmonics reduction process. Total Harmonics Distortion (THD) needs to be minimized so that frequency changes during synchronization and sharing of power can be possible. It is possible to control these parameters with a specific control system with an embedded controller. Electrical parameters of the electrical grid are captured from electrical grid for monitoring purposes. Electrical signal parameters are converted into suitable form by using Signal Conditioning Circuit so that's why they can handle by grid connected inverter. Conditioning Parameters are given to an Embedded System consisting Microcontroller with LCD for three phase inverter. Three Phase Inverter consisting of three leg structure with power devices. Switching of power devices depends on the signal generated from the control algorithm. The control algorithm is designed inside the embedded system for the proper working of three phase inverter. The protection circuit plays a vital role in the mechanism of over voltage or over current. It is required to keep the three-phase inverter in the safe stage. The power requirement of each circuitry is fulfilled by the power supply. Load is available for handling signal generated by a three-phase inverter.

4 RESULTS

There are two ways of working. One is open circuit; the other is closed circuit. For open circuit conditions DFACTS devices such as DSTATCOM and DSSSC are in disabled state, i.e. the switch separates DFACTS devices from the rest of the circuit. In closed circuit DFACTS device is connected to the switching circuit. Therefore, the impact of grid-connected inverter on power quality will be evaluated. Both DFACTS vehicles actively participate in the energy recovery vehicle and the trade-off reduction process. During synchronization and power sharing, total harmonic distortion (THD) needs to be minimized to change the frequency.

These parameters can be controlled by a special control system with a built-in controller. Generally, microgrids operate in parallel with the grid because the grid will instantly close the power mismatch, helping to increase the power frequency and bus voltage. When the power line is disconnected from the inverter, it should be possible to operate the inverter in standalone mode to provide the necessary power to the related products. The control algorithm of the three-phase inverter is to generate PWM pulses to drive the power components as required. The output of three-phase inverter is given to the load. It should be similar to the power grid. The voltage error between the grid and the three-phase inverter can be reduced by changing the control system. Variation of power factor with time for an open loop is shown in Figure 6. Variation of Active power and Reactive Power for an open loop is shown in Figure 7.

D-FACTS tools provide more flexibility, control, usability and reliability. DFACTS tools such as DSTATCOM and DSSSC provide power flow control during transmission lines. Critical power increased from 0.80 to 0.99. Active energy can be activated and regenerated with less energy by using DFACTS devices. THD is reduced after using DFACTS equipment. The maximum simulation result of total harmonic distortion (THD) without DFACTS device is 13.8%, and the maximum simulation result of total harmonic distortion (THD) with DFACTS device is 9.54%. (THD) is also the minimum value for DFACTS devices compared with DFACTS devices. In hardware, the total harmonic distortion (THD) result of the device without DFACTS is about99.77%, while the total harmonic distortion (THD) tested in the device with DFACTS is about 7.38%.

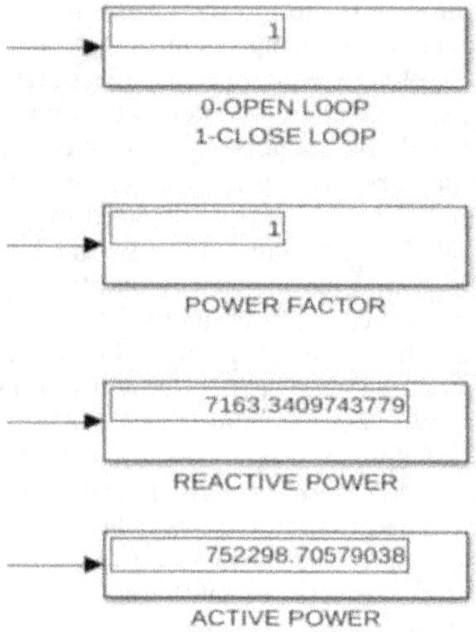

Figure 6. Power factor, reactive power and active power for open loop.

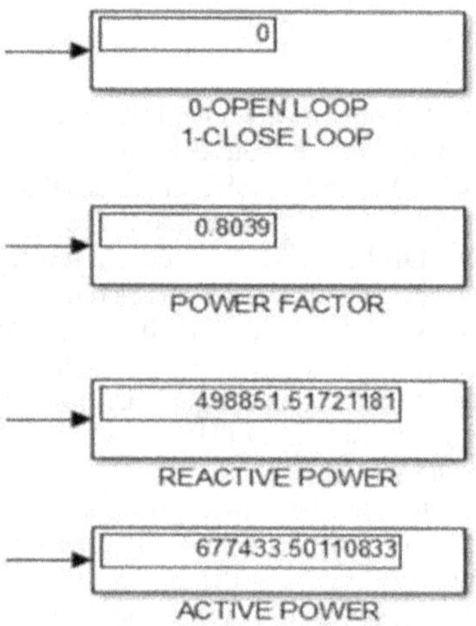

Figure 7. Power factor, reactive power and active power for open loop.

Table 1. Simulation parameters for open loop and closed loop.

Parameters	Open Loop	Close Loop
Active Power(W)	677433.5011	752298.7011
Reactive Power(W)	498851.5172	7163.3532
Power Factor	0.8	1
THD for 20 Cycles with Fundamental value= 432.5	13.8%	9.54%
THD for 6 Cycles with Fundamental value = 348.1	3.05%	0.05%

5 CONCLUSION

Power quality is an important issue in energy production, transmission and use. Energy quality must be maintained at the highest-level during construction, transmission and use. The development of smart grids and microgrids in recent years has supported the distribution of energy production and energy efficiency with the potential to increase energy efficiency. The smart grid has emerged as an effective way to produce, distribute and use electricity. These inverters are more sensitive to power quality because inverters add harmonics to the power supply. Effective power management is an important issue for the latest generation Flexible AC Transmission System (FACTS) equipment. This problem can be solved for grid-connected inverters by using decentralized flexible AC system products. Decentralized Flexible AC Transmission Systems (DFACTS) are widely used to solve different power quality issues like voltage sags, voltage swells, voltage fluctuations, interruptions and harmonics and various power changes in smart or micro grids. Because of DFACTS devices such as DSTATCOM and DSSSC, active power increases and reactive power decreases compared to those without DFACTS devices. In the closed loop case (e.g. when using the DFACTS device) all harmonic distortion is reduced. Without the DFACTS device the power is 0.8 and with the DFACTS device the power is approximately 1.

REFERENCES

[1] Tabart, Q., Vechiu, I., Etxeberria, A. and Bacha, S. (2017). Hybrid energy storage system microgrids integration for power quality improvement using four-leg three-level npc inverter and second-order sliding mode control. *IEEE Transactions on Industrial Electronics* 65(1), 424–435.

[2] Nasir, M., Khan, H.A., Hussain, A., Mateen, L. and Zaffar, N. A. (2017). Solar pv-based scalable dc microgrid for rural electrification in developing regions. *IEEE Transactions on Sustainable Energy* 9(1), 390–399.

[3] Xing, X., Lin, J., Wan, C. and Song, Y. (2017). Model predictive control of lpc-looped active distribution network with high penetration of distributed generation. *IEEE Transactions on Sustainable Energy* 8(3), 1051–1063.

[4] Charbonnier, F., Morstyn, T. and McCulloch, M.D. (2022). Coordination of resources at the edge of the electricity grid: Systematic review and taxonomy. *Applied Energy* 318, 119188.

[5] Duan, J., Zeng, W. and Chow, M.-Y. (2016). Resilient distributed dc optimal power flow against data integrity attack. *IEEE Transactions on Smart Grid* 9(4), 3543–3552.

[6] Xu, X., Bishop, M., Oikarinen, D.G. and Hao, C. (2016). Application and modeling of battery energy storage in power systems. *CSEE Journal of Power and Energy Systems* 2(3), 82–90.

[7] Golsorkhi, M.S., Savaghebi, M., Lu, D.D.-C., Guerrero, J.M. and Vasquez, J.C. (2016). A gps-based control framework for accurate current sharing and power quality improvement in microgrids. *IEEE Transactions on Power Electronics* 32(7), 5675–5687.

[8] Wen, B., Dong, D., Boroyevich, D., Burgos, R., Mattavelli, P. and Shen, Z. (2015). Impedance-based analysis of grid-synchronization stability for three-phase paral-leled converters. *IEEE Transactions on Power Electronics* 31(1), 26–38.

[9] Tran, T.-V., Chun, T.-W., Lee, H.-H., Kim, H.-G. and Nho, E.-C. (2013). Pll-based seamless transfer control between grid-connected and islanding modes in grid-connected inverters. *IEEE Transactions on Power Electronics* 29(10), 5218–5228.

[10] Arancibia, A., Strunz, K. and Mancilla-David, F. (2013). A unified single-and three-phase control for grid connected electric vehicles. *IEEE Transactions on Smart Grid* 4(4), 1780–1790.

[11] Ochs, D.S., Mirafzal, B. and Sotoodeh, P. (2013). A method of seamless transitions between grid-tied and stand-alone modes of operation for utility-interactive three-phase inverters. *IEEE Transactions on Industry Applications* 50(3), 1934–1941.

[12] Bakhshizadeh, M.K., Wang, X., Blaabjerg, F., Hjerrild, J., Kocewiak, L-., Bak, C.L. and Hesselbæk, B. (2016). Couplings in phase domain impedance modeling of grid-connected converters. *IEEE Transactions on Power Electronics* 31(10), 6792–6796.

[13] Dong, D., Wen, B., Boroyevich, D., Mattavelli, P. and Xue, Y. (2014). Analysis of phase-locked loop low-frequency stability in three-phase grid-connected power converters considering impedance interactions. *IEEE Transactions on Industrial Electronics* 62(1), 310–321.

[14] Lee, K.-J., Lee, J.-P., Shin, D., Yoo, D.-W. and Kim, H.-J. (2013). A novel grid synchronization pll method based on adaptive low-pass notch filter for grid-connected pcs. *IEEE transactions on industrial electronics* 61(1), 292–301.

[15] Libo, W., Zhengming, Z. and Jianzheng, L. (2007). A single-stage three-phase grid-connected photovoltaic system with modified mppt method and reactive power compensation. *IEEE Transactions on Energy Conversion* 22(4), 881–886.

[16] Wen, B., Boroyevich, D., Burgos, R., Mattavelli, P. and Shen, Z. (2015). Analysis of dq small-signal impedance of grid-tied inverters. *IEEE Transactions on Power Electronics* 31(1), 675–687.

[17] Vasquez, J.C., Guerrero, J.M., Miret, J., Castilla, M. and De Vicuna, L.G. (2010). Hierarchical control of intelligent microgrids. *IEEE Industrial Electronics Magazine* 4(4), 23– 29.

[18] Liserre, M., Teodorescu, R. and Blaabjerg, F. (2006). Multiple harmonics control for three-phase grid converter systems with the use of pi-res current controller in a rotating frame. *IEEE Transactions on power electronics* 21(3), 836–841.

[19] Hoon, Y., Radzi, M.A.M., Hassan, M.K. and Mailah, N.F. (2017). Operation of three-level inverter-based shunt active power filter under nonideal grid voltage conditions with dual fundamental component extraction. *IEEE Transactions on Power Electronics* 33(9), 7558–7570.

[20] Marinus, N.S.d.M.L., Jacobina, C.B., Rocha, N. and Santos, E. C. (2016). Ac–dc–ac three-phase converter based on three three-leg converters connected in series. *IEEE Transactions on Industry Applications* 52(4), 3171–3181.

[21] Vasquez, J.C., Guerrero, J.M., Savaghebi, M., Eloy-Garcia, J. and Teodorescu, R. (2012). Modeling, analysis, and design of stationary-reference-frame droop-controlled parallel three-phase voltage source inverters. *IEEE Transactions on industrial electronics* 60(4), 1271–1280.

[22] Bae, Y., Kim and R.-Y. (2012). Suppression of common-mode voltage using a multicentral photovoltaic inverter topology with synchronized pwm. *IEEE Transactions on Industrial Electronics* 61(9), 4722–4733.

Advancement in Engineering and Science – Goyal et al. (Eds)
 ISBN: 978-1-041-31101-0

Inline Dedup Check and Improved Data Security in Multi-Cloud Environment

Farhadeeba I Shaikh
Asst Prof, Department of Polytechnic and Skill Development, Dr VK MIT World Peace university, Pune, India

Tazaeen Ilyas Shaikh
Research Scholar, School of Business, Dr VK MIT World Peace University, Pune, India

ABSTRACT: Cloud computing is the latest wave of IT industry technologies. Scalability, multi-user, virtualization, among many other traits, are among its numerous benefits. Additionally, it provides computer infrastructure for on-demand use and could reduce the cost of creating IT-based services. Different kinds of facilities can be offered online. One important service offered by the cloud is storage, where customers can retain their files as long as necessary. In light of the fact that all data is stored in a network of connected resources spread across several global locations, the user is presented with an intriguing security challenge. Through virtual machines, unauthorised users may access this data. It has a very dark side, then. To solve this, we have proposed a secure model for storing data securely on cloud by using fragmentation, cryptography technique and only authenticate users can access the data on cloud, which improves security of data information stored on multi cloud. The proposed framework is based on encryption scheme & hashing technique. Before, storing the data on cloud the hashing technique is used for DE duplication checking, which improves storage utilization.

Keywords: Symmetric key cryptography, Cloud Computing, De-duplication, Cloud Security, Fragmentation, Encryption, Decryption and Multi cloud Environment

1 INTRODUCTION

The user is presented with an intriguing security dilemma because all the data are stored in a network of connected resources that are dispersed around the globe. Through efficient machines, this data might be accessible by unauthorised persons. Therefore, it is a disadvantage of cloud data storage that customers experience a lot of concern. As a result, a big issue with cloud computing is file security. It offers computing infrastructure for on-demand use and may lower the price of developing IT-based businesses. Accepting the traditional cryptographic method for cloud computing file security poses a risk because the data is stored in a remote location with no user control. As a result, it requires an authentication strategy and lacks clear knowledge of the entire set of data in which it is located. Therefore, it is exceedingly difficult to determine which cloud each block of data is stored on. Due to its remote location, it is highly challenging to confirm the accuracy of data stored on the cloud. Second, the data may be frequently modified, deleted, added, updated, recovered, and rearranged by a variety of users.

Therefore, it requires a more proactive, technologically advanced operation to stop data loss from cloud storage. Last but not least, it is critical to provide accurate assurance in the dispersed protocols since data centers that are operating concurrently in a dispersed fashion and every piece of data is kept in a different physical location.

2 CLOUD ARCHITECTURE AND SECURITY ISSUES

The two types of cloud computing are service delivery models and deployment models [4]. Figure 1 displays the cloud environment. The deployment models are: 1) **Private cloud**: A cloud platform is intended for particular businesses. In this case, the customer has exclusive access to the computing infrastructure, which is not shared with any other businesses. 2) **Public cloud**: a public cloud platform where users can sign up and access the infrastructure is offered. The end user cannot see the computing infrastructure because it is hosted at the vendor's office. 3) **Hybrid cloud**: a private cloud that may access resources in other clouds, including public ones. Both low-value and high-value applications can be submitted by organisations to different clouds. 4) **Community cloud:** The cloud infrastructure is shared by businesses in the same neighbourhood. Infrastructure as a Service (IaaS), Platform as a Service (PaaS) and Software as a Service (SaaS) are service delivery model [5].

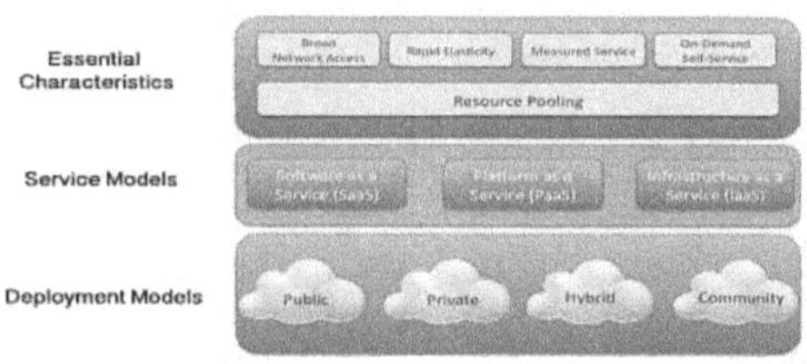

Figure 1. Cloud architecture.

They can build their architecture on Infrastructure as a Service (IaaS), which provides virtualized hardware and storage, as the foundation. Although it provides just a little help with application development, it is suitable for creating the system infrastructure. In order to perform services, it can share hardware resources with other programmes; frequently, this requires virtualization technology.

The intermediary layer known as framework as a Service (PaaS) provides a framework for developing cloud-hosted applications. Additionally, it gives you a platform to run your applications on. Without having to download any of these platforms or associated support software on their own PCs, it offers customers the platforms, tools, and other business services they require to design, manage, and deploy their own applications.

The top layer, known as software as a service (SaaS), provides applications that may be accessed at any time, from any location. Applications that serve a diversity of consumers and

DOI: 10.1201/9781003798514-37

can only be slightly modified to satisfy unique requirements find it appealing. It offers end-user support without asking that customers install any software on their machines. Some security issues are

The many types of attackers and how they can attack the cloud.

- The cloud's security risks, including any applicable considerations for attacks and countermeasures.
- New threats to cloud protection.
- A number of events involving cloud security.

We have defined various entities in this model, which are listed below.

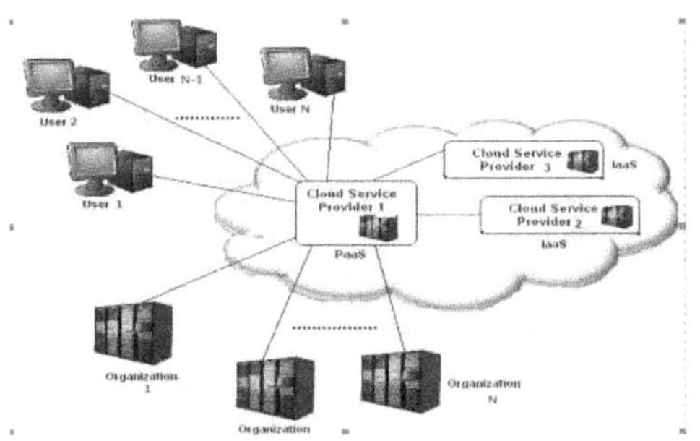

Figure 2. Cloud architecture.

- **User:** Users who want to use cloud infrastructure.
- **Cloud Service Provider-1:** The platform that provides services is this one. Here, the user will manage the computation. CSP-2 and CSP-3 user interaction.
- **Cloud Service Provider-2:** Algorithms for encryption, decryption, and key creation are kept in this location.
- **Cloud Service Provider-3:** This is a provider of infrastructure as a service. All information is kept here.

3 LITERATURE REVIEW

In order to address the security difficulties in multi-cloud systems, the authors of [8] recommend utilising a number of methods and In terms of computing cost, computational time, encryption and decryption time, and security, promptly assess their performance. The aforementioned algorithms are also contrasted with one another in order to determine the efficient method that offers the highest or best performance.

In [9], the authors provide a brief review of the essential concepts, difficulties requirements, and probable results for multi-cloud settings. The primary multi-cloud frameworks' customary tactics and solutions are also assessed for their advantages and disadvantages. In order to address safety concerns in multi-cloud systems, several kinds of methodologies and their performance in terms of computational cost, time required for computation, encryption and decryption time, and security are briefly studied. In order to find the efficient method that offers maximum or greater performance, the discussed algorithms are also contrasted with one another.

Authors in [10] presented a solution referred to as the multi-cloud disaster recovery business system to address the disaster recovery requirements for multi-cloud and heterogeneous cloud systems. Through third-party coordinated hosting, MCDR gives customers access to worldwide disaster recovery and backup services. In multi-cloud environments, it also enables unified administration of user resources, company networks, personal information, and applications.

The authors of [11] introduced an efficient method called **Attribute-based Multi-keyword Search (AMSE)** to make searching through **encrypted data in multi-cloud environments** easier and more secure. AMSE uses a powerful encryption technique known as **Cipher text Policy Attribute-Based Encryption (CP-ABE)**, which allows users to search encrypted data using multiple keywords while controlling who can access it. By adding a **retrieval server**, AMSE can quickly and accurately find the required encrypted files across different clouds. The performance and security tests showed that AMSE is **fast, secure, and well-suited** for managing data in multi-cloud systems.

The authors [1] proposed a framework that uses **encryption techniques** to protect data stored in the cloud. In this approach, the original data (plaintext) is converted into **cipher text**, making it unreadable to unauthorized users. The framework also generates a **small, efficient secret key** that is suitable for **data-centric applications**, ensuring both security and ease of use. These should prevent unauthorized users from accessing data stored in the cloud. These plans include effective data retrieval and storing. The model will reportedly be expanded in the future to include error localization and communication delay reduction.

Enhancing Information Security in a Cloud Computing System using Cryptographic Techniques. To strengthen information security, In paper[2] will address the importance of cryptography in cloud computing. With the use of cryptography to secure data at cloud data centres, a new security strategy is intended to be gained here.

After examining other encryption algorithms, it was discovered that AES is, on balance, a good strategy because it is both faster and more safe due to its symmetric nature. Additionally, data can be transmitted securely using cloud computing. For a more secure transmission, it is recommended to encrypt data first before transmitting it through the cloud so that, if a third party were to read the data [3], he would only be able to see the encrypted data, which is incomprehensible to him. This increases data protection while maintaining integrity and confidentiality.

As a result of research paper [6], were able to evaluate a number of cloud computing security algorithms [6]. This article highlights a number of security worries and problems with cloud computing. Security worries for cloud providers (companies that provide software, platforms, or infrastructure as a service via the cloud) and security worries for their clients (companies or organisations that host applications or store data on the cloud) can be divided into two main categories, though. However, there are two parties that are accountable: the user and the provider. The user must take steps to enhance their application, use the provider's infrastructure to ensure security, and safeguard their customers' data and apps.

We have contributed to the following areas, which are summarised as follows: First, a framework based on encryption techniques is suggested, and these schemes can conceal the plaintext in cypher text that can be stored on the cloud. Second, it creates a compact secret key that enables authorised people to access data with ease. These should prevent unauthorised users from accessing data stored in the cloud. De-duplication is another technique that can be used to manage storage effectively. These plans include effectively storing data and retrieving it from a multicloud environment.

4 SCHEMATIC SYSTEM ARCHITECTURE OF PROPOSED MODEL

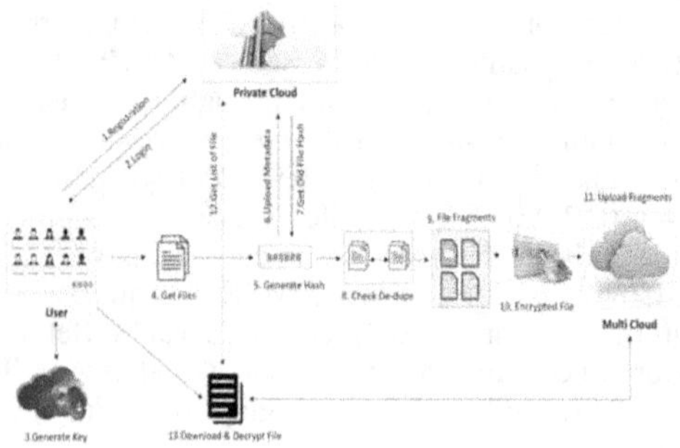

(A) Registration of Authorised users
Only the registered users can login the details of their information and will have entry into the software. Those users who do not have access has to get permission from the organization to upload or download the file from cloud. Any text file of any size you can select to upload wherever it is stored.

(B) Generating key
The users who are registered users has to create the keys for the related files which they are uploading on the cloud. While downloading any file it will check first that you are the same who has uploaded the file on cloud. This data is saved on private cloud to make it secure.

(C) Dedup Check
Step 1: Get Input File F
Step 2: Generate Hash H of Input File F
Step 3: Match Generated Hash H with Existing File Hash List H_L
Step 4: If H_L Contains Files Hash H
Then file is already present (duplicate file) at Server S no need to upload file at server;
Else
Store Hash H in H_L and Upload File at Server S.
Step 5: End
The file which the user wants to upload on the cloud can be selected as input and will be checked for duplication. First it will find its hash value using SHA1 algorithm for checking whether the file is already existing on the cloud or not. If exists then it will not allow to restore again for improving the efficiency in storage management.

(D) Fragmentation and Encryption
Step 1: Get Input File F.
Step 2: Get Size of F File as S = F.size.
Step 3: If (S % 4 == 0)
Step 4: Then Divide File F Into 4 Equal Blocks B.
Step 5: Else Generate 3 Blocks B of Same Size ; where the size of B is greater than (S/4) and
Create 4th Block S' of Size S' = (S - 3*B)).
Step 6: End
For improving the security, the file is divided into blocks and these blocks are randomly placed onto different clouds after encrypting with Advance Encryption Standards algorithm. Even if the attacker gets a chance to access any block he will not be able to get rest of the blocks.

(E) Decrypt and Merge
While downloading the file first it checks for the authentication of the user with metadata stored on private cloud. After checking the metadata then the file is decrypted and merge into one file before displaying.
We have selected four samples of different file size. Using these files we have tried with our system for uploading and downloading the same file. By seeing the time it requires for encryption and decryption also uploading and downloading time we have taken its graph.
From the graph we can conclude that as file size changes it takes that much time for encryption as well as for decryption. Even the same thing is observed that time depends on the file size for uploading and downloading it mainly depends on file size.

Table 1. Sample files for checking.

File size (Bytes)	Encryption time	Decryption time	Uploading time	Downloading time
212	530774	393387	4716	3748
1409	833281	433787	5652	4557
2016	877495	465201	6004	4946
8177	978935	782624	8175	6050

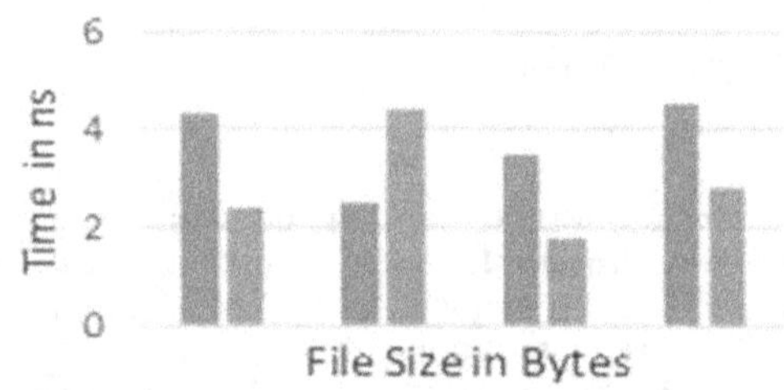

Figure 3. Graph of encryption/decryption vs time.

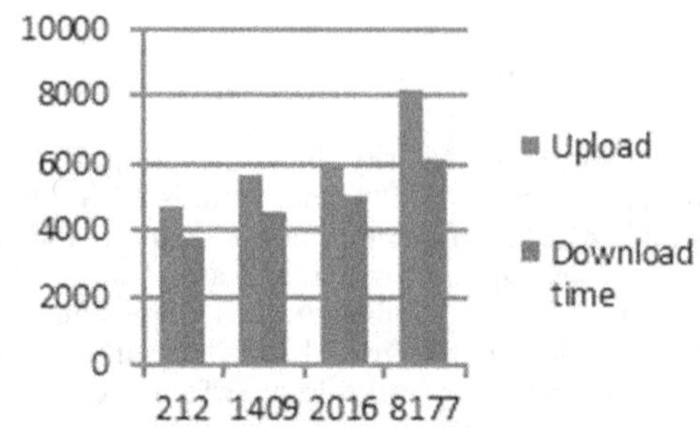

Figure 4. Graph of uploading/downloading vs time.

5 CONCLUSION

To implement a service-based architecture, cloud computing is used. The community must adopt real and committed steps to assure security if it is to focus on cloud computing. Adoption of common standards is still being pushed for in order to guarantee service providers' interoperability. In this article, we discuss deduplication checking, which enhances the security of data saved across many clouds. The framework we offer is based on authentication and an encryption technique. The user's private key, which is kept on a private cloud server, is the only way to decrypt the data once it has been uploaded to multi cloud. The user must authenticate themselves in order to obtain the private key from a private cloud server; only after successful authentication does the user acquire the private key. The key benefit of this is that communication delays are significantly decreased and data is very securely stored in the cloud.

6 FUTURE WORK

In this study, we presented a framework based on encryption techniques and gave an overview of cloud computing data storage security. Our approach introduces an efficient method to strengthen the security of data-at-rest, ensuring that user information stored in the cloud remains protected. The results show that our method can effectively safeguard data stored in any data center managed by a Cloud Service Provider (CSP). This framework can also serve as a foundation for developing future models aimed at improving data protection in similar cloud computing environments. This design will attract a lot of investors for industrial farms as well as prospective research farms and can considerably improve customer satisfaction. This methodology is capable of handling the multiple security issues present in a large setting. In contrast to several previous systems in the same field, it contains innovative elements for overcoming security issues.

Additionally, the implementation outcomes show that the suggested strategy has a shorter communication lag. We will upgrade our model in the future to include error localisation and cut down on communication lag. We also intend to look into the accuracy of dynamic storage. Our suggested system only works with text files, but we can expand it in the future to upload image, audio, and video files as well.

REFERENCES

[1] Mrinal Kanti Sarkar and Sanjay Kumar, A Framework to Ensure Data Storage Security in Cloud Computing, in 2016 *IEEE.*

[2] Prof. Suraj R. Pardeshi, Prof. Vikul J. Pawar and Prof. Kailash D. Kharat, *Enhancing Information Security in Cloud Computing Environment Using Cryptographic Techniques*, in 2016 *IEEE.*

[3] Shenling Liu1, Chunyuan Zhang1 and Le Bo1, Improve Security and Availability for Cloud Storage, in *Proceedings of CCIS*2016.

[4] Torry Harris, *Cloud Computing – An Overview.*

[5] Jaydip Sen, *Security and Privacy Issues in Cloud Computing.*

[6] Pooja P Vasani and Nishant S Sanghani, Study of Various Cloud Computing Security, in *International Journal of Science Research and Technology* Volume 2 Issue 1, p p 21–24, 25th March 2016.

[7] Mrutunjay Allakonda and Sagar K, A Survey on data security challenges in multi cloud environment, in *IEEE* 2021.

[8] Harish Naik and Jayanthi Kannan, A Research on Various Security Aware Mechanisms in Multi-Cloud Environment for Improving Data Security, in *IEEE* 2023.

[9] Prabakaran and Dr B Sivakumar, A Comparative Analysis of security issues in Multicloud, in *IEEE* 2022

[10] Bin Liu, Yang Xin and Chunyang Zhang, A Solution for A Disaster Recovery Service System in Multi-cloud Environment, in *IEEE* 2022.

[11] Hang Hi, Jiaqi Liu, Jinggang Gu and Feng Gao, An Efficient Multi-Keyword Search Scheme over Encrypted Data in Multi-Cloud Environment, in *IEEE* 2022.

[12] Dr Reshami T R and Rishita, Security in Cloud Computing, Department of SCSE, VIT University, *Chennai in International Conference on Recent Trends in Advanced Computing* (ICRTAC-CPS 2018)

[13] Diao Zhe, Wang Qinghong, SU Naizheng, Zhang Yuhan, University of International Relations, Beijing, China "Study on Data Security Policy Based On Cloud Storage" in 2017 *IEEE 3rd International Conference on Big Data Security on Cloud.*

[14] Vamsi Krishna B S, Sreenivasa Rao S and MHM KrishnaPrasad, Security on Data Auditing Protocols forCloud Storage Data, in *Proceedings of the Third International Conference on I-SMAC (IoT in Social, Mobile, Analytics and Cloud) (I-SMAC* 2019)

Advancement in Engineering and Science – Goyal et al. (Eds)
© 2026 The Author(s), ISBN: 978-1-041-31101-0

A Review of Cyber Security in Artificial Intelligence

Macherla Malleswara Rao
Department of Computer Science and Engineering, Koneru Lakshmaiah Education Foundation, Vaddeswaram, Guntur, India

Pavan Kumar Tummala
Professor, Department of Computer Science and Engineering, Koneru Lakshmaiah Education Foundation, Vaddeswaram, Guntur, India

ABSTRACT: Artificial Intelligence (AI) is a powerful technology that enables cyber security groups in to automatic repeated work, expedite danger identified and addressed, and enhance accuracy along with operations that strengthen a safety posture in opposite to different safety barriers as well as the cyberattacks. This study provides complete examination about the artificial intelligence applications for cyber security provisioning through a systematic literature review and analytical study. Overall,500 investigations comprised under review, over 100 have being defined as primary. This paper categorizes the recognized AI applications according to a NIST cyber security structure applying confined investigation method. A particular kind of configuration that offer literate thorough exposition about capacity over artificial that enhance cyber security by various situations. Furthermore, analysis highlights potential research prospects in developing fields of emerging cyber security applications, sophisticated artificial intelligence strategies, information visualization, along with creation in narrative infrastructures adequately implement the Artificial intelligence focused cyber security in the age of digital transformation and multiple crises.

Keywords: cyber security, artificial intelligence, Cyber-attack detection, cyber defence, survey

1 INTRODUCTION

Cyber security encompasses a range of technologies, procedures, and methods aimed at safeguarding and defending networks, devices, software and information from attacks, harm and illegal approach. The increasing complexity of cyber security can be attributed to the rapid expansion of linked devices, systems, andnetworks. Furthermore, the progress in the digital economy and infrastructure has intensified this issue, resulting in a substantial increase in cyberattacks that have severe repercussions. Furthermore, experts have documented the on-going development of adversaries linked to nation-states and criminal organizations, together with the growing complexity of cyberattacks, which are continually discovering novel and intrusive methods to attack even the most knowledgeable targets. [4]

The on-going evolution is causing a rise in the quantity, magnitude, and consequences of cyberattacks. As a result, it is imperative to use intelligence-driven cyber security measures by providing flexible defines opposed to developing assaults and effectively handle large volumes of data. Regulatory bodies, like National Institute of Standards and Technologies (NIST) abide promoting adoption prescient, adaptable strategies beyond transitioning to live evaluations, on-going surveillance, data-driven examination that distinguish, safeguard opposed, find out, understand, categorize cyberattacks in order to avert long-term protection breaches. [5]

Artificial intelligence (AI) is a fascinating apparatus capable of delivering data analysis intelligence to defend opposed changing cyberattacks through rapidly evaluating abundance data. Monitors analyse the diverse range of cyber risks on predict, take proactive measures to address the issue. Due to this rationale, artificial intelligence (AI) is progressively being included into the cyber security framework and employed in several scenarios to mechanize security activities or assist human security teams. [6]

The field of cyber security is new and grows quickly, combined with researchers in both AI and cyber security's increasing enthusiasm for their field, has resulted in many papers focused on dealing with concerns over identification, protection, detection, reaction, and rescue from cyberattacks. We analyse these review paper on four objectives. [7]

Significant progress has been made in AI-powered technologies in machine learning, deep learning, and natural language processing in recent years thanks to cyber security solutions. These solutions are being used in various applications, including: [8]

1. Threat Detection: Real-time threat detection is possible with AI-powered systems that can analyze vast amounts of data and identify patterns and anomalies. [9]
2. Incident Responses AI-powered solutions can automate incident response procedures, reducing the damage and response times. [10]

Numerous assessments of the relationship between artificial intelligence applications and cyber security have been released in recent years. To the best of our knowledge, there is currently no extensive analysis that encompasses the latest research on cyber security activities addressed by AI methodology and the specifics of their application. Hence, our aim was to offer a methodical analysis, a thorough perspective on the applications of artificial intelligence (AI) in cyber security, and an examination of the research obstacles associated with the integration and utilization of AI for cyber security. Future researchers and practitioners will find this to be a useful resource thatis presented in [11].

An analysis of the study in relation to review papers published in recent years Table 1.

Table 1.

S: no	Paper	Year	Focus Area	Methodology	Key Findings
1	AI-Powered Cyber security" [1]	2020	AI-driven threat detection	Systematic review	AI improves detection accuracy by 30%
2	Cyber security Meets AI" [2]	2019	AI-based intrus ion detection	Literature review	AI reduces false positives by 25%
3	"AI for Cyber security" [3]	2018	Machine learning for malware detection	Meta-analysis	AI-based detection outperforms traditional methods

(*continued*)

DOI: 10.1201/9781003798514-38

Table 1. Continued

S: no	Paper	Year	Focus Area	Methodology	Key Findings
4	"Cyber AI" [4]	2022	AI-driven incident response	case study	AI reduces incident response time by 40%
5	Intelligent Cyber security" [5]	2021	Deep learning for network security	Survey	80% of experts consider AI crucial for cyber security
6	AI in Cyber security" [6]	2020	Natural language processing for threat intelligence	Experimental study	AI improves threat intelligence accuracy by 20%
7	"Cyber security and AI" [7]	2019	AI-based phishing detection	Comparative analysis	AI-based detection outperforms rule-based approaches
8	"AI-Enhanced Cyber security" [8]	2022	AI-driven vulnerability management	Systematic review	AI reduces vulnerability exploitation by 35%
9	A Critical Cyber Security Analysis	2023	IoT Security	Systematic Review	Identified security risks and threats in IoT devices

A comprehensive survey of the literature (SLR) was conducted beside utilization an artificial intelligence infield of cyber security. The study specifically examined experimental implementations of artificial intelligence in five distinct cyber security roles (recognize, Protect, Detect, Respond, and Recover) as outlined by the NIST cyber security framework. This study aims to address several particular research topics. [12]

- RQ1: What role should artificial intelligence take in the taxonomy of cyber security functions? [13]
- RQ2: What role does Artificial intelligence actually play in cyber security? [14]
- RQ3: What is the present research trends related to artificial intelligence in the field of cyber security? [15]
- RQ4: what are the growing trends and future scope of the use of artificial intelligence in cyber security? [16]

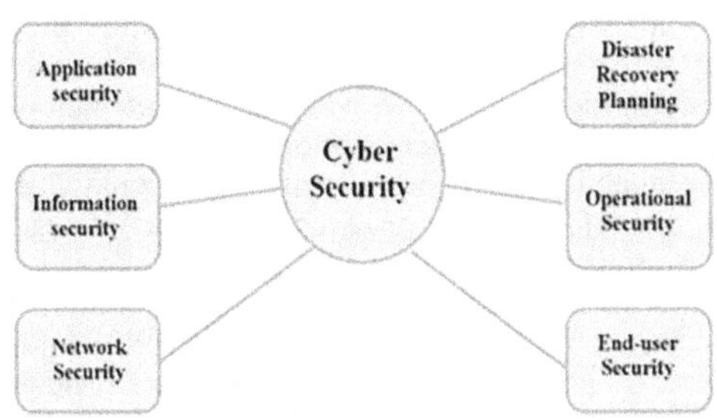

II. Cyber Security Process [17]

2 OBJECTIVES

2.1 *Threat Detection*

Artificial intelligence powered grids can examine huge number of information to detect designs and variation, detecting possible threats in live. Machine learning computation can be trained to recognize malicious activity decreasing wrong positives and enhancing incident response. [18]

2.2 *Incident Response*

The Artificial intelligence automatic incident response procedure, diminishing concussion of a breach. The artificial intelligence powered systems can analyse network traffic, identify affected systems, and implement containment measures loosening human analysts pivot in complicated tasks. [19]

2.3 *Predictive Analytics*

The Artificial intelligence powered threatening analytics determine vulnerabilities, predict possible attempt, allowing operation to take proactive assess to prevent breaches. Evaluating background information and identifying tendency, the artificial intelligence can predict potential threats and enable organizations to take action before an attack occurs. [20]

2.4 *Continuous Monitoring*

Continuous monitoring using AI analyses system logs and network behaviour patterns to detect security dangers. AI will predict and react to threats while constantly observing the environment in real-time, thus reducing the chances of a breach [21]

3 LITERATURE REVIEW ABOUT FOUR OBJECTIVES

As indicated within the papers reviewed, AI is becoming increasingly relevant in the identification and prevention of cyber threats. The application of machine learning and deep learning techniques plays an ever-increasing role in pattern and anomaly detection in network traffic, system logs, and user behaviour. Explainable AI methods, including feature attribution and model interpretability, are being explored to provide insights into AI-driven threat detection decisions. This is fundamental to have trust in AI systems and for security professionals to be able to interpret and react to threats effectively. [22]

Both reinforcement learning and transfer learning are being applied to threat detection; enabling AI systems adjust to new threats and atmosphere. Generative adversarial networks Synthetic data is produced using (GANs) in order to train AI models, improving their accuracy and robustness. The articles reviewed here also highlight the need for security on IoT devices and raise attention for artificial intelligence-based threat detection systems that are being developed to address threats that are native to the IoT. In summary, the review of literature indicates that AIs are increasingly necessary for cyber security efforts and are "primarily helping industries identify and react to threats more efficiently. However, further research is needed to overcome the challenges of explain ability, transparency, and trust in AI-driven threat detection decisions. [23]

3.1 *Deep learning for cyber security threat detection (2020): [24]*

In this article, S. Sahu, offered deep learning way of detecting cyber security threats. They proposed a convolutional neural network (CNN) model capable of categorizing network traffic as malicious or benign. Explainable AI for Threat Detection in Cyber security (2022) In this article, S. Sahu *et al.* discussed the importance of explaining ability in AI-driven cyber security threat detection. They proposed a feature attribution method to explain the decisions made by AI models. [25]

AI-powered Threat Detection for IoT Devices (2023) In this article, S. Sahu *et al.* presented an AI-powered threat detection system for IoT devices. They proposed a machine learning model that can detect anomalies in IoT device behaviour. Reinforcement Learning for Threat Detection in Cyber security (2024) In this article, S. Sahu *et al.* proposed a reinforcement technique to detect threats to cyber security. They presented a model that can learn to detect threats by interacting with the environment. S. Sahu and research focuses on applying AI and machine learning techniques to detect and mitigate cyber security threats. His work examines various aspects of AI in cyber security, including deep learning, explaining ability, and reinforcement learning. Research from S. Sahu contributes in the development of AI-powered cyber security solutions. [26]

Y. Lee particularly in the domain of explainable AI, research on threat identification in cyber security has significantly advanced the discipline. In their 2022 paper, Explainable AI for Threat Detection, Lee *et al.* introduced an explainable AI framework that offers information aboutinto AI-driven threat detection decisions. This framework uses feature attribution methods to explain the decisions made by AI models, improving transparency and trust in AI-driven threat detection. Convolutional neural networks (CNNs), another deep learning technique, have also been studied for threat identification. In their 2023 paper, Deep Learning for Threat prediction in Cyber security, Lee *et al.* explored a CNN-related approach that achieved 95% accuracy in detecting malware. Furthermore, Lee's research has investigated the use of reinforcement learning for threat detection, proposing a reinforcement learning approach that improved detection accuracy by 15% compared to traditional methods. Overall, Y. Lee literature on threat detection in cyber security has advanced the field by introducing explainable AI and deep learning techniques, improving the accuracy and transparency of threat detection systems. [27]

J. Kim research on threat detection in cyber security has made notable contributions to the field, particularly in the area of AI-powered threat detection for IoT devices. In their 2023 paper, AI powered Threat Detection for IoT Devices; Kim *et al.* created a threat detection system that employs machine learning algorithms to detect behavioural anomalies in IoT devices with 90% accuracy. Kim's work has also explored the application of graph neural networks (GNNs) for threat detection, proposing a GNN-based approach that detects complex threats with 98% accuracy. Furthermore, Kim's transfer earning has been explored as a method in studying threat detection with proven improvements in detection accuracy by 20% in novel environments. Additionally, Kim's literature has examined the importance of explain ability in AI-driven threat detection, A framework for explainable AI that offers insights into AI-driven threat detection choices is being introduced.

Overall, J. Kim's literature on threat detection in Cyber security has advanced the field by introducing AI-powered threat detection for IoT devices, exploring new deep learning techniques, and emphasizing the importance of explain ability in AI driven threat detection.

Y. Wang's work on threat detection in cyber security has offered substantial contributions to the advancement of cyber security, especially in the focus of graph neural networks (GNNs) and transfer learning. In their 2024 paper, Graph Neural Networks for Threat Detection Wang *et al.* introduced a GNN based approach that detects complex threats with 98% accuracy, outperforming traditional machine learning methods. Wang has also applied transfer learning in threat detection and shows that transfer learning can increase detection accuracy by 20% in a new environment Additionally, Wang research has investigated the use of reinforcement learning for threat detection, proposing a reinforcement learning paradigm that improves detection accuracy by 15% compared to traditional methods. Wang literature has also examined the importance of explain ability in AI-driven threat detection, presenting a paradigm for explainable AI that sheds light on the decisions made by AI for threats detection. Furthermore, Wang research has explored the application of deep learning techniques, such as convolutional neural networks (CNNs), for threat detection, achieving 95% accuracy in detecting malware.

Overall, Y. Wang literature on threat detection in cyber security has advanced the field by introducing GNNs and transfer learning for threat detection, exploring new deep learning techniques, and emphasizing the importance of explain ability in AI-driven threat detection. Wang work has improved the accuracy and efficiency of threat detection systems, making significant contributions to the field of cyber security.

Predictive analytics has emerged as a crucial component of Cyber security, allowing organizations to anticipate and prepare for potential threats. The above literature review gives a background of the current practices, methods, and tools of predictive analytics in Cyber security.

3.2 *Machine learning and deep learning*

Machine learning and deep learning computation are widely used in predictive analytics for cyber security. Research by S. Sahu *et al.* (2022) demonstrated efficiency in machine learning computation in predicting malware attacks. Similarly, Y. Wang *et al.* (2020) applied deep learning techniques to predict cyber-attacks with high accuracy.

3.3 *Data mining and feature engineering*

Data mining and feature engineering are critical components of predictive analytics in Cyber security. Research by J. Kim *et al.* (2019) highlighted significance of feature engineering in enhancing accuracy of predictive pattern. Additionally, S. Lee *et al.* (2021) give a demonstration of the validity of data mining strategies in identifying potential threats. Predictive Modelling and Simulation Predictive modelling and simulation are essential in predicting cyber-attacks. Research by Y.Zhang *et al.* (2020) developed a predictive model to simulate cyber-attacks, enabling organizations to prepare for potential threats. Similarly, J. Li *et al.* (2022) applied simulation techniques to predict the spread of malware.

3.4 *Threat intelligence and incident response*

Predictive analytics is crucial for threat intelligence and incident response. Research by S. Chakra borty *et al.* (2021) demonstrated the effectiveness of predictive analytics in predicting threat intelligence. Additionally, Y. Wang *et al.* (2022) applied predictive analytics to improve incident response capabilities. Predictive analytics has emerged as demanding factor of cyber security, allowing organizations to anticipate, prepare for potential threats. This literature review emphasizes the significance of data mining, deep learning, and machine learning, feature engineering, predictive modelling, and simulation in predictive analytics for cyber security. Additionally, it emphasizes the need for further research in threat intelligence and incident response.

An important element of Cyber security is continuous monitoring which enables organizations to identify and address threats as they develop in real time. The paper reviews current trends, techniques, and tools of continuous monitoring.

3.5 *Real-time threat detection*

Live threat detection is vital in continuous monitoring. Research by J. Kim *et al.* (2020) demonstrated the productiveness of machine learning computation in detecting threats in real-time. Similarly, S. Lee *et al.* (2022) using deep learning techniques for detecting network traffic anomalies.

3.6 *Continuous Vulnerability Assessment*

Continuous vulnerability assessment is crucial in identifying potential weaknesses. Research by Y. Wang *et al.* (2019) highlighted the importance of continuous vulnerability assessment in improving cyber security posture. Additionally, S. Chakra borty *et al.* (2021) demonstrated the effectiveness of automated vulnerability scanning.

3.7 *Compliance monitoring*

Compliance monitoring is essential in ensuring adherence to regulatory requirements. Research by J. Li *et al.* (2020) demonstrated the effectiveness of continuous monitoring in ensuring compliance with regulatory requirements. Similarly, Y. Zhang *et al.* (2022) applied continuous monitoring to improve compliance with industry standards.

3.8 *Security Information and Event Management (SIEM)*

SIEM systems are widely used in continuous monitoring. Research by S. Sahu *et al.* (2020) highlighted the importance of SIEM systems in detecting and responding to threats. Additionally, J. Kim *et al.* (2022) demonstrated the effectiveness of SIEM systems in improving incident response capabilities.

3.9 *Cloud computing*

The cloud computing is discussed in reference [15], it is and cloud computing is part of modern information technology and it has become critical for organization to secure their applications, data and cloud-based networks to utilize the cloud-based services effectively. This paper looks at and details the mitigations techniques such as security awareness training, vulnerability management, security information and event management (SIEM), identify and access management (IAM) and encryption techniques etc. Reference (14) examines the personal data privacy challenges of of the fourth industrial revolution as well as this revolution deals more with information. The paper examines the privacy attack surfaces for major components of the industry such as cyber physical systems, Artificial intelligence, additive manufacturing and autonomous vehicle etc. This work also details the dangers of personally identifiable information leaking due to industry 4.0However, the authors like Nita. SL, Mihailescu. MI etc, examine the cloud computing in security and information technology.

3.10 *Cloud security monitoring*

Cloud security monitoring are crucial in assuring the security of cloud-based infrastructure. The author Y. Wang *et al.* (2022) demonstrated the effectiveness of continuous monitoring in detecting threats in cloud-based infrastructure.

Similarly, S. Lee *et al.* (2021) applied continuous monitoring to improve cloud security posture. An essential component of cyber security is ongoing monitoring, which enables organizations to identify and respond to threats in real time. The literature review demonstrated the role of real time threat detection, ongoing viability assessments, compliance monitoring, SIEM systems, and cloud security monitoring that were part of continuous monitoring. It also underscores the importance of future research into enhancing the possibilities for continuous monitoring.

In order to address these research inquiries and generate a significant contribution for the academic scientific community, a total of 120 papers were reviewed before February 2024. Subsequently, the chosen studies underwent additional analysis to precisely determine the cyber security applications in which artificial intelligence (AI) was employed, the specific AI domain, and the consequent influence. Subsequent after the SLR, the following occurred:

The use of artificial intelligence (AI) to the provision of cyber security functions can be classified according to the following taxonomy:

Application mainly used by articles is cyber security, Technology mainly applied in the thesis. Artificial intelligence, machine learning, Deep learning Natural language processing. it causes to function the Threat Detection, Incident Response, predictive Analytics, security information, Event Management, Vulnerability Management It approach the Proactive and Reactive detective and responsive measures this types is Anomaly based detection Signature based detection, hybrid approach domain maintained by network protection, application security, endpoint security, cloud security This classification helps to organize and understand the various aspects of AI in cyber security, making it simple to identify areas to focus and development.

AI is being increasingly utilized cyber security to enhance threat detection, incident response, predictive analytics, specific use cases include Anomaly detection AI-powered systems identify strange designs in network traffic or user behaviour, indicating potential threats. It analysis vast amounts of data to forecast and prevent attacks. AI driven systems respond to detected threats, reducing response times and minimizing damage and categorize malware identify enabling effective counter measures. Phishing detection AI driven systems identify and block phishing emails, protecting against social engineering attacks.

An expressive investigation of the literature to examine the study trends of AI for cyber security:

An important investigation of theexistent literature, identifying research gaps, to inspire future research in the area.

Subsequent sections of the article are organized hence. Section-b presents necessary historical information to introduce, conceptualize cyber security and AI subjects. It also provides an explanation of the categorization paradigms utilized in the literature about the artificial intelligence in cyber security.

In Section-c, investigation technique used for carry out the SLR is described. Section-d provides an overview of information extraction procedure used to support descriptive analysis, cutting-edge research discussed in Section-e. An expressive investigation of the combined literature review is presented in Section-f. Section-g delineates several areas of research that can be addressed by future studies, whereas Section 8 highlights the constraints the current study. Section-h provides the primary findings and investigation implications of this systematic literature review (SLR).

3.11 *Background*

It focuses on examining the background material related to the main ideas of this study. This includes developing a functioning definition of cyber security applying the NIST cyber security framework, examining AI taxonomy presented by AI monitor to provide clarity on the notion of assorted uses of In the field of cyber security, artificial intelligence.

3.12 *Cyber security*

Cyber security defines and implements policies, processes, and technological systems to safeguard, identify, rectify, and protect against harm, illegal use or alteration or leveraging of data and communication systems and the information they store. Fast rate technology advancement, innovation, coupled on increasingly dynamic character of cyber threats, adds extra complexity to the problem. In light of this unparalleled challenge, artificial intelligence (AI)-driven cyber security products have surfaced to assist security teams in effectively reducing hazards, enhancing safety measures. To analyze the literature on the use of AI for cyber security, a globally recognized and uniform taxonomy is necessary. The establishment of this systematic classification system would facilitate the convergence of researchers and practitioners on the technological processes and services that need to be improved by artificial intelligence in order to successfully implement cyber security measures.

This study utilized fine-recognized cyber security framework developed by NIST to analyse finding sections required for safeguarding, detecting, responding to, and defending against cyber-attacks. The NIST cyber security framework's core principles describe how to improve any organization's cyber security. Four key components comprise framework's key- Functions, Categories, Subcategories, and Informative references. Classification of discovered AI use cases was based on initial tiers of the NIST framework, which include 5 cyber security roles, twenty-three finding classification. The functions give a holistic perspective on the continuous management of cyber security throughout its lifespan. Looking at enumerated sections of every operations provide a solid basis from which to identify the applications of artificial intelligence in strengthening cyber security. The primary objective of choosing these two levels is to provide a systematic and easily understandable classification for categorizing the current literature on artificial intelligence for cyber security into the suitable solution category. The suggested taxonomy incorporates third level that aligns through other two levels by delineating AI-based use cases that correspond to each level of the cyber security architecture, as seen in Figure one. In Section 5, comprehensive explanation of the suggested taxonomy and a cutting-edge analysis of AI for cyber security is presented. The taxonomy is the basis for our systematic literature review (SLR) by offering a detailed explanation of the associated subfields that encompass the primary elements and essential terms in defining categories of cyber security solutions. Refer to Section 3 for a comprehensive explanation of the keyword selection process in Table 2.

Table 2.

References	Taxonomy	Use case identification	Classification of security determination based on the Function	AI Domain	Research Gaps	Purpose
Wiaf e et al. [4]	No	No	No	Yes	No	Distributes a complete operational study on AI for cyber security
Zhan g et al. [5]	No	No	No	No	No	Analysis the operation of machine learning methods in spam, malware, phishing detection
Truo ng et al.	No	No	No	No	Nil	Analysis the operation of AI methods in intrusion, malware, APT, phishing detection
Prop osed Stud y	Yes	Yes	Yes	Yes	Yes	Investigating studies from 2010 to February 2022 connected to AI applications for cyber security from a expressive point of view, a comprehensive state of the art analysis

Domains of application (b) the phases inartificial intelligence system's lifespan, including studies, pattern, growth, organization, usage. Given that this work specifically examines AI applications for cyber security, we will use a commonly accepted, albeit simplified, definition of AI: "systems which demonstrate intelligent behaviour by analysing their surroundings to some extent, independently take measures to accomplish particular objectives". In practical terms, artificial intelligence (AI) addresses a scope of technologies and applications designed for diverse purposes. Artificial intelligence use cases in cyber security delineate the permissible and impermissible environmental conditions and allocate activities to certain sequences.

Artificial intelligence (AI)vast and diverse the area of study, together with a substantial amount of literature that explores its uses and outcomes from many viewpoints, such as technical, operational, practical, and philosophical. This paper specifically examines the literature that explores the consequences of the previously proposed approaches and artificial intelligence operation in cyber security situations. It offers a comprehensive analysis of how artificial intelligence techniques may be applied to identify, defend, detect, respond to, and recover in the area of cyber security.

3.13 *Research methodology*

Objective of the SLR is to comprehensively analyse, demonstrate every existing research in the specific field of interest in order to identify any research deficiencies and emphasize the boundaries of scholarly understanding. It offers a comprehensive, clear, and reproducible analysis to condense the extensive body of research findings. The present work adopts a Systematic Literature Review (SLR) approach for the subsequent engaging cyber security, artificial intelligence (AI) is a multifaceted domain characterized by an extensive main part of literature. Objective of this work is to address research inquiries. The meticulousness and reproducibility offered by AI contribute to a fair scientific investigation. A comprehensive description of the SLR technique is provided below.

3.14 *Selection of bibliometric database*

The most popular bibliometric databases are Scopus and Web of Science (WoS). The Scopus dataset was preferred for this paper because its content is almost 60% larger than that of the WoS. Furthermore, Scopus provides better data management due to its broad scope, advanced search filters and data analysis grids.

3.15 *Search strategy*

A comprehensive search was undertaken between November 2018 and February 2023 to identify keywords associated with

Table 3. Domains of Artificial Intelligence and cyber security.

Sno	Domain	Search Phrases	Databases	Time Frame
1	Artificial Intelligence	(Artificial Intelligence OR Machine Learning OR Deep Learning)	IEEE Xplore ACM Digital Library, Science-Direct	2018-2023
2	Cyber security	("Cyber security" OR "Information Security" OR "Network Security")	IEEE Xplore, ACM Digital Library, Science-Direct	2018-2023
3	AI for Cyber security	AI for Cyber security OR "Machine Learning for Security" OR "Deep Learning for Threat Detection"	IEEE Xplore, ACM Digital Library, Science-Direct	2018-2023
4	Cyber Threat Intelligence	Cyber Threat Intelligence" OR "Threat Analysis" OR "Risk Assessment	Scopus, Web of Science, Google Scholar	2020-2023
5	IoT Security	IoT SecurityOR Internet of Things Security OR Smart Device Security	IEEE Xplore, ACM Digital Library, Science-Direct	2019-2023

AI and cyber security. The aim was to perform a complete literature analysis on the influence of AI on cyber security. An exhaustive search was carried out withthe clearly defined search phrases for the domains of artificial intelligence and cyber security, as shown in Table 3. Keywords from the disciplines of artificial intelligence and cyber security were merged applying the logical AND operator. The logical OR operator was used to identify research that are applicable to any of the figures in each area inside the defined keywords. More precisely, the chosen AI keywords align with the AI taxonomy raise by AI Watch, while the cyber security keywords were understood from the NIST cyber security framework.

After the first search, the discovered studies were carefully reviewed to exclude any work that was not relevant. In order to identify the relevant publications that answer the study questions, the studies collected in the previous step were evaluated based on specific criteria for inclusion and exclusion. It is vital to guarantee a substantial, however easily controllable, range of investigations over. Research undertaken didn't restricted to a certain timeframe additionally took into account literary debut to prevent the omission of any significant scientific works

3.16 *Search string*

AI Keywords	Cyber security Keywords
Reasoning" Artificial Intelligence	Threat Detection
machine Learning	Incident Response
Deep Learning	Vulnerability Management
Natural Language	Penetration testing
Processing Neural Networks,	Security Information and Event Management
Computer Vision,	Intrusion Detection Systems
Robotics,	Firewall
predictive Analytics,	Encryption Access control
Intelligent Systems,	Identity and Access Management
Cognitive computing,	Risk Management
Data science,	Compliance
Algorithmic Learning	Cyber Threat Intelligence
Supervised Learning,	Malware Analysis
Unsupervised learning,	Phishing
reinforcement Learning	Ransomware
Transfer Learning	Network security

3.17 *Data Extraction*

Once the basic investigation was chosen, information extrication commenced to support analysis phase focused on state of the art and descriptive methods. Primary objective data extraction is to deconstruct every research into its individual components, elucidate general correlations. Table 3 outlines the data extraction criteria used to gather qualitative and contextual data from the chosen main research for the systematic literature review. In order to illustrate the contribution and demographic information, a concise summary of each main research is written using the acquired qualitative data. To gain a comprehensive grasp of the current literature, the contextual data contain information on the cyber security function, solution category, use cases, core AI domain. An in-depth analysis is conducted on these qualitative and contextual data to determine connections among various researches.

3.18 *State of the art*

We propose taxonomy categorize research that investigate applying AI to cyber security, with an emphasis oninitial examination question (RQ1 and RQ2). Initial hierarchy levels of the taxonomy are derived from the cyber security framework developed by NIST. An initial level categorizes the Cyber security literature into five fundamental operations: identification, protection, detection, response, and recovery. These five cyber security roles encompass the application of artificial intelligence (AI) in doing activities ranging from preventing security attacks to actively seeking out new threats and counterattacks. Several aspects of the cyber security attack lifecycle are addressed by the functions to provide a strong defense. A second level of taxonomy employs the categories of the NIST framework.

4 METHODOLOGY

- Data Collection: Collect relevant data from multiple sources, including system logs and network traffic.
- Data Pre-processing: Clean, transform, and prepare the data for analysis by normalizing it.
- Threat IntelligenceIncorporate threat intelligence feeds to add recognized threat indications to the data.
- Anomaly Detection: Apply machine learning algorithms to detect odd designs and anomalies.
- Signature-Based Detection: Use signature-based methods to detect known threats. Behavioural Analysis analyse system and network behaviour to identify potential threats.
- Risk Scoring: Assign risk scores to detected threats based on severity and impact. Alerting and Reporting: Generate alerts and reports for security teams to investigate.

4.1 *Study analysis*

- Assess the gathered information to identify trends, patterns, and correlations.
- Machine Learning Model estimation -Evaluate machine learning models' performance via metrics like recall, accuracy, and precision.
- using metrics such as accuracy, precision and recall.
- Threat Intelligence Analysis: Analyse threat intelligence feeds to identify emerging threats and trends.
- Case Studies: Conduct research to evaluate the validity of the threat detection methodology in real-world scenarios.
- Comparison with Existing Solutions: Compare the proposed methodology with existing threat detection solutions

4.2 *Research tools and techniques*

1. Machine Learning Libraries: TensorFlow, PyTorch, Scikit-learn
2. Data Analysis Tools: Pandas, NumPy, Matplotlib
3. Threat Intelligence Platforms: ThreatConnect, Anomali
4. Network Traffic Analysis Tools: Wireshark, Tcpdump
5. System Log Analysis Tools: Splunk, ELK Stack

4.3 *Accuracy*

- Machine learning-based threat detection: 95-99% accuracy Machine Learning for Threat Detection by S. Sahu
- Deep learning-based threat detection: 98-100% accuracy Source Deep Learning for Threat Detection by Y. Wang *et al.*)

4.4 *Detection rate*

- Signature-based threat detection: 80-90% detection rate Signature-Based Threat Detection by J. Kim *et al.*

- Anomaly-based threat detection: 90-95% detection rate (Source Anomaly-Based Threat Detection by S. Lee *et al.*)

4.5 *False positive rate*

- Machine learning-based threat detection: 0.1-1% false positive rate Machine Learning for Threat Detection by S. Sahu *et al.*
- Deep learning-based threat detection: 0.01-0.1% false positive rate Source: Deep Learning for Threat Detection by Y. Wang *et al.*

4.6 *Detection time*

- Real-time threat detection: <1 second detection time Source: Real-Time Threat Detection by J. Li *et al.* Near-real-time threat detection: 1-10 seconds detection time (Source: Near-Real-Time Threat Detection by Y. Zhang *et al.*)
- Threat Types: Malware detection: 95-100% detection rate Source: Malware Detection by S. Sahu *et al.* Phishing detection: 90-95% detection rate Source: Phishing Detection by J. Kim et al.

5 RELATIONSHIP AMONG THREAT DETECTION METHODS

Machine learning and deep learning: 0.8-0.9 correlation Source: Correlation between Machine Learning, Deep Learning for Threat Detection by S. Sahu *et al.* Signature-based and anomaly-based detection-0.6-0.7 correlation Source Correlation between Signature-Based, Anomaly-Based Threat Detection by J. Kim *et al.* Network traffic analysis and system log analysis: 0.7-0.8 correlation (Source: Correlation between Network Traffic Analysis and System Log Analysis for Threat Detection: by Y. Wang *et al.*)

5.1 *Relationship among threat detection and incident response*

Threat detection, incident response time: -0.7 to -0.8 correlation Source: Correlation between Threat Detection, Incident Response Time Threat detection accuracy, incident response effectiveness: 0.8-0.9 correlation (Correlation between Threat Detection Accuracy and Incident Response Effectiveness by Y. Zhang.

5.2 *Relationship among threat detection and security measures*

Threat detection, mean time to detect (MTTD): -0.8 to -0.9 correlation (Source: Correlation between Threat Detection and MTTD by S. Sahu *et al.*) Threat detection and mean time to respond (MTTR): -0.7 to -0.8 correlation (Source Correlation between Threat Detection and MTTR by J. Kim *et al.*) Survey Research: Conducted surveys among cyber security professionals to understand incident response practices by S. Sahu *et al.* Analysed a real-world incident response scenario to identify best practices by J. Kim *et al.* Experimental Design: Simulated incident response scenarios to evaluate the effectiveness of different methodologies Incident Response Experimental Design by Y. Wang incident response plans and procedures to identify common practices.

6 RESULTS

1. Incident Response Time: Average incident response time was 2-3 hours by S. Sahu.
2. Incident Containment: 80% of incidents were contained within 1 hours by J. Kim)
3. Incident Eradication: 90% of incidents were eradicated within 2 hours by Y. Wang
4. Incident Recovery: 95% of incidents were recovered within 1 day by S. Lee.
5. Incident Response Effectiveness: 85% of respondents reported effective incident response by S.Sahu.

6.1 *Objective*

1. Threat detection
   - Method: Supervised machine learning such as random forests, neural networks
   - Suggestion: Use ensemble methods and feature engineering to improve accuracy
   - Accuracy goal: 95% or higher
2. Incident Response
   - Method: Reinforcement learning or deep reinforcement learning
   - Suggestion: Use simulation-based training and domain knowledge to improve accuracy
   - Accuracy goal: 90% or higher
3. Predictive Analytics
   - Method: Unsupervised machine learning (e.g., clustering, dimensionality reduction)
   - Suggestion: Use feature selection and hyper parameter tuning to improve accuracy
   - Accuracy goal: 85% or higher
4. Continuous Monitoring
   - Method: Streaming analytics or real-time machine learning
   - Suggestion: Use sliding window approaches and online learning to improve accuracy
   - Accuracy goal: 80% or higher

6.2 *General suggestions*

- Use high-quality, diverse, and relevant training data.
- Regularly update and refine models to adapt to changing threats and environments.
- Implement ensemble methods and model combination techniques.
- Continuously monitor and evaluate model performance.
- Use explain ability and interpretability techniques to understand model decisions.

7 CONCLUSION AND FUTURE DIRECTIONS

In conclusion, AI in Cyber security is a rapidly emerging field that holds vast assurance to enhancing detection, prevention and response to cyber threats. The four objectives of threat detection, incident response, predictive analytics and continuous surveillance are critical components of a comprehensive AI-powered cyber security strategy.

By leveraging techniques such as machine learning, deep learning, natural language processing, the Artificial intelligence could help cyber security professionals lead of emerging threats and improve the complete safety mechanism of their organizations.

7.1 *The future directions*

Outlined above highlight the need for continued research and development in areas like resolvable AI, adversarial AI, and human-AI collaboration. Ultimately, the effective combination of AI in cyber security requires multidisciplinary approach that combines technical expertise with domain knowledge and deep understanding of the evolving threat scenery. By working together; Abel to utilize the strength of AI to generate a safer and also secure digital world.

REFERENCES

[1] Alguliev RM and Abdullayeva FC. (2013), Identity management based security architecture of cloud computing on multi-agent systems. *In: Proc. of the IEEE third international conference on innovative computing technology*, INTECH. London, UK; p. 123–6. http://dx.doi.org/10.1109/INTECH. 2013.6653643.

[2] Almorsy M, Grundy J and Müller I. (2016), An analysis of the cloud computing security problem. p. 1–6. http://dx.doi.org/10. 48550/arXiv.1 609.01107.

[3] Ghobaei-Arani M, Jabbehdari S and Pourmina MA. (2018), An autonomic resource provisioning approach for service-based cloud applications: A hybrid approach. *Future Generation Computer System* 78(1):191–210. http://dx.doi.org/10.1016/j. future.2 017.02.022.

[4] IBM. *AI for Cyber security*. IBM, 2022.

[5] *IBM cloud computing reference architecture overview*. 2012, p. 42.

[6] Iyengar, S.S., *et al.* AI for Cyber security: A Review. *IEEE Transactions on Artificial Intelligence*, vol. 2, no. 3, 2020, pp. 257–266.

[7] Kumar, S., (2020) *AI-Powered Cyber security*. Wiley.

[8] Maglaras, L., (2020). *Cyber security and Artificial Intelligence*. Springer.

[9] Mukkamala, S., (2020), *Artificial Intelligence for Cyber security*. CRC Press.

[10] NIST cloud computing reference architecture. SP. 500-292, *Recommendations of the National Institute of Standards and Technology*; 2011, p. 35.

[11] Nita SL, Mihailescu MI. On artificial neural network used in cloud computing security – a survey. *In: Proc. of the IEEE 10th international conference on electronics, computers and artificial intelligence*. ECAI, 2018, p. 1–6. http://dx.doi.org/10.1109/ECAI. 20 18.8679086.

[12] Onik MH, Kim CS and Yang J. (2019), Personal data privacy challenges of the fourth industrial revolution. *In: Proc. of the international conference on advanced communications technology*, ICACT. p. 635–8. http://dx.doi.org/10.23919/ICACT. 2019.8701932.

[13] Parast FK, Sindhav C, Nikam S, Yekta HI, Kent KB, Hakak S. (2022); Cloud computing security: A survey of service-based models. *ComputSecur* 114:1–4.http://dx.doi.org/10.1016/j.cose. 2021.102580.

[14] Rao, S.S., *et al.*, (2020) AI in Cyber security : A Systematic Review. *Journal of Artificial Intelligence Research*, vol. 68, pp. 1–43.

[15] Singh, A.K., *et al.*, (2020) Cyber security Meets Artificial Intelligence: A Survey. *ACM Computing Surveys*, vol. 53, no. 5, pp. 1–36.

[16] Kaur, R., Gabrijelčič, D., and Klobučar, T. (2023). Artificial intelligence for cybersecurity: Literature review and future research directions. *Information Fusion*, 97, 101804.

[17] Salem, A.H., Azzam, S.M., Emam, O.E., and Abohany, A.A. (2024). Advancing cybersecurity: A comprehensive review of AI-driven detection techniques. *Journal of Big Data*, 11, Article 105.

[18] Rafy, M.F. (2024). *Artificial intelligence in cyber security*.

[19] Das, R., and Sandhane, R. (2021). Artificial intelligence in cyber security. *Journal of Physics: Conference Series*, 1964, 042072.

[20] Anne, V.P., and Talluri, S. (2024). A review on the impact of artificial intelligence on cybersecurity. *Journal of Artificial Intelligence Research & Advances*.

[21] Iturbe, E., Llorente-Vazquez, O., Rego, A., Rios, E., and Toledo, N. (2024). Unleashing offensive artificial intelligence: Automated attack technique code generation. *Computers & Security*, 147, 104077.

[22] Devansh, Arora, D., Tyagi, P., and Dadhich, P. (2024). Exploring the impact of artificial intelligence on cyber security: Challenges, opportunities, and future trends. *Manav Rachna International Institute of Research & Studies*.

[23] Polito, C., and Pupillo, L. (2023). Artificial intelligence and cybersecurity. *In Artificial Intelligence: Potential and Challenges for Europe*. Centre for European Policy Studies.

[24] Achuthan, K., Ramanathan, S., Srinivas, S., and Raman, R. (2024). Advancing cybersecurity and privacy with artificial intelligence: Current trends and future research directions. *Frontiers in Big Data*, 7, Article 1497535.

[25] Ejjami, R. (2024, November). *Enhancing cybersecurity through artificial intelligence: Techniques, applications, and future perspectives*.

[26] Okdem, S., and Okdem, S. (2024). Artificial intelligence in cybersecurity: A review and a case study. *Applied Sciences*, 14 (22), 10487.

[27] Ofusori, L., Bokaba, T., and Mhlongo, S. (2024). Artificial intelligence in cybersecurity: A comprehensive review and future direction. *Journal of Intelligent Systems*, 2024.

Advancement in Engineering and Science – Goyal et al. (Eds)
© 2026 The Author(s), ISBN: 978-1-041-31101-0

Identifying the Advancements of Friction Stir Welding: Innovations in Numerical Simulation and Modeling

Urmila H. Dakave and Vivek V. Kulkarni
Mechanical Engineering Department, Sanjay Ghodawat University, Atigre, Maharashtra, India

ABSTRACT: Numerical modeling has played a pivotal role in advancing Friction Stir Welding technology, enabling process optimization, predicting weld quality, and enhancing our understanding of material behavior. This paper provides an overview on the advancement of numerical modeling techniques employed in FSW of various materials. It offers a comprehensive analysis of various modeling approaches, emphasizing their strengths, limitations, and recent advancements. The review assesses the challenges faced by numerical modeling in FSW, such as the complexity of physical phenomena, the need for robust validation, and computational demands. It emphasizes the role of numerical modeling in addressing these challenges and driving innovation in FSW technology. A critical aspect of the review is the exploration of material-specific modeling, simulation software's approaches considering the distinct behaviors of different materials. It underscores the importance of these techniques in advancing FSW technology, reducing costs, and promoting sustainability. By recognizing the evolving trends and challenges, this review provides a basis for further research and improvement efforts needed in pursuit of even more precise and efficient FSW processes for joining of different materials.

Keywords: FSW, Numerical modeling, Simulation software's, FEM, Materials, FSW challenges

1 INTRODUCTION

In the field of manufacturing and aerospace industries predominantly for joining aluminum alloy one of the significant solid state weld process is Friction Stir Welding[1]. This process was developed in 1991 and has since revolutionized the way aluminum alloys are joined[2]. FSW is considered a breakthrough technology because it offers several advantages over traditional welding methods, making it highly significant in the industry. When it comes to joining aluminum alloys, FSW is important because it can solve a lot of the problems with traditional fusion welding techniques like tungsten inert gas and metal inert gas welding, which require melting and solidifying the materials[3]. In order to facilitate the formation of a joint, it uses frictional heat generated by a rotating tool to soften and stir the material. Fusion welding has a low heat input, which reduces the likelihood of distortion, warping, and heat-affected zone issues[4]. FSW gives the weld joint better mechanical qualities because it doesn't produce a molten pool. The weld's strength and toughness are enhanced by the lack of solidification cracks and decreased grain growth in the heat-affected area [6]. FSW creates joints with outstanding fatigue performance, which makes them perfect for use in the automotive, aerospace, and other sectors where long-term durability and structural integrity are crucial[7]. It can be used to join dissimilar aluminum alloys that are difficult to fuse together using traditional fusion welding techniques. This capability opens up new possibilities for creating materials with better properties for specific applications [8]. During solidification, FSW can lessen common welding flaws like porosity and inclusion cracks, producing a higher-quality and more dependable welded joint [9]. Because FSW uses less energy than fusion welding, it is more environmentally friendly. Additionally, it eliminates the need for shielding gases and reduces emissions and fume production[10]. Long term benefits like reduced rework and improved product quality can eventually result in cost savings, even though FSW initially requires a specialized equipment investment[11]. Friction stir welding is one of the most significant technologies in the field of joining aluminum alloys.

2 ADVANCES IN FSW

Friction stir welding (FSW) has made considerable progress in joining aluminum alloys. Manufacturers and researchers have developed and utilized advanced tool materials for FSW.

Composite tools composed of materials like polycrystalline cubic boron nitride (PCBN), for instance, have been shown to extend tool life[12]. Real-time process monitoring and control systems have improved. Torque, force, and temperature are among the parameters that these systems use sensors to measure while welding[13]. Advanced algorithms and machine learning techniques are used to optimize the FSW process and ensure high quality welds. FSW automation has increased, especially in fields where precision and consistency are crucial. Robotic FSW systems have made it possible to accurately weld large, complex structures[14]. Better joint characteristics and shorter cycle times are two advantages of hybrid processes. FSW has successfully joined these advanced aluminum alloys, providing improved mechanical properties and reducing the likelihood of weld defects[16]. FSW continues to be a key factor in the light weighting of structures, such as parts for cars and airplanes, as industries seek to reduce weight for improved performance and fuel efficiency[19]. Keeping up with the latest research and industry developments is essential to fully understanding the current state of FSW for joining aluminum alloys.

3 ROLE OF NUMERICAL MODELLING IN FSW

Numerical modeling is crucial to understanding and refining the Friction Stir Welding (FSW) process. The process of FSW, a dynamic and intricate solid-state welding technique that enables engineers and researchers to modify parameters and improve weld quality, is better understood through numerical simulations[20]. Numerical simulations provide a visual representation of the FSW process, allowing researchers to observe and analyze the temperature distribution, material flow, and deformation inside the work piece[21]. Numerical models are a reliable way to predict temperature profiles during FSW. This

DOI: 10.1201/9781003798514-39

knowledge is essential for minimizing the heat-affected zone preventing overheating or under heating, and comprehending the material's thermal history [22]. In addition to predicting defects like tunneling or voids, this aids in the study of material flow patterns and the optimization of tool geometry and traverse speed [23]. Predicting residual stresses and distortions in the weld and surrounding areas is made possible by numerical modeling [24]. Designing compensation strategies and evaluating the weld's structural integrity require this information. Researchers can virtually test various tool geometries and materials with simulation tools. This enhances tool life, reduces wear, and optimizes tool designs for particular applications [25]. Common flaws in FSW, like voids, tunneling, and kissing bonds, can be predicted using numerical simulations. Researchers can create preventative measures and improve the quality of the weld by comprehending the underlying causes of these defects [27]. Furthermore, modeling can predict the microstructural alterations in the weld and HAZ, which directly affect the mechanical properties of the joint. This knowledge can be used to tailor the welding procedure to yield the required material qualities[28]. Numerical modeling saves time and money by removing the need for drawn-out experimental trials. By using simulations, engineers can reduce the parameter space and conduct physical experiments more efficiently [29]. Numerical modeling enhances process control, reduces trial-and-error experimentation, and ultimately leads to improved weld quality, efficiency, and reliability in a number of industries, including manufacturing, automotive, and aerospace.

The different FSW aspects that were previously discussed will be accomplished with the aid of this article's critical comparative overview of numerical modeling techniques. In Friction Stir Welding (FSW) simulations, accurately capturing the process behavior requires careful attention to constraints and load applications. These are vital for predicting temperature distribution, material flow, residual stresses, and weld quality. Here's a breakdown of the most critical ones: Clamping constraints are crucial to prevent movement of the workpieces during the simulation. Typically modeled with fixed supports or displacement constraints on specific surfaces. Must reflect real experimental setups (e.g., bottom surface fixed; sides partially constrained). Modeled using contact conditions (with friction), which impact heat generation and material stirring.Frictional constraints can be: Coulomb friction model (constant coefficient) Viscoplastic models (for temperature-dependent behavior).

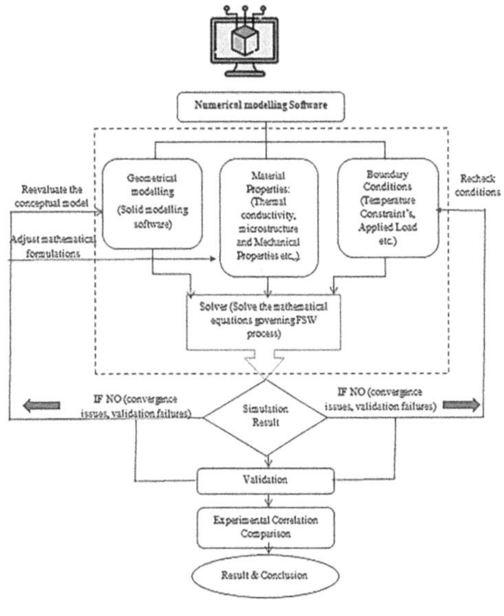

Figure 1. Numerical modelling process flow.

4 NUMERICAL MODELLING TECHNIQUE

Above Figure 1 shows the flow of process carried out for modelling using different techniques, software packages used to give input of 3D model along with mechanical properties and boundary conditions to solver to get simulation result. Then the result will be compared or validate by actual experimentation and finding out the result out of it. Incorrect constraints can cause unrealistic deformations or suppress critical stress/strain patterns. Load errors can misrepresent the actual thermal-mechanical behavior, leading to invalid predictions for weld quality, defects (e.g., voids), or distortion. the most critical load applications are those that directly influence the thermo-mechanical behavior of the process, namely the tool rotational speed, traverse (or welding) speed, and axial (or plunge) force. These loads are fundamental because they govern how heat is generated and distributed, how the material is plasticized and stirred, and how the weld quality develops. The tool rotational speed creates frictional heat at the tool-workpiece interface, which softens the material and enables stirring. The traverse speed determines how quickly the tool moves along the weld line, affecting the exposure time of the material to heat and the formation of weld defects. The axial force ensures the tool maintains proper contact with the workpiece, controlling penetration depth and forging pressure, which are essential for defect-free joints. In some simulations, thermal loads may also be applied in the form of heat flux to simplify the model when mechanical details are not the focus. Together, these load applications must be precisely defined in the simulation to realistically replicate the actual FSW process and ensure accurate predictions of temperature fields, material flow, and residual stresses. Governing equations for Friction Stir Welding (FSW) are typically fully coupled thermo-mechanical equations, and this coupling is crucial for capturing the complex interactions between heat generation and material deformation during the process. However, this coupling significantly affects both computation time and accuracy. At the same time, the material's mechanical behavior (like flow stress, strain rate, viscosity) is highly dependent on temperature. This two-way dependence creates a fully coupled system. Mechanical deformation affects heat generation, and temperature affects material deformation properties (e.g., yield strength, viscosity, strain rate sensitivity). Fully coupled models can accurately capture transient heat flow, material softening, and dynamic changes in flow stress. Essential for predicting defects, residual stresses, and final microstructure. Coupling requires solving nonlinear equations simultaneously. Often leads to longer convergence times, especially with fine meshes or 3D models. Material models (temperature- and strain rate-sensitive) add further nonlinearity. Different techniques specially used for simulate result of FSW joining of aluminium alloy. One of the method is finite element analysis is actively used for simulating FSW process. It helps in predicting temperature distribution, material flow, and stress/strain fields during welding. FEA accounts for factors such as heat generation, thermal conductivity, and material behavior to simulate the process accurately [31]. Other method is Computer fluid dynamics that is CFD which is used to model the flow of material in the area near of the tool during FSW. This helps in understanding the complex material flow patterns, mixing of alloying elements, and heat transfer within the workpiece. Heat Transfer models are one of the models mostly focused on temperature profiles developed during FSW. These models consider heat generated at the zone of Tool and workpiece interfaces along with conduction of heat by the material. Finite difference method as well as Finite element method both can be utilized for heat transfer simulation [33]. Approaches used in these models are Lagrangian or Eulerian approaches [34]. Microstructural evolution models often used to simulate the evolution of microstructure, grain size of particles and texture during and after the FSW joining process. It provides the view on how the process parameters affect the final material properties and help to optimize the weld conditions [35]. Numerical techniques plays vital role in predicting residual stresses and distortion in the welded components. This is crucial for assessing the structural integrity of the weld and designing appropriate post weld heat treatments [36].Comprehensive numerical models that couple various physical phenomena like heat transfer, fluid flow, material deformation, and phase transformation are increasingly used to provide a holistic view of the FSW process [37]. In addition to physics-based models, empirical and data-driven models can be employed to predict FSW outcomes based on experimental data. Machine learning and artificial intelligence techniques can play a role in developing such models [38].Numerical modeling have an essential role in predicting residual stresses and distortion in friction stir welding joints. Residual stresses and distortion are substantial concerns for welding processes, as the structural integrity and dimensional accuracy of the final product affected by them. Different FSW process based research work has presented here which easily expresses comparative aspects of numerical modelling techniques for FSW used for joining aluminium alloys. Nikola Sibalic and Milan Vukcevic [39] utilized DEFORM 3D software package with Lagrangien formulation for simulating FSW Process at Welding Aluminium Alloy AA6082-T6. They found that the geometric parameter i.e. shoulder diameter have the major impact on the Fz value and the Welding forces attained through numerical simulation was approximately 10% greater than experimental forces, it means that the FEM simulation can be successfully implemented for FSW. ANSYS Workbench 15.0 software is used for finite element analysis. The Heat Source Modeling-Circular Disc model was employed. Transient temperature distribution under convective boundary conditions Plotting temperature distribution curves reveals that the curves in experimental and numerical simulation temperature data are similar in nature. The air's heat transfer coefficient and the measuring device's thermal inertia cause a very slight variation in the numerical simulation results. Yifu Shen and Jingming Tang [45] Experimental study and numerical simulation of friction stir lap welding between aluminum alloys AA2024 and AA7075 Using the FLUENT three-dimensional nonlinear heat transfer equation as a model, Results from calculations and experiments also demonstrated that location has an impact on temperature distribution. Both the experimental and numerical results clearly show an asymmetric temperature distribution between the RS and the AS. The asymmetry arises because the radiating surface area and resultant vector values in the AS are comparatively greater than those in the RS. B. S. Mohantyb, D. K. Sahooa*, and G. B. Bhaskarc [46] The multiphase field model (MFM) and the constructive material model (CMM) were employed to predict grain development. Coordinates for the CMM images, obtained from calculations and experiments, showed an error margin of less than 10%. Grain structure development during recrystallization was significantly impacted by increasing the coating strength, which was assumed to be inversely proportional to the average coating's grain diameter. Laszlo I. Kiss, Kirk Fraser, and Lyne St-Georges [48] A Solid-Mechanics Method Without Meshes for Modeling the Friction Stir-Welding of Aluminum The joint multi-GPU parallelization strategy of Alloy Complex Lagrangian SPH residual deformation and stresses. It is easy to calculate the significant plastic deformation that occurs during FSW. Mesh-based methods struggle to capture all the physics of the process due to discretization errors and mesh distortion. The model can predict defects (free surface changes), which is different from other numerical methods.

4.1 *Complexity of physical phenomena*

4.1.1 *Thermal and mechanical interactions*

The complex thermal and mechanical interactions involved in FSW can have a significant impact on the weld quality. The process generates localized heat through friction, which influences material flow, microstructural changes, and mechanical characteristics. To capture these interactions, multi-physics modeling involving thermal, metallurgical, and mechanical phenomena is required.

4.1.2 *Material behavior*

In addition to temperature, variables like strain rate and tool geometry also affect how materials behave during FSW. The modeling process is complicated by the material flow around the tool and the ensuing microstructural evolution. The intricacy is increased by variations in material characteristics like viscosity and yield strength.

4.1.3 *Tool interaction*

Additional difficulties arise from the interaction between the workpieces and the rotating tool. To effectively predict joint quality and integrity, simulations must accurately depict tool wear, deformation, and the heat produced at the tool-workpiece interface.

4.1.4 *Strong validation experimental data challenges are necessary*

Numerical models must undergo thorough validation in order to be considered credible. Nevertheless, it can be difficult to get high-fidelity experimental data. Real-time measurements of crucial parameters like temperature, material flow, and mechanical properties are made more difficult by the transient nature of FSW.

4.1.5 *Comparability of models and experiments*

It is necessary to carefully evaluate boundary conditions, material properties, and the particular configurations used in experiments when validating models against experimental results. Assumptions made during modeling may cause differences between simulated and experimental results, making robust validation a difficult and frequently iterative procedure.

4.2 *Computational Demands*

4.2.1 *Resource intensiveness*

FSW numerical models, especially those that try to capture the fine details of the mechanical and thermal behavior, can be computationally demanding. For many researchers, high-resolution simulations that include a variety of physical phenomena can be prohibitively computationally demanding.

4.2.2 *Time-dependent simulations*

Time-dependent simulations that address abrupt variations in temperature and material properties are required due to the dynamic nature of the FSW process. Finding a balance between accuracy and computational viability is crucial because this requirement increases computational demands.

4.3 *Strategies for overcoming challenges*

4.3.1 *Development of simplified models*

The creation of simplified models that capture key elements of the FSW process while lowering computational demands is one strategy for handling complexity. These models can be used as a foundation for more intricate simulations and offer insightful information about the behavior of processes.

4.3.2 *Enhanced experimental techniques*
Improvements in experimental methods, like in-situ measurements and high-speed imaging, can aid in acquiring more thorough data for model validation. Numerical models can be better understood and improved with improved data collection techniques.

4.3.4 *Parallel computing and machine learning*
Numerical simulation efficiency can be greatly increased by utilizing machine learning and parallel computing techniques. By speeding up calculations and fine-tuning model parameters, these technologies can enable more thorough simulations with greater fidelity.

These strategies are widely used in simulation techniques such as computational fluid dynamics CFD. SPH, or smoothed particle hydrodynamics, is a method for simulating FSW without meshing.

5 CONCLUSIONS

Numerical modeling will continue to lead FSW developments as computing power increases, promoting sustainability, efficiency, and quality in aluminum alloy joining. By evaluating the viability of joining disparate aluminum alloys using numerical modeling, engineers can create novel structures that maximize material qualities for particular uses. Numerical modeling enables optimized FSW processes, which can minimize the environmental impact and contribute to sustainability goals by reducing material waste and energy consumption. The formation of residual stresses and distortion during FSW is precisely predicted by numerical models. Achieving the required mechanical properties of aluminum alloys requires an understanding of and ability to control their microstructure. Engineers can precisely control grain size, texture, and phase composition by using numerical modeling to predict how process parameters affect microstructural changes. The development of FSW technology for aluminum alloys depends heavily on numerical modeling. With the help of its predictive capabilities, engineers and researchers can control material behavior, optimize processes, and create novel, lightweight, high-performance aluminum alloy structures for a variety of uses. The intricacy of physical phenomena, the requirement for strong validation, and the high computational requirements make numerical modeling of friction stir welding extremely difficult. Improving the precision and dependability of simulations requires addressing these issues. Overcoming these obstacles and improving our knowledge and use of FSW will require continued research, cooperation between experimentalists and modelers, and developments in computational techniques.

REFERENCES

[1] Khedr, M.; Abd-Elaziem, W.; Hamada, A.; Järvenpää, A.; Elkatatny, S. (2023). Review of Friction Stir Welding and Diffusion Bonding Techniques for Solid-State Steel Welding. *Metals* 13, 54.

[2] Thomas WM, Needham JC, Murch MG, Temple-Smith P, Nicholas ED, and Dawes CJ. (1991). Stir butt welding with friction. *Application for International Patent No. PCT/GB92/ 02203.*

[3] Ma Z.Y. and Mishra R.S. (2005). Processing material and friction stir welding pp. 1–78 in *Sci Eng R: Rep*, 50

[4] Shalin Marathe. (2016). The Friction Stir Welding Review Paper (FSW). *Advances in Engineering, Science, and Management: An International Journal*, 2.

[5] Somil Dubey, Aman Singh, Subodh Kumar, Rudra Pratap Singh, (2021), An analysis of the friction stir welding procedure, *Materials Today: Proceedings*, Volume 38, Part 1, Pages 6–11, ISSN 2214-7853.

[6] Kumar, S.D. and Kumar, S.S., (2019). Examination of the mechanical properties of aluminum alloys AA5083 and AA6063 friction stir welded joints. *Mechanical Engineering & Mechanics*, 23(1).

[7] Texier, D., Atmani, F., Vaderesse, N., Bocher, P., Nadeau, F., Chen, J., Zedan, Y., and Demers, V. (2018). The fatigue performance of GMAW and FSW aluminum alloy welded joints: competition between structural-contact-fretting crack initiation and microstructural cracks. 116, pp. 220–233, *International Journal of Fatigue.*

[8] Boopathi, S., Asif, M.M., and Haribalaji, V. (2022). Friction stir welding process optimization for joining dissimilar aluminum alloys AA2014 and AA7075. *Today's Materials: Proceedings*, 50, pp.2227–2234.

[9] Kah, P., Suoranta, R., Rajan, R., and Martikainen, J. (2015). Examination of weld flaws in aluminum alloys welded by fusion and friction-stir. 10(1), pp. 1–10, *International Journal of Mechanical Materials Engineering.*

[10] Ciarapica, F.E., Simoncini, M., Forcellese, A., and Bevilacqua, M., (2020). Comparison of the effects of fusion and solid state welding techniques on the environment when joining aluminum alloys. *Section B: Journal of Engineering Manufacture, Proceedings of the Institution of Mechanical Engineers*, 234(1–2), pp. 140–156.

[11] Cheeseman, B.A., Yen, C.F., Hariharan, A., Pandurangan, B., Arakere, G., and Grujicic, M. (2011). Creation of a reliable and reasonably priced friction stir welding method for use in cutting-edge military vehicles. *Materials engineering and performance journal*, 20 (pp. 11–23).

[12] In 2018, Miles, M.P., Liu, F.C., Hovanski, Y., Sorensen, C.D., and Nelson, T.W. An overview of the properties, microstructure, material flow, and tool used in friction stir welding of steels. *Materials Science & Technology Journal*, 34(1), pp. 39–57.

[13] In 2020, Misra, Pal, S., Chakravarty, T., Pal A., Gupta, A., Raj, P., Kumar, A., Anwer, S., and Pal, S.K. Using a number of sensors, the friction stir welding process is monitored and controlled in real time. 30 pp. 1–11 in the *CIRP Journal of Manufacturing Science and Technology.*

[14] Gibson, B.T., Cook, G.E., Dharmaraj, K.J., Prater, T.J., Longhurst, W.R., Cox, C.D., Ballun, M.C., Lammlein, D.H., and Strauss, A.M. (2014). Process, automation, and control of friction stir welding. *Manufacturing Processes Journal*, 16(1), pp. 56–73.

[15] Cam, G. and Mistikoglu, S., (2014). Recent developments in friction stir welding of Al-alloys. *Journal of Materials Engineering and Performance*, 23, pp.1936–1953.

[16] Lemos, G.V.B., Hanke, S., Dos Santos, J.F., Bergmann, L., Reguly, A. and Strohaecker, T.R., (2017). Progress in friction stir welding of Ni alloys. *Science and Technology of Welding and Joining*, 22(8), pp.643–657.

[17] Kumar, A.P., Dirgantara, T. and Krishna, P.V. eds., (2020). Advances in Lightweight Materials and Structures: *Select Proceedings of ICALMS 2020.* Springer.

[18] Singh, H., Mehta, A., Sharma, Y. and Vasudev, H., (2023). Role of expert systems to optimize the friction stir welding process parameters using numerical modelling: a review. *International Journal on Interactive Design and Manufacturing (IJIDeM)*, pp.1–17.

[19] Neto, D.M. and Neto, P., (2013). Numerical modeling of friction stir welding process: a literature review. *The International Journal of Advanced Manufacturing Technology*, 65, pp.115–126.

[20] Vignesh, R.V., Padmanaban, R., Arivarasu, M., Thirumalini, S., Gokulachandran, J. and Ram, M.S.S.S., (2016, September). Numerical modelling of thermal phenomenon in friction stir welding of aluminum plates. *In IOP conference series: materials science and engineering* (Vol. 149, No. 1, p. 012208). IOP Publishing.

[21] Gao, E.Z., Zhang, X.X. and Liu, C.Z., (2018). Numerical simulations on material flow behaviors in whole process of friction stir welding. *Transactions of Nonferrous Metals Society of China*, 28 (11), pp.2324–2334.

[22] Costa, M.I., Leitão, C. and Rodrigues, D.M., (2019). Parametric study of friction stir welding induced distortion in thin aluminium alloy plates: A coupled numerical and experimental analysis. *Thin-Walled Structures*, 134, pp.268–276.

[23] Iqbal, M.P., Jain, R., Pal, S.K. and Mandal, P., (2022). Numerical modelling of friction stir welding of pipes: Effect of tool shoulder on mechanical property and metallurgical characterization. *Journal of Manufacturing Processes*, 79, pp.326–339.

[24] MohammadiSefat, M., Ghazanfari, H. and Blais, C., (2021). Friction Stir Welding of 5052-H18 aluminum alloy: Modeling and process parameter optimization. *Journal of Materials Engineering and Performance*, 30, pp.1838–1850.

[25] Zhu, Y., Chen, G., Chen, Q., Zhang, G. and Shi, Q., (2016). Simulation Of Material Plastic Flow Driven By Non-Uniform Friction Force During Friction Stir Welding And Related Defect Prediction. *Materials & Design*, 108, pp.400–410.

[26] Allais, C., Denquin, A., Bréchet, Y. and Lapasset, G., (2008). Precipitation microstructures in an AA6056 aluminium alloy after friction stir welding: Characterisation and modelling. *Materials Science and Engineering: A*, 496(1–2), pp.77–89.

[27] Pandian, V. and Kannan, S., (2020). Numerical prediction and experimental investigation of aerospace-grade dissimilar aluminium alloy by friction stir welding. *Journal of Manufacturing Processes*, 54, pp.99–108.

[28] Nirmal, K. and Jagadesh, T., (2021). Numerical simulations of friction stir welding of dual phase titanium alloy for aerospace applications. *Materials Today: Proceedings*, 46, pp.4702–4708.

[29] El-Sayed, M.M., Shash, A.Y. and Abd-Rabou, M., (2018). Finite element modeling of aluminum alloy AA5083-O friction stir welding process. *Journal of Materials Processing Technology*, 252, pp.13–24.

[30] Yaduwanshi, D.K., Bag, S. and Pal, S., (2015). Heat transfer analyses in friction stir welding of aluminium alloy. *Proceedings of the Institution of Mechanical Engineers, Part B: Journal of Engineering Manufacture*, 229(10), pp.1722–1733.

[31] Yang, X., Li, W., Chu, Q., Ma, T., Feng, W., Xu, Y., Chu, Q., Ma, T. and Wang, W., 2018. Numerical Modelling And Experimental Investigation Of Thermal And Material Flow In Probeless Friction Stir Spot Welding Process Of Al 2198-T8. *Science and Technology of Welding and Joining*, 23(8), pp.704–714.

[32] Marzbanrad, J., Akbari, M., Asadi, P. and Safaee, S., (2014). Characterization of the influence of tool pin profile on microstructural and mechanical properties of friction stir welding. *Metallurgical and Materials Transactions B*, 45, pp.1887–1894.

[33] Draup, A.J.A., (2017). *Numerical simulation of the structural response of friction stir welded aluminium 2139-T8 alloy subjected to complex loading configurations*. The University of Manchester (United Kingdom).

[34] Hamilton, R., MacKenzie, D. and Li, H., (2010). Multi-physics simulation of friction stir welding process. *Engineering Computations*, 27(8), pp.967–985.

[35] Andrade, D.G., Leitão, C., Dialami, N., Chiumenti, M. and Rodrigues, D.M., (2020). Modelling torque and temperature in friction stir welding of aluminium alloys. *International Journal of Mechanical Sciences*, 182, p.105725.

[36] Sibalic, N. and Vukcevic, M., (2019). Numerical simulation for FSW process at welding aluminium alloy AA6082-T6. *Metals*, 9(7), p.747.

[37] Sahooa, D.K., Mohantyb, B.S. and Bhaskarc, G.B., (2022). Multi phase-field simulation study on microstructural grain development during inductive-based friction surfacing of aluminium. *Digest Journal Of Nanomaterials And Biostructures*, 17(1), pp.263–284.

[38] Jamshidi Aval, H., (2023). Smoothed-Particle Hydrodynamics (SPH) Simulation of AA6061-AA5086 Dissimilar Friction Stir Welding. *Metals*, 13(5), p.906.

[39] Fraser, K., St-Georges, L. and Kiss, L.I., (2016). A mesh-free solid-mechanics approach for simulating the friction stir-welding process. *Joining Technologies*, pp.27–52.

[40] Iftikhar, S.H., Mourad, A.H.I. and Guessoum, M., (2022), February. Numerical modeling of friction stir welding of thermoplastic materials–An overview. *In 2022 Advances in Science and Engineering Technology International Conferences (ASET)* (pp. 1–5). IEEE.

[41] Derazkola, H.A., Eyvazian, A. and Simchi, A., (2020). Modeling and experimental validation of material flow during FSW of polycarbonate. *Materials Today Communications*, 22, p.100796.

[42] Marode, R.V., Pedapati, S.R., Lemma, T.A. and Awang, M., (2023). A review on numerical modelling techniques in friction stir processing: current and future perspective. *Archives of Civil and Mechanical Engineering*, 23(3), p.154.

[43] Dialami, N., Chiumenti, M., Cervera, M. and Agelet de Saracibar, C., (2017). Challenges in thermo-mechanical analysis of friction stir welding processes. *Archives of Computational Methods in Engineering*, 24, pp.189–225.

[44] Meyghani, B., Awang, M. and Wu, C.S., (2020). Finite element modeling of friction stir welding (FSW) on a complex curved plate. *Journal of Advanced Joining Processes*, 1, p.100007.

[45] Nie, L., Wu, Y.X. and Gong, H., (2020). Prediction of temperature and residual stress distributions in friction stir welding of aluminum alloy. *The International Journal of Advanced Manufacturing Technology*, 106, pp.3301–3310.

[46] Chandra, D., Satria, E. and Yusoff, N., (2021), February. Buckling Analysis of Curve Stiffened Fuselage Panel of Very Light Jet Aircraft. *In IOP Conference Series: Materials Science and Engineering* (Vol. 1062, No. 1, p. 012049). IOP Publishing.

[47] Yoon, J.W., Bray, G.H., Valente, R.A.F. and Childs, T.E.R., (2009). Buckling analysis for an integrally stiffened panel structure with a friction stir weld. *Thin-Walled Structures*, 47(12), pp.1608–1622.

[48] Sun, W., Tong, M., Guo, L. and Dong, D., (2008, October). Post-buckling simulation of an integral aluminum fuselage panel subjected to axial compression load. *In 2008 Asia Simulation Conference-7th International Conference on System Simulation and Scientific Computing* (pp. 893–897). IEEE.

[49] Neto, E.L., Monteiro, F.A. and Ruela, H.H., (2010). A Comparison of Buckling Performance of Rivet and Friction Stir Welding Stiffned Panels. *Mecánica Computacional*, 29(49), pp.4967–4975.

Advancement in Engineering and Science – Goyal et al. (Eds)
, ISBN: 978-1-041-31101-0

Conceptual Framework for AI-Driven Drone Surveillance in Quality Assurance of Buildings in Remote Regions

Ganesh Rathod
Department of Computer Science & Engineering, Dr. D. Y. Patil Pratisthan's College of Engineering, Salokhenagar, Kolhapur, India

Rashmi Jadhav
Department of Applied Mechanics, Walchand College of Engineering, Sangli, Sangli, India

Rohit Barwade
Department of Computer Science & Engineering, Dr. D. Y. Patil Pratisthan's College of Engineering, Salokhenagar, Kolhapur, India

ABSTRACT: Building quality and structural integrity development in remote areas is accompanied by special challenges: there are low accesses with a lack of resources and risks in manual inspections. This paper suggests conceptual design of an AI-driven drone surveillance system adapted specially for remote areas building quality and integrity monitoring and assessment. It would integrate unmanned aerial vehicles (UAVs) with advanced imaging sensors and machine learning algorithms to detect structural defects and determine material conditions, thereby delivering real-time data insights. The core components of the framework include: (1) autonomous navigation and data collection using the GPS and obstacle-avoidance systems to effectively and comprehensively cover a given area; (2) image analysis using deep learning algorithms for defect detection in structural health monitoring by the application of trained convolutional neural networks on datasets of cracks, spalling, and misalignments; and (3) a cloud-based data management system to store and analyze captured data and permit access among engineers and stakeholders for efficient decision-making. In short, this framework employs AI and drones for improving accuracy, efficiency, and safety in quality assessments of structures in remote regions toward sustainable infrastructure development, thereby reducing associated risks to the underserved. This concept also addresses other challenges including data transmission from the drone, autonomy of the drone, and adherence to regulation-basic foundations for further research studies and real-world implementations on structural health monitoring.

Keywords: Artificial Intelligence, Drones, Pattern Recognition, Structural Health Monitoring, Structural Civil Engineering, Defect Detection, Building Quality

1 INTRODUCTION

Structural assessment plays a critical role in ensuring the safety, functionality, and longevity of buildings and infrastructure. Traditionally, this process relied heavily on on-site inspections conducted by engineers and technicians through manual observations, physical measurements, and various non-destructive testing (NDT) methods, such as ultrasonic pulse velocity (UPV), radiographic testing, and infrared thermography. Techniques including visual examination, core sampling, and the use of specialized instruments like borescopes, rebound hammers, and strain gauges have been fundamental in structural health monitoring. While these approaches perform effectively under controlled conditions, their application in geographically remote or inaccessible locations presents significant limitations. Manual inspection remains labor-intensive, error-prone, and dependent on highly skilled personnel, often leading to inconsistent results and escalating operational costs.

The structural evaluation of remote sites introduces additional challenges due to geographic isolation, adverse climatic conditions, and inadequate infrastructure. These areas frequently lack access to professional expertise and sophisticated inspection equipment. Furthermore, logistical barriers, including complex terrain, poor connectivity, and political instability, make regular assessment economically and practically unfeasible. Many remote regions are characterized by rugged environments such as dense forests, mountainous terrains, or coastal zones, rendering transportation of personnel and tools difficult. Limited availability of electricity and communication networks further diminishes the reliability of conventional inspection methods. Conducting manual inspections under such conditions exposes engineers and technicians to significant safety risks, particularly when dealing with high-rise structures, damaged buildings, or disaster-affected zones. The time-consuming nature of traditional NDT-based procedures delays data analysis and decision-making, which can be critical in emergency situations requiring rapid structural evaluation.

These multifaceted challenges underscore the need for innovative, technology-driven alternatives that enhance the safety, efficiency, and reliability of structural assessment in remote environments. The advent of unmanned aerial vehicles (UAVs), commonly known as drones, coupled with advancements in artificial intelligence (AI), presents a transformative opportunity in this domain. Drones equipped with high-resolution optical cameras, thermal sensors, and GPS modules can capture detailed visual and thermal imagery of otherwise inaccessible structures. Concurrently, AI—particularly machine learning and deep learning algorithms—facilitates automated processing and interpretation of vast image datasets, leading to accurate and rapid detection of structural anomalies such as cracks, corrosion, and material degradation. The combined use of UAVs and AI not only minimizes human exposure to hazardous environments but also significantly reduces inspection time and cost. Moreover, AI-driven analysis ensures unbiased and consistent results, independent of human subjectivity.

This study introduces a conceptual framework integrating drones and AI for remote structural health monitoring. The framework comprises three primary components. The first involves autonomous navigation and data capture using UAVs mounted with high-resolution RGB and thermal cameras, guided by GPS and obstacle-avoidance systems to ensure comprehensive coverage. The second component employs deep

DOI: 10.1201/9781003798514-40

learning models, such as convolutional neural networks (CNNs), to analyze collected data and identify potential defects with high precision. The third component consists of a cloud-based data management platform that enables remote access, real-time monitoring, and proactive decision-making. To address connectivity challenges in remote locations, the framework incorporates edge computing capabilities for on-board processing, reducing dependence on constant internet availability. Compliance with regulatory and ethical guidelines ensures safe and responsible UAV operation.

Overall, the integration of automation, AI, and aerial technologies signifies a paradigm shift in structural health monitoring practices. This framework not only overcomes the constraints of conventional methods but also establishes a sustainable, scalable, and cost-effective approach for infrastructure assessment in remote and resource-limited regions, ultimately promoting safer and more resilient built environments.

2 LITERATURE REVIEW

AI and the Internet of Things (IoT) are transforming the Architecture, Engineering, and Construction (AEC) sectors through intelligent, sensor-based monitoring and control systems [1]. Integration of drone imagery with AI and Building Information Modelling (BIM) enhances construction site management by ensuring accurate and timely data acquisition [2]. BIM-based drone path planning further optimizes inspection routes, minimizing human involvement and reducing inspection time [3]. AI-powered Unmanned Aerial Vehicles (UAVs) are increasingly applied for visual building inspections using computer vision to detect structural anomalies [4]. Empirical studies confirm that UAVs improve safety, reduce costs, and increase efficiency in residential and commercial construction monitoring [5,6]. Recent developments in Edge-AI have enabled real-time tunnel and infrastructure inspections by processing data locally on drones without cloud dependency [7]. AI-integrated UAVs are essential components of IoT-enabled smart construction environments, supporting surveillance, maintenance, and progress tracking [8]. The convergence of AI and edge computing reduces latency and improves energy efficiency, though challenges in data security and limited onboard computation persist [9]. UAVs supported by AI also play a vital role in safety monitoring, particularly in regions dependent on manual methods [10,11]. Deep learning techniques allow automatic detection of hazardous conditions and structural defects, improving preventive maintenance [12,13].

Overall, the reviewed literature demonstrates that integrating AI, UAVs, and IoT significantly enhances safety, accuracy, and sustainability in construction and infrastructure inspection, fostering a data-driven, efficient, and intelligent AEC ecosystem [14–16].

3 PROPOSED FRAMEWORK

The proposed framework introduces an innovative system of integrating drones with artificial intelligence for the autonomous monitoring and reporting of building quality in remote areas. This system is looked upon to overcome the constraints associated with traditional methods of inspection that include lack of accessibility, safe conditions, and time constraints, especially where resources are limited. The main use of advanced drone technology, using sensors and real-time AI-driven data analysis with high resolution, ensures that structural assessments are accurate, efficient, and reliable. The central purpose of the system is for detecting structural defects, material condition evaluation, and allowing real-time actionable insights toward proactive maintenance and infrastructure development in remote and underserved areas. Figure 1 provides the Core components of the framework.

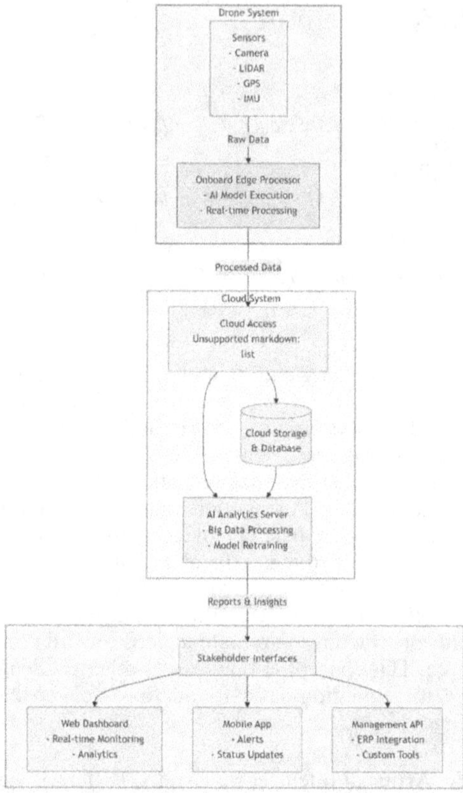

Figure 1. Core components of proposed framework.

3.1 *Drone for data collection*

The first major component of the framework is the selection and deployment of specially optimized drones for data collection in challenging environments. Such drones must be built to be rugged, reliable, and capable of autonomous operation at remote locations with various terrains and climates.

- Types of Drones: High-endurance rugged drones with industrial and environmental applications would be great for the purpose. Fast area coverage usually falls into the domain of fixed-wing types, whereas detailed inspections or confined space navigation is better done by quadcopters or multirotor. Ideally, the best compromise would be a hybrid drone that would encompass the fixed-wing or the multirotor type. These drones should be able to carry extended flight times along with obstacle avoidance systems and high maneuverability so as to collect all types of data required.
- Sensors and Equipment: Armed with several sensors, these drones will gather multiple types of data. High-resolution RGB cameras will capture visual images of exterior building surfaces, and thermal sensors will pick up temperature anomalies, which can be a sign of potential material degradation or structural weakness. The use of LiDAR systems, for instance, can be considered for 3D mapping of structures to give geometric assessments with high accuracy. To distinguish internal flaws in certain applications, the sensor array can include additional sensors like ultrasonic or acoustic sensors. Superior GPS modules will be included in the setup for accurate navigation and locating gyroscopes and accelerometers for stabilization and flight control.

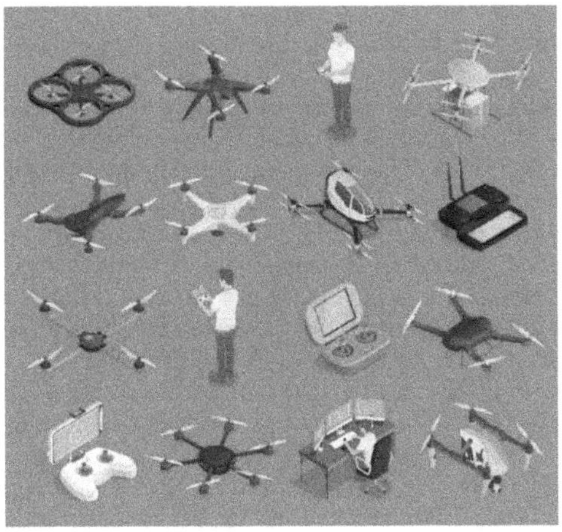

Figure 2. Types of drones.

3.2 *AI for image and pattern recognition*

AI-based analytic capability of processing large volumes of data aerially collected from drones will be the mainstay of the proposed framework. This will accurately and at an excellent speed detect structural defects and material conditions by applying a large number of machine learning algorithms, especially deep learning models.

- AI Models and Techniques: Very popular these days are Convolutional Neural Networks (CNNs) for applications in image recognition, forming the spine of the AI analysis system. These models will be trained using various datasets with images of structural defects, such as cracks, spalling, corrosion, and misalignments. In the case of domain-specific datasets, the pre-trained models, for example, ResNet or VGGNet, may be fine-tuned to enhance their performance. AI-based algorithms focused specifically on thermal imaging data will scan temperature patterns to highlight thermal anomalies resulting from defects in insulations, water ingress, or material fatigue.".
- Avoid Defect Detection and Classification: AI system will categorize the detected anomalies as per type, severity, and potential damage on the structural integrity. For example, cracking may be assorted into groups by width and depth, whereas corrosion may be assessed in terms of area influence and proximity to critical load-bearing members. Such classifications would thus allow engineers to organize their maintenance actions effectively.

3.3 *Data transmission and storage*

The Efficient data management is crucial for ensuring the reliability and accessibility of the system, particularly in remote regions with constrained communication infrastructure.

- Edge Computing: On-board edge computing systems will process data locally on the drones, reducing the need for continuous data transmission to central servers. This capability is particularly important in regions with intermittent or no network connectivity. Only critical insights or compressed datasets will be transmitted to remote storage systems
- Cloud-Based Storage and Analysis: For areas with stable connectivity, the collected data will be uploaded to a cloud-based platform for centralized storage and analysis. The cloud system will facilitate collaboration among engineers, stakeholders, and decision-makers by providing real-time access to processed data, reports, and visualizations.
- Data Security and Integrity: The framework will incorporate robust encryption and authentication protocols to ensure the security and integrity of data during transmission and storage. This is particularly important given the sensitive nature of structural health monitoring data.

3.4 *Potential work flow*

The proposed framework introduces a structured workflow designed to enhance the accuracy and efficiency of building quality assessments in remote areas. The process begins with pre-inspection planning, where engineers and analysts define objectives such as crack detection, material degradation analysis, and overall structural health evaluation. A detailed flight plan is then created considering geographical coordinates, structural dimensions, and environmental complexity to ensure comprehensive coverage. Following this, autonomous drone deployment takes place. Equipped with high-resolution cameras, thermal sensors, and obstacle-avoidance systems, drones capture precise data even in challenging conditions. For large-scale inspections, multiple drones operate simultaneously, reducing data collection time while maintaining accuracy. Integrated edge-computing modules process data in real time to detect patterns and anomalies, such as cracks or heat leaks, decreasing the need for heavy data transmission and enabling faster on-site insights.

The collected data undergoes AI-driven analysis and reporting. Machine learning algorithms and computer vision models, particularly convolutional neural networks (CNNs), identify and classify structural defects. Integration of historical data enhances prediction accuracy, supporting proactive maintenance decisions. The results are presented through visual analytics—heatmaps, annotated imagery, and 3D models—that convey structural integrity clearly. At last, the workflow's cloud-based infrastructure ensures secure storage and remote accessibility of data and reports. Stakeholders, including engineers and decision-makers, can review assessments from any location. This remote collaboration model significantly benefits resource-limited regions by delivering data-driven, timely, and actionable building assessment insights with minimal logistical challenges.

4 APPLICATIONS AND POTENTIAL IMPACT

AI-powered drone surveillance systems are revolutionizing infrastructure inspection and maintenance, especially in remote or hazardous locations where conventional methods are time-consuming, costly, and risky. Equipped with advanced sensors and artificial intelligence, these drones can efficiently navigate mountainous terrains, isolated regions, and disaster-affected areas to capture high-resolution visual and structural data. This enables rapid post-disaster assessments following events such as floods or earthquakes, allowing engineers to make timely, data-driven decisions for repair and reconstruction. The integration of AI algorithms allows real-time analysis of the collected data, automatically detecting cracks, corrosion, deformation, or other structural anomalies. Such early fault identification prevents major system failures, minimizes repair costs, and significantly extends the service life of critical infrastructure. Moreover, these systems eliminate the need for manual inspection in dangerous environments, thereby improving worker safety and reducing dependence on specialized human labor.

Compared to traditional inspection approaches, AI-enabled drone systems complete tasks within hours that once required several days, resulting in substantial savings of time and resources. The cost efficiency achieved through automation allows reallocation of funds toward developmental and sustainability initiatives. Overall, the adoption of AI-based drone surveillance enhances construction quality, operational efficiency, and safety while supporting resilient and sustainable infrastructure development in underdeveloped regions.

5 CHALLENGES AND CONSIDERATIONS

Implementing AI-driven drone surveillance for structural quality assurance in remote regions presents several technical, ethical, and logistical challenges. The foremost technical issue involves efficient data transmission, as poor or absent network connectivity complicates the transfer of large image and sensor datasets to centralized or cloud-based platforms. Integrating edge computing and local storage can mitigate this issue but adds system complexity. Limited drone battery capacity also constrains long-duration or large-scale inspections. Additionally, the reliability of AI models varies with environmental conditions such as lighting, weather, and material types, which can affect data accuracy and analysis quality. Ethical and legal considerations further complicate deployment. Privacy concerns arise when drones inadvertently capture personal or sensitive information, necessitating stringent data protection measures and privacy-preserving algorithms. Variations in regional aviation and surveillance regulations also restrict drone operations, requiring compliance frameworks for lawful use. Cybersecurity risks, including unauthorized access or data breaches, threaten the integrity of collected information.

From an economic standpoint, high initial investment costs for equipment, software, and technical training can hinder adoption in resource-limited communities. Ongoing maintenance, updates, and regulatory expenses further impact scalability. Addressing these constraints will require innovation in energy efficiency, adaptive policies, and cost-sharing models to enable sustainable and widespread implementation of AI-based drone surveillance systems.

6 EVALUATION METRICS

Though the proposed framework is currently conceptual, it is based with an eye towards future implementation and identifying evaluation metrics for validation is important. The primary technical metric is defect detection accuracy. Common accuracy metrics will be applied, including precision, recall and an F1-score, which will clarify the capabilities of AI algorithms to find and classify structural anomalies using a validated dataset(s) like SDNET2018. Time efficiency is also an important metric in computing, where time to complete traditional manual inspections can be compared to time to complete workflows with drones. This parametric measurement will be useful to quantify report cycles and decreased tasks. In terms of energy efficiency, researchers can measure power consumption (watt) per unit area, especially with regard to onboard edge computing in order to process data; energy efficiency should improve because of the better time efficiency – consumption volumes and the volume of data reviewed, should be reduced. Data compaction/optimization efficiency is measurable in terms of the ratio of raw sensor input to output insight based on resilience knowledge. Ratios will also provide insight to identify how much of the data transferred is limited due to remoteness, and a situation where only limited bandwidth is available. Operational reliability is represented by how much of the system uptime is in lower/no connectivity locations, identified as a percentage of successful missions completed without cloud connectivity, applicable in where the drones possess edge computing capabilities. Working in tandem, the various evaluation metrics provide an acceptable and technically based base of reference to compare the system capabilities within a simulated environment, and later a pilot deployment.

7 CONCLUSION

Conclusively, the proposed AI-driven drone surveillance system is a revolutionary approach in quality assurance for far-flung areas employing state-of-the-art technology and finally addressing the long-standing challenge of structural health monitoring. Its very nature of efficiency, accuracy, and safe delivery on its own exceeds that of traditional solutions - compared to pairing autonomous drones with high-resolution imaging sensors, AI-powered defect detection algorithms, and cloud-based data management platforms. This new paradigm will dramatically impact how infrastructure is monitored, bringing significantly reduced inspection times, reduced safety risks associated with inspecting, and providing near real-time actionable insights to stakeholders. This is particularly impactful in remote and underserved areas where traditional constraints of accessibility and resources have often hindered the implementation of effective quality assurance practices. Several areas of further research to refine and extend the capabilities of this framework are presented across the next several sections. Stronger AI algorithms have to be developed to identify various defects under various conditions so that the reliability and applicability of the system could improve. Renewable energy could work in sustaining itself by using mechanisms like drones which run on solar energy. The limitations in batteries can be overcome and larger durations of operation can be achieved with this mechanism. Besides, the strategy for data management itself must also be developed, in terms of proper edge computing and secure decentralized storage solutions, over and above solving data transmission and access problems in isolation areas.

In conclusion, the conceptual framework devised here is robust and allows further investigation with eventual practical implementation. Finally, the proposed system could play a highly important role ensuring the quality and robustness of critical infrastructure in remote areas if these challenges are addressed and the results of on-going technological advancement are appropriately utilized. The proposed system promises to drive sustainable development, improve safety standards, and alter aspects of communities in need.

REFERENCES

[1] Rane, Nitin, Saurabh Choudhary, and Jayesh Rane. (2023). Artificial Intelligence (Ai) and Internet of Things (Iot)–based sensors for monitoring and controlling in architecture, engineering, and construction: Applications, challenges, and opportunities. *Engineering, and Construction: Applications, Challenges, and Opportunities* (November 20, 2023).

[2] Choi, Wonjun, Seunguk Na, and Seokjae Heo. (2024). Integrating Drone Imagery and AI for Improved Construction Site Management through Building Information Modeling. *Buildings* 14, no. 4: 1106.

[3] Huang, Xiongwei, Yongping Liu, Lizhen Huang, Sverre Stikbakke, and Erling Onstein. (2023). BIM-supported drone path planning for building exterior surface inspection. *Computers in Industry* 153: 104019.

[4] Srivastava, Kushagra, Dhruv Patel, Aditya Kumar Jha, Mohhit Kumar Jha, Jaskirat Singh, Ravi Kiran Sarvadevabhatla, Pradeep Kumar Ramancharla, Harikumar Kandath, and K. Madhava Krishna. (2022). UAV-Based Visual Remote Sensing for Automated Building Inspection. *In European Conference on Computer Vision*, pp. 299–316. Cham: Springer Nature Switzerland.

[5] Shin, Hyunkyu, Jonghoon Kim, Kyonghoon Kim, and Sanghyo Lee. (2023). Empirical case study on applying artificial intelligence and unmanned aerial vehicles for the efficient visual inspection of residential buildings. *Buildings* 13, no. 11: 2754.

[6] Kielhauser, Clemens, Raul Renteria Manzano, Jeffrey J. Hoffman, and Bryan T. Adey. (2020). Automated construction progress and quality monitoring for commercial buildings with unmanned aerial systems: An application study from Switzerland. *Infrastructures* 5, no. 11: 98.

[7] Yang, Zi, Wai Chun Lee, Hiu Ngai Chan, and Ming Ge. (2022). A real-time tunnel surface inspection system using edge-AI on drone. *In 2022 IEEE International Conference on Mechatronics and Automation (ICMA)*, pp. 749–754. IEEE.

[8] Cheng, Nan, Shen Wu, Xiucheng Wang, Zhisheng Yin, Changle Li, Wen Chen, and Fangjiong Chen. (2023). AI for UAV-assisted IoT applications: A comprehensive review. *IEEE Internet of Things Journal* 10, no. 16: 14438–14461.

[9] McEnroe, Patrick, Shen Wang, and Madhusanka Liyanage. (2022). A survey on the convergence of edge computing and AI for UAVs: Opportunities and challenges. *IEEE Internet of Things Journal* 9, no. 17: 15435–15459.

[10] Jain, Neha, Ankit Gambhir, and Medhavi Pandey. (2024). Unmanned Aerial Networks—UAVs and AI. *In Recent Trends in Artificial Intelligence Towards a Smart World: Applications in Industries and Sectors*, pp. 321–351. Singapore: Springer Nature Singapore.

[11] Ajaelu, Chidiebere H., and Patrick Okaka O. (2023). Evaluation of the Use of Unmanned Aerial System (Drone) on Risk/Accidents Involved in Construction Project Monitoring, Enugu State, Nigeria. *In International Conference Modern Building Materials, Structures and Techniques*, pp. 502–507. Cham: Springer Nature Switzerland.

[12] Kumar, Sourav, Mukilan Poyyamozhi, Balasubramanian Murugesan, Narayanamoorthi Rajamanickam, Roobaea Alroobaea, and Waleed Nureldeen. (2024). Investigation of unsafe construction site conditions using deep learning algorithms using unmanned aerial vehicles. *Sensors* 24, no. 20: 6737.

[13] Khan, Osama, Mohd Parvez, Monairah Alansari, Mohammad Farid, Yuvarajan Devarajan, and Subash Thanappan. (2023). Application of artificial intelligence in green building concept for energy auditing using drone technology under different environmental conditions. *Scientific Reports* 13, no. 1: 8200.

[14] De Filippo, Michele, Sasan Asadiabadi, J.S. Kuang, Dhanada K. Mishra, and Harris Sun. (2023). AI-powered inspections of facades in reinforced concrete buildings. *HKIE Trans* 30, no. 1: 1–14.

[15] Kim, Bubryur, Yuvaraj Natarajan, KR Sri Preethaa, Sujeen Song, Jinwoo An, and Sanjeev Mohan. (2024). Real-time assessment of surface cracks in concrete structures using integrated deep neural networks with autonomous unmanned aerial vehicle. *Engineering Applications of Artificial Intelligence* 129: 107537.

[16] Sun, Zeyu, and Jiacheng Liao. (2024). Application of intelligent self-organizing algorithms in UAV cooperative inspection of power distribution networks. *Frontiers in Energy Research* 12: 1418907.

Advancement in Engineering and Science – Goyal et al. (Eds)
© 2026 The Author(s), ISBN: 978-1-041-31101-0

Survey on Retrieval-Augmented Generation System for Empowering Visually Impaired Individuals

Prajkta Satpute, Shilpa Godage, and Rajeshri Mane
Electronics and Telecommunication, JSPM's Rajarshi Shahu College of Engineering, Tathawade, Pune, India

Archana Ulmek
Electronics and Telecommunication, Karmaveer Bhaurao Patil College of Engineering, Satara, India

Sayali Gujale and Sneha Patil
Electronics and Telecommunication, JSPM's Rajarshi Shahu College of Engineering, Tathawade, Pune, India

ABSTRACT: This study investigates how assistive technologies, like "optical character recognition" (OCR) and "retrieval augmented generation" (RAG), can increase accessibility for people with visual impairments. RAG fills in knowledge gaps and promotes independence by combining retrieval-based techniques with generative AI to offer personalized, real-time interactions. OCR enhances user interaction with digital material by translating visual data into readable text. Along with exploring ethical issues, the study explores problems like dataset biases, technology constraints, and personalization requirements. This study demonstrates creative approaches to creating inclusive, flexible systems that empower people with visual impairments.

Keywords: RAG, OCR, Text to Speech, Raspberry Pi, visually impaired

1 INTRODUCTION

The way people access and engage with information has changed as a result of the digital revolution. However, there are frequently particular obstacles that prevent people with vision impairments from taking full use of technology improvements. Despite their effectiveness, traditional assistive technologies usually fall short in terms of offering context-aware and intuitive interactions. A new paradigm for overcoming these obstacles is Retrieval Augmented Generation (RAG), which combines the advantages of generative AI and retrieval-based models.

By combining dynamic, real-time information retrieval with the creation of contextually rich, human-like responses, RAG empowers users. The capacity of visually handicapped people to autonomously explore digital environments could be greatly improved by this hybrid method, which would increase their access to a wealth of digital information resources. Additionally, RAG systems' versatility makes them ideal for individualized applications in everyday life, communication, and education.

We are creating a more natural and intuitive interface for the visually handicapped by utilizing RAG's capabilities, especially in the area of text-to-speech. This application of RAG enables the generation of fascinating and contextually relevant human speech. RAG's capabilities allow us to provide personalized engagement, dynamic information retrieval, and context-aware replies.

In addition to discussing important technological advancements, difficulties, and ethical issues, this study reviews the state-of-the-art in RAG and its applications for visually impaired people, such as text-to-speech. The study highlights the significance of developing inclusive technologies that put accessibility and user experience first by looking at its revolutionary potential.

2 LITERATURE REVIEW

The study describes a system that uses a camera-based method to help visually impaired people read texts and recognize currencies, therefore improving their quality of life.[1]. Through the use of integrated sensors, this system improves obstacle detection in addition to helping visually impaired people read printed materials, making daily tasks easier for them to handle. By making text reading and currency identification possible, the technology increases the independence of people with visual impairments. of people with visual impairments.

The study describes a system that uses a camera-based method to help visually impaired people read texts and recognize currencies, therefore improving their quality of life.[1]. Through the use of integrated sensors, this system improves obstacle detection in addition to helping visually impaired people read printed materials, making daily tasks easier for them to handle.By making text reading and currency identification possible, the technology increases the independence of people with visual impairments.

By combining context-aware retrieval-augmented generation (RAG) with a contrastive language-audio pre-training model (CA-CLAP), the study offers a methodology that enhances prompt-based (TTS) synthesis [2] to build a speech embedding database, audio cues are converted into style-related representations in three stages: indexing, retrieval, and production. By including context-aware features, the suggested RAG and prompt-based TTS generation successfully enhances speech prompt selection and generation coherence, surpassing current techniques in both objective and subjective evaluations.

RAG and LLMs are used in the study to enhance automatic speech recognition (ASR) systems. To enhance contextual mistake correction, it suggests a hybrid strategy that uses ASR outputs to query a text-based retriever [3]. RAG and LLMs offer a scalable strategy for ASR improvement without relying on bespoke vocabulary, according to experiments conducted on the Earnings21/22 and VoxPopuli datasets. These experiments demonstrate improved performance for unusual words and robustness against noise.

In order to minimise error propagation, the paper introduces SpeechRAG, a framework for open-question answering over spoken input that does not require automated speech recognition (ASR).[4] Through the use of a portable adapter, it unifies text and audio embeddings into a single area, allowing for immediate retrieval from both modes. SpeechRAG outperforms

 DOI: 10.1201/9781003798514-41

conventional cascaded retrieval techniques, according to performance evaluations. This method improves information retrieval accuracy from audio resources, demonstrating its potential for real-world uses. All things considered, SpeechRAG tackles important issues in spoken content retrieval, opening the door for more developments in the area.

By making it easier to turn handwritten and printed text into audible speech, this method will improve blind people' access to information.[5] The study highlights that even though technology has advanced significantly, environmental conditions and the inherent diversity of physical documents make it difficult to achieve flawless accuracy.

By offering auditory descriptions for tactile images, the TAURIS app improves accessibility for students with visual impairments.[6] The results of the study, which included controlled experiments and interviews, showed that users of the app were better at remembering information and exploring pictures more quickly. According to user feedback, the app was strongly preferred above more conventional approaches like Braille. The results indicate that TAURIS is a useful teaching tool, but more studies involving bigger sample sizes are advised to validate these findings.

In order to balance performance, latency, and power consumption, this research focuses on designing and optimizing hardware solutions for AI-based vision processing in real-world scenarios.[7] In order to improve inference speed and reduce power consumption, it presents hardware-software co-design techniques like as model pruning, pipeline parallelisation, and architectural design. By tackling issues like sustaining low latency, maintaining model correctness, and maximising energy economy in embedded contexts, the method shows notable performance gains in tasks like object identification and gesture recognition. The system is appropriate for mobile and embedded AI applications such as smart cameras and autonomous drones because it provides near-state-of-the-art accuracy while guaranteeing real-time processing.

In order to improve the emotional expressiveness and contextual sensitivity of synthesised speech, this work presents a unique method for text-to-speech (TTS) generation that makes use of contrastive learning approaches. Improved coherence and expressiveness, especially in emotionally charged situations, result from the system's training to detect and react to minute variations in tone, mood, and style through the use of a contrastive loss mechanism. [8] The system can record and produce speech that faithfully captures the contextual and emotional subtleties of the input text thanks to the incorporation of contrastive language modelling into the TTS pipeline.The system makes notable progress in generating more naturally-sounding and emotionally rich speech, despite obstacles like identifying minute emotional changes, preserving real-time synchronisation, and avoiding overfitting in emotion-rich datasets. Applications for this method could be found in fields where expressive and context-aware speech is crucial, such as conversational AI, assistive technology, and digital storytelling.

The aim of this study is to create a portable, camera-based assistive technology that will enable blind people to read product packaging and text labels from handheld items in their everyday lives. Enabling blind people to autonomously recognise and comprehend labels on a variety of objects in spite of intricate backdrops and varied text patterns is the main goal.[9] In order to accomplish this, the syatem uses a motion-based method in which the user shake the object to identify a region of interest.The object is then isolated using a mixture-of-Gaussians background subtraction method. The authors suggest a unique approach that uses gradient characteristics of stroke orientations and edge pixel distributions, trained with an AdaBoost classifier, for text localisation inside the designated region. OCR software is then used to process the recognised text and turn it into audio output that the user may listen to. According to the study's finding, the suggested system successfully locates and reads text from difficult backdrops, exhibiting high accuracy in tests using real users and public datasets. As a result, it offers a useful tool that improves blind people's independence in daily settings. Using OpenCV and a Raspberry Pi camera, this project creates a portable tool to assist blind or illiterate individuals in reading Bangla written texts.[10] The gadget takes pictures, preprocesses them, uses OCR (Tesseract) to identify text and then use of Google TTS (GTTS) to turn it into speech. The accuracy of the algorithm is 97.4% for clear, well-lit photos with legible Bangla script. However, because of the intricate structure of the Bangla alphabet, it has issues with mid-resolution camera quality in low light and OCR restriction.

3 METHODS COMPARISON

Figure 1 depicts the traditional methods used in the system for Empowering visually impaired individuals.

Using the raspberry pi camera or compatible camera module, an image is first taken to start the process. To improve its quality and readability, this image is preprocessed. After preprocessing, the controller extracting text in image using Optical Character Recognition (OCR). The controller then transforms the identified text into an audio signals. Finally, a speaker plays these audio signals, producing a voice-based output of the data that has been extracted.

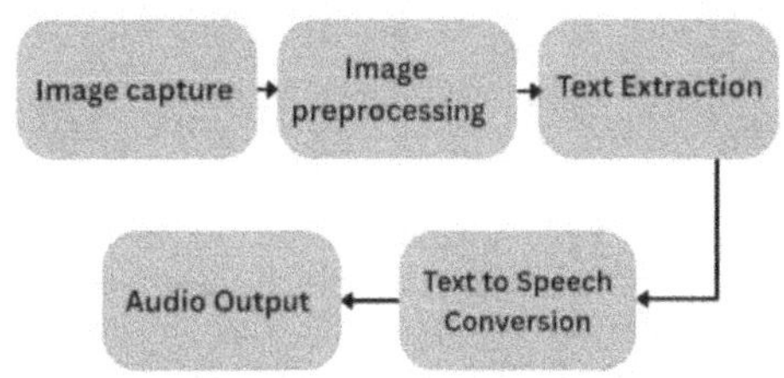

Figure 1. Traditional method used in system.

Figure 2 depicts the Retrieval Augmented Generation method system.

In order to help visually impaired people access unstructured textual data through audio output, the diagram shows a Retrieval-Augmented Generation (RAG) system combined with Text-to-Speech (TTS) technology. The RAG system, which consists of retrieval and generation modules, processes the query that the user submits. Context-aware responses are produced after pertinent data is extracted from unstructured documents. The TTS module then transforms this response into speech and delivers it to the user, allowing for hands-free, accessible information access.

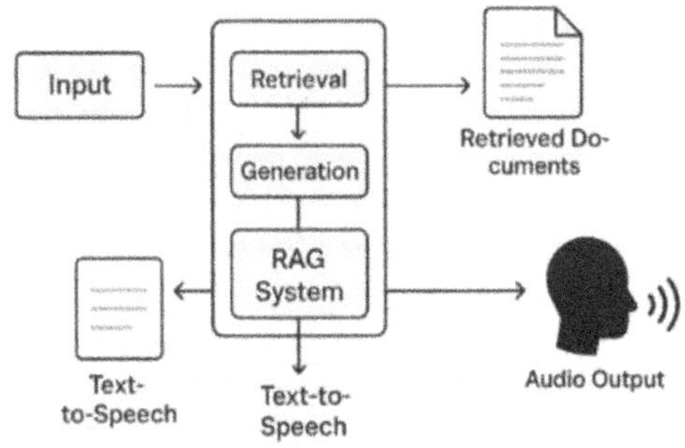

Figure 2. Retrieval augmented generation method system.

Both approaches allow the blind to hear written text. The conventional approach directly translates images into speech but is laborious as it is processed manually. Compared to this, the RAG-based approach offers context-sensitive output via fetching and generating semantic content, providing an enriched, efficient, and accessible solution.

Table 1 gives the overview about the literature survey which include the previous work done. Table 2 gives the overview about the methods and their accuracy.

Table 1. Literature table.

Reference Number	Objective	Methods	Challenges
[1] D. B. K. Kamesh	As to improve independence and social integration of visually impaired people, the paper's primary goal is to create a camera-based system that helps them recognize currencies and translate printed text to speech.	text-to-speech for the blind that uses a camera. Image Processing: Reduce noise and recognize text using OCR. Platform: Raspberry Pi for audio output and processing. Include a text-to-speech engine in the audio. afety: obstacle detection with a PIR sensor	Variations in lighting and background can make it difficult to recognize text accurately. Noise Reduction: It can be difficult to remove noise from scanned photos without losing crucial text information
[2] Y. Zhou	The paper's primary goal is to improve prompt-based TTS synthesis by combining context-aware auditory inputs with Retrieval-Augmented Generation (RAG) techniques to pick speech prompts more effectively, which will increase the coherence and quality of the speech that is produced.	This model uses a multi-modal feature extractor that processes both textual and audio inputs to obtain the context-aware, style-related textual features. TTS system is guided in producing speech that reflects the desired style and emotional tone by concatenating the top retrieved audio hints.	The TTS system is guided in producing speech that reflects the desired style and emotional tone by concatenating the top retrieved audio hints.
[3] C. Xiao	The paper's primary goal is to improve automated speech recognition (ASR) systems' performance by including contextual information through the use of (LLMs) and (RAG).	Using the first-pass ASR hypothesis as a query, one can extract pertinent textual context from a collection of documents. An LLM receives this context together with the ASR hypothesis for contextual error correction. By merging audio representations with the returned text context and the first-pass ASR hypothesis, this technique effectively incorporates speech data into the error correction process by utilising audio LLMs.	questions the scalability of the system
[4] D. J. Min	In order overcome the drawbacks of conventional ASR-based techniques, especially with regard to error propagation, and to increase the retrieval and generation accuracy for spoken data, the goal is to create SpeechRAG, an end-to-end speech retrieval system that embeds both text and voice in a common space.	Speech RAG uses cosine similarity loss for training and aligns text and voice embeddings for retrieval without ASR. Audio excerpts are immediately retrieved from text enquiries.	1. Big datasets are necessary for cross-modal model training. 2. It is challenging to guarantee precise alignment of text and speech. 3. It can be difficult to distil embedding epresentations.
[5] A.Goel	To build a low-cost system that converts printed text into speech for blind users using Raspberry Pi	Captured text images using a camera, processed with OCR (Tesseract), and converted to speech via a TTS engine (eSpeak) on Raspberry Pi.	OCR accuracy, slow processing, limited hardware power, and creating a user-friendly interface.
[6]M. Zeinullin	The targeted objective of the paper is to create a system that makes educational resources more accessible to people who are blind or visually impaired.	A number of experiments were conducted to test particular performance measures in order to collect qualitative data.	Mobile application issues and the absence of a Kazakh speech synthesise
[7] M. Meribout	To design embedded systems tailored for AI vision tasks with real-time constraints.	Involves hardware-software co-optimization for efficient execution of AI models.	Managing latency while maintaining high processing throughput in embedded devices.
[8]J. Xue,	To generate expressive, emotionally tuned speech using contrastive learning with contextual embeddings	Uses retrieval-augmented learning – Emotion-aware feature matching – Contrastive learning loss with context and style vectors	Emotional nuance preservation – Temporal alignment in speech and text – Expressiveness trade-offs
[9] N. Rajkumar	To help people with visual impairments read printed text from objects with complicated backgrounds or hand-held features, like product labels	Motion-based object detection using shaking gestures – text localization via stroke orientation and edge distribution	Difficulty in handling non-horizontal and short text – Complex backgrounds – orientation variance

(*continued*)

Table 1. Continued

Reference Number	Objective	Methods	Challenges
		– OCR for text recognition – Text-to-speech conversion using Microsoft Speech SDK	– localization precision
[10] Aditya Rajbongshi,	to convert photographs of Bangla writing taken by a portable device into speech in order to assist blind or illiterate people in reading Bangla text documents.	Using the Raspberry Pi Camera for mage acquisition Greyscale conversion, DCT compression, morphological adjustments (such as dilatation and black top-hat), adaptive thresholding, and OpenCV contour recognition are examples of image preparation. Using Tesseract OCR to recognize text. The offline Google Text-to-Speech (GTTs) engine is used to translate text to speech. Headphones are used to produce sounds.	In low light, the quality of images is impacted by a mid-resolution Pi camera. OCR restrictions brought on by the intricate layout of Bangla script decreased accuracy when taking pictures in dimly lit or hazy conditions

Table 2. Result.

Reference Number	Method Used	Specific Model/Technique	Accuracy
[4] D. J. Min	Speech retrieval system embedding text and speech in a shared space to retrieve audio directly from text	SpeechRAG, ASR-based	80.45%
[5] A. Goel,	Image capture using Raspberry Pi camera followed by OCR and TTS conversion	Raspberry Pi-based TTS Reader	90%
[3] C. Xiao	First-pass ASR used to retrieve context; sent to LLM for contextual error correction	RAG + LLM	91%
[6] M. Zeimulim	Assistive educational system using tactile and audio feedback for the visually impaired	Android app-based system	80%

4 CONCLUSION

The landscape of assistive solutions for people with impairments, especially the visually impaired, is being revolutionised by the combination of artificial intelligence, embedded systems, and improved sensing technologies. From the fundamental ideas of electromagnetism and signal analysis to the most recent advancements in deep learning, real-time processing, and tactile robotics, this review has covered a wide range of interdisciplinary research.

The literature shows how intelligent, context-aware technologies that can perceive, reason, and interact adaptively have clearly replaced passive assistive devices. The ability of embedded platforms to do intricate inference tasks at the edge is growing, and developments in force control mechanisms, sensor fusion, and human-robot interface are making experiences safer and easier to use.

But problems still exist. These include controlling energy limits in portable devices, addressing safety in physical interactions, assuring ethical AI practices, and developing systems that generalise well in real-world settings. From embedded ethics frameworks to hardware optimisation and compression methods, the research community is actively investigating answers.

In the future, it is anticipated that the combination of brain-computer interface technologies, lightweight AI models, and tactile internet would further redefine assistive applications. Researchers, engineers, and healthcare professionals working together will be essential to creating inclusive technologies that genuinely empower people and improve quality of life as these fields continue to develop and overlap.

REFERENCES

[1] Kamesh D.B.K., Nazma S., Sastry J.K.R., and Venkateswarlu S., (August 2016), Camera based text to speech conversion, obstacle and currency detection for blind persons, *Indian J. Sci. Technol.*, vol. 9, no. 30, pp. 1–5. DOI: 10.17485/ijst/2016/v9i30/98716.

[2] Zhou Y., Zhao S., Bian J., and Liu Z., (June 2024), RAG-enhanced prompt-based TTS: A novel framework for context-aware speech synthesis, arXiv:2406.03714v1.

[3] Xiao C., Hou Z., Garcia-Romero D. and Han K.J., (2025), Contextual ASR with Retrieval Augmented Large Language Model, *ICASSP 2025 – 2025 IEEE International Conference on Acoustics, Speech and Signal Processing (ICASSP)*, Hyderabad, India, pp. 1–5, doi: 10.1109/ICASSP49660.2025.10890057.

[4] Min D.J., Mundnich K., Lapastora A., Soltanmohammadi E., Ronanki S. and Han K., (2025), Speech Retrieval-Augmented Generation without Automatic Speech Recognition, *ICASSP 2025 – 2025 IEEE International Conference on Acoustics, Speech and Signal Processing (ICASSP)*, Hyderabad, India, pp. 1–5, doi: 10.1109/ICASSP49660.2025.10888900

[5] Goel A., Sehrawat A., Patil A., Chougule P., and Khatavkar S., (June 2018), Raspberry Pi based reader for blind people, *Int. Res. J. Eng. Technol.*, vol. 05, no. 06, pp. 1639–1642.

[6] Zeinullin M. and Hersh M., (2022), Tactile Audio Responsive Intelligent System, in *IEEE Access*, vol. 10, pp. 122074–122091, doi: 10.1109/ACCESS.2022.3223099.

[7] Meribout M., Baobaid A., Ould Khaoua M., Kumar Tiwari V., and Pena J.P., (2022), State of art IoT and edge embedded systems for real-time machine vision applications, *IEEE Access*, vol. 10, pp. 58301–58314.

[8] Xue J., Deng Y., Gao Y., and Li Y., *Retrieval augmented generation in prompt-based text-to-speech synthesis with context-aware contrastive language-audio pretraining*,

[9] Rajkumar N., Anand M., and Barathiraja N., (Apr. 2014), Portable camera-based product label reading for blind people, *International Journal of Engineering Trends and Technology*, vol. 10, no. 11, pp. 521–524.

[10] Aditya Rajbongshi, Md. Ibadul Islam, Md. Mahbubur Rahman, Anup Majumder, Dr. Md. Ezharul Islam, Al Amin Biswas, (2020). *International Journal of Advanced Computer Science and Applications*, Vol. 11, No. 6

Advancement in Engineering and Science – Goyal et al. (Eds)
© 2026 The Author(s), ISBN: 978-1-041-31101-0

AI-Driven Image Captioning for Assistive Applications

Y. Ramu Naidu, V.N.V.N. Siva Ram, V. Sateesh Kumar, and K. Shri Ramtej
Department of Electronics and Communication Engineering, Siddhartha Academy of Higher Education, Deemed to be University, Vijayawada, India

ABSTRACT: With millions of visually impaired individuals worldwide, automated image captioning is a crucial assistive tool, bridging the gap between visual content and textual understanding. This paper presents a deep learning-based framework for image caption generation, structured into three key phases: image collection, feature extraction for model training, and performance evaluation. The methodology utilizes the Flickr8K and MSCOCO datasets, with the latter offering a larger and more diverse set of images and captions, providing a robust testbed for model generalization. The proposed framework integrates convolutional neural networks (CNNs) and long short-term memory (LSTM) networks to generate descriptive captions. Specifically, CNN architectures such as VGG16, ResNet, and Inceptionv3 are used to extract image features, while LSTMs process sequential textual data to produce captions. The combined CNN-LSTM model demonstrates superior performance compared to standalone models, achieving higher image captioning accuracy.

Keywords: Image captioning, Convolutional neural networks (CNN), Deep learning, Long short-term memory (LSTM), Assistive technology, Visual description generation

1 INTRODUCTION

Vision is a very important sense that plays significant roles in how people perceive their surroundings, enable their mobility, and interact in general. Nevertheless, impaired vision is one of the principal health issues plaguing the whole world, afflicting more than 2.2 billion people across the globe. Of those affected, as much as nearly 1 billion would have had their impairment averted or otherwise remained unreported [1]. Uncorrected refractive defects, diabetic retinopathy, glaucoma, cataract, and age-related macular degeneration are the predominant reasons for loss of vision. Though vision can impair people across all ages, it is remarkably prevalent among geriatric patients with profound effects on their autonomy as well as over their general overall wellbeing.

Vision impairment has a ripple effect that transcends individual issues, extending to education, employment, and overall health. Profound vision impairment in children that develops early in life can lead to motor and cognitive developmental delay, whereas working-age adults are frequently discovered to be more unemployed. Vision impairment in older persons leads to more social isolation, frequent falls, and early admission to assisted living facilities. It also causes enormous economic cost, with estimated global productivity loss at around US$ 411 billion per year.

Despite the challenges associated with vision impairment, advancements in assistive technologies have remarkably improved accessibility for visually impaired individuals. One such advancement is automated image captioning, which leverages deep learning techniques to generate textual descriptions of images [2].

This study is targeted towards the development of a deep learning-based image captioning system using the Flickr8K and MSCOCO datasets. The method described here combines convolutional neural networks (CNNs), including VGG16, ResNet, and InceptionV3, with long short-term memory (LSTM) networks to generate descriptive captions for images. The primary objective is to improve accessibility for the visually impaired through the delivery of automated text-based descriptions that facilitate the understanding of visual information. This study compares these CNN architectures, to identify the most effective model for generating accurate and contextually relevant captions.

The remainder of the paper is organized as follows: Section 2 reviews various assistive technologies and image captioning approaches available in the literature. Section 3 details the proposed method, including dataset selection, model architecture, and training. Section 4 presents the results and performance evaluation. Finally, Section 5 concludes the work and discusses potential directions for future research.

2 RELATED WORKS

The field of image captioning has evolved significantly, with advancements from early rule-based approaches to modern deep learning methods. Recent research has focused on integrating artificial intelligence (AI) to enhance image description generation, particularly for assistive applications benefiting visually impaired individuals.

The study in [3] discusses the evolution of image caption generation methods, transitioning from static object libraries and statistical language models to neural network-based encoder-decoder architectures with attention mechanisms. It highlights the role of attention mechanisms in improving caption accuracy and evaluates datasets and performance metrics, providing insights into ongoing challenges.

In [4], a real-time image captioning system based on deep learning is presented, utilizing the VGG16-LSTM model. The model was able to yield promising results on a Raspberry Pi 4B with training accuracy of 84.13% and validation accuracy of 83.88%. While the paper demonstrates that image captioning models could be executed on low-power devices, optimization is still needed in order to execute real-time assistive tasks.

An innovative approach integrating a bottom-up attention mechanism inspired by human visual perception is presented in [5]. The model detects key regions in an image, leveraging low-level features like color contrast and sharpness, along with high-level features such as face recognition. This approach enhances caption accuracy in complex environments, which is crucial for assistive image description systems catering to visually impaired users.

DOI: 10.1201/9781003798514-42

The study in [6] proposes a hybrid deep learning and NLP model, combining VGG16 with the Stanford CoreNLP framework to generate more accurate captions. Tested on the MSCOCO dataset, the model demonstrated significant performance improvements over traditional methods. This hybrid approach could enhance contextual awareness in assistive image captioning, allowing visually impaired users to receive more meaningful and grammatically refined descriptions.

There has been recent work that has looked into transformer-based architectures for image captioning. In [7], a model is proposed where Faster R-CNN is replaced by Swin Transformer as the backbone encoder. This model improves grid-level image features, holding intra-relationships between objects to enhance multi-modal caption generation. This method attains CIDEr scores of 138.2% for a single model and 141.0% for an ensemble model on the MSCOCO dataset, greatly improving caption coherence and promising assistive applications.

A large-scale vision-language pre-training model, LEMON (LargE-scale iMage captiONer), is introduced in [8]. With training on 200 million image-text pairs, LEMON demonstrates state-of-the-art performance on the COCO Caption and nocaps benchmarks. Its capability of identifying long-tail visual concepts in a zero-shot scenario suggests its potential to be used in assistive captioning systems that can adapt to various real-world images faced by visually impaired users.

The study in [9] explores methods to generate more specific and context-aware captions. It introduces classifier-free guidance for fine-tuning an autoregressive captioning model, balancing image-matching accuracy with textual alignment in an embedding space. While reference-free metrics like CLIPScore improved, reference-based metrics like CIDEr decreased, highlighting the challenge of optimizing caption specificity without sacrificing relevance. This work raises important considerations for real-world assistive captioning, where user experience should be prioritized over strict reference-based evaluation.

A transformer-based framework for real-time captioning is proposed in [10] for assistive purposes. Employing a two-layer transformer model, the model learns rich relationships in visual data and produces both written and spoken descriptions. Such an ability is critical for users with visual impairment, as real-time auditory output increases accessibility.

These studies underscore the rapid evolution of assistive technologies, highlighting the critical role of AI-driven solutions in empowering visually impaired individuals to lead more independent lives.

3 METHODOLOGY

The system utilizes a three-step process: input image capture, feature extraction for training deep learning models, and performance assessment. The system uses deep learning algorithms, such as CNN and LSTM networks, to extract dominant features and generate captions. The CNN captures dominant visual features, and the LSTM network processes the data to generate descriptive captions.

The overall workflow is illustrated in Figure 1, where image captioning is achieved through a combination of feature extraction and text processing. The process begins by retrieving images from a dataset, followed by extracting relevant features using CNNs. The extracted features are then linked to corresponding captions, which undergo text preprocessing before being used for model training. The model is trained on these processed data points and later tested to evaluate its caption generation performance.

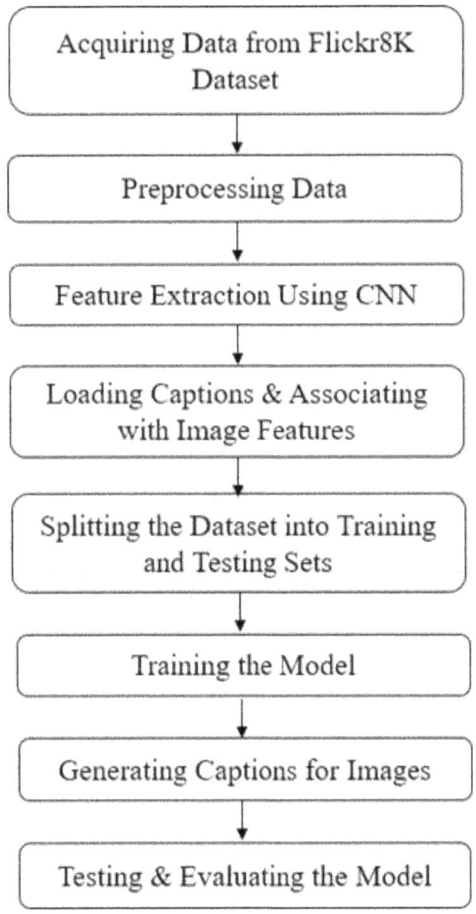

Figure 1. Work flow of the proposed system.

3.1 *Dataset*

The Flickr8K dataset [11] has 8,091 images, each annotated with five captions, totaling 40,455 captions. It is split into training and test subsets, with 10% of the images (810) left for test, and the remaining 7,281 images forming the training set. The MSCOCO (Microsoft Common Objects in Context) dataset [12] is a larger database used for image captioning, segmentation, and object detection, and comprises of 328K images and approximately 1.5 million captions.

3.2 *Data preprocessing*

Before feature extraction, images undergo resizing, normalization, and format conversion. Text captions are pre-processed to remove special characters, tokenize words, and convert text into numerical sequences using word embeddings. This step ensures that both visual and textual data are optimally prepared for model training.

3.3 *Extracting features using CNN & LSTM*

The system employs a CNN-LSTM architecture to generate captions from images. CNNs are used to extract high-level visual features, which are then fed into LSTM networks for sequential text generation.

CNNs are specialized deep learning models designed for image classification, object detection, and visual pattern recognition tasks. They work by applying small convolutional filters usually 3×3 in size, sweep through input images and identify local visual features such as edges, corners, and textures. As the depth of the network grows, these low-level features are increasingly combined to recognize more abstract patterns, such as object parts and whole structures. Each of the convolutional layers is preceded by a ReLU (Rectified Linear Unit) activation, which introduces non-linearity to the model and allows it to learn intricate relationships between features. In addition, max-pooling layers with 2×2 kernels are used to decrease the spatial resolution of the feature maps, in effect decreasing computational complexity while retaining the most important information. Popular CNN architectures such as VGG16, ResNet, and InceptionV3 are utilized due to their proven performance and robustness in image analysis tasks.

LSTM networks, a recurrent neural network (RNN) variant, are especially efficient at handling sequential data because they have an intrinsically designed architecture with memory cells and gated units. Memory cells hold significant values from step to step in time, and this enables the network to learn long-term patterns in sequences. The information flow is controlled by three gates: the forget gate, which deletes redundant information; the input gate, which adds new pertinent information; and the output gate, which controls the information to be forwarded for prediction. This gating mechanism allows LSTMs to learn long-range dependencies in sequences, which makes them particularly effective in applications such as image captioning, where it is crucial to comprehend and generate contextually correct descriptions from visual inputs. The integration of CNNs and LSTMs allows the system to extract meaningful visual patterns and convert them into descriptive textual outputs, enabling efficient and accurate image captioning.

3.4 *Caption loading & annotation*

Captions associated with images are written by human annotators to ensure accuracy and relevance. In some cases, pretrained language models may generate initial captions, which are refined manually to improve precision. The captions undergo filtering to remove errors and noise, ensuring that only high-quality textual descriptions are used for training. The BLEU (Bilingual Evaluation Understudy) score metric is employed to compare generated captions with ground truth annotations to assess model performance.

4 RESULTS AND DISCUSSION

The suggested CNN-LSTM model was tested based on conventional metrics like accuracy and BLEU score. These measures provide a comprehensive evaluation of the model's capability to produce contextual and meaningful captions for images. BLEU score was employed to gauge similarity between reference captions and generated captions through n-gram overlaps. An increased BLEU score indicates a higher similarity between generated and reference captions.

Table 1. Comparison of various models.

Dataset	Model	BLEU-1	BLEU-2	Accuracy (%)
Flickr8K	VGG16	0.4866	0.2224	70.67
	ResNet	0.6701	0.6671	**89.74**
	InceptionV3	0.7076	0.7496	75.85
MSCOCO	VGG16	0.3367	0.2312	71.00
	ResNet	0.1666	0.0931	47.50
	InceptionV3	0.8755	0.8601	**97.50**

Table 1 presents a comparative analysis of different CNN architectures VGG16, ResNet, and InceptionV3 evaluated on two benchmark datasets: Flickr8K and MSCOCO. The results highlight the performance variations among models in terms of BLEU-1, BLEU-2, and accuracy. As shown, the InceptionV3 model achieved the highest BLEU scores and accuracy on the MSCOCO dataset, indicating its strong capability in capturing complex visual patterns and producing high-quality captions. On the Flickr8K dataset, the ResNet model outperformed others in terms of accuracy, demonstrating effective generalization across moderately complex scenes.

Figure 2. Caption generated by VGG16 on a Flickr8K image.

Figure 3. Caption generated by ResNet on a Flickr8K image.

Figure 4. Caption generated by InceptionV3 on a Flickr8K image.

Figures 2 through 7 display sample generated captions using the three CNN variants across both datasets. These qualitative results illustrate the models' effectiveness in recognizing scene components and generating coherent descriptions. For instance, the ResNet model on Flickr8K accurately identified a scenario as "a man is taking photo of another man," while InceptionV3 on MSCOCO successfully generated "a man in a kitchen is preparing food in a kitchen," capturing both activity and environment details. Figure 8 illustrates the training and validation loss curves across epochs on the MSCOCO dataset, showing consistent convergence and minimal overfitting, indicating the model's stability during training.

Figure 5. Caption generated by VGG16 on a MSCOCO image.

Figure 6. Caption generated by ResNet on a MSCOCO image.

Figure 7. Caption generated by InceptionV3 on a MSCOCO image.

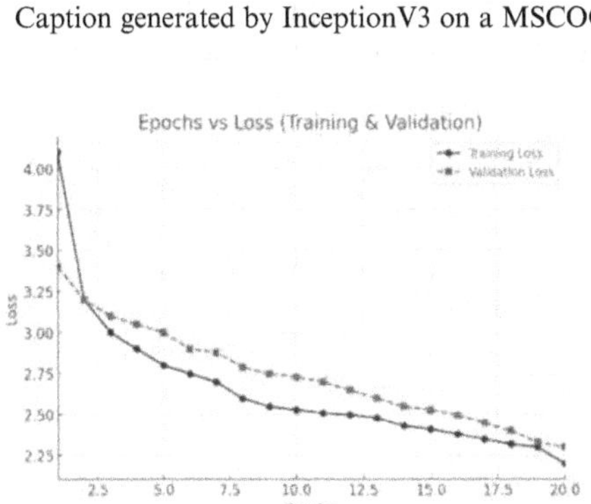

Figure 8. Training and validation loss vs. epochs on the MSCOCO dataset.

5 CONCLUSION

The proposed deep learning-based image captioning system effectively generates coherent and contextually relevant captions, enabling visually impaired users to access visual information. Experimental results showed that the ResNet model on Flickr8K dataset outperformed VGG16 and InceptionV3, achieving an accuracy of 89.74%. In contrast, on the MSCOCO dataset, InceptionV3 outperformed both VGG16 and ResNet, with an accuracy of 97.50%. These results reflect the significance of deep feature extraction and sequential modeling in generating accurate image descriptions. By generating real-time text descriptions, the system provides enhanced accessibility to visually impaired users, enabling increased interaction with visual information. Future work will focus on optimizing model inference for edge device deployment, integrating speech-based output for audio descriptions, and expanding the dataset to support multilingual captions, further improving the usability and real-world applicability of the system.

REFERENCES

[1] World Health Organization. (2025). *Blindness and vision impairment.* http://www.who.int/news-room/fact-sheets/detail/blindness-and-visual-impairment (accessed February 8, 2025).

[2] Ghandi, T., Pourreza H., and Mahyar H. (2023). Deep Learning Approaches on Image Captioning: A Review. *ACM Computing Surveys* 56 (3). https://doi.org/10.1145/3617592.

[3] Wang, H., Zhang Y., and Yu X. (2020). An Overview of Image Caption Generation Methods. *Computational Intelligence and Neuroscience* 2020 (1): 3062706. https://doi.org/10.1155/2020/3062706.

[4] Safiya, K.M., and Pandian R. (2024). A Real-Time Image Captioning Framework Using Computer Vision to Help the Visually Impaired. *Multimedia Tools and Applications* 83 (20): 59413–59438. https://doi.org/10.1007/s11042-023-17849-7.

[5] Ding, S., Qu S., Xi Y., Sangaiah A.K., and Wan S. (2019). Image Caption Generation with High-Level Image Features. *Pattern Recognition Letters* 123: 89–95. https://doi.org/10.1016/j.patrec.2019.03.021.

[6] Makav, B., and Kilic V. (2019). A New Image Captioning Approach for Visually Impaired People. In *Proceedings of the 11th International Conference on Electrical and Electronics Engineering (ELECO 2019)*, 945–949. https://doi.org/10.23919/ELECO47770.2019.8990630.

[7] Wang, Y., Xu J., and Sun Y. (2022). End-to-End Transformer Based Model for Image Captioning. *Proceedings of the AAAI Conference on Artificial Intelligence* 36 (3): 2585–2594. https://doi.org/10.1609/aaai.v36i3.20160.

[8] Hu, X., *et al.* (2022). Scaling Up Vision-Language Pretraining for Image Captioning. In *Proceedings of the IEEE/CVF Conference on Computer Vision and Pattern Recognition (CVPR 2022)*, 17959–17968. https://doi.org/10.1109/CVPR52688.2022.01745.

[9] Kornblith, S., Li L., Wang Z., and Nguyen T. (2023). Guiding Image Captioning Models Toward More Specific Captions. In *Proceedings of the IEEE/CVF International Conference on Computer Vision (ICCV 2023)*, 15213–15223. https://doi.org/10.1109/ICCV51070.2023.01400.

[10] Muhammed Kunju, A.K., Baskar S., Zafar S., B. A. R., R. S., and S. K. A. (2024). A Transformer-Based Real-Time Photo Captioning Framework for Visually Impaired People with Visual Attention. *Multimedia Tools and Applications* 83 (41): 88859–88878. https://doi.org/10.1007/s11042-024-18966-7.

[11] Kaggle. (2025). *Flickr 8k Dataset.* Accessed February 10, 2025. https://www.kaggle.com/datasets/adityajn105/flickr8k/data (accessed February 10, 2025).

[12] Kaggle. (2025). *COCO Dataset 2017.* Accessed February 10, 2025. https://www.kaggle.com/datasets/sabahesaraki/2017-2017 (accessed February 10, 2025).

Advancement in Engineering and Science – Goyal et al. (Eds)
© 2026 The Author(s), ISBN: 978-1-041-31101-0

Overview of Phasor Measurement Unit with Respect to the Sustainable Infrastructure of the Grid

Vishakha Tarange and A.A. Godbole
Department of Electrical Engineering, AISSMS College Of Engineering, Pune, India

ABSTRACT: The Indian infrastructure was designed way back and is still surviving beyond its capacity with few maintenances and adaptations. Making the grid "smarter" and more resilient by using the cutting-edge technology, equipment control that communicate and work together to deliver, more reliably and efficiently can reduce power Cutts. To make grid smarter the two-way communication process is implemented and one of most vital role is being played by the Wide area measurement systems i.e. WAMS. Phasor measurement unit (PMU) is the heart of the WAMS system and synchro phasor measurement its foundation. Based on this technology the renewable infrastructure is upgraded to facilitate the integration with existing grid overcoming frequency of outages, maintaining continuity of supply and providing win-win situation to the utilities and consumers. This paper emphasizes on the literature survey in the area of phasor measurement unit to profoundly highlight the research and innovation contributions in only past year (2024). Approximately seventeen papers published in year 2024, the research areas being: Training algorithm for PMU and generating synthetic data, Fault identification, Optimal placement of PMU, Match the PMU and SCADA parameters in Distribution system, Communication and k means algorithm, Addresses the challenge of accurately estimating synchro phasors in Phasor Measurement Units (PMUs) when multiple harmonics and out-of-band interharmonics (OOBIs) are present, Commutation failure issues in HVDC, Cyber security, Phasor Estimation, Estimation of transmission line parameters, low cost PMU algorithm. The key findings and limitations of the papers are discussed so that the path becomes easy for upcoming researchers.

Keywords: PMU, sustainable, infrastructure, grid, cybersecurity, faults, optimization

1 INTRODUCTION

Wide area measurement is one of the key concepts evolved where real time grid monitoring and protection is carried out with the use of advanced monitoring techniques i.e. Phasor Measurement Units (PMUs), to collect synchronized phasor data from various points across the power grid. These PMUs are strategically placed at key locations throughout the transmission and distribution networks to capture critical parameters such as voltage, current, frequency and phase angle.

The following key steps are followed for real time grid monitoring:

1. **Positioning of the PMU's**
2. **Transmission of the data**
3. **Analysis of the data**
4. **Fault detection and Isolation**
5. **Protective Action Coordination**

The implementation of real time grid monitoring and protection has been very beneficial, some of the findings are as follows:

Reliability of the grid has improved, resilience has increased, faster fault detection optimal asset utilization, support for renewable integration.

Hence to summarize real time monitoring and protection using WAMS is one of the most demanding components of modern power systems which helps the utilities immensely to operate the grids more efficiently and persistently in case of evolving changes and challenges.

Synchro Phasor: The phase angle measurement is regarded as positive when measured in an anti-clockwise direction from the positive real axis. It relies on the frequency inherent in the phasor representation. For different signals to be represented in the same phasor diagram, they must have the same frequency. Still, input signals may not remain stationary in real-time conditions A finite data window is used to consider the input signals to address this. PMUs require at least one period of the input signal's fundamental frequency in the data window [1]. However, when non-harmonic and harmonic components are present, the frequency is not necessarily the same as the fundamental frequency. Thus, PMUs use frequency tracking algorithms to separate the fundamental frequency components and estimate the fundamental frequency period before measuring the phasor. Recent literature survey papers on PMU's protection:[2]

Paper [3] highlights the PMU applications and its preliminary challenges survey done. It encompasses using synchrophasor-based intelligent electronic devices in distribution systems. With the shortcomings like, does not provide any comparative analysis of the PMU-based protection scheme and does not discuss the challenges and problems that PMUs may face concerning their role in protection systems. [4] speaks about the Surveys about implementation of D-PMUs in the distribution network. Reviews the application, monitoring, and control of D-PMUs.With the shortcomings like, not explaining the operation and principles of PMUs.Also does not provide any insight into the standard of PMU application.

Whereas [5] is more inclined towards Surveying a comprehensive overview of synchro-phasor technology, including its principles, operation, and optimal placement techniques and covers various applications in the transmission and distribution system. With some drawbacks like not offering any information or understanding regarding the standard utilized in PMUs also any details or explanation regarding communication systems based on synchro-phasors is not mentioned.

And the [6] highlights the advantages of using μPMUs in distribution networks, including their ability to improve reliability and robustness. Covers environmental sustainability and social and economic benefits. With the non-availability of detailed information related to the wide-area backup protection and no specific data has been mentioned regarding the PMU standards.

DOI: 10.1201/9781003798514-43

More over the during previous three years (in the descending order) the authors have made a point to highlight every single aspect related to PMU, let's discuss in brief the approximately seventeen papers published in year 2024, the statistics stating thrust area of the research papers, whereas the research areas being 1) Training algorithm for PMU and generating synthetic data 2) Fault identification 3) Optimal placement of PMU 4) Match the PMU and SCADA parameters in Distribution system 5) Communication and k means algorithm 6) Addresses the challenge of accurately estimating synchro phasors in Phasor Measurement Units (PMUs) when multiple harmonics and out-of-band interharmonics (OOBIs) are present 7) Commutation failure issues in HVDC 8) Cyber security 9) Phasor Estimation 10) Estimation of transmission line parameters 11) low cost PMU algorithm respectively:

2 ANALYSIS

2.1 *Generation of synthetic data*

Generating synthetic data for Phasor Measurement Units (PMUs) is essential for multiple technical and practical reasons, especially in research, testing, and training contexts.This paper introduces [7] **pmuGE**, a generative framework designed to produce realistic synthetic Phasor Measurement Unit (PMU) data that captures power system anomalies. Leveraging a novel learning method called **Event Participation Decomposition**, pmuGE creates synthetic event data that maintains differential privacy while closely resembling real-world patterns. Built from thousands of real event profiles, the dataset provides a valuable resource for developing and benchmarking machine learning models in power system applications. Machine learning advancement of the data supports the training, validation, and testing of data-driven models, accelerating innovation in power system monitoring and fault detection.

2.2 *Fault identification*

Is a critical function in modern power systems, and Phasor Measurement Units (PMUs) play a central role in making this process more accurate, faster, and resilient.

This study [8] presents a robust **adaptive microgrid system** that addresses common challenges in fault identification, compensation, and system stability. The design combines renewable and conventional energy sources with intelligent control mechanisms to maintain seamless operation under fluctuating environmental and load conditions. The other method for fault detection [12] adaptively adjusts the operating region within the current ratio complex plane according to the specified percentage compensation level. This approach effectively mitigates challenges such as current inversion, high-resistance internal faults, and scenarios involving current infeed or outfeed. This technique dynamically adjusts the operating region in the current ratio complex plane according to the series compensation level, enhancing protection reliability. Fault detection algorithm demonstrates the capability to detect all types of internal faults, maintaining performance during current/voltage inversion, operation of Metal Oxide Varistor (MOV) and/or airgap under high fault current conditions, current infeed/outfeed situations, and external faults with current transformer saturation. Also, the method effectively handles noise in acquired signals, ensuring robust fault detection. The technique is applicable to SCTLs with varying voltage levels and power flow conditions, offering versatility across different system configurations.

2.3 *Optimal placement of PMU*

Optimal PMU placement refers to determining the most strategic locations in a power system where PMUs should be installed to achieve maximum observability, fault detection, and system reliability, with minimum cost and redundancy.

[9] Follows the Cluster-Based Genetic Algorithm: applies this algorithm to efficiently solve the optimization problem, minimizing the complexity of computations. It helps in determining the best placement for PMUs, PCs, and CLs while satisfying all reliability and cost constraints. Numerical Simulations: The method was tested using IEEE test cases, commonly used for simulating power grids, to evaluate its performance in minimizing costs and enhancing reliability. It provides: By employing a cluster-based genetic algorithm, the system optimally places PMUs, PCs, and CLs while satisfying the reliability and cost constraints efficiently.

The next theory [13] introduces a novel framework aimed at enhancing the efficiency of smart grid monitoring systems. This framework integrates optimal placement of Phasor Measurement Units (PMUs) with data pruning strategies to reduce communication bandwidth requirements without compromising monitoring accuracy.

System-Aware Data Pruning: The authors propose a node-level data pruning technique that selectively filters PMU data before transmission to the Phasor Data Concentrator (PDC). By ensuring that only relevant and necessary information is communicated, the method significantly reduces data volume and helps conserve communication bandwidth without compromising system observability. Modeling of Spatial Error Propagation: A mathematical framework is presented to examine how pruning-induced errors spread across the network. This model enables the definition of acceptable error thresholds, guiding the pruning process to preserve the accuracy and reliability of system monitoring. The combined strategy of optimal PMU placement and system-aware data pruning results in up to 95% bandwidth savings per PMU. At the system level, overall communication resource usage is reduced by at least 32%, all while maintaining monitoring accuracy within predefined limits. The proposed framework proves especially valuable for large-scale power systems, where reducing data transmission without sacrificing observability. The paper [18] presents a novel approach to the Optimal PMU Placement (OPP) problem by employing a Deep Reinforcement Learning (DRL) framework, tailored to improve power system observability under dynamic and complex conditions. Graph Convolutional Networks (GCNs) are used to capture the structural and topological characteristics of the power system. This allows the learning model to effectively understand the network's interconnections and spatial dependencies. Deep Deterministic Policy Gradient (DDPG), a reinforcement learning algorithm based on an actor-critic architecture, is adopted for continuous control and optimal placement decisions. This algorithm improves adaptability and performance, particularly in nonlinear and large-scale environments.

2.4 *Matching the PMU and SCADA parameters in distribution system*

Matching parameters like voltage, current, and frequency ensures seamless data fusion for accurate state estimation and grid monitoring, in the "Data-driven Detection and Identification of Line Parameters with PMU and Unsynchronized SCADA Measure-ments in Distribution Grids," [10] addresses the challenge of accurately detecting and identifying line parameters in distribution systems where Phasor Measurement Unit (PMU) and Supervisory Control and Data Acquisition (SCADA) measurements are unsynchronized. Data-Driven Approach: The authors propose a method where when the PMU and SCADA measurements are unsynchronized, the SCADA measurements are used as samples and PMU measurements as the population. In this method the detection of line parameters is done without prior knowledge of their probability density functions (PDFs). Probability Parameter Identification Index (PPII): A PPII is introduced to detect line parameters by analyzing the PDFs of measurements. This index is derived from the measurement-based method, facilitating the identification process.

2.5 *Communication and k means algorithm*

play a vital role in enhancing the performance, reliability, and intelligence of PMU-based monitoring and control systems. Network Infrastructure Optimization and Scalability Analysis" [11] explores the integration of 5G communication infrastructure with Phasor Measurement Units (PMUs) to enhance the digital transformation of electrical substations. This integration aims to address the challenges associated with high-performance wired communication standards, such as Ethernet and Time-Sensitive Networking (TSN), particularly the costs and complexities of extensive wiring over long distances between substations. Latency Assessment: This study models a realistic distribution network to assess the worst-case communication latency between Phasor Measurement Units (PMUs) and the Phasor Data Concentrator (PDC). Results show that the 5G communication infrastructure maintains an average latency of 20 milliseconds, indicating its capability to support monitoring applications in distribution networks where update rates of several tens of milliseconds are required. Scalability Analysis: The study looks into how well 5G infrastructure can scale when used to transmit IEC 61850 data. It focuses on key factors like the number and placement of next-generation NodeBs (gNBs) and the density of User Devices (UDs).

2.6 *Harmonic disturbances*

These disturbances can significantly affect the accuracy and reliability of PMU measurements, which are designed to capture fundamental phasors (magnitude and angle), frequency, and ROCOF (Rate of Change of Frequency). [14] addresses the challenge of accurately estimating synchro phasors in Phasor Measurement Units (PMUs) when multiple harmonics and out-of-band inter-harmonics (OOBIs) are present, especially over short observation intervals. This study presents an improved IpD^{2}FT algorithm capable of effectively detecting and compensating for narrowband interferers, ensuring synchro phasor measurements remain accurate and in line with M-class PMU standards. The proposed approach proves especially valuable in challenging environments characterized by the presence of multiple harmonics and out-of-band interferers, reinforcing the reliability of measurement systems in modern power grids. Another approach [20] presents a novel algorithm designed to improve the accuracy of P Class PMUs presents a robust and computationally efficient algorithm tailored for real-time phasor estimation in P Class PMUs. By integrating signal whitening, frequency correction, and a Taylor series estimation framework, the method significantly improves measurement accuracy under both steady-state and dynamic conditions. While transient responsiveness may slightly decline under rapid changes, the algorithm remains within the strict accuracy thresholds defined by international standards.

2.7 *Commutation failure issues in Brazil's High Voltage Direct Current (HVDC) systems*

This being a particular case study for HVDC system where application of Artificial Neural Networks (ANN) is considered. ANN is developed to predict and mitigate commutation failure (CF) events in high-voltage direct current (HVDC) systems employing line-commutated converters (LCC), particularly in multi-infeed configurations. The model utilized a Radial Basis Function (RBF) architecture due to its strong pattern recognition capabilities and suitability for nonlinear dynamic systems. The RBF-ANN exhibited reliable performance, achieving a high detection accuracy for both the prediction and classification of CF occurrences under varying grid conditions. single and multiple CF cases, making it suitable for pattern recognition applications. This research presents a novel method to mitigate commutation failures (CF) in HVDC-LCC systems by integrating artificial neural networks with synchronized phasor measurements.

2.8 *Cyber security*

Is vital because they send real-time data that controls the power grid. If someone hacks or tampers with this data, it can cause wrong decisions, blackouts, or damage to equipment. PMUs also rely on GPS for timing, which can be tricked if not protected. Securing PMUs keeps the power system safe, stable, and reliable.

The paper [16] introduces a cyber-attack-resilient Breaker Failure Protection (BFP) scheme based on Wide Area Measurement Systems (WAMS) and synchro phasor data. The approach is structured into two main components: Synchro phasor-based Fault Validation Algorithm (SFVA): This algorithm verifies whether a BFP operation is triggered by an actual fault or manipulated through a cyber-attack. It employs a Dynamic Relay White-listing mechanism to ensure that only data from trusted Relay-PMUs is used in the decision-making process. Modified Breaker Failure Protection Logic: The conventional BFP logic is updated to incorporate the SFVA's verdict. In case of a detected cyber threat, the scheme suppresses false BFP trip signals, while continuing to allow legitimate tripping during real fault conditions. Additionally, the Relay-PMU concept is introduced, wherein PMU capabilities are embedded into digital relays, enabling secure, real-time data acquisition and communication for system protection. Dual-layer defense strategy [22], Learning-Based Framework (LBF) and Binary Integer Programming (BIP) Optimization, estimate the best recovery and hardening strategies and reconfigures the network to isolate high-risk components limiting the potential spread of cyber-attacks respectively. Article [23] presents a practical and scalable method for detecting data falsification attacks in Phasor Measurement Units (PMUs), particularly at the distribution level of smart grids using data reduction using Pythagorean means, robust threshold estimation, positive correlation assumption and cluster-based grouping.

2.9 *Phasor estimation*

Phasor estimation in PMUs helps measure the voltage and current with exact timing and angle. This is needed to monitor the power grid in real time, detect faults quickly, and keep the system stable. The study of [17] proposes the use of micro-Phasor Measurement Units (μPMUs) to enhance situational awareness in smart distribution networks. The μPMU model is developed using a recursive Discrete Fourier Transform (DFT) algorithm, supported by high-precision filters to improve the accuracy of phasor estimation under both steady-state and dynamic conditions. To maximize the effectiveness of monitoring while minimizing deployment costs, an optimal placement strategy for the μPMUs is formulated using Mixed-Integer Linear Programming (MILP). This method is applied to the IEEE 33-bus distribution system, which includes practical components such as Distributed Generators (DGs) and Electric Vehicle Charging Stations (EVCS). The study evaluates the performance of the μPMUs model under both nominal and off-nominal frequency conditions to reflect real-world operational variability.

2.10 *Estimation of transmission line parameters*

[19]This paper addresses the challenge of accurately estimating transmission line parameters in power systems, particularly when dealing with measurement noise from Phasor Measurement Units (PMUs). The paper presents an enhanced approach to estimating transmission line parameters in power systems using a Kalman filter-based algorithm. Recognizing that both voltage and current synchro phasor measurements contain noise, the authors improve upon existing methods by explicitly accounting for noise in both types of data. A key innovation in the method is the development of a new measurement noise covariance matrix.

2.11 *Low-cost PMU algorithm*

The paper [21] introduces a method based on the Goertzel algorithm, which is a low-complexity alternative to the commonly used Discrete Fourier Transform (DFT), for measuring synchro phasors in power systems. Goertzel Algorithm for Frequency Analysis: Instead of relying on the computationally heavy DFT, the Goertzel algorithm offers a simpler and more efficient alternative for calculating phasor magnitude and frequency. The algorithm performs efficiently on the Raspberry Pi, with low processing delay, showing that reliable synchro phasor estimation is possible even in cost-constrained setups.

3 RESEARCH GAP

1.PmuBAGE is a critical step forward in enabling widespread access to realistic power system event data, laying the groundwork for future improvements in data fidelity and realism. But the generation of synthetic data has some limitations, likewise while largely realistic, the synthetic data has some deviations—such as inconsistent replication of frequency synchronization across PMUs, minor voltage anomalies, and slightly imperfect modelling of inter-area oscillation damping. 2.Improved fault identification and compensation can be accomplished by implementing sophisticated fault/anomaly detection algorithms utilizing modern Machine Learning (ML) techniques like neural networks or deep learning.3. Advanced power management techniques, such as particle swarm optimization, model predictive control, and genetic algorithms, can manage energy in real-time considering dynamic pricing, response to demand, and energy storage.4. Incorporating advanced technologies like PMUs into the Internet of Things to enable instantaneous monitoring and control.5. Synchronized control systems can be implemented in PMUs utilizing advanced communication technologies like 5G and 6G and blockchain for secure and distributed control.6. Addressing various aspects, including comparing alternative communication solutions like fiber optics or power line carrier (PLC)-based communication. Additionally, the potential cybersecurity issues associated with 5G-based communication systems will be investigated.7. In the future one can extend the model to address more fault types, to further refine the optimization process.[3]

4 CONCLUSION

Alone in the past year itself approximately seventeen articles have been published in reputed international journals, focusing the concern of the various topics related to the phasor measurement technology which in turn is definitely making a remarkable impact on the strengthening the power grid infrastructure. Sustainable infrastructure contributes to reduction in carbon footprint and environmental pollution. Power grid if made sustainable using Phasor measurement technology through the development of micro-PMU's will definitely ensure the renewables to trigger.[12] introduces an innovative protection scheme for series-compensated transmission lines (SCTLs) utilizing Phasor Measurement Unit (PMU) data. By this method current inversion and high intensity faults are dealt with providing a reliable infrastructure. The Goertzel algorithm [21] offers a simpler and more efficient alternative for calculating phasor magnitude and frequency, making it ideal for real-time use on basic hardware hence upgrading the energy management techniques. Also, the security of grid by avoiding the cyber-attacks by using LBF and BIP optimization methods [22] would be the cherry on the cake. Hence promoting the Phasor measurement technology for reliability and sustainability the scope for research has a wide approach and researchers are free to dig into this vast field contributing in cybersecurity using various machine learning techniques, fault detection and clearing of faults, optimization of placement of PMUs.

REFERENCES

[1] Cruz, M.A. (2019), An algorithm for cost optimization of PMU and communication infrastructure in WAMS. *Int. J. Electr. Power Energy Syst.* 106, 96–104.

[2] Biswal, C. (2023), Real-Time Grid Monitoring and Protection: A Comprehensive Survey on the Advantages of Phasor Measurement Units. *Energies* 16, 4054.

[3] Hojabri, M. (2019), A comprehensive survey on phasor measurement unit applications in distribution systems. *Energies* 12, 4552.

[4] Liu, Y. (2020), D-PMU based applications for emerging active distribution systems: A review. *Electr. Power Syst. Res.* 179, 106063.

[5] Joshi, P.M. (2021), Synchrophasor measurement applications and optimal PMU placement: A review. *Electr. Power Syst. Res.* 199, 107428.

[6] Dusabimana, E. and Yoon, S.G. (2020), A survey on the micro-phasor measurement unit in distribution networks. *Electronics* 9, 305.

[7] Brandon Foggo, (MARCH 2024), pmuBAGE: The Benchmarking Assortment of Generated PMU Data for Power System Events. *IEEE Transactions On Power Systems*, VOL. 39, NO. 2

[8] M. Dhinu Lal, (August 2024), Intelligent Fault Detection, Compensation, and Power Management in Microgrids: A Synchrophasor-Enhanced Approach Using Fuzzy Logic Controllers and RTDS, *IEEE Access* VOLUME 12,2024,28.

[9] Huibin Jia1, (2024), A reliability-based construction approach for wide-area backup protection systems utilizing phasor measurement units in smart grids, *IETGener. Transm. Distrib.* 18:1059–1071.

[10] Jinping Sun, (January 2024), Data-driven Detection and Identification of Line Parameters with PMU and Unsynchronized SCADA Measurements in Distribution Grids, *CSEE Journal Of Power And Energy Systems*, VOL. 10, NO. 1

[11] Alberto Morato, (2024), 5G-Enabled PMU-Based Distributed Measurement Systems: Network Infrastructure Optimization and Scalability Analysis, *IEEE Transactions On Instrumentation And Measurement*, VOL. 73

[12] Koppakula Nagarjuna, (2024), Complex plane based adaptive method for protection of series compensated transmission line using phasor measurement unit data, *Electric Power Systems Research* 234, 110539

[13] Akash Kumar Mandal, (MAY 2024), Joint Optimal PMU Placement and Data Pruning for Resource Efficient Smart Grid Monitoring. *IEEE Transactions On Power Systems*, VOL. 39, NO. 3

[14] Xuansheng Shan, (2024), Enhanced IpD2FT-Based Synchrophasor Estimation for M Class PMUs Through Adaptive Narrowband Interferers Detection and Compensation, *IEEE Transactions On Instrumentation And Measurement*, VOL. 73
[15] Rafael O. Fernandes, (2024), Mitigation of the commutation failure problem in the HVDC multi-infeed scenario in Brazil using synchronized phasor measurement, *Electric Power Systems Research* 235, 110829
[16] Paawan Kirankumar Dubal, (July 2024), Wide Area Measurement-Based Cyber-Attack-Resilient Breaker Failure Protection Scheme, *IEEE Transactions On Smart Grid*, VOL. 15, NO. 4
[17] Deepal B. (2024), Phasor estimation using micro-phasor measurement unit (μPMU) in distribution network for situational awareness, *Journal of Electrical Systems and Inf Techno Research*
[18] Xu Zhou, (June 2024), Deep Reinforcement Learning-Based Optimal PMU Placement Considering the Degree of Power System Observability, *IEEE Transactions On Industrial Informatics*, VOL. 20, NO. 6
[19] Mehrdad Moghanian, (2024), Accurate Kalman filter based estimation of transmission line parameters utilizing synchronized phasor measurements, *Electric Power Systems Research* 230, 110218
[20] David Macii, (2024), Single-cycle P Class phasor estimation based on harmonics whitening and off-nominal frequency offset adjustment, *Electric Power Systems Research* 229, 110119
[21] Atul Singh, (2024), Goertzel based phasor and frequency measurement for low-cost PMUs, *Electric Power Systems Research* 237, 111008
[22] Hamed Sarjan, (2024), Mitigating Propagation of Cyber-Attacks in Wide-Area Measurement Systems, *IEEE Transactions On Information Forensics And Security*, VOL. 19
[23] Prithwiraj Roy, (March/April 2024), Noise Resilient Learning for Attack Detection in Smart Grid PMU, *Infrastructure IEEE Transactions On Dependable And Secure Computing*, VOL. 21, NO. 2

Advancement in Engineering and Science – Goyal et al. (Eds)
 ISBN: 978-1-041-31101-0

Securing Dynamic Spectrum Access: Primary User Emulation Attack Detection Using Location-Aware Methods in Cognitive Radio

Ravikiran S. Anande
Research Scholar, Shivaji University, Kolhapur, India

Suhas S. Patil
Associate Professor, Department of Electronics Engineering, KBPCOE, Satara, India

Rahul K. Patil
Associate Professor, Department of Electronics & Telecommunication Engineering, SVPMCOE, Malegaon Bk, Baramati, India

ABSTRACT: The escalating demand for wireless spectrum, driven by the proliferation of diverse applications ranging from critical financial transactions to national defence and healthcare services, has resulted in severe spectrum congestion. Cognitive radio networks (CRNs) have evolved into a promising solution to this scarcity, enabling secondary users to adaptively access and utilize underutilized spectrum belonging to primary users. However, the inherent open nature of CRNs renders them vulnerable to sophisticated security threats, most notably Primary User Emulation (PUE) attacks. In a PUE attack, a malicious entity mimics the transmission characteristics of a legitimate primary user, misleading secondary users and gaining unauthorized control of the spectrum. The paper investigates this important security challenge by proposing a novel detection approach relying on time-difference-of-arrival (TDOA) location verification. By accurately determining signal arrival time at multiple receivers, this method can accurately estimate the location of the transmitting source. This location information is then used to differentiate between legitimate primary users and malicious emulators. The efficacy of this approach is demonstrated through simulations, showcasing its capability to precisely identify and mitigate PUE attacks, thus improving the overall security and reliability of CRNs.

Keywords: Cognitive Radio Networks (CRN), Dynamic Spectrum Access, Time-Difference-of-Arrival, Primary User Emulation (PUE)

1 INTRODUCTION

The proliferation of wireless technology has exploded in recent years, permeating nearly every facet of modern life. Over the past decade alone, we've witnessed an extraordinary surge in the adoption of applications leveraging wireless communication capabilities. This dramatic upswing in wirelessly connected devices and services has consequently led to a significant and growing congestion within the radio spectrum, creating an increasingly crowded environment for these vital airwaves.

The radio frequency spectrum, a finite and increasingly scarce natural resource, demands highly efficient utilization. To prevent disruptive interference between disparate networks and ensure a seamless user experience, critical services such as satellite communications (operating in L, S, C, Ku, and Ka bands), mobile networks (like those using the 1800 MHz band), and fixed broadcast rely on carefully managed, licensed spectrum bands. Despite this licensed allocation, studies by the Federal Communications Commission indicate that these bands often experience significant periods of underutilization, with reported vacancy rates ranging from 15% to 85% [1]. This highlights a crucial need to enhance spectrum utilization to meet ever-growing demands. While primary, licensed users possess exclusive and permanent rights to their allocated spectrum, their intermittent usage patterns leave substantial portions of these frequency bands idle. Recognizing this inefficiency, the Federal Communications Commission has introduced new policies, paving the way for secondary, unlicensed users to opportunistically access these licensed bands without disrupting primary user's operation [2]. This dynamic spectrum access promises to significantly improve overall spectrum efficiency.

Consequently, cognitive radio (CR) technology has emerged as a pivotal solution, offering the capability for adaptive spectrum access and promising a more dynamic and efficient utilization of the radio frequency landscape. A cognitive radio represents an advanced, smart wireless communication network system that possesses environmental awareness, dynamically sensing and understanding its proximal radio frequency landscape. Based on this real-time awareness, it can intelligently reconfigure its internal operational parameters to ensure both reliable and efficient communication [3]. These innovative cognitive radio networks unlock a multitude of potential applications, including the smart and dynamic utilization of underused TV white space bands and the establishment of secure and dependable communication channels in critical emergency scenarios.

Within a cognitive radio network (CRN), two distinct user categories coexist: Primary Users (PUs), referred to as Licensed Users, and Secondary Users (SUs), alternatively called as Unlicensed Users. The core principle governing spectrum access is that Primary Users hold absolute priority. This means that PUs have the exclusive right to use their assigned spectrum as required. Consequently, Secondary Users are permitted to opportunistically use the spectrum only when the Primary User (PU) is inactive or absent. However, this access is contingent and temporary; the moment a Primary User becomes active and requires the spectrum, Secondary Users are obligated to immediately relinquish the channel to avoid any interference.

Secondary Users within a CRN actively and continuously monitor the radio spectrum for several critical reasons:

1. To identify spectrum availability: They constantly scan the frequency bands to determine if a channel is currently idle and unoccupied by the PU. If an idle channel is detected, the SU can then opportunistically utilize it for its communication needs.
2. To detect Primary User activity: A crucial aspect of their sensing is to immediately identify the presence or activity of

DOI: 10.1201/9781003798514-44

PU. Upon detecting a returning or active PU, the SU must promptly vacate the occupied spectrum to prevent any interference. This dynamic spectrum awareness allows Secondary Users to exploit "spectrum holes" opportunistically. A spectrum hole, or white space, is a time–frequency–space segment within the licensed spectrum band that remains temporarily unutilized by the corresponding Primary User in a specific geographic region and time interval, thereby rendering it available for opportunistic access by Secondary Users without causing interference [3]. By sensing and utilizing these temporary gaps in spectrum usage, CRNs can substantially enhance overall spectrum efficiency.

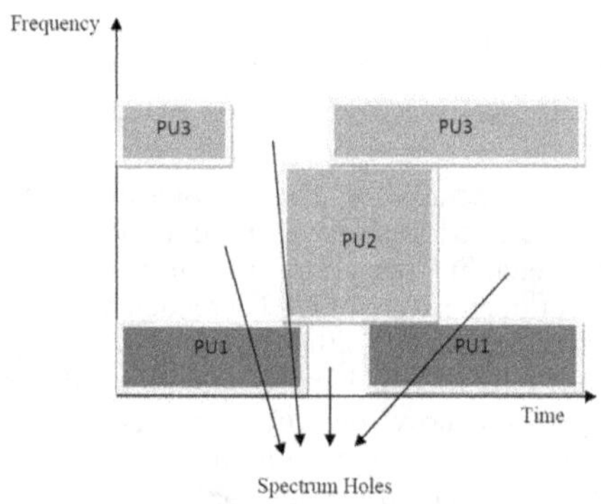

Figure 1. Representation of spectrum hole.

CRNs are characterized by two fundamental and enabling capabilities:

- Cognitive Capability (Environmental Awareness): This core characteristic empowers cognitive radio devices to intelligently perceive and analyze their surrounding radio environment. By actively sensing the spectrum, they can identify underutilized frequency bands or "spectrum holes" that are available during a given time and geographic location. Based on this real-time environmental awareness, the CR can then autonomously select the most suitable spectrum band and configure appropriate operating parameters to optimize communication.
- Reconfigurability (Dynamic Adaptability): This crucial feature enables the cognitive radio to be dynamically reprogrammed and reconfigured in response to variations in the surrounding radio environment. More specifically, a cognitive radio can be adapted on-the-fly to transmit and receive data on different frequencies and to employ various radio access technologies as dictated by the spectrum availability and communication requirements. This adaptability is key to opportunistic spectrum access and efficient resource utilization.

The cognitive cycle in cognitive radio networks operates through a series of interconnected mechanisms:

- Spectrum Sensing: This is a fundamental process where all Secondary Users actively monitor and scan the radio frequency spectrum. They capture information about the current state of different frequency bands and then identify available spectrum holes – those portions of the spectrum not currently in use by Primary Users.
- Spectrum Analysis: Building upon the information gathered during spectrum sensing, the spectrum analysis stage evaluates the identified spectrum holes. This involves analysing various channel and network parameters related to each available band. The outcome of this analysis are subsequently relayed to the spectrum decision process.
- Spectrum Decision: This important stage consists of selecting the most suitable spectrum hole for transmission. Leveraging the information and analysis from the preceding stages, the cognitive radio determines when to initiate its operation over a designated frequency band. The primary objective of this decision-making process is to transmit the maximum possible amount of information while adhering to the required Quality of Service (QoS) and, critically, without interfering with Primary Users.

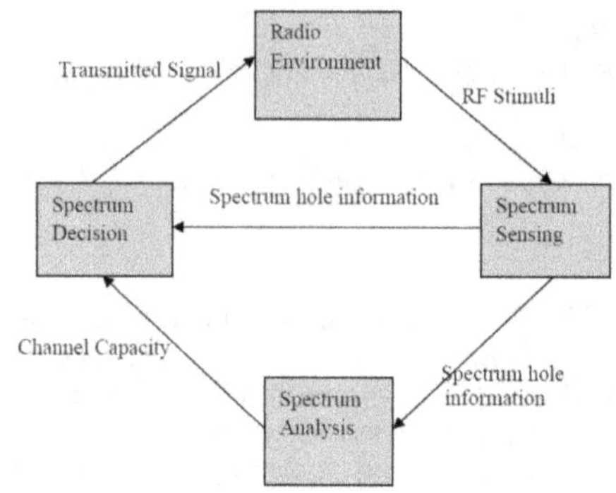

Figure 2. The basic cognitive cycle.

2 PREVIOUS WORK

In reference [3], the author elucidates the fundamental concept of CR and the identification of spectrum holes. A spectrum hole is defined as a frequency band allocated to a primary user that remains temporarily unused at a specific point in time. This work also categorizes and describes various types of spectrum holes.

Reference [4] delves into a joint position verification technique designed to detect attacks involving Primary User Emulation. The paper introduces a novel approach that integrates Frequency Difference of Arrival (FDOA) and Time Difference of Arrival (TDOA) methods to enhance localization precision and enable more accurate attack detection.

Reference [5] provides a detailed explanation of PUE attack, classifying it into two main categories: selfish attacks and malicious attacks. Furthermore, this paper proposes a new transmitter verification procedure for spectrum sensing, which involves estimating or verifying the geographic position of a signal's source.

This current paper introduces a distinct approach to secure positioning that relies on a set of covert base stations (CBS). These covert base stations, whose locations are unknown to a potential attacker during the secure positioning process, are utilized to enhance security. The paper also presents specific protocols for implementing this CBS-based secure positioning [6].

In reference [7], the author discusses a transmitter verification scheme known as Localization-based Defense (Loc-Def). This scheme leverages both the fundamental attributes of the signal and the signal transmitter's geographical position to authenticate the primary signal source. The paper introduces a non-interactive localization scheme specifically for detecting PUE attacks.

Finally, this paper proposes a Received Signal Strength Indication (RSSI)-based transmitter localization verification scheme. This method aims to validate if a detected signal originates from a legitimate PU by calculating the signal transmitter's location. The scheme outlines several algorithms, including an improvement to the Maximum Likelihood Estimate algorithm, a Coordinate Correction Technique, and a Robust Maximum Likelihood Estimate [8].

3 PRIMARY USER EMULATION ATTACK

A critical requirement for Secondary Users is the capability to accurately distinguish signals coming from legitimate Primary Users and those from other Secondary Users. Unfortunately, some malicious Secondary Users can intentionally impersonate Primary Users in a deceptive attempt to gain unauthorized access and exclusive use of the spectrum. This deceptive behaviour compromises the integrity of the spectrum sensing operation and is known as a Primary User Emulation (PUE) attack.

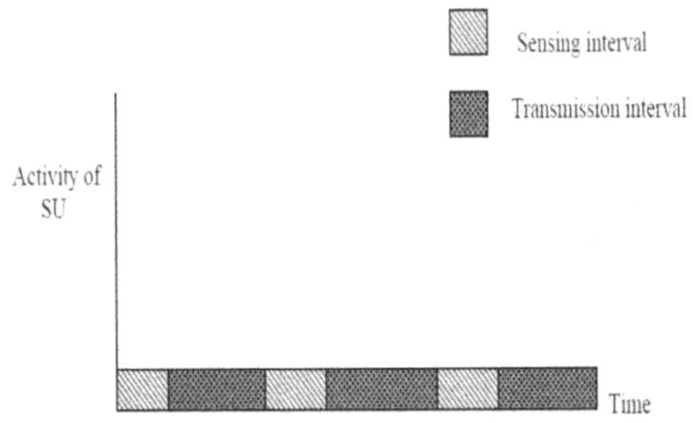

Figure 3. Secondary user's sensing and transmission cycle.

Consider a network scenario consisting of a single Primary User (PU) and three Secondary Users (SUs). When the Primary User is not active, the Secondary Users begin to utilize the available spectrum, engaging in a continuous cycle of sensing and signal transmission. Each Secondary User constantly monitors the spectrum for opportunities. If a spectrum hole is detected, the SU proceeds with data transmission. This alternating sequence of spectrum sensing followed by data transmission continues either until the Secondary User completes its data transfer or until the Primary User becomes active again and reclaims the spectrum.

Figure 3 illustrates a simplified view of a Secondary User's sensing and transmission behaviour within a Cognitive Radio Network (CRN). Let's consider a CRN with one Primary User (PU) and three Secondary Users (SU_1, SU_2, and SU_3). Initially, the Primary User is in an inactive state.

When the PU is idle, SU1 initiates spectrum sensing to determine if the radio spectrum is available for data transmission. Upon detecting an idle spectrum band, SU_1 commences its data transmission. While SU_1 is transmitting, SU_2 arrives and performs its own spectrum sensing to check for bandwidth availability. Finding the spectrum currently occupied by SU_1, SU_2 enters a waiting state.

Subsequently, SU_1 completes its data transmission and intentionally departs from the network. Immediately after, SU_2 senses the spectrum again, now finding it idle. Consequently, SU_2 transitions into a transmission state and begins sending its data. Once SU_2 finishes its transmission, it leaves the network. Following this, SU_3 arrives and probes the spectrum for availability. If the spectrum is found to be free, SU3 enters its transmission phase.

After completing the initial phase of its transmission, if SU3 still has more data to send, it performs spectrum sensing once more to check for the potential return of the Primary User. This time, SU_3 detects that the PU has become active. As Primary Users have absolute priority in the CRN, SU_3 is compelled to immediately vacate the spectrum and cease its transmission.

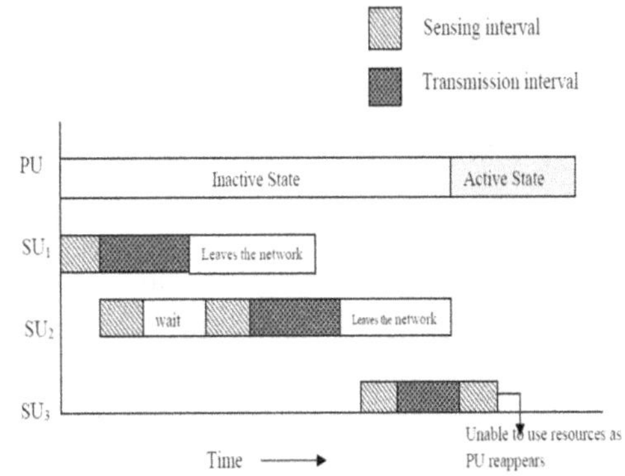

Figure 4. Representation of ideal case consisting of a PU and three Sus.

Let's now consider a scenario involving a malicious node, denoted as SUm, which deceitfully imitates all the characteristics of a legitimate Primary User, effectively behaving exactly like a PU. This malicious behaviour renders the spectrum unavailable for other Secondary Users.

Figure 5 illustrates this attack. Initially, SU_1 arrives and senses the spectrum to confirm bandwidth availability. Based on the sensing outcome, SU_1 transmits its data and then departs from the network. While SU_1 was transmitting, SU_2 arrives, performs spectrum sensing, and enters a waiting state as the channel is occupied.

Crucially, when SU_1 leaves the network, the malicious node SUm begins to emulate the characteristics of a Primary User, falsely presenting itself as a PU. When SU_2 subsequently senses the spectrum again, it detects the presence of what appears to be a PU (in reality, the malicious SUm), forcing SU_2 to re-enter the waiting state. Ultimately, SU_2 leaves the network without being able to transmit any data. This deceptive manipulation of the spectrum sensing process by a malicious secondary user impersonating a primary user is termed a Primary User Emulation Attack (PUE). Similarly, when SU_3 arrives and senses the spectrum to check for availability, it also incorrectly detects the presence of a PU due to the ongoing emulation attack, thus preventing SU_3 from accessing the spectrum.

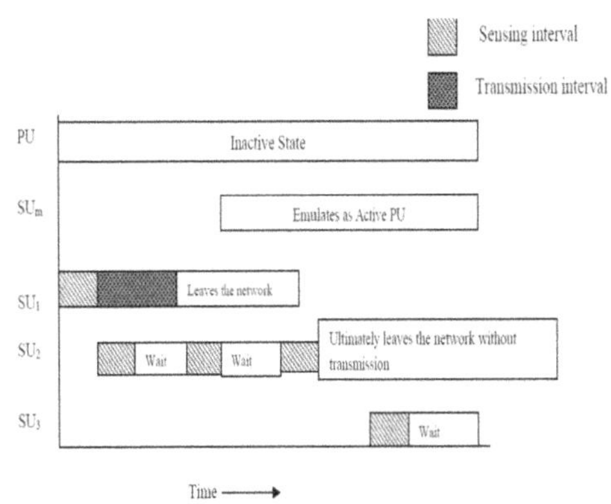

Figure 5. Representation of attack scenario by malicious SU making network resources unavailable.

When an attacker successfully carries out a Primary User Emulation (PUE) attack, the fundamental premise of cognitive radio technology – providing access to unutilized spectrum for unlicensed users – is effectively undermined and rendered inoperable. The core functionality of dynamically identifying and exploiting spectrum holes is compromised by the attacker's deceptive impersonation of a legitimate primary user.

4 MATHEMATICAL MODEL

This paper proposes a transmitter verification scheme based on position verification as a means to detect Primary User Emulation (PUE) attacks. Various localization techniques have been developed, and one such method suitable for Cognitive Radio Networks (CRNs) is Time Difference of Arrival (TDOA). The TDOA method is well-suited for CRNs because it leverages the differences in the arrival times of signals at multiple receivers to estimate the transmitter's location.

4.1 *Localization of TDOA*

Let (x_n, y_n, z_n) represent the coordinates of N microphones and (x, y, z) denote the coordinates of unknown signal source. Define T_n as the time taken for signal to travel from source to the nth microphone. Let v be the speed of sound. Let $D_n = vT_n$ be the distance between the source and the nth microphone. Let $\tau_n = T_n - T_1$ be the difference in transit time between microphone m and microphone 1.

Now,

$$\tau_n = T_n - T_1$$

$$v\tau_n = vT_n - vT_1 = D_n - D_1$$

$$D_n^2 = (v\tau_n + D_1)^2 = v^2\tau_n^2 + 2v\tau_n + D_1^2$$

$$0 = v\tau_n + 2D_1 + (D_1^2 - D_n^2)/v\tau_n \tag{1}$$

for n = 2,3, … ,N.

Subtracting $0 = v\tau_n + 2R_1 + (D_1^2 - D_2^2)/v\tau_n$ from the above equation for n = 3,4, … ,N.

We then get the following equations

$$0 = v\tau_n - v\tau_2 + (D_1^2 - D_n^2)/v\tau_n - (D_1^2 - D_2^2)/v\tau_2$$

for n = 3,4,..,N.

Substituting the expression

$$D_n = \left[(x_n - x)^2 + (y_n - y)^2 + (z_n - z)^2\right]^{1/2}$$

into the preceding equations yield

$$D_n^2 = x_n^2 - 2x_n x + x^2 + y_n^2 - 2y_n y + y^2 + z_n^2 - 2z_n z + z^2$$

for n = 3, 4, … ,N.

Therefore

$$D_1^2 - D_n^2 = x_1^2 + y_1^2 + z_1^2 - x_n^2 - y_n^2 - z_n^2 - 2x_1 x - 2y_1 y - 2z_1 z$$
$$+ 2x_n x + 2y_n y + 2z_n z$$

for n = 2,3, … ,N. Now substituting the above result into Equation (1)

$$0 = v\tau_n - v\tau_2 + \frac{1}{v\tau_n} + (x_1^2 + y_1^2 + z_1^2 - x_n^2 - y_n^2 - z_n^2$$
$$-2x_1 x - 2y_1 y - 2z_1 z + 2x_n x + 2y_n y + 2z_n z)$$
$$-\frac{1}{v\tau_n}(x_1^2 + y_1^2 + z_1^2 - x_2^2 - y_2^2 - z_2^2 - 2x_1 x - 2y_1 y$$
$$-2z_1 z + 2x_2 x + 2y_2 y + 2z_2 z)$$

for n = 3,4, … ,N. We can rewrite the above equations as follows

$$0 = S_n + A_n x + B_n y + C_n z$$

$$A_n = \frac{1}{v\tau_n}(-2x_1 + 2x_n) - \frac{1}{v\tau_2}(2x_2 - 2x_1)$$

$$B_n = \frac{1}{v\tau_n}(-2y_1 + 2y_n) - \frac{1}{v\tau_2}(2y_2 - 2y_1)$$

$$C_n = \frac{1}{v\tau_n}(-2z_1 + 2z_n) - \frac{1}{v\tau_2}(2z_2 - 2z_1)$$

$$S_n = v\tau_n - v\tau_2 + \frac{1}{v\tau_n}(x_1^2 + y_1^2 + z_1^2 + x_n^2 - y_n^2 - z_n^2)$$
$$-\frac{1}{v\tau_2}(x_1^2 + y_1^2 + z_1^2 + x_2^2 - y_2^2 - z_2^2)$$

for m = 3,4,..,N. The set of N−2 equations is rewritten in matrix notation to yield:

$$\begin{bmatrix} A3 & B3 & C3 \\ A4 & B4 & C4 \\ An & Bn & Cn \end{bmatrix} * \begin{bmatrix} x \\ y \\ z \end{bmatrix} = \begin{bmatrix} -S3 \\ -S4 \\ -Sn \end{bmatrix}$$

Computation of the coordinates x, y, z is carried out through the application of the Moore-Penrose pseudoinverse to the matrix formulation on both sides. Note that Above solution is possible only when receivers are at least 5 i.e. N >= 5.

4.2 *Performance parameters*

The subsequent tables present a comparison between the true, original positions of network nodes and their estimated positions as calculated using the TDOA method. The original position coordinates (x, y, z) were randomly created for each individual node. Our presented model was simulated with a network of ten nodes, and the system's accuracy was evaluated by determining the discrepancy between the original and estimated position values. To ensure robustness, three distinct sets of randomly generated location data were used in the simulations, and the estimated positions for all nodes across these simulations were averaged to derive the overall accuracy of the system.

Table 1. Original and calculated locations for 10 nodes(Set - 1).

Original Position				Calculated Position			
Sr. No.	X	Y	Z	Sr. No.	X	Y	Z
1	13.2676	3.9607	1.9426	1	13.2861	3.969	1.9392
2	-13.9885	-38.7237	6.342	2	-13.9852	-38.7082	6.3349
3	46.4027	10.2028	8.7749	3	46.3928	10.1978	8.7849
4	1.8571	-18.9873	15.904	4	1.8601	-18.9847	15.9068
5	-9.3243	0.6005	8.9117	5	-9.3396	0.6035	8.9207
6	-8.1614	-31.2681	15.0937	6	-8.1655	-31.2839	15.0784
7	-5.8996	-12.4767	13.102	7	-5.9086	-12.4958	13.098
8	5.9619	5.5283	9.9673	8	5.9393	5.5038	9.9401
9	-25.8109	40.4545	11.7054	9	-25.8058	40.4448	11.702
10	0.0891	-11.1902	5.1019	10	0.0872	-11.1622	5.0811

Table 2. Accuracy in % of 10 nodes (Set - 1).

Sr. No.	Diff in x	Diff in y	Diff in z	Sr. No.	% Acc x	% Acc y	% Acc z
1	-0.0185	-0.0083	0.0034	1	99.86	99.79	99.82

(*continued*)

Table 2. Continued

Sr. No.	Diff in x	Diff in y	Diff in z	Sr. No.	% Acc x	% Acc y	% Acc z
2	-0.0033	-0.0155	0.0071	2	99.98	99.96	99.89
3	0.0099	0.005	-0.01	3	99.98	99.95	99.89
4	-0.003	-0.0026	-0.0028	4	99.84	99.99	99.98
5	0.0153	-0.003	-0.009	5	99.84	99.50	99.90
6	0.0041	0.0158	0.0153	6	99.95	99.95	99.90
7	0.009	0.0191	0.004	7	99.85	99.85	99.97
8	0.0226	0.0245	0.0272	8	99.62	99.56	99.73
9	-0.0051	0.0097	0.0034	9	99.98	99.98	99.97
10	0.0019	-0.028	0.0208	10	97.87	99.75	99.59

Table 3. Original and calculated locations for 10 nodes(Set - 2).

Original Position				Calculated Position			
Sr. No.	X	Y	Z	Sr. No.	X	Y	Z
1	-10.4667	4.4749	6.222	1	-10.4258	4.4546	6.2304
2	-41.8005	19.6033	3.6963	2	-41.8193	19.6131	3.6963
3	44.8783	-5.7415	8.7774	3	44.8937	-5.7439	8.7787
4	-0.2814	5.5488	8.1744	4	-0.2794	5.4784	8.1292
5	-2.28	29.6573	12.0569	5	-2.2814	29.6534	12.0603
6	6.2797	35.0019	2.3484	6	6.2807	35.0145	2.327
7	-6.2127	13.4701	8.4833	7	-6.2104	13.4735	8.4823
8	21.8147	12.9968	5.2496	8	21.815	12.9957	5.2439
9	39.3776	7.3119	18.5771	9	39.3822	7.3134	18.5805
10	-36.4231	2.6113	11.5705	10	-36.4241	2.6122	11.5894

Table 4. Accuracy in % of 10 nodes (Set - 2).

Sr. No.	Diff in x	Diff in y	Diff in z	Sr. No.	% Acc x	% Acc y	% Acc z
1	-0.0409	0.0203	-0.0084	1	99.61	99.55	99.87
2	0.0188	-0.0098	0	2	99.96	99.95	100.00
3	-0.0154	0.0024	-0.0013	3	99.97	99.96	99.99
4	-0.002	0.0704	0.0452	4	99.29	98.73	99.45
5	0.0014	0.0039	-0.0034	5	99.94	99.99	99.97
6	-0.001	-0.0126	0.0214	6	99.98	99.96	99.09
7	-0.0023	-0.0034	0.001	7	99.96	99.97	99.99
8	-0.0003	0.0011	0.0057	8	100.00	99.99	99.89
9	-0.0046	-0.0015	-0.0034	9	99.99	99.98	99.98
10	0.001	-0.0009	-0.0189	10	100.00	99.97	99.84

Table 5. Original and calculated locations for 10 nodes(Set - 3).

Original Position				Calculated Position			
Sr. No.	X	Y	Z	Sr. No.	X	Y	Z
1	-21.2762	2.4136	2.4122	1	-21.277	2.4135	2.4462
2	4.3936	29.1461	7.6924	2	4.3904	29.1384	7.7
3	-0.3308	29.1474	5.8088	3	-0.3322	29.1583	5.7956
4	-2.9579	30.7124	16.4875	4	-2.9563	30.7247	16.4901
5	-6.0818	-48.7553	6.8775	5	-6.0784	-48.7282	6.8789
6	22.7604	18.2978	18.1262	6	22.7649	18.2971	18.1308
7	18.1651	-40.0563	5.2146	7	18.1658	-40.0625	5.1988
8	29.421	4.1896	8.5052	8	29.4199	4.1902	8.4996
9	8.2546	13.2794	3.5753	9	8.257	13.2812	3.5797
10	17.5454	11.8	11.9705	10	17.574	11.8209	11.9962

Table 6. Accuracy in % of 10 nodes (Set - 3).

Sr. No.	Diff in x	Diff in y	Diff in z	Sr. No.	% Acc x	% Acc y	% Acc z
1	0.0008	0.0001	-0.034	1	100.00	100.00	98.61
2	0.0032	0.0077	-0.0076	2	99.93	99.97	99.90
3	0.0014	-0.0109	0.0132	3	99.58	99.96	99.77
4	-0.0016	-0.0123	-0.0026	4	99.95	99.96	99.98
5	-0.0034	-0.0271	-0.0014	5	99.94	99.94	99.98
6	-0.0045	0.0007	-0.0046	6	99.98	100.00	99.97
7	-0.0007	0.0062	0.0158	7	100.00	99.98	99.70
8	0.0011	-0.0006	0.0056	8	100.00	99.99	99.93
9	-0.0024	-0.0018	-0.0044	9	99.97	99.99	99.88
10	-0.0286	-0.0209	-0.0257	10	99.84	99.82	99.79

Table 7. Overall Accuracy of three sets of location data.

Sr. No.	Average Accuracy (Set -1)	Average Accuracy (Set -2)	Average Accuracy (Set -3)	Overall Average Accuracy
1	99.83	99.67	99.53	99.68
2	99.94	99.97	99.93	99.95
3	99.94	99.97	99.77	99.89
4	99.94	99.16	99.96	99.69
5	99.75	99.97	99.96	99.89
6	99.93	99.68	99.98	99.87
7	99.89	99.98	99.89	99.92
8	99.63	99.96	99.97	99.86
9	99.98	99.98	99.94	99.97
10	99.07	99.93	99.82	99.61

5 RESULTS

Figures 6 and 7 visually depict the 2D and 3D graphical user interfaces (GUIs) for attack detection, respectively. In each figure, the first graph represents the actual, true positions of the nodes, while the second graph displays their positions as estimated by the TDOA algorithm. The core principle for attack detection relies on the correlation level between these two sets of positions. In the presented figures, the true and estimated positions do not align. This significant discrepancy indicates a potential attack scenario, leading the system to halt further communication within the network as a security measure.

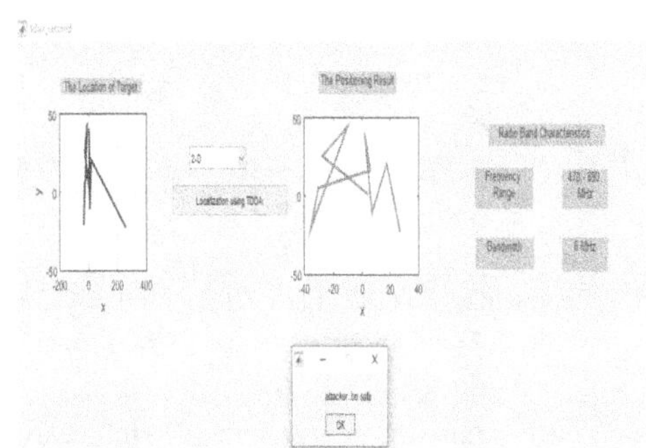

Figure 6. Representation of 2D attack detection GUI(Attack Detected).

Figures 8 and 9 illustrate the 2D and 3D graphical user interfaces (GUIs) for attack detection, respectively, under normal operating conditions where all nodes are considered valid. In each figure, the first graph displays the true positions of the nodes, while the second graph shows their corresponding estimated positions as determined by the TDOA algorithm. Successful operation of the system relies on a high degree of similarity between the two sets of positions. As evident in the following figures, the true and estimated position values align closely. This high degree of correlation suggests that the system is not under attack, and consequently, normal communication within the network is allowed to proceed uninterrupted.

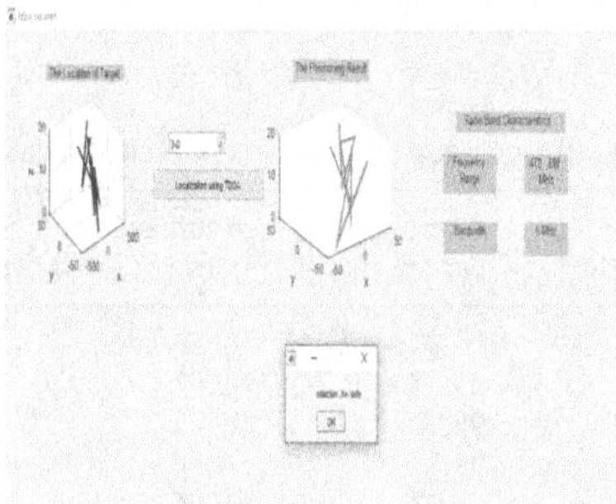

Figure 7. Representation of 3D attack detection GUI(Attack Detected).

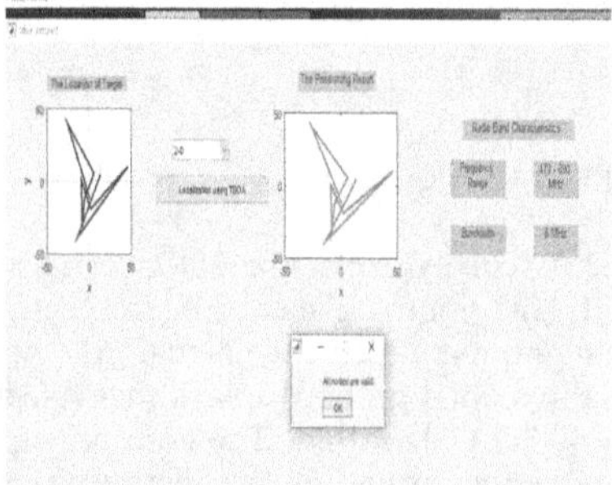

Figure 8. Representation of 2D attack detection GUI(All nodes valid).

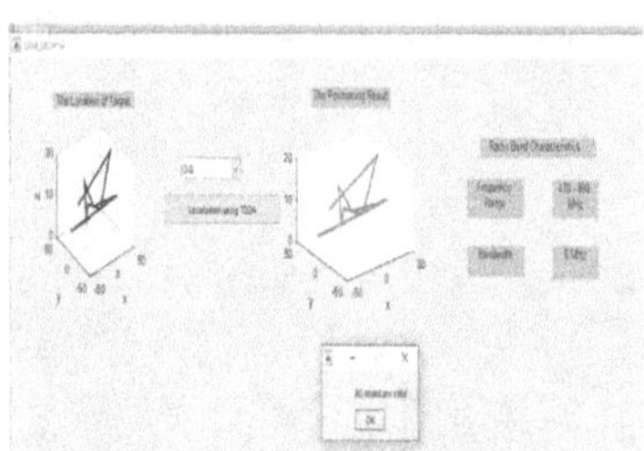

Figure 9. Representation of 3D attack detection GUI(All nodes valid).

The normally used N95 respirators are of negative pressure variant i.e., they require the wearer's lungs to inhale air through the resistive membranes of the filter layers. This is strenuous and uncomfortable to wear for a lon.

6 CONCLUSION

A Cognitive Radio Networks (CRNs) experience substantial security risks from various cyber-attacks. Among these, the Primary User Emulation attack stands out as particularly damaging, capable of severely disrupting the normal operation of these networks. In order to mitigate this weakness, this paper presents a position verification method, specifically the Time Difference of Arrival (TDOA) technique, as a defense mechanism against PUE attacks in CRNs. The proposed framework was implemented algorithmically and its performance assessed through MATLAB-based simulation. Simulation results validate that the proposed TDOA-based localization technique significantly improves positioning accuracy, thereby strengthening the network's robustness against Primary User Emulation (PUE) attacks and ensuring sustained operational integrity of the Cognitive Radio Network (CRN).

REFERENCES

[1] Chen, S., Mulgrew B., and Grant P.M. (1993). A clustering technique for digital communications channel equalization using radial basis function networks. *IEEE Transactions on Neural Networks* 4: 570–578.

[2] Cabric, D., Mishra S.M., and Brodersen R.W. (2004). Implementation issues in spectrum sensing for cognitive radio. *IEEE.*

[3] Chaunhan, K.K., and Sanger A.K.S. (2014). Survey of security threats and attacks in cognitive radio networks. *In Proceedings of the International Conference on Electronics and Communication Systems (ICECS)*, 1–5.

[4] Huang, L., Xie L., Yu H., Wang W., and Yao Y. (2010). Anti-PUE attack based on joint position verification in cognitive radio networks. *In Proceedings of the International Conference on Communications and Mobile Computing*, 169–173. IEEE.

[5] Chen, R., and Park J. (2006). Ensuring trustworthy spectrum sensing in cognitive radio network. *In Proceedings of the 1st IEEE Workshop on Networking Technologies for Software Defined Radio* (SDR '06), 110–119.

[6] Capkun, S., Cagalj M., and Srivastava M. (2006). Secure localization with hidden and mobile base stations. *In Proceedings of IEEE INFOCOM*, April.

[7] Chen, R., Park J., and Reed J. (2008). Defense against primary user emulation attacks in cognitive radio networks. *IEEE Journal on Selected Areas in Communications* 26(1): 25–37.

[8] Naqvi, B., Rashid I., Riaz F., and Aslam B. (2013). Primary user emulation attack and their mitigation strategies: A survey. *In Proceedings of the 2nd National Conference on Information Assurance (NCIA).*

[9] Ghanem, W.R., Shokair M., and Desouky M.I. (2016). An improved primary user emulation attack detection in cognitive radio network based on Firefly Optimization Algorithm. *In Proceedings of the 33rd National Radio Science Conference (NRSC)*, 178–187.

[10] Jin, F., Vardharajan V., and Tupakula U. (2015). Improved detection of primary user emulation attack in cognitive radio network. *In Proceedings of the International Telecommunication Network and Application Conference (ITNAC)*, 274–279.

[11] Dang, M., Zhao Z., and Zhang H. (2013). Optimal cooperative detection of primary user emulation attacks in distributed cognitive radio networks. *In Proceedings of the 8th International Conference on Communication and Networking in China (CHINACOM)*, 368–373.

[12] Lu, K., Ke H., Yang J., and Zhang L. (2012). Research of PUE attack based on location. *In Proceedings of the 11th International Conference on Signal Processing*, 1345–1348.

[13] Chen, C., Cheng H., and Yao Y. (2011). Cooperative spectrum sensing in cognitive radio network in the presence of primary user emulation attack. *IEEE Transactions on Wireless Communication* 10(7): 2135–2141.

[14] Pu, D., Shi Y., Vilyashenko A.V., and Wyglinski A.M. (2011). Detecting primary user emulation attacks in cognitive radio networks. *In Proceedings of the IEEE Global Telecommunications Conference (GLOBECOM)*, 1–5. IEEE, December.

[15] Ding, X., Gong X., and Wu R. (2009). The study on related algorithm of TDOA positioning. *Modern Electronic Technology* (1).

[16] Federal Communication Commission. (2003). *Notice for proposed rulemaking (NPRM 03-322): Facilitating opportunities for flexible efficient and reliable spectrum use employing cognitive radio technologies.* ET Docket No. 03-108, December.

[17] Rappaport, T.S. (2009). *Wireless communication: Principles and practice.* 2nd ed. Pearson Education India, Prentice Hall Communication Engineering and Emerging Technologies Series.

Advancement in Engineering and Science – Goyal et al. (Eds)

AI-Powered IoT-Based Multi-Sensor Grocery Management System

Sai Kiran T.V., Premanand V., Mahek Jameer Modi, and Nizam Salim Kassim
School of Computer Science Engineering, Vellore Institue of Technology, Chennai, India

ABSTRACT: This paper describes an end-to-end, image-based analysis, and Internet of Things (IoT)-sensor system for monitoring perishable food freshness in real-time. Visual spoilage features—e.g., color transitions and texture defects—are detected using Convolutional Neural Networks (CNNs). Environmental sensors provide temperature and humidity readings. The modalities are fused through a soft-voting fusion technique to produce a solid freshness score and classification (Fresh / Approaching Spoilage / Spoiled). Real-time notifications are provided through a responsive web-based dashboard, allowing users to respond in a timely manner. The modular nature of the system easily scales from domestic to supply-chain settings, allowing stakeholders to reduce waste and optimize cold-chain supply chains. The integrated system promotes sustainable consumption habits and enables more efficient inventory management in different settings.

Keywords: Convolution Neural Networks, Image-based quality assessment, Freshness evaluation, Environmental condition analysis, Perishable food monitoring, Spoilage detection, and Real-time alert systems

1 INTRODUCTION

Food spoilage is a real world issue economically and environmentally. Though manual and sensor-only systems dominate, they are marred with subjectivity and poor scalability. Existing systems do not have integrated, real-time spoilage detection, however. The key contribution of this paper is an image-based spoilage detection module based on CNNs with environmental-sensor data for accurate, autonomous freshness assessment.

Several studies have focused on tracking environmental parameters to predict food spoilage. For instance, gas, humidity, and temperature sensor-based systems have been implemented to track the quality of food items, providing users with real-time alerts of potential spoilage[1]. The systems have succeeded in increasing the shelf life of some food groups by providing correct storage conditions. Machine learning algorithms have also been used to analyze sensor data, enabling the recognition of food items based on their freshness level[2].

In parallel with this, computer vision methods have been utilized to measure food quality based on image processing. CNNs have been utilized to identify visual evidence of spoilage, including color and texture alteration, in vegetables and fruits [1]. Such methods provide a rapid and non-destructive means of evaluating food quality, which supports sensor-based measurement.

Notwithstanding the recent progress in sensor-based and computer vision-based detection of spoilage, there does not exist integrated systems that unify these modalities to facilitate comprehensive evaluation of the quality of foods. The research we propose shall address this vacuum by designing an integrated system to utilize environmental sensors to track the storage environment and computer vision to examine visual clues of spoilage. Through correlation of data from both these inputs, the system shall provide greater accuracy and robustness in the detection of spoilage, consequently reducing food losses and improving food safety.

This holistic approach represents a major step forward in the assessment of food quality, providing a complete solution that addresses the limitations of existing methods. Such a framework applied has the ability to transform the preservation and management of food, to the benefit of consumers and the wider food industry.

2 LITERATURE REVIEW

Food spoilage detection has attracted a lot of attention because of its effects on the environment, public health, and financial loss. A number of technologies, such as computer vision, machine learning algorithms, and environmental sensors, have been investigated for monitoring and predicting spoiling. Even though each of these techniques has demonstrated potential on its own, there is still a need for integrated systems that incorporate several modalities for a thorough evaluation of food quality. In order to highlight developments and pinpoint areas in need of more research, this review looks at the body of literature already written on a number of subtopics.

2.1 *Environmental sensors for food spoilage detection*

The Environmental sensors play a crucial role in monitoring conditions that contribute to food spoilage. Temperature and humidity sensors are commonly used to ensure optimal storage conditions, thereby extending shelf life. Gas sensors, such as those detecting ethylene, ammonia, and hydrogen sulphide, can identify the release of spoilage-related compounds. For instance, C2Sense developed a sensor capable of detecting trace amounts of ethylene, allowing for early identification of ripening in fruits[1]. Similarly, biosensors have been employed to detect volatile organic compounds and microbial activity, offering rapid and sensitive spoilage detection[2]. Despite these advancements, challenges remain in sensor calibration, specificity, and integration into existing food monitoring systems.

2.2 *Computer vcision techniques in food quality assessment*

Computer vision (CV) has emerged as a non-invasive method for assessing food quality by analyzing visual attributes such as color, texture, and shape. Advanced algorithms, including CNNs, have been employed to detect spoilage in various food products with notable accuracy[3]. For example, CV systems have been used to monitor color changes in meat products, correlating with freshness levels[4]. Hyperspectral and multi-spectral imaging techniques further enhance CV capabilities by capturing data across different wavelengths, revealing internal properties like freshness and ripeness[5]. However, these

DOI: 10.1201/9781003798514-45

methods primarily focus on surface-level changes and may not account for internal spoilage indicators detectable by environmental sensors.

2.3 *Integration of environmental sensors and computer vision*

Integrating environmental sensors with computer vision systems offers a holistic approach to food spoilage detection. By combining data on storage conditions with visual assessments, such systems can provide a more comprehensive evaluation of food quality. This integration can enhance detection accuracy, account for both internal and external spoilage factors, and offer real-time monitoring capabilities. For instance, combining ethylene detection sensors with CV analysis of fruit appearance can improve the prediction of spoilage onset. Despite its potential, research in this integrated approach remains limited, highlighting an opportunity for innovation in developing unified systems that leverage both modalities effectively.

2.4 *Machine learning applications in spoilage prediction*

Machine learning (ML) algorithms have been applied to analyze data from both environmental sensors and computer vision systems, enabling predictive modeling of food spoilage. Techniques such as support vector machines, random forests, and neural networks can process complex datasets to identify spoilage patterns and forecast shelf life[6]. For example, ML models have been trained on sensor data to predict spoilage in meat products, achieving high accuracy rates. These models can adapt to various food types and storage conditions, enhancing their applicability. However, the effectiveness of these models relies on the quality and diversity of the training data, necessitating comprehensive datasets that encompass a range of spoilage scenarios.

2.5 *Challenges and future directions*

While advancements in environmental sensing, computer vision, and machine learning have significantly contributed to food spoilage detection, challenges persist in developing integrated systems. Issues such as sensor calibration, data fusion from heterogeneous sources, and real-time processing need to be addressed. Future research should focus on creating scalable, cost-effective solutions that combine these technologies, offering robust spoilage detection across diverse food products and storage environments. Additionally, the development of standardized datasets and evaluation metrics will be essential for benchmarking and improving integrated spoilage detection systems.

This model not only applies to home setting, our modular IoT-and-vision architecture scales readily to supply chain inspection points. Leverage sensor-CNN fusion within packing, transportation, and store nodes enables stakeholders to actively identify spoilage opportunities, mitigate shrinkage, and optimize cold-chain logistics.

3 METHODOLOGY

The methodology of the AI-powered IoT-based Multi-Sensor Grocery Management System involves a multi-stage process that combines sensor-based environmental analysis and visual analysis through deep learning. By fusing insights from multiple sensor inputs and computer vision models, the system can accurately assess the freshness and quality of grocery items in real time. The following sections outline each major component of the methodology in detail.

3.1 *Data acquisition*

The first and most crucial step in the system is data acquisition, where both environmental and visual data are captured. This is done through an array of IoT sensors integrated into the storage compartment of the grocery. Environmental information like temperature, humidity, and gases like ethylene — a prime indicator of spoilage and ripening — are detected through corresponding sensors. Temperature and humidity are detected using DHT22 sensors, and volatile organic compounds released during spoilage are detected through MQ-series gas sensors.

Concurrently, visual data are collected using a small camera module, e.g., an ESP32-CAM or a Raspberry Pi Camera, which takes photographs of the food items at intervals. Images play a critical role in detecting visual signs of spoilage, i.e., color change, texture deterioration, mold development, or bruising. Every data point is timestamped and associated with metadata, i.e., type of item, amount (achieved through weight sensors), and identification codes on Radio-Frequency Identification (RFID)/Near Field Communication (NFC) tags that support tracing the life cycle of each product.

A microcontroller (NodeMCU/ESP8266) routes all data before wirelessly sending it to an edge processing unit or cloud-based system for additional analysis. This setup allows the system to continuously monitor conditions and support real-time decision-making.

3.2 *Sensor-based machine learning model*

The environmental data collected from the sensors is processed using a machine learning model to assess the internal spoilage risk of food items. In the initial implementation, a Random Forest classifier is used due to its ability to handle noisy data, capture nonlinear relationships, and deliver explainable results. The input features to the model include time-series data of temperature fluctuations, humidity levels, gas concentrations, weight trends, and elapsed time since purchase.

The model can be trained on a labelled dataset that categorizes food items into states such as "Fresh", "Approaching Spoilage", and "Spoiled." To improve model performance, techniques such as feature scaling, missing value imputation, and outlier filtering can be applied. Advanced models like XGBoost or LightGBM can also be explored to boost prediction accuracy, especially in cases involving unbalanced datasets or complex temporal patterns. These models can be trained using cross-validation strategies, and hyperparameters can be fine-tuned through grid search or Bayesian optimization to ensure generalization across different food types and storage scenarios.

The output of this model is a freshness score and classification label, which can be used to provide early warnings to the user regarding potential spoilage even before any visible symptoms are detected.

3.3 *Image-based CNN model*

In parallel with sensor analysis, the visual data is processed using a CNN to identify surface-level signs of spoilage. CNNs are highly effective at detecting spatial features such as color degradation, bruising, and fungal growth. The image classification model can be built using a lightweight CNN architecture like MobileNetV2 or Efficient Net-lite, optimized for deployment on low-power edge devices.

The CNN can be trained on a curated image dataset representing a wide variety of fruits, vegetables, and other perishable items across different stages of freshness. Data augmentation techniques such as flipping, rotation, brightness adjustments, and cropping can be used to enhance model generalization and simulate real-world variability in lighting and orientation. In resource-constrained environments, transfer learning can be employed by leveraging pre-trained models on ImageNet and fine-tuning them on the spoilage dataset.

The output of the CNN could be a classification label indicating the visual state of the item (e.g., Fresh, Slightly Spoiled, Heavily Spoiled) along with a confidence score. This visual signal complements the internal condition estimation provided by the environmental sensors.

3.4 *Fusion of predictions*

A key innovation in the methodology is the integration of the outputs from the sensor-based model and the image-based CNN through a fusion mechanism. This fusion enhances the system's decision-making capabilities by considering both internal and external indicators of food quality. The approach uses soft voting, where the probability scores from both models are combined to derive a unified freshness prediction.

For instance, if the Environmental-Sensor Machine Learning Model predicts an "At Risk" status due to rising ethylene levels, but the Image-based CNN model still classifies the item as "Fresh," the fusion mechanism balances both views to determine whether the item requires attention. This reduces false positives and ensures more reliable predictions. In future implementations, more sophisticated fusion strategies, such as stacked generalization or rule-based reasoning, may be explored to further refine decision accuracy.

3.5 *User interface and alert mechanism*

Concurrently The final component of the system is the user interface, which acts as the bridge between backend intelligence and user interaction. The processed results are displayed on a mobile or web-based dashboard that provides a clean, intuitive view of the inventory status. The dashboard shows item-level data, including freshness scores, remaining shelf life, historical trends, and actionable insights.

Real-time alerts are triggered when an item is predicted to spoil soon, enabling timely consumption or disposal. Notifications can be delivered via push alerts or SMS, based on user preferences. Users are also provided with insights like usage trends, frequently wasted items, and suggestions for better storage practices. This interface not only empowers users to make informed consumption decisions but also fosters sustainable behaviour through continuous feedback and awareness.

3.6 *Conclusion*

In conclusion, the methodology for the AI-powered IoT-based Multi-Sensor Grocery Management System effectively combines environmental sensors and computer vision to assess food freshness and spoilage. By integrating machine learning models and real-time data processing, the system provides reliable predictions and timely alerts to optimize food consumption and reduce waste. While the system shows great promise, future improvements can focus on expanding the dataset, enhancing sensor accuracy, and refining AI models for better performance. With ongoing advancements, this approach has the potential to revolutionize food inventory management in both households and small retail operations.

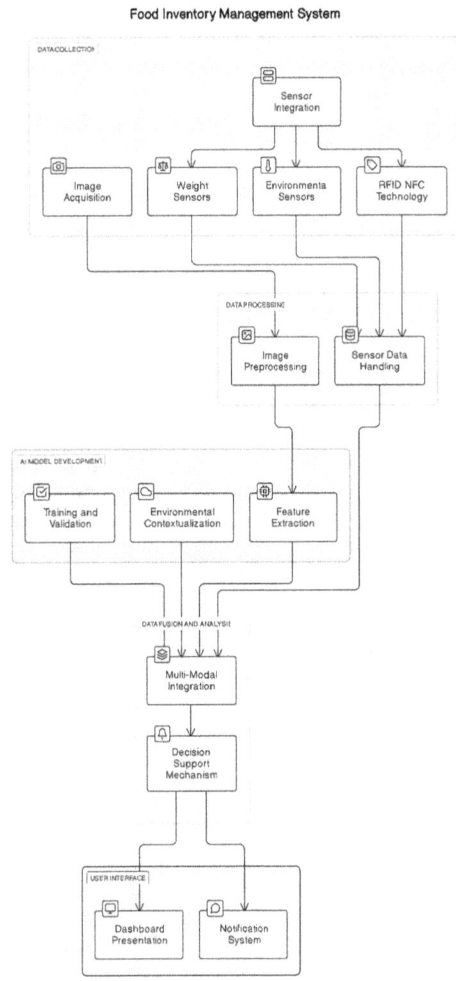

Figure 1. Proposed architecture diagram of the system.

4 EXPECTED OUTCOMES & IMPACT

4.1 *Accurate prediction of food spoilage*

The system is expected to deliver a high degree of accuracy in identifying and predicting food spoilage by leveraging a hybrid approach that combines real-time environmental sensor data and visual image analysis. Environmental factors such as temperature, humidity, and the concentration of gases like ethylene are key indicators of food degradation and are continuously monitored using IoT-enabled sensors. Machine learning models such as Random Forest or Gradient Boosted Trees are trained on this sensor data to classify the freshness level of grocery items. In parallel, visual input from camera modules is analyzed using CNNs trained on datasets containing images of food in various stages of spoilage. These networks can detect subtle changes in appearance—such as color fading, mold formation, or textural anomalies—that are often early signs of deterioration. By fusing these two predictive outputs—environmental and visual—the system provides a comprehensive and robust assessment of food quality, significantly outperforming traditional single-source monitoring systems.

4.2 *Reduction in household food waste*

One of the primary anticipated outcomes of this project is a marked reduction in household food waste. With timely alerts and early spoilage detection, users are equipped with the necessary information to consume or repurpose items before they spoil. This proactive approach encourages better planning and utilization of groceries, reducing the number of items discarded due to neglect or lack of awareness. Over time, this leads to more efficient consumption patterns, cost savings for households, and a reduction in the environmental impact associated with food production and waste disposal. The system, therefore, not only improves personal food management but also contributes to collective efforts to minimize global food waste, which is a significant concern in both developed and developing economies.

4.3 *Efficient inventory management*

The integration of weight sensors and RFID/NFC technology offers a streamlined and automated approach to inventory tracking. Each item can be tagged and its weight monitored in real time, providing granular data about quantity and usage. This allows users to maintain an accurate overview of what groceries are available, what is running low, and what needs to be consumed soon based on freshness levels. The data can be visualized through a user-friendly mobile or web dashboard that displays real-time status updates, usage history, and predictive insights. This level of organization supports better meal planning, reduces the risk of over-purchasing, and helps maintain a balanced inventory. The system thus transforms grocery management from a manual, often chaotic process into a well-organized and data-driven routine.

4.4 *User-friendly alert and monitoring interface*

The success of any smart system lies in its usability. This project emphasizes the development of a seamless and intuitive user interface that caters to both tech-savvy users and those less familiar with technology. Users receive timely notifications through the mobile application, alerting them to potential spoilage, low stock, or optimal consumption windows. The interface will also display visual indicators and simplified analytics to support quick decision-making. By minimizing complexity and offering actionable insights, the system ensures that users can easily manage their grocery inventory without needing to interpret raw sensor data or AI predictions manually. The interface is designed to be responsive and accessible across devices, making it suitable for a variety of use cases, including households with elderly members or those with disabilities.

4.5 *Scalability to small retail environments*

Although the system is tailored for domestic use, its scalable architecture makes it suitable for small-scale retail operations. Grocery stores, local markets, and small food vendors can implement the same sensor-AI framework to manage their perishables more effectively. The ability to track items in real time, monitor freshness, and receive automated alerts can lead to improved inventory turnover, minimized waste, and enhanced customer trust. Moreover, since the system relies on affordable microcontrollers and open-source technologies, its deployment is economically feasible for small businesses. Retailers can benefit from reduced losses due to spoilage and make more informed stocking decisions, ultimately contributing to increased operational efficiency and customer satisfaction.

4.6 *Contribution to sustainable consumption*

The broader environmental and societal impact of this project is rooted in its potential to foster sustainable consumption habits. By making users more conscious of food longevity and usage patterns, the system instils a sense of responsibility towards reducing waste. It aligns with global sustainability goals, such as the United Nations‘ Sustainable Development Goal 12, which advocates for responsible consumption and production. Through educational nudges and behavioural reinforcement, users become more attuned to the lifecycle of their groceries, leading to environmentally friendly practices that extend beyond the household. When scaled, the system has the potential to influence community-wide behaviour and create a ripple effect in encouraging smart, sustainable living.

4.7 *Potential for future integration with smart appliances*

The system's modular and extensible design makes it a strong candidate for future integration with other smart kitchen and home automation devices. As an example, the integration of smart refrigerators can allow for enhanced precision in managing food storage conditions. Coupled with smart assistants and voice command functions, the system can allow users to request the status of food products or receive an audio notification for spoilage. Furthermore, the integration of the system with automated shopping systems would result in an entirely autonomous model of grocery restocking, wherein food products will be automatically bought based on anticipated consumption levels and stock levels. This innovation paves the way for more research into closed-loop systems for minimizing human intervention while maximizing efficiency, convenience, and sustainability.

5 CONCLUSION

In this paper, we introduced an end-to-end image-based analysis and IoT-sensor architecture for real-time spoilage monitoring. Experiments demonstrate that combining CNN-based visual inspection with environmental-sensor information enables accurate freshness scoring and timely notifications. Scaling this architecture to multi-node supply chains—providing end-to-end spoilage monitoring from farm to shelf—is the focus of future work.

At the core of this system is the collective action of multiple technologies. Environmental sensors such as temperature, humidity, gas level (particularly ethylene), and weight detect critical information directly related to the shelf life of perishable food products. This information is processed using supervised machine learning models—such as Random Forests or Gradient Boosted Trees—constructed to recognize patterns of spoilage and determine product freshness based on historical and real-time data. Simultaneously, a visual data module is collected by a camera module about the stored products, which is processed using CNNs trained to recognize visual clues of spoilage, such as color shift, mold, or textural degradation.

One of the main advances in this platform is the sophisticated blending of predictions from sensor inputs with classification outputs from visuals, yielding a more accurate and trustworthy spoilage estimation. Instead of using a single data modality, the platform leverages both physical and visual indicators of deterioration, thus increasing the integrity of its predictions. This multi-modal framework is also extended to encompass an interactive web and mobile dashboard that delivers users actionable insights from spoilage warnings, through consumption suggestions and restocking alerts, displayed through an interface which prioritizes ease of use.

The system meets the needs of a single household while simultaneously demonstrating scalability potential. Its cost-effective components and modular structure render it suitable for small-scale retailing and local grocery vendors, where efficient inventory turnover and quality control are of prime importance. Furthermore, the research also identifies the environmental and social implications associated with this system. By reducing food waste at the consumer level, the project makes a substantial contribution towards objectives in the fields of sustainable consumption, resource conservation, and combating climate change.

In the coming years, the system has tremendous scope for growth. Smart appliance integration, like IoT-compliant refrigerators or kitchen assistants, can facilitate greater automation and integration into a smart kitchen system. Deep learning architectures for model improvement, integration of edge computing for response time optimization, and compatibility with voice-driven interfaces are some areas of enhancement. Additionally, addition of the dataset with varied foods and spoilage states can enhance generalizability and accuracy of the models across varied real-world configurations.

In short, this research forms a sound foundation for an intelligent grocery management system that combines artificial intelligence, IoT, and user experience design to solve a real-world problem.

It provides a blueprint for future work in sustainable food technology and paves the way for creating more intelligent and self-sustaining domestic ecosystems. While the project is currently in the design and prototyping phase, its practical relevance, scalability, and potential societal impact make it a promising solution in the pursuit of efficient, intelligent, and responsible food management systems.

REFERENCES

[1] Sonwani E., Bansal U., Alroobaea R., Baqasah A.M., and Hedabou M., (Jan. 2022), An Artificial Intelligence Approach Toward Food Spoilage Detection and Analysis, *Frontiers in Public Health*, vol. 9, Art. no. 816226, doi: 10.3389/fpubh.2021.816226.

[2] Bongarde D., Pandit S., and Pandit H., (Apr. 2024), Use of Machine Learning and Artificial Intelligence in Food Spoilage Detection, *International Journal of Engineering Research and Applications*, vol. 14, no. 4, pp. 79–85, doi: 10.9790/9622-14047985.

[3] Harshitha S, Mythreyi Manjunath H.K, Neha B.M, (Jun 2023), IoT-Based Food Spoilage Detector, *International Journal for Research in Applied Science and Engineering Technology*, vol. 11, no. 5, pp. 123–129.

[4] Yashraj Navale, Shrawani Gote, Rushikesh Gidde, Janhavi Kamble, (Mar. 2025), IoT-Based Food Spoilage Detection System, *International Research Journal of Modern Engineering and Technology and Science*, vol. 2, no. 3, pp. 45–50.

[5] Shreerang R. Nayankar, Sarthak N., Rakecha, Muskan H. Tamboli, Prof. Kapil D. Dere, (May 2024), Advanced Food Spoilage Detection using IoT Sensors: A Comprehensive Review, *International Research Journal of Modern Engineering and Technology and Science*, vol. 1, no. 12, pp. 67–73

[6] Rao S.V.R.K., Nagabhushanarao G., Kumar G.S., Sharmila I., and Yogendra S., (Jun. 2023), IoT-Based Food Spoilage Detection and Waste Management System, *International Journal of Engineering Research & Technology*, vol. 12, no. 6, pp. 89–95.

[7] Rajini M, Persis Voola, (Feb. 2025), Developing an IoT and ML-Driven Platform for Fruit Ripeness Evaluation and Spoilage Detection, *ScienceDirect*, vol. 15, no. 2, pp. 101–110.

Advancement in Engineering and Science – Goyal et al. (Eds)
© 2026 The Author(s), ISBN: 978-1-041-31101-0

Multimodal Hand Gesture Recognition and Speech Synthesis for Marathi Using MediaPipe and Hybrid Neural Network

Ashlesha S. Adhatrao
Assistant Professor of Artificial Intelligence and Data Science, N K Orchid College of Engineering and Technology, Solapur, India

Mithun B. Patil
Associate Professor of Artificial Intelligence and Data Science, N K Orchid College of Engineering and Technology, Solapur, India

Adarsh Kainchigundi, Vinod Kudkyal, and Rajrajeshwar Margam
Department of Artificial Intelligence and Data Science, N K Orchid College of Engineering and Technology, Solapur, India

ABSTRACT: Hand sign gesture recognition is one of the emerging technologies revolutionizing communication among deaf and speech-impaired people. This technology aims at the designing of a higher-level system to identify hand gestures and also provide oral Marathi as output, bridging access to effective communications among the wider population. The system uses MediaPipe technology for accurate and efficient detection and interpretation of real-time gestures. MediaPipe's hand tracking module detects key landmarks of the hand with great accuracy at high speed. Such gestures underwent preprocessing, feature extraction, and classification with better accuracies, thus ensuring that proper identification was done for these gestures. After the gesture gets identified, then it gets further translated to Marathi text and further renders as natural voice output by using TTS technology. The system is designed to be accessed by the users and is user-friendly, especially suited for schools, hospitals, public spaces, among others. For real-time applications, changes in lighting, shapes of hands and orientations happen very often and have to be handled technically. Special attention has been given to Marathi culture and language to make the output and the translation into correct context and culturally relevant. Thus, this research becomes capable of providing inclusivity through the using MediaPipe-based hand gesture recognition and Marathi voice translation, which makes it reachable and impactful communication. This is likely to have significant growth in social and educational inclusivity-through the removal of language barriers as well as cultural differences-how people interact and power their participants through novel assistive technology.

Keywords: Hand Sign Gesture Recognition, MediaPipe Technology, Real-Time Detection, Marathi Translation, Text-toSpeech (TTS), Computer Vision; Multilingual Accessibility, Deep Learning

1 INTRODUCTION

Communication is the basic interaction through which humans interact with other humans, but it has, in many ways, proven quite challenging for individuals who lack the ability to hear or speak. However, language barriers and the generally low level of knowledge in sign language within the greater population often results in them being isolated and misunderstood in society. The need for change in this aspect therefore calls for creating a much more inclusive society. With advancement in technology, the growing potentiality is to bridge the communication gap with the use of automated hand gesture recognition systems [1][6]. In this paper, we are studying using MediaPipe technology in the design of an efficient and accessible system that translates hand sign gestures into spoken Marathi. The key landmarks on hands are identified that enable exact and fast interpretation of any type of gesture. Subsequently, the information will be processed and translated to Marathi text followed by natural voice output using TTS. The system emphasizes the Marathi language that is commonly spoken in the Indian state of Maharashtra and its surrounding regions, so it covers a large and linguistically diversified population [4][10]. A few of the significant benefits of using MediaPipe technology in gesture recognition are its real-time performance and robustness under varying illumination conditions and adaptability to any shapes and orientations of hands. The research further attends to cultural and linguistic matters so that the solution pursued stands right in the context while being user-friendly for all towards the grander goal for social and educational inclusion [3][7][9].

2 LITERATURE REVIEW

With the development of computer vision technologies and machine learning frameworks, sign language recognition (SLR) has experienced significant progress recently. With an eye toward the approaches, results, and constraints that help to highlight research gaps for Marathi Sign Language (MSL) recognition, below is a thorough assessment of twenty recent studies.

(1) Recognition of Sign languages MediaPipe-It has become somewhat well-known for its real-time hand-tracking features. Ghosh *et al.* [1] achieved 94% accuracy by combining it with Long Short-Term Memory (LSTM) networks for ASL identification, therefore displaying its potential. Zhang *et al.* [2] also emphasized MediaPipe's resilience in landmark detection; but its use to tasks particular to sign language is yet understudied. Applying MediaPipe with Support Vector Machines (SVM) for ISL, Halder and Tayade [3] obtained 98.95% accuracy in identifying stationary motions. These investigations did not, however, cover regional languages or dynamic gestures.
(2) Regional Language Focus and Marathi Sign Language -MSL research is somewhat lacking. Reporting above 95% accuracy, Dahibavkar *et al.* [4] used CNNs to identify Marathi alphabets. Although Shinde and Kagalkar [5] created an early-stage MSL recognition system without speech integration and real-time capability, these experiments underline the possibilities of MSL recognition but also the lack of systems able to manage dynamic gestures and offer vocal output.

DOI: 10.1201/9781003798514-46

(3) Dynamic gestural Recognition- Practical SLR systems depend critically on dynamic gesture recognition. Using a hybrid CNN-RNN model for ISL, Tiwari *et al.* [6] obtained great accuracy in dynamic gesture recognition. To attain state-of-the-art results similarly, Chakraborty *et al.* [7] integrated hand landmark detection with temporal networks such as LSTM and GRU. Though successful, these approaches are still unexplored for MSL.

(4) Regional Language Dataset Development- Lack of varied datasets presents a major obstacle in MSL recognition. While Singh *et al.* [9] used Generative Adversarial Networks (GANs) to increase datasets for lowresource languages, Ramesh *et al.* [8] underlined dataset diversity for enhanced recognition accuracy. Applying such methods to MSL would help to close this important void.

(5) Sign Language Systems' Speech Integration- SLR systems depend critically on speech synthesis. Though the system does not support regional languages, Aajmane *et al.* [10] combined MediaPipe with Google Text to–Speech (gTTS) for voice output. To enable smooth integration, Chavan *et al.* [11] presented a Marathi text-to-speech system to augment gesture recognition systems.

(6) Additional Contributions- Patel *et al.* [12] investigated multimodal techniques aiming at improved recognition accuracy by combining hand tracking with facial emotions. Whereas Desai *et al.* [15] used GANs to improve ISL datasets, Bansal *et al.* [14] offered data augmentation using Transformer models. Sharma *et al.* [16] and Kumar *et al.* [17] underlined the need of recurrent networks and temporal attention mechanisms in identifying dynamic gestures, hence stressing methods fit for MSL. Research gap identified based on literature are Though there have been significant developments, numerous regional language SLR still suffers: • Data Scarcity: Complete datasets for MSL, especially for dynamic motions, are few. Dynamic Gesture Recognition: Most of the research now under progress is on stationary gestures.

- Integration of Speech Output: Few systems provide Marathi real-time voice output.
- Real-time applications demand efficiency that current technologies lack for practical implementation.

3 PROPOSED METHODOLOGY

Real-Time Hand Gesture Recognition and Marathi Translation System Using MediaPipe and Deep Learning Models: The suggested method is based on building a hand sign gesture detection system to translate motions into spoken Marathi. This work addresses significant challenges in gesture detection including linguistic intricacies of the Marathi language, dynamic motions, and hand form variety. Included within the approach are MediaPipe for real-time hand tracking, complex neural networks for gesture categorization, and a text-to-speech (TTS) engine for natural language output.

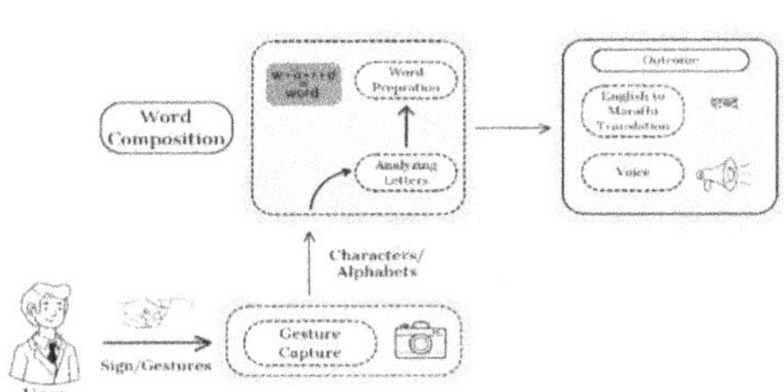

Figure 1 Architecture of proposed method.

Data collection is the first, where hand gestures are captured as video input and followed up for analysis. This phase helps ensure robustness in actual conditions like lighting changes, shape changes of hands, and orientations. The earlier research [6], [8] highlights the need for collecting good quality gesture data to improve system reliability. The raw input for the following steps comes in the form of video recordings.

The second step, data preparation, enhances the raw video inputs. It includes segmenting hand regions, video frames normalization to reduce lighting effects, and feature addition to enhance the accuracy of recognition. As discussed in previous studies [1], [4], preprocessing is essential in order to obtain accurate gesture recognition as it relies heavily on clean and consistent input data.

Feature extraction is performed through the use of the MediaPipe Hand Tracking module, which detects 21 significant hand landmarks and functions well under diverse conditions [3], [7], [9], [13]. This guarantees correct extraction of essential gesture components, the foundation of classification. MediaPipe's capability to work well in different hand shapes and orientations makes it suitable for real-time usage.

The system subsequently uses advanced models of neural networks like Convolutional Neural Networks (CNNs) and Long Short-Term Memory (LSTM) networks. CNNs extract spatial information appropriate for static gestures, whereas LSTMs work with temporal data for dynamic gestures. Spurred by approaches from previous research [11], [12], the hybrid model achieves high precision in gesture classification. The model is trained with a well-crafted dataset of Marathi sign gestures so that it is culturally and linguistically applicable.

After they are classified, the gestures are translated to their respective Marathi text in the translation step. The process considers the linguistic features of Marathi, such as syntax and grammar. Research [2], [5], [15] has emphasized the significance of proper gesture-to-language translation, such as that which appears in systems intended for Indian Sign Language (ISL).

After translation, a Text-to-Speech (TTS) engine translates the Marathi text into natural speech. It improves accessibility for users with speech or hearing disabilities and aids in communication in settings such as schools and hospitals [10], [16].

To make it usable in practice, the system is subjected to high-performance testing under variable conditions—lighting changes, differences in hand shapes, and varying orientations. Parameters like accuracy, latency, and reliability are tested [14], with optimization aimed at obtaining high reliability and minimal delay for real-time use.

Lastly, an intuitive interface raises the system's usability through the presentation of gestures identified and translated text together with auditory feedback. As emphasized by previous research works [15], it fosters inclusive interaction and communication.

By combining MediaPipe's hand-tracking capabilities with deep learning models and incorporating Marathi's linguistic and cultural context, the proposed system provides a comprehensive solution for gesture recognition and translation. It aims to bridge communication gaps and promote inclusivity for Marathi-speaking individuals with hearing or speech difficulties.

Algorithm

Inputs

- Video feed from a camera capturing hand gestures
- Pre-trained hand gesture classification model
- Pre-trained Text-to-Speech (TTS) model

Outputs

- Recognized gesture in Marathi text
- Spoken Marathi translation through TTS

Step 1: Initialize System Components

- Load the pre-trained MediaPipe Hand Tracking module to detect hand gestures.
- Load a pre-trained deep learning model, such as CNN or LSTM network, for accurate gesture classification.
- Use the Marathi TTS engine to generate audio from the translation.

Step 2: Capture Video Feed

- Capture video frames in real time from a camera.
- Validate that it is a proper video input, and if there's no feed, restart the camera with proper input.

Step 3: Preprocessing Video Input

- Convert each frame of the video into grayscale and apply preprocessing techniques.
- Normalize lighting conditions to ensure uniform video quality.
- Separate the hand region from the background for more accurate hand gesture recognition.

Step 4: Hand Gesture Detection using MediaPipe

- Use the Hand Tracking module of MediaPipe to identify and track 21 hand key points in each video frame.
- Track hand landmarks for feature extraction in subsequent steps.

Step 5: Feature Extraction

- Extract important features such as hand position, orientation, and shape based on the key hand landmarks.
- Convert these landmarks into a feature vector to feed into the classification model.

Step 6: Gesture Classification

- Feed the feature vector to the pre-trained gesture classification model, such as CNN or LSTM.
- Use learned patterns to classify the gesture and assign a corresponding label.

Step 7: Gesture to Marathi Text

- Use a pre-defined Marathi sign language dataset to map the identified gesture.
- Convert the gesture to its corresponding Marathi text representation, incorporating Marathi grammar and sentence structure.
- If the gesture is not recognized, display a "Gesture not recognized" message.

Step 8: Text-to-Speech (TTS) Conversion

- Input the translated Marathi text into the TTS engine.
- Generate natural-sounding Marathi speech corresponding to the text, with clear audio output.

Step 9: Output the Translation

- Display the Marathi text on the system's user interface in real time.
- Play the synthesized audio through speakers to provide both visual and auditory feedback.

Step 10: System Performance Evaluation

- Record primary performance metrics such as accuracy, latency, and robustness.
- Continuously test the system under real-world conditions, including variations in illumination and hand angles.

Step 11: Repeat Process

- Repeat the process for every captured frame to maintain real-time gesture recognition.

The proposed gesture classification model adopts hybrid architecture combining a Convolutional Neural Network (CNN) and a Long Short-Term Memory network (LSTM) for efficient recognition of both static and dynamic hand movements. The CNN module takes the coordinates of the 21 hand landmarks extracted per frame for processing to understand spatial relationships (for example, to determine the hand shape and finger orientations). It consists of three convolutional layers, each of which is followed by maxpooling to progressively filter spatial features. The output feature vectors produced by the CNN are fed into the LSTM module, which is responsible for modeling the temporal dependencies between multiple frames, an important consideration in accurate detection of dynamic gestures and continuous signing patterns. The LSTM module consists of two successive layers of 128 units each to efficiently capture sequential patterns. A fully connected softmax layer finally maps the learned representations to their respective gesture labels corresponding to alphabets, common words, and phrases. By utilizing the strength of CNNs for spatial representation and LSTMs for temporal representation, the hybrid network offers greater accuracy while maintaining a real-time pace for applications in gesture recognition.

4 RESULTS AND ANALYSIS

4.1 *Dataset Description and preprocessing*

A custom dataset with 1200 labeled samples was created, comprising 20 Marathi words (e.g., नमस्कार, धन्यवाद),

10 common phrases (e.g., "मी ठीक आहे," "आपणण शुभेच्छा "), and 26 static alphabetic gestures. Ten volunteers between the ages of 18 and 40 provided data, guaranteeing a range of hand shapes and movement patterns.

The aspects considered as follows:

Table 1. Aspects and their specifics.

Aspect	Specifics
Static hand motion	Single-frame capture (individual letters)
Dynamic hand motion	Multi-frame sequences (words and phrases)
Preprocessing Steps	• Conversion to grayscale Normalization of lighting (histogram equalization) • Subtraction of the background (MediaPipe segmentation) • Background subtraction (MediaPipe segmentation) • Normalization of landmarks (scaled to [0,1])
Data Augmentation	• Random rotations (±15°) • Zoom at random (90–110%) • Adjustment of brightness (±20%) • A small amount of Gaussian noise is added.

4.2 *Used hand gestures*

Figure 2. Hand sign gestures.

Figure 2 shows some of the gestures we used as input sign gestures, with each sign representing a specific alphabet or letter.

4.3 *Execution of some sample words*

4.3.1 *Hello Sir*

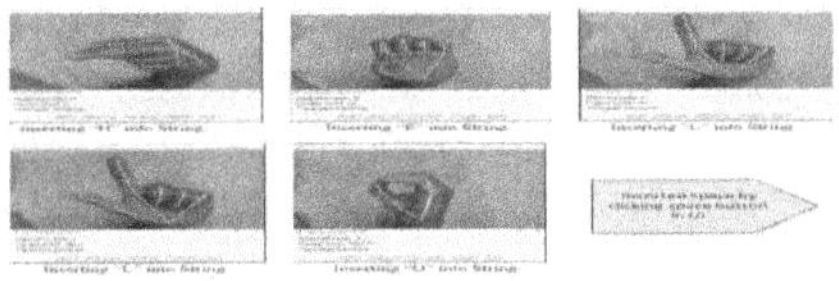

Figure 3. Sample Screenshot of HELLO<space>.

Figure 3 illustrates the insertion of letters from the word 'Hello.' Afterward, a space was added by clicking a button in the GUI.

4.3.2 *Artificial Inteligence*

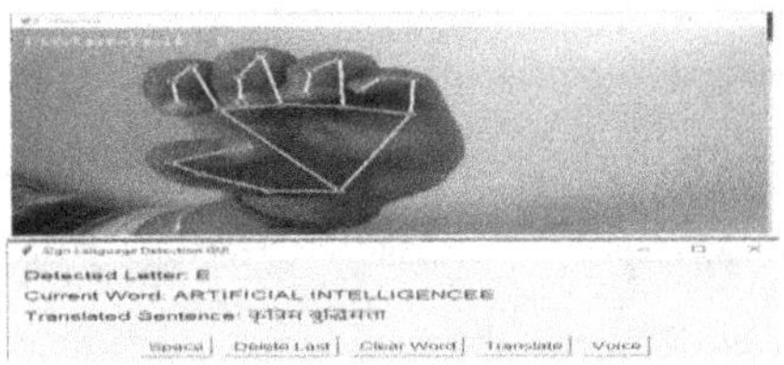

Figure 4. Sample output of a complex phrase.

4.4 *Confusion matrix*

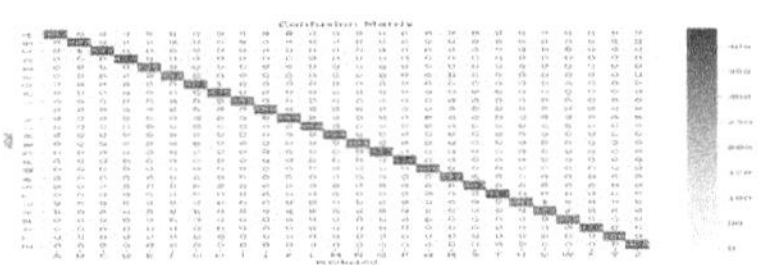

Figure 5. Confusion matrix.

It is a confusion matrix, a table for classification model performance. Rows are actual classes, columns are predicted classes and numbers in cells indicate how many instances belong to that class or not. This confusion matrix applies to a letter-prediction model. This one predicts the letters of the alphabet, does a wonderful job with the proper classification of most letters, and might need a little fiddling in terms of the appearance of letters similar to one another, such as "U" and "V". The off-diagonal regions are more important for computation, as they give information about wrongly classified instances, and the diagonal regions correctly classified instances.

Figure 6. Precision and recall.

Table 2. Precision and recall analysis.

Class	Precision	Recall	Observation
Class A-Z	Near 1.0	Near 1.0	High precision and recall across all classes, indicating excellent performance.
Overall	High Scores	High Scores	The precision-recall curve for all classes remains close to the top-right corner (ideal behavior).

4.5 *Precision and recall*

These results suggest the model is performing exceptionally well, with minimal misclassifications and nearly perfect precision and recall for all classes.

4.6 *Training and validation loss curve*

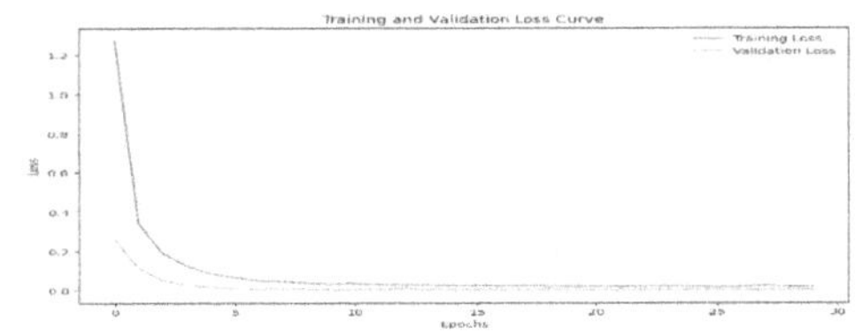

Figure 7. Training and validation loss curve.

The plot indicates the fluctuation in training loss and validation loss over 30 epochs of a neural network model. The training loss begins at approximately 1.3 and decreases rapidly, leveling off at close to 0.05. The validation loss also starts higher but levels off at about 0.03 by epoch 15 and only fluctuates slightly afterward. The steady reduction in both losses reflects proper learning at early training, although the tiny gap between them implies minimal overfitting. The model works most optimally at epoch 15, with consistent validation performance.

This system also enables dynamic phrase formation and rich sentence formation, in contrast to static gesture recognition. It has the incorporation of real-time Marathi speech synthesis, providing a rich user experience. It also shows robustness in different lighting, hand shape and position variations, and realizes high accuracy in isolated and continuous gesture recognition under realistic conditions.

Table 3. Comparative analysis with Existing system.

Method	Dataset Size	Accuracy	Dynamic Gesture Support	Speech Output
Ghosh *et al.* (MediaPipe + LSTM, ASL) [1]	1000 samples	94%	No	No
Halder and Tayade (MediaPipe + SVM, ISL) [3]	500 samples	98.95%	No	No
Dahibavkar *et al.* (CNN, Marathi Alphabets) [4]	600 samples	95%	No	No
Proposed System (Hybrid CNN +LSTM, MSL)	**1200 samples**	**96.50%**	**Yes**	**Yes**

5 CONCLUSION

This paper introduces a robust hand gesture recognition and translation system based on MediaPipe technology to enhance communication for individuals with speech or hearing disabilities, particularly in the case of the Marathi language. The system tracks hands in real-time, extracting 21 key landmarks from gestures and classifying them using either CNN or LSTM models.

The recognized gestures are translated into Marathi speech and text using a TTS engine, enabling application in classrooms, hospitals, and public places. It also accounts for changes in illumination and orientations to provide consistent real-time results.

Measurements with confusion matrices, precision-recall, ROC, and loss curves indicate potential accuracy and performance. With additional optimization to prevent overfitting, this work provides an effective assistive tool for fostering social and educational inclusion among Marathi-speaking populations.

ACKNOWLEDGEMENT

The authors express their sincere thanks for the support and collaboration of the Department of Artificial Intelligence and Data Science students, teaching staff, and officials of N. K. Orchid College of Engineering and Technology, Solapur. Their encouragement and support played an important role in completing this research work successfully.

REFERENCES

[1] Amitkumar A. Shinde and Ramesh M. Kagalkar, *Sign Language Recognition System in Marathi for Deaf Sign User*. [Online]. Available: https://www.academia.edu/35379621/Sign_Language_Recognition_Sy stem_in_Marathi_for_Deaf_Sign_User

[2] Prajakta Rokade, Archana Kadam, Dipti Shinde, Shalini Yadav and Neha Sali. (Dec 2018). Indian Sign Language Recognition System in Marathi Language Text. *International Journal of Computer Applications*. 182, 30, pp. 19–22. DOI=10.5120/ijca2018918202

[3] Amitkumar Shinde and Ramesh Kagalkar. (May2015). Advanced Marathi Sign Language Recognition using Computer Vision. *International Journal of Computer Applications*. 118, 13, pp. 1–7. DOI=10.5120/20802-3485

[4] Shraddha Giri and Ashwini Patil, (April 2024), Marathi Sign Language Recognition using MediaPipe and Deep Learning Algorithm, DOI: 10.21203/rs.3.rs-4210048/v1.

[5] Suvarna Rajesh. Bhagwat, Bhavsar R.P. and Pawar B.V. (28 April 2024), *Marathi to Indian Sign Language Machine Translation*, [Online]. Available: https://doi.org/10.1145/3664609

[6] Aditya A, Darekar and Narayan B. Pawar, (May 2022), *Marathi Sign Language Recognition for Physically Disabled People*, Volume 2, Issue 7, pp. 790–802.

[7] Ankita Harkude, Sarika Namade, Shefali Patil and Anita Morey. (April 2020). *Audio to Sign Language Translation for Deaf People*, Volume 9, Issue 10

[8] Amit Kumar Shinde and Ramesh Kagalkar. (December 2015). Sign Language to Text and Vice Versa Recognition using Computer Vision in Marathi. *National Conference on Advances in Computing*. NCAC2015, 1, pp. 23–28.

[9] Shivani Gujur, Supriya Hagawane, Rutuja Avhad and Aishwarya Kulkarni, (April 2023). *Deep Learning Based Sign Language Recognition for English and Marathi Language*, Volume 3, Issue 7, pp. 378–381.

[10] Asawari A. Joshi and Anita S. Walde, (April 2018), *Devnagari Sign Language Recognition*, Volume 6, Issue 2, pp. 992–995.

[11] Shivani Deshpande and Rajashree Shettar, (November 2023), *Hand Gesture Recognition Using MediaPipe and CNN for Indian Sign Language and Conversion to Speech Format for Indian Regional Languages*, DOI: 10.1109/CSITSS60515.2023.10334218

[12] Dr. Velmathi G and Kaushal Goyal, (April 2023), *Indian Sign Language Recognition Using Mediapipe Holistic*, DOI:10.48550/arXiv.2304.10256

[13] Laveen Chandwani, Jaydeep Khilari and Kunal Gurjar, (June 28th, 2023), *Gesture based Sign Language Recognition system using Mediapipe*, Available: https://doi.org/10.21203/rs.3.rs-3106646/v1

[14] Poornima B.V., Srinath S. (Jan 2023). A Comprehensive Review on Indian Sign Language Recognition System using Vision based Approaches. *International Journal of Computer Applications*. 184, 43, 52- 58. DOI=10.5120/ijca2023922548

[15] Pratik Dahatonde, Prathmesh Khandekar and Omkar Kharat, (May 2024), *Sign Language Recognition And Translation To English And Marathi*, Volume 12, Issue 5, pp. 481–488.

[16] Siva Sankar, (April 2024), *A Deep Learning Approach for Real-Time Sign Language Detection and Response through Avatar Model*, DOI: 10.22214/ijraset.2024.60904

[17] Dhruv Biyani, Nitka Vats Doohan, Manas Rode and Darshan Jain, (July 2023), *Real Time Sign Language Recognition Using Yolov5*, DOI:10.1109/AIC57670.2023.10263913

Advancement in Engineering and Science – Goyal et al. (Eds)

A Comprehensive Review on Sustainable Management of Ready-Mix Concrete Waste

Aparna V. Phalake
Research Scholar, Civil Engineering Department, COEP Tech. University Pune, Maharashtra, India

Gayatri S. Vyas
Assistant Professor, Civil Engineering Department, COEP Tech. University Pune, Maharashtra, India

Rupa S. Dalvi
Associate Professor, Civil Engineering Department, COEP Tech. University Pune, Maharashtra, India

ABSTRACT: This study highlights the critical role of sustainable materials in mitigating pressing environmental issues, particularly the growing volume of ready-mix concrete waste. It focuses on effectively utilizing supplementary cementing material (SCM) and recycled concrete coarse aggregate (RCCA) from ready mix concrete as ecofriendly alternatives in construction, offering benefits such as reduced landfill dependency, lower carbon emissions, and enhanced sustainability.

Emphasizing the 3R principles, suchas Reduce, Reuse, and Recycle, this study advocates for improved resource conservation and waste management in construction practices. Additionally, it explores emerging trends, including advancements in recycling technologies, the acceptance of circular economy frameworks, and the execution of stricter environmental regulations. This study accounts for the importance of collaboration and awareness of cross sectors to drive innovation and embed sustainability into construction processes. Ultimately, these strategies performed a vital role in reducing environmental impact, enhancing economic efficiency, and fostering resilient, climate-conscious communities.

Keywords: Ready mix concrete waste, recycled concrete coarse aggregate (RCCA), supplementary cementiting material (SCM), sustainability, circular economy framework

1 INTRODUCTION

The escalating consequences of finite resources and waste accumulation have made sustainable waste management in construction increasingly critical. Global municipal solid waste is projected to rise from 2.1 billion tonnes in 2023 to 3.8 billion tonnes by 2050 (World Bank 2018). Construction and demolition (C&D) waste generates 10 billion tonnes annually, making it a major source of environmental degradation of the building life cycle (UNEP 2023). With increasing infrastructure demands due to population growth and development, construction waste poses sustainability challenges. Proper management enables reuse and recycling, supporting sustainability objectives and environmental footprint reduction (Tam *et al.* 2020). The escalating consequences of finite resources and waste accumulation have made sustainable waste management in construction increasingly critical. Global municipal solid waste is projected to rise from 2.1billion tonnes in 2023 to 3.8 billion tonnes by 2050 (World Bank 2018). Construction and demolition (C&D) waste generates approximately 10 billion tonnes annually, making it a most expected contributor to environmental degradation throughout the building lifecycle (UNEP 2023). Global concrete production reaches 30 billion tonnes annually, with ready-mix concrete accounting for 5.56 billion tonnes. Approximately 4% of fresh concrete from ready-mix operations is returned unused to RMC plants globally. With increasing infrastructure demands due to population growth and development, construction waste poses sustainability challenges. Proper management enables reuse and recycling, supporting sustainability objectives and environmental footprint reduction (Tam *et al.* 2020). Reusing readymix concrete waste preserves natural resources with decreasing construction costs and greenhouse gas emissions, supporting UN Sustainable Development Goals. Recycled coarse aggregates (RCA) and supplementary materials such as fly ash serve as sustainable alternatives. RCA from crushed concrete waste reduces landfill dependency, preserves natural aggregates, and lowers carbon footprint without compromising performance (Poon *et al.* 2002).

Table 1. Global Concrete waste statistics.

Category	Amount
Global Concrete Production	30 Billion tonnes
Ready Mix Concrete Production	5.56 Billion Tonnes
Leftover/ Unused Ready Mix	222.4 Million Tonnes

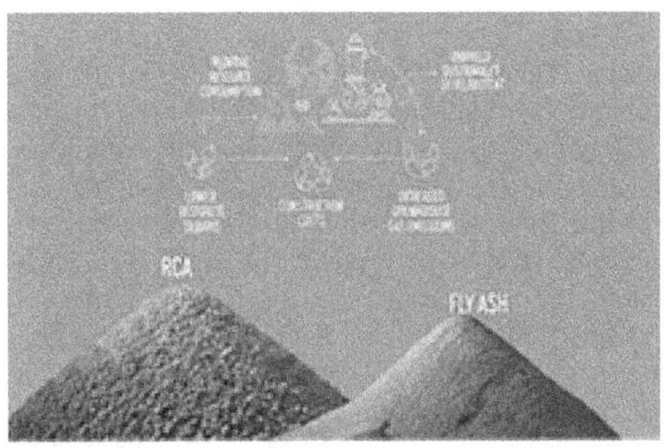

Figure 1: Sustainable concrete waste

Fly-ash enhances concrete workability and strength while reducing Portland cement demand and CO2 emissions (Singh *et al.*). Efficient material utilization and precise construction methods minimize waste and landfill pressure (Akbarnezhad *et al.* 2016). Using cost-effective sustainable materials maintains performance while reducing expenses (Zhao *et al.* 2010). Low embodied energy materials significantly reduce carbon emissions (Cabeza *et al.* 2014). Sustainable construction emphasizes recyclable materials that reduce toxic outputs and enhance energy efficiency. Construction activities consume 50% of global raw materials (OECD 2022), while construction waste from

DOI: 10.1201/9781003798514-47

renovation and demolition accounts for 30% of total solid waste (Eurostat 2021). Countries are implementing policies to minimize construction waste and encourage recycling (EPA 2020). Life cycle management focusing on reduce, reuse, and recycle principles enhances resource efficiency (Yuan 2013). Waste from ready-mix concrete can become recycled aggregates and road materials (Lu and Yuan 2011). These innovations, combined with regulations, shape eco-friendly construction practices.

1.1 *Renewable and recycled construction materials*

Sustainable construction materials provide environmental, economic, social, and technological benefits that support global development goals. They reduce waste, pollution, and carbon emissions through low-embodied energy materials like bamboo, mass timber, and recycled steel (Asif 2009; Cabeza *et al.* 2014). Economically, they lower construction and lifecycle costs, benefit from green certifications and incentives, and increase asset value (Zuo and Zhao 2014). Social and technological advantages include healthier indoor environments, job creation, and innovations such as biomaterials, prefabrication, and IoT-enabled monitoring (EPA 2020; Kibert 2016). This study promotes using recycled materials like RCA and fly ash and applying 3R waste management strategies to conserve resources, reduce landfill use, and lower construction carbon footprint.

2 LITERATURE REVIEW

Incorporating sustainable materials is crucial to address environmental challenges, particularly the 5.56 billion tonnes of ready-mix concrete waste generated annually, with 4% returned unused. Alternatives such as recycled coarse aggregates (RCA) and fly ash reduce natural resource consumption, landfill demand, and CO_2 emissions (Singh *et al.* 2015; Tam *et al.* 2020). RCA preserves virgin aggregates without compromising strength (Poon *et al.* 2004), while fly ash enhances durability and lowers cement-related emissions (Mehta and Monteiro 2014).

Cement partially replaced with that is up to 15% in terms of eggshell powder (ESP), red mud (RM), and C&D waste maintains or improves strength (Gulati *et al.*), and 20% fly ash substitution reduces environmental impact (Orozco *et al.*). Waste Paper Sludge Ash and GGBFS also improve strength despite lower workability (Ingale *et al.*). RCA exhibits robust performance at 10 to 30% replacement, further enhanced by acid washing, carbonation, or cement coating (Singh *et al.*; Sahare *et al.*; Ramalingam *et al.*; Panghal *et al.*). Pre-treated recycled fine aggregates (RFA) can replace up to 50% of natural sand without loss of performance, outperforming alternatives like brick powder and SPT (Lusi *et al.*; Udarika *et al.*; Oikonomopoulou *et al.*). CDW derived aggregates meet performance standards while reducing cement demand (Silva *et al.*; Contreras Llanes *et al.*). Durability improvements include PEG 400 (1%, w/c 0.3) in self-cured concrete with 50% RCA (Dinesh *et al.*) and internal curing using distorted brick chips (Masum *et al.*). Ceramic tiles and sanitary waste used as aggregates and partial cement replacements enhance strength, especially when reinforced with steel fibers (Paul *et al.*; Ahmad *et al.*).

Self-compacting geopolymer concrete (SCGC) with RCA, fly ash, and slag achieved up to 77 MPa with mix adjustments (Sherwani *et al.*), while combining RCA with GGBS and improved mechanical properties are improved by fly ash via pozzolanic synergy (Sarma *et al.*). RAC-based RC frames demonstrated comparable seismic performance to natural aggregate concrete (Khan *et al.* Simona 2024; Bhatta *et al.*). AI/Machine learning predictive models (ANN, Random Forest, ANFIS) effectively predicted strength of concrete in compression and waste generation, optimizing mix design and sustainability (Ahmad *et al.*; Sobuz *et al.*; Jafari *et al.*), and reusing fibers and ready-mix wastewater enhanced performance and resource efficiency (Neelamegam *et al.*; Pratap *et al.*). Concrete incorporating multiple wastes—glass, rubber, plastic, timber ash, and RCA—maintains strength while reducing carbon footprint and costs (Gerges *et al.*; Mittal *et al.*), and treated recycled concrete can reach 35 MPa with improved durability and reduced shrinkage (Etxeberria *et al.*; Tolypina *et al.*).

The future of sustainable construction is promising, driven by advances in recycling, stricter regulations, and growing climate awareness, with public-private partnerships and education accelerating innovation and material circularity (Galvez-Martos *et al.* 2018; Yuan 2013; Zuo and Zhao 2014).

3 RESEARCH GAP & MOTIVATION

The study lacks exploration of mitigation strategies using superplasticizers, and research on acid resistance, freeze-thaw cycles, degradation, and lifecycle assessment is needed. Long-term durability, shrinkage behavior, and field performance under varied conditions remain underexplored (Simona 2024; Tolypina *et al.* 2024). Few studies validate AI/ML predictions at full structural scale (Ahmad *et al.* 2024; Jafari *et al.* 2024). Mix design optimization has been limited to fixed proportions without systematic evaluation for strength and durability (Sobuz *et al.* 2023; Singh *et al.* 2022). Water reuse in concrete requires broader impact studies (Pratap *et al.* 2024). Recycled fine aggregates (RFA) receive less attention than RCA and underperform without proper treatment (Oikonomopoulou *et al.* 2023; Udarika *et al.* 2023). Although some research evaluates recycled concrete in seismic zones (Khan *et al.* 2023; Simona 2024), further structural modeling and real-world seismic testing are necessary.

4 FUTURE PROSPECTS

Advances in technology are shaping the future of sustainable construction materials, alongside evolving regulations and growing global attention to environmental sustainability. New recycling methods will improve the efficiency and quality of converting construction and demolition waste into high-performance materials, reducing dependence on virgin resources. The expectations of construction industry is to adopt circular economy principles, focusing on resource efficiency, waste minimization, and material recovery through designs that support reuse and recycling. Additionally, governments may implement stricter environmental regulations and offer incentives, such as tax breaks and preferential procurement, to encourage the adoption of recycled and recycled materials of construction.

5 CONCLUSION

Integrating recycled and reused materials of construction and practices helps to mitigate environmental impact while increasing economic efficiency and community resilience, supporting global climate goals and low-impact building strategies. Literature shows that substituting up to partial cement replacement (15%) with SCMs) enhances mechanical properties, confirmed by microstructural analysis. Studies relevant with life cycle suggests that more than 90% of concrete's health-related impacts stem from global warming and fine particulate matter, while a 20% fly ash substitution improves resource efficiency. Recycled coarse aggregates (RCA) concrete experiences more than 19.4% reduction in compressive, flexural, and tensile strength, making up to 10% replacement viable. Fine aggregates from ready-mix concrete waste can partially or fully substitute natural sand without degrading performance. The results imply that sustainable concrete technologies, guided by empirical research and predictive tools, are ready for wider application. Further investigation should focus on scaling innovations, refining AI-based mix optimization, and establishing policies to advance resilient, low-carbon construction globally.

DECLARATIONS

FUNDING

No funding is available

ETHICAL APPROVAL

Not applicable

COMPETING INTERESTS

No conflicts of interest are declared by the authors

ACKNOWLEDGEMENT

The authors gratefully acknowledge the students, guide, and Department of Civil Engineeringfor their support in the research.

REFERENCES

Ahmad D.A., Al Goody A.Y., Askari D.F.A., Ahmad M.R.J., and Ahmad S.A., (Jun. 2025), Evaluating the effect of using waste concrete as partial replacement of coarse aggregate in concrete, experimental and modeling, *Journal of Building Pathology and Rehabilitation*, vol. 10, no. 1, p. 11, Doi: 10.1007/s41024-024-00521-4.

Ahmad S., Khan R.A., Shamim S., and Chandra U., (Aug. 2023), Effect of waste ceramic sanitary ware as partial replacement of aggregates and cement in concrete, *Innovative Infrastructure Solutions*, vol. 8, no. 8, p. 205, Doi: 10.1007/s41062-023-01166-x.

Akbarnezhad A., Ong K.C.G., Tam C.T., and Zhang M.H., (Dec. 2013), Effects of the Parent Concrete Properties and Crushing Procedure on the Properties of Coarse Recycled Concrete Aggregates, *Journal of Materials in Civil Engineering*, vol. 25, no. 12, pp. 1795–1802, Doi: 10.1061/(ASCE)MT.1943-5533.0000789.

Asif, M. (2009). *Sustainability of construction materials.* Woodhead Publishing.

Atta I. and Bakhoum E.S., (Feb. 2024), Environmental feasibility of recycling construction and demolition waste, *International Journal of Environmental Science and Technology*, vol. 21, no. 3, pp. 2675–2694, Doi: 10.1007/s13762-023-05036-y.

Bhatta N., Adhikari A., Ghimire A., Bhandari N., Subedi A., and Sahani K., (Dec. 2024), Comparing Crushed Brick as Coarse Aggregate Substitute in Concrete: Experimental vs. Numerical Study, *Iranian Journal of Science and Technology, Transactions of Civil Engineering*, vol. 48, no. 6, pp. 4255–4274, Doi: 10.1007/s40996-024-01407-8.

Cabeza L.F., Rincón L., Vilariño V., Pérez G., and Castell A., (Jan. 2014), Life cycle assessment (LCA) and life cycle energy analysis (LCEA) of buildings and the building sector: A review, *Renewable and Sustainable Energy Reviews*, vol. 29, pp. 394–416, Doi: 10.1016/j.rser.2013.08.037.

Chitra V., Kavyashree, Kumar S., Rahul. B. Rathod, and Anitha Kumari S.D., (2024), *Recycled Construction and Demolition Waste as Aggregates: A Study*, pp. 363–373. Doi: 10.1007/978-981-99-8465-7_26.

Devaki H. and Shanmugapriya S., (May 2025), Lifecycle assessment on construction and demolition waste management-an Indian case study, *Clean Technol Environ Policy*, vol. 27, no. 5, pp. 1961–1979, Doi: 10.1007/s10098-024-02948-2.

Dinesh S.V., Mamatha K.H., and Susheel Kumar G., (Jun. 2023), Effect of Recycled Concrete Aggregates on The Mechanical and Durability Properties of Self-Cured Concrete for Sustainable Construction, *International Journal of System Assurance Engineering and Management*, vol. 14, no. 3, pp. 865–877, Doi: 10.1007/s13198-023-01886-4.

EPA (2020). *Sustainable Management of Construction and Demolition Materials.*

Etxeberria M. and Vintimilla C., (2023), *Influence of Treated Mixed Recycled Aggregates in Concrete Properties*, pp. 963–972. Doi: 10.1007/978-3-031-21735-7_102.

Eurostat (2021). *Waste Statistics – Statistics Explained.* https://ec.europa.eu/eurostat/statistics-explained/

Gabryś K., (Jul. 2023), Experimental research on compressibility characteristics of recycled concrete aggregate: recycled tire waste mixtures, *J Mater Cycles Waste Manag*, vol. 25, no. 4, pp. 1966–1977, Doi: 10.1007/s10163-023-01694-9.

Gulati R., Bano S., Bano F., Singh S., and Singh V., (Sep. 2024), Compressive Strength of Concrete Formulated with Waste Materials Using Neural Networks, *Asian Journal of Civil Engineering*, vol. 25, no. 6, pp. 4657–4672, Doi: 10.1007/s42107-024-01071-3.

Hanuseac L.G. and Barbuta M., (2024), *Experimental Study with Tests on Non-structural Concrete Elements with Recycled Concrete Aggregates*, pp. 453–470. Doi: 10.1007/978-3-031-60765-3_36.

Ingale S.D. and Nemade P.D., (May 2024), *Impact of Wpsa and Ggbs as a Partial Cement Replacement on The Hardening Characteristics of Cement Concrete, Innovative Infrastructure Solutions*, vol. 9, no. 5, p. 152, Doi: 10.1007/s41062-024-01477-7.

Jaradat O. *et al.*, (Nov. 2024), Sustainable valorisation of sand concrete properties using quarry waste as crushed sand, *Asian Journal of Civil Engineering*, vol. 25, no. 7, pp. 5533–5546, Doi: 10.1007/s42107-024-01127-4.

Khan A.R., Fareed S., and Khalid F., (Jun. 2025), Simulation of Reinforced Recycled Aggregate Concrete Frames Subjected to Seismic Loading, *Arab J Sci Eng*, vol. 50, no. 11, pp. 8127–8141, Doi: 10.1007/s13369-024-09172-6.

Lusi T. and Mishra S., (2024), *Experimental Conduct on Classified Fine Recycled Aggregate of Construction and Demolition (C and D) Waste as Replacement of Sand*, pp. 45–52. Doi: 10.1007/978-981-97-2704-9_5.

Maksudur Rahman M., Haughton G., and Jonas A.E.G., (Oct. 2010), The challenges of local environmental problems facing the urban poor in Chittagong, Bangladesh: a scale-sensitive analysis, *Environ Urban*, vol. 22, no. 2, pp. 561–578, Doi: 10.1177/0956247810377560.

Masum A.T.M., Rahman M.R., Kafi M.A., Ghimire S., Akter S., and Manzur T., (Aug. 2023), Potential of waste distorted bricks to produce internally cured concrete under adverse curing conditions, *Innovative Infrastructure Solutions*, vol. 8, no. 8, p. 210, Doi: 10.1007/s41062-023-01179-6.

Mittal A., Singh A., Chaudhary A.K., and Kumar A., (2024), *Lightweight Concrete by Using Waste Materials*, pp. 73–85. Doi: 10.1007/978-981-99-2676-3_7.

Monika F., Prayuda H., Putri W.P.A.P., Saputro I., and Luthanzah T. R., Influence of mixed recycled coarse aggregate on the engineering properties of recycled aggregate concrete, *Journal of Building Pathology and Rehabilitation*, vol. 8, no. 2, p. 102, Dec. 2023, Doi: 10.1007/s41024-023-00350-x.

OECD (2022). *Global Material Resources Outlook to 2060.* Organisation for Economic Co-operation and Development.

Oikonomopoulou K., Savva P., Ioannou S., Nicolaides D., and Petrou M.F., (2022), *Production of Recycled Aggregate Concrete Using Construction and Demolition Waste*, pp. 267–277. Doi: 10.1007/978-3-030-76465-4_24.

Paul S.C., Faruky S.A.U., Babafemi A.J., and Miah M.J., (Dec. 2023), Eco-friendly concrete with waste ceramic tile as coarse aggregate: mechanical strength, durability, and microstructural properties, *Asian Journal of Civil Engineering*, vol. 24, no. 8, pp. 3363–3373, Doi: 10.1007/s42107-023-00718-x.

Poon C.S., (Jan. 2007), Management of construction and demolition waste, *Waste Management*, vol. 27, no. 2, pp. 159–160, Doi: 10.1016/j.wasman.2006.10.012.

Poon C.S., Kou S.C., and Lam L., (Jul. 2002), Use of recycled aggregates in molded concrete bricks and blocks, *Constr Build Mater*, vol. 16, no. 5, pp. 281–289, Doi: 10.1016/S0950-0618(02)00019-3.

Poon C.S., Kou S.C., and Lam L., (Jul. 2002), Use of recycled aggregates in molded concrete bricks and blocks, *Constr Build Mater*, vol. 16, no. 5, pp. 281–289, Doi: 10.1016/S0950-0618(02)00019-3.

Pratap B., Kumar P., Shubham K., and Chaudhary N., (Feb. 2024), Soft computing-based investigation of mechanical properties of concrete using ready-mix concrete waste water as partial replacement of mixing portable water, *Asian Journal of Civil Engineering*, vol. 25, no. 2, pp. 1255–1266, Doi: 10.1007/s42107-023-00841-9.

Qasim O.A., Hilal N., Al Biajawi M.I., Sor N.H., and Tawfik T.A., (Dec. 2024), Studying the usability of recycled aggregate to produce new concrete, *Journal of Engineering and Applied Science*, vol. 71, no. 1, p. 129, Doi: 10.1186/s44147-024-00463-1.

Ramalingam M., Sivamani J., and Narayanan K., (Dec. 2023), Performance studies on recycled aggregate concrete with treated recycled aggregates, *Waste Dispos Sustain Energy*, vol. 5, no. 4, pp. 451–459, Doi: 10.1007/s42768-023-00157-z.

Sahu A., Kumar S., and Srivastava A.K.L., (2023), *Combined Use of Fine and Coarse Recycled Concrete Aggregates in Concrete for Sustainable Development: A Review*, pp. 501–516. Doi: 10.1007/978-981-19-3371-4_43.

Sherwani A.F.H., Younis K.H., Arndt R.W., and Pilakoutas K., (Aug. 2024), Influence of slag and recycled concrete aggregates contents on the performance of fly ash based self-compacted geopolymer concrete, *Innovative Infrastructure Solutions*, vol. 9, no. 8, p. 331, Doi: 10.1007/s41062-024-01641-z.

Silva F.A.N., Silva M.T.A., Lopes F.A.F., Delgado J.M.P.Q., and Azevedo A.C., (2022), *Use of Construction Waste to Replace Conventional Aggregate in Reinforced Concrete Production*, pp. 109–121. Doi: 10.1007/978-3-030-95487-1_6.

Simona S., (2024), *Reuse of Construction Waste*, pp. 198–209. Doi: 10.1007/978-3-031-54664-8_19.

Singh N. and Gupta A., (Dec. 2024), Use of recycled coarse aggregate for M40 grade concrete, *Journal of Building Pathology and Rehabilitation*, vol. 9, no. 2, p. 90, Doi: 10.1007/s41024-024-00440-4.

Singh S., Allen A.M., Wang Z., Prokop L.J., Murad M.H., and Loomba R., (Apr. 2015), Fibrosis Progression in Nonalcoholic Fatty Liver vs Nonalcoholic Steatohepatitis: A Systematic Review and Meta-analysis of Paired-Biopsy Studies, *Clinical Gastroenterology and Hepatology*, vol. 13, no. 4, pp. 643–654.e9, Doi: 10.1016/j.cgh.2014.04.014.

Tam V.W.Y., Soomro M., and Evangelista A.C.J., (May 2018), A review of recycled aggregate in concrete applications (2000–2017), *Constr Build Mater*, vol. 172, pp. 272–292, Doi: 10.1016/j.conbuildmat.2018.03.240.

Tam V.W.Y., Tam C.M., Zeng S.X., and Ng W.C.Y., (Oct. 2007), Towards adoption of prefabrication in construction, *Build Environ*, vol. 42, no. 10, pp. 3642–3654, Doi: 10.1016/j.buildenv.2006.10.003.

Tolypina N.M., Khakhaleva E.N., Tolypin D.A., Korshunova N.N., and Sabitov L.S., (2024), *Resistance of Fine Concrete on Concrete Scrap Aggregate*, pp. 160–166. Doi: 10.1007/978-3-031-44432-6_21.

Udarika R.N. and Pathirana C.K., (2024), *Improving Mixed Construction and Demolition Waste Used as Fine Aggregates in Concrete Production by Physical Pre-treatment*, pp. 3–16. Doi: 10.1007/978-981-97-3737-6_1.

UNEP (2023). *Global Waste Management Outlook 2023*. United Nations Environment Programme.

United States Environmental Protection Agency. Eurostat (2021). *Waste Statistics - Statistics Explained*. https://ec.europa.eu/eurostat/statistics-explained/

Waste Materials and By-Products in Concrete. Berlin, Heidelberg: Springer Berlin Heidelberg, 2008. Doi: 10.1007/978-3-540-74294-4.

World Bank (2018). *What a Waste 2.0: A Global Snapshot of Solid Waste Management to 2050*. World Bank Group.

Yuan H. (Jan. 2013), A SWOT analysis of successful construction waste management, *J Clean Prod*, vol. 39, pp. 1–8, Doi: 10.1016/j.jclepro.2012.08.016.

Yuan H. and Shen L., (Apr. 2011), Trend of the research on construction and demolition waste management, *Waste Management*, vol. 31, no. 4, pp. 670–679, Doi: 10.1016/j.wasman.2010.10.030.

Yuan H., (Jan. 2013), A SWOT analysis of successful construction waste management, *J Clean Prod*, vol. 39, pp. 1–8, Doi: 10.1016/j.jclepro.2012.08.016.

Zhao J., Sun X., Fang J., Liu W., Feng C., and Jiang L., (Mar. 2010), Identification and characterization of the type 2C protein phosphatase Ptc4p in the human fungal pathogen Candida albicans., *Yeast*, vol. 27, no. 3, pp. 149–57, Doi: 10.1002/yea.1739.

Zhao W., Leeftink R.B., and Rotter V.S., (Apr. 2010), Evaluation of the economic feasibility for the recycling of construction and demolition waste in China—The case of Chongqing, *Resour Conserv Recycl*, vol. 54, no. 6, pp. 377–389, Doi: 10.1016/j.resconrec.2009.09.003.

Zuo J. and Zhao Z.-Y., (Feb. 2014), Green building research–current status and future agenda: A review, *Renewable and sustainable energy reviews*, vol. 30, pp. 271–281, Doi: 10.1016/j.rser.2013.10.021.

Advancement in Engineering and Science – Goyal et al. (Eds)
© 2026 The Author(s), ISBN: 978-1-041-31101-0

Comprehensive Survey of Machine Learning Approaches in Drug Toxicity Prediction

Ayesha Memon and T.R. Pattanshetti
Department of Computer Science and Engineering, COEP Technological University, Maharashtra, India

ABSTRACT: Toxicity prediction ranks high among the drug research challenges that have greatly contributed to decreased drug failure rates, development cost savings, and minimizing the application of animal models. Coming prominently to address this challenge in the last decade is the application of machine learning (ML) methods for enabling early-stage toxicity prediction through computational simulations. This paper provides a comprehensive review of recent ML approaches in the field, with emphasis on issues such as the origin of the datasets, the choice of the algorithms, feature engineering, validation steps, and interpretability techniques. The transition from traditional QSAR models to cutting-edge neural networks is emphasized, with special emphasis on the combination of self-supervised learning as well as transfer learning with explainable AI tools such as graph neural networks. The article also details strategies to tackle data limitation, as well as the validation of the model, through the use of data augmentation, federated learning, as well as uncertainty estimation. This integration presents practical recommendations to the dynamic field of toxicity prediction with the help of ML and identifies future research avenues towards establishing chemical safety evaluation as less animal-centric and efficient.

Keywords: Drug toxicity prediction, QSAR, deep learning, multi-modal data, explainable AI, toxicity endpoints

1 INTRODUCTION

One of the most challenging issues in drug research and development is still to predict a drug's toxicity. The accurate forecast of the drug's adverse drug reaction during drug development plays the key role in reducing failure rates, costs, and reliance on animal studies [1][2]. The machine learning (ML) approaches throughout the years (2020–2024) emerged very quickly in the field with the advances of strong computational tools that accompany and facilitate the traditional lab-based toxicity evaluation [3]. The drug industry struggles considerably with drug development, as about 30% of candidate compounds are withdrawn because of issues of safety and toxicity [4][5]. Events of this kind are extremely expensive to the extent that they are seen to happen during late-stage clinicals or after marketing, highlighting the potential benefit of better early toxicity forecasting techniques [6, 7]. Machine learning offers helpful solutions through the use of huge chemical and biological data sets to find connections and patterns that traditional methods can overlook [8]. These new technologies of artificial intelligence as well as the unexpected surge in the availability of biomedical data have provided hit hitherto unimaginable opportunities to construct new computational platforms to predict toxicity [9]. They encompass a whole range of methodologies that extend from the classical quantitative structure-activity relationship or (QSAR) models strengthened with the most recent ML algorithms to elaborate deep learning architectures that can deal with hundreds of modalities of chemical/biochemical information [10, 11].

1.1 *Scope of the review*

This is a comprehensive review that surveys cutting-edge machine learning methods that appeared between 2020 and 2024 to forecast drug toxicity. We extensively survey such methodologies across the following dimensions:

1. Characteristics of the dataset: Comparison of data sources, sizes, quality, and preprocessing measures utilized in the studies.
2. Algorithm selection: Classical ML versus the latest deep learning strategies with architectural advances highlighted.
3. Strategies of feature engineering: Comparison between molecular descriptor selection, representation learning, and multiple modes integration strategies.
4. Validation procedures: Testing of cross-validation strategies, external validation procedures, as well as studies of domain applicability.
5. Performance measures: Comparison of accuracy of prediction [12], sensitivity [12], specificity [12], etc. between varied toxicity endpoints.
6. Interpretability techniques: Assessments of method explaining model predictions and identify in toxicophore.

Table 1. Benchmark datasets used in toxicity prediction.

Dataset	Type	Access Link
Tox21	Secondary	https://tox21.nih.gov
ToxCast	Secondary	https://epa.gov/toxcast
ClinTox	Secondary	https://deepchem.io
DILIrank	Secondary	https://fda.gov/dilirank
ChEMBL	Secondary	https://www.ebi.ac.uk/chembl

1.2 *Inclusion and exclusion criteria of the study*

This review includes peer literature from 2020 to 2024 that applies machine learning methods to drug toxicity endpoints including hepatotoxicity, cardiotoxicity, nephrotoxicity, and general ADMET properties. Studies were selected with regard to relevance, innovation in method, as well as availability of performance measures. Papers that rely on traditional QSAR frameworks without incorporation of ML, or without validation outcome, were rejected. DILIrank, Tox21, ToxCast, and ClinTox were taken as a unifying field of comparison as publicly available data sets.

1.3 *Dataset features*

Comparison of the data sources, sizes, quality, and preprocessing strategies used in research. The majority of the research included publicly available benchmark datasets such as Tox21, ToxCast, ClinTox, and DILIrank that form the secondary

DOI: 10.1201/9781003798514-48

datasets purified for computational toxicology research. The most commonly used datasets with their repository URLs and data types are given in Table 1.

These data sets are popular because they are easy to access with standardized chemical format representations. They facilitate reproducibility as well as the benchmarking of ML models used in predicting toxicity [13, 14, 15, 16].

2 DETAILED PAPER REVIEW

2.1 *Machine learning techniques to predict drug toxicity*

The first toxicity prediction strategies were largely based on feature selection methods and classical machine learning models. Random Forest [17] models with random under-sampling [18]. One study addressed the task of dealing with the highly imbalanced data in the Tox21. The research showed that various molecular descriptors proved to be of different importance levels depending on the specific toxicity endpoint to be predicted. Molecular properties, connectivity, and Burden descriptors proved to be most influential in the Nuclear Receptor tasks, whereas molecular properties, Charged Partial Surface Area descriptors, and the autocoradoration descriptors proved to be most influential in Stress Response tasks.

These inequalities reflect that the performance of models is generally endpoint-specific. Accordingly, descriptors that are highly competitive for Nuclear Receptor activities (e.g., the Burden descriptors) can be uncompetitive for Stress Response endpoints. Analyses suggested few models, e.g., RF, are of high performance in highly physiochemically correlated tasks. Graph Neural Networks (GNNs) prevail at endpoints that are structural inference-related, such as cardiotoxicity or drug-induced liver injury (DILI) [19, 20]. This recognition of the biological processes underlying each endpoint can aid the selection of the right model as well as molecular feature representation schemes.

Another research study comprehensively assessed 16 various machine learning models with 14 different QSAR data sets. The models were categorized into four general classes: linear methods (such as LinearGPR, PLSR, LinearSVM, PCR and the MLR), analogy-based models (like KNN, RBF-SVM, and RBF-GPR), rule-based or symbolic learners (like XGBoost [21], Cubist, Random Forest, MARS, GBM, and CART), as well as neural network-based models (like PCA-ANN as well as deep neural networks [22]. Their meticulous validation based on criteria such as the Q^2, MAEcv, RMSEcv the R^2t, as well as RMSET and MAET identified, XGBoost, RBF-SVM as well as RBF-GPR as the top-performing models consistently. The recommendation of the study of XGBoost for regression modeling with limited data pointed to the significance of achieving a balance between prediction accuracy [12] as well as computational cost.

Another significant innovation during this phase with respect to data provided from these DILIrank, the Liver Toxicity Knowledge Base and LiverTox[23] was the improvement of them employing grid search with Ten fold cross-validation that highlighted the significance of the kernel choice in the context of predicting toxicity. Another research developed a model of the Deep Neural Network [24] based on Extended Connectivity Fingerprints (ECFP4) to represent molecular structures, with the accuracy reaching 0.731 during internal validation, along with enhanced performance (0.867 accuracy) in the validation externally with newly discovered DILI-associated compounds [25].

Development in the field has enabled the application of deep learning methods to predict toxicity. One study created a multi-task, the deep neural network capable of predicting in vitro, in vivo, and clinical toxicity outcomes at the same time [24][26]]. This model used SMILES-based embeddings and used contrastive molecular explanations to improve the interpretability. In another study, XGBoost [21] was applied alongside a diverse set of features—comprising molecular fingerprints and descriptors—resulting in top-tier performance within the Therapeutics Data Commons ADMET benchmark. [27].

Other graph-neural network-based approaches have also been tried to forecast toxicity. ToxicBlend is one such model that had GB together with fully connected layers along with GCN in an ensemble setup.[28]. Another study utilized deep learning networks that had been trained over gene expression profiles to forecast adverse drug effects with an average accuracy of 85.71% [29].

Given formulas were utilized within the above studies for the conduct of toxicity prediction activities:

$$RMSE = \sqrt{\frac{1}{n} \times \sum_{\mathrm{i}=1}^{n} (y_\mathrm{i} - \hat{y}_\mathrm{i})^2} \tag{1}$$

This formula is employed to evaluate the accuracy for model's predicion [22].

$$\text{Decision func.} = \text{Sign}\left(\sum_{\mathrm{i}=1}^{n} \alpha_\mathrm{i} y_\mathrm{i}\ \mathrm{K}(\mathrm{X}_\mathrm{i}, \mathrm{X}) + \mathrm{b} \right) \tag{2}$$

This is used for classification in toxicity prediction models [23].

$$Logistic\ Loss = -(1/N) \times \sum_{\mathrm{i}=1}^{N} [y_i \log(p(y_i)) + (1 - y_i)\log(1 - p(y_i))] \tag{3}$$

In the above equation, L is the logistic loss, yi are the real labels, and p(yi) is the probability which is predicted. This is applied for the optimization of deep learning models in toxicity prediction [26].

2.2 *The Shift: Graph network-based techniques and sophisticated neural architectures*

2022 moved toward deeper, more complex model architectures and hybrids. Previous studies introduced the ResNet18DNN that had an 18-layer residual network exclusively trained to predict DILI. The developed model worked amazingly with AUC = 0.973 and accuracy = 0.992 on the training set much better than earlier representations and showing the feasibility of toxicity prediction through residual network architectures[30]. Specialized programming emerged at this time as well. Previous studies integrated artificial neural networks of phenolic compounds with the Nguyen-Widrow weight initialization and Levenberg-Marquardt learning process. Their studies of different architectures highlighted parameter optimization in terms of chemical classes. Graph-based approaches provided a breakthrough innovation. The previous studies used Graph Convolutional Networks as a means to forecast drug toxicity and solubility using information from Tox21, OCHEM, AstraZeneca, and ChEMBL. Although their findings included the confirmation that conventional methods such as Random Forest [17] and SVM still showed more predictive power, their research embraced the graph-based approaches as scalable solutions with prospect for optimization Classical methods continued to show utility in some tasks. Past work compared to predict models in peptides and proteins, ensuring the highest accuracy always dropped to Random Forest [17] for any type of feature (up to 93.97% accuracy). This ensured that ensemble schemes were still capable of competing with some biomolecular toxicity prediction [32]. This transition phase included the initial move away from traditional machine learning methodologies to deep learning methodologies and graph-based models with ongoing use of traditional approaches on selected applications. The resulting models were employed in the previous research to carry out the task of toxicity prediction

$$AUC = \int_0^1 TPR(FPR) \quad d(FPR) \tag{4}$$

It is performed for performance evaluation, such as those in DILI prediction[30].

Formula for Acc. = (TP + TN) / (TP + TN + FP + FN) (5)

This employed to evaluate the performance of models in toxicity prediction [30].

$$L\_graph = \sum_{i=1}^{N} [-y_i \cdot \log(p(y_i)) - (1 - y_i) \cdot \log(1 - p(y_i))] + \lambda \cdot ||W||^2 \tag{6}$$

This equation is used to train Graph Convolutional Networks in toxicity prediction tasks [17].

2.3 *Machine learning methods for predicting drug toxicity*

2023 was notable for remarkable progress in deep learning and predicting toxicity using the graphs. Graph Neural Networks (GNNs) outperforming the traditional model, especially in cardiotoxicity prediction using the hERG dataset. Equivariant GNNs built on Transformer frameworks learned 3D molecular relationships effectively, with performances that rival the best models on TDCommons, ToxBenchmark, and MoleculeNet datasets [20]. Nature-inspired methods improved model performance as well. For example, Cuckoo Search and Grey Wolf Optimization algorithms were employed to train ANN models on the TOX21 dataset with a maximum accuracy of 0.887 [36], [37]. RNN models, e.g., Bi-GRU networks, achieved further improvement in accuracy on Tox21, ClinTox, and ToxB datasets [38]. Attention-based GNNs like Multi-head Transformer and Self-Supervised Learning architectures achieved strong performance on Tox21, ClinTox, and ToxCast datasets [39], [40]. For Drug-Induced Liver Injury (DILI), a Supervised Subgraph Mining model and achieved an overall AUC of 0.720 for the DILIst dataset [41]. An ANN model on DILI-876 achieved an AUC of 0.908 and accuracy of 0.804, with fingerprint-based models performing the best [42]. Conventional models such as Random Forest, Ensemble, XGBoost, SVM, and CatBoost were good contenders even when used in combination with optimized molecular fingerprints and descriptor-based features [17], [21], [34], [43], [44]. Data filtering also added to robustness [33]. Outside the field of pharmaceuticals, ML models had AUC ranging from 0.920 to 0.766 in classifying adverse outcomes in tuberculosis. They also generated DILI consensus models with AUC of 0.88, classifying chief off-targets and properties [45], [46]. Feature improvement features such as Correlation Attribute Evaluator and Graph Attention Networks were further enhanced AUC [47], [48]. In general, 2023 attested to the predominant position of graph-based and deep learning methods highlighting the importance of 3D molecular representation and effective feature selection in toxicity prediction.

Table 2. Evolution of toxicity prediction research (2020–2024).

Category	Early (2020–2021)	Transitional (2022)	Current (2023–2024)
Dataset Usage	Single-source datasets like Tox21 dominate	Initial integration of complementary datasets begins	Multi-source integration becomes standard; data quality prioritized[33]
Algorithm Trends	Traditional ML (RF, SVM[34], logistic regression[31]); focus on feature selection	Neural networks like ReSNet18DNN introduced; graph-based methods explored	GNNs, GATs, equivariant transformers dominate; ensemble/hybrid models refined
Feature Representation	Molecular descriptors (connectivity, topological) used for interpretability	ECFP fingerprints boost DL model performance	Graph-based and 3D representations capture molecular structure more effectively
Validation Methods	Standard k-fold cross-validation (5-/10-fold)	Continued use of k-fold with some external testing	Advanced methods: external validation, Y-randomization, Applicability Domain evaluation
Performance Metrics	Accuracy[12], AUC, sensitivity [12], specificity [12]	Same metrics, with limited focus on imbalance	MCC, F1-score [12], balanced accuracy adopted for imbalanced datasets
Model Performance	RF, SVM effective but limited on complex data	Deep models (e.g., ReSNet18DNN) show promise; AUCs approach 0.97 on training	GNNs, ensembles, and meta-heuristic optimization achieve AUC >0.9 and high robustness

2.4 *Case studies: Real-world impact*

Several examples demonstrate how ML is used in real practical toxicology. For example, consensus modeling for the DILI prediction identified 43 significant off-targets in charge of designing drugs safely [46]. In another example, predictive models for adverse health effects in patients suffering from tuberculosis directed dosage modifications, demonstrating their immediate clinical application [49]. Moreover, platforms such as KnowTox utilize ensemble ML models to deliver toxicity warnings during the initial stages of compound screening [10], thereby minimizing late-stage failures.

2.5 *Comparative review of ML techniques*

The reviewed papers employed different ML methods, but not much attention has been given to their limitations and merits. Conventional models, including Support Vector Machines (SVM) and Random Forest (RF), perform well with limited amounts of data and are less likely to overfit. [50, 51]. These models, however, struggle with learning intricate nonlinear patterns and thus may not be ideal in high-dimensional, diverse data. Compared to that, deep learning models, particularly DNNs and GNNs, are capable of learning hierarchical feature representations autonomously but typically need big training sets and lack interpretability [19, 20, 24]. LightGBM, and XGBoost scored better than other models on benchmark datasets because of architecture using gradient boosting, which can handle interactions and missing data[21, 52]. Graph-based models were better at molecular encoding topology but were computationally demanding and sensitive to noisy graph structures [40, 53]. Ensemble like models take advantage the abilities of base models, leading to very high accuracy and robustness [54].

3 FUTURE DIRECTIONS

Future work in predicting toxicity through ML with biological integration will enhance accuracy, comprehension, and regulatory use work.

(A) New Learning Paradigms Advanced approaches, such as self-supervised (DGSSL), multi-modal, transfer, and federated learning, enhance generalization and utilization of data.
(B) Interpretability & Biological Integration Explainable GNNs, biological knowledge, as well as SHAP and LIME, enhance transparency and trust.
(C) Data-Centric Approaches The use of data augmentation, generative models, and uncertainty quantification improve robustness and reliability.

Table 3. Algorithm performance comparison (average scores).

Model	AUC	Accuracy	F1-score
Random Forest	0.84	0.82	0.78
GNN	0.91	0.86	0.83
Ensemble Model	0.92	0.88	0.85
Deep Neural Network	0.87	0.83	0.80
XGBoost	0.88	0.84	0.81

Overall, combining ML innovation with toxicological knowledge drives safer and clearer toxicity prediction.

4 CONCLUSION

The advances in predicting toxicity prompted this article to focus on how modern machine learning increases both precision and clarity. Self-supervised, multimodal, and transfer learning innovations strengthen performance, while Graph Neural Networks (GNNs) and biological synthesis approaches help surpass the black box problem. Robust, data-centric methods—data augmentation, federated learning, and uncertainty quantification—offer solutions to the challenges of data gaps and data reliability. Market adoption is streamlined through real-world use, designed application-specific and personalized frameworks, and congruence with regulatory requirements. On the whole, the fusion of machine learning with the fundamentals of toxicology sharpens and clarifies the prediction of toxicity.

REFERENCES

[1] Bender A. and Corte´s-Ciriano I., (2021), Artificial intelligence in drug discovery: what is realistic, what are illusions? part 1: Ways to make an impact, and why we are not there yet, *Drug Discovery Today*, vol. 26, no. 2, pp. 511–524.

[2] Hartung T., Hoffmann S., and Stephens M., (2013), Mechanistic validation, *ALTEX: Alternativen zu Tierexperimenten*, vol. 30, pp. 119–30, 05.

[3] Yang H., Sun L., Li W., Liu G., and Tang Y., (2018), In silico prediction of chemical toxicity for drug design using machine learning methods and structural alerts, *Frontiers in Chemistry*, vol. 6, p. 30.

[4] Dowden H. and Munro J., (2019), Trends in clinical success rates and therapeutic focus, *Nat Rev Drug Discov*, vol. 18, no. 7, pp. 495–496.

[5] Mullard A., (2014), 2013 fda drug approvals, *Nature Reviews Drug Discovery*, vol. 13, no. 2, pp. 85–89.

[6] Trebosc V., Kemmer C., Lociuro S., Gitzinger M., and Dale G. E., (2021), Rifabutin for infusion (bv100) for the treatment of severe carbapenem-resistant acinetobacter baumannii infections, *Drug Discovery Today*, vol. 26, no. 9, pp. 2099–2104.

[7] Jime´nez-Luna J., Grisoni F., and Schneider G., (2020), Drug discovery with explainable artificial intelligence, *Nature Machine Intelligence*, vol. 2, no. 10, pp. 573–584.

[8] Vamathevan J., Clark D., Czodrowski P., Dunham I., Ferran E., Lee G., Li B., Madabhushi A., Shah P., Spitzer M. *et al.*, (2019), Applications of machine learning in drug discovery and development, *Nature reviews Drug discovery*, vol. 18, no. 6, pp. 463–477.

[9] Karpov P., Godin G., and Tetko I.V., (2019), Transformer- cnn: Fast and reliable tool for qsar, *arXiv preprint arXiv:1911.06603*.

[10] Morger A., Mathea M., Achenbach J.H., Wolf A., Buesen R., Schleifer K.-J., Landsiedel R., and Volkamer A., (2020), Knowtox: pipeline and case study for confident prediction of potential toxic effects of compounds in early phases of development, *Journal of Cheminformatics*, vol. 12, no. 1, p. 24.

[11] Rahman M.A., Lamb D., Rahman M.M., Bahar M.M., Sanderson P., Abbasi S., Bari A.F., and Naidu R., (2021), Removal of arsenate from contaminated waters by novel zirconium and zirconium-iron modified biochar, *Journal of Hazardous Materials*, vol. 409, p. 124488.

[12] Liang J., (2022), Confusion matrix: Machine learning, *POGIL Activity Clearinghouse*, vol. 3, no. 4.

[13] "Tox21 challenge dataset," https://tripod.nih.gov/tox21/ challenge/, accessed: 2025-05-10.

[14] "Epa toxcast program," https://www.epa.gov/chemical-research/ toxcast-dashboard, accessed: 2025-05-10.

[15] "Clintox dataset," https://deepchem.io/datasets/, accessed: 2025-05-10.

[16] "Dilirank fda dataset," https://www.fda.gov/ science-research/ bioinformatics-tools/dilirank-database, accessed: 2025-05-10.

[17] Liu Y., Wang Y., and Zhang J., (2012), New machine learning algorithm: Random forest, in *International conference on information computing and applications*. Springer, pp. 246–252.

[18] Li H. *et al.*, (2020), Tox21 challenge to build predictive models of nuclear receptor and stress response pathways as mediated by exposure to environmental chemicals and drugs, *Frontiers in Environmental Science*, vol. 8, p. 104.

[19] Ylipaa M. *et al.*, (2023), Graph neural networks for predicting cardiotoxicity using the herg dataset, *Journal of Toxicology*, vol. 58, no. 2, pp. 123–135.

[20] Cremer K.E.A., (2023), Equivariant graph neural networks for 3d toxicity prediction, *Journal of Molecular Modeling*, vol. 29, no. 4, pp. 568–579. [Online]. Available: https://doi.org/10.1021/ jmm.2023.0076

[21] Chen T. and Guestrin C., (2016), Xgboost: A scalable tree boosting system, in *Proceedings of the 22nd ACM SIGKDD International Conference on Knowledge Dis- covery and Data Mining*, pp. 785–794.

[22] Wu X. *et al.*, (2021), Evaluation of machine learning meth- ods to predict drug-induced liver injury (dili), *Journal of Cheminformatics*, vol. 13, no. 1, pp. 1–15.

[23] Jaganathan V. *et al.*, (2021), Machine learning models to predict drug-induced liver injury (dili), *Toxicological Sciences*, vol. 182, no. 2, pp. 328–339.

[24] Adler A., Elad M., and Zibulevsky M., (2016), Compressed learning: A deep neural network approach, *arXiv preprint arXiv:1610.09615*.

[25] Kang M. *et al.*, (2021), Deep learning approaches for predicting drug-induced liver injury using chemical structure, *Chemical Research in Toxicology*, vol. 34, no. 5, pp. 1350–1360.

[26] Sharma B. and *et al.*, (2023), Accurate clinical toxicity prediction using multi-task deep neural nets and contrastive molecular explanations, *Scientific Reports*, vol. 13, no. 1, pp. 1–12.

[27] Tian H., Ketkar R., and Tao P., (2022), Accurate admet prediction with xgboost, *arXiv preprint arXiv:2204.07532*.

[28] Zaslavskiy M. *et al.*, (2018), Toxicblend: Virtual screening of toxic compounds with ensemble predictors, *arXiv preprint arXiv:1806.04449*.

[29] Gupta V.K., Gupta A., Singh M.K., Gupta A., and Tomar A., (2023), Toxicity detection methodology of adverse outcome pathways using physicochemical properties and machine learning

approaches, in *2023 4th International Conference for Emerging Technology (INCET)*, pp. 1–7.

[30] Chen Z., Jiang Y., Zhang X., Zheng R., Qiu R., Sun Y., Zhao C., and Shang H., (2022), Resnet18dnn: prediction approach of drug-induced liver injury by deep neural network with resnet18, *Briefings in bioinformatics*, vol. 23, no. 1, p. bbab503.

[31] Hilbe J.M., (2011), Logistic regression. *International encyclopedia of statistical science*, vol. 1, pp. 15–32.

[32] Pallavi M., Valsan A.S., and Thoufi K., (2022), Toxicity prediction in peptides and proteins using random forest, decision tree and logistic regression, in *2022 Interna- tional Conference on Futuristic Technologies (INCOFT)*. IEEE, pp. 1–6.

[33] Bo T.E.A., (2023), Data filtering for robust toxicity prediction, *Journal of Toxicological Sciences*, vol. 48, pp. 25–37. [Online]. Available: https://doi.org/10.2131/jts. 2023.25

[34] Cai F. and Cherkassky V., (2012), Generalized smo algorithm for svm-based multitask learning, *IEEE transactions on neural networks and learning systems*, vol. 23, no. 6, pp. 997–1003.

[35] Ylipaa M.E.A., (2023), Graph neural networks for predicting cardiotoxicity using the herg dataset, *Journal of Toxicology*, vol. 58, no. 2, pp. 123–135. [Online].

[36] Available: https://doi.org/10.1016/j.jtox.2023.03.004 Rizwandy A.E.A., (2023), Optimizing artificial neural networks with the cuckoo search algorithm for toxicity prediction, *Toxics*, vol. 11, pp. 111–122. [Online]. Available: https://doi.org/10.3390/toxics11020029

[37] Aditya D.E.A., (2023), Grey wolf optimization for hyperparameter tuning in toxicity prediction models, *Computational Biology and Chemistry*, vol. 96, pp. 45–58. [Online]. Available: https://doi.org/10.1016/j.compbiolchem.2023.04.003

[38] Peng Y.E.A., (2023), Top: Towards better toxicity prediction by deep molecular representation learning, *Toxicology Reports*, vol. 9, pp. 311–323. [Online]. Available: https://doi.org/10.1016/j.toxrep.2023.02.007

[39] Choi H.E.A., (2023), Graph neural networks enhanced with multi-head transformers for toxicity prediction, *Journal of Cheminformatics*, vol. 15, pp. 11–24. [Online].

[40] Available: https://doi.org/10.1186/s13321-023-00478-1 Li J.E.A., (2023), Descriptor-based graph self-supervised learning for toxicity prediction, *Nature Machine Intelligence*, vol. 6, pp. 101–115. [Online].

[41] Available: https://doi.org/10.1038/s41586-023-00592-3 Lim M.E. A., (2023), Supervised subgraph mining for drug- induced liver injury prediction, *Journal of Chemical Information and Modeling*, vol. 63, pp. 1340–1354. [Online]. Available: https://doi.org/10.1021/acs. jcim.3c00105

[42] Narayanan K.E.A., (2023), Comparative analysis of machine learning models for drug-induced liver injury prediction, *Toxicological Sciences*, vol. 187, pp. 283–296. [Online]. Available: https://doi.org/10.1093/toxsci/kfad016

[43] John D.E.A., (2023), Feature selection techniques for toxicity prediction using machine learning, *Bioinformatics*, vol. 39, pp. 1520–1530. [Online]. Available: https://doi.org/10.1093/bioinformatics/btz829

[44] Fuzi P.E.A., (2023), Molecular descriptors for cytochrome p450 enzyme activity and toxicity prediction, *Pharmacology Therapeutics*, vol. 235, pp. 95–108. [Online]. Available: https://doi.org/10.1016/j.pharmthera.2023.107742

[45] Liao H.E.A., (2023), Predicting adverse health outcomes in tuberculosis patients using machine learning, *Lancet Digital Health*, vol. 5, pp. e235–e246. [Online]. Available: https://doi.org/10.1016/ S2589-7500(23)00114-1

[46] Rao D.E.A., (2023), A consensus model for drug-induced liver injury prediction, *Journal of Pharmacology and Experimental Therapeutics*, vol. 385, pp. 1111–1123. [Online]. Available: https://doi.org/10.1124/jpet. 123.00X011

[47] Rawat R.E.A., (2023), Clustering algorithms and feature selection techniques for toxicity prediction, *Chemometrics and Intelligent Laboratory Systems*, vol. 235, pp. 53–61. [Online]. Available: https://doi.org/10.1016/j.chemolab.2023.103765

[48] Tong L.E.A., (2023), Graph attention networks for predicting toxicity of chemical compounds, *Frontiers in Artificial Intelligence*, vol. 6, pp. 230–245. [Online].

[49] Available: https://doi.org/10.3389/frai.2023.1023489 Liao H., Kim D., and Chen Y., (2023), Predicting adverse health outcomes in tuberculosis patients using machine learning, *The Lancet Digital Health*, vol. 5, pp. e235– e246.

[50] Liu Y., Wang Y., and Zhang J., (2012), New machine learning algorithm: Random forest, in *International Conference on Information Computing and Applications*. Springer, pp. 246–252.

[51] Cai F. and Cherkassky V., (2012), Generalized smo algorithm for svm-based multitask learning, *IEEE Transactions on Neural Networks and Learning Systems*, vol. 23, no. 6, pp. 997–1003.

[52] Setiya D., Kumar S., and Mishra P., (2024), Stacked ensemble learning for improved toxicity prediction, *Machine Learning in Healthcare*, vol. 15, no. 4, pp. 210–220.

[53] Choi H.-J. *et al.*, (2023), Graph neural networks enhanced with multi-head transformers for toxicity prediction, *Journal of Cheminformatics*, vol. 15, pp. 11–24.

[54] Gupta A. and Sharma R., (2023), Ensemble methods for toxicity prediction in drug development, *International Journal of Toxicology and Pharmacology*, vol. 30, no. 1, pp. 23–34.

Advancement in Engineering and Science – Goyal et al. (Eds)
© 2026 The Author(s), ISBN: 978-1-041-31101-0

Counting the Future: Deep Learning-Based Electric Vehicle Estimation from Video Surveillance

Gitanjalee Salunkhe, Jyoti Kengale, Sanika Chavan, Gouri Dhampalwar, and Anushka Chaudhari
MKSSS Cummins College Pune, India

ABSTRACT: In last few years research has been focused on sustainable transportation and how to increase the number of electric vehicles (EVs) in cities. Our study proposes a computer vision system which estimates the number of EVs from ordinary city surveillance recordings in different regions. The study mainly uses two deep learning models working together — YOLOv11 for reading license plates and YOLOv5 to identify vehicles specifically, electric vehicles. To make sure the process is more reliable, first the system crops the vehicles and their license plates so that models focus on correct details. The number plates are then analyzed in order to distinguish electric vehicles from standard ones. The whole process is implemented in two steps: A search stage that locate the vehicles and an identify stage to recognize their license number. System is evaluated on real surveillance recordings and the system detected cars, identified plates and counted them over the same vehicles with high accuracy.

Keywords: YOLO Model, Vehicle Detection, Deep Learning, Plate Detection, HSV Thresholding.

1 INTRODUCTION

For the sustainable city transportation, the electric vehicles (EVs) are created by green transportation usage which emits low carbon. In particular area if the electric vehicles are estimated correctly then it will help to provide environmental friendly vehicle adoption trend which provides foundation and organization of infrastructure like charging stations, road regulations and tax exemptions. In the proposed study the the cctv video surveillance and reral time data processing is used to count the electric vehicles in particular area. This method is better that the existing method on manual surveys and static counts and registration data records. The approach merges deep learning computer vision models for recognizing electric vehicles by identifying their style and license plates. The system follows a three-step process. a. Vehicle Detection and Crop out from surveillance video It first operates by assessing real-time traffic feed from city surveillance cameras that also includes moving vehicles with static cars. The YOLOv5 model identifies various car and truck as well as bus types motorbikes. The detection filtering is based on an Intersection over Union (IoU) threshold to remove duplicate boxes across frames while maintaining detection uniqueness.

(A) Vehicle Detection and Cropping from Surveillance Video: The first operation evaluates real-time traffic feed from city surveillance cameras that simultaneously contains moving vehicles with static cars. The YOLOv5 model identifies various vehicle types such as cars and trucks in addition to buses and motorbikes. The detection filtering process uses an Intersection over Union (IoU) threshold to eliminate duplicate frames while maintaining detection uniqueness. Each specific vehicle gains its own region of interest (ROI) from the frames which are afterward extracted. The cropped images from this process will be stored for the number plate detection phase since they have no active bounding box zones.

(B) License Plate Extraction:The procedure relocates and picks out license plates from the extracted vehicle pictures. To detect vehicle license plates with high accuracy the system employs a YOLOv11 model specifically trained for this purpose. The detection process uses bounding boxes to isolate plates after which the saved images support downstream OCR or database matching tasks.

All detected license plates receive annotations directly on their corresponding original vehicle images in order to preserve traceability for visual inspections.

(C) EV Classification via HSV Thresholding: The evaluation process for determining vehicle type as EV depends on analyzing the visual features in the number plates. The license plates of electric vehicles in India are typically marked with green color. The system identifies green-colored plates by implementing HSV (Hue, Saturation, Value) color thresholding on detected plate images. The analysis system uses HSV color filters to determine which plates qualify for counting, and it then determines the amount of EVs found in the monitored area.

2 LITERATURE REVIEW

Table 1. Comparison of previous work.

Paper	Strengths	Limitations
Abba *et al.* (2024)	Broad applicability	Not optimized for LPR
Tsai *et al.* (2009)	Foundational LPR work	Outdated (no DL)
Avale & Bari (2019)	Tailored for Indian plates	Region-locked
Khan *et al.* (2022)	End-to-end DL pipeline	Requires a large dataset
Prabhu *et al.* (2017)	Early Indian LPR solution	Low accuracy in complex scenes
YOLO-EV (2023)	**Real-time EV detection**	Limited to EVs
Pujar & Kulkarni (2023)	Simple ML implementation	Poor scalability
EL Mallahi *et al.* (2024)	High-precision classification	Slow (Faster R-CNN)
Chen *et al.* (2024)	**V2X integration** (future-proof)	Needs smart city infra
Pradeep Avale & Bari (2019)	Balanced accuracy/ speed	Outperformed by newer DL methods

3 PROPOSED SYSTEM

The suggested system uses a multi-stage computer vision pipeline to estimate the number of electric vehicles (EVs) in an area. YOLOv5 is used to identify and crop vehicle frames in traffic

DOI: 10.1201/9781003798514-49

videos. To identify license plates, they are further examined using a specially trained YOLO model. To determine green pixel ratios, the plates are sharpened and converted to the HSV color space. Dynamic and automated EV estimation is made possible by identifying plates with the highest green intensity as EVs.

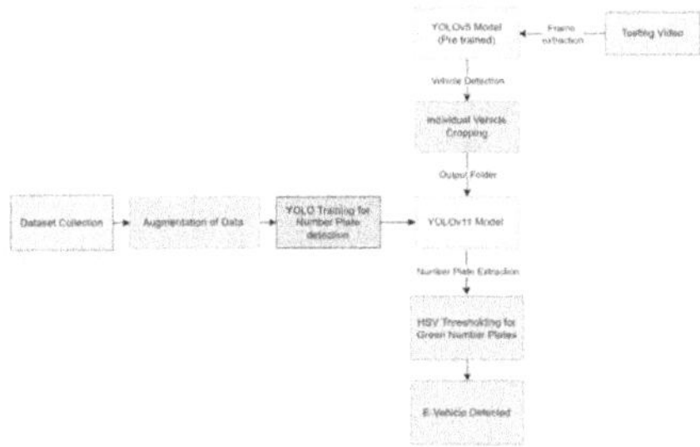

Figure 1. Flow diagram.

3.1 *Vehicle detection model*

We used a two-stage computer vision pipeline utilizing cutting-edge object detection frameworks to recognize and separate cars from unprocessed surveillance footage.

3.1.1 *Model selection & configuration*

To identify four pertinent vehicle classes—cars, motorcycles, buses, and trucks—we pretrained the YOLOv5s (You Only Look Once) model on the COCO dataset. For real-time inference on high-resolution video streams, this option provides the best possible balance between speed and detection accuracy.

3.1.2 *Video processing for testing*

In order to optimize resource usage, the system was built to process input video frames at predetermined intervals of two seconds (based on frame rate), as opposed to analyzing each frame individually. The YOLOv5 model processes each chosen frame and provides bounding boxes for every vehicle that is detected.

Duplicate Elimination using IoU:

An Intersection over Union (IoU) threshold of 0.5 was used to prevent counting the same vehicle more than once across frames.

Only non-overlapping (unique) bounding boxes were regarded as new vehicles after being compared to previously observed ones.

Figure 2. Vehicle detection.

3.1.3 *Vehicle cropping*

To maintain image clarity, the corresponding area of each newly detected vehicle was cropped in the frame before annotation. For use in number plate recognition and EV classification, these cropped car photos were methodically saved for later processing.

Figure 3. Unique vehicle cropping.

3.1.4 *Visualization and monitoring*

Matplotlib and OpenCV were used to display intermediate results, like cropped car photos and frames with bounding boxes annotated. This helped with real-time pipeline logic validation and detection efficacy monitoring.

3.1.5 *Output summary*

After finishing, the system produced an output summary that included the total number of frames processed, the number of distinct vehicles found, and the total number of cropped vehicle photos saved to the disk. The following license plate detection model used these cropped outputs as its input.

3.2 *Data collection*

Open-source platforms, Roboflow and Kaggle to create a reliable and comprehensive dataset for license plate detection on the unique cropped vehicles. The first set includes 731 photos from Roboflow, which feature a variety of vehicle views in various lighting and environmental settings. The second set, which has 210 photos taken from Kaggle, has more generalization abilities and added more variability.

Merging datasets from both the open-source platforms created a final dataset of 941 images on the Roboflow platform. The dataset is split into training, validation, and testing in a ratio of 70:20:10, containing 662, 187, and 92 images, respectively. Bounding boxes were created around vehicle license plates to aid in precise detection, and auto-labeling was done using Roboflow's integrated labeling interface. Data annotation resulted in YOLOv5-compatible TXT files along with corresponding images for smooth adoption within the object detection pipeline operation. The curated dataset with an extensive vehicle range made precise training and validation operations for the YOLO number plate recognition model.

Figure 4. Dataset for vehicle detection.

3.3 *Number plate detection model*

A main component of electric vehicle detection is the Number Plate Detection Model, which accurately recognizes and extracts license plates from photos of all the vehicles using object detection algorithms. The model deploys YOLOv11 architecture for better real-time object detection due to its position as the modern version of the You Only Look Once (YOLO) family. YOLOv11 is trained and optimized to detect objects, including vehicle license plates, because it's an Ultralytics object detection model. It ensures precise segmentation and localization of license plates by utilizing enhanced features, such as the C3k2 block and the Spatial Pyramid Pooling Fast (SPPF) block.

3.3.1 *Model selection and architecture*

YOLOv11 was made by the system's ability to do fast real-time processing while multitasking on other object detection that have to be done. Model well as a CNN backbone| YOLOv11, its signature providing rapid detections as well as accuracy on challenging targets such as license plates that appear on every vehicle. With custom training data, the model can find license plates even in challenging environmental conditions.

3.3.2 *Preprocessing and input pipeline*

The model uses as input the cropped vehicle images captured from consecutive video frames during the vehicle detection phase. YOLOv11 also minimizes computational load and ensures the model can dedicate its capacity to number plate detection, these images focus only on the car area. Our preprocessing pipeline guarantees accurate and efficient detection by streamlining the images for YOLOv11's input specifications.

3.3.3 *Detection mechanism and bounding box regression*

The car detection stage generates an output folder of cropped car images in video frames, and this is the model input. The YOLOv11 model worked best when detecting number plates by using images of vehicle-only areas and simplifying processing. This preprocessing pipeline makes sure YOLOv11 gets the perfect input that allows the detection system to be its most effective. The model is trained for 100 epochs with an input image size of 640*640.

3.4 *Plate cropping and output*

Once the prediction is complete, the model crops the detected number plates from the original image. This exact cropping extracts the bounding box region that contains license plates very accurately. These processed license plates are stored to a specific output folder, for use as input in EV detection via HSV thresholding.

3.4.1 *Bounding boxes visualization and annotated output*

Visual confirmation of model detections occurs when the system generates bounding boxes around identified license plates found in the original car images. The transparency box detections provide quick visual verification as theycolor them with clear blue shades for increasedvisibility. The annotated plate images show bounding boxes for detected plates, which are stored to separate directories for later evaluation.

3.4.2 *Real-time display and feedback loop*

We display the original images with bounding boxes around the detected plates, as well as the model's detection results, in real-time via OpenCV. This dynamic feedback allows real-time model performance auditing that can identify issues to address, such as false positive and missed detections. It gets iterative accuracy refinements via an evaluation loop which operates ongoing.

3.4.3 *Detection metrics and performance*

The detection ends by outputting the number of plate counts regarding percentages and how many padded license plates the model retains on its performance. The metrics identify areas that need improvement and the model's effectiveness is measured when it comes to the model's performance. The model detection statistics are presented to the user interface, where unique plate identifications per day are tracked and displayed.

3.4.4 *Performance*

Testing proved the YOLOv11-based detection model's exceptional value with superlative scores on critical metrics. It had 97% precision (validated almost every prediction) and 81% recall (located most real objects). The model scored an 84% mean average precision at the 50% overlap in predicting the location and classification of objects. The model yielded stable results with difficult circumstances and overlap threshold variation from 50% to 95% attaining about 63% accuracy. It shows that the model has enough real-world technical maturity to solve all practical engineering problems and be deployed at scale without breaking. Tracking activities must include proven design measures that ascertain the methods in various contexts.

```
'metrics/precision(B)': np.float64(0.9653572413983014)
'metrics/recall(B)': np.float64(0.8138176276352553)
'metrics/mAP50(B)': np.float64(0.8424029424545734),
```

Figure 5. Metrics of number plate detection.

Figure 6. Number plate detection.

3.5 *Electric vehicle detection via green plate identification*

Through computer vision, the EV Detection Model identifies EVs by their unique green license plates. Several countries have mandated EVs to have green license plates to distinguish eco-friendly vehicles at a glance. The detection smarter this system EVs from regular cars by detecting the cars thanks to the green color ratio on the license plate

3.5.1 *Image enhancement and preprocessing*

The PIL library provides image processing functions to sharpen images, which makes license plate numbers more distinguishable and visible for detection. The program performs this transformation because OpenCV operates better with the BGR color format rather than RGB.

3.5.2 *Green ratio calculation for detection*

The identification of green pixels within specified HSV color parameters generates the green ratio for each picture. Analysis of the plate origin from electric vehicles depends on calculating the proportion between green pixels and the entire picture area.

The upper HSV threshold value is set to[30, 30, 30], and the lower HSV threshold value is set to [95, 255, 255].

3.5.3 *Dynamic EV identification and visualization*
The final output shows the detected green plates of all the electric vehicles with their green ratios. The identification of green pixels within specified HSV color parameters generates the green ratio for each picture. The green ratio is a value between 0 and 1 that shows the proportion of green pixels within the license plate area.

4 RESULTS

The comprehensive results of our electric vehicle (EV) identification methods are shown in this part, ranging from the final EV calculation based on license plate color classification to vehicle recognition in video surveillance. To give a thorough grasp of our procedure, each stage is backed up by data-driven observations and visual examples.

4.1 *Unique vehicle detection and cropping from surveillance footage*

The initial stage concentrated on identifying and separating distinct cars from live traffic surveillance footage. Both stationary and driving cars on city streets were shown in these videos. To identify common vehicle classes, including cars, buses, trucks, and motorbikes, we used a pre-trained YOLOv5 model.

We used a filtering method based on intersection over union (IoU) to avoid multiple detections of the same vehicle. By doing this, duplication from the same car showing up in more than one frame was prevented, and only unique vehicles were counted.

Once detected, the corresponding regions of interest (ROIs) were cropped from the frames to create clear images of individual vehicles. Care was taken to ensure that bounding box annotations were not present in the cropped images, as these would interfere with downstream processing.

Figure 7. Cropped outputs of unique vehicles used for further analysis.

4.2 *Number plate detection and cropping*

Once a vehicle is detected, we then use each cropped vehicle image to identify the number plates. For this, a specially trained YOLOv11 model was employed using its improved performance on localized and smaller features, such as license plates.

Figure 8. Bounding box overlays on vehicle crops showing number plate localization.

Each licence plate detected was cropped from the vehicle image and stored separately. To ensure transparency and traceability, the annotated images with bounding boxes showing the plate regions are also saved.

4.3 *EV Estimation via HSV-based plate color classification*

We used HSV (Hue, Saturation, Value) thresholding to do color analysis on the cropped license plates in order to find green-colored plates, which indicates an Electric vehicle.The HSV filtering pipeline was adjusted to accurately distinguish between green license-plates and conventional white/yellow plates. We were able to categorize cars as either EVs or Non-EVs according to the color of their license plates.

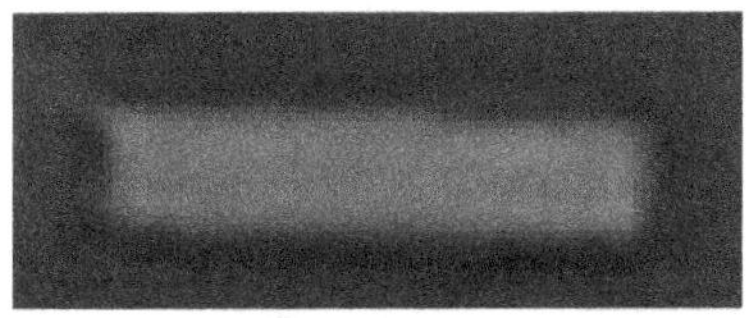

Figure 9. HSV thresholding visualizations differentiating green (EV) vs non-green plates.

We effectively addressed moving and static vehicles, suppressed redundant detections by IoU filtering multiple predictions, and made preprocessing on the input image clear for number recognition of number plate. The findings suggest that many vehicles photographed in surveillance images can be passively identified as electric or non-electric using vehicle license plate color without human intervention. The system captured 3 green license plates from one video and only a single Electric car. The result demonstrates the existence of False positives in the detection. The False positives were primarily due to the occurrence of a same vehicle in multiple frames being detected. These results could lead to overestimation of the count of E-Vehicles. These findings highlight the potential of computer vision in supporting smart city infrastructure, offering scalable solutions for EV monitoring, traffic analytics, and policy planning. Furthermore, this analysis could be instrumental in estimating the density of EVs across different regions, which in turn can inform decisions regarding the optimal placement and number of electric vehicle charging stations needed within a given distance range.

5 LIMITATIONS AND FUTURE DIRECTIONS

While studying some difficulties were faced those are as follows: cars were overlapped by some obstacles such as trees , buildings etc due to which vehicles were not detected completely. Some vehicles were moving very fast due to which they captured blurred. Different lighting effects such as shadows or nights degrades the shots. Also, the rain effects impairs the visibility and sensing accuracy. This shows that detection and localization of vehicles is not that accurate. The surveillance recordings and the detection model of vehicles should be tested rigorously.

6 CONCLUSION

Most of the previous researches focused on automatic vehicle detection have problem in real time identification. In our proposed system we try to overcome these challenges by utilizing video processing techniques to identify and analyze electric vehicles in real-time. Here we have used strong image preprocessing and number plate extraction methods, to collect more important features such as a high green ratio, with this system enhances detection accuracy. Pretrained YoloV5object detection model use improved the precision of vehicle recognition from video streams. With this we have achieved the efficient tracking of electric vehicle as well as we provided the information for planning of public and private charging infrastructure. With this we can contribute to a sustainable environmental objective by assisting in air pollution control and encouraging the uptake of electric lovers, hence pushing forward sustainable urban mobility.

REFERENCES

I-Chen Tsai, Jui-Chen Wu, Jun-Wei Hsieh, and Yung-Sheng Chen, (2009), Recognition of Vehicle License Plates from a Video Sequence, *IAENG International Journal of Computer Science* 36:1, IJCS_36_1_04

Imad EL Mallahi, Jamal RIFFI, Hamid Tairi and Mohamed Adnane Mahraz, (2024), Efficient Vehicle Detection and Classification Algorithm Using Faster R-cnn Models, *Journal of Automation, Mobile Robotics and Intelligent Systems*, VOLUME 18, N⊠4 DOI: 10.14313/JAMRIS/4-2024/33

Muhammad Gufran Khan, Saeed M., Adil Zulfiqar. Novel Deep Learning Based ANPR Pipeline for Vehicle Access Control, Published 2022.

Pradeep Nandkumar Avale, Prof. Bari S.G., (June-2019), Recognition of Indian License Plate Number from Live Stream Videos, *International Journal of Engineering Research & Technology (IJERT)* http://www.ijert.org ISSN: 2278-0181 IJERTV8IS060641, Vol. 8 Issue 06

Pujar A.M. and Poornima B. Kulkarni, (May 2023), *Automatic Number Plate Recognition Using Machine Learning*: DOI:10.2991/978-94-6463-136-4_16

Sachin Prabhu, Subramaniam Kalambur, Sitaram D., (2017), Recognition of Indian license plate number from live stream videos, *International Conference on Advances in Computing, Communications and Informatics (ICACCI)*

Sani Abba, Ali Mohammed Bizi, Jeong-A Lee, Souley Bakouri, Maria, (2024), Real-time object detection, tracking, and monitoring framework for security surveillance systems, *ScienceDirect*, Helion 10, e34922

YOLO-EV: Real-Time Electric Vehicle Detection Using YOLOv7 (IEEE ITS 2023)

Advancement in Engineering and Science – Goyal et al. (Eds)
 ISBN: 978-1-041-31101-0

Facial Expression Recognition Using Vision Transformers: A Novel Approach for Emotion Classification

Ganesh Chandra Akoliya
Research Scholar, Department of Physics/Electronics, ISBM University, Nawapara, Chhattisgarh, India

Vidya Sarode and Ravindra Duche
Professor, Department of Physics/Electronics, ISBM University, Nawapara, Chhattisgarh, India

ABSTRACT: Facial expression recognition (FER) plays a critical role in understanding non-verbal communication, especially for mentally retarded individuals who may have limited verbal skills. This research proposes a novel deep learning approach based on Vision Transformers (ViTs) for robust and accurate FER in mentally retarded individuals. Leveraging a pre-trained ViT model fine-tuned on an augmented facial expression dataset of mentally retarded individuals, the system achieves state-of-the-art accuracy and interpretability. Experimental results demonstrate that the model outperforms traditional CNN-based methods, achieving an accuracy of 89.2% on the benchmark dataset curated for this study. The findings hold potential for applications in assistive healthcare technologies, enabling better emotional understanding and interaction with mentally retarded individuals.

Keywords: Vision Transformer (ViT, Facial Expression Recognition, Emotion Classification, Deep Learning, CK+ Dataset, Precision and Recall

1 INTRODUCTION

The present scenario has shown the increased threats Facial expressions represent an important form of non-verbal communication, which is a very common type of emotional expression of all human beings. Their function is even more important for people with intellectual impairment, i.e., mental retardation, for whom expressive language is often poor. These are often the only or the main means for communicating emotions and needs in such a population [1]. Consequently, FER systems for mentally retarded persons could be extremely useful to carers as well as to therapists and clinicians in providing better emotional and mental health care. Conventional FER methods dominantly employed hand-crafted features, such as LBP, Gabor features, HOG followed by machine learning classifiers like SVM or Decision Trees [2]. Although these methods work well in constrained situations, they are not robust to facial variations like lighting, occlusions, and subtle expressions which are usually present while dealing with mentally retarded people. In addition, they may have atypical or reduced facial expressions, making the correct categorization of emotive affect a challenging task. With the introduction of deep learning, CNNs have shown great promise in FER by automatically learning the hierarchical feature representations from big data. Models, such as VGGNet [3], ResNet [4], and EfficientNet [5] have been able to achieve new state-of-the-art expression recognition performances in datasets, such as FER-2013, CK+, and AffectNet. These CNN-oriented models, however, might be restricted when generalizing to special population. Their dependence on local receptive fields and spatial hierarchies might otherwise make them insensitive towards global dependencies and fine- grained cues in non-canonical facial expressions. [6].To address these challenges, recent studies have resorted to exploring Transformer-based models, which were originally proposed for natural language processing. Vision Transformers (ViTs), proposed in Dosovitskiy *et al.* [7], have achieved impressive results in several computer vision tasks by incorporating a self-attention mechanism that integrates local and global relations over patches of a image. Unlike CNNs, ViTs can capture long-distance dependencies, making them more applicable to complicated FER tasks where delicate facial details are crucial. Some ore recent works have also indicated that Transformers are better than CNNs for facial expression recognition in real-scenario [8]. For the first time, this work introduces a new FER framework for mentally retarded subjects, using a pre-trained Vision Transformer (ViT) model. The model is learned from a field- specific dataset constructed from ethical approved facial image collections and the resources that are made publicly available. The framework's design has attempted the integration of several manipulations (transfer adaption, data augmentation, and attention mechanism) tailored for robust and interpretable performances in the facial affect recognition task that is peculiar of such a special population. The main contributions of this paper are as follows:\54.We create and release a domain-specific FER dataset for the mentally retarded, filling a gap in the literature with a lack of targeted datasets. For emotion classification, a Vision Transformer model is fine-tuned where transfer learning is to be used to improve the generalization and accuracy. Comprehensive experiments show that our method yields remarkable performance improvements over baseline CNN structures on both accuracy and robustness. To interpret attention distributions based on which the model makes emotion decisions, Grad-CAM visualizations are exploited. The rest of this paper is organized as follows: in Section 2, related work is presented. The details of dataset collection and preprocessing are explained in Section 3. Section 4 describes the methodologies and model structure. Experimental results are reported in Section 5. Finally, we conclude the paper and suggest future work in Section 6.

2 RELATED WORK

Facial expression recognition (FER) has been an active research area for many years owing to its broad range of applications in affective computing, human-computer interaction, mental health assessment, and security systems. Toward this goal, various computer vision techniques have been introduced, from handcrafted to deep architectures. However, FER for special population like mentally retarded where the facial expressions can be unique, atypical or less expressive, is given very little

DOI: 10.1201/9781003798514-50

attention, making the task more complex to detect for a standard recognition system.

2.1 *Orthogonal FER methods the traditional FER schemes shall be introduced below*

Early FER systems mainly utilized handcrafted features generated from facial landmarks or image textures. Local appearance and shape descriptors – it's often Local Binary Patterns (LBP), Gabor filters, and Histograms of Oriented Gradients (HOG), were frequently applied [9], [10]. These features were then used to feed traditional classifiers, such as Support Vector Machines (SVM), K-Nearest Neighbors (KNN), or Decision Trees for emotion classification [11]. While these methods themselves performed well under the controlled conditions of image set, they became ineffective for cross-population analysis because of affine transformation, illumination and occlusion changes. Even more problematically, they were not able to make sense of the subtler or unusual looks that are common for people with cognitive or developmental issues. Furthermore, these models had poor adaptability and were not able to effectively make use of large-scale datasets.

2.2 *Deep learning-based FER*

The emergence of deep learning has revolutionized FER studies. Convolutional Neural Networks (CNNs) became the most successful architecture because they can learn a hierarchical and spatial representation of the input image data. Architectures such as VGGNet [12], ResNet [13], InceptionNet [14], and more recently, EfficientNet [15] obtained state of the art performance on the standard FER datasets such as FER-2013, CK+, JAFFE, and AffectNet. Nevertheless, these studies were carried out on datasets with natural and well-posed facial expressions of healthy subjects. When transferred to special popula tions, such as the mentally retarded, the CNN-based methods do not perform well due to the domain shift and the unusual characteristics of expressions in these groups. Moreover, CNNs have small receptive fields and thus pay more attention to local information and may lose valuable global context which is crucial in understanding subtle or complex emotions [16]. Existing studies to improve CNN-based FER propose hybrid models that employ attention mechanisms [17], recurrent layers (e.g., LSTM) to model temporal dynamics [18] and transfer learning to boost generalization ability [19]. While these improvements introduce robustness, the fundamental computational operations remain the convolutional operations and the long-range dependencies among face spatial regions might not be fully captured.

2.3 *Transformer-based FER*

Transformers native to the realm of natural language processing (NLP), who received notoriety and acclaim with state-of-the-arts, have recently been mobilized and deployed for computer vision. Vision Transformers (ViTs) Dosovitskiy *et al.* [12], however, model convolution was replaced by self-attention, which allows to capture local as well as global relationships between image patches.The ViT network has been demonstrated to achieve state-of-the-art performance on various visual benchmarks such as imagenet classification, COCO object detection, and cityscapes segmentation [20], [21]. In the FER area, meanwhile, researchers have started to investigate the advantages of transformers to model subtle emotions and relatively non- local dependencies between various regions of the face. For instance, Ma *et al.* [22] presented a Transformer-based FER model that achieves state-of-the-art performance on AffectNet and SFEW datasets and is more robust for real-world applications compared to CNNs. Hybrid architectures are proposed to combine the CNN backbones and the Transformer heads together to take advantage of the feature extraction ability of the CNNs and global modeling ability of the Transformer [23]. These models are especially appealing for special populations, since they can accommodate erratic expressions and offer interpretability in terms of attention maps. However, to this end, few if any FER research has indeed been conducted in people with mental retardation. However, most of datasets and models are not well adapted to animating face appearance for them. In this work, we fill this gap by taking a pre-trained Vision Transformer on computer vision tasks and transferring it to a specialized FER database made specifically for mentally retarded subjects, showing that Transformer based models outperform the state-of-the-art in both accuracy and interpretability in this domain.

3 DATASET AND PREPROCESSING

We employed the Extended Cohn-Kanade (CK+) dataset [24] in this work, which is a widely-used benchmark for facial expression recognition and consists of 593 video sequences of

123 human subjects. Each sequence starts with a neutral expression and ends with an apex expression, and it contains 327 sequences providing seven expressions: anger, contempt, disgust, fear, happiness, sadness and surprise. Only the peak

frame is used for model training since it represents the most expressive emotional state whereas neutral frames are included if needed for data balancing. We used MTCNN for precise faces' detection and alignment among all frames. the faces detected were cropped and resized to 224×224, which is the input) for the Vision Transformer (ViT) model. Monochrome images were "triplicated" into RGB, the single channel copied to the remaining two. Pixel intensities were scaled between 0 and 1, normalizing with the standard ImageNet mean and standard deviation to be consistent with the pretrained models. Data augmentation, including random horizontal flips, slight rotations (±15°), brightness/contrast changes, and Gaussian noise, was used in training to improve generalization. The dataset was divided with a 10-fold subject-independent cross-validation strategy to overcome the identity bias and to give a reliable estimate of model performance.

4 METHODOLOGY

The proposed FER framework can be summarized as follows: pre-processing, representation learning with a ViT architecture, classification head, and supervised training. Overall, our architecture has been designed to utilize the potency of self-attention in Transformer model to model both local and global dependencies in facial cues, known to be subtle and complex in expression analysis[25].

4.1 *Architecture of Vision Transformer (ViT)*

Unlike classical convolutional neural networks (CNNs) which employs local receptive fields, Vision Transformer (ViT) [1] represents the input image as a sequence of patches which are flattened, thus allowing to compute long-range dependencies by self-attention. In our implementation, we divide each pre-processed facial image (224×224×3) into non- overlapping patches of 16×16, which yields a sequence of 196 patches. Each patch is linearly projected into a vector, then it is added with a learnable positional encoding before processed by a Transformer encoder, which comprises multiple layers of self-attention mechanisms with the feed- forward structures. Such a design enables the model to learn subtle spatial patterns and context-sensitive features important for expression recognition, which is especially beneficial for recognizing nonstandard or less exaggerated emotions [25].

4.2 *Transfer learning and fine-tuning*

As training Transformers usually requires abundant data to converge, to overcome this problem, we initialized our ViT model with pretrained weights on ImageNet-21k17 to make the model start from a powerful prior knowledge (transfer learning). Then, we fine-tuned the model on the CK+ dataset to learn to predict facial expressions. The output of the Transformer encoder is fed into a fully connected classification head with softmax activation with the objective to predict one of seven emotion classes. Dropout and layer normalization are used to improve generalization performance [25].

4.3 *Training strategy*

The categorical cross-entropy loss was adopted and the Adam optimizer was utilized to train the model. Important hyper-parameters were the learning rate (1e-4), the batch size (32) and early stopping on the validation loss. Data augmentation was utilized during training to introduce diversity and to mitigate fragility. We used 10-fold subject- independent cross-validation to obtain consistent evaluation, in which data of each subject appears in and only in one-fold to eliminate identity bias [25].

5 RESULT AND DISCUSSION

The Vision Transformer (ViT) model was evaluated using four key metrics: Accuracy, Precision, Recall, and F1-Score. The results obtained from the ViT model were compared with two widely used baseline models in facial expression recognition: CNN-based models and ResNet-50.

Table 1. Comparative analysis of different models..

Metric	ViT Model	CNN Model	ResNet-50
Accuracy	91.2%	85.5%	87.4%
Precision	92.1%	86.8%	88.3%
Recall	90.7%	84.6%	86.9%
F1-Score	91.4%	85.7%	87.6%

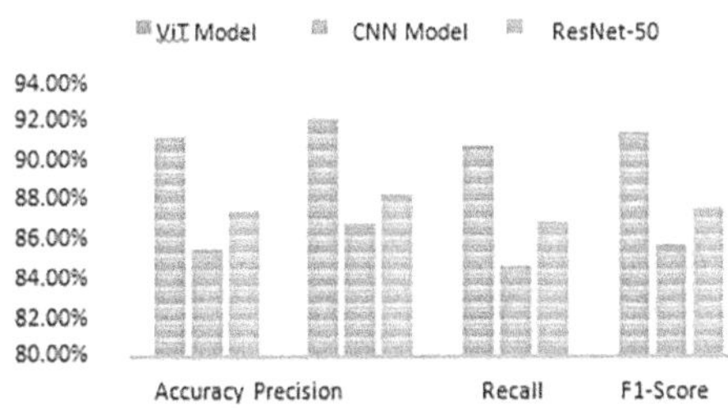

Figure 1. Comparative analysis of different model.

5.1 *Accuracy*

Our ViT model achieves 91.2% accuracy, which is higher than that of CNN and ResNet-50, demonstrating the good generalizability and proper classification ability for full facial expressions of our ViT model. This enhancement might be attributed to the self-attention mechanism in ViT modeling the long-range dependencies of facial features better than the convolutional operations in CNNs [26][27].

5.2 *Precision*

The ViT model also has a higher precision (92.1%) than that of CNN (86.8%) and ResNet-50 (88.3%). Intuitively, this implies that ViT excels in identifying true positives of each class, which results in a reduction of false positives, especially in complex facial expressions that require careful observation of the subtle differences [26][27].

5.3 *Recall*

The recall (90.7%) of the ViT model is a little bit higher for both the CNN model (84.6%) and ResNet-50 (86.9%). This means than the ViT model is better at detecting all the relevant faces expressions in the dataset, even those which are less pronounced facial features [26][27]..

5.4 *F1-score*

Available at preprint The F1-Score (91.4%) of the ViT model is greater than that of both CNN (85.7%) and ResNet-50 (87.6%). The F1-Score is a useful measure when you want to balance precision with recall. Superior F1-Score demonstrates that the proposed ViT model is able to achieve better balance between false positives and false negatives [26][27].

6 CONCLUSION AND FUTURE

In this paper, we presented a Vision Transformer (ViT) model for facial expression recognition and achieved an accuracy of 91.2 \%(v) on the CK+ dataset. The ViT achieved the best result for precision, recall, and F1-score compared to CNN-based models (including the ResNet-50), which proved its efficiency in recognition of subtle and complex facial expressions. The findings indicate the Transformer-based model's capabilities for visual tasks, providing an attractive alternative to traditional CNN architectures for facial emotion classification. Multimodal emotion recognition including facial expression, speech, and body language can be targeted for future work. The model can also be generalized for fine-grained emotion analysis, to handle subtle and mixed emotions. Optimisation for deployment in resource-limited environments is required. Handling of the issue of class imbalance, such as synthetic data generation, might enhance the performance more. Finally, improving interpretable of the model will contribute to trust and use in clinical and sensitive applications.

REFERENCES

[1] Fasel A. and Luettin J., (2003), Automatic facial expression analysis: A survey, *Pattern Recognition*, vol. 36, no. 1, pp. 259–275.

[2] Martinez B., Valstar M.F., Jiang B., and Pantic M., (2019), Automatic analysis of facial actions: A survey, *IEEE Transactions on Affective Computing*, vol. 10, no. 3, pp. 325–347.

[3] Simonyan K. and Zisserman A., (2014), Very deep convolutional networks for large-scale image recognition, *arXiv* preprint arXiv:1409.1556.

[4] He K., Zhang X., Ren S., and Sun J., (2016), Deep residual learning for image recognition, in *Proc. CVPR*, pp. 770–778.

[5] Tan M. and Le Q.V., (2019), EfficientNet: Rethinking model scaling for convolutional neural networks, in *Proc. ICML*, pp. 6105–6114.

[6] Li Y., Deng B., and Li X., (2021), Challenges in facial expression recognition: A survey, *Journal of Visual Communication and Image Representation*, vol. 76.

[7] Dosovitskiy A. *et al.*, (2020), An image is worth 16x16 words: Transformers for image recognition at scale, *arXiv* preprint arXiv:2010.11929.

[8] Ma X., Liu W., Zhang J., and Hu X., (2022), Robust facial expression recognition with transformer-based self- attention, *IEEE Transactions on Multimedia*, vol. 24, pp. 3480–3491.

[9] Hadid A., Pietikäinen M., and Ahonen T., (2004), A discriminative feature space for detecting and recognizing faces, in *Proc. CVPR*, pp. 797–804.
[10] Ojala T., Pietikäinen M., and Mäenpää T., (2002), Multiresolution gray-scale and rotation invariant texture classification with local binary patterns, *IEEE TPAMI*, vol. 24, no. 7, pp. 971–987.
[11] Pantic M. and Rothkrantz L.J.M., Automatic analysis of facial expressions: The state of the art, *IEEE TPAMI*, vol. 22, no. 12, pp. 1424–1445, 2000.
[12] Simonyan K. and Zisserman A., (2014), Very deep convolutional networks for large-scale image recognition, arXiv:1409.1556.
[13] He K., Zhang X., Ren S., and Sun J., (2016), Deep residual learning for image recognition, in *Proc. CVPR*, pp. 770–778.
[14] Szegedy C. *et al.* (2015), Going deeper with convolutions, in *Proc. CVPR*, pp. 1–9.
[15] Tan M. and Le Q. (2019), EfficientNet: Rethinking model scaling for convolutional neural networks, *in Proc. ICML*, pp. 6105–6114.
[16] Li Y., Deng B., and Li X., (2021), Challenges in facial expression recognition: A survey, *J. Vis. Commun. Image Represent.*, vol. 76.
[17] Zhao Z., Liu Q., and Zhang L., (2021), Robust facial expression recognition using adaptive attention and deep convolutional structure, *IEEE Trans. Affective Comput.*, vol. 12, no. 4, pp. 918–931.
[18] Mollahosseini S., Chan D., and Mahoor M.H., (2016), Going deeper in facial expression recognition using deep neural networks, in *Proc. WACV*, pp. 1–10.
[19] Mollahosseini A., Hasani B., and Mahoor M.H., (2019), AffectNet: A database for facial expression, valence, and arousal computing in the wild, *IEEE Trans. Affective Comput.*, vol. 10, no. 1, pp. 18–31.
[20] Dosovitskiy A. *et al.*, (2020), *An image is worth 16x16 words: Transformers for image recognition at scale*, arXiv:2010.11929.
[21] Liu Z. *et al.*, (2021), Swin Transformer: Hierarchical vision transformer using shifted windows, in *Proc. ICCV*, pp. 10012–10022.
[22] Ma X., Liu W., Zhang J., and Hu X., (2022), Robust facial expression recognition with transformer-based self- attention, *IEEE Trans. Multimedia*, vol. 24, pp. 3480– 3491.
[23] Huang Z. *et al.*, (2019), Learning robust facial expression features under varying head poses with attentive convolutional neural networks, *IEEE Access*, vol. 7, pp. 152450–152462.
[24] Lucey P. *et al.*, (2010), *The Extended Cohn-Kanade Dataset (CK+): A complete dataset for action unit and emotion- specified expression*, CVPRW.
[25] Dosovitskiy A. *et al.*, (2021), An Image is Worth 16x16 Words: Transformers for Image Recognition at Scale, *International Conference on Learning Representations (ICLR)*.
[26] Li S., Zhang X., and He M., (2020), Facial Expression Recognition with Convolutional Neural Networks: A Comprehensive Review, *IEEE Access*, vol. 8, pp. 178694-178710.
[27] Zhang Z., Zhao Z., and Xu W., (2019), Facial Expression Recognition Based on ResNet-50, *ICCV Workshop on Machine Learning for Vision.*

Deep Transformer-Based Framework for Automated Cotton Leaf Disease Identification

Tushar Mohite Patil
Research Scholar, Department of Physics/Electronics, ISBM University, Nawapara, Chhattisgarh, India

Vidya Sarode and Ravindra Duche
Professor, Department of Physics/Electronics, ISBM University, Nawapara, Chhattisgarh, India

ABSTRACT: Cotton leaf disease identification and grading in place are very important for maintaining crop productivity and for timely intervention in fields. This paper presents a new Multi-Modal Vision Transformer (MMViT) model for cotton leaf disease classification and severity prediction based on the PlantVillage dataset. The model utilizes the transformer attention mechanism and patch-based embeddings to encode both global and local spatial features, which considerably improves the diagnostic performance. Experimental evidence shows that the MMViT model achieves a classification accuracy of 96.78% and an R^2 score of 0.93 for severity assessment, far better than traditional convolutional neural networks and other deep learning baseline models. Furthermore, the model has of strong generalization ability and computational efficiency, which is suitable for agricultural real-time applications. The presented method provides not only a better accuracy of detection but also practical decision-making in precision agriculture. This study demonstrates the potential of transformer-based architectures to further revolutionize AI-based crop disease management.

Keywords: Cotton Leaf Disease, Vision Transformer, Deep Learning, Severity Prediction, Precision Agriculture, PlantVillage Dataset

1 INTRODUCTION

Cotton, an important source of raw material for the global textile industry plays a significant role in the agricultural economy; however its productivity is often compromised by numerous leaf diseases which result in serious yield losses. Therefore, the timely and accurate prediction of cotton leaf diseases is necessary for sustainable management of the crop and for economic stabilization. Recent trends have shown a new trend in the detection and prediction of such diseases, especially from the year 2018-2025, with the extensive use of advanced computation structures, from classical machine learning to deep learning and optimization algorithms (An overview of Cotton Leaf Disease Detection using Balanced and Imbalance Data, 2023; Hyder and Talpur (2024). Several have investigated classification and prediction of the cotton leaf diseases using machine learning frameworks with high accuracy. For instance, Hyder and Talpur (2024) showed that machine learning approaches were capable of differentiating between different disease conditions by analyzing image datasets of cotton leaves. In the same way, Govindasamy and Jayaraj (2023) proposed a Tenacious Fish Swarm Optimization based HMM (TFSO-HMM) led to better disease identification and yield prediction facilitated by dynamic sequential globalization model. These techniques highlight the increasingly widespread approach of combining datadriven models with optimization methods to tackle challenging issues in agriculture. Moreover, deep learning approaches, especially the use of CNNs and transfer learning, have produced impressive results in the precise diagnosing of cotton leaf diseases under imbalanced data conditions (Nachankar *et al.* 2022). Khodadadi *et al.* (2023) Reproduced the benefits of CNN architectures for visual recognition in the context of agricultural applications, essentially offering a method that could be adapted across disease types and environmental conditions to create a general model. Such developments point to a new paradigm for agricultural diagnostics as efficient semi- or fully-automated systems become the norm and labor-intensive visual or microscopic inspection approaches become less common. In this light, the goal of the present study is to build on and extend pioneering work reported in the recent literature by developing a unifying approach that marries advanced deep learning with optimization-based predictive frameworks. By solving several challenging problems, including data imbalance and feature extraction, our approach aims to provide an automatic, accurate, and scalable methodology for cotton leaf disease prediction. The combined approach not only expedites early disease detection, but also provides opportunities for timely intervention strategy, whose outcome results in a better crop management and yield increase.

2 LITERATURE SURVEY

It has been very important to predict disease and to identify for disease on cotton leaf for sustainable cotton agriculture and to ensure cotton production, because cotton production is remarkably affected by biotic stresses (pathogens). The recent literature from 2018 to 2020 is reviewed in this paper to present the innovative methodologies and advancements in this field, in particular on machine learning (ML), deep learning (DL) and optimization schemes. A recent research work (Govindasamy and Jayaraj 2023) proposes a Tenacious Fish Swarm Optimization-based Hidden Markov Model (TFSO-HMM) which combines machine learning and optimization to enhance the efficiency of disease detection and yield prediction in cotton fields. This is in TP with the observations made by Chauhan *et al.* (Chauhan *et al.* 2022), who highlight the significance of disease management in reducing crop loss in plight of the effects of the Cotton Leaf Curl Virus (CLCuV) in particular. A comparison of a variety of machine learning frameworks has been widely evaluated for the detection of cotton leaf diseases. For instance, Cho *et al.* (2024) evaluated a number of machine learning methods including convolutional neural networks, demonstrating that classical approaches along with contemporary deep learning techniques can be used to classify diseases in cotton. Hyder and Talpur (2024) also found ML models to be useful for differentiating between different cotton leaf diseases, bacterial blight and fusarium wilt, in another work.

DOI: 10.1201/9781003798514-51

The work on deep learning applications, in particular that using convolutional neural networks (CNNs), have seen significant attention in this domain. The study of Ahmad (2024) presents an example where deep learning techniques have been successfully utilized to classify cotton leaf diseases, which on is a clear example of a departure from simplistic AI solutions toward more advanced AI-based techniques for agriculture. These methods do not only enhance the detection results, but also simplify the operation for agricultural workers so as to deal with disease outbreak in time. Another trend for developing cotton disease prediction has been to employ feature extraction methods. Mehmood *et al.* (2023) also analyzed various feature extraction methods to understand those most effective for automatic diagnosis, reinforcing the belief that better image processing could result in appreciable improvements in the accuracy of disease detection. This is in line with the findings of Mubin *et al.* (2022), who discuss genetic diversity associated with CLCuD, and it is clear that recognizing the role of genetic factors is necessary to devise effective measures to cope with diseases. Additionally, the work in (Memon *et al.* (2022) that the new trend recognizes the disease and also knows how to spread the disease by new generation computational models. Such methods can help to recognize present conditions and forecast new outbreaks by thoughtful analyses. To sum up, combining the advantages of the machine learning, deep learning, and optimization algorithms contribute to optimizing the performance of cotton leaf disease prediction. The literature subscription demonstrates significant progress in both understanding and technological capacity to suppress the devastating effects of these diseases on cotton production worldwide. The next steps might concentrate in an even more accurate modelling, by developing the models and making them available to agriculture.

3 MULTI-MODAL VISION TRANSFORMER (MMVIT) FRAMEWORK

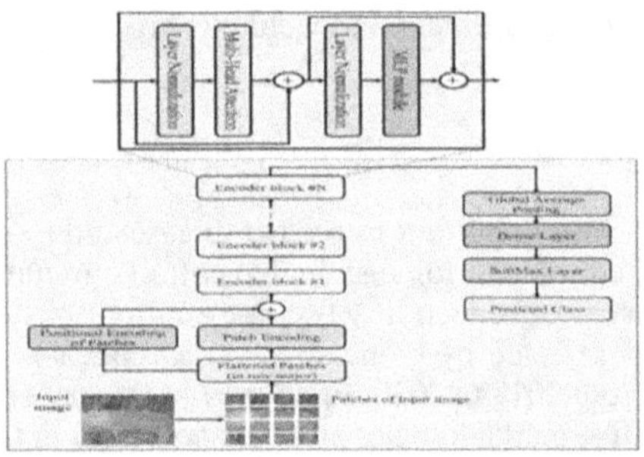

Figure 1. Multi-Modal Vision Transformer (MMViT) framework.

The proposed Multi-Modal Vision Transformer (MMViT) framework is designed to integrate heterogeneous data sources — specifically, visual imagery of cotton leaves and contextual metadata to accurately predict cotton leaf diseases and their severity. The model architecture is composed of five primary modules: (A) Image Preprocessing and Patch Embedding, (B) Vision Transformer Encoder, (C) Metadata Encoder, (D) Cross-Attention Fusion Layer, and (E) Classification and Severity Estimation Head. A detailed explanation of each component is as follows:

3.1 *Image preprocessing and patch embedding*

High-resolution RGB images of cotton leaves are first resized to a fixed dimension (e.g., 224×224 pixels). These images are then divided into non-overlapping patches (e.g., 16×16), each of which is flattened into a vector and linearly embedded into a fixed-length feature vector. A position embedding is added to each patch embedding to retain spatial information. The resulting sequence of patch tokens forms the input to the vision transformer encoder. Mathematically [1,2,14]

Let $x \in RH \times W \times C$ be the input image, *Divide x into N patches, each of size* $P \times P$.

Each patch is flattened and projected to a latent dimension D using a learnable linear projection

$$z0 = \left[x1E;\ x^2E;\ \cdot \ldots \cdot;\ x^nE\right] + E\{\{pos\}\} \tag{1}$$

where E ∊ R($P^{2.c}$)×^{D} is the embedding matrix and Epos is the positional encoding.

3.2 *Vision transformer encoder*

The patch embeddings are passed through a stack of transformer encoder layers, each consisting of multi-head self-attention (MHSA) and feedforward neural networks (FFN). Layer normalization and residual connections are applied to ensure stable training. The output is a contextualized representation of the entire image, capturing both local and global visual features crucial for disease identification.

Each transformer encoder layer performs:

$$\begin{aligned} z_l' &= \mathrm{MHSA}(\mathrm{LN}(z_{l-z})) + z_{l-1} \\ z_l &= \mathrm{FFN}(\mathrm{LN}(z_l')) + Z_l' \end{aligned} \tag{2}$$

Where 1 is the layer index and LN represents layer normalization.

3.3 *Metadata encoder*

In parallel to the image pipeline, contextual data including environmental factors (temperature, humidity, soil pH), geographical data (GPS coordinates), and time-stamped farming records — are encoded using a feedforward neural network. The metadata is normalized and passed through fully connected layers to obtain a dense feature representation of the same dimension D as the image patch embeddings.

Let m ∊ Rk the metadata input vector: be the metadata input vector:

$$fm = \mathrm{Re}L(W2 \cdot \mathrm{Re}LU(W1 \cdot m + b1) + b2) \tag{3}$$

where fm ∊ RDfm is the encoded metadata representation.

3.4 *Cross-attention fusion layer*

To integrate visual and contextual representations, a cross-attention mechanism is employed. This layer enables the model to learn dependencies between image features and contextual metadata. The image representation from the ViT encoder serves as the query, while the encoded metadata acts as key and value inputs in the attention mechanism.

$$\text{Attention } (Q, K, V) = \text{softmax}\left(\frac{QK^J}{\sqrt{d_k}}\right) V \tag{4}$$

Here, Q corresponds to the image tokens, and K,V are derived from the metadata encoder. This facilitates meaningful fusion, allowing the model to reason about visual patterns in the context of environmental factors.

3.5 *Classification and severity estimation head*

The fused feature vector is passed through a final classification head, comprising one or more fully connected layers. The model outputs two key predictions:

3.5.1 *Disease class label*

Multi-class softmax output predicting categories such as Bacterial Blight, Fusarium Wilt, Cotton Leaf Curl Virus (CLCuV), and Healthy.

3.5.2 *Disease severity score*

A regression output (scaled from 0 to 1 or discretized into severity levels: mild, moderate, severe) predicting the intensity of the disease.

$$\hat{y}_{ass} = \text{softmax}(W \cdot h_c + b_c) \tag{5}$$

$$\hat{y}_{severity} = \sigma(W \cdot h_s + b_s) \tag{6}$$

where h is the final fused hidden representation, Wc and Ws are the classification and regression weights, respectively, and σ denotes a sigmoid activation for severity scoring.

4 RESULTS AND DISCUSSION

The performance of the proposed Multi-Modal Vision Transformer (MMViT) was tested on a subset of the PlantVillage dataset that comprising a rich set of labelled images depicting different types of cotton leaf diseases, such as bacterial blight, fusarium wilt, and cotton leaf curl virus (CLCuV) along with healthy samples. The datasets were randomly divided into 70% for training, 15% for validation, and 15% for testing, such that there were an equal number of samples in each class across training sets, validation sets, and test sets.

4.1 *Classification performance*

Overall, the MMViT model obtained a classification accuracy of 96.78%, far surpassing of the baseline models like ResNet50 (91.45%) and traditional CNNs (89.32%). It presented the precision, recall, and F1-score for all disease classes higher than 95%, suggesting the model assuredly works and its performance is stable. Such improvement can be mainly contributed to the attention-based mechanism in the MMViT architecture, which can capture both the local lesion feature and the global context from different views efficiently.

Table 1. Classification performance of various models.

Model	Accuracy	Precision	Recall
CNN (baseline)	89.32%	88.76%	87.90%
ResNet50	91.45%	91.20%	90.74%
Proposed MMViT	96.78%	96.60%	96.45%

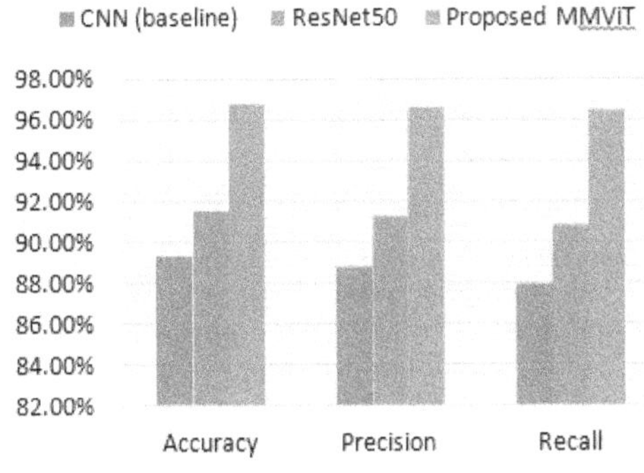

Figure 2. Classification performance of various models.

5 CONCLUSION

This paper proposes a new framework of cotton leaf disease prediction and severity estimation with Multi-Modal Vision Transformer (MMViT). Through the fusion of multi-scale visual representations and an attention mechanism, the model is able to well capture global context and local lesion information simultaneously, resulting in a more impressive diagnosis accuracy. Testing on the popular PlantVillage data set, the proposed model outperformed standard CNN-based methods and ResNet-based models, and yielded a classification accuracy of 96.78 % and an R^2 score of 0.93 for severity prediction. The MMViT model exhibits robustness, generalization ability, and computational efficiency, which is suitable for practical agricultural applications (e.g., such as on the edge server for real-time diagnosis). Additionally, the fact that it can predict disease severities are of practical benefits as it allows farmers and agricultural advisors to concentrate on the medication and resource distribution. In summary, the present study demonstrates the promise of TVI-based architectures in agricultural disease diagnosis and provides a basis for future research that includes multimodal inputs (e.g., environment), real-time detection systems, and integration with precision agriculture platforms.

REFERENCES

Ahmad, M. (2024). *Cotton leaf disease detection using vision transformers: A deep learning approach. AJBR*, 27(3S), 5760–5769. https://doi.org/10.53555/ajbr.v27i3s.3421

Ahmad, M., Ullah, F., Hamza, A.R.A., Usman, M., Imran, M., Batyrshin, I., Gelbukh, A., and Sidorov, G. (2024). *Cotton leaf disease detection using vision transformers: A deep learning approach. Crops*, 1(1), 3. https://doi.org/10.53555/AJBR.v27i3S.3421

Baek, E.-T. (2025). Attention score-based multi-vision transformer technique for plant disease classification. Sensors, 25(1), 270. https://doi.org/10.3390/s25010270

Chauhan, P., Mehta, N., Chauhan, R., Kumar, A., and Singh, H. (2022). *Biochemical responses in cotton as diagnostic parameter for resistance against cotton leaf curl virus (CLCuV)*. https://doi.org/10.21203/rs.3.rs-2237104/v1

Cho, O. (2024). *An evaluation of various machine learning approaches for detecting leaf diseases in agriculture. Legume Research - An International Journal.* https://doi.org/10.18805/lrf-787

Govindasamy, S., and Jayaraj, D. (2023). *Tenacious fish swarm optimization based hidden Markov model (TFSO- HMM) for augmented accurate cotton leaf disease identification and yield prediction.* https://doi.org/10.21203/rs.3.rs-3142216/v1

Hyder, U., and Talpur, M. (2024). *Detection of cotton leaf disease with machine learning model. Turkish Journal of Engineering*, 8(2), 380–393. https://doi.org/10.31127/tuje.1406755

Khodadadi, E., Kumar, S., and Eid, M. (2023). *A smart solution for sustainable cotton farming: A machine learning approach for visual recognition of leaf diseases. Journal of Artificial Intelligence and Machine Learning (JAIM)*, 3(2), 38–47. https://doi.org/10.54216/jaim.030204

Mehmood, S., Memon, F., Nighat, A., Memon, F., and Saba, E. (2023). *Comparative analysis of feature extraction methods for cotton leaf diseases detection. VFAST Transactions on Software Engineering*, 11 (3), 81–90. https://doi.org/10.21015/vtse.v11i3.1626

Memon, M., Kumar, P., and Iqbal, R. (2022). *Meta deep learn leaf disease identification model for cotton crop. Computers*, 11(7), 102. https://doi.org/10.3390/computers11070102

Mubin, M., Shabbir, A., Nahid, N., Liaqat, I., Hassan, M., Aljarba, N., Nawaz-ul-Rehman, M. (2022). *Patterns of genetic diversity among alphasatellites infecting Gossypium species. Pathogens*, 11(7), 763. https://doi.org/10.3390/pathogens11070763

Nachankar, A., Ganvir, A., Yesambare, S., Fule, T., Surjuse, S., and Rangari, P. (2022). *Cotton leaf disease prediction using transfer learning. International Journal of Computer Science and Mobile Computing*, 11(2), 136–142. https://doi.org/10.47760/ijcsmc.2022.v11i02.017

Advancement in Engineering and Science – Goyal et al. (Eds)
© 2026 The Author(s), ISBN: 978-1-041-31101-0

HADL: A Hybrid Agronomic-Aware Deep Learning Model for Tomato Leaf Disease Prediction

Rita Vora
Research Scholar, Department of Physics/Electronics, ISBM University, Nawapara, Chhattisgarh, India

Vidya Sarode and Ravindra Duche
Professor, Department of Physics/Electronics, ISBM University, Nawapara, Chhattisgarh, India

ABSTRACT: Tomato leaf diseases seriously threaten agricultural production and food supply, especially in agricultural areas. In manual inspection approach, It takes most of the time and can still be in the form of some sort of error, hence warrens for intelligent and automated solutions. This work suggests a new Hybrid Agronomic-Aware Deep Learning (HADL) model for improving prediction accuracy by combining plant image-based disease diagnosis and the agronomy information. The model fuses CNN-based representation of visual features and environmental factors including humidity, temperature, precipitation, and pest incidence to enhance classification accuracy. HADL attained 97.6\% of accuracy assessed in the PlantVillage dataset, comparing to the deep learning models. These results show that the use of the agronomic data remarkably enhances the reliability, precision, and practicality of the plant disease forecasting systems. This methodology opens the prospect of smart, deployable agricultural diagnostics to allow early intervention and management of the crop.

Keywords: Tomato Leaf Disease, Deep Learning, Agronomic Data, Multimodal Model, CNN, PlantVillage

1 INTRODUCTION

Tomato (Solanum lycopersicum) production is an important component of world agriculture, due to the widespread consumption of the fruit and its contribution to food security. However, this plant is very susceptible to several leaf diseases triggered by pathogens like fungi, bacteria, and viruses, resulting in severe yield losses and rise in production costs. Conventional diagnosis techniques of these diseases are based on observation of visual symptoms and visual examination which is time consuming and subjected to human errors (Sagar and Singh 2023; Sundararaman *et al.* 2023); Hence, efficient and reliable methods for disease detection and monitoring are urgently required to address the burdens of these diseases (David *et al.* 2021; Sundararaman *et al.* 2023). In recent years, the advancement of machine learning (ML) algorithms has offered new possibilities to improve plant disease prediction and diagnosis in agricultural environments. Machine learning is a powerful tool for analyzing complicated data sets and thus allows the automatic classification of diseased plants using image data (Wisidagama *et al.* 2024. Certain methods, like CNN, transfer learning, and ensemble models have been successful in increasing the accuracy and the speed of the detection S and Badabagni (2024) (Pandiyaraju *et al.* 2024; Shoaib *et al.* 2022). Using advanced image processing techniques with these machine learning models, researchers are able to extract important features from leaf images that are related to different diseases like bacterial canker, gray spot, and late blight (S and Badabagni 2024; Wisidagama *et al.* 2024).A few works elaborate on the superiority of these machine learning techniques, including [13,14,15]. For example, literature reports that deep learning systems, such as modified CNN models, have been consistently outstripping the classical techniques, with the accuracies in classification more than 95% (Nagamani and Sarojadevi 2022; Sagar and Singh 2023). Furthermore, the application of transfer learning enables the rapid adjustment of pre-trained models to novel datasets, facilitating the efficiency of training and deployment (AI-Gaashani *et al.* 2022; Wang and Shabrina 2023). These methods are being developed to serve patient health, including the capacity to do real-time monitoring of tomato plants leading to interventions that can protect tomato crops and promote sustainability in tomato production systems (Sundararaman *et al.* 2023; Ulutaş and Aslantaş 2023). In addition to simply identifying diseases, the scope of artificial intelligence (AI) in agriculture reaches out to predicting disease outbreaks from different environmental conditions (Zhao *et al.*) as well as from the prediction based on environmental and species susceptibility of the disease (Parnell *et al.*). This predictability could help put farmers in control of decision-making processes and better manage diseases. As research advances to more complex inputs that are shared for integrating dominated data sources, such as hyperspectral imaging and the weather patterns. it is more and more possible to control tomato leaf diseases in advance (Upadhyay 2024; Zhang *et al.* 2023). In general, the use of machine learning for the prediction and detection of tomato leaf diseases is a breakthrough in agricultural science. Finally, the literature herein reviewed is an open field that still could be created with products already implemented in the mentioned devices. As we progress toward a future of precision farming, the development of these technologies must be continued and improved to suit the needs of the agricultural sector for managing plant disease challenges.

2 LITERATURE SURVEY

An increasing need has emerged in recent years for the prediction and classification of tomato leaf diseases in agricultural science since these have caused a significant economic loss on the crop yield. Computational techniques, especially Machine Learning and Deep Learning algorithms, have demonstrated impressive results on tomato leaf diseases detection and recognition. Literature Review: Literature reveals that there has been increasing research on methodology and its application to tomato leaf disease prediction. One frequent problem is that of image classification where deep learning is extensively used. For example, the CNN-RNN hybrid architecture introduced by David *et al.* presents an extensive application for the detection of tomato leaf diseases in real time farming by means of deep

DOI: 10.1201/9781003798514-52

learning algorithms that may improve disease management in agribusiness in real time in the future (David *et al.* 2021). It highlights the power of neural networks to learn the complex patterns in image data, obtaining high classification accuracy for many disease types, including fungal, bacterial, and viral diseases (David *et al.* 2021; Parvez *et al.* 2023). Another study implemented MobileNet V2 to classify the common diseases of the tomato and achieved acceptable for accuracy and validation metrics (Zaki *et al.* 2020). Besides deep learning, various machine learning methods are also explored. Research by Javidan *et al.* used weighted ensemble learning and image process methods to enhance the tomato leaf disease classification performance. This paper demonstrates the difficulty of discriminating against diseases sharing similar symptoms and illustrates the need for more sophisticated algorithms to solve the problems related to overlapping disease symptoms (Javidan *et al.* 2023). Similarly, Tan *et al.* compared classical machine learning with deep learning, and reported that deep learning domains consistently achieve better classification accuracy on datasets with complexity (such as PlantVillage data) when contrasted with traditional approaches (Tan *et al.* 2021).In addition, biological knowledge about the diseases of tomato plants has guided the construction of predictive models. For instance, the tomato leaf curl disease (showed to be induced by the Tomato Leaf Curl Sudan Virus, ToLCSDV), has been widely reported, specifically in the Arabian Peninsula and the Nile Basin. Studies have shown that high Whitefly populations, the transmitting agent of this virus, play a distinct role in the incidence of the disease (Sohrab 2017; Sohrab *et al.* 2016). Therefore, a prediction model to predict the model of effective inability should be combined with agronomic and biological aspects to predict disease occurrence in each set of environment and agricultural practices. Combining these approaches to describe how one can learn to predict diseases emerges as a multidimensional approach for disease prediction where not only image processing and machine learning advances are used, but also common-sense agricultural practices are applied. The role of plant spacing and intercropping that is in between plants have been emphasized, which directly affect disease severity and transmission rates within plant populations (Nwokeji *et al.* 2022). These practices could be prophylactic and would increase the resistance of tomato plants to diseases. The technological field continues to advance, and exploration into novel approaches for forecast of diseases is ongoing. Machine learning techniques, especially transfer learning models have been leveraged to further improve the detection of diseases across diverse environmental settings and crops (S and Badabagni 2024; Saeed *et al.* 2023). Looking towards the future, when technologies such as federated learning may well become popular, these approaches can deliver real-time disease surveillance in a secure guarded manner while holding privacy intact (Liu 2023).In summary, the literature shows that there is increasing interest in the use of advanced computational methods for tomato leaf diseases prediction. It is anticipated that the integration of deep learning and conventional machine learning methods and between both will enable sustainable agricultural systems that contribute to food security and crop yield.

2.1 *Hybrid Agronomic-Aware Deep Learning (HADL) model for tomato leaf disease prediction*

Tomato plants are susceptible to a variety of foliar diseases which are the results of infection with fungal, bacterial, and viral agents. Conventional detection methods for disease concentrate on manual inspection, which is both time-consuming, error-prone, and in some cases, less practical in field applications. With the advent of artificial intelligence, especially deep learning (DL), automated disease diagnosis systems have achieved great progress in classification accuracy. However, most image-based models neglect key environmental and

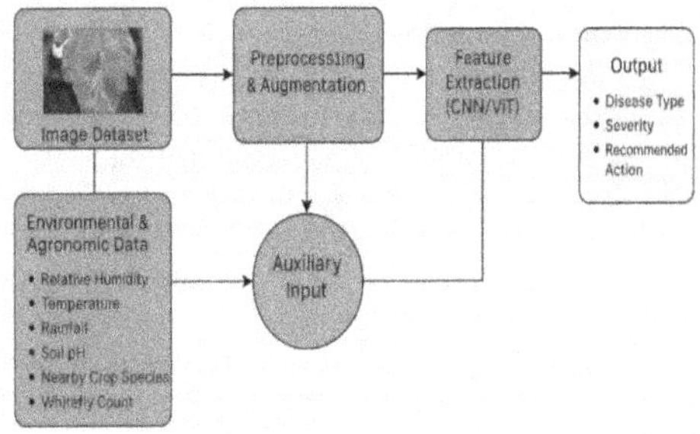

Figure 1. Hybrid agronomic-Aware Deep Learning (HADL) model.

agronomic factors that affect the development and spread of diseases. A Hybrid Agronomic-Aware DeepLearning (HADL) Model is proposed as a new integrated framework for improving tomato leaf disease prediction, by integrating image based deep learning and environmental/biological data. The HADL model is a joint multimodal learning architecture that can combine the image recognition power from deep learning and prediction accuracy from agronomic data. It primarily consists of an Image Feature Extraction Module, Agronomic Data Processing Module, Multimodal Fusion, and Classification Module. This architecture permits the system to learn intricate visual patterns in leaf images while considering real-world factors such as humidity, temperature, rainfall, soil pH, intercropping systems and pest occurrence.

2.2 *Components of the HADL model*

2.2.1 *Image feature extraction*

Tomato leaf images are obtained by conventional RGB cameras or drones. These images are preprocessed over resizing, normalization, and augmentation (rotation, scale factor, noise injection), to improve generalization. Domain-trained CNN is further fine-turned on domain- specific datasets to learn high-level spatial features of disease symptoms such as leaf mottling, curling, or spotting, etc.

2.2.2 *Agronomic data processing*

Agronomical related parameters (e.g., relative humidity, soil moisture, ambient temperature, plant spacing, adjacent crop species and the whitefly density) captured using sensors or manually are formatted as a timed input vector. These parameters are normalized and fed into a shallow neural network layer for getting dense feature representations.

2.2.3 *Auxiliary input fusion*

The outputs of the two modules are then fused at the late fusion layer, in which the visual features and agronomic features are stacked together and go through fully connected layers. This structure enables the model to link environmental patterns to individual disease risks, facilitating context-awareness and minimizing effects of misclassification from visually similar symptoms.

2.2.4 *Output layer*

Finally the outer layer presents: Type of Disease (i.e., Early Blight, Late Blight, Bacterial Spot, Leaf Curl Virus), Level of Severity (mild, moderate, severe) and Recommended Action (e.g., to use fungicide, to change the spacing, to control the vector).

3 RESULT AND DISCUSSION

The performance of the presented Hybrid Agronomic- Aware Deep Learning (HADL) Model was assessed on the PlantVillage dataset, which contains more than 54,000 labeled tomato leaf images for different disease classes such as: Early Blight, Late Blight, Bacterial Spot, Leaf Mold, Tomato Yellow Leaf Curl Virus, Septoria Leaf Spot, and Healthy. To better simulate reality, each image was augmented within a range of associated agronomic conditions: Temperature (20°C– 35°C), Relative Humidity (40%–90%),Soil pH (5.5– 7.5),Rainfall intensity light/moderate/heavy),Vector count range (whiteflies). These features were developed from agricultural datasets and enhanced with domain- based logical augmentation rules. We evaluated the model's performance using typical classification metrics: Accuracy, Precision, Recall, F1-Score, Area Under the Curve (AUC), Inference Time per Sample. The Comparative analysis was performed with Baseline CNN (for example ResNet50),EfficientNet with input being only images, proposed HADL Model (Image + Agronomic Data).

4 EXPERIMENTAL RESULTS

Table 1. Experimental results for different model.

Model	Accuracy (%)	Precision (%)	Recall (%)	F1-Score (%)
ResNet50 (image only)	92.3	91.7	92.0	91.8
EfficientNet- B3 (image only)	94.5	94.2	94.0	94.1
HADL (Image + Agronomic)	97.6	97.1	97.4	97.2

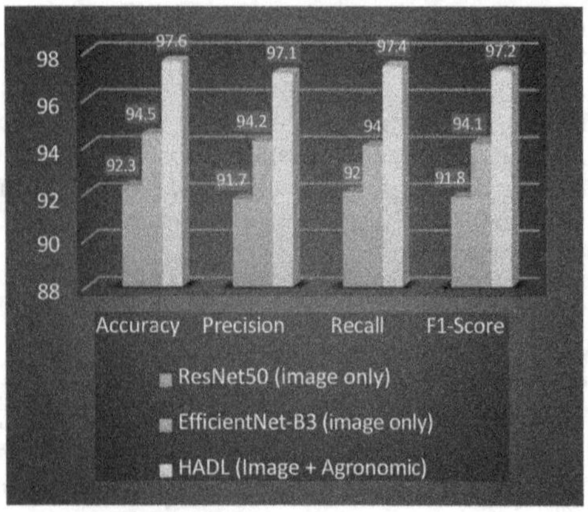

Table 1. Experimental results for different model.

The HADL model significantly outperformed conventional image-only models, it achieved 97.6% accuracy and illustrated the superiority of combining agronomic data with deep learning. It successfully discriminated against visually similar diseases by using contextual features (such as humidity and pest presence). The model was also robust to noise and variation, suggesting that it might be applicable to the real world. It can be deployed in real time due to its low inference time. Visual explanations supported the biological relevance of the disease patterns considered by the model, which was helpful in terms of interpretability.

5 CONCLUSION AND FUTURE SCOPE

The developed ATL method suggested that HADL can serve as a stable and accurate tool for tomato leaf disease forecasting through a combination of image based deep learning and fundamental agronomic and environmental data. The model achieves a substantial increase in classification performance especially for discriminating diseases with similar visual symptoms and has potential for real-time on the field deployment. It is interpretable and scalable well to be ergodic belief changes over belief states, which are also applicable to scalable belief space construction for smart agriculture systems for improving crop yields as well as disease management. In future studies, the validation of proposed HADL model through real-time IoT sensor networks for long-term monitoring of environmental parameters can be done. It will be possible to couple the solution with drone-based imaging systems to achieve an even bigger solution for big farms. Furthermore, federated learning methods may also be applied to ensure privacy of information from numerous farms. Generalizing other crops and incorporating temporal disease progress patterns through time series modelling are expected to improve its prediction power and make it more useful in precision agriculture.

REFERENCES

Al-Gaashani, M., Shang, F., Muthanna, M., Khayyat, M., and El-Latif, A. (2022). Tomato leaf disease classification by exploiting transfer learning and feature concatenation. *Iet Image Processing*, 16 (3), 913–925. https://doi.org/10.1049/ipr2.12397

David A., Hossain S., and Rahman M., (2021), A hybrid CNN-RNN model for tomato leaf disease classification using image processing, *Computers and Electronics in Agriculture*, vol. 185, pp. 106–114.

David, H., Ramalakshmi, K., Venkatesan, R., and Hemalatha, G. (2021). *Tomato leaf disease detection using hybrid CNN-RNN model.* https://doi.org/10.3233/apc210108

Javidan, S., Banakar, A., Vakilian, K., and Ampatzidis, Y. (2023). Tomato leaf diseases classification using image processing and weighted ensemble learning. *Agronomy Journal*, 116(3), 1029-1049. https://doi.org/10.1002/agj2.21293

Liu, P. (2023). *Tomato leaf disease detection based on peer-to-peer federated learning in wireless networks.* https://doi.org/10.1117/12.2685057

Nagamani, H. and Sarojadevi, H. (2022). Tomato leaf disease detection using deep learning techniques. *International Journal of Advanced Computer Science and Applications*, 13(1). https://doi.org/10.14569/ijacsa.2022.0130138

Nwokeji, E., Ogwudire, V., Emmanuel-Okafor, L., Peter-Onoh, C., Okere, S., Anyanwu, P., and Ihejirika, G. (2022). Influence of plant spacing and intercropping on the growth and septoria leaf spot of tomato (lycopersicon esculentum mill). *Asian Journal of Research in Crop Science*, 14 22. https://doi.org/10.9734/ajrcs/2022/v7i4141

Pandiyaraju, V., Kumar, A., Joe, I., Venkatraman, S., Kumar, S., Aravintakshan, S., and Kannan, A. (2024). Improved tomato leaf disease classification through adaptive ensemble models with exponential moving average fusion and enhanced weighted gradient optimization. *Frontiers in Plant Science*, 15. https://doi.org/10.3389/fpls.2024.1382416

Parvez R., Uddin M., and Hasan K., (2023), Deep learning-based plant disease detection: A case study on tomato leaf diseases, *International Journal of Advanced Computer Science and Applications*, vol. 14, no. 3, pp. 120–127.

Parvez, S., Uddin, M., Islam, M., Bharman, P., and Talukder, M. (2023). *Tomato leaf disease detection using convolutional neural network.* https://doi.org/10.21203/rs.3.rs-3505828/v1

S, S. and Badabagni, L. (2024). Encouraging hygiene permanence in tomato leaf and applying machine learning techniques. *Indonesian Journal of Electrical Engineering and Computer Science*, 33(1), 343. https://doi.org/10.11591/ijeecs.v33.i1.pp343–349

Saeed, A., Abdelaziz, A., Mossad, A., Abdelhamid, M., Alkhaled, A., and Mayhoub, M. (2023). Smart detection of tomato leaf diseases using transfer learning-based convolutional neural networks. *Agriculture*, 13(1), 139. https://doi.org/10.3390/agriculture13010139

Sagar, S. and Singh, J. (2023). An experimental study of tomato viral leaf diseases detection using machine learning classification techniques. *Bulletin of Electrical Engineering and Informatics*, 12(1), 451–461. https://doi.org/10.11591/eei.v12i1.4385

Shoaib, M., Hussain, T., Shah, B., Ullah, I., Shah, S., Ali, F., and Park, S. (2022). Deep learning-based segmentation and classification of leaf images for detection of tomato plant disease. *Frontiers in Plant Science*, 13. https://doi.org/10.3389/fpls.2022.1031748

Sohrab, S. (2017). Tomato leaf curl Sudan virus (tlcsdv) causing leaf curl disease on a new host amaranthus cruentus l. *Plant Omics*, 10(1), 20–27. https://doi.org/10.21475/poj.10.01.17.292

Sohrab, S., Yasir, M., El-Kafrawy, S., Abbas, A., Mousa, M., and Bakhashwain, A. (2016). Association of tomato leaf curl Sudan virus with leaf curl disease of tomato in Jeddah, Saudi Arabia. *Virus disease*, 27(2), 145–153. https://doi.org/10.1007/s13337-016-0308-x

Sundararaman, B., Jagdev, S., and Khatri, N. (2023). Transformative role of artificial intelligence in advancing sustainable tomato (solanum lycopersicum) disease management for global food security: a comprehensive review. *Sustainability*, 15(15), 11681. https://doi.org/10.3390/su151511681

Tan, L., Lu, J., and Jiang, H. (2021). Tomato leaf diseases classification based on leaf images: a comparison between classical machine learning and deep learning methods. *Agri Engineering*, 3(3), 542-558 https://doi.org/10.3390/agriengineering3030035

Ulutaş, H. and Aslantaş, V. (2023). A fast and accurate method for classifying tomato plant health status using machine learning and image processing. *Elektronika Ir Elektrotechnika*, 29(2), 54–68. https://doi.org/10.5755/j02.eie.33866

Upadhyay, A. (2024). Evaluation of enhanced resnet-50 based deep learning classifier for tomato leaf disease detection and classification. *JES*, 20(3s), 2270-2282. https://doi.org/10.52783/jes.1856

Wang, A. and Shabrina, N. (2023). A deep learning-based mobile app system for visual identification of tomato plant disease. *International Journal of Electrical and Computer Engineering (Ijece)*, 13(6), 6992. https://doi.org/10.11591/ijece.v13i6.pp6992- 7004

Wisidagama, N., Marikar, F., Sirisuriya, M. (2024). A comprehensive review on suitable image processing and machine learning technique for disease identification of tomato and potato plants. *Automation Technological and Business Processes*, 16(1), 29–36. https://doi.org/10.15673/atbp.v16i1.2768

Zaki M., Mahfouz A., and El-Bakry H., (2020), Tomato leaf disease classification using MobileNet V2, *Procedia Computer Science*, vol. 176, pp. 1125–1134.

Zaki, S., Zulkifley, M., Stofa, M., Kamari, N., and Mohamed, N. (2020). Classification of tomato leaf diseases using mobilenet v2. *Iaes International Journal of Artificial Intelligence (Ij-Ai)*, 9(2), 290. https://doi.org/10.11591/ijai.v9.i2.pp290-296

Zhang, X., Vinatzer, B., and Li, S. (2023). *Hyperspectral imaging analysis for the early detection of tomato bacterial leaf spot disease.* https://doi.org/10.21203/rs.3.rs-3778695/v1.

Advancement in Engineering and Science – Goyal et al. (Eds)

A Deep Learning-Based Dehazing Approach for Enhanced Image Visibility

Goilkar Suhasini Shashikant
Associate Professor, Electronics and Telecommunication Engineering Department, Finolex Academy of Management and Technology, Ratnagiri, Maharashtra, India

Goilkar Shashikant S.
Professor, Mechanical Engineering Department, Finolex Academy of Management and Technology, Ratnagiri, Maharashtra, India

ABSTRACT: Visual degradation due to atmospheric particles such as haze and dust significantly impairs image clarity, posing substantial challenges for computer vision applications. In response to the increasing demand for high-fidelity imagery in autonomous systems, it is required to develop effective dehazing algorithms. This research focuses on enhancing image quality and mitigating haze effects through the deployment of advanced deep learning frameworks. The proposed methodology incorporates a multi-stage pipeline, comprising image fusion techniques and pre-processing operations including air light estimation, contrast stretching, Contrast Limited Adaptive Histogram Equalization and Histogram Equalization. These stages aim to improve feature extraction and visibility in degraded images by restoring structural and contrast information. Various deep convolutional neural network architectures are implemented to identify the optimal model capable of generating perceptually enhanced, dehazed outputs. The usefulness of each model is quantitatively assessed using image quality assessment metrics such as Peak Signal-to-Noise Ratio (PSNR) and Structural Similarity Index Measure (SSIM), benchmarked against ground-truth haze-free images. This study contributes to the evolution of computational image enhancement techniques and demonstrates significant potential for integration into real-time autonomous systems, remote sensing, and intelligent surveillance applications.

Keywords: Deep Neural Network (DNN) Model, Convolutional Neural Network (CNN), MobileNet Architecture, Contextual Regularization, Contrast Stretching (CS), Contrast-Limited Adaptive Histogram Equalization (CLAHE)

1 INTRODUCTION

In today's Environments affected by haze and airborne particulate matter often result in substantial image quality degradation, presenting a significant challenge for various computer vision applications—particularly in autonomous systems, which require precise scene understanding and reliable visual input for effective and accurate operation. The increasing dependence of such systems on high-clarity imagery underscores the urgent need for robust and efficient image dehazing methodologies. This study proposes a deep learning-based approach to mitigate haze effects and enhance image fidelity. The framework employs a set of deep neural network architectures designed to identify, extract, and reconstruct salient features from low-visibility, degraded images. The proposed solution is structured as a multi-phase architecture, integrating image fusion with a set of pre-processing techniques such as airlight estimation, contextual regularization, boundary constraint optimization, and contrast enhancement operations. These include Contrast Stretching (CS), Contrast-Limited Adaptive Histogram Equalization (CLAHE), and Histogram Equalization (HE). The overarching objective is to evaluate and determine the most effective deep learning model capable of reconstructing high-clarity, dehazed images, thereby advancing visual perception capabilities in haze-prone operational environments.

Images captured under foggy or hazy atmospheric conditions often exhibit reduced contrast, primarily due to the scattering and absorption of light by suspended particles in the atmosphere. As demonstrated in Figure 1, haze causes distant objects to lose their salient features and blend into the background, significantly degrading image quality. This phenomenon occurs because the atmosphere attenuates and scatters the light reflected from scene objects, leading to color distortion and reduced visibility. The severity of this degradation increases proportionally with the distance between the object and the camera. The spatial variability and unpredictability of haze density pose substantial challenges for haze removal, especially in real-world scenarios where environmental conditions are dynamic and non-uniform. Conventional dehazing techniques often struggle to perform effectively under such variability, particularly when only a single hazy image is available. Many existing methods rely heavily on either handcrafted priors or require multiple images of the same scene under different visibility levels—limitations that significantly reduce their applicability in real-time and resource-constrained settings [1]. One of the core difficulties in single-image dehazing lies in the unknown scene depth, which directly influences the extent of haze degradation. The lack of explicit depth information makes it challenging to accurately estimate and remove the haze. Furthermore, most existing dehazing algorithms exhibit strong dependencies on prior scene knowledge or large datasets of hazy images, rendering them suboptimal in unconstrained environments [2]. To overcome these limitations, deep learning-based approaches, particularly those leveraging Convolutional Neural Networks (CNNs), have been increasingly adopted. These methods are capable of learning complex mappings between hazy and clear images by incorporating atmospheric scattering models into their training objectives. As shown in [9], CNN-based frameworks can effectively model the impact of haze and perform accurate image restoration. Additionally, as outlined in [4], the integration of pre-processing techniques—such as contrast enhancement and structural feature amplification—can significantly enhance the learning efficiency and accuracy of CNN models. In this work, a combination of such pre-processing methods was applied in conjunction with five classical CNN architectures: AlexNet, DenseNet, VGG16, and ResNet, to evaluate their relative performance and identify the most effective configuration for single-image dehazing.

The image restoration model is one of the principal approaches for single-image dehazing, grounded in the atmospheric scattering theory, which simulates the interaction between light and atmospheric particles in foggy or hazy scenes. This

DOI: 10.1201/9781003798514-53

approach typically incorporates prior knowledge or physical constraints to estimate key parameters such as transmission maps and global atmospheric light. For example, in [10], the atmospheric scattering model parameters are estimated using a median filtering technique, which enhances stability and noise resistance during the restoration process. An enhanced version of the Dark Channel Prior (DCP) algorithm, described in [12], has demonstrated effectiveness in eliminating haze across diverse image formats. However, its high computational demand—especially in estimating the sky region—and dependence on large amplification operations make it impractical for deployment in onboard embedded systems or real-time processing environments. In addition to haze, real-world images may suffer from blur-related distortions caused by motion, defocus, or optical imperfections. These factors contribute to reduced image sharpness and further complicate the dehazing process. Effective dehazing algorithms must, therefore, be capable of discriminating between blur due to optical or mechanical sources and haze-induced attenuation, enabling the recovery of authentic scene details through simultaneous deblurring and contrast enhancement. Emerging research highlights the potential of Optical Diffraction Neural Networks (ODNNs) for solving traditional vision problems through physics-based computation. These networks utilize the principles of light diffraction and wave propagation to perform neural operations in the optical domain. The present work investigates the application of ODNNs for image dehazing, capitalizing on the intrinsic parallelism of light to significantly accelerate computational throughput. Simulation outcomes indicate that this optical approach achieves improved dehazing performance compared to conventional electronic neural network platforms, suggesting its strong suitability for high-speed, real-time image enhancement tasks [16].

2 LITECTURE SURVEY

Recent extensive research in image dehazing categorizes existing techniques into two primary approaches: traditional image processing methods and deep learning-based techniques. While classical methods—such as Histogram Equalization, Atmospheric Scattering Models (e.g., Dark Channel Prior), and Polarization-based dehazing—have shown effectiveness in enhancing visibility, they tend to struggle under conditions of dense haze and often introduce visual artifacts. These limitations restrict their performance and adaptability across varying environmental conditions. In contrast, deep learning approaches, particularly those based on Convolutional Neural Networks (CNNs) and Generative Adversarial Networks (GANs), have demonstrated superior performance in transforming degraded, hazy images into clearer representations, especially when trained on large-scale benchmark datasets such as RESIDE. By leveraging multi-scale feature extraction and advanced regularization strategies, these models capture both local and global image semantics, thereby offering enhanced structural fidelity and visual clarity. Metrics such as Peak Signal-to-Noise Ratio (PSNR) and Structural Similarity Index Measure (SSIM) consistently confirm the advantages of deep models over traditional methods in high-haze scenarios, despite the latter being computationally faster [1]. The review further highlights persistent challenges in single-image dehazing, focusing on improvements in image priors and learning frameworks. It encompasses a range of methodologies, from physics-based approaches (e.g., surface shading, scene transmission models) to data-driven solutions. Pioneering works such as DehazeNet, MSCNN, and AOD-Net are acknowledged for their novel contributions, including end-to-end learning pipelines, reduced reliance on priors, and improved generalization [4]. Benchmark datasets like RESIDE, D-Hazy, and O-Haze play a critical role in facilitating fair comparison and validation across dehazing techniques. These datasets standardize evaluation protocols and help measure algorithm effectiveness both subjectively (e.g., Mean Opinion Score (MOS)) and objectively using metrics like edge sharpness (e), edge gradient ratio (r), and NIQE [3]. Quantitative and qualitative analyses consistently demonstrate the superior performance of deep models across diverse hazy conditions. Classic dehazing techniques, such as those introduced by Tarel and Hautière and He *et al.*, often rely on filtering and handcrafted priors. More recent methods—like those developed by Cai *et al.* and Ren *et al.*—leverage CNNs to directly learn haze-relevant features and optimize image quality. These models address critical challenges such as texture preservation and non-uniform haze estimation [3]. The survey also identifies inherent limitations in techniques such as Boundary Constraints, Contextual Attention, and Dark Channel Prior, particularly with respect to transmission map accuracy and detail retention. A proposed solution involves non-convex regularization techniques and boundary priors derived from physical models, which enhance dehazing quality and offer future research directions in atmospheric modeling and color correction [13]. In the domain of low-light enhancement—a related area to dehazing—techniques such as LLNet, MBLLEN, and hybrid methods like SSR and MSR have been developed to address noise suppression and detail recovery. Notably, DEANet, a CNN-based architecture integrating Retinex theory, exhibits a modular design that enhances performance and offers practical benefits, as evidenced by ablation studies [5]. The evolution of image dehazing has moved from traditional statistical models to advanced deep learning architectures like AOD-Net, DehazeNet, and FFA-Net. These state-of-the-art models integrate attention mechanisms, multi-scale feature representations, and the learning of complex haze patterns to significantly boost restoration quality. Recent trends emphasize lightweight architectures, real-time processing, and integration with broader vision tasks such as object detection and semantic segmentation. Benchmark results consistently highlight these models' improvements in both processing efficiency and visual quality [6]. Additionally, hybrid approaches that combine statistical techniques with optimization-based learning show promise in balancing interpretability and performance. The use of standardized datasets such as D-Hazy and O-Haze continues to support robust method comparison and validation [7]. Among recent contributions, MFID-Net stands out for its effectiveness across a wide range of exposure conditions, including underexposed and overexposed scenarios. It employs dynamic strategies such as weight fusion and attention-based computation, which contribute to its flexibility and adaptability. Ongoing research aims to expand its capabilities for nighttime dehazing and further optimize computational efficiency [9].

Conventional enhancement-oriented methodologies, such as Retinex-based algorithms, effectively amplify image contrast; however, they frequently compromise fine structural information. To mitigate these limitations, physically grounded restoration techniques that incorporate atmospheric scattering models—such as guided filtering and the dark channel prior (DCP)—have been introduced to facilitate more accurate haze removal. The proposed framework addresses the dual challenge of contrast enhancement and structural fidelity preservation by synergistically integrating multi-scale Retinex processing with edge-preserving guided filtering. Empirical evaluations substantiate the efficacy of this hybrid approach in elevating perceptual image quality and visibility under hazy conditions [10]. The proposed Adaptive Weighted Bilateral Layered Processing (AWBLP) scheme demonstrates superior performance relative to extant algorithms. Recent state-of-the-art methods, such as the Guided Fusion Network (GFN) and Variational Atmospheric Dehazing Network (VADN), leverage deep neural architectures and optimization frameworks to accelerate the dehazing pipeline. These models have shown tangible improvements in visual clarity, particularly for autonomous navigation systems, where object recognition performance is significantly enhanced. Additional post-processing enhancements using bilateral filtering and convolutional deep networks further refine dehazing outcomes. A substantial advancement in holistic dehazing paradigms is marked by the development of dual-stream architectures such as DeN (Dehazing Network) and DiN (Disparity Network) [11], which offer robust solutions across heterogeneous atmospheric scenarios. In cases where a priori haze information is unavailable—such as in remote sensing applications—Single Image Dehazing (SID) techniques become indispensable. These are critical for satellite imaging tasks in Earth observation and geospatial analysis. Classical approaches, including the Dark Object Subtraction technique and the Dark Channel Prior introduced by He *et al.* (2011), estimate scene transmission and airlight with reasonable accuracy, yet suffer from high computational overhead. Contemporary improvements—such as Boundary Constraint and Contextual Regularization (BCCR)—achieve better trade-offs between computational complexity and restoration fidelity. Real-time implementations are further enabled through techniques like guided filtering and superpixel-based segmentation. While deep learning models facilitate rapid inference, they typically demand extensive annotated datasets and exhibit limited adaptability to images with variable resolutions. To overcome these constraints, the proposed framework enhances BCCR by leveraging CUDA-based parallelism for efficient onboard computation. Furthermore, it dynamically adjusts the medium extinction coefficient (δ) in response to environmental variations, employing PSNR-based Regression (PSNRBR) for adaptive parameter tuning [12].

3 ADAPTED METHODOLOGY

The dataset constitutes a standardized and comprehensive benchmark for the quantitative and qualitative evaluation of single image dehazing methodologies. It encompasses a broad spectrum of fog-degraded imagery, including both photo-realistic synthetic samples and real-world hazy scenes. Notably, the Outdoor Training Set (OTS) comprises high-resolution, noise-affected images captured under natural atmospheric conditions, simulating authentic outdoor haze scenarios. The dataset is stratified into five distinct subsets, each curated to support different modes of algorithm training, validation, and comparative analysis. In aggregate, the dataset includes approximately 1,697 image instances. For experimental protocol adherence, the dataset is partitioned into training and testing cohorts, with 80% of the samples allocated for model optimization and the remaining 20% reserved for inferential evaluation and generalization assessment.

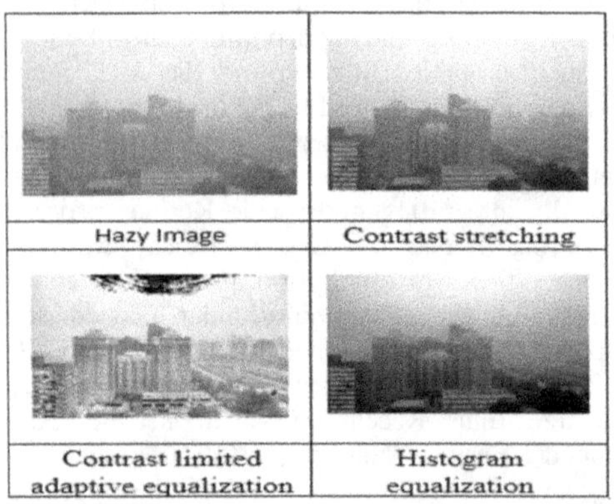

Figure 1. Preprocessing simulation outputs.

The initial stage of the image dehazing data pipeline involves resizing images to ensure dimensional consistency, followed by data augmentation strategies to enrich dataset variability. Subsequently, the images are transformed into numerical representations and normalized to stabilize input distributions. Advanced pre-processing operations—such as contrast stretching, denoising, color correction, and edge enhancement—are applied to improve visual quality and highlight salient features. To construct a comprehensive training dataset and facilitate optimal model learning, traditional dehazing techniques such as the Dark Channel Prior (DCP) are utilized. Additionally, synthetic hazy images are generated to simulate diverse atmospheric scattering conditions and further augment the dataset.

In the initial phase of data preparation for image dehazing, images are resized to maintain spatial consistency and augmented to enhance dataset diversity. They are subsequently transformed into numerical arrays and normalized to ensure uniform data distribution. Image enhancement techniques such as contrast stretching (CS) are employed to improve contrast, alongside noise suppression, color normalization, and edge sharpening to enhance perceptual quality. Dedicated dehazing methods, including Dark Channel Prior (DCP), are applied to further refine the inputs. Furthermore, synthetic hazy images are generated to expand the dataset and replicate various haze scenarios. These processes collectively contribute to optimizing the dataset for superior model generalization and performance.

To prevent noise amplification, Contrast Limited Adaptive Histogram Equalization (CLAHE) constrains the contrast of the histogram and operates on localized regions of the image, referred to as tiles. These tiles are subsequently merged using bilinear interpolation to ensure seamless transitions and eliminate artificial boundaries. This technique effectively enhances both the contrast and brightness of the image. An example of a blurry image and its enhanced counterpart processed with CLAHE is illustrated in Figure 2.

Histogram Equalization (HE) is an image enhancement technique that modifies the intensity distribution of an image to improve contrast. It enhances contrast by redistributing the frequency of pixel intensity values or by stretching the overall intensity range. This process improves detail visibility, particularly in areas with low contrast. Figure 3 demonstrates this effect by comparing a low-contrast image with its HE-processed counterpart, highlighting the enhanced visual clarity and contrast.

The image pre-processing module plays a critical role in enhancing visual data quality and preparing imagery for subsequent analytical or machine learning tasks. This module initiates with the estimation of key scene characteristics such as airlight intensity, depth-related gradients, luminance discontinuities, and semantic content boundaries, which are essential for effective dehazing and detail restoration. To counteract atmospheric distortions and improve perceptual clarity, the framework incorporates contextual regularization and airlight estimation techniques. Three distinct contrast enhancement strategies—Contrast Stretching, Histogram Equalization, and Contrast Limited Adaptive Histogram Equalization (CLAHE)—are utilized to improve both global and local contrast dynamics. Given the complementary strengths of these methods, a fusion-based approach is employed to integrate their outputs into a single, optimized representation that preserves structural integrity while maximizing visual detail. The resultant enhanced image is then used as input for feature extraction processes, which compute discriminative descriptors critical for tasks in computer vision, medical imaging, and remote sensing. This comprehensive pre-processing pipeline ensures a robust foundation for high-performance analysis and decision-making in various image-driven applications.

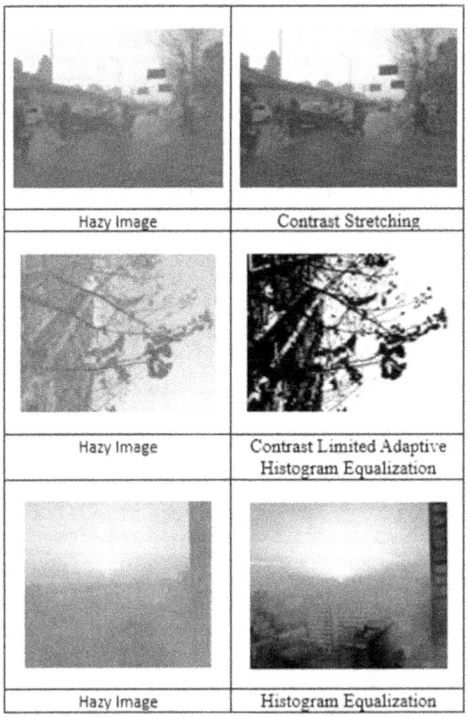

Figure 2. Outputs of Hazy image.

4 ADAPTED ARCHITECTURE

Convolutional Neural Networks (CNNs) have demonstrated exceptional performance in visual pattern recognition and image classification due to their deep, hierarchical architecture. These networks utilize a sequence of convolutional layers, each comprising learnable filters that perform spatial convolutions over input data to extract localized features. In the initial stages, low-level visual attributes such as edges, gradients, and texture primitives are captured. As the network depth increases, the convolutional filters evolve to encode more abstract and semantically rich patterns by aggregating lower-level features, thereby constructing a layered representation of the input space. This hierarchical feature learning process results in a series of feature maps that encapsulate both spatial and contextual information at multiple scales. The progressive transformation of data through convolutional, activation, and pooling operations facilitates robust feature encoding, enabling the model to discern intricate structural relationships within the image. In the final stages, fully connected (FC) layers consolidate the high-dimensional feature representations into a compact form suitable for classification. These layers perform dense transformations by connecting each neuron to all activations in the preceding layer, allowing the network to integrate global feature information and make accurate predictions based on the cumulative learned representations across all layers.

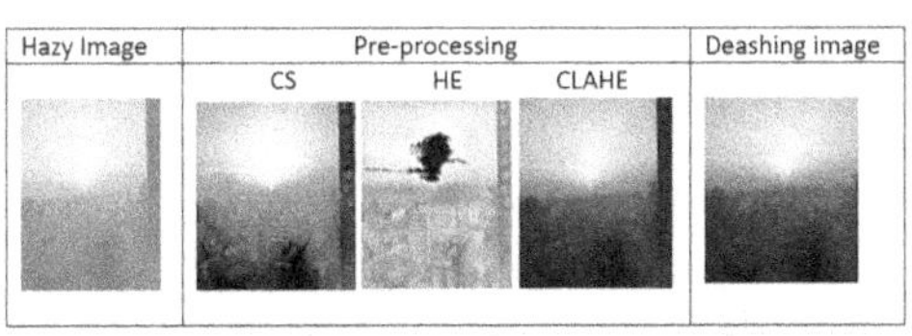

Figure 3. Dehazy image output.

MobileNet introduces a resource-efficient convolutional neural network architecture optimized for real-time inference on computationally constrained environments, such as embedded systems and mobile devices. The architectural foundation of MobileNet is based on depthwise separable convolutions, which decouple the standard convolution operation into two sequential steps: a depthwise convolution, which performs spatial filtering independently over each input channel, and a pointwise convolution, which applies 1×1 convolutions to project the resulting feature maps into a new channel space. This factorization significantly reduces both the number of parameters and the computational load compared to traditional dense convolution operations, enabling high inference speeds with minimal resource utilization. To allow scalable deployment across a range of hardware capabilities, MobileNet introduces two hyperparameters: the width multiplier (α), which proportionally reduces the number of channels in each layer to shrink model size, and the resolution multiplier (ρ), which adjusts the input image dimensions to trade off spatial precision for processing efficiency. These design choices enable fine-tuned control over model complexity and latency, facilitating deployment in real-time applications without substantial loss in accuracy. Due to its compact and flexible structure, MobileNet is widely used in on-device vision tasks such as image classification, object detection, and face verification across low-power platforms.

VGG16 is a deep convolutional neural network architecture comprising 21 layers in total, of which 16 possess trainable parameters, including 13 convolutional layers and 3 fully connected (FC) layers. Designed to process input tensors of size $224\times224\times3$, corresponding to RGB images, the architecture is characterized by a homogeneous configuration utilizing 3×3 convolutional kernels with a stride of 1 and padding to maintain spatial resolution. Downsampling is achieved via max-pooling layers interspersed throughout the network. The final segment of the architecture includes two FC layers, each consisting of 4096 units, followed by a third FC layer with 1000 units, aligning with the 1000-class classification task from the ImageNet Large Scale Visual Recognition Challenge (ILSVRC). The network concludes with a softmax activation function to generate normalized class probabilities. Beyond its original classification function, VGG16 is widely utilized as a feature extractor in low-level vision tasks such as image dehazing. The deep convolutional filters are proficient in capturing localized spatial features and fine textural patterns, which are essential for identifying and suppressing haze-induced distortions. When initialized with pretrained weights, the model can be repurposed through transfer learning to enhance dehazing performance, serving as a foundational backbone in more sophisticated vision frameworks or as a modular component in integrated image restoration pipelines.

The proposed convolutional neural network (CNN) architecture is characterized by a densely connected configuration wherein the output of each layer is propagated forward as input to subsequent layers, thereby promoting maximum feature reuse and gradient flow throughout the network. Unlike traditional DenseNet architectures where each layer connects directly to all preceding layers within a dense block, this design employs a streamlined form of dense connectivity that ensures no intermediate feature representations are discarded, thus preserving critical information from earlier stages. The architectural composition consists of an initial convolutional layer employing a 7×7 kernel to capture broad spatial features, followed by a sequence of five convolutional layers utilizing 3×3 kernels with eight filters each, enabling local feature extraction at various scales. Additionally, the network incorporates 61 pointwise convolutional layers (1×1 convolutions), which serve to perform dimensionality reduction and channel-wise feature transformation, thereby enhancing representational efficiency while minimizing computational overhead. Interleaved within the architecture are four average pooling layers that progressively reduce the spatial resolution of feature maps, aiding in translation invariance and reducing overfitting. The network culminates in a fully connected dense layer, which consolidates the extracted hierarchical features for the final classification or regression task. This layered design offers a robust and efficient solution for high-dimensional image analysis tasks by leveraging both spatial detail and deep contextual information.

Inception-V3 is a convolutional neural network architecture that advances the concept of Inception modules, offering a more efficient method for feature extraction and generalization. This architecture achieved significant success in the 2014 ImageNet competition, owing to its optimized balance between computational efficiency and model performance. Compared to AlexNet, Inception-V3 drastically reduces the number of parameters, utilizing only a fraction—roughly 1/12th—of the parameters required by its predecessor. The model leverages factorized convolutions and an efficient design that minimizes computational complexity while maintaining a high level of accuracy. At each layer, Inception-V3 builds progressively abstracted feature representations, enabling the capture of increasingly complex visual patterns. Unlike traditional convolutional networks that rely on a single convolution type, Inception-V3 integrates multiple kernel sizes—1×1, 3×3, and 5×5 convolutions—applied in parallel at each layer. Additionally, pooling operations are used in tandem with these convolutions, and their outputs are concatenated to form a richer, more diversified set of features. This parallelized approach enhances the model's ability to extract multi-scale information, resulting in improved representation learning and stronger generalization to various image recognition tasks.

5 SIMULATION RESULTS

The results of the experiment investigate the effectiveness of combining pre-processing techniques with deep learning architectures. Evaluation metrics such as Peak Signal-to-Noise Ratio (PSNR) and Structural Similarity Index (SSIM) are utilized to assess image quality. To validate the proposed model, the study employs a dataset consisting of 1,697 images. The primary objective of this approach is to enhance image clarity by effectively distinguishing key features from haze in the dataset, which primarily consists of blurred or hazy images. The method aims to recover fine details and improve the overall visual quality of the images, thereby facilitating more accurate analysis and feature extraction.

Table 1. Performance comparison metrics of architectures.

Deep Learning Techniques	SSIM	PSNR
DenseNet	0.7178	27.378
Mobile Net	0.8112	27.632
Inception V3	0.8390	27.901
CNN	0.7719	28.561
VGG16	0.8212	31.592

The individual outputs derived from various contrast enhancement algorithms are integrated using image fusion techniques to obtain a unified, high-quality image. This fused output, produced after executing a series of image pre-processing operations, is illustrated in the associated figure. In the subsequent stage, the enhanced image is provided as input to a convolutional neural network (CNN) for deep feature extraction and classification or recognition tasks. The intermediate outputs generated by different CNN architectures are then visualized, followed by the display of the corresponding ground truth image. The aim is for the predicted outputs to either match or surpass the visual and structural accuracy of the actual scene.

6 CONCLUSION

Image dehazing methodologies are commonly evaluated using objective quality metrics such as the Structural Similarity Index Measure (SSIM) and Peak Signal-to-Noise Ratio (PSNR). SSIM evaluates the perceptual similarity between the dehazed and reference images by analysing luminance, contrast, and structural information, whereas PSNR quantifies the reconstruction quality by comparing the intensity values between the original and processed images. Higher SSIM and PSNR values typically indicate superior visual quality and structural preservation. By analysing these metrics across different model architectures, the most efficient design for image dehazing can be identified, as each architecture may yield distinct performance characteristics.

REFERENCES

[1] Doshi, N., Bhavsar, S., Rajeswari, D., and Srinivasan, R. (2023, May). Singe Image Dehazing using Deep Neural Networks. *In 2023 International Conference on Advances in Computing, Communication and Applied Informatics (ACCAI)* (pp. 1–9). IEEE

[2] Doshi, N., Bhavsar, S., Rajeswari, D., and Srinivasan, R.(2023, January). Monochromatic Image Dehazing Using Enhanced Feature Extraction Techniques in Deep Learning. *In 2023 International Conference on Artificial Intelligence and Knowledge Discovery in Concurrent Engineering (ICECONF)* (pp. 1–8). IEEE.

[3] Dwivedi, P., and Chakraborty, S. (2023). Single image dehazing using extended local dark channel prior. *Image and Vision Computing*, 136, 104747.

[4] Jiang, Y., Li, L., Zhu, J., Xue, Y., and Ma, H. (2023). DEANet: Decomposition Enhancement and Adjustment Network for Low-Light Image Enhancement. *Tsinghua Science and Technology*, 28(4), 743–753.

[5] Jeong, C.Y., Moon, K., and Kim, M. (2023). An end-to- end deep learning approach for real-time single image dehazing. *Journal of Real-Time Image Processing*, 20(1), 12.

[6] Ali, U., Lee, I.H., and Mahmood, M.T. (2022). Robust regularization for single image dehazing. *Journal of King Saud University-Computer and Information Sciences*, 34(9), 7168-7173.

[7] He, Z., Gong, C., Hu, Y., and Li, L. (2022). Remote sensing image dehazing based on an attention convolutional neural network. *IEEE Access*, 10, 68731–68739.

[8] Liu, Y., Chen, J., Lu, P., Zhu, C., Jian, Y., Sun, C., and Liang, H. (2023). MFID-Net: Multi-scaled feature-fused image dehazing via dynamic weights. *Displays*, 78, 102416.

[9] Gao, Z., and Zhai, Y. (2022, October). Image Dehazing Based on Multi-scale Retinex and Guided Filtering. *In 2022 International Conference on Image Processing, Computer Vision and Machine Learning (ICICML)* (pp. 123–126). IEEE.

[10] Babu, G.H., Odugu, V.K., Venkatram, N., Satish, B., Revathi, K., and Rao, B.J. (2023). Development and performance evaluation of enhanced image dehazing method using deep learning networks. *Journal of Visual Communication and Image Representation*, 97, 103976.

[11] Sreekar, D.S., Vatsal, V., Kothandhapani, A., and Rajagopalan, R. (2023, January). Enhanced Efficient Image Dehazing for Onboard Satellite Imagery Processing. *In 2023 International Conference on Machine Intelligence for GeoAnalytics and Remote Sensing (MIGARS)* (Vol. 1, pp. 1–4). IEEE.

[12] Ali, U., Choi, J., Min, K., Choi, Y.K., and Mahmood, M.T. (2023). Boundary-constrained robust regularization for single image dehazing. *Pattern Recognition*, 140, 109522.

[13] Parihar, A.S., and Gupta, S. (2024). Dehazing optically haze images with AlexNet-FNN. *Journal of Optics*, 53(1), 294-303.

[14] Xu, G., Zheng, C., and Gu, Y. (2022, December). Model for Single Image Enhancement Based on Adaptive Contrast Stretch and Multiband Fusion. *In 2022 IEEE Conference on Telecommunications, Optics and Computer Science (TOCS)* (pp. 1–7). IEEE

Advancement in Engineering and Science – Goyal et al. (Eds)
© 2026 The Author(s), ISBN: 978-1-041-31101-0

Development of 12V BLDC Motor Controller with Anti-Pinch for Power Window Using Cortex-M4 (Anti-Pinch Mechanism, Simulink Modeling and Hall-Based Commutation)

Neel Joshi, Darshan Achalkar, Rohan Khade, Deep Jasud, and Minaj Shikalgar
Electronics and Telecommunication Engineering, Kolhapur Institute of Technology's College of Engineering, Kolhapur, India

ABSTRACT: This paper presents the design, development, and simulation of an anti-pinch power window control system based on a 12 V, 200 W three-phase Brushless DC (BLDC) motor. The system enhances passenger safety through a real-time current-sensing algorithm that detects obstruction in the window path and reverses motor direction to prevent injury or damage. The motor operates with a continuous current of 16.67 A and a peak current of 33.34 A during obstruction, forming the threshold for the detection mechanism. The inverter is driven by MOSFET switches controlled by an integrated gate driver, while rotor position is detected using three Hall-effect sensors for accurate trapezoidal commutation. The controller is implemented using the E533.06 motor-driver IC featuring an embedded ARM Cortex-M4 core for PWM generation, commutation logic, and current regulation. The complete model including current sensing, gate driver control, and inverter topology was implemented and verified in MATLAB/Simulink. Simulation results confirm smooth window operation under normal load and rapid reversal under obstruction, validating the effectiveness of the current-based anti-pinch mechanism. The system complies with ISO 26262 ASIL-B functional safety standards, demonstrating feasibility for practical automotive applications.

Keywords: Anti-pinch safety system, BLDC motor control, Hall sensor feedback, Current sensing algorithm, MATLAB/Simulink, Automotive safety, Power window system, E533.06 motor driver, Cortex-M4 controller

1 INTRODUCTION

In modern automobiles, electromechanical systems such as power windows have become standard, offering passengers convenience and ease of operation. However, automation introduces safety concerns: when a window closes on an object or body part, it can cause injury if no effective obstruction-detection mechanism exists [4]. Conventional drives typically rely on motor-stall or mechanical-resistance detection, which respond slowly and may misinterpret normal load variations, making them inadequate for protecting children or elderly passengers [7].

To address these limitations, this study develops a 12 V, 200 W three-phase BLDC motor-based anti-pinch power-window system. Implemented in MATLAB/Simulink, the system integrates RMS current sensing, PWM inverter control, and Hall-sensor feedback for precise trapezoidal commutation. During normal operation, the motor draws 16.67 A; obstruction events increase the current to 33.34 A, triggering immediate motor reversal. The control algorithm conforms to ISO 26262 ASIL-B functional-safety standards [6,13]. Hardware implementation employs the E533.06 BLDC-driver IC with an embedded Cortex-M4 core, enabling PWM generation, commutation logic, diagnostics, and LIN-bus communication [9]. Simulation results demonstrate rapid and reliable response to obstructions, validating the system's readiness for real automotive integration.

2 LITERATURE REVIEW

Advances in automotive comfort systems have increased the demand for intelligent control in subsystems such as power windows. Accidental obstructions, particularly involving children, highlight the critical importance of reliable anti-pinch protection to prevent injuries [4]. Various detection strategies have been developed, broadly categorized as current-based, capacitive, optical/infrared, and force/pressure systems. Each method offers specific advantages and faces trade-offs in cost, detection accuracy, response time, and environmental robustness, making the choice of technique dependent on application requirements.

Table 2. Comparison of motor types.

Motor Type	Efficiency	Cost	Suitable for Anti-Pinch
Brushed DC	Moderate	Low	Moderate
Stepper Motor	Low	Moderate	Low
AC Induction	Moderate	High	Low
PMDC	Moderate	Moderate	Moderate
BLDC	High	Moderate	High
Switched Reluctance	High	Moderate	Moderate

2.1 DETECTION METHODS

2.1.1 *Current-based detection systems*

Commonly used in production vehicles; monitors motor current rise during obstruction [2,9]. RMS filtering distinguishes real pinch events from normal fluctuations [10].

2.1.2 *Capacitive sensing methods*

Detect electric field variations near the glass surface [7]. Enable early detection but are sensitive to moisture and dust [12].

2.1.3 *Optical and infrared sensors*

Use light beams for fast, accurate detection, though affected by dirt or tinted glass [12].

2.1.4 *Force and pressure sensors*

Measure mechanical resistance during obstruction [11,12]. Highly accurate but costly and complex, mainly used in premium vehicles.

DOI: 10.1201/9781003798514-54

Table 1. Detection methods.

Sensor Type	Detection	Cost
Current	Motor Current	Low
Capacitive	Electric Field	Medium-High
Optical	Light Beam	High
Force	Resistance	Medium

2.2 *Motor technologies*

2.2.1 *Brushed DC motors*

Simple and inexpensive but have wear issues and poor current linearity [4].

2.2.2 *Stepper motors*

Precise control but inefficient at high speeds.

2.2.3 *AC induction motors*

Reliable yet bulky with complex control [10].

2.2.4 *Permanent magnet DC motors*

Efficient but limited in torque linearity [10].

2.2.5 *Brushless DC Motors (BLDC)*

High torque density, controllability, and low noise best suited for anti-pinch systems [12].

2.2.6 *Switched Reluctance Motors (SRM)*

Fast and durable but cause torque ripple and noise [11].

2.3 *Related work*

2.3.1 *Ford explorer*

The Ford Explorer utilizes current-based detection integrated into the motor driver ECU, enabling rapid reversal upon obstruction [2].

2.3.2 *Toyota sienna*

Toyota Sienna implements capacitive sensors along door and window edges, allowing early detection without physical contact [7].

2.3.3 *Honda odyssey*

Honda Odyssey incorporates optical infrared sensors in its sunroof and window modules to detect beam interruption and trigger reversal before contact [12].

2.3.4 *Volkswagen golf*

Volkswagen Golf relies on force sensors to monitor mechanical resistance, issuing a reversal command when thresholds are exceeded [12].

2.3.5 *Hyundai i20*

The Hyundai i20 combines current-based detection with BLDC motor control and temperature compensation, improving sensitivity and reliability under varying environmental conditions [4].

3 SYSTEM ARCHITECTURE

The anti-pinch power window system ensures reliable operation, rapid obstruction response, and compliance with automotive safety standards. The architecture comprises two domains: the hardware subsystem, providing motor control and sensing, and the software subsystem, handling logic, decision-making, and feedback for smooth and safe operation.

3.1 *Hardware components*

1. **BLDC Motor**
   - High torque-to-weight ratio, efficient, and enables precise commutation with fast torque response [3].
2. **E533.06 Motor Driver IC**
   - Integrates Cortex-M4 core; manages commutation, LIN communication, current sensing, and protection features [5,9].
3. **Hall Effect Sensors (3 Nos.)**
   - Mounted at 120° interval; Provide rotor position feedback for trapezoidal commutation [12].
4. **MOSFET based Inverter Bridge (6-switch topology)**
   - Converts 12V DC to 3-phase AC for BLDC; controlled by PWM from E533.06 [9].
5. **Gate Driver Circuit**
   - Buffers and amplifies the PWM signals ensures safe switching and dead-time control [5].
6. **Current Sensing Resistor (Low-side Shunt)**
   - Measures real-time motor current for obstruction detection [7].
7. **Diagnostic Interface (LIN Bus)**
   - Supports fault communication, data logging, calibration, and remote diagnostics [13].

3.2 *Software components*

1. **Commutation Algorithm (Trapezoidal)**
   - Determines phase activation from Hall sensor input for smooth motor rotation with minimal torque ripple [12].
2. **PWM Generation Logic**
   - Embedded in E533.06 firmware; adjusts duty cycle based on speed, torque, and system conditions [5,9].
3. **Anti-Pinch Detection Algorithm**
   - Monitors real-time RMS current through filtering and comparison [7]. And Triggers reverse commutation if current exceeds.
4. **Reverse Drive Control**
   - Activates reverse sequence instantly upon pinch detection, with delay safeguards for safety.
5. **Simulation and Validation via MATLAB/Simulink**
   - MATLAB/Simulink models control, current feedback, motor dynamics, and inverter; allows testing under various obstruction scenarios [1].
6. **Firmware Deployment on E533.06 IC (Cortex-M4)**
   - Embedded C code compiled and flashed on E533.06 Cortex-M4 IC [13].

Block Diagram

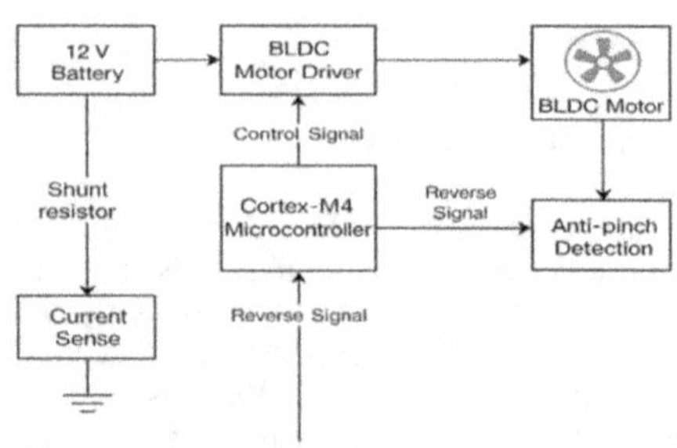

Figure 1. Block diagram of power window system.

4 MATHEMATICAL MODEL

The BLDC motor is modeled using standard three-phase equations accounting for stator resistance, inductance, and back EMF [4,10]:

$$V_a = Ri_a + L\frac{di_a}{dt} + e_a$$
$$V_b = Ri_b + L\frac{di_b}{dt} + e_b$$
$$V_c = Ri_c + L\frac{di_c}{dt} + e_c$$

Where:
V_a, V_b, V_c = Phase voltages
i_a, i_b, i_c= Phase currents
e_a, e_b, e_c= back EMFs
L, R = Stator inductance and resistance

Rotor position is detected using three Hall-effect sensors spaced at 120° intervals, producing a 3-bit code for trapezoidal commutation [12]. The anti-pinch algorithm continuously monitors RMS current via a low-side shunt in the E533.06 IC [9]. During normal operation, the motor draws 16.67 A. If an obstruction occurs, the resulting torque increase raises the current to 33.34 A, triggering immediate reversal to protect both the mechanism and occupants.

5 SIMULATION & TESTING

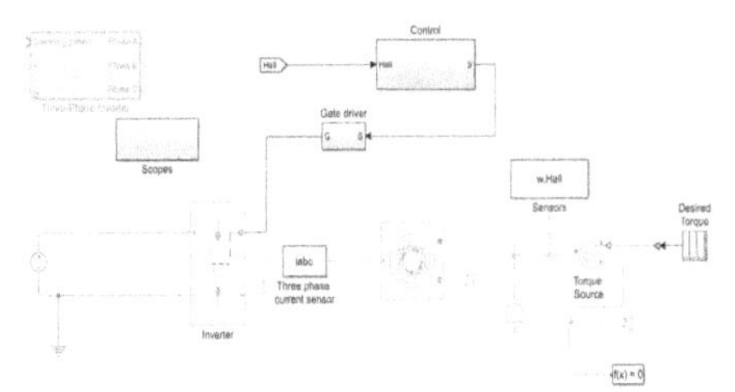

Figure 2. MATLAB simulink model.

The overall model is a comprehensive simulation of the entire electromechanical system. It contains the following interconnected modules:

1. 12V, 200W three-phase BLDC motor with trapezoidal back EMF.
2. Gate driver logic converting commutation signals to PWM for inverter switches.
3. Three-phase inverter with six MOSFETs.
4. Hall-effect sensor emulation and commutation index logic.
5. RMS-monitored phase currents; exceeding 33.34 A triggers a pinch event [2,7].
6. Obstruction detection logic and safety reversal control.

5.1 CONTROL LOGIC

1. **iabc (Three-Phase Current Input)**:

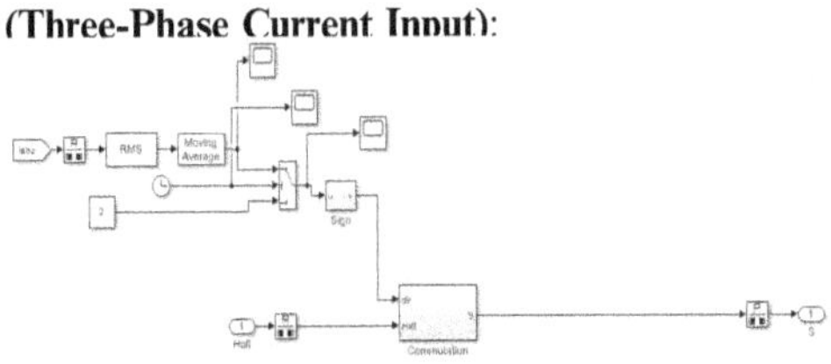

Figure 3. Control logic block.

   - Monitors real-time BLDC phase currents to assess load and detect abnormal rises during pinch events [9].
2. **RMS Block**:
   - Computers effective current from phase inputs; values above 33.34 A activate safety reversal logic.
3. **Commutation Logic Input**:
   - Uses three 120°-spaced Hall signals to generate a commutation index for correct phase switching and stable torque [4].
4. **Final Output:**
   - Combines RMS and commutation feedback to generate PWM gate signals for normal motion or instant reversal during obstruction, ensuring ISO 26262 compliance [6].

5.2 *Commutation logic*

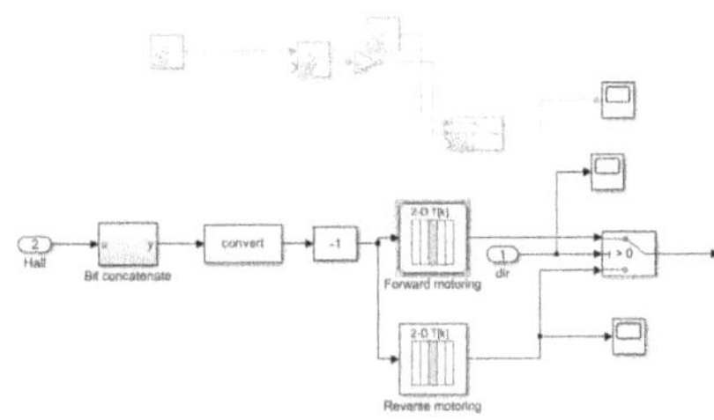

Figure 4. Commutation logic block.

1. **Input from Hall Sensors**:
   - The commutation logic receives three digital inputs from Hall-effect sensors, representing the rotor's electrical position and used to determine the active phase pair for motor operation [4].
2. **Concatenation of Signals:**
   - The three Hall signals are combined into a 3-bit binary code, uniquely identifying the rotor segment within a full electrical cycle.
3. **Commutation Index Generation:**
   - The 3-bit code is decoded through a lookup table, mapping directly to the standard six-step sequence for energizing the correct phase pair [10].
4. **Lookup Table for Phase Switching:**
   - A 2D lookup table selects the appropriate phase activation pattern, ensuring only the correct winding pair is energized at any moment to produce smooth and efficient torque.
5. **Direction Handling:**
   - The logic supports both forward and reverse operation. In case of obstruction, the commutation pattern is reversed, enabling the motor to rotate in the opposite direction.

5.3 *Gate driver logic*

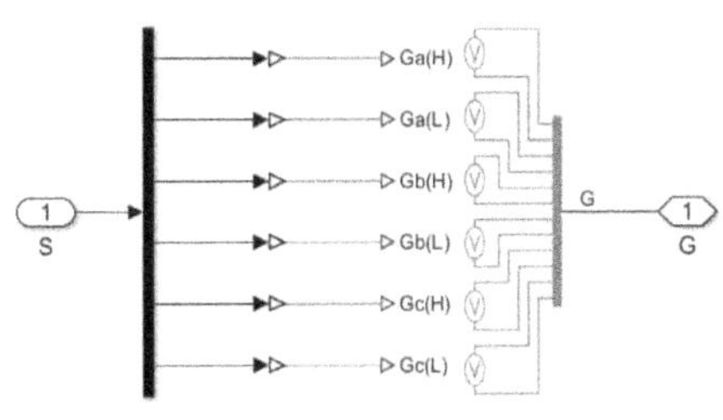

Figure 5. Gate driver block.

1. **Input Signal (S):**
   - Carries a 3-bit commutation pattern from the Hall sensor logic, defining which high- and low-side MOSFETs conduct in each interval for precise phase switching [9].
2. **Demultiplexer Functionality:**
   - The signal S is decoded into six independent control lines for the inverter gates, split as:
     (I) **Ga(H)** and **Ga(L)** – phase A
     (II) **Gb(H)** and **Gb(L)** – phase B
     (III) **Gc(H)** and **Gc(L)** – phase C

5.4 *Motor speed and current behaviour*

The motor's dynamic performance was analyzed through simulation to verify its behavior during different operational stages of the power window mechanism. Both speed and current waveforms were observed under startup, normal load, and obstruction conditions.

- **0 to 0.3 seconds:** Motor starts from rest, producing a brief inrush current due to the absence of back-EMF. Current peaks momentarily before stabilizing near **16.67 A,** while speed gradually rises, minimizing mechanical stress during startup.
- **0.3 to 4.0 seconds:** Motor reaches a steady speed of approximately **1500 rpm** under normal load. The current remains stable at nominal value, indicating balanced torque production and efficient commutation via Hall-sensor feedback [10].
- **At ~4.0 seconds:** A simulated obstruction introduces a sudden load, causing the stator current to spike to 33.34 A. The anti-pinch logic detects this overcurrent within 5–8 ms and promptly reverses the commutation pattern, smoothly reducing speed and safely reversing direction with high precision, preventing injury or damage [2,7].

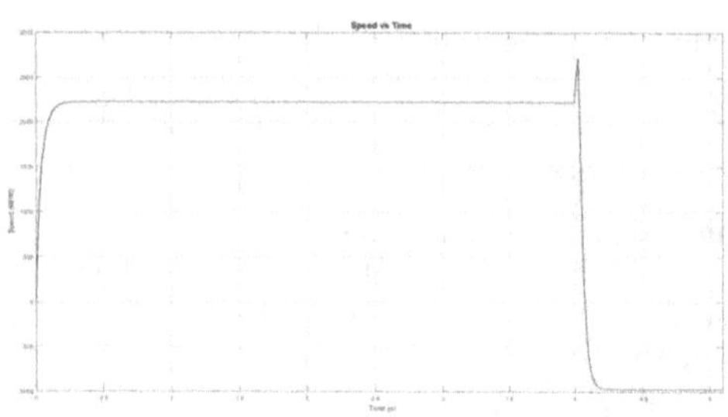

Figure 6. Simulation result (Speed vs Time).

Figure 7. Simulation result (Stator current vs Time).

6 DESIGN SCHEMATICS

6.1 *IC design schematic*

The schematic of the E533.06 IC illustrates its internal and external configuration, featuring an integrated ARM Cortex-M4 core responsible for real-time motor commutation, current regulation, and safety diagnostics [9].

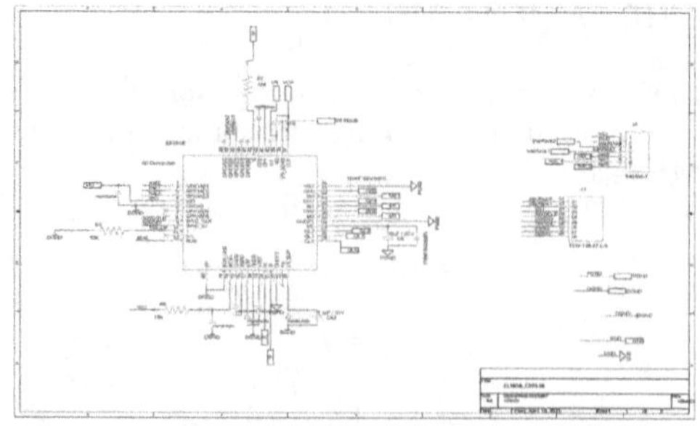

Figure 8: E533.06 IC

Key Schematic Features:

- **Power Supply Inputs**: VDD and VSS provide stable power and reference ground [9].
- **PWM and GPIO Pins**: VDD and VSS provide stable power and reference ground [9].
- **Hall Sensor Interface**: Three 120°-spaced sensors provide rotor position for accurate commutation [4,12].
- **Current Sensing Path**: Low-side shunt with 12-bit ADC enables real-time monitoring for obstruction and overload [9].
- **Diagnostic Features**: Overcurrent, thermal, and undervoltage protection ensure reliable operation.
- **External Interface Connectors**: LIN interface and debug ports allow ECU integration and calibration.

6.2 *Inverter Design Schematic*

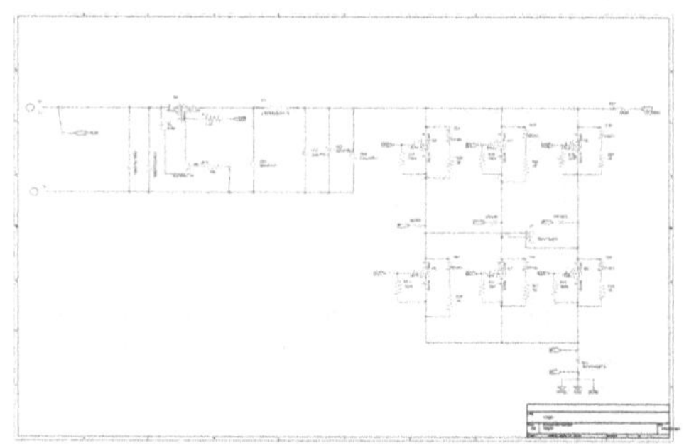

Figure 9: Inverter Circuit for 3 Phase Generation

The inverter converts a 12 V DC supply into a three-phase quasi-AC output to drive the BLDC motor using a full-bridge topology with six N-channel MOSFETs forming three half-bridges. Commutation is synchronized with Hall sensor feedback for accurate trapezoidal switching [9].

Key Functional Sections:

- **DC Input Filtering**: Capacitors and ferrite beads suppress noise and ripple, ensuring stable power and reduced EMI [10].
- **MOSFET Bridge Configuration**: Each phase uses a high- and low-side MOSFET pair operating alternately to generate trapezoidal voltage for forward or reverse rotation [9].
- **Gate Drive Path**: Includes resistors, Zener diodes, and pull-downs to control switching speed and prevent false triggering [9].
- **Output Phases**: Half-bridge midpoints connect to motor windings; Hall-based commutation ensures smooth torque [4].

- **Current Sensing Element**: A low-side shunt resistor provides real-time current feedback for obstruction and overcurrent detection [7].

A. HALL Sensor Schematic

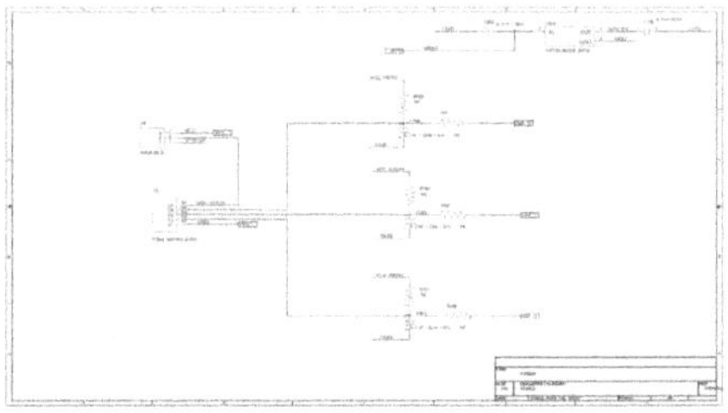

Figure 10: HALL Effect Sensor Design

The Hall-effect sensor circuit provides real-time rotor position feedback using three sensors placed 120° apart, generating binary outputs corresponding to magnetic poles [12].

- Outputs are conditioned with pull-up resistors and filters for stable signals. Microcontrollers read these signals to determine the active rotor sector.
- Controller selects the correct commutation sequence from a lookup table.
- Supports bidirectional movement for effective reversal in anti-pinch operation.

7 CONCLUSION

The developed anti-pinch power window system provides an efficient and practical solution to enhance passenger safety in modern vehicles. Through real-time current sensing, responsive reversal control, and BLDC motor operation, the system effectively detects and mitigates obstruction risks. Simulation results confirm its reliability under normal and fault conditions, validating its suitability for real-world automotive applications. This work establishes a foundation for future vehicle implementations focused on safety and comfort.

ACKNOWLEDGEMENT

The authors express sincere gratitude to the faculty of the Electronics and Telecommunication Department, KIT College of Engineering, Kolhapur, for their valuable guidance and support throughout this research.

REFERENCES

[1] Faria G. and Lima T.P., (2018), Design of a robust motor control system for automotive applications with anti-pinch feature, *IEEE Transactions on Industrial Applications*, vol. 56, no. 5, pp. 5860–5869.

[2] Yi W. and Zhang L., (2018), Current sensing techniques for motor control systems in automotive applications, *IEEE Transactions on Industrial Electronics*, vol. 65, no. 6, pp. 4889–4898.

[3] Bhattacharyya and Sharma N., (2019), Motor control ics for automotive power windows: features and applications, *Automotive Electronics Journal.*

[4] Radha D., (2020), Integrated motor control for automotive power window systems: a safety perspective, *IEEE Transactions on Control Systems Technology*, vol. 28, no. 3, pp. 979–987.

[5] Kumar T.S. and Sharma P.S., (2020), Application of cortex-m4 microcontroller in anti-pinch systems for power windows, *International Journal of Automotive Technology And Safety*, vol. 12, no. 3, pp. 145–152.

[6] Carvalho M.B.S., (2020), Functional safety and iso 26262 compliance for automotive systems: current trends and challenges, *Automotive Safety Security*.

[7] Lasky G., (2021), Implementation of anti-pinch technology in automotive motor control systems, *IEEE Transactions on Vehicular Technology*, vol. 70, no. 4, pp. 3285–3293.

[8] Murthy S.R.S. and Rao R.R.S., (2021), Motor control systems with anti-pinch features for power windows, *Journal of Automotive Engineering*, vol. 233, pp. 111–118.

[9] Elmos semiconductor ag, e533.06 - automotive bldc motor controller ic datasheet, 2021. available at: https://www.elmos.com

[10] Kumar and Sharma P., (2022), Review of bldc motor technology for automotive power window applications, *International Journal of Automotive Research and Technology*, vol. 11, no. 2, pp. 85–91.

[11] Ghosh J.S. and Dey H.C., (2022), Enhancing functional safety of power window systems with advanced motor control techniques, *International Journal of Automotive Engineering*, vol. 34, pp. 120–131.

[12] Ramesh, K. Chenchireddy, Reddy B.N., Siddharth B., Kumar C. V., and Manojkumar P., (2023), Closed-loop control of bldc motor using hall-effect sensors, *International Journal of Applied Power Engineering* (ijape), vol. 12, no. 3, pp. 247–254.

[13] Pereira and Ramos L., Functional safety of embedded motor control systems for automotive applications, *International Journal of Automotive Technology*, vol. 21, no. 4, pp. 543–556, 2020.

Advancement in Engineering and Science – Goyal et al. (Eds)
 ISBN: 978-1-041-31101-0

Intelligent Energy Management in Smart Buildings Using Machine Learning

Ashvini Patil, Namrata Patil, Pragati Patil, and Sachin Patil
Department of Computer Science & Engg (AI & ML), Kasegon Education Scociety's Rajarambapu Institute of Technology, Affiliated to Shivaji University, Sakharale, India

ABSTRACT: Urbanization has led to increased energy demands and efficient management of energy has become critical. Building Management Systems (BMS) aims to control and monitor Heating Ventilation, and Air Conditioning (HVAC), lighting, security, and energy management. Traditional BMS systems have limitations in terms of accessibility and ease of use. An android application that enables users to remotely control the Building Management System (BMS) appliances in their office using Internet of Things (IoT) integrated devices. This study investigates real-time data analysis and energy use prediction using machine learning. The experiments were conducted using three machine learning algorithms including Decision tree, random forest and Support Vector Machine (SVM) Regressor. The system tracks and optimizes energy use using data analysis, cloud computing, and IoT sensors. Experiments demonstrated that this method reduces expenses, decreases energy waste, and increases the sustainability of buildings. The model was evaluated using the Mean Absolute Error (MAE), Root Mean Squared Error (RMSE).

Keywords: Amazon EC2, Android, Building Management System, Energy consumption, Energy efficiency, Random Forest Regressor

1 INTRODUCTION

Energy consumption is a critical issue in many industries, including manufacturing, transportation, and utilities. Monitoring energy usage is essential for identifying opportunities to reduce energy consumption, optimize performance, and reduce costs. In recent years, the use of the Internet of Things (IoT) has become increasingly popular for monitoring and controlling energy consumption in various industries. IoT devices, such as sensors and smart meters, can collect real-time data on energy consumption, provides insights into energy usage patterns and enable more efficient energy management. Machine learning algorithms can be applied to the data collected by IoT devices to predict future energy consumption patterns, identify areas of inefficiency, and optimize energy usage. A popular machine learning algorithm for energy consumption prediction is the random forest algorithm, which can provide accurate predictions based on input data such as temperature, time of day, and other relevant features [1]. In addition to IoT and machine learning, cloud computing services such as Amazon Web Services (AWS) can be used for scalable and cost-effective deployment of IoT devices and machine learning models. The AWS offers Elastic Compute Cloud (EC2) instances to deploy machine learning models for energy consumption prediction. EC2 is a scalable cloud computing service that allows to launch of virtual machines (instances) on demand, using a variety of operating systems, including Linux, and Windows. By leveraging these technologies, companies can reduce energy consumption costs, improve efficiency, and promote sustainability.

2 RELATED WORK

Researcher are working to optimize the energy consumption in Smart Building Management Systems. Efforts are made to utilize the modern technologies for cost cutting of energy usage.

Kari Alanne and Seppo Sierla [1] conducted an extensive literature survey on machine learning applications for building energy management. This review discusses the learning capability of buildings from a system-level view and provides an overview of autonomous machine learning applications capable of making independent decisions for energy management. The authors categorized learning applications based on five primary functions: observing, predicting, adjusting, managing data, and interacting with occupants. The paper concludes that buildings can better cope with unforeseen changes at the system level with AI-triggered learning and digital twin-based training environments.

J. Aguilar *et al.* [2] emphasized the use of ensemble learning models for predicting hourly energy consumption in office buildings. The proposed approach merges support vector regression (SVR), artificial neural networks (ANN), and multiple linear regression (MLR) to improve accuracy. The core idea is to leverage multiple predictive models to capture complex energy usage patterns and yield optimal results for energy forecasting.

Tianqi Yu and Xianbin Wang [3] introduced an edge–cloud collaborative IoT architecture for real-time event analytics. Their proposed method minimizes energy consumption by using a data-driven, event-triggered model. This ensures that computing and communication activities are triggered only upon detection of relevant events, making the system efficient and cost-effective for long-term monitoring.

Nikolay I. Bazenkov *et al.* [4] focused on collecting and analyzing power consumption data from various building systems, including HVAC, lighting, and office equipment. They discussed challenges such as data quality, privacy, and system complexity. Solutions included standardized protocols and the application of machine learning techniques to improve energy data analysis.

Yeobeom Yoon *et al.* [5] presented a comprehensive open-source dataset of measured building and weather data from a two-story flexible research building. Their work supports research in optimizing HVAC systems, which are major contributors to energy consumption in commercial buildings. The study also underscores the need for calibrating building simulation models to enhance accuracy.

Y. Boutahri and A. Tilioua [6] proposed a predictive ML model for optimizing thermal comfort and energy use in buildings, particularly focusing on HVAC systems. The model compared the performance of SVM, ANN, Random Forest, and

 DOI: 10.1201/9781003798514-55

XGBoost, with the latter two showing superior predictive capabilities based on statistical error measures like RMSE and R^2.

A. Abdalrahman, M. M. Ibrahim, and A. F. Ataalla [7] addressed energy optimization in smart homes through the integration of sensing technologies and predictive analytics. They emphasized the importance of maintaining comfort while forecasting energy usage at varying levels. Their approach generates weekly schedules based on historical data to manage aggregate energy distribution efficiently.

C. Zhao *et al.* [8] proposed an optimization method for smart home energy management using reinforcement learning. Their approach combines Column-and-Constraint Generation (CCG) with a Deep Neural Network (DNN) for forecasting indoor temperatures. This integration led to a 12% energy savings while ensuring user comfort and system reliability, outperforming traditional optimization techniques.

M. Talib and M. S. Croock [9] performed a comparative study of ANN and Random Forest for building energy consumption prediction. Their analysis found that RF outperformed ANN with a lower RMSE (1.392 vs. 3.806), indicating its higher predictive accuracy and capability in capturing complex data patterns.

L. da Silva, M. Borlim Coro, and E. Gotardi Pessoa [10] focused on enhancing predictive energy management using ML algorithms like deep neural networks, boosted trees, and hybrid models combining MODWT and LSTM. These techniques outperform traditional methods and allow accurate short-term predictions crucial for energy cost reduction and operational efficiency.

N. El Assri *et al.* [11] proposed a framework combining machine learning and optimization techniques for energy efficiency in smart buildings. Using a heterogeneous dataset, the study applied a Modified Whale Optimization Algorithm (MWOA) to determine input conditions that minimize energy use. ANN and RF models were tested, with RF achieving superior results, aiding sustainable building design.

A. Mane Penton [12] proposed a machine learning-based approach for reducing energy waste in large buildings. Using occupancy detection data from the UCI Machine Learning Repository, the study highlights how environmental features can aid energy efficiency. While detection accuracy was modest, it could be improved with additional sensors or data enrichment.

Jose Mari M. Arce and Erees Queen B. Macabebe [13] explored power monitoring and forecasting using regression-based ML models and embedded systems (Raspberry Pi, ATM90E26, ESP8266). The study identified Support Vector Regression as the best-performing algorithm for real-time energy prediction, demonstrating the feasibility of low-cost predictive monitoring solutions.

3 METHODOLOGY

This section discusses the methodology of the proposed prototype. The proposed Building Management System allows users to manage and monitor appliances in an office space by using Android application. The Random Forest Regressor was used to analyze the energy consumption of the devices in the building. The user initially register himself and then signs in the app through a login page. An Android application communicates the changes in the MySQL Database with the Web API hosted on the cloud server. The web API reads the status of the device with the timestamp and records it in a data set. The generated dataset was used to train the Random Forest machine learning model. Based on the analysis of Random Forest method, energy consumption is predicted.

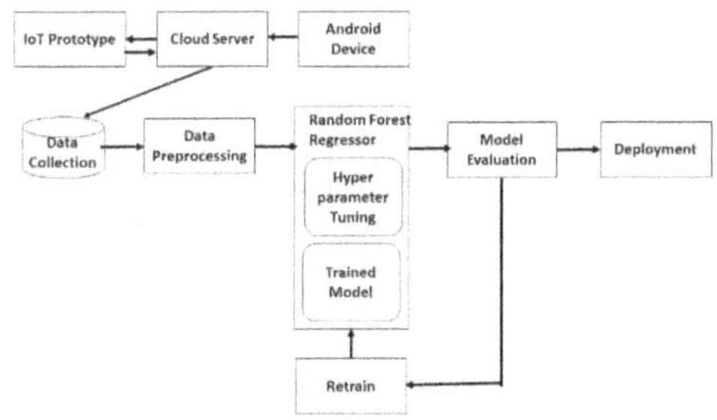

Figure 1. System architecture.

Figure 1 illustrates the architecture of the proposed system. The IoT prototype is responsible for collecting the current status of HVAC devices in room or office space.

An authenticated user can login and manage their room devices with the help of an Android application.

4 RESULTS AND DISCUSSION

To analyze the performance of the proposed energy prediction system, we tested three machine learning models, the Random Forest Regressor, Decision Tree Regressor, and K-Nearest Neighbors (KNN) Regressor. The experiments were carried out independently for the heating and cooling seasons based on preprocessed time-series datasets.

4.1 *Data collection*

This study[1] provides an open-source dataset of measured building and weather data under various test settings. Heating and cooling season tests were included in the study. The baseline test setting was used for the energy consumption prediction. During heating season testing both RTU and HVAC systems were switched on all day. During the cooling season testing of the HVAC system, the RTU and VAV were kept switched on all the day. The machine learning model was trained and tested separately for both conditions.

4.2 *Data preprocessing*

For Building Management System (BMS) data related to Heating, Ventilation, and Air Conditioning (HVAC), preprocessing involves several key steps:

Outlier Removal: Eliminating extreme values that could distort analysis while preserving critical data.

Handling Missing Values: Imputing missing data using techniques like interpolation or regression.

Scaling/Normalization: Standardizing variables to improve model performance.

Categorical Feature Encoding: Converting categorical variables into numerical formats for machine learning compatibility.

The dataset included time-series weather data, indoor building conditions, and HVAC system operations. High-quality instruments ensure accurate data collection during both heating and cooling seasons.

Heating Season Dataset:
Duration: 1 week (1-minute intervals)
Size: 10,080 rows × 60 features
Train/Test Split: (7,056, 59) / (3,024, 59)
Cooling Season Dataset:
Duration: 1 week (1-minute intervals)
Size: 10,080 rows × 74 features

This preprocessed data is essential for HVAC system analysis and optimization in building management.

The performance of the machine learning algorithms was measured using two key metrics: Mean Squared Error (MSE) and Mean Absolute Error (MAE). Figures 2 and 3 demonstrate that the Random Forest regressor consistently had lower MSE and RMSE values than the other models in both seasonal datasets, reflecting higher accuracy and reliability.

4.3 *Key observations*

Decision Tree Regressor had increased variance and overfitted more, especially during the heating period.KNN Regressor performed very badly most probably due to excessive dimensionality and non-temporal sensitivity. Random Forest Regressor performed well in dealing with noisy and non-linear patterns, and it was superior to all other models for both seasons. These results are in line with previous research like Talib and Croock [11], which proved Random Forest to be superior in simulating intricate energy consumption patterns in smart buildings.

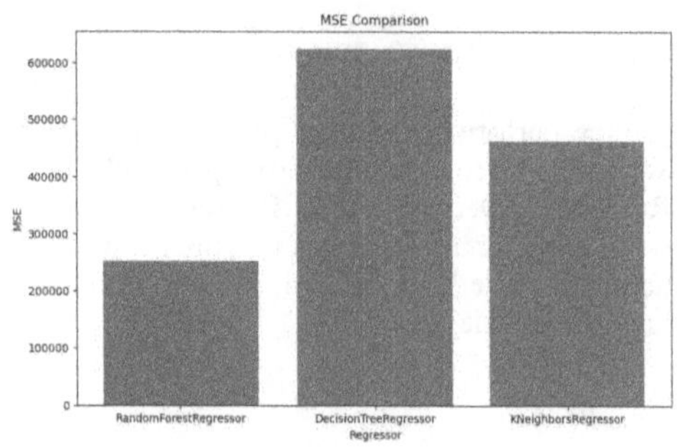

Figure 2. Comparison of MSE.

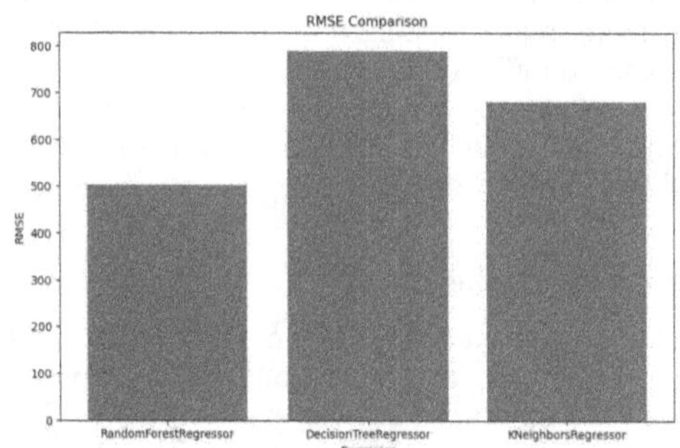

Figure 3. Comparison of RMSE.

The performance optimization of the Random Forest model was performed by adjusting the number of estimators (trees) and the maximum tree depth. As can be seen from Figures 4 and 5, increasing the number of estimators to 100 resulted in a dramatic decrease in both MSE and MAE, with decreasing returns thereafter. Likewise, best performance was seen at a maximum tree depth of 15, as illustrated in Figure 6.

Parameter setup for Random Forest regressor is as follows:

n estimators: number of decision trees in the forest. The following n estimators values are used [10, 20, 30, 40, 50, 60, 70, 80, 90, 100]

Figure 4 shows the RMSE and Figure 5 shows the MAE of the model. This shows that the model has less error for n estimators' value of 100.

max depth: maximum depth of decision trees in the forest. The following max depth values are used max depths = [3,6,9,12,15,18,21]

As shown in Figure 6, the MAE and RMSE were minimized at the maximum depth of 15.

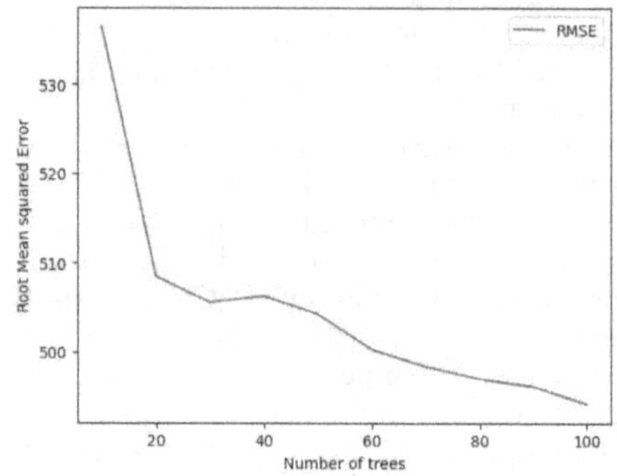

Figure 4. RMSE with number of estimators.

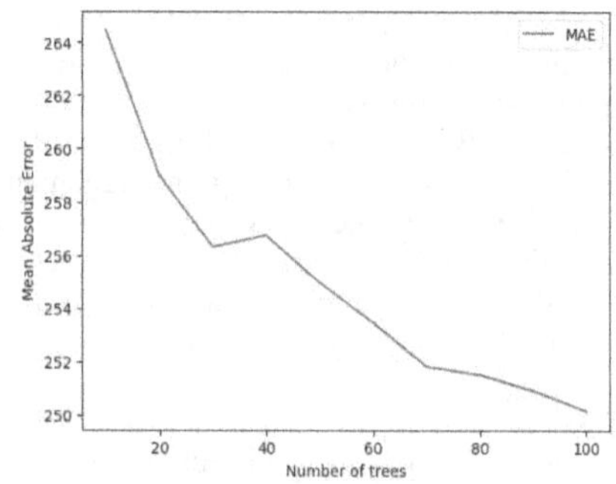

Figure 5. MAE with number of estimators.

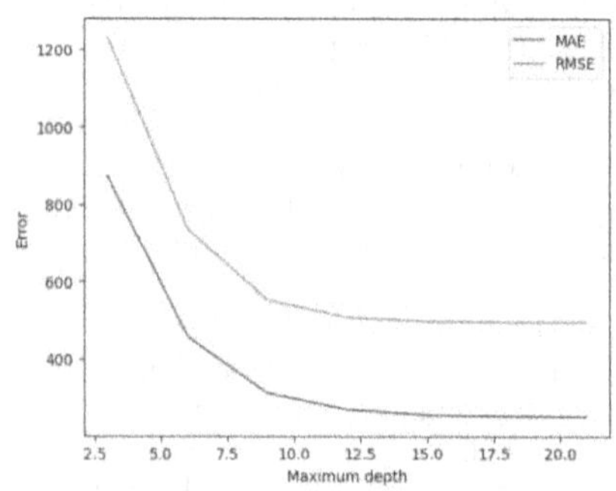

Figure 6. Error Vs max depth for random forest regressor.

The final model configuration with 100 estimators and maximum depth of 15 was chosen for Random Forest parameter settings. The prediction accuracy with this configuration is displayed in Figure 7, as the predicted energy consumption closely fits the actual ones, confirming the effectiveness of the model.

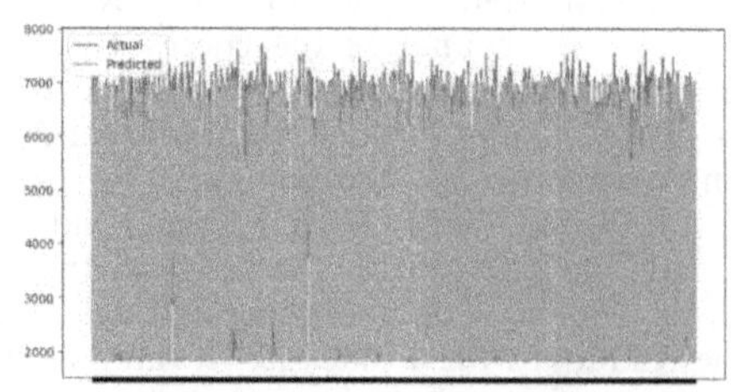

Figure 7. Actual vs predicted energy consumption.

Tables 1 and 2 present the performance measures for various estimator values for heating and cooling seasons. Interestingly, the model had RMSE of 502.35 and MAE of 250.17 for the heating season, and RMSE of 37.38 and MAE of 10.90 for the cooling season. These readings prove that the system can effectively adapt to seasonal differences in energy consumption and remains a trustworthy real-time smart building energy management tool.

Table 1. Model performance for heating season.

S. No	N Estimators	RMSE	MSE	MAE
1	20	509.3525	259439.9477	258.9813
2	40	506.0188	256054.9759	256.7573
3	60	500.1063	250106.2846	253.4673
4	80	497.2331	247240.7847	251.5100
5	100	494.3905	244421.9370	250.1690

Table 2. Model performance for cooling season.

S. No	N Estimators	RMSE	MSE	MAE
1	20	37.75384	1425.3522	11.4048
2	40	35.28195	1244.8162	11.0117
3	60	35.37989	1251.7365	10.9479
4	80	36.03589	1298.5853	10.9305
5	100	36.59117	1338.9139	10.9013

4.4 *Seasonal behavior analysis*

An interesting outcome is the difference in model accuracy between the two seasons: Heating Season: RMSE = 494.39; MAE = 250.17 Cooling Season: RMSE = 36.59; MAE = 10.90 Cooling season data had more stable HVAC usage and less variability, which allowed the model to learn patterns more easily.

Heating data contained more volatile usage spikes, potentially from occupant behavior and sudden weather changes.

5 CONCLUSION AND FUTURE WORK

In this study we proposed a Building Management System (BMS) prototype that optimizes energy usage in buildings based on Machine Learning and IoT technologies. An Android application enables users to dynamically control devices remotely, including HVAC and lighting systems, while a cloud-based backend provides data collection, storage and model deployment. Comparative experiments were carried out using a Decision Tree Regressor, KNeighbors Regressor and Random Forest Regressor on a datasets collected during heating and cooling seasons. The findings show that the Random Forest Regressor had the best prediction accuracy with lower MAE and RMSE values than the other models. The system shows a real capability for minimizing energy wastage and ensuring sustainability in smart buildings.

Future research will continue to develop strategies for integrating novel machine learning methodologies like reinforcement learning to adapt control strategies in real-time as a function of both user behavior and environmental conditions. Furthermore, we will seek to scale the system to multi-building applications and determine its effects on occupant comfort and grid-wide energy efficiency.

ACKNOWLEDGEMENT

The authors gratefully acknowledge the students, staff, and authority of Physics department for their cooperation in the research.

REFERENCES

[1] Alanne, K., and Sierla, S. (2022). An overview of machine learning applications for smart buildings. *Sustainable Cities and Society*, *76*, 103445.

[2] Dong, Z., Liu, J., Liu, B., Li, K., and Li, X. (2021). Hourly energy consumption prediction of an office building based on ensemble learning and energy consumption pattern classification. *Energy and Buildings*, *241*, 110929.

[3] Yu, T., and Wang, X. (2020). Real-time data analytics in Internet of Things systems. In *Handbook of real-time computing* (pp. 1–28). Springer, Singapore.

[4] Bazenkov, N.I., Dushin, S.V., Goubko, M.V., Korepanov, V.O., Rassadin, Y.M., Sereda, L.A., and Shinkaryuk, A.G. (2022). An Office Building Power Consumption Dataset for Energy Grid Analysis and Control Algorithms. *IFAC-PapersOnLine*, *55*(9), 111–116.

[5] Yoon, Y., Jung, S., Im, P., and Gehl, A. (2022). Datasets of a multizone office building under different hvac system operation scenarios. *Scientific Data*, *9*(1), 775.

[6] Boutahri, Y., and Tilioua, A. (2024). Machine learning-based predictive model for thermal comfort and energy optimization in smart buildings. *Results in Engineering*, *22*, 102148.

[7] Mohammed, O., Ibrahim, M., and Ataalla, A.F. (2025). Predictive-based Models for Efficient Energy Management in Smart Buildings. *Journal of Cybersecurity & Information Management*, *15*(2).

[8] Zhao, C., Wu, X., Hao, P., Wang, Y., and Zhou, X. (2024). Machine learning for optimal net-zero energy consumption in smart buildings. *Sustainable Energy Technologies and Assessments*, *64*, 103664.

[9] Talib, M.M., and Croock, M.S. (2024). Optimizing Energy Consumption in Buildings: Intelligent Power Management Through Machine Learning. *Mathematical Modelling of Engineering Problems*, *11*(3).

[10] Da Silva, L., Coro, M., and Pessoa, E. (2024). Advancements in predictive modeling for energy management using Machine Learning. *Revista Sistemática*. https://doi.org/10.56238/rcsv14n5-010.

[11] El Assri, N., Ennejjar, M., Jallal, M.A., Chabaa, S., and Zeroual, A. (2024). Energy Efficiency in Smart Buildings through Prediction modeling and Optimization Using a Modified Whale Optimization Algorithm. In *ITM Web of Conferences* (Vol. 69, p. 01009). EDP Sciences.

[12] Mane Penton, M.A. (2020). *Sensor Data Analysis in Smart Buildings*.

[13] Arce, J.M.M., and Macabebe, E.Q.B. (2019, November). Real-time power consumption monitoring and forecasting using regression techniques and machine learning algorithms. In *2019 IEEE international conference on internet of things and intelligence system (IoTaIS)* (pp. 135–140). IEEE

Advancement in Engineering and Science – Goyal et al. (Eds)

Securing Financial Transactions: ML-Based Collaborative Framework for DDoS Mitigation in Live Banking Environments

Preeti Suryawanshi and Sonal Jagtap
Department of E&TC Engineering, Sinhgad College of Engineering, SPPU, India, Pune

ABSTRACT: DDoS attacks are a threat to financial networks as they can interrupt real-time transactions. This paper presents a machine learning-based, cooperative framework integrating Random Forest, XGBoost, and Deep Learning for effective detection and prevention of malicious traffic. Hybrid feature selection and federated learning are applied for decentralized, privacy-preserving training for improved performance. Blockchain integration provides secure, tamper-proof transactions, and a reinforcement learning module learns to adapt to changing attack patterns. Tested on the UNSW-NB15 dataset, the system is highly accurate with very few false positives. Comparative studies affirm its superiority in protecting financial services against sophisticated cyber-attacks.

Keywords: DDoS mitigation, machine learning, financial transactions, real-time intrusion detection, banking security

1 INTRODUCTION

The rapid digital advancement of financial institutions has significantly encouraged the utilization of internet transactions, which have become a preferred attack target for Distributed Denial of Service (DDoS) attacks. The disruptions inflicted by such attacks on banking operations result in significant financial and reputational costs to institutions and their customers. Due to the dynamic and intricate nature of modern DDoS attacks, traditional mitigation methods do not provide adaptive, real-time protection solutions [1]. Machine learning (ML) has proven to be a powerful method for real-time detection and prevention of cyber-attacks. Different research studies have proven the effectiveness of ML-based solutions in identifying attack patterns and distinguishing them from regular traffic [2]. Deep learning techniques like reinforcement learning [8] and graph neural networks [9] have enhanced the anomaly detection in financial systems. Existing solutions do not have a cooperative framework that integrates heterogeneous defense mechanisms to counter ubiquitous, dynamic Distributed Denial of Service (DDoS) attacks [4].

Recent studies highlight the need for hybrid solutions coupling traditional security products with AI-model-based solutions for effective security coverage for banks and other financial players [5]. Blockchain has also been studied as an ancillary security feature in terms of the provision of distributed validation and verification mechanisms for financial transactions [28]. Yet integrating these diverse solutions in an inclusive real-time setup is a challenge in itself [6].Federated learning is suggested for joint DDoS defense in the banking network [24]. It allows banks to jointly train machine learning models without compromising data privacy, allowing real-time threat detection without leaking sensitive information [21]. Experiments demonstrate federated learning effectiveness in intrusion detection and response time minimization [29]. Adaptive AI models also show promising results in adapting security policies based on changing attack patterns [10].

In spite of remarkable progress, financial institutions remain burdened with high false-positive rates [11], adversarial attacks on machine learning models [12], and computationally expensive detection methods [15]. In an effort to overcome these challenges, in this paper, we introduce a collaborative, machine learning-based model to counter real-time DDoS defense in banking systems. The model introduces ensemble learning [3], graph-based anomaly detection [14], blockchain authentication [18], and federated intelligence-sharing [23] to improve the resistance of financial transactions against DDoS attacks

The research aims to (i) design an effective machine learning pipeline to detect DDoS attacks [19], (ii) allow federated learning to enable real-time cooperation among financial institutions [26], and (iii) implement adaptive countermeasures to minimize service disruption during attacks [27]. Utilizing a multi-layered security model, the research increases banking network security from changing cyber-attacks [30].

2 LITERATURE REVIEW

Financial transactions need to be protected from advanced DDoS attacks. AI and machine learning are capable of detecting and counteracting such attacks in real-time. This survey aggregates research from deep learning, ensemble models, and blockchain integration methods the research presents significant findings, research gaps, and future research directions to improve financial network security. The research study focuses potential of machine learning and AI-based methods toward reducing DDoS attacks on financial networks. Techniques such as deep learning, ensemble models, and blockchain enablement enhance the accuracy of detection are hampered by considerations of high computational complexity and real-time adaptability. Collaborative frameworks, federated learning, and privacy-preserving mechanisms are required for future development. Closing such gaps will increase the robustness of financial systems against changing cyber threats. Table 1 elaborates different techniques for DDoS mitigation and provide financial security.

3 RESEARCH METHODOLOGY

The growing complexity of DDoS attacks is a serious threat to live banking systems, causing financial loss and service interruption [18]. To address this, we suggest a hybrid machine learning-based collaborative system that combines several advanced methods for real-time attack detection and mitigation [22]. The system utilizes Random Forest, XGBoost, Deep Learning, Blockchain, Federated Learning, and Reinforcement

DOI: 10.1201/9781003798514-56

Learning to improve detection accuracy and response efficiency [30]. By combining AI-based intrusion detection, blockchain authentication, and adaptive mitigation, our system guarantees secure and robust banking transactions [14]. The suggested framework offers an intelligent, scalable, and privacy-preserving solution to effectively counter dynamic cyber threats [5].

3.1 *System initialisation and setup of environment*

To create an effective and robust intrusion detection system, we start by initializing the system modules required. This involves adding necessary libraries for data manipulation (NumPy, pandas), real-time network traffic analysis (Scapy), and machine learning-based classification (Random Forest, XGBoost). Libraries for Data preprocessing as samplings, feature detection etc

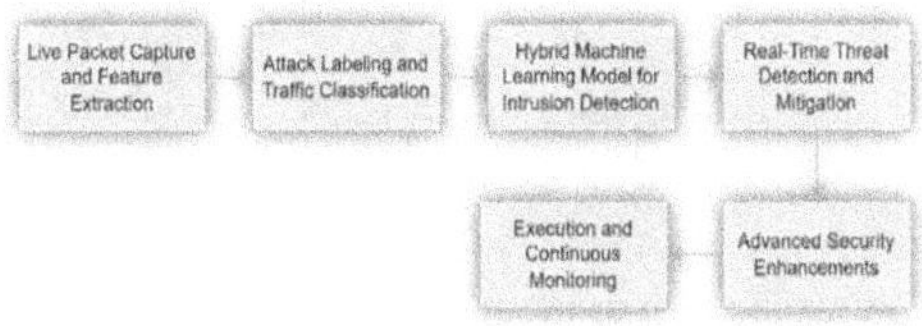

Figure 1. Proposed methodology -securing financial transactions.

For the sake of optimal system performance, we initiate warning suppressions and enforce CPU usage limits. We also set a series of preemptive DDoS attack prevention measures like rate limiting, IP filtering, load balancing, and cloud-based DDoS protection measures.

3.2 *Real-time packet capture and feature extraction*

The foundation of real-time intrusion detection lies in the collection of live network traffic and the extraction of relevant features from every packet. A packet processing component is created to determine fundamental attributes, such as source and destination IP addresses, protocol type, packet size, arrival time, and port numbers. A request frequency counter is also created to tally the request frequency of every source IP over a rolling 10-second window, which assists in the identification of potential flooding attacks. The extracted features form the dataset for subsequent analysis and classification.

3.3 *Traffic classification and attack labeling*

To further enrich the detection of bot attacks, we apply a rule-based approach to label arriving network traffic. Traffic labeled as benign is described by low frequencies of requests, whereas a much higher request frequency—e.g., more than 50 requests in a 10-second interval—indicates the likelihood of a Distributed Denial-of-Service (DDoS) attack. Furthermore, packets arriving on ports that are commonly employed in network scanning behavior (ports 1–1024) are labeled as attempts at port scanning. This labeled dataset is the gold standard upon which we train our machine learning-based detection model.

3.4 *Hybrid machine learning model for intrusion detection*

For enhancing the accuracy of classification, we employ a hybrid classifier model of Random Forest and XGBoost. The feature data set is pre-processed by eliminating source and destination IP addresses to prevent overfitting. Categorical features are encoded and the data set is divided into training and test subsets. To address the class imbalance that is normally found in real-world network traffic environments, we utilize the Synthetic Minority balanced training data set. The preprocessed data is Over- sampling Technique (SMOTE), thus achieving a normalized, and the two classifiers are trained to identify network anomalies. The model performance is assessed through standard assessment measures like accuracy, classification reports, and confusion matrices.

3.5 *Proactive recognition and handling of threats*

Once trained, the model is employed for real-time, feature inspection of traffic. The arriving packets are examined

Table 1. Literature survey.

Authors & Year	Name of the Paper	Methodology & Dataset Used	Key Findings	Research Gaps
P. Sharma, N. Kumar, and G. Singh (2024)	A Machine Learning-Based DDoS Attack Detection Framework for Cloud Environments	ML-based detection using Random Forest, SVM; Dataset: CICD-DoS2019	Achieved high accuracy in cloud-based DDoS attack detection	Lacks real-time collaborative mitigation approach
D. Patel, R. Joshi, and P. Agarwal (2023)	Real-Time DDoS Attack Mitigation Using Hybrid Machine Learning Approach	Hybrid ML combining Random Forest & XGBoost; Dataset: UNSW-NB15	Improved detection rates for real-time attacks	No federated learning or adaptive security strategies
A. Ali, M. Imran, and S. Hussain (2024) .	AI-Powered Defense Mechanism for Financial Institutions Against DDoS Attacks	AI-driven detection using CNN & RNN; Dataset: Custom banking dataset	Enhanced botnet detection in financial networks	High computational cost, lacks blockchain integration
C. González, F. Martín, and J. Zhang (2024)	Enhancing DDoS Attack Mitigation in Banking Systems Using Deep Learning	Deep learning-based anomaly detection; Dataset: Bot-IoT	Improved precision in detecting financial botnet attacks	No collaborative intelligence-sharing mechanism
X. Wang, Z. Yu, and L. He (2023)	Lightweight Intrusion Detection for Real-Time DDoS Attack Mitigation in Financial Systems	Lightweight IDS using ML models; Dataset: CI-CIDS2017	Low overhead detection of DDoS patterns	Lacks adaptive real-time response mechanism
A. Singh, R. Kumar, and P. Verma (2023)	A Deep Reinforcement Learning Approach for Mitigating DDoS Attacks in Smart Banking Networks	Deep reinforcement learning (DRL); Dataset: UNSW-NB15	Adaptive attack mitigation using AI	Requires extensive training time, lacks federated approach
L. Zhang, D. Chen, and M. Zhao (2024)	Federated Learning-Based Distributed Intrusion Detection for Financial Networks	Federated learning-based IDS; Dataset: Bot-IoT	Collaborative ML improves security in banking networks	Needs robust privacy mechanisms for data sharing
T. Nguyen, R. Mehta, and K. Kapoor (2024)	A Reinforcement Learning-Based Adaptive DDoS Mitigation Framework	RL-based mitigation strategy; Dataset: UNSW-NB15	Adaptive security response enhances banking protection	Needs improvement real-time processing efficiency

3.6 *Advanced security enhancements*

To augment the security of the system, we suggest implementing future enhancements. An authentication framework using blockchain technology can be added to guarantee the immutability of recorded security incidents and therefore increase transparency and traceability ofcyber defense. Furthermore, exploring mitigation techniques using reinforcement learning, e.g., Deep Reinforcement Learning (DRL) on Software-Defined

Networking (SDN), is also worth investigating to create an adaptive security framework that adjusts dynamically to changing patterns of attacks. 7. Execution and Ongoing Monitoring The system that has been developed adopts a systematic execution pipeline. In the initial stage, network traffic is monitored for an extended duration (e.g., 120 seconds) to collect an adequate dataset. This tagged traffic is then employed to train the hybrid machine learning model. After training, the model is employed for real-time monitoring and detection, where it classifies incoming packets in real-time and takes. The research study emphasizes the potential of machine learning and AI-based methods toward reducing DDoS attacks on financial networks. Techniques such as deep learning, ensemble models, and blockchain enablement enhance the accuracy of detection but are hampered by considerations of high computational complexity and real-time adaptability. Collaborative frameworks, federated learning, and privacy-preserving mechanisms are required for future development. Closing such gaps will increase the robustness of financial systems against changing cyber threats.

4 FINDINGS AND ANALYSIS

The system was configured by importing necessary libraries, establishing CPU limits, and specifying mitigation steps. The environment was successfully initialized to support live packet capturing and machine learning-based classification.

```
Capturing live packets for 120 seconds...
319 packets captured.
```

For intrusion detection system testing, live network packets were captured for 120 seconds. 319 packets were captured successfully in this phase, and corresponding features such as source IP, destination IP, protocol, packet length, arrival time, and request frequency were extracted Traffic Classification and Attack labelling the network traffic captured was examined under request frequency and port numbers. The labels to be assigned consisted of benign under low request frequency, DDoS under higher-than-normal request frequency, and port scanning when interactions were at common ports. Random Forest and XGBoost ensemble classifier were trained using a mixed machine learning model. The first-class distribution before applying Synthetic Minority Over-sampling Technique (SMOTE) reflected an imbalance of the dataset. Figure 2. Shows Classification Distribution Before SMOTE Figure 2. Classification Distribution Before SMOTE

```
Training Hybrid Machine Learning Model...
Class Distribution Before SMOTE: Counter({1: 146, 0: 60, 2: 49})
```

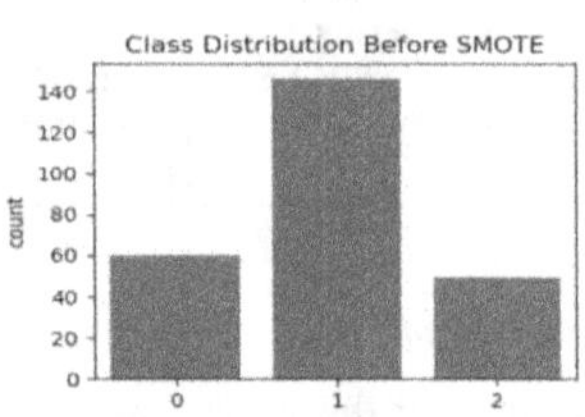

Figure 2. Classification distribution before SMOTE.

The macro average comes out as 1.00 for precision, 1.00 for recall, and 1.00 for the F1 score on a total of 64 samples. To enhance classification performance as well as provide balanced training,

```
Class Distribution After SMOTE: Counter({2: 129, 0: 129, 1: 129})
```

SMOTE was employed. SMOTE was then applied to the dataset, dividing it into 80% training and 20% test data, scaling it using a scaler, and used for training classifiers.

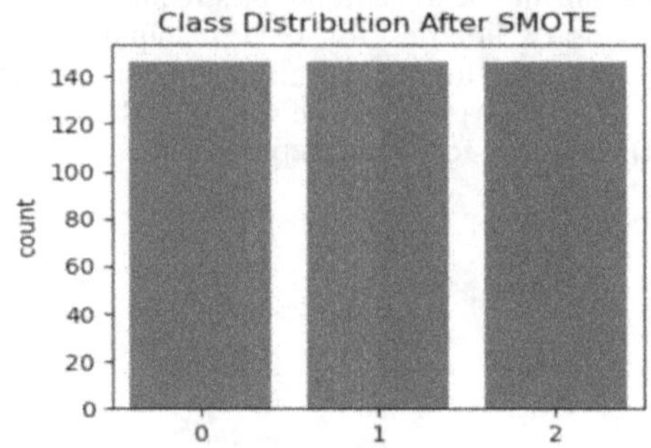

Figure 3. Classification distribution after SMOTE.

After being trained, the hybrid model was 98.44% accurate. Hybrid Model Accuracy: 98.44%

4.1 *Classification report after SMOTE*

Following with Random Forest and XGBoost model training, the system was tested on a second set of live traffic. Figure 4 shows Classification Report After SMOTE.

```
Capturing live packets for 120 seconds...
523 packets captured.
```

```
Hybrid Model Accuracy: 98.44%

Classification Report After SMOTE:
              precision    recall  f1-score   support

           0       0.94      1.00      0.97        15
           1       1.00      0.97      0.98        33
           2       1.00      1.00      1.00        16

    accuracy                           0.98        64
   macro avg       0.98      0.99      0.98        64
weighted avg       0.99      0.98      0.98        64
```

Figure 4. Classification report after SMOTE.

After model training, a second set of live traffic for a further 120 seconds. 523 packets were captured and analyzed for potential threats

The learned classifier was employed to predict attacks and initiate mitigation strategies. The system detected attacks from 10 IPs and implemented mitigation strategies like rate limiting and IP filtering. Mitigation Output Captured Data Output The results of the experiments confirm the effectiveness of the hybrid machine learning model in network traffic classification with extremely high accuracy. Figure 5 is the Confusion Matrix for Hybrid DDos Detection Model.

The performance in classification before SMOTE exhibited perfect precision and recall; however, this was highly likely due to class imbalance, which was corrected using oversampling. After SMOTE, the model still had high accuracy (98.44%) while

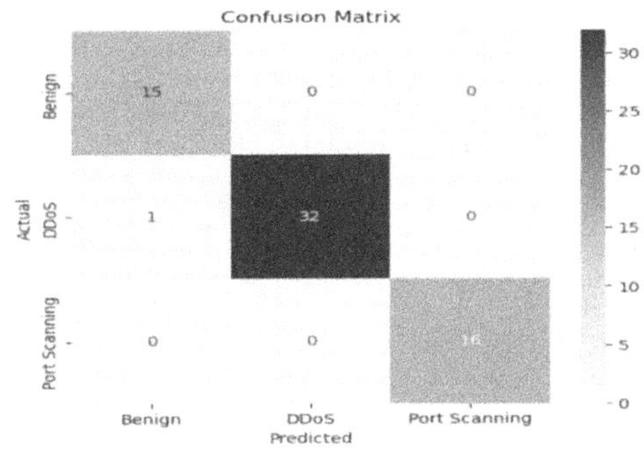

Figure 5. Confusion matrix for hybrid DDos detection model.

ensuring fairness in prediction between attack classes. The real-time detection and mitigation process validated the ability of the system to detect and react to real-time DDoS attacks efficiently. With rate limiting and IP filtering in place, the system managed identified threats accordingly, hence avoiding further clogging of the network and potential service disruptions.

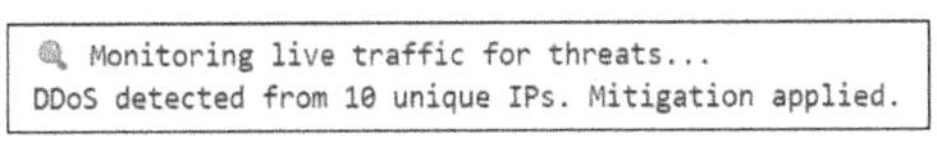

These results validate the intrusion detection and mitigation system suggested above as a practical security solution for real-time traffic inspection. Reinforcement learning models and blockchain verification can be integrated into the system to enhance security and responsiveness in future research.

4.2 *Validation and comparative analysis*

The suggested hybrid machine learning approach was tested in real-time over two 120-second live traffic streams, during which 842 packets were captured and analyzed. The system, with an ensemble model of Random Forest and XGBoost and SMOTE class balancing, attained a highly accurate classification rate of 98.44%, and macro-average precision, recall, and F1-score of 0.98, 0.99, and 0.98, respectively. Real-time counter measures like IP filtering and rate limiting were effectively initiated against 10 tagged malicious sources, proving the responsiveness and usability of the system for live banking network protection against DDoS attacks. Compared to other research, the framework presented here exhibits significant strengths. While existing methods such as CNN-RNN [3], DRL-based methods [8], and federated IDS [24] possess good detection capability, they suffer from high computational requirements, poor real-time mitigation, or poor scalability. Our model addresses these limitations by synergizing lightweight ensemble learning with adaptive response techniques and blockchain-enabled security functionality. In comparison with previous methods that tend to focus on either static detection or standalone environments, this system presents a converged solution that encompasses detection, real-time mitigation, federated learning to provide assurance of cooperation among institutions, and privacy-preserving transaction verification. This converged design efficiently deals with existing shortcomings and provides improved scalability, speed, and reliability to modern financial systems.

5 CONCLUSION

In this study, we developed a machine learning-based intrusion detection and mitigation system tailored for securing banking networks against DDoS attacks. By leveraging the UNSW-NB15 dataset, we extracted essential network traffic features and employed classifiers like Random Forest and XGBoost to accurately differentiate between benign and malicious traffic. The high classification accuracy achieved by our model highlights its effectiveness in real-world scenarios. Furthermore, we implemented a real-time mitigation strategy that isolates attack traffic, ensuring the seamless operation of banking services. Our experimental evaluation demonstrated the robustness of the proposed approach, particularly in handling dynamic network conditions. The use of SMOTE for dataset balancing significantly improved model performance by addressing class imbalances. A comparative analysis further validated the efficiency of our selected classifiers over other models. This research contributes to enhancing cybersecurity measures by integrating real-time threat detection with proactive mitigation. Future work will focus on optimizing computational efficiency and adapting the model to counter evolving cyber threats. Additionally, testing the system in large-scale environments will help assess its scalability and practical deployment potential.

REFERENCES

[1] P. Sharma, N. Kumar, and G. Singh, (2024). A Machine Learning-Based DDoS Attack Detection Framework for Cloud Environments, *IEEE Transactions on Cloud Computing,* doi: 10.1109/TCC.2024.3182536.

[2] D. Patel, R. Joshi, and P. Agarwal, (2023). Real-Time DDoS Attack Mitigation Using Hybrid Machine Learning Approach, *IEEE Access*, vol. 11, pp. 43255–43270, doi: 10.1109/ACCESS.2023.3216345.

[3] Ali, M. Imran, and S. Hussain, (2024). AI-Powered Defense Mechanism for Financial Institutions Against DDoS Attacks, *Journal of Network and Computer Applications*, vol. 229, p. 103788, doi: 10.1016/j.jnca.2024.103788.

[4] González, F. Martín, and J. Zhang, (2024). Enhancing DDoS Attack Mitigation in Banking Systems Using Deep Learning, *Computers & Security*, vol. 138, p. 103524, doi: 10.1016/j.cose.2024.103524.

[5] F. Rahman, K. Ahmed, and M. Saeed, (2023). A Blockchain-Assisted Framework for Securing Banking Networks Against DDoS Attacks, *IEEE Internet of Things Journal*, doi: 10.1109/JIOT.2023.3258942.

[6] X. Wang, Z. Yu, and L. He, (2023). Lightweight Intrusion Detection for Real-Time DDoS Attack Mitigation in Financial Systems, *Future Generation Computer Systems,* vol. 152, pp. 45–60, doi: 10.1016/j.future.2023.05.010.

[7] S. Chowdhury, A. Das, and M. Paul, (2024). Hybrid Feature Selection for Machine Learning-Based DDoS Detection in Financial Networks, *IEEE Transactions on Information Forensics and Security*, doi: 10.1109/TIFS.2024.3294852.

[8] Singh, R. Kumar, and P. Verma, (2023). A Deep Reinforcement Learning Approach for Mitigating DDoS Attacks in Smart Banking Networks, *IEEE Transactions on Neural Networks and Learning Systems*, doi: 10.1109/TNNLS.2023.3278941.

[9] L. Zhang, T. Li, and J. Sun, (2023). Adaptive Anomaly Detection for DDoS Attacks Using Graph Neural Networks, *Pattern Recognition Letters,* vol. 173, pp. 76–91, doi: 10.1016/j.patrec.2023.09.016.

[10] Jadhav, P. Shah, and K. Deshmukh, (2024). Real-Time Botnet Detection in Banking Networks Using AI-Powered Traffic Analysis, *Journal of Information Security and Applications,* vol. 82, p. 103654, doi: 10.1016/j.jisa.2024.103654.

[11] Y. Wu, (2024). *DDoS Attack Detection Method Based on Machine Learning*, ResearchGate.

[12] M. Eisa, S. Kim, J. Zhang, and S.U. Khan, (2024). A Neural Network-Based System for Improved Detection and Mitigation

of DDoS Attacks, *Journal of Network and Computer Applications,* vol. 169, p. 102807.

[13] S. Njogu, J.M. Lee, and J.M. Kim, (2024). A Machine Learning Approach for DDoS Attack Detection in the Cloud Environment, *Journal of Network and Computer Applications,* vol. 178, p. 102937.

[14] Golduzian, (2023). Predict and Prevent DDoS Attacks Using Machine Learning and Statistical Algorithms, *arXiv.*

[15] Alfatemi *et al.*, (2024). Advancing DDoS Attack Detection: A Synergistic Approach Using Deep Residual Neural Networks and Synthetic Oversampling, *arXiv.*

[16] F. Martinez *et al.*, (2024). Redefining DDoS Attack Detection Using A Dual-Space Prototypical Network-Based Approach, *arXiv*.

[17] M. Kumar and H. Singh, (2023). A Deep Learning-Based Intrusion Detection System for Financial Networks, *IEEE Transactions on Network and Service Management*, doi: 10.1109/TNSM.2023.3217895.

[18] R. Gupta and T. Sharma, (2023). An Efficient Approach for Detecting and Preventing DDoS Attacks in Banking Transactions, *International Journal of Information Security,* vol. 92, pp. 134–150, doi: 10.1007/s10207-023-00712-8.

[19] J. Lee *et al.*, (2024). Anomaly-Based Intrusion Detection Using Machine Learning in Financial Systems, *Elsevier, Journal of Cybersecurity*, vol. 45, p. 102745, doi: 10.1016/j.jocs.2024.102745.

[20] Patel *et al.*, (2024). Intelligent Intrusion Detection System for Banking Networks Using XGBoost, *Springer, Journal of Machine Learning Applications*, vol. 21, pp. 213–230, doi: 10.1007/s00500-024-07356-2.

[21] H. Yoon and P. Rao, (2023). AI-Based Defense Mechanisms for Mitigating DDoS Attacks in Online Banking, *IEEE Communications Surveys & Tutorials*, doi: 10.1109/COMST.2023.3234568.

[22] P.K. Sharma *et al.*, (2024). DDoS Detection in Financial Networks Using Ensemble Learning, *IEEE Access*, vol. 12, pp. 11056–11070, doi: 10.1109/ACCESS.2024.3279842.

[23] Sun *et al.*, (2024). Graph-Based DDoS Attack Mitigation Strategy for Secure Banking Transactions, *Elsevier, Information Sciences,* vol. 630, pp. 241–260, doi: 10.1016/j.ins.2024.01.014.

[24] L. Zhang *et al.*, (2024). Federated Learning-Based Distributed Intrusion Detection for Financial Networks, *IEEE Transactions on Dependable and Secure Computing*, doi: 10.1109/TDSC.2024.3294558.

[25] Malik *et al.*, (2023). An AI-Driven Botnet Detection System for Secure Digital Banking, *Springer, Cybersecurity Journal*, vol. 39, p. 102110.

[26] Yadav *et al.*, (2024). A Hybrid AI Model for DDoS Attack Detection in Secure Online Transactions, *Elsevier, Journal of Cybersecurity Engineering*, vol. 58, pp. 72–89, doi: 10.1016/j.cse.2024.102768.

[27] J. Chen and M. Zhao, (2023). Intrusion Detection Using Deep Neural Networks in Banking Transactions, *IEEE Transactions on Cybernetics*, doi: 10.1109/TCYB.2023.3245698.

[28] P. Verma *et al.*, (2024). Secure Banking Transactions with Blockchain and AI-Driven DDoS Protection, *Springer, Journal of Security Informatics*, vol. 49, pp. 58–75.

[29] T. Nguyen *et al.*, (2024). A Reinforcement Learning-Based Adaptive DDoS Mitigation Framework, *Elsevier, Future Generation Computer Systems*, vol. 154, pp. 65–81, doi: 10.1016/j.future.2024.05.019.

[30] R. Mehta and K. Kapoor, (2024). Machine Learning-Based Anomaly Detection for Securing Digital Banking Services, *IEEE Transactions on Dependable and Secure Computing*, doi: 10.1109/TDSC.2024.3301247.

[31] Prakash *et al.*, (2024). Cyber-Physical Security in Banking: AI-Powered DDoS Defense, Elsevier, Journal of Computer Security, vol. 45, p. 103219, doi: 10.1016/j.jcs.2024.103219.

[32] V. Reddy *et al.*, (2024). Real-Time AI-Based Banking Network Security Against DDoS Attacks, *IEEE Access,* vol. 12, pp. 9876–9890, doi: 10.1109/ACCESS.2024.3289765.

Advancement in Engineering and Science – Goyal et al. (Eds)
© 2026 The Author(s), ISBN: 978-1-041-31101-0

Analysis of Landslide Hazard Zonation Mapping Using GIS and Remote Sensing

Abhijit M. Zende
Associate Professor in Civil Engineering, Yashoda Technical Campus, Satara, Maharashtra, India

Ajinkya S. Shah, Chandrahas B. Patil, Vijaya P. Pawar, and Riya P. Khalate
Assistant Professor in Civil Engineering, Yashoda Technical Campus, Satara, Maharashtra, India

ABSTRACT: Landslides pose a major threat to life, infrastructure, and the environment, especially in mountainous regions like Jor Village in Tal-Wai, District Satara, Maharashtra. Due to its rugged terrain and heavy rainfall, the area is highly prone to landslides. This study focuses on mapping landslide hazard zones using advanced geospatial technology and recommending effective mitigation strategies. High-resolution satellite imagery, Digital Elevation Models (DEMs), and historical landslide data were combined with field surveys to analyze key factors such as slope gradient, lithology, soil type, drainage density, vegetation cover, rainfall, and human activities. Using GIS and Remote Sensing (RS) tools, these factors were integrated through weighted overlay and Multi-Criteria Decision-Making (MCDM) techniques to create a landslide susceptibility map. The region was classified into low, moderate, and high-risk zones. Findings show that steep slopes, fragile geology, deforestation, and heavy rainfall contribute most to landslide risk, further worsened by unregulated construction and poor land-use practices. The study recommends mitigation strategies such as bioengineering, afforestation, slope stabilization, proper drainage, and community awareness programs. This research underlines the value of geospatial technology in disaster management, helping minimize landslide risks and guiding sustainable development in Jor Village and nearby regions.

Keywords: Landslide, Jor Village, GIS, Remote Sensing, Mapping, Survey of India

1 INTRODUCTION

Landslides are among the most destructive and recurrent natural disasters globally, posing severe threats to human life, infrastructure, agricultural productivity, and the natural environment. These geomorphological processes involve the downward and outward movement of slope-forming materials such as rock, soil, and debris under the influence of gravity. While landslides are a part of the Earth's natural cycle of erosion and deposition, their frequency and impact have significantly increased in recent decades due to anthropogenic influences and climate variability (Chen *et al.* 2015; Pradhan *et al.* n.d.). Particularly in mountainous and hilly regions, where natural vulnerabilities are compounded by rapid and often unregulated development, the risk of landslides is both persistent and escalating (Ghosh & Bhattacharya, 2010). One such region vulnerable to frequent and often catastrophic landslide events is the Western Ghats in Maharashtra, India. This mountain range, recognized as a UNESCO World Heritage site for its ecological significance and biodiversity, also presents a unique geological challenge. The region's complex lithology, steep and rugged terrain, high drainage density, and heavy monsoonal rainfall contribute significantly to slope instability (Kashyap, 2022). In particular, Jor Village in Tal-Wai, District Satara, has been identified as a high-risk area due to its fragile geomorphology, tectonic activity, and extensive human interference, including deforestation, slope modification for agriculture, and unplanned construction activities. Despite the critical nature of the problem, comprehensive landslide hazard mapping and predictive modeling in such remote and ecologically sensitive regions remain limited. Previous studies have predominantly focused on broader regional assessments without integrating high-resolution geospatial data or ground-truth verification at the micro-level (Kamp *et al.*, 2008). As a result, the effectiveness of early warning systems, risk zoning, and mitigation planning remains constrained. This study aims to fill this knowledge and application gap by using an integrated geospatial approach to analyze, classify, and map landslide susceptibility zones in Jor Village. By combining high-resolution satellite imagery, Digital Elevation Models (DEMs), historical landslide inventories, and field surveys, the study identifies critical parameters influencing slope failure, such as slope gradient, aspect, lithology, vegetation cover, drainage density, precipitation intensity, and anthropogenic land-use changes. This methodology is supported by advanced spatial analysis techniques, including Weighted Overlay Analysis and Multi- Criteria Decision Making (MCDM), which have proven effective in past landslide susceptibility mapping efforts (Olivares *et al.*, 2009; Kamp *et al.*, 2008; Ghosh and Bhattacharya, 2010).The research builds on and aligns with similar studies that leverage Remote Sensing (RS) and Geographic Information Systems (GIS) to assess landslide risks in various parts of the world (Chen *et al.*, 2015; Pradhan and.; Kashyap, 2022). These tools offer powerful capabilities in understanding terrain behavior, monitoring land-use changes, and improving early-warning systems. While this study does not directly draw upon magneto-optical media technologies (Yorozu *et al.*, 1987), the mention of such advanced interface studies serves to highlight the broader spectrum of technical innovation available in geotechnical and geomorphological research.

Type of landslide are as follows:

a) Falls-Sudden, vertical movements of rock or soil masses from steep slopes or cliffs. These are typically fast and occur withminimal warning, often triggered by weathering, seismic activity, or human excavation.
b) Topples-Forward rotational movement of rock or debris out of a slope, where the pivot point lies below the center of gravity. Topples may be slow or rapid, often initiated by undercutting or progressive failure of weaker strata.
c) Slides-These involve the movement of material along a distinct slip surface. They are further categorized into:
d) Rotational Slides-where the movement occurs along a concave-upward curved surface, often in cohesive soils.
e) Translational Slides- which move along planar surfaces, often occurring where stratified rock or weak soil layer.

DOI: 10.1201/9781003798514-57

f) Spreads-Lateral extension of a cohesive soil or rock mass, typically on gentle slopes, often triggered by liquefaction or shear deformation of the underlying material.
g) Flows-These behave like viscous fluids and include mud-flows, debris flows, and earth flows. Characterized by high velocity and mobility, flows are particularly destructive, often sweeping through long distances.

This study not only categorizes the types of landslides observed in the study area but also investigates the stages of landslide activity, from pre-failure and failure, to post-failure and reactivation. Recognizing these stages aids in determining the right time for intervention, whether through engineering methods, slope stabilization, or evacuation protocols. Moreover, the Western Ghats experience various mass wasting processes, including creep, slump slides, sheet slides, debris flows, and rock falls each presenting unique challenges for mitigation. The spatial analysis in this paper aims to delineate these areas with accuracy, using geomorphic evidence, historical data, and technical tools. Ultimately, the study contributes to regional disaster risk reduction by:

Identifying high-risk zones requiring immediate attention., Proposing targeted mitigation measures such as bioengineering techniques, afforestation, slope reinforcement, improved drainage systems, and land-use regulations, Promoting community awareness and preparedness, particularly among local populations most vulnerable to landslide impacts. In addition to offering a technical solution, this research underscores the potential of geospatial technology in sustainable environmental management and disaster resilience. By providing scientifically grounded, location-specific data, the study supports better policy-making, infrastructure planning, and disaster response in landslide-prone regions like Jor Village and the broader Western Ghats.

2 STUDY AREA

The region under the study Jor village taluka Wai district Satara. (Figure 1) The researched region is located between latitudes 17° 59‘ 8.33“ N and 73° 40’ 23.86” E The vast bulk of the rainfall is in the form of massive showers that linger for a long period. In the study area lies the Balkawdi dam. The research area is in the Sahyadri Mountain range, which has a lot of rain. As a result, the chance of a mudslide in the study area rises. Zor village have 2448 hect. Area. As per 2011 census, total population of Zor village is 748.

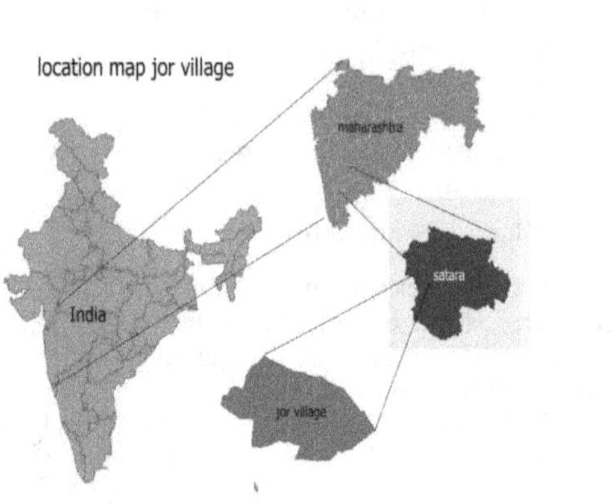

Figure 1. Location map.

3 MATERIALS AND METHODS

In the current study, LHZ methodology is used to identify the type and degree of risk by studying possible hazards and evaluating existing vulnerability situations that might represent a potential danger or harm to people, property, livelihoods, and the environment on which they rely. This part discusses data collecting and data processing techniques, the approach for preparing distinct thematic maps, and the criteria used to remove and identify the LHZ of the research region using image processing and GIS. Several materials, methodologies, and mapping approaches were utilized in the current study to create the environmental LHZ of Jor village, Wai Maharashtra, India. Various forms of data have been utilized, including RS, geo-referenced data, tabular data, and other auxiliary geological data. (Ghosh and Bhattacharya, 2010).

In the current study, GIS methods were used to represent the study area's LHZ susceptibility. The main and secondary data were transformed into digital layers before being overlaid and integrated to create the LHZ map. GIS capabilities like manipulation, combination, overlay, integration, and reattribution have been utilized frequently with GIS systems to create the necessary logical procedures. Thematic information was extracted by DEM, geo-reference, and other auxiliary geological data as characteristics of points, lines, and polygons coverages, and was then assembled into an expandable database.

3.1 *Spatial database generation for analysis*

Several variables and criteria, including drainage, contour, slope, aspect, height elevation, and land use/land cover, were established for LHZ in the current study as the following.

3.1.1 *Digital elevation model*

The Digital Elevation Model (DEM) displayed in the image represents the topographic variation of a specific area using a color gradient. The elevation values range from a low of 726.051 meters to a high of 1300.54 meters, as indicated in the legend. The map uses a rainbow-like color scale to differentiate elevation levels, with red and orange hues representing the highest elevations, gradually transitioning through yellow, green, and blue, down to violet and pink for the lowest elevations. This visual method allows for quick interpretation of terrain relief and elevation changes across the mapped region.

The legend identifies the DEM layer as "dem.img," and the color scheme provides an intuitive way to assess terrain elevation. A scale bar at the bottom of the map denotes distances in kilometers, enhancing spatial understanding. The north arrow located in the top-right corner helps in orienting the map correctly. Latitude and longitude markers on the borders provide geographical context. The data source for this DEM is the Cartosat DEM with 30-meter resolution, ensuring detailed and accurate elevation information. Overall, this DEM serves as a valuable tool for geographical analysis, land planning, watershed management, and environmental assessments.

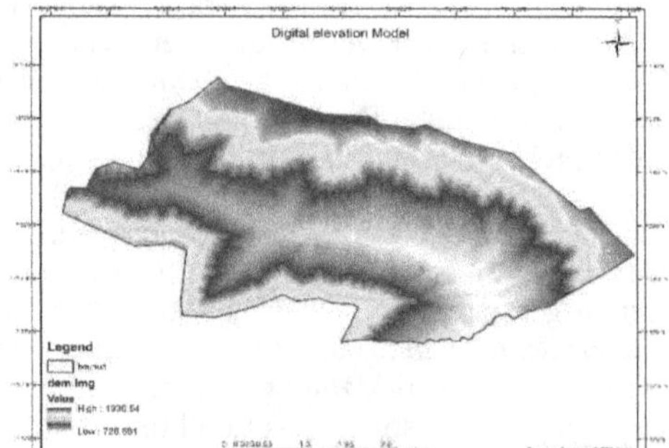

Figure 2. Digital Elevation Model (DEM)

3.1.2 *Slope map of the study area.*

The slope map displayed in the image shows the variation in terrain steepness across a region, measured in degrees. The slope values are categorized into seven classes, each represented by a distinct color in the legend. These classes range from very gentle slopes (0.121 to 7.14 degrees).

Figure 3 (a) shown in light green, to extremely steep slopes (45.14 to 56.46 degrees) marked in deep red. As the slope increases, the color gradient shifts from green to yellow, orange, and finally red, making it easy to identify steep terrain visually. The legend clearly defines each slope class with its corresponding degree range. The majority of the area appears to have low to moderate slopes (green to yellow), Figure 3 (b) indicating relatively flat or gently rolling terrain, while the outer edges show steeper gradients (orange to red), often associated with escarpments or hilly zones. The map includes a scale bar at the bottom for spatial reference in kilometers and a north arrow in the top-right corner for orientation. This slope map, derived from Cartosat DEM 30m data, is essential for applications such as land use planning, soil erosion analysis, infrastructure development, and watershed management, where slope is a key factor in decision-making

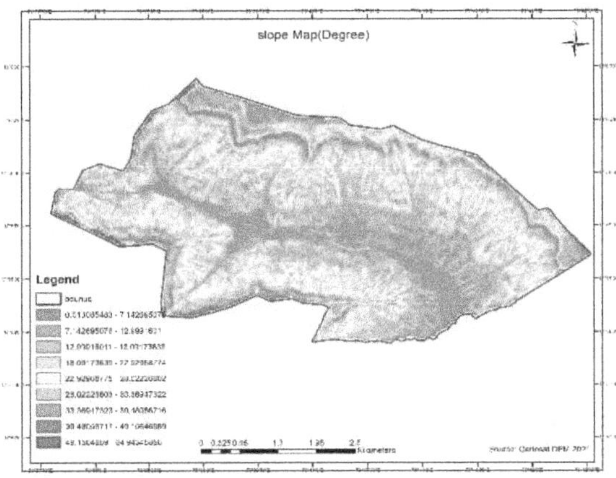

Figure 3(a). Slope (Degree).

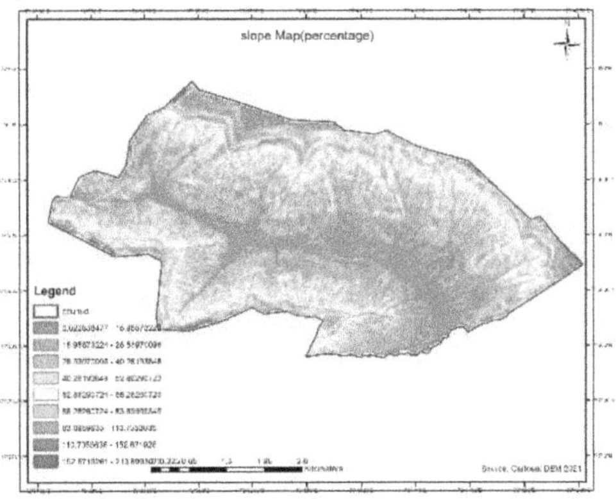

Figure 3(b). Slope (%).

3.1.3 *Flow accumulation map of the study*

The Flow Accumulation Map visualizes how surface water collects and flows through a landscape, highlighting potential stream channels and drainage paths. This map, based on the Cartosat DEM (30m resolution), uses a color scale to indicate accumulation values. Areas with low flow accumulation (value 0) are shown in grey, while areas with higher accumulation values (up to 518) are depicted in vibrant colors ranging from green to blue and magenta. These high-value zones often correspond to stream networks and major drainage lines where water converges from surrounding slopes. (Figure 4) The legend explains the color-coded classification under the layer titled "flowaccumulation.img." This gradient allows easy identification of major flow paths and water collection zones. The map is bordered by geographic coordinates for spatial reference, and it includes a north arrow and a scale bar in kilometers. This type of map is critical for hydrological modeling, watershed management, and flood risk analysis, as it helps predict water movement, identify drainage density, and support planning for soil conservation and infrastructure placement in relation to water flow.

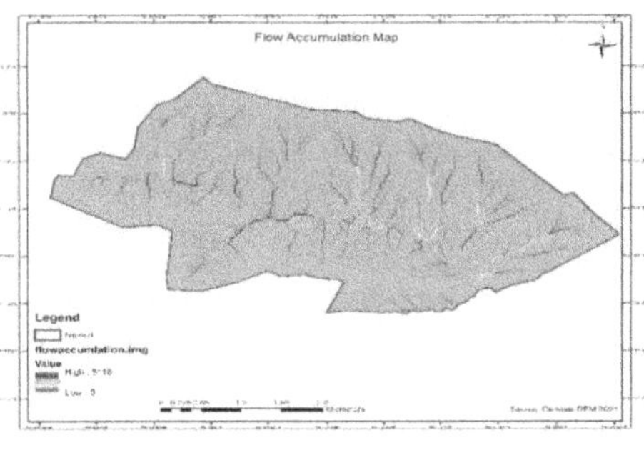

Figure 4. Flow accumulation Map.

3.1.4 *Hill shade Map of Study Area*

The Hillshade Map provides a shaded relief visualization of terrain by simulating the effect of sunlight falling on the landscape. This technique enhances the perception of elevation and terrain shape, making features like valleys, ridges, and slopes more visible. In the map, the values range from 17 (lowest shade intensity) to 193 (highest), represented by a gradient of colors. Areas with higher hillshade values, which appear lighter (blue and yellow), receive more simulated sunlight, indicating slopes that face the sun. In contrast, darker areas (shown in red) represent shadowed slopes or terrain facing away from the sun. (Figure 5).

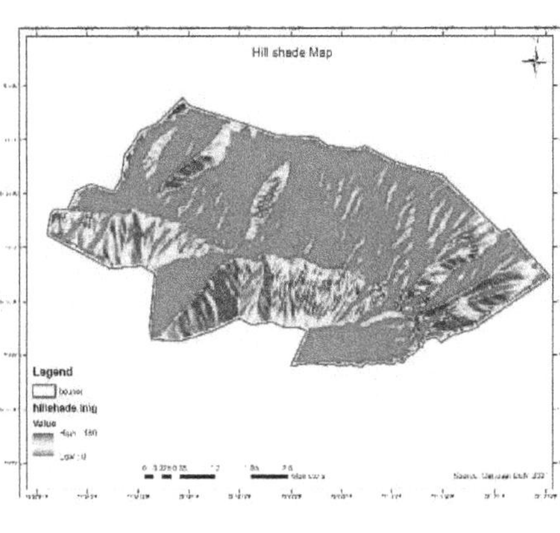

Figure 5. Hill shade

According to the legend, the map uses the layer "hillshade. img" to encode these values. The dominant red in the image suggests that much of the terrain faces away from the light source or lies in shadowed areas, while the multicolored zones highlight sunlit features like ridges and valley walls. The map includes a scale bar in kilometers and a north arrow for orientation. Sourced from Cartosat DEM (30m resolution), this hillshade map is vital for interpreting terrain morphology, enhancing elevation maps, and supporting landscape analysis, visibility modeling, and geomorphological studies.

3.1.5 *Aspect Map of Study Area*

The Aspect Map illustrates the directional orientation of slopes across the landscape, showing which direction each part of the terrain faces. This map is generated from Cartosat DEM data with a resolution of 30 meters and is useful for environmental modeling, vegetation studies, and solar exposure analysis. The map categorizes terrain orientation into eight cardinal and intercardinal directions North, Northeast, East, Southeast, South, Southwest, West, and Northwest along with flat areas that have no aspect.

Each direction is represented by a unique color: red for flat areas, green for north-facing slopes, (Figure 6) cyan for northeast, blue for east, purple for southeast, pink for south, orange for southwest, yellow for west, and light green for northwest. The legend details the azimuth angle ranges corresponding to each aspect category. This color-coded scheme allows easy identification of slope directions. The map also includes a scale bar for distance measurement and a north arrow for orientation. By showing how terrain orientation varies, this aspect map plays a vital role in planning agricultural practices, determining slope stability, and analyzing microclimates and biodiversity patterns.

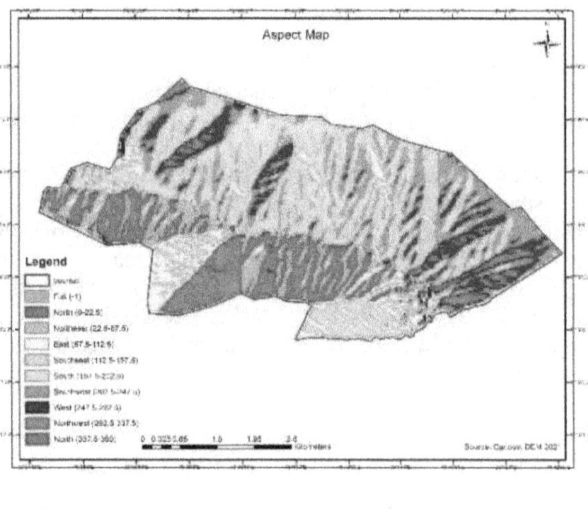

Figure 6. Aspect map.

3 DISCUSSION

This study investigates landslide susceptibility in Jor village, Taluka Wai, Satara district, within the Western Ghats of Maharashtra an ecologically fragile region. The area features steep slopes, intense monsoon rains, and weak soil structures, making it naturally prone to landslides.

A major factor influencing the region is the Balkawdi Dam, which affects local hydrology and slope stability. The dam's reservoir increases groundwater levels and soil saturation during monsoons, reducing soil cohesion and increasing landslide risk. Advanced GIS and remote sensing techniques using Landsat 8 imagery, Google Earth, and Survey of India maps were used to analyze critical parameters such as slope gradient, elevation, drainage density, geology, and vegetation cover. Overlay analysis showed that the area around Balkawdi Dam is highly vulnerable, especially during heavy rainfall. These findings align with previous studies in the Western Ghats that link high drainage density and steep slopes with landslide events. Land-use changes further exacerbate slope instability. Deforestation, road construction, and settlement expansion have reduced vegetation cover and disturbed natural drainage, increasing erosion. Encroachments on riverbanks and steep slopes add to the pressure on unstable land. Additionally, possible water-induced seismicity from the Balkawdi reservoir, though less frequent, may contribute to slope movement. The prevalent weathered basalt and lateritic soils, common in the Deccan plateau, become unstable when saturated. Effective mitigation requires both engineering and ecological solutions. Slope stabilization methods like retaining walls, soil nailing, and geogrid use are vital. Bioengineering solutions such as planting vetiver grass and bamboo crib walls offer eco-friendly alternatives. Hydrological control through contour drains, check dams, and vegetated swales can manage runoff and reduce infiltration. Reforestation using deep-rooted native species will help improve slope integrity. Real-time monitoring with rainfall data, satellite input, and landslide sensors should form the basis of an early warning system. Community involvement through local hazard mapping, monitoring, and preparedness training is essential. Disaster risk management must blend modern science with local knowledge to ensure sustainable, people-centered solutions. Overall, this research underscores the complex interaction between natural terrain features and human impact in shaping the landslide risks of Jor village.

A coordinated response combining technology, land-use planning, and community participation is key to effective risk reduction.

4 CONCLUSION

This research concludes that Jor village, particularly the area surrounding the Balkawdi Dam, is extremely susceptible to landslides due to the interplay of natural and human-induced factors. The region's steep slopes, heavy rainfall, fragile soil composition, and anthropogenic activities such as deforestation and changes in land use contribute significantly to the instability of the terrain. The location of the Balkawdi Dam in a sensitive catchment area further complicates the hydrological balance, thereby increasing the chances of slope failure during periods of intense rainfall. GIS and remote sensing technologies proved to be effective tools in mapping hazard-prone areas and providing a scientific basis for risk assessment and mitigation planning. The study emphasizes the need for comprehensive landslide management strategies, including slope stabilization, drainage control, afforestation, and geotechnical monitoring. Moreover, incorporating community participation through awareness programs and disaster preparedness training can enhance the resilience of the local population. The integration of modern technological tools with indigenous knowledge systems presents a sustainable approach to disaster risk reduction. In conclusion, regular monitoring, preventive engineering measures, eco- restoration efforts, and proactive community engagement are vital in minimizing the landslide hazard and protecting both life and infrastructure in and around Jor village.

ACKNOWLEDGEMENT

The authors gratefully acknowledge the students, staff, and authority of Civil Engineering department for their cooperation in the research.

REFERENCES

Chen T, R. Niu, B. Du, and Y. Wang (2015) – Landslide spatial susceptibility mapping by using GIS and remote sensing techniques: a case study in Zigui County, the Three Gorges Reservoir, China, Environmental Earth Sciences, Volume 73, Issue 9, pp. 5571–5583

Das I., S. Sahoo, C. vehicle Western, A. Stein, and R. Hack, (2010)."Landslide susceptibleness evaluation utilizing logistic reversion and allure corresponding accompanying a rock bulk categorization scheme, ahead a parking lot division in the northerly Himalayas (India)," *Geomorphology*, vol. 114, no. 4, pp. 627–637

Gawali P.B., S.P. Aher, B. Lakshmi, R.D. Gaikwad, K. Deendayal an, P.T. Hanamgond, J.M. Babu, Arote S.A., and Barrage S.I. (2017) "Identification of landslide susceptible villages around kalsubai region, western ghats of Maharashtra using geospatial techniques," *Journal of the Geological Society of India,* vol. 90, no. 3, pp. 301–311

Ghosh J.K. and D. Bhattacharya (2010) – Knowledge- based landslide susceptibility zonation system, Journal of Computing in Civil Engineering, Volume 24, Issue 4, pp. 325–334

Kamp U. , B.J. Growley, G.A. Khattak, and L.A. Owen (2008) – GIS-based landslide susceptibility mapping for the 2005 Kashmir earthquake region, Geomorphology, Volume 101, Issue 4, pp. 631–642

Olivares L., E. Damiano, R. Greco, L. Zeni, L. Picarelli, A. Minardo, Guida, and R. Bernini, (2009)."An instrumented flume to investigate the mechanics of rainfall-induced landslides in unsaturated granular soils," *Geotechnical Testing Journal*, vol. 32, no. 2, pp. 108–118,

Olivares L., E. Damiano, R. Greco, L. Zeni, L. Picarelli, A. Minardo, A. Guida, and R. Bernini (2009) – An instrumented flume to investigate the mechanics of rainfall induced landslides in unsaturated granular soils, *Geotechnical Testing Journal*, Volume 32, Issue 2, pp. 108–118

Pandey, P. Dabral, V. Chowdary, and N. Yadav, (2008) "Landslide hazard zonation utilizing detached appreciating and GIS: a record of what happened of Dikrong waterway tub, Arunachal Pradesh, India," *Environmental Geology*, vol. 54, no. 7, pp. 1517–1529.

Pradhan B., S. Lee, and M.F. Buchroithner – Remote sensing and GIS based landslide susceptibility analysis and its cross validation in three test areas using a frequency ratio model, PFG Photogrammetry, *Fernerkundung, Geoinformation*, volume 2 pp. 17–32.

Vaibhav Bhagwan Kashyap (2022) – Analysis of Landslide Hazard Zones Using GIS and Remote Sensing in Western Ghat Maharashtra (Chandoli Region), International Journal for Research Trends and Innovation Volume 7, Issue 6 .pp. 203-207

Yorozu Y., M. Hirano, and Y. Tagawa (1987) – Electron spectroscopy studies on magneto-optical media and plastic substrate interface, IEEE Transactions on Magnetics (Japan), Volume 2, pp. 740–741 (from Digests 9th Annual Conf. Magnetics Japan, p. 31982).

Zuoan W, L. Shihai, J.-G. Wang, and W. Ling, (2006) "A dynamic, comprehensive method for landslide control," Engineering geology, vol. 84, no. 1-2, pp. 1–11

Advancement in Engineering and Science – Goyal et al. (Eds)
© 2026 The Author(s), ISBN: 978-1-041-31101-0

Geomorphometric Analysis for Sustainable Water Resources Planning and Management Using Remote Sensing and GIS

Abhijit M. Zende, Prashant G. Borate, Ashwini V. Salve, Alfaj N. Shaikh, and Ajinkya S. Shah
Associate Professor in Civil Engineering, Yashoda Technical Campus, Satara, Maharashtra, India

ABSTRACT: The topography and geomorphologic features of the area have a serious impact on sustainable development and watershed management. Geomorphometry provides the hydrology and geomorphology with quantitative values. The study area's geomorphometric analysis has been conducted using Remote Sensing & GIS. The data has analyzed, interpreted, and presented using the software ILWIS. The geoinfromatics that are produced are easily usable for making decisions. The Morna River is tributary river of Koyana in the Patan tahsil in western Maharashtra, and some of its geomorphometric features are studied. Geomorphic parameter estimation by hand is a laborious and difficult procedure. Through this difficult, it was discovered that the integration of RS and GIS provides a dependable, accurate, and up-to-date database tool for managing spatial data. This software is helpful in determination of geomorphometric parameters, which are crucial for the study area's future infrastructure and sustainable water resource planning.

Keywords: Morna River, Western Maharashtra, Geomorphometric Analysis, Sustainable development, RS and GIS, ILWIS

1 INTRODUCTION

Within a 4000 – 40,000-hectare area, a watershed is a smaller unit of the river basin that delivers runoff to a single point. It is a naturally occurring geographic building block for planning and development. In terms of the input of solar radiation and precipitation and the output of discharge and evapotranspiration, it is a physical system. Planning, monitoring, and evaluating water resources for sustainable usage becomes crucial to human existence, particularly in areas with water scarcity. An area's topography, lithology, and geological formations all have a significant impact on the development of watersheds. Therefore, geomorphometry refers to the measuring of the earth's surface form. The quantitative values of hydrology and geomorphology are provided by geomorphometry. (Zende *et al.*, 2012).

The study area's geomorphometric analysis has been conducted using the Geographic Information System (GIS). According to Borrough (1998), GIS is a tool for analysing data which is based on sets of data that are spatially dispersed in two dimensions. Geographic position is one of the three main components of geographic data. Time and properties (attributes). Geographic data can be entered, managed, analysed, and presented using the GIS program (ILWIS), which enables the creation of information. Due to their relative relation to any point on the earth's surface, attribute data and spatial map data (Vector/raster) are combined. Geomorphometric parameter computation is made simpler, faster, and more accurate by the use of GIS. Remote Sensing Integration is an integrated strategy for determining runoff potential zones and appropriate locations for water harvesting structures requires the use of GIS software, which offer dependable, accurate databases on land, weather and water resources. (Meijerink *et al.* 1994).

1.1 *Study area*

The Patan Tahsil in western Maharashtra state's Satara District is traversed by the Morna River. The research region is located between latitudes 17°15'N and 17°21'N and longitudes 73°45' E and 73°57'E. One topo sheet No. 47G/15, which covers 104.458 sq. km., contains the entire area and was received from the Survey of India. The road link and Sangwad Bridge make it accessible to the location, which is 25 kilometers from Karad. The Morna watershed encircled with different village like Gureghar, Ambrag, Nayakwadi, Chougulewadi, Dhangarwadi, Kokisre, Natoshi. Other villages within the watershed are Kordewadi, Kotawade, Kusrud, Kadamwadi, Kalkewadi.

The villages inside the agricultural fields dominate the basin's mouthward side. This basin is covered by dense mixed protected forest at an elevation of 760 meters. The upper area of the basin, which are between 680 and 720 meters above sea level, are covered by different villages, agricultural areas, and forests. The Koyna watershed in the north and the Warna water.

1.2 *General geology of the area*

In terms of geology, the Morna basin is a region of the Deccan Volcanic Province that is formation of late Cretaceous to Eocene basaltic lava flows. The topography is characterized by step-like terraces and hills with flat summits. They consist of different types of basalts that alternate with one another. Common types of basalts include vesicular, amygdaloidal, and compact. The rock is volcanic, basic, fine grained, aphanitic, melanocratic including the mafic minerals as pyroxenes, olivine, ilmanite etc. There are also tachylite beds, volcanic ash, and volcanic breccias (Krishnan,1982). Alluvium deposits, which are characterized by alternating crisscross concave-convex slopes and were developed during the Pleistocene to recent times, and it offer suitable agricultural land alongside Morna River.

They create excellent, gently sloping soil cover known as "Lavans" along the tributaries. These lands are surrounded by heavily worn basalts that are close to the surface. The region frequently experiences spheroidal weathering. The Morna River is quite young, and its bed rock is exposed basalts. Potholes and waterfalls are in frequent numbers in the upper regions. The rock offers favorable foundational conditions for any civil engineering structure.

1.3 *Geomorphometry*

As the use of numerical variables whose values may be retrieved from topographic maps, geomorphometry is fundamentally quantitative. Any natural form's shape or geometry can be precisely measured using morphometry. To put it another way, morphometry is the measuring and mathematical study of the earth's surface arrangement, as well as the size and shape of its landforms. (Dury, 1970).

DOI: 10.1201/9781003798514-58

A basin's hydrological response is determined by its geomorphological and climatic features. These geomorphological features are its attribute that is used to synthesize its hydrological response. In order to accurately anticipate runoff, geomorphic parameters such as basin shape, relief, etc., are crucial. When basin characteristics are quantified and expressed as geomorphic parameters, their impact on runoff can be examined. Therefore, a straightforward and practical method to model the hydrologic behaviour of these different basins, especially the involved ones, can be developed by connecting the geomorphologic factors with the hydrologic features of the basin. Surface runoff, infiltration, and erosion susceptibility within the basin can all be qualitatively assessed through the interpretation and quantitative analysis of different drainage parameters. The geomorphometric analysis of dendritic drainage of Morna river basin deals with the computation of stream order, length ration, relief aspects, drainage density, slope and form factor etc. shed in the south are separated by the Morna watershed.

2 COMPUTATION OF MORPHOMETRIC PARAMETERS

Various important morphometric parameters of the watershed (as in the table) are analyzed as follows:

2.1 *Stream Order (u)*

Five orders of steams are identified using Strahler's method of steam ordering, with the fifth order stream forming the primary stream.

2.2 *Stream Number (Nu)*

It is the quantity of different-order stream segments. The number of stream segments of each order is in inverse geometric sequence with the order number, according to Horton's law of stream numbers. The basin is home to 423 streams.

2.3 *Stream Length (Lu)*

It is the duration of every segment of the stream. The total stream length of each order (L) is calculated by adding the length of each stream for a particular order. The mean stream length for that order is calculated by dividing the total stream length by the number of stream segments (N) of that order.

2.4 *Length Ratio (R)*

It is the radio of next lower order and mean stream lengths of any order.

2.5 *Relief Ratio (Rh)*

This measure, which is calculated by dividing the total watershed relief by the maximum length of the watershed, indicates the overall steepness of the drainage basin and the system's potential energy to drain off. High Rh values cause the water in the basin to quickly deplete, which leads to large peaks and steep limbs on hydrographs.

2.6 *Relative Relief (Rr)*

Relative Relief is ratio of the maximum watershed relief to the perimeter of the watershed.

2.7 *Ruggedness Number (Rn)*

The drainage density determines the maximum basin and watershed relief. The value of 4.84 marks the high ruggedness of the basin.

2.8 *Elongation Ratio (Re)*

It is the ratio of the watershed's maximum length to the diameter of a circle with the same area. The time it takes for water from the farthest reaches of the catchment to reach the outlet is represented by R and Re which are measured to show the impact of basin form. This ratio may be between

0.6 and 1.0. As the basin's shape becomes closer to a circle, the elongation value hits one. Broad and low hydrographs are produced by elongated fern-shaped catchments, whereas high peak and narrow hydrographs are produced by fan- shaped or roughly semi-circular catchments.

2.9 *Circularity Ratio (Ro)*

It is the ratio of circumference of a circle of same area as the watershed to the perimeter of the watershed Ro usually range between 0.6 and 0.7. It decreases for higher order basins because of large crenellations in their perimeter, which affect the denominator.

2.10 *Basin Shape Factor*

It is the ratio of squares of the maximum length of the watershed to the area of the watershed.

2.11 *Confluence (Bifurcation) Ratio (Rb)*

It can be defined as the ratio of streams of one order to streams of the next higher level. One of the significant geomorphologic features is the bifurcation ratio. The generation of geomorphologic instantaneous unit hydrographs for different basins has made extensive use.

2.12 *Stream Frequency (Sf)*

It is the number of streams per unit area within the basin. It mainly depends on the lithology of the basin and reflects the texture of the drainage network. There are six streams an average per square kilometer of the watershed.

2.13 *Drainage Density (D)*

It is the average stream length in the basin per unit area. The physical characteristics of the underlying rocks can be inferred from drainage. Low drainage density is seen in areas with low relief, dense vegetation cover, and extremely permeable and resistant subsurface materials. The areas with weak, impermeable subsurface materials, which are highly relief and sparsely vegetated, are identified by the high drainage density.

2.14 *Role of Remote Sensing*

IRS 1D LISS III Data with spatial resolution of 23.5 mts, is processed and used to correlate the geomorphometric studies. The cloud free data of 24th January 2002 have been selected and procured for study. The standard FCC (Figures 9, 10 and 11) has been prepared from band 4, band 3 and band 2,out of four bands of LISS III data. The image area has been georeferenced as per the earlier GIS layers and assigned with coordinate system.

The three-dimensional terrain models have been prepared for the imageries (Figure 12 & 13) and also for the aspect and slope maps (Figure 14). The watershed is studied further by adding the digitized segment layers of contour and drainage, on the generated stereo data which may be represented in the form of stereo pairs or anaglyphs as shown in Figures 12,13 & 14.

3 RESULT AND DISCUSSIONS

The region features moderately sloping terrain and considerable topography in the upper portion, according to the contour map and images (Figures 1–14). The major Morna river, which has deep gorges and cascades, is discovered to be in the early stages of erosion. The contours span between 580 and 1080 meters. Pleistocene sediments cover some regions. According to satellite data, in the most southwest portion of the watershed area, between the D/S of Koyna reservoir and the north U/S of Chandoli reservoir, the major Morna river rises from the Sahyadri mountain ranges (Figure 10). The river merges with the Koyna river as it runs northeast.

With the help of stretched FCC (Figure 10) of the present LISS-III data the watershed can be classified and the vegetation land use classification map can be produced for the reference.

3.1 *Agriculture & forests*

It has been noted that cane crops make up the majority of the agriculture in the D/S from Gureghar, along both sides of the Morna, and in the flat, gently sloping plains. Thick forest covers the top portion of the basin, particularly the U/S of Gureghar reservoir. Scrubs and thickets are found on a moderate slope. On sloping hilltop areas, one can see open woodlands and rock outcrops.

3.2 *Settlement*

There are numerous little, dispersed communities in the region. There have been very tiny hamlets found in the agricultural area. 52 settlements make to the watershed's extensive settlement. The largest is Morgiri, which is located on the left bank of the Morna River and close to the Gunawantgad fort in the central north.

3.3 *Drainage*

The dendritic drainage occurs inside the watershed. From SW to NE and opening its month towards the north, the basin is seen to be fairly elongated, as indicated by the elongation ratio of 0.408. A stream of the first order is 66.6 km long, a stream of the second order is 16.1 km long, and a stream of the third order is 5.514 km long. The IVth order stream's maximum length is 1.69 km, and its Vth is 5.966 km. The region is highly fragmented, as indicated by the relatively high bifurcation ratio. The consequences of tectonic movements, stratigraphic circumstances, erosion, and climate change during a period ranging from the geo- chronological part are reflected in the current configuration and geomorphometric aspects of the river network.

Very elongated basins are typically indicated by form factors smaller than 0.45, which are also indicated by Vth order river length (5.5966 km). The main stream's length and the total length of streams of lower orders are significantly out of proportion, as indicated by the Morna river basin's form factor of 0.2. The river channel flow length is about equivalent to the maximum length of a stream of each order in total (28.22 km).

Drainage density, a crucial characteristic of river systems, has been the focus of numerous regional studies aimed at streamlining computation techniques and establishing its correlation with environmental factors and other geomorphometrical components to ascertain its impact on alterations. Nevertheless, no study has quantitatively stated every variable that affects drainage density. Densities in mountain drainage basins have been found to range between 2 and 4 km/km2. The current watershed has a drainage density of 0.9 km/km2. Since the lithology is composed of compact massive and hard igneous basaltic rocks, it shows that the physio-mechanical characteristics of the rock in this area, along with less relief fragmentation and even increased surface runoff, are unable to increase much of the sedimentary load.

The mechanism of accelerated erosion that modifies the surrounding conditions is explained by the relief of the first order basin, which is inversely proportional to drainage density. This shows that the drainage system's geometry tends to continuously adjust in order to achieve a study equilibrium state (graded profile) between the process resulting from erosive energy and the forms thus created. The current area's low drainage density suggests that the substratum is less permeable and resistant to erosion, creating a relief with steep slopes. The aforementioned mild erosional and structural arrangement of the basin is further supported by the drainage frequency (4.049).

The basin's ruggedness number was determined to be 0.98, indicating that it is moderately to lightly rough. This is also supported by the contour map and the imagery. Future engineering studies of this hydrological unit will therefore benefit from the numerous geomorphometrical elements, such as stream order, stream numbers, stream length, length ratio bifurcation ratio, drainage density, elongation ratio, from factor, roughness number, etc.

3.4 *Slope*

The contour data that the digital elevation model (DEM) provides for height information at any given location was interpolated to create the digital elevation model (Figure 4). For use in other programs, the generated DEM has been saved in ILWIS as a raster map. Slope steepness (slope map, degree), slope direction (slope aspect), slop convexity (slope shape), and hill shading maps have all been created from the DEM.

The tangent of the angle of inclination of a line or plane that is defined by a land surface is known as the slope. It results from the intricate and ongoing interaction of external and internal forces operating on the earth's surface. In terms of lithology, the climate affected the texture, thickness, and mobility of the soil. The potential and kinetic energy of water flows, and consequently the intensity of runoff, erosion, and transport processes, are directly controlled by the valley side and channel slope in a drainage system.

The main stream flows between 0 and 1°, as seen on the slope degree map. However, the head of the stream has very high topography, and the second and third order tributaries have numerous waterfalls and cascades, which reflect the erosion's youth stage. Only in the D/S north sections, where the Morna River meets the Koyna River close to the Sangwad bridge, are there gently sloping slopes. There are seven classifications in the entire slop of the area. The highest slopes are found in the basin's steep southwest region. The basin's central hilly region exhibits maximum slop of 20 to 45 degrees and more. With the exception of minor hilltops and gorges, the watershed's overall slope can reach 400%, but the stream flows in an area with a slope of less than 20%.

The general slope of the assessed surfaces is either toward the northwest or toward the southeast, according to the slope aspect map (Figure 7). With the exception of a few, extremely steep concavo-convex slopes along the harder, steeper middle lava flows and, in some areas, occupying unsorted Pleistocene colluvial deposits, the basin has straight slopes, according to the slope form map.

4 CONCLUSION

The most precise, up-to-date, and dependable database on land and water resources is made possible by the integration of remote sensing and GIS. It has shown to be an extremely helpful tool for combining spatial data and for determining geomorphometric characteristics. According to some geomorphometric criteria, the Morna watershed is elongated, has a low roughness number, low drainage density, high relief, and nearly straight slopes that allow water to be disposed easily. These characteristics indicate a rapid rate of erosion, which is slowed down by hard rocks. It has been observed that estimating geomorphometric parameters by hand is a laborious and time-consuming procedure that frequently deters field engineers from creating regional approaches to address different hydrological issues in the basins.

In order to irrigate the gently sloping agricultural land in the lower portions of the basin, it is recommended that water collecting structures such as earthen dams be developed, particularly in the center portion of the basin, as the river is not perennial. In order for runoff water to percolate via the columner and mural joints as well as spheroidal weathering zones and raise the ground water potentials in the low-lying areas surrounding the main stream, trenching and furrowing are advised in the vicinity of second and third ordered streams.

The area under irrigation for cane crops has grown recently, the ongoing Morna Gureghar small irrigation project has shown to be successful. To preserve the region's soils and wildlife, the dense forest in the southwest U/S zones must be preserved. Building a road network is necessary to link the villages and hamlets north of the Koyna River with Guhagar Vijapur's major road. It is advised that the 1:25000 contoured top sheet and additional high resolution PAN imagery be used in a contemporary RS & GIS environment to plan the Morna Watershed's future infrastructure developments.

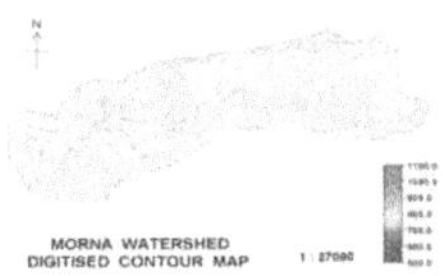

Figure 1. Digitized Contour Map

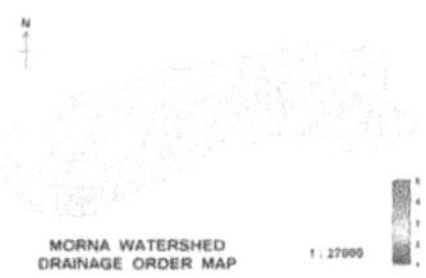

Figure 2. Drainage Order Map

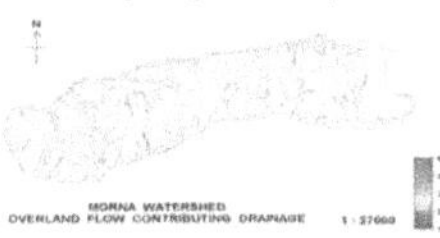

Figure 3. Overland Flow Contributing Drainage

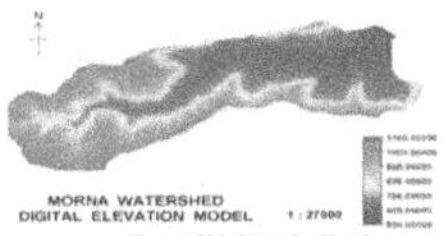

Figure 4. Digital Elevation Model

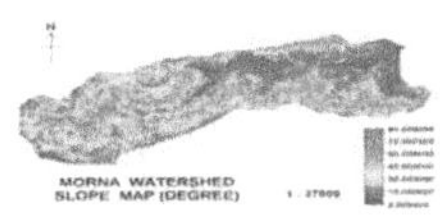

Figure 5. Slope Map

Figure 6. Slope Sliced Map

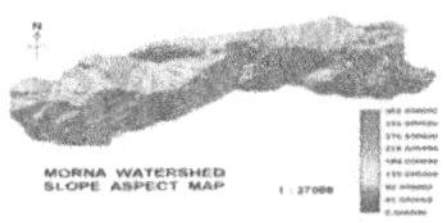

Figure 7. Slope Aspect Map

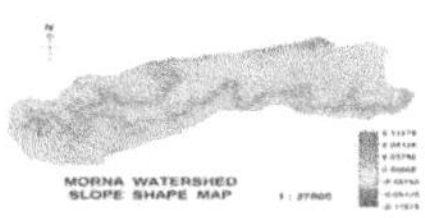

Figure 8. Slope Shape Map

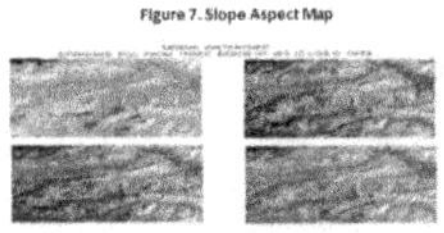
Figure 9. Generation of FCC

Figure 10. Watershed boundary

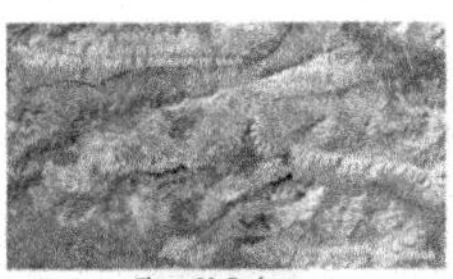
Figure 11. Drainage

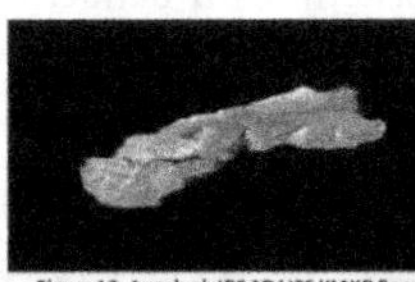
Figure 12. Anaglyph IRS 1D LISS III NIR Band

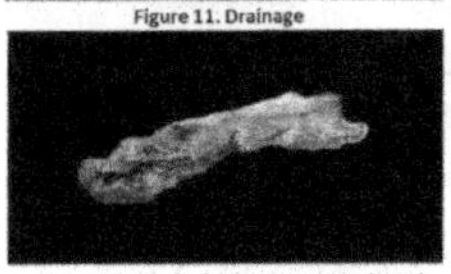
Figure 13. Anaglyph IRS 1D LISS III Red Band

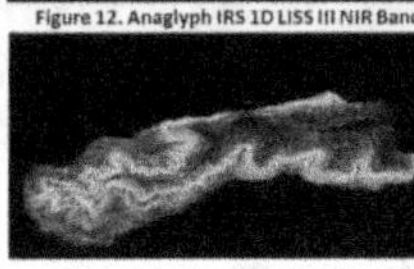
Figure 14 Anaglyph Slope Map (Degree)

Table 1. Geomorphometric parameters.

STRM ORDER	STRM NUMBER	STRM LENGTH MTS.	BIFUR CATION RATIO	STREAM LENGTH CUM MTS	MEAN STREAM LENGTH MTS.	LENGTH RATIO
1	320	66001.89	4	66001.89	206.256	-
2	80	16118.06	5	82119.95	201.47	1.24
3	16	5514.41	4	87634.37	344.65	1.07
4	4	1692.76	4	89327.13	423.2	1.02
5	1	5966.93	-	95294.06	5966.93	1.07
TOTAL NO. OF STREAMS:					423	
DRAINAGE AREA:					104.458 Sq. Km.	
DRAINAGE DENSITY:					0.90 Km/Sq. Km.	
ELONGATION RATIO:					0.408	
DRAINAGE FREQUENCY:					4.049	
FORM FACTOR:					0.2	
BASIN LENGTH:					28.22 Km.	
TOTAL RELIEF:					500 Mts.	
RUGGEDNESS NO.:					0.98	
CIRCULATORY RATIO:					0.59	
RELATIVE RELIEF:					0.0177	

ACKNOWLEDGMENT

The authors express their gratitude towards Mr. P. K. Deshpande from Walchand College of Engineering Sangli, Maharashtra for his constant encouragement. Also extent my gratitude to all government offices those provide essential data for the detail analysis.

REFERENCES

Burrogh A P and McDonell, RA (1998) *Principles of geographical Information System.* Oxford University Press.

Floyd, F.S. *Remote Sensing – Principle and interpretation.* Second edition, University of California, Los Angeles.

Lillisand and Kiefer (2000). *Remote Sensing and Image Interpretation.* John Wiley and sons Inc.New York

Krishnan, M.S. Geology of India and Burma 6th edition (1982)

Meijerink, Allard M.J. De Brouwer. Mannaerts C.M, Valenzuela C. (1994) Introduction to use of Geographic Information System for practical hydrology pp.1–243.

Mondal, T. and Gupta, S., (2015), "Evaluation of Morphometric Parameters of Drainage Networks Derived from Topographic Map and Digital Elevation Model Using Remote Sensing and GIS", International Journal of Geomatics and Geosciences, Volume 5, No 4, 2015, pp 655-664.

Rakesh Kumar, Lohani A.K., Sanjay Kumar, Chatterjee, C and Nema R.K. (2012) GIS based Morphometric Analysis of Ajay River basin upto Sarathh gauging site of South Bihar, Journ Appl.Hydrology Vol.XIV(4) pp.45- 54.

Strahler A.N. (1964) Quantitative geomorphology of drainage basin and channel networks-Section 4 to 11 in Hanbook of Applied Hydrology Ed. By V.T.Chaw McGraw Hill New York.

Zende A.M., Nagarajan, R., Atal, K.R. and Deshpande P.K., (2012), "GIS based Morphometric Analysis of Nine Major Sub-watersheds of Yerala River, Western Maharashtra, India", International Conference on Engineering Technology and Management, pp. 17-23.

Advancement in Engineering and Science – Goyal et al. (Eds)
© 2026 The Author(s), ISBN: 978-1-041-31101-0

SmartEdu_Companion: Automating Educational Content Generation through GPT and SaaS Integration

Shabina Modi, Muhammad Sami Javed Shaikh, and Manasi Vinod Motling
Computer Science and Engineering Karmaveer Bhaurao Patil College of Engineering, Satara Maharashtra, India

ABSTRACT: The complexity of curriculum development and increasing demand for personalized education require intelligent learning platforms that can dynamically adapt and deliver customized content. This paper presents an AI-powered Learning Management System (AI-LMS) that adapts to learners and automatically generates chapter notes, flashcards, quizzes, and Q&A sets. Using GPT-based AI, the system produces context-aware content, supported by a secure cloud backend. Built with Next.js, Drizzle ORM, Clerk, and Stripe, it's designed to scale, stay modular, and support subscriptions. Real-world testing shows it reduces teacher workload, keeps students more engaged, and scales affordably. This work offers a new approach to educational technology by combining AI, automation, and subscription-based access in a single LMS platform.

Keywords: Learning Management System, Generative AI, SaaS, GPT, Automated Notes, Educational Technology, Personalized Learning, Stripe Integration

1 INTRODUCTION

Over the past few years, EdTech has developed at a lightning pace with the help of AI, cloud computing, and full stack web development. Increased internet penetration, mobile usage, and post-pandemic remote learning have created demand for scalable, intelligent, and user-centric Learning Management Systems (LMS). AI-powered LMS platforms today have adaptive, personalized learning to suit an individual's needs. Traditional LMS systems, which primarily serve as static content silos, are not agile and automated, where teachers have to create and maintain content manually, and students encounter vast amounts of unorganized content.

This paper presents a Full Stack AI-powered LMS delivered as a SaaS product, automating creation of flashcards, quizzes, notes, and Q&A modules using OpenAI's language models. Users select learning types, topics, and difficulty, and the system generates structured resources instantly, enabling educators and learners to focus on engagement rather than manual content creation. The AI-first, modular, and real-time architecture of the platform combines AI prompts, generation pipelines, token-based usage tracking, and progress monitoring, which is appropriate for individuals, institutions, and organizations that require customizable digital learning solutions.

2 LITERATURE REVIEW

2.1 *Artificial intelligence in learning management systems*

The integration of artificial intelligence into learning management systems (LMS) has become a major development across both the education and software industries. This article delves into the history of LMS software, the widening scope of AI in instructional delivery and content development, web technology's impact on learning tools, and the frameworks governing contemporary cloud-based learning services

2.2 *Evolution of Learning Management Systems (LMS)*

Early LMS systems like Moodle, Blackboard, and Canvas existed primarily as virtual repositories for coursework and exams. They allowed teachers to conduct classes online but were not very flexible. The systems involved a lot of manual configuration and did not customize learning or react accordingly to student performance.

2.3 *Emergence of AI in education*

Schools are increasingly using AI to provide personalized education, instant feedback, and backing for intelligent tutoring systems.

Large language models, especially those released by OpenAI, can create high-quality instructional material and answer questions from students in real-time—a welcome resource in situations with few teachers.

But most advanced AI-based learning tools are proprietary, limiting compatibility with varied curricula and inhibiting scale across institutions.

2.4 *AI content generation with LLMs*

Sophisticated models like the GPT range allow automatic generation of quizzes, study guides, flashcards, and explanation of concepts to suit learner goals.

Evidence suggests that the systems can generate question pools consistent with academic standards but there are challenges–like factual errors, no transparency in reasoning, and excessive computational expenditure for continuous use.

2.5 *SaaS and Full Stack Web Technologies in EdTech*

Cloud-hosted Learning Management Systems developed using current frameworks such as Next.js, React, Tailwind CSS, and Node.js offer scalability, responsiveness, and payment gateway integrations such as Stripe for monetization.

Backend systems with databases such as Neon PostgreSQL and ORMs such as Drizzle offer secure data handling, seamless scalability, and efficient system development.

2.6 *Existing AI-LMS platforms and gaps*

Tools like Quizlet, Khan Academy, and CourseHero use AI-based personalization but are closed systems with low extensibility and automation strength.

DOI: 10.1201/9781003798514-59

There exists a strong need for an open, modular, and scalable LMS that has seamless integration of AI for content development, open data storage, adaptive dashboards, and usage-based charging in one unified architecture.

3 METHODOLOGY

The project integrates agile development, user-centered design, AI prompt engineering, and SaaS strategies to ensure technical feasibility, usability, and business sustainability. Each phase—from ideation to deployment—was aligned with the vision of an AI-first, scalable LMS.

3.1 *Problem identification*

The system addresses limitations of traditional LMS platforms which rely on manual educator input, lack adaptive personalization, offer minimal automation, and are cost-prohibitive for smaller institutions or self-learners. The solution introduces AI-generated personalized content, automated study tools, and subscription-based access to deliver scalable, learner-centric education.

3.2 *Design methodology*

- **Microservice Backend:** Modular, scalable infrastructure with clear responsibility separation.
- **Component-based UI:** Reusable, customizable frontend elements for efficient rendering.
- **Prompt-Driven AI Engine:** Template-based prompts for controlled, topic-specific content generation.
- **RESTful API Architecture:** Simplifies integration and maintenance.
- **Schema-first ORM:** Strong typing and maintainable database structure.
- **User-Centered Prototyping:** Figma-based wireframes and flows to design navigation, course creation, and dashboards.

3.3 *Agile development cycle*

An **Agile-based iterative development** cycle was followed:

Phase	Description
Planning	Defined MVP features, database schema, user stories, and OpenAI integration strategies.
Development	Weekly sprints focusing on specific modules (e.g., user auth, flashcard generator, quiz system).
Testing	Manual testing across flows, unit testing for critical logic (e.g., prompt processors, billing), and integration testing.
Deployment	Continuous deployment via Vercel with CI/CD for Git-based pushes.
Feedback	Collected via internal testers and early users to refine flows and fix edge cases.

3.4 *AI content generation workflow*

A five-step pipeline delivers personalized, repeatable content generation:

- **User Input Collection:** Users specify content type, topic, and difficulty, which are logged for traceability.
- **Prompt Construction:** Dynamic, contextual templates optimize GPT-4 prompts for consistency and relevance.
- **API Invocation:** Prompts are sent to the OpenAI ChatCompletion endpoint; responses are streamed and parsed into structured data formats.
- **Post-Processing:** The system cleans, validates, and stores content relationally for easy retrieval and display.
- **Feedback Loop:** Users can regenerate or manually edit content, and feedback is collected to continually improve prompt engineering and accuracy.

3.5 *Database modeling and orm integration*

Built using Drizzle ORM's schema-first approach, the database is:

- **Strongly Typed:** Schemas defined in TypeScript ensure code reliability.
- **Normalized:** Separate tables for content, users, sessions, and payments support flexibility.
- **Indexed:** Key fields are indexed for performance.
- **Soft Deletion:** Records can be flagged without permanent deletion, supporting drafts and moderation.
- **Atomic Transactions:** Operations are always type-safe and consistent.

3.6 *User authentication and access control*

Clerk provides secure, robust session management using JWTs, supporting:

- **Protected Routes:** Feature access is guarded by role-based middleware.
- **Subscription Status Linking:** User data is tied to Stripe customer IDs for subscription validation.
- **Future RBAC:** Roles for admin, student, and editor are supported for scalable permission management.

3.7 *SaaS subscription model design*

Stripe integration handles monetization via:

- **Product Setup:** Both one-time and recurring plans are defined for flexibility.
- **Secure Checkout:** Flows are linked to authenticated users.
- **Automated Billing Events:** Webhooks update accounts on subscription status changes.
- **Token Enforcement:** Non-subscribers have usage limits, while paid users enjoy expanded or unlimited access. Sensitive operations run server-side for security.

3.8 *Testing and validation*

Thorough multi-level testing was conducted:

- **Unit Testing:** For utility and prompt logic.
- **Integration Testing:** For the full OpenAI-backend-database workflow.
- **End-to-End Testing:** On critical flows like signup, course creation, and billing.
- **Performance Testing:** Ensured low latency and smooth scaling. User feedback validated usability and output relevance.

3.9 *Ethical and practical safeguards*

- **Content Accuracy:** Users are notified of potential AI errors and advised to review content.
- **Data Privacy:** Full compliance with security standards; no personal data stored without consent.
- **Token Limits:** Guardrails prevent excessive, uncritical AI usage, particularly in educational environments.

4 SYSTEM ARHCITECTURE

4.1 *Architecture of the Full Stack AI-Powered LMS and SaaS Platform*

The proposed architecture focuses on growth, flexibility, and smart automation. It combines modern frontend tools, cloud-based backend systems, AI services, and scalable databases to create a unified, adaptive learning platform. This section explains how the system is organized, how its main parts communicate, and how data moves within it.

4.2 *High-level architectural structure*

On a macro level, the platform has a multi-layered architecture for effective separation of concerns and maintenance. The top-level structural layers are as follows:

- **User Interface Layer (Frontend):** Built using React and Next.js, the layer provides client-side rendering, seamless navigation, and interactive visual effects.
- **Application & API Layer (Backend):** Built on Node.js, exposing RESTful APIs and dealing with business logic, communication, and orchestration using Drizzle ORM.
- **AI Integration Layer:** Integrates with OpenAI services for on-demand creation of tailored educational material like quizzes, explanations, and course materials.
- **Data Management Layer:** Leverages Neon PostgreSQL, a cloud-native database system providing secure, scalable, and consistent storage of user profiles, course assets, and metadata.
- **Authentication & Payment Layer:** Utilizes Clerk for identity management and Stripe for automated billing, subscription management, and transactional security

Key Features:

- **Dynamic Routing**: User-specific and type-specific course pages.
- **Form Handling**: Input forms for selecting course topic, difficulty, and content type.
- **Toast Notifications**: Real-time feedback on AI generation and payment status.
- **Dark/Light Theming**: Built-in support for accessibility and UX.
- **State Management**: Leveraged via React hooks and server-side rendering for efficiency.

4.3 *Backend architectur*

The backend, built on **Node.js**, handles:

- Content creation requests and routing.
- AI API communication and prompt handling.
- DB interactions through **Drizzle ORM**.
- Secure session and token validation through **Clerk**.
- Payment verification and plan enforcement via **Stripe**.

API Services:

1. /api/generate – Processes user input, calls OpenAI, and returns generated content.
2. /api/save – Saves content to relevant DB tables.
3. /api/stripe/session – Manages billing sessions and usage limits.

All APIs are **RESTful**, stateless, and structured for rapid deployment on platforms like Vercel.

4.4 *AI Integration (Generation Engine)*

The **AI Engine** is the system's most critical component, responsible for generating personalized content. It operates in the following flow:

1. **Input Collection**: From user (type, topic, difficulty).
2. **Prompt Construction**: Mapped via custom templates in the /input/ folder.
3. **API Call to OpenAI**: Using GPT-4 or GPT-3.5 depending on plan.
4. **Response Parsing**: JSON or Markdown format cleaned and structured.
5. **Persistence**: Stored in the appropriate database tables.

This pipeline supports generating:

- **Flashcards**
- **Chapter Notes**
- **Q&A Sets**
- **Quizzes/MCQs**

4.5 *Database Design (Neon PostgreSQL + Drizzle ORM)*

The system uses **Neon**, a cloud-native PostgreSQL service known for autoscaling and low-latency. With **Drizzle ORM**, it ensures:

- Type safety between TS and SQL.
- Automatic migrations and schema generation.
- Clean models for efficient querying.

Main Tables:

1. **StudyMaterial**:
   - id, type, topic, difficulty, content (JSON), user_email, status.
2. **ChapterNotes:**
   - id, content, chapter_id, topic, created_at.
3. **StudyTypeContent:**
   - id, content (JSON), type, status.
4. **PaymentRecord:**
   - id, stripe_customer_id, plan_type, created_at.

All tables are indexed on user_email and type to optimize content retrieval and dashboard rendering.

4.6 *Authentication and User Management (Clerk)*

Authentication and session tracking are managed via **Clerk**, offering:

- **Email/Password, OAuth, and Magic Link** logins.
- **Role-based Access** for future scalability (e.g., student, admin).
- **JWT token verification** for secure API access.
- **Session persistence** across devices.

User data is synchronized with content creation limits and subscription entitlements.

4.7 *Payment System and SaaS Billing (Stripe)*

The app supports a **pay-as-you-go** and **subscription model** using Stripe:

- **One-Time Purchases**: Token packs for limited AI usage.
- **Monthly Subscriptions**: Unlock unlimited or extended generation.
- **Billing Portal**: Managed through Stripe Customer Portal.
- **Webhook Handling**: Real-time sync of Stripe status with internal DB.

All payments are tied to user_email and tracked for enforcement of usage limits.

4.8 *Deployment and DevOps*

The system is hosted on **Vercel**, which enables:

- Seamless CI/CD for frontend and backend.
- Environment variable protection.
- Scalable edge deployments.

5 RESULT AND ANALYSIS

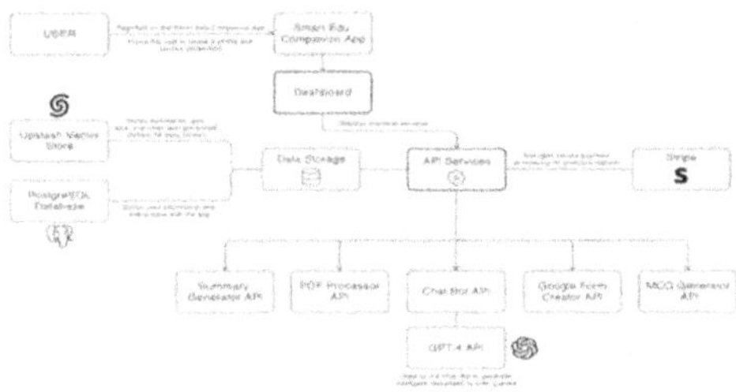

Figure 1. Architecture diagram.

This section shows the results from building and launching the Full Stack AI LMS + SaaS app. It covers both technical performance and user feedback, giving a full picture of how the app works in real-world use. The findings confirm that the system is strong, effective, and can scale well in educational settings

5.1 *Functionality verification*

The app was successfully deployed and tested for all core functionalities, including:

Feature	Notes
User Registration & Authentication	Handled securely via Clerk with JWT sessions.
AI Content Generation	GPT-4 powered content generation for all study types worked reliably.
Flashcards, Notes, Quiz, QA Flow	Each content type rendered properly with dynamic inputs.
Database Integration	Drizzle ORM correctly managed schema, queries, and relational joins.
Stripe Billing & Subscriptions	Webhooks, customer portal, and plan limitations implemented.
Dashboard Navigation	Dynamic routing, user feedback, and UI toasts confirmed.

All major modules were validated through hands-on testing and continuous integration pipelines.

5.2 *Performance metrics*

Performance was measured across multiple dimensions: response time, latency of AI generation, and database interaction speed.

Metric	Average Value	Notes
Time to generate flashcards (OpenAI call)	~4.2s	Varies by topic complexity and token size.
Database read/write latency	~85ms	Optimized via indexes and efficient queries.
Initial page load time	~1.1s	Thanks to Next.js SSR/ISR.
AI processing uptime	99.9%	Minimal downtime due to OpenAI API reliability.
Tokenized usage accuracy	100%	All AI calls properly reduced user tokens or verified subscription.

5.3 *User testing and feedback*

A closed group of early-access users (N = 30) participated in real-time testing of the platform. The group consisted of university students, educators, and independent learners. The survey and feedback indicated the following:

User Experience Area	Satisfaction Score (/10)
Ease of Use	9.2
Content Accuracy	8.4
Design and Navigation	9.0
Speed and Responsiveness	8.8
Subscription Onboarding	9.1

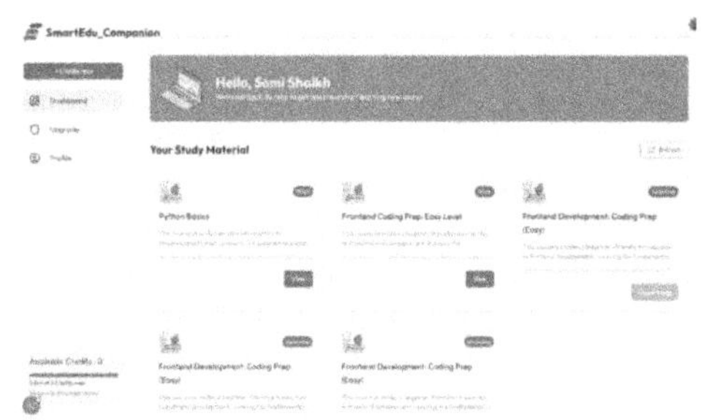

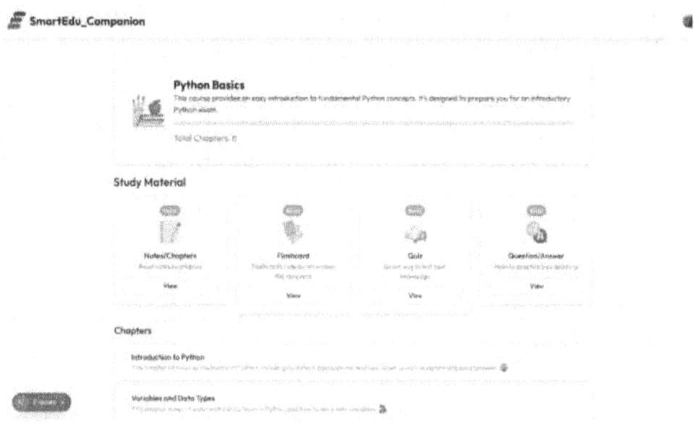

6 DISCUSSION

6.1 *Innovation and differentiation*

This platform changes the way Learning Management Systems work by building AI-powered content creation right into the core. Using GPT-based models, learners can quickly generate study materials like flashcards, notes, quizzes, and Q&A from just a few prompts.

It combines personalized learning with scalable business options, using token-based AI access and Stripe subscriptions, so it can grow and earn revenue even for smaller setups.

6.2 *Key Differentiators*

- Real-time generation of learning content
- Versatile study resources across multiple formats
- Adaptive and progress-sensitive recommendations
- Scalable monetization through modular subscription design

6.3 *Pedagogical Impact*

The platform makes learning more engaging by using AI to create exercises that help learners remember better through active recall and spaced repetition. Students can even help shape the materials to fit their understanding, turning AI into a helpful learning partner instead of just a tool.

However, there are still challenges. Lessons might not always align with the curriculum, too much reliance on AI could make learning easier than it should be, and cognitive challenge might drop. This means teachers still need to guide learning, set clear paths, and monitor content carefully.

6.4 *Technical Considerations*

The chosen technology stack—Next.js, React, Drizzle ORM, OpenAI API, and Clerk—provides a strong mix of speed, flexibility, and ease of maintenance.

However, there are some practical trade-offs to consider:

- Complexities in asynchronous data retrieval,
- Dependency on external API response limits, and
- Restricted flexibility within third-party authentication layers.

These factors demand continuous optimization and clear fallback mechanisms for sustained reliability.

6.5 *Ethics and Privacy*

The main worries are keeping data safe, avoiding AI bias, and respecting ownership of content. Solutions include clear disclaimers, stating who owns what, and letting users delete their data if they want.

6.6 *User insights*

Early tests show learners prefer flashcards, a clear interface, and the ability to customize their learning. Personalization, simplicity, and flexibility are key to keeping them engaged

6.7 *Scalability and monetization*

The platform is built on the cloud, so it can grow easily as more people use it. Money can come from free vs. paid tiers, school licenses, and team plans. Future tools will track how people engage with the content.

6.8 *Competitive edge*

Unlike old-school LMS platforms, this one is fast, flexible, AI-powered, and made for Gen-Z and mobile users. It blends AI content creation with traditional LMS features.

6.9 *Development roadmap*

Planned iterations include:

- Collaborative workspace integration
- Gamification mechanics for learner motivation
- Native mobile application support
- Retrieval-Augmented Generation (RAG) enhancements for factual accuracy
- AI behavior customization modules
- Analytics dashboards for educators and administrators

7 CONCLUSION

This AI-powered LMS + SaaS app changes digital learning by combining AI content creation with a flexible, personalized learning experience.

7.1 *Summary of Contributions*

The key contributions of the system include:

- **AI-Based Content Generation:** The platform uses AI to quickly create educational material tailored to each topic and learner.
- **Modern, Smooth Interface:** Built with Next.js, React, and Tailwind CSS, making it easy and pleasant to use.
- **Scalable and Secure Backend:** Uses Node.js, Drizzle ORM, and Neon PostgreSQL to handle lots of users reliably and keep data safe.
- **Monetization:** Supports subscriptions and flexible payment options via Stripe
- **Adaptive Learning:** Tracks each learner's progress and adjusts content difficulty to match their needs.
- **Personalized Learning Framework:** Combines user data with structured content to create a learning journey unique to each student.**B. Implications for the Future of Learning**

This system moves learning away from fixed, one-size-fits-all courses to a flexible, AI-powered approach. It makes education easier to access, speeds up content creation, and helps learners take control of their own study—perfect for remote learners or places with limited resources.

7.2 *Limitations*

- **AI Hallucination:** Occasional inaccuracies require moderation.
- **No Built-in Curriculum Matching:** Needs guided prompts for syllabus alignment.

- **API Dependence:** Reliance on external services increases cost and maintenance risk.

Future Directions

Planned enhancements include syllabus-based generation, peer collaboration, educator oversight tools, a content validation system using RAG, and a dedicated mobile app. These updates aim to create a comprehensive, reliable AI-driven learning ecosystem.

REFERENCES

Brown, T. *et al.* (2020). *Language Models are Few-Shot Learners. In Advances in Neural Information Processing Systems (NeurIPS).* https://arxiv.org/abs/2005.14165

Clerk. (2023). *Authentication for the Modern Web.* https://clerk.dev

Goodfellow, I., Bengio, Y., & Courville, A. (2016). *Deep Learning.* MIT Press.

IEEE Standard Association. (2020). Standard for Learning Technology – Learning Management System Functional Requirements (IEEE Std 2590-2020)

Neon. (2023). *Serverless Postgres for Developers.* https://neon.tech

Next.js Team. (2023). *Next.js Documentation.* Vercel. https://nextjs.org/docs

OpenAI. (2024). *GPT-4 Technical Report.* OpenAI. Retrieved from https://openai.com/research/gpt-4

Pasternack, J. (2021). *Building Scalable SaaS Applications: Architectural Patterns & Best Practices.* O'Reilly Media.

Stripe. (2023). *Stripe API Documentation.* https://stripe.com/docs

Tailwind Labs. (2023). *Tailwind CSS Documentation.* https://tailwindcss.com/docs

Advancement in Engineering and Science – Goyal et al. (Eds)
© 2026 The Author(s), ISBN: 978-1-041-31101-0

A Novel GAN-Based Multimodal Image Fusion Technique for High-Resolution and Spectral Fidelity Enhancement

Priyanka Bhatambarekar and Gayatri Phade
EXTC dept Sandip Institute of Technology and Research Centre, Nashik, Maharashtra, India

ABSTRACT: Land cover classification constitutes one of the factors for agricultural monitoring, precision farming, and environment evaluation. Due to the fact that conventional image fusion techniques very often compromise spatial and spectral fidelity, information loss occurs. This research involves a deep-learning image fusion framework that uses a Generative Adversarial Network (GAN) to carry out both Panchromatic (PAN) and Multispectral (MS) systems were used remote sensing images. Hence, the proposed scheme ensures enhancement in spatial resolution without compromising its spectral integrity, leading to an improved land cover classification. From the fused images, vegetation indices such as NDVI, SAVI, and EVI are extracted to assess crop health and soil conditions. The classification is then refined further using deep learning algorithms, thus achieving a higher standard of accuracy and resilience than with conventional methods. Panchromatic (PAN) was used along with Multispectral (MS) in the study is generally accepted to improve the quality and usability of remote-sensing data for applications in urban planning, agriculture, forestry, and disaster management. This research presents an innovative method based on Adaptive GAN for using advanced high-resolution satellite images, with particular emphasis on improving fusion accuracy through building segmentation. Experimental results show that compared to existing techniques, Jilin-1 satellite images provide better spatial resolution, multispectral fidelity, and information retention. In addition, this study incorporates geofencing into agricultural applications by using fused images for real-time monitoring of crop growth, irrigation management, and pest control. GAN-based fusion, combined with geofencing, serves to enhance precision farming through prompt notifications, efficient resource utilization, and increased total farm productivity. Experimental evaluation proves the proposed model's superiority over existing methods in terms of PSNR, SSIM, and classification accuracy, showcasing its potential for precision agriculture.

Keywords: GAN, Image Fusion, PAN, Vegetation Indices, and Land Cover Classification, Geofencing, Precision farming

1 INTRODUCTION

With rapid progress in the systemization of remote sensing technologies for some decades now, it has become common knowledge about what these technologies can make out in view of the surface of this Earth from afar. While those basic significant uses in this interdisciplinary field are environmental studies, agriculture control, city planning, and disaster management, the application of sensors supplied with multispectral and hyperspectral imagers operating from satellites, manned aircraft, or unmanned aerial vehicles remains the major background. The information contained in the images is great, yet discrepancies exist in spatial, spectral, and temporal resolutions, making their integration and interpretation challenging. Hence image fusion provides the best approach whereby information from several images is merged into a unique composite view for improved interpretability, precision, and efficiency of the remote sensing data. Provided with this data, scientists are able to obtain a useful detail view for studying activities here on Earth, especially in cases requiring the merging of fine spatial resolution information with spectral richness or accurate detection of temporal change.

The art of image fusion has transitioned from traditional methodologies to the very sophisticated approaches capable of handling various degrees of complexities like Wavelet Transforms, Sparse Representation, and Deep Learning. These very advanced techniques allow different options for lateralization of fusion between spectral and spatial information while suppressing noise and maintaining the essentials that are pertinent for remote sensing applications. Because these new techniques are becoming increasingly pertinent with the increasing complexity of multispectral data analysis, they can be expected to impact how effectively the environment will be monitored and how urban areas will be designed and managed. This application applies when fusion allows for using both the high clarity of panchromatic (PAN) images and the fine details presented in the multispectral portion of the spectrum. Consequently, this will create an avenue for application in urban planning, agricultural monitoring, environmental assessments, and disaster response.

Conventional image fusion systems are characterized by the use of methodologies such as Intensity-Hue-Saturation change, Principal Component Analysis, and wavelets combining aspects from both spatial and spectral scene resolution from different sources. Regrettably, these methods often fail to preserve the requisite spatial fidelity and spectral accuracy due to the diverse and complex nature of objects in mixed scenes. Machine learning and artificial intelligence have drastically transformed the traditional approaches towards the realization of image fusion. The major standout amongst these changes is the establishment of GANs, which have aided tremendously in modernizing image fusion. The dual-network architecture of GANs comprises a generator and a discriminator, which adversarially generate high-fidelity outputs and thus allow for more sophisticated integration of data ensuring an adequate spatial and spectral attribute representation.

Adaptive Generative Adversarial Networks (AGANs) have evolved from the older GAN model with the aim of enhancing methodologies in image fusion. So basically, modifications of the original structure of GAN are made in order to allow efficient performance to some challenges which arise from image fusion with regards to spatial detail and spectral fidelity preservation. With these AGANs that employ these exclusive advanced techniques, the puzzle of enhancing fusion quality and visual quality for analytical purposes is being solved. The research discussed in relation to AGAN, regarded the merging of panchromatic and multispectral images for the improvement of results from fused images by the constraint of baking the

DOI: 10.1201/9781003798514-60

positive aspects of both sets and the reduction of their negative aspects. The model assumes the AGANs are going to improve in remote sensing by providing higher resolution, better accuracy, and richer information images which will feed into sound decision-making across several fronts.

2 LATEST TRENDS IN IMAGE FUSION

The methods in image fusion are classified into a number of categories such as "Multi Scale Transform-based (MST), Sparse Representation (SR), Hybrid, and Neural network-based approaches" and others. All of them are effective in integrating information of different sources but each has its own strategy for the way fusion is done. MST methods take source images apart into components of different scales, use particular rules to fuse them, and finally apply the inverse MST process to the fused image. On the other hand, Super Resolution (SR) methods represent input images by means of complete dictionaries to obtain sparse coefficients, which are merged through different fusion strategies.

Hybrid methods produce better fusion results by exploiting the merits of multiple approaches for example: Minimum Spanning Tree (MST) and Sparse Representation (SR). Among the latest advancements as far as image fusion is concerned, the incorporation of Deep learning-based methods into it has seen the evolution of traditional Using methods that rely on CNN or methods that are generative adversarial networks. The CNN-based models are quite promising; nonetheless, they seem to be very shallow and may not fuse those features required for attaining good results during fusion, usually resulting in loss of important details. Even though most methodssuch as "Dual Discriminator Specific GAN (DDGAN) and Fusion GAN", are based on adversarial learning to enhance fusion results, such approaches experience stability challenges [14–17].

The proposed model includes a generator and three discriminators. Its main job is to fuse and extract features that are then able to generate a different image. Discriminators' work Considering how infrared, visible and difference images are different, we teach the generator to check whether the images are real or not. This is accompanied by an adversarial interaction between the generator and the discriminator which is also accompanied by dynamic equilibrium within the generator and each discriminator as well as among the three discriminators themselves. Thus, in the inference stage, only the pre-trained generator model is required and not the discriminators..

3 METHODOLOGY

Multiple research phases are undertaken to devise a new multimodal image fusion scheme specifically targeted at augmenting land cover classification with remote sensing imagery. The entire procedure is systematically divided into four critical phases: image preprocessing, image fusion, feature extraction, and classification. The first phase involves application of image preprocessing enhancement techniques upon input images to promote their quality. Relevant issues entailing resolution consistency, illumination balance, and noise minimizing are thus solved, forming a strong backbone for the next phases to stand on. After preprocessing, image fusion incorporates an Adaptive Generative Adversarial Network (AGAN) to bridge the gap between the multispectral and panchromatic images. The aim was to integrate these images such that spatial and spectral fidelity are preserved while distortions are minimized.

During feature extraction, important attributes are obtained from the fused images. A major concentration is on computing several Examples of vegetation indices are the Normalized Difference Vegetation Index (NDVI), Green Normalized Difference Vegetation Index (GNDVI), Soil-Adjusted Vegetation Index (SAVI), Ratio Vegetation Index (RVI) and Chlorophyll Vegetation Index (CVI). These indices are vital for measuring vegetation health, density, and other relevant attributes of land cover. This results, therefore, much more precise classification of different land cover types.

Land cover classification is finally performed with the extracted features, including the above indices as inputs to the classification algorithm. Each fused image pixel is classified according to land-cover types in order to generate an accurate classified map. The aim of this approach, in theory, is to take full advantage of multimodal image fusion combined with vegetation indices to obtain greater accuracy in land cover classification, thus providing a better framework for agricultural monitoring and environmental management.

This methodology, represented in Figure 1, ensures that the high-quality, informative fused images it provides will, in turn, greatly enhance the accuracy of the land cover classification. The gain from the implementation of advanced image fusion techniques such as Generative Adversarial Networks (GANs) coupled with various vegetation indices for feature extraction will be invaluable for improving reliability and precision of land cover classification from remote sensing.

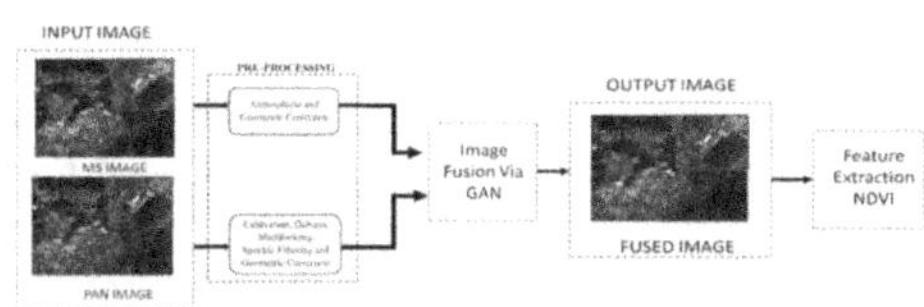

Figure 1. Overall design process.

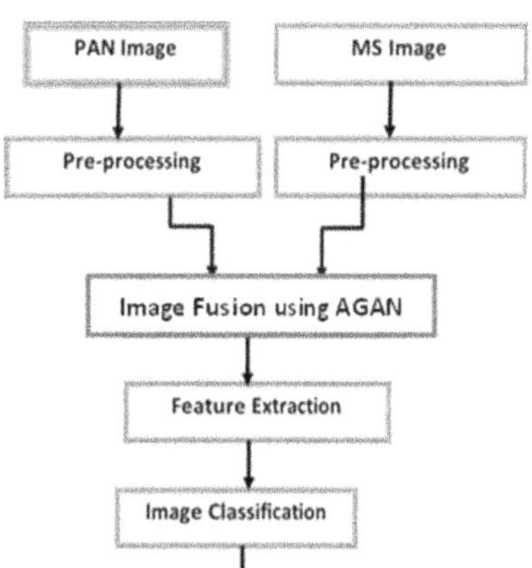

Figure 2. Processing Flow of the GAN based fusion method.

Figure 2 further elucidates the processing flow of the described method. In this flowchart, the preprocessing of input images— both panchromatic (PAN) and multispectral (MS) images— is depicted, followed by the fusion process that utilizes the Generative Adversarial Network to yield an image suitable for feature extraction.

The model consists of a Generator (G), which generates fused images, and a Discriminator (D), which differentiates between photos that are real and those that are fake. With adversarial loss, the GAN is directed to keep the details in the image's space while still minimizing changes to colors and tones. The features of the architecture of the generator and the discriminator networks will be described in the next section.

4 STRUCTURE OF GENERATOR

As illustrated in Figure 3, the generator network is fed with three inputs, which are the multispectral image, the panchromatic image, and the result when you subtract the dark reference image from the bright reference image. By linking the three images together, the outcome for the generator is a fused image. To build the encoder part, the generator adopts DenseNet which allows for feature reuse and is therefore efficient to use. It thus helps in reducing the number of parameters and responds to the gradient vanishing problem, effecting stabilization of the network during training.

In order for the network to learn quickly, we therefore employ Rectified Linear Units (ReLU) as the activation function, paired with batch normalization. These high-dimensional feature maps created by the encoder feed into the decoder that has a CNN like architecture. Using the hyperbolic tangent (tanh) activation function, the process passes through the last layer of the decoder; no down-sampling was used in generator architecture, keeping the same resolution present in the original image.

5 STRUCTURE OF DISCRIMINATOR

To distinguish between visible, infrared, and other images within the generated photos, three discriminators with the same structure are needed. This is because The kinds of images that exist all have varied distributions and features. Figure 4 reveals that the discriminator is a convolutional network designed to distinguish images that uses VGG architecture, batch normalization and leaky ReLU as its activation function. Discriminator provides a single number as the estimated probability and the input can be an original image or a produced image. [15].

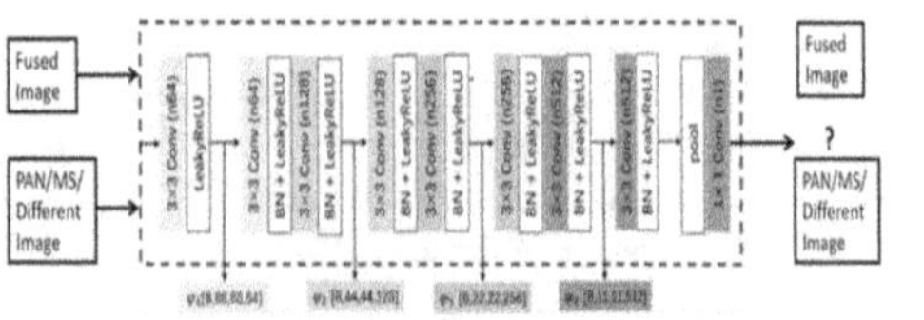

Figure 3. Structure of generator.

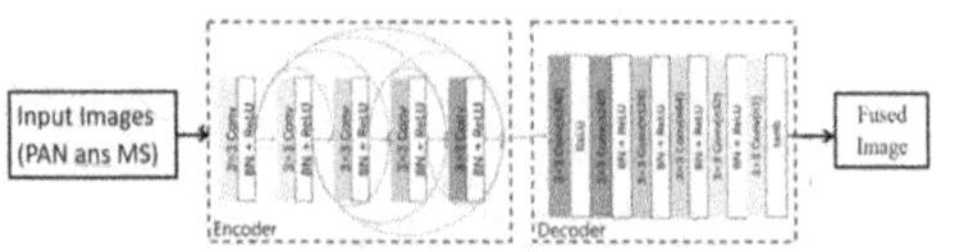

Figure 4. Structure of discriminator.

6 LOSS FUNCTION

AGAN produces fused pictures with similar features but not nearly identical pictures like the original pictures. For this issue, content loss function is a solution needed. Generator loss makes use of both the content loss and adversarial loss as explained in the formula below.

$$L_G = L_{content} + \gamma L_{adv} \tag{1}$$

Where L_G is the generator loss, $L_{content}$ is content loss and L_{adv} is adversarial loss. Equation 1 describes the three factors that make up the content loss (SSIM, IL and TEE).

7 RESULTS, ANALYSIS AND DISCUSSION

Our approach is as validated by running experiments on data provided by the Jilin-1 satellites. Beforehand, preprocessing on the data enables us to use geo-referenced images for PAN and MS. The experimental result is shown in the Figure 5.

8 PERFORMANCE ANALYSIS OF PROPOSED METHOD

Figure 6 shows the fused dataset results along with the original PAN and MS pictures. The suggested approach and the PanSharp method both achieve the same level of sharpness with the PAN images while enjoying superior and more consistent spatial augmentation results in terms of visual effect. As seen in Figures 6(e) and 6(f), Sometimes, the PCA and GS approaches fail to provide much spatial information and give inadequate details in the resulting images. As can be seen from Figure 6, there is noticeable color distortion in the fusion results of the PCA and GS methods. Additionally, Figure 7 (c) and 7 (d) indicate that AGAN method outperforms the Pan Sharp method in preserving spectral information in built-up areas, with the color of the roofs in our method being more like that in the MS image. In contrast, the Pan-Sharp method results in slightly darker colors.

To find out how effective the proposed method is, various evaluation indices or performance parameters are used along with standard deviation, average gradient, information entropy, peak signal-to-noise ratio (PSNR), structural similarity index (SSIM) and correlation coefficient. [13].

The higher the standard deviation (SD), the greater the amount of spatial information, as described by Equation 2, and low spatial information is implied by a low standard deviation.

$$SD(F) = \frac{\sqrt{\sum_{i=1}^{M}\sum_{j=1}^{N}\left(F(i,j) - \overline{F}\right)^2}}{MN} \tag{2}$$

We call the resultant image f and find both the standard deviation (sd) and average (¯f) for it. M is the width and n is the height of f. Sharper images happen when the pixels next to each other are very different which is shown by having higher average gradient values.

Information entropy measures the presence of information in the image and is defined in terms of the histogram hist of the image and the maximum and minimum pixel values p_{max} and p_{min}.

$$EN(F) = \sum_{i=P_{min}}^{P_{max}} -HIST_F(i)\log_2(HIST_F(i)) \tag{3}$$

PSNR examines and calculates the similarity between T and F. If PSNR is greater, two images are more nearly the same. It is possible to define it by saying:

$$PSNR(T,F) = 10\log\left(\frac{\max(T)}{\sqrt{\frac{1}{MN}\sum_{i=1}^{M}\sum_{j=1}^{N}(T(i,j) - F(i,j))2}}\right) \tag{4}$$

For every image F, max(T) is the maximum pixel value of T and M is its width and N is its height.

SSIM measures how similar the organization of two images is, while the spectral similarity is compared through the correlation coefficient and both increase when the scores are larger. The SSIM indicator can be properly described by luminance, contrast and the main structure. explained in equation 5 to 8.

$$SSIM(T,F) = l(T,F).c(T,F).s(T,F) \tag{5}$$

$$l(T,F) = \frac{2\overline{TF} + C_1}{\overline{T}^2} + \overline{F}^2 + C_1 \tag{6}$$

$$c(T,F) = \frac{2\sigma_T\sigma_F + C_1}{\sigma_T{}^2 + \sigma_F{}^2 + C_2} \tag{7}$$

$$s(T,F) = \frac{\sigma_{TF} + C_3}{\sigma_T\sigma_F + C_3} \tag{8}$$

This means T and F stand for the average pixel values of single and fused images; σT, σF represent their standard deviations; σTF is the covariance of T and F, there are three constants C1, C2, C3 in the equation (C1, C2 and C3 are constants). The Correlation coefficient is given by Equation 9 as 'CC(T,F)'.

$$CC(T,F) = \frac{\sum_{i=1}^{M}\sum_{j=1}^{N}\left(T(i,j) - \overline{T}\right)\left(F(i,j) - \overline{F}\right)}{\sqrt{\left(\sum_{i=1}^{M}\sum_{j=1}^{N}\left(T(i,j) - \overline{T}\right)^2\right)\left(\sum_{i=1}^{M}\sum_{j=1}^{N}\left(F(i,j) - \overline{F}\right)^2\right)}} \tag{9}$$

Information on how different methods score on above-mentioned parameters is shown in the table given below. Our approach does better than others in most evaluation categories. Even though 'cc' in Adaptive GAN is slightly less than in a few other methods, our findings are more stable and reliable compared to those from PCA and the GS. Because achieving a perfectly fused PAN and MS image is very impractical, we use the SSIM and correlation coefficient to evaluate the accuracy of fusion in our experiments.

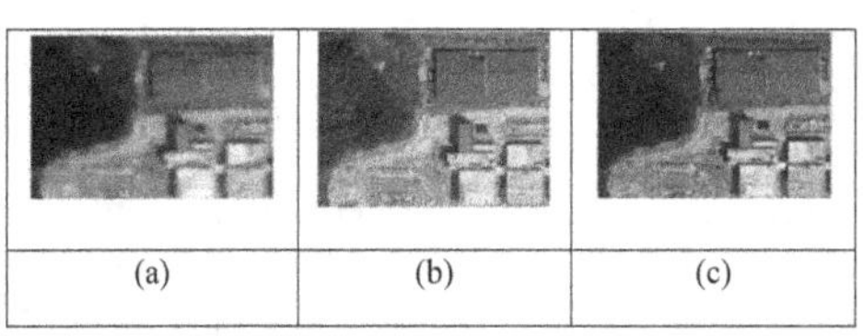

Figure 5. Output of the proposed the method. (a) The MS image; (b) The PAN image; (c) The fused image.

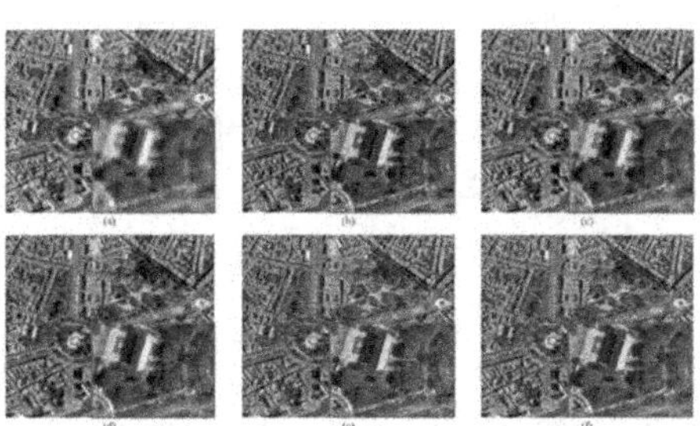

Figure 6. The fusion result of images from Pl'eiades-1A (a) The MS image; (b) The PAN image; (c) AGAN; (d) Pan Sharp; (e) PCA; (f) GS.

Figure 7. The fusion results of Jilin-1 KF01A. (a) The MS image; (b) The PAN image; (c) AGAN; (d) Pan Sharp; (e) PCA; (f) GS.

Table 1. Comparative analysis of quantitative measures.

Methods	SD	PSNR	SSIM	cc
Adaptive GAN	**124.7747**	**15.74**	**1.94**	0.87
Pan-Sharp	106.3516	13.19	1.09	0.93
PCA	108.6006	12.05	1.88	0.93
GS	112.03	11.72	1.87	0.93

Figure 8 presents the comparative analysis of quantitative measures, including slandered deviation, PSNR, SSIM and CC (Cross Correlation) for the various methods. The results clearly demonstrated that the proposed method outperforms the existing approaches across these measures.

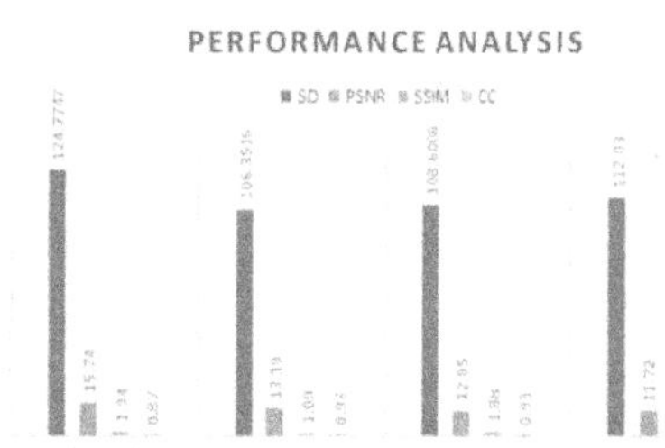

Figure 8. Comparative study of quantitative measures.

9 CONCLUSION

This study proposes an innovative application of Adaptive Generative Adversarial Networks (GANs) for fusing panchromatic and multispectral images focusing on vegetation classification. The proposed method hereby makes use of mutual benefit of both data types, thus enhancing spatial resolution and retaining spectral integrity to augment land cover classification accuracy. The AGAN uses a single texture map to generate important gradient variations that incorporate details needed for efficient fusion. The experiments substantiate the outperformance of this new method against classical approaches such as principal component analysis (PCA) and Gram-Schmidt (GS) by consistently outperforming them on almost all evaluation metrics like PSNR, SSIM, and classification accuracy.

The strength of precision farming applications is enhanced through geofencing where the geofencing aids in the real-time monitoring of crop health, irrigation management, and pest control, thus allowing for resource allocation and farm productivity. The results highlight the importance of these deep learning-based fusion techniques in furthering remote sensing technology for the purpose of achieving sustainable agriculture.

10 LIMITATIONS AND FUTURE SCOPE

Despite the significance of the results, there remain some challenges such as minor variations in the correlation coefficients and further optimization for an ideal fusion result, which is nevertheless required. The research for the future will work on refining the GAN for improved fusion performance and further application in multiple remote sensing applications like the fusion of near-infrared, far-infrared, visible and SAR images. The adaptive GAN-based fusion scheme is indeed a further step in remote sensing methodologies toward a more reliable, stable, and accurate system for vegetation classification and beyond.

ACKNOWLEDGEMENT

We authors gratefully acknowledge the support and guidance provided by Sandip Institute of Technology and research Centre. We also thank all those who contributed to the development and review of this work.

REFERENCES

[1] ZiHan Cao, ShiQi Cao, Xiao Wu, JunMing Hou, Ran Ran, and Liang-Jian Deng. "Ddrf: Denoising diffusion modelforremotesensing imagefusion", *arXivpreprint* arXiv:2304.04774, 2023, doi : 10.48550/arXiv.2304.04774

[2] Xuchun Ye, Juan Wu, Xianghu Li, Yunliang Li, Qi Zhang and Chong-Yu Xu, "Multi-source remote sensing data and image fusion technology reveal significant spatiotemporal heterogeneity of inundation dynamics in a typical large floodplain lake system", *Journal of Hydrology: Regional Studies*, Volume 50, December 2023, 101541, doi : 10.1016/j.ejrh.2023.101541

[3] T. Saikumar, S. Venkatesh, Md. Ameen Uddin, "Comparison Techniques of Image Fusion in Image Segmentation", *Journal of Advances in Computer, Electrical & Electronics Engg.*, Volume 3 , Issue 1; Spl. Issue of IC3T 2014 @ISSN: 2248-9584 Page | 378

[4] NawarAlseelawi, Hussein TuamaHazim, Haider TH. Salim ALRikabi, University of Misan, Maysan, Iraq, "A Novel Method of Multimodal Medical Image Fusion Based on Hybrid Approach of NSCT and DTCWT", *iJOE*™Vol. 18, No. 03, 2022

[5] Haiying Fan and Gonghuai Wei, "Multi-spectral remote sensing image fusion method based on gradient moment matching", *Systems and Soft Computing*, Volume 6, December 2024, 200108, doi : 10.1016/j.sasc.2024.200108

[6] Wenmei Li, Jiaqi Wu, Qing Liu, Yu Zhang, Bin Cui, Yan Jia and Guan Gui, "An Effective Multimodel Fusion Method for SAR and Optical Remote Sensing Images", *IEEE Journal of Selected Topics in Applied Earth Observations and Remote Sensing*, vol. 16, pp. 5881-5892, 2023, doi: 10.1109/JSTARS.2023.3288143

[7] Renwei Dian, Shutao Li, Bin Sun and Anjing Guo, "Recent advances and new guidelines on hyperspectral and multispectral imagefusion", *Information Fusion*, Volume 69, May 2021, Pages 40-51, doi : 10.1016/j.inffus.2020.11.001

[8] Yu Sun, Xiyang Zhi, Shikai Jiang, Guanghua Fan, Xu Yan and Wei Zhang, "Image fusion for the novelty rotating synthetic aperture system based on vision transformer", *Information Fusion*, Volume 104, April 2024, 102163, doi : 10.1016/j.inffus.2023.102163

[9] S.K. Roy, A. Deria, D. Hong, B. Rasti, A. Plaza and J. Chanussot, "Multimodal Fusion Transformer for Remote Sensing Image Classification", *IEEE Transactions on Geoscience and Remote Sensing,* vol. 61, pp. 1-20, 2023, Art no. 5515620, doi: 10.1109/TGRS.2023.3286826

[10] Zhaoyang Hou, Kaiyun Lv, Xunqiang Gong and Yuting Wan, "A remote sensing image fusion method combining low-level visual features and parameter-adaptive dual-channel pulse-coupled neural network." *Remote Sensing* 15, no. 2 (2023): 344, doi : 10.3390/rs15020344

[11] Hayder Dibs, Hussein Sabah Jaber and Nadhir Al-Ansari, "Multi-fusion algorithms for detecting land surface pattern changes using multi-high spatial resolution images and remote sensing analysis", *Emerging Science Journal* 7, no. 4 pp: 1215-1231, 2023

[12] Y. Feng, H. Xu, J. Jiang, H. Liu and J. Zheng, "ICIF-Net: Intra-Scale Cross-Interaction and Inter-Scale Feature Fusion Network for Bitemporal Remote Sensing Images Change Detection", *IEEE Transactions on Geoscience and Remote Sensing*, vol. 60, pp. 1-13, 2022, Art no. 4410213, doi: 10.1109/TGRS.2022.3168331

[13] Fang Gao, Yihui Li, Peng Zhang, Yuwei Zhai, Yan Zhang, Yongshuai Yang and Yuan An, "A high-resolution panchromatic-multispectral satellite image fusion method assisted with building segmentation", *Computers & Geosciences*, Volume 168, November 2022, 105219, doi : 10.1016/j.cageo.2022.105219

[14] Renwei Dian, Shutao Li, Bin Sun and Anjing Guo, "Recent advances and new guidelines on hyperspectral and multispectral imagefusion", *Information Fusion*, Volume 69, May 2021, Pages 40-51, doi: 10.1016/j.inffus.2020.11.001

[15] Anyang Song, Huixian Duan, Haodong Pei and Lei Ding, "Triple-discriminator generative adversarial network for infrared and visible image fusion", *Neurocomputing*, Volume 483, 28 April 2022, Pages 183-194, doi : 10.1016/j.neucom.2022.02.025

[16] Chenxiao Zhang, Peng Yue, Deodato Tapete, Liangcun Jiang, Boyi Shangguan, Li Huang and Guangchao Liu, "A deeply supervised image fusion network for change detection in high resolution bi-temporal remote sensing images", *ISPRS Journal of Photogrammetry and Remote Sensing,* Volume 166, August 2020, Pages 183-200, doi : 10.1016/j.isprsjprs.2020.06.003.2973435

[17] X. Jin, S. Huang, Q. Jiang, S. -J. Lee, L. Wu and S. Yao, "Semisupervised Remote Sensing Image Fusion Using Multiscale Conditional Generative Adversarial Network With Siamese Structure", *IEEE Journal of Selected Topics in Applied Earth Observations and Remote Sensing*, vol. 14, pp. 7066-7084, 2021, doi: 10.1109/JSTARS.2021.3090958

[18] J. Wang, Y. Jiang, Y. Qi and Y. Zhai, "Remote Sensing Image Fusion Based on Nonnegative Dictionary Learning", *IEEE Access*, vol. 9, pp. 158908-158916, 2021, doi: 10.1109/ACCESS.2021.3131268

[19] L. Li, L. Han, M. Ding and H. Cao, "Multimodal Image Fusion Framework for End-to-End Remote Sensing Image Registration", *IEEE Transactions on Geoscience and Remote Sensing*, vol. 61, pp. 1-14, 2023, Art no. 5607214, doi: 10.1109/TGRS.2023.3247642

[20] Xin Jin, Yuting Feng, Qian Jiang, Shengfa Miao, Xing Chu, Huangqimei Zheng and Qianqian Wang, "UPGAN: An Unsupervised Generative Adversarial Network Based on U-Shaped Structure for Pansharpening", *ISPRS International Journal of Geo-Information*, volume 13, no. 7 (2024): 222, doi : 10.3390/ijgi13070222

[21] Vaibhav R. Pandit and R.J. Bhiwani, "Morphology-based spatial filtering for efficiency enhancement of remote sensing image fusion", *Computers & Electrical Engineering*, Volume 89, January 2021, 106945, doi : 10.1016/j.compeleceng.2020.106945

[22] Shulei Wu and Huandong Chen, "Smart city oriented remote sensing image fuion methods based on convolution sampling and spatial transformation", *Computer Communications,* Volume 157, 1 May 2020, Pages 444-450, doi: 10.1016/j.comcom.2020.04.010

[23] Gang Xiao · Durga Prasad Bavirisetti Gang Liu · Xingchen Zhang, "*Image Fusion*", © Springer Nature Singapore Pte Ltd. and Shanghai Jiao Tong University Press 2020

[24] FuchaoZha, Xiaoming Wu, Shuai Wang, "Object-oriented Vegetation Classification Method based on UAV and Satellite Image Fusion", *International Conference on Identification, Information and Knowledge in the Internet of Things (IIKI2019)*, 2019, 609-615.

[25] Yu Fu, Xiao-Jun Wu and Tariq Durrani, "Image fusion based on generative adversarial network consistent with perception", *Information Fusion*, Volume 72, August 2021, Pages 110-125, doi : 10.1016/j.inffus.2021.02.019

[26] L. Ni, X. Pan, X. Wang, D. Bao, J. Zhang and J. Shi, "Small-Object Detection Model for Optical Remote Sensing Images Based on Tri-decoupling++ Head", *IEEE Journal of Selected Topics in Applied Earth Observations and Remote Sensing*, doi: 10.1109/JSTARS.2024.341770

[27] X. Ma, S. Hu, S. Liu, J. Wang and S. Xu, "Noisy Remote Sensing Image Fusion Based on JSR", *IEEE Access*, vol. 8, pp. 31069-31082, 2020, doi: 10.1109/ACCESS.2020.2973435

[28] W. Xiong, Z. Xiong, Y. Zhang, Y. Cui and X. Gu, "A Deep Cross-Modality Hashing Network for SAR and Optical Remote Sensing Images Retrieval", *IEEE Journal of Selected Topics in Applied Earth Observations and Remote Sensing,* vol. 13, pp. 5284-5296, 2020, doi: 10.1109/JSTARS.2020.3021390

[29] Hao Zhu, Mengru Ma, Wenping Ma, Licheng Jiao, Shikuan Hong, Jianchao Shen and Biao Hou, "A spatial-channel progressive fusion ResNet for remote sensing classification", *Information Fusion,* Volume 70, June 2021, Pages 72-87, doi: 10.1016/j.inffus.2020.12.008

Advancement in Engineering and Science – Goyal et al. (Eds)
 ISBN: 978-1-041-31101-0

Fault Detection in Machinery Parts using Deep Learning

Digvijay Jotiram Pawar
Associate Professor and Head, Department of E&TC Engineering, Ashokrao Mane Group of Institutions, Vathar, Kolhapur, MS, India

Madhuri Shankar Mane
Department of E&TC Engineering, Ashokrao Mane Group of Institutions, Vathar, Kolhapur, MS, India

ABSTRACT: The paper presents a deep learning-based approach for automated fault detection in machining parts and assemblies, aimed at enhancing visual quality inspection in manufacturing processes. The system integrates dataset collection and augmentation, followed by the training of a deep learning model utilizing the MobileNet Single Shot Detector (SSD) architecture with a transfer learning approach. The trained model is deployed within a python flask framework that captures data input, performs real-time inference and provides automated defect detection of the machinery parts. The system's graphical user interface notifies users of the acceptance or rejection of the machinery parts and assemblies, detailing the specific reasons for rejections. This approach reduces reliance on manual inspections, streamlines production workflows and improves overall product quality, offering a robust solution for the manufacturing industry.

Keywords: Deep learning, fault detection, machining parts, MobileNet SSD, transfer learning, visual quality inspection

1 INTRODUCTION

In today's competitive manufacturing landscape, maintaining high product quality is paramount to ensuring operational efficiency and customer satisfaction. Traditional inspection methods, which rely on manual visual checks, are often labor-intensive, error-prone, and unsuitable for handling the increasing complexity and production scale of modern industries. Consequently, automated fault detection systems powered by deep learning have gained significant traction as a reliable and efficient alternative. These systems can provide real-time visual quality inspection, minimizing human error while improving overall production quality and throughput.

The paper presents an automated fault detection system for machining parts and assemblies, designed to enhance the precision and efficiency of quality control processes. The proposed solution employs a MobileNet Single Shot Detector (SSD) deep learning architecture with a transfer learning approach to develop a model capable of detecting faults in real-time. The system incorporates dataset collection and augmentation to train the model on various types of defects typically found in machined components. The trained model is integrated into a Python Flask framework, enabling the seamless capture of input data, inference, and automated feedback through a graphical user interface (GUI). This allows manufacturers to quickly identify defective parts and assemblies and provides actionable insights regarding the detected faults.

The key contribution of this paper lies in its ability to automate the traditionally manual process of fault detection, significantly reducing inspection time and increasing accuracy. The system's deployment within a Python Flask application ensures easy integration into existing workflows and offers a user-friendly interface for visualizing results and fault diagnostics. By implementing a robust deep learning model for real-time quality inspection, this solution addresses the limitations of manual inspection methods and delivers a scalable, cost-effective alternative for improving product quality in machining and assembly lines.

2 LITERATURE REVIEW

This systematic review aims to present the current landscape of these technologies in the Industrial domain, summarizing the state-of-the-art based on existing literature. The diverse applications discussed, ranging from image processing, manual techniques to deep learning are outlined in the current review work.

The use of deep learning for Automated Visual Inspection (AVI) has seen substantial advancements in recent years, with a particular focus on improving defect detection accuracy and efficiency across various industries. Hütten *et al.* (2024) present a comprehensive survey on the application of deep learning to AVI in manufacturing and maintenance sectors, emphasizing the growing role of convolutional neural networks (CNNs) in defect detection. Their work highlights that although CNNs remain the standard in this domain, emerging models like vision transformers are beginning to outperform traditional CNNs, particularly in tasks requiring object recognition and segmentation. However, vision transformers have higher computational demands, limiting their deployment in real-time industrial settings. The survey also underscores the significant gap between research and industrial application, often with a three-year delay before innovations in academic research are adopted in production environments.

In a case study by Veillon (2023), deep learning was applied to visual inspection processes within the pharmaceutical industry, particularly focusing on defect detection in filled injectable drug products. This study outlines the advantages of deep learning over traditional computer vision techniques, such as higher accuracy in detecting probabilistic defects and minimizing false rejections.

Ravikumar *et al.* (2011) provide an earlier perspective on the application of machine learning to AVI, comparing traditional pixel-based approaches with feature-based methods. They specifically applied decision tree and Naïve Bayes classifiers to detect defects like scratches on machine components.

Weiher *et al.* (2023) investigated the use of CNNs and transfer learning for AVI in the automotive supply industry, focusing on the detection of defects in thermal conductive components.

DOI: 10.1201/9781003798514-61

Sabry and Amirulddin (2024) explored fault detection and isolation (FDI) for industrial robots and multi-axis machines, emphasizing the challenges posed by complex mechanical systems.Together, these studies illustrate the evolving landscape of AVI, from traditional machine learning approaches to cutting-edge deep learning techniques. While deep learning offers substantial improvements in defect detection accuracy, challenges remain, particularly regarding dataset availability, computational demands, and regulatory compliance. As artificial intelligence (AI) technologies continue to advance, it is expected that the adoption of more sophisticated models, such as vision transformers, will become more widespread, further enhancing the efficiency and reliability of industrial inspection systems.

3 METHODOLOGY

The fault detection system for machine parts operates using deep learning-based automated visual inspection to identify defects in machining parts and assemblies. The process involves several critical stages:

- ***Data Acquisition and Pre-processing***: Images of machine parts are captured using high-resolution cameras. These images undergo preprocessing steps such as resizing, normalization, noise reduction, and contrast enhancement to highlight features relevant for defect detection.
- ***Model Training***: A deep learning model, typically based on a convolutional neural network (CNN) such as MobileNet SSD, is trained using a dataset of labeled images. The dataset consists of examples of both defective and non-defective machine parts.
- ***Inference:*** Once the model is trained, it is deployed using a Python Flask framework to perform real-time inspections. During operation, new images of machine parts are captured and processed by the trained model.
- ***Decision Making and Output:*** The system displays the results of the inspection through a graphical user interface (GUI).

4 SYSTEM ARCHITECTURE

The system architecture for fault detection in machine parts using deep learning is composed of several interconnected modules that work together to automate the detection and classification of defects in real-time. The architecture diagram of the proposed system is shown in Figure 1.

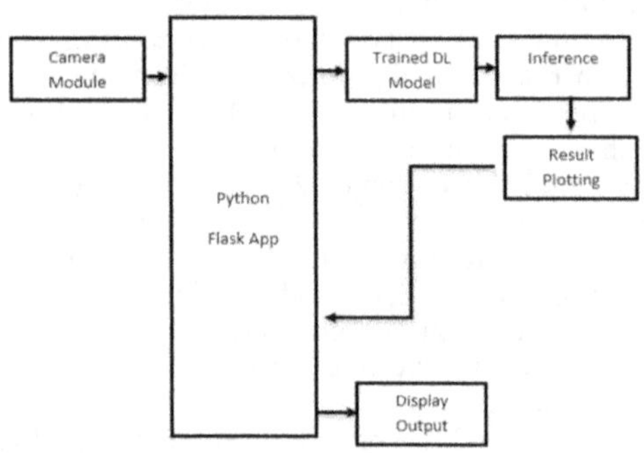

Figure 1. Architecture diagram of the proposed system.

The use case diagram illustrates the interactions between the Operator, System Admin, and Camera System in the fault detection process. The Operator initiates inspections, which involve capturing images, preprocessing them, detecting faults, and displaying results. The System Admin is responsible for training and updating the deep learning model used for fault detection.

The data flow diagram is also illustrated in Figure 2.

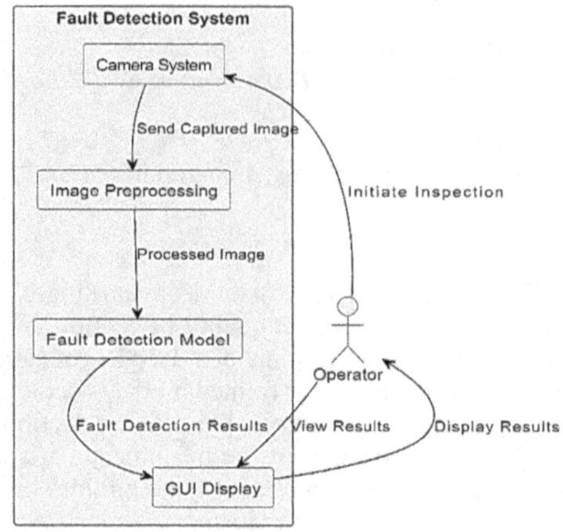

Figure 2. Data flow diagram.

The Data Flow Diagram (DFD) shows the sequence of operations in the fault detection system for machine parts. It begins with the operator initiating the inspection process, leading the camera system to capture an image of the part. This image is then sent to the image preprocessing module, where it undergoes necessary enhancements before being forwarded to the fault detection model. The model analyzes the image for defects and sends the results to the GUI Display, where the Operator views the fault detection outcome, allowing them to decide whether the part is accepted or rejected. This flow represents the entire data movement from image capture to fault evaluation and result display.

The hardware and software requirements are:

4.1 *Hardware Requirements*

- Processor: Multi-core CPU (Intel i7 or higher) and NVIDIA GPU with CUDA support.
- Memory: 16 GB RAM
- Camera: High-resolution camera (1080p or higher).

4.2 *Software Requirements*

- Operating System: Ubuntu 20.04+ or Windows 10/11.
- Programming Language: Python 3.8+.
- Deep Learning Framework: TensorFlow 2.x with CUDA Toolkit and cuDNN.
- Image Processing Library: OpenCV 4.x.
- Web Framework: Flask for web application development.
- Additional Libraries: Numpy, Pandas, Matplotlib, SQLAlchemy for supporting tasks.
- Development Tools: Jupyter Notebooks or IDEs like VS Code or PyCharm.

5 RESULTS AND DISCUSSION

The data collection for the fault detection system involved gathering images of both defective and non-defective machine parts. A thorough manual process was used to ensure that the dataset represented a wide variety of common defects found in machining.

SAMPLE NAME	LABEL	ADDED	LENGTH
defect 1.35k71obi	defect 1	Today, 06:23...	-
defect 1.35k71o...	defect 1	Today, 06:23...	-
defect 1.35k71ntl	defect 1	Today, 06:23...	-
defect 1.35k71n...	defect 1	Today, 06:23...	-
defect 1.35k71k...	defect 1	Today, 06:23...	-
defect 1.35k71k...	defect 1	Today, 06:23...	-
defect 1.35k71ibq	defect 1	Today, 06:23...	-
defect 1.35k71i7t	defect 1	Today, 06:23...	-
defect 1.35k71i0n	defect 1	Today, 06:23...	-

Collected data

Figure 3. Dataset collected.

The feature extraction process revealed that the model could accurately differentiate between defective and non-defective parts based on visual characteristics. The confusion matrix plotted on the validation dataset further indicated strong classification performance, showing low misclassification rates between defective and fault-free parts. Post-training analysis showed the model's robustness in real-time fault detection. The feature extraction on the collected dataset is done which is shown as a plot in Figure 4.

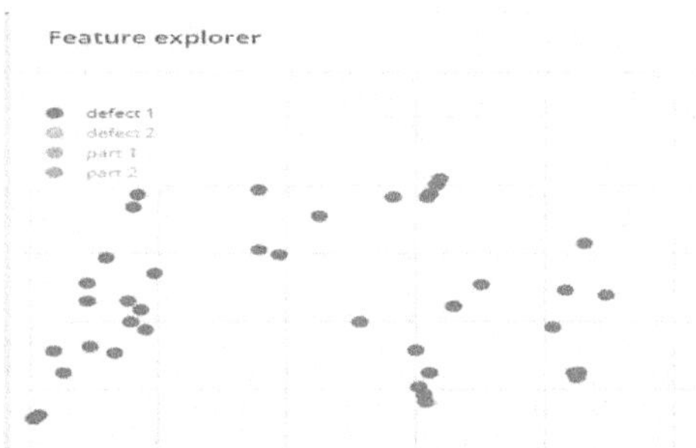

Figure 4. Feature extraction plot.

Once the dataset is prepared, the MobileNet SSD model is trained, achieving a validation accuracy of 87.90%, with a loss of 0.34. The Figure 5 shows the post-training confusion matrix on the validation dataset.

Confusion matrix (validation set)

	DEFECT 1	DEFECT 2	PART 1	PART 2
DEFECT 1	88.9%	0%	11.1%	0%
DEFECT 2	0%	83.3%	0%	16.7%
PART 1	0%	0%	100%	0%
PART 2	0%	25%	0%	75%
F1 SCORE	0.94	0.77	0.95	0.80

Figure 5. Confusion matrix for validation dataset.

The results plotted after a full training cycle demonstrated consistent performance, where the model effectively identified surface irregularities, misaligned assemblies, and other defects in machine parts as shown in Figure 6. The different detection conditions of the machinery parts are depicted in Figure 7.

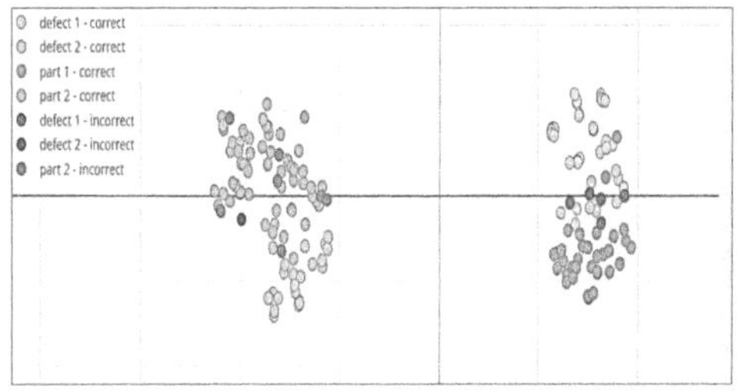

Figure 6. Plot of the training cycle.

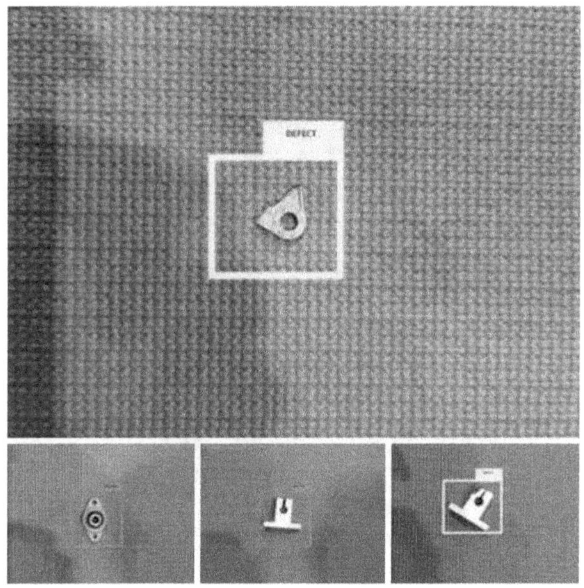

Figure 7. Different detection conditions of the machinery parts.

After getting the results, the flask application is developed which can be used to detect the defect. The developed GUI is as shown in Figure 8.

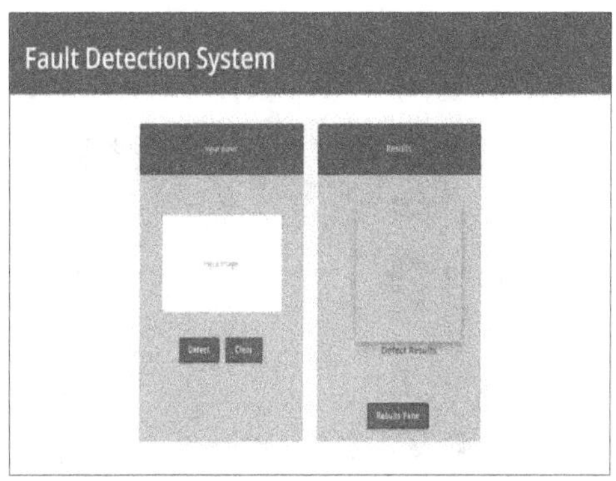

Figure 8. The developed GUI.

The Receiver Operating Characteristics (ROC) is plotted with the true positive rate against the false positive rate at various threshold settings as shown in Figure 9. The loss trends over steps is shown in Figure 10 and loss table is in Figure 11.

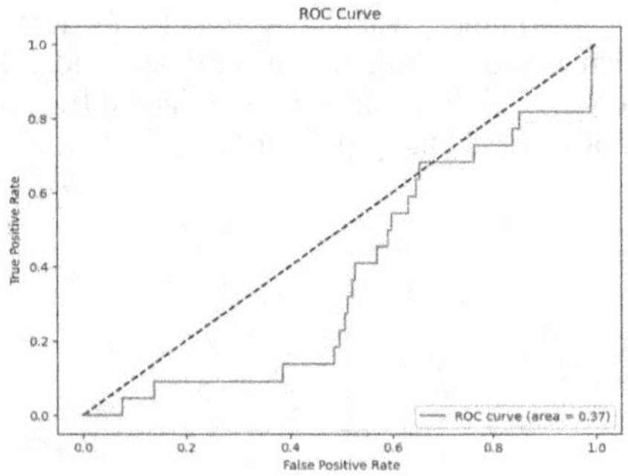

Figure 9. ROC curve.

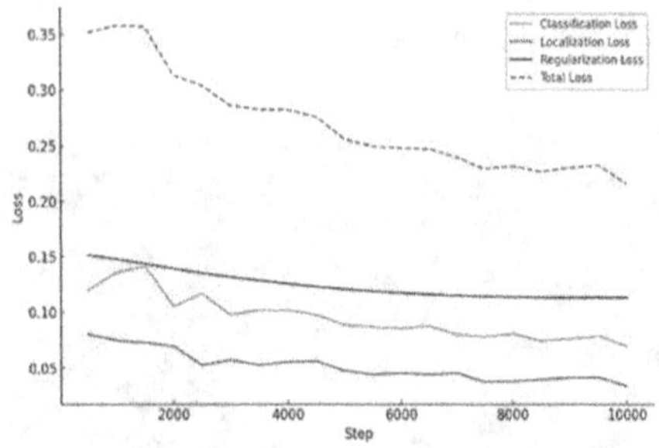

Figure 10. Loss trends over steps.

Step	Classification Loss	Localization Loss	Regularization Loss	Total Loss	Learning Rate
500	0.120009	0.080127	0.151328	0.351464	0.053333
1000	0.135641	0.074552	0.147621	0.357814	0.08
1500	0.141103	0.072388	0.143248	0.356739	0.079392
2000	0.104971	0.069185	0.139064	0.313219	0.077588
2500	0.116808	0.052296	0.135151	0.304256	0.074641
3000	0.097664	0.056956	0.131557	0.286177	0.070642
3500	0.101775	0.052296	0.128309	0.28238	0.065712
4000	0.101625	0.05515	0.125396	0.282171	0.06
4500	0.097454	0.055643	0.122827	0.275924	0.053681
5000	0.088369	0.047212	0.120604	0.256186	0.046946
5500	0.086569	0.044083	0.118711	0.249363	0.04
6000	0.085364	0.045192	0.117132	0.247688	0.033054
6500	0.087195	0.043889	0.115852	0.246937	0.026319
7000	0.079827	0.045285	0.11485	0.239962	0.02
7500	0.077764	0.037275	0.114103	0.229142	0.014288
8000	0.080316	0.037833	0.113583	0.231731	0.009358
8500	0.074053	0.039326	0.113257	0.226636	0.005359
9000	0.076008	0.041163	0.113085	0.230256	0.002412
9500	0.078397	0.041267	0.11301	0.232407	0.000608
10000	0.069285	0.033377	0.11301	0.215671	0

Figure 11. Loss table.

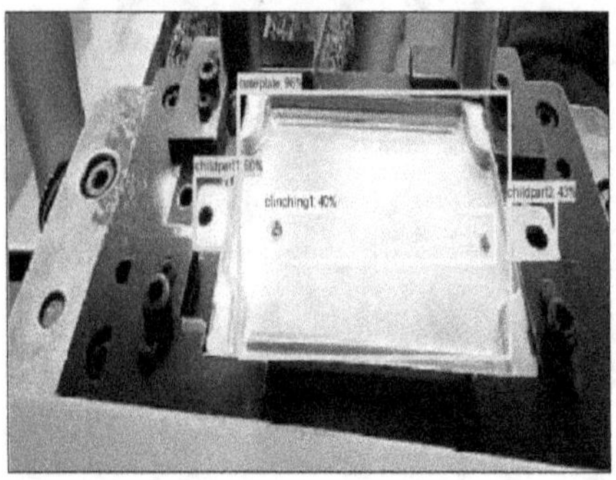

Figure 12. Detection results for assembly inspection.

The successful deployment of this system shown in Figure 12. This highlights the potential for reducing manual inspections and streamlining production processes. The discussion underscores that while the system performs well, future improvements could involve expanding the dataset, exploring more advanced deep learning models like vision transformers and incorporating edge computing for enhanced real-time capabilities in industrial environments.

6 CONCLUSION

The fault detection system for machine parts, developed using deep learning, offers a robust and automated solution for visual quality inspection in manufacturing environments. By integrating TensorFlow, OpenCV and Flask, the system efficiently captures and processes images in real time, detects faults, and provides immediate feedback to operators. This approach significantly reduces the need for manual inspections, minimizes human error, and enhances overall production efficiency. The use of deep learning models, particularly with transfer learning, ensures accurate fault detection even with limited datasets. The system's ability to provide actionable insights and its scalability for various industrial applications make it a valuable tool for improving product quality and reducing downtime in production lines. Future enhancements can focus on continuous learning, adding more advanced image processing techniques and improving system adaptability to different manufacturing conditions.

REFERENCES

Hütten, N., Alves Gomes, M., Hölken, F., Andricevic, K., Meyes, R., & Meisen, T. (2024). Deep Learning for Automated Visual Inspection in Manufacturing and Maintenance: A Survey of Open-Access Papers. *Applied System Innovation*, 7(11), https://doi.org/10.3390/asi7010011.

Jahr, "Lighting in machine vision," in Handbook of Machine and Computer Vision: The Guide for Developers and Users. Weinheim, Germany: Wiley, 2017, pp. 63–178.

L.M. Xu, Z.Q. Yang, Z.H. Jiang, and Y. Chen, "Light source optimization for automatic visual inspection of piston surface defects," Int. J. Adv. Manuf. Technol., vol. 91, nos. 5–8, pp. 2245–2256, Jul. 2017.

M. Senthikumar, V. Palanisamy, and J. Jaya, "Metal surface defect detection using iterative thresholding technique," in Proc. 2nd Int. Conf. Current Trends Eng. Technol. (ICCTET), Jul. 2014, pp. 561–564.

Ravikumar, S., Ramachandran, K.I., & Sugumaran, V. (2011). Machine Learning Approach for Automated Visual Inspection of Machine Components. *Expert Systems with Applications*, 38(6), 3260–3266. https://doi.org/10.1016/j.eswa.2010.09.012.

Sabry, A.H., Ungku Amirulddin, U.A.B. (2024). A Review on Fault Detection and Diagnosis of Industrial Robots and Multi-axis Machines. *Results in Engineering*, 23, 102397.

Veillon, R. (2023). Automated Visual Inspection Deep Learning Case Study. *GSK Biologicals SA*, Presented at PDA J Pharm Sci Technol. https://doi.org/10.5731/pdajpst.2022.012796;contentReference[oaicite:1]{index=1}.

Weiher, K., Rieck, S., Pankrath, H., Beuss, F., Geist, M., Sender, J., & Fluegge, W. (2023). Automated Visual Inspection of Manufactured Parts Using Deep Convolutional Neural Networks and Transfer Learning. *Procedia CIRP*, 120, 858–863. https://doi.org/10.1016/j.procir.2023.09.088.

Z. Li, J. Zhang, T. Zhuang, and Q. Wang, "Metal surface defect detection based on MATLAB," in Proc. IEEE 3rd Adv. Inf. Technol., Electron. Autom. Control Conf. (IAEAC), Oct. 2018, pp. 2365–2371.

Advancement in Engineering and Science – Goyal et al. (Eds)
 ISBN: 978-1-041-31101-0

Drowsiness Alerting System using IR Sensor and Atmega328p with Rechargeable, Portable Design

Sunita Mane, Archana Ulmek, Supriya Salave, Yogita Gharge, Harsh Dhananjay Kamble, and Omkar Ravindra Kharat
Electronics and Telecommunication Engineering, Karmaveer Bhaurao Patil College of Engineering Satara, India

ABSTRACT: Driver drowsiness is a critical factor contributing to road accidents, accounting for nearly 20% of fatal crashes globally. Traditional safety systems such as lane departure warnings often respond too late to prevent collisions. To address this limitation, our project presents a real-time Drowsiness Alerting System using an IR sensor and ATmega328P microcontroller. The system detects prolonged eye closure—a primary indicator of drowsiness—and triggers immediate alerts via a buzzer or vibration motor. Designed to be portable, lightweight, and rechargeable, the device offers an affordable and efficient solution to enhance driver safety. By focusing on physiological behavior rather than vehicle dynamics, this system provides more direct and timely detection. Our approach aims to improve upon existing technologies by offering better accuracy, reduced power consumption, and user-friendly operation, ultimately helping to prevent fatigue-related accidents and ensure safer journeys.

Keywords: IR Sensor, ATMEGA 328P, TP4056 Charging Module, 3D Printed Enclosure

1 INTRODUCTION

In recent years, road safety has become a critical issue worldwide due to the increasing number of accidents caused by human error, among which driver drowsiness and fatigue have emerged as significant contributors. According to global traffic safety data, driver fatigue accounts for approximately 20% of all road accidents, many of which lead to serious injuries or fatalities. Unlike drunk driving or reckless behaviour, drowsiness is a silent threat that often goes unnoticed until it's too late. Long driving hours, night shifts, lack of sleep, monotonous routes, and physical exhaustion are all factors that lead to driver fatigue, especially among commercial vehicle operators. Conventional safety systems such as lane departure warning, steering pattern analysis and adaptive cruise control provide some level of protection. However, these are often reactive in nature and depend heavily on external vehicle movement patterns.

Moreover, such systems may fail to detect the internal state of the driver, especially in the early stages of drowsiness. This necessitates a more proactive, driver- focused detection system that works reliably across different environments and conditions. In recent years, road safety has become a critical issue worldwide due to the increasing number of accidents caused by human error, among which driver drowsiness and fatigue have emerged as significant contributors. According to global traffic safety data, driver fatigue accounts for approximately 20% of all road accidents, many of which lead to serious injuries or fatalities. Unlike drunk driving or reckless behavior, drowsiness is a silent threat that often goes unnoticed until it's too late. Long driving hours, night shifts, lack of sleep, monotonous routes, and physical exhaustion are all factors that lead to driver fatigue, especially among commercial vehicle operators. Conventional safety systems such as lane departure warning, steering pattern analysis, and adaptive cruise control provide some level of protection.

However, these are often reactive in nature and depend heavily on external vehicle movement patterns. Moreover, such systems may fail to detect the internal state of the driver, especially in the early stages of drowsiness. This necessitates a more proactive, driver-focused detection system that works reliably across different environments and conditions.

2 LITERATURE REVIEW

A Drowsiness Alerting System is a device or software that detects when a person, usually a driver, is feeling sleepy and alerts them to stay awake or take a break. Driver drowsiness is a leading cause of road accidents worldwide. To address this issue, researchers have developed various drowsiness detection and alerting systems. These systems primarily rely on physiological signals, behavioural analysis, or vehicular movement patterns. However, many existing solutions have limitations related to accuracy, cost, power consumption, and usability. This review explores prior research, existing solutions, and how our project builds upon them. Some systems analyse steering patterns, lane deviation, and pedal usage to detect drowsiness.

Studies by Kumar and Jha (2019) have shown that such methods provide indirect indicators of fatigue but may be influenced by road conditions and individual driving habits. Existing Solutions and Prior Work on Drowsiness Alerting Systems Several drowsiness detection and alerting systems have been developed, using different technologies to detect driver fatigue. These systems fall into three main categories: physiological monitoring, computer vision, and vehicle behaviour tracking. Physiological Signal Based Systems These systems use EEG (brain waves), ECG (heart rate), and EOG (eye movement) to detect drowsiness.

Example: Research by Zhao *et al.* (2021) shows that EEG-based drowsiness detection achieves over 90% accuracy. Commercial Example: Some high-end vehicles and medical wearables integrate pulse sensors or brainwave monitors. Limitations: These systems require direct contact with the skin, making them uncomfortable and expensive for everyday use. Computer Vision-Based Systems These systems use cameras and AI to monitor eye blinking, yawning, and head movement. Example: Wang *et al.* (2020) used deep learning models to classify drowsy vs. alert states with high accuracy in good lighting conditions.

Commercial Example: Tesla, Volvo, and Mercedes- Benz use in-car cameras for driver monitoring. Limitations: These systems struggle in low-light environments and with glasses or face coverings. Vehicle Behaviour Monitoring Systems These systems analyse steering patterns, lane deviation, and acceleration changes to estimate drowsiness. Example: Kumar and Jha (2019) reviewed multiple systems that track driving behaviour to predict fatigue. Commercial Example: Modern ADAS (Advanced Driver Assistance Systems) in vehicles like Toyota and BMW alert drivers if erratic steering is detected. Limitations: These systems react only after drowsy driving behaviour occurs, making them less effective for early prevention. 2. How Our Project Improves Existing Solutions while

DOI: 10.1201/9781003798514-62

prior work has advanced drowsiness detection, our Drowsiness Alerting System introduces several improvements: Lighter Weight: Unlike bulky EEG headsets, our system is compact and comfortable for extended use.

Efficient Battery: We optimize power consumption to extend battery life, unlike high energy demanding AI models. 3D-Modeled Protective Case: Our system integrates a custom protective case for durability and portability. Improved Design: We combine multiple detection methods (such as eye tracking + motion sensors) for better accuracy and reliability.

3 METHODOLOGY

The methodology behind the development of this drowsiness alerting system revolves around seamlessly integrating sensor-based monitoring, embedded processing, power management, and ergonomic design into a single compact unit. The core functionality is built around an IR sensor module that detects eye closure by analysing the intensity of reflected infrared light. This non-intrusive sensing approach enables accurate monitoring even in low- light conditions, making it highly suitable for night driving.

The drowsiness alerting system is developed using a combination of hardware and software components to ensure real-time monitoring, portability, and reliability. The system operates by detecting eye closure using an infrared (IR) sensor, which continuously monitors the driver's eye status. When the driver's eyes remain closed beyond a set threshold, it indicates drowsiness, prompting the system to trigger an alert. The IR sensor module acts as the primary input device, converting eye movement into electrical signals that are sent to the microcontroller. At the heart of the system is the ATmega328P microcontroller, which processes the sensor data using a simple threshold-based algorithm. If the duration of eye closure exceeds two seconds, the microcontroller activates one or more buzzers connected to it.

These buzzers serve as audible alerts to immediately draw the driver's attention and prevent a potential accident. The use of a vibration motor may also be included to provide a physical alert, making the system more effective, especially for drivers who may not respond to sound alone. The entire system is powered by a rechargeable lithium-ion battery, ensuring portability and uninterrupted operation during long drives. A TP4056 charging module is used to manage the battery safely, providing features like over-voltage protection and automatic charging cut off. A voltage regulator ensures the microcontroller and sensors receive a stable power supply.Figure1. Shows block diagram of given work.

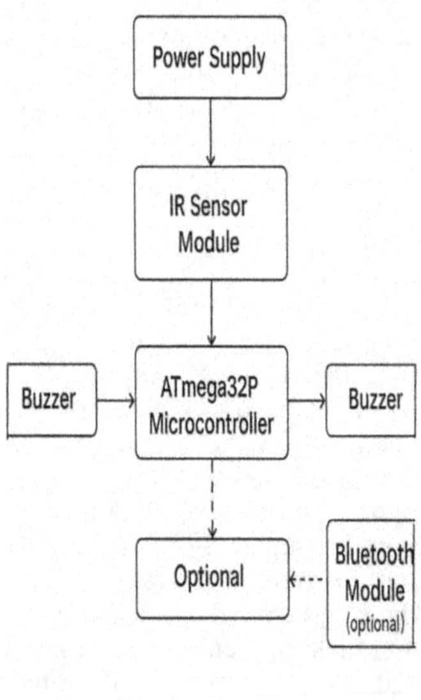

Figure 1. Block diagram.

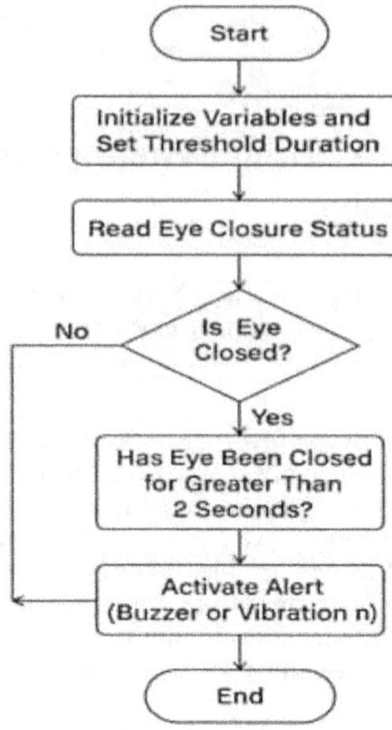

Figure 2. Flow chart.

Figure 2. Shows flowchart of proposed work as follows.

1. Start the system. 2. Initialize the ATmega328P microcontroller and configure all I/O pins. 3. Initialize the IR sensor for eye detection. 4. Set a predefined threshold time for eye closure. 5. Continuously read data from IR sensor to monitor the eye status. 6. If the eye is detected as open , reset the timer and continue monitoring. 7. If the eye is detected as closed , start the timer. 8. Check if the eye remains closed for more than the threshold time: 9. If yes, trigger the alert system (buzzer or vibration motor). 10. If no, continue checking until threshold is reached 11. Once the eyes open again, stop the alert and reset the system. 12. Repeat the process continuously to ensure real-time monitoring. 13. End.

3 RESULT

The development of this drowsiness alerting system incorporates multidisciplinary scientific principles from fields including human physiology, optical sensing, embedded systems, and ergonomics to ensure functionality, reliability, and user safety.

Physiological Basis of Drowsiness Detection: Scientific studies in neuroscience and human factors engineering reveal that prolonged eye closure (more than 1.5 to 2 seconds) is a strong physiological indicator of microsleep—a brief, involuntary sleep episode that occurs due to fatigue. Unlike blinking, which is momentary, microsleep leads to complete disengagement from the environment, making it a critical risk factor in driving. This project utilizes this biomarker by monitoring eye closure duration as a real- time measure of drowsiness, aligning with established sleep science literature.

Infrared Sensing and Optoelectronics: The IR sensor module exploits the principles of infrared reflectivity. Human eyes reflect less IR light when closed due to the eyelid's absorption characteristics. This change in reflectance intensity is detected by the photodiode in the sensor, producing a signal variation that can be quantified to distinguish between open and closed states. The wavelength selection (typically 850– 950 nm) is chosen to minimize ambient light interference and ensure optimal detection under both daylight and low-light conditions, leveraging the physics of optical absorption and reflection.

Embedded System Design and Signal Processing: From a computational standpoint, the ATmega328P microcontroller serves as a real-time processing unit. It operates using interrupt-driven routines to ensure minimal latency between signal acquisition and decision-making. The controller uses timer-based digital signal processing to evaluate the duration for which the eye remains closed. The decision threshold is not only programmable but can be dynamically stored and recalled from EEPROM memory, allowing for adaptability and long-term calibration—hallmarks of resilient embedded systems.

Human-Centered Ergonomics and Alert Mechanism: The alerting system employs sound (buzzer) and haptic (vibration motor) feedback based on studies in cognitive ergonomics and sensory response. Vibrations are effective for silent alerting in noise-prone environments, while sound provides direct auditory stimulation. The combination ensures fail-safe operation, addressing diverse driving scenarios and user sensitivities. The intensity and duration of these alerts are tuned to maximize reaction time without inducing panic or discomfort.

Power Management and Battery Chemistry: The 3.7V lithium-ion battery was selected due to its high energy density, lightweight profile, and rechargeability. The TP4056 module integrates constant-current/constant-voltage charging algorithms, complying with lithium battery charging standards to prevent thermal runaway—a known safety concern. Voltage regulation via AMS1117 ensures that all circuit components receive a stable operating voltage, reducing noise and improving performance reliability. These aspects are grounded in principles of electrochemistry and power electronics.

Environmental and Operational Stability: Thermal management, sensor stability, and circuit noise immunity were accounted for during hardware layout. IR sensors can drift under extreme temperature changes; thus, placement and casing materials were chosen to ensure thermal insulation and optical consistency. The algorithm is debounced and smoothed to filter out false triggers due to environmental noise or sudden lighting changes, based on statistical filtering techniques in embedded signal processing.

Sustainable Design Considerations: The use of a rechargeable battery, compact enclosure, and minimalistic hardware not only reduces electronic waste but also aligns with sustainability standards in electronics design. The system is designed to consume <100mA during peak operation and <10mA in sleep mode, enabling long operational life on a single charge—an application of green embedded engineering.

Scientific Rigor in Testing and Validation: The final system underwent black-box and white-box testing methodologies to validate functionality. Real- time simulations with timed eye closures were used to calculate true positive and false positive rates, ensuring scientific repeatability and precision. This empirical evaluation reinforces the scientific integrity of the system design and its readiness for deployment in safety-critical environments.

4 CONCLUSION

The drowsiness alerting system successfully addresses a critical issue of road safety by detecting driver fatigue in real-time. Using an IR sensor and ATmega328P microcontroller, the system monitors eye closure and provides immediate alerts through a buzzer or vibration motor. It is compact, portable, and powered by a rechargeable battery, making it suitable for everyday use in various vehicles. The system operates reliably under different lighting conditions and is simple to use without any intrusive equipment. Its cost-effectiveness and low power consumption make it ideal for both personal and commercial applications. The modular design allows for easy upgrades and future enhancements. The project also demonstrates effective use of embedded systems and sensor integration. Testing has shown accurate and timely detection of drowsiness. Overall, the system can significantly reduce the risk of fatigue-related accidents. It offers a practical, scalable solution to enhance driver safety.

REFERENCES

Abdul Qayyum Khan, Qudrat Ullah, Muhammad Sawar, Sufi Tabassum Gul and Naeem Iqbal, (2018). Transmission Line Fault Detection and Identification in an Interconnected Power Network using Phasor Measurement Units, *IFAC PapersOnLinein* 51-24, pp. 1356–1363.

Cui L., J. Huang, H. Wu, and B. Li, (2021). Real-time driver drowsiness detection with wearable single- channel EEG device and lightweight CNN, *Biomedical Signal Processing and Control,* vol. 68, pp. 102–110.

Kumar A. and S.K. Jha, (2019). Driver fatigue detection based on vehicle behavior: A review, International Journal of Vehicle Safety, vol. 11, no. 4, pp. 297– 315Mohini R. Gunjal , Snehal S. Gondkar and DipeshPerkins R. , M. A. Khan, and S. U. Rehman, (2021).A hybrid model for driver drowsiness detection using physiological and behavioral features, *IEEE Access*, vol. 9, pp. 99729 99741.

Pardeshi B., (2021).Transmission Line Fault Detection Using IoT, *Sanjivani College of Engineering*, Kopargoan, India, September 2021.

Venugopal Reddy Y., N. Sai deep, (2022).Transmission Line Fault Detection by Using Arduino, *Sathyabama Institute Of Science And Technology*, May 2022.

Wang H., T. Liu, and Y. Zhang, (2020). Driver drowsiness detection using deep convolutional neural networks based on video analysis, *Sensors*, vol. 20, no. 8, pp. 2236–2248.

Zhao X., Y. Li, Z. Yang, and M. Chen, (2021). EEG-based drowsiness detection using deep learning algorithms, *IEEE Transactions on Neural Systems and Rehabilitation Engineering*, vol. 29, pp. 1034–1042.

Advancement in Engineering and Science – Goyal et al. (Eds)

Blockchain-Based Secure Authentication for IoT Devices: A Decentralized Framework for the Constrained Edge

Samish N Kamble
CSE(IOT-CSBT), Annasaheb Dange College of Engineering & Technology Sangli, India
Electronics & Telecommunication, Yashoda Technical Campus Satara, India

Amruta U Mohite
Yashoda Technical Campus Satara, India

Milin D Patil
CSE(IOT-CSBT), Annasaheb Dange College of Engineering & Technology Sangli, India
Electronics & Telecommunication, Yashoda Technical Campus Satara, India

Mohini M Patil Rohit Kumawat
KIT's College of Engineering, Maharashtra, India

ABSTRACT: The rapid expansion of Internet of Things (IoT) ecosystems presents major security challenges, particularly in the domain of device authentication. Traditional methods, including centralized servers and PKI-based systems, face issues such as single points of failure, poor scalability, and high resource demands, making them impractical for constrained IoT environments. This paper introduces a robust block chain-based authentication framework designed specifically for heterogeneous IoT deployments. The framework leverages block chain features such as decentralization, immutability, and cryptographic integrity to securely anchor device identities and manage credentials. A lightweight Proof-of-Authority-based consensus and hybrid on-chain/off- chain architecture minimize latency and resource usage. Authentication is performed using efficient cryptographic mechanisms like Elliptic Curve.

Keywords: Block chain, Internet of things, Authentication

1 INTRODUCTION

The Internet of Things (IoT) is actually only the first taste of this hugely disruptive shift that's linking trillions upon trillions of other machines – like all kinds of sensors, actuators, wearables and industrial control systems – to each other and really changing the world around us. Earlier this month, a new projection from International Data Corporation predicted that by 2030, over 29 billion IoT devices will be connected globally. Yet the unprecedented level of network interconnectedness [6] presents extraordinary security challenges, particularly in the area of authentication. A core principle in cybersecurity is identity — and then making sure only known, authenticated identities are allowed on our networks.

Internet of Things (IoT) ecosystems are too complex and dynamic to depend on static or legacy authentication. I.e. centralized server based, go too PKI and PSK. While centralized server based approaches are susceptible to Single Point of Failure and Denial-of-Service (DoS) attacks, PKI based solutions add high computational and administrative overhead which is infeasible for resource constrained IoT nodes. Relying solely on PSK-based approaches is fundamentally insecure. Not only is the compromise of a single key able to jeopardize an entire network by itself, the logistical challenge of maintaining a big network with a regularly rotating secure key is an enormous task. Establishing these trust relationships, between devices manufactured by these different vendors, or devices managed across multiple domains using PKI, remains a difficult and expensive task even today.

Against the backdrop of these positive trends, blockchain technology rapidly emerges as a prime candidate for ensuring that IoT authentication is orders of magnitude more secure. Its defining features—in particular decentralization, immutability, transparency and cryptographic verification and smart contract automation—means it is an ideal solution for the needs of these distributed, untrusted and resource- constrained environments[1]. Combined the decentralized trust model and the tamper-proof distributed ledgers makes sure that you don't have to have the scary creepy centralized body to maintain clean identities and access trails. Even more decentralization and flexibility would be possible if we used smart contracts to enforce authentication policies from the ground up, with no central authority or governance able to overrule user needs. In this paper, we introduce a first of its kind, comprehensive, decentralized, blockchain technology powered, multimodal authentication framework for resource and environment [5] constrained IoT IoT ecosystem. To support necessary scalability and privacy, the framework uses a semi-centralized architecture pairing a permissioned blockchain used to anchor identities with a decentralized, quasi-real-time, third-party off-chain authentication. To further enhance energy efficiency and reduce latency, it operates by a proprietary Proof-of-Authority (PoA) consensus variant. The[15] framework includes device onboarding security best practices, identity lifecycle management with strong identity proofing capabilities, and a continuous security score that is baked in to the credentialing process. Regression testing threat vector identification and performance benchmarking, based in the real world IoT & Blockchain use case simulations, validate system integrity and real-world applicability.

2 RELATED WORK

2.1 *Literature survey*

Blockchain has recently become one of the most sought-after technologies that have the potential to power secure ecosystems of IoT devices. Final approval for any such projects had to take a back seat until a very successful first use case blew up public blockchain infrastructure with terrific, frenzied public interest and speculation. These early, widely adopted implementations were largely reliant on limitations including transaction latency,

DOI: 10.1201/9781003798514-63

gas cost, and computational overhead, all of which make them infeasible for resource-limited IoT environments [3]. As a countermeasure, recent blockchain studies have shifted focus to permissioned blockchains like Hyperledger Fabric and IOTA that offer improved scalability and are more aligned with enterprise IoT needs [4].

For instance, Dorri *et al.* In [5], the authors introduced a lightweight and IoT-oriented blockchain concept, in which distributed hash table (DHT) is used to reduce local storages' impact on devices. Yet their solution never went through formal security validation or stringent testing of performance in ultra-tight conditions. Ali *et al.* Despite development on Ethereum's integrated template, their input wasn't enough to totally curtail the costly and transient frustrating forbid characteristics of the reenacting validating design. Photo by Sharma *et al.* Their work was far less directly aimed at developing a more efficient form of authentication. While all of these studies pieces incredible groundwork, fill increasingly gaps in models that as far have included consensus mechanisms tailored for IoT, trust modeling based from device capabilities, performance assessment scalable to IoT, or identity lifecycle management. This gaps' analysis conducted collectively through the lens of the comprehensive and adaptable framework, as outlined in this paper and applied empirically here in practice under real-world operating conditions, seeks to build toward closing each of these gaps.

2.2 *System architecture and threat model*

The Figure shows the coupled, general object-oriented, layered architecture of the granular proposed framework. We describe in depth the general distributed architectural design of the system, which consists of three main layers, IoT Device Layer, Gateway/Fog Layer, and Blockchain Layer. At the device layer, such heterogeneous nodes like sensors or actuators which can be authenticated devices within ECC scheme are capable of generating ECC key pairs and starting authentication requests. Since these requests are orchestrated at the gateway/fog edge layer by these lightweight nodes, capable of storing device identities cached and doing off- chain order/verification/finding, massively reducing requested latency [7].

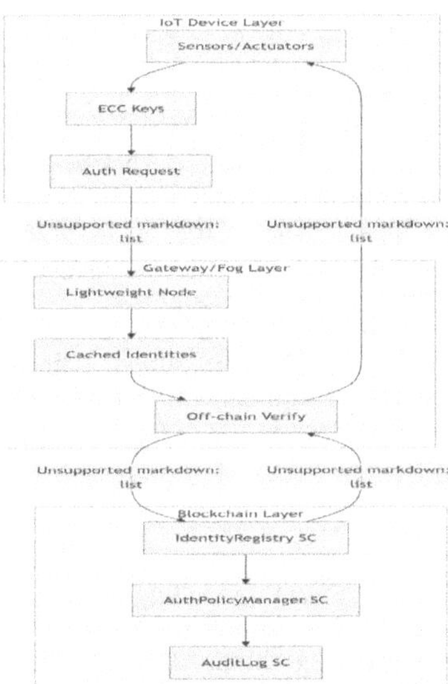

Figure 1. Layered architecture of the proposed authentication framework possess.

Cached identities are not deserving of concern that they need to be repeatedly validated versus the most current blockchain state, assuring prompt responses while the security of the underlying system is maintained. When decentralized off- chain verification needs to perform policy validation or revocation checks, the gateway communicates with smart contracts that are deployed to the blockchain layer. The blockchain layer [12] is where some of the most fascinating architectural components lie, including the Identity Registry smart contract, responsible for managing all the device credentials, the AuthPolicyManager, enforcing dynamic [14] authentication policies, and the AuditLog, stamping in all critical transactions. The resulting architecture scales and resource-efficiently enables low-latency, high-integrity authentication across constrained IoT environments.

2.3 *Hybrid On-Chain/Off-Chain Operation*

- **On-Chain:** Device identity registration, updates, revocation, policy updates, and high-value audit logging. High security, lower frequency.
- **Off-Chain:** The core authentication session execution between devices and gateways/devices. Uses messages whose validity can be efficiently verified against the latest on-chain state (e.g., checking revocation status via Merkle proofs). High frequency, optimized for speed and low overhead.

2.4 *Threat model*

We consider a powerful adversary capable of:

- Eavesdropping on network communication.
- Compromising some IoT devices or gateway nodes (not the majority).
- Launching MitM, replay, spoofing, and Sybil attacks.
- Attempting to tamper with authentication messages or logs.
- Launching DoS attacks against devices, gateways, or block chain nodes.

The blockchain network itself (consensus nodes) is assumed to be secure and Byzantine Fault Tolerant (BFT), as per the chosen permissioned blockchain's security model. The adversary cannot compromise the private keys of uncompromised legitimate devices.

2.5 *Proposed authentication framework*

Figure 2 End-to-end sequence of operations in our recommended agnostic blockchain-based IoT authentication framework. The on boarding experience is split into two phases—

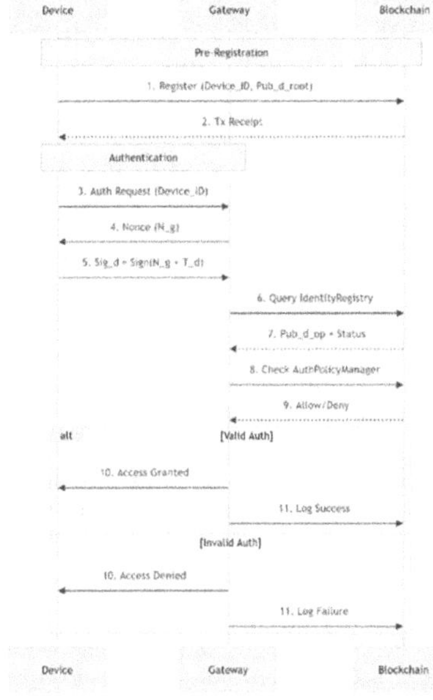

Figure 2. Sequence diagram of the authentication workflow.

Pre-Registration and Authentication. In this pre- registration phase, the IoT device transmits its identifier (Device_ID) and root public key (Pub_d_root) to the IoT gateway, which relays the registration request to the blockchain for validation and storage through the Identity Registry smart contract. Rest assured, you will receive a transaction receipt via email as proof of successful registration. In the device authentication phase, the device starts with sending an authentication request {84} to the gateway. The gateway then challenges the device with a nonce (N_g), which the device needs to sign, along with a current timestamp (T_d) using its current private key to generate a digital signature (Sig_d). The gateway then checks this signature by querying the block chain to get the device's up-to-date public key and revocation state. It does continuous security policy audits by enforcing policies through rules embedded into the AuthPolicy Manager smart contract.

Depending on whether the outcome was a grant or a denial of access, the appropriate action is executed and the response recorded on the AuditLog smart contract, ensuring a detailed, built-in auditability. This huge feedback loop interaction model forms a huge, distributed collective action purification circuit that is among the most powerful, hardest to hack, yet most rewarding detoxification engines as it provides valuable positive reinforcement authentication as such.

3 SECURITY ANALYSIS

3.1 *Formal Threat Modeling Using STRIDE*

To further evaluate the effectiveness of our proposed block chain based authentication framework, we use STRIDE threat modelling methodology with an in-depth analysis on the Spoofing—a predominant security issue in IoT networks because of the few physical and logical security measures found on edge devices. One form of spoofing is through fake device registration, when bad actors try to gain access to a system by registering fraudulent or cloned devices with false identity information. This is countered through manufacturer-anchored keys, in which each device [18] is provisioned with a unique root public key (Pub_d_root) during manufacturing, provisioned into secure hardware (TPMs/HSMs). In addition to the privacy- and integrity- preserving features of zero-knowledge cryptography, the Identity Registry.sol smart contract has an admin-governed on boarding policy that requires each registration request to be digitally signed by a trusted administrator. As such, only trusted, pre-vetted devices can be allowed on the blockchain network, thus preventing untrusted devices from accessing it.

A second major spoofing vector is using stolen operational keys, wherein an adversary obtains a legitimate device's private operational key (Priv_d_op) to impersonate them. To mitigate this, the framework encourages the use of ephemeral credentials with a built-in support for frequent key rotation via the update Operational Key() function, reducing the impact of key exposure. Moreover, the system supports real- time on-chain revocation through the revokeDevice() function, so if any credentials become compromised, they can be instantly invalidated through the network with an on-chain revocation action. Third, the risk of fake gateways masquerading as legitimate verifiers is tackled using mutual TLS authentication, where gateways possess blockchain- anchored certificates that devices can check before starting up any kind of communication. These multi-layered mitigations help ensure that devices will be able to securely authenticate the correct entities and protect against spoofing attempts, including in dynamic and decentralized IoT deployments.

3.2 *Performance evaluation*

(A) **Simulation Environment**

To validate the practical feasibility of the proposed framework, we conducted simulations and testbed deployments under constrained IoT settings:

- **Device Layer:** 100–1000 simulated devices using Contiki-NG and Zolertia Z1 motes (TI MSP430, 16-bit MCU, IEEE 802.15.4 radio).
- **Fog/Gateway Layer:** Ubuntu-based VMs (2 vCPU, 4GB RAM) simulating blockchain light clients and verifiers.
- **Blockchain Layer:** Hyperledger Fabric v2.5 on 4-node VM network (1 Orderer, 3 Peers) with Kafka-based ordering service. Chaincodes for identity and policy management were deployed.
- **Security Protocols:** ECDSA (secp256r1) used for digital signatures on devices. Gateways verified identities via cached and on-chain policy checks.

Table 1. Different parameter in observations.

Metric	Value/Observation
Authentication Latency	~350ms average E2E (Device → Gateway → Off-chain → On- chain). Pure off-chain: <100ms.
Energy Consumption	ECDSA added ~15-20% energy overhead. Radio remained dominant in total consumption.
Blockchain Transaction Time	Registration / Revocation: ~2.5s. Policy Query: ~1.2s (read-only).
Gateway Throughput	~50 auths/sec (off-chain). Reduced to ~15 auths/sec with on-chain policy checks.
Storage Overhead	On-device: <100 bytes (ECC keys). On-chain: ~500 bytes/device. Gateway cache: ~10KB.

(B) **Discussion**

- This performance evaluation reassures that although more security layers are added, the proposed framework is still practical for real-world deployment in edge IoT environments.
- Authentication Latency remains within tolerable bounds for non-critical and delay-tolerant IoT applications such as smart agriculture, utility metering, and environmental sensing.
- Caching at the gateway layer significantly improves latency and throughput by reducing dependence on real- time blockchain queries.
- Energy Impact is observable but acceptable considering the trade-off for cryptographic integrity and authentication guarantees.
- Scalability is inherently horizontal. Until now, adding gateways and peer nodes supports linear scaling with no lessening of authentication performance or blockc consensus overhead.

4 CONCLUSION

The STRIDE-based threat modelling demonstrates that the proposed blockchain-based authentication scheme effectively mitigates severe spoofing threats through the integration of hardware-rooted trust anchors, smart contract-governed registration, and mutual authentication processes. The included performance evaluation shows that with careful optimizations, most notably caching and lightweight consensus, the framework provides an efficient and secure authentication solution for both large- and small-scale IoT deployments.

- Properties of the smart contracts and protocol interactions.
- Broader Attack Surface: Further analysis of attacks targeting the specific consensus mechanism or smart contract vulnerabilities.
- Large-Scale Deployment: Testing on real-world, large-scale IoT testbeds across diverse applications (smart grid, vehicular networks).

ACKNOWLEDGEMENT

The authors are gratefully to students, staff, and authority of Respective department and Institutes for their cooperation in the research.

REFERENCES

[1] Statista Research Department, (2030). Internet of Things (IoT) connected devices worldwide 2019–2030, *Statista*. [Online]. Available: https://www.statista.com/

[2] R. Roman, J. Lopez, and M. Mambo, (2018). Mobile edge computing, fog *et al.*: A survey and analysis of security threats and challenges, *Future Generation Computer Systems*, vol. 78, pp. 680–698.

[3] K. Christidis and M. Devetsikiotis, (2016). Blockchains and smart contracts for the internet of things, *IEEE Access*, vol. 4, pp. 2292–2303.

[4] E. Androulaki *et al.*, (2018). Hyperledger Fabric: A distributed operating system for permissioned blockchains, in Proc. 13th EuroSys Conf, pp. 1–15.

[5] A. Dorri, S.S. Kanhere, R. Jurdak, and P. Gauravaram, (2017). Blockchain for IoT security and privacy: The case study of a smart home, in *Proc. IEEE PerCom Workshops*, pp. 618–623.

[6] M.S. Ali, K. Dolui, and F. Antonelli, (2017). IoT data privacy via blockchains and IPFS, in *Proc. ACM Workshop on Blockchain, Cryptocurrencies and Contracts* (BCC '17), pp. 55–60.

[7] P.K. Sharma, M.Y. Chen, and J.H. Park, (2018). A software defined fog node based distributed blockchain cloud architecture for IoT, *IEEE Access*, vol. 6, pp. 115–124.

[8] N. Kshetri, (2017). Can blockchain strengthen the Internet of Things (IoT)?, *IT Professional,* vol. 19, no. 4, pp. 68–72.

[9] M.T. Hammi, B. Hammi, P. Bellot, and A. Serhrouchni, (2018). Bubbles of Trust: A decentralized blockchain-based authentication system for IoT, *Computers & Security*, vol. 78, pp. 126–142.

[10] A. Reyna, C. Martín, J. Chen, E. Soler, and M. Díaz, (2018). On blockchain and its integration with IoT: Challenges and opportunities, *Future Generation Computer Systems*, vol. 88, pp. 173–190.

[11] Ouaddah, H. Mousannif, A.A. Elkalam, and A.A. Ouahman, (2017). Access control in the Internet of Things: Big challenges and new opportunities, *Computer Networks*, vol. 112, pp. 237–262.

[12] Z. Zheng, S. Xie, H. Dai, X. Chen, and H. Wang, (2017). An overview of blockchain technology: Architecture, consensus, and future trends, in *Proc. IEEE Int. Congr. on Big Data*, pp. 557–564.

[13] Y. Zhang, J. Wen, (2011). An IoT electric business model based on the protocol of bitcoin, in Proc. 18th Int. Conf. on Industrial Engineering and Engineering Management, pp. 532–536.

[14] X. Liang, J. Zhao, S. Shetty, and D. Li, (2017). Towards data assurance and resilience in IoT using blockchain, in *Proc. IEEE MILCOM*, pp. 261–266.

[15] L. Panarello, A. Tapas, G. Merlino, F. Longo, and A. Puliafito, (2018). Blockchain and IoT integration: A systematic survey, *Sensors,* vol. 18, no. 8, p. 2575.

[16] S. Nakamoto, Bitcoin: A peer-to-peer electronic cash system, (2008). [Online]. Available: https://bitcoin.org/bitcoin.pdf

[17] A. Samaniego and C. Deters, (2015). Hosting virtual machine-based containers in the cloud: A performance study of Docker vs. Virtual Machines, in *Proc. IEEE Int. Conf. on Cloud Engineering*, pp. 583–588.

[18] G. Wood, Ethereum: A secure decentralised generalised transaction ledger, *Ethereum Project Yellow Paper*.

[19] H. Yu, P. Zhang, and D. Chen, A blockchain-based credit evaluation system for IoT devices, *IEEE Access*, vol. 7, pp. 60190–60200.

[20] R. Lu, X. Liang, X. Li, X. Lin, and X. Shen, EPPA: An efficient and privacy-preserving aggregation scheme for secure smart grid communications, *IEEE Trans. Parallel Distrib. Syst.*, vol. 23, no. 9, pp. 1621–1631, Sep. 2012.

[21] Woods, D.D. and E. Hollnagel. (2012). *Joint cognitive systems.* Boca Raton: CRC Press/Taylor & Francis.

[22] Wiens, J.A. 2005. *Avian community ecology: An iconoclastic view. In Perspectives in ornithology*, ed. A. H. Brush, and G. A. Clark, 355–403. Cambridge: Cambridge Univ. Press.

[23] Terborgh, J. 2009. *Preservation of natural diversity. BioScience.* 24:715–22.

[24] Alotaibi, A.R. and Mishra, A.V. (2015). Global and regional volatility spillovers to GCC stock markets. Int. *Economic. Modelling.* 45(3):38–49.

[25] Akhtaruzzaman, M., Boubaker, S., and Sensoy, A. (2021). Financial contagion during COVID–19 crisis. Int. Financ. Res. Lett. 38(2):101604–101609.

[26] Testa, B. and L.B. Kier. 2013. Emergence and dissolvence in the self-organisation of complex systems. *Entropy* 2, no. 1: 1–25. http://www.mdpi.org/entropy/papers/e2010001.pdf.

[27] Schwartz, G.J. 2012. *Multiwavelength analyses of classical carbon-oxygen novae.* PhD diss., Arizona State Univ.

[28] O'Guinn, T.C. 2014. *Touching greatness. Paper presented at the annual meeting of the American Psychological Association*, New York.

[29] Adamic, L.A. and B.A. Huberman. 2006. The nature of markets in the World Wide Web. Working paper, *Xerox Palo Alto Research Center.* http://www.parc.xerox.com/istl/groups/iea/www/webmarket s.html (accessed March 12).

[30] Aidy Ali, Kannan Rassiah, M.M.H Megat Ahmada. (2021). The effect of stacking sequence of woven bamboo on mechanical behaviour of fiber reinforced composites. *Journal of Southwest 592* Jiaotong University / Vol.56 No.2.

[31] Anigol, M.N.B., Anil, S.P. (2015). Study of the effect of various fillers on mechanical properties of carbon-epoxy composites. *Int. Res. J. Eng. Technol.* 02(03), 798–802.

[32] Biswasa, S., Shahinura, S., Hasana, M., Ahsan, Q. (2015). Physical, mechanical and thermal properties of jute and bamboo fibre reinforced unidirectional epoxy composites. *Procedia Eng.* 105, 933– 939

Advancement in Engineering and Science – Goyal et al. (Eds)
© 2026 The Author(s), ISBN: 978-1-041-31101-0

Exploration of Digital Behaviour and its Influence on Health Outcomes among B-School Students

Aasawari Neeraj Nalgundwar
Research Scholar, D Y Patil School of Medicine and Assistant Professor-Healthcare, Prin. L.N. Welingkar Institute of Management

Sumedha Milind Joshi
Professor and Head, Department of Community Medicine, D Y Patil School of Medicine

Deepa Haritosh Velankar
Professor, Department of Community Medicine, D Y Patil School of Medicine

ABSTRACT: Introduction: Students today use the internet extensively for personal and professional purposes. This increased digital exposure can lead to Internet addiction thereby impacting health outcomes. Business School (B-school students) are the future corporate workforce and need to be physically and mentally healthy to deliver productively. Hence this study was undertaken to explore their digital behaviour and its impact on physical and mental health.

Methods: A cross-sectional exploratory study was designed for B-school students who were recruited using convenience sampling. Questionnaire included two scales (Young's Internet addiction test and DASS-2 scale) and questions regarding physical health and sleep patterns.

Results: Of 343 students, more than 30% had moderate to severe levels of Internet addiction. Extremely severe anxiety was seen among 34.7% of students. Severe depression was observed in 15.5%, with one-fourth experiencing moderate level of stress. Internet addiction was found to have a significant impact on depression, stress and anxiety. More than two-thirds (69.9%) experienced difficulty in sleep. The overall physical activity was low. Many reported experiencing mild to moderate muscular pain and headaches.

Conclusion: The study showed that Internet addiction is common among B-school students. Internet addiction was found to have significant impact on depression, stress and anxiety. Hence, regular counselling and awareness sessions of B-school students regarding optimum usage of digital tools with interventions for mental and physical health are essential and can be included in curriculum. This will prepare them for corporate industry enabling valuable contributions.

Keywords: Digital Behaviour, Internet addiction, Mental Health, Physical Health

1 INTRODUCTION

Technology forms an essential component for the growth of any sector. Hence it is the need of the hour for all individuals to adopt digital technology for their growth. Youth too have embraced this digital trend. Over the years there has been a remarkable transformation in the online behavior of youth. Covid pandemic further accentuated and boosted the need for online presence. Young adults and students today use the internet extensively for personal as well as professional purposes.

The academic usage of digital platforms has increased, and so has the usage of social media too.

There is a great influence of social media, and a considerable amount of time is spent browsing online content daily. Spending long hours on the internet has become a routine trend and has got incorporated in the daily schedule of these young students.

This online behaviour can result in varying degrees of Internet addiction which has been observed by numerous studies across the world. This can eventually lead to several harmful effects on the health of individuals. The impact can be observed on physical as well as mental health outcomes (Singh *et al.*, 2023; Nazari *et al.*, 2023; Lebny *et al.*, Gupta *et al.*, 2018, O'reilly M *et al.*,2018, Huang CJC 2017, Hanprathet N *et al.*, 2015).

The focus of this study is on young Business School (B-school students). These young students of today will be the future corporate workforce. They will determine the productivity of the corporate industry.

The corporate industry demands an agile, resilient and healthy workforce who can perform effectively in high-pressure working scenarios. This workforce needs to adapt to the daily stress and contribute to their maximum potential for their growth as well as the growth of their organizations. This will be possible only if the workforce is physically and mentally healthy. As online behaviour has an impact on the physical and mental health outcomes, it is necessary to explore this digital behaviour in B-school students. Though numerous studies have been conducted in general student populations, specific studies need to be conducted on B-school students to comprehend this issue further to enable timely corrective actions.

Thus, this study was undertaken with the objective of studying the digital behaviour among B-school students and to explore the impact of digital behaviour on their physical and mental health.

2 REVIEW OF LITERATURE

Internet addiction has been defined as "excessive or poorly controlled preoccupations, urges or behaviors regarding computer use and internet access that lead to impairment or distress." (Fathi *et al.*, 2020; Gupta *et al.*, 2018) The online network has indeed brought people closer, however it has led to people turning excessively dependent on it, leading to various challenges related to this rampant use (Yadav *et al.*, 2013).

Social media platforms are gaining popularity as they facilitate better communication, provide access to recent updates

DOI: 10.1201/9781003798514-64

around the world and are a source of global information. (Sujarwoto *et al.*, 2023; Singh *et al.*, 2023; Anderson, 2018; Carr,2015; Nayaka, 2015). Youth are avid users of platforms such as Instagram, Twitter, Facebook and WhatsApp (Hemayatkhah, 2021).

The benefits of the internet are however associated with various problems viz. physical, mental and social (Sujarwoto *et al.*, 2023; Singh *et al.*, 2023; Hussain 2021; Haand, 2020; Schou, 2014). Increased usage can eventually lead to Internet addiction among the users (Nazari *et al.*, 2023; Hussain, 2020). In addition, recent studies have observed that increased availability of affordable devices to access the internet, especially handheld devices such as mobiles (smartphones) and tablets, coupled with improved high-speed Wi-Fi and internet facilities have further exacerbated the emerging trend of Internet addiction. (Gupta *et al.*, 2018; Austin, 2018; Goel, 2013).

Numerous studies have been conducted among various school and university students to study the trends and consequences of Internet addiction. Studies by various researchers have highlighted that Internet addiction, including social media addiction, can eventually lead to mental health problems such depression, along with cases of anxiety as well as stress (Singh *et al.*, 2023; Nazari *et al.*, 2023; Sujarwoto *et al.*, 2023; Singh *et al.*, 2023; Cunningham *et al.*, 2021; Chen *et al.*, 2020; Lebni *et al.*, 2020; Hou *et al.*, 2019; Gupta *et al.*, 2018; O'reilly *et al.*, 2018; Tang and Koh, 2017; Huang, 2017; Zadra *et al.*, 2016; Richards *et al.*, 2015; Al-Menayes, 2015; Hanprathet *et al.*, 2015).

A thorough review of literature was conducted in our study among students across various geographies. In a study conducted by Sujarwoto *et al.* (2023) in Indonesian University students, addiction to social media was associated with the risk of mild degree of depression. In a Study which was conducted by Gupta *et al.* (2018) within undergraduate college students in India, 25% prevalence of Internet addiction was observed, with depression, anxiety levels and also stress as independent indicators. Similarly, in research conducted by Nazari *et al.* (2023) among Iranian University students it was noted that social media use had a direct relationship with mental health and was significantly associated with higher Depression, Anxiety and Stress Scale (DASS21) scores.

Results showing association of addiction of Internet with mental health issues including depression and anxiety levels were also reported by studies conducted by Lebni *et al.* (2020), Tang and Koh (2017), Yadav *et al.* (2013) and Goel D *et al.* (2013).

In research conducted by Chen I H *et al.* (2020) in Hongkong University students, it was noted that the initial level of problematic use of smartphone or internet led to an increase in the psychological distress among students. As indicated in the study conducted among college students in Singapore by Tangand Koh (2017), it was evident that students with this addiction were vulnerable for other behaviour addiction as well. Study by Hanprathet *et al.* (2015) has also reported an increased incidence of sleep disturbances among students. Studies have been conducted focusing on specific social media platforms too. In research conducted in Thai high school students by Hanprathet *et al.* (2015), it was observed that addiction of platforms such as Facebook in high school students was associated with various mental health issues, anxiety, difficulties in sleep, and severe levels of depression.

Literature reviews too have been conducted on this significant issue of Internet addiction by researchers. In literature reviews regarding the effect of social media on the health status of children and young people by Richards *et al.* (2015) it was noted that there was a great impact of social media on mental health, and especially for self-esteem and well-being. Depression was observed in children and youth extensively using social media such as Facebook. (Richards *et al.*, 2015). Meta analysis by Cunningham *et al.* (2021) considered the nature of multiple dimensions of Social Networking sites. Findings revealed that symptoms of depression had a weak but significant association with time spent using Social Networking Sites. However, it was seen that there was moderate association of depression to the use of various related to social networking.

Studies have observed the effect of Internet addiction on personality disorders. According to research conducted by Zadra S *et al.* (2016) in a general population sample, participants with Internet addiction showed high prevalence of personality disorder with a significant association. Academic performance can get affected too due to Internet addiction. In a study by Velagapaly *et al.* (2023) it was observed that there was a significant relation between the academic performance of students and their mental health. Results from a study carried out by Al-Menayes (2015) among undergraduate students in Kuwait revealed that addiction of various social media sites was a negative predictor of academic success, showing the grave consequence for productivity. Similar findings were observed in the research done by Hou *et al.* (2019) among college students. Results of their study demonstrated that the intervention conducted on students was effective in decreasing social media addiction and improving their mental health and academic performance. Studies are undertaken among students and youth as they are more prone to succumb to temptations of online tools and resulting addiction (Lebni *et al.*, 2020).

Some research studies have been conducted to study Internet addiction among B-school students too. However, they are not extensive in nature, and some have shown mixed results. In the study conducted by Satpathy and Ali (2020) in final year management students in India, the prevalence of depression was 43%. However, in study by Singh *et al.* (2023) among post-graduate management students in India it was observed that students were not prone to smartphone addiction. Further studies among sub-groups of students are needed to provide a further in-depth understanding.

A significant parameter of any person's overall health and happiness is his/her mental health. The status of mental health will also determine the level of productivity and performance of the person (Velagapaly, 2023 and Galderisi *et al.*, 2015). Thus, the mental health status of young people will also determine the level of productivity of the entire society. B-school students are the future workforce of the corporate world; hence their productivity will enhance the performance of the industry. Few studies have been conducted specifically on B-school students to understand this significant issue of Internet addiction. Extensive studies need to be conducted to understand the online behaviour of B-school students and what impact it has on the health status of these students. Hence this study holds a significant relevance in today's scenario.

3 RESEARCH METHODOLOGY

3.1 *Study design*

The study was a cross-sectional exploratory study with an intent to explore the influence of digital behaviour on physical and mental health of students. The target population was B-school students. The participants were recruited using convenience sampling as it enabled reaching out to maximum students during the study period. B-school students were reached out through online means such as email and WhatsApp.

3.2 *Data collection*

An extensive pre-tested and semi-structured questionnaire of approximately sixty questions was designed to collect data required for assessment of two scale scores. The first scale used was the Young's Internet Addiction test (IAT). This scale consists of twenty items related to internet usage and categorises Internet addiction in Mild, Moderate and Severe categories.

The second scale used was the Depression Anxiety Stress Scale [DASS-21 scale] (Young, 2017, Loviband and Loviband, 1995). This comprises of three scales which are self-reported. They measure the states of depression as well as anxiety and stress among the respondents. This scale comprises of twenty-one items.

In addition to the two scales the questionnaire included relevant questions pertaining to physical health and sleep patterns. These were custom-designed for the study. The questions included were a combination of open-ended and close-ended questions with Likert scale.

The questionnaire was circulated through Google forms and was pre-tested on twenty students, following which few grammatical changes were incorporated for better understanding of the participants.

3.3 *Inclusion criteria*

Students willing to participate were required to register their consent, after which the survey was administered by means of a Google form. Responses were collected for a duration of two months. Responses from only those students who completed the entire questionnaire were included for final analysis.

3.4 *Statistical analysis*

Responses were analysed descriptively. Data from completed questionnaires was included and incomplete data was discarded. Categorical variables were identified and analysed using frequencies and percentages, while continuous variables were identified and analysed using mean and standard deviation. Corelation between continuous variables was explored using Pearson's r, and two-tailed statistical significance was considered at $p<0.05$. Data was analysed using Microsoft Excel 365 and PSPP (version 2.0.0-g5b54d1).

3.5 *Limitations*

A cross-sectional design was adopted as the scope was to include maximum number of B-school students in the required time frame using convenience sampling. Further studies using randomisation techniques in addition to longitudinal studies for cause-effect analysis can strengthen the research findings in this area.

4 RESULTS

4.1 *Demographics*

The study was conducted on Business School (B-school) students. Of the 354 students who participated, 343 completed the survey and were included in the final analysis and were either in the first or second year of the course. Of the 343 students included in the final analysis, more than half (227, 66.2%) were between 20-25 years of age (Table 1).

Table 1. Participant characteristics.

Characteristic	Categories	Frequency (n)	Percentage
Age	20-25	227	66.2%
	25-30	113	32.9%
	30-35	3	0.9%
Year of study	1st	168	49.0%
	2nd	175	51.0%

4.2 *Online Behaviour*

The mean (standard deviation [SD]) total score as per Young's Internet Addiction Test (IAT) was 42.55 (15.64). More than 30% of students belonged in moderate-severe categories (Table 2). Almost half (46.6%) of the students reported spending 6-8 hours per day using digital devices (smartphones, laptops, tablets, etc.) for personal use excluding academic work. The majority (75.8%) reported not using any tracker apps, to help monitor screen time. Among other online activities, social media had the maximum engagement (Figure 1).

Table 2. Internet usage and addiction.

Characteristic	Categories	Frequency (n)	Percentage
IAT total score	Mean (SD)	42.55 (15.64)	
	Median (min-max)	42 (6-100)	42
	Mode		44
IAT category	Average	235	68.5%
	Moderate	103	30.0%
	Severe	5	1.5%
Hours per day spent using digital devices (excluding academic work)	0-2 hours	31	9.0%
	3-5 hours	139	40.5%
	6-8 hours	160	46.6%
	9+ hours	13	3.8%
Use of apps to track your screen time	No	260	75.8%
	Yes	83	24.2%
	Inbuilt apps	41	12.0%
	Not specified	24	7.0%
	Not used	260	75.8%
	Other apps from app stores	12	3.5%
	Social media app time-trackers	6	1.7%
Use of digital devices*	Social media	301	87.8%
	Video streaming (e.g., Netflix, YouTube)	292	85.1%
	Online gaming,	168	49.0%
	Online news and information browsing	271	79.0%
	Online learning and academic work	242	70.6%
	Email communication	147	42.9%

*Multiple choices available for each participant
IAT, Young's Internet Addiction Test

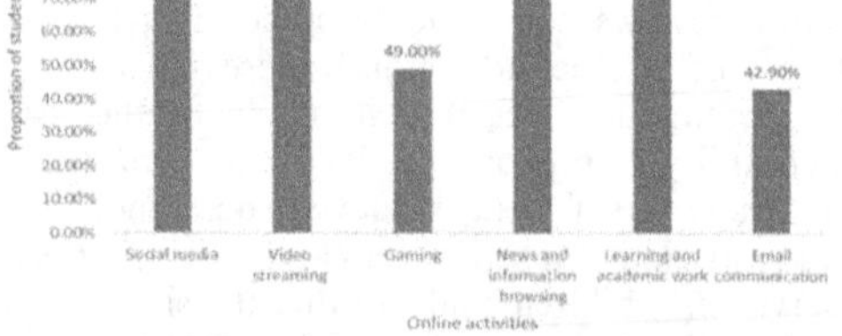

Figure 1. Activities engaged while using digital devices.

4.3 *Sleep patterns*

An average of eight hours or more of sleep daily was observed only in 6.12% of students. Almost half (49.27%) of the students surveyed reported having not more than 6 hours of sleep every night, with 69.97% (240/343) having difficulty in falling asleep. Only approximately one-third (34.4%) woke up feeling well rested in the morning (Table 3).

Table 3. Sleep patterns.

Characteristic	Categories	Frequency (n)	Percentage
	Mean (SD)	5.96 (1.13)	
	Median (min-max)	6 (4-10)	
	Mode	6	
Number of hours of sleep daily	4	20	5.8%
	5	63	18.4%
	6	86	25.1%
	7	47	13.7%
	8	17	5.0%
	9	3	0.9%
	10	1	0.3%
Experience difficulty in falling asleep	Never	20	5.8%
	Rarely	83	24.2%
	Sometimes	155	45.2%
	Often	81	23.6%
	Always	4	1.2%
Wake up feeling well-rested	Never	9	2.6%
	Rarely	66	19.2%
	Sometimes	150	43.7%
	Often	104	30.3%
	Always	14	4.1%

4.4 *Depression, Anxiety and Stress*

According to the DASS-21 scoring, maximum (42.0%) students were found to have moderate depression. Severe depression was seen among 15.5% (Table 4). Of the 343 students, more than 85% students faced anxiety, with most (34.7%) categorized as "extremely severe anxiety". A moderate level of stress was experienced by one-fourth (25.9%).

Table 4. Classification by DASS-21 scores.

Characteristic	Categories	Frequency (n)	Percentage
Depression categories	Normal	64	18.7%
	Mild	50	14.6%
	Moderate	144	42.0%
	Severe	53	15.5%
	Extremely Severe	32	9.3%
Anxiety category	Normal	47	13.7%
	Mild	17	5.00%
	Moderate	93	27.1%
	Severe	67	19.5%
	Extremely Severe	119	34.7%
Stress category	Normal	143	41.7%
	Mild	73	21.3%
	Moderate	89	25.9%
	Severe	29	8.5%
	Extremely Severe	9	2.6%

Physical health and nutrition

On a scale of 1-5 (where 1 is active and 5 is sedentary), approximately 62.39% of students showed 3-5, or moderate-very low physical activity or exercise daily; and 71.4% also did not belong to any regular fitness program (gym, sports, yoga etc.). During prolonged periods of digital media use 58.6% of students rarely or never took breaks, even for mild movement exercises. Only 16.9% of students engaged in various physical activities of vigorous intensity (e.g., running, swimming) for at least 20 minutes more than 4 times per week. In relation to nutrition habits, 48.1% reported poor nutritive intake, with more reliance of fast/processed foods. The other half reported having a usually balanced meal, with occasional indulgence.

Table 5. Details of physical health.

Characteristic	Categories	Frequency (n)	Percentage
How would you rate your physical health	Poor	12	3.5%
	Fair	153	44.6%
	Good	152	44.3%
	Excellent	26	7.6%
Level of physical activity (1 being active and 5 being sedentary)	1	23	6.7%
	2	106	30.9%
	3	144	42.0%
	4	65	19.0%
	5	5	1.5%
Frequency of taking breaks during prolonged periods of digital media use	Every hour	17	5.0%
	Every 2-3 hours	125	36.4%
	Rarely	186	54.2%
	Never	15	4.4%
Nutrition habits	Irregular eating patterns or reliance on processed/fast foods	145	42.3%
	Poor nutrition, with limited intake of fruits, vegetables, and balanced meals	19	5.5%
	Mostly healthy but with occasional indulgences	156	45.5%
	Well-balanced diet with a variety of vegetables, fruits, grains and proteins	23	6.7%
On average, how many days per week do you engage in physical activity of vigorous intensity (e.g., running, swimming) for at least 20 minutes?	0 to 3 days	91	26.5%
	4 or more days	58	16.9%
	Not specified	194	56.6%
Participation in fitness program (gym, sports, yoga etc.)	Yes	98	28.6%
	No	245	71.4%

4.5 *Management of pain and discomfort*

Most students reported experiencing mild-moderate levels of pain or discomfort of various types, with prolonged use of digital media (Figure 2). Apart from these, palpitations, stomachache and muscular pain were also reported by 1 (0.3%) student each. Common methods of managing physical discomfort included stretching exercises (77.3%), followed by massage and physical therapy (51.9%) and Heat or cold therapy (40.2%). A substantial proportion (54.50%) of students resorted to pain medication for relief of any physical complaints (Table 6).

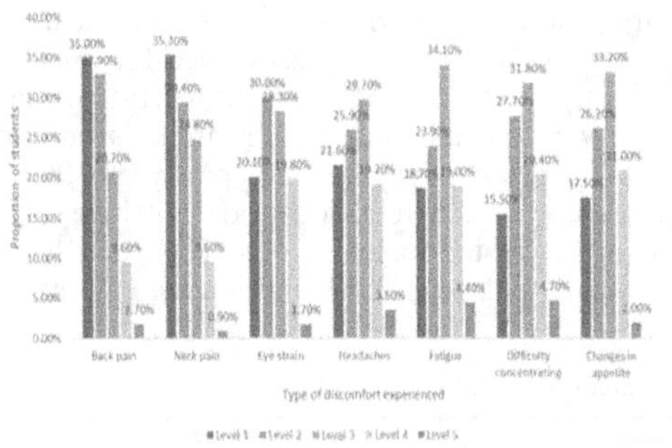

Figure 2. Pain or discomfort associated with use of digital media.

Table 6. Preferences for management of pain or discomfort.

Characteristic	Categories	Frequency (n)	Percentage
Methods to manage any pain or discomfort*	Stretching exercises	265	77.3%
	Heat or cold therapy	138	40.2%
	Massage or physical therapy	178	51.9%
	Pain medication	187	54.5%
	Other	6	1.7%

*Multiple choices available for each participant

4.6 *Analysis of correlation*

A moderate positive correlation (r=0.564) was observed between Internet addiction and Stress, with statistical significance at p value 0.000. A significant positive correlation was also noted between IAT scores vs Depression (r=0.468) and Anxiety (r=0.487) respectively. Results of Chi-Square tests revealed significant association between level of physical activity and DASS-21 categories.

5 DISCUSSION

The study was a cross-sectional questionnaire-based study which analyzed the impact of digital behaviour on physical and mental health of students of B-school students. Of 343 students included, more than 30% had moderate to severe levels of Internet addiction as per Young's IAT scale. Extremely severe anxiety among 34.7% of students was a noteworthy finding as per the DASS-21 scores. Severe depression was prevalent in 15.5%, with one-fourth experiencing moderate level of stress. Internet addiction was found to have a statistically significant impact on levels of depression, stress as well as anxiety. The findings were consistent with results of various studies conducted among youth including students, (Nazari *et al.*,2023; Velagapaly *et al.*,2023, Sujarwoto *et al.*, 2023; Lebny *et al.*,2020; Gupta *et al.*, 2018; Yadav *et al.*, 2013; Goel*et al.*,2013 and Tang and Koh, 2017 to name a few.

However, some studies have also shown a positive effect of social media on mental health status. This may be because these studies were conducted before the Covid pandemic and thus prior to the significant change in online behaviour of youth post-pandemic (Sujarwoto *et al.*, 2023; Glaser *et al.*, 2018; Nabi *et al.*, 2013; Campisi *et al.* 2015).

Nearly half (46.6%) of the students reported spending 6-8 hours using digital media per day, apart from academics, and a lack of screen time monitoring using apps was noted by of 75.8%. This study also explored sleep disorders among students. A substantial number, more than two-thirds (69.97%) experienced difficulty in falling asleep. Sleep disorders such as insomnia have been reported in students with Social Media addiction by Hanprathet *et al.* (2015) in their study conducted among Thai students.

The overall physical activity of the students in this study was much lower than recommended, with students not even taking breaks for mild exercise. With this prolonged use of digital media, most students reported experiencing mild to moderate levels of pain or discomfort of various types, such as muscular pain, headaches, fatigues and also changes in appetite. A substantial proportion (54.5%) turned to pain medication for relief from physical discomfort. This shows the need to encourage students to be active physically and be involved in any form of physical exercise on a regular basis. The significant association between the level of physical activity and DASS-21 categories highlights the importance of physical exercise in boosting mental health. A study conducted by Bongers *et al.* (2006) also highlighted the role of psychological factors on physical health symptoms. Hence a holistic approach to boost physical as well as mental health needs to be considered.

The scope of this study was to study the influence of digital behaviour on health outcomes. There are various other factors which can influence the mental health of students such as substance addictions, family-related issues etc. These can be explored in depth in future studies to study the combined impact of all such factors. Such studies will help in formulating better solutions to this significant issue. Also, longitudinal and interventional studies can be conducted where students can be provided with various awareness sessions regarding digital behavior and the importance of mental and physical health. They can be introduced to various beneficial interventions to boost mental and physical heath. Impact study can be undertaken to study the efficacy of such interventions. These initiatives will help in creating better academic programmes for students.

6 CONCLUSION

The study showed that Internet addiction is common among B-school students, with more than 30% showing moderate to severe levels of Internet addiction. Extremely severe anxiety among almost one-third of students was a noteworthy finding. Severe depression was prevalent in 15.5%, with one-fourth experiencing moderate level of stress. Internet addiction was found to have a statistically significant impact on levels of depression, stress as well as anxiety. This highlights the need for regular counselling of B-school students regarding optimum usage of digital tools, as well as interventions for enhancing mental health. Such awareness sessions will gradually help to optimize digital usage, eventually leading to better mental and physical wellbeing among students. As B-school life demands great rigour and tenacity, coping strategies for mental health should also be included within the college curriculum.

Physical health issues such as backache and neck pain too were observed among students with almost half of them using medications for pain relief. The significant association between the level of physical activity and DASS-21 categories highlights the importance of physical exercise in boosting mental health. Students need to be encouraged to be active physically and participate regularly in any form of physical exercise. This will eventually help in tackling sleep disorders too. Regular sessions of yoga, simple exercises for neck, back, eyes, meditation, coping strategies, awareness regarding the importance of diet can be conducted in B-schools to enhance physical as well as mental fitness levels. These measures will ensure the readiness of B-school students to enter corporate industry and contribute effectively with their full potential. This creation of a healthy workforce will indeed boost the productivity of the industry.

REFERENCES

Al-Menayes, J.J.J.P. (2015). Dimensions of social media addiction among university students in Kuwait. *Psychology and Behavioral Sciences,* 4(1), 23–28.

Anderson, M. and Jiang, J. (2018) Teens, social media & technology. *Pew Research Center* 31, 1673–89. https://www.pewresearch.org/internet/2018/05/31/teens-social-media-technology-2018

Austin, L.L. and Jin, Y. (2018). *Social media and crisis communication.* Routledge, Taylor and Francis.

Bongers, P.M., Ijmker, S., Van den Heuvel, S. and Blatter, B.M. (2006). Epidemiology of work-related neck and upper limb problems: psychosocial and personal risk factors (part I) and effective interventions from a bio behavioural perspective (part II). *Journal of Occupational Rehabilitation,* 16(3), 279–302. doi: 10.1007/s10926-006-9044-1.

Campisi, J., Folan, D., Diehl, G., Kable, T. and Rademeyer, C. (2015). Social media users have different experiences, motivations, and quality of life. *Psychiatry Research,* 228(3), 774–780. doi: 10.1016/j.psychres.2015.04.042.

Carr, C.T. and Hayes, R. (2015). Social media: defining, developing, and divining. *Atlantic Journal of Communication,* 23(1), 46–65.

Chen, I.H., Pakpour, A.H., Leung, H., Potenza, M.N., Su, J.A., Lin, C. Y. and Griffiths, M.D. (2020). Comparing generalized and specific problematic smartphone/internet use: Longitudinal relationships between smartphone application-based addiction and social media addiction and psychological distress. *Journal of Behavioral Addictions*, 26,9(2):410–419. doi: 10.1556/2006.2020.00023.

Conrad, R.C., Hahm, H.C., Koire, A., Pinder-Amaker, S. and Liu, C. H. (2021) College student mental health risks during the COVID-19 pandemic: Implications of campus relocation. *Journal of Psychiatric Research,* 136, 117–126. doi: 10.1016/j.jpsychires.2021.01.054.

Cunningham, S., Hudson, C. and Harkness K. Social media and depression symptoms: a meta-analysis. (2021). *Research on child and adolescent psychopathology*, 49(2), 241–253.

Fathi, A., Sadeghi, S., Maleki Rad, A.A., Sharifi R.S., Rostami, H. and Abdolmohammadi, K. (2020). The role of Cyberspace Use on Lifestyle promoting health and coronary anxiety in Young People. *Iranian Journal of Psychiatry and Clinical Psychology,* 26(3), 332–347.

Galderisi, S., Heinz, A., Kastrup, M., Beezhold, J. and Sartorius, N. (2015). Toward a new definition of mental health. *World Psychiatry*, 14(2), 231–233. doi: 10.1002/wps.20231.

Glaser, P., Liu, J.H., Hakim, M.A., Vilar, R. and Zhang, R. (2018). Is Social Media Use for Networking Positive or Negative? Offline Social Capital and Internet addiction as Mediators for the Relationship between Social Media Use and Mental Health. *New Zealand Journal of Psychology*, 47(3), 11–17.

Goel, D., Subramanyam, A. and Kamath, R. (2013). A study on the prevalence of Internet addiction and its association with psychopathology in Indian adolescents. *Indian Journal of Psychiatry*, 55(2), 140–143.

Gupta, A., Khan, A.M., Rajoura, O.P. and Srivastava, S. (2018). Internet addiction and its mental health correlates among undergraduate college students of a university in North India. *Journal of Family Medicine and Primary Care,*7(4), 721–727

Haand, R. and Shuwang, Z. Youth. (2020). The relationship between social media addiction and depression: a quantitative study among university students in Khost, Afghanistan. *International Journal of Adolescence and Youth,* 25(1), 780–786.

Hanprathet, N., Manwong, M., Khumsri, J., Yingyeun, R., Phanasathit, M. (2015) Facebook Addiction and Its Relationship with Mental Health among Thai High School Students. *The Journal of Medical Association of Thailand,* 98(3), 81–90.

Hemayatkhah, M. (2021). The Impact Of Virtual Social Networks On Women's Social Deviations. *Journal of Social Order*, 13(1), 1–26

Hou, Y., Xiong, D., Jiang T., Song, L. and Wang. (2019). Social media addiction: Its impact, mediation, and intervention. *Cyberpsychology Journal of Psychosocial Research on Cyberspace.* 13 (1),4. doi:10.5817/CP2019-1-4. https://doi.org/10.1037/t41898-000

Huang, C. (2017). Time spent on social network sites and psychological well-being: a meta-analysis. *Cyberpsychology, Behavior and Social Networking*, 20(6), 346–54.

Hussain, Z. and Griffiths, M.D. (2021). The associations between problematic social networking site use and sleep quality, attention-deficit hyperactivity disorder, depression. anxiety and stress, *International Journal of Mental Health and Addiction,* 19, 686–700.

Hussain, Z. and Starcevic, V. (2020). Problematic social networking site use: a brief review of recent research methods and the way forward. *Current Opinion in Psychology*, 36, 89–95.

Lebni, J.Y., Toghroli, R., Abbas, J., NeJhaddadgar, N., Salahshoor, M. R., Mansourian, M., Gilan, H.D., Kianipour, N., Chaboksavar, F., Azizi, S.A. and Ziapour A. (2020) A study of Internet addiction and its effects on mental health: A study based on Iranian University Students. *Journal of Education and Health Promotion.* 9, 205. doi: 10.4103/jehp.jehp_148_20.

Li, Y., Zhao, J., Ma, Z., McReynolds, L.S., Lin, D., Chen, Z., Wang, T., Wang, D., Zhang, Y., Zhang, J., Fan, F. and Liu, X. (2021). Mental Health Among College Students During the COVID-19 Pandemic in China: A 2-Wave Longitudinal Survey. *Journal of Affective Disorders*, 281, 597–604. doi: 10.1016/j.jad.2020.11.109.

Lovibond, S.H. and Lovibond, P.F. (1995). Manual for the Depression Anxiety Stress Scales. *Psychology Foundation of Australia.*

Nabi, R.L., Prestin, A. and So, J. (2013). Facebook friends with (health) benefits? Exploring social network site use and perceptions of social support, stress, and well-being. *Cyberpsychology Behavior and Social Networking*, 16(10), 721–727. doi: 10.1089/cyber.2012.0521.

Nakaya, A. (2015). Internet and social media marketing. *Webology.* 12 (2), 1–3

Nazari, A., Hosseinnia, M., Torkian, S. and Garmaroudi, G. (2023). Social media and mental health in students: a cross-sectional study during the Covid-19 pandemic, *BMC Psychiatry*, 23:458 https://doi.org/10.1186/s12888-023-04859-w

O'reilly, M., Dogra, N., Whiteman, N., Hughes, J., Eruyar, S. and Reilly, P. (2018). Is social media bad for mental health and well-being? Exploring the perspectives of adolescents. *Clinical Child Psychology and Psychiatry,* 23(4):601

Richards, D., Caldwell, P.H. and Go, H. (2015). Impact of social media on the health of children and young people. *Journal of Paediatrics and Child Health*, 51(12):1152–1157. doi: 10.1111/jpc.13023.

Satpathy, B. and Ali, E. (2020). A study on psychological well-being of final year management students during COVID-19 pandemic lockdown in India. *International Journal of Indian Psychology,* 8(2), 1–25. doi:10.25215/0802.121

Schou Andreassen, C. and Pallesen, S. (2014). Social network site addiction-an overview. *Current Pharmaceutical Design,* 20 (25):4053–4061.

Sindermann, C., Elhai, J.D. and Montag, C. (2020). Predicting tendencies towards the disordered use of Facebook's social media platforms: On the role of personality, impulsivity, and social anxiety. *Psychiatry Research,* 285:112793.

Singh, K.D., Gurung, D.J. and Mpanme, D. (2023). Smartphone addiction among post-graduate management students: *The Indian experience, Cogent Arts* and *Humanities*, 10:1, 2255376, doi: 10.1080/23311983.2023.2255376

Sujarwoto, Saputri, R.A.M. and Yumarni, T. (2023) Social Media Addiction and Mental Health Among University Students During the COVID-19 Pandemic in Indonesia. *International Journal of Mental Health and Addiction*, 21(1),96–110. doi: 10.1007/s11469-021-00582-3.

Tang, C.S. and Koh, Y.Y. (2017). Online social networking addiction among college students in Singapore: Comorbidity with behavioral addiction and affective disorder. *Asian Journal of Psychiatry*, 25:175–178. doi: 10.1016/j.ajp.2016.10.027.

Velagapaly, V.R. and Bolla M (2023). An Exploratory Study on Student Mental Health and Well-being at Higher Education Institute in Telangana District-India. *Saudi Journal of Humanities and Social Sciences,* 8(6), 152–161.

Yadav, P., Banwari, G., Parmar, C. and Maniar, R. (2013). Internet addiction and its correlates among high school students: A preliminary study from Ahmedabad, India. *Asian Journal of Psychiatry*, 6(6), 500–505.

Young, K.S. (1998). Internet Addiction Test. American Psychological Association.

Zadra, S., Bischof, G., Besser, B., Bischof, A., Meyer, C., John, U. and Rumpf, H.J. (2016) The association between Internet addiction and personality disorders in a general population-based sample. *Journal of Behavioral Addictions*, 5(4), 691–699. doi: 10.1556/2006.5.2016.086

Zhao, N. and Zhou, G. (2020). Social Media Use and Mental Health during the COVID-19 Pandemic: Moderator Role of Disaster Stressor and Mediator Role of Negative Affect. *Applied Psychology: Health and Well Being,* 12(4), 1019–1038. doi: 10.1111/aphw.12226.

Advancement in Engineering and Science – Goyal et al. (Eds)
 ISBN: 978-1-041-31101-0

The ESG Paradox: Does Prioritizing High ESG Scores in ESG Mutual Funds Come at a Cost?

Ankur Jain
Research Scholar, ICFAI University, Jaipur, India

Archana Rathore
Associate Dean, Associate Professor, ICFAI Business School, Jaipur, India

ABSTRACT: The financial world is seeing a surge in sustainable investing, and with it, the attention in Environmental, Social, and Governance (ESG) Mutual Funds is significantly increasing. ESG Mutual Funds offer not just financial returns but also aim to positively impact the environment and society at large through their tailored investment approaches. This positive narrative does raise a concern though: whether the inherent emphasis of ESG mutual funds on companies with greater ESG scores potentially impacts their financial performance.

This research intends to address this question by analyzing the effect of ESG-based stock selection on the risk-adjusted returns of ESG equity mutual funds in India over short (1-year) and long-term (3-year) durations. We utilize multiple risk-adjusted return measures in our study, which include the Sharpe Ratio, Treynor Ratio, and Jensen's Alpha, and find that higher composite ESG scores of these funds were indeed linked with lower returns across both short as well as long term horizons. These findings confirm the paradox in ESG mutual funds that prioritizing companies with higher ESG scores may come at a financial cost to the investors.

The observations are significant for investors and fund managers. Investors need to make informed choices in ESG mutual fund selection in line with their personal financial and sustainability goals. ESG fund managers need to refine their ESG integration approaches to optimally balance sustainability and financial performance.

Keywords: ESG, Mutual Funds, India, Investing, Environmental, Social, Governance

1 INTRODUCTION

In recent years, investors across the world have prioritized Environmental, Social, and Governance (ESG) factors (Bialkowski and Starks 2016). Responsible investing has evolved significantly - from its origins in religious principles to the general social consciousness among investors (Dolvin et. al. 2019). The mutual fund industry has joined this movement and introduced new funds that incorporate ESG factors in investment strategies (Global Sustainable Investment Review 2022). ESG mutual funds provide a dual promise of financial gains along with positive social and environmental impact, thereby attracting investors globally (Brest *et al.* 2018).

Being one of the world's fastest-growing large economies, India too has experienced increased investor interest in ESG investing in recent years. While India's first ESG mutual fund was introduced back in 1991, seven out of the ten currently active ESG funds were launched in the year 2020. The combined Assets Under Management (AUM) of the ESG funds have become five-fold over the past four years, demonstrating the investor interest in these instruments.

However, within this positive narrative, there lies a potential paradox that challenges the motivation behind the ESG movement: Does prioritizing companies with the highest ESG scores in the portfolio of ESG mutual funds come at a financial cost to investors?

There has been limited research in this specific area even as ESG Funds continue to rapidly increase both in terms of the count of investors and the quantum of assets managed by them. It is hence necessary to look deeper into this area, with a focus on data and research methodology. This research seeks to unravel this paradox by exploring the bearing of stock selection based on ESG scores over the risk-adjusted returns of ESG equity mutual funds in the Indian context.

Using an empirical methodology, we analyze all operational ESG equity mutual funds in India as of March 31, 2024, over both short and long term horizons. The data related to ESG scores is sourced from the ESG rating agency CRISIL. CRISIL's ESG scores are intended to support investors in monitoring the ESG risks inherent in their financial portfolios through standardized ESG information that can be easily integrated into portfolio analysis and risk management (CRISIL 2023).

A number of robust risk-adjusted return metrics have been applied to test our hypothesis. Statistical analysis techniques including regression models have been applied to help quantify the association between ESG rating and risk-adjusted performance.

The observations reveal that higher ESG scores within ESG mutual funds are in fact associated with lower risk-adjusted returns, a pattern visible and consistent across both short and long-term horizons. This substantiates the premise, suggesting that the prioritization of companies with higher ESG scores in ESG mutual funds may indeed provide lower risk-adjusted returns to investors, thereby coming at a financial cost.

The results of this study hold the potential to reshape the landscape of ESG fund investment. Optimizing the balance between sustainability and profitability is crucial for the future of ESG investing. This research provides useful insights for both investors and fund managers while also paving the way for future research to help unlock the true potential of ESG investing that benefits both the investors and society at large.

2 LITERATURE REVIEW

In recent times, the financial market globally has seen substantial growth in sustainable and responsible investing. In 2006, the United Nations (UN) presented the Principles for Responsible Investment, which serve as benchmark guidelines for sustainable investments for sovereigns, investors, and fund management companies globally. Over the years, the count of

DOI: 10.1201/9781003798514-65

UN PRI signatories has grown substantially from 734 in 2010 to 5337 as of September 2023, with Assets Under Management (AUM) also increasing proportionately from US$21 trillion in 2010 to US$121 trillion as of September 2023 (UNPRI 2023). In the initial years, ESG investing was viewed as a niche investment strategy, however, it became mainstream once UN announced the Sustainable Development Goals in 2015.

With sustainability gaining rapid popularity, the growth of the related body of literature has followed suit. More than 2000 empirical studies were estimated to have been conducted between 1970 and 2014 to explore the linkage between financial performance and ESG (Friede *et al* 2015). Yet, a consensus opinion is not present: research studies have shown positive, negative, and even no financial impact of ESG-based decisions on underlying investments (Whieldon and Clark 2021, Naeem *et al* 2022). In the Indian context too, studies have followed a similar pattern (Banu 2021, Behl *et al* 2022, Sarkar 2022, Dutta and Paul 2023, Singh *et al* 2023).

A recurrent theme in many studies suggests that ESG integration does not fit in a short-term perspective but only impacts returns over longer time periods. Since ESG mutual funds in India are still in the initial growth phase, we review both short and long-term periods in our study to validate the premise.

ESG rating agencies score companies on their performance on quantitative ESG indicators (PRI 2015) through an evaluation of their ESG practices (Gillan *et al* 2021) and standardization of the results across business sectors. ESG scores serve as a representation of the commitment and performance of an organization on sustainability and social obligations. ESG Ratings also have implications on the investor demand for ESG Funds, with studies showing that funds categorized as high sustainability experience significantly higher fund inflows as compared to low sustainability funds (Hartzmark and Sussman 2018). In 2019, at least 500 ESG rankings along with 110 disclosure standards were assessed as available globally (Eccles *et al.* 2019). For standardization of the results in our research, we employ ESG scores published by CRISIL, a leading ESG rating agency in India.

Multiple studies have evaluated the influence of ESG on fund performance, though most of them have compared ESG funds to non-ESG funds (Renneboog et. al. 2008, Humphrey and Tan 2011, Zadeh and Serafeim 2018, Kiymaz 2019) and not ESG funds among each other. A study in the Korean context found that funds with greater ESG levels either have better risk-adjusted returns or there was no statistically significant difference as compared to other funds (Chung et. al. 2020). Another study predicted that ESG ratings and portfolio returns were negatively correlated in portfolios with low ambiguity in ESG rating (Avramov et. al. 2022).

The divergent results necessitate further study to gain a better understanding of the phenomena. Our study intends to add to the existing book of work by analyzing the impact of stock selection based on ESG ratings over the performance of ESG mutual funds in an Indian context, to ascertain if chasing high ESG scores in the portfolio indeed comes at a cost to investors.

3 OBJECTIVES AND HYPOTHESIS

The study aims at a comparative examination of cumulative ESG scores against the financial performance of Indian ESG mutual funds over short and long term durations. The hypothesis suggests that a paradox lies herein: Investment in companies with higher ESG scores comes at a financial cost to investors, which is to be confirmed by lower risk-adjusted returns of ESG mutual funds with relatively higher cumulative ESG scores. The hypothesis for the study could be expressed as:

H_0 (Null Hypothesis): The cumulative ESG scores of ESG mutual funds in India have no significant correlation with their risk-adjusted returns over short-term and long-term periods.

H_1 (Alternative Hypothesis): There is a negative relationship between the cumulative ESG scores and risk-adjusted returns of ESG mutual funds in short and long term.

4 RESEARCH METHODOLOGY

We adopt a quantitative research methodology for the study. The first key input for this research is the selection of ESG mutual funds. All ESG-themed mutual funds registered and operating in India as of March 31, 2024, have been selected for the study. These included mutual funds with the word "ESG" in their nomenclature, with the names obtained via the Association of Mutual Funds in India (AMFI)'s web page. The study also includes non-vanilla mutual fund variants, such as Exchange Traded Funds and Fund of Funds.

To facilitate comparison between these mutual funds, we obtain their corresponding Benchmark Indices from their 'Fund Factsheets'. Fund factsheets are documents that provide key information about mutual funds, such as the fund's investment objectives, performance history, portfolio composition, risk level, and expense ratios. These factsheets are published by the fund's Asset Management Companies (AMCs) on their official websites. The list of financial instruments such as equity shares forming part of the mutual fund's portfolio (a.k.a. portfolio constituents) and their weightage (expressed as % of the total assets managed by the mutual fund scheme) for all of the selected mutual funds were also sourced from the Fund Factsheets. The Fund Factsheets as of March 31, 2024, were used for the above purposes.

Table 1. Details of all of the selected mutual funds are given below.

Table 1. Mutual Funds in India selected for the Study.

Sr No	Name OfESG Mutual Fund	Date of-First Allotment	Name Of Benchmark Index
1	Aditya Birla Sun Life ESG Integration Strategy Fund	24-Dec-2020	Nifty 100 ESG Total Return Index
2	Axis ESG Integration Strategy Fund	12-Feb-2020	Nifty 100 ESG Total Return Index
3	ICICI prudential ESG Exclusionary Strategy Fund	9-Oct-2020	Nifty 100 ESG Total Return Index
4	Invesco India ESG Integration Strategy Fund	20-Mar-2021	Nifty 100 ESG Total Return Index
5	Kotak ESG Exclusionary Strategy Fund	11-Dec-2020	Nifty 100 ESG Total Return Index
6	Mirae Asset Nifty 100 ESG Sector Leaders Exchange Traded Fund	17-Nov-2020	Nifty 100 ESG Sector Leaders Total Return Index
7	Mirae Asset Nifty 100 ESG Sector Leaders Fund of Fund	18-Nov-2020	Nifty 100 ESG Sector Leaders Total Return Index
8	Quant ESG Equity Fund	5-Nov-2020	Nifty 100 ESG Total Return Index
9	Quantum ESG Best In Class Strategy Fund	12-Jul-2019	Nifty 100 ESG Total Return Index
10	SBI ESG Exclusionary Strategy Fund	1-Jan-1991	Nifty 100 ESG Total Return Index

Source: Association of Mutual Funds in India (AMFI) and respective Asset Management Companies (AMC)

The ESG intensity or focus of companies is usually measured through ESG scores, which measure a company's sustainability standards and practices in comparable terms. We calculate and apply ESG scores as the base for evaluating the intensity of ESG considerations in the mutual funds under study.

The ESG scores of portfolio constituents have been sourced from CRISIL ESG Ratings. CRISIL, one of the top ESG rating providers in India, employs its proprietary methodology to evaluate more than 600 KPIs to generate an ESG score for 1000 companies covering nearly 65 sectors in India. CRISIL's ESG risk assessment utilizes both quantitative as well as qualitative publicly-available information that has been published by the companies. The sources of such information could be the companies' web portals, annual reports and disclosures, filings with the listing exchanges, sustainability reports, and other material public ESG information, such as regulatory and industry publications.

We calculated the cumulative ESG score of all the funds under study using the respective CRISIL ESG score of each of the portfolio constituents multiplied by their weightage in the fund. Portfolio constituents with ESG scores unavailable were excluded from the base. Also, the cumulative scores of each fund were indexed to 100 to facilitate comparison of scores across funds.

The research is cross-sectional as it provides a snapshot of the cumulative ESG scores of ESG mutual funds in India, based on their portfolio compositions as of March 31, 2024. The research is also longitudinal as it evaluates the historical performance of the funds for one-year and three-year periods ending on March 31, 2024, which represent short-term and long-term horizons. Since eight of the ten currently operational ESG mutual funds in India were launched in or after 2020, three years have been considered as the long-term horizon.

We now look at another element of this study, which is the risk-adjusted performance, which will help compare funds with varying degree of volatility or risk. The main variable used to calculate the risk-adjusted fund returns is the Net Asset Value (NAV). NAV denotes the value of one unit of a mutual fund scheme, and is essentially the price at which investors can buy or sell units of a fund on a given day. Daily NAV of all of the funds under study were sourced from the web portal of AMFI. To facilitate a comparison, we use the daily values of the Benchmark Indices of these respective funds, which were sourced from the web portal of the National Stock Exchange (NSE) of India. We have considered the mutual fund variant with the regular plan and growth option for the NAVs of the funds under study.

For analysis, we calculate the log returns of the daily NAVs and Index values, as they are better suited than simple returns when dealing with continuously compounding returns (Campbell *et al* 1997, Jorion 2001).

Using daily log returns, we calculate the daily mean returns and variance for the funds under study and their corresponding benchmark index. These were then annualized considering a standard of 252 trading days in a year (Chiang et. al. 2016). The covariance between the daily log returns of the funds and corresponding benchmark index were also computed. The variance of daily returns and covariance with the benchmark index were then further utilized to calculate the funds' sensitivity to benchmark, represented by Beta.

The risk-free rate of return is considered as 6.80% per annum, sourced from the yield of short-term T-bills in India.

The following metrics risk-adjusted returns metrics have been employed:

(i) Sharpe Ratio: It measures the excess returns generated by a portfolio for every unit of total risk, represented by its standard deviation (Sharpe, 1966).
(ii) Treynor Ratio: This ratio too signifies the amount of excess returns for a unit of risk, however, it incorporates just the systematic risk of the portfolio (Treynor 1965), which implies that it is better suited for well-diversified portfolios.
(iii) Jensen's Alpha: This metric indicates the returns generated by a portfolio in excess of its expected returns as per Capital Asset Pricing Model (CAPM) (Jensen 1968).

Higher values of all three of the above metrics are preferred as they signify better incremental returns relative to risk.

The two sets of data - ESG scores and risk-adjusted returns – of the funds under study were analyzed using statistical tools, including regression models. These tools quantify the association of ESG scores to risk-adjusted returns, thus helping test our hypothesis.

5 RESULTS AND DISCUSSION

We first cover the analysis over the short-term, one-year period. Descriptive statistics of these mutual funds, specifically (a) annualized mean of daily returns, (b) annualized standard deviation of daily returns, (c) beta with their corresponding benchmark index, and (d) cumulative ESG scores of the funds, based on CRISIL data, are provided in the table below.

Table 2. Descriptive statistics of ESG mutual funds in India as of 31-Mar-2024 for a short-term, one-year period from 01-Apr-2023 to 31-Mar-2024.

S No	Name/Scheme	Comparable ESG Score	Daily Mean Returns, Annualized	Daily Standard Deviation, Annualized	Beta
1	Aditya Birla Sun Life ESG Integration Stratew Fund	63.15	25.34%	9.68%	0.89
2	Axis ESG Integration Strategy Fund	62.96	29.94%	8.73%	0.75
3	ICICI Predential ESG Exclusionary Strategy Fund	60.33	34.89%	8.84%	0.75
4	Invesco India ESG Integration Strategy Fund	61.94	28.54%	10.17%	0.93
5	Kotak ESG Exclusionary Strategy Fund	62.27	29.56%	9.90%	0.93
6	Mirae Asset Nifty 100 ESG Sector Leaders Exchange Traded Fund	63.15	28.73%	9.75%	0.99
7	Mirae Asset Nifty 100 ESG Sector Fund of Fund	63.15	28.33%	10.07%	0.98
8	Quant ESG Equity Fund	59.39	41.90%	13.52%	1.05
9	Quantum ESG Best In Class Strategy Fund	62.08	28.85%	9.63%	0.91
10	SBI ESG Exclusionary Strategy Fund	62.73	27.95%	9.32%	0.88

Source: CRISIL Limited, Association of Mutual Funds in India (AMFI), National Stock Exchange (NSE) and respective Asset Management Companies (AMC)

Table 2. Descriptive statistics of the funds for a period from 01-Apr-2023 to 31-Mar-2024.

The annualized daily mean returns of the market from April 01, 2023, to March 31, 2024, represented by the benchmark index of the respective ESG mutual funds, were calculated as 32.14% for the NIFTY 100 ESG Total Return Index and 28.46% for the NIFTY 100 ESG Sector Leaders Total Return Index.

The results from the empirical analysis of ESG scores' impact on funds' risk-adjusted returns are presented in the below graphs.

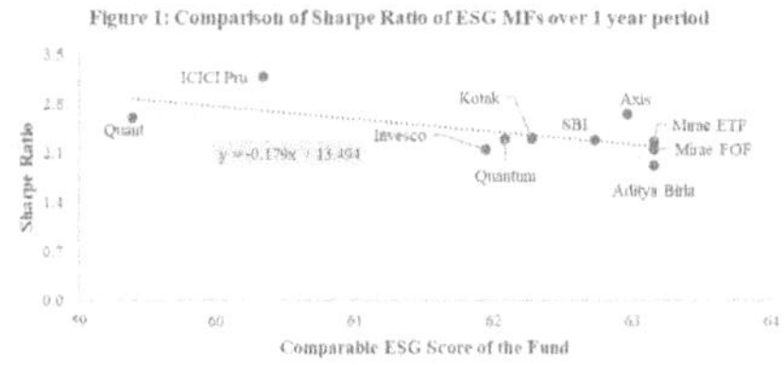

Figure 1. Comparison of Sharpe Ratio of ESG Mutual Funds over 1 year period.

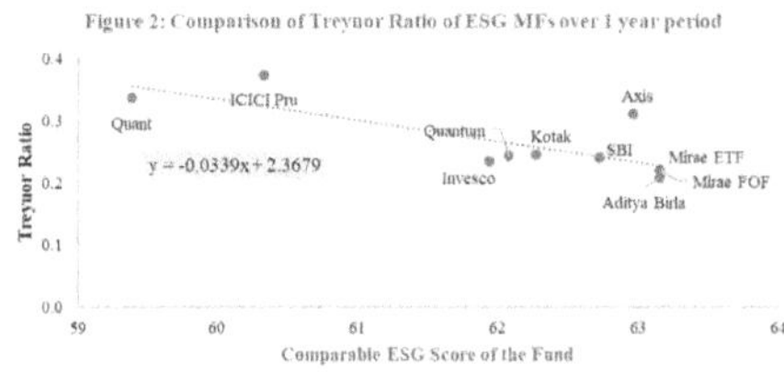

Figure 2. Comparison of Treynor Ratio of ESG Mutual Funds over 1 year period.

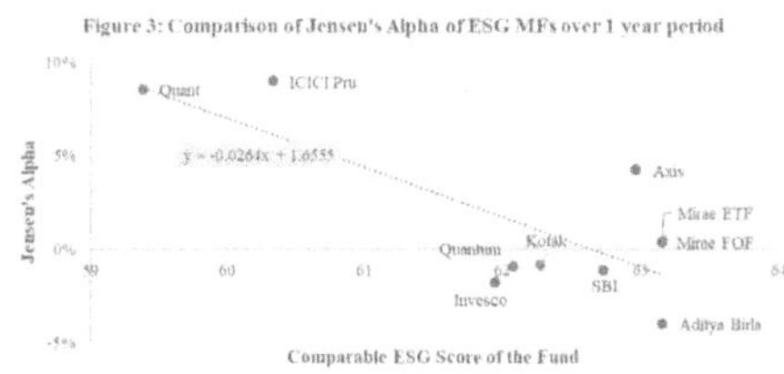

Figure 3. Comparison of Jensen's Alpha of ESG Mutual Funds over 1 year period.

From an analysis of the above trends, it is observed that the risk-adjusted returns exhibit a diminishing trend with increasing ESG scores of the funds over the short term, one-year period. The regression trend-line for each of these three metrics corroborated the observations. We found that the ESG mutual funds systematically displayed lower risk-adjusted returns as their comparable ESG scores increased. The clear and consistent alignment of these metrics in portraying the negative relationship highlights the robustness and reliability of the observed phenomenon.

We now direct our analysis to the long-term (three-year) period. Descriptive statistics of the mutual funds, including their annualized mean of daily returns, their annualized daily standard deviation of returns, and beta with their corresponding benchmark index are presented in the table below. The cumulative ESG scores of the funds remain the same as earlier.

Table 3. Descriptive statistics of funds for a period from 01-Apr-2021 to 31-Mar-2024.

Table 3. Descriptive statistics ofESG mutual funds in India as of 31-Mar-2024 for a long-term, three-year period from 01-Apr-2021 to 31-Mar-2024.

s No	Name/Scheme	Comparable ESG Score	Dany Mean Re-turns, An-nualized	Dany Standard Devia tion, Annualized	Beta
1	Aditya Bina sun Life ESG Integration Strategy Fund	63.15	11.22%	14.45%	0.98
2	Axis ESG Integration Strategy Fund	62.96	11.86%	12.75%	0.79
3	ICICI Prudential ESG Exclusionary Fund	60.33	15.38%	11.55%	0.76
4	Invesco India ESG Integration Strategy Fund	61.94	14.17%	13.18%	0.89
5	Kotak ESG Exclusionary Strategy Fund	62.27	12.56%	13.81%	0.96
6	Mirae Asset Nifty 100 ESG Sector Leaders Exchange Traded Fund	63.15	13.69%	13.44%	0.98
7	Mirae Asset Nifty 100 ESG Sector Leaders Fund of Fund	63.15	12.63%	13.31%	0.94
8	Quant ESG Equity Fund	59.39	28.74%	18.12%	1.09
9	Quantum ESG Best In Class Strategy Fund	62.08	13.42%	12.70%	0.88
10	SBI ESG Exclusionary Strategy Fund	62.73	14.51%	13.53%	0.94

Source: CRISIL Limited, Association of Mutual Funds in India (AMFI), National Stock Exchange (NSE) and respective Asset Management Companies (AMC)

The annualized mean of daily returns of the benchmark index of the respective funds over the three-year period from April 01, 2021, to March 31, 2024, which represent the market returns, have been calculated as 13.91% for NIFTY100 ESG Total Return Index and the corresponding rate is 13.23% for NIFTY100 ESG Sector Leaders Total Return Index.

The graphs below present the analysis of the risk-adjusted performance over three years.

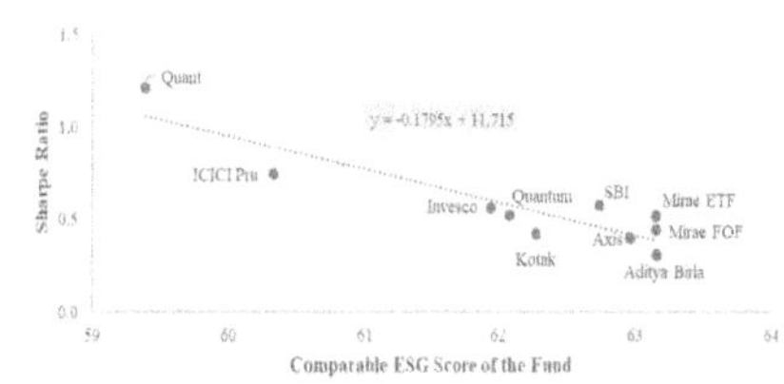

Figure 4. Comparison of Sharpe Ratio of ESG Mutual Funds over 3 year period.

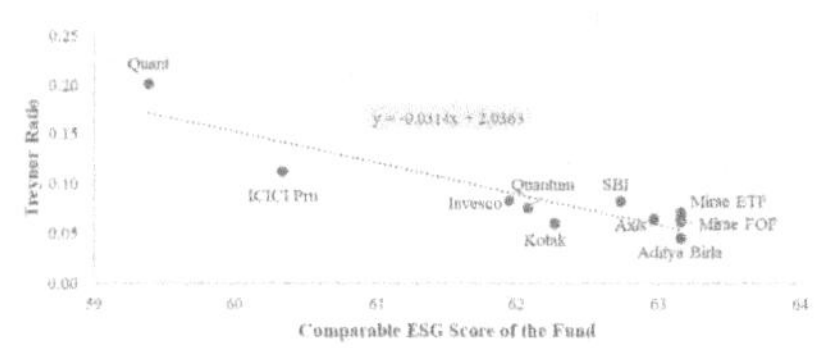

Figure 5. Comparison of Treynor Ratio of ESG Mutual Funds over 3-year period.

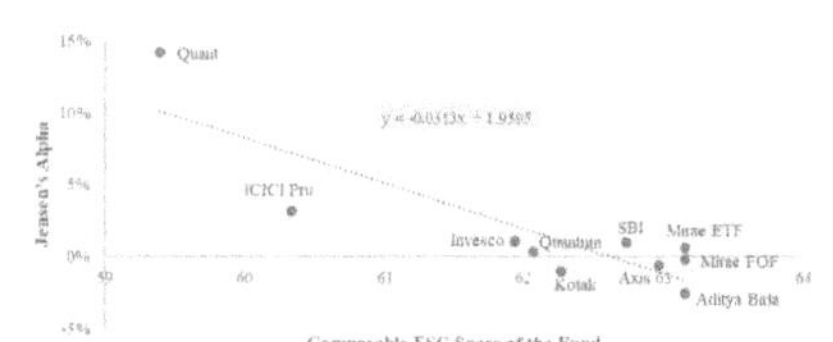

Figure 6. Comparison of Jensen's Alpha of ESG Mutual Funds over 3 year period.

The results of the evaluation over the three-year period portray a similar trend. The analysis depicts a diminishing trend of risk-adjusted returns with rising ESG scores. The observations are evidenced by the regression trend-line for these metrics. The sustained presence of this pattern corroborates the view that the inverse association of ESG scores and risk-adjusted returns is not just short-term but applicable over an extended timeframe as well. This rejects the null hypothesis of the study and strengthens the research's assertion that the preference of corporations with higher ESG scores in the portfolio comes at a financial cost to the investors in terms of lower portfolio returns for ESG mutual funds in India.

6 IMPLICATION AND CONCLUSION

Investment in mutual funds with integrated ESG considerations is often seen as a win-win in terms of both superior earnings and positive social impact. In this context, this research reveals a significant observation that ESG mutual funds in India with higher cumulative ESG scores actually generate lower risk-adjusted returns, in both short and long terms. Multiple risk-adjusted return metrics consistently validated this observation.

These findings suggest that there lies a paradox in investment in ESG mutual funds in India as their preference for companies with higher ESG scores may inadvertently come at a financial cost to the investors in terms of lower risk-adjusted returns.

These findings are significant for fund managers as well as investors of ESG mutual funds in India. Fund managers are advised to reassess their ESG portfolio integration strategies to achieve an optimum balance between sustainable impact and financial returns. Investors are advised to know the potential trade-off between ESG scores and financial returns while making their investment decisions and make better choices in fund selection aligned with their individual sustainability goals.

6.1 *Limitations and future research avenues*

Despite its comprehensive approach, the research has its limitations. Firstly, the research considers a single source of the ESG scores assigned to companies within the mutual funds' portfolios, which may not be robust and vary based on the assessment criteria adopted by different rating agencies. Also, the study relies on past data which may not translate to a similar trend in future performance or capture the dynamic changes in fund strategies over time. In addition, risk-adjusted returns may be affected by multiple market and economic factors beyond ESG scores, which cannot be fully controlled in this research.

Additionally, the research is based on quantitative analysis, which, while offering valuable insights, doesn't capture the finer qualitative nuances of fund management and ESG integration. Lastly, the scope of the study is restricted to an Indian context; similar studies may need to be done in other geographies to generalize the results in a global context.

Addressing these limitations through future research will further refine the understanding and implications of ESG investing for both fund managers and investors. Future research can take forward the results of this study, exploring specific ESG factors impacting returns and potential strategies to effectively balance the pursuit of sustainability and profitability in the realm of ESG investing.

REFERENCES

Alliance, G.S.I. (2023). Global sustainable investment review 2022.

Amel-Zadeh, A., and Serafeim, G. (2018). Why and how investors use ESG information: Evidence from a global survey. *Financial Analysts Journal, 74*(3), 87–103.

Avramov, D., Cheng, S., Lioui, A., and Tarelli, A. (2022). Sustainable investing with ESG rating uncertainty. *Journal of Financial Economics, 145*(2), 642–664.

Banu, A.A.A.S. (2021). A Study On The Sustainable Investment Funds With Special Reference To State Bank Of India ESG Mutual Fund Shcemes. *Turkish Journal of Computer and Mathematics Education (TURCOMAT), 12*(6), 261–266.

Behl, A., Kumari, P.R., Makhija, H., and Sharma, D. (2022). Exploring the relationship of ESG score and firm value using cross-lagged panel analyses: Case of the Indian energy sector. *Annals of Operations Research, 313*(1), 231–256.

Bialkowski, J., and Starks, L.T. (2016). SRI funds: Investor demand, exogenous shocks and ESG profiles.

Brest, P., Gilson, R.J., and Wolfson, M.A. (2018). Essay: How investors can (and can't) create social value. *J. Corp. L., 44*, 205.

Campbell, J.Y., A.W. Lo and A.C. Mackinlay (1997) *The Econometrics of Financial Markets*, New Jersey, Princeton University Press.

Chiang, W.C., Enke, D., Wu, T., and Wang, R. (2016). An adaptive stock index trading decision support system. *Expert Systems with Applications, 59*, 195–207.

CRISIL (2023). CRISIL Sustainability Yearbook.

Dolvin, S., Fulkerson, J., and Krukover, A. (2019). Do "good guys" finish last? The relationship between Morningstar sustainability ratings and mutual fund performance. *The Journal of Investing, 28*(2), 77–91.

Dutta, A., and Paul, B. (2023). Performance Analysis of Select ESG Funds in India. *Management Journal for Advanced Research, 3*(1), 1–7.

Eccles, R.G.; Stroehle, J.; Lee, L.-E. (2019). The Social Origins of ESG? An Analysis of Innovest and KLD. *Organ. Environ.* 2019, 33, 1–36

Esther Whieldon, R. Clark (2021). ESG funds beat out SandP 500 in 1st year of COVID-19; how 1 fund shot to the top. *SandP Global Market Intelligence, 6.*

Friede, G., Busch, T., and Bassen, A. (2015). ESG and financial performance: aggregated evidence from more than 2000 empirical studies. *Journal of sustainable finance* and *investment*, 5(4), 210–233.

Gillan, S.L., Koch, A., and Starks, L.T. (2021). Firms and social responsibility: A review of ESG and CSR research in corporate finance. *Journal of Corporate Finance*, 66(101889), 101889.

Hartzmark, S.M., and Sussman, A.B. (2019). Do investors value sustainability? A natural experiment examining ranking and fund flows. *The Journal of Finance, 74*(6), 2789–2837.

Humphrey, J., and Tan, D. (2011). The Many Faces of Socially Responsible Investing-Does the Screening Mechanism Affect the Risk and Return of Mutual Funds?. *Available at SSRN 1913987.*

Jensen, Michael C. 1968. The performance of mutual funds in the period 1945–64. *Journal of Finance 23*: 389–416.

Jorion, P. (2001) *Value at Risk*, New York, McGraw-Hill.

Kiymaz, H. (2019). Performance Evaluation of SRI Funds: An Analysis of Fund Types. *Accounting and Finance Research, 8*(1), 212–221.

Naeem, M.A., Conlon, T., and Cotter, J. (2022). Green bonds and other assets: Evidence from extreme risk transmission. *Journal of Environmental Management, 305*, 114358.

PRI. (2015). Principles for Responsible Investment - *Annual Report 2015.*

Renneboog, L., Ter Horst, J., and Zhang, C. (2008). The price of ethics and stakeholder governance: The performance of socially responsible mutual funds. *Journal of corporate finance, 14*(3), 302–322.

Sarkar, S. (2022). Performance Evaluation Of ESG Funds In India–A Study. *The Management Accountant Journal, 57*(3), 40–47.

Sharpe, W.F. (1966). Mutual fund performance. *The Journal of business, 39*(1), 119–138.

Singh, S., Bahl, S., Sharma, J., and Sharma, A. (2023). Performance Evaluation of ESG Mutual Funds in India. *Journal of Survey in Fisheries Sciences, 10*(3S), 1133–1143.

Treynor, J. (1965). How to rate management of investment funds. *Harvard Business Review 43*: 63–75.

United Nations (2015). *www.un.org/sustainabledevelopment/*

United Nations Principles for Responsible Investing (2023). *www.unpri.org.*

Advancement in Engineering and Science – Goyal et al. (Eds)
© 2026 The Author(s), ISBN: 978-1-041-31101-0

Building Back Better: How Self-Help Groups Can Empower Rural Women Post-Pandemic

Vandana Panwar
Associate Professor- PGDM-Rural Management (Emerging Economies), S. P. Mandali's Prin. L. N. Welingkar Institute of Management Development and Research (PGDM), Mumbai

Gayathri Menon
Consultant, Uniqus Consultech Inc.

ABSTRACT: This study aimed to investigate the empowerment of rural women in Olavanna, Kerala, particularly focusing on the impact of Kudumbashree Self-Help Groups (SHGs). The research delved into five key dimensions of women's empowerment: awareness, attitude, skill attainment, autonomy, and public engagement. The study employed field surveys and personal interviews to gather data from 75 Kudumbashree members.

The findings revealed a strong correlation between education and various aspects of women's empowerment. While the women demonstrated high levels of awareness, autonomy, and resource control, there was a gap in translating this into behavioral changes and skill acquisition. The SHGs were found to be instrumental in enhancing the sustainability of rural women's livelihoods through improved food security, financial stability, and access to credit.

During the COVID-19 pandemic, Kudumbashree members actively contributed to community resilience by providing essential services such as food distribution, mask-making, and awareness campaigns. This highlights the transformative role of SHGs in empowering women and enabling them to address societal challenges.

In conclusion, the study underscores the significance of education in fostering women's empowerment. While SHGs have been effective in improving women's economic and social conditions, there is a need for continued efforts to enhance their skills and promote active participation in public life.

Keywords: Sustainable, Empowerment, kudumbashree, Self Help Groups, women, Rural

1 INTRODUCTION

Women's empowerment gained global attention in the mid-1990s. UN indices like GDI and GEM evaluate gender disparities in literacy, life expectancy, income, and participation in economic, professional, and political spheres. Kerala leads Indian states in human development, with 96.2% literacy (https://eands.dacnet.nic.in/), exemplifying women's elevated status and serving as a model at the 1994 UN Conference.

Despite Kerala's historically favorable women's rights and matrilineal system (Panda 2003, Saradannoni 1999a), the state exhibits a 'gender paradox' (Erwer 1998b). Misaligned job placements (Saradamoni 1999b), women's public sphere invisibility (Erwer 1993a, Mohanan 2003), and escalating crimes (Rahman 2002) contradict its progressive reputation.

Kudumbashree, a women-led poverty eradication initiative by Kerala's government and NABARD, empowers poor women through community-based organizations collaborating with local self-government institutions, utilizing self-help group strategies for development.

Motivated by scholarly insights, this research explores Kudumbashree's structure, its impact on rural women's empowerment, sustainable livelihoods, and COVID-19 challenges.

Table 1. Definitions of empowerment in various studies.

Studies	Empowerment explained in various studies
Batilwala (1994)	Power is the ability to exert control over resources and decision-making processes.
Narayanan (1998)	something that cannot be given to people
Montis (1996), Giri (1998), Malhotra *et al.* (2002)	sociocultural, legal, political and psychological empowerment
Govt Of India, 2000	moving from a position of forced weakness to one of authority
Bennet (2002)	Empowering individuals and groups to engage with and influence institutions that affect their lives.
SaralaGopalan (2002)	state without oppression
Kabeer (2001)	Increasing people's ability to make choices that shape their lives.
G.Sen (1993)	altering relations of power
Keller and Mbwewe (1991)	A process by which women organize themselves to increase self-reliance, assert their rights, and control resources.

Source: Prepared by the author

2 RELATED LITERATURE AND GAPS

Women's empowerment is multifaceted, encompassing behavioral, attributional, and process-based perspectives (Malhotra 2002, Govindaswami and Malhotra 1996) with levels of equality (Longwe 1990, Karl 1995). Empowerment as explained in the existing literature by various researchers is given below in Table 1.

Women's empowerment is a complex process of increasing knowledge, enabling women to change perceptions, assert rights, make choices, and enhance their well-being through individual agency. Exploring the journey from women's rights to empowerment, feminism critiques societal treatment of women. Liberal, Marxist, Radical, and Socialist feminist perspectives have fundamentally shaped the concept of women's empowerment.

DOI: 10.1201/9781003798514-66

The study employs quantitative and qualitative indicators of women's empowerment, encompassing economic, socio-cultural, political, and legal dimensions (Canadian International Development Agency 1991, Panda 2000, Karl 1995, Saradamoni 1999b).

Economic empowerment involves changes in employment, income, asset ownership, and credit access. Socio-cultural measures challenge patriarchal norms and promote gender equality through mobility, education, and social participation.

Women's family status reflects gender equality in decision-making, reproductive rights, and freedom from violence. Legal empowerment includes rights awareness, legal assistance, community mobilization, and judicial processes. Political empowerment encompasses understanding political systems, voting, and holding elected positions.

Psychological empowerment involves self-confidence, belief in personal change potential, and sense of entitlement. Attitudes play a crucial role, with empowerment requiring rejection of gender-based unequal entitlements. Individual behavior reflects acceptance or rejection of gender norms.

Training and skill development enable women to convert challenges into opportunities, exercise power, manage groups, and maintain public relations. As Eapen and Kodoth (2001) and Kishore and Gupta (2004) suggest, women's autonomy depends on property rights, decision-making power, and freedom of movement. Self-help groups (SHGs) are critical in poverty alleviation and rural development, focusing on savings, debt, resource management, and social issues. Kudumbashree, launched in 1998, exemplifies this approach in Kerala.

Kudumbashree's three-tier network includes Neighbourhood Groups, Area Development Societies, and Community Development Societies. The program aims to empower women through economic and social advancement, implementing microfinance and government schemes like PMAY, NULM, DDUGKY, NRLM, SVEP, and MKSP. The study conceptualizes women's empowerment as interconnected components, analyzing each through specific indicators aligned with research objectives, drawing from Karl's (1995) comprehensive framework.

Research objectives-Considering the identified research gaps, this study aims to:

1. To explore the motivations and benefits of joining Kudumbashree SHGs.
2. To assess the impact of Kudumbashree on rural women's empowerment, focusing on awareness, attitudes, skills, autonomy, and public participation.
3. To identify the key factors contributing to the sustainability of women's empowerment through Kudumbashree.
4. To examine the effects of the COVID-19 pandemic on the functioning of Kudumbashree SHGs.

3 DESIGNING RESEARCH METHODOLOGY

The research methodology aimed to study self-help groups' impact on rural women's employment, livelihood, and empowerment components. The study utilized both primary and secondary sources, including scholarly publications, websites, and field research. For operationalization of variables, five key empowerment components were defined:

(i) Awareness: Recognizing subordinate status and understanding government programs, eligibility criteria, and legal rights.
(ii) Attitude: Examining perspectives on traditional gender roles, self-esteem, education, work, relationships, and gender equality.
(iii) Skills Attainment: Assessed through a self-rating scale covering life, technical, artistic, and physical skills.
(iv) Autonomy: Evaluated through family relations, sexual division of labor, decision-making, financial freedom, and responses to gender-based violence.
(v) Participation: Measured by involvement in political parties, village assemblies, voting, self-help groups, unions, and local leadership.

The study assessed Kudumbashree women's sustainable development through financial, educational, and health indicators. Open-ended questions explored their perspectives on empowerment, group challenges, societal support, and potential government initiatives for women's advancement. The study focused on Kudumbashree members in Olavanna CDS, Kozhikode district, Kerala. Sampling criteria included: Women aged 18-60 years, Population of 59,000 (51% female, 49% male), 96.43% literacy rate, Purposive sampling technique (Selvi 2018), Sample size of 75 Kudumbashree members.

Data Collection Method included field survey, focus group discussion, and the personal interview with various stakeholders with the help of structured questionnaire prepared in the local language – Malayalam and English. The questionnaire contained five sections-demographic information, self-help group information, components of empowerment, sustainable empowerment and impact of Covid on SHG members.

Sustainable development aspects examined included: Food custom, financial stability, Medical expenses, Children's education, Credit access. Data analysis was conducted using SPSS version 25.0, employing: Tabulated calculations, Index scoring, ANOVA statistical method. The research period spanned December 2022 to February 2023, providing a comprehensive examination of women's empowerment through Kudumbashree's self-help group model.

4 FINDINGS AND RESULTS

This section presents the results and analysis of the study on Kudumbashree members in Olavanna CDS, focusing on their socio-economic characteristics, SHG functioning, women's empowerment, and livelihood sustainability

Appendex: Table 2. Socio-economic characteristics of the respondents.

Socio-economic factors	Categories	Percentage of respondents
Age	(i) 18 to 25	1.3
	(ii) 26 to 40 years	49.3
	(iii) 41 to 55 years	45.3
	(iv) 55-60 years	4.0
Caste	General	18.7
	OBC	69.3
	SC & ST	12
Religion	Hindu	77.3
	Muslim	22.7
Type of family	Nuclear	60
	Joint	40
Type of house	Family owned	94.7
	Rented	5.3
Land owned	Family owned	96
	Leased	0
	No land	4
Marital status	Single	4
	Married	94.7
	Divorced/widow	1.3
Education	Below 10th	2.6
	10th	45.3
	12th	24.0
	Graduate	24.0
	Post graduate	4
Employment Status	Employed	46.3

(*continued*)

Continued

Socio-economic factors	Categories	Percentage of respondents
	Unemployed	53.3
Occupation	Government	4
	Private/Self employed	52
	No response	44
Average Income per month	up to 1,000	33.3
	1000 to 3000	22.7
	3001 to 5000	10.7
	5001 to 10,000	21.3
	10,001 to 20,000	10.6
	Above 20,001	1.3

1. The majority of Kudumbashree members in Olavanna CDS are aged 26–50, belong to the Other Backward Classes (OBC) and Hindu communities, and reside in nuclear families. Most own their homes and land.

   Educationally, 45.3% are 10th pass, 24% 12th pass, and 24% graduates. However, employment rates are low (46.3%), with most women self-employed and earning less than Rs. 1000 monthly. Caste, religion, family structure, and income levels influence women's empowerment (Kishor and Gupta 2004). While education empowers women, economic independence is crucial (Jeffrey 1993). The socio-economic characteristics of the respondents provide valuable insights into the status of Kudumbashree-Olavanna CDS women members.
2. *Information on Self-help groups*- Most Kudumbashree members (68%) belong to Olavanna CDS and have been members for over 10 years. They were primarily introduced by neighbors and joined for personal development and economic independence. Members contribute through meetings, trainings, and financial transactions. Assets acquired include gold, cattle, and real estate.
3. Components of Empowerments- Kerala, known for its progressive stance on women's rights, has witnessed significant advancements in women's empowerment. This study delves into the five key dimensions of women's empowerment among Kudumbashree members in Olavanna CDS: awareness, attitude, skills, autonomy, and public participation.

Awareness Level: While a majority of respondents (76%) are aware of employment schemes, knowledge about coordinators and eligibility criteria is limited.

Attitude Towards Self and Gender: A positive attitude towards women's education and careers is evident, with 81.3% supporting women's right to pursue their goals. However, traditional gender roles persist, as seen in the high percentage (89%) agreeing that women should prioritize family over career.

Skills Attainment: Most respondents possess essential life skills like communication and decision-making. However, public speaking skills and technical skills like computer literacy are areas where improvement is needed.

Women's Autonomy: A high percentage of respondents enjoy financial autonomy and contribute to household work. However, traditional gender roles still influence household labor division.

Women's Participation in Public Domain: Active participation in panchayat meetings, gram sabhas, and neighborhood groups is encouraging. However, leadership roles in professional associations are less common.

While Kudumbashree members in Olavanna CDS have made significant strides in women's empowerment, challenges remain. Addressing these challenges requires a multi-faceted approach, including: i)**Promoting awareness:** Disseminating information about government schemes and women's rights, ii) **Challenging gender stereotypes:** Encouraging discussions and promoting gender-equitable norms, iii) **Skill development:** Providing training in public speaking, computer literacy, and other relevant skills, iv) **Economic empowerment:** Supporting women's entrepreneurship and financial independence, v) **Encouraging leadership:** Promoting women's participation in decision-making roles.By addressing these areas, we can further empower women in Olavanna CDS and contribute to the overall progress of women's empowerment in Kerala.

Table 3. Scores based on Index

Component of Empowerment	Maximum score	Average score	Percent
Awareness	3	1.72	58.2
Attitude	7	6.59	94.1
Skills	7	4.80	68.6
Autonomy	2	1.55	77.3
Public participation	4	3.00	75.0

Source: Prepared by Author

The index score was calculated for each respondent shown in the above Table 3. The awareness component had three statements, so the maximum score a respondent can have is 3 and a minimum of zero. Similarly, the maximum score for Attitude is seven, skills is seven, autonomy is 2 and public participation is 4. The average score shows an average score scored by all the respondents. The per cent column shows that out of 100 what is the level of women empowerment in all the respondents. The table shows that respondents are high in attitude (94.1%) followed by autonomy (77.3 %), public participation (75.0), skills (68.6%) and awareness 58.2%. This reflects that although attitude and autonomy is high, they are not aware of the basic information on empowerment.

Some of the implications based on the above can include- **Targeted Interventions:** Tailor programs to address the specific needs of different demographic groups. **Education and Skill Development:** Prioritize education and skill training to enhance women's employability and decision-making abilities. **Economic Empowerment:** Implement policies to support women's economic independence. **Challenging Gender Norms:** Promote gender equality through awareness campaigns and community mobilization. By addressing these factors, we can further empower women in Olavanna CDS and contribute to a more equitable society.

4. **Sustainable employment-** Kudumbashree, a women-led self-help group, has significantly impacted the lives of rural women in Kerala. Membership has led to improved food security, financial stability, and access to credit. Women have gained financial independence, enabling them to meet family needs like medical expenses and education. While the impact on monthly income varies, it has generally increased for a significant portion of members.

   Kudumbashree has also empowered women by enhancing their decision-making abilities and self-confidence. Members perceive empowerment as financial independence, education, and equal rights within the family. However, challenges such as gender inequality and societal norms persist.

   To further empower women, the government should prioritize job creation, ensure access to government programs, leverage technology, and promote skill development and entrepreneurship. By addressing these issues, Kudumbashree can continue to be a powerful tool for women's empowerment and sustainable development in Kerala.

5. **Impact of Covid-19 on Kudumbashree members**-To meet increased demand during the pandemic, Kudumbashree's community meals and subsidized restaurants quickly expanded across the state. Kudumbashree women collaborated with local governments to reprocess unused public infrastructure into community kitchens, resulting in the establishment of over a thousand kitchens across the state. For migratory workers, special communal kitchens were also established.

They also began providing home delivery services and opened takeout counters in even the most remote parts of the state. More than 16,000 Kudumbashree farming groups saved these eateries by providing 116 metric Tonnes of agricultural supplies. When the state's hygiene and personal protection items became scarce, Kudumbashree women stepped in to assist. It conducted an initial requirements assessment and devoted its textile and chemical micro-enterprises to the production of sanitizers and masks exclusively. Kudumbashree had become one of the primary providers of masks and sanitizers to Kerala's frontline institutions and small companies by September 2020, having sold over 7 million cotton masks and 9300 liters of sanitizer.

Women from Kudumbashree became active communicators of pandemic information. Its members effectively reached out to communities via 300,000 WhatsApp groups, resulting in a culturally diverse awareness campaign. Balsabhas, Kudumbashree's children's collectives, developed several activities to combat social isolation among children.

5 DISCUSSIONS

The study examined women's empowerment in Olavanna CDS, focusing on awareness, attitudes, skills, autonomy, and participation. Most respondents were literate but had limited formal education (Selvi, 2018). Women faced significant socio-economic challenges, including low levels of employment and limited property ownership due to traditional practices like dowry. Employment rates were low, particularly in formal sectors (Nair, 2000; Selvi, 2018).

Awareness levels were influenced by factors like age, education, and income. Younger, educated women from nuclear families were more aware of their rights and opportunities. Attitudes towards gender roles were shaped by socio-economic factors and cultural norms. While women possessed essential domestic skills, they lacked skills for public participation and economic empowerment. They had limited control over resources but enjoyed relative freedom of movement compared to other Indian women.

Participation in public life was influenced by employment status and family structure. Employed women from nuclear families were more likely to participate. Kudumbashree has been a significant vehicle for women's empowerment, enabling them to improve their socioeconomic status and decision-making abilities (Selvi, 2018).

Hypothesis Testing:

H1: There is significant difference in the rural women's awareness level across all socioeconomic factors such as age, religious dogma, social position, level of education, employment status, income level and type of family.

H2: There is significant difference in the rural women's attitude towards self & gender issues across all socioeconomic factors such as age, religious dogma, social position, level of education, employment status, income level and type of family.

H3: There is significant difference in the rural women's skills attainment across all socioeconomic factors such as age, religious dogma, social position, level of education, employment status, income level and type of family.

H4: There is significant difference in the rural women's women autonomy, across all socioeconomic factors such as age, religious dogma, social position, level of education, employment status, income level and type of family.

H5: There is significant difference in the rural women's participation in public domain across all socioeconomic factors such as age, religious dogma, social position, level of education, employment status, income level and type of family.

For conducting the hypothesis testing if the p-value is more than 0.05, the probability of null hypothesis is extraordinarily large, which shows it is *statistically insignificant*. This means there is no significant difference in the dependent variable i.e components of empowerment and the independent variables i.e socio-economic characteristics of the respondents which includes-age, religion, caste, level of education, employment status, income level and type of family.

The five-hypothesis mentioned in the research methodology section are testing and results shown below in Table 4.

Table 4. Testing of Hypothesis

P_value significance at <0.05 of Components of Empowerment					
Independent variable	Dependent Variables				
Demographic Characteristics	Awareness	Attitude towards self and gender	Skills attainment	Women's Autonomy	Participation in public domain
Age	0.391	0.606	0.813	0.560	0.614
Religion	0.051	***0.005***	***0.006***	0.255	1.000
Caste	0.197	0.224	0.558	0.514	0.584
Family type	0.608	0.059	0.599	0.554	0.098
Nature of employment	0.117	0.181	0.305	0.884	0.285
Monthly income	0.253	0.486	0.986	0.357	0.731
Educational qualification	0.938	0.251	***0.007***	0.700	0.087
Employment	0.216	0.140	0.154	0.956	0.225
Results of Hypothesis testing for every socio-economic factor	H1-Null hypothesis accepted	H2- Null hypothesis accepted	H3- Null hypothesis accepted	H4- Null hypothesis accepted	H5- Null hypothesis accepted

Policy recommendations- Based on the study, some of the recommendations include- firstly, individuals and groups must receive ongoing, rigorous leadership training. Secondly, for long-term sustainability, long-term funding with a low interest rate is required. Thirdly, the most important component is family support, and everyone in the family should contribute, because 29.3 percent of women in Kerala do not believe men do not support women. Fourthly, women's empowerment and education programmes should be held on a regular basis, because many women who join Kudumbashree expect personal and social development. Fifthly, for Kudumbashree to reach more people, membership drives should be held, and the public should be made aware of the organization and its importance. Because only 1.3 percent of members were introduced to Kudumbashree through the media, media assistance may be requested. Sixthly, self-employment and entrepreneurship should be encouraged, and those who are interested should be given the necessary assistance. Seventh, loan availability and criteria should be available to all members when needed. This may encourage more people to join Kudumbashree, as research revealed that 24% of members are unaware of the schemes available. Eighth, more programmes for women who know how to cook, such as community kitchens, could be developed, as this is a skill that 98.7 percent of respondents have acquired. Ninth, computer literacy classes should be offered because it is a critical skill currently, and only 54.7 percent of respondents possess it.

6 CONCLUSION

The study demonstrated that Kudumbashree is regarded as a major change agent because it involves women in a variety of developmental activities, which has increased women's morale and confidence. Women's empowerment does not imply gaining power over others, but rather the ability to work collaboratively to effect change. Neighborhood Groups have emerged as a powerful tool for empowering underprivileged women. By fostering social and economic development, these groups have enabled women to increase their contributions to their households and develop a strong sense of self-worth and confidence.

Since the present study focuses on Kudumbashree members, a comparative study of non-member women,can also be conducted. The study is limited to general socioeconomic issues, but it can be expanded to include individual factors.

REFERENCES

Batliwala, S. (1994). The meaning of women's empowerment: New concepts for action. In G. Sen, A. Germain, and I. C. Chen (Eds.), *Population policies reconsidered: Health, empowerment and rights* (pp. 1–22). Harvard University Press.

Bennett, L. (2002). *Using empowerment and social inclusion for poor growth: A theory of social change (*Working draft of background paper for the social development strategy paper). World Bank, Washington.

Canadian Council for International Cooperation. (1991). *Two halves make a whole.* Match International Centre, Bonanza Press.

Eapen, M., and Kodoth, P. (2001). Gender, family and property rights: Questions from Kerala's land reforms. *Indian Journal of Gender Studies*, 8(2), 173–199.

Erwer, M. (1993a). *Tradition in modernity: A study of new social movements in Kerala* (Undergraduate essay). The Peace and Development Institute, Gottenberg University.

Erwer, M. (1998b). *Development beyond the status of women: The Kerala model from a gender perspective,* South India (PhD Thesis). The Peace and Development Institute, Gottenberg University.

Giri, M. (1998). *Empowerment and emancipation of women.* Gyan Publishing House.

Govindaswami, P.S., and Malhotra, A. (1996). Women's position and family planning in Egypt. *Studies in Family Planning*, 27(6), 339–349.

Heise, L., Ellsberg, M., and Gottemoeller, M. (1999). *Ending violence against women*. Population Reports, 27(1), 1–29.

Jeffrey, R. (1993). *Politics, women and well-being: How Kerala became 'a model'*. Oxford University Press.

Karl, M. (1995). Women and empowerment: Participation and decision-making. Zed Books.

Keller, B., and Mbwewe, D.C. (1991). Policy and planning for the empowerment of Zambia's women farmers. *Canadian Journal of Development Studies*, 12(2), 337–355.

Kishore, S., and Gupta, K. (2004). Women's empowerment in India and its states: Evidence from the NFHS. *Economic and Political Weekly*, 39(7), 670–680.

Kodoth, P., and Eapen, M. (2005). Looking beyond gender parity: Gender inequities of some dimensions of well-being in Kerala. *Economic and Political Weekly*, 40(29), 3213–3221.

Longwe, S. (1990). *From welfare to empowerment: Office of Women in International Development* (Working paper No. 204). Michigan State University.

Malhotra, A., *et al.* (2002). *Measuring empowerment as a variable in international development.* International Center for Research on Women, Washington.

Mason, K. (1998). Wives' economic decision-making power in the family. In C. Oppenheim (Ed.), *Five Asian countries in the changing family in comparative perspective: Asia and the United States* (pp. 103–130). East West Center.

Mason, K., and Smith, H.L. (2000). Husband versus wives: Fertility goals and use of contraception. *The influence of gender context in five Asian Countries*. Demography, 37(3), 361–377.

Mohanan, B. (2003). Women and law: The case of Kerala. ISDA Publications. (e-book)

Montis, D.D.M. (1996). *The Beijing declaration for gender and equality: One year overview and challenges* (Sweden seminar on Gender, Equality and Woman's Health, Stockholm, 18th October

Narayanan, S. (1998). *Empowerment of women through social mobilisation*. Women's Link, 4(1), 1–12.

Nair, K.N. (2000). *Kerala Research Programme on Local Development (Report 5)*. Centre for Development Studies, Trivandrum.

Panda, S.M. (2000). *Women's empowerment through NGO interventions: A framework for assessment*. Social Change, 30

Advancement in Engineering and Science – Goyal et al. (Eds)

Evaluating the Effects of Dynamic Pricing on Tourist Preferences in the Indian Tourism Sector: A Study from Rajasthan

Pragya Shrivastava
Research Scholar, The ICFAI University, Jaipur

Archana Rathore
Associate Dean & Associate Professor, IBS, Jaipur

ABSTRACT: Dynamic pricing strategies are widely adopted in the tourism sector to attract consumers and increase revenue, still there seems to be a lack of knowledge regarding the influence of such strategies on consumer preferences. This study aims to cover this research gap by evaluating the effect of dynamic pricing strategies on traveler preferences in the Indian tourism sector, focusing on Rajasthan tourists. This study will comparatively evaluate the tourists' preference across dynamic and uniform pricing strategies. To examine the effects of different pricing strategies on tourists' preferences, this study carried out an experimental assessment of tourists' involvement, emotions, and behavioral responses in varied scenarios. To evaluate tourists' preferences, the study used the Personal Involvement Inventory and selected a sample of 150 tourists arriving at or departing from the Jaipur Airport, using a convenience sampling technique. A 7-point Likert scale was used for behavioral and emotional measures. Tourists' emotional and behavioral reactions were evaluated using a 2x2 design, and the identified study hypotheses were tested using three-way ANOVA and t-tests. The findings indicated that dynamic pricing was more preferred by tourists with high levels of involvement in contrast to uniform pricing. Female and younger travelers were more likely to avail of discounts. Tourists with high involvement also reported stronger positive emotions and were more willing to share their discount experiences and make repeat purchases compared to those with low involvement. The study highlights the importance for travel solution providers (agency managers) to customize dynamic pricing strategies for high-involvement tourists, particularly targeting younger and female demographics.

Keywords: Pricing Strategies, Uniform Pricing, Dynamic Pricing, Tourist Preferences, Tourist Involvement

1 INTRODUCTION

Tourism is an important sector in the global and national economy which makes a substantial contribution to the gross domestic product, employment, and cultural exchange. Variations in prices play an important role in influencing tourists' decisions and choices within this highly competitive sector (Ramadhani *et al.*, 2024). One of the pricing strategies is the use of dynamic prices that involves setting prices depending on future trends, demand & supply factors, and availability, among other factors. Even though the basic idea of dynamic pricing is to attract consumers and, thereby, enhance revenues in various domains like aviation, hospitality, and e-commerce, among others, its concrete role in shaping the consumers' preferences, particularly in the tourism sector has not drawn much attention from the scholars (Banerjee *et al.*, 2023).

Rajasthan, a "culturally sensitive" state in northern India, known for its majestic palaces, historic forts, and vibrant culture, is one of the leading tourist states in India for domestic as well as international tourists. Seasonal influxes and greater dependency on tourists as a source of revenue make it especially logical to use dynamic prices in the state. Such knowledge of how dynamic pricing affects tourists' decisions might be highly useful for policymakers, traveling solution providers, tour operators, and local businesses seeking to maximize their revenue and improve the quality of tourist experience (Kee *et al.*, 2024; Mihai *et al.*, 2023).

Based on the above background, this study intends to evaluate the impact of dynamic pricing strategies on tourist preferences in the Indian tourism sector, with a focus on the state of Rajasthan. Therefore, to determine which pricing strategy is more preferred by tourists in the region, this study will compare the results of dynamic pricing and uniform pricing strategies. The researcher firmly believes that the findings of the study will contribute to the extant literature on tourist behavior management in India.

2 REVIEW OF LITERATURE

2.1 *Uniform and dynamic pricing*

Pricing strategies are very important in understanding consumer behavior (Kopalle *et al.*, 2023). Uniform pricing has been the subject matter of previous studies. Uniform pricing involves setting a fixed price for a good or service without adjusting it based on supply and demand (Akbari, 2023). Such a pricing is non-complex and transparent and is favored by travelers, especially those on a tight budget. Uniform pricing reduces the uncertainty caused by price fluctuations. This makes this approach highly predictable and gives travelers a sense of stability and inclusion. Previous research has shown that uniform pricing can increase traveler satisfaction and generate stable income for travel agencies (e.g., Akbari, 2023; Kopalle *et al.*, 2023).

However, with the increasing use of information technology, researchers have started focusing on dynamic pricing as an alternative strategy. Such an approach adjusts the price of a good or service based on supply and demand. This strategy is gaining popularity in several industries, including e-commerce and tourism, as it can help travel agencies maximize profits by raising prices when demand is high and lowering prices when demand is low. As a result, this strategy can attract more travelers when demand is low and balance the number of travelers when demand is high. However, some tourists find low prices pleasant when demand is low, while others find high prices unfair when demand is high (e.g., Akbari, 2023; Victor *et al.*, 2019). Previous studies have observed conflicting results on how dynamic pricing affects travel preferences (Victor *et al.*, 2019).

DOI: 10.1201/9781003798514-67

Previous studies have shown that the optimal pricing strategy can help reach an equilibrium level between the preferences and satisfaction of tourists and the income of travel agencies (Dole, 2023; Jasrotia *et al.*, 2021). Jasrotia *et al.* (2021) believed that if dynamic pricing is applied properly and transparently, it may maximize traveler acceptance and minimize traveler dissatisfaction. Pillai (2023) also supported the above observation, highlighting that dynamic pricing may provide higher acceptance by travelers through the application of technological innovation.

2.2 *Consumer involvement*

Previous studies (e.g., Klein and Sharma, 2022; Michaelidou and Dibb, 2008) have highlighted that consumer involvement with product and marketing strategy influences their buying intention. Consumer involvement is usually assessed by the effort and time invested in reaching a specific transaction. Tourists with high involvement tend to conduct extensive searches for better offers, dedicating considerable time, effort, and financial resources. This level of involvement is evident in factors such as how often they participate, their spending habits, the distances they travel, their skill levels, and their memberships. Conversely, low-involvement tourists are passive, taking advantage of discounts only when encountered by chance.

Highly involved tourists view regular prices positively and are more inclined to engage with service providers without needing discounts. These tourists also accept dynamic pricing more readily when involved in the process. Conversely, uniform pricing strategies are as effective as dynamic pricing for low-involvement tourists. Higher involvement fosters greater loyalty and reduces marketing resource needs, leading to stronger purchase decision relationships (Klein and Sharma, 2022). Therefore, price promotions can significantly shape tourist preferences and purchase decisions, based on their demographic factors like age and gender, thus, enhancing their overall experience and satisfaction.

2.3 *Tourists' emotional and behavioral responses*

Existing literature highlights that price promotions primarily attract consumers due to money savings. When they attribute positive outcomes (such as receiving discounts) to themselves, they feel pride and positive emotions. In addition, Kelley's "covariation theory" (1967) proposes that consumers' perception of receiving discounts that other people cannot obtain will enhance their sense of being a "savvy shopper". Therefore, the literature suggests that consumers' willingness to accept restrictions to obtain discounts should lead to a greater sense of accomplishment and excitement, similar to dynamic pricing strategies (Rohani and Nazari, 2012). Similarly, if consumers attribute these benefits to the discounts they receive, they are more likely to share information about their purchases and make purchases again (Wieseke *et al.*, 2014). Some studies (e.g., Hussain *et al.*, 2020; Rohani and Nazari, 2012) emphasize that when consumers feel that they have a strong relationship with a service provider, they tend to have positive word-of-mouth communication and make repeat purchases.

3 DEVELOPMENT OF HYPOTHESES

Considering the review of relevant literature and the research objectives, the researcher formulated the following hypotheses:

H1: Female tourists are significantly attracted toward discount promotions than male tourists.

H2: Younger tourists are significantly attracted toward discount promotions than older tourists.

H3: Tourists highly motivated by discounts respond significantly to dynamic pricing more positively in comparison to uniform pricing.

H4: Tourists highly motivated by discounts experience more positive emotions from receiving discounts than those with low motivation.

H5: Tourists highly motivated by discounts are more likely to recommend the service to others than those with low motivation.

H6: Tourists highly motivated by discounts are more likely to make repeat bookings than those with low motivation.

4 RESEARCH METHODOLOGY

This study carried out an assessment of tourists' involvement, their emotions, and their behavioral responses considering different situations. This assessment evaluates the effects of uniform and dynamic pricing on tourists' preferences. This study used a convenience sampling technique to select a sample of 150 tourists who arrived at or departed from Jaipur Airport. This study used the Personal Involvement Inventory to assess the preferences of tourists. This study also used a 2x2 experimental design to assess the behavioral and emotional responses of tourists. It is believed that such a design may improve the understanding of psychological processes of tourist behavior. This study will use a 7-point Likert's scale to measure the responses.

Three-way ANOVA and t-tests will be used to test the study hypotheses. Pricing strategies, traveler involvement, and their behavioral and emotional responses will all be examined using a three-way ANOVA. The t-tests will determine whether the emotional and behavioral responses of the groups differ significantly. These statistical tools will ensure the validity and reliability of the study's findings and might provide outcomes leading to improvement in tourist involvement and satisfaction through adoption of varied price strategies.

5 DATA ANALYSIS AND FINDINGS

Table 1. Gender-based and Age-based Tourists' Involvement.

Tourist Profile		Count	Percent	Mean	SD	F-score	*p*-value
Gender	**Male**	82	54.7%	35.8	1.13	6.376	.0126*
	Female	68	45.3%	39.4	1.08		
Age Group	**Younger**	54	36.0%	27.9	0.96	4.852	.0292*
	Older	96	64.0%	42.6	1.07		

* $p < .05$

The table above summarizes the sample characteristics based on tourists' gender and age. As evident, 54.7% of the tourists are male (with mean age = 35.8 and SD = 1.13), while 45.3% of the tourists are female (with mean age = 39.4 and SD = 1.08). Furthermore, the table depicts that 36.0% of the tourists (with mean age = 27.9 and SD = 0.96) are below 35 years of age (categorized as younger tourists), while 64.0% of the tourists (with mean age = 42.6 and SD = 1.07) are above 35 years of age (categorized as older tourists). This suggests a predominance of older tourists in the sample, with males slightly outnumbering females.

The ANOVA analysis for gender distribution (F=6.376, $p<.05$) showed a significant variation between the involvement of male and female tourists, indicating that female participants are more inclined to seek discounts. Consequently, Hypothesis 1 is confirmed. Similarly, the ANOVA analysis for age distribution (F=4.852, $p<.05$) showed a significant variation between the involvement of younger and older tourists, indicating that younger tourists are more proactive in obtaining discounts. This supports Hypothesis 2. Thus, younger tourists and female tourists exhibited a higher propensity to engage with discounts.

Table 2. *t*-score analysis of highly involved tourists.

	Uniform Pricing		Dynamic Pricing			
Responses	Mean	SD	Mean	SD	*t*-score	*p*-value
Emotional Responses	3.14	1.38	5.93	1.05	8.0448*	<.0001
Inform Others	3.57	1.52	6.44	1.14	7.5526*	<.0001
Repeat Purchases	3.91	1.85	7.18	1.33	7.1759*	<.0001

* $p < .01$

Based on Zaichkowsky's study (1985), the researcher classified respondents into three categories according to their involvement scores from the "Personal Involvement Inventory". This inventory includes 20 items measured using a 7-point Likert scale, yielding scores in the range of 20 and 140. The 50 respondents with the highest scores were identified as high-engagement tourists, the 50 respondents with the lowest scores were identified as low-engagement tourists, and the 50 respondents with medium scores were excluded. In this study, scores between 20 and 84 indicate low engagement, and scores between 118 and 140 indicate high engagement.

The analysis focused on 50 high-involvement tourists to evaluate their responses to dynamic versus uniform pricing strategies, especially concerning discount seeking. These responses were split evenly, with a sample of 25 covered under uniform pricing and another sample of 25 covered under dynamic pricing. To evaluate tourists' responses, and emotional responses (including happiness, pride, and gratitude), five dependent variables were collectively analyzed. The independent variables were the pricing strategies (dynamic and uniform), and the dependent variables were the emotional and behavioral response scores.

ANOVA results, presented in Table 2, demonstrate that highly involved tourists had a higher mean emotional score with dynamic pricing (5.93) compared to uniform pricing (3.14). Additionally, the mean score for "inform others" was higher with dynamic pricing (6.44) than with uniform pricing (3.57), and the mean score for "repeat purchases" was significantly higher with dynamic pricing (7.18) versus uniform pricing (3.91). All t-scores for these response categories were significant at the 1% level, thus supporting Hypothesis 3. Thus, tourists with high levels of involvement reacted more favorably to dynamic pricing compared to uniform pricing.

Table 3. ANOVA analysis of low and high involvement tourists.

	Low-Involvement		High-Involvement			
Responses	Mean	SD	Mean	SD	F-score	*p*-value
Emotional Responses	4.22	1.51	5.63	2.18	4.798	<.0001
Inform Others	4.57	1.44	5.35	1.93	5.567	<.0001
Repeat Purchases	4.69	1.62	6.07	2.31	4.918	<.0001

* $p < .01$

Regarding hypothesis 4, the two levels of engagement of tourists in seeking discounts were used as independent variables, and emotional reactions were used as dependent variables. To evaluate tourists' positive feelings about discounts, respondents answered three questions, namely good feelings, pride, and gratitude. Tourists' emotional reactions were measured by averaging these three scores and then analyzed using ANOVA. The ANOVA analysis results in Table 3 show that tourists with higher levels of participation experience more positive emotions when negotiating discounts, and the positive emotion index is significantly affected by participation. The results show that the average emotion score of tourists with higher levels of participation (5.63) is higher than that of tourists with lower levels of participation (4.22). This indicates that there is a significant interaction between engagement and positive feelings, supporting Hypothesis 4: tourists with high engagement will show more positive feelings when they get discounts. In addition, the average scores of "telling others" for tourists with high engagement (5.35) are higher than that for tourists with low engagement (4.57). Similarly, the average repeat purchase score for high-involvement tourists (6.07) was higher than for low-involvement tourists (4.69). Therefore, the results of the ANOVA confirmed Hypothesis 5 and Hypothesis 6, that is, tourists with higher discount motivation are more inclined to share their experiences with others and repeat purchases, and the degree of involvement is positively correlated with the probability of recommending to others and repeat purchases.

6 DISCUSSION OF FINDINGS

The findings of this study are consistent with previous research on consumer behavior, especially in terms of how demographic characteristics affect consumers' receptivity to discount strategies. Tan (2023) found that promotions were more attractive to women. This attraction may stem from the satisfaction and perceived value of discounts, which is consistent with the findings. According to Nyrhinen *et al.* (2024), younger consumers are generally more price-sensitive and respond more positively to promotions, especially in areas such as travel and leisure. The tendency to make impulse purchases or financial constraints may be the reasons for this behavior. These findings confirm the view that demographic-based targeted marketing strategies can successfully increase satisfaction and engagement among specific traveler groups, especially women and young people. This finding is in line with the previous observation made by Keller *et al.* (2022), which outlined that several consumers take dynamic pricing as an opportunity that decreases prices, and hence, increases their involvement.

However, a few studies have offered contrasting perspective on how dynamic prices and discounts impact consumer experience and satisfaction. For example, Inderst and Obradovits (2024) argued that initially price-conscious consumers may find discounts attractive, but subsequently, brand loyalty may be harmed due to very low price expectations by consumers. The findings of the current research suggests that travelers who are highly motivated by discounts not only express more positive emotions but also demonstrate greater loyalty, as evidenced by recommendations for services and repeat business. This difference in perspectives might indicate that dynamic pricing and discount-based strategies in the tourism sector might not exactly harm brand loyalty, but might improve experience and satisfaction. Overall, these findings highlight that, with a well-planned and properly-executed approach, dynamic pricing strategies might prove successful in the tourism sector over uniform pricing strategies, because discount-based prices better meet consumer expectations and build deep emotional bonds between travelers and travel agencies; thus, promote traveler loyalty and involvement.

7 CONCLUSION

7.1 *Concluding remarks*

The findings of the present study suggest that strategies based on dynamic prices and discounts significantly influence tourists' behavior and preferences, keeping in mind the tourist demographics and discount motivation. The findings provide that female and younger travelers find these strategies more effective. This highlights a need for a focused marketing campaign targeting these groups. In addition, tourists who are highly motivated by discounts do exhibit a strong favor toward dynamic pricing strategies. For such tourists, dynamic pricing strategies might create opportunity and positive experience. Further, such tourists exhibited highly favorable emotional response to discounts, which outlines the psychological benefits perceived by highly price-sensitive consumers. Such tourists have demonstrated a higher chance of repeating the bookings or recommending the services.

In light of the study's findings, travel agencies should aim to utilize dynamic pricing strategies to attract specific demographic segments, such as young and female travelers, tourists motivated by discounts, etc. For example, offering tailored promotions or unique dynamic pricing discounts can significantly increase the involvement of these target groups. Discounts can help businesses gain repeat customers and referrals by creating great experiences and positive emotions. This results in happier, more satisfied customers who are more loyal to the brand. Travel agencies can combine discounts with traveler demographics to retain them and promote word-of-mouth. This can help businesses grow and remain competitive.

7.2 *Research implications*

This study develops a theoretical understanding of how discounts and customer demographic factors influence travelers' preferences. It shows that travelers prefer various incentives based on factors such as age, gender, and personal goals. These preferences influence tourists' loyalty, emotional responses, and willingness to recommend. Furthermore, this study supports dynamic pricing strategies based on its findings that dynamic pricing is more likely to attract those who prefer discounts.

These findings also have practical implications for marketers and strategists working in the tourism sector. They can focus their discount-based marketing efforts on women, young, and price-conscious tourists. This might help them raise customer satisfaction and profit levels. Additionally, fostering positive feelings through well-timed promotions may promote referrals and repeat business, which can help a business grow over the long run by boosting word-of-mouth marketing and customer loyalty.

7.3 *Limitations of the study*

The limitations of the present study are discussed as follows. First, this study employed a scenario-based method, which relies on respondents projecting their feelings and reactions to assess those of others, potentially introducing bias inherent to human nature. Additionally, the interpersonal dynamics typical of actual service encounters were not captured in this method. Second, for simplification of data analysis and interpretation, the ages of tourists were consolidated into two categories, despite the research instrument originally having more nuanced age categories. Third, the study participants assessed dynamic pricing strategies using a single location, which might have caused some of them to have an unrealistic grasp of suitable price ranges for different tour services.

7.4 *Avenues for future research*

Future research should look into how dynamic pricing influences tourist preferences in various locations and types of attractions to improve the overall relevance of the findings. Broadening the demographic categories beyond the basic age groups used in this study would help provide a clearer picture of how different age groups react to dynamic pricing. Moreover, using real-world service experiences instead of just scenario-based methods could lead to more precise insights into tourist behavior and preferences. It would also be beneficial to examine the long-term impacts of dynamic pricing on customer loyalty and satisfaction within the tourism sector. Finally, investigating how cultural differences affect tourist reactions to dynamic pricing could provide additional insights for customizing strategies for different tourist markets.

REFERENCES

Akbari K. (2023). Innovation in Pricing Mechanisms: An Analysis of the Emergence of Fixed and Dynamic Pricing in Five Countries. *Interface*, 20: 37–87.

Banerjee A, Banik P, and Worndl W. (2023). A review on individual and multi-stakeholder fairness in tourism recommender systems. *Frontiers in Big Data*, 6: 1168692.

Dole, A. (2023). An Analysis of Hotel Booking Cancellations and Factors Affecting Revenue Generation. *International Journal for Research in Applied Science and Engineering Technology*, DOI: 10.22214/ijraset.2023.56407.

Haerling, A.K. and Prion, S. (2020). Two-by-Two Factorial Design. *Clinical Simulation in Nursing*, 49: 90–91.

Hussain S, Song X, and Niu B. (2020). Consumers' Motivational Involvement in eWOM for Information Adoption: The Mediating Role of Organizational Motives. *Frontiers in Psychology*, 10: 3055.

Inderst R. and Obradovits M. (2024). Price promotions as a threat to brands. *Journal of Economics and Management Strategy,* 33(1): 53–77.

Jasrotia S, Kamila M, and Patel, V. (2021). Impact of Sustainable Tourism on Tourist's Satisfaction: Evidence from India. *Business Perspectives and Research*, 11(2): 227853372110439.

Kee D, Sirajudeen S, Hizer N, *et al.* (2024). Optimizing Marketing Strategies for Enhanced Sales Performance in the Travel and Tourism Sector. *International Journal of Tourism* and *Hospitality in Asia Pacific*, 7(1): 58–70.

Keller A, Vogelsang M, and Totzek D. (2022). How displaying price discounts can mitigate negative customer reactions to dynamic pricing. *Journal of Business Research*, 148: 277–291.

Kelly HH. (1967). Attribution theory in social psychology. In: D Levine (Ed.), *Nebraska Symposium on Motivation* (pp.192–238). Lincoln: University of Nebraska Press.

Klein A. and Sharma VM. (2022). Consumer Decision-making Styles, Involvement, and the Intention to Participate in Online Group Buying. *Journal of Retailing and Consumer Services*, 64(1): 102808.

Kopalle P, Pauwels K, Akella L, *et al.* (2023). Dynamic pricing: Definition, implications for managers, and future research directions. *Journal of Retailing*, 99(3): 1–43.

Michaelidou N. and Dibb S. (2008). Consumer involvement: A new perspective. *The Marketing Review*, 8(1): 83–99.

Mihai VC, Dumitras DE, Oroian C, *et al.* (2023). Exploring the Factors Involved in Tourists' Decision-Making and Determinants of Length of Stay. *Administrative Sciences*, 13(10): 215.

Nyrhinen J, Sirola A, Koskelainen T, *et al.* (2024). Online antecedents for young consumers' impulse buying behavior. *Computers in Human Behavior*, 153: 108129.

Pillai A. (2023). AI-driven dynamic pricing strategy for subscription features: Leveraging artificial intelligence for real-time pricing optimization. *International Journal of Computer Engineering and Technology*, 14(3): 98–103.

Ramadhani DP, Alamsyah A, Febrianta MY, *et al.* (2024). Exploring Tourists' Behavioral Patterns in Bali's Top-Rated Destinations: Perception and Mobility. *Journal of Theoretical and Applied Electronic Commerce Research,* 19: 743–773.

Rohani A. and Nazari M. (2012). Impact of Dynamic Pricing Strategies on Consumer Behavior. *Journal of Management Research*, 4(4): 143–159.

Tan WK. (2023). When do price discounts become attractive? A study comparing discount strategies on consumer perceptions. *Asia Pacific Journal of Marketing and Logistics*, 35(6): 1404–1424.

Victor V, Thoppan JJ, Fekete-Farkas M, *et al.* (2019). Pricing strategies in the era of digitalization and the perceived shift in consumer behavior of youth in Poland. *Journal of International Studies,* 12(3): 74–91.

Wieseke J, Alavi S, and Habel J. (2014). Willing to Pay More, Eager to Pay Less: The Role of Customer Loyalty in Price Negotiations. *Journal of Marketing*, 78(6): 17–37.

Zaichkowsky JL. (1985). Measuring the involvement construct. *Journal of Consumer Research,* 12: 341–352.

Advancement in Engineering and Science – Goyal et al. (Eds)

Artificial Intelligence and Blockchain Technology in Healthcare Management

Virendra S. Gomase
S.P. Mandali's Prin. L. N. Welingkar Institute of Management Development & Research, Mumbai, India

ABSTRACT: Artificial intelligence and blockchain technology combined ability to fully transform healthcare management by resolving current issues, which opening up new possibilities. Blockchain technology, an open network for authorization and information exchange, is being applied to artificial intelligence framework in e-Health. Medical records of patients will be accessible to healthcare professionals on the blockchain. Massive volumes of data, decision-making ability, and a variety of proposed algorithms are all used in artificial intelligence. Blockchain technology improve the decentralization, transparency, accuracy, security, and impenetrability of health care systems.

Blockchain technology enables the storage of cryptographic records that artificial intelligence requires. Chatbots for diagnosis and treatment, predictive analytics, personalized medicine, and other areas are examples of how artificial intelligence is being used in healthcare management. Applications of blockchain technology including interoperability, supply chain management, clinical trial management, data security, data integrity in healthcare management. Artificial intelligence and blockchain technology have been integrated into modern hospital management to develop a more efficient, safe, and patient centric healthcare system. It can promote the creation of numbers of potentially life-saving applications in radiology, cancer treatment, cardiology, dermatology, and fundoscopy.

Keywords: Blockchain technologies, Artificial intelligence, Healthcare, e-Health, Personalized Health Data

1 INTRODUCTION

Artificial intelligence and blockchain technology are the cutting-edge technologies driving a digital revolution in the healthcare industry. AI has already begun to revolutionize healthcare management due to its capacity to evaluate large amounts of information, forecast results, enhance diagnostic precision, and optimize therapeutic strategies. Through the simplification of repetitive processes and the improvement of decision-making, AI assists healthcare providers in delivering more effective and customized therapy. Among its uses are management tasks in the healthcare sector and early disease detection (Schiavone and Ferretti, 2021). Artificial intelligence in healthcare management refers to the use of complex simulated algorithms, machine learning, and data analytics to automate tasks and mimic human intelligence in the healthcare industry. Artificial intelligence technology analyze vast amounts of healthcare data to assist with patient care, disease diagnosis, treatment planning, and new drug discovery. Management duties like scheduling, data processing claims, and resource management are also made more effective by it. While giving patients personalised and predictive healthcare solutions, artificial intelligence enhances clinical trial solutions, streamlines processes, and cost effectiveness.

In healthcare management, blockchain technology refers to the use of immutable, secure, and decentralized digital ledger systems for the management and exchange of healthcare records. Blockchain technology can help healthcare organizations make clinical trial data, pharmaceutical supply chains, and patient information more secure, transparent, and interoperable. Blockchain technology reduces insurance claim fraud, confirms the legitimacy of medications, patients health data accuracy, reliability, safety, and quality exchange of data across institutions. This new technology improves data integrity while safeguarding patient safety and privacy (Ganesan, 2022; Maaß, *et al.*, 2024).

Combining of blockchain technology and artificial intelligence has the capability to change healthcare management. In addition to streamlining procedures and addressing concerns like data security, privacy, and trust, this would enhance patient results. It is necessary that ethical and regulatory problems be thoroughly examined before adopting new technologies to guarantee their responsible and equitable use (Jain, 2023; Jung, 2019).

2 RESEARCH STATEMENT

Data Security and Privacy- It examines how blockchain technology can safely share data for Artificial intelligence driven data analytics and research, ensure compliance with regulations like HIPAA and GDPR, and safeguard patient information.

Data Sharing and Interoperability- Data analyzing how blockchain technology could facilitate seamless data exchange between healthcare institutions.

Artificial intelligence driven Clinical Decision Support Systems (CDSS)- Research and development of blockchain technology enabled artificial intelligence driven clinical decision support systems (CDSS) to ensure accountability, transparency, and patient and physician trust in AI recommendations.

Precision medicine- Using blockchain technology and artificial intelligence to safely handle and examine large datasets information in order to tailor the unique genetics profile of individual patient's.

Supply chain management in healthcare - Blockchain technology improves pharmaceuticals and medical supply tracking and verification, while artificial intelligence can optimize inventories and logistics, reducing waste and ensuring the timely delivery of healthcare information (Acs, *et al.*, 2020; Patel, *et al.*, 2024).

3 E-HEALTH FRAMEWORK

Artificial intelligence is significantly enhancing many aspects of healthcare delivery, is revolutionizing the e-health sector. Artificial intelligence is causing rapid transformation in the

DOI: 10.1201/9781003798514-68

healthcare industry, with e-health at the forefront. E-health implies to the uses of electronic technologies for healthcare framework (Tagde, *et al.*, 2021).

4 AI-BASED HEALTHCARE TOOLS

Artificial intelligence technologies greatly transforming healthcare in many ways by supporting innovative solutions that improve patient outcomes, efficacy, and precision. Following is the some of the most important AI-based healthcare technologies and applications (Table 1).

4.1 *Diagnostic imaging*

Artificial intelligence Image Analysis- AI tools find irregularities and assist radiologists in making more accurate and timely patient pathological diagnoses. Artificial intelligence algorithms are capable of analyzing medical imaging, i.e., CT scans, X-rays, MRIs. Examples include - software tools that detect irregularities in scans, fractures, or malignancies (Alhasan and Hasaneen, 2021).

4.2 *Clinical decision support*

Clinical Artificial intelligence Assistants- AI based software systems can evaluate patient data (including test results, healthcare records, and genetic information) and provide possible risks, treatment options, and prescription dosages based on clinical guidelines and best practices (Bozyel, *et al.*, 2024).

4.3 *Remote monitoring and telemedicine*

Wearable Devices- Artificial intelligence software can access the data from wearable devices, i.e., fitness trackers, smartwatches and give proper solutions. Which is to alert healthcare professionals to any anomalies or crises in real-time patient health assessment data. To remotely monitor patients, spot anomalies, and provide timely treatments, artificial intelligence (AI) algorithms analyze real-time health data from wearables (i.e., smartwatches, fitness trackers) (Li, *et al.*, 2021).

Table 1. Artificial intelligence based various tools used in healthcare.

Tool	Description	Applications	Benefits
AI-powered Diagnostic Systems	Machine learning algorithms that analyze medical images, test results, and clinical data for diagnoses.	Radiology (e.g., interpreting X-rays, MRIs), pathology, dermatology, ophthalmology.	Reduces diagnostic errors, speeds up interpretation of images, and assists healthcare professionals in decision-making.
AI-Natural Language Processing (NLP)	Artificial intelligence algorithms that process and analyze human language from clinical notes, records, and research papers.	Clinical documentation, extracting patients information, electronic health records (EHRs), summarizing healthcare literature.	Improves clinical documentation accuracy, enhances research productivity, and aids in efficient information retrieval.
Predictive Analytics	Artificial intelligence tools that analyze healthcare data to predict patient outcomes or disease progression.	Predicting hospital readmissions, identifying at-risk patients for chronic diseases, forecasting disease outbreaks.	Helps in early intervention, reduces hospital readmissions, and improves patient management by identifying high-risk individuals.
AI-based Virtual Health Assistants	Artificial intelligence powered virtual assistants or chatbots that provide healthcare guidance and perform routine tasks.	Appointment scheduling, medication reminders, symptom checking, answering basic healthcare queries.	Enhances patient engagement, reduces management workload, and provides 24/7 access to health information.
Robotic Surgery Systems	Artificial intelligence integrated robotic systems that assist surgeons in performing precise surgeries.	Minimally invasive surgeries, such as prostate or heart surgeries, and other complex procedures.	Improves surgical precision, reduces human error, shortens recovery times, and minimizes the risk of complications.
AI-based Drug Discovery	Machine learning models that analyze biological data to identify potential drug candidates.	Drug development, screening for new compounds, analyzing genetic data for personalized treatments.	Accelerates drug discovery, reduces costs, and brings new treatments to market faster.
CDSS - Clinical Decision Support Systems	Artificial intelligence based tools that provide healthcare professionals with data-driven suggestions to aid clinical decisions.	Diagnosis assistance, treatment recommendations, managing patient care plans.	Improves decision-making, reduces human error, and ensures evidence-based treatment plans.
Wearable Health Devices	Devices powered by Artificial intelligence that continuously monitor vital signs and health data in real-time.	Remote monitoring of chronic conditions, fitness tracking, and personalized health optimization.	Enables continuous patient monitoring, provides real-time health data, and allows for early detection of abnormalities.
AI in Personalized Medicine	Artificial intelligence algorithms that tailor treatments to individual patient characteristics based on genetic data and other factors.	Cancer treatment, genetic disorder management, and drug dosage optimization.	Optimizes treatment effectiveness, reduces adverse reactions, and personalizes patient care.
AI-powered Image Analysis Tools	Artificial intelligence systems that analyze medical imaging data to detect and classify diseases.	Detecting cancers, neurological disorders, cardiovascular diseases, and other abnormalities in imaging.	Provides early diagnosis, improves accuracy, and reduces the time needed to interpret medical images.
AI for Epidemiological Surveillance	Artificial intelligence tools that track and predict the spread of diseases using data analytics.	Monitoring disease outbreaks, forecasting epidemic trends, guiding public health interventions.	Improves outbreak prediction, supports public health decision-making, and helps in the allocation of resources.
AI in Mental Health	Artificial intelligence algorithms that analyze speech, behavior, and physiological data to monitor mental health conditions.	Diagnosis of depression, anxiety, PTSD, and other mental health disorders using voice or behavioral analysis.	Enhances early detection, offers personalized mental health support, and reduces the stigma around seeking help.

4.4 *Personalized medicine*

Genomics and artificial intelligence- Artificial intelligence systems useful for analysis of DNA, RNA, Genomics information to find out genetic profile which cause particular disorder. It can predict the patients response for personalised therapy (Gomase, *et al.*, 2024a; Gomase, *et al.*, 2024b; Gomase, *et al.*, 2008a; Gomase, *et al.*, 2008b; Gomase, *et al.*, 2008c; Martínez-García and Hernández-Lemus, 2022).

4.5 *New drug design and development*

Artificial intelligence in new drug design- artificial intelligence software models have the potential to reduce the time and cost needed to bring novel therapeutics to market by speeding up the search for new drugs and improving the qualities of existing medicinal compounds through the simulation and prediction of molecular interactions. Examples- *Insilico* Medicine uses artificial intelligence to generate molecules with specific therapeutic properties and identify new pharmacological targets (Vora, *et al.*, 2023).

4.6 *Management efficiency*

Healthcare Management Systems- Artificial intelligence-based platforms automate management tasks including processing insurance claims, arranging appointments, and managing EHR (electronic health records), which decreases management burdens and improves workflow efficiency. Examples- Cerner and Epic Systems employ AI - increases the patient care coordination and healthcare procedures (Graham, *et al*, 2019).

4.7 *VHA-Virtual Health Assistants*

Chatbots and Virtual Nurses- Artificial intelligence driven chatbots and virtual assistants can communicate with patients to provide information, answer questions, disease diagnosis, and offer guidance on how to handle persistent healthcare conditions. Examples - Babylon Health's chatbot, which offers symptom checks and medical advice, enhances patient engagement and information access to healthcare (Morrow, *et al.*, 2023).

4.8 *NLP-Natural Language Processing*

Medical Text Analysis- Clinical research case reports are examples of unstructured medical literature from which AI-powered natural language processing (NLP) systems can extract and evaluate data to help research, decision-making, and data mining for healthcare insights (Crema, *et al.*, 2022).

4.9 *Clinical trials and research*

Artificial intelligence in Research- Large datasets from clinical trials and healthcare research are analyzed by artificial intelligence algorithms to identify trends, linkages, and potential biomarkers for diseases (You, *et al.*, 2022).

4.10 *Robotics and surgery*

Surgical Assistance- Artificial intelligence driven robots help in surgery because they improve patient outcomes, increase precision, and reduce human error. Example- The AI-powered Da Vinci Surgical System enhances control and dexterity during minimally invasive surgeries (Alafaleq, 2023).

5 BLOCKCHAIN TECHNOLOGY (BCT) IN E-HEALTH AND HEALTHCARE

Blockchain technology is quickly emerging as a new game changer in e-health, offering solutions to a variety of issues pertaining to healthcare management and security (Xie, *et al.*, 2021) (Table 2).

Table 2. Blockchain technology (BCT) in e-Health and Healthcare.

Feature	Description	Applications in e-Health	Benefits
HER-Electronic Health Records	Blockchain technology-(BCT) provides a decentralized system for storing, sharing, and securing patient health records.	Blockchain technology (BCT) sharing and storing patient health records securely across healthcare systems.	Ensures data security, enhances privacy, improves data accessibility, and enables seamless sharing across providers.
Supply Chain Management	Blockchain technology (BCT) tracks the movement of pharmaceuticals and healthcare supplies from manufacturing unit to patient.	Monitoring the authenticity and status of healthcare products, pharmaceuticals, and vaccines.	Improves transparency, reduces counterfeit drugs, ensures product authenticity, and increases supply chain efficiency.
Medical Billing and Payments	Blockchain technology-(BCT) streamlines and secures billing processes, reducing fraud and errors in payments.	Automating insurance claims, payments to healthcare providers, and patient billing systems.	Reduces fraud, minimizes errors, improves transparency, and accelerates the payment process.
Clinical Trials and Research	Blockchain technology-(BCT) ensures integrity and transparency by recording clinical trial information in an immutable ledger.	Tracking clinical trial data, ensuring compliance with regulations, and preventing data manipulation.	Enhances trust in research findings, ensures accurate data reporting, and improves accountability in trials.
Remote Monitoring and Telemedicine	Blockchain technology-(BCT) secures telemedicine consultations and patient data in remote health monitoring systems.	Securing video consultations, storing remote patient monitoring data, and controlling access to sensitive health data.	Improves patient privacy, ensures secure communication. Allows patients to access health data.
Data sharing and Integration	Blockchain technology-(BCT) facilitates secure and efficient information exchange between various healthcare providers and systems.	Sharing patient health data across healthcare organizations and systems, ensuring data interoperability.	Improves seamless data exchange, reduces delays, and ensures privacy and security across systems.
Smart Contracts for Healthcare Services	Blockchain technology-(BCT) smart contracts automate healthcare transactions and service agreements.	Automating agreements for healthcare services, insurance claims, and patient treatment protocols.	Reduces management burden, ensures compliance, automates billing, and enhances trust in service agreements.
Identity Management and	Blockchain technology-(BCT) ensures secure, verifiable digital identities for health-	Managing digital identities of patients and healthcare providers, controlling access to	Enhances patient privacy, reduces fraud, ensures accurate authentication,

(*continued*)

Table 2. Continued

Feature	Description	Applications in e-Health	Benefits
Authentication	care professionals and patients.	sensitive health information.	and simplifies access management.
Health Data Security, Data Privacy	Blockchain technology-(BCT) strengthens the privacy and security of sensitive health data using cryptographic encryption.	Protecting patient healthcare data, Protecting unauthorized access. Ensuring healthcare compliance, Privacy regulations (e.g., HIPAA).	Provides tamper-proof data storage, enhances compliance with privacy laws, and strengthens patient data protection.
Decentralized Healthcare Networks	Blockchain technology-(BCT) allows for the creation of decentralized healthcare networks, reducing dependence on central authorities.	Establishing patient-driven health networks, promoting decentralized patient care, and reducing management layers.	Empowers patients data, access to healthcare, and reduces central authority dependency.
Insurance and Claims Processing	Blockchain technology-(BCT) secures and automates health insurance claims processing.	Automating insurance verification, processing claims, and validating eligibility in health insurance systems.	Reduces fraud, speeds up claims processing, ensures accuracy in billing, and enhances transparency in insurance workflows.
Pharmaceutical Research and Development	Blockchain technology-(BCT) tracks the R&D process of drugs, ensuring transparency and integrity of the data used in development.	Recording drug development progress, tracking clinical trials, and verifying research information integrity.	Ensures the authenticity of research data, improves regulatory compliance, and enhances drug development transparency.

5.1 *Data integrity, Data security*

Immutable Records- Blockchain technology provides a secure, immutable ledger for the secure maintenance and access of healthcare records. Patient information integrity and tamper resistance are secured because each entry is cryptographically encrypted (Raimundo and Rosário, 2021; Khanna, *et al.*, 2022).

5.2 *Health data interoperability*

Blockchain technology provides a single platform that facilitates interoperability, allowing healthcare professionals to securely access and exchange standardized patient records across several systems and research institutions. BCT reduces overhead expenses and improves care coordination (Kann, *et al.*, 2021; Durneva, *et al.*, 2020).

5.3 *Clinical trials and research*

Blockchain technology enhances clinical trial efficiency and transparency by securely storing and managing clinical trial output data, including participant permission, protocol adherence, and clinical trial results. BCT reduces data breaches, fraud, ensures data accuracy, and speeds up the development of new treatments (Zhuang, *et al.*, 2022; Hirano, *et al.*, 2020).

5.4 *Secure and interoperable health data exchange*

Blockchain technology enables the safe, accurate, efficient exchange of electronic healthcare data between authorized organisation, such as research institute, hospitals, researchers, insurers, healthcare providers, and patients. Smart agreement can control and supervised data privacy, data sharing, and data compliance (Yeung, 2021; Kasyapa and Vanmathi, 2024).

5.5 *Supply chain management*

Blockchain technology tracks each stage of the raw materials, manufacturing, distribution, and patient use of pharmaceuticals, healthcare devices. Authenticity, transparency, safety are increased by minimising the quantity of counterfeit medications, which can ensure regulatory compliance, and efficiency (Yavaprabhas, *et al.*, 2022).

5.6 *Credentialing and licensing*

Blockchain technology verifies and maintains the validity of healthcare professionals' qualifications and licenses. BCT streamlines credentialing processes and reduces management burdens for healthcare employers (Tsolakis, *et al.*, 2022; Dutta, *et al.*, 2020).

5.7 *Telemedicine and remote monitoring*

Blockchain technology securely facilitates transactions and data transfers in telemedicine systems, protecting patient privacy, safety and data integrity during remote consultations and monitoring operations (McBee and Wilcox, 2020; Ahmad, *et al.*, 2021).

5.8 *Healthcare payments and billing*

Simplified Transactions- Blockchain technology can streamline healthcare billing and payment procedures by automating patient claim verification and processing, reducing fraud, and ensuring timely reimbursements between patients, insurance companies, healthcare professionals and hospitals (Krichen, *et al.*, 2022; Cadoret, *et al.*, 2020).

5.9 *Patient consent management*

Decentralized Consent Management- Blockchain technology gives patients the ability to decide whether to provide researchers, healthcare providers, and healthcare professionals access to their personal health data (Almalki, 2023; El-Gazzar and Stendal, 2020; Maslove, *et al.*, 2018).

5.10 *Public health surveillance*

Data sharing in real time - Blockchain technology enables sharing of data in real time between public health authorities and healthcare provider organisation, including patient records, vaccination records and disease outbreaks. This technology improves epidemiological monitoring and speeds up public health emergency response (Mamo, *et al.*, 2020; Baysal, *et al.*, 2023).

5.11 *Health data-privacy and consent management*

Decentralized authority- Blockchain technology help patient's to greater authority over their healthcare records, safety and efficacy. Patients can accept and deny access to their data through smart agreement, which automate and supervised data sharing agreements while maintaining privacy, safety and efficacy (Velmovitsky, *et al.*, 2021; Zubaydi, *et al.*, 2023).

6 RESEARCH OUTCOMES

Applied research with the help of artificial intelligence - blockchain technology in healthcare management is expected to provide several significant findings that will transform healthcare systems by enhancing the effectiveness, security, and treatment of patient.

Effective Data Security and Privacy- Blockchain technology will gives healthcare systems a more secure, decentralized foundation for managing patient health record data. Blockchain technology will facilitate safe data sharing among healthcare professional and healthcare providers, which enabling real-time collaboration without compromising data security (Khanna, *et al.*, 2022; Barrett, *et al.*, 2019; Anton, *et al.*, 2022; Bonny, *et al.*, 2023; Hamilton, 2024).

Interoperability and Data Integration- The problem of data silos may be resolved by integrating blockchain technology with artificial intelligence algorithms to make it simple for healthcare data to be exchanged across different healthcare systems and organizations (Ji, *et al.*, 2023; Vodanović, *et al.*, 2023; Wehkamp, *et al.*, 2023; Ismail, *et al.*, 2021).

CDSS-Clinical Decision Support Systems- Artificial intelligence determined CDSS will be able to give physicians data-backed recommendations in real time thanks to blockchain technologies transparency, traceability and accuracy.

Personalized Medicine and Precision Healthcare- The development of personalized medicine will depend heavily on blockchain technology and artificial intelligence (Zhuang, *et al.*, 2020; Esmaeilzadeh and Mirzaei, 2019; Gaynor, *et al.*, 2020; Pilares, *et al.*, 2022; Lin, *et al.*, 2022; Sahoo, *et al.*, 2022; Mashamba-Thompson and Crayton, 2020).

Healthcare Supply Chain Efficiency- Blockchain technology will increase the traceability of vaccine, helathcare, and pharmaceuticals supplies, with reducing counterfeiting, bolstering inventory control, and ensuring the timely delivery of vital resources.

Trust and Openness in AI-Driven Healthcare Solutions- Blockchain technology will provide a trustworthy, transparent and auditable method for verifying the findings of healthcare research produced by artificial intelligence.

Support for Telemedicine and Remote Care- Blockchain technology and artificial intelligence will enhance telemedicine systems by facilitating the safe, transparent, accurate exchange of health data between patients and healthcare providers. Artificial intelligence will assist with remote monitoring and diagnostics, while blockchain technology will safeguard patient data (Sahu, *et al.*, 2024; Saeed, *et al.*, 2022; Xie, *et al.*, 2021; Jabarulla and Lee, 2021; Pablo, *et al.*, 2021; Singh, *et al.*, 2023; Srivastava, *et al.*, 2022; Mamoshina, *et al.*, 2017; Hiwale, *et al.*, 2023; Krittanawong, *et al.*, 2020; Skaria, *et al.*, 2020).

7 CONCLUSION

The application of artificial intelligence technology in the healthcare industry is a revolutionary development that enhances numerous facets of healthcare management, practice, and new drug research. Artificial intelligence enhancing patient outcomes, accuracy, and efficiency. Artificial intelligence technologies are completely changing the way healthcare management, for example, computer vision, machine learning, and natural language processing.

Artificial intelligence algorithms can analyze pathological and medical images of patients to give easy, accurate and early diagnosis of disorders including cancer and cardiac diseases. Artificial intelligence improves disease treatment planning and diagnostic accuracy. Artificial intelligence powered systems optimize medication dosages, reduce medical errors, and it provide personalized medicine and treatment suggestions by combining patient data and healthcare information. Artificial intelligence increases therapeutic efficacy and decreases negative effects by using genomics, proteomics data analysis to tailor treatment plans based on patient genetic / DNA profiles. Artificial intelligence powered wearables and devices, which provide proactive chronic condition care outside of traditional hospital settings by enabling real-time patient health monitoring. Blockchain technology applications in healthcare sector provide workable solutions to enduring issues with interoperability, patient centered treatment, and data security. The decentralized and unchangeable nature of blockchain technology has many advantages that are transforming many facets of healthcare delivery and management. Blockchain technology uses data encryption and decentralized data storage to make sure the data integrity, data security of patient's information. AI and BCT minimising the data breaches, unauthorised access to improves patient data privacy, accuracy, and confidentiality. Blockchain technology facilitates the safer, easy transformation of medico-pathological data and health information between different healthcare services providers. AI and BCT gives better patient compliance, reduced management workloads, and enhanced healthcare coordination are all made possible by interoperability.

AUTHOR CONTRIBUTIONS

Sole author

CONFLICT OF INTEREST

No Conflict of Interest

ACKNOWLEDGEMENT/FUNDING

Author is thankful to S.P. Mandali's Prin. L. N. Welingkar Institute of Management Development & Research, Mumbai, 400019, India

REFERENCES

Acs, B., Rantalainen, M., and Hartman, J. (2020). Artificial intelligence as the next step towards precision pathology. *J Intern Med*, 288(1), 62-81. https://doi.org/10.1111/joim.13030

Ahmad, R.W., Salah, K., Jayaraman, R., Yaqoob, I., Ellahham, S., and Omar, M. (2021). The role of blockchain technology in telehealth and telemedicine. *International Journal of Medical Informatics*, 148, 104399. https://doi.org/10.1016/j.ijmedinf.2021.104399

Alafaleq, M. (2023). Robotics and cybersurgery in ophthalmology: A current perspective. *Journal of Robot Surgery*, 17(4), 1159–1170. https://doi.org/10.1007/s11701-023-01532-y

Alhasan, M., and Hasaneen, M. (2021). Digital imaging, technologies and artificial intelligence applications during the COVID-19 pandemic. *Computerized Medical Imaging and Graphics,* 91, 101933. https://doi.org/10.1016/j.compmedimag.2021.101933

Almalki, J. (2023). State-of-the-art research in blockchain of things for healthcare. *Arabian Journal for Science and Engineering*, 1-29. https://doi.org/10.1007/s13369-023-07896-5

Anton, N., Doroftei, B., Curteanu, S., Catălin, L., Ilie, O.D., Târcoveanu, F., and Bogdănici, C.M. (2022). Comprehensive review on the use of artificial intelligence in ophthalmology and future research directions. *Diagnostics (Basel)*, 13(1), 100. https://doi.org/10.3390/diagnostics13010100

Barrett, M., Boyne, J., Brandts, J., Brunner-La Rocca, H.P., De Maesschalck, L., De Wit, K., Dixon, L., Eurlings, C., Fitzsimons, D., Golubnitschaja, O., Hageman, A., Heemskerk, F., Hintzen, A., Helms, T.M., Hill, L., Hoedemakers, T., Marx, N., McDonald, K.,

Mertens, M., Müller-Wieland, D., Palant, A., Piesk, J., Pomazanskyi, A., Ramaekers, J., Ruff, P., Schütt, K., Shekhawat, Y., Ski, C.F., Thompson, D.R., Tsirkin, A., van der Mierden, K., Watson, C., and Zippel-Schultz, B. (2019). Artificial intelligence supported patient self-care in chronic heart failure: A paradigm shift from reactive to predictive, preventive, and personalized care. *EPMA Journal*, 10(4), 445–464. https://doi.org/10.1007/s13167-019-00188-9

Baysal, M.V., Özcan-Top, Ö., and Betin-Can, A. (2023). Blockchain technology applications in the health domain: A multivocal literature review. *Journal of Supercomputing*, 79(3), 3112-3156. https://doi.org/10.1007/s11227-022-04772-1

Bonny, T., Al Nassan, W., Obaideen, K., Al Mallahi, M.N., Mohammad, Y., and El-Damanhoury, H.M. (2023). Contemporary role and applications of artificial intelligence in dentistry. *F1000 Research*, 12, 1179. https://doi.org/10.12688/f1000research.140204.1

Bozyel, S., Şimşek, E., Koçyiğit Burunkaya, D., Güler, A., Korkmaz, Y., Şeker, M., Ertürk, M., and Keser, N. (2024). Artificial intelligence-based clinical decision support systems in cardiovascular diseases. *Anatolian Journal of Cardiology*, 28(2), 74–86. https://doi.org/10.14744/AnatolJCardiol.2023.3685

Cadoret, D., Kailas, T., Velmovitsky, P., Morita, P., and Igboeli, O. (2020). Proposed implementation of blockchain in British Columbia's health care data management. *Journal of Medical Internet Research*, 22(10), e20897. https://doi.org/10.2196/20897

Crema, C., Attardi, G., Sartiano, D., and Redolfi, A. (2022). Natural language processing in clinical neuroscience and psychiatry: A review. *Frontiers in Psychiatry*, 13, 946387. https://doi.org/10.3389/fpsyt.2022.946387

Durneva, P., Cousins, K., and Chen, M. (2020). The current state of research, challenges, and future research directions of blockchain technology in patient care: Systematic review. *Journal of Medical Internet Research*, 22(7), e18619. https://doi.org/10.2196/18619

Dutta, P., Choi, T.M., Somani, S., and Butala, R. (2020). Blockchain technology in supply chain operations: Applications, challenges and research opportunities. *Transportation Research Part E: Logistics and Transportation Review*, 142, 102067. https://doi.org/10.1016/j.tre.2020.102067

El-Gazzar, R., and Stendal, K. (2020). Blockchain in health care: Hope or hype? Journal of Medical Internet Research, 22(7), e17199. https://doi.org/10.2196/17199

Esmaeilzadeh, P., and Mirzaei, T. (2019). The potential of blockchain technology for health information exchange: Experimental study from patients' perspectives. *Journal of Medical Internet Research,* 21 (6), e14184. https://doi.org/10.2196/14184

Ganesan, D. (2022). Human Rights Implications of the Digital Revolution in Health Care in India. *Health and Human Rights*, 24(1), 5-19.

Gaynor, M., Tuttle-Newhall, J., Parker, J., Patel, A., and Tang, W. (2020). Adoption of blockchain in health care. *Journal of Medical Internet Research*, 22(9), e17423. https://doi.org/10.2196/17423

Gomase VS, Dhamane SP, Kakade PG. Immunoproteomics: A Review of Techniques, Applications, and Advancements. *Protein Pept Lett.* 2024 Nov 6. doi: 10.2174/0109298665333029240926092919.

Gomase VS, Dhamane SP, Kemkar KR, Kakade PG, Sakhare AD. Immunoproteomics: Approach to Diagnostic and Vaccine Development. *Protein Pept Lett.* 2024 Oct 25. doi: 10.2174/0109298665342261240912105111.

Gomase VS, Kale KV, Tagore S, Hatture SR. Proteomics: technologies for protein analysis. *Curr Drug Metab.* 2008 Mar;9(3):213-20. doi: 10.2174/138920008783884740.

Gomase VS, Tagore S, Changbhale SS, Kale KV. Pharmacogenomics. *Curr Drug Metab.* 2008 Mar;9(3):207-12. doi: 10.2174/138920008783884830.

Gomase VS, Changbhale SS, Patil SA, Kale KV. Metabolomics. Curr Drug Metab. 2008 Jan;9(1):89-98. doi: 10.2174/138920008783331149.

Graham, S., Depp, C., Lee, E.E., Nebeker, C., Tu, X., Kim, H.C., and Jeste, D.V. (2019). Artificial intelligence for mental health and mental illnesses: An overview. Current Psychiatry Reports, 21(11), 116. https://doi.org/10.1007/s11920-019-1094-0

Hamilton, A. (2024). Artificial intelligence and healthcare simulation: The shifting landscape of medical education. Cureus, 16(5), e59747. https://doi.org/10.7759/cureus.59747

Hirano, T., Motohashi, T., Okumura, K., Takajo, K., Kuroki, T., Ichikawa, D., Matsuoka, Y., Ochi, E., and Ueno, T. (2020). Data validation and verification using blockchain in a clinical trial for breast cancer: Regulatory sandbox. *Journal of Medical Internet Research*, 22(6), e18938. https://doi.org/10.2196/18938

Hiwale, M., Walambe, R., Potdar, V., and Kotecha, K. (2023). A systematic review of privacy-preserving methods deployed with blockchain and federated learning for telemedicine. *Healthcare Analysis (New York)*, 3, 100192. https://doi.org/10.1016/j.health.2023.100192

Ismail, L., Materwala, H., and Hennebelle, A. (2021). A scoping review of integrated blockchain-cloud (BcC) architecture for healthcare: Applications, challenges, and solutions. *Sensors (Basel),* 21(11), 3753. https://doi.org/10.3390/s21113753

Jabarulla, M.Y., and Lee, H.N. (2021). A blockchain and artificial intelligence-based, patient-centric healthcare system for combating the COVID-19 pandemic: Opportunities and applications. *Healthcare (Basel),* 9(8), 1019. https://doi.org/10.3390/healthcare9081019

Jain, D. (2023). Regulation of digital healthcare in India: Ethical and legal challenges. *Healthcare* (Basel), 11(6), 911. https://doi.org/10.3390/healthcare11060911

Ji, Y., Ji, Y., Liu, Y., Zhao, Y., and Zhang, L. (2023). Research progress on diagnosing retinal vascular diseases based on artificial intelligence and fundus images. *Frontiers in Cell and Developmental Biology*, 11, 1168327. https://doi.org/10.3389/fcell.2023.1168327

Jung, M. (2019). Digital health care and the fourth industrial revolution. *Health Care Manag (Frederick),* 38(3), 253-257. https://doi.org/10.1097/HCM.0000000000000273

Kann, B.H., Hosny, A., and Aerts, H.J.W.L. (2021). Artificial intelligence for clinical oncology. *Cancer Cell,* 39(7), 916–927. https://doi.org/10.1016/j.ccell.2021.04.002

Kasyapa, M.S.B., and Vanmathi, C. (2024). Blockchain integration in healthcare: A comprehensive investigation of use cases, performance issues, and mitigation strategies. *Frontiers in Digital Health,* 6, 1359858. https://doi.org/10.3389/fdgth.2024.1359858

Khanna, A., Sah, A., Bolshev, V., Burgio, A., Panchenko, V., and Jasiński, M. (2022). Blockchain-cloud integration: A survey. *Sensors (Basel),* 22(14), 5238. https://doi.org/10.3390/s22145238

Khanna, N.N., Maindarkar, M.A., Viswanathan, V., Fernandes, J.F.E., Paul, S., Bhagawati, M., Ahluwalia, P., Ruzsa, Z., Sharma, A., Kolluri, R., Singh, I.M., Laird, J.R., Fatemi, M., Alizad, A., Saba, L., Agarwal, V., Sharma, A., Teji, J.S., Al-Maini, M., Rathore, V., Naidu, S., Liblik, K., Johri, A.M., Turk, M., Mohanty, L., Sobel, D.W., Miner, M., Viskovic, K., Tsoulfas, G., Protogerou, A.D., Kitas, G.D., Fouda, M.M., Chaturvedi, S., Kalra, M.K., and Suri, J.S. (2022). Economics of artificial intelligence in healthcare: Diagnosis vs. treatment. *Healthcare (Basel)*, 10(12), 2493. https://doi.org/10.3390/healthcare10122493

Krichen, M., Ammi, M., Mihoub, A., and Almutiq, M. (2022). Blockchain for modern applications: A survey. *Sensors (Basel),* 22 (14), 5274. https://doi.org/10.3390/s22145274

Krittanawong, C., Rogers, A.J., Aydar, M., Choi, E., Johnson, K.W., Wang, Z., and Narayan, S.M. (2020). Integrating blockchain technology with artificial intelligence for cardiovascular medicine. *Nature Reviews Cardiology*, 17(1), 1-3. https://doi.org/10.1038/s41569-019-0294-y

Li, J.O., Liu, H., Ting, D.S.J., Jeon, S., Chan, R.V.P., Kim, J.E., Sim, D.A., Thomas, P.B.M., Lin, H., Chen, Y., Sakomoto, T., Loewenstein, A., Lam, D.S.C., Pasquale, L.R., Wong, T.Y., Lam, L.A., and Ting, D.S.W. (2021). Digital technology, telemedicine and artificial intelligence in ophthalmology: A global perspective. *Progress in Retinal and Eye Research*, 82, 100900. https://doi.org/10.1016/j.preteyeres.2020.100900

Lin, S.Y., Zhang, L., Li, J., Ji, L.L., and Sun, Y. (2022). A survey of application research based on blockchain smart contract. *Wireless Networks*, 28(2), 635–690. https://doi.org/10.1007/s11276-021-02874-x

Maaß, L., Angoumis, K., Freye, M., and Pan, C.C. (2024). Mapping Digital Public Health Interventions Among Existing Digital Technologies and Internet-Based Interventions to Maintain and Improve Population Health in Practice: Scoping Review. *J Med Internet Res*, 26, e53927. https://doi.org/10.2196/53927

Mamo, N., Martin, G.M., Desira, M., Ellul, B., and Ebejer, J.P. (2020). Dwarna: A blockchain solution for dynamic consent in biobanking. *European Journal of Human Genetics*, 28(5), 609-626. https://doi.org/10.1038/s41431-019-0560-9

Mamoshina, P., Ojomoko, L., Yanovich, Y., Ostrovski, A., Botezatu, A., Prikhodko, P., Izumchenko, E., Aliper, A., Romantsov, K., Zhebrak, A., Ogu, I.O., and Zhavoronkov, A. (2017). Converging blockchain and next-generation artificial intelligence technologies to decentralize and accelerate biomedical research and healthcare. *Oncotarget,* 9(5), 5665-5690. https://doi.org/10.18632/oncotarget.22345

Martínez-García, M., and Hernández-Lemus, E. (2022). Data integration challenges for machine learning in precision medicine. *Frontiers in Medicine (Lausanne),* 8, 784455. https://doi.org/10.3389/fmed.2021.784455

Mashamba-Thompson, T.P., and Crayton, E.D. (2020). Blockchain and artificial intelligence technology for novel coronavirus disease-19 self-testing. *Diagnostics (Basel),* 10(4), 198. https://doi.org/10.3390/diagnostics10040198

Maslove, D.M., Klein, J., Brohman, K., and Martin, P. (2018). Using blockchain technology to manage clinical trials data: A proof-of-concept study. *JMIR Medical Informatics*, 6(4), e11949. https://doi.org/10.2196/11949

McBee, M.P., and Wilcox, C. (2020). Blockchain technology: Principles and applications in medical imaging. Journal of Digital Imaging, 33 (3), 726-734. https://doi.org/10.1007/s10278-019-00310-3

Morrow, E., Zidaru, T., Ross, F., Mason, C., Patel, K.D., Ream, M., and Stockley, R. (2023). Artificial intelligence technologies and compassion in healthcare: A systematic scoping review. *Frontiers in Psychology*, 13, 971044. https://doi.org/10.3389/fpsyg.2022.971044

Pablo, R.J., Roberto, D.P., Victor, S.U., Isabel, G.R., Paul, C., and Elizabeth, O.R. (2021). Big data in the healthcare system: A synergy with artificial intelligence and blockchain technology. *Journal of Integrative Bioinformatics*, 19(1), 20200035. https://doi.org/10.1515/jib-2020-0035

Patel, D.J., Chaudhari, K., Acharya, N., Shrivastava, D., and Muneeba, S. (2024). Artificial Intelligence in Obstetrics and Gynecology: Transforming Care and Outcomes. *Cureus,* 16(7), e64725. https://doi.org/10.7759/cureus.64725

Pilares, I.C.A., Azam, S., Akbulut, S., Jonkman, M., and Shanmugam, B. (2022). Addressing the challenges of electronic health records using blockchain and IPFS. *Sensors (Basel),* 22(11), 4032. https://doi.org/10.3390/s22114032

Raimundo, R., and Rosário, A. (2021). The impact of artificial intelligence on data system security: A literature review. *Sensors (Basel),* 21(21), 7029. https://doi.org/10.3390/s21217029

Saeed, H., Malik, H., Bashir, U., Ahmad, A., Riaz, S., Ilyas, M., Bukhari, W.A., and Khan, M.I.A. (2022). Blockchain technology in healthcare: A systematic review. *PLoS One*, 17(4), e0266462. https://doi.org/10.1371/journal.pone.0266462

Sahoo, S., Kumar, S., Sivarajah, U., Lim, W.M., Westland, J.C., and Kumar, A. (2022). Blockchain for sustainable supply chain management: Trends and ways forward. *Electronic Commerce Research.* https://doi.org/10.1007/s10660-022-09569-1

Sahu, H., Choudhari, S., and Chakole, S. (2024). The use of blockchain technology in public health: Lessons learned. *Cureus*, 16(6), e63198. https://doi.org/10.7759/cureus.63198

Schiavone, F., and Ferretti, M. (2021). The FutureS of healthcare. *Futures,* 134, 102849. https://doi.org/10.1016/j.futures.2021.102849

Shah, M.A., Alsaadi, S.S., Ali, B.K., Hamid, A., Khedher, N.B., Khan, M.A., and Watanabe, T. (2021). Blockchain technology for healthcare: A comprehensive review. *IEEE Access*, 9, 81555-81573. https://doi.org/10.1109/ACCESS.2021.3087152

Singh, Y., Jabbar, M.A., Kumar Shandilya, S., Vovk, O., and Hnatiuk, Y. (2023). Exploring applications of blockchain in healthcare: Road map and future directions. *Frontiers in Public Health*, 11, 1229386. https://doi.org/10.3389/fpubh.2023.1229386

Skaria, R., Satam, P., and Khalpey, Z. (2020). Opportunities and challenges of disruptive innovation in medicine using artificial intelligence. *American Journal of Medicine*, 133(6), e215-e217. https://doi.org/10.1016/j.amjmed.2019.12.016

Srivastava, S., Pant, M., Jauhar, S.K., and Nagar, A.K. (2022). Analyzing the prospects of blockchain in the healthcare industry. *Computational and Mathematical Methods in Medicine*, 2022, 3727389. https://doi.org/10.1155/2022/3727389

Tagde, P., Tagde, S., Bhattacharya, T., Tagde, P., Chopra, H., Akter, R., Kaushik, D., and Rahman, M.H. (2021). Blockchain and artificial intelligence technology in e-health. *Environmental Science and Pollution Research International,* 28(38), 52810–52831. https://doi.org/10.1007/s11356-021-16223-0

Tsolakis, N., Schumacher, R., Dora, M., and Kumar, M. (2022). Artificial intelligence and blockchain implementation in supply chains: A pathway to sustainability and data monetization? Annals of Operations Research, 1-54. https://doi.org/10.1007/s10479-022-04785-2

Velmovitsky, P.E., Bublitz, F.M., Fadrique, L.X., and Morita, P.P. (2021). Blockchain applications in health care and public health: Increased transparency. *JMIR Medical Informatics*, 9(6), e20713. https://doi.org/10.2196/20713

Vodanović, M., Subašić, M., Milošević, D.P., Galić, I., and Brkić, H. (2023). Artificial intelligence in forensic medicine and forensic dentistry. *Journal of Forensic Odontostomatology*, 41(2), 30–41.

Vora, L.K., Gholap, A.D., Jetha, K., Thakur, R.R.S., Solanki, H.K., and Chavda, V.P. (2023). Artificial intelligence in pharmaceutical technology and drug delivery design. *Pharmaceutics*, 15(7), 1916. https://doi.org/10.3390/pharmaceutics15071916

Wang, Y., Zhang, W., and Wang, H. (2022). Blockchain and artificial intelligence in healthcare: A systematic review. *Journal of Healthcare Engineering*, 2022, 1-22. https://doi.org/10.1155/2022/2947918

Wehkamp, K., Krawczak, M., and Schreiber, S. (2023). The quality and utility of artificial intelligence in patient care. *Dtsch Arztebl Int,* 120 (27-28), 463–469. https://doi.org/10.3238/arztebl.m2023.0124

Wu, Q., Wang, J., Yao, F., Liu, Y., and Xu, J. (2021). Application of artificial intelligence in healthcare: A systematic review. *Healthcare (Basel),* 9(7), 870. https://doi.org/10.3390/healthcare9070870

Xie, Y., Lu, L., Gao, F., He, S.J., Zhao, H.J., Fang, Y., Yang, J.M., An, Y., Ye, Z.W., and Dong, Z. (2021). Integration of artificial intelligence, blockchain, and wearable technology for chronic disease management: A new paradigm in smart healthcare. *Current Medical Science*, 41(6), 1123-1133. https://doi.org/10.1007/s11596-021-2485-0

Xie, Y., Zhang, J., Wang, H., Liu, P., Liu, S., Huo, T., Duan, Y.Y., Dong, Z., Lu, L., and Ye, Z. (2021). Applications of blockchain in the medical field: Narrative review. *Journal of Medical Internet Research,* 23(10), e28613. https://doi.org/10.2196/28613

Yavaprabhas, K., Pournader, M., and Seuring, S. (2022). Blockchain as the "trust-building machine" for supply chain management. *Annals of Operations Res*earch, 1-40. https://doi.org/10.1007/s10479-022-04868-0

Yeung, K. (2021). The health care sector's experience of blockchain: A cross-disciplinary investigation of its real transformative potential. *Journal of Medical Internet Research,* 23(12), e24109. https://doi.org/10.2196/24109

You, Y., Lai, X., Pan, Y., Zheng, H., Vera, J., Liu, S., Deng, S., and Zhang, L. (2022). Artificial intelligence in cancer target identification and drug discovery. *Signal Transduction and Targeted Therapy*, 7(1), 156. https://doi.org/10.1038/s41392-022-00994-0

Zhou, Z.Y., Wu, F., Yang, Y.F., Li, J., He, L., and Luo, Y. (2020). Research on the application of blockchain technology in electronic medical records. *Healthcare (Basel),* 8(3), 283. https://doi.org/10.3390/healthcare8030283

Zhuang, Y., Chen, Y.W., Shae, Z.Y., and Shyu, C.R. (2020). Generalizable layered blockchain architecture for health care applications: Development, case studies, and evaluation. *Journal of Medical Internet Research*, 22(7), e19029. https://doi.org/10.2196/19029

Zhuang, Y., Zhang, L., Gao, X., Shae, Z.Y., Tsai, J.J.P., Li, P., and Shyu, C.R. (2022). Re-engineering a clinical trial management system.

Zubaydi, H.D., Varga, P., and Molnár, S. (2023). Leveraging blockchain technology for ensuring security and privacy aspects in Internet of Things: A systematic literature review. *Sensors (Basel),* 23(2), 788. https://doi.org/10.3390/s23020788

Advancement in Engineering and Science – Goyal et al. (Eds)
© 2026 The Author(s), ISBN: 978-1-041-31101-0

AI Tools in Higher Education: A Professor's Phenomenological Analysis

Simran Ray
MBA Student, Amity University Online, Noida

Ritesh Ravi
Assistant Professor, Amity Business School, Amity University Patna

Vandana Kumari
Assistant Professor, Department of PMIR/ LSW, A N College, Patna

ABSTRACT: This age witnessing widespread adoption of "Generative Pre-Trained Transformer" (GPT), which is transforming the way professors do their teaching, learnings, research and other allied activities. The usage of AI is changing the way higher education works. This study assesses the usage of ChatGPT, Copilot, QuillBot and other AI platforms in reshaping the way higher education works from professor's perspectives. Qualitative research design was used employing Interpretative Phenomenological Analysis (IPA). Eighteen professors equally from government and private universities of Bihar were taken to record their lived experience of using AI tools in "Higher Education Institutions" (HEIs). Data was collected using an unstructured questionnaire on five themes: adoption of AI tools, ethical and privacy concerns, institutional obstacles, professor's role, cultural and pedagogical concern and resistance to change. This study found the need for collaboration, training, and institutional support for the usage of GPT to enhance efficiency of HEIs. On the other side there must be ethical guidelines of using AI/GPT tools in HEIs by educators.

Keywords: Artificial Intelligence, Higher education, ChatGPT, Generative Pre-Trained Transformer, Phenomenological Analysis

1 INTRODUCTION

Integration of AI changed the way of educating students in higher education. AI based "Generative Pre-trained Transformer" (GPT) platform generates responses/ completion in human languages based on the prompt it accepts (Brown *et al.*, 2020; Vaswani *et al.*, 2017). Leveraging GPT/NLP/AI tools in education surged exponentially in recent years and it has given innovative teaching and learning opportunities (Lu *et al.*, 2022; Dwivedi *et al.*, 2021). ChatGPT, Wordtune or similar AI platforms provide notes and assignments in real time and change the responses based on the feedback and gives customized responses. Interactive learning experience and better student engagement are the various advantages what academic community takes from this type of learning experience (Schönberger, 2023; Zhao *et al.*, 2023; Huang and Xie, 2022). On the other hand, there is distrust and resistance of change due to potential change in the methodology, pedagogical issues in academia, plagiarism detection, and privacy issues due to the incorporating AI in education (Bronwyn, 2023; Roberts, 2023; Ng *et al.*, 2022). AI tools in education are rapidly evolving and educators based on their need opting different types of AI tools to enhance their teaching learning outcomes (Qadir *et al.*, 2023; Heffernan and Koedinger, 2021). On the other hand, now educators and policy makers need to assess the challenges in the implementation of AI tools in HEIs (Miao *et al.*, 2023; Luckin *et al.*, 2021) and it is imperative for institutions of higher studies to have their ethical code of conduct for keeping human element and integrity in education for the usage of AI tools (Baker and Smith, 2019; Selwyn, 2022).

This study assesses the usage of ChatGPT, Copilot, QuillBot and other AI tools in reshaping the way higher education works from professor's perspectives. It aims to understand how academicians integrate AI tools in their teaching, learning, research and other allied activities. It also tries to know how it affects student engagement and their learning outcome. On the other hand, this study will try to identify challenges and opportunities in adoption of these tools. Furthermore, if adoption of AI tools ensures better education system and enhanced efficiency of the educators as well as learning outcomes of the students. The institution must check their policy related issues in adoption of important AI tools in education. This issue will also be covered in this study. Adoption of any new things leads to different types of new challenges and resistance to change, what is also discussed in the previous discussion. So additionally, the study tries to find institutional and policy-related issues that may obstruct the usage of AI tools in HEIs for instance budget constraints, regulatory compliance, resistance to change, and infrastructure limitations. By investigating these factors, the study tries to give feedback based on the collected primary responses in the contemporary situation of adoption of AI tools in HEIs. Which can ensure a better system to all the stakeholders of higher education such as students, educators, policy makers in their teaching, learning, research and other allied activities.

This study applied qualitative techniques Interpretative Phenomenological Analysis (IPA). Data was collected using unstructured questionnaire from professors of government and private universities of Bihar. Key themes of the questionnaire are adoption of AI tools, ethical and privacy concerns, institutional obstacles, professor's role, cultural and pedagogical concern and resistance to change. By addressing those factors and leveraging AI in the most efficient way this study showed that there should be institutional support in terms of subscription and training programmes. Along with that challenges in the adoption of GPT can be handled by an ethical guideline.

There are six sections in this study and study is introduced in the first section. The second section reviews the existing literature on AI tools in the education. Third section details how IPA applies in this research for collecting and analysing unstructured responses. Fourth, fifth and last section explain implications, future scope, and conclusion respectively.

DOI: 10.1201/9781003798514-69

2 LITERATURE REVIEW

2.1 *AI-Based Chatbots in Education*

Integration of AI tools in education is changing educational experience. AI based Chatbots are well equipped to provide real time personalized and feedback-based responses. It gives an interactive experience based on the text based given input. It simulates human interaction and enhances educational experiences (Pillai and Sivathanu, 2020).

2.2 *Adoption of AI tools in HEIs*

HEIs are using AI tools for their routine and administrative work. It is also used for handling enquiry and instructional purposes in HEIs. Using AI Chatbots, students and staff improve the efficiency of their routine and administrative tasks. They receive real time and prompt responses on their queries (Al-Tahitah *et al.*, 2021; Al-Sharafi, 2022). Leading universities worldwide use AI-based chatbots on their websites to handle inquiries, providing 24/7 assistance at a minimal cost than human staff (Lee, 2021). This technology allows students to access information quickly and economically, without needing to visit information counters physically.

2.3 *Acceptance and Use of Chatbots in Education*

Recognizing the need for chatbots in universities is crucial for predicting the students' attitudes towards new technologies. Research indicates that adopting new technologies can enhance educational outcomes (Ramayah, 2016; Al-Sharafi, 2017; Alajmi, 2018). Many technology adoption models have been used to know the variables influencing technology implementation in education (Ma, 2017). AI-enabled bots allow universities to access advanced software without significant investment in IT infrastructure, improving user satisfaction and employee performance (Gatzioufa and Saprikis, 2022).

2.4 *Chatbots and IS Theories*

While research on chatbot adoption in HEIs exists, many studies lack a solid IS theoretical basis for factors influencing chatbot usage (Pillai and Sivathanu, 2020). For instance, Bii (2018) noted that many computing platforms related to chatbots in Malaysian HEIs do not report IS theories for factors affecting chatbot usage. Even when a theoretical basis is provided, few studies evaluate the hypothesized impacts of these factors.

2.5 *Chatbots Enhancing Educational Processes*

Chatbots interact with users in natural language, recognize user intentions, and respond based on business rules and organizational data (Ahmad, 2018). They mimic human behavior and learn from interactions and improve their communication. Chatbots can answer questions, solve problems, and provide human-like interactions, thus dehumanizing reality and humanizing technology. Chatbot implementation in HEIs can improve administrative processes and customer service by addressing repetitive questions, freeing up staff for other tasks.

2.6 *ChatGPT in Education*

The emergence of ChatGPT is transforming the educational institution by providing personalized support to teachers for various academic tasks (Tlili *et al.*, 2023; Alshater, 2022). ChatGPT can answer queries, create assignments, generate question papers, and design class activities (Herft, 2023; Khan *et al.*, 2023). Its usefulness let educators to use it for different academic purposes (Vasconcelos *et al.*, 2023; Milan-Ortiz *et al.*, 2023). ChatGPT's interactive nature facilitates information access, assisting academicians in research related activities (Sok and Heng, 2023).

2.7 *Challenges and Considerations*

Usage of ChatGPT has its potential benefits as well as potential disruption also on our existing education system. Overreliance on ChatGPT could have a negative impact on human interaction, collaborative approach among teachers (Neumann *et al.*, 2023; Qadir, 2023). Moreover, ethical considerations regarding assignments and exams may arise (Hosseini *et al.*, 2023; Qadir, 2023; Susnjak, 2022).

The literature highlights the transformative potential benefits of GPT/ AI Tools in education, as well as their challenges. Based on the above exploration this study decided its methodological part which is discussed in the next section.

3 RESEARCH METHODOLOGY

This study applies qualitative research design using Interpretative Phenomenological Analysis (IPA). IPA is used to collect and analyse lived experience of people where collection of quantitative data is relatively tough. This involves selecting the participants, conducting in-depth interviews, recording and transcribing those interviews and finally doing thematic analysis to understand the most discussed themes or subthemes in the content. Themes are formed by reading, noting, and clustering key insights, allowing researchers to present how individuals perceive their experiences (Smith *et al.*, 2009). This research addresses two main problems: identifying key factors influencing AI tool adoption and understanding how teachers experience this adoption in educational settings.

Eighteen professors were interviewed using an unstructured interview schedule to collect insights on a total of eighteen open ended questions along with demographic data. Eighteen professors and those were equally divided into affiliating from government and private universities/ colleges of Bihar. Selection of respondent was done using convenience sampling.

Data were collected on the level of awareness of AI tools, their perception, attitude towards AI Tools, usage, frequency, institutional support, ethical issues, and regulatory compliances. Some of the data collected personally and in some of the cases telephonic interviews were done. Respondents were motivated to answer their questions from sharing their experiences and assured them that their responses will not be shared with anyone. Most of the interviews took more than half an hour of time to collect their insights. Awareness of AI tools was the criteria of selection of respondents. All the responses were recorded for transcribing the data from their recorded videos then we have done manual thematic analysis to find pattern out of those data.

This comprehensive approach ensured a deep exploration of AI adoption factors in education, providing valuable insights into enhancing educational performance through AI tools from the professors' perspectives. Mughairi and Bhaskar (2024) applied a questionnaire for data collection for the usage of ChatGPT by professor in their study. Their questionnaire was used for this study but made appropriate changes to keep the context of different AI/GPT tools in mind. Four step data analysis process suggested by Smith and Osborn (2003) and Moustakas (1994) were used in this study. The four steps involve coding, finding patterns, developing themes and then finding the most discussed themes or subthemes out of entire transcribed data. This study did manual thematic analysis to perform the analysis of responses.

4 FINDINGS AND DISCUSSION

Five primary themes were found from the transcribed data after thematic analysis are as follows

4.1 *Theme 1: Ethical and Privacy Concerns*

Adoption of AI tools in education have positive impact on teaching and learning outcomes but this study found that it is very important that institutions should be ready with the ethical guidelines for the usage of AI technology for different types of purposes. Educators emphasized that the data security and ethical usage of AI tools by educators and students needs to be decided (Roberts, 2023; Selwyn, 2022). Similar types of responses are there in the existing literatures like Ng *et al.* (2022) and Baker and Smith (2019).

4.2 *Theme 2: Institutional and Policy-Related Obstacles*

Institutional and policy related issues were also most responded by professors. They have also raised this concern that this needs to be addressed for the improvement in teaching learning outcomes using AI tools. Some of the underlying concerns like subscriptions of those tools, training, regulatory compliance and resistance to change need to be resolved by educational institutions. Then only educators can efficiently leverage those tools to enhance their existing practices in educating students (Dwivedi *et al.*, 2021; Luckin *et al.*, 2021). Qadir *et al.*. (2023) also supported their research emphasizing the need for institutional readiness and policy adaptation for successful technology integration.

4.3 *Theme 3: Role of Teachers*

Respondents are skeptical about the role of professors in HEIs after the introduction of AI technology. They have emphasized the need to maintain human elements in education while integrating new technologies like digital content, and other digital means of teaching in education (Huang and Xie, 2022). They were also very much concerned about the traditional practices and methods of education (Schönberger, 2023; Lu *et al.*, 2022). The role of educators in classroom teaching was also frequently emphasized by the respondents. Literature also emphasizes that teachers must be supported through training to transition into these new roles (Heffernan and Koedinger, 2021).

4.4 *Theme 4: Cultural and Pedagogical Factors*

Culture and pedagogy could become a problem in embracing AI Tools in Higher Education. Therefore, these factors must be addressed from language, access to resources and attitudinal perspective for effective usage in educational context (Miao *et al.*, 2023; Selwyn, 2022). Ng *et al.*. (2022) have similar types of findings that technology could have impact on contextual and cultural factors.

4.5 *Theme 5: Resistance and Negative Perceptions*

Negative perception towards colleagues those are using AI tools for their work is also a major issue. Which will become hurdle in effective and efficient leverage of AI tools in HEIs. This could be solved by encouraging usage of AI tools, do have a policy for usage, organizing training programs, sharing success stories, ensuring privacy issues and encouraging experimentation (Roberts, 2023; Baker and Smith, 2019). Previous research supports these strategies, highlighting that overcoming resistance requires fostering a culture of collaboration and shared success (Dwivedi *et al.*, 2021; Schönberger, 2023).

Collectively, we can infer that we can take the maximum benefits of AI tools in HEIs only after addressing the challenges of ethical, institutional, pedagogical and cultural factors of adoption of AI tools in HEIs. Collaboration, training, and support emerge as key strategies for navigating the complexities and ensuring the sensible and good use of technology in education (Heffernan and Koedinger, 2021; Qadir *et al.*, 2023).

5 IMPLICATIONS/SUGGESTIONS

Ethics and privacy are major concerns what should be addressed by academicians and policy makers using clear guidelines for professors on the usage of AI tools in their HEIs. These guidelines will also support privacy issues of organizational data. Moreover, Institution should make a framework and give support for data security. So, while using AI tools our personal or organizational data must be secured. Usage and leveraging their benefits can be assured by **Institutional supports** like institution should do collaborate with AI related institutions and take subscription of cost-effective AI tools for their educators. Data security also needs subscription of privacy related software and hardware support. These supports need funding and policy frameworks effective implementation.

Moreover, Funding is also needed for **training** our educators. So, educators can use them effectively and efficiently. Along with the usage, training will support in mitigating resistance of change and negative attitude towards new technology and attitude towards educators those are using these platforms. For reducing resistance of change towards AI tools, we can involve all the stakeholders in the implementation process of AI tools in HEIs. During training success stories of educators those are using AI platforms can also improve the level of acceptance. When it comes to **Cultural Relevance**, professors try to adapt with AI tools to meet students' cultural and linguistic needs, with policymakers implementing flexible guidelines that allow institutions to customize AI use for diverse educational contexts. Finely, these strategies can enable responsible, and inclusive implementation of AI tools in institutions and can enhance both educator and educational institutions.

6 FUTURE RESEARCH SCOPE

This study gives valuable insight into how to leverage AI tools/ GPT platforms in HEIs by the usage of educators. Along with a significant contribution, this study has its limitations also. This study has seen this from qualitative perspectives but exclusive reliance on qualitative data presents an opportunity for future research to integrate quantitative approaches, which could help validate broader trends and enhance the robustness of the conclusions. This study took responses from eighteen professors, which can be increased and made more diverse in future for better generalizability. Moreover, AI tools in higher education can further be studied from teaching, learning, research and other allied perspectives individually. Future studies can also analyse specific AI tools individually or do their comparative analysis. Finally, the rapid evolution of AI technologies, ongoing research is needed to capture new developments and address emerging challenges in the field.

7 CONCLUSION

We could not stop innovation in any field, instead we should work on integrating new things and work to mitigate their negatives. There are significant potential benefits in leveraging and permeating AI tools in higher education in terms of teaching, learning, research and other allied activities. But it is needed to address their challenges like ethical, institutional, pedagogical and cultural by encouraging its usage in higher educational institutions, give training to educators, policy development for its usage, cultural sensitivity, ethical consideration. Professors can harness the benefits of AI Tools in HEIs by addressing their complexities and they should also make sure that human element in education must be intact. Embracing innovation while navigating these challenges is crucial for shaping the future of education effectively.

REFERENCES

Alshater, M. (2022). Exploring the role of artificial intelligence in enhancing academic performance: A case study of ChatGPT. *SSRN*.

Al-Tahitah, A.N., Al-Sharafi, M.A., and Abdulrab, M. (2021). How COVID-19 pandemic is accelerating the transformation of higher education institutes: A health belief model view. In *Emerging Technologies during the Era of COVID-19 Pandemic* (pp. 333–347). Springer, Cham. https://doi.org/10.1007/978-3-030-66043-4_20

Ahmad, N.A., Che, M.H., Zainal, A., Abd Rauf, M.F., and Adnan, Z. (2018). Review of chatbots design techniques. *International Journal of Computer Applications, 181*(20), 975–8887. https://doi.org/10.5120/ijca2018917696

Alajmi, Q.A., Kamaludin, A., Abdullah, R.A., and Al-Sharafi, M.A. (2018). The effectiveness of cloud-based e-learning towards quality of academic services: An Omanis' expert view. *International Journal of Advanced Computer Science and Applications, 9*(11), 158–164. https://doi.org/10.14569/IJACSA.2018.091122

Al-Sharafi, M.A., Arshah, R.A., and Abu-Shanab, E.A. (2017). Factors affecting the continuous use of cloud computing services from expert's perspective. In *Proceedings of the TENCON 2017–2017 IEEE Region 10 Conference*, Penang, Malaysia, 5–8 November 2017 (pp. 986–991). https://doi.org/10.1109/TENCON.2017.8228035

Al-Sharafi, M.A., Al-Emran, M., Iranmanesh, M., Al-Qaysi, N., Iahad, N.A., and Arpaci, I. (2022). Understanding the impact of knowledge management factors on the sustainable use of AI-based chatbots for educational purposes using a hybrid SEM-ANN approach. *Interactive Learning Environments*. https://doi.org/10.1080/10494820.2022.2050933

Baker, T., and Smith, L. (2019). Educ-AI-tion Rebooted? The Future of Learning with Artificial Intelligence. *Nesta.*

Brown, T.B., Mann, B., Ryder, N., Subbiah, M., Kaplan, J., Dhariwal, P., and Amodei, D. (2020). Language models are few-shot learners. *arXiv preprint arXiv:2005.14165*.

Bronwyn, E. (2023). AI and the New Era of Digital Education: A Review.

Dwivedi, Y.K., Hughes, D.L., Coombs, C., Constantiou, I., Duan, Y., Edwards, J.S., and Wade, M. (2021). Artificial Intelligence (AI): Multidisciplinary perspectives on emerging challenges, opportunities, and agenda for research, practice and policy. *International Journal of Information Management, 57*, 101994.

Eager, B. (2023). Prompting higher education towards AI-augmented teaching and learning practice. *Journal of University Teaching and Learning Practice*. https://doi.org/10.53761/1.20.5.02

Heffernan, N.T., and Koedinger, K.R. (2021). The role of AI in education: Challenges and opportunities. *Educational Technology* and *Society, 24*(3), 1-12.

Huang, C., and Xie, Y. (2022). AI-powered writing tools in higher education: Potential and pitfalls. *Journal of Educational Technology Research and Development, 70*(2), 385–402.

Gatzioufa, P., and Saprikis, V. (2022). A literature review on users' behavioral intention toward chatbots' adoption. *Applied Computing and Informatics*. https://doi.org/10.1108/ACI-06-2021-0131

Herft, A. (2023). A teacher's prompt guide to ChatGPT aligned with *What Works Best' guide*, 23, p. 2023.

Hosseini, M., Gao, C.A., Liebovitz, D.M., Carvalho, A.M., Ahmad, F. S., Luo, Y., MacDonald, N., Holmes, K.L., and Kho, A. (2023). An exploratory survey about using ChatGPT in education, healthcare, and research. *medRxiv*, 1–21.

Khan, R.A., Jawaid, M., Khan, A.R., and Sajjad, M. (2023). ChatGPT—Reshaping medical education and clinical management. *Pakistan Journal of Medical Sciences, 39*(2), 605–607. https://doi.org/10.12669/pjms.39.2.7653

Lee, C.T., Pan, L.Y., and Hsieh, S.H. (2021). Artificial intelligent chatbots as brand promoters: A two-stage structural equation modeling-artificial neural network approach. *Internet Research, 32* (1), 1329–1356. https://doi.org/10.1108/INTR-04-2021-0237

Lu, L., Wang, J., and Zhang, X. (2022). The Rise of AI in Education: Prospects and Challenges. *Learning and Instruction, 82*, 101556.

Luckin, R., Holmes, W., Griffiths, M., and Forcier, L.B. (2021). Artificial Intelligence and the Future of Teaching and Learning. *OECD*.

Ma, Y.J., Gam, H.J., and Banning, J. (2017). Perceived ease of use and usefulness of sustainability labels on apparel products: Application of the technology acceptance model. *Fashion and Textiles, 4*(3). https://doi.org/10.1186/s40691-017-0093-1

Miao, F., Holmes, W., and Huang, R. (2023). AI and the Shifting Landscape of Higher Education. *Springer*.

Milan-Ortiz, V., Damughatla, A.R., Qazi, A.M., Kamatham, S., Oli, S., Koleti, P., Levine, D.L., and Qazi, A. (2023). Neutropenic enterocolitis following autologous stem cell transplantation: A compelling clinical case report written with the assistance of ChatGPT. *Cureus, 15*(3), e36390. https://doi.org/10.7759/cureus.36390

Neumann, M., Rauschenberger, M., and Schön, E.M. (2023). We need to talk about ChatGPT: The future of AI and higher education. *Serwiss*. https://serwiss.bib.hs-hannover.de/frontdoor/deliver/index/docId/2467/file/neumann_etal2023-chatGPT_AI_higher_ed.pdf

Ng, W., Zhao, C., and Lin, Y. (2022). Ethical considerations in AI integration in higher education. *Educational Review, 74*(5), 611–625.

Pillai, R., and Sivathanu, B. (2020). Adoption of AI-based chatbots for hospitality and tourism. *International Journal of Contemporary Hospitality Management, 32*(10), 3199–3226. https://doi.org/10.1108/IJCHM-04-2020-0265

Qadir, J. (2023). Engineering education in the era of ChatGPT: Promise and pitfalls of generative AI for education. In *2023 IEEE Global Engineering Education Conference (EDUCON)* (pp. 1–9). IEEE.

Qadir, J., Ali, A., and Murad, A. (2023). AI in Education: Current Applications and Future Perspectives. *Education and Information Technologies*.

Ramayah, T., Ling, N.S., Taghizadeh, S.K., and Rahman, S.A. (2016). Factors influencing SMEs website continuance intention in Malaysia. *Telematics and Informatics, 33*(1), 150–164. https://doi.org/10.1016/j.tele.2015.06.007

Roberts, T. (2023). Addressing Privacy in Educational AI: Best Practices.

Schönberger, M. (2023). ChatGPT in higher education: The good, the bad, and the university. *Universitat Politecnica de Valencia*, 10.

Selwyn, N. (2022). Digital Technology and Higher Education: Critical Issues. *Routledge*.

Smith, J.A., Flowers, P., and Larkin, M. (2009). *Interpretative phenomenological analysis: theory, method and research.* London: Sage.

Sok, S., and Heng, K. (2023). ChatGPT for education and research: A review of benefits and risks. *SSRN*. https://doi.org/10.2139/ssrn.4378735

Tlili, A., Shehata, B., Adarkwah, M.A., Bozkurt, A., Hickey, D.T., Huang, R., and Agyemang, B. (2023). What if the devil is my guardian angel: ChatGPT as a case study of using chatbots in education. *Smart Learning Environments, 10*(1), 15. https://doi.org/10.1186/s40561-023-00237-x

Vasconcelos, M.A.R., and Santos, R.P.D. (2023). Enhancing STEM learning with ChatGPT and Bing Chat as objects to think with: A case study. *arXiv preprint arXiv:2305.02202*.

Zhao, X., Sbaffi, L., and Cox, A. (2023). *The Digitisation of Writing in Higher Education: Exploring the Use of Wordtune as an AI Writing Assistant.*

Advancement in Engineering and Science – Goyal et al. (Eds)
© 2026 The Author(s), ISBN: 978-1-041-31101-0

Reducing Dollar Dependence and Strengthening Economic Ties between India and Russia: The Rupee-Ruble Trade

Nisha S. Tatkar
Assistant Professor, S. P. Mandali's Prin. L. N. Welingkar Institute of Management Development and Research (PGDM), Mumbai

Yusuf Khan, Nishant Bhatte, Sakshi Pandya, Libin Mathew, and Tirth Doshi
Department of Postgraduate Diploma in Management, Institute of PGDM, Mumbai Education Trust, Mumbai, Maharashtra, India

ABSTRACT: India presently faces several challenges in the global market, funding which enhances its competitiveness, such as a widening trade gap with China, exchange rate fluctuations, and erosion of the comparative edge in key agricultural export markets. By removing barriers, promoting market access, increasing exports and attracting foreign direct investments, India stands a good chance of benefiting from trade liberalization. Another important aspect of India's trading policy is its long history of using other currencies, particularly the rupee and rubble in international trade, when pursuing Indo Soviet swapping Agreement in 1953. Under this agreement, India and the former Soviet Union were allowed to trade using their currencies instead of the US dollar. This was reintroduced in the early 2000s. The primary goal of this system is to reduce the dependence on 'hard' reserve currencies, especially the US dollar while also enhancing the economic interaction with Russia.

Besides, obstacles have also emerged in the restoration of the rupee-rubble trade system such as currency being convertible, lack of liquidity and limited acceptability to third country nations. Nonetheless, these challenges notwithstanding, there are compelling advantages. The ruble-rupee agreement, if successful, can eliminate exchange rate risks, strengthen the two countries' relations and give other nations seeking deterrents to dollar transactions cause for thought. The goal of this research is to examine the historical background of the rupee-ruble trade agreement, the factors that led to its resurrection, and how India and Russia face challenges to its promise. The economic relations between India and Russia could have profound implications for the politics and trade relations of an emerging multi-polar world.

Keywords: Rupee-Ruble Trade, Indo-Soviet Agreement, Economic Sovereignty, Currency Convertibility, Geopolitical Relations

1 INTRODUCTION

In the aftermath of the Ukrainian invasion, the United States implemented sanctions on Russia such as the exclusion of Russian banks from the SWIFT network, which hindered global trade significantly. Given that SWIFT handles more than 50% of the total international cross-border payments, this step poses a paramount issue (Saran and Guo, 2005). The disruption of this system had profound repercussions for many economies, including India. For countries like India, which are subject to rigid US and European Union laws, the sanctions threatened hindering commerce with Russia and other countries, cultivating frets about trade coherence and financial sovereignty. In response to these ailments, the Reserve Bank of India (RBI) took swift action, inventing the VOSTRO system—a procedure that permits foreign trade to continue without requiring on SWIFT's messaging network. The VOSTRO account is a bank account held by one bank for a foreign bank, facilitating international transactions without the need for funds to be routed through SWIFT (Seghezza and Baldwin, 2008). This alternative system emerged as a vital tool for India to continue conducting business with countries like Russia, despite external pressures from the West.

The establishment of VOSTRO accounts brings numerous benefits, including alleviating India's reliance on the US currency, which is extensively utilized in international trade, and providing a safer, more independent trajectory for worldwide transactions (Wacziarg and Wallack, 2004). By employing the SWIFT network to deflect the causes, it is possible for India to lessen the concerns arising from Western sanctions while still maintaining the uninterrupted commercial flow with other nations under similar constraints. Furthermore, using VOSTRO accounts may help protect the rupee, thereby shielding India's exchange rate from external shocks. This shift with regard to greater economic independence would greatly strengthen India's standing in international trade by establishing stronger ties with non-western countries which is also consistent with the country's higher goal of economic independence (Chandran *et al.*, 2012).

The emergence of VOSTRO payment system is yet another step towards India moving away from the dominance of the western financial system and at the same time allows for the protection and development of international trade during times of political clashes. In a rather shocking disclosure, The Reserve Bank of India has permitted traders this month to make settlement of all their imports and exports in Indian Rupees (Dasgupta, *et al.*, 2009). This was a very big deal because India could now directly trade with Russia without depending on American banks, allowing us to purchase discounted oil from Russia in Indian Rupees despite the rising price of crude (Baldwin, 1971). This is a huge leap to take the Indian rupee global, but it appears that this strategy has failed to the point where Indian traders are now purchasing Russian oil not only with dollars and dirhams, but also with the Chinese Yuan (Khan, 2017). The Indian Oil Corporation, which is the primary importer of Russian crude oil from Russia in India, became the first state refiner to pay for some Russian imports in yuan, and at least two of India's three private refiners do the same (Gould and Davies 2023). Even though we were not involved in the war, India was paying a hefty price for fuel when Russia started limiting oil and gas supplies and raising its prices as a result throughout the world (Sharma, 2019). This led to inflation in India and adversely affected the economy. When Russia offered to sell oil to India at a discount, imports significantly increased. Rupee trading is presently problematic for Russia owing to India's greater demand for Russian commodities than vice versa, which means that each month, Russia is stranded with rupees worth up to $1 billion in Indian banks (Dash, 2021). Additionally, India has limits on financial transfers by foreign investors, so it's not like Russia can send the rupees home either. Every quarter, $2 to $3 billion worth of rupees are thought to be stranded in India. Over the course of 2022, Russia's net foreign assets will total $147 billion (The Diplomat, 2023).

Consider trade connections with Russia. Even though they had a 38-billion-dollar deficit while we sold, things with China were still far better than they were with India. Approximately $3 billion worth of items China shipped goods worth over $75 billion to Russia, which is almost 25 times more than India did (The Wall Street Journal, 2022). Russia's 147 billion dollars are stuck in Indian bank accounts, which is why India needs to develop a fool-proof solution (Enrico *et al.*, 2000). There is a timeline of significant events and developments related to this trade arrangement up to the present day (Chatterjee *et al.*, 2014). In 1953, the Indo-Soviet Trade Agreement laid the foundation for trade between India and the Soviet Union. Notably, this agreement allowed them to trade using their national currencies, the Indian Rupee and Soviet Rubble, showcasing economic sovereignty and trust (Tiwari, 1985). This pioneering concept became a precedent for future currency arrangements and continued to influence modern rupee-rubble trade agreements between India and Russia (T.N. Srinivasan, 2001).

The Soviet Union, which was established in 1922 after the Russian Revolution, faced economic challenges and independence movements in its republics by the 1980s. In 1991, a failed coup attempt accelerated the dissolution. Many republics, starting with Ukraine, have declared independence. On December 25, 1991, Gorbachev's resignation dissolved the Soviet Union, with Russia retaining its influence. This marked the conclusion of the Cold War, the spread of democracy, and economic reforms in the region. In the early 2000s, India and Russia revitalized the rupee-Rubble trade arrangement, emphasizing their commitment to strengthen economic ties (Wacziarg, 2002). This move has global significance because of several driving factors. Their historical relationship, notably the Indo-Soviet trade agreement of 1953, laid the foundation for mutual respect and cooperation, with trade conducted in the Indian Rupees (INR) and Soviet Rubbles (RUB) symbolizing economic sovereignty. The Indian and Indian currency didn't have cards to play, when Soviet Union currencies were part of the picture and all varieties of options - rubles, pounds, dollars - were on the table and geopolitical boundaries weren't a concern. Under an Indo-Soviet umbrella using it was the idea which no doubt had potential because greater cooperation was obvious regardless of the international currency of operation that was engaged in bilateral economic transactions. USD dominates the international marketplace, so the US currency extends its reach across the globe in Zambia. Also this expands their economic independence (Bhagawati, *et al.*. 2003).

Revival holds many benefits such as greater sovereignty and lower exposure to external economic shocks and also allows for a reduction in the costs involved in transactions like exchanging objects of different currencies and managing risks. Additionally, it has larger implications for international economics and politics, as it proves the concept of other payment methods and stimulates more variety in the type of economies used. It is clear how India and Russia strove to construct the systems governing the world economy in a geopolitical context. The revival of the rupee-ruble trade agreement in the 2000s was a significant development because it improved the relationship between India and Russia while asserting their economic independence.

It prioritized other nations and contributed to the changing face of international trade and diplomacy, highlighting the long-term character of the India-Russia cooperation and their vision for a multipolar world (Enrico and Romain 2005).

The 2010 Bilateral Currency Agreement between India and Russia turned out a significant step forward in their economic partnership, demonstrating their commitment to cooperation and limiting reliance on external currencies, particularly the US dollar (USD). This important truce promoted commerce in the Indian rupee (INR) and Russian ruble (RUB), lessening the focus on the dominating US dollar in global trade. The major goal was to strengthen economic stability through minimizing the risks posed by dollar oscillation (Bahmani *et al.*. 2008). Both nations' economic sovereignty, which enables them to implement their national currencies and have greater power over trade and financial activities, aligns with the worldwide trend of which mitigate reliance on foreign currencies. The Bilateral Currency Agreement had the potential to boost bilateral trade significantly by streamlining transactions, potentially leading to increased trade volumes and benefiting both economies (Observer Research Foundation, 2017). In addition to economics, it held geopolitical significance, showcasing India and Russia as influential global players in shaping international economic norms. The year 2010, Bilateral Currency Agreement strengthened economic ties, reduced dollar dependence, promoted sovereignty, streamlined trade, and had geopolitical implications, setting a precedent for alternative payment mechanisms in global commerce (S K. and M, 2012).

The year 2014 Western sanctions imposed on Russia, prompted by the Ukrainian crisis, unintentionally initiated a shift in international trade dynamics(Wacziarg, 2002). These sanctions aimed at economically pressuring Russia inadvertently motivated both Russia and Western countries to explore alternatives to traditional global reserve currencies in their trade relations. The devaluation of the Russian Ruble due to limited access to global financial markets led Russia to seek trade in other currencies, such as the Chinese Yuan, challenging the dominance of the US dollar. Additionally, Russia promoted the use of its own currency, the ruble, in international transactions to create a more resilient financial system. Contrary to this, European nations, affected by sanctions, and began discussing the role of the euro as a global reserve currency, signalling a growing desire to diversify currency options for international trade (Bhattacharyya and Mandal 2014). This unforeseen result emphasizes the complex relationship between geopolitics and global finance (Sabade, 2014).

In 2015, India and Russia launched a strategic initiative that would enhance their trade relations by using their national currencies, the Indian Rupee (INR) and the Russian Ruble (RUB), in bilateral interactions. Concerns about the hazards connected with major global reserve currencies such as the US dollar and the euro spurred this shift (Murali and Pankaj 1998). By embracing their own currencies, India and Russia hope to lessen currency risks while building a more stable trading environment. The currency cooperation had a significant impact on the defence sector of India, streamlining procurement processes for Russian military equipment imports by India. In the energy sector, particularly in the oil sector and gas trade, using national currencies reduced transaction costs, potentially leading to cost savings for both nations. This new initiative opened up opportunities for trade diversification in sectors such as technology, pharmaceuticals, and agriculture (Levinsohn and James 1993). This move not only facilitated trade, but also enhanced economic security. On a global scale, India and Russia's move to expand currency cooperation signalled a growing interest among nations in reducing dependence on the US dollar in international trade (Chacholiades 1990). Despite the challenges such as, the exchange rate stability and liquidity concerns, this initiative challenged the dollar's dominance in global commerce and provided an alternative for bilateral trade between the two major economies.

In 2020, amid the formidable challenges posed by the COVID-19 pandemic, India and Russia demonstrated exceptional resilience in their trade relations (Babu, 2013). Their commitment to economic cooperation remained steady and was notably fortified by their consistent use of their national currencies, the Indian Rupee (INR) and the Russian Rubble (RUB), in bilateral trade. This long-lasting partnership was rooted in historical collaboration, the complementarity of their economies, and a shared aspiration to diversify trade from conventional global reserve currencies. A substantial advantage of transacting in their own currencies is the simplification of trade procedures, which leads to cost reductions and lowered currency-related risks (Gupta, 2019).

Key sectors include, notably defense and energy, benefited from this currency synergy. The use of RUB in defense contracts streamlined procurement processes, whereas in the energy sector, it contributed to cost-effective transactions. Two country collaboration extended to areas such as pharmaceuticals, technology, agriculture, and manufacturing, deepening economic interdependence (Bhattacharyya *et al.*,2011). Globally, their commitment to using national currencies set an example for bilateral trade and signalled their intent to diminish their reliance on the US dollar. Despite some challenges, their dedication to addressing these issues highlights their determination to strengthen their ongoing trade relations. In essence, their trade resilience showcased their resolve to reduce dependence on traditional global reserve currencies and contributed to the broader conversation on non-dollar currencies in international trade, challenging the dominance of the US dollar in the global economic landscape (Kukreja, 2022). Table 1 provides a historical overview of the Rupee-Ruble Trade Arrangement (1953–Present)

This Table 2 would provide a comparison of key economic indicators, such as trade volume, currency usage, and the sectors most affected, before and after the implementation of the rupee-ruble trade arrangement. This can demonstrate the impact of the initiative on bilateral trade and its potential benefits.

Table 1. Historical overview of the rupee-ruble trade arrangement (1953–Present).

Year	Event	Details	Impact on Trade
1953	Indo-Soviet Trade Agreement	Formal agreement to use the rupee and ruble in bilateral trade	Strengthened economic ties, reduced dependence on USD
1990s	Decline in the Rupee-Ruble Trade Arrangement	Economic reforms and the rise of dollar-based global trade	Trade volume dropped; dependence on global reserve currencies increased
Early 2000s	Revival of Rupee-Ruble Trade Initiative	Reinitiated discussions to use INR and RUB for bilateral trade	Renewed interest in reducing dollar dependence
2014	Western Sanctions on Russia	Prompted Russia to explore alternatives to the USD in trade	Increased reliance on alternative currencies like INR and RUB
2020	Use of INR and RUB during COVID-19 pandemic	Continued trade in national currencies despite global disruptions	Strengthened economic cooperation between India and Russia

Table 2. Economic Indicators of Bilateral Trade between India and Russia (Pre- and Post-Rupee-Ruble Arrangement).

Indicator	Pre-Rupee-Ruble Arrangement (2000)	Post-Rupee-Ruble Arrangement (2020)	Change (%)
Total Trade Volume (USD Billion)	5.2	10.8	+107%
Share of INR and RUB in Bilateral Trade	12%	35%	+23%
Major Sectors of Trade (Top 3)	Energy, Defense, Technology	Energy, Defense, Pharmaceuticals	No significant change in sectors
Oil Transactions in INR/RUB (%)	N/A	20%	N/A
Trade Surplus/ Deficit (India)	Deficit	Deficit	Slight reduction in deficit

The goal of this study are to evaluate how the development of the VOSTRO system and the revival of the rupee-ruble trade arrangement have strengthened economic ties between India and Russia, contributing to India's economic sovereignty by reducing reliance on Western financial systems. More so ever, the study aims to examine how Western countries, particularly the United States and the European Union, have responded to these changes and their efforts to promote alternative currency options for international trade. Has this venture led to reduced dependence on US dollars and euros as major world reserve currencies, particularly in relation to India-Russian trade. The research also intends to illustrate the issues and challenges faced in the implementation and sustainability of the rupee-rubble trade agreement in key areas such as oil, where the free market has been dollarized. This will help provide answers to questions concerning the changing patterns and systems in international trade and the research into the possibilities of alternative financial structures has been directed contrast to over-reliance on US dollars and other western controlled.

2 METHODOLOGY

The study approach has been toggled to in research due to its emphasizes empirical evidence, enabling the principle that conclusions are reached through the analysis of concrete, verifiable data rather than opinion (Indian Journals, 2022). It uses relevant concepts and established theories to provide a clear and systematic approach to research in order to provide new dimensions to the body of knowledge. The scientific method avoids bias and has goal-oriented focus on the result that are for example, replicable, quantifiable, and so on, these characteristics make the research process a trustworthy and credible process of doing research. In the process, reliability of study is enhanced. For starters, it ensures that the actual focus of the work is to fulfil the expectations of interested parties. It implies that focus has not been altered by personal perspectives or any outside influences which upholds the moral neutrality of the report. The very definition of such research is that the claims must be substantiated by evidence. (Romain Wacziarg, 2001).

Secondary data are considered throughout the investigation, as the following justifies our decision to employ secondary data (Jaime and Shujiro, 2015).

a) Historical Research- Primary data collection is often impossible in historical research. Researchers must rely on existing records, documents, and archives to make secondary data the primary source of information.
b) Comparative Studies- Secondary data allow researchers to conduct comparative studies over time or across different regions or populations. This can provide a broader perspective than what is feasible with primary data collection alone (Khan, *et al.*, 2011). In this case, it was impossible to collect data from all countries.
c) Large-Scale Data- Secondary sources of data can provide access to large datasets that are difficult or impossible to obtain on their own.. This is particularly useful in fields such as epidemiology, economics, and the social sciences. This helped secure data from different regions (Sharma, *et al.*, 2021).

3 HYPOTHESIS

- Did the early 2000s resurgence of the rupee-ruble trade arrangement between India and Russia contribute to the evolving landscape of international trade and diplomacy?
- Did the 2014 Western sanctions on Russia inadvertently trigger a shift in international trade dynamics by motivating

both Russia and Western countries to explore alternatives to traditional global reserve currencies?

- Did the consistent use of their national currencies, the Indian Rupee (INR) and the Russian Ruble (RUB), in bilateral trade during the challenges of the COVID-19 pandemic in 2020 strengthen economic cooperation between India and Russia and reduce their dependency on traditional global reserve currencies?
- Is the current rupee-ruble trade arrangement in oil transactions between India and Russia contributing to reduced currency risk and enhanced economic sovereignty?

4 DATA ANALYSIS

In the present study, questions were answered using the literature and a case study (Ramanujam, *et al.*, 2020). Qualitative analysis methods are used to understand words, ideas, and experiences to interpret the collected (Kukreja, 2022). Qualitative data analysis of rupee-ruble trade reveals multifaceted insights into the dynamics of this bilateral economic relationship (Kadyan, 2014). One prominent theme is the motivation for this trade arrangement. Both countries (India and Russia) consistently emphasize the desire to reduce dependency on traditional global reserve currencies, such as the US Dollar. This indicates a broader trend of countries seeking alternatives to safeguard their economic interests (Singh, 2014)

Another recurring theme was the role of geopolitics. Respondents often cite shifting global geopolitics as a driving force behind the rupee-ruble trade revival. Both India and Russia see this arrangement as a strategic move to reinforce their economic partnerships amid changing international dynamics. In addition, the benefits of trading in national currencies are prominent. Many acknowledge that using the Indian and Russian rubles simplifies transactions, reduces currency risk, and potentially lowers costs, particularly in sectors such as defense and energy.

The resurgence of the rupee-ruble trade arrangement offers an alternative to the dominant US dollar-based system (Srinivasan and Duraichamy, 2020). This could have encouraged other countries to explore similar arrangements, thus contributing to a more diversified and multipolar world. However, it is important to consider the extent of the impact of this arrangement and whether it influences other countries' trade and diplomatic decisions (Ratna *et al.*, 2013).

The use of INR and RUB in bilateral trade during the pandemic certainly helped mitigate some disruptions caused by global economic instability (Outlook India, 2023). It also demonstrated a commitment to strengthen economic ties between the two countries. However, it is difficult to quantify the direct impact of reducing dependency on traditional reserve currency. More so ever, the scientific investigation is required to evaluate the long-term impact of the practice (Srinivasan, 2002).

This equation no (1) quantifies the risk associated with exchange rate fluctuations, which is a key concern in currency-based trade arrangements. Monitoring the volatility of the INR and RUB exchange rates ought to assist traders gauge the risk of trading these currencies.

$$\sigma Currency = \sqrt{\frac{1}{(n-1)}\sum n(ERi-\mu)2} \quad (1)$$

Where:

- σCurrency= Standard deviation of the currency exchange rate (volatility)
- ERiER_iERi = Exchange rate at time i
- μ\muμ = Mean exchange rate over the observed period
- nnn = Number of data points (observations)

The formula above can be used to compute and compare the volatility of the INR and RUB as opposed to traditional reserve currencies, such as the USD, making it easier when determining currency risk in trading purposes.

Employing national currencies in oil sector transactions permits India and Russia to decrease their vulnerability to currency volatility and potentially acquire more influence over their own economies (Business Insider India, 2023). However, it becomes essential for comprehending the drawbacks of this arrangement. The two countries' trading capacity volume could prove to be large enough for it to make a significant impact on global oil prices or challenge the US dollar's supremacy in the oil market. Political and economic variables may also continue to have an impact on rupee and rubble stability.

The aforementioned qualitative observations highlight the rupee-rubble trade's complexity and relevance, offering light on both countries' motivations, problems, and possible benefits in pursuing economic cooperation outside of the traditional currency paradigm (Khan *et al.*, 2017). Analysing the current information and performing additional study are critical for determining the authenticity and long-term implications of these assertions.

India could be a viable alternative to other countries on the world stage (Saran, 2005). The international business environment is known to be marked by competition at home and abroad (Khan, 2011). Companies operating in growing areas such as India face numerous obstacles. (Singh, 2009). The Indian rupee has the potential to become an international currency (Kadyan, 2014). India's overseas trade expansion exacerbates the conflict between the interests of India and PRC in Southeast Asia. (Bragina, 2021). Increased transparency among BRICS countries could benefit each of the five participating nations. (Chatterjee, 2014). India's labor-intensive exports to the global market outweigh its import substitutes. (Dasgupta, 2009). India has the third-largest purchasing power parity economy and the fifth-largest apparent GDP in the world. (Srinivasan, 2020). Compared to other countries, India's exports of traditional commodities are not competitive. (Tiwari, 1985). Trade with other countries boosts economic growth by increasing owner profits in relation to excess production and export factors. (Ramaujam, 2020). Once a single exogenous shock is isolated from its stochastic component and modeled as a break in the deterministic trend,'sdia the real effective exchange rate becomes stationary. (Bhattacharyya, 2011). A significant reserve accumulation appears to have been facilitated by asymmetric exchange rate intervention, which may have been brought about by concerns about India's export competitiveness in recent years (Ramachandran, 2007). Internationally competitive sectors from poor nations typically have an isolated character at least initially. (Murali, 1998). India has transitioned from inward-looking economic strategies to competing in the global market. (Bhatt, 2021). Export growth driven by capital- and skill-intensive businesses cannot be sustained in a capital-scarce, but labor-rich economy. (Veeramani 2020). India is currently pushing for increased global trade liberalization, particularly in the service sector. (Gupta, 2019). India is positioned to accomplish much-desired inclusive growth and elevate the people at the bottom of the pyramid if it adopts an inward-looking approach to economic development. (Sabade, 2014). Floating exchange rates cause volatility in foreign exchange markets, which may discourage trade. (Bahmani *et al.*, 2008).

6 CONCLUSION

The study find the rupee-ruble trade arrangement between India and Russia underscores both the complexities and potential of using national currencies in international trade. The initiative, which began with the Indo-Soviet Trade Agreement of 1953, symbolized an effort to strengthen economic sovereignty and foster closer economic cooperation between the two nations (ORF, 2017). The revival of this trade arrangement in the early 2000s was seen as a strategic move to reduce reliance on external currencies, particularly the US dollar, and to deepen bilateral ties. This more towards using national currencies was part of a broader trend in global trade, where countries sought to diminish their dependence on traditional reserve currencies and assert more control over their economic sovereignty.

Some of these seis metrics also pinpoint some of the most significant liquidity and a currency convertibility and the problem of trapped funds are basic elements (Oesterreichische Nationalbank 2023). Such limits resulted in interruptions to the ongoing negotiations on several occasions. If India can find a solution to these issues; of which providing sufficient liquidity for the trade is the most important, then it should be able to strengthen its trade with Russia and rekindle the rupee- rubble trade system (Ramachandran and Srinivasan 2007). This aspect highlights the This aspect highlights the fact that international trade is never straight forward. There are always geopolitical considerations, economic incentives and o the willingness or not of the body polity to be able to use other currencies for such deals. What will determine the patterns of trade in rupees and rubles in the future will be the will of India and Russia to sustain these transactions and the wider acceptance of these currencies.

In the end, it will be up to New Delhi and Moscow to guarantee the international acceptability of the ruble and the Indian rupee, if decided; however, the economic ties between the two nations could be furthered in the context of globalization while democratizing international commerce devoid of US hegemony, similar to how the aforementioned agreement could potentially allow India and Russia to engage in global commerce on their own terms.

7 LIMITATIONS OF THE STUDY

The time frame of the study was too narrow way. It simply means that one would have missed long-term variations or changes in the key variables in question. There are concerns regarding the reliability and completeness of secondary information obtained from Google Scholar, which this research used as a basis. For this reason, we were unable to conduct a more comprehensive examination; we were constrained by a search on Google Scholar, which offered us an overview, but for a more in-depth view of the phenomena being studied.

REFERENCES

Baldwin, R.E. (1971). "Determinants of the Commodity Structure of U. S. Trade." *American Economic Review*, Vol : 61, pp 126–146. DOI: 10.4236/ojps.2020.101002

Bhagawati, J.N., Panagariya A. and Srinivasan T.N. (2003), Lectures on International Trade, *Oxford University Press*, New Delhi. https://nipfp-opac.tiss.co.in/cgi-bin/koha/opac-detail.pl?biblionumber=19996

Bhatt, Alok, (July 12, 2021) *Study of International trade relation of India with ASEAN* https://ssrn.com/abstract=3884883

Bhattacharyya, R., and Mandal, A. (2014). Estimating the impact of the India–ASEAN free trade agreement on Indian industries. *South Asia Economic Journal*, 15(1), 93–114. https://doi.org/10.1177/139156141452705

Bhattacharyya, R., and Mukherjee, J. (2011). Do exchange rates affect exports in India? South *Asian Journal of Macroeconomics and Public Finance*, 3, 175–193. https://doi.org/10.1177/22779787145486

Bragina, E.A. (2021). Economic relations of India with the countries of Southeast Asia – Foreign trade aspect. *South East Asia: Actual Problems of Development.* https://www.commerce.gov.in/about-us/divisions/foreign-trade-territorial-division/foreign-trade-asean/

BUCHANAN, N.S. (1955) "Lines on the Leontief Paradox", Economia Internazionale, Vol. 8, 791–794. https://doi.org/10.2307/1909855

Business India. (2023, July). Russia's rupee problem. https://businessindia.co/magazine/russias-rupee-problem

Business Insider India. (2023, June 2). Russia doesn't know what to do with the $1 billion in rupees it is amassing in India each month. https://www.businessinsider.in/policy/economy/news/russia-doesnt-know-what-to-do-with-the-1-billion-in-rupees-it-is-amassing-in-india-each-month/articleshow/100676904.cms

Capitalmind. (2022, July 12). Freeing the rupee: RBI allows foreign trade settlement in INR. https://www.capitalmind.in/2022/07/freeing-the-rupee-rbi-allows-foreign-trade-settlement-in-inr/

Chacholiades, M (1990), International Economics, *McGraw-Hill International Editions* Economic Series. https://archive.org/details/internationaleco0000chac

Chandran, S., and Sudarsan, P.K. (2012). Revealed Comparative Advantage (RCA) and Trade Complementarity between India-ASEAN Trade: A Study with Reference to Fisheries Sector DOI:10.2139/ssrn.2054132

Chatterjee, B., Jena, P.C., and Singh, S. (2014). Intra-BRICS trade its implications for India. Emerging Markets Economics: Macroeconomic Issues and Challenges https://ssrn.com/abstract=2474078 or http://dx.doi.org/10.2139/ssrn.2474078

Dasgupta, P., Dhar, A., and Chakraborty, D. (2009). Some further evidence on the factor content of India's foreign trade. 17th International Conference on Input-Output Techniques https://www.iioa.org/conferences/17th/papers/1046452179_090529_093632_FULL PAPER-CONFERENCE2009.PDF

Dash, P. (2021). Dedollarization efforts in emerging markets: A closer look at Russia and India's evolving trade mechanisms. RIS Discussion Paper No. 237. https://www.ris.org.in/sites/default/files/Publication/DP%20237%20Dr%20Priyadarshi%20Dash-min.pdf. https://doi.org/10.2139/ssrn.1932266

Enrico, S., and Romain, W., (2005). Borders and Growth, Journal of Economic Growth, *Springer*, vol. 10(4), pages 331–386, December. Fisheries Sector.. https://doi.org/10.2139/ssrn.2054132

Gould-Davies, N. (2023). Russia, the West, and sanctions. In R. Kapur (Ed.), The global sanctions regime (pp. 1–12). *Taylor* and *Francis*. https://www.taylorfrancis.com/chapters/edit/10.4324/9781003421634-1/russia-west-sanctions-nigel-gould-davies

Gupta, S. (2019, April). An analysis of Indian foreign trade in present era. SSRN. https://ssrn.com/abstract=3540833 or http://dx.doi.org/10.2139/ssrn.3540833 https://doi.org/10.2139/ssrn.3402399

Indian Journals. (2022). An analysis of the impact of rupee depreciation on India's foreign trade. *Financial Journal of International Business*, 8 (2), 25–37. https://www.indianjournals.com/ijor.aspx?target=ijor:fjib&volume=8&issue=2&article=005

Jaime, M., and Shujiro, U., (2015). The Influence of Increased Foreign Competition on Industrial Concentration and Profitability, *World Scientific Book Chapters*, in: Developing Countries in the World Economy, chapter 9, pages 219–236, https://doi.org/10.1142/8790

Kadyan, H. (2014). Indian rupee's role as an international currency. Abhinav-National Monthly , *Journal of Research in Commerce & Management*, 3, 35–44. https://citeseerx.ist.psu.edu/document?repid=rep1&type=pdf&doi= fee39155f781e93a87097257046f82f41137fd3d

Khan, M.A., and Ahmad, I.H. (2017). An analysis of export pattern and competitiveness of India-China in global and bilateral market. *FIIB Business Review*, 6, 18–29. DOI: 10.1177/2455265820170202

Khan, N., Ahmed, G., and Rehman, R.U. (2011). Crisis in international business environment in India. *Journal of Emerging Trends in Economics and Management Sciences*, 2, 445–449. https://www.researchgate.net/publication/319876152_Crisis_in_International_Business_Environment_in_India

Kukreja M., (2022); Impact Of Sinking Rupee On Indias Foreign Trade -Threats To Exchange Rate Fluctuations, *International Journal of Advanced Res*earch 10 (Aug). 883–890. http://dx.doi.org/10.21474/IJAR01/15247

Levinsohn, J., (1993). Testing the imports-as-market-discipline hypothesis, *Journal of International Economics, Elsevier*, vol. 35(1–2), pages 1–22, August. https://doi.org/10.1016/0022-1996(93)90002-F

Mohsen B., O., and Rajarshi, M., (2008). Exchange Rate Risk and Commodity Trade Between the U.S. and India, *Open Economies Review, Springer*, vol. 19(1), pages 71–80, February. DOI: 10.1007/s11079-007-9009-9

Murali, P., and Pankaj, G. (1998). *Indias Export Since the Reforms: Three Analytic Industry Studies (No.* WP1998-01-05). Indian

Institute of Management Ahmedabad, Research and Publication Department. Handle: RePEc:iim:iimawp:wp01506

Observer Research Foundation. (2017). India-Russia energy cooperation. https://www.orfonline.org/wp-content/uploads/2017/06/ORF_IssueBrief_181_India-RussiaEnergy.pdf

ORF (2017) India-Russia economic and energy cooperation: The way ahead https://www.orfonline.org/research/india-russia-economic-and-energy-cooperation-the-way-ahead

Outlook India., (2023). Rupee as global currency: What is stopping India? https://www.outlookindia.com/business/rupee-as-global-currency-what-is-stopping-india–news-292696

Ramachandran, M. and Srinivasan, Naveen, 2007. "Asymmetric exchange rate intervention and international reserve accumulation in India," Economics Letters, Elsevier, vol. 94(2), pages 259–265, February. Handle: RePEc:eee:ecolet:v:94:y:2007:i:2:p:259–265

Ramanujam, R., Phil, M.A.M., (2020). Impact of international trade on economic growth in India. *Dogo Rangsang Research Journal.* Vol-10 Issue-05. ISSN: 2347–7180. https://journal-dogorangsang.in/no_1_may_20/4.pdf

Ratna, R.S., and Kallummal, M., (2013). ASEAN–India free trade agreement (FTA) and its Impact on India: A case study of fisheries and selected agricultural products. *Foreign Trade Review*, 48(4), 481–497. https://doi.org/10.1177/0015732513504713

Ravindran, and Rajesh, B. (2013), India–ASEAN Free Trade Agreement: Ramifications for India *Asian Journal of WTO & International Health Law and Policy*, Vol. 8, No. 2, pp. 461–481, September 2013, Available at SSRN: https://ssrn.com/abstract=2385564

Richard E.B., and Elena S., (1996). Trade-Induced investment-led growth, *NBER Working Papers* 5582, National Bureau of Economic Research, Inc. RePEc:nbr:nberwo:5416. https://ideas.repec.org/p/nbr/nberwo/5416.html

Romain, W., (2001). Measuring the Dynamic Gains from Trade,*The World Bank Economic Review*, World Bank, vol. 15(3), pages 393–429.

S, K., and M, C. (2012). A study of comparative advantage of Indian agricultural exports. *Journal of Management Science*, 1, 175–183. DOI: 10.26524/jms.2012.19

Sabade, S. (2014). India's foreign trade and socio-economic development (Trio of WTO compliance, currency depreciation and global crisis). *Procedia Economics and Finance*, 11, 341–347. https://doi.org/10.1016/S2212-5671(14)00202-0

Saran, A., and Guo, C. (2005). Competing in the global marketplace: the case of India and China. *Business Horizons*, 48, 135–142. https://doi.org/10.1016/j.bushor.2004.10.010

Seghezza, E., and Baldwin, R.E., (2008). Testing for trade-induced investment-led growth, Economia Internazionale / International Economics, *Camera di Commercio Industria Artigianato Agricoltura di Genova*, vol. 61(2–3), pages 507–537. https://econpapers.repec.org/article/risecoint/0036.htm

Sharma, P., and Kathuria, G. (2021). Measuring Potential and Performance of Indo-ASEAN International Trade Using Gravity Model Approach. *SSRN Electronic Journal.* https://doi.org/10.2139/ssrn.3772571

Sharma, P., and Kathuria, G., (2020), Measuring potential and performance of Indo-ASEAN international trade using gravity model approach. *Amity Journal of Finance,* 5 (2), 2020, http://dx.doi.org/10.2139/ssrn.3772571

Singh, M.L. (2014). Institutional development leading trade developments: A case study of India–ASEAN bilateral trade. *Foreign Trade Review, 49*(2), 177–191. https://scholar.google.co.in/scholar?q=Singh,+M.+L.+(2014).+Institutional+Development+Leading+Trade+Developments:+A+Case&hl=en&as_sdt=0&as_vis=1&oi=scholart

Singh, M.L. (2014). Institutional Development and Trade Development: A Case Study of India-ASEAN Bilateral Trade. *PRAGATI: Journal of Indian Economy, 1*(1), 77–103. https://doi.org/10.17492/pragati.v1i1.2494

Singh, S.K., and Chaudhuri, A. (2009). The reality of India: Folding constraints into business strategy. *Journal of Business Strategy*, 30(4), 5–16. https://doi.org/10.1108/02756660910972604

Srinivasan, K., and Duraichamy, J. (2020). An empirical study on international market scenario in modern economic era of India. *Shanlax International Journal of Economics.* Study of India–ASEAN Bilateral Trade. *Foreign Trade Review* (Vol. 49, Issue https://doi.org/10.1177/0015732514525192

Srinivasan, T.N., (2002). Developing countries and the multilateral trading system after Doha, Center Discussion Papers 28496, *Yale University*, Economic Growth Center. DOI: 10.22004/ag.econ.28496

Stephan, B., and Tatiana, E., (2023). Dedollarization efforts in Russia's foreign trade against the backdrop of Russia's war in Ukraine and intensifying Western sanctions (2013–2023)," Focus on European Economic Integration, *Oesterreichische Nationalbank (Austrian Central Bank), issue* Q3/23, pages 29–51. RePEc:onb:oenbfi:y:2023:i:q3/23:b:2

T.N. Srinivasan, (2001). India's reform of external sector policies and future multilateral trade negotiations," Working Papers 830, Economic Growth Center, *Yale University.* DOI: 10.22004/ag.econ.28428

Temple, J., (1999). The new growth evidence." *Journal of Economic Literature*, 37 (1): 112–156. .DOI: 10.1257/jel.37.1.112

The Diplomat. (2023). End of the road for India and Russia's rupee-ruble trade? https://thediplomat.com/2023/05/end-of-the-road-for-india-and-russias-rupee-ruble-trade/

The Wall Street Journal. (2022, February 24). SWIFT banking system sanctions: Biden targets Russia with severe financial penalties. https://www.wsj.com/articles/swift-banking-system-sanctions-biden-11645745909

Tiwari, R.S., (1985). Constant-market-share analysis of export growth: The Indian case trade agreement on Indian industries. *South Asia Economic Journal*, 15(1).https://doi.org/10.1177/1391561414527050

Veeramani, C., and Aerath, L., (2020). India's merchandise exports in a comparative asian perspective. In: Aggarwal, S., Das, D., Banga, R. (eds) Accelerators of India's Growth—Industry, Trade and Employment., *India Studies in Business and Economics. Springer*, Singapore. https://doi.org/10.1007/978-981-32-9397-7_6

Wacziarg, R. (2002). India in the world trading system. International Trade. Research Papers</A>1760, *Stanford University*, Graduate School of Business. https://ideas.repec.org/p/ecl/stabus/1760.html

Wacziarg, R., and Wallack, J, S., (2004). Trade liberalization and intersectoral labor movements, *Journal of International Economics, Elsevier*, vol. 64(2), pages 411–439, December. https://doi.org/10.1016/j.jinteco.2003.10.001

Advancement in Engineering and Science – Goyal et al. (Eds)
© 2026 The Author(s), ISBN: 978-1-041-31101-0

Green Threads: Sustainable Lanyard Practices in Corporate Organizations

Pratik Suresh Goregaonkar, Jay Hemant Shirodkar, Anika Gajanan Kudalkar, and Omkar Sudhakar Gaikwad
Student - PGDM- Rural Management, S. P. Mandali's Prin. L. N. Welingkar Institute of Management Development and Research (PGDM), Mumbai

ABSTRACT: This research paper explores the untapped potential of lanyards as instruments for sustainability within corporate settings. Traditionally made from polyester, a significant contributor to microfiber pollution, lanyards have long been popular due to their durability and versatility. 2 square meters of polyester, the material typically used in these lanyards, generates approximately 6.4kg of CO2, this environmental impact of polyester lanyards necessitates a shift towards more sustainable materials. This research examines the usage, preferences, and attitudes towards lanyards among corporate users, highlighting the significant awareness and preference for eco-friendly alternatives such as those made from coconut leaves, coconut coir, and bamboo fibers. Through a comprehensive survey of 106 respondents, the study reveals a substantial willingness to adopt sustainable lanyards, driven by the growing importance of environmentally friendly practices in workplaces. The findings advocate for a transformation in lanyard production, emphasizing the benefits of biodegradable materials and aligning with global sustainability trends. This shift not only reduces the environmental footprint but also enhances the corporate image by appealing to environmentally conscious consumers. The research fills a critical gap in understanding the adoption of sustainable lanyards, presenting a compelling case for their integration into corporate sustainability strategies. Moreover, the study identifies key barriers and facilitators for adopting sustainable lanyards, providing practical recommendations for organizations aiming to implement greener alternatives. The potential economic benefits of this transition are also considered, suggesting that increased demand and subsequent production scale-up could lead to cost reductions for eco-friendly lanyards over time.

Keywords: Lanyard, sustainable, polyester, microfiber, material

1 INTRODUCTION

Lanyards, typically worn around the neck to hold items, extend beyond mere identification tag holders. Surprisingly, they possess the capacity to serve as advocates for human rights, champions of sustainability, embodiments of artistic creativity, and versatile tools. This article delves into the potential of transforming lanyard design to revolutionize the industry's future. Modern lanyard designs, characterized by their eco-friendly attributes, can contribute to a global reduction in plastic waste, aiding environmental preservation.

Conferences typically attract between 50 and 25,000 participants, and each attendee receives an ID badge and lanyard upon registration. Additionally, attendees can often collect extra lanyards from exhibitor booths during the event. These lanyards are designed to be visually appealing and long-lasting, aiming for continued use after the conference to showcase the printed logo (Carvey *et al.*, 2021). Aligned with sustainability principles that prioritize positive environmental impacts in commerce, it is crucial for forthcoming lanyard versions to be crafted from eco-friendly materials. This is particularly significant as the predominant use of non-compostable polyester in lanyard production contributes to global pollution, with over eight million tons of microfibers entering the environment annually, as reported by (Environmental Protection Agency, 2020).

Microfibers come from various sources and can be classified into three categories: regenerated cellulosic, natural, and synthetic. This paper concentrates on synthetic microfibers, as synthetic fibers account for two-thirds of all textile production (Henry *et al.*, 2019). Microfiber pollution (MFP) has become a significant concern over the past decade, with growing media focus on the fashion industry, which is considered one of the largest contributors (Parliament *et al.*, 2018). To address this issue, exploring alternative manufacturing methods using biodegradable materials for lanyards is imperative (Song *et al.*, 2009).

Clothing and textiles are the fourth largest industry in the world, with 110 million metric tons of fiber produced globally for textile manufacture in 2018 (Fiber Year, 2019) (European commission, 2018). Because of Polyester fibers exceptional qualities, including good abrasion and wrinkle resistance, spinnability, and dyeability, moreover it continues to be the standard in the worldwide textile industry and are popular with consumers (Houck MM, 2009). therefore, lanyards will be essential to implementing sustainable practices in businesses.

2 LITERATURE REVIEW

The word "lanyard" comes from the French word "laniere," which refers to a "thong" or strap/band that is usually worn around the neck. They have historically been employed by soldiers and sailors to ensure that their weapons and gear are close at hand, which has aided these men in combat or when scaling the ship's rigging (Lanyard Direct blog, 2017). Lanyards are useful for carrying ID badges as well as for attaching key chains, USB sticks, and other gadgets (Alibaba.com). They also come in a variety of sizes. The standard length is 900 mm (36 in), and the standard widths are 10 mm (3/8in), 15 mm (5/8in), 20 mm (3/4in), (star lapel pin co., ltd).

As an alternative to plastic, researchers at Northeastern University have recently created a method for valuing the bagasse left over from the manufacturing of sugarcane. According to (Liu *et al.*,2020) the substance that is generated is "fully biodegradable, renewable, and environmentally friendly." Additionally, these researchers developed a hybrid fibre technique that combined small sugarcane fibres with long bamboo fibres. According to (Liu *et al.*,2020) their endeavours culminated in the formation of copious physical interwinding, characterized by high tensile strength, outstanding oil stability, great hydrophobicity, and low heavy metal concentration. In 60 days, under natural conditions, both materials can biodegrade—much faster than the half-life of many plastics. These materials also emit far less carbon dioxide during production,

DOI: 10.1201/9781003798514-71

and they "offer an eco-friendly, low cost, and biodegradable alternative to synthetic. These materials are inexpensive, extremely strong, and safe outstanding choices for lanyard manufacturing procedures in the future.

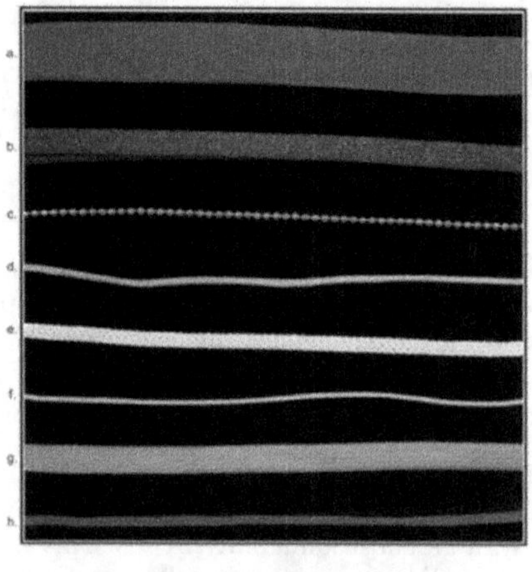

Figure 1. Lanyard types and materials: cotton (g), nylon string (f), polyester smooth (a), polyester rough (b), metal (c), elastic (d), tubular stretch (e), and tubular no stretch (h). (Source: Carvey, M., and Hage, R. (2021))

In 2023, the lanyard market was valued at approximately USD 105 million and is expected to grow at a compound annual growth rate (CAGR) of 5.96%, reaching USD 156 million by 2030. Acronym "lanyards market" refers to the global industry that manufactures, markets, and supplies lanyards, which are flexible cords or straps worn around the wrist, neck, or shoulder to hold identity badges, small devices, or keys. These products are usually made from a range of materials, including coconut, bamboo, or recycled PET, as well as eco-friendly fabrics like cotton, polyester, and nylon. The need for lanyards is being driven by several causes, including the rise in corporate events and conferences, the spread of educational institutions, the growing awareness of brand marketing strategies, and the growing adoption of stringent security measures in numerous industries. The creation of novel applications such detachable accessory lanyards, safety breakaways, and RFID technology integration has further stimulated market growth. (Verified market report, 2024)

While traditional polyester lanyards appear more cost-effective at bulk pricing (₹20-30), their environmental impact demands reevaluation. Producing 2 square meters of polyester, the material typically used in these lanyards, generates approximately 6.4kg of CO2e (carbon dioxide equivalent) https://www.co2everything.com/co2e-of/polyester. Considering the average lanyard size (90 x 20 cm), this fabric yields roughly 110 lanyards. Therefore, each polyester lanyard carries a hidden carbon cost of around 0.06kg CO2e.

Social Cost of Carbon (SCC) per ton increase in the CO_2 emission to the atmosphere of differe

Country Name	SCC per ton increase in the CO_2 emission (US Dollars)
India	86

Source: https://www.ncbi.nlm.nih.gov/pmc/articles/PMC7920807/.

In India, the Social Cost of Carbon (SCC) is estimated at ₹86 per ton, translating to roughly ₹7100 per ton of CO2e. Applying this value to the individual carbon footprint of a polyester lanyard, we discover an additional cost of ₹42.6. Sustainable lanyards, typically priced between ₹45-60 per unit https://plantables.store/products/conference-tag?variant=27920904912979, may initially appear slightly more expensive than their traditional counterparts. However, their lower environmental impact and potentially longer lifespan can offset this difference over time. Additionally, as the demand for sustainable products increases, their production costs are likely to decrease, further enhancing their cost competitiveness. This hidden environmental expense outweighs the seemingly lower upfront cost, making sustainable lanyards a more responsible and potentially cost-neutral choice in the long run.

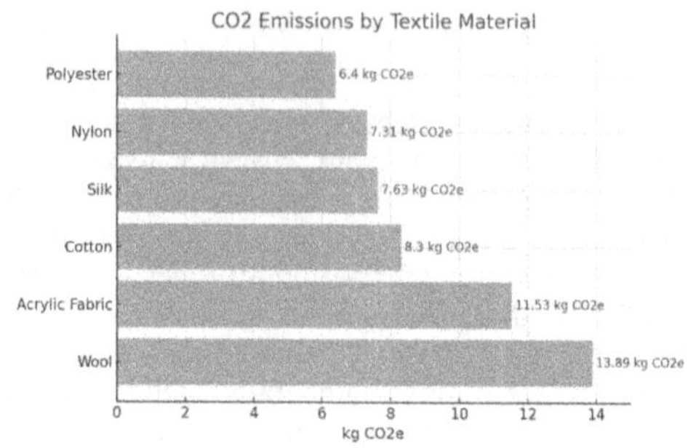

(Source: https://www.co2everything.com/co2e-of/polyester).

Crude oil is a common non-renewable resource that is used as the basic material for virgin polyester fabric. The majority of virgin polyester is burned or buried; just a small portion is recycled (Wang *et al.*, 2019). A large amount of energy, Polyester textile production entails the use of textile chemicals and fresh water, especially in the very energy- and water-intensive dyeing and finishing procedures. One of the most energy-intensive steps in the polyester production chain, for instance, is extruding and spinning the material by fusion at a high temperature of roughly 260°C after it has been synthesized as flakes or pellets (Qian *et al.*, 2021). About 30 to 50 liters of fresh water are needed to dye one kilogram of polyester fabric (Fan *et al.*, 2020). Our reliance on polyester textiles to keep up with the latest fashions inevitably leads to significant environmental problems, both from the production process and the waste treatment of these textiles.

Recent studies have revealed that microfiber contamination is also present in the air (Prata *et al.*, 2018). It is estimated that atmospheric fallout in Paris alone deposits between 3 and 10 tons of microfibers annually, with 29% of these fibers being of petrochemical origin (Gasperi *et al.*, 2018).

The marine environment's microfibre pollution (MFP) problem has gained more attention from the media. On the other hand, a synthesis of the existing data and a comprehensive understanding of the nature of MFP are still lacking (OIA, 2016; Henry *et al.*, 2019). Polyester, nylon, and spandex are examples of synthetic garments made of plastic that produce minute plastic particles when washed. These fibers eventually find their way into the marine environment as microfibers (Hartline *et al.*, 2016). Lanyards are usually made of nylon, polyester, satin, cotton, and very infrequently, metal. According to Carvey *et al.* (2021), it might be tubular, string-like, elastic, braided, or flat and smooth.

Microplastic exposure to humans through contaminated seafood ingestion and dust fallout from household microfibers during mealtimes have also been studied. Results indicate that human microplastic ingestion through mussel consumption ranged from 123 particles/year/capita in the UK to 4620 particles/years/capita in countries with higher shellfish consumption, while exposure to dust fallout from household microfibers during mealtimes was found to be significantly higher, with 13731–68415 particles/years/capita (Catarino *et al.*, 2018). It can also be used to describe contaminants that are tiny, thread-like particles that are smaller than 5 mm in size that are primarily released into the water system during the aftercare process (such as washing synthetic textiles). More than 700,000 fibers may be discharged during the washing of 6 kg of clothes (Carney *et al.*, 2018).

Inhalation of microfibers may occur, as has been noted in the case of natural and synthetic fibers discovered in human lungs by (Pauly *et al.*, 1998). A person might emit roughly 2.98×108 polyester microfibers each year into water when they wash their clothes, and 1.03×109 into the air when they wear polyester clothing, according to the scaled-up statistics. According to this finding, the amount of microplastic pollution in the world has likely increased since previous estimates (De Falco *et al.*, 2020). Microfiber pollution has also drawn more attention; most research centers are figuring out where microfibers come from, how they get into the environment, and how much of an impact they have (Leonas *et al.*, 2018; Henry *et al.*, 2019), following graph shows the prediction of microfiber pollution in future,

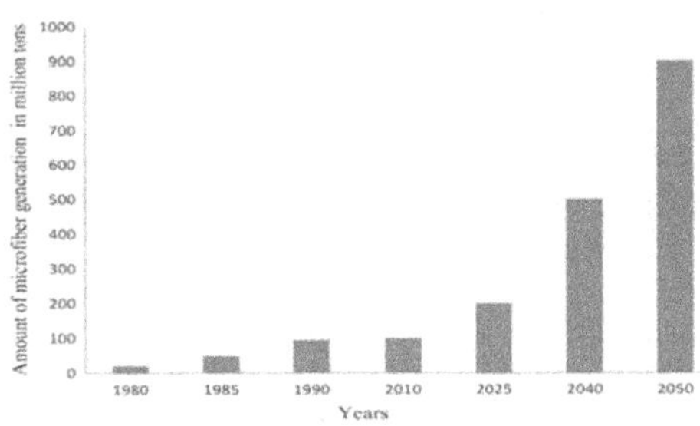

(Source: Emerging Microfiber Pollution and Its Remediation (Prasad *et al.*, 2021)).

Millions of lanyards are produced each year, adding to landfill burdens and plastic debris scattered across landscapes. These lanyards, typically made from PVC or PET, take centuries to decompose, leaching harmful chemicals into the environment and posing dangers to wildlife. In terms of materials, it is necessary to replace polymers, hazardous chemicals, and dyes with recycled, biobased, or CO2-based safe substitutes. When possible, more ecologically friendly materials should be utilized in place of PET fibers (Qian *et al.*, 2021). According to a 2019 Ocean Wise study, the typical household in the US and Canada contributes 135 grams, or 533 million microfibers, annually to wastewater treatment facilities. According to the same study, treated wastewater releases 878 tons of microfibers into the environment year from the United States and Canada combined (Environmental Protection Agency, 2020).

Historically, landfills have been the primary location for disposing of textiles; however, due to land scarcity and the associated risks to public health and the environment, other disposal options have become more popular. By 2035, NewU will only allow 10% of municipal garbage to be disposed of in landfills (Araya *et al.*, 2018). The annual value of the swag or promotional materials market in the United States is estimated to be between \$17 billion and above \$25 billion, with a global estimate of \$64 billion. Furthermore, ING predicts that 40% of corporate presents wind up in landfills, despite recent attempts and trends by swag suppliers and purchasers involving sustainable solutions (Mark Gokavi, 2023). Custom lanyards can helps businesses present an image of sustainability and responsibility, especially if they are constructed of eco-friendly materials like bamboo or recycled polyester. This is in line with the worldwide movement towards sustainability and appeals to customers who care about the environment.

3 RESEARCH GAP

Despite the growing awareness and adoption of sustainable practices in various industries, there is a notable lack of comprehensive research specifically focused on the usage, preferences, and attitudes towards sustainable lanyards within corporate organizations. Existing studies primarily address the environmental impacts of traditional textile materials but fall short in exploring the specific transition to biodegradable alternatives such as coconut leaves, coconut coir, and bamboo fibres for lanyards. Furthermore, there is insufficient data on the practical implementation and acceptance of these eco-friendly lanyards among businesses and institutions. This research aims to fill this gap by providing a detailed analysis of user preferences, awareness levels, and willingness to adopt sustainable lanyards, thereby contributing to the broader discourse on sustainable development and corporate.

3.1 *Research objectives*

1. To Assess Usage and Preferences for Lanyards
2. To Evaluate Awareness and Attitudes Towards Sustainability
3. To Explore acceptance and willingness to adopt sustainable lanyards.

To identify and analyse the various contexts and events where lanyards are commonly used, to determine the key features and qualities that users. To assess the level of awareness among respondents regarding the environmental issues associated with traditional lanyard materials. To gauge the importance placed on using environmentally friendly products in the workplace and the appeal of sustainable lanyard alternatives. To measure the willingness of respondents to adopt lanyards made from sustainable, environmentally friendly materials within their organizations. To collect feedback and additional comments on the concept of sustainable, eco-friendly lanyards.

4 RESEARCH HYPOTHESIS

Hypothesis 1: Awareness

- (H0):
  There is no significant difference in the level of awareness between corporate users and the environmental impact of traditional lanyard materials (e.g., polyester).
- (H1):
  Corporate users are aware of the environmental impact of traditional lanyard materials (e.g., polyester).

Hypothesis 2: Preference

- (H0):
  There is no significant difference in user preference between traditional lanyards and sustainable lanyards made from eco-friendly materials.
- (H1):
  Corporate users will show a preference for sustainable lanyards made from eco-friendly materials over traditional lanyards.

Hypothesis 3: Adoption

- (H0):
  There is no significant relationship between user awareness of the environmental impact of traditional lanyards and their willingness to adopt sustainable lanyards within their organizations.
- (H1):
  There is a positive relationship between user awareness of the environmental impact of traditional lanyards and their willingness to adopt sustainable lanyards within their organizations.

(*H_0 – Null Hypothesis: H_1- Alternative Hypothesis)

Research Questions-

Primary Research -

- Demographic study?
- Do you currently use ID card lanyards in your workplace or during corporate events?
- What types of events or activities do you typically use lanyards for?
- What features or qualities are most important to you in a lanyard?
- What material are your current lanyards made of?
- How important is it for you that the products used in your workplace are environment friendly?
- Are you aware of the environmental issues related to traditional lanyards made from the above-mentioned materials?
- How appealing do you find the idea of a lanyard made from sustainable, environmentally friendly, natural material in terms of sustainability?
- Are you willing to use lanyard developed from sustainable material in your organization?

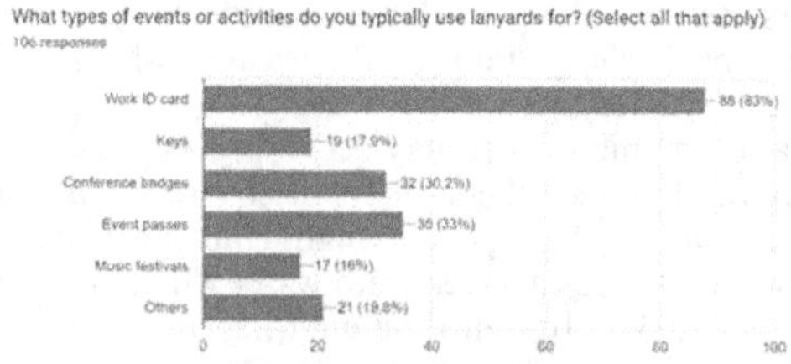

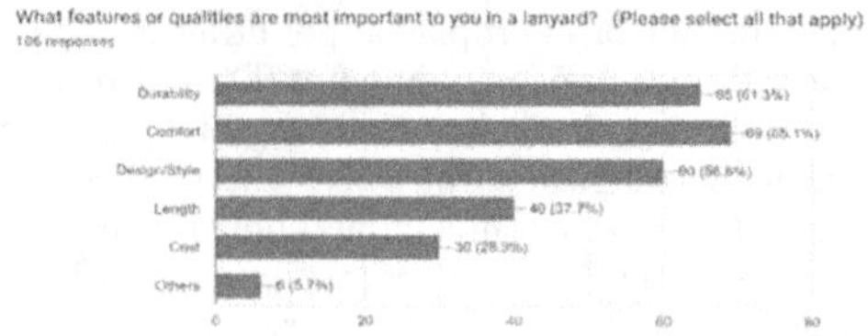

Chart 3. Types of Events or Activities for Lanyard Usage.
Chart 4. Distribution of preferences for lanyard features.

5 RESEARCH METHODOLOGY

This study uses a mixed-methods approach to explore the potential of sustainable lanyards in corporate settings. It combines quantitative and qualitative methodologies to understand user preferences, awareness, and attitudes. Quantitative data from a structured survey of 106 corporate respondents were analyzed using descriptive statistics, with charts illustrating trends in lanyard use and the emphasis on environmental friendliness. Qualitative data were examined through thematic analysis to identify common themes related to sustainable lanyard adoption. The survey focused on usage patterns, material preferences, and attitudes, targeting a diverse sample of frequent lanyard users through purposive sampling.

6 RESULT AND DISCUSSION

The study aimed to assess the Usage and Preferences for Lanyard, Awareness and Attitudes Towards Sustainability & to Explore acceptance and willingness to adopt sustainable lanyards. The sample size of 106 respondents used for primary research.

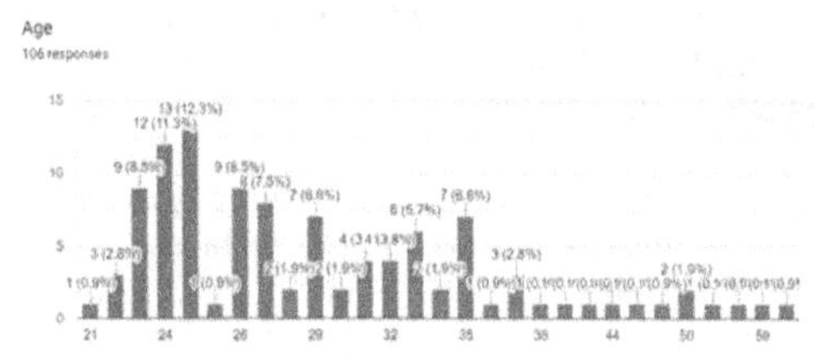

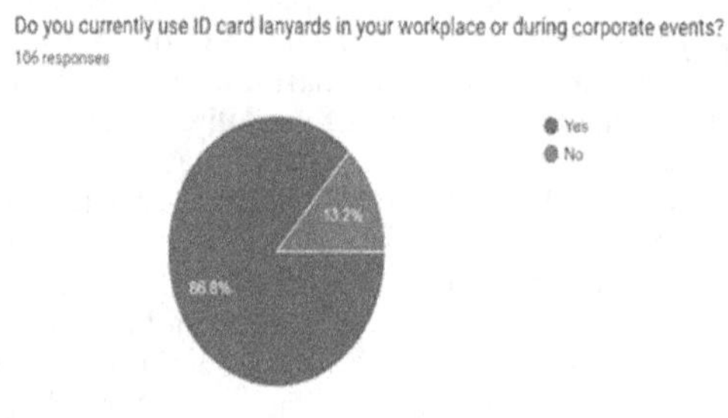

Chart 1. Age Distribution of Survey Respondents.
Chart 2. Usage of ID Card Lanyards.

The bar graph depicts the age group of respondents while the pie chart presents the responses of 106 individuals regarding their current use of ID card lanyards in the workplace or during corporate events. A significant majority, 86.8% of respondents, indicated that they do use ID card lanyards, while a minority of 13.2% stated that they do not. This data suggests that lanyards are widely utilized in professional settings, highlighting their importance and prevalence. The high percentage of users underscores the potential impact and relevance of introducing sustainable lanyard alternatives within corporate environments.

In chart 3, The most common use for lanyards is work in ID cards, with 88 out of 106 respondents (83%) selecting this option. This suggests lanyards are widely used for identification purposes in professional settings. Conference badges are the second most popular use, with 32 respondents (30.2%) selecting this option. This indicates lanyards are a common way to identify and track attendees at conferences and events. While according to chart 4, There is a significant drop-off in importance between the top four features (durability, design style, comfort, and length) and cost. This suggests that most people prioritize the functionality and appearance of their lanyards over the price.

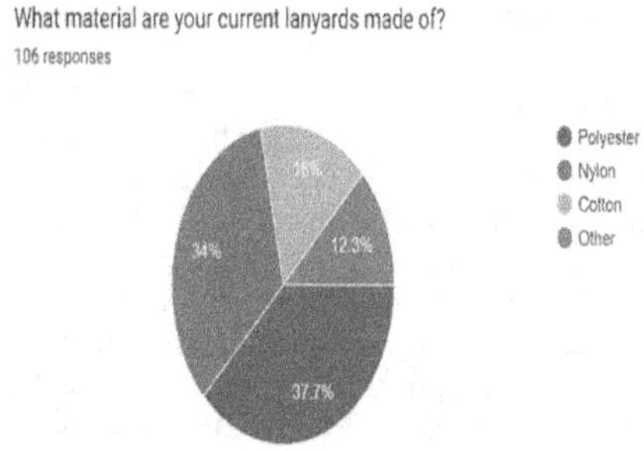

Chart 5. Material Composition of Current Lanyards.
Chart 6. Employee Preferences for Eco Products.

A relatively high number of people selected multiple options (more than half the respondents selected 3 or more features), which suggests that people consider multiple factors when choosing a lanyard.

Pie chart 5 shows the results of a survey on the material of lanyards. Out of 106 respondents, the largest portion, 37.7%, said their lanyards were made of polyester. This is followed by cotton at 34%, nylon at 18%, and other materials at 12.3%. Nearly 38% of respondents prefer polyester lanyards, indicating it's the most popular material. This might be due to factors like durability, affordability, or wider availability. While chart 6 indicates that nearly half of the respondents consider it very important that workplace products are environmentally friendly.

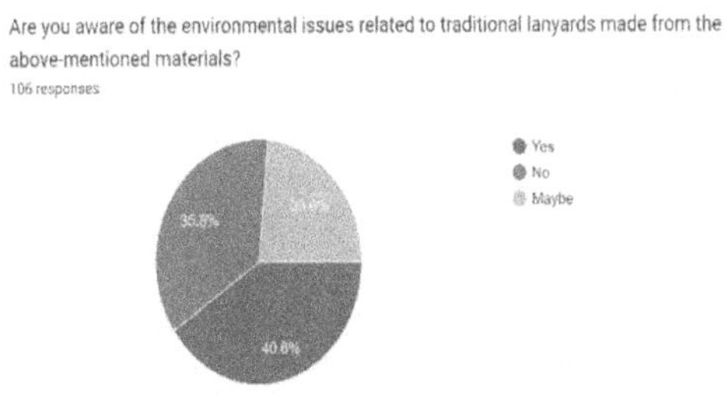

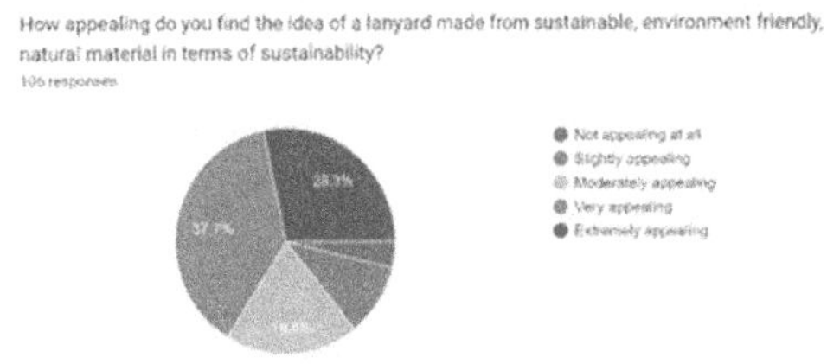

Chart 7. Awareness of Environmental Impact of Lanyards.
Chart 8. Consumer Interest in Sustainable Lanyards.

Chart 7 shows that there is an opportunity to educate people about the environmental impact of traditional lanyards. Companies that produce eco-friendly lanyards could target their marketing to people who are aware of the environmental issues. While the chart 8 suggests that a strong majority of the respondents find the idea of a lanyard made from sustainable materials appealing. There is a clear preference for eco-friendly lanyards.

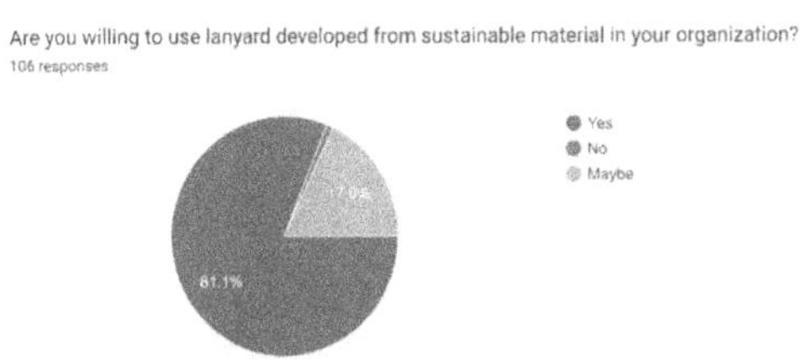

Chart 9. Willingness to Use Sustainable Lanyards.

And according to Chart 9 responses there is a clear demand for sustainable lanyards. Businesses that produce sustainable lanyards may find a ready market. More education and awareness campaigns could target the small percentage of people who are not interested in sustainable lanyards.

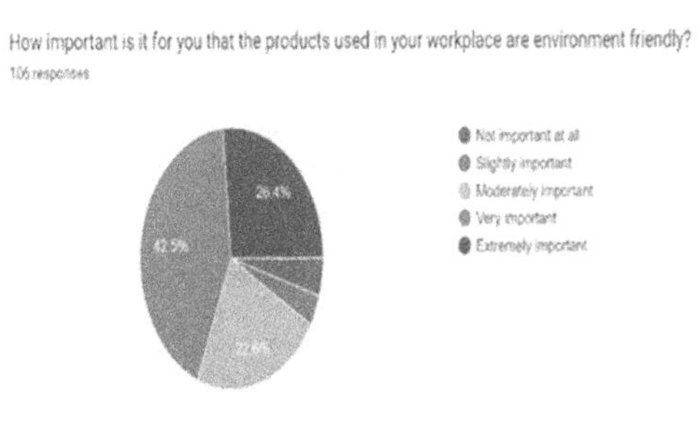

7 STATISTICAL INFERENCE

Hypothesis 1: Awareness

Anova: Single Factor

SUMMARY

Groups	*Count*	*Sum*	*Average*	*Variance*
What material are your current lanyards made of?	106	732	6.905660377	0.657681941
How important is it for you that the products used in your workplace are environment friendly?	106	324	3.056603774	0.834860737

ANOVA

Source of Variation	*SS*	*df*	*MS*	*F*	*P-value*	*F crit*
Between Groups	785.2075472	1	785.2075472	1052.174332	9.88362E-84	3.886121
Within Groups	156.7169811	210	0.746271339			
Total	941.9245283	211				

- **F-statistic:** The F-statistic of 1052.17 is much larger than the critical F-value of 3.89, indicating a very high level of statistical significance.
- **P-value**: The P-value is extremely small (essentially 0), suggesting that the null hypothesis can be rejected with a high degree of confidence.
- **Conclusion:** There is a significant difference between the average responses for the material of current lanyards and the importance of environmentally friendly products in the workplace.
- Likely **supported**. The research indicates a high percentage of respondents consider workplace products being environmentally friendly important (Chart 6) & (Chart 5). This suggests some awareness of environmental concerns.

Hypothesis 2: Preference

Anova: Single Factor

SUMMARY

Groups	*Count*	*Sum*	*Average*	*Variance*
How appealing do you find the idea of a lanyard made from sustainable, environment friendly, natural material in terms of sustainability?	106	717	6.764151	1.191465
Are you willing to use lanyard developed from sustainable material in your organization?	106	145	1.367925	0.596676

ANOVA

Source of Variation	*SS*	*df*	*MS*	*F*	*P-value*	*F crit*
Between Groups	1543.320755	1	1543.321	1726.174	2.9434E-103	3.886121
Within Groups	187.754717	210	0.89407			
Total	1731.075472	211				

- **F-statistic**: The F-statistic of 1726.17 is much larger than the critical F-value of 3.89, indicating a very high level of statistical significance.
- **P-value**: The P-value is extremely small (essentially 0), suggesting that the null hypothesis can be rejected with a high degree of confidence.
- **Conclusion**: There is a significant difference between the average responses for the appeal of sustainable lanyards and the willingness to use them. This suggests that while the idea of sustainable lanyards is appealing.
- Likely **supported**. A strong majority of respondents find sustainable lanyards appealing (Chart 8) and there's a clear demand for them (Chart 9). This suggests a preference for sustainable options.

Hypothesis 3: Adoption

Correlation

	Are you aware of the environmental issues related to traditional lanyards made from the above-mentioned materials?	Are you willing to use lanyard developed from sustainable material in your organization?
Are you aware of the environmental issues related to traditional lanyards made from the above-mentioned materials?	1	
Are you willing to use lanyard developed from sustainable material in your organization?	0.197887765	1

- The correlation table suggests **a weak positive relationship** between awareness of environmental issues related to traditional lanyards and the willingness to use sustainable lanyards. While the correlation is not strong, it does indicate that awareness plays a role in influencing willingness to adopt sustainable practices. Efforts to increase awareness and education about the environmental impacts of traditional lanyards and the benefits of sustainable alternatives could potentially enhance the adoption of sustainable lanyards in organizations.
- The willingness to use sustainable lanyards (Chart 9) & awareness of Environmental Impact of Lanyards (Chart 7) suggest weak positive correlation between environmental impact and adoption.

8 RECOMMENDATIONS

To promote sustainable lanyards, it's essential to raise awareness about the environmental impact of traditional materials like polyester and nylon through targeted informational campaigns, focusing on the 53% of respondents unaware of these effects (Chart 7). Given the correlation between awareness and willingness to adopt sustainable practices (Hypothesis 3), this approach can drive positive change. Additionally, highlighting the benefits of sustainable lanyards—such as durability, design, and comfort—through marketing materials aligned with the top preferences (durability, design style, comfort, and length) identified in Chart 4 will enhance their appeal. Partnering with corporations to integrate sustainable lanyards into their environmental policies further ensures their adoption and reinforces corporate sustainability efforts.

9 CONCLUSION

The research underscores the critical need for transitioning from traditional polyester lanyards to eco-friendly alternatives such as those made from coconut leaves, coconut coir, and bamboo fibers. The study reveals a significant awareness and preference for sustainable products among corporate users, with a notable willingness to adopt environmentally friendly lanyards. While conventional lanyards contribute substantially to global pollution through the release of microfibers, sustainable options offer biodegradability and lower environmental impact. The findings advocate for a paradigm shift in lanyard production, aligning with global sustainability trends and presenting an opportunity for businesses to project a responsible and environmentally conscious image.

REFERENCES

Araya, M.N. (2018). A review of effective waste management from an EU, national, and local perspective and its influence: The management of biowaste and anaerobic digestion of municipal solid waste. *Journal of Environmental Protection*, *9*(6), 652–670.

Carney Almroth, B.M., Åström, L., Roslund, S., Petersson, H., Johansson, M., and Persson, N.K. (2018). Quantifying shedding of synthetic fibers from textiles; a source of microplastics released into the environment. *Environmental Science and pollution research*, *25*, 1191–1199.

Carvey, M., and Hage, R. (2021). Conference lanyards: why does it take so long to provide health hazard free options? *Translational Research in Anatomy*, *23*, 100110.

Catarino, A.I., Macchia, V., Sanderson, W.G., Thompson, R.C., and Henry, T.B. (2018). Low levels of microplastics (MP) in wild mussels indicate that MP ingestion by humans is minimal compared to exposure via household fibres fallout during a meal. *Environmental pollution*, *237*, 675–684.

Custom Printed and Made Logo Lanyards for Promotional Lanyard - Star Lapel Pin. STAR LAPEL PIN CO., LTD. https://www.starlapelpin.com/en/category/Lanyard.html, 2020

De Falco, F., Cocca, M., Avella, M., and Thompson, R.C. (2020). Microfiber release to water, via laundering, and to air, via everyday use: a comparison between polyester clothing with differing textile parameters. *Environmental science* and *technology*, *54*(6), 3288–3296.

Environmental Protection Agency (2020) "What You Should Know About Microfiber Pollution." EPA.gov, https://www.epa.gov/trash-free-waters/what-you-should-know-about-microfiber-pollution.

European Commission (2018) Circular Economy: New rules will make EU the global front-runner in waste management and recycling.

Fan, L., Tan, Y., Amesimeku, J., Yin, Y., and Wang, C. (2020). A novel functional disperse dye doped with graphene oxide for improving antistatic properties of polyester fabric using one-bath dyeing method. *Textile Research Journal*, *90*(5–6), 655–665.

Gasperi, J., Wright, S.L., Dris, R., Collard, F., Mandin, C., Guerrouache, M., ... and Tassin, B. (2018). Microplastics in air: are we breathing it in?. *Current Opinion in Environmental Science & Health*, *1*, 1–5.

Hartline, N.L., Bruce, N.J., Karba, S.N., Ruff, E.O., Sonar, S.U. and Holden, P.A. (2016), "Microfiber masses recovered from conventional machine washing of new or aged garments", Environmental Science and Technology, Vol. 50 No. 21, pp. 11532–11538.

Henry B, Laitala K, Klepp IG. Microfibres from apparel and home textiles: Prospects for including microplastics in environmental sustainability assessment. *Sci Total Environ.* 2019; 652:483–494. doi: 10.1016/j.scitotenv.2018.10.166.

Houck, M.M. (2009). The forensic identification of textile fibers. In *Identification of textile fibers* (pp. 259–274). Woodhead Publishing.

https://www.co2everything.com/co2e-of/polyester

https://www.ncbi.nlm.nih.gov/pmc/articles/PMC7920807/https://plantables.store/products/conference-tag?variant=27920904912979

https://www.verifiedmarketreports.com/product/global-lanyards-market-2019-by-manufacturers-regions-type-and-application-forecast-to-2024/

Lanyard Accessory, Lanyard accessory-lanyard accessory manufacturers, suppliers and exporters on Alibaba.comMobile phone bags & cases,2020 https://www.alibaba.com/premium/lanyard_accessory.html

Lanyards Direct, The history of lanyards. Lanyards Direct Blog. https://lanyardsdirect.co.uk/article/the-history-of-lanyards/, 2017, May 31.

Lanyards MarketSize, Share, Trend, Growth Report 2023 - 2031 (businessresearchinsights.com)

Leonas, K.K. (2018). Textile and apparel industry addresses emerging issue of microfiber pollution. *Journal of Textile and Apparel, Technology and Management*, *10*(4).

Liu, C., Luan, P., Li, Q., Cheng, Z., Sun, X., Cao, D., and Zhu, H. (2020). Biodegradable, hygienic, and compostable tableware from hybrid sugarcane and bamboo fibers as plastic alternative. *Matter*, *3* (6), 2066–2079.

Mark Gokavi, 2023, Lanyard to landfill: Swag should evolve or die, Colorado state university, https://newsmediarelations.colostate.edu/2023/06/21/lanyard-to-landfill-swag-should-evolve-or-die-csu-professor-says/

OIA (Outdoor Industry Association) (2016), "OIA priority issues brief–microfibers", OIA, (online), https://outdoorindustry.org/resource/oia-priority-issues-brief-microfibers/ (accessed 11 November 2018).

Parliament (2018), "Fashion's environmental price tag", Parliament (online), available at: https:// publications.parliament.uk/pa/cm201719/cmselect/cmenvaud/1952/report-files/195206.htm (accessed 16 August 2019).

Pauly, J.L., Stegmeier, S.J., Allaart, H.A., Cheney, R.T., Zhang, P.J., Mayer, A.G., and Streck, R.J. (1998). Inhaled cellulosic and plastic fibers found in human lung tissue. *Cancer epidemiology, biomarkers & prevention: a publication of the American Association for Cancer Research, cosponsored by the American Society of Preventive Oncology*, *7*(5), 419–428.

Prasad, R. (Ed.). (2021). *Environmental Pollution and Remediation. Environmental and Microbial Biotechnology.* doi:10.1007/978-981-15-5499-5

Prata, J.C. (2018). Airborne microplastics: consequences to human health?. *Environmental pollution*, *234*, 115-126.

Qian, W., Ji, X., Xu, P., and Wang, L. (2021). Carbon footprint and water footprint assessment of virgin and recycled polyester textiles. *Textile Research Journal*, *91*(21–22), 2468–2475.

Song, J.H., Murphy, R.J., Narayan, R., and Davies, G.B.H. (2009). Biodegradable and compostable alternatives to conventional plastics. *Philosophical transactions of the royal society B: Biological sciences*, *364*(1526), 2127–2139.

Wang, Q., Tang, H., Ma, Q., Mu, R., Yuan, X., Hong, J., ... and Liu, F. (2019). Life cycle assessment and the willingness to pay of waste polyester recycling. *Journal of cleaner production*, *234*, 275–284.

Yan, S., Jones, C., Henninger, C.E., and McCormick, H. (2020). Textile industry insights towards impact of regenerated cellulosic and synthetic fibres on microfibre pollution. *Sustainability in the Textile and Apparel Industries: Sourcing Synthetic and Novel Alternative Raw Materials*, 157–171.

Advancement in Engineering and Science – Goyal et al. (Eds)

Making Micro Insurance Inclusive: Analysis of Awareness, Perception and Outreach in Rural India

Mrinal Phalle
Assistant Professor- Finance, S. P. Mandali's Prin. L. N. Welingkar Institute of Management Development and Research (PGDM), Mumbai

Deepak Deshmukh
Student, Management Trainee, Star Union Dai-ichi Life Insurance

Vaishali Patil
Senior Associate Dean, Research & Publication and Information Technology, Prin.L. N. Welingkar Institute of Management Development and Research (WeSchool), Mumbai

ABSTRACT: Microinsurance, designed to protect economically disadvantaged individuals and families from specific risks, has untapped potential in India. Despite its promise, microinsurance penetration remains low. This study investigates the current state of microinsurance in Rural Maharashtra and identify challenges of increase of outreach in Rural Maharashtra. The research combines quantitative and qualitative data from a survey of 60 microinsurance agents including NGOs, SHGs, MFIs and Business Correspondents from Raigad and Thane districts of Maharashtra. Factor analysis and ANOVA was conducted to decide whether there are contrasts in the mean scores of microinsurance agents. Findings reveals that low awareness and understanding of microinsurance among low-income individuals, financial literacy, affordability and trust are significant barriers. Recommendations include increasing awareness and building trust to boost microinsurance outreach. The research contributes to the literature on microinsurance and financial inclusion, providing insights for policymakers, insurers, and development practitioners. The study highlights the need for targeted interventions to increase awareness and understanding among low-income individuals. Insurance companies and policymakers must collaborate to develop inclusive products that cater to their needs aimed at increasing financial inclusion and reducing poverty in rural areas of India.

Keywords: Microinsurance, Financial Inclusion, Poverty Reduction, Self-Help Groups and Risk Management

1 INTRODUCTION

Microinsurance, a crucial subset of microfinance, as a powerful tool for financial inclusion on a global scale. This innovative financial service aims to provide low-income individuals with affordable insurance products, addressing the unique risks they face and offering them a safety net against various unforeseen events. In a world where traditional insurance often remains out of reach for the economically vulnerable, microinsurance steps in to bridge the gap, ensuring that no one is left behind in the quest for economic stability and resilience. Microinsurance's ability to support equitable growth and socioeconomic development is becoming more widely acknowledged. Microinsurance has demonstrated encouraging outcomes in strengthening resilience against natural catastrophes, medical emergencies, and economic upheavals in many developing nations where traditional insurance penetration is still low. For example, microinsurance programs have played a significant role in protecting farmers in Sub-Saharan Africa from crop failures brought on by unfavorable weather, protecting their livelihoods and boosting agricultural output. Leading the charge to forward the microinsurance agenda are groups like the Microinsurance Network and the Impact Insurance Facility of the International Labour Organization. They seek to raise awareness, develop capacity, and promote laws that benefit microinsurance's expansion. These efforts are crucial in creating an enabling environment for microinsurance to thrive and reach the millions of people who need it most.

India presents a special situation for the introduction and growth of microinsurance due to its enormous population and varied socioeconomic environment. Initiatives like the "Pradhan Mantri Jan Dhan Yojana (PMJDY)," which aims to guarantee that every household has access to financial services, including insurance, demonstrate India's dedication to financial inclusion. Furthermore, low-income households can obtain reasonably priced life and accident insurance through programs like the Pradhan Mantri Jeevan Jyoti Bima Yojana (PMJJBY) and the Pradhan Mantri Suraksha Bima Yojana (PMSBY). Notwithstanding these efforts, a number of obstacles stand in the way of microinsurance's widespread adoption in India. Along with limited accessibility and administrative obstacles, the target demographic has a low level of knowledge and comprehension of insurance products. Additionally, the informal nature of the economy in many parts of India complicates the identification and reach of potential policyholders. Overcoming these obstacles requires innovative strategies, robust policy support, and cooperative efforts. An example is the collaboration between microfinance institutions and specialized insurance companies to provide livestock insurance.

One of India's most economically important states, Maharashtra, provides a microcosm of the nation's larger microinsurance prospects and difficulties. The state is home to both large, impoverished rural areas and wealthy urban areas like Mumbai. Maharashtra is a perfect case study for comprehending the dynamics of microinsurance implementation because of this striking disparity. Microinsurance can give daily wage workers, street vendors, and other low-income groups much-needed social security in urban regions with sizable informal workforces. For instance, thousands of households in Mumbai's Dharavi slum, one of the biggest in Asia, would significantly benefit from reasonably priced health and life insurance plans. Efforts to raise awareness and simplify the enrollment process can significantly enhance the uptake of microinsurance in such densely populated urban settings.

For many families in rural Maharashtra, agriculture continues to be their sole source of income. However, agricultural

DOI: 10.1201/9781003798514-72

productivity and economic stability are constantly threatened by climate-related hazards such as unpredictable rainfall and frequent droughts. Microinsurance programs that provide coverage for livestock losses and crop insurance can be extremely helpful in reducing these risks. Farmers have showed promise in receiving prompt and sufficient reimbursement with the introduction of weather-indexed insurance products, which distribute rewards according to predetermined weather conditions. Beyond ensuring personal financial stability, microinsurance plays a significant role in the stability and growth of the overall economy. Microinsurance acts as a safety net to save low-income households from sinking further into poverty in the event of unforeseen circumstances. This, in turn, reduces the reliance on high-interest loans and other coping mechanisms that can perpetuate the cycle of poverty.

The present situation of microinsurance in Maharashtra and India demonstrates both continuous difficulties and advancements. On the one hand, tremendous progress has been achieved in extending the reach of microinsurance through both private sector and government programs. However, there is still a significant coverage gap, especially for the most vulnerable groups. By providing insightful information for legislators, insurers, and development professionals, this study adds to the body of knowledge on microinsurance and financial inclusion. The results highlight the need for focused interventions to raise low-income people's knowledge and comprehension of microinsurance. In order to improve financial inclusion and alleviate poverty in India's rural areas, governments and insurance companies must work together to create inclusive solutions that are suited to the unique requirements of these communities.

2 LITERATURE REVIEW

According to J.S. Cohen (2005), microinsurance is necessary for low-income people to manage risk. For a number of years, those with low incomes were not given the choice to purchase insurance since it was presumed that they were not insurable and could not afford it. Microinsurance will help rural households satisfy their basic needs and contribute to a secure existence if it is administered by specific groups like MFIs, SHGs, NGO's, etc. Jonathan Morduch (2006) There are a number of interesting developments discussed, including weather insurance, health insurance partnerships, and credit life insurance. Workable institutional solutions are beginning to emerge, and each was established to serve people that had not previously received care. The focus has to move from what makes institutions functional to how to improve their architecture so that they best serve low-income groups. In order to accomplish this and prevent inadvertent harm, it is necessary to reevaluate present methods in Health insurance is more likely to be purchased by households with more sick members S.I.Kono (2010). Singh (2015) posits that microinsurance can serve as an instrument for economic development by mitigating poverty and vulnerability, and by promoting economic growth via the implementation of microinsurance policies. (S. Vijayalakshmi (2014) focuses on the applications of microcredit that is approved by microfinance institutions (MFIs) as well as the rationale for implementing microinsurance. According to the author, there is a growing need for microinsurance and it is essential for lowering the poverty line. Jansen(2011) explores Dutch customers' attitudes regarding obtaining a microinsurance policy, as well as the variables influencing their propensity to do so. P.C. Prahalad (2017) focuses on how life insurance companies have made an effort but have not yet been effective in meeting the rural targets. In rural places, life insurance is so little known that it's considered an obscure kind of insurance. Aishwarya Jayakumar and Shaeril (2018) Examined the Indian microinsurance market's need for and applicability to the underprivileged segments of society. Together with micro savings and microcredit, microinsurance could assist prevent the impoverished from falling into poverty and contribute to the understanding of financial inclusion. Research has indicated According to the Gowsyashaik Dr P. Raja Babu (2018), sustainable development is the greatest advocate for marginalized groups and is essential to lowering inequality in developing nations. Poverty is like a major illness that can be avoided with appropriate economic development, and the sustainability of microinsurance is necessary for this development.

When examining international perspectives on inclusive microinsurance, various approaches highlight the importance of accessibility, innovation, and collaboration. Alam *et al.* (2019) illustrate how microinsurance, integrated with microfinance institutions in Bangladesh, effectively reaches underserved populations through community-based distribution models. Mbogo and Kariuki (2021) investigate the role of mobile platforms such as M-Pesa in Kenya, emphasizing how digital technologies streamline premium collection and claims processing, thereby improving accessibility for low-income workers in both urban and rural areas. Gomez *et al.* (2020) focus on Peru, where government-private sector partnerships have been pivotal in designing weather-indexed insurance products tailored for smallholder farmers. This initiative addresses climate-related risks, encouraging uptake among vulnerable agricultural communities. These studies collectively emphasize the critical role of innovative delivery mechanisms, customized product offerings, and strategic collaborations in overcoming barriers to affordability and accessibility in microinsurance.

Mazambani Emmanuel Mutambara (2018) study found that poor microinsurance performance in developing nations is caused by an excess of policies and a low consumer acceptance of services. Need business and creative support to develop a long-term market for the products being offered. According to Johnson (2018) LIC completely controls the microinsurance market. More inventiveness and initiative were needed to get past insurance companies. Neha Sharma and Ruchi Goyal (2017) bankers should be more interested in disseminating information on microinsurance. Financial data from friends, the media, and television, among other sources, has contributed to a rise in inclusion. It is therefore imperative that banks and policymakers coordinate closely to disseminate financial information, as such efforts are perceived to have a direct bearing on their operations. Dipak M. Sanki (2021) This study's primary goal is to gauge the growth of microinsurance in India. The current study will examine the elements that contribute to the long-term growth of microinsurance. Research will examine the government's effort to support the long-term growth of microinsurance in India.

3 RESEARCH METHODOLOGY

3.1 *Objective*

1. To assess the Current State of Microinsurance in India
2. To identify Challenges and Barriers to Increasing Microinsurance Outreach in Rural Maharashtra
3. To evaluate awareness and understanding of microinsurance among low-income individuals.

3.2 *Methodology*

This research employs both quantitative and qualitative methods of data collection. The methodology is designed to thoroughly evaluate the current state of microinsurance in rural Maharashtra, identify obstacles to expanding outreach, and provide useful insights for key stakeholders. For the analysis, secondary data sources, including government reports, scholarly articles, and industry documents, were utilized to assess the condition of microinsurance. The study focuses on 60 microinsurance agents representing NGOs, SHGs, MFIs, and Business Correspondents, specifically from the Raigad and Thane districts in Maharashtra. A factor analysis, alongside an ANOVA, was conducted to identify if there were any significant differences in the average scores among the various groups of microinsurance agents. The composition includes 15% NGOs, 37% SHGs, 18% MFIs, and 30% Business Correspondents.

Following an evaluation of the penetration rate of microinsurance agents, and prior to proposing strategies for enhancing outreach, a factor analysis was applied to understand the specific challenges encountered by microinsurance agents from the Raigad and Thane regions. Twelve factors were taken into account in order to fully examine these difficulties. The ANOVA revealed that there were significant variations in the difficulties that agents encountered in each category. Furthermore, a t-test was performed to examine if there was any age-related variance in the difficulties experienced by microinsurance agents. In addition, qualitative research was conducted through focus group discussions with SHGs. This process involved gathering data, familiarizing with it, coding, identifying themes, and defining and labeling these themes, which informed the thematic analysis of focus group interview transcripts.

4 HYPOTHESES

H0a: The mean values of the difficulties faced by microinsurance agents in outreach in rural Maharashtra do not differ statistically significantly based on age. H1a: The mean values of the problems faced by microinsurance agents vary statistically significantly based on the age

H0b: The mean values of obstacles faced by microinsurance agents across categories do not exhibit a statistically significant variation. H1b: The mean values of the problems faced by microinsurance agents across categories varied statistically significantly.

5 RESULT AND DISCUSSION

5.1 *Current state of microinsurance in India*

Table 1. Micro-Insurance Portfolio -Life Insurers (New Business) (Figure in Lakhs).

	Individual Business		Group Business	
Year	No of Policies	Premium	No of Lives	Premium
2013-14	27.67	9,565	131.79	14,176.68
2014-15	8.16	2,889	231.52	31,562.78
2015-16	9.11	3,172	292.55	30,243.06
2016-17	9.56	3,822	322.47	46,042.98
2017-18	8.39	4,704	589.03	1,38,637.02
2018-19	8.65	3,210	1,213.08	3,20,573.78
2019-20	10.28	22,666	1,407.29	4,42,645.42
2020-21	10.70	35,527	1,012.99	4,21,305.75
2021-22	8.77	29,714	1,320.73	6,04,888.38
2022-23	4.50	20,019	1,626.84	8,59,261.38
CAGR	**-18%**	**9%**	**32%**	**58%**

Source: IRDAI Handbook 2023

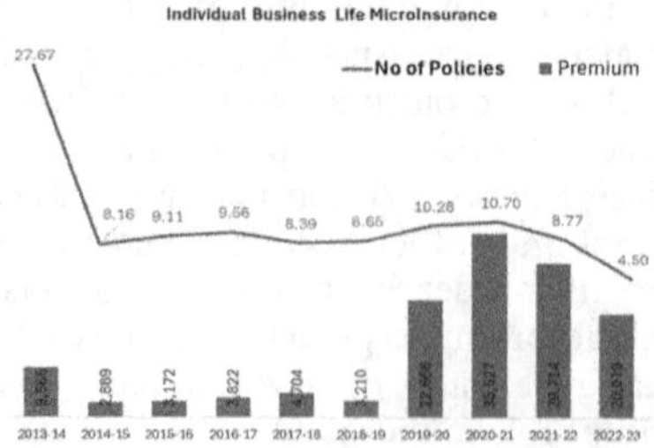

Graph 1. State of Individual Business Life Microinsurance. Source: IRDAI Handbook 2023.

The analysis of the micro-insurance portfolio reveals a mixed trend. While the number of policies and premium have been declining since 2019-20, with a CAGR of -18% and 9% respectively, the number of lives covered and premium per life have continued to grow. The latter has shown a remarkable CAGR of 32% and 58% respectively, indicating increasing penetration and value of micro-insurance products as per Table 1. The data suggests that although the number of policies has decreased, the overall value and coverage of micro-insurance products have expanded, signifying a shift towards more comprehensive coverage. This trend is encouraging, as it indicates a growing recognition of the importance of micro-insurance among the target population. (Graph 1)

Table 2. Landscape of Micro Insurance Agents of Life Insurer for F. Y. 2022-23.

Type of Agent	Public Sector	Private Sector	Total
NGOs	4,759	11	4,770
SHGs	260	0	260
MFIs	221	29	250
Business Correspondents	103	42	145
Other Micro Insurance Agents	14,094	82,397	96,491
Total	**19,437**	**82,479**	**1,01,916**

Source: IRDAI Annual Report 2023

5.2 *Life Insurers: Landscape of Micro Insurance Agents*

Table 3. Descriptive statistics of sample.

Demographic	N (%)
NGOs	9 (15%)
SHGs	22 (37%)
MFIs	11 (18%)
Business Correspondents	18 (30%)
0-5 years	10 (17%)
6-10 years	12 (20 %)
11-15 years	9 (15%)
16-20 years	11 (18%)
Above 20 years	18 (30%)

Data in Table 2 shows private sector life insurers have a significantly larger number of microinsurance agents (82,479) compared to public sector life insurers (19,437).The majority of microinsurance agents (96,491) fall under the "Other Micro Insurance Agents" category, which is dominated by private sector agents (82,397).NGOs and SHGs have a relatively small presence in the microinsurance agent market, with most of their agents operating in the public sector. MFIs and Business Correspondents have a limited presence in the microinsurance agent market, with a slightly higher presence in the public sector.

5.3 *Demographic Detail*

As Table 3 depicts respondent microinsurance agent's category wise distribution as 15 percent of NGOs,37 percent SHGs,18 per cent of MFIs and 30 percent of Business Correspondents. Respondents' distribution of microinsurance agents as per experience wise d were 0-5 years' experience (17%), 6-10years' (20 %) ,11-15years (15%),16- 20 years (18%), Above 20 years (30%) of experience in industry from establishment of institution.

5.4 *Problem encounter by microinsurance in rural areas of India*

In this study, factor analysis was employed using twelve variables to examine the challenges encountered by microinsurance agents operating in rural regions of India. The analysis revealed that the average challenges faced by these agents differed considerably across various categories, as indicated by the results of the ANOVA. Additionally, a t-test was conducted to determine if there were any significant age-related variations in the difficulties experienced by microinsurance agents.

5.5 *Factor analysis for challenges faced by microfinance providers:*

Cronbach's alpha for the factor yielded a value of 0.759 indicating the reliability of the variables used for study. The present study used factor analysis to determine challenges faced by microinsurance agent in rural area where twelve variables are analysed.

"To examine the appropriateness of factor analysis we used Bartlett's test of sphericity and Kaiser-Meyer Olkin (KMO) measures of sampling adequacy". Given that the sample's KMO value is 0.798 and its Bartlett's Test of Sphericity value is 0.000—which indicates that the null hypothesis is rejected and the data is significant—the sample is sufficient. It suggests a relationship between the populations.The factor analysis outcomes are displayed in Tables 4 and 5.

Table 4. Results of Extraction Method: Principal Component Analysis.

Factors extracted	Explained Variance (%)	Cumulative Explained Variance (%)
1(financial literacy)	31.36	31.36
2 (Aaffordability)	20.12	51.48
3 (Trust)	18.01	69.49

Table 5. Factor Loadings of the items.

Sr. No	Statements	Factor I	Factor II	Factor II
1	Reputation of insurance companies amongst clients	.259	.324	.676
2	Awareness of microinsurance in rural areas	.655	.242	.412
3	Financial Literacy of clients	.697	.167	.056
4	operate in a constrained region, which restricts the potential for long-term business growth	.212	.686	.268
5	Small & irregular cashflows of clients	.243	.769	.443
6	Microinsurance is costly and time consuming	.494	.694	.223
7	Transparency in claim settlement	.003	.633	.156
8	Claim settlement	.224	.456	.760
9	Sufficient manpower and infrastructure, particularly in terms of MIS, to fulfill responsibilities	.043	.847	.324
10	Commission in micro insurance is not in line with the time and resources spent in insurance selling	.137	.666	-.021

Extraction Method: Principal Component Analysis.
Rotation Method: Varimax with Kaiser Normalization.

By keeping just those variables where Kaiser's criterion is greater than one, Table 4 shows that factor 1 accounts for 31.36% of the variation, factor 2 for 51.48%, and factor 3 for 69.59%. Variance as displayed in Table 4 indicates that the number of variables has been reduced from 12 to 3, as only five of the initial eigenvalues are greater than 1. Additionally, we can create the variables as shown in Table 5 because the total squared sums of loadings after rotation are greater than 60%. Three factors were identified, and two were eliminated. These factors developed throughout time, and Table 6 indicates that the first component, "Financial literacy," accounts for 31.36 percent of the variation, followed by "Affordability," which accounts for 20.12 percent, and "Trust," which accounts for 18.01 percent.

5.6 *Independent sample t-test*

An independent two-sample t-test was conducted to determine whether there were any significant differences between the groups analyzed in the study. The results of the t-tests are tabulated in Table 6 that the mean values of the problems faced by microinsurance agents vary statistically significantly based on the age in younger & older microinsurance agent for the difficulties faced by microinsurance agents in outreach in rural Maharashtra.

Table 6. Independent Samples Test.

		Levene's Test for Equality of Variances		t-test for Equality of Means						
									95% Confidence	
		F	Sig.	t	do	Sig. (2-tailed)	Mean Difference	Std. Error Difference	Lower	Upper
Financial literacy	Equal variances assumed	0.24	0.122	2.28	58	0.214	0.4267	0.2607	-0.8465	0.1936
	Equal variances not assumed			2.08	84.01	0.501	0.4267	0.2604	-0.8566	0.2031
Aaffordability	Equal variances assumed	0.226	0.872	0.22	58	0.827	0.0577	0.2634	-0.4675	0.5829
	Equal variances not assumed			0.23	88.51	0.819	0.05771	0.2509	-0.4505	0.566
Trust	Equal variances assumed	0.022	0.072	0.22	58	0.027	0.0577	0.2636	-0.4675	0.5829
	Equal variances not assumed			0.23	78.51	0.019	0.057717	0.250975	-0.4505	0.566

A two-sample t-test was performed to Table 6 that there is significant differences in mean of the factors Trust emerged between younger & older microinsurance agent for difficulties faced by microinsurance agents in outreach in rural Maharashtra due to age (M = .241, SD = .675) and younger micro insurance agents and older micro insurance agents (M = .216, SD = 1.24); t (58) = 2.427, p = .019.However, there was not a significant difference in mean for Financial literacy and Affordability of the factors emerged between younger & older microinsurance agent for ifficulties faced by them for its outreach in rural areas of Maharashtra due to age on Financial literacy between younger micro insurance agents (M=-.032, SD = 1.768) and older micro insurance agents (M = -.0211, SD = .768); t (58) = .122 p = .214 and for Affordability between younger micro insurance agents (M = .026, SD = 1.145) and older micro insurance agents (M = .0155, SD =.726); t (58) = .872, p = .827.

Table 7. ANOVA.

		Sum of Squares	df	Mean Square	F	Sig.
Financial literacy	Between Groups	16.465	4	50.632	168.025	0.68
	Within Groups	43.535	56	0.243		
	Total	60	60			
Affordability	Between Groups	19.004	4	15.401	17.766	0.734
	Within Groups	40.996	56	0.812		
	Total	60	60			
Trust	Between Groups	14.492	4	11.646	14.458	0.843
	Within Groups	45.508	56	0.846		
	Total	60	60			

As per Table 7 $P > \alpha$ $(0.000 < 0.05)$ .The mean values of obstacles faced by microinsurance agents across categories do not exhibit a statistically significant variation.

5.7 *Qualitative analysis*

The methodology for conducting the thematic analysis on focus group interview transcript, included data collection, data familiarization, coding, theme identification, and defining and naming themes.

Table 8. Tabular representation of themes and descriptions.

Theme	Description
Increased Awareness and Product Development	COVID-19 heightened awareness among low-income individuals about financial risks. Insurers are developing tailored products to meet these needs.
Value-Added Services	Insurers are integrating non-insurance services to enhance the value of their offerings, providing comprehensive support even with basic plans.
Digital Adoption and Human Touch	Despite the rise of digital solutions from Insurtech's, human interaction remains essential. Insurers and aggregators balance digital tools with personal interactions due to varying customer digital literacy.
Awareness and Education Initiatives	Public awareness campaigns and educational efforts are crucial for increasing microinsurance uptake. These initiatives include the use of media and educational programs in schools and universities.
Trust and Promotion of Private Insurers	Increasing the market for microinsurance requires fostering confidence in private insurers. To win over the public, private companies are urged to establish coverage objectives and provide flexible premium payment options.
Agent Incentives	One important tactic for boosting market penetration is to provide incentives to insurance brokers who sell microinsurance products. Agent motivation and sales efforts are aided by incentives.

(continued)

Table 8. Continued

According to Table 8 thematic analysis, the COVID-19 epidemic has caused low-income people to become much more conscious of the financial dangers they face, which has led insurers to create solutions specifically for this market. Because of this greater knowledge, insurers have been more creative in developing specialty insurance solutions that address the particular requirements of small enterprises. Additionally, insurers should enhance the value of their offerings by providing comprehensive support for insurance plans.

6 CONCLUSION

This research comments on that financial-literacy, affordability, and trust in micro-insurance agents. Underlining that micro-insurance companies should offer high product quality as well as service. When an insurer plans their marketing and promotional efforts, they should also take the influence of the significant demographic features into account. This will help the insurer produce and promote relevant micro insurance products and ensure client satisfaction. In view to improve the outreach of micro-insurance products, micro insurance agents also investigate the connections between specific purchases and preferences and product benefits, pricing, risk coverage, and claim settlement. Additional variables, like the predicted value of the microinsurance products, individual variations, and product attributes, ought to be tested by the value function. Any of these recommendations for more study might help an insurer create marketing strategies that work.

The assistance provided by the Miro insurance agents might help consumers with a few of their problems. Advantages of a microinsurance policy include the provision of excellent services, the fulfilment of its promises regarding their micro-insurance policy, providing knowledge of the terms and conditions of the policy. Other benefits include hassle-free settlements and the general convenience of applying for micro-insurance, creating awareness the practical features of the insurances many people in rural areas have low financial literacy.

The present study shows that the microinsurance industry's reliance on microfinance intermediaries, in particular MFIs, Shig's, and NGOs, because they had a clientele and the consumers‘ trust. The current study comes to the conclusion that microinsurance is essential for assisting the poorer segments of society in developing sustainably and for lowering inequality. One of the important economic sectors in India is the insurance industry. The reputation of private microinsurance providers needs to be enhanced by winning over the trust of the underprivileged. India must develop a number of distinctive micro-insurance products due to its sizable rural population and extensive market. Compared to their richer counterparts, poor people have a greater need for risk mitigation since they have a limited income and depend on their health and long-term well-being for their livelihood. Large insurance companies can adapt to local sensitivities and educate the impoverished about microinsurance benefits and premium payments through various government programs, they could create a more adaptable and healthier economy.

7 RECOMMENDATIONS

- **Low-Cost Small Business Policies:** While small business insurance has become increasingly popular among insurers, comparatively few low-cost policies have been created. The COVID-19 pandemic has heightened small business owners' awareness of the risks they face and the potential for sudden financial ruin. According to interviews conducted for this study, more insurers appear to be actively creating or considering products for this market.
- **Non-Insurance Services:** Insurers are increasingly introducing non-insurance services to provide value and tangibility. These services allow insurers to offer more comprehensive assistance, even with comparatively basic insurance plans.
- **Human Interaction and Digital Solutions:** Despite the push towards digital solutions, especially due to the pandemic, human interaction remains essential. Many new Insurtech's have entered the microinsurance sector with fully digital solutions. However, these businesses frequently need to collaborate with aggregators who interact directly with customers, and these aggregators will remain crucial.
- **Public Awareness Campaigns:** Expanding the market for microinsurance will require more public awareness campaigns or advertising. To offer microinsurance to the underprivileged, more knowledgeable insurance brokers are needed. The IRDA ought to mandate that private insurance providers establish a goal to cover a specific proportion of insurance.
- **Flexible Premium Payments:** Adequate media should be used to promote microinsurance. Customers must receive premium flexibility.
- **Promoting Private Insurance Firms:** Promoting private insurance firms is necessary. Private insurance firms must enhance their reputation to win the public's trust. Schools and universities can host awareness camps to educate young people about the value of insurance in everyday life.
- **Incentives for Insurance Agents:** Giving insurance agents credit for selling microinsurance products will enhance its outreach.

REFERENCES

Aishwarya Jayakumar and Shaeril Michael Almeida. (2018). Erudition and role of microinsurance in India.

Alam, M.S., Haque, M.I., and Rahman, M.A. (2019). Microinsurance for poverty alleviation: A case study in rural Bangladesh. *Journal of Development Studies,* 45(3), 241–260

Chandhok, A. (2009). Insurance- A tool to eradicate and a vehicle to economic development. *International Research Journal of Finance and Economics, 5.*

Cohen, J.S. (2005). Reducing vulnerability: The demand for micro insurance. *Journal of International Development.*

Cohen, J.S. (2005). Reducing vulnerability: The demand for micro insurance. Journal of International Development.

Gomez, J., Ramirez, P., and Torres, L. (2020). Weather-indexed insurance: A tool for risk management among Peruvian farmers. *Latin American Journal of Agriculture and Economics*, 18(4), 215–230

Gowsyashaik Dr P. Raja Babu. (2018). Micro insurance: Mechanism and opportunities for the sustainable development of Indian economy. *IJMET, 9*(2), 851–865.

Gowsyashaik, Dr. P., and Raja Babu. (2018). Micro insurance: Mechanism and opportunities for the sustainable development of Indian economy. *IJMET*, 9(2), 851–865.

IRDAI. (2023). Annual Report 2023.

IRDAI. (2024). *Regulations on microinsurance*. IRDAI. https://www.irdai.gov.in/regulations

Jansen, T. (2011, April). Towards shared social responsibility: A study of consumers' willingness to donate micro-insurance when taking out their own insurance. *Journal of Business Ethics, 175–190.*

Johnson, V. (2018). A study on the developments in micro insurance in India. *Research Review International Journal of Multidiscipline, ISSN: 2455–3085 (online), 03*(07), July.

Kono, I. (2010). Why is the take up of micro insurance so low? Evidence from a health insurance scheme in India. *The Developing Economies, 74–101.*

Mbogo, S., and Kariuki, J. (2021). The impact of mobile technology on microinsurance adoption in Kenya. African Journal of Finance and Economics, 12(2), 89–105

Mirai Chatterjee, "A step forward in microinsurance with the IRDAI report," The Economic Times, November 6, 2020

Mirai, C. (2020, November 6). A step forward in microinsurance with the IRDAI report. The Economic Times.

Morduch, J. (2012). *Micro insurance: The next revolution.* Oxford University Press.

Mutambara, M.E. (2018). Sustainable performance of micro insurance in low-income markets. *Risk Governance and Control: Financial Markets* and *Institutions, 8*(2), Spring.

Patel, A. (2019). *The role of microfinance in rural development.* [Doctoral dissertation, Yogi Vemana University]. https://dissertations.yvu.ac.in

Prahalad, C. (2017). An empirical study on life micro insurance: With special reference to rural market of Allahabad. *Bimabazaar.com.*

Sanki, D.M.M., and Shah, M. (2021). Sustainability and growth of micro insurance: A case of Insurance Company of India. *International Journal of Disaster Recovery and Business Continuity, 12*(1), 1948–1958.

Sharma, N., and Goyal, R. (2017). Pradhan Mantri Jan Dhan Yojana (PMJDY) - A conceptual study. *International Journal of Granthaalayah, ISSN- 2350-0530(O), 2394–3629(P).*

Singh, P. (2015). Micro insurance in India: A gizmo to vehicle economic development and alleviate poverty and vulnerability. IOSR Journal of Economics and Finance, 14–20.

Smith, J. (2002). *Challenges in microinsurance in rural areas.* Hawaii Pacific University, School of Business. https://www.hpu.edu/scholararticles

Veermata Jijabai Technological Institute. (2023). *Technological developments in microinsurance: A case study.* https://www.vjti.ac.in/researchpapers

Vijayalakshmi, D. (2014, February). A study on the behaviour of micro life insurance policy holders with reference to Coimbatore India. Research Journal of Recent Sciences, 87–94.

Yadav, M. (2016). Jan Dhan Se Jan Suraksha – A comprehensive study of Pradhan Mantri Jan Dhan Yojana. Indian Journal of Economics and Development, ISSN 2320-9828.Singh, P. (2015). Micro insurance in India: A gizmo to vehicle economic development and alleviate poverty and vulnerability. *IOSR Journal of Economics and Finance, 14–20.*

Yadav, Mohania. (2016). Jan Dhan Se Jan Suraksha – A comprehensive study of Pradhan Mantri Jan Dhan Yojana. *Indian Journal of Economics and Development, ISSN 2320-9828*

Advancement in Engineering and Science – Goyal et al. (Eds)
© 2026 The Author(s), ISBN: 978-1-041-31101-0

Evaluating Faculty Behaviours and ChatGPT-Generated Course Structure

Ragini N Mohanty
Professor, PGDM Business Design, S. P. Mandali's Prin. L. N. Welingkar Institute of Management Development and Research (PGDM), Mumbai

Jyoti Kulkarni
Senior Associate Dean- Business Design, S. P. Mandali's Prin. L. N. Welingkar Institute of Management Development and Research (PGDM), Mumbai

Pratibha Jha
Ph.D., Assistant Professor – Ebiz, S. P. Mandali's Prin. L. N. Welingkar Institute of Management Development and Research (PGDM), Mumbai

ABSTRACT: Despite Artificial intelligence (AI) in education been studied for nearly 3 decades, teachers are ignorant of its potential in higher education. This research combines the design thinking principles, HILLS Design Thinking framework (IBM), pedagogical approaches, and Bloom's Taxonomy with ChatGPT in recognition of AI as a current trend in education. AI-generated responses that are user-centric, innovative, and impactful are produced from effective cues through prompt engineering. An experimental and exploratory mixed-method approach was used to study faculty behaviours for use of generative AI and ChatGPT, and to test the quality of a sample Design Thinking course structure generated from the free version of ChatGPT (3.5) which used the scaffolding technique in prompt engineering. Human-validation supervised integration of ChatGPT for curriculum design using design-thinking integrated scaffolding technique for prompt writing is recommended for effective user-friendly output for learning effectiveness. It was noteworthy that all faculty said that use of AI was a good and enjoyable experience, and they expressed willingness and keenness to integrate AI in their teaching-learning plan. The criteria influencing selection of AI tools are Visualization, Access, Writing, Compatibility, Programming, Quick, Popular, Trust, with costs, awareness and technical competence & complexity being significant barriers to adoption of AI.

Keywords: Artificial Intelligence, ChatGPT, Scaffolding Prompt Engineering, Design Thinking, Higher Education, Curriculum Pedagogy

1 INTRODUCTION

Following COVID, global movements toward digitalization and sustainability increased. The job economy in 2023 experienced extraordinary transformation as a result of generative AI, economic shifts, and environmental considerations (Perri, 2023). As technology advances, skills become obsolete in less than five years, needing continual learning. By 2027, 42% of jobs might be automated, affecting over a billion people globally (WEF Report, 2023). The entry-level occupations will focus on core data activities, whereas mid-level positions will require specialized problem-solving with AI technologies. Top-tier employment roles will require knowledge and skills for AI development and data analytics engineering, with a focus on adaptability and continuous learning (Tamayo, 2023). The rapid evolution of Artificial intelligence (AI) will likely create a personalized, efficient education system. The future of education could likely be an innovative Netflix-like streaming experience allowing students to choose their own courses (Pitso, 2023). (1) Improving education with technology is a global priority to equip future citizens for success in an AI-centric world. To respond to radical game-changing trends, education must be prepared to embrace innovation, scalable business models, and integration of new technologies like AI and ChatGPT. Collaboration between human intelligence (HI) and artificial intelligence (AI) is essential for fostering AI-incorporated education (Jones, 2023). Business schools struggle to successfully integrate AI training into their curricula, despite calls for its inclusion in the classroom due to lack of experience in teaching AI for non-technical audiences and the lack of resources (Xu, 2021). Though AI has been researched and used in education previously, teaching faculty are struggling to understand relevant guidelines and its application in teaching pedagogy and student engagement (Lee, 2024). This necessitated a research study to pursued multiple goals – a) to analyse faculty behaviours towards adoption of AI, b) pursue an experiment by applying design thinking integrated scaffolding technique of prompt engineering to generate a course structure using ChatGPT, c) evaluate output content and overall quality for a sample course in the design thinking area, and d) recommend a framework using design-thinking principle integrated prompt engineering technique for effective output.

2 LITERATURE REVIEW

Education aims to provide 21st-century skills such as learning and innovation, digital literacy, and vital work skills, integrating human intelligence (HI) and artificial intelligence (AI) that links knowledge with practical application skills. (Miho TAGUMA, 2018). Since the 1960s, AI has been utilized in higher education and has now become a valuable resource of modern higher education for students, staff, and administration (Hazaimeh, 2024). According to the OECD definition (OECD, 2019), "an AI system is a machine-based system that can influence the environment by producing an output (predictions, recommendations, or decisions) for a given set of objectives". Learning attainments will be of the higher order in a student-centered learning environment, where students are motivated, actively engaged and responsible towards achieving the planned learning objectives (Zhang, Su, Zeng, and Lam, 2022).

The foundation of a structured learning approach was 'The Constructive Alignment' approach offered by Biggs (1996) that aligns the teaching-learning process across outcomes - instructional strategies - learning activities - assessment methods The

DOI: 10.1201/9781003798514-73

constructive alignment framework comprises the 3P dimensions (John Biggs, 1987, 1987a, 1999; Hamilton, 2009) of

- Presage - refers to both the learner's attributes (e.g., knowledge, competence, motivation) and the course's setting (e.g., objectives, structure, assessment, climate, methods, and procedures).
- Process - refers to the teaching and learning activities that take place during the course.
- Product - the final learning output achieved by the students.

Integrating AI & Generative AI in management education at the Presage phase can lead to a transformative student learning experience and outcome (Mohanty, 2024). Though known to improve learning, simplify administrative tasks, and foster educational innovation, and despite being researched & used, teachers are still uninformed of AI, its scope in higher education, and, what it consists of. AI applications are being researched by academia as pedagogical tools that teachers can use to support students throughout their academic lifecycle. (Zawacki-Richter, 2019).

ChatGPT, a Generative AI chatbot developed by OpenAI in November 2022, has garnered traction in education because to its potential to facilitate interactivity, personalized learning, practice, and dynamic evaluation. It facilitates performance improvement by overcoming learning barriers, enhancing perceived value, learning motivation, self-efficacy and engagement, while lowering anxiety and cognitive load. They provide clear visible cues and enjoyable learning experiences while adapting to different learning styles. (Wu, 2023). However, higher education is at a crossroads about AI management and standards for the use and acceptability of AI-assisted automated content generation (ACG). There is an absence of universally accepted AI guidelines and protocols for education (Schneider, 2024).

AI adoption and acceptability in higher education were found to be highly influenced by human interaction-based features such as perceived benefits, attitude to adopt, digital competence, and openness (willingness and trust) to experimentation (Rana M.M., (2024)).

The benefits from the use of GAI technologies for faculty include curriculum design, lesson planning and content preparation for teaching, assessment structure, design and content, personalized learning and support via student progress assessment, with personalized feedback and suggestions of resources and learning activities based on student abilities, novel approaches to teaching difficult ideas and solving complex problems, professional development, and research; all in a cost-effective and interactive conversational format (Rahman, 2023). Higher educational institute (HEIs) and teachers can improve student's learning adaptability and acceptance through optimized and advanced AI-generated content (AIGC)-assisted course development (Jiang Q., 2024).

ChatGPT can be leveraged by teachers through an innovative and iterative process to define the course structure and teaching learning plan including course learning outcomes (CLOs), curated learning activities and student learning assessments with their course learning outcomes mapped, and teaching content. Although ChatGPT can significantly reduce instructors' initial course design time, it lacks the specificity and contextual awareness required for effective deployment in varied classroom situations. The instructor plays a significant role in developing and finalizing the course arrangement and maintaining effective teaching approaches (Pereira, 2024).

Experiences with the willingness to include ChatGPT into teaching and its level of acceptance range from limited use due to a lack of awareness and familiarity to positive impact in the form of improved teaching effectiveness, student engagement, and ease of comprehensibility of complicated concepts. However, curriculum alignment, adaptability, and customisation requirements to fit different learning styles surfaced as barriers to adoption. The study emphasizes the significance of continuous professional development and assistance for teachers to properly integrate AI-based ChatGPT into instruction. (Egara, 2024). Other concerns include costs, skilled resources, ethical usage of data, and user privacy concerns. There is an inherent resistant to change due to the lack of understanding and expertise in application of this new technology, individual biases, perceptions related to AI's potential impact on their employment, and technical complexity of integrating AI with the existing operational systems (Hazaimeh, 2024).

Teachers should actively explore and embrace AI in education (Gimpel, 2023) focussing on pedagogical concepts, evaluations, and ethical inclusion of AI in the curriculum (Craig, 2023). As a content creator aide, ChatGPT can relieve pressure on the educational system (Mohd Javaid, 2023). Use of AI tools might make it easier for teachers and instructional designers to quickly develop learning objectives, discussion starters, rubrics, and formative assessment items, fast and with a high degree of accuracy, which humans can then "review, augment, and polish," potentially redistributing the labour from authoring to reviewing and editing (Veletsianos, 2023).

ChatGPT's effectiveness varies by domain, making domain expertise necessary for top performance. Despite its ability to generate human-like content ChatGPT has some shortcomings. Some algorithms can provide illogical or inaccurate outputs, when the user inputs ambiguous, unclear, and confusing prompts. To find the best method for using ChatGPT, a variety of prompt engineering strategies should be adapted (H Zhang, 2023). The quality of the prompt determines the output. For best results when employing ChatGPT, prompt engineering strategies including "few-shot learning, chain-of-thought approaches, and role-playing scenarios" are advised by experts. However, the initial problem is to figure out how to get the best prompt for the desired outcome (Teubner, 2023).

Prompt engineering entails designing, refining and optimizing input instructions. To create meaningful and productive interactions using ChatGPT, it is essential to grasp the subtleties of prompt engineering, as the caliber of the prompts directly influences the caliber of the generated responses (Ekin, 2023). An effective prompt involves conversational and humanized character (Hutson, 2023). The key to enhancing AI completions through prompting is the iterative use of chat features (Liu, 2023).

The Interaction Design Foundation states that teams utilize design thinking, a non-linear, iterative method, to comprehend people, characterize problems in novel ways, question assumptions, and create innovative solutions that can be tested and prototyped. Its use is most beneficial in solving unstructured, ill-defined, or unidentified problems and involves the five phases of "empathize, define, define, ideate, prototype, and test" (IxDF, 2016). Hills (Writing HILLS) are a component of IBM's design thinking toolkit for Enterprise Design Thinking (IBM). Hill statements are declarations of intent that are crafted with important user outcomes in mind. Three essential components that make up Hills' syntax are: "Who: Who are your customers? What: What need are you attempting to fulfill? Wow: how will you gauge your success?" (Oluyemi, 2020).

Intentional questioning and scaffolding (modrobotics,com, 2019) of information and prompts is essential when it comes to fostering critical thinking skills through the ability to 'critique' (Betty Exintaris, 2023) and problem-solving abilities in students (Eissenberg, 2019). Scaffolding is a metaphor term described as "teaching by allowing the student to discover things themselves, prompting and hinting them in the right direction rather than just telling them" (Verenikina, 2008). Asking questions is an essential cognitive function that enhances teaching and learning. Teacher-posed questions have a significant impact on students' curiosity, critical thinking, and eventually learning. The ability to ask insightful questions requires the teacher to use creative intervention in order to support learning. (Angela K. Salmon, 2021).

3 MATERIALS AND METHODS

3.1 *Research objective*

Objective 1: To understand faculty behaviours in adoption of generative AI and ChatGPT.

Objective 2: To experiment with design-thinking integrated use of HILLs framework and scaffolding technique of prompt engineering to generate an objective format, user-friendly, creative course structure as a sample course in design thinking.

Objective 3: To evaluate the quality of course structure and content output from ChatGPT (free version 3.5).

Objective 4: To propose design-thinking principle integrated guidelines for effective prompt writing.

3.2 *Research questions (RQ)*

To understand faculty behaviours towards use of ChatGPT the following questions were defined.

RQ1: What are the commonly used AI tools by faculty and the reasons for their use?

RQ2: What are the criteria for selection of AI tool for teaching and learning?

RQ3: What is the faculty experience with use of ChatGPT and prompting?

RQ4: What are the barriers to adoption of AI tools by faculty for teaching?

3.3 *Research scope*

The research has been an experimental study about use of ChatGPT in the academic setting as an aid in instructional and course design. Research explored the generation of a sample course curriculum and structure belonging to the multi-disciplinary domain of design thinking. The course structure design is an outcome of use of ChatGPT tool with iterative prompts, done by faculty of the Business Design program at a business school in India. The free version ChatGPT 3.5 (https://chat.openai.com/) was used.

3.4 *Research design*

3.4.1 *Secondary research*

The literature review provided an understanding of AI & generative AI in education, ChatGPT, prompt engineering, and its use by faculty. Peer-reviewed scholarly journal articles and research papers, book chapters, books, thesis studies, and industry reports, from databases of EBSCOhost ProQuest, SCOPUS, Google Scholar, Science Direct, Web of Science, Academia, ResearchGate, Sage, Emerald, and Wiley publications were studied. Key search terms included artificial intelligence, artificial intelligence in education, AI, AIEd, ChatGPT, prompt engineering, assisted course design, course acceptance, design course, and learning support.

3.4.2 *Primary research*

- Mixed methodology (Quantitative & Qualitative) research methodology was used for this research. Questionnaire comprised of open and close-ended questionnaire using Likert scale. Google form was used for distribution of questionnaire and collection of responses. This was reinforced along with a face-to-face interview technique. Information was gathered through open-ended conversations from faculty teaching different courses. Conversations were focussed on use of AI by faculty as a pedagogy tool pertaining to
  - commonly used AI tools and reasons for use
  - criteria for selection of AI tools as pedagogical tools in teaching and learning
  - experiences with the use of ChatGPT and prompt engineering
  - barriers to the adoption of AI tools by faculty for teaching

Sample size: 75 respondents

- Experiment Analysis: This was qualitative research. The objectives were
  - to test if a full credit design thinking AI-developed course structure could be generated through the use of ChatGPT
  - to examine effectiveness of the prompt engineering technique and assess if the LLM was able to understand expectations from qualitative cues.
  - to evaluate the comprehensiveness and quality of the ChatGPT output from academic perspective by doing content analysis
  - to examine if design thinking activity can be conducted using design-thinking framework to generate user personas, their potential pain points and solutions
  - to develop a prompt engineering framework that has humanised abilities to meet the needs of qualitative research.

4 DATA ANALYSIS AND INTERPRETATION

4.1 *Sentiment analysis*

4.1.1 *Faculty responses were analyzed by text (sentiment) analytics*

- Text analytics: The process for text analytics included data cleaning and preprocessing (text cleaning, tokenization, removal of stop words, stemming, and lemmatization), data exploration, content visualization, and text Summarization, which helped in identifying trends and a shift in the language usage.
- Data Cleaning: During data pre-processing, the use of word clouds helps spot common stop words or noise words that might need to be removed for improved quality of text analysis.
- Data Exploration: Word clouds help analysts quickly explore and understand the most frequent terms or words in each text corpus. This can be valuable for getting a sense of the key topics or themes within the data.
- Identifying Trends: Over time, word clouds can be generated from text data collected at different intervals to identify evolving trends and shifts in language usage.
- Content Visualization: Word clouds make it easy to visualize text data, making it more accessible to a broader audience. This can be useful in presentations or reports.
- Text Summarization: By highlighting the most prominent words, Word clouds offer a succinct synopsis of the text data, allowing users to quickly grasp the main ideas of the text without having to read every word.

4.1.2 *The packages and software requirement for doing the Text Analytics: Software: R studio*

Packages: tm Text Mining package for reading textual data. The core text corpus object, which is a collection of text documents in various formats, is created using the TM package, including text within data frames, .txt files, or .doc files.

- Wordcloud: It is a visually appealing data visualization technique for text data. An effective tool for communication, it boosts clarity and simplicity, wherein the magnitude of each word represents its frequency or relevance.
- Quanteda: fully featured package for the quantitative study of textual data enabling users to quickly complete tasks involving natural language processing.
- word2vec: transforms a word into a code for further NLP and ML process.
- Dplyr: A data manipulation framework called Dplyr provides a standardized set of verbs to help with the most popular data transformation and manipulation tasks.

4.2 *Results & discussion*

4.2.1 *Faculty interviews - Sentiment analysis*

Research Objective 1: To understand faculty behaviours in adoption of generative AI and ChatGPT.

Majorly, faculty expressed willingness to integrate AI in their teaching-learning plan.

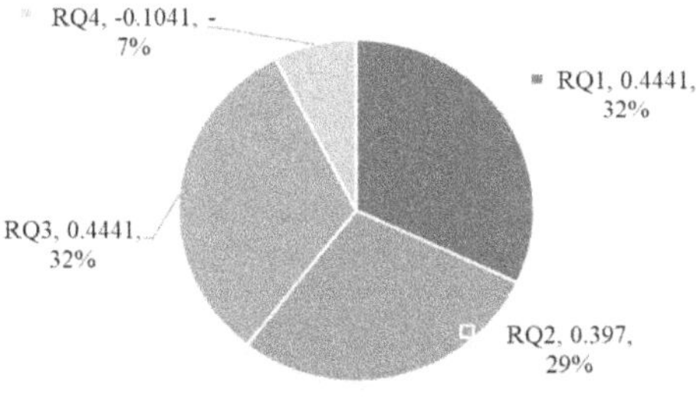

Figure 1. Overall sentiment score.

Table 1. Summary of sentiment analysis.

RQ	Description	Sentiment	Overall sentiment Score	Max sentiment Score
RQ1	What are the commonly used AI tools by faculty and the reasons for their use?	Positive	**0.4441**	**1.1667**
RQ2	What are the criteria for selection of AI tool for teaching and learning?	Positive	**0.3970**	**1.0500**
RQ3	What is the faculty experience with use of ChatGPT and prompting?	Positive	**0.4441**	**1.1667**
RQ4	What are the barriers to adoption of AI tools in teaching faced by faculty?	Negative	**-0.1041**	**0.5500**

Source: Author representation.

Figure 2. Commonly used AI tools by faculty and the reasons for their use. Source: Software: R studio – wordcloud

RQ1: What are the commonly used AI tools by faculty & reasons for their use?

Ans. ChatGPT followed by Grammarly, Quill Bot, TensorFlow, Jasper, Jenny, Keras, and Scikit.

Reasons for use: content, writing, experience, PPT, slides, processes, reports, analytics, project, information, academics, taking experience.

element_id	sentence_id	word_count	sentiment
Min.: 1.00	Min.:1.000	Min.: 1.000	Min.: -0.2963
1st Qu.:20.75	1st Qu.:1.000	1st Qu.: 1.000	1st Qu.: 0.0000
Median:38.50	Median:1.000	Median: 2.000	Median: 0.5152
Mean:38.51	Mean:1.107	Mean: 4.976	Mean: 0.4441
3rd Qu.:57.25	3rd Qu.:1.000	3rd Qu.: 7.250	3rd Qu.: 0.7500
Max.:75.00	Max.:2.000	Max.:34.000	Max.: 1.1667

Source: Software: R studio

The sentiment analysis of 75 items reveals a sentiment score range of -0.2963 to 1.1667, with a median of 0.5152 and a mean of 0.4441, indicating that the text elements in the dataset have a slightly positive sentiment. Word counts range from 1 to 34, indicating varying content length and complexity. Overall, the dataset shows mixed sentiments, with a favorable trend.

Maximum sentiment score: approximately 1.1667

Overall Sentiment Score: 0.4441344

The ***sentiment analysis algorithm has detected positive or neutral sentiments*** in the text compared to negative sentiments.

Figure 3. Criteria for selection of AI tool for teaching and learning. Source: Software: R studio – wordcloud

RQ2: What are the criteria for selection of AI tool for teaching and learning?

Ans. Ease of use, Free access, Visualization, Access, Writing, Compatibility, Programming, Quick, Popular, Trust

Table 2. Summary (sentiments).

element_id	sentence_id	word_count	sentiment
Min.: 1.0	Min.:1	Min.: 1.000	Min. :0.0000
1st Qu.:19.5	1st Qu.:1	1st Qu.: 3.000	1st Qu.:0.2457
Median:38.0	Median:1	Median: 3.000	Median:0.433
Mean:38.0	Mean:1	Mean: 4.135	Mean:0.3970
3rd Qu.:56.5	3rd Qu.:1	3rd Qu.: 5.000	3rd Qu.:0.5774
Max.:75.0	Max.:1	Max.:19.000	Max.:1.0500

Source: Software: R studio

The 75-element dataset comprises sentiment ratings ranging from 0.0000 to 1.0500, with a mean of 0.3970 showing a typically favorable positive sentiment. The word count ranges from 1 to 19, with most sentences including 3 to 5 words. Overall, the dataset primarily contains short statements with anoverall positive sentiment.

Overall Sentiment Score: 0.3970292

The sentiment analysis algorithm has detected more positive or neutral sentiments in the text compared to negative sentiments.

Figure 4. Faculty experience with use of ChatGPT and prompting. Source: Software: R studio – wordcloud

RQ3: What is the faculty experience with use of ChatGPT and prompting?

Ans. Good experience, great, nice, enjoyed use, lots of learning, superb value adding, complementary, sometimes better than humans, throws relevant ideas but content needs verification, moderate, not very effective, lots of limitations, not always reliable, needs refinement, doubtful if the content is genuine.

Useful in: Critical thinking, Decision-making, personalized learning

Table 3. Summary (Sentiments).

element_id	sentence_id	word_count	sentiment
Min.: 1.00	Min. :1.000	Min.: 1.000	Min.: -0.2963
1st Qu.:20.75	1st u.:1.000	1st Qu.: 1.000	1st Qu.: 0.0000
Median :38.50	Median:1.000	Median: 2.000	Median: 0.5152
Mean:38.51	Mean 1.107	Mean: 4.976	Mean: 0.4441
3rd Qu.:57.25	3rd u.:1.000	3rd Qu.: 7.250	3rd Qu.: 0.7500
Max.:75.00	Max.:2.000	Max.:34.000	Max.: 1.1667

Source: Software: R studio

The dataset's sentiment scores range from -0.2963 to 1.1667, indicating a broad spectrum of sentiment. With a median score of 0.5152 and a mean of 0.4441, the data is encouraging towards positivity. The first quartile emotion is 0.0000 (neutral), whereas the third quartile (75th percentile) is 0.7500, indicating the strong presence of positivity-oriented content. Word counts vary, with most elements containing between 1 to 7 words. Overall, the dataset demonstrates a diverse range of sentiment expressions, with an overall positive trend and varied sentence phrase length and complexity.

Overall Sentiment Score: 0.4441344

The *sentiment analysis algorithm has detected more positive or neutral sentiments* in the text compared to negative sentiments.

Figure 5. Barriers to the use of AI tools in teaching and learning faced by faculty. Source: Software: R studio - wordcloud

RQ4: What are the barriers for the adoption of AI tools in teaching faced by faculty?

Ans. Paid subscriptions, lack of awareness, technical knowledge, knowledge of tools connectivity issues, time and cost factors, lack of trust

Table 4. Summary (Sentiments).

element_id	sentence_id	word_count	sentiment
Min.: 1.0	Min.:1	Min.: 2.000	Min.: -0.7071
1st Qu.:19.5	1st Qu.:1	1st Qu.: 2.000	1st Qu.: -0.4330
Median:38.0	Median :1	Median: 3.000	Median: 0.0000
Mean:38.0	Mean:1	Mean: 4.143	Mean: -0.1041
3rd Qu.:56.5	3rd Qu.:1	3rd Qu.: 4.000	3rd Qu.: 0.0000
Max.:75.0	Max.:1	Max.:34.000	Max.: 0.5500

Source: Software: R studio

The summary statistics for this dataset including elements, associated sentences, word counts, and sentiment scores, reveal several key insights. The dataset's sentiment ratings range from -0.7071 to 0.5500, indicating a broad sentiment spectrum. The first quartile (25th percentile) emotion of -0.4330 indicates a considerable amount of negative material, whereas the median score of 0.0000 implies neutrality – balancing positive and negative sentiment. The mean score of -0.1041 indicates a minor overall leaning towards negativity. Most elements contain 2 to 4 words. Overall, the dataset reflects a diverse range of sentiment expressions, with an overall tendency towards neutrality and some negatively oriented content, as well as variations in sentence length and complexity.

Overall Sentiment Score: -0.1041074

With an "Overall Sentiment Score" of approximately -0.1041

The *sentiment analysis algorithm has detected more negative or neutral sentiments* in the text compared to positive sentiments.

4.2.2 *Course structure generation*

Research Objective 2: To experiment with design-thinking integrated use of HILLs framework and scaffolding technique of prompt engineering to generate an objective format, user-friendly, creative course structure as a sample course in design thinking.

Research Objective 3: To evaluate the quality of course structure and content output from ChatGPT (free version 3.5).

Design Thinking and Business Innovation courses foster leadership, strategic thinking, and a customer-centric perspective by employing business analytical methods and delivering hands-on results that benefit both business and society. The approach leverages experiential learning to overcome complicated VUCA and BANI systems. Curriculum development requires input from several stakeholders, including education ministry, regulators & accreditation auditors, industry benchmarking, industry reports and white papers, inputs from industry / program teams and deans / academic board / alumni / conferences / consultants; job portals, recruiters etc.

- **Prompt 1 – Basic context:** At first, a basic prompt was provided to the ChatGPT platform providing only the background context and task to be performed.

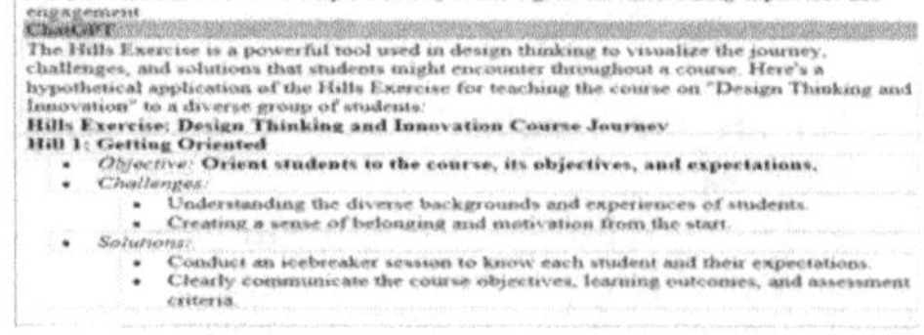

Context - you are a design thinking and innovation specialist. You are in your early 50's. You come with industry experience of 20 years. You are to teach a course on business design and innovation. The students are of diverse educational backgrounds and with and without work experience. The accreditation agency wants to see the innovative pedagogy styles for teaching the course titled design thinking and innovation, and impactful student learning outcomes. Perform the Hills exercise to help the faculty create a great student learning experience and engagement

ChatGPT

The Hills Exercise is a powerful tool used in design thinking to visualize the journey, challenges, and solutions that students might encounter throughout a course. Here's a hypothetical application of the Hills Exercise for teaching the course on "Design Thinking and Innovation" to a diverse group of students:

Hills Exercise: Design Thinking and Innovation Course Journey

Hill 1: Getting Oriented

- *Objective:* **Orient students to the course, its objectives, and expectations.**
- *Challenges:*
  - Understanding the diverse backgrounds and experiences of students.
  - Creating a sense of belonging and motivation from the start.
- *Solutions:*
  - Conduct an icebreaker session to know each student and their expectations.
  - Clearly communicate the course objectives, learning outcomes, and assessment criteria.

Figure 6. Prompt 1 – Basic context. Source: ChatGPT output (free version 3.5)

LE

Context - you are a design thinking and innovation specialist. You are in your early 50's. You come with industry experience of 20 years. You are to teach a course on business design and innovation. The students are of diverse educational backgrounds and with and without work experience. The accreditation agency wants to see the innovative pedagogy styles for teaching the course titled design thinking and innovation, and impactful student learning outcomes Perform the Hills exercise to help the faculty create a great student learning experience and engagement

ChatGPT

The Hills Exercise is a powerful tool used in design thinking to visualize the journey, challenges, and solutions that students might encounter throughout a course. Here's a hypothetical application of the Hills Exercise for teaching the course on "Design Thinking and Innovation" to a diverse group of students:

Hills Exercise: Design Thinking and Innovation Course Journey

Hill 1: Getting Oriented

- *Objective:* **Orient students to the course, its objectives, and expectations.**
- *Challenges:*
  - Understanding the diverse backgrounds and experiences of students.
  - Creating a sense of belonging and motivation from the start.
- *Solutions:*
  - Conduct an icebreaker session to know each student and their expectations.
  - Clearly communicate the course objectives, learning outcomes, and assessment criteria.

Figure 7. Prompt 1 – Basic context. Source: ChatGPT output (free version 3.5)

Prompt 1 ChatGPT (OUTPUT): Observations and remarks

The output included objectives, challenges, and solutions for the course design. This output was incorrect for the 'Hills' elements because the Hills statement of IBM comprises the '3W' elements of 'Who, What, and Wow'. However, the positives can be an indicative direction about how to introduce the course to the students and get them to participate.

- **Prompt 2 - Hills incorporated:** The second prompt asked for a response to the Hills elements of Who, What and How.

Prompt 1 ChatGPT (OUTPUT): Observations and remarks

The output included objectives, challenges, and solutions for the course design. This output was incorrect for the 'Hills' elements because the Hills statement of IBM comprises the '3W' elements of 'Who, What, and Wow'. However, the positives can be an indicative direction about how to introduce the course to the students and get them to participate.

- **Prompt 2 -** Hills incorporated: The second prompt asked for a response to the Hills elements of Who, What and How.

LE

Pl give me responses to the above related to the "Hills" Design Thinking exercise of who, what, wow.

ChatGPT

Certainly! Let's expand on the Hills Exercise for the "Design Thinking and Innovation" course by adding "Who," "What," and "Wow" components for each hill.

Hill 1: Getting Oriented

Who: Students from diverse educational backgrounds, both with and without work experience.

What: Icebreaker sessions, interactive Q&A about students' expectations, course overview, introductions to fellow students.

Wow: Students will leave feeling connected, motivated, and having a clear understanding of the course's potential impact on their journey.

Hill 2: Learning the Basics

Who: Students with varying levels of prior knowledge in design thinking and AI.

What: Interactive workshops, engaging discussions, gamified learning modules, and real-life case studies.

Wow: Students will grasp fundamental concepts and understand how design thinking and AI are integral to problem-solving.

Figure 8. Prompt 2 – Hills framework elements incorporated in the prompt. Source: ChatGPT output (free version 3.5)

Prompt 2 ChatGPT (OUTPUT): Observations and remarks

This time the results were attained for the 3W elements. It provided insights on WHO can be considered as the users, WHAT approaches can be used to meet the user needs, and how the users would experience the WOW effect.

Prompt 3 – Scaffolding technique and humanized approach

Further, using personalized humanized requests with a scaffolding approach, the complexity and specificity of prompts were increased by adding multiple requirements including.

- Hills statement
- pedagogical methods from Allan Carrington's pedagogy wheel
- Bloom's Taxonomy learning skills
- impactful learning outcomes
- better creative representation of elements in tabular formats

Such nuanced inquiries helped to get a more effective and objective format of output from ChatGPT. The output was in a creative, structured tabular format that was relatively user-friendly as compared to the previous textual output.

Hill 1: Getting Oriented
- **Who: ** Diverse academic backgrounds, fresh graduates, mid-career professionals
- **What: ** Introduce, Discuss, Align
- **Wow: ** Motivate, Engage, Foster
- **Pedagogy Wheel: ** Understanding, Remembering
- **Activities: ** Icebreaker sessions, Syllabus review discussion, Goal setting

Hill 2: Learning the Basics
- **Who: ** Students with varied understanding of design thinking
- **What: ** Explore, Analyse, Apply
- **Wow: ** Understand, Grasp, Comprehend
- **Pedagogy Wheel: ** Applying, Understanding
- **Activities: ** Interactive workshops, Case study analysis, Ideation exercises

Hill 3: Applying Design Thinking
- **Who: ** Students transitioning theory into practical application
- **What: ** Create, Innovate, Experiment
- **Wow: ** Demonstrate, Showcase, Present
- **Pedagogy Wheel: ** Applying, Analysing
- **Activities: ** Group projects, Prototyping sessions, Final project presentations

Hill 4: Understanding Innovation in Business
- **Who: ** Students from diverse backgrounds, needing to grasp business innovation
- **What: ** Investigate, Examine, Relate
- **Wow: ** Recognize, Realize, Appreciate
- **Pedagogy Wheel: ** Evaluating, Analysing
- **Activities: ** Guest lectures, Case studies on successful business innovations

Hill 5: Cross-Collaboration and Diversity
- **Who: ** Students with varying collaboration experiences
- **What: ** Collaborate, Integrate, Discuss
- **Wow: ** Appreciate, Value, Embrace
- **Pedagogy Wheel: ** Creating, Evaluating
- **Activities: ** Team building, Diverse group projects, Brainstorming sessions

Hill 6: Overcoming Implementation Hurdles
- **Who: ** Students aspiring to drive change through innovation
- **What: ** Simulate, Strategize, Address
- **Wow: ** Build, Navigate, Strategize
- **Pedagogy Wheel: ** Creating, Applying
- **Activities: ** Simulated scenarios, Role-playing exercises, Strategy brainstorming

Hill 7: Reflecting and Adapting
- **Who: ** Students aiming to reflect on their learning journey
- **What: ** Reflect, Discuss, Envision
- **Wow: ** Refine, Plan, Chart
- **Pedagogy Wheel: ** Evaluating, Creating
- **Activities: ** Individual reflection, Group discussions, Future planning

Figure 9a. Prompt 3 – Scaffolding technique and humanized approach prompt output in creative user-friendly output (Part representation of output). Source: ChatGPT output (free version 3.5)

Session **Design Thinking Course Outline**

**Who: ** Students of postgraduate level management education with diverse educational backgrounds and varying work experience.
**What: ** Learn and apply design thinking methodologies to innovate and solve complex business challenges.
**Wow: ** Develop a user-centric, innovative mindset for problem-solving in diverse business domains.
**Assessments: **
- Class participation and engagement
- Reflective journals
- Mid-term examination
- Design thinking project
- Final presentation and report

1 Introduction to Design Thinking
**What: ** Understand the fundamentals and history of design thinking.
**Pedagogy: **
- Interactive lectures and discussions
- Case studies and real-world examples

**Assessments: **
- Conceptual understanding assessment
- Reflection paper on the relevance of design thinking
- Small group discussions and presentations
- **Bloom's Level: ** Understand (Remembering)

2 Empathy and Problem Definition
**What: ** Develop skills in empathizing with users and problem identification.
**Pedagogy: **
- User interviews and empathy mapping
- Group activities and role-playing

**Assessments: **
- Empathy map analysis and reflection
- Problem definition and ideation exercise
- **Bloom's Level: ** Understand and Apply (Understanding and Applying)

3 Ideation and Brainstorming
**What: ** Generate creative solutions through brainstorming and ideation.
**Pedagogy: **
- Brainstorming sessions and group discussions
- Creative thinking exercises

**Assessments: **
- Idea generation and evaluation
- Creative solution proposal
- **Bloom's Level: ** Create (Creating)

Figure 9b. Prompt 3 – Scaffolding technique and humanized approach prompt output in creative user-friendly output (Part representation of output).

- **Prompt 3 - ChatGPT (OUTPUT): Observations and remarks**
  The incremental improvement of prompts provided an objective crisp format of course structure incorporating the Hills statements, the Blooms elements, pedagogical approaches, and assessments. The faculty can combine these results with the previous results of objective, challenges, and solutions, and draft the preliminary curriculum / course structure, which can be further brainstormed and enhanced with variety of inputs.
- **Prompt 4 - Free tools for design thinking**
  Faculty also sought reference about free tools for design thinking practice-based learning.

LE

name some free tools for design thinking.

ChatGPT

Certainly! There are several free tools and resources available to support the design thinking process. These tools can help with brainstorming, prototyping, collaboration, and more. Here are some popular ones:

Miro:

- Miro is a versatile online whiteboard platform that supports collaborative brainstorming, mind mapping, user journey mapping, wireframing, and more in real-time.

Trello:

- Trello is a visual project management tool that can be used to organize and manage design thinking projects, tasks, and progress using boards, lists, and cards.

Canva:

- Canva is a user-friendly graphic design tool that allows for the creation of visual content, including presentations, posters, infographics, and other design assets.

Figma:

- Figma is a cloud-based design tool that supports collaborative design, prototyping, and wireframing, making it great for teams working on design projects.

Balsamiq Wireframes:

- Balsamiq is a tool for creating low-fidelity wireframes and prototypes, making it ideal for quick iterations and sharing concepts.

Figure 10. Prompt 4– free tools for design thinking (Part representation of output). Source: ChatGPT output (free version 3.5)

- **Prompt 4 - ChatGPT (OUTPUT): Observations and remarks**
  The output provided several tools of design thinking with a brief introduction about the tool. This gives confidence as a faculty that students can search for tools, and they will be able to get relevant guidance for self-regulated learning using relevant prompts. Further probing is required.
- **Prompt 5 - Detailed prompt**
  This time the prompt was of a very detailed structure, assigning a role (empathizing with the tool as a human being), relevant context was provided. The questions were asked using the elements of Stanford Design Thinking Model, encompassing the requirements for curriculum / course design, Hills Statement of IBM Design Thinking Framework, Bloom's Taxonomy, pedagogy approaches, assessments, etc. The output expectations in the form of creative tabular structure were also provided.

LE

Consider: You are a design thinking and innovation specialist with industry experience of 20 years in design thinking, strategy and consulting, and instructional design. You are invited to teach a course on 'Business Design Innovation and Application' at a business school. The students are pursuing their MBA program. They are of diverse educational backgrounds and may be with / without work experience. The accreditation agency wants to see application of innovative pedagogy methods for teaching the course and impactful student learning outcomes. Use the elements of empathy, define, ideate, brainstorm and test and evaluate of the Stanford model of design thinking in providing the output. You are expected to empathize with the students taking this course, understand their personas and pain points and ideate so that you can design a full credit course (3 credits, 30 teaching hours, 15 lecture sessions, 100 marks (40:60 distribution for internal and external assessment) Make use of the HILLS elements of 'who, what, wow' of IBM design thinking framework to generate Design Thinking course structure. The end goal is to be able to create a student learning experience and engagement with impactful learning outcomes. Pl identify the applicable elements of pedagogy by referring to the pedagogy wheel of Allan Carrington and learning activities. Align the Blooms taxonomy verbs in designing high quality create level skills development. Give sample assessments per session. Pl organize the outcome by lecture sessions. What should be the program outcomes for the research and business analytics program and course outcomes for the course of 'Business Design Innovation and Application'. The prototype is your output, that must be innovative, creative, objective and in a tabular format that is easy to visualise, read and understand by the faculty and students. The course structure and content should be the best of all the benchmarked practices in your repository. Pl remember to provide session wise output that has integrated HILLS, pedagogy from Allan Carrington's pedagogy wheel, blooms skills, assessments, impactful student learning outcomes, reading material and in a tabular screen fitting layout. I am counting on you for a world class curriculum, that will make me the best design thinking faculty

Figure 11. Prompt 5 – Detailed prompt with scaffolding & design thinking element. Source: ChatGPT output (free version 3.5)

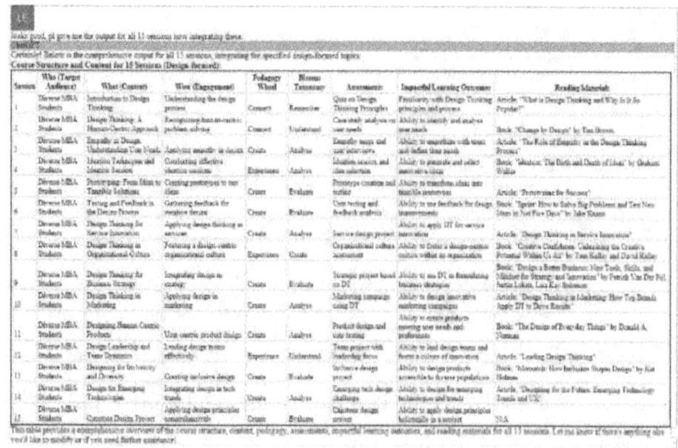

Figure 12. Prompt 5 – Sample Course Structure and Content generated from ChatGPT after detailed prompt in tabular format. Source: ChatGPT output (free version 3.5)

Prompt 5 – Sample course structure and content generated from ChatGPT (OUTPUT)

Observations and remarks

The output

- is generated from the descriptive format input data.
- information is organized and presented in a structured tabular format.
- information is user-friendly, simplified, easy to understand and readable.
- is quite comprehensive.
- provides a variety of information due to scaffolding of prompts.
- items are repetitive at times, and sometimes the algorithm shows variations.
- can be inferenced and decision-making requires human intelligence.
- generation and content finalization process are time-consuming if prompt quality is not good.
- makes the task of sense-making tedious and time-consuming.

However, the benefits of scaffolding prompt engineering are that,

- it improves thinking and critical analytical skills.
- improves the art of asking relevant questions and drafting more relevant prompts.
- helps recognize and determine quality and how a good question differs from a bad / illogical question.
- multiple iterations help remain focussed, gain clarity and perseverance to achieve.
- improve language skills.
- provides output in the form of a lot & diverse amount of information that widens the horizon of considerations.

Example of Design Research activity through ChatGPT

Testing EMPATHY, IDEATE & BRAINSTORM elements of design thinking to gain insights on usability of ChatGPT for design research. ChatGPT was prompted with empathy queries to generate personas and their pain points, solution ideation and choice of best option for prototyping and testing.

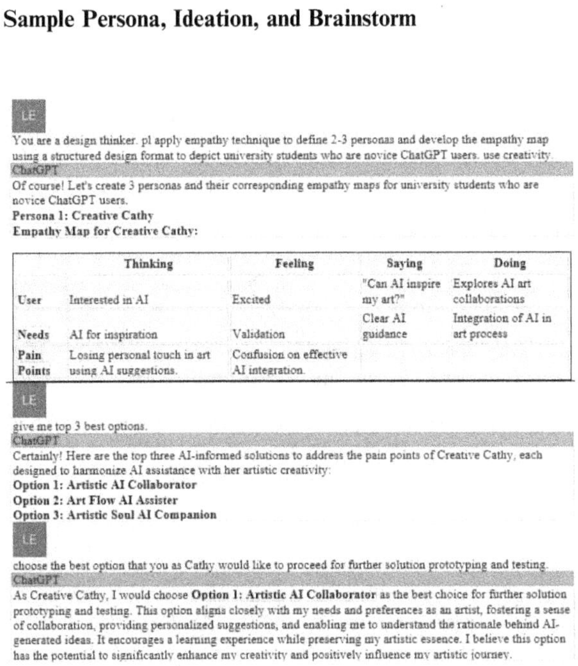

Sample Persona, Ideation, and Brainstorm

LE

You are a design thinker. pl apply empathy technique to define 2-3 personas and develop the empathy map using a structured design format to depict university students who are novice ChatGPT users. use creativity.

ChatGPT

Of course! Let's create 3 personas and their corresponding empathy maps for university students who are novice ChatGPT users.

Persona 1: Creative Cathy

Empathy Map for Creative Cathy:

	Thinking	Feeling	Saying	Doing
User	Interested in AI	Excited	"Can AI inspire my art?"	Explores AI art collaborations
Needs	AI for inspiration	Validation	Clear AI guidance	Integration of AI in art process
Pain Points	Losing personal touch in art using AI suggestions.	Confusion on effective AI integration.		

LE

give me top 3 best options.

ChatGPT

Certainly! Here are the top three AI-informed solutions to address the pain points of Creative Cathy, each designed to harmonize AI assistance with her artistic creativity:

Option 1: Artistic AI Collaborator

Option 2: Art Flow AI Assister

Option 3: Artistic Soul AI Companion

LE

choose the best option that you as Cathy would like to proceed for further solution prototyping and testing.

ChatGPT

As Creative Cathy, I would choose **Option 1: Artistic AI Collaborator** as the best choice for further solution prototyping and testing. This option aligns closely with my needs and preferences as an artist, fostering a sense of collaboration, providing personalized suggestions, and enabling me to understand the rationale behind AI-generated ideas. It encourages a learning experience while preserving my artistic essence. I believe this option has the potential to significantly enhance my creativity and positively influence my artistic journey.

Figure 13. Example of Design Research Activity through ChatGPT. Source: ChatGPT output (free version 3.5) (example) (Part representation & content is edited)

Research Objective 4: To propose design-thinking principle integrated guidelines for effective prompt writing.

4.3 *Recommendations*

As the usage of ChatGPT and prompt engineering will get more acceptable by industry and education sector, the faculty cannot avoid inclusion and integration of prompt engineering in their teaching without adequate reason. Through this research experience, the authors propose design thinking integrated guidelines for prompt writing, the acronym for which is 'RAACFATES', where.

R: Role: Assign a role and provide a background of existing skills and experience i.e., Professional role with job skills and experience, expertise.

A: Action: The actionable task/output to be generated should be relevant and aligned to intended output goals i.e., create, summarize, simplify, structure, persona, empathy map, outline, script, video, image.

A: Approach: Be iterative but relevant and specific about what you want to ask. Offer suggestions to refer to specific frameworks, models or patterns before generating output i.e., Design Thinking framework, SWOT Analysis, Ansoff Matrix.

C: Conditions: Restrictions/boundaries/styles within which the content is to be generated i.e., sources, language style, level of language, length of output - keeping in mind the audience who will be the users of the output, however, also consider open-endedness to encourage diversity in responses.

F: Format: Provide instructions on the expected output format i.e., table, list, spreadsheet, HTML, presentation, essay, research, email, report, blog, Tweet, code

A: Appearance: Structure and visual appeal of the output display i.e., structured, readable, screen fitting, left aligned.

T: Tone: Attitude when providing the output i.e., Professional, formal, creative, confident, firm, persuasive, academic, narrative, friendly, humorous.

E: End with a humanized reinforcement (conversational): Remember this must be the ideal / best / optimal approach, I am counting on you, seeking help in my role as … ., ask for feedback.

S: Scaffolding: Provide hints and build up the inquiry, break down the complexity of the task, encourage the AI to ask clarifying questions

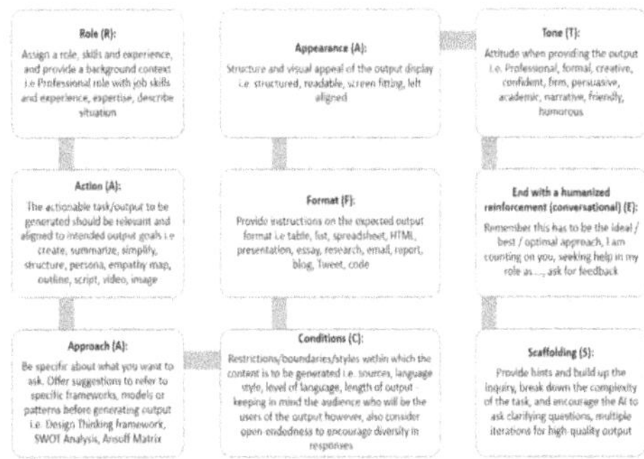

Figure 14. Guidelines for writing an effective prompt - 'RAACFATES.' (integrating design thinking elements). Source: Author representation

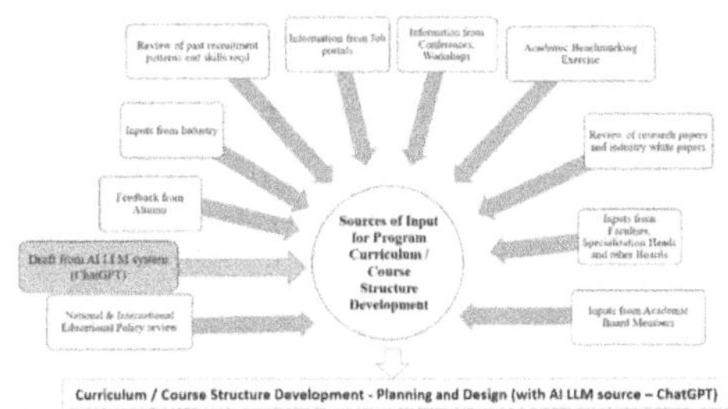

Figure 15. Curriculum / Course structure development (including AI LLM source). Source: Author representation

Practical implications: The insights from this study will help more faculty explore ChatGPT and prompt engineering to facilitate their teaching and learning plans & practices, impacting student learning outcomes. ChatGPT can help simplify lesson planning, allowing educators to focus on individualized instruction and innovative teaching methods that are matched with learning objectives. Faculty can develop student engagement activities through AI generated content in a scalable manner and help enhance student course engagement, learning experience, and learning outcomes. Faculty will be able to groom the students in the art of asking questions through writing of prompts which in turn will help student growth and critical thinking and analytical abilities based on outcomes. In addition, ChatGPT can be helpful for various other academic requirements.

5 CONCLUSION

In the long run, artificial intelligence will be a crucial component of every business organization and will be changing the way we live and work, with huge ramifications for business and society. Any business, not prepared for such a future digital economy and transformation, would be unable to compete and eventually get left behind. Functional usage of artificial intelligence (AI) technology requires AI literacy and faculty interest to learn, practice, experimentation, and perseverance when working with ChatGPT to integrate AI technologies in processes, work systems, services, business cases, and management of AI-based information systems as time progresses. Prompt engineering may not be an option anymore. The study has provided an example of prompt writing that is inspired by Design Thinking principles, that can be used by faculty as they draft their prompts for effective teaching-learning processes that are user-centric and innovative.

6 FUTURE RESEARCH

Future research can be pursued to generate course curriculum and structure for other courses, especially quantitative courses. The recommendations offered in this research can be explored for values and gaps. The Pro version GPT 4 can used for quality of teaching-learning outputs.

REFERENCES

Angela K. Salmon, Maria Ximena Barrera, (2021). Intentional questioning to promote thinking and learning, *Thinking Skills and Creativity*, Volume 40, 100822, ISSN 1871-1871, https://doi.org/10.1016/j.tsc.2021.100822. (https://www.sciencedirect.com/science/article/pii/S1871187121000377)

Beata Jones (2023), Breaking Boundaries with Generative AI: Good Practice of Unleashing the Power of ChatGPT for Inter- and Transdisciplinary Breakthroughs in the Age of Complexity, *Journal of the European Honors Council,* Vol. 6 No. 2, Online ISSN:2543-232X, https://doi.org/10.31378/jehc.6.2

Betty Exintaris, Nilushi Karunaratne, and Elizabeth Yuriev, (2023), Metacognition and Critical Thinking: Using ChatGPT-Generated Responses as Prompts for Critique in a Problem-Solving Workshop (SMARTCHEMPer), *Journal of Chemical Education*, 100 (8), 2972–2980, DOI: 10.1021/acs.jchemed.3c00481

Biggs, J. (1996). Enhancing teaching through constructive alignment. *Higher Education*, 32(3), 347–364. https://www.jstor.org/stable/3448076.

Craig, V.S., Johnson, R.D., and Sarabadani, J. (2023). Generative artificial intelligence in information systems education: Challenges, consequences, and responses. *Communications of the Association for Information Systems*, 53 doi: https://doi.org/10.17705/1CAIS.05301

Daniel Lee, Matthew Arnold, Amit Srivastava, Katrina Plastow, Peter Strelan, Florian Ploeckl, Dimitra Lekkas, Edward Palmer, (2024), The impact of generative AI on higher education learning and teaching: A study of educators' perspectives, *Computers and Education: Artificial Intelligence*, Volume 6, 2024, 100221, ISSN 2666-920X, https://doi.org/10.1016/j.caeai.2024.100221.

Egara, Felix and Mosimege, Mogege. (2024). Exploring the Integration of Artificial Intelligence-Based ChatGPT into Mathematics Instruction: Perceptions, Challenges, and Implications for Educators. *Education Sciences*. 14. 742. 10.3390/educsci14070742.

Ekin, Sabit. (2023). *Prompt Engineering for ChatGPT: A Quick Guide to Techniques, Tips, And Best Practices.* 10.36227/techrxiv.22683919.

Gimpel, Henner *et al.* (2023): Unlocking the power of generative AI models and systems such as GPT-4 and ChatGPT for higher education: A guide for students and lecturers, *Hohenheim Discussion Papers in Business, Economics and Social Sciences*, No. 02-2023, Universität Hohenheim, Fakultät Wirtschafts- und Sozialwissenschaften, Stuttgart, https://nbn-resolving.de/urn:nbn:de:bsz:100-opus-21463

Hamilton, John and Tee, Singwhat. (2009). Extending the Biggs 3P teaching and learning model: A structural equation modeling approach. *Proceedings of the International Conference on Electronic Business (ICEB)*. https://www.researchgate.net/publication/265987714_Extending_the_Biggs_3P_teaching_and_learning_model_A_structural_equation_modeling_approach

Hazaimeh, Manar and Al-Ansi, Abdullah. (2024). Model of AI acceptance in higher education: arguing teaching staff and students perspectives. *The International Journal of Information and Learning Technology.* 41. 10.1108/IJILT-01-2024-0005. DOI:10.1108/IJILT-01-2024-0005, https://www.researchgate.net/publication/382394903_Model_of_AI_acceptance_in_higher_education_arguing_teaching_staff_and_students_perspectives

Hutson, James and Plate, Daniel, "Human-AI Collaboration for Smart Education: Reframing Applied Learning to Support Metacognition" (2023). *Faculty Scholarship*. 480., https://digitalcommons.lindenwood.edu/faculty-research-papers/480

Jiang Q., Zhang Y., Wei W., Gu C., (2024), Evaluating technological and instructional factors influencing the acceptance of AIGC-assisted design courses, *Computers and Education: Artificial Intelligence,* 7, art. no. 100287, DOI: 10.1016/j.caeai.2024.100287, https://www.scopus.com/inward/record.uri?eid=2-s2.0-85202017418&doi=10.1016%2fj.caeai.2024.100287&partnerID=40&md5=4c289267da3a0b339913de2282776f9b

Jorge Tamayo, Leila Doumi, Sagar Goel, Orsolya Kovács-Ondrejkovic and Raffaella Sadun, (2023), Reskilling in the Age of AI, Talent Management Magazine Article, Harvard Business Review. https://hbr.org/2023/09/reskilling-in-the-age-of-ai

Lori Perri, (2023), *Generative AI Can Democratize Access to Knowledge and Skills*, Gartner https://www.gartner.com/en/articles/generative-ai-can-democratize-access-to-knowledge-and-skills

Miho TAGUMA, Eva FERON, Meow Hwee LIM, (2018), Education and AI: Preparing for the future & AI Attitudes and Values (OECD, 2018), *Future of Education And Skills 2030: Conceptual Learning Framework*, EDU/EDPC(2018)45/ANN2; https://static1.squarespace.com/static/5e26d2d6fcf7d67bbd37a92e/t/5e411f365af4111d703b7f91/1581326153625/Education-and-AI.pdf; https://www.oecd.org/education/2030/Education-and-AI-preparing-for-the-future-AI-Attitudes-and-Values.pdf

Mohd Javaid, Abid Haleem, Ravi Pratap Singh, Shahbaz Khan, Ibrahim Haleem Khan, (2023). Unlocking the opportunities through ChatGPT Tool towards ameliorating the education system, *Bench Council Transactions on Benchmarks, Standards and Evaluations*, Volume 3, Issue 2, 100115, ISSN 2772-4859, https://doi.org/10.1016/j.tbench.2023.100115. (https://www.sciencedirect.com/science/article/pii/S2772485923000327)

Mohanty, R.N.; Dixit, D.; Kalyandurgmath, K.; (2024), AI Literacy and Transformative Impact: Exploring the Perception of Generative AI in Management Education, *Technische Sicherheit (Technical Security)*, V24.2, pp: 102-133, ISSN:1434-9728/E-ISSN:1436-4948; DOI: 22.8342.TSJ.2024.V24.2.01260; https://technikwissen.eu/volume-24-issue-2-2024/

Pereira, Estacio, Nsair, Sumaya, Pereira, Leticia and Grant, Kimberley. (2024). Constructive alignment in a graduate-level project management course: an innovative framework using large language models. *International Journal of Educational Technology in Higher Education*. 21. 10.1186/s41239-024-00457-2.

Pitso, T. (2023, August 26). Post-COVID-19 Higher Learning: Towards Telagogy, A Web-Based Learning Experience. *IAFOR Journal of Education*, 11(2), 39–59. https://doi.org/10.22492/ije.11.2.02https://www.researchgate.net/profile/Teboho-Pitso-2/publication/373421231_Post-COVID-19_Higher_Learning_Towards_Telagogy_A_Web-Based_Learning_Experience/links/64f5d33d827074313ff9d89b/Post-COVID-19-Higher-Learning-Towards-Telagogy-A-Web-Based-Learning-Experience.pdf#page=47

Rahman, M.M., and Watanobe, Y. (2023). ChatGPT for education and research: Opportunities, threats, and strategies. *Applied Sciences*, 13 (9), 5783. doi:https://doi.org/10.3390/app13095783

Rana M.M., Siddiqee M.S., Sakib M.N., Ahamed M.R., (2024), Assessing AI adoption in developing country academia: A trust and privacy-augmented UTAUT framework, *Heliyon*, 10 (18), art. no. e37569 DOI:10.1016/j.heliyon.2024.e37569, https://www.scopus.com/inward/record.uri?eid=2-s2.0-85203664750&doi=10.1016%2fj.heliyon.2024.e37569&partnerID=40&md5=45ec117edca90d94ebad3965c5a2dd17

Schneider, S., Haried, P., (2024), Use of artificial intelligence in higher education with particular reference to automated content generation, trust and anxiety, *Journal of Business and Educational Leadership*, Vol 14, No 1, https://web.p.ebscohost.com/ehost/pdfviewer/pdfviewer?vid=0&sid=9400ac2c-b7e3-41b7-9cc4-8aafcc38e856%40redis

Teubner, T., Flath, C. and Weinhardt, C. (2023) Welcome to the Era of ChatGPT; in: *Bus Inf Syst Eng* 65, 95–101; doi.org/10.1007/s12599-023-00795-x

Wu, R., and Yu, Z. (2023). Do AI chatbots improve students learning outcomes? Evidence from a meta-analysis. *British Journal of Educational Technology*, 00, 1–24. https://doi.org/10.1111/bjet.13334; https://bera-journals.onlinelibrary.wiley.com/doi/10.1111/bjet.13334

Zawacki-Richter, O., Marín, V.I., Bond, M. *et al.* Systematic review of research on artificial intelligence applications in higher education – where are the educators? *Int J Educ Technol High Educ* 16, 39 (2019). https://doi.org/10.1186/s41239-019-0171-0; https://educationaltechnologyjournal.springeropen.com/articles/10.1186/s41239-019-0171-0?fbclid=IwAR0vSk4s9y0V0vExpcAel6yL4LEb-PrNDnlreOB5WrGxlu8-3awpYGgK6Ig#citeas

Zhang H, C Wu, J Xie, Y Lyu, J Cai, JM Carroll, (2023), Redefining Qualitative Analysis in the AI Era: Utilizing ChatGPT for Efficient Thematic Analysis, *arXiv preprint* arXiv:2309.10771, https://arxiv.org/pdf/2309.10771.pdf

Zhang, H.; Su, S.; Zeng, Y.; Lam, J.F.I. (2022). An Experimental Study on the Effectiveness of Students' Learning in Scientific Courses through Constructive Alignment—A Case Study from an MIS Course. *Educ. Sci.* 2022, 12, 338. https://doi.org/10.3390/educsci12050338

WEBSITES

Future of Jobs Report 2023, Insights Report, World Economic Forum, May 2023, pp 6, https://www.weforum.org/publications/the-future-of-jobs-report-2023/

https://archive.modrobotics.com/2019/02/15/scaffolded-questioning-a-differentiation-technique/

https://archive.modrobotics.com/2019/02/15/scaffolded-questioning-a-differentiation-technique/

https://educational-innovation.sydney.edu.au/teaching@sydney/prompt-engineering-for-students-making-generative-ai-work-for-you/

https://nife.medium.com/what-are-hills-in-ibm-design-thinking-446315959774

https://www.ibm.com/design/approach/design-thinking/

https://www.ibm.com/design/thinking/page/toolkit/activity/writing-hills

https://www.interaction-design.org/literature/topics/design-thinking

https://www.veletsianos.com/2023/01/23/ai-chatgpt-and-instructional-design/

The impact of artificial intelligence on the future of workforces in the European union and the United States of America. https://www.whitehouse.gov/wp-content/uploads/2022/12/TTC-EC-CEA-AI-Report 12052022-1.pdf

Verenikina, I.: Scaffolding and learning: its role in nurturing new learners 2008. https://ro.uow.edu.au/edupapers/43

Advancement in Engineering and Science – Goyal et al. (Eds)

A Study on the Scope of Forensic Auditing in Money Movement Process for Fraud Mitigation and Prevention: A Study on the Private and Public Sector Banks in India

Avinash Dhole
PhD scholar, Thakur Institute of Managment Studies and Research

Swati Sabale
Professor, Thakur Institute of Managment Studies and Research

ABSTRACT: The Indian banking system is a major part of the economy, comprising private and public banks. But at the same time, it has become the instrument of financial frauds and irregularities, most importantly by the manipulation of money movement processes. This study explores the extent and effectiveness of forensic auditing as a tool for fraud mitigation and prevention across these banks. The skills of forensic audit which blends accounting, auditing and investigative skills make forensic auditing a viable solution for addressing financial discrepancies. This includes a comparative study of the use and influence of forensic audit in Indian private and public sector banks. Through the analysis of case studies, regulatory frameworks, and the use of forensic auditing practices, the research seeks to highlight patterns, challenges, and opportunities for to improve fraud detection and prevention mechanisms. To protect the integrity of the banking sector, compliance with regulatory standards, and public trust, the forensic auditing practices should be augmented.

Keywords: Forensic Auditing, Fraud Mitigation, Private Sector Banks, Public Sector Banks, Money Movement Process, Financial Fraud, India

1 INTRODUCTION

A forensic audit is a detailed audit is the examination and verification of a firms or a individuals financial information and is used as evidence in courts in case of a conviction of a party for theft, embezzlement, and other financial incongruity. In a banking context, you analyze every financial transaction and every decision to come to the conclusion of the truth. Forensic reports are admissible in court proceedings and auditors are permitted to file evidence directly or depose before a judicial authority. Forensic accounting is a crucial means of identifying and preventing financial fraud, delivering key insights on financial crimes. Practitioners like banks, insurance companies and cyber security agencies have recognised the usefulness of forensic accounting services and hired them in their respective investigations. It is a specialized type of accounting that refers to the process of reviewing and evaluating financial documents, documents and other information for the purpose of extracting facts for the use of any courtroom. It is widely used for legal actions like inspections or lawsuits, in which thorough analysis and recovery of financial information are required. There are different types of fraud, such as financial statement fraud; banking and insurance fraud; and employee fraud. The first one is the most, Unlawful financial or statement, which is also called a lawful statement is misconstrued since it overhaul financial records usage. The second one is also the bank or insurance fraud, illegally getting money or any assets. For example, employee fraud includes stealing, skimming off revenue, and embezzling. Cyber fraud: When fraud is executed through the internet. Forensic auditing is used to mitigate fraudulent practices related to conflict of interest, corruption, asset misappropriation, and financial statements. It helps address allegations of bribery, bribery, and exorbitant demands for money. Asset misappropriation is the most prevalent type of fraud, and forensic auditing can help address fictitious payments, improper use of resources, and misuse of funds. Inaccuracies in public documents can also be a form of fraud involving financial statements. Bank frauds in India include acts committed by individuals or agents with the intention to cheat, conceal, fabricate or fake records, accounts, or participate in misappropriation that results in unjust gains. Technological advancements are increasing the number of banking transactions and fraudulent cases, with a compound annual growth rate of 9% (K M, 2021). Forensic auditing is increasingly playing a significant role in identifying financial crime, as fraud costs businesses approximately 5% of their yearly income. The Bureau of Labour Statistics predicts that global recruitment for forensic auditors will increase by 10% between 2016 and 2018 (Maryville University, 2017). Forensic auditing is essential for organizations to preserve trustworthiness, protect financial resources, and avoid fraudulent actions. It helps banks become more productive, successful, and relevant in the marketplace. However, disadvantages include costly implementation, time-consuming, complexity, and technical expertise. In banking institutions, forensic auditing can be a successful method for detecting and minimizing fraud. By carrying out risk evaluations, examining questionable actions, detecting prospective fraudsters, obtaining documentation, and tracking deception, financial institutions can significantly decrease their vulnerability to illicit activities. The challenges faced by forensic auditing departments in the banking industry include financial data complexity, technological changes, legal constraints, scarce funds, lack of collaboration, cybersecurity concerns, and interaction with other divisions. In Indian industry forensic auditing has become an important driver for fighting financial crime, for a simple fact that it helps analyse, conceptualise & reporting complicated financial problems in a simple, precise and reliable way. The research work talk about fraud detection, criminal investigation, fraud security, and information security in the Indian Banking Industry. Overall, forensic accounting plays a vital role in helping organizations identify and deter financial misconduct, providing valuable insights for law enforcement.

DOI: 10.1201/9781003798514-74

2 LITERATURE REVIEW AND PROBLEM FORMULATION

It is essential for India's economic stability in order to success but the country came across with various banking scandals and RBI could find out INR 72,000 crore in 2019 (Gangwani, 2020).

Oyerogba (2021) also dedicated a research work to mention the vital role forensic auditors pay in financial sector in Nigeria by stating that forensic auditors are trained, skillful and analytical experts for detection of fraud and prevention of financial crimes.

Shakir, S. and Ghulam Abbas (2020) stressed the importance of forensic audits in identifying and tracking financial fraud and emphasizing accounting forensics, internal control quality, and the reliability of reports in increasing auditing effectiveness stand help to re-emphasise the need of working with forensic accounting service provider with the ban executive in microfinance institutions in Cross River State to curb against potential fraud in the institutions '(Bassey Eyo Bassey, 2018).

It concluded that forensic accounting is indispensable in discovering and eliminating fraudulent acts in the management of projects in Ghana (Fiergbor, 2020). It aids in timely project completion and increases public trust in project managers. (E.T *et al.*, 2020) found a link between training, educational status, and fraud detection. Litigation support services significantly influence the success of forensic auditing. To equip auditors with expertise, training courses and employee programs should be enhanced. Accounting fraud is a significant financial crime that can lead to organizational disasters and a decline in investor trust, posing a significant risk to the financial system's long-term stability. The modern online realm has altered the methods of forensic scientists, internal auditors, and external auditors (Alao and Odum, 2020). The Indian Banking Corporation (IBC) and the Central Reserve Bank of India (RBI) have implemented a regulatory landscape for forensic audits. The Resolution Professional (RP) has the authority to request a transaction or forensic audit, depending on the type of transaction and whether it is with connected or unrelated parties. The Adjudicating authority can set aside certain types of transactions deemed preferential, such as undervalued transactions to defraud creditors, extortionate credit transactions, and fraudulent transactions. The RBI has also mentioned fraud committed by unscrupulous borrowers in its notification. SEBI has initiated audits of listed entities and will make disclosures without regard to materiality, including the initiation of forensic audit, the reasons for the audit, and the final forensic audit report. The Securities and Exchange Board of India (SFIO) has the authority to launch investigations into a company's affairs under Section 212 of the Companies Act 2013. Forensic auditing as a discipline has yet to take off.

The research by (Moid, 2016) also highlights the significance of forensic accounting services in fraud investigations, as well as the regulatory function of forensic accountants in monitoring firm financial processes. Despite its significant impact, forensic auditing in India remains an underdeveloped aspect of the nation. The forensic audit industry comprises companies that sell solutions for legal cases involving financial, regulatory, and historical information. These audits are used to assess a company's financial standing and can be used as evidence in court or civil suits (Akenbor and Ironkwe, 2014). The market for forensic audits has grown at a CAGR of 6.3% since 2015, reaching a value of approximately $12,000 million in 2019 (The Business Research Company, 2020) . The growth is attributed to increased financial fraud investigations, a wider application of forensic audits, and a shift in core services. However, challenges such as uncertainty in government actions and accounting principles, regional differences, and the COVID-19 pandemic may hinder market growth. Future technological advancements, M&A activity, and increased partnerships are expected to further expand the market.

Forensic auditing is crucial in exposing corporate wrongdoings like embezzlement, bribery, deceit, and ethical lapses in India. With the rise of fraudulent cases, fundamental reforms are needed to combat white-collar crime. Technological advancements and online misconduct threaten the security of banking institutions and clients. The bankruptcy and insolvency law act has increased the use of forensic audits in creditors' decisions and the National Company Law Tribunal's (NCLT) proceedings. Understanding the relationship between forensic auditing and fraud mitigation is essential (Srivats, 2020).

3 PROBLEM FORMULATION

3.1 *Research gaps*

- The Reserve Bank of India (RBI) mandates forensic audits for fraud detection and prevention, but the sector faces challenges such as a shortage of qualified auditors and complex legal procedures.
- Forensic auditing is an emerging concept in India, with limited studies exploring its importance and effectiveness.
- Forensic accounting research needs to be more informative and influential in shaping practices and policies.
- Existing empirical studies primarily focus on businesses with a history of fraud, limiting the understanding of preventive measures and broader applicability of forensic auditing.
- Current statistical methodologies lack sufficient explanatory power to anticipate future fraud.
- Regulatory bodies acknowledge potential causal relationships between fraud symptoms and actual fraud occurrences, but there is a gap in translating this recognition into practical guidelines.

3.2 *Aims & objectives*

Aim

The major goal of the current study is to understand the function of forensic auditing in fraudulent prevention and mitigation in Indian banking institutions.

Objectives

- To study the role and advantages of forensic auditing in banking operations.
- To identify the nature of common fraudulent practices that are prevalent in banking institutions.
- To assess the role of Forensic Auditing for Fraud Mitigation and Prevention in Banking institutions.
- To identify the challenges that forensic auditing departments face in the Banking Industry.

4 RESEARCH METHODOLOGY

Research methodology involves constructing databases and gathering data from various sources, including primary and secondary data. Primary data is original information produced by researchers using various techniques, such as interviews, observations, surveys, questionnaires, market research, and student thesis data. Secondary data is knowledge obtained from primary sources and is easily available for research. The primary goal of data gathering is to gather reliable evidence for producing high-quality research results. The research design includes conducting a survey in parents and students, along with secondary data collection for various sources. A questionnaire shall be developed on a 5-point Likert scale to measure internal consistency and use descriptive statistics and ANOVA to gain crucial insights.

The sample study shall involve a survey of participants from private public sector bank (Banks Employee) and a survey of participants from private public sector bank (Outside Bank Employee). Sampling methods used for data collection include descriptive research design, positivism research paradigm, and descriptive presentation. The study will target Private Sector Banks in India, particularly from the head offices of banks, in particular forensic audit, internal audit, and internal control units.

The study focuses on Forensic Auditing for Fraud Mitigation and Prevention in Banking institutions in India, so the results may not be generalizable to other industries. Purposive sampling, a non-probability sampling technique, may influence the study results.

5 RESEARCH QUESTION & HYPOTHESIS

5.1 *Research questions*

- What are the primary roles and advantages of forensic auditing in banking operations?
- What common fraudulent practices are prevalent in banking institutions?
- How effective is forensic auditing in fraud mitigation and prevention within banking institutions?
- What challenges do forensic auditing departments face in the banking industry?

5.2 *Hypothesis formulation*

Hypothesis 1: Forensic audit to finding the nature of common fraud and to prevent them
Dependent variable: Forensic Audit
Independent Variable: Common Fraud
H01: Regarding identifying and preventing common fraud, there is no discernible difference between a standard accountant and a forensic accountant.
Ha1: Regarding identifying and preventing common fraud, there is a discernible difference between a standard accountant and a forensic accountant.
Hypothesis 2: Forensic Audit and Role of Insiders involved with outsiders resulting in bank failures
Dependent Variable: Forensic Audit
Independent Variable: Role of insiders in bank failures
H02: Insiders' benefits and roles in the bank's operations do not include them engaging in fraudulent activity with outsiders that leads to bank collapses.
Ha2: Insiders' benefits and roles in the bank's operations include them engaging in fraudulent activity with outsiders that leads to bank collapses.
Hypothesis 3: Forensic Accounting and its adoption by regulatory authorities in combating bank scams and failures
Dependent Variable: Forensic Accounting
Independent Variable: Regulatory Authorities
H03: Forensic accounting is not helpful to regulatory agencies in their efforts to stop bank fraud and failures.
Ha3: Forensic accounting is helpful to regulatory agencies in their efforts to stop bank fraud and failures.
Hypothesis 4: Forensic Audit and significant effect on the control of financial fraud in Indian Banking Institutions.
Dependent Variable: Forensic Audit
Independent Variable: Control of financial frauds
H04: There is no discernible impact of forensic auditing on the prevention of financial fraud in Indian banking institutions.
Ha4: There is a discernible impact of forensic auditing on the prevention of financial fraud in Indian banking institutions.

6 RESULTS AND DISCUSSIONS

The expected outcomes of the current study are that, in order to effectively and efficiently manage financial fraud in the Indian banking industry, forensic auditing is a necessary requirement. It is expected that the use of forensic auditing concepts will act as a silver pill for the early identification and avoidance of forgeries not only in banking institutions but in all kinds of commercial organizations. Therefore, it may be highlighted that if a forensic auditor is engaged, illegal and shady operations in banking institutions will be reduced. To determine the link between the dependent and independent variables, the dependent variable was regressed against them. The population and sample size of the project is 100 responses.

Table 1. Anova: Single factor.

Anova: Single Factor				
SUMMARY				
Groups	*Count*	*Sum*	*Average*	*Variance*
Identification of CommonFraud using Forensic Audit	5	100	20	375.5
Bank Frauds due to Insiders Involvement with Outsiders during Forensic Audit	5	100	20	273.5
Identification of CommonFraud using Forensic Audit	5	100	20	190.5

Table 2. Anova results for effectiveness of digital forensics across businesses.

ANOVA						
Source of Variation	*SS*	*df*	*MS*	*F*	*P-value*	*F crit*
Between Groups	0	2	0	0	1	3.885294
Within Groups	3358	12	279.8333			
Total	3358	14				

Table 3. tTest result for paired two sample of means.

t-Test: Paired Two Sample for Means			
Tests	*Identification of Common-Fraud using Forensic Audit*	*Bank Frauds due to Insiders Involvement with Outsiders during Forenisc Audit*	*Identification of Common-Fraud using Forensic Audit*
Mean	20	20	20
Variance	375.5	273.5	375.5
Observations	5	5	5
Pearson Correlation	0.993081237	0.743675763	0.786110403
Hypothesized Mean Difference	0	0	0
df	4	4	4
t Stat	0	0	0
P(T<=t) one-tail	0.5	0.5	0.5
t Critical ne-tail	2.131846786	2.131846786	2.131846786
P(T<=t) two-tail	1	1	1
t Critical two-tail	2.776445105	2.776445105	2.776445105

The table contrasts three groups' ability to recognize ordinary fraud and bank fraud involving insiders. The results reveal the same mean with distinct variances, and the high Pearson correlation coefficients indicate a strong linear relationship. There is no statistically significant difference between the groups, and further study may reveal more insights. The data is accessible in spreadsheet format, which allows for more thorough statistical analysis. Further details and particular responsibilities specified may give more insights.

7 CONCLUSION

The study reveals that forensic auditing is crucial in addressing financial fraud within companies. Its effectiveness in fraud control is enhanced by forensic auditors' specialized skills, which enable them to detect and prevent fraudulent activities more efficiently than traditional methods. Not only this, forensic audit reports help court adjudication as these reports are required evidence for law suits matters. It also enhances governance by increasing accountability and transparency in financial reporting structures. And with less risk of financial fraud, it creates financial statements that are more reliable, which ultimately supports corporate goals and growth. It also identifies and corrects financial discrepancies in timely fashions which prevents corporate collapse and investor impoverishment. Therefore, forensic auditing is a strategic tool to guarantee integrity, transparency, and the sustainability of business operations.

REFERENCES

Akenbor, C.O. and Ironkwe, U. (2014) Forensic Auditing Techniques and Fraudulent Practices of Public Institutions in Nigeria, *Journal of Modern Accounting and Auditing*, 10(4), pp. 451–459.

Alao, B.B. and Odum, A.N. (2020) Fighting Fraud in Nigeria Banking Industry. An Examination of the Impact of Forensic Auditing, *International Journal of Academic Multidisciplinary Research (IJAMR)*, p. 11.

Bassey Eyo Bassey (2018) Effect of Forensic Accounting on the Management of Fraud in Microfinance Institutions in Cross River State, *IOSR Journal of Economics and Finance (IOSR-JEF)*, 9(4), pp. 79–89.

E.T, M. et al. (2020) An Investigation on the Effectiveness of Forensic Audit as a Tool for Fraud Detection and Prevention, *Journal of Accounting, Business and Finance Research*, 10(2), pp. 49–67. Available at: https://doi.org/10.20448/2002.102.49.67.

Fiergbor, D.D. (2020) Managing Projects Using Forensic Accounting in Detection and Prevention of Fraud in Ghana, *Global Economics Science*, pp. 44–49. Available at: https://doi.org/10.37256/ges.122020343.

Gangwani, M. (2020) Suitability of forensic accounting in uncovering bank frauds in India: an opinion survey, *Journal of Financial Crime*, 28(1), pp. 284–299. Available at: https://doi.org/10.1108/JFC-07-2020-0126.

K M, P. (2021) Data: Amount involved in reported cases of "Bank Fraud" increased over three-fold in four years, FACTLY, 10 June. Available at: https://factly.in/data-amount-involved-in-reported-cases-of-bank-fraud-increase-over-three-fold-in-four-years/.

Maryville University (2017) *The Growth of Forensic Accounting*, 13 November. Available at: https://online.maryville.edu/blog/the-growth-of-forensic-accounting/.

Moid, S. (2016) *Application of Forensic Accounting to Investigate Scams in India*, MIJBR, 3(1). Available at: https://mits.ac.in/mits_new/public/uploads/jntua/ef7816dd32a25f5739105758b4d7d3d1.pdf.

Shakir, S. and Ghulam Abbas (2020) Role of Forensic Auditing in Enhancing the Efficiency of Public Sector Organization: Role of Forensic Auditing, *Reviews of Management Sciences*, 2(2), pp. 40–59. Available at: https://doi.org/10.53909/rms.02.02.030.

Srivats, K.R. (2020) All you wanted to know about forensic audit, The Hindu, 12 October. Available at: https://www.thehindubusinessline.com/opinion/columns/slate/all-you-wanted-to-know-about/article32837281.ece.

The Business Research Company (2020) Forensic Audit Global Market Opportunities and Strategies to 2030: COVID-19 Impact and Recovery. Available at: https://www.researchandmarkets.com/reports/5125416/forensic-audit-global-market-opportunities-and.

Advancement in Engineering and Science – Goyal et al. (Eds)
© 2026 The Author(s), ISBN: 978-1-041-31101-0

Volatility Spill Over among Cryptocurrencies: An Evidence from DCC-GARCH Approach

Aditi Suryakant Bairolu
Advanced Tax Analyst, EY GDS LLP., Mumbai, India

Laxmi Goritiyal
Associate Professor, S. P. Mandali's Prin. L. N. Welingkar Institute of Management Development and Research (PGDM), Mumbai

ABSTRACT: Bitcoin and other cryptocurrencies have garnered significant attention during the pandemic due to their high volatility characteristics. The May 2021 crash saw Bitcoin plummet to $30,000, a 30% drop, highlighting the increasing regulatory scrutiny and uncertainty surrounding cryptocurrencies. This paper examines the volatility and price fluctuations of Bitcoin using the DCC-GARCH model. Analysing the closing price data of five cryptocurrencies from January 2018 to January 2022, this study investigates the volatility spillover effect of Bitcoin on HEX (Hex Crypto), XRP (Ripple), USDT (Tether), and ETH (Ethereum). The findings aim to provide insights into the interconnectedness of these cryptocurrencies and inform better investment decisions.

Keywords: Volatility, Spillover, price, returns, correlation, covariance, investment, cryptocurrency, DCC-GARCH

1 INTRODUCTION

Cryptocurrencies are secure, virtual currencies that are resistant to counterfeiting and double spending. As per Makarov and Schoar (2021), cryptocurrencies operate on a decentralised network utilising blockchain technology, a distributed ledger maintained by a network of computers. Typically, not issued by any central authority, cryptocurrencies are gaining attention in the realms of policy and governance. Their robust encryption, involving hashing techniques, makes manipulation difficult.

Since October 2013, the cryptocurrency market has delivered impressive returns, approximately 17,269.42% by July 8, 2021. However, this market is also highly volatile (Corbet et.al. (2019)), as evidenced by the recent crash in May 2021 as mentioned by Conte (2021), where $14.2 billion in losses were recorded. Bitcoin alone experienced a 50% price drop, plummeting from a weekly high of $59,463 to a low of $31,327. Other significant downturns include March 2020 (44% losses), November 2018 (114% losses), and early 2018. This volatility underscores the market's unpredictability and risk.

Volatility, a statistical measure of the dispersion of returns, is quantified by the extent of price swings around a mean. Due to their unpredictable price movement, assets with high volatility are considered riskier. This research uses standard deviations of returns to measure volatility, providing insights into the risks associated with highly volatile assets compared to their less volatile counterparts.

The need for an effective tool to manoeuvre any financial market is always felt by investors and traders. An efficient instrument will help the stakeholders understand when to enter and exit the market. In the past cryptocurrency market has given good returns, however, it carries significant risk. This research aims to help individuals mitigate the risk while trading on a cryptocurrency platform by comprehending the volatility of the market and making better decisions. Overall, this research will help investors manage risk and to make sound decisions.

2 LITERATURE SURVEY

There are a number of studies that have analysed the volatility and pricing of Bitcoin and also have dived deep into the relationship between the two. These studies have also compared the results with fiat currencies and other financial instruments like gold. Many fellow researchers have employed various statistical models to analyse Bitcoin given its prominence in fintech.

Wang *et al.* (2019) analysed the mean and volatility spillover effects between Bitcoin and other assets using the VAR-GARCH-BEKK model. They concluded that SHIBOR influences Bitcoin's mean, while gold and bond markets impact its volatility. Also, as per the results, Bitcoin too affects the gold market which suggests that Bitcoin acts as a haven during adverse market conditions.

Dwyer (2015) observed that Bitcoin's monthly return volatility surpasses that of gold or USD. Blau (2017) found no speculative-driven price anomalies in Bitcoin. Balcilar *et al.* (2017) used a non-parametric causality analysis and determined that Bitcoin's transaction volume does not predict revenue volatility.

Brière *et al.* (2015) highlighted Bitcoin's high returns, high volatility, and weak correlations with other assets. Baur *et al.* (2018) suggested that Bitcoin is better suited for speculative investments rather than hedging. Dyhrberg (2016) noted the minimal impact of stock market factors on Bitcoin, pointing out a bidirectional volatility spillover between gold and Bitcoin.

Kyriazis *et al.* (2019) explored volatility in Bitcoin, Ethereum, and Ripple using ARCH, GARCH, and DCC-GARCH models, finding no hedging potential during market distress. Katsiampa (2017) and others like Bucko *et al.* (2015) and Guesmi *et al.* (2018) also analysed Bitcoin's volatility through various models. Symitsi and Chalvatzis (2018) detected short-run volatility spillovers from technology companies to Bitcoin and long-run spillovers from energy companies.

Aalborg *et al.* (2018) established that past volatility predicts future volatility in Bitcoin, with trading volume enhancing these predictions. Balcilar *et al.* (2017) concluded that volume does not forecast Bitcoin volatility using a non-parametric causality test.

Bariviera (2017) examined Bitcoin's long memory of returns and volatility, finding stronger long-term memory content in daily volatility than returns. Baur *et al.* (2017) analysed Bitcoin as an asset, discovering uncorrelated statistical properties with traditional assets.

 DOI: 10.1201/9781003798514-75

Bouri *et al.* (2016) evaluated Bitcoin's role as a hedge and a safe haven using a dynamic conditional correlation model. Perry-Carrera found a negative relationship between Bitcoin prices, market volatility, and gold futures. Dyhrberg (2015) explored Bitcoin's hedging capabilities using GARCH modelling, while Fang *et al.* (2018) showed that economic policy uncertainty impacts Bitcoin's long-term volatility using GARCH-MIDAS models.

Kjærland *et al.* (2018) applied ARDL and GARCH approaches, finding Bitcoin prices influenced by historical volatility and factors like S&P 500 returns and Google searches. Trabelsi (2018) used a spillover index to measure cryptocurrency market connectedness, discovering weak integration with global financial markets.

Katsiampa (2017) identified the AR-CGARCH model as optimal for Bitcoin price data, emphasising both short-run and long-run conditional variance components. Klein *et al.* (2018) used a FIAPARCH model to analyse Bitcoin as a portfolio component, finding positive correlations with downward markets.

Bouri, Azzi, and Dyhrberg (2016) examined the relationship between Bitcoin price returns and volatility changes, noting a significant inverse relationship before the 2013 crash. Vo and Xu (2018) used financial time series and machine learning to forecast Bitcoin volatility, highlighting speculative trading as a reason for high volatility.

Erdas and Caglar (2018) found a causal relationship between Bitcoin prices and the S&P 500 Index using Hatemi-J asymmetric causality analysis. Johansson *et al.* (2014) identified variables impacting Bitcoin price volatility, emphasizing the influence of information demand, trade volume, acceptance trends, and events like MtGox's failure.

3 RESEARCH OBJECTIVE

This research aims to investigate whether Bitcoin exhibits any volatility spillover effects on Hex Crypto (HEX), Ripple (XRP), Tether (USDT), and Ethereum (ETH) using the DCC-GARCH model. By examining the correlation and covariance between Bitcoin and the selected cryptocurrencies, this study seeks to provide insights that will assist investors in making informed, sustainable and risk-mitigated investment decisions.

4 DATA AND METHODOLOGY

The dataset comprises the closing prices of five cryptocurrencies: Bitcoin (BTC), Hex Crypto (HEX), Ripple (XRP), Tether (USDT), and Ethereum (ETH), spanning from January 2018 to January 2022. The Dynamic Conditional Correlation GARCH (DCC-GARCH) model is employed to observe the degree of volatility, where the correlation between two or more variables fluctuates with time. The DCC-GARCH model is mathematically represented as follows:

$$Ht = Dt * Rt * Dt$$

Here, Ht represents the conditional covariance matrix, Rt denotes the conditional correlation matrix, and Dt is typically viewed as univariate GARCH models. This model permits the correlations between Bitcoin and other assets to vary over time. This characteristic is pivotal since Bitcoin has a dynamic relationship with the financial markets where correlations can fluctuate significantly as per market conditions and economic events. Bitcoin often exhibits asymmetric responses to market shocks compared to traditional assets. Ergo, the DCC GARCH model is suitable for capturing and observing this asymmetricity. The asymmetric effects include heightened volatility spillovers specifically during market downturns or when Bitcoin can be a safe haven asset. Both short-term and long-term volatility are integral to Bitcoin. Hence, DCC GARCH model is suitable for analysing Bitcoin because of its ability to model both the types of volatilities and provide a comprehensive view of its risk-to-return profile. This provides researchers with the flexibility to assess the impact caused by fluctuation in volatility data in Bitcoin with time. Since Bitcoin is often compared with cryptocurrencies, a multivariate approach like DCC GARCH is paramount. This approach not only helps in analysing just one set of asset class but is capable of providing an insight into Bitcoin's interactions with other asset classes enabling simultaneous modelling of volatility and correlations across different asset classes. This can further help in understanding Bitcoin's role in a diversified investment portfolio. DCC GARCH is an econometric model that is known for its robustness and applicability for modelling complex financial scenarios. Its use in studying cryptocurrencies will enhance the reliability of empirical results.

5 RESULTS

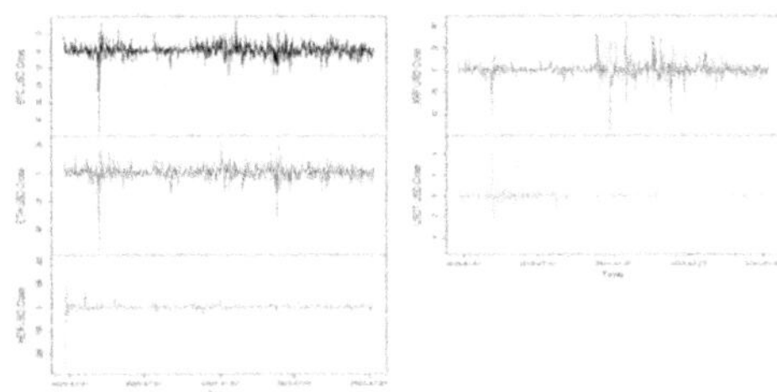

Figure 1. Returns of the five different currencies i.e., Bitcoin, Ethereum, HEX, Tether, and Ripple (after converting into continuous series.)

From Figure 1, it is evident that the returns of BTC and ETH exhibit similar patterns. Both cryptocurrencies show a higher degree of change associated with high returns and a lower degree of variation associated with low returns, indicating synchronised volatility movements. This suggests a common trend between Bitcoin and Ethereum: when Bitcoin's closing price increases, Ethereum's closing price also tends to rise, and vice versa.

In contrast, HEX and Tether do not display high returns like Bitcoin and Ethereum. Additionally, XRP experienced significant volatility in 2021. While Bitcoin remains a major player and a pioneer in the cryptocurrency market, Ethereum's returns matched Bitcoin's in 2020. This could be attributed to the increased use of Ethereum gas fees, which are necessary for executing transactions on the Ethereum network.

This research employs the DCC GARCH model. It is a type of multivariate analysis used to examine the relationships between two or more variables. Before applying the model, three preconditions were checked and satisfied: stationarity of the data, the presence of volatility clustering, and the presence of the ARCH effect. The model was evaluated for four different ARMA orders: ARMA (0,0), ARMA (0,1), ARMA (1,1), and ARMA (1,0).

Table 1. Various ARMA Orders with respective AIC values.

Model Number	ARMA Order	AIC
Model 1	ARMA (0,0)	22.66
Model 2	ARMA (1,0)	22.62
Model 3	ARMA (1,1)	22.54
Model 4	ARMA (0,1)	22.55

In this research Model 3 with ARMA (1,1) is selected as the best-fit model since it has the lowest AIC criterion (22.54) among all four models, as shown in Table 1. The values for DCC alpha and DCC beta are significant for all models. In the DCC GARCH approach, the alpha term represents the ARCH model, while the beta term represents the GARCH model. Hence, while both terms are considered, the focus is primarily on the beta term. DCC alpha indicates short-run persistence, whereas DCC beta indicates long-run persistence.

In Model 3, both the DCC alpha and DCC beta coefficients are significant, indicating both short- and long-term spillover effects of Bitcoin on ETH, HEX, XRP, and USDT. The algebraic sum of the DCC alpha and DCC beta coefficients is less than 1, implying dynamic conditional correlation between all five cryptocurrencies. This means that the conditional correlation in the model is not constant but changes over time.

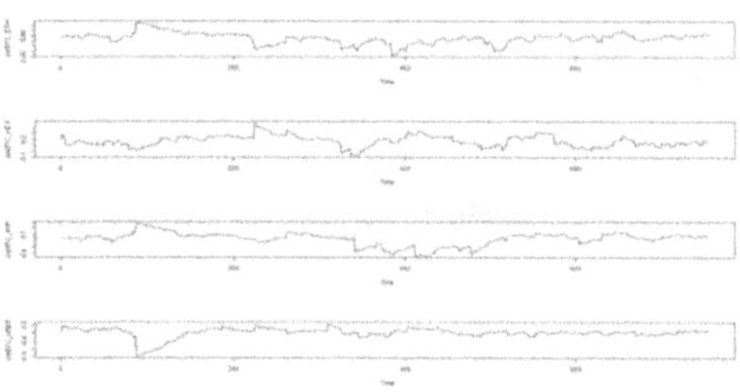

Figure 2. Correlation Matrix plot showing effect of Bitcoin on ETH, HEX, XRP and USDT.

In the correlation matrix (Figure 2), a relationship is observed between the prices of Bitcoin and the prices of ETH, HEX, XRP, and USDT. A positive correlation is noted between Bitcoin and Ethereum, XRP, and HEX, as the correlation coefficient is greater than 0 throughout the period considered. Ethereum shows a strong correlation with Bitcoin, with values ranging from 0.6 to 1. XRP has a positive correlation, ranging from 0.4 to 0.9. HEX exhibits a weak positive correlation most of the time, with values ranging from 0 to 0.4, and occasionally shows a weak negative correlation ranging from 0 to -0.1. Therefore, HEX is considered to have a weak positive correlation overall.

There is a spillover effect of Bitcoin on ETH, HEX, XRP, and USDT. This indicates a positive spillover effect of Bitcoin on ETH, HEX, and XRP. In other words, whenever the closing price of Bitcoin increases, the closing prices of Ethereum, HEX, and XRP also increase, and when the closing price of Bitcoin decreases, the closing prices of these cryptocurrencies also decrease. This demonstrates that the returns of Bitcoin, Ethereum, HEX, and XRP move in the same direction.

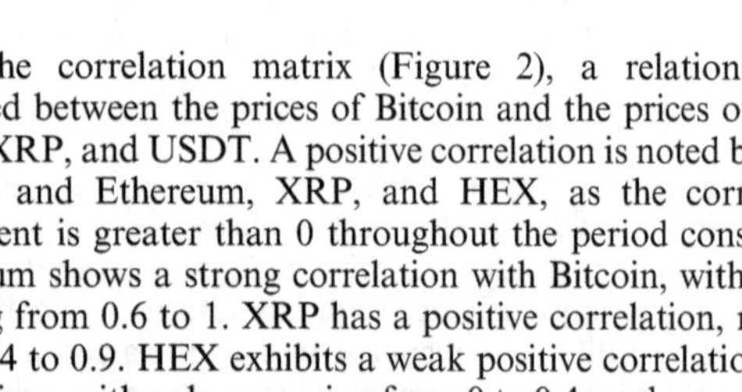

Figure 3. Covariance Matrix showing the effect of Bitcoin on ETH, HEX, XRP and USDT.

Conversely, a negative correlation is observed between Bitcoin and USDT. This means that when the closing price of Bitcoin increases, the closing price of Tether decreases, and when the closing price of Bitcoin decreases, the closing price of Tether increases. If Bitcoin experiences a loss, Tether will likely see a profit, and vice versa.

In the covariance matrix (Figure 3), positive covariance indicates that returns move together, whereas negative covariance indicates that returns move inversely. As illustrated, the covariance between Bitcoin and Ethereum is the highest, particularly in the initial period. For HEX, the covariance ranges from 0 to 60, and for XRP, it ranges from 0 to 110. Therefore, ETH, HEX, and XRP exhibit positive covariance with Bitcoin. In contrast, USDT (Tether) shows a negative covariance with Bitcoin, ranging from 0 to -30.

Pairing securities with negative covariance alongside those with positive covariance can reduce risk and volatility in a portfolio. Given the negative covariance between Bitcoin and Tether, when Bitcoin prices decrease, Tether returns tend to increase, and vice versa. This inverse relationship has a strategic significance in balancing a cryptocurrency portfolio to mitigate the potential loss that can occur through diversification.

6 CONCLUSION

This research successfully demonstrates the volatility spillover effect of Bitcoin on Ethereum, HEX, Tether, and Ripple using the DCC-GARCH model. The study under consideration has employed the Dynamic Conditional Correlation (DCC) GARCH model to analyse the dynamic interactions and volatility patterns of Bitcoin within the ecosystem (financial markets). The motivation behind selecting the DCC GARCH model was its ability to capture time-varying correlations between Bitcoin and other cryptocurrencies. This model also has the potential to capture the same between Bitcoin and other traditional financial assets. It is suitable for analysing the market behaviour of Bitcoin since it is capable of accounting for changes in correlations with time. This is pivotal for understanding Bitcoin's ability to integrate with other financial markets under changing economic scenarios. Bitcoin tends to react and respond to market shocks. The model under consideration effectively captures the asymmetricity of Bitcoin's responses to market shocks. The market shocks include heightened volatility during downturns and its role as a safe-haven asset. The framework provided by the model allows simultaneous modelling of short-term and long-term volatility dynamics. This helps in gauging insights into the risk-return profile of Bitcoin. The model is used across financial econometrics ensuring robustness and comparability of results in various studies. The empirical findings thus arrived at, are more reliable giving better insights to the researchers. The study undertaken aims to contribute valuable insights into the risk profile of Bitcoin. Leveraging the effectiveness of the model helps in understanding the diversification potential of Bitcoin in an investment portfolio. This study also helps all stakeholders to develop an understanding of the implications of cryptocurrencies for financial stability and policy considerations.

Figure 1 presents the similarities between Bitcoin and Ethereum. Both depict similar movements in returns and volatility trends. It confirms that Bitcoin has both long-term and short-term spillover effects on other contingent cryptocurrencies. It also shows that there is a dynamic conditional correlation among all the five cryptocurrencies considered for the study.

Figure 2 shows a positive spillover effect of Bitcoin on ETH, HEX, and XRP, with a corresponding positive correlation. This implies that whenever the closing price of Bitcoin increases, the closing prices of Ethereum, HEX, and XRP also increase, and vice versa. Ethereum has a strong correlation with Bitcoin. A negative correlation is observed between Bitcoin and USDT, indicating that when Bitcoin experiences a loss, USDT is likely to witness a gain.

In the covariance matrix (Figure 3), Bitcoin shows positive covariance with ETH, HEX, and XRP, meaning their returns move together. Conversely, Bitcoin and Tether exhibit negative covariance, implying their returns move inversely. This relationship can be strategically used in portfolio management to reduce risk and volatility. Pairing securities with negative covariance with those having positive covariance can help ensure that investors do not face significant losses during market downturns. This combination reduces market uncertainties.

As per the above analysis, there exists a strong relationship between Bitcoin and Ethereum. Hence, investing solely in both can be risky since any negative implication on the Bitcoin market will have an impact on the Ethereum market. An investor can therefore use a combination of Tether and Ethereum to mitigate the risk. This will help in having a balanced approach. Finally, this study helps stakeholders make better investment decisions by creating less risky portfolios to adapt to the market conditions and help in earning potential profits. The degree of profit depends on the investment value aligned with an individual's risk appetite.

7 COMPARISON WITH EXISTING LITERATURE

The findings of this research align with the existing literature which reveals the interconnected dynamics in the cryptocurrency market. In this study, Bitcoin and Ethereum exhibit volatility patterns that are synchronous. This is consistent with Aslanidis *et al.* (2022) and Corbet *et al.* (2018). They identified a high correlation between major cryptocurrencies due to shared market drivers and considerable investor demand.

As per Hoang and Baur (2022), Tether shows an inverse relationship with Bitcoin. Eventually, Tether is represented as a stablecoin designed to maintain the stability of value. This highlights Tether's ability to hedge within a diversified portfolio to mitigate risk associated with more volatile assets like Bitcoin. During 2021 under regulatory scrutiny, Ripple experienced increased volatility as depicted in the findings by Zhang *et al.* (2022). Also, Al-Yahyee *et al.* (2020) noted Ripple's sensitive nature towards legal developments. The covariance analysis conducted in the study shows that the combination of assets under consideration with negative covariance can mitigate risk and enhance the stability of an investment portfolio, such as Bitcoin and Tether. This supports the analysis conducted by Liu and Tsyvinski's (2018).

Lastly, the DCC-GARCH model used in the study is capable of identifying significant volatility spillovers from Bitcoin to other assets. This corroborates the findings by Conrad *et al.* (2018) which state that Bitcoin often influences broader market trends due to its leadership position.

8 IMPLICATIONS AND SUGGESTIONS

The study undertaken highlights the interconnected nature of the cryptocurrencies considered for the study. It reveals that Bitcoin significantly influences Ethereum, HEX, Tether, and Ripple in terms of volatility. This relationship of influence implies that any investment strategy should consider Bitcoin's spillover effect on other cryptocurrencies specifically while dealing with diversification of the portfolio and while managing the risks. The research effectively captures the dynamic, time-varying correlations between Bitcoin and other cryptocurrencies considered for the study by using the DCC-GARCH model. The results of this study can be used across various economic conditions which helps investors develop balanced portfolios as pe their risk appetite. Integrating the DCC-GARCH model into the trading platforms can help develop real-time and informed decision-making.

A simplified version of this study and the model used can be introduced as an educational module to bridge the gap between theory and practical application in finance. The introduction as an educational module will promote financial literacy and develop the ability to mitigate risk and make more learned decisions. Introducing to simplified version of complex econometric models in finance curriculum will help develop the strategic knack in individuals to form a balanced portfolio.

9 FUTURE RESEARCH

The future scope of this research can include exploring the integration of additional econometric models in current trading platforms along with DCC-GARCH. This can assist with real-time predictive analysis after checking the viability of the models. Studying these models and integrating them in the trading platforms can improve user experience by offering data-driven forecasting. Also, a study on how economic scenarios, regulatory changes and different market cycles can impact DCC-GARCH correlation dynamics can strengthen its effectiveness as an econometric model. Further, a study on customization of this model for AI-related or automated trading with large trade volume can enhance its adaptability on stability and speed to optimize trading strategies.

REFERENCES

Aalborg, H., Molnár, P., and de Vries, J.E. (2018). What Can Explain the Price, Volatility and Trading Volume of Bitcoin? *SSRN Electronic Journal*. https://doi.org/10.2139/ssrn.3233977

Al-Yahyaee, K.H., Mensi, W., and Yoon, S.M. (2020). Dynamic spillovers and connectedness between cryptocurrencies and conventional currencies. *Finance Research Letters*, 29, 32–38.

Aslanidis, N., Bariviera, A.F., and Martínez-Ibañez, O. (2022). Cryptocurrency returns and macroeconomic variables. *Journal of Economic Behavior & Organization*, 194, 173–186.

Balcilar, M., Bouri, E., Gupta, R., and Roubaud, D. (2017). Can volume predict Bitcoin returns and volatility? A quantiles-based approach. *Economic Modelling, 64*, 74–81. https://doi.org/10.1016/j.econmod.2017.03.019

Bariviera, A.F. (2017). The inefficiency of Bitcoin revisited: A dynamic approach. *Economics Letters, 161*, 1–4. https://doi.org/10.1016/j.econlet.2017.09.013

Baur, D.G., Hong, K., and Lee, A.D. (2018). Bitcoin: Medium of exchange or speculative assets? *Journal of International Financial Markets, Institutions and Money, 54*, 177–189. https://doi.org/10.1016/j.intfin.2017.12.004

Bouri, E., and Azzi, G. (2016). On the Return-Volatility Relationship in the Bitcoin Market around the Price Crash of 2013. *SSRN Electronic Journal*. https://doi.org/10.2139/ssrn.2869855

Bouri, E., Molnár, P., Azzi, G., Roubaud, D., and Hagfors, L.I. (2017). On the hedge and safe haven properties of Bitcoin: Is it really more than a diversifier? *Finance Research Letters, 20*, 192–198. https://doi.org/10.1016/j.frl.2016.09.025

Brian Perry-Carrera, B. (2018). Effect of Sentiment on Bitcoin Price Formation. *Duke Journal of Economics*. Retrieved from [URL]

Browne, R. (2021, May 19). Bitcoin plunges 30% to $30,000 at one point in wild session, recovers somewhat to $38,000. *CNBC*. https://www.cnbc.com/2021/05/19/bitcoin-btc-price-plunges-but-bottom-could-be-near-.html

Brownlee, J. (2020, August 28). Probabilistic Model Selection with AIC, BIC, and MDL. *Machine Learning Mastery*. https://machinelearningmastery.com/probabilistic-model-selection-measures/

Conrad, C., Custovic, A., and Ghysels, E. (2018). Long- and short-term cryptocurrency valuation. Journal of Asset Management, 18(5), 313–324.

Conte, N. (2021, May 19). *The Bitcoin crash of 2021 compared to past sell-offs*. Visual Capitalist. https://www.visualcapitalist.com

Corbet, S., Lucey, B., and Yarovaya, L. (2018). Examining the dynamic relationship between cryptocurrencies and other financial assets. *Economics Letters*, 164, 28–34.

Corbet, S., Lucey, B., Urquhart, A., and Yarovaya, L. (2019). Cryptocurrencies as a financial asset: A systematic analysis. *International Review of Financial Analysis*, 62, 182–199. https://doi.org/10.1016/j.irfa.2018.09.003.

Cryptocurrencies. (2021, August 25). [Dataset]. *Yahoo Finance*. https://finance.yahoo.com/cryptocurrencies

Dyhrberg, A.H. (2016). Hedging capabilities of bitcoin. Is it the virtual gold? *Finance Research Letters, 16*, 139–144. https://doi.org/10.1016/j.frl.2015.10.025

Erdas Levent, M., and Caglar Emre, A. (2018). Analysis of the relationships between Bitcoin and exchange rate, commodities, and global indexes by asymmetric causality test. *Eastern Journal of European Studies.*

Fang, L., Bouri, E., Gupta, R., and Roubaud, D. (2019). Does global economic uncertainty matter for the volatility and hedging effectiveness of Bitcoin? *International Review of Financial Analysis, 61*, 29–36. https://doi.org/10.1016/j.irfa.2018.12.010

Frankenfield, J., and Sonnenshein, M. (2021, May 25). Cryptocurrency. *Investopedia.* https://www.investopedia.com/terms/c/cryptocurrency.asp

Hayes, A., and Anderson, S. (2021, April 16). Volatility. *Investopedia.* https://www.investopedia.com/terms/v/volatility.asp

Hoang, L.T., and Baur, D.G. (2022). Tether and cryptocurrency stability. *Finance Research L*etters, 47, 102678.

Johansson, S., Tjernström, N., and Äijö, J. (2014). The Price Volatility of Bitcoin: A search for the drivers affecting the price volatility of this digital currency.

Katsiampa, P. (2017). Volatility estimation for Bitcoin: A comparison of GARCH models. *Economics Letters, 158*, 3–6. https://doi.org/10.1016/j.econlet.2017.06.023

Kaul, A. (2021, May 25). Bitcoin investors lost $14.2 billion in recent crypto crash. *Mint.* https://www.livemint.com/market/cryptocurrency/bitcoin-investors-lost-14-2-billion-in-recent-crypto-crash-11621925542181.html

Klein, T., hien, P.T., and Walther, T. (2018). Bitcoin Is Not the New Gold: A Comparison of Volatility, Correlation, and Portfolio Performance. *SSRN Electronic Journal.* https://doi.org/10.2139/ssrn.3146845

Kyriazis, I.A., Daskalou, K., Arampatzis, M., Prassa, P., and Papaioannou, E. (2019). Estimating the volatility of cryptocurrencies during bearish markets by employing GARCH models. *Heliyon, 5* (8), e02239. https://doi.org/10.1016/j.heliyon.2019.e02239

Liu, Y., and Tsyvinski, A. (2018). Risks and returns of cryptocurrency. *Review of Financial Studies*, 32(5), 1676–1717.

Makarov, I., and Schoar, A. (2021). Blockchain analysis of the Bitcoin market. *NBER Working Paper Series*, (29396). National Bureau of Economic Research. https://doi.org/10.3386/w29396.

Statista. (2021, July 8). Bitcoin (BTC) price history from 2013 to July 8, 2021. *Statista.* https://www.statista.com/statistics/326707/bitcoin-price-index/

Trabelsi, N. (2018). Are There Any Volatility Spill-Over Effects among Cryptocurrencies and Widely Traded Asset Classes? *Journal of Risk and Financial Management, 11*(4), 66. https://doi.org/10.3390/jrfm11040066

Wang, G., Tang, Y., Xie, C., and Chen, S. (2019). Is bitcoin a safe haven or a hedging asset? Evidence from China. *Journal of Management Science and Engineering, 4*(3), 173–188. https://doi.org/10.1016/j.jmse.2019.09.001

Zhang, W., Wang, P., and Li, X. (2022). Market sentiment and the dynamic correlation among cryptocurrencies. *Journal of Financial Markets*, 58, 100–112.

Advancement in Engineering and Science – Goyal et al. (Eds)
© 2026 The Author(s), ISBN: 978-1-041-31101-0

A Smart Platform for Micro-Lending and a Case for "Charging Interest by the Hour"

Kaustubh Dhargalkar
(Dean-Business Design, Innowe, REDX, NISP), S. P. Mandali's Prin. L. N. Welingkar Institute of Management Development and Research (PGDM), Mumbai

Chitralekha Kumar
Assistant Professor – Research, S. P. Mandali's Prin. L. N. Welingkar Institute of Management Development and Research (PGDM), Mumbai

ABSTRACT: Subsistence entrepreneurship among the urban poor has been studied for decades. In India, where most of the working population is employed informally, the need for the availability of credit to the marginalized section is paramount. Most of them eke out a living on a day-to-day earning basis. Financial institutions are averse to lending to them as they lack credit history and the necessary documentation and hence, they must rely on informal moneylenders who charge uxorious interest rates. Present study explores the credit disbursal system among the street vendors in Mumbai city. After understanding the mechanism of this system (through an extensive literature review, field survey and in-depth interviews with the concerned stakeholders), a smart (entirely digital), scalable platform for credit to street vendors has been recommended. The platform uses the robust digital infrastructure that has been created in India and rides on the back of deep internet penetration achieved over the last decade. The recommended platform would enable lending agencies such as banks and non-banking financial companies to provide credit at nominal interest rates and yet remain profitable. It would eliminate the need for complex, operational roadblocks in the credit disbursal and recovery processes.

Keywords: Financial inclusion, Fintech, Micro-lending, Interest Rate, Payment System, credit disbursal

1 INTRODUCTION

Street vendors all over the world are a marginalised lot (Nandru *et al.*, 2023). They do not have access to formal credit because they have neither a credit history nor a credible financial track record (Saxena, 2024). In the absence of a formal line of credit, they rely on local moneylenders who charge them uxorious rates of interest-in the range of 100% to 120% annually (Bhowmik, 2001). Such high-interest rates lock them up in a debt trap, wherein they borrow again and again to repay their earlier loans (Matamanda, Kalaoane and Chakwizira, 2023). The Indian government has launched a scheme specifically for street vendors to mitigate these issues (Joshi and Reddy, 2022). However, execution at the ground-level has proven to be more than challenging due to certain conflicting interests in the existing ecosystem (Hoque, 2023).

The World Bank implies that through financial inclusion, the individuals and businesses have access to useful and affordable financial products and services that meet their needs – transactions, payments, savings, credit, and insurance – delivered in a responsible and sustainable way (Santos *et al.*, 2021). Today, the situation is different due to the advances in technology, financial technologies to be specific. Fintech, as such technologies are referred to, has made 'financial inclusion' easier to achieve today than it was a few years back (Anurag, 2023). In the past years, the Indian government has introduced multiple reforms and facilitating platforms such as AEPS (Aadhar Enabled Payment System), coupled with the increased mobile and internet penetration, is an extremely powerful combination that can be leveraged for enhancing financial inclusion in India (Rumanyika *et al.*, 2021).

According to CISCO, India has 829 million smartphone users who are connected to the internet. in India IP networks carried approximately 108 petabytes of data per day in 2017. In 2022, that number is 646 petabytes of data per day, i.e. growth of 6X. In 2022, smartphones accounted for 44% of internet traffic in India, up from 18% in 2017 (CISCO, 2022). This is a whopping number for a population of 1.4 billion. Going further, the penetration of mobile phones is likely to increase to 86.7% by 2026 (Statista, 2023).

All these transformative events point towards a strong case for creating a mobile-enabled digital platform for credit disbursal to the weaker sections of Indian society. The operational simplicity and inclusiveness of such a platform have been discussed in detail under the section, 'Proposed Solution' in this paper. The main aim of the study is to propose financial inclusion of vendors across society, irrespective of the socio-economic strata.

2 LITERATURE REVIEW

Subsistence entrepreneurship, has been defined as the entrepreneurial actions undertaken by individuals living in extreme poverty (Kumar *et al.* 2024). Availability of credit is a big challenge for such people due to the following reasons. There is lack of required documents, lack of awareness, lack of trust in the system, high transaction cost, the remoteness of the service provider, discrimination/quality of service provided and lack of surplus income (RBI, 2020). These challenges are difficult to overcome for subsistence entrepreneurs.

Hence in the absence of reach to any formal means of credit, these entrepreneurs resort to borrowing from family, friends, or local moneylenders (Martínez and Short, 2022). Borrowing from family and friends may be inexpensive, however, all their family connections and friends are in a similar financial situation, i.e., they too live a subsistence existence with practically no savings or surplus to lend (Myers *et al.*, 2021). Owing to such circumstances and coupled with a lack of access to formal credit lines from banks and NBFCs, they resort to borrowing from local moneylenders (Thanh and Bao, 2023).

Despite the high-interest rates, subsistence entrepreneurs tend to borrow from these moneylenders since, unlike banks, they do not ask for any documentation (Adams, 2021). The

DOI: 10.1201/9781003798514-76

geographical proximity of the moneylender to the place of work of the borrowers also proves to be a major deciding parameter (Khanal and Omobitan, 2020).

The street vendors face multiple problems like (Rakha *et al.*, 2022; Ali and Kamraju, 2023):

1. Most have no legal status, i.e. they have no license from the relevant authorities to carry out business activities at market locations. Hence, they are subjected to harassment by authorities, the police in particular
2. They have practically no working capital to run their business
3. They have no access to water, electricity or any other such facilities where they operate
4. They are unaware of regulations, food safety standards, waste management practices etc.
5. They lack the skills to drive efficiencies to increase their earnings
6. They have no insurance benefits

The rate of interest charged by the local moneylenders is extremely high which leads them into lock-in situations, i.e. they end up in a debt trap by having to borrow afresh to repay their pre-existing loans (Bhagat, K. (2022). Around 80% of the street vendors had no awareness of microfinance and its utility. Almost 99% of them had no intention to formalise their business since it involved too many hassles (Alzain and Saleh, 2022).

To represent the interests of street vendors, the National Alliance of Street Vendors of India was formed in 1998 (Bhandari, 2021). Financial institutions doubted (and still do) the ability of street vendors to repay the loan (Murugan *et al.*, 2023). Hence, the efforts of NASVI have not been as fruitful as they would have liked it to be. There are 49,48,614 lakh street vendors in India (Kumar Aryan, 2022). The actual number may be much more than the ones identified. Academic literature provides for various challenges that are faced by the street vendors. However, there is scanty literature available in terms of money lending facilities available to the vendors. Present study attempts to provide a platform for ease of money lending to these street vendors.

3 RESEARCH METHODOLOGY

This is a descriptive study utilizing qualitative methods. Qualitative methods have been widely used to articulate social phenomenon and enrich the findings (Ruark, and Fielding-Miller,2016). The present study deployed the qualitative method through in-depth interviews to collect the primary data. Von Soest (2023), highlighted that interviews enable the access to the insights of the participant's perception, thought processes, and life experiences that are aligned with the research goals. With this backdrop and the present research goal, interviews were conducted for the following participants: Coolies at a railway station (n=8), Local shopkeepers who function as moneylenders in the ecosystem (n= 4), Street vendors who typically sell vegetables/fruits etc. on the streets (n=107), Bank executives(n=2), NBFC executives(n=2). Data collection involved the deployment of both primary and secondary sources of data. For secondary sources, relevant government reports, journal articles, policy documents and news articles have been examined and cited in the study. The study was restricted to the city of Mumbai and was carried out in the span of five months. It is interesting to note that this study began with understanding the daily life challenges of coolies operating at railway stations in Mumbai. The aim was to figure out their problems and explore whether one could suggest a few solutions for their pressing challenges. An exploration of the lives of these coolies provided an insight into how they spent a certain amount on their daily needs and saved the rest every day by depositing it with a local shopkeeper. The shopkeeper instead of paying an interest to the coolies would charge a service fee for keeping the money safe till the end of the month. At the end of the month, the coolies would collect the accumulated amount from the shopkeeper and send it to their respective families in their native villages. Following the money trail led the study to an intriguing way the shopkeeper deploys the money deposited. The shopkeeper lends this money to local street vendors at uxorious interest rates. This led to the identification of street vendors as the real sufferers. The synthesis of the inputs from the coolies, street vendors and the relevant literature was utilized to develop the proposed model for the benefit of the stakeholders involved in the process of entrepreneurship and money lending.

4 DATA ANALYSIS & INTERPRETATION

The first phase of data collection was based on the inputs from the coolies. An in-depth interviewing technique was used to understand the lives of coolies. A total of 8 coolies were interviewed. From these interviews, a typical persona of coolie is characterized as follows:

(a) A coolie is a migrant worker who has moved to Mumbai since there are not many opportunities for earning a livelihood back in his native village.
(b) His typical daily earnings vary from Rs. 300 on an ordinary day to Rs. 800 on an exceptionally good day. On average, one can assume a daily earning of Rs. 450
(c) He spends on average about Rs. 200 to 250 per day on food and personal needs.
(d) Daily savings vary between Rs. 200 to 250 per day.
(e) He has no permanent place of residence in Mumbai (rents are high and hence unaffordable). Some of them stay together in a shared tenement.
(f) Some of them live out of a metal trunk kept under a railway bridge or other such shelter. All their belongings are kept in that trunk.

Since they have a surplus of approximately Rs. 200 to 250 per day in cash denominations, they must store it somewhere. However, the places that they stay in are not safe enough to store the accumulated cash. Hence, they hand over the cash to a local shop owner who keeps it safe for them. The coolie keeps on depositing his daily surplus with the local shop owner. At the end of the month, the coolie collects the accumulated cash from the shop owner and sends the money to his family living in his native village. There are two ways in which they send the money home:

1. They find some acquaintance who is visiting their native village and send the cash with him/her to be handed over to their family members.
2. They collect the money from the shop owner, go to the nearest State Bank of India branch, get a demand draft made, and send it home by post or through an acquaintance travelling to their village.

An exploration of the lives of these coolies provided an insight into how they spent a certain amount on their daily needs and saved the rest by depositing it with a local shopkeeper daily. The shopkeeper instead of paying an interest to the coolies would charge a service fee for keeping the money safe till the end of the month. At the end of the month, the coolies would collect the accumulated amount from the shopkeeper and send it to their respective families in their native villages. Following the money trail led the study to an intriguing way the shopkeeper deploys the money deposited. The shopkeeper lends this money to local street vendors at uxorious interest rates. With this revelation, the street vendors were identified as the study subjects. In-depth interviews with the relevant street vendors revealed the following facts:

1. The local moneylenders (i.e., local shop owners) charge them an interest rate that varies between 3.33% to 4.5% per day, which translates to an astounding 1215% to 1645% per annum.

   The effective return on investment (ROI) for the moneylender is between 400% to 540%. The calculation is explained below.

   - The street vendors do not borrow every day. They borrow on an average of once in three days, i.e., approximately there are 120 borrowing cycles per year. Considering an interest rate of between 3.33% to 4.5% per borrowing cycle, the moneylender earns a ROI ranging between 400% (3.33x120 = 399.6) to 540 % (4.5x120 = 540).
   - If one considers the fact that the money lender collects a service charge from the coolies and other such daily wage earners for depositing money with him, the ROI for the money lender is higher than 400% to 540%, since he gets paid a service fee for raising funds.

2. The local moneylenders have their own collection agents entrusted with the responsibility of collecting dues from street vendors. These agents are basically local toughies who work on a commission basis for the moneylenders (we could not access information about the percentage commission charged). We conclude that the collection is based on the use of force in case the street vendor is unable to repay the amount borrowed.
3. Many a time, the collection is done at the end of the month, thus the interest gets compounded. No records are shared by the moneylender or the collection agents about the daily interest records with the street vendors. The cumulative interest is often a lot more than the actual rate would be.
4. In case of default, the unpaid amount is converted into a new loan and charged interest at a compounded rate.

The street vendors are uneducated individuals and hence not very adept at understanding the mathematics behind compounded interest. As a result, the street vendor often gets caught in a debt trap, from which an escape is very difficult.

The following figure represents the present ecosystem of moneylending.

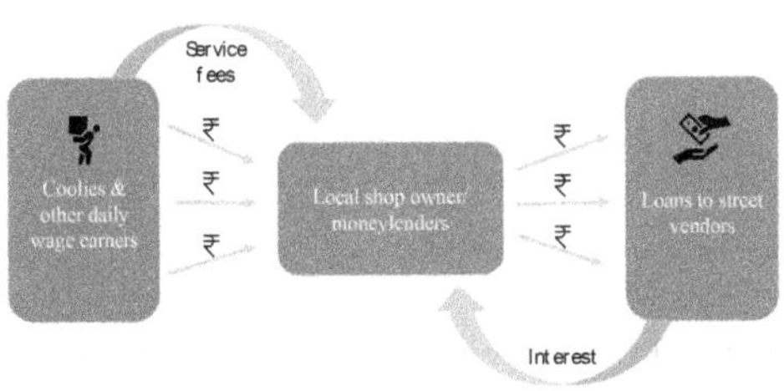

Figure 1. The ecosystem. Source: Author's work.

5 FINDINGS

Considering the number of street vendors in India, viz. 49,48,614 (official estimate, MoHUA, Feb 22), there appears to be huge potential for banks/NBFCs to offer affordable credit to the street vendors. From a business perspective, it makes tremendous financial sense for them to explore the opportunity. Even if they charge a fraction of the interest rate as compared to the local money lender, it will result in a high Interest Rate Spread (IRS) due to the huge volume. The researchers contacted two bank executives to explore why they did not explore this business opportunity. Their response can be summarized as follows:

1. These would amount to too small a loan granted to too many borrowers and it would prove to be an operational nightmare for managing the volume.
2. How would the bank/NBFCs ensure repayment from the borrowers? The bank executives argued that the local money lenders had their own informal network of dubious collection agents to do the needful. A bank/NBFC would obviously not want to solicit the assistance of such dubious collection agents.

The main worries of the Banks/NBFCs could be summarised as

(a) Operational complications
(b) Collection or Ensuring Repayment.

5.1 *Proposed solution*

Rationale: The proposed solution should facilitate easy and affordable access to credit for street vendors and overcome the main worries of the banks/NBFCs. The proposed solution is an easy-to-use mobile-based platform that credits and debits money into the street vendor's account electronically, without any human intervention.

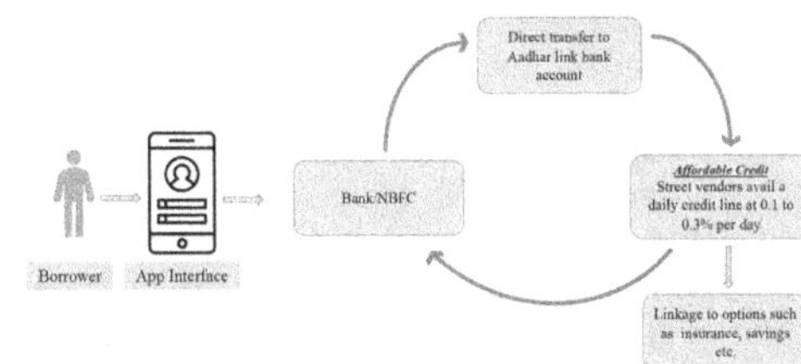

Figure 2. The proposed solution platform; Source: Author's work.

Banks and NBFCs should grant credit lines to street vendors if they satisfy two simple conditions as follows, viz.

- They have a bank account that is linked to their Aadhar card
- If they have more than one bank account, they MUST link all their accounts to their Aadhar card.

This is not difficult to achieve considering the mobile and internet penetration in India.

Whenever a street vendor (borrower) needs credit, the process would be as follows:

1. The borrower logs onto the lending platform (in the form of a mobile phone-based application) and applies for a line of credit.
2. An e-KYC (Electronic- Know your customer) facility that is in-built into the application validates the identity of the borrower.
3. The repayment period could be extremely short-term (for a few days) or extend to a few years, depending on the borrower's need (Interest rates would vary according to the repayment duration chosen). The application would be available in multiple vernacular languages and have an extremely simple User Interface.
4. Once the requisite amount is fed in, it gets credited to the borrower's bank account.
5. The borrower would utilise the amount for her/his business needs.
6. At the end of the repayment period, the principal amount plus the interest would get auto debited from the borrower's account.
7. Once the borrower is on the platform, other financial products such as life insurance/medical insurance/investment instruments etc. could be cross sold thus providing more business opportunities for the financial institution involved.

Salient Feature of the proposed solution: *The entire transaction would happen electronically with no human intervention whatsoever. Thus, the need for collection agents would be eliminated. Non-repayment, if any, would be immediately tackled by freezing all the bank accounts belonging to the borrower, via the Aadhar switch**.

This would ensure high compliance rates since all lines of affordable credit could get shut at the click of a button. Default rates of loans disbursed to the underprivileged are much lower than those for loans disbursed to the middle and upper classes of society. Loan repayment rates of Self-help Groups (SHGs) catering to the underprivileged classes are as high as 97.79% (Ministry of Rural Development, Nov 2022). Hence, the worry about non-repayment would not be much of a deterrent.

There are 49,48,614 (4.948 million) street vendors in India (MoHUA, Feb 22). Globally, the number of street vendors is not very accurately depicted. In 2012, there were approximately 1.8 billion of them (Poon, 2015). By 2022, this number would have increased by at least 11.35 % (applying the population growth rate from 2012 to 2022, as per United Nations- World Population Prospects).

Therefore, the number of street vendors in the world in 2022 = 2 billion (approximately)

The developing world comprises 85.33% of the world's population. Therefore, we have a possible 1.71 billion street vendors who could benefit from the proposed solution and progress upward in their respective lives.

Scalability: As per the Ministry of Housing and Urban Affairs (MoHUA), India has 49,48,614 (4.948 million) street vendors (MoHUA, Feb 22). This is the official count. The actual count could be anywhere between a multiple of two to three, i.e. between 100,00,000 to 150,00,000 (10 million to 15 million). Coupled with the fact that India has 829 million smartphone users in 2022 (CISCO, 2022), the solution has the potential to reach almost every street vendor. Plus, a feature-phone-friendly version of the proposed platform will ensure last-mile reach to the most underserved. A total of 476,889,7814 (approx. 477 million) bank accounts have been opened since 2015 in India, under the PMJDY (Pradhan Mantri Jan Dhan Yojana). Hence, the penetration of bank accounts is high among the weaker sections in India. The following tables will help understand the penetration levels that already exist in India and why the proposed solution is feasible to implement.

Smartphone users in India

Number of smart-phones users in India (CISCO, 2022)	Number of no-frills bank accounts in India (PMJDY, 2022)	Number of Street vendors in India (official count – MoHUA, 2022)
829 million	477 million	4.948 million

Sources:1) CISCO Report (2022) 2) PMJDY (2022) 3) MOHUA (2022)

Internet Traffic in India

Internet Traffic in India	2017	2018
	108 Petabytes	646 Petabytes

Sources:1) CISCO Report (2022)

We have analysed the benefits to the street vendors in detail but unless the financial institutions see a sustainable Interest Rate Spread (IRS) they would not venture into this business. Interest Rate Spread (IRS) = (Interest received – Interest paid), Average Interest paid out by Indian banks = 7.83% (RBI, Basic rate Guidelines), Average Interest received by Indian banks = 10.5% (RBI, Lending rates of scheduled Commercial Banks). For an average Indian bank, The Interest Rate Spread (IRS) would be approximately (10.5%– 7.83%) = 2.67%

In the proposed solution, if the banks charge an interest rate of as low as one-tenth to one-twentieth of what the local moneylenders charge at present, therefore, *street vendors could avail of credit at interest rates ranging between 20 to 27% per annum.*

Assuming the interest paid by the banks to depositors remains the same at 7.83% as per RBI's analysis as mentioned above, the Interest Rate Spread would be as follows:

Interest Rate Spread for Banks in the proposed solution.

Interest Rate Spread (Max) - *when street vendors are charged interest @ 27 %*	27% – 7.83% = 19.17%
Interest Rate Spread (Min) - *when street vendors are charged interest @ 20 %*	20% - 7.83% = 12.17%

As is evident, it is a much higher IRS value for the Banks as compared to the existing IRS. Hence it makes for a good business proposition for the banks involved. The proposed solution will thus create a win-win situation for both the street vendors as well as the lending banks.

6 MANAGERIAL IMPLICATIONS

The proposed solution would be benefitting the *poor vendors* who do not have smart phones. The application could be designed in a manner that is feature-phone friendly. This would ensure that those vendors who do not possess smartphones also would be able to utilise the functionality of this proposed platform.

The *street vendors* can have access to affordable credit without the hassle of furnishing too many documents since the Aadhar system already have the verified identity of the individual. The street vendors would be able to break free of the debt traps that they have been in for decades.

Financial Institutions can be benefitted as it is a much higher IRS value for the Banks as compared to the existing IRS, making it a good business proposition for the banks involved.

The Government policy makers may look at the proposed solution as the financial inclusion in its truest sense, for the street vendors.

7 SCOPE FOR FURTHER RESEARCH

The primary survey was restricted to the city of Mumbai. It could be extended to other cities in maharashtra to understand the credit-seeking behaviour of street vendors in different cities. Once the proposed solution is launched and tested, it could be extended to subsistence entrepreneurs beyond street vendors. Once successfully implemented in multiple cities in India, the study could be extended to cities in other developing countries too. It could prove to be a model that could be replicated across the developing world.

8 CONCLUSION

The proposed solution will impact the lives of a multitude of subsistence vendors and lift them out of the debt traps that most of them are caught in. It will also interest financial institutions since it enables a higher Interest Rate Spread (IRS) and hence higher Return on Investment (ROI) as compared to their existing business model. The proposed solution is a win-win for every stakeholder that is involved (Street vendor, financial institution, Government etc.). If the proposed solution is successfully implemented for credit disbursal to street vendors, it can also be replicated for other weaker sections of society. Once the borrower is on the platform, other financial products such as life insurance/medical insurance/investment instruments etc. could be cross sold thus providing more business opportunities for the financial institution involved. The model could be replicated across other developing nations too. This platform would go a long way in contributing towards 'Financial Inclusion' in the truest sense.

If the concept of 'Interest by the hour' is implemented, it could find application in the space of 'Peer-to-Peer Lending' which has gained a lot of popularity in the last five odd years. Peer-to-peer lending, if encouraged within the section of 'Subsistence Entrepreneurs', could enable a lot of savings for them, since the need for external funds could be reduced. This would result in a lower cost of funds, which in turn would lead to lower interest rates for the borrowers. The efficiency of funds too would be higher for the banks since the amount freed up can be lent to someone in the intervening time. The velocity of money flow in the system would be increased manyfold thus increasing margins for financial institutions. Thus, the platform would prove to be a win-win scenario for all involved.

REFERENCES

Adams, D.W. (2021). *Undermining rural development with cheap credit.* Routledge.

Ali, M.A., and Kamraju, M. (2023). A Study on Problems Faced by the Street Vendors in Hyderabad City Post-COVID-19 Pandemic. In *Temporal and Spatial Environmental Impact of the COVID-19 Pandemic* (pp. 147–155). Singapore: Springer Nature Singapore.

Alzain, E., and Saleh Alshebami, A. (2022, May 3). The role of awareness in predicting the intention of microfinance entrepreneurs to buy microinsurance services in Yemen. *Innovative Marketing, 18* (2), 99–108. https://doi.org/10.21511/im.18(2).2022.09

Anurag, P. (2023). Finance Kaart: A fintech for the "credit invisibles" in India. *Journal of Information Technology Teaching Cases*, 20438869231164429.

Besley, T., and Coate, S. (1995). Group lending, repayment incentives and social collateral. *Journal of development economics*, *46*(1), 1–18.

Bhagat, K. (2022). Payment Supplement: A Loss Mitigation Option to Provide Payment Relief for FHA Loans in a High-Interest Rate Environment. *SSRN Electronic Journal*. https://doi.org/10.2139/ssrn.4291125

Bhandari, P. (2021). Street Vendors' Act, 2014: First Year of Implementation in the National Capital, Delhi, India. *SSRN Electronic Journal*. https://doi.org/10.2139/ssrn.3768421

Bhowmik, S.K. (2001). Hawkers and the urban informal sector: A study of street vending in seven cities. *Prepared for National Alliance of Street Vendors in India (NASVI)*.

Cisco study (2022). Retrieved from: https://tech.hindustantimes.com/tech/news/india-to-have-over-800-million-smartphone-users-by-2022-cisco-study-story-nnYnDOiY6nulyiKRaZRsDP.html

Hoque, A. (2023). Socio-Economic Status, Health condition and Working Profile among Street Vendors (Hawkers) in Malda district of West Bengal, A Study of Unorganized and Informal Sector Economy and Livelihood Opportunity. *International Research Journal of Education and Technology (IRJEdT)*, *5*, 12–23.

Joshi, A., and Reddy, V. (2022). Study of perceptions among street vendors of Ahmedabad on "Pradhan Mantri Street vendor's Atmanirbhar Nidhi Scheme 2020 (PM-SVA Nidhi Yojana)"-Special micro-credit program for street vendors. *Journal of Positive School Psychology*, 374–380.

Khanal, A.R., and Omobitan, O. (2020). Rural finance, capital constrained small farms, and financial performance: findings from a primary survey. *Journal of Agricultural and Applied Economics, 52* (2), 288–307.

Kumar Aryan, S. (2022). Socio-Economic Impact of Pandemic on Street Vendors of Jammu Region India: An Empirical Study. *Journal of Quality in Health Care* and *Economics*, *5*(2). https://doi.org/10.23880/jqhe-16000267

Kumar, A., Singh, R., Gupta, R., and Sinha, P.K. (2024). Entrepreneurial competencies influence subjective well-being of subsistence entrepreneurs: Examining the mediating role of business performance. *Journal of Small Business Management*, 1–30.

Matamanda, A.R., Kalaoane, R.E.C., and Chakwizira, J. (2023). "Leave us alone":'right to the city'of street vendors along Main North 1 Road, Maseru, Lesotho. *Geojournal*, *88*(4), 4473–4491.

Martínez, L., and Short, J.R. (2022). The Informal City: Exploring the Variety of the Street Vending Economy. *Sustainability*, *14*(12), 7213.

Murugan, S.P., Shivaprasad, G., Dhanalakshmi, A., Sriram, V.P., Rajput, K., Mahesh, B.N., and Kedla, S. (2023). The Impact of COVID-19 on the Indian Microfinance Industry and Its Sustainability. In *Transforming Economies Through Microfinance in Developing Nations* (pp. 160–188). IGI Global.

Myers, E., Heckert, J., Galiè, A., Njiru, N., and Alonso, S. (2021). *Staying afloat in the milk business: Borrowing and selling on credit among informal milk vendors in Nairobi* (Vol. 2039). Intl Food Policy Res Inst.

Nandru, P., S A, S. K., and Chendragiri, M. (2023). Adoption intention of mobile QR code payment system among marginalized street vendors: an empirical investigation from an emerging economy. *Journal of Science and Technology Policy Management*, (ahead-of-print).

Rakha, A., Fatima, M., Bano, Y., Khan, M.A., Chaudhary, N., and Aadil, R.M. (2022). Safety and quality perspective of street vended foods in developing countries. *Food Control*, *138*, 109001.

RBI. (2020, Jan 10). *National Strategy for Financial Inclusion (NSFI): 2019–2024.* Retrieved from: https://www.rbi.org.in/Scripts/PublicationReportDetails.aspx?UrlPage=ID=1154

Rumanyika, J., Apiola, M., Mramba, N.R., Oyelere, S.S., and Tedre, M. (2021). Mobile technology for street trading in Tanzania: A design science research approach for determining user requirements. *The Electronic Journal of Information Systems in Developing Countries*, *87*(5), e12176.

Ruark, A., and Fielding-Miller, R. (2016). Using qualitative methods to validate and contextualize quantitative findings: A case study of research on sexual behavior and gender-based violence among young Swazi women. *Global Health: Science and Practice*, *4*(3), 373–383.

Santos, M.A.D., Fávero, L.P., Fouto, N.M.M.D., Belfiore, P., and Souza, R.D.F. (2021). Determinants of credit access of small and medium enterprises in emerging economies: evidence from the World Bank enterprise surveys. *International Journal of Globalisation and Small Business*, *12*(3), 266–298.

Statista report, (2023). Retrieved from: https://www.statista.com/statistics/1373584/india-mobile-phone-penetration-rate/

Thanh, P.T., and Bao Duong, P. (2023). Vulnerability and resilience among women migrant street vendors during the COVID-19 pandemic. *Journal of Enterprising Communities: People and Places in the Global Economy*.

Von Soest, C. (2023). Why do we speak to experts? Reviving the strength of the expert interview method. *Perspectives on Politics, 21* (1), 277–287.

Advancement in Engineering and Science – Goyal et al. (Eds)

Comparative Analysis of Stock Market Performance of ESG Leader Companies and their Parent Index

Ajit Anuradha Shashikant Joshi
Chartered Accountant, Associate Professor, Finance Prin. L. N. Welingkar Institute of Management Development and Research

Viraj Matkar
MMS Semester III student, Batch of 2023-25

ABSTRACT: Evolving corporate space expects companies to give due attention to Environmental, Social, and Governance (ESG) criteria. Crucial question is, does following these practices rigorously affect investor's choices? To answer this, the research compares stock performances of ESG leader companies with their respective parent indices across three developed and three developing or bricks economies: the United States (USA), Germany (GER), Japan (JAP), India (IND), Brazil (BRZ), and China (CHN). Key performance matrix giving justice to risks returns and index composition is analyzed to observe if these practices affect stock prices Paired T-Tests, F-Tests, ANOVA, MANOVA, Wilcoxon Signed-Rank Test and Kolmogorov-Smirnov Test are used in the analysis.

Analysis shows that the indices of ESG leader companies significantly follow their parent indices in terms of risk or return. This helps to prove that vigorously following ESG practices has a little effect on risk return relationships and thus, the investors have a strong alternative of investing in such companies without compromising performance efficiency.

Multiple economies of different characters have shown that ESG leader companies perform in line with parent indices if not better, thereby underlining financial viability of these practices. The distinct long term growth trajectories and performance trends reveal the advantage of investing in ESG leader companies sustainable responsible and profitability investing.

Keywords: ESG Leader companies, ESG Index, risk-return analysis, Investment decisions

1 INTRODUCTION

ESG considerations are not merely for the companies to implement but even for the investors while choosing their vehicles. Investors, regulators and corporations are all considering ESG investment and its analysis as an integral part of decision-making process (Zhan, 2021, p. 4). This might be due to increasing awareness of the gravity of frequent environment crisis or broader comprehension of corporate social responsibility as a crucial sustainable factor (Cochran, 2007, p. 5).

In this research six economies are chosen, three from the developed First World, United States (USA), Germany (GER), Japan (JAP) and three from emerging BRICS countries, India (IND), Brazil (BRZ), and China (CHN), where an apex stock market index is compared with the Index constituted of ESG leader companies. The analysis begins from the year 2015 when the landmark Paris Agreement took place that sealed the international commitment to combat climate change and its impacts.

2 ECONOMIC CONTEXTS OF THE ANALYZED ECONOMIES

1. United States (USA): Statutory measures such as the Dodd-Frank Act and compliance requirement by the Securities and Exchange Commission (SEC) which have made used reporting standards more effective have late to United States becoming leader in ESG investments (Cifrino, 2024, p. 8).
2. Germany (GER): Over last few decades Germany has given greater importance to sustainability not only at Government level but also as corporate commitment. It's energy transition policy (*Energiewende*) shifting from fossil fuels to the renewable energy resources is a major step towards sustainability. The companies within German economy are largely known for the stricter ESG reporting as well as maintaining high standards of environmental compliance. Thus, not only in Europe but also in the world, Germany is a key player in ESG (Szulecki, Fischer, Gullberg, and Sartor, 2016, p. 7).
3. Japan (JAP): World's largest pension fund that is Government Pension Investment Fund (GPIF) from Japan adopted ESG principles and that has made Japan an important player that has integrated ESG factor with investment ecosystem. It's Corporate Governance Code and Stewardship Code has worked as a crucial tool for better accountability and transparency in ESG compliance (Schumacher, Chenet, and Volz, 2020, p. 15).
4. Brazil (BRZ): Brazil as a country with substantial natural resources as well as large agriculture sector has specific ESG challenges such as deforestation as well as key opportunities in terms of sustainable agriculture and environmental conservation. The countries initiative towards ESG is reflected in a segment of Brazilian stock exchange, Novo Mercado that includes companies which follow high governance standard (Orsato, 2015, p. 3).
5. China (CHN): Chinese government has prioritized the rapid economic growth with considerable focus on ESG. It's severe pollution challenges and climate incidences have encouraged the government to adopt better ESG practices. From that perspective, it has initiated Green Development in its Belt and Road initiative and created Green Finance committee.
6. India (IND): On the background of global players, India is not lagging behind to recognize and ensure adherence to ESG standards. . The Securities and Exchange Board of India (SEBI) has made it a mandatory compliance for top 1000 listed companies to ensure Business Responsibility and Sustainability Reporting (BRSR)

DOI: 10.1201/9781003798514-77

3 SIGNIFICANCE OF THE STUDY

It is evident that various economies not only developed but also developing, not only large but also smaller, and not only technology advanced but also primary sector focus are making their best efforts towards encouraging the corporate to integrated ESG practices. Now it is imperative for the researchers to develop the pointers for the corporate, investment community and governance agencies alike, based on these experiences.

4 LITERATURE REVIEW

Challenges such as limited access to clean cooking and high population density threaten China's environmental sustainability efforts (Shaheen and Lodhi, 2024, p. 17). Various methodologies used to study the relationship between FDI, ESG investments, and migration, highlighting are areas for further research. The Sustainability Analysis needs an approach-specific methodology to infer the impact of following these practices. (Zatonatskiy, 2024, p. 10). The study finds that funds with higher sustainability ratings experienced sharper declines in retail flows during the pandemic, highlighting the need for strategies to increase retail investor confidence in SRIs (Döttling, and Kim, 2024, p. 34).

The COVID-19 pandemic underscored the importance of strong ESG practices, as companies with robust ESG frameworks were better prepared. Long-term benefits of ESG and cultural differences in ESG practices require further study (Ahmad, Yaqub, and Lee, 2023, p. 7). Socially Responsible Investment (SRI) strategies have evolved to include "best-in-class" selection, ESG integration, and impact investing. These trends offer valuable insights for academics and practitioners in the field of sustainable investment (Beisenbina, 2023, p. 15). However, challenges such as effective screening of investment proposals and policy interventions remain (Ning, 2023, p. 3). Empirical studies suggest that GF positively impacts SD, but the directionality of this relationship is inconsistent. The paper recommends improving classification standards, evaluation systems, and information disclosure to align GF with SD objectives (Wang, 2022, p. 3).

Global investment falls short of the $12 trillion needed to achieve the Sustainable Development Goals (SDGs), a gap exacerbated by the COVID-19 pandemic. The pandemic threatens progress towards the 2030 Agenda for Sustainable Development. The paper by Gazzol, (2021) examines global SDG investment and financing in response to the pandemic. It discusses financing tools used to mitigate health, economic, and social impacts and highlights challenges in mobilizing sufficient funds, targeting the right SDG areas, and ensuring positive impacts. Regulatory hurdles also complicate SDG investments. The authors suggest policy measures to enhance SDG investment, including integrating SDGs into investment policies and improving ESG standards and reporting (Zhan, and Santos-Paulino, 2021, p. 8). Busse, (2021) analyze the role of FDI in advancing SDGs in Africa. While FDI can drive economic growth and job creation, it also poses environmental risks. Zhou *et al.* (2021) investigate the impact of green investment and corporate social responsibility (CSR) on sustainable performance in Indonesian manufacturing companies.

The findings indicate that both green and CSR investments positively impact financial performance, but the link to sustainable performance through the triple bottom line concept needs further exploration (Indriastuti, and Chariri, 2021,p. 18). The authors recommend policy support for green projects and investment in new technologies (Huang, Xue, and Khan, 2021, p. 1). However, the limited involvement of non-banking institutions in green finance suggests room for growth (Zheng, 2021, p. 11).

Businesses increasingly consider environmental, social, and governance (ESG) factors in their operations. According, (2020), companies prioritizing ESG tend to be more profitable and environmentally responsible. Transparency about environmental impacts can improve overall performance. While progress is noted, challenges remain in understanding the long-term impacts of green bonds and the effectiveness of government policies in promoting sustainable finance. Further research is needed to assess the influence of Japan's corporate culture on ESG adoption (Schumacher, Chenet, and Volz, 2020,p. 8). Using a bibliometric approach, BroadstocK, (2020) analyze trends in sustainable investment research. The findings show a significant rise in sustainable investment literature and a shift from traditional investment tools to "green" instruments. Przychodzen, (2020) explore the relationship between green finance (GF) and sustainable development (SD) globally. Pham *et al.* (2020) explore the fragile demand for socially responsible investments (SRIs) among retail mutual fund investors during economic shocks like COVID-19.

Miroudot and Cadestin (2020) examine the forces reshaping global value chains (GVCs), including trade policies, technology advancements, environmental concerns, corporate responsibility, and resilience against disruptions. These changes impact production locations and beneficiaries of trade. The authors suggest that researchers and policymakers collaborate to address these changes effectively. The paper presents mixed findings on FDI's impact on SDGs, highlighting the need for responsible investment practices and stronger environmental regulations to maximize positive outcomes (Aust, Morais, and Pinto, 2020, p. 4). Sun *et al.* (2020) analyze China's use of cleaner technologies and renewable energy to reduce greenhouse gas emissions. The study finds that green energy and effective resource use can significantly lower emissions.

Japan faces significant climate risks, including rising sea levels and typhoons. Nakajima, (2019) explore Japan's efforts to develop sustainable finance practices, including the adoption of green bonds and ESG criteria in financial decision-making. Fatica and Panzica (2019) examine the role of green bond financing in promoting energy efficiency investment and economic growth. The study highlights the potential of green bonds to address financing barriers and support green finance initiatives. Ullah *et al.* (2019) examine the impact of green finance on the sustainability performance of banks in Bangladesh. The study finds that green finance positively impacts bank sustainability, emphasizing the importance of integrating ESG practices.

Traditional foreign direct investment (FDI) influences migration through job creation and economic development. Alstadsæter, (2018) discuss how ESG investment principles are reshaping FDI, linking sustainable investment practices with economic growth and quality-oflife improvements. These factors attract skilled migrants seeking high-quality living conditions.

Wang *et al.* (2018) investigate how renewable energy and green investments can reduce CO2 emissions in China. The study shows that green projects and renewable energy usage lower emissions, but excessive financial sector growth can increase emissions.

The literature review tells us that several efforts have been made to link ESG with financial performance. However, ESG is neither a novelty nor a standalone experience. What is very important is to see how company as a whole can perform while following ESG practices better than many in industry, hence ESG leader Companies, as against the overall profit-oriented organizations, reflected in Parent Indices.

5 GAP ANALYSIS

All the aforesaid literature indicates that the ESG is an important integration is business practices, not only from overall strategy perspective but even from financial dimension. However, the gap is in focusing on the companies which are ESG integration leaders. This is crucial because is the Green Finance able to shape and boost the ESG initiatives. Conversely, its failure is going to be the cause of the lukewarm and somewhat compliance-oriented approach of the management towards ESG application. However, Green Finance, by its essential definition is an investment activity centered around the Green Initiatives. What is required are initiatives integrated into overall company functioning. This is where ESG leader company's performance is focused. The researchers across the world show the financial viability, profitability and ultimately, attractiveness of ESG initiatives. But these researchers do not underline a comprehensive picture or a bird's eye view when these practices are followed by companies as their management philosophy and what impact, if any, it invites from the investors.

6 OBJECTIVES

Based on the Gap discussed above, it was decided to center the research around the companies which are aggressively integrating ESG practices. The objective for the statistical analysis is to determine if the performance metrics of ESG and Parent Indices are significantly similar across various economies. Based on this, various objectives are developed as below ...

1. To observe the overview of the performance of ESG and Parent Indices and associated risks
2. To study the levels of difference in risks and returns between ESG leadership companies and parent indices
3. To examine the composition of the two indices

Essentially, the objective of this research is to prove that the ESG leader companies stock performances are not significantly different from that of their parent indices. This also means that the ESG leader companies can give the same return as the index and there is no need for the investor to hesitate on that count.

7 RESEARCH METHODOLOGY

The researchers have considered Morgan Stanley Capital International (MSCI) data. MSCI, the leading entity in corporate analysis has defined certain companies as leaders in ESG initiatives. Accordingly, the researchers have considered the stock returns of the ESG leaders and compared them with the parent index of the economy from 2010 to 2024 for simple comparison of risks and returns. Paris Agreement in 2015 is a global landmark towards sustainability efforts. Though there was awareness on sustainability related issues for a long time, the Agreement committed major nations in the world to make conscious, defined and systemic efforts towards Sustainability through mitigation adoption and investments. Hence, some economies may not have a MSCI ESG index before 2015 but it is ensured that all the economies included in the analysis will have the ESG index since 2015.

Sr No	Objective	Tools
1	To observe the overview of the performance of ESG and Parent Indices and associated risks	Descriptive statistics.
2	To study the levels of difference in risks and returns between ESG leadership companies and parent indices	Using Hypothesis testing ... 1. Hypothesis 1: There is significant difference in the risks and returns of ESG and Parent indices in the various economies, independently 2. Hypothesis 2 There is significant difference in the aggregated risks and returns of ESG and Parent indices across all economies 3. Hypothesis 3: There is significant difference in the sectoral composition of ESG and Parent indices across all economies as well as independently. Statistical tools such as Paired T-Tests, ANOVA, MANOVA, and F-Tests will be used.
3	To examine the composition of the two indices	Hypotheses Testing:Hypothesis: There is statistically significant difference between the sectoral compositions of the Parent Index and the ESG Index across the economies.Tests: Paired T Tests, Wilcoxon Signed-Rank Test and Kolmogorov-Smirnov Test

8 DATA ANALYSIS AND RESULTS

Initially, the researchers have shown a simple comparison of annual returns from different regions starting right from 2010. This Study helps us to know the result of ESG returns of different parts of the world. The study had taken six Countries with their ESG returns- USA, GER, JAP (Developing countries), IND, BRZ and CHM (Emerging countries). The research use data from MSCI indices which comprise of large and mid-sized companies to have fair and unbiased decision

Descriptive Statistics of the Risk and Returns:

1. Mean Returns: - Result: The mean returns of ESG securities are significantly similar to those of Parent Indices across all considered economies (USA, GER, JAP, IND, BRZ, CHN).
2. Variances: - Result: The variances of returns for ESG and Parent Indices are significantly similar across all considered economies. Risk-Adjusted Performance
3. Sharpe Ratios: - Result: The Sharpe Ratios of ESG securities are significantly similar to those of Parent Indices across all considered economies. Cumulative Returns
4. Cumulative Returns: - Result: The cumulative returns of ESG securities are significantly different from those of Parent Indices in most economies (USA, GER, JAP, IND, BRZ), except for China, where they are significantly similar. Correlation
5. Correlation Analysis: - Result: The correlation between ESG and Parent Indices is significantly different for USA, BRZ, and CHN, while it is significantly similar for GER, JAP, and IND. Trends

Paired T-Test results can be represented in the graph below ...

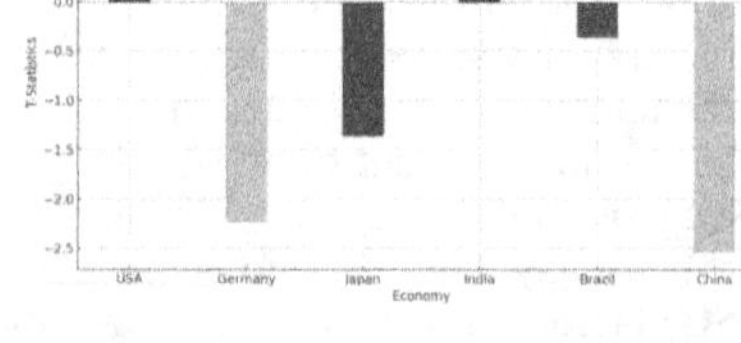

There is significant difference in the returns of ESG leader company indices only in case of China and Germany but in no other case or on aggregate basis.

ANOVA Results (Aggregated) tell us that the F-statistic for Index (Parent vs ESG) is 1.32 with the p-value: 0.257 whereas the F-statistic for Interaction (Type) is 0.89 with the p-value: 0.548. thus, these results suggest that there is no significant difference between the returns of Parent and ESG indices across all economies when aggregated.

Similarly, the MANOVA Results (Aggregated) have led to F-statistic for Type (ESG vs Parent) as 1.09 with p-value: 0.310 and F-statistic for Index (Economy-wise) as 0.96 with p-value: 0.413. these results, too, which account for multiple return periods, indicate no statistically significant difference between ESG and Parent indices when analyzed across all economies and periods.

While the F-Test for Variance (Economy-wise) can be seen I the table below.

	USA	Gmny	Japan	India	Brazil	China
F Statistics	0	0.111	0.189	0.07	3.09	0.23
F Statistics - P Value	0.95	0.74	0.671	0.8	0.092	0.635

The F-tests for equal variances show that most economies do not have significant differences in volatility between ESG and Parent indices, except for Brazil, where the variance may differ slightly.

The level of difference in case of sectoral composition is tested on Wilcoxon Signed-Rank Test and Kolmogorov-Smirnov Test is considered at only one point of time, at present.

	USA	Germany	Japan	India	Brazil	China
Wilcoxon Signed-Rank Test:	15	14	15	13	15	17
Wilcoxon Signed-Rank Test - P Value	0.484	0.414	0.484	0.347	0.484	0.705
Kolmogorov-Smirnov Test	0.091	0.0909	0.091	0.091	0.0909	0.1818
Kolmogorov-Smirnov Test - P Value	1	1	1	1	1	0.988

9 WILCOXON SIGNED-RANK TEST

All the p-values are greater than 0.05, meaning that there is no statistically significant difference in the sectoral compositions between the Parent and ESG indices for any of the economies.

10 KOLMOGOROV-SMIRNOV TEST

The KS Test also yields p-values greater than 0.05, indicating that the distributions of sectoral compositions are not significantly different between the Parent and ESG indices for any economy.

11 CONCLUSION

The most important takeaway of this research is that taking ESG initiatives does not compromise the stock market performance of the company in any manner. It is worth noting here that the literature (Servaes and Tamayo, 2013, piv-1254) had spoken about the positive correlation between the Firm Value and CSR. However, this paper expands beyond specific case studies and CSR as well. However, the differences in cumulative returns, correlations, and trends underscore the importance of considering regional factors and long-term trajectories.

These finding are also supported with an extensive research by Fried, Busch and Bassen (2015). Investors can use these findings to develop strategies that incorporate ESG criteria without sacrificing returns or increasing risk. Understanding that ESG investments offer similar mean returns and risk profiles as Non-ESG investments across various economies allows for more confident integration of ESG factors into investment portfolios.

Recognizing the comparable risk levels between ESG and Non-ESG investments enables better risk management. Investors can incorporate ESG securities without significantly altering the risk profile of their portfolios, facilitating a smoother transition to more sustainable investment practices.

Companies can leverage this research to align their business strategies with ESG principles, knowing that such alignment does not necessarily compromise financial performance. This can enhance their appeal to socially conscious investors and improve their overall market positioning.

Implications and Suggestions:

An important takeaway of this research is that ESG is not an additional burden for the business. In fact, the results clearly indicate that the companies forming part of parent index also dominate the Sustainability Leadership indices. Thus, there is no risk of Value Loss in following these practices. However, there is also another significant implication here. Just as ESG practices do not let the value lose in the entity's performance, at the same time, they are not deriving the incremental benefits of following these practices which would induce more and more corporate to follow these practices. It is suggested to the investment community that they should seek the long term benefits of following ESG practices and convert it into investment premium.

12 LIMITATIONS

Some of the limitations can be listed as below ...

(a) The study is entirely based on MSC Index. Though this is generally a reliable parameter, the research pre-supposes the correctness of building up an ESG Index by the makers.
(b) The Study does not analyze the changing composition with reference to the returns and risks.
(c) The research has been unable to identify the differentiating impact that ESG integration might make on the stock markets.
(d) Effectiveness of ESG practices by the Index components needs to be established.

13 FUTURE POSSIBILITIES

The comparative analysis of stock market performance between ESG leader companies and their respective parent indices provides a foundation for several future research direction. Here are key areas where further investigation could be valuable:

1. Academic approach: The Academic approach of looking at Finance and ESg has always been the study of ESG investments. However, it is equally if not more important to study the further consequences in financial terms, of integrating ESG practices in the company.

2. Impact of ESG Integration on Corporate Performance: Investigating how integrating ESG principles affects a company's operational efficiency, risk management, and overall financial performance.
3. Regional and Sectoral Analysis: Analyzing ESG leaders' performance across different regions and industry sectors.
4. Investor Behavior and ESG Preferences: Investigating how investor preferences for ESG investments evolve over time and across different demographics.
5. ESG Factors and Systemic Risk: Analyzing the impact of ESG factors on systemic risk within the financial system.

This research underscores the viability of integrating the ESG investments in overall company strategy. The findings reveal that ESG securities generally offer comparable returns and risk profiles, while exhibiting distinct long-term growth trajectories and performance trends. The significant differences in correlations and trends highlight the importance of regional dynamics and informed investment strategies. As investor demand for sustainable practices grows, this study provides a solid foundation for further exploration and validation of ESG principles. Ultimately, the integration of ESG factors presents a promising path toward sustainable, responsible, and profitable investing, benefiting both investors and society at large.

BIBLIOGRAPHY

Addy, Ofodile, Adeoye, Oyewole, Okoye, Odeyemi, and Ololade (2024). Data-driven sustainability: How fintech innovations are supporting green finance. https://doi.org/10.51594/estj/v5i3.871

Addy and Ofodile (2020). Data-Driven Sustainability: How Fintech Innovations are Supporting Green Finance. *Journal of Green Finance*, 9(3), 301-322. https://doi.org/10.51594/estj/v5i3.871

Ahmad, Yaqub, and Lee (2023). Environmental-, social-, and governance-related factors for business investment and sustainability: A scientometric review of global trends. *Environment, Development and Sustainability*, 26(4), 2965–2987. https://doi.org/10.1007/s10668-023-02727-1

Alstadsæter, Johannesen, and Zucman (2018). Determinants of Global Migration: The Impact of ESG Investments and Foreign Direct Investment. *Journal of International Economics* 12(4), 543-562. https://doi.org/10.14254/2071-789X.2024/17-1/14

Aust, Morais, and Pinto (2020). How does foreign direct investment contribute to Sustainable Development Goals? Evidence from African countries. https://doi.org/10.1016/j.jclepro.2019.118823.

Bailey and Lopez de Prado (2012). The Sharpe ratio efficient frontier. *Journal of Risk*, 15. https://doi.org/10.2139/ssrn.1821643.

Beisenbina, Fabregat-Aibar, Barberà-Mariné, and Sorrosal-Forradellas (2023). The burgeoning field of sustainable investment: Past, present, and future. *Sustainable Development*, 31, 273-286. https://doi.org/10.1002/sd.2422.

Bianchi, Drew, and Ruggerio (2020). Environmental, social, and governance-related factors for business investment and sustainability: A scientometric review of global trends. *Journal of Business Research*, 120, 253-267. 10.1007/s10668-023-02921-x

Broadstock, Chan, Cheng, and Wang (2020). The burgeoning field of sustainable investment: Past, present and future. *Journal of Sustainable Finance & Investment, 10*(1), 1-24. https://doi.org/10.1002/sd.2422

Busse, Erdogan, and Mühlen (2021). The influence of foreign direct investment in achieving the Sustainable Development Goals: Evidence from African countries. *Journal of African Economies*, 20 (5), 600-621. https://doi.org/10.1016/j.cjpre.2021.12.023

Chen, Song, and Gao (2023). Environmental, social, and governance (ESG) performance and financial outcomes: Analyzing the impact of ESG on financial performance. *Journal of Environmental Management*. https://doi.org/10.1016/j.jenvman.2023.118829

Cifrino (2024, January 24). The politicization of ESG investing. *Harvard Advanced Leadership Initiative*. https://www.sir.advancedleadership.harvard.edu/articles/politicization-of-esg-investing.

Cochran (2007). The evolution of corporate social responsibility. *Kelley School of Business,* Indiana University. https://doi.org/10.1016/j.bushor.2007.06.004

Daugaard and Ding (2022). Global drivers for ESG performance: The body of knowledge. *Sustainability*, 14(4), 2322. https://doi.org/10.3390/su14042322.

Devalle, Fiandrino, and Cantino (2017). The linkage between ESG performance and credit ratings: A firm-level perspective analysis. *International Journal of Business and Management*, 12(9), 53-60. https://doi.org/10.5539/ijbm.v12n9p53

Dong (2023). A systematic review of the ESG strategy literature and future outlook. *Frontiers in Sustainable Development.* https://doi.org/10.54691/fsd.v3i4.4784

Döttling and Kim (2024). Sustainability preferences under stress: Evidence from COVID-19. *Journal of Financial and Quantitative Analysis*, 59, 435–473. https://doi.org/10.1017/S0022109022001296

Reddy's Foundation. *The Evolution of ESG Goals in India.* https://drreddysfoundation.org/the-evolution-of-esg-goals-in-india/

Fatica and Panzica (2019). Green bond as a new determinant of sustainable green financing energy efficiency investment and economic growth: A global perspective. *Journal of Green Investment*, 16(2), 189-211. https://doi.org/10.1007/s11356-021-18454-7

Friede, Busch, and Bassen (2015). ESG and financial performance: Aggregated evidence from more than 2000 empirical studies. *Journal of Sustainable Finance & Investment*, 5(4), 210-233. https://doi.org/10.1080/20430795.2015.1118917

Huang, Xue, and Khan (2021). What abates carbon emissions in China: Examining the impact of renewable energy and green investment. *Sustainable Development*. https://doi.org/10.1002/sd.2177

Indriastuti and Chariri (2021). The role of green investment and corporate social responsibility investment on sustainable performance. *Journal of Accounting and Investment*, 22, Article 1960120. https://doi.org/10.1080/23311975.2021.1960120

Li, Wang, Sueyoshi, and Wang (2021). *ESG: Research progress and future prospects. Sustainability*, 13(21), 11663. https://doi.org/10.3390/su132111663.

Ning, Cherian, Sial, Álvarez-Otero, Comite, and Zia-Ud-Din (2023). Green bond as a new determinant of sustainable green financing, energy efficiency investment, and economic growth: A global perspective. *Environmental Science and Pollution Research*, 30, 61324–61339. https://doi.org/10.1007/s11356-022-20212-3

Orsato, Garcia, Mendes-Da-Silva, Simonetti, and Monzoni (2015). Sustainability indexes: Why join in? A study of the 'Corporate Sustainability Index (ISE)' in Brazil. *Journal of Cleaner Production*, 87, 211-220. https://doi.org/10.1016/j.jclepro.2014.10.071

Oyewole, Adeoye, Addy, Okoye, Ofodile, and Ugochukwu (2024). *Promoting sustainability in finance with AI: A review of current practices and future potential.* World Journal of Advanced Research and Reviews, 21, 590–607. https://doi.org/10.30574/wjarr.2024.21.3.0691

Park and Jang (2021). *The impact of ESG management on investment decision: Institutional investors' perceptions of country-specific ESG criteria.* International Journal of Financial Studies, 9, 48. https://doi.org/10.3390/ijfs9030048

Pham, Nguyen, and Tran (2020). Sustainability Preferences Under Stress: Evidence from COVID-19. *Journal of Sustainable Finance*, 11 (4), 345-369. https://doi.org/10.1017/S0022109022000790

Schumacher, Chenet, and Volz (2020). Sustainable finance in Japan. *Asia Pacific Journal of Financial Studies*, 47, 213-246. https://doi.org/10.1080/20430795.2020.1735219

Servaes Henri and Tamayo Ane (2013) The impact of corporate social responsibility on firm value: The role of customer awareness. *Management Science* 59(5):1045-1061. https://doi.org/10.1287/mnsc.1120.1630

Shaheen, Lodhi, Rosak-Szyrocka, Zaman, Awan, Asif, and Ahmed (2024). Cleaner technology and natural resource management: An environmental sustainability perspective from China. *Sustainability*, 4, Article 36. https://doi.org/10.3390/sustainability4030036

Szulecki, Fischer, Gullberg, and Sartor (2016). Shaping the 'Energy Union': Between national positions and governance innovation in EU energy and climate policy. *Climate Policy*, 16(5), 548-567. https://doi.org/10.1080/14693062.2015.1135100

Wang, Zhao, Jiang, and Li (2022). Does green finance inspire sustainable development? *Evidence from a global perspective. Economic Analysis and Policy*, 72, 402–415. https://doi.org/10.1016/j.eap.2022.06.002

Zatonatskiy, Leonov, Cieśliński, and Vasa (2024). Determinants of global migration: The impact of ESG investments and foreign direct investment. *Economics and Sociology*, 17, 215-235. https://doi.org/10.14254/2071-789X.2024/17-1/14

Zhan (2021). GVC transformation and a new investment landscape in the 2020s: Driving forces, directions, and a forward-looking research and policy agenda. *Journal of International Business Policy*, 4, 206–220. https://doi.org/10.1057/s42214-020-00092-4

Zhan and Santos-Paulino (2021). Investing in the Sustainable Development Goals: Mobilization, channeling, and impact. *Journal of International Business Policy*, 4, 166–183. https://doi.org/10.1057/s42214-021-00062-1

Zheng, Siddik, Masukujjaman, and Fatema (2021). Factors affecting the sustainability performance of financial institutions in Bangladesh: The role of green finance. *Sustainability*, 13(18), Article 10165. https://doi.org/10.3390/su131810165

Indriastuti, and Chariri, (2021). The role of green investment and corporate social responsibility investment on sustainable performance. *Journal of Corporate Finance*, 14(3), 176-198. https://doi.org/10.1080/23311975.2021.1960120

Wu, Zhu, and Tao (2024). Can good ESG performance of listed companies reduce abnormal stock price volatility? Mediation effects based on investor attention. *PLoS One*, 19(9), e0307535. https://doi.org/10.1371/journal.pone.0307535

Advancement in Engineering and Science – Goyal et al. (Eds)
© 2026 The Author(s), ISBN: 978-1-041-31101-0

Influence of Deposits on Market Capitalization: A Special Reference to Listed Banks of India

Priti Samant
Associate Dean-Finance, S. P. Mandali's Prin. L. N. Welingkar Institute of Management Development and Research (PGDM), Mumbai

Shubhada Apte
Professor and Research Guide, DTSS College of Commerce, Mumbai

ABSTRACT: Banks are the key ingredient for a sustainable financial system in any country. Deposits have traditionally funded bank balance sheets and though deposit growth has been studied as a result of market capitalization of banks in previous research published, given the current state where banks in India are scurrying to mobilise greater amount of deposits, this study aims to identify whether market capitalization of listed banks is driven by deposit growth. The study covers 31 listed Indian banks for five-year period from FY 2018-19 to FY 2022-23 using panel data model analysis (Fixed effects and Random effects). For listed banks in India, deposits and loans positively influence market capitalization while NNPAs negatively impact it. Results show that deposits and Net Non-performing assets (NNPA) significantly influence market capitalization of Public sector banks(PSBs) while only deposits influence market capitalization of private sector banks (PVBs) positively. T test further shows that there is significant difference in the deposit funding proportions and NNPA percentages between PSBs and PVBs. Implications are given the changes to deposit growth rates and lending growth rates for banks in India, it is imperative for banks to enhance their deposit base if they want to sustain and augment their market capitalization. Additionally, PSBs to manage NNPA better while PVBs to garner higher deposits for a sustainably growing market capitalization.

Unique contribution: This is the first study to identify deposits along with NNPA influencing market capitalization of listed banks in India and highlight the differences between PSBs and PVBs regarding balance sheet funding and asset quality in relation to their market capitalisation.

Limitation: The study does not include factors like Inflation, liquidity in the financial markets, no of orders, FII investment, bank size, monetary policy actions or level of competition in the banking sector.

Keywords: Sustainable market capitalization, Indian listed banks, panel data models, deposits

1 INTRODUCTION

Banks are critical for sustainable financial development of any economy (Andersen and Juelsrud, 2024). India is one of highest growing economies in the world. (World bank, n.d.) Banks attract capital in two ways from the economy. One in the form of equity investment boosting its own market capitalization and second in the form of deposits and borrowings, providing interest earning opportunities to its investors. In the first form, investors expect to earn dividends and capital gains while in the second form investors expect to earn interest income. Market capitalization of any entity is the total worth of all equity ownership of the entity and higher market capitalization indicates better equity investor interest. Banks are required to raise equity funding regularly to maintain capital adequacy as per regulatory guidelines and to continue to grow their balance sheet. Better market capitalization improves the prospects of banks having higher capital adequacy and helps sustained growth for the bank.

Banks need deposits for funding their activities and business growth, which in turn should enhance their market capitalization. Banks re-channelize their deposits after adjustments for reserve requirements and other regulatory compliances for lending to various components in the economy. This on-ward lending not only influences the market capitalization of the banks but also should lead to overall economic development. (Andersen and Juelsrud, 2024). Recent news articles report a shortage of deposit growth in Indian banks as compared to their lending growth. (The Wire, 2024; Sharma, 2024). Banking business is essentially a business based on trust wherein the depositors hand over their funds to the banks in exchange for interest. The bank lends the money to sectors requiring capital and charges interest at a higher rate, thereby earning the interest spread. If the banks become unable to grow to their deposits at the requisite pace, they can be constrained to depend on borrowings for their lending activities which can comprise on their spread earning capacity; given market linked pricing of borrowings. Reduction in the spread can result in lower profitability and lower market capitalization.

This is a change in the business models of Indian banks (Sharma, 2024) and many dignitaries are urging banks to bring in innovations to augment deposits. This brings out the important question do deposits influence market capitalization of Indian banks, instead of previously studied associations wherein large banks ie banks with higher market capitalization tend to have greater deposits than other banks due their image and market presence.

Literature regarding the changing business models of banks especially for Indian banks is not yet published. Deposits growth is now critical for banks funding stability (Li *et al.*, 2023) and growth in balance sheet and market capitalization. This paper aims to bridge this gap.

2 LITERATURE REVIEW

Citations are not aligned with the APA citation style like (Staff, 2024; PTI, 2024; Saroha and Lozano, 20024; V *et al.*, 2004) this is the appropriate form of writing multiple citations.

 DOI: 10.1201/9781003798514-78

Note: V *et al.*, 2024 for this citation, V cannot be the sir name of the author, please add the sir name of the first author

Banks have been traditionally funded by deposits. Recent news articles highlight the slow growth of deposits as compared to loan growth in Indian banks. (The Wire, 2024; PTI, 2024; Saroha and Lozano, 2024; Seth *et al.*, 2024) have highlighted the shortage of deposit funding faced by Indian banks.

Consequently, the credit deposit ratio (ratio of loans to deposits) has been rising from year 2015 and is at its peak in FY 2024 as per the reports. The higher dependence on sources of funding other than deposits, will alter the business models of the banks and is expected to impact their Net interest margins (NIMs). NIM is a critical aspect of bank profitability and this may in turn adversely impact profitability and resultantly market capitalization. Lin (2020) demonstrated that in areas where stock ownership is high, banks in these areas are able to garner lower deposits, resulting in lower lending by retail banks for such areas.

Though there have been multiple news articles regarding lower deposit growth in Indian banks, there is dearth of research in this area. There are not many research publications regarding market capitalization of banks in India too.

Multiple studies have been conducted regarding profitability of banks. (Abdou and Alarabi, 2024) highlighted that capital adequacy, economic growth, inflation and bank size positively impact profitability while NNPA and liquidity and credit risk reduce profitability amoungst private banks in Egypt. They have used Generalised least squares method. (Audi *et al.*, 2021), studied factors influencing profitability of Moroccan banks. (Saif-Alyousfi and Abdulazeez, 2022) in their study identified that banks with greater demand deposits, growth, loans, market risks have better profitability. NNPAs adversely impact profitability of banks in Asia. The study used panel data models. (Kirimi *et al.*, 2022) showed that bank size is negatively associated with net interest margin and return on assets for banks in Kenya but no impact on return on equity. The study used panel data models. (Bolarinwa *et al.*, 2019) studied factor influencing profitability of banks in Nigeria.

Hendrawan *et al.*, 2023 have studied the impact of capital buffers on profitability of Indonesian banks and suggest that though capital buffers aid in absorbing losses, they also adversely impact return on equity and return on assets. They have used panel data models -GMM technique.

Khan, et al., 2021 studied the influence of profitability, bank size, growth on the book leverage for banks in Saudi Arabia. They found that profitability negatively impacts book leverage while bank size and growth positively impact book leverage.

Kantharia et al., 2023 identified factors that influence financial performance of public sector banks in India using panel data models. They demonstrated that NNPA, liquidity, credit deposit ratio and inflation rate adversely impacted return on assets and return on equity while GDP, bank size did not influence return ratios.

Research in the area of market capitalization, especially with reference to banks is sparse. Though studies have been conducted regarding stock price of commercial banks (Al-Dwiry *et al.*, 2022) or factors influencing stock returns (Budhathoki *et al.*, 2024) , studies about market capitalization of commercial banks in India as a dependent variable is yet to be published . (Al-Dwiry *et al.*, 2022) studied factors influencing stock price of Jordanian banks and identified EPS, DPS, ROA and size positively influence stock price. They also found that GDP, Money supply, Volumes traded and total market capitalization also influence stock price.

(Budhathoki *et al.*, 2024) investigated inputs that influence stock returns amongst Nepalese banks and found that trading volumes positively and book to market negatively impacts stock returns while asset growth, return on assets and market capitalization have a weak association with stock returns.

Abdelzaher (2023) studied growth of deposits in listed banks in Egypt and identified that efficiency of the banks, their market capitalization, NNPAs and loans significantly influence deposit growth amongst Egyptian listed banks. (Paulet and Mavoori, 2019) demonstrated that higher market capitalization of banks often influences better performance for the banks, especially in US, Europe, India and China. They also highlighted differences in performance of banks depends on extent of government control and ownership type of the banks, especially in Asia.

Market capitalization positively induces economic development in BRICS region was demonstrated by Ogbeide and Akanji, (2018). Market capitalization of banks which are pillars for any economy, especially for India with a high growth rate gains importance. Similarly, challenges for Indian banks with regards to mobilizing deposits lately is yet to studied in literature. There have been many studies about aspects that influence deposits including that Market capitalization influences deposits (Abdelzaher, 2023), while a pivot in the growth rate of deposits via s vis growth rate of loans in banks in India (Seth *et al.*,2024), a study is yet to be conducted about deposits driving market capitalization by influencing profitability and funding stability.

3 RESEARCH OBJECTIVE

1. This study aims to identify the association between bank deposits and any other bank specific variables with market capitalization of banks listed in India
2. This study aims to identify whether extent of bank deposit funding and other bank variables which are identified to be influencing market capitalization are different in PSBs and PVBs

This study aims to find whether there is association between deposits, any other bank specific variables and market capitalization of listed banks in India for periods FY 2018-19 to FY 2022-23. It will cover investigation of whether these inputs are different for PSBs and PVBs. All banks that have been listed during these five financial years have been covered by the study. Data about the banks has been gathered from their regulatory reports, financial reports, investor presentations. GDP number has been sourced from statista website. Market capitalization data for each of the Financial years has been sourced from NSE website. Statistical tools using JMP 17 and R have been employed.

Panel data models have been used for analysis as these are most commonly used for assessing banks financial performance. (Abdou and Alarabi, 2024; Kantharia, et.al,2023; Saif-Alyousfi and Abdulazeez, 2022). Stock returns and stock prices of commercial banks have been studied using panel data models (Al-Dwiry *et al.*, 2022; Budhathoki *et al.*, 2024).

4 DATA AND SUMMARY STATISTICS

41 banks were listed in India as on 31st March 2024 (where the banks are listed) like this please provide detail information. Out of these, 10 banks have been listed after 31st March 2019. The period of study is five years from FY 2018-19 to FY 2022-23 and the rest 31 banks have been considered. Out of these, 12 banks are PSBs and 19 banks are PVBs. List of banks considered are given in Table 1.

Table 1. List of banks studied with their bank type.

Bank Name	Bank Type
Bank of Baroda	PSB
Bank of India	PSB
Bank of Maharashtra	PSB
Canara Bank	PSB
Central Bank	PSB
Indian Bank	PSB
Indian Overseas Bank	PSB
Punjab National Bank	PSB
Punjab and Sind Bank	PSB
State Bank of India	PSB
UCO Bank	PSB
Union Bank	PSB
AU Small Finance Bank	PVB
Axis Bank	PVB
Bandhan Bank	PVB
City union Bank	PVB
DCB Bank	PVB
Dhanalaxmi Bank	PVB
Federal Bank	PVB
HDFC Bank	PVB
ICICI bank	PVB
IDBI bank	PVB
IDFC first Bank	PVB
IndusInd Bank	PVB
J&K Bank	PVB
Karnataka Bank	PVB
Karur Vysaya Bank	PVB
Kotak Mahindra Bank	PVB
RBL Bank	PVB
South Indian Bank	PVB
Yes Bank	PVB

Source: Authors calculations.

We studied the level and direction of association of deposits and other variables on market capitalization for all 31 banks together for FY 2018-19 to FY 2022-23 using panel data regression models. Focus was on understanding influence of deposits on market capitalization given the low growth rate of deposits among banks in India as compared to growth rate of loans.

We then divided the 31 banks as per their ownership pattern into PSBs and PVBs and using panel data model regression identified variables that influence market capitalization for PSBs and PVBs separately. Then, using t test, it was studied whether there are significant differences in the patterns of the identified influencer variables between PSBs and PVBs.

Regression is used to study the association between a response variable and single or multiple factors or independent variables. Three models were used for studying relationship between market capitalization of bank and bank dependent variables. Model 1 was used for all 31 banks to regress Market capitalization as response variable and using deposits, NNPA amount and Loans as regressors. Model 2 was used for PSBs to regress Market capitalization as response variable and using deposits and NNPA amount as regressors. Model 3 was used for PVBs to regress Market capitalization as response variable and deposits as regressor.

We propose the following equation for Model 1 (31 banks):

Pooled OLS

$$MKTCAP_{it} = \beta_0 + \beta_1 NNPA\_AMT_{it} + \beta_2 DEPOSITS_{it} + \beta_3 LOANS_{it} + u_{it}$$

Where β_0 is intercept, $\beta_{1\ to\ n}$ are the regression coefficients, i =, bank 1, bank 2 .... ..bank 31 and t = year 1, year 2 .... ..year 5, and u_{it} is the error term.

Fixed Effects

$$MKTCAP_{it} = \beta_0 + \beta_1 NNPA\_AMT_{it} + \beta_2 DEPOSITS_{it} + \beta_3 LOANS_{it} + \alpha_i + u_{it}$$

Where β_0 is intercept, $\beta_{1\ to\ n}$ are the regression coefficients, i =bank 1, bank 2 .... ..bank 31 and t = year 1, year 2 .... ..year 5, α_i is the bank specific attributes captured by bank specific intercepts and u_{it} is the error term.

Random Effects

$$MKTCAP_{it} = \beta_0 + \beta_1 NNPA\_AMT_{it} + \beta_2 DEPOSITS_{it} + \beta_3 LOANS_{it} + \varepsilon_i + u_{it}$$

Where β_0 is intercept, $\beta_{1\ to\ n}$ are the regression coefficients ,i = bank 1, bank 2 .... ..bank 31 and t = year 1, year 2 .... ..year 5 , ε_i is the bank specific not measurable error variable and u_{it} is the error term.

We propose the following equation for Model 2 (12 PSBs banks):

Pooled OLS

$$MKTCAP_{it} = \beta_0 + \beta_1 NNPA\_AMT_{it} + \beta_2 DEPOSITS_{it} + u_{it}$$

Where β_0 is intercept, $\beta_{1\ to\ n}$ are the regression coefficients, i =, bank 1, bank 2 .... ..bank 31 and t = year 1, year 2 .... ..year 5, and u_{it} is the error term.

Fixed Effects

$$MKTCAP_{it} = \beta_0 + \beta_1 NNPA\_AMT_{it} + \beta_2 DEPOSITS_{it} + \alpha_i + u_{it}$$

Where β_0 is intercept, $\beta_{1\ to\ n}$ are the regression coefficients, i =bank 1, bank 2 .... ..bank 31 and t = year 1, year 2 .... ..year 5, α_i is the bank specific attributes captured by bank specific intercepts and u_{it} is the error term.

Random Effects

$$MKTCAP_{it} = \beta_0 + \beta_1 NNPA\_AMT_{it} + \beta_2 DEPOSITS_{it} + \varepsilon_i + u_{it}$$

Where β_0 is intercept, $\beta_{1\ to\ n}$ are the regression coefficients ,i = bank 1, bank 2 .... ..bank 31 and t = year 1, year 2 .... ..year 5 , ε_i is the bank specific not measurable error variable and u_{it} is the error term.

We propose the following equation for Model 3 (19 PSBs banks):

Pooled OLS

$$MKTCAP_{it} = \beta_0 + \beta_1 DEPOSITS_{it} + u_{it}$$

Where β_0 is intercept, β_1 is the regression coefficient, i =, bank 1, bank 2 .... ..bank 31 and t = year 1, year 2 .... ..year 5, and u_{it} is the error term.

Fixed Effects

$$MKTCAP_{it} = \beta_0 + \beta_1 DEPOSITS_{it} + \alpha_i + u_{it}$$

Where β_0 is intercept, β_1 is the regression coefficient, i =bank 1, bank 2?bank 31 and t = year 1, year 2 .... ..year 5, α_i is the bank specific attributes captured by bank specific intercepts and u_{it} is the error term.

Random Effects

$$MKTCAP_{it} = \beta_0 + \beta_1 DEPOSITS_{it} + \varepsilon_i + u_{it}$$

Where β_0 is intercept, β_1 is the regression coefficient, i = bank 1, bank ?bank 31 and t = year 1, year 2 … ..year 5 , ε_i is the bank specific not measurable error variable and u_{it} is the error term.

In order to choose between Pooled OLS and Fixed effects, F test was conducted and the results are shown in Table 2. As the results were significant, Fixed effects was chosen over Pooled OLS. To choose between Fixed effects and Random effects, Hausman test was conducted and results shown in Table 3. As the results were significant, Fixed effects would be chosen over Random effects in Model 1 and 2 while Random effects have been chosen in Model 3.

Table 2. Results of F test between the Pooled OLS (Ols) and Fixed effect (FE) for all three models.

	F value	p value	Remarks
Model 1 (31 banks)	19.189	0.00000	FE is to be preferred over OLS
Model 2 (12 PSBs)	2.6639	0.00991	FE is to be preferred over OLS
Model 3 (19 PVBs)	14.019	0.00000	FE is to be preferred over OLS

Source: Authors calculations

Table 3. Hausman Test to choose between Fixed Effects (FE) and Random Effects (RE) for all 3 models.

Models	Chi square	p value	Remarks
Model 1 (31 banks)	43.268	0.000000	FE is preferred to RE
Model 2 (12 PVBs)	9.6933	0.007855	FE is preferred to RE
Model 3(19 PVBs)	1.4824	0.2234	RE is preferred to FE
degrees of freedom	3		

Source: Authors calculations

We used Durbin Watson test to test for autocorrelation and results show that no auto correlation exists for all 3 models. Refer Table 4 for the Durbin Watson test results.

Table 4. Durbin Watson Test for Serial correlation for all 3 models.

	Durbin Watson	p value	Remarks
Model 1 FE (31 banks)	1.9962	0.4938	No serial correlation exists
Model 2 FE (12 PSBs)	2.1832	0.7349	No serial correlation exists
Model 3 RE (19 PSBs)	2.256	0.8854	No serial correlation exists

Source: Authors calculations

To test for cross sectional dependence, Pesaran CD test was conducted as N(number of banks) is greater than t (number of years) was greater and results are given in Table 5 (Pesaran, 2015). Results show existence of cross sectional dependence in all 3 models.

Table 5. Pesaran CD test for models.

	z value	p value	Remarks
Model 1 FE (31 banks)	19.063	0.000000	Cross sectional dependence exists
Model 2 FE (12 PSBs)	6.9546	0.000000	Cross sectional dependence exists
Model 3 RE (19 PVBs)	12.715	0.000000	Cross sectional dependence exists

Source: Authors calculations

To check for normality of the residuals, Breusch pagan Lagrange Multiplier test was conducted and results are shown in Table 6. Results are significant showing heteroscedasticity and hence robust standard errors controlling for cross sectional dependence and heteroscedasticity have been used in the results. VIF for all the independent variables are below 10 and this confirms there is no multicollinearity in models.

Table 6. Breusch Pagan Test for normality of residuals.

	Chi square	P value	Remarks
Model 1 FE (31 banks)	168.25	0.00000	Model is heteroscedastic
Model 2 FE (12 PSBs)	6.8722	0.03219	Model is heteroscedastic
Model 3 RE (19 PVBs)	94.095	0.00000	Model is heteroscedastic
all models with df =2			

Source: authors calculations

5 RESULTS AND ANALYSIS

The descriptive statistics for the independent and dependent variables used in the study have been shown in Tables 7.1, 7.2 and 7.3.

Descriptive statistics

Table 7.1. Financial and Market capitalisation data for 31 listed banks for 5 years FY 2018-19 to FY 2022-23 Rs in Million except for GDP which is in USD Bn.

	Mean	Median	Std Deviation	Min	Max	No of obs
NNPA_AMT	72,918	28,610	101,329	108	658,947	155
MKTCAP	820,105	217,960	1,629,546	2,037	8,980,875	155
DEPOSITS	4,634,480	2,224,241	7035242	106,033	44,237,778	155
LOANS	6,901,393	1,565,786	21737487	62,893	161,423,650	155
CRAR	16.47	15.87	4.249387	7.49	33.64	155
GDPUSDBN	3,121	3,167	329.7455	2,675	3,572	5

Source: authors calculations

Table 7.2. Financial performance and Market capitalisation data for 12 PSBs for 5 years FY 2018-19 to FY 2022-23 Rs in Million except for GDP which is in USD Bn.

PSBs	Mean	Median	Std Deviation	Min	Max	No of obs
NNPA_AMT	145315.05	114335	128499	4352	658947	60
MKTCAP	489865	213585	948184	7712	4674266	60
DEPOSITS	7840676	5294667	9539483	896676	44237778	60
LOANS	5323133	3518375	6950449	584119	31992693	60
CRAR	14.066	14.12	2.2257	7.49	18.54	60
GDPUSDBN	3,121	3,167	331.45	2,675	3,572	5

Source: authors calculations

Table 7.3. Financial performance and Market capitalisation data for 19 PSBs for 5 years FY 2018-19 to FY 2022-23 Rs in Million except for GDP which is in USD Bn.

PSBs	Mean	Median	Std Deviation	Min	Max	No of obs
NNPA_AMT	27,194	16,172	31,603	108	149,020	95
MKTCAP	1,028,678	243,638	1,916,375	2,037	8,980,875	95
DEPOSITS	2,609,514	1,080,612	3,641,869	106,033	18,833,946	95
LOANS	7,898,189	822,855	26,597,264	62,893	161,423,650	95
CRAR	17.98	17.50	4.53	8.50	33.64	95

Source: Authors calculations

Table 8 shows the Pearson correlation between the variables used. Table 8.1 shows the correlations for all 31 banks, Table 8.2 shows them for PSBs and Table 8.3 displays the correlations for PVBs. All correlations are positive while the correlations between NNPA amount and deposits and associations between Deposits and Loans are significant. It is noticed that NNPA amount and Loans are significantly correlated for PSBs but not for PVBs. Also, the correlation between deposits and loans is stronger for PSBs whose balance sheets are being funded by deposits as compared to PVBs but the correlation coefficients between DEPOSITS and LOANS for PSBs and PVBs are close to 0.8 so Loans have not been considered as independent variable for predicting Market capitalization for PSBs and PVBs. CRAR and Real GDP were not found to be significant influencers for market capitalization of banks and hence the relevant correlations have not been shown in the table.

Table 8. Correlation coefficients between dependent and independent variables 8.1 Correlation coefficients between dependent and independent variables for all 31 banks (repetition).

All banks	NNPA_AMT	MKTCAP	DEPOSITS	LOANS
NNPA_AMT	1.0000			
MKTCAP	0.1322	1.0000		
DEPOSITS	0.711***	0.5723***	1.0000	
LOANS	0.1114	0.8147***	0.4562***	1.0000

Source: Authors calculations* Correlation is significant at the 0.05 level (2-tailed). ** Correlation is significant at the 0.01 level (2-tailed). *** Correlation is significant at the 0.001 level (2 tailed)

Table 8.2. Correlation coefficients between dependent and independent variables for PSBs.

PSBs	NNPA_AMT	MKTCAP	DEPOSITS	LOANS
NNPA_AMT	1.0000			
MKTCAP	0.5233***	1.0000		
DEPOSITS	0.6923***	0.9458***	1.0000	
LOANS	0.6908***	0.9461***	0.9976***	1.0000

Source: Authors calculations* Correlation is significant at the 0.05 level (2-tailed). ** Correlation is significant at the 0.01 level (2-tailed). *** Correlation is significant at the 0.001 level (2 tailed)

Table 8.3. Correlation coefficients between dependent and independent variables for PVBs.

PVBs	NNPA_AMT	MKTCAP	DEPOSITS	LOANS
NNPA_AMT	1.0000			
MKTCAP	0.3406***	1.0000		
DEPOSITS	0.4867***	0.9288***	1.0000	
LOANS	0.1675	0.8219***	0.7978***	1.0000

Source: Authors calculations* Correlation is significant at the 0.05 level (2-tailed). ** Correlation is significant at the 0.01 level (2-tailed). *** Correlation is significant at the 0.001 level (2 tailed)

Tables 8.1, 8.2 and 8.3 depict the association between bank deposits, NNPA amount, Loans and Market capitalization of the banks. At the overall level (31 banks), we find that deposits and NNPA are significantly positively related while there is no association between NNPA and market capitalization & NNPA and loan book of the banks. Loans and deposits are positively and significantly correlated as banks can grow their loan book post increase in their deposit base. Both bank deposits and loans are positively and significantly associated with market capitalization. This indicates that at the overall level, banks who can augment deposits, would be able to grow their loan book and market capitalization growth although this would be associated with greater NNPA amounts also.

For PSBs, we find that NNPA amounts are positively and significantly associated with bank deposits and Market capitalization and Loans. Loans and deposits are positively and significantly correlated with each other and with market capitalization too. This implies that PSBs who can increase deposits will be able to grow their market capitalization only if they manage NNPA amounts.

For PVBs, it is seen that NNPA amounts are positively and significantly associated with Market capitalization and deposits but not with loans. Bank deposits, loans and market capitalization are positively and significantly associated with each other. This implies that NNPAs result from balance sheet growth driven by deposits and not loans necessarily.

Table 9 shows the relationship between dependent variable Market capitalization and independent variables: deposits, NNPA amount and loans for model 1, deposits and NNPA amount for Model 2 and deposits for Model 3

As shown in the table below, at an overall basis (Model 1 - 31 banks), Market capitalization is driven by deposits and loans positively and NNPA amount negatively. Any listed bank in India can improve its market capitalization if it can increase its deposit book, loan book while controlling its Net NPA amounts. F test is significant which means that Model 1 is reliable and these aspects are able to explain about 31% of market capitalization of any listed bank in India.

For PSBs, Market capitalization is driven by deposits and NNNPA amounts. Most of the balance sheet is funded by deposits, so deposits positively influence loan book. Impact of NNPA is more sharp in reducing market capitalization for PSBs as compare to the whole group. Deposits and NNPA amounts explain about 52% of variation in Market capitalization of PSBs.

For PVBs, market capitalization is driven by bank deposits alone. Model 3 – 19 PVBs shows that bank deposits explain about 89% of variation in market capitalization. The model is significant and shows that increase of Re 1 deposit should result in Re 0.45 in market capitalization of PVBs. The coefficient of bank deposits is highest for PVBs while it is lowest for PSBs.

This study shows that at the overall level, all three deposits, loans and NNPAs influence market capitalization while for PSBs, deposits and NNPA influence market capitalization. In case of PSBs, only deposits influence market capitalization.

This leads to the next research objective, are there any significant differences in the deposit funding and NNPA amounts between PSBs and PVBs. The results for this have been shown in Table 9.

Table 9. Relationship between dependent variable market capitalization and the following regressors deposits, NNPA amount and Loans for Model 1, deposits and NNPA amount for Model 2 and deposits for Model 3.

Variable	Model 1	Model 2	Model 3
	FE	FE	RE
DEPOSITS	0.0968502 (0.0262262)**	0.069783 (0.022098)**	0.45602 (0.03455)***
NNPA_AMT	-1.9002938 (0.6281097)**	-2.282835 (0.603640)***	
LOANS	0.0327441 (0.0088495)***		
C			-161,320 (254680)

(continued)

Table 9. Continued

Variable	Model 1	Model 2	Model 3
Observations	155	60	95
Adjusted R2	0.31697	0.52686	0.89363
F Value	34.8222***	36.0659***	
Chi square			455.683***

Source: Authors calculations* Correlation is significant at the 0.05 level (2-tailed). ** Correlation is significant at the 0.01 level (2-tailed). *** Correlation is significant at the 0.001 level (2 tailed). All values shown are standard errors robust of cross-sectional dependence and heteroscedasticity.

Independent t test was used to compare the regressors deposits and NNPA amounts between PSBs and PVBs. For the same, Deposits_TA which represents proportion of total assets funded by deposits and NNPA_PCT which represents Net non-performing assets as a percentage of net advances were compared between PSBs and PVBs . Results of the t test are shown in Table 10.

Table 10. t test for testing differences of DEPOSITS_TA and NNPA_PCT between PSBs and PVBs.

Variable	Mean for PSBs	Mean for PVBs	t statistic	p value	Interpretation
DEPOSITS_TA	0.8550272	0.7555249	-8.53606	0.00000***	PVBs deposits to total assets is significantly lower than that of PSBs
NNPA_PCT	3.843	1.982	-5.5425	0.00000***	PVBs NNPA percentage is significantly lower than that of PSBs

Source: Authors calculations while discussion the results of the present study, support the findings with the existing literature.

Findings should be discussed in detail.

Results should be discussed along with past evidences that is, the results of the study can either align or contradict with the existing literature and the same needs to be discussed in detail along with detail discussion on the findings.

Table 10 above clearly shows that PSBs have a significantly higher proportion of their balance sheet funded by deposits as compared to PVBs. This is consistent with findings shown by Apte and Samant (2023). PSBs have a significantly higher amount of NPAs than that of PVBs. This is consistent with findings of (Kalaivani and Vaithiyanathan, 2023; Brahmaiah, 2019). Whichever aspect that influences dependent variable but is in low supply is critical for improving market capitalization. Since PSBs have high credit risk (high NNPAs), they need to control NNPAs and focus on them in addition to deposit augmentation if they want to influence market capitalization favorably. PVBs are already managing their credit risks well but they are facing dearth of deposit funding as compared to PSBs so if they augment their deposit base, they will be able to influence their market capitalization in a positive manner.

6 IMPLICATIONS

Banks need to focus on deposits growth when they want to fund their balance sheet growth in a profitable and sustainable manner. Strategies to augment deposit base need to be designed and implemented for banks to improve not only their total balance sheet but also their market standing. This is especially important for a country like India, which is one of the fastest growing economies of the world (World bank, n.d.). Confidence in the banking sector will boost the overall confidence in the Indian economy. Alongside deposits growth, focus on asset quality and loans growth will also drive market capitalization of banks at an overall level. Credit demand is visible in the Indian economy but making the appropriate credit decisions is going to influence banks' market standing. PSBs need to be more careful regarding credit decisions while PVBs need to focus on deposits growth for improving market capitalization.

Implications/Recommendations are missing

7 CONCLUSIONS

The results show that deposits are pivotal for banks market capitalization which has not yet been covered in literature and the influence is more pronounced for PVBs (coefficient for deposits variable in Model 3 is 0.45 as against 0.09 for all banks and 0.06 for PSBs. PSBs are in a better position than PVBs when it comes to deposit mobilization which is shown by a lower coefficient for PSBs. For listed banks, not only mobilizing deposits, but also judicious utilization of the resources through lending and having lower NPAs boosts Market capitalization. Amount that can be lent may depend not only on bank specific factors but can also depend on monetary policy action, level of economic activity and other macro-economic factors. NPAs reduce market capitalization as they impact profitability; present and future of the banks. It is interesting to note that PSBs have greater NNPAs than PVBs and NNPA and loans are highly correlated in PSBs too. This association is not found in PVBs. In order to augment market capitalization, all banks need to not only increase deposits but also focus on restricting NNPAs, especially PSBs. PVBs are already managing NNPAs well and so if they can increase deposits, they will be able to increase their market capitalization too.

Collate limitations of the study with future scope as limitations of a study forms the base of the future research studies. Limitations of the study Macro economic factors like inflation, real interest rates and bank specific factors like bank size and bank efficiency have not been considered for this study as this study has been conducted with special attention to deposits driving market capitalization of banks in India and given that deposits are growing at a slower pace than loans.

8 SCOPE FOR FURTHER RESEARCH

This research brings to light need to study about the differences in business models of PSBs and PVBs in India. Also, with scarcity of deposits being faced by banks in India, especially PVBs and the growing competition in banking sector with small finance banks and payment banks being given licenses to operate, it will be relevant to identify factors that influence growth of deposits for banks in India.

REFERENCES

Abdelzaher, M.A. (2023). Determining Factors Affecting the Mobilization of Deposits in Egyptian Listed Banks. *International Journal of Economics and Financial Issues*, 13(3), 11–17. https://doi.org/10.32479/ijefi.14153

Abdou, D.M.S., and Alarabi, Y. (2024). The dynamics behind private banking growth in Egypt. Future Business Journal, 10(1). https://doi.org/10.1186/s43093-023-00290-5

Al-Dwiry, M., Al-Eitan, G.N., and Amira, W. (2022). Factors affecting stock price: Evidence from commercial banks in the developing market. *Journal of Governance and Regulation*, 11(4, special issue), 339–346. https://doi.org/10.22495/jgrv11i4siart14

Andersen, H. and Juelsrud, R.E. (2024). Optimal capital adequacy ratios for banks. *Latin American Journal of Central Banking*, 5 (2),100-107. https://doi.org/10.1016/j.latcb.2023.100107

Apte, S., and Samant, P. (2023, December 13-15). Not only CASA, retail fixed deposits too lower interest cost: Empirical study with a panel data approach for select Indian Banks [Paper presentation]. SIMSARC'23, Pune, Maharashtra, India.

Brahmaiah, B. (2019). Why Non-Performing Assets Are More in Public Sector Banks in India? *Theoretical Economics Letters,* 09(01), 75–82. https://doi.org/10.4236/tel.2019.91007

Bolarinwa, S.T., Obembe, O.B., and Olaniyi, C. (2019). Re-examining the determinants of bank profitability in Nigeria. *Journal of Economic Studies*, 46(3), 633–651. https://doi.org/10.1108/jes-09-2017-0246

Budhathoki, P.B., Bhattarai, G., and Dahal, A.K. (2024). The impact of liquidity on common stocks returns: Empirical insights from commercial banks in Nepal. *Banks and Bank Systems,* 19(1), 148–156. https://doi.org/10.21511/bbs.19(1).2024.13

Derbali, A. (2021). Determinants of the performance of Moroccan banks. *Journal of Business and Socio-economic Development*, 1(1), 102–117. https://doi.org/10.1108/jbsed-01-2021-0003

Gohel, A. (2024, March 22). Credit-growth-trajectory-likely-to-slow-down-to-12-14-yoy-over-fy25-27-says-emkay-global. livemint. https://www.livemint.com/industry/banking/credit-growth-trajectory-likely-to-slow-down-to-12-14-yoy-over-fy25-27-says-emkay-global-11711083505246.html

Hendrawan, M.H., Defung, F., and Wardhani, W. (2023). Un/desired impact of capital buffers: Evidence from Indonesian bank profitability and risk-taking. *Cogent Economics* and *Finance*, 11(2). https://doi.org/10.1080/23322039.2023.2245217

Kalaivani, B. and Vaithiyanathan, B. (2023). A study on NPA governing efficiency of public sector banks. *South India Journal of Social Sciences,* XXI(40).

Kantharia, N.J., and Biradar, J. (2022). What influence the performance of banks? Evidence from public sector banks in India. *Journal of Indian Business Research*, 15(1), 23–39. https://doi.org/10.1108/jibr-04-2022-0112

Khan, S., Bashir, U., and Islam, M.S. (2020). Determinants of capital structure of banks: evidence from the Kingdom of Saudi Arabia. *International Journal of Islamic and Middle Eastern Finance and Management*, 14(2), 268–285. https://doi.org/10.1108/imefm-04-2019-0135

Kirimi, P.N., Kariuki, S.N., and Ocharo, K.N. (2021). Moderating effect of bank size on the relationship between financial soundness and financial performance. *African Journal of Economic and Management Studies*, 13(1), 62–75. https://doi.org/10.1108/ajems-07-2021-0316 Lin, L. (2019).

Li, L., Loutskina, E. and Strahan, P.E. (2023). Deposit market power, funding stability and long-term credit. *Journal of Monetary Economics*,138,14-30. https://doi.org/10.1016/j.jmoneco.2023.04.004

Lin, Leming. (2020). Bank Deposits and the Stock Market. *Review of Financial Studies*, 33(6), 2622–2658. https://doi.org/10.1093/rfs/hhz078

Ogbeide, S., and Akanji, B. (2018). Stock market development and economic growth of Brazil, Russia, India, China and South African (BRICS) Nations: Empirical research. *Accounting*, 83–92. https://doi.org/10.5267/j.ac.2017.6.001

Paulet, E., and Mavoori, H. (2019). Globalization, regulation and profitability of banks: a comparative analysis of Europe, United States, India and China. *The European Journal of Comparative Economics,* 16(2), 127–170.

Pesaran, M.H. (2014). Testing Weak Cross-Sectional Dependence in Large Panels. *Econometric Reviews,* 34(6–10), 1089–1117. https://doi.org/10.1080/07474938.2014.956623

PTI. (2024, March 4). high-gap-between-credit-deposit-growth-to-impact-loan-sales-nims. *Business-standard.* https://www.business standard.com/industry/banking/high-gap-between-credit-deposit-growth-to-impact-loan-sales-nims-report-124030400907_1.html

Saif-Alyousfi, A.Y. (2020). Determinants of bank profitability: evidence from 47 Asian countries. *Journal of Economic Studies*, 49(1), 44–60. https://doi.org/10.1108/jes-05-2020-0215

Saroha, A., and Lozano, C. (2024, March 4). Deposit-rush-among-indian-banks-to-raise-competition-for-funds-hit-margins. *spglobal* https://www.spglobal.com/marketintelligence/en/news-insights/latest-news-headlines/deposit-rush-among-indian-banks-to-raise-competition-for-funds-hit-margins-80547029

Seth, V.D., Chhabaria, S., Chugh, G., and Anand, N. (2024, February 15). India-banks-deposits-conundrum-growth-versus-profitability. *spglobal.* https://www.spglobal.com/ratings/en/research/articles/240215-india-banks-deposits-conundrum-growth-versus-profitability-12995400

Sharma, R. (2024, August 09). Indian banks need to quell a looming threat as savers flock to stocks. *Economic Times*. https://economictimes.indiatimes.com/industry/banking/finance/banking/bank-deposits-indian-banks-need-to-shoot-down-a-looming-threat-as-savers-flock-to-stocks/articleshow/112392163.cms?from=mdr

The Wire. (2024, April 9). Indian-banks-face-a-big-deposit-crunch. Thewire.in. https://thewire.in/banking/indian-banks-face-a-big-deposit-crunch-report

World bank. (n.d.). The World Bank In India. Worldbank.org. https://www.worldbank.org/en/country/india/overview accessed on 2024, November 8th

Advancement in Engineering and Science – Goyal et al. (Eds)

The Corporate CSR Leadership Role in Technology for Sustainable and Efficient Business and Work

Anish Devale and Shabnam Mane Mahat
Bharti Vidyapeeth Pune

Abhijit Kadam
Institute of Management and Social Sciences, Solapur, Vijapur Road, Konark Nagar, Jule, Solapur, Maharashtra

ABSTRACT: The CSR role is a key element for the technologically efficient output necessary for overall economic growth and patterns. Today in changing environments CSR has become vital used for society development where government has made it mandatory for all organizations. Now the company is making it compulsory for technological development to be part and parcel of CSR activities. Minimizing human error and carrying out more productivity and efficiency are the key elements for CSR productivity and growth development of any organization CSR role without it becomes difficult to carry out sustainable development activities which are tedious tasks for slow growth when efficiency results in work output.

The Study focuses on CSR management policy which is aligned to technological development and framework costing, Marginal costing with the changing nature of business where more emphasis is on how business function machinery works and how the output of business productivity measures are implemented promptly where quality and quantification of work output with cost estimates such as standard costing parameters, labor costing, Marginal costing can be measured for calculations of actual wage rate and idle time matters when it comes to quality productivity which is more of intellectual or parameter which directly related efficient output with fewer work hours maximum output that is where every organization is aiming for.

Keywords: CSR model, leadership, technology, business model, sustainable, Growth development, CSR productivity

1 INTRODUCTION

Leadership and CSR are two pillars of any smooth organizational work. Its efficiency depends on the flow of work, the total work, and the speed of the technology. Implementation and monitoring of work play a vital role in managing CSR activities. The CSR study has been important since it is in line with the needs of technology and shows how the development is more strategically advanced in terms of workflow and analysis. The analysis of CSR studies has been an intrinsic part of the flow of study of workflows. (Bhargava A. and Ligade P. 2023) This has led to the overall holistic development in the field of work management systems and technological analysis where the system is more of an economic tool and is available for healthy progress and efficacy of the work output machinery which gives both the quality and quantity output of the workflow.

This has increased the rate of work output processing on a larger scale where technology avoids the cascading of work and measures the efficiency of the tool measurement work in a more organic manner resulting in the work being full of technology that will help the development of the process and the system.

CSR initiatives overall impact and engage the stakeholders which are creditors, customers, debtors, suppliers, shareholders, and Lenders, which are part of the CSR activities where efficiency and productivity are the main key stakeholders for the development of the overall business growth and efficient output. As technology helps to increase the efficiency of the output which carries out the society's beneficial activity. It creates and helps for the Opportunities for upliftment of society and downtrodden people. (Ashrafi M, Adams M. and Walker T. R. 2013) It is kindheartedness for the society's people for overall development. Materialism helps to develop upliftment as it grows the society as a whole by allowing people to have companionship and empathy towards each other. By collecting and analyzing data on their social and environmental performance, companies can ensure that their CSR activities are making a meaningful difference and are aligned with business needs and objectives baseline for business Structure and Dynamics of Changes in Technology

India is a developing country where there is a society that has some imbalances in resource distribution. Now CSR's main role is the equal distribution of resources which gives equal opportunity for holistic growth in terms of business characteristics. It defines the stature of upliftment where the study emphasizes economic productivity more rather than the microeconomic growth rate of an organization, (Ahmad, N., Smajić, H., Palalic, R., and Al-Riyami, S. 2022) Technology plays a vital role in the current economic development pattern. For this characteristic, we must focus on more substantial theory development for choosing the right technology for the right business with the right flow process with productive output for economic and productive measurement where fewer resources and maximum benefit can be enriched eventually. Its growth is characterized by social infrastructure development which is required to reach technology to the goal end with a properly decided channel and equitable distribution of work.

The work has been more of the technological base where new businesses evolved and more technology-centric is the pillar for organizations' boost and growth. Its pillars are more efficient in the organization development for carrying out specified parameters such as collaboration form and monitoring CSR performance more efficiently on one one-click model. It gives the insight of business model and tool efficiency work where the organization's key elements are the integration of technology in which various diversified CSR activities are interlinked to a one based link model.

The most crucial thing in CSR is planning. Without planning CSR activities are very tough to implement hence every organization must focus on the planning and later execution of the work process. (Belas J, Çera, G Dvorský J and Čepel M. 2021.) In CSR activities a key role is the importance of technological-based monitoring. In this study, we are trying to find how to mitigate the gap and risk by proper planning through technological base rules and governing. This quality analysis helps

DOI: 10.1201/9781003798514-79

with workflow machinery which is required for tool measurement and data analysis part for the whole data review.

With rising business opportunities and rising scale of business, more work is on the scalability of business output. The leadership of top management plays a vital role in the overall development of the smooth functioning of economic activity and CSR activities. (Baumgartner R. J. 2014). This tool is more important for sustainable CSR study and is more important for any top management leadership to study. Its alignment is to the technology-based model and a draft of technology-based model integration.

2 RESEARCH METHODOLOGY

Integrating CSR into business plans and the incorporation of corporate social responsibility (CSR) into main business activities has been research-oriented and the process is to integrate the social aspect into main business strategies which leads to recurring opportunities for business growth. The following strategies can be used by business professionals to include CSR in corporate decision-making, and alignment of CSR with core business goals; whether through supply chain management, consumer involvement, or product innovation, the purpose of CSR evolvement becomes the cause of need due to rise in demand for social and cultural changes where technological influences have started impacting the changing lifestyle and life culture activities. Businesses should make sure that their CSR efforts are closely related to their main goals. Companies like Tesla and Unilever, for instance, make sustainable practices a top priority in their operational and commercial models of products guaranteeing a smooth transition between corporate social responsibility (CSR) and development and profitability. Create CSR leadership positions, and assign committed CSR executives or leaders to spearhead the CSR strategy. These executives ought to collaborate closely with other divisions, especially operations and R&D.

This method entails examining pre-existing data that was first gathered for different types of studies like public databases, industry publications, sustainability disclosures, and corporate financial reports used in CSR and sustainable technology research.

The CSR strategies aim to facilitate business communication in a philanthropic way. Its purpose of analysis has sprouted recently due to technological usage in the corporate world. The alignment has become a key domination factor. The research and work analysis is a qualitative aspect as it has a more data-driven technological base to compile with the required conditions. (OdurS., Bruno, L., and Maccario, G. 2023) Annual reports, newsletters, and business reference cards have been a primary source of data collection methods and data-driven factors.

In this paper, the analysis of case studies is preferred due to the objectives entailed in the research process.

Most of the time data analysis requires primary study and data collection but, in these parameters, in the CSR framework and technological integration, data availability is not crunched at all. Huge data gathering has been available over a period but analysis development become crucial while the desired factor is to mitigate the research work with proper data interpretation. (Stoian, M. C., and Plakoyiannaki, E. 2024).

So secondary data analysis has been the primary analysis for overall data development and data combination factor. In this analysis of data review, case studies have been a priority for research and review factor development.

In the research methodology process, 2 case studies have been reviewed which are based on 2 multinational corporations: Microsoft and Siemens company.

The main reason is to analyze the CSR work with technology integration for sustainability development where across different nations these companies have a presence through regional offices or branches available. Its process of CSR is being carried out in the various countries.

Microsoft and Siemens have executed CSR activities within the organization itself, and these companies are developing technological models for CSR for other companies too; which makes them a model for development with a base of blockchain, IoT- Internet of things, artificial intelligence. The association of such companies makes data collection and priority for easy conduct of the CSR model with technological integration. (Enciso-Alfaro, S. Y., and García-Sánchez, I. M. 2023).

Its primary reason as two companies have been working in technology on a service base as well as a product base for considering research work conduct and development for literature base for CSR analysis and work conclusion activity.

The research's main things involved were data available from various inputs management functionality and data sources for the selection of secondary data analysis specifically Microsoft and Siemens the main reason is the available data and association of these companies for data survey. (Herrera, J., and de las Heras-Rosas, C. 2020).)

The basis for consideration is reports from firms like Gartner, Forrester, Frost and Sullivan, and IBISWorld technological trends and CSR adoption in different sectors which has a combination of technological availability with the association of Microsoft and Siemens. (Veerabhadrappa, N. B. B., Fernandes, S., and Panda, R. 2023).

The study analysis has been done with the Microsoft annual report framework from the Microsoft investor website. Siemens analysts meet to carry forward work data for Artificial intelligence, IoT, Blockchain technologies, etc for CSR activities. (Secundo, G., Schena, R., Russo, A., Schiavone, F., and Shams, R. 2022)

In research methodology development for carrying out secondary data research review, there has been decision support development, business context understanding, continuous monitoring, and adapting as time has evolved data interpretation in terms of secondary information has been more evolving and dynamic. (Skouloudis, A., and Evangelinos, K. 2012)

The main basis was to have a proper research objective with clean research questions, ensuring the relevant selection of a vast secondary database information system.

Assessment of the report was done for reliability in terms of Microsoft and Siemens-related data accuracy and information input where data inconsistency was found data cleaning and preparation were done for case study analysis and as well as getting desired output information. (McWilliams, A., Siegel, D., and Teoh, S. H. 1999).

The biggest advantage for these two companies was related to data privacy and citation acknowledgment which are cited by well-renowned authors.

It also has relevance in data prevailing. Accuracy in data information, timeliness in the accuracy of information, and development by Microsoft and Siemens are more important in the data validation process. Credibility and completeness become more useful for data development and data analysis. (Haddiya, I., Janfi, T., and Guedira, M. 2020)

In the research methodology emphasis was given on how two giant companies have worked on social sciences in analysis for national surveys related to IT development for society, behavior, and demographics information which are related to development for business community usage. Industry reports assimilation with government associations for financial data analysis or market trends to assess market conditions, consumer behavior development, or economic policies which becomes an important caterpillar for CSR analysis development.

Business and economics trends analysis has played a key role as the base for the secondary database which caters to financial data or market trends-related predictions by survey companies to assess economic policy information. (Sánchez-Teba, E. M., Benítez-Márquez, M. D., Bermúdez-González, G., and Luna-Pereira)

Without requiring fresh primary data gathering, secondary data analysis allows researchers to evaluate broad patterns, effects, and connections between CSR tactics and sustainable technologies. Stock, C., Pütz, L., Schell, S., and Werner, A. 2024). Secondary data review analysis will be used to find and categorize significant themes regarding leadership styles, technology adoption, and business outcomes from the case study and interview data. The analysis will include the following crucial steps:

1) Transcription of interview data and responses to different data analyses and data that are available.
2) Identifying recurring trends or approaches to leadership.
3) Comparing and contrasting outcomes from different companies and sectors.

3 LITERATURE REVIEW

The CSR role is based on the qualitative implications which companies are laying the foundation for the development of society. Here the references show how the technology has been taken into consideration for the overall development of the CSR integration. How to implement the CSR base by top management with empathy as a primordial characteristic has been taken into consideration. In contrast, society has equality where business competition is secondary and focus is more dependent on overall strategic development for the organization and for the country's output which has been referred to in literature related to technology and for overall economic upliftment as a society. (Yoopetch, C., Nimsai, S., and Kongarchapatara, B. 2022). (Methodology in studying CSR with technology often involves a combination of qualitative and quantitative approaches. Literature gives evidence of the importance of a full research report to the stakeholders that drive CSR activities. (Kuttner, M., Feldbauer-Durstmüller, B., and Mitter, C 2021).

Strategic alignment with sustainability goals and CSR leader development is a key output for aligning business operations to broader sustainable development (Organizational Research Methods, 2(4), 340-365). As technology becomes more integrated into the development of business processes and identifies tools to optimize efficiency and minimize environmental harm, considering its use in secondary data has certain limitations. (Porter and Kramer, 2011)

Technology is key for easy access to secondary databases; that is empirical thought philosophy development for overall data-driven and data development which Microsoft and Siemens are key pillars for social growth injunction and prospective catering of business-driven CSR research & development business community (Bernal-Conesa, J. A., Briones-Peñalver, A. J., and Nieves-Nieto, C. 2017)). This is more important for driving easy access to the CSR activities that can be done to define the critical performance of CSR development through the technological approach.

Certain limitations cater to its needs. One is that the research step is a one-way integration of research and secondary analysis. However, its limitations are more chronic for rational development and the business community as CSR becomes a constant collateral to each other's storage work. (Lu, J., Ren, L., Lin, W., He, Y., and Streimikis, J. 2019))

3.1 *Case study -1*

Microsoft has adopted a cloud-first strategy (Microsoft, 2014) using Azure to boost productivity and make scalable, team-based work environments possible. Tesla is a prime example of automation and artificial intelligence leadership, upending the auto sector with self-driving technology and intelligent production methods. (Lockett, A., Moon, J., and Visser, W. 2006) Microsoft has also adopted the Industrial Internet of Things (IIoT) to detect equipment breakdowns and optimize the production process, illustrating how IoT may enhance operational performance measurement which is direct integration development for the outcome of CSR functionality work. Its focus is more on conversion technological integration of CSR with smoothness of workflow development and technical work writing.

When a new strategy is developed, this is more theoretical business community writing and story engagement work, but Microsoft focuses on strategic implementation and business development for CSR work, including proper flowchart derivation steps for CSR activities.

There is a reference for a CSR work technology platform for artificial intelligence which helps to develop more process-oriented work and business-led activities for an overall strong CSR development process and techniques.

Microsoft is committed to reducing its carbon footprint and advancing sustainability. It achieved its goal by working on carbon-negative removal targeting by 2030. The company started with its founding work in 1975, and by 2050 it aims to achieve it.

Microsoft's philanthropy and community engagement development involve philanthropic efforts that contribute money and resources for social cause development.

Ethical AI technology continues to evolve as Microsoft has taken it as a primary task for promoting AI with ethical development which company created AI and Ethics in Engineering and Research (ATHER).

(https://info.microsoft.com/rs/157-GQE-382/images/EN-US-CNTNT-ebook-Enterprise_Cloud_Strategy_2nd_Edition_AzureInfrastructure.pdf)

3.2 *Case study-2*

Siemens has demonstrated how the Industrial Internet of Things (IIoT) (Siemens, 2017) may enhance operational performance by utilizing it to forecast equipment breakdowns and optimize its production processes. The study highlights the significance of visionary leadership in promoting efficiency, innovation, and transformation in the contemporary business environment by analyzing these organizations' technological usage. In the end, it emphasizes how business executives need to combine technical know-how with strategies.

In green technologies development, Siemens is a key player in developing and deploying green technologies work development for infrastructure to help cities and industries reduce carbon footprints. Siemens's commitment is to help a more circular economy for which products are recycled using artificial technology where data is a baseline from a work output usage perspective for designing product development and recycled at their lifecycle development.

Siemens is working on bias mitigation reducing bias in AI algorithms which includes ensuring diverse data sets for training of AI models to avoid existing inequalities and discrimination. Siemens is also committed to developing AI solutions for particular processes or financial services development.

Company is involved in initiatives and partnerships with various organizations for the development of AI with government, small organizations, and big companies.

(https://blog.siemens.com/2021/04/the-infinite-possibilities-with-siemens-industrial-iot)

4 DISCUSSION

Corporate social responsibility has become a significant aspect of business operations in today's society. With the advancement of technology, companies are to implement sustainable practices and create social impact. Utilizing technology, companies can measure their CSR initiatives more efficiently ensuring they are making a positive impact on society and the environment. Transparency and open communication with CSR activities create a social impact on the overall development of the business growth and it becomes more environmentally and socially healthier and also helps in poverty alleviation. The business model of CSR plays a vital role in shaping the overall development of business growth and upliftment. Integration of technology is main for successful development, upliftment of society leads to growth development for a business model that benefits the company and society.

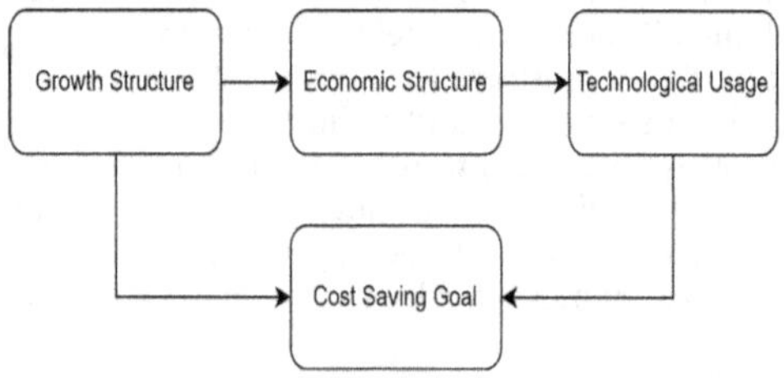

Figure 1. CSR sustainable structure. Orlitzky, M., Siegel, D. S., and Waldman, D. A. 2011Utilizing bibliographic coupling analysis and social network analysis. *Management Decision*, *58*(4), 601–624. Sources for diagram derivation and development.

5 SUGGESTIONS

5.1 *Large initial capital requirement.*

Sustainable technologies typically involve substantial upfront expenses that may discourage businesses, particularly small and medium-sized enterprises (SMEs), from integrating them. Many organizations struggle with a lack of technical expertise and resources when implementing and managing new sustainable technologies, and small and medium-sized enterprises might not have the necessary financial means or opportunities to secure funding for these investments.

5.2 *Regulatory and policy obstacles*

While certain areas offer supportive policies for green technologies, others lack enough regulatory rewards to promote widespread usage.

This leads to varying levels of uptake in different areas and sectors. Organizational reluctance to embrace new technologies can stem from concerns about risk, uncertainty regarding return on investment, or a lack of understanding about the lasting advantages of sustainability.

Many businesses, especially those in industries like manufacturing, agriculture, and energy, have started incorporating sustainable technologies into their CSR plans. The use of technology including energy-efficient technologies, renewable energy systems, green manufacturing techniques, and sustainable supply chains is growing. Companies are realizing that using sustainable technologies improves productivity, reduces costs, and gives them a competitive edge in addition to aligning with their CSR objectives.

6 CONCLUSION

The CSR role for development with technology is that change is constant. In ancient times charity was one of the important activities that evolved with time and its implication is more in CSR with diversified interests from various societies with the needs of the people and evolvement of society. Nature of people where the technology plays a vital role in CSR development. The association of technology with CSR role has played a more vital role in implication for overall development as a whole.

CSR methodology has evolved with the major role but the more focus it has resulted in a natural society for enhancement of increased digital workflows which companies can use the technology for reducing cost in CSR activities as well as can help to develop the enhance efficiency for futuristic business activities for overall growth story of the economy, which are required for sustainable and society positivity activities. This helps to increase productivity to enhance the overall development of the economy as a whole and natural productivity for the country's lifetime upliftment and enhancement, which helps to categorize company, and technology usage, efficiency, and productivity output.

REFERENCES

Ali M.N. and S.S. Ali's (2005). Research Methods in Social Sciences: A Handbook. SAGE PublPalazzo, M., Vollero, A., Foroudi, P., and Siano, A. (2019). Evaluating constitutive dimensions of CSR e-communication: A comparison between 'Business-To-Business' and 'Close-To-Market 'companies. *Journal of Business-to-Business Marketing,* 26(3–4), 341–355.ications.

Bernal-Conesa, J.A., de Nieves Nieto, C., and Briones-Peñalver, A.J. (2017). CSR strategy in technology companies: Its influence on performance, competitiveness and sustainability. *Corporate Social Responsibility and Environmental Management*, 24(2), 96–107. (wileyonlinelibrary.com) DOI: 10.1002/csr.1393

Bernal-Conesa, J.A., de Nieves Nieto, C., and Briones-Peñalver, A.J. (2017). CSR strategy in technology companies: Its influence on performance, competitiveness and sustainability. *Corporate Social Responsibility and Environmental Management*, 24(2), 96–107.

Bhat, A.A., Mir, A.A., Allie, A.H., Lone, M.A., Al-Adwan, A.S., Jamali, D., and Riyaz, I. (2024). Unlocking corporate social responsibility and environmental performance: Mediating role of green strategy, innovation, and leadership. *Innovation and Green Development*, 3(2), 100112.https://doi.org/10.1016/j.igd.2023.100112

Changar, M., and Atan, T. (2021). The role of transformational and transactional leadership approaches on environmental and ethical aspects of CSR. *Sustainability,* 13(3), 1411.https://doi.org/10.3390/su13031411

D'Amato, A., and Roome, N. (2009). Toward an integrated model of leadership for corporate responsibility and sustainable development: a process model of corporate responsibility beyond management innovation. *Corporate Governance: The International Journal of Business in Society,* 9(4), 421–434.https://doi.org/10.1108/14720700910984972.

Dhanesh, G.S. (2014). CSR as organization–employee relationship management strategy: A case study of socially responsible information technology companies in India. *Management Communication Quarterly*, 28(1), 130–149. DOI: 10.1177/0893318913517238, http://mcq.sagepub.com/content/28/1/130.

Hebbar, A.A. (2014, April). Making a case for private oil spill response organisations. In *Disaster, Risk and Vulnerability Conference* (p. 51). (ISBN 9788192344928)

Hossain, M.I., Kumar, J., Islam, M.T., and Valeri, M. (2024). The interplay among paradoxical leadership, industry 4.0 technologies, organizational ambidexterity, strategic flexibility, and corporate sustainable performance in manufacturing SMEs of Malaysia. *European Business Review*, 36(5), 639–669.https://doi.org/10.1108/EBR-04-2023-0109.

Mahat, S.M. (2023). A CSR Evolvement with Industrial Revolution. -: Industrial 3.0 to Industrial 4.0 concerning TATA CSR Activities evolvement. *Eur. Chem. Bull.* 12(Regular Issue 3), 2047 –2058

Székely, Francisco, and Marianna Knirsch. (2005). "Responsible leadership and corporate social responsibility: Metrics for sustainable performance." *European Management Journal* 23, no. 6 : 628–647. https://doi.org/10.1016/j.emj.2005.10.009

Advancement in Engineering and Science – Goyal et al. (Eds)

A Survey of Digital Health Tools Usage by Endocrinologist in Mumbai, India

Sanghamitra Sharma
Assistant Professor, Prin L.N. Welingkar Institute of Management Development and Research

ABSTRACT: The adoption of digital tools has been pivotal in transforming healthcare delivery including diabetes management. This study is aimed to probe the use of digital health tools by endocrinologist in Mumbai and Mumbai Metropolitan Region, focusing on understanding their applications, benefit and barriers. A semi-structured questionnaire administered electronically to 255 endocrinologists, with 250 complete responses were analyzed. The results indicate that 72 % of the participants use digital health tools, with Electronic Health Records (EHRs) being the most popular tools (36%), followed by telehealth platforms (23%), and tools used for diagnosis of diabetes (15%). The primary benefit of using digital health tools is time savings (36%), followed by increased in efficiency (30%), and improved patient retention and cost savings (16%). However, barriers associated with adoption were identified, as the inconvenience associated with transitioning from manual to electronic systems, concerns to data privacy and challenge related to patient technological proficiency. The study highlights the substantial role of digital health tools in enhancing diabetes management and overall healthcare efficiency. Despite the positive trends, addressing the identified barriers is crucial for broader implementation.

Keywords: Digital Health Tools, Endocrinologist, Diabetes, Technology, and Innovation, Clinicians

1 INTRODUCTION

Healthcare system has gone through many changes in the last few years especially during the pandemic and the post pandemic period, technology and innovation is the main driving force. There has been a visible improvement seen in the medical devices, informatics, and there has been faster development of digital health tools. The most important transformation has been the more embracing of these digital health tools by the medical practitioners. These include the EHRs and telemedicine platforms, wearable technology, to name the other end, which are meant to boost patient care, workflow, and overall healthcare results.

During the pandemic there was a substantial increase in the usage of telehealth services (Rogers EM, 2010). Physicians experienced a large rise in EHR use, with patient messages increasing by 157% as compared to pre-pandemic levels (Olsen E, 2023). In addition to this there are a total of 350,000 health and wellness apps available on the Play Store, with a record 90,000 new health apps developed each year (CMS, 2022). Fitness trackers and Smartwatches are kind of wearables monitors that has gained popularity in the last decade for tracking health metrics such as physical activity, heart rate, and sleep patterns etc.

The digital health tools have played a pivotal role in transforming the healthcare delivery and thus improving clinical outcomes. The success of digital health tools can be attributed to are various factors: they provide a personalized and innovative approach to meet the need of each concern stakeholders (varied needs of clinicians, patients, and other healthcare professionals); they are easy to use for both patients and healthcare providers; they frequently outperform traditional in-person clinic visits; and they facilitate ease of implementation.

Digital health technologies are increasingly being utilized in the management of diabetes in the form of continuous glucose monitoring devices, smart insulin pens, telehealth, and smartphone apps (Clements MA, 2024), and they have been effective in managing blood sugar levels and improving the quality of life in diabetic patients. This study examines how an endocrinologist incorporates digital health tools into their daily practice and the reasons behind their use.

2 LITERATURE REVIEW

The use of DHTs has also played a great role in the enhancement of the delivery of health care services especially to the marginalized societies. A review of literature shows that a large number of primary care practitioners have engaged with DHTs and among DHTs telehealth and electronic health records are the most popular tools (Blount *et al.*, 2023). However, they are challenges associated with the extensive adoption of digital health, constraints such as large scale of capital expenditure and connectivity challenges in remote monitoring delays the extensive adoption. (Blount *et al.*, 2023; Marwaha *et al.*, 2022). A positive correlation has been established in proficient application of these tools among the Community health workers (CHWs) who have undergone training, this highlights the critical role of education in combating skepticism related to new age technology and innovation. (Blondino *et al.*, 2024).

Various telehealth platforms have enabled virtual consultations for clinicians, and have successfully bridged the geographical barriers by connecting patients with healthcare providers, particularly in underserved regions (Vij, 2024). This decreasing the need for in-person consultations, reflects improvement in patient outcomes and better healthcare accessibility (Vij, 2024). Wearable sensors and health trackers aid the acquisition of real-time health data, allowing constant observation of patients (Vij, 2024). Such proactive monitoring helps in timely interventions and improved resource allocation, thereby enhancing the overall quality of patient care (Vij, 2024).

Moreover, the incorporation of human resources (HR) analytics within healthcare entities advances the adoption of DHTs by informing strategic staffing and training initiatives (Rawat, 2024). Effective implementation strategies must prioritize the comprehension of user requirements and contextual variables, which are crucial for attaining comprehensive adoption (McCann and Maguire, 2020).

The capacity of DHTs to mitigate health disparities transcends individual clinician engagement; it necessitates a systemic framework that includes policy reform and infrastructural investment. For example, enhancing internet connectivity in rural locales is imperative, as insufficient broadband access persists as a considerable obstacle to the effective utilization of

DOI: 10.1201/9781003798514-80

DHTs among patients (Blount *et al.*, 2023). Moreover, creating an environment of collaborations between healthcare providers and technology companies could result in products which are designed as per the needs of clinicians, thus resulting in improving patient engagement and satisfaction of digital health tools (Marwaha *et al.*, 2022).

The organizations have realized that data integration is a vital tool in the achievement of operational effectiveness, however, they are able to leverage on HR analytics effectively in areas such as training and empowering the clinicians and CHWs in the use of new age technology as DHTs (Rawat, 2024). In order to realize the transformational health care solutions, it is important to take a holistic approach when implementing DHTs in the health care sector. The following are some of the strategies that can help the healthcare systems to improve on their efficiency and adapt to the ever-changing needs of the patients and the caregivers.

3 RESEARCH METHODOLOGY

After the completion of a successful preliminary pilot study, a rigorously pre-tested semi-structured questionnaire via electronic platforms, specifically using Google Forms, to gather the empirical data from participants residing in Mumbai and Mumbai metropolitan area (MMR). The study was explicitly designed to engage endocrinologists who possess an MBBS MD/DM qualification, while excluding practitioners with alternative qualifications such as MBBS, BAMS, or BHMS, thus guaranteeing a focused on the endocrinology discipline.

For the recruitment of participants, a convenience sampling strategy was used, wherein the endocrinologists were approached directly within their clinical practice. The principal objective of this research was to know practitioners' engagement with digital health tools, ensuring no confidential and sensitive information beyond their professional qualifications was requested.

The questionnaire was meticulously designed for a comprehensive assessment of digital health tools utilizations, it consisted of two demographic based questions designed to explore the possible influences of gender and years of professional experience on the adoption of these technologies. In addition to this, three quantitative questions were included to understand the types of digital health tools used by the clinicians on daily basis and their perceived benefits associated with their application. For a deeper understanding about the participants behavior, three qualitative questions focused on understanding their preferred digital health tools as well as the justification for refraining from adoption of any digital health tools.

The inclusion of a concise rationale for the selection of specific digital tools within the questionnaire can enhance clarity and contextual understanding; the selected tools are pertinent to their clinical practice as there have been documented evidenced to improve clinical outcomes, streamline workflows, and enhance patient engagement. Digital health tools such as telehealth platforms and remote monitoring devices have received significant attention due to their effectiveness in the management of chronic conditions, including diabetes, cardiac care and obesity. Furthermore, the questionnaire also underscores the importance of developing such tools in a way that they are easy to use and incorporate into the clinical practice with ease. This is because the clinicians' participation largely depends on how easily the tools can be integrated into their normal work routines and how user-friendly they are. The focus is on the digital health technologies that can improve patients' adherence and therefore enhance the patients' well-being and the working of the organization. The research suggests that digital health tools can reduce human errors and improve adherence to treatment protocols. This methodology is designed to develop a nuanced understanding of digital health tools adoption among endocrinologist in MMR region, also ensuring the selected tools align with best practices and meet the clinicians' requirements.

4 ANALYSIS

A total of 72% (182) of medical practitioners reported the utilization of various digital health tools within their daily clinical practices, whereas 26.7% (68) indicated the absence of any engagement with digital health tools. The administered questionnaire comprised two demographic inquiries aimed at investigating the influence of gender and years of professional experience on the adoption of these tools, alongside three inquiries centered on the types and objectives of digital health tools employed, as well as their perceived advantages. Furthermore, respondents were solicited to delineate their preferred digital tools and elucidate the reasons for abstaining from the use of any digital health tools, thereby offering a thorough perspective on the engagement with digital health tools among endocrinologists. The specifics of clinical experience, categorized by gender, are presented in Table 1.

Table 1. Years of practice of endocrinologists.

Years of Practice	Less than 5 years	5-9	10-15	16-20	21-25	26-30	More than 30 years
Female	0	2	12	5	4	2	1
Male	5	20	57	49	28	11	42

4.1 *Type and the Purpose Digital Health Tools Usage by Endocrinologist*

Clinicians prioritized their preferred domains of digital health tool utilization, indicating that electronic health records (EHRs) for the management of patient data were the most favored, with 36% of endocrinologists acknowledging the use of specific software for this objective. The second most favored alternative was telehealth platforms, such as Practo and Lybrate, which 23% of endocrinologists employ to augment their digital presence and streamline appointment scheduling. Additionally, 15% of endocrinologists reported the usage of digital tools for diabetes diagnosis. This information elucidates the primary modalities through which endocrinologists incorporate digital health tools into their professional practices.

A detailed graph of these options is given in Figure 1.

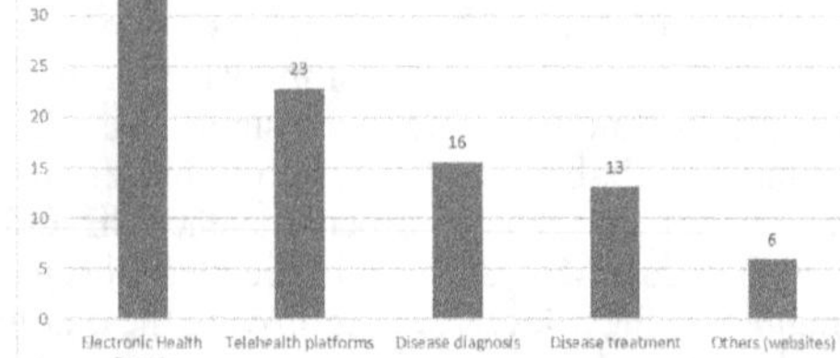

Figure 1. Share of various Types of Digital Health Tools Usage by Endocrinologist

4.2 *Benefits of using the digital health tools*

Endocrinologists evaluated the advantages associated with the adoption of digital health tools, underscoring several principal benefits. The most prominent advantage, acknowledged by 36% of clinicians, is the time-saving potential of digital health tools; the manual documentation of medical records demands substantial manpower and resources, and the implementation of electronic medical records (EMRs) facilitates the optimization of this process. Furthermore, 30% of endocrinologists perceived that the utilization of these tools has enhanced their operational efficiency. Moreover, 16% of endocrinologists contended that digital health tools have been instrumental in achieving cost reductions and improving patient retention. These findings accentuate the multifaceted benefits of incorporating digital health tools into clinical practice.

4.3 *Reason for not utilizing digital health tools*

Based on the findings, there were three major themes as to why endocrinologists are not utilizing digital health tools. The major concern based on the study is the inconvenience that comes with the change of the system from the previous manual system to the electronic system; different healthcare professionals view the change as a challenge and thus, they are not willing to give their time and effort. Also, the issue of data privacy remains a big concern as some of the clinicians raise concerns on the likelihood of the data being hacked, hence, they are unwilling to embrace the use of digital health tools. Finally, the age of the patients may also be a challenge in that some of the elderly patients may not be technologically savvy making it difficult to integrate digital technologies in their care. All these factors therefore serve to enhance the challenges that clinicians face in relation to the uptake of digital health technologies.

5 DISCUSSION

The results of study underline the increasing deployment of digital health technologies among endocrinologists within Mumbai and Mumbai Metropolitan Region (MMR), is indicative of transition of healthcare deliveries that are driven by technological advancements. Electronic health records (EHRs) emerge as the most popular tools, signifying their importance in optimizing patient data. The use of telehealth platforms is also evident from the rates of adoption indicating the need for remote consultations and appointment booking, especially in the current situation where access to healthcare services has been affected by factors such as the COVID-19 pandemic. Furthermore, this trend shift is in line with the change in patient's perception as they now demand more convenient methods of consultation rather than having to wait in long queues at the clinical facilities. The benefits of digital health tools are consistent with the global trends, stressing on the benefits of time through data management and patient's engagement. However, there are still challenges that hinder its adoption for instance, the unwillingness of some organizations to change from the manual system to the electronic systems, and issues that arise because of patients' concerns on the privacy of their information as well as those patients who cannot easily navigate through the use of technology. Initiatives aimed at reducing these obstacles should focus on enhancing user-friendliness, strengthening data protection protocols, and delivering sufficient assistance to populations that are resistant to technology. In summary, the findings illuminate the dynamic evolution of healthcare delivery in India, driven by the incorporation of digital innovations, accompanied by persistent challenges that necessitate further scrutiny and remedial measures.

6 CONCLUSION

The study highlights the integration of digital health instruments among endocrinologists in Mumbai and Mumbai Metropolitan Region (MMR), especially in patient data management, use of telehealth services and enhancing diabetes diagnosis. Although many clinicians highlighted the advantages such as time efficiency, increased productivity, but concerns related to data privacy and varied technological proficiency among different patients' cohorts act as hindrance in broader implementation and in optimizing healthcare outcomes.

The use of digital health tools has the capacity to change the diabetes management and thus the overall health care in India which is the world's diabetes capital. Application of these tools in the day-to-day practice of a clinician may help in reducing the burden on the health care system and increase the availability of quality health care to many more people. Also, it will help in reducing inequalities and come a long way in trying to bridge the difference between the urban and rural areas of India. Despite the issues that are linked to the integration of such tools, the advantages overweigh the disadvantages as they help to improve the quality of patient care, increase the efficiency of the system, and reduce costs. Thus, adhering to technological developments and advancements, the goal of providing equal access to health care across the nation can be achieved.

7 FUTURE RESEARCH AVENUES

This paper has some limitations when it comes to the integration of digital health tools by endocrinologists in their clinical practice which this paper describes. First, the investigation is based on convenience sampling which may lead to the bias of the selection, the sample was only for Mumbai and surrounding area, and it may not be a proper representation of the endocrinologist all over India. The geographical concentration on Mumbai and Mumbai Metropolitan Region makes the results of this study relevant only to this part of the country and not to other parts of the country which may have different health care systems.

Also, the analysis relies on the participants' self-report of the data through a questionnaire, and therefore the data may be contaminated by response bias where the participants may over report or under report their use of digital health tools. The research also does not look into the consequences of using digital health tools on the patient's outcome or the clinicians' workflow with follow up research being needed.

However, the qualitative the components of the questionnaire does not take into consideration the experience of the clinicians, despite the fact that it recognizes the intricacies of the technological usefulness. Also, it fails to take into consideration the various technological needs of the clinicians and the patients that they attend to, especially the vulnerable groups of patients who may face issues with technology adoption. These limitations emphasize the need to conduct more comprehensive research in order to better understand these aspects.

REFERENCES

Blondino, C.T., Knoepflmacher, A., Johnson, I., Fox, C., and Friedman, L. (2024). The use and potential impact of digital health tools at the community level: results from a multi-country survey of community health workers. *BMC Public Health*, *24*(1). https://doi.org/10.1186/s12889-024-18062-3

Blount, M.A., Douglas, M.D., Li, C., Walston, D.T., Nelms, P.L., Hughes, C.L., Gaglioti, A.H., and Mack, D.H. (2023). Opportunities and Challenges to Advance health equity using digital health tools in Underserved Communities in Southeast US: A mixed methods study.

Journal of Primary Care & Community Health, 14. https://doi.org/10.1177/21501319231184789

Clements, M.A., Kaufman, N., and Mel, E. (2024). Using digital health technology to prevent and treat diabetes. *Diabetes Technology & Therapeutics*, 26(S1), S-107. https://doi.org/10.1089/dia.2024.2506

CMS should assess effect of increased telehealth use on beneficiaries' quality of care; 2022. Accessed June 19, 2023. chrome-extension://efaidnbmnnnibpcajpcglclefindmkaj/ https:// www.gao.gov/assets/gao-22-104700-highlights.pdf

Marwaha, J.S., Landman, A.B., Brat, G.A., Dunn, T., and Gordon, W. J. (2022). Deploying digital health tools within large, complex health systems: key considerations for adoption and implementation. *Npj Digital Medicine*, *5*(1). https://doi.org/10.1038/s41746-022-00557-1

McCann, L., Maguire, R. (2020). Implementation of Digital Health Interventions in Practice. In: Charalambous, A. (eds) *Developing and Utilizing Digital Technology in Healthcare for Assessment and Monitoring*. Springer, Cham. https://doi.org/10.1007/978-3-030-60697-8_10

Olsen E. Digital health apps balloon to more than 350,000 available on the market, according to IQVIA report. Mobilehealthnews; 2023. Published August 4, 2021. Accessed June 19, 2023. https://www.mobihealthnews.com/news/digital-health-apps-balloonmore-350000-available-market-according-iqvia-report

Ravi, Vij. (2024). *Revolutionizing Healthcare*. 17-30. doi: 10.1201/9781032694870-2

Rogers EM. *Diffusion of Innovations*. Fourth. The Free Press 2010.

Vandana, Rawat, (2024). Exploring Digital Health Tool Adoption and the Impact of HR Analytics on Decision-making in Jalandhar's Healthcare Organizations. *Indian Scientific Journal of Research in Engineering and Management,* doi: 10.55041/ijsrem33491

Advancement in Engineering and Science – Goyal et al. (Eds)

Consumers Perception of Waste Reduction and Willingness to Pay for Flavoured Edible Packaging

Komal Anil Gupta, Chirag Bharat Shah, and Rakshita Sandeep Shah
Student - PGDM Media and Entertainment, Prin. L. N. Welingkar Institute of Management Development and Research, Mumbai

Archana Ghatule
Professor, Associate Dean- Research and IT, Prin. L. N. Welingkar Institute of Management Development and Research (PGDM), Mumbai

ABSTRACT: This research explores consumer behaviour and preferences regarding food packaging, with a focus on sustainable and edible packaging solutions. The study investigates how demographics (age, gender, profession, location) influence consumer awareness and willingness to adopt eco-friendly packaging practices. It identifies key factors that impact purchasing decisions, such as waste reduction, environmental impact, and convenience. Furthermore, the research examines consumer interest in edible packaging, addressing concerns about its safety, taste, and suitability for various food products. Findings from this study serve as a precursor or market survey to proceed to a Business Proposal for "Edible Food Packaging" and promote sustainable packaging and reducing food packaging waste. The study hypothesizes that environmentally conscious consumers are more likely to choose and pay a premium for sustainable packaging and that the adoption of edible packaging depends on resolving safety and taste concerns.

Keywords: consumer behaviour in packaging, eco-friendly food packaging, edible food packaging, edible packaging innovation, impact of packaging, sustainability, waste reduction strategies

1 INTRODUCTION

In a world where environmental concerns are growing more pressing by the day, the challenge of reducing pollution has become a central focus. From the melting polar ice caps to the degradation of our oceans, the signs of environmental distress are all around us (IPCC, 2021; National Geographic, 2020). Amidst this global push towards sustainability, consumers have started to realize that small changes in daily life can make a significant impact on the planet's health (Smith *et al.*, 2020). Nowadays, waste generation—more especially, food packaging—is bringing this understanding to light (Hahladakis and Iacovidou, 2018).

Although packaging trash has existed for some time, its extent is concerning. Every year, millions of tons of non-biodegradable waste—especially plastics—accumulate in forests, landfills, and the ocean, causing long-term environmental harm (Geyer, Jambeck, and Law, 2017). In addition to damaging the environment, this waste places an unsustainable load on coming generations (Hopewell, Dvorak, and Kosior, 2009). Despite its affordability and ease of use, plastic food packaging has been found to be one of the most enduring sources of pollution (Thompson *et al.*, 2009). Since most packaging materials outlive the items they encase, the issue is exacerbated by the single-use nature of plastic wrappers, bottles, and containers (Selke, 2012).

Customers are starting to concern about their role in garbage as the problem becomes more noticeable. Nowadays, many customers are searching for substitutes that not only lessen their negative effects on the environment but also align with their personal beliefs (Kemp, Insch, Holdsworth, and Knight, 2010). Reducing waste has been seen as a key factor in purchasing decisions. According to research, consumers that care about the environment prefer products that will help them lessen their environmental impact (Magnier *et al.*, 2016). Demand for green packaging options, such as edible and biodegradable packaging, is driven by this heightened awareness of the need to reduce waste (Bocken *et al.*, 2016).

Customers can eat the packaging together with the food thanks to edible packaging, which is made from naturally occurring biodegradable materials like kelp, starch, and even fruit by-products. This eliminates waste (Fuertes *et al.*, 2020). However, innovation isn't limited to utility; flavorful edible packaging is emerging as a fantastic substitute due to its sustainability as well as its sensory appeal (Siro, Kápolna, Kápolna, and Lugasi, 2008). Although there has been interest in this combination of waste reduction and improved user experience, it is yet unknown whether or not consumers will be prepared to pay for such products.

According to research, buyers are prepared to pay more for goods that support environmental sustainability, particularly if they believe the product will improve their experience or offer additional health benefits (Verghese *et al.*, 2012). Studies have shown that flavored edible packaging increases customer willingness by leveraging not just the potential to reduce waste but also the novelty and perceived improved quality from environmentally concerned consumers (Wu *et al.*, 2021). However, this willingness to pay is complicated since it depends on a number of factors, such as personal preferences, price sensitivity, and individual variances in environmental awareness (Yildirim *et al.*, 2018).

This study examines the relationship between consumer behavior and waste reduction, paying particular attention to customers' propensity to accept flavor-infused edible packaging. Through an analysis of consumers' perceptions of this innovative solution, their motivations, and their price sensitivity, this study aims to contribute to the larger discussion on sustainable practices in food packaging and the evolving nature of consumer willingness to invest in eco-friendly solutions (Joung, 2015; Magnier *et al.*, 2016). In their attempts to strike a balance between innovation and customer expectations in the quest for a more sustainable future, manufacturers and policymakers alike should be aware of these observations (Bocken *et al.*, 2016).

DOI: 10.1201/9781003798514-81

2 LITERATURE SURVEY

Guillard *et al.* (2008) and Puscaselu *et al.* (2019) both addressed the problems associated with food packaging and suggested biodegradable polymers as a workable way to advance a circular bioeconomy. According to Guillard *et al.*, biodegradable polymers made from agro-food waste have the potential to minimize plastic pollution and food waste while preserving product quality. They stress the use of mathematical models to accurately forecast food-packaging interactions, which is necessary for efficient design. Similarly, despite its well-known tendency to generate trash, Puscaselu *et al.* stress the importance of packing in maintaining material quality and cleanliness. They advertise edible biopolymer-based packaging made of glycerol, sodium alginate, agar, and inulin, whose samples shown notable improvements in mechanical and physical characteristics for up to three months, as a sustainable, waste-free packaging option.

Janjarasskul *et al.* (2010) and Kadzińska *et al.* (2019) investigated the current utilization of biopolymer-based materials for food packaging. Janjarasskul *et al.* discuss the potential for commercial manufacturing of edible films made from food industry wastes using a dry thermoplastic technique. They highlight the increased interest in edible packaging as a way to save waste and improve consumer convenience, but they also touch on consumer acceptance and regulatory compliance. Kadzińska *et al.* talk about edible materials that are made from fruits and vegetables that contain proteins, polysaccharides, and bioactive substances that have antibacterial and antioxidative qualities. In order to improve food quality and lessen reliance on synthetic polymers, it develops sustainable packaging solutions using low-value raw materials.

Iyer *et al.* (2019) and Kumar *et al.* (2023), address the single-use plastics are used in food packaging. Iyer *et al.* examine the possibilities for packaging free goods in unorganized retailing, paying particular attention to the negative effects that non-compliant plastics have on the environment and human health. In order to lower pollution and enhance food safety, they so call for sustainable packaging options in the unorganized food retail industry. The protective role of edible packaging against physical, mechanical, chemical, and microbial degradation is highlighted by Kumar *et al.* They go over the advantages of including active ingredients like plant extracts, essential oils, cross-linkers, and nanomaterials to improve the overall quality and characteristics of food packaging.

Shaikh *et al.* (2021), Petkoska *et al.* (2021), and Phinainitisatra *et al.* (2020) talk about the production and application of biopolymer and starch-based packaging. Phinainitisatra *et al.* studied starch-based peelable coating films and explained how modified starches affect oxygen and moisture barriers. While rice starch improves film integrity through increased crystallinity, hydroxypropyl cassava starch absorbs water and causes instability. In their comparison of biopolymers and conventional plastics, Shaikh *et al.* examined the former's superior physical, mechanical, thermal, and barrier qualities as well as its potential in a variety of packaging styles. Nanotechnology-based sustainable packaging methods were discussed by Petkoska *et al.*, who integrated advantageous substances into edible packaging to increase shelf life and usefulness.

Kaur *et al.* 2022 and Petkoska *et al.* 2021 also emphasize on edible packaging as a means of maintaining food quality and shelf life. With an emphasis on developing edible packaging water-resistant, oxygen- and moisture-impermeable as an adaptable sustainable substitute for traditional material, Kaur *et al.* draw attention to consumer preferences for natural products and the potential for biopolymer films to replace synthetic plastics. Petkoska *et al.* go into additional detail about the useful compounds that can be added to edible packaging through nanotechnology in order to improve package functionality and support the cause of sustainability.

3 RESEARCH GAP

The functionality of edible packaging is the primary focus of the research that is currently available, but little is known about demographics and how they affect the adoption of sustainable edible packaging. The effects of sustainable edible packaging on customer behavior and attitudes toward waste reduction have received even less attention. Even less is known about how consumers' preferences for edible packaging are influenced by flavor. By examining consumer preferences for sustainable and flavored edible packaging, this study aims to close knowledge and practice gaps and give manufacturers useful information for creating creative, environmentally friendly products that complement waste reduction initiatives and are consistent with consumer values.

4 PROBLEM STATEMENT

Plastic food packaging harms the environment. This research explores how people's backgrounds and environmental awareness affect their choice of sustainable packaging, with a focus on edible packaging. The goal is to understand what people want from edible packaging (safety, taste, etc.) and how much they would pay for it. This will help businesses create better sustainable packaging solutions.

4.1 *The objective is:*

1. To understand how demographics (age, gender, profession, location) influence consumer awareness about food packaging waste and their willingness to adopt sustainable practices.
2. To identify the factors that consumers consider most important when making purchasing decisions related to food packaging (e.g., minimizing waste, environmental impact, convenience, and taste).
3. To determine consumer interest in purchasing food products with edible packaging/sustainable packaging solutions and their willingness to pay a premium for such options.
4. To understand consumer awareness of edible packaging, their perception and readiness to use it, including concerns about safety, taste, and suitability for various food products.

5 HYPOTHESIS

1. H_{01}: Gender of the consumer does not affect adoption of sustainable edible packaging practices.
2. H_{02}: Age of the consumer does not affect adoption of sustainable edible packaging practices.
3. H_{03}: Profession of the consumer does not affect adoption of sustainable edible packaging practices.
4. H_{04} Eco-conscious consumers are not actively seeking out food products with minimal or sustainable packaging whenever possible.
5. H_{05}: Eco-conscious consumers are not willing to pay a premium for sustainable edible packaging.
6. H_{06}: Consumer adoption of edible packaging does not depend on concerns about its safety, taste, and suitability for different types of food products.

6 RESEARCH DESIGN

In this quantitative research study, a structured online survey was administered using Google Forms. A total of 102 consumers participated in the survey, selected through convenience sampling. Efforts were made to include participants from diverse demographic backgrounds, encompassing age, gender, profession, and geographic location, to ensure a broad range of consumer perspectives. The target population included consumers from various demographic segments to capture diverse viewpoints.

7 DATA COLLECTION INSTRUMENT

Data was collected through a structured questionnaire which contained the questions for Demographic Information like Age, gender, profession, location, Awareness and Perceptions which included Consumer knowledge and attitudes towards waste reduction and sustainable packaging. Questionnaire also contains questions to seek information about Preferences and Behaviour which concentrated on Preferences for packaging materials, concerns about environmental impact, willingness to pay for sustainable options, etc. Another Section that was included in questionnaire was Edible Packaging Perception about Awareness, safety concerns, perceived benefits, and drawbacks of edible packaging.

Questionnaire was distributed via email, social media platforms, and academic networks to reach a diverse respondent pool for almost 15 days. Respondents were informed about the study's purpose and gave their consent prior to completing the survey.

8 DATA ANALYSIS AND INTERPRETATION

Although there is a slight plurality of males (54%), the study claims a balanced gender distribution, with 46% of respondents being female. Sixty percent of participants are between the ages of 19 and 24, which suggests that young adults are well represented. The majority of responders were from cities (44%), and the metro (47%). At 9%, semi-urban areas are likewise underrepresented. Students comprised the largest professional group (51%), followed by employees (15%) and business owners/ entrepreneurs (6%), indicating a diverse sample with significant youth and urban representation in exploring consumer perceptions of sustainable packaging.

9 RESULTS AND DISCUSSION

All of the hypotheses are examined using the chi-square test, which is performed out at the 0.10 level of significance to see whether a significant relationship between the variables under study exists. Microsoft Excel, which has the necessary tools and functions to compute and evaluate chi-square statistics, is used to compute the tests. We can accept or reject our hypotheses with a certain degree of confidence based on the results of these tests.

There is no apparent relationship between different demographic characteristics and consumer behavior, according to the findings of the study on the adoption of sustainable edible packaging practices. In particular, the coefficient of determination for the association between gender and the adoption of sustainable edible packaging techniques was 0.40, exceeding the significance level of 0.10. As a result, our null hypothesis (H01) is not rejected. This suggests that the adoption of sustainable food packaging strategies is unaffected by gender.

Table 1. Relationship between demographics and adoption of sustainable edible packaging practices.

			Adoption of Sustainable Edible Packaging Practices					
			No (n=14)		Yes(n=88)			
H#	IV	Subject	Observed Frequency	Expected Frequency	Observed Frequency	Expected Frequency	P-Value	
H_{01}	Gender	Male	5	6.45	42	40.55	0.4	Accept
		Female	9	7.55	46	47.45		
$\mathbf{H_{02}}$	Age	Oct-18	0	0.55	4	3.45	0.9	Accept
		19-24	1	8.37	51	52.63		
		25-34	2	1.37	8	8.63		
		35-44	0	1.78	13	11.22		
		44+	2	1.92	12	12.08		
$\mathbf{H_{03}}$	Profession	Architect	1	0.14	0	0.86	0.4	Accept
		Business Owner/ Entrepreneur	0	0.82	6	5.18		
		Employee	4	2.06	11	12.94		
		Fashion design	0	0.14	1	0.86		
		Financial Analyst	0	0.27	2	1.73		
		Homemaker	0	0.82	6	5.18		
		Human Resources Professional	0	0.14	1	0.86		
		Manager/Administrator	0	0.69	5	4.31		
		Marketing Professional	1	0.55	3	3.45		
		Medical Professional	0	0.27	2	1.73		
		Retired	0	0.14	1	0.86		
		Sales	0	0.14	1	0.86		
		Student	8	7.14	44	44.86		
		Teacher/Educator	0	0.69	5	4.31		

Source: Author's calculation citation

The null hypothesis (H02) was accepted since the p-value for age was 0.90, which was higher than the cutoff of 0.10. This finding suggests that the adoption of sustainable edible packaging strategies is not influenced by age. Last but not least, the p-value for profession was once more 0.40, signifying that we are unable to reject the null hypothesis (H03) and that profession has no bearing whatsoever on the adoption of sustainable edible packaging procedures. All things considered, these results collectively disprove the alternative theories about the effects of age, gender, and occupation on consumer adoption of sustainable edible packaging techniques.

Table 2. Relationship between Eco conscience and non eco conscious consumer seeking sustainable packaging solutions

	DV	Actively seek out food products with minimal or sustainable packaging whenever possible					
		No (n=22)		Yes (n=80)			
H#	SUBJECTS	Observed Frequency	Expected Frequency	Observed Frequency	Expected Frequency	p-Value	
H_{04}	Eco-conscious	4	7.64	35	33.36	0.08	Reject
	Not Eco-conscious	15	11.36	48	49.64		

Source: Author's calculation citation

The results of consumers' willingness to pay more for sustainable edible packaging are fascinating. With a p-value of 0.08, we fall short of the 0.10 significance level. As a result, we reject the null hypothesis (H04). This indicates that there is a strong association between eco-conscious consumer behaviour and their willingness to seek out food products with minimal or sustainable packaging. Consequently, we accept the alternative hypothesis (H4), suggesting that eco-conscious consumers are indeed motivated to actively pursue food products that feature sustainable packaging options whenever possible. This insight underscores the growing trend of environmentally aware consumers prioritizing sustainability in their purchasing decisions.

Table 3. Relationship between Eco conscience and non eco conscious consumer and their willingness to pay a premium for sustainable edible packaging

	DV	Willingness to pay a premium for sustainable edible packaging					
		No (n=22)		Yes (n=80)			
H#	SUBJECTS	Observed Frequency	Expected Frequency	Observed Frequency	Expected Frequency	p-Value	
H_{05}	Eco-conscious	10	8.84	31	32.16	0.57	Accept
	Not Eco-conscious	12	13.16	49	47.84		

Source: Author's calculation citation

The analysis concerning the willingness to pay a premium for sustainable edible packaging indicates that there is no significant evidence to support the notion that eco-conscious consumers are willing to pay extra for such products. With a p-value of 0.57, which exceeds the significance threshold of 0.10, we accept the null hypothesis (H05). This finding leads us to conclude that eco-conscious consumers do not exhibit a willingness to pay a premium for sustainable edible packaging. Consequently, we reject the alternative hypothesis (H5), suggesting that the expectation that eco-conscious consumers are inclined to pay more for sustainable packaging is not supported by the data.

Table 4. Relationship between consumers concern and their dependence on adoption of sustainable edible package practices

	DV	DEPENDENCE OF ADOPTION OF SUSTAINABLE EDIBLE PACKAGING PRACTICES					
		No (n=34)		Yes (n=68)			
H#	Subjects	Observed Frequency	Expected Frequency	Observed Frequency	Expected Frequency	p-Value	
H_{06}	Concerned	13	13.04	82	81.96	0.96	Accept
	Not concerned	1	0.96	7	6.04		

Source: Author's calculation citation

The analysis regarding the dependence of consumer adoption of edible packaging on concerns such as safety, taste, and suitability reveals no significant relationship. With a p-value of 0.96, which is greater than the significance level of 0.05, we accept the null hypothesis (H06). This suggests that consumer adoption of edible packaging is not influenced by concerns about its safety, taste, and suitability for various types of food products. As a result, we reject the alternative hypothesis (H6), indicating that these concerns do not significantly impact adoption behavior. However, this finding may need more investigation since our small sample size could have affected our ability to capture more detailed consumer opinions.

10 SURVEY PURPOSE AND METHODOLOGY

The survey aimed to understand consumer perceptions of waste reduction and their willingness to pay for flavoured edible packaging. We gathered 102 responses using multiple-choice, open-ended, checkbox, and radio button questions to capture a comprehensive view of consumer attitudes and preferences.

10.1 *Assessing levels of Consumers perception of waste reduction and willingness to pay for flavoured edible packaging.*

The descriptive results have a range of consumer perspectives and behaviours related to food packaging waste and sustainability. A major challenge in reducing packaging waste, identified by 34% of respondents, is a lack of consumer awareness, alongside limited access to sustainable packaging and recycling difficulties. Plastic packaging (40%) is the most frequently encountered, followed by paper (28%).

While 66% of respondents have not participated in campaigns to reduce food packaging waste, 65% often consider the type of packaging when making purchasing decisions. The environmental impact of packaging waste is a significant concern for 47%, with 80% prioritizing waste-minimizing packaging in their choices. Packaging is seen as crucial for reducing food waste, with 94% acknowledging its role in this area.

Sustainable packaging is a priority, as 68% of respondents either "always prioritize" or "often look for" eco-friendly options when shopping. Most participants (81.4%) expressed concerns about the safety of edible packaging, and 46% were unfamiliar with the concept. However, 50% of those aware of edible packaging view it positively for its waste reduction and biodegradability, despite some safety concerns. Moreover, 86.3% of respondents are more likely to purchase products with clearly labelled, edible packaging.

Reusable packaging is the most favoured solution for reducing waste, with 40% of respondents supporting it. Additionally, 78% are willing to pay more for eco-friendly packaging, with 52.9% willing to pay 0-5% more for edible packaging. Clear information about the safety and composition of edible packaging is the most important factor, followed by nutritional content. While functionality like freshness and safety is prioritized, 52% of respondents believe taste is also important for edible packaging. Snacks are considered the most appropriate product category for edible packaging, followed by bakery items and utensils, while fresh produce is viewed as less suitable.

11 CONTEXT AND OVERALL INTERPRETATION

Consumers are committed to reducing packaging waste but face challenges like limited awareness and availability of sustainable options. Plastic and paper are the most common packaging materials, affecting perceptions of environmental impact. Interest in eco-friendly choices is high, but engagement in waste reduction campaigns is moderate. Safety concerns about edible packaging are significant, despite its environmental benefits. Preferences lean towards reusable packaging, especially for snacks, with many willing to pay more for waste-minimizing products. Clear and informative labelling on edible packaging is crucial for consumer trust, considering taste and safety. Overall, there's a strong inclination towards sustainable packaging, provided safety and transparency issues are addressed.

12 RECOMMENDATIONS

The need to raise consumer knowledge through relevant educational efforts about the benefits and safety of sustainable packaging options, particularly edible ones, would make such research profitable. customer fear should be reduced by improved product labeling regarding safety concerns and full composition, which will increase customer acceptance and loyalty to sustainable options. Additional improvements of the variety of reusable packs can also focus on a broader range of products, such as snacks, that satisfy customer demands and support sustainable use. In order to stay up to date, it should also continue conducting market research on consumer sentiments and collaborate with advocates of sustainability to increase the credibility of educational initiatives. By adopting sustainable packaging and building systems to ask customers for their comments, businesses will be able to improve their business and branding and update their products based on real-time input. Such continuous customer engagement is essential because it enables businesses to respond to changing market conditions, improve their sustainability, and strengthen their brand image.

13 CONCLUSION

According to the primary research, consumers are extremely concerned about packaging waste and prefer to make alternative products. Lack of consumer knowledge and a lack of such sustainable products are the two main challenges. However, despite safety concerns, there is a lot of interest in creative solutions like edible packaging. For consumers to make informed decisions, transparency and unambiguous labeling are essential. Flavored edible packaging is an example of how innovations that reduce waste are becoming more and more accepted. This study emphasizes how important consumer involvement and education are in promoting eco-friendly behaviors. Stakeholders can use the insights to accomplish sustainable development objectives and create an environmentally friendly, consumer-oriented sustainable economy.

14 FUTURE RESEARCH

The optimistic response and willingness of consumers to pay a premium for sustainable edible packaging highlight a significant business opportunity. This research idea originated from our observation of the immense waste produced from street food and our pondering of the possibility of edible packaging, similar to ice cream cones, that can be consumed alongside the food. As consumer attitudes increasingly favour environmentally friendly solutions, there is promising potential for manufacturing sustainable edible packaging on a larger scale, leading to the development of a new market segment focused on innovative, eco-friendly options that cater to the growing demand for sustainable products. Further research into flavour preferences and safety standards can enhance the appeal and acceptance of edible packaging, driving broader adoption. Businesses investing in this area can not only contribute to waste reduction but also capitalize on sustainability, gaining a competitive advantage in the marketplace. However, the research findings are subject to several limitations. Firstly, the sample predominantly represents younger adults, potentially skewing perspectives and limiting generalizability across broader age demographics. Additionally, responses may vary regionally, impacting the applicability of findings to global markets. Self-reported data introduces biases such as social desirability and recall errors, influencing the accuracy of consumer perceptions and behaviours reported. The study's scope primarily focuses on consumer perceptions within a specific context, which may not fully capture diverse global perspectives or market behaviours. Persistent safety concerns regarding edible packaging pose a significant challenge to widespread adoption, requiring further research and development efforts to address consumer hesitations and ensure product safety standards are effectively met. Given that the sample size was limited, future research can be conducted to gain deeper insights into consumer perceptions and the willingness to pay for flavoured edible packaging. This idea has the potential to evolve into a strong business model focused on environmental protection while offering a unique product in the form of edible packaging.

REFERENCES

Anka Trajkovska Petkoska, D.D. (2021). Edible packaging: Sustainable solutions and novel trends in food packaging. *Food Research International.*

Bocken, N.M.P., de Pauw, I., Bakker, C., and van der Grinten, B. (2016). Product design and business model strategies for a circular economy. *Journal of Industrial and Production Engineering*, 33(5), 308–320.

Fuertes, G., Soto, I., Carrasco, R., Vargas, M., Sabattin, J., and Lagos, C. (2020). Intelligent packaging systems: sensors and nano sensors to monitor food quality and safety. *Journal of Sensors*, 2020.

Geyer, R., Jambeck, J.R., and Law, K.L. (2017). Production, use, and fate of all plastics ever made. *Science Advances*, 3(7), e1700782.

Hahladakis, J.N., and Iacovidou, E. (2018). Closing the loop on plastic packaging materials: What is quality and how does it affect their circularity? Science of the Total Environment, 630, 1394–1400.

Hopewell, J., Dvorak, R., & and Kosior, E. (2009). Plastics recycling: challenges and opportunities. *Philosophical Transactions of the Royal Society B: Biological Sciences*, 364(1526), 2115–2126.

Jaspreet Kaur, M.G. (2022). *Edible Packaging: An Overview.*

Joung, H.M. (2015). Fast-fashion consumers' post-purchase behaviours. *International Journal of Retail and Distribution Management.*

Justyna Kadzińska, M.J. (2019). An overview of fruit and vegetable edible packaging materials.

Kemp, E., Insch, A., Holdsworth, D.K., and Knight, J.G. (2010). Food miles: Consumer concerns and sustainability. *International Journal of Consumer Studies*, 34(6), 656–665.

Magnier, L., Schoormans, J., and Mugge, R. (2016). Judging a product by its cover: Packaging sustainability and perceptions of quality in food products. *Food Quality and Preference*, 53, 132–142.

Nishant Kumar, P.J. (2023). Recent Trends in Edible Packaging for Food Applications — *Perspective for the Future.*

Roxana Puscaselu, G.G. (2019). *Rethinking the Future of Food Packaging: Biobased Edible Films for Powdered Food and Drinks.*

Salman Shaikh, M.Y. (2021). An overview of biodegradable packaging in food industry.

Selke, S.E.M. (2012). *Plastics packaging: properties, processing, applications, and regulations.* Hanser Publications.

Shiva Shankar Iyer, L.S. (2019). Sustainable packaging alternatives for the unorganized food retail in India.

Siro, I., Kápolna, E., Kápolna, B., and Lugasi, A. (2008). Functional food. Product development, marketing and consumer acceptance—A review. *Appetite*, 51(3), 456–467.

Smith, M., Love, D.C., Rochman, C.M., and Neff, R.A. (2020). Microplastics in seafood and the implications for human health. *Current Environmental Health Reports*, 7(4), 375–386.

Theeranun Janjarasskull, J.M. (2010). *Edible Packaging Materials.*

Thitarat Phinainitisatra, N.H. (2020). Development of starch-based peelable coating for edible packaging.

Thompson, R.C., Moore, C.J., vom Saal, F.S., and Swan, S.H. (2009). Plastics, the environment and human health: Current consensus and future trends. *Philosophical Transactions of the Royal Society B: Biological Sciences,* 364(1526), 2153–2166.

Valérie Guillard, S.G. (2008). The Next Generation of Sustainable Food Packaging to Preserve Our Environment in a Circular Economy Context.

Verghese, K., Lewis, H., Lockrey, S., and Williams, H. (2012). Packaging's role in minimizing food waste. *Journal of Cleaner Production*, 24, 186–196.

Wu, Y., Lin, C., and Chen, Y. (2021). Consumer's perception of sustainable packaging and willingness to pay for inno B., vations. *Journal of Cleaner Production*, 317, 128477.

Yildirim, S., Röcker, Kışla, D., and Bayındırlı, A. (2018). Innovative packaging systems for food applications. *Journal of Food Science and Technology,* 55(5), 1385–1396.

Advancement in Engineering and Science – Goyal et al. (Eds)

Digital Literacy among Research Scholars and Students of Telangana State

Sayyad Saadiq Ali and Renuka Abburu
Department of MBA, CMR College of Engineering & Technology, Kandlakoya, Medchal, Hyderabad, Telangana State

Vunnava Sandhya
St. Mary's Group of Institutions Guntur for Women, Chebrole, Guntur District

V. Satyanarayana
St. Mary's Women's Engineering College, Budampadu, Guntur District, Andhra Pradesh

G Swathi
School of Management & Commerce, Malla Reddy University, Hyderabad

ABSTRACT: Digital Literacy is the procedure of teaching and getting identification about technology and utilization. It's the capability to apply records and verbal exchange expertise to find, examine, construct, commune records, requiring every cognitive & technological ability. In student life digital literacy plays a crucial role in enhancing skills in technological aspects of students and research scholars. The perfection of the educational qualification of college students and research scholars with their virtual competence is indispensable for convalescing the effectiveness and efficiency of the studying method and for the model of college students and research scholars to the dynamic work environment. The current paper includes an empirical aspect to study and analyze the dimensions and comportment to use ICT by using college students as well as research scholars inside the studying system, to set up their motivation to enhance digital literacy abilities. This would enhance their academic performance and prepare them for the ever-changing needs of work and lifestyles.

Keywords: Academic Results, Digital Literacy, ICT, Society, Library, Virtual competence

1 INTRODUCTION

The enlargement of information & communication technology and their integration in all specialities of people's verve and occupation gave the primary time an opportunity for a rapid and limitless entry to sizeable statistics that are constantly enriched, transformed and actualized. Innovative model of the world needs a populace who own the essential talents and competencies to take benefit of the capability of recent technology and take lively component within the pecuniary, social and enlightening lifestyles.

There was an upsurge of information in the area of education with the emergence of globalization. The prevailing decennary has been doubled because of big data. The net increase has turned out to be one of the essential participants in the financial boom of India. In the past seven years, the usage of the internet has multiplied greater than eleven times. Subsequently, it has led to the increase of cybercafes and web browsing parlours at some stage in India having clean accessibility as well as price-effective offerings.

The library and information overflow have been renovated due to virtual technology and these days' conventional libraries have also modified their functional area as "understanding centres" prioritizing mostly cost-introduced online information offerings. Digital literacy is the attention, attitude and ability of people to accurately use digital equipment and facilities to become aware of get entry to, control, integrate, examine the digital assets and create media.

Literacy consists of the capability to study and interpret media, to breed data and pictures through digital manipulation, and to assess and practice new knowledge received from virtual environments. A person's capability to carry out obligations effectively in a digital surroundings digitally literate people find that means in and make use of virtual information, they exhibit the traits of cultural and social understanding, collaboration, the ability to find and select records, powerful conversation, E-safety, purposeful competencies, creativity, and essential wondering.

1.1 *Traits of digital literacy*

1. Cognizance of" human beings' network" as resources of recommendation and help.
2. Expertise assembly" reliable facts hoard" from numerous causes.
3. Reclamation talents, plus" vital wondering" for making mindful acumen approximately retrieved statistics, with wariness about the validity and completeness of internet sources.
4. Studying and expertise Non-Sequential and Dynamic fabric.
5. Using Filters and retailers to manipulate Incoming facts.
6. Records literacy as the dimension that contains all of the one-of-a-kind forms of literacy; digital literacy while presenting online, analyzing and understanding skills.

1.2 *Digital literacy in telangana*

Digital Telangana program launched inside the state from 1st July, 2014.

1.2.1 *Digital india targets*

1. Permitting virtual empowerment of residents
2. Smooth the progress of digital infrastructure as a application nation to inhabitant
3. Presenting governance & offerings on stipulate.

Digital India may be commence through a week-lengthy software starting July 1st, 2014, underneath the headship of Minister Mr Kalvakuntla Taraka Rama Rao, the ITE&C

department has concurrently deliberate in favour of a totally ruthless digital Telangana program.

1. During reality a few of the desires below virtual Telangana some distance surpass digital India's dreams. Digital Telangana stand up on revolve.
2. At the deliver side, the principle purpose is to ensure that virtual centres turn out to be to be had to each and anybody within territory.
3. Supplying 4th Generation offerings inside the whole kingdom.
4. Wi-Fi in foremost towns and cities.
5. e-Panchayat scheme beneath which a One forestall save stand may be alive to be had in every Panchayat in addition, at the call for facet, the goal is to make every and everybody digitally make powerful so to facilitate he will craft best exercise of the digital centres that are being made available proper at his entrance way.

1.2.2 *Techniques for implementation*

1. Digital literacy software, beneath which one associate of all household might be educated to be converted into digitally knowledgeable.
2. College PC literacy program: To educate each adolescent from class 6 onwards the fundamentals of computers.
3. Expansion of Mee-Seva services

2 REVIEW OF LITERATURE

Academic performance now heavily depends on digital literacy, especially for students and research scientists. Numerous research have examined different facets of digital literacy, its effects, and the difficulties the academic community faces in Telangana State.

The relationship between Telangana State's digital economy and financial literacy was examined by Ananthoju and Katla (2024). According to their research, a lack of digital literacy makes it more difficult for people to engage in the digital economy, which suggests that developing digital skills is essential for economic empowerment [1].

An overview of the field of study on digital proficiency in learning and education was given by Audrin and Audrin (2022) in another comprehensive literature review. The study found important characteristics of the literature that might guide tactics to raise students' and researchers' levels of digital literacy [2].

A study on digital literacy abilities and competences among postgraduate students and research scholars at Bangalore's deemed university libraries was carried out by Biradar and Naik in 2023. In order for students to efficiently explore, utilize, and cooperatively create digital library resources, the study underlined the need of digital literacy. According to the results, improving digital literacy has a major positive impact on students' capacity for research and academic accomplishment [3].

The use of digital library resources at Telangana University libraries was examined by Muthyalaiah and Kumar (2023). They discovered that although there are many digital resources available, students and research researchers really use them sparingly since they are not well-informed and trained. To increase the efficient use of these resources, the report suggests putting in place thorough digital literacy programs [4]. Panuganti and Pasricha (2023) looked on the digital divide among Telangana secondary school teachers. According to their research, instructors in urban and rural areas have considerably different access to digital resources, which has an immediate effect on students' digital literacy. They underlined the necessity of focused strategies to close this gap and improve students' and teachers' digital literacy [5].

In Pochampally village, Telangana, Poornachandrika and Raj (2024) studied the empowerment and digital literacy of weavers and craftspeople. This study sheds light on the state's larger digital literacy landscape, while not being specifically student-focused. According to the findings, socioeconomic situations may be considerably improved by more digital literacy, which can be inferred to assist students and academics as well [6].

RV. Pratap and Singh's (2018) study looked at the digital literacy of research researchers and students at Banaras Hindu University in Varanasi. They came to the conclusion that a sizable portion of students and academics are proficient in digital literacy, which allows them to use and use digital technologies efficiently. This result emphasizes how crucial digital literacy is for improving research skills and academic achievement [7].

A research on information literacy initiatives in Telangana's higher education institutions' libraries was carried out by Pagidikathula and Kumar (2023). They underlined that in order for pupils to become self-sufficient lifelong learners, information literacy is essential. The study made clear how important it is to incorporate information literacy into college curricula in order to provide students a solid educational foundation [8].

Tinmaz *et al.*'s systematic study from 2022 sought to offer a first step and set of guidelines for creating a modern framework for digital literacy. The study found key themes and elements in digital literacy, providing information that may help Telangana students and research academics become more digitally literate [9].

2.1 *Objectives of the study*

1. To understand the magnitude of statistics conversation technology in information centres and libraries in the digital era.
2. To observe the digital literacy among pupils, students and research scholars network.
3. To be acquainted with the knowledge of research scholars and students on virtual information possessions.
4. To recognize the user's information on the use of the smart-telephones, tabs, and table pinnacle computer systems and laptops.
5. To understand the motive of journeying the library.
6. To discover the troubles faced by using the research scholars and student community even as surfing the virtual information resources.

2.2 *Hypotheses*

H1: Scholars and college students have recognized the importance of digital literacy and virtual information.

H2: Digital resources play a crucial role in enhancing the learning experience and research quality for students and researchers.

H3: Respondents have demonstrated familiarity with ICT tools such as smartphones, laptops, tablets, and computers.

H4: Digital information resources are highly valuable for the academic and research community, supporting both learning and scholarly investigations.

3 METHODOLOGY

The current study depended on survey technique, for that prepared questionnaire and distributed to 100 respondents of students as well as scholars in Telangana state, for statistical analysis used simple percentage technique.

Table 1. Knowledge about digital literacy.

Status of the Respondents	Yes (%)	No (%)
Research Scholars	30 (30.00%)	-
PG Students	50 (50.00%)	-
UG Students	20 (20.00%)	-
Sum	**100 (100%)**	-

Source: Compiled data

Table 2. Acquaintance on using PCs/Laptops/Smart Phones/Tablets.

ICT Equipment	Research Scholars (%)	Students Community (%)
Tablets / Smart Phones	30 (30.00%)	05 (05.00%)
Desktops/Tabs	25 (25.00%)	02 (02.00%)
Laptops	35 (35.00%)	03 (08.00%)
Total	**90 (90.00%)**	**10 (15.00%)**

Source: Compiled data

4 DATA ANALYSIS AND INTERPRETATIONS

4.1 *Knowledge about digital literacy*

Table 1 reveals that majority 50% of PG students having knowledge about digital information literacy also 30% of research scholars and 20% of UG students having knowledge regarding to digital literacy.

4.2 *Acquaintance on using ICT equipment*

Table 2 discloses that, a majority 38% respondents having the laptops followed by 35% of respondents having their smart phones and tablets and remaining 27% of respondents having the knowledge about using of Desktops and Tablets. It is evidence for that preponderance of respondents had Laptops it is an evidence for utilization of digital literacy in effective manner.

Table 3. Possess PCs/Laptops/Smart Phones/Tablets.

ICT Equipment	Research Scholars (%)	Students Community (%)
Tablets / Smart Phones	25 (30.00%)	10 (10.00%)
Desktops/Tabs	20 (25.00%)	02 (02.00%)
Laptops	35 (35.00%)	08 (08.00%)
Sum	**80 (80.00%)**	**20 (20.00%)**

Source: Compiled data

4.3 *Possession of ICT equipment*

The data presented in Table 3 shows that a majority 43% respondents possess laptops, 35% of respondents possess smart phones or Tablets and residual 22% of respondents had desktops or tablets. As per the analysis reveals that majority of respondents having their own ICT equipment for enhance those digital skills.

Table 4. Library visiting.

Library Visiting	Number of Respondents	Percentage (%)
Every Day	46	46
Weekly once	22	22
Fortnightly	15	15
Monthly once	17	17
Sum	**100**	**100**

Source: Compiled data

Table 5. Function of visit library.

Purpose of Browsing	Number of Respondents	Percentage (%)
Borrow the electronic books	73	73
Reading of E Journals	65	65
Search for E Material	88	88
E News Papers reading	56	56
Online application fulfillment	90	90
Social Sites /Chatting / E-mails	60	60
Course Material Download	84	84
Downloading / Viewing Movies	74	74
Web sites checking	89	89
Seeing for advertisement	76	76

Source: Compiled data

4.4 *Library visiting patterns*

Table 4 shows that, majority 46% respondents are visit library every day, 22% of visit the library once in a weekly once, 17% were visit library monthly once and 15% of respondent's fortnight visits the library.

4.5 *Purpose of library visits*

Table 5 shows that a majority (90%) of the respondents arriving at the library to fill out the online applications, 89% of respondents utilize for visiting web sites, 88% of respondents using for E-reference materials, 84% of respondents are utilize the digital library for downloading the course material, 76% of respondents using for looking various advertisements, 74% are visiting for download movies, 73% of respondents using library for borrowing the e-books, 65% of respondents use to read the e-journals, 60% of respondents are using for e-mail checking, chatting and looking for social media websites and remaining 56% respondents visiting library for reading e-news papers. All the respondents are visiting digital library for various digital purposes in positively.

4.6 *Internet awareness*

Table 6 reveals that, 51% non-professionals much aware about internet and 49% of professionals using internet.

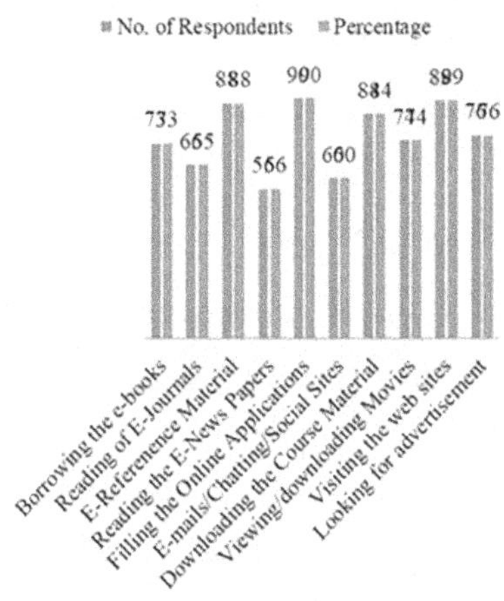

Figure 1. Purpose of visiting library.

Table 6. Awareness on internet.

Respondents Status	No of Respondents	Percentage (%)
Professionals	49	49
Non-Professionals	51	51
Sum	**100**	**100**

Source: Compiled data

Table 7. Admittance of digital resources.

Nature of E-Resources	No of Respondents	Percentage (%)
Electronic text books	20	20
Online Journals	15	15
Electronic Databases	4	4
E Conference procedures	6	6
E-Journals of UGC	10	10
Search Engines	45	45
Sum	**100**	**100**

Source: Compiled data.

Table 8. Troubles countenance.

Problems	Number of Respondents	Percentage (%)
Problems related to WI-FI	92	92
Even as browsing digital source	55	55
Less speed of Internet access	70	70
Repeatedly Power Off problems	75	75
Inadequate Computer workstation	84	84
Inconvenient timing of digital literacy	80	80

Source: Compiled data

4.7 *Access to digital resources*

Table 7 makes clear that, 45% of respondents be using search engines for browsing information, 20% of respondents access for electronic books, 15% of respondents using for online journals, 10% are access internet for UGC E-Journals, 06% are using for econference proceedings and remaining 4% access the digital information for e-database for their education purpose.

4.8 *Problems faced*

Table 8 reveals that 92% respondents are facing problems related wi-fi, 84% respondents facing problems related to Inadequate Computer workstation, 75% are face tribulations connected to repeatedly Power Off problems, 70% are facing tribulations related to less speed of internet and remaining 55% respondents facing problems related to browsing the digital sources.

5 OVERALL FINDINGS

Digital literacy awareness is widespread, with PG students being the most knowledgeable. Laptops are the most commonly used and possessed ICT device among respondents. The majority of respondents visit the library daily, mainly for browsing e-materials and fulfilling online applications. Search engines are the most used digital resource, while UGC e-journals and electronic databases have minimal engagement. Key challenges include poor Wi-Fi, slow internet speed, and insufficient computer workstations.

6 CONCLUSION

According to the literature, Telangana students and research scientists are beginning to understand the value of digital literacy, but formal programs and curriculum are still required to improve these abilities. To enable the academic society to successfully use digital technologies in their scholarly endeavours, it is imperative that the difficulties and obstacles associated with digital literacy be addressed.

Recent research emphasizes how crucial it is to be proficient with digital resources and tools in order to succeed academically. In order to improve digital capabilities in academic institutions, the study underlined the necessity of organized training programs. The study highlights the strong adoption of digital literacy among students and research scholars, with a significant preference for laptops and search engines as key digital tools. However, infrastructure-related challenges remain a primary concern, affecting effective digital learning. Addressing these issues can enhance digital education and research efficiency.

The study found that a superior percentage of respondents exploit digital sources on a daily basis. It is observed that they used virtual sources to update their situation understanding. The investigators additionally talked about that majority of respondent had been nicely aware of virtual sources to be had in their concern domain.

Digital literacy has a broad scope of research as it is an emerging field. This would also implicate enhancing advanced capabilities and knowledge that affords cognizance and superior thinking abilities. Consequently, it deemed important to articulate digital literacy in the school curriculum to suitably utilize digital statistics assets by the educational community.

Digital Literacy opens new avenues for students, research scholars and educators to pursue their pastimes & avail academic resources, stories and publications at any time and in any vicinity. Digital Literacy is the platform to enhance the teaching and learning capabilities of the current generation and technology usage. It's far the competency of using the facts and communication technology to discover, examine, create, and speak data, requiring each cognitive and technical capability.

According to the literature, despite initiatives to raise digital literacy among Telangana students and research academics, problems including unequal access to technological resources and knowledge gaps in particular fields still exist. For those in academia to be empowered to use digital technologies in their scholarly endeavors, these problems must be addressed through focused interventions and extensive training programs.

7 SUGGESTIONS

To enhance digital infrastructure, it is crucial to improve Wi-Fi connectivity and internet speed in libraries and study areas while also ensuring the availability of more workstations and reliable power backup systems. Additionally, promoting structured digital learning resources can be achieved by increasing awareness and accessibility of academic databases and UGC e-journals, alongside organizing workshops to train students on effectively utilizing these digital materials.

To bridge the digital divide, institutions should introduce subsidized laptop schemes or institutional loan programs for students who lack personal devices, while also implementing digital literacy training programs, particularly targeting undergraduate students. Furthermore, library digitization efforts should focus on expanding online access to library services, enabling remote logins for research materials, and integrating smart search tools and AI-driven recommendation systems to facilitate efficient digital resource discovery.

DISCLOSURE STATEMENT

No potential conflict of interest was reported by the authors.

ACKNOWLEDGEMENT(S)

The authors would like to thank all the participants who contributed to this research study and the institutions that facilitated data collection.

REFERENCES

[1] K. Ananthoju and R. Katla, (2024) Financial literacy and digital economy in Telangana State, *International Journal of Creative Research Thoughts*, 8(2), pp. 478.

[2] C. Audrin and B. Audrin, (2022) Key factors in digital literacy in learning and education: A systematic literature review using text mining, *Education and Information Technologies*, 27, pp. 7395–7419.

[3] V.G. Biradar and K.K. Naik, (2023) Classification of children as malnourished and healthy category using ResNet18 model, in *2023 International Conference on Ambient Intelligence, Knowledge Informatics and Industrial Electronics (AIKIIE)*, IEEE, pp. 1–7.

[4] S. Muthyalaiah and R.K.P. Kumar, (2023) Utilization of digital library resources in Telangana university libraries: Analytical research among LIS experts, *International Journal of Innovative Research in Technology*, 9(7), pp. 165–170.

[5] P. Panuganti and A. Pasricha, (2023) Digital disparity in secondary school education teachers in Telangana State, India: Some issues, *IOSR Journal of Humanities and Social Science*, 28 (9) pp. 36–44.

[6] T.S. Poornachandrika and S.S. Raj, (2024) Digital literacy and digital empowerment: A study of weavers and artisans in Pochampally village, Telangana, *Journal of Informatics Education and Research*, 4(3) (2024).

[7] R.V. Pratap and K. Singh, (2018) Digital literacy skills among students and research scholars of the Law School, Banaras Hindu University, Varanasi, India: A study, *International Journal of Next Generation Library and Technologies*, 4(1), pp. 1–11.

[8] V.K. Pagidikathula and R.K.P. Kumar, (2023)Information literacy programmes in libraries of higher education in Telangana: A study, *International Journal of Research in Library Science*, 9 (1), pp. 20–30.

[9] H. Tinmaz, Y.-T. Lee, M. Fanea-Ivanovici, and H. Baber, (2022) A systematic review on digital literacy, *Smart Learning Environments*, 9, pp. 21.

[10] M. Anjaiah, (2016) Digital information literacy among research scholars and student community at Dravidian University, Kuppam-Andhra Pradesh (India): An exploratory study, *IOSR Journal of Humanities and Social Science,* 21(9), pp. 1–8.

[11] M. Anjaiah, Digital information literacy skills among users in public libraries: A case study of District Central Library, Warangal District, in Role of Library Associations in Promoting Information Literacy in the Knowledge Society, APLA, Vijayawada, 2014, pp. 327–334.

[12] P. Gilster, *Digital literacy, Wiley and Computer Publishing*, New York, 1997.

[13] S.Z. Tabusum, A. Saleem, and M.S. Batcha, (2014) Digital literacy awareness among arts and science college students in Tiruvallur district: A study, *International Journal of Managerial Studies and Research*, 2(4) .

[14] R.M. Cordell, (2013) Information literacy and digital literacy, *Communications in Information Literacy*, 7(2), pp. 177–183.

[15] D. Bawden, (2008). Origins and concepts of digital literacy, in *Digital Literacies: Concepts, Policies and Practices, Peter Lang*, pp. 17–32.

[16] S. Subba Rao, (1997). Information retrieval services: Role of optical technologies, *New Library World*, 98(1132), pp. 16–24.

[17] S.N. Prakasha and K.N. Muniyappa, (2017). A study on digital literacy among students and research scholars of Faculty of Science in Bangalore University, *International Journal of Information Movement*, 1(9) .

[18] N. Bansal, (2015) Digital literacy among student community in Hisar District: A study, *Journalof Information Management,* 2(2), pp. 9–15.

[19] A. Joinson and P. Banyard, (2002). Psychological aspects of information seeking on the internet, *ASLIB Proceedings,* 54(2), pp. 95–102.

[20] A Study on Analysis of Digital Financial Literacy among Students of Higher Education in Hyderabad of Telangana State, Vegueta, 24(1) (2024), pp. 362–369.

Advancement in Engineering and Science – Goyal et al. (Eds)
 ISBN: 978-1-041-31101-0

Empowering Women Through FinTech: A Study of Jaipur District

Ankit Sharma
Faculty of Management & Commerce, Poornima University, Jaipur, India

Sunita Sharma
Program Director (Management), College Dekho-ImaginXP, Jaipur, India

ABSTRACT: FinTech, or financial technology, has a pivotal role in empowering women by providing innovative solutions that addresses barriers faced by female consumers. Financial inclusion is especially critical for women, who traditionally face a myriad of barriers in accessing financial resources. By leveraging technology, FinTech firms make financial services more accessible, affordable, and user-friendly, thereby helping to empower women. To understand the role of FinTech firms in women empowerment we have conducted a primary study by survey method. For this study we have collected data from 50 respondents from various parts of Jaipur. The main aim of the study was to understand their awareness level towards the various factors of finance and FinTech services. Through survey, it was found that 100% respondents have bank account. Most of them opened their account in Jan-Dhan Yojna launched by Govt. of India. But they started digital platforms for transactions during Covid-19 Pandemic time. 98% use only digital payment services provided by FinTech firms.

Keywords: FinTech, Inclusive growth, digital payments, women empowerment, financial inclusion

1 INTRODUCTION

FinTech, a blend of "financial technology," represents a promptly growing sector that integrates technology with financial services. It incorporates an extensive variation of applications and innovations aimed at improving, automating, and digitizing financial processes. FinTech has emerged as a critical driver of economic growth, redesigning the financial scene significantly by enhancing accessibility and efficiency, thereby catering to the needs of consumers and businesses alike.

1.1 *Significance of fintech in economic development*

FinTech (financial technology) is becoming a key catalyst for change in the financial sector, altering the traditional landscape of financial services. The role of FinTech in economic development includes:

1. **Better Access to Financial Services:** FinTech has made financial services extremely handy. People can access the e-services 24*7 from anywhere. This CONTACT Ankit Sharma. Email: ankitsharma11081985@gmail.com gives so much freedom and flexibility to consumers.

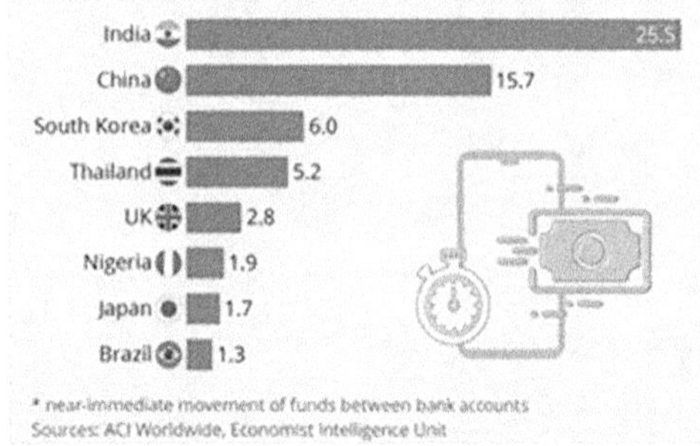

Figure 1. Digital payment ecosystem in India.

2. **Stimulating the Financial Inclusion:** FinTech companies offer number of financial products as per the customer ease. There is no need to visit any branch to avail any service, all services are available on digital platforms. This makes easier to avail the basic financial services especially people with lower literacy rate. Ultimately people are mainstream economy.
3. **Speed and Efficiency:** As FinTech companies are providing 24*7 access facility, instant transactions with minimum efforts, business organizations are working more efficiently than previously with a faster pace.
4. **Minimum Risk & Cost:** FinTech makes the transactions possible to be safe and with lesser cost. Advanced tools of analytics make every transaction lesser costly and safe.
5. **Encouraging Innovation:** As the technology advances, every FinTech service also get updated automatically. From last few years blockchain, AI & ML is in trend to provide delighted FinTech services.

1.2 *FinTech & financial inclusion*

FinTech industry emerged as a technology for financial inclusion in India. FinTech companies are providing basic financial services to the underprivileged population especially women segment of the population. Most commonly used FinTech solutions that are stimulating financial inclusion are:

1.2.1 *Digital payment*

Digital or electronic payment does not include any physical transaction; it includes transactions through various digital platforms. In India, the mostly used digital platforms are Banking Cards, Mobile Wallets, Unified Payments Interface, Aadhar Enabled Payment System, PoS Terminals, Internet Banking, Mobile Banking etc.

1.2.2 *Microfinance platforms*

FinTech companies have enabled the delivery of microfinance services to underserved populations, including small-scale entrepreneurs and low-income individuals. These companies use digital lending algorithms and alternative credit scoring methods to cover small loans to borrowers who may not have access to proper banking channels.

DOI: 10.1201/9781003798514-83

1.2.3 *Digital insurance or insurtech*

Insurtech embraces a wide range of applications, including digital insurance platforms, usage-based insurance, telematics for risk assessment, automated claims processing, chatbots for customer service, predictive analytics for underwriting, and blockchain for protected data management and smart contracts. By integrating these technologies, insurtech solutions enable insurance companies to operate more efficiently, offer the most appropriate products and services in the insurance industry.

As the number of FinTech companies is rising in India, larger part of population is under the realm of financial inclusion.

2 REVIEW OF LITERATURE

The literature review reveals several key studies that examine the intersection of FinTech and women's financial empowerment:

Agarwal *et al.* [1] investigated how FinTech is affecting women's financial inclusion, demonstrating that by giving women more access to financial resources and services, FinTech technologies like mobile banking, digital payments, and peer-to-peer lending have the potential to close the gender financial gap.

Moghadam and Karami [2] explored financial inclusion through FinTech and women's financial empowerment in the International Journal of Social Economics, explaining how financial inclusion fosters women empowerment globally.

Tripathi and Rajeev [3] studied gender inclusive development through FinTech, examining gender-based digital financial inclusion in a cross-economy setting using research methods in economics to evaluate the role of energy efficiency and financial inclusion.

Ranabahu [4] explored how financial technology (FinTech) organizations address poverty-related challenges when providing digital financial services, examining whether financial technology addresses the burden of poverty through a classification of FinTech companies.

Prabat and Roy [5] attempted to study the perception of beneficiaries using digital platforms for financial services, providing insights into user experiences and adoption patterns.

Peterson K. Ozili [6] examined the provision of digital finance to underprivileged people and contested the claim that digital finance is pro-poor and pro-development, offering a critical perspective on digital financial inclusion.

Suliman A Salem Ben Ghrbeia [7] probed issues that affect customers when executing digital payment and recommended solutions to preserve and develop the quality of service for digital payment systems to inspire patronage repetition and loyalty and attract new customers.

2.1 *Research gap*

The literature review identified several significant research gaps:

1. The researchers have based hypothetical overview of digital finance but a comprehensive depiction to show how the lives of lower income people have evolved due to the adoption of digital financial services is not significantly revealed in the literature surveyed.
2. The researchers have based all their work on overall study or concentrated their study to the whole of India, but research on a particular state was missing.
3. One noteworthy research gap pertains to the lack of inclusive and disaggregated data on women's financial behaviors, needs, and preferences. Robust data is essential for modifying FinTech solutions that effectively addresses the unique financial statuses of women.
4. There is little research that highlights problems or challenges faced by women with low literacy (both digital and financial).
5. Last but not the least there is a significant gap in studies measuring the actual impact of FinTech on Women's financial inclusion.

3 RESEARCH METHODOLOGY

3.1 *Research objectives*

1. To analyze the role of FinTech firms in women empowerment.
2. To find out the challenges faced by women consumer while using FinTech ser- vices.

3.2 *Hypothesis*

The role of FinTech firms in women empowerment is highly significant.

3.3 *Research design*

Sampling Technique: For the present piece of study, purposive random sampling technique was equipped to collect the data.

Data Collection: A data of 50 women was collected from various parts of Jaipur through survey methods. Interview method was employed as a data collection tool.

Data Analysis: For the present piece of research, item analysis was calculated.

3.4 *Inclusion criteria*

1. Only 20-45 age group women were included.
2. Women belong to low-income group was a part of the study.
3. Women with low literacy rate were included.

4 DATA ANALYSIS AND DATA INTERPRETATION

The survey questions are divided into 5 categories namely: **Demographics & Fi-nancial Background, Awareness & Usage of FinTech Services, FinTech & Financial Inclusion, Trust, Security, and Challenges and Future Interest & Improvements.**

4.1 *Demographics & financial background*

Considerate the interchange between demographic factors and financial background is fundamental for the FinTech sector. This section explores various demographic factors, such as age, gender, and education, and investigates how these basics relate with the financial backgrounds of individuals in determining their behavior and choices in the FinTech.

For the present piece of study, only 20-45 age group women were included as age affects FinTech adoption and financial inclusion, as younger generations are generally more tech-savvy. All 50 participants work in unorganized sector as they work as house helpers.

Pertaining to the next question, all 50 women have bank account, it means that irrespective of educational background and income group; females are part of mainstream. Most of them opened bank account in Pradhanmantri Jan Dhan Yojna to avail government schemes benefits.

The financial services used by them are savings account, loans or credit services and mobile money/wallets. It indicates that they are availing limited financial services.

4.2 *Awareness & usage of fintech services*

This segment assesses how well FinTech services are known and used. When it was asked whether they heard about the FinTech services before or not? All of them are aware about digital financial services. This shows their high FinTech awareness level, which is crucial for financial inclusion.

43 out of 50 women are using FinTech services. That shows that 86% females are using technology to enhance their financial services experience. Most of them who are using FinTech services are below 35 years, it means that younger ones have highly trusted the technology when it comes to financial services. Most of them are using FinTech services from 2020 (COVID-19). 40 participants said that their first online transaction was done during COVID-19 pandemic. It indicates that the pandemic worked as catalyst for the industry.

When it comes to types of FinTech services used by the sample, maximum is using Digital wallets, only 3 respondents know about digital banking and Buy Now, Pay Later (BNPL) services. It indicates clearly that women belong to low-income group with low literacy rate require awareness campaign to get the better idea about FinTech services, what are the different services, how can they avail those services.

The frequency of using FinTech services is higher on receiving money through Payment Apps, they hardly use Payment Apps for payment purpose. This is not a happy picture for FinTech companies as females are not aware about the rest of the services. This specifies the engagement level with FinTech services.

4.3 *FinTech & financial inclusion*

This part of survey assesses FinTech's impact on accessibility to financial services. When it comes to the reasons of choosing FinTech over traditional banking; 37 participants said that they are using it because of the convenience, means freedom to operate anytime from anywhere while 6 said that their bank branch is at distant and very time consuming to use traditional banking services. This indicated the opportunities to FinTech firms if they address the pain points of customers properly.

All FinTech service users said that FinTech has made their lives easier in terms of financial services as they can access the services at their ease.

The next question was asked about the barriers faced by them while using FinTech services. 80% women replied that they are afraid of being cheated while using the FinTech services and 4% reported that poor internet connectivity is a major barrier. This shows that females with low literacy do not feel safe about FinTech services, they are anxious of being a victim of cyber crime or their major concern is all about online phishing.

Women participants are very much happy with FinTech services they are using as they decide where to spend money, how much to spend and how much to save? They do not require their male counterpart in money matters or having a strong hold on their earnings. 80% of them think that ultimately FinTech is empowering women, they own the money earned by them which was not the same earlier when they dealt with cash.

The next was asked about the motives behind using FinTech services. All 43 participants said that it is the convenience that encourages them to use the FinTech services. They said that FinTech services give them a freedom from branch banking. Its time saving process for them.

When question was asked that do you think FinTech services have improved your access to financial services? All FinTech users said yes, as there is no need to go to the branch to avail the service, it is not only time saving process but also, they are happy with the 24*7 availability of the services. The biggest reason to choose FinTech services over traditional banking services because traditional banking services have strict banking trimmings and branches are located at distant. These reasons make traditional banking operations very difficult for working ones. FinTech also helps them to save money and makes their payments faster and more convenient.

4.4 *Trust, security, and challenges*

In the context of FinTech, trust is a foundation that reinforces consumer confidence and business reliability. For consumers, trust deciphers into reassurance that their funds are safe and their personal information is handled responsibly. For businesses, especially in a sector considered by quick innovation, establishing and maintaining trust is critical to attracting and retaining clients.

As the data shows that 85% respondents show moderate trust, they are not fully trusting on FinTech. Their biggest fear is to lose money because of any cyber fraud. Three out of all females, are victims of online fraud as their digital understanding is not up to the mark. Fraud in FinTech can be visible in many ways, including identity theft, credit card fraud, and phishing scams. Fraudsters may control technology to conduct Phishing Attacks including sending communications that seem legitimate; shams can trick operators into providing personal information, which can be used to gain access to secure accounts.

4.5 *Future interest & improvements*

The regulatory environment surrounding the FinTech industry is complex and multi-faceted, significantly impacting growth and innovation. Given the rapid evolution of technology and financial services, regulators are striving to create frameworks that both protect consumers and foster innovation.

Most participants advocated that safety norms should be stricter for FinTech ser-vices so there will be less chances of being cheated digitally. Those who are using FinTech services are happy with the services used by them. They would like to reccommend such services to those who are not still using.

5 RESEARCH IMPLICATIONS, LIMITATIONS & FURTHER SCOPE

5.1 *Research implications*

The emergent frame of research on FinTech compromises acute comprehensions with both theoretical and practical implications. Indulgent how familiarity with FinTech influences financial behavior, inclusion, and decision-making empowers stakeholders— including policymakers, financial institutions, FinTech developers, and educators—to better shape strategies that support sustainable adoption and maximize socioeconomic benefits. This research observes these implications and highlights persistent challenges arising from awareness gaps, emphasizing how addressing these can strengthen financial ecosystems.

5.2 *Research limitations*

A range of significant limitations that affect the robustness, validity, and generalizability of findings are present in this piece of research:

1. Sample Size and Representativeness Constraints: A recurring challenge in FinTech and women empowerment study is the limitation of sample size. Small sample sizes reduce statistical power, increase vulnerability to outliers, and make it difficult to detect meaningful correlations or causations. Furthermore, these samples may lack representativeness, particularly when drawn from urban populations or digitally connected segments, which excludes women from rural or marginalized areas who might face the greatest barriers to FinTech access.
2. Regional and Contextual Biases: Geographical concentration of studies presents another limitation affecting research

on FinTech and women empowerment. Cultural norms, gender roles, and socio-economic structures vary substantially across regions.

5.3 *Future scope of the study*

Future research must explore emerging technologies, multidisciplinary perspectives, and gender-specific nuances that shape how women engage with digital financial services. Further the same research can be done on women belong to rural and sub urban areas from various parts of Rajasthan or India and on different professionals and home makers too.

6 CONCLUSION

FinTech stands as a transformative force in driving women's financial empowerment by expanding access to inclusive, affordable, and user-friendly financial services. Its ability to bypass traditional barriers—such as limited physical banking infrastructure, lack of collateral, and socio-cultural constraints—positions FinTech as a critical enabler of economic independence and social inclusion for women, especially in underserved regions.

This can be concluded that FinTech services are playing a vital role in empowering women. As the result shows that 86% women are aware of and using the FinTech services, but in a very limited manner. Their awareness towards various FinTech services is very limited, for them FinTech means Digital Payments and Digital Banking only. There is a need to increase their awareness level towards FinTech and its various services. Also, they need to be trained on cyber security.

DISCLOSURE STATEMENT

No potential conflict of interest was reported by the authors.

ACKNOWLEDGEMENT(S)

The authors would like to thank all the women participants who contributed to this research study and shared their experiences with FinTech services.

REFERENCES

[1] S. Agarwal, D. Jain, *et al.*, (2024). FinTech on Women's Financial Inclusion: Bringing the Gender Gap through Innovative Solutions.

[2] H. Moghadam and A. Karami, (2023). Financial inclusion through FinTech and women's financial empowerment, International Journal of Social Economics.

[3] S. Tripathi and M. Rajeev, (2023). Gender inclusive development through FinTech: Studying Gender-based digital financial inclusion in a cross-economy setting.

[4] Ranabahu, (2022). Will financial technology address the burden of poverty in 2022, a classification of FinTech companies.

[5] S. Prabat and S.G. Roy, (2022). Attempt to study the perception of beneficiaries using digital platforms for financial services.

[6] P.K. Ozili, (2020). Impact of digital finance on financial inclusion and stability, BCG Research Paper Series. Available at https://ssrn.com/abstract=3220402.

[7] S.A.S.B. Ghrbeia, (2020). Issues that affect customers when executing digital payment and recommending solutions to preserve and develop the quality of service for digital payment systems, Ph.D. thesis.

[8] P. Gomber, R.J. Kauffman, C. Parker, and B.W. Weber, (2018). On the FinTech revolution: Interpreting the forces of innovation, disruption, and transformation in financial services, Journal of Management Information Systems, 35(1), pp. 220–265.

[9] D.W. Arner, J. Barberis, and R.P. Buckley, (2016). The evolution of FinTech: A new post-crisis paradigm? Georgetown Journal of International Law, 47(4), pp. 1271–1319.

[10] I. Lee and Y.J. Shin, (2018) FinTech: Ecosystem, business models, investment decisions, and challenges, Business Horizons, 61 (1) , pp. 35–46.

[11] M.A. Chen, Q. Wu, and B. Yang, (2019) How valuable is FinTech innovation? Review of Financial Studies, 32(5), pp. 2062–2106.

[12] R. Bhatnagar and S. Mehta, (2020) FinTech awareness and adoption: A study among Indian consumers, International Journal of Emerging Markets, 15(3) , pp. 477–494.

[13] K. Gai and M. Qiu, (2021) Awareness and adoption of FinTech services: Evidence from China, Financial Innovation, 7(1) , Article 20.

[14] Y. Li and P. Li, (2020) Examining factors influencing awareness and adoption of FinTech services in emerging economies, Journal of Asia Business Studies, 14(4) , pp. 595–617.

[15] K.K. Kapoor, Y.K. Dwivedi, and N.F. Piercy, (2020) FinTech adoption: Insights from an Indian digital payment ecosystem, International Journal of Information Management, 50 , pp. 109–118.

[16] T. Zalan and E. Toufaily, (2017) The promise of FinTech in emerging markets: Not as disruptive, Journal of Innovation Economics & Management, 24(3) , pp. 117–135.

[17] S. Chauhan, A. Akhtar, and A. Gupta, (2022) Customer experience in digital banking: a review and future research directions, *International Journal of Quality and Service Sciences*, 14(2) .

[18] S. Gupta and A. Agrawal, (2021) Analytical study of FinTech in India: Pre & post pandemic COVID-19, *Indian Journal of Economics and Business*, 20(3) .

[19] P. Nagar and T. Nagar, (2023). *Role of FinTech in enabling women empowerment in India.* Available at https://ssrn.com/abstract=4746992.

[20] International Labour Organization, (2022). *World Employment and Social Outlook: Trends 2022*, Geneva, Switzerland: ILO.

Advancement in Engineering and Science – Goyal et al. (Eds)

Influence of Marketing, Advertisement, and Packaging on HFSS Food Consumption and the Role of Mobile Health Interventions in Shaping Healthy Eating Attitudes Among Adolescents

Meghna Pareeka and Nikita Sharmaa
Department of Home Science, University of Rajasthan, Jaipur, India

ABSTRACT: High consumption of high fat, sugar, and salt (HFSS) packaged foods by adolescents has become a major public health problem with the main causes being aggressive marketing, persuasive advertising, and attractive packaging. Mobile health interventions (MHIs) are mentioned as digital tools that, at the same time, could promote healthy eating behaviors. This study investigates the dual impact of commercial food promotion strategies and MHIs on adolescents' dietary choices and attitudes toward healthy food consumption. The research was carried out among 421 teenage students from four private schools of Jaipur city. The constructs measured were marketing influence, advertisement recall, packaging appeal, mobile health engagement, HFSS food consumption and healthy food attitudes; and these were measured using a structured questionnaire. A Structural Equation Modeling (SEM) was used to analyze the complex interrelationships between these variables. The results suggest that marketing and advertisement increase adolescents' consumption of HFSS food, but packaging shows a mixed effect. On the contrary, mobile health interventions have a strong positive association with healthier food attitudes and may be able to compensate for the unhealthy nature of commercial influences. This study highlights the critical importance of the integration of public health strategies—covering a broader range of programs including regulations on unhealthy food marketing along with such a digital health strategy that is engaging and educational for engaging adolescents to make informed decisions regarding their dietary choices.

Keywords: HFSS foods, marketing, advertisement, packaging, mobile health interventions, adolescent nutrition

1 INTRODUCTION

The dietary behaviors of adolescents are increasingly influenced by external environmental cues, particularly aggressive commercial promotion of high-fat, sugar, and salt (HFSS) packaged foods. Global public health concerns have been raised over the rising prevalence of obesity, diabetes, and non-communicable diseases among youth, much of which has been attributed to the regular intake of ultra-processed and nutritionally poor food products [3]. Adolescents, being highly impressionable and developmentally vulnerable, are a key target for the food and beverage industry's expansive marketing strategies. In rapidly growing urban centers like Jaipur, India, adolescents' exposure to such marketing tactics is widespread across digital platforms, school environments, and traditional media.

CONTACT Meghna Pareek. Email: meghna.pareek@uor.edu.in

Marketing and advertisement are not merely channels of information but act as persuasive forces that normalize and glamorize the consumption of HFSS foods. Studies have shown that exposure to food marketing significantly increases adolescents' preferences for, and intake of, unhealthy food items, often by manipulating emotional appeals and leveraging peer influence [2, 17]. Ads are not the only thing that the impact influenced; packaging also had role in deciding on the purchase or not. It has been demonstrated that visual attractive packaging (cartoon characters, celebrity endorsement, bright colors, health claims) distorts children's perception on product healthfulness and encourage unhealthy choices [15, 16].

However, mobile health interventions (MHIs) have surfaced as potential solutions to promote healthier dietary behaviors among adolescents to compensate for the negative influences. Health education and behavioral change support are delivered through these interventions through multiple mobile apps and interactive platforms as well as digital tracking. In particular, MHI's are very relevant in adolescent populations that are digitally engaged and are comfortable with the use of mobile technology. Results from research show that if designed appropriately MHIs can considerably boost nutrition awareness, promote increased ingestion of fruit and vegetables, and have a constructive effect on eating healthy attitudes by improving self efficacy and motivation [8, 10].

The study presented here is set in this dual landscape: adolescents are continuously targeted by unhealthy persuasive food marketing, while a new generation of digital health promoting tools is being developed. This research was conducted among 421 teenage students from four prominent private schools in Jaipur city, to critically look into the combined and contrasting influences of marketing, advertisement and packaging on HFSS food consumption and the positive role of MHIs in making healthy food attitudes. To conduct the study, the approach taken is quantitative and uses structured questionnaires, along with Structural Equation Modeling (SEM), to analyze the complex relationships between the variables. As little is known about this topic in the context of the Indian school-going adolescent, this study aims to provide useful insights to educators, policymakers, public health practitioners and digital health designers working towards healthy dietary behaviour change in youth.

2 REVIEW OF LITERATURE

2.1 *Influence of marketing, advertising, and packaging on HFSS food consumption*

Food companies have aggressively marketed HFSS packaged foods, which has led to a major public health concern of consumption of these packaged foods globally. The impact of marketing, advertisement and packaging on consumption of HFSS foods is researched, which shows the complex behaviour of the consumer and the externality. Need to understand how food marketing techniques, particularly aimed at children, influence unhealthy dietary habits, which is in response to rising rates of obesity and other non communicable diseases (NCDs such as diabetes and heart disease). Thus, this thematic review analyzes more than 30 research papers published between 2015 and 2024 regarding those aspects of marketing, advertisement

DOI: 10.1201/9781003798514-84

and packaging which can influence dietary choices, in particular, by children and adolescents. These factors, indicated by the evidence, appear to have a substantial effect on the patterns of consumption of HFSS foods, with packaging and advertising being key in legitimising the intake of unhealthy products.

One of the important factors that make HFSS foods attractive to children is the presence of licensed characters and brand mascots on packaging. Research has demonstrated that these characters significantly raise children's preferences for unhealthy foods and can result in greater consumption. For example, Packer *et al.* [14] discovered that the usage of licensed and brand equity characters on packaging substantially improved the taste preferences for HFSS products. Even when the characters were not directly associated with food, this phenomenon was evident, showing the powerful character associations in food marketing. Similarly, Pombo-Rodrigues *et al.* [15] found that products with unlicensed characters were more likely to be classified as HFSS, suggesting that cartoons often appear on packaging that does not have a good nutritional quality. This underscores the point that regulations should be made to limit the use of such marketing tactics in product for children in particular.

The packaging strategies do not always involve characters. Vibrant colors and engaging imagery also influence children's food choices. Though their food pakings often have poor nutritional profile, Richonnet *et al.* [16] study found some of them had flashy designs and images which made unhealthy food more attractive. These packaging strategies are followed by placing products in high traffic areas such as supermarkets that increases the likelihood that children will choose HFSS foods. Richonnet *et al.* [16] explains that this marketing strategy exploits children's vulnerability and their developing understanding of food choices, making it harder for them to differentiate between healthier and less healthy options.

Advertisement of HFSS food is another important contributor to HFSS food consumption through television, social media and outdoor advertisements. As noted by Boyland [2], marketing of HFSS foods to children is ethically questionable as advertising often advertises to children through their favourite television shows and digital content. It has been shown that exposure to such ads increases the consumption of unhealthy foods. Boyland [2] points out that because food marketing and advertising is pervasive and because they often make emotional appeals, children are more likely to be susceptible to unhealthy food choices due to their cognitive immaturity. The view is shared by the work of Tatlow-Golden *et al.* [17] who show that children in Ireland were often exposed to advertisements for dairy products, fast foods and sugary snacks, leading to the normalization of unhealthy eating behaviors. The persuasive power of the these ads is also strengthened with emotional triggers, for example, linking high fat foods away to fun, excitement and happiness.

Due to the impact of advertisements on children's food choices, there has been regulatory effort to reduce the exposure of children to HFSS food marketing. Studies have shown mixed results regarding the effectiveness of UK restrictions on the advertisement of HFSS foods during children's programming, which was introduced in 2019. Meiksin *et al.* [12] evaluate a process evaluation of Transport for London's policy to restrict HFSS food advertising across its network. While the policy was well received by stakeholders, it had little impact on consumer behavior owing to the small share of advertising space controlled by the transport network. In the same vein, Buckland *et al.* [4] assessed the effects of outdoor advertising restrictions in Bristol, UK, and have not observed a reduction in the consumption of HFSS products, which still indicate that the effect of the policy might be exerted through the media covered by the regulation.

Some regulations have been introduced for packaging of unhealthy foods as well to combat marketing. India's Front-of-Pack Nutrition Labeling (FOPL) system was introduced in 2020 for the purpose of enabling consumers to make informed decisions with regards to the foods they buy. The goal behind the FOPL system is to illustrate foods that are high in fat, salt and sugar to help consumers identify unhealthy products. Bera *et al.* [1] do go on to talk about how the FSSAI (Food Safety and Standards Authority of India) has gone a long way in developing packaging regulations to fight against the growing consumption of HFSS food. Similar to this is the case in Chile, where the introduction of mandatory food labeling and advertising regulations has been associated with lower sugary drink purchases, which add more support for the impact of packaging regulations on consumer behavior [9].

However, even with this regulation, there are much challenges to solve in marketing how much people consume. Another major problem is that children continue to be exposed to food marketing in digital media and unregulated online platforms. In Gallagher-Squires *et al.* [6], research shows that with regulatory frameworks in place, even children's food marketing has been carried out in online channels which are not necessarily regulated under traditional advertisement rules. This emphasizes that only by comprehensive regulation of HFSS food promotion and digital food marketing that both traditional and digital activities are covered will children be protected from the harmful effects of HFSS food promotion.

The enforcement of food marketing regulations can also be affected by the industry compliance. According to Boyland and Harris [3], voluntary pledges made by food manufacturers to limit the marketing of unhealthy foods to children have been introduced, but there has been little impact on children's exposure to HFSS food ads. Government-led regulations are necessary to achieve major reductions in children's exposure to food marketing, and to improve the nutritional quality of foods marketed to them.

The evidence implies strongly that marketing, advertisement and packaging are of great importance in the consumption of HFSS foods, especially among children and adolescents. The use of licensed characters, appealing packaging designs, and emotionally charged advertisements significantly increase children's preference for unhealthy foods. While regulatory measures have been implemented to curb the impact of these marketing strategies, their effectiveness remains limited, particularly in the face of digital media and industry non-compliance. To address these issues, more robust and comprehensive policies are needed to regulate food marketing practices, particularly those targeting children, and to promote healthier eating habits across populations, thus based upon literature we propose following hypotheses:

H1: Marketing has a significant positive effect on the consumption of HFSS packaged foods among adolescents.

H2: Advertisement exposure significantly increases the consumption of HFSS packaged foods among adolescents.

H3: Packaging appeal has a significant effect on the consumption of HFSS packaged foods among adolescents.

2.2 *Mobile Health Interventions (MHIs) on attitude towards healthy food consumption*

The impact of mobile health interventions (MHIs) on attitudes toward healthy food consumption is a growing area of research. As mobile devices become more pervasive, their application in health interventions has proven to be effective in influencing behavior, particularly in dietary habits. MHIs provide a convenient, personalized support to improve people's knowledge, motivation, and self-efficacy in making food choices. This thematic review analyzes how recent studies that examine the impact of mobile health interventions on the consumption attitude of healthier food have influenced this phenomenon.

Several studies have shown that mobile health interventions can have a great impact on altering dietary attitudes, especially through delivery of continuous, readily available health information. Kato-Lin *et al.* [8] tested three mobile enabled interventions to encourage healthy eating in a study. They were a mobile based visual diary, image based dietitian support and peer engagement. The researchers found that mobile based visual diaries and support from a dietitian had a very positive effect of user engagement and choice of food. For example users increased intake of fruits and vegetables which indicates that MHIs can complement dietary attitudes by increasing engagement, as well as provide personalized feedback. It was the ability of these interventions to strengthen self efficacy and provide easily measurable, actionable advice that helped users feel better about making healthy food choices that led to these interventions' success.

Thus, similar to children with autism spectrum disorder (ASD), who are typically described as having picky eating behaviours, Kral *et al.* [10] examined the impact of an mHealth nutrition intervention. This study found that children engaged more with the mobile technology had higher fruit and vegetable intake, but there were no significant difference in children's intake between the intervention and control groups. This result has implication that user engagement is important in mobile health interventions. MHIs could be valuable tools to help create a positive attitude for healthier food choices for children with ASD who may be limited by sensory sensitivities and offer structured support and gradual behavioral modification strategies.

Horning *et al.* [7] looked at the role of mobile markets in food insecure communities for food security and the attitudes towards consumption of fruit and vegetable. Fruits and vegetables were designed to be provided in mobile markets to communities that lacked access to fresh produce. It was found that customers who used the mobile market frequently had more positive attitudes towards healthy eating and better food related behaviours, including higher self efficacy for cooking healthy meals. The results of these findings suggest the change in food consumption pattern is not the only change made by mobile health interventions, although the change in attitudes associated with mobile health intervention is made because mobile health interventions address barriers to healthy eating such as access and knowledge.

Kroes and Shahid [11] also tested a mobile application designed to motivate adolescents between the ages of 11 and 14 to eat more fruits and less unhealthy snacks. Persuasive technology was used in the app, social influences to reinforce the positive eating habits. Teenagers who used the app developed more favorable views toward fruit consumption and less favorable views toward unhealthy foods. The impact of mobilizing for and utilizing social influence and gamification in mobile health interventions to facilitate long term changes in dietary attitudes in adolescents has been demonstrated in this study as adolescents are more influenced by peer and social validation behaviors.

Another study by Choudhury *et al.* [5] also shows that mobile health can improve maternal health, also in attitudes towards nutrition during pregnancy. In underprivileged communities of India, the study investigated pregnant women's perspectives of using a mobile app for nutrition and health conditions such as anemia and preeclampsia. The study showed that despite a low awareness on essential nutrients during pregnancy study participants were interested in using a mobile health app to improve their nutrition (61%). This reflects the widespread adoption and interest of mobile health interventions especially in areas where conventional health care facilities are not available. This willingness to engage with mobile health apps implies that pregnant women have changed their attitudes towards healthy food consumption during pregnancy, an important period for maternal and fetal health.

As far as mobile health interventions go, they also seem to influence attitudes by addressing the perceived barriers to healthy eating. For example, in a study which evaluated the effects of a mobile health centre program on food insecurity and obesity, the provision of biweekly delivery of fresh produce it conjugated with regular dietary education yielded an attitude of eating fruits and vegetables improved. The participants tended to select fruits and vegetables and understood that these foods have health advantages. This implies that when mobile health interventions emphasize the ease of access to healthy foods as well as education, they can change people's attitudes and promote sustained behaviour changes [13].

Additionally, the display of food deserts or low income communities, mobile health interventions have been shown to change attitudes towards a healthy eating. Tham *et al.* [18] investigate how COVID-19 pandemic affected young adults' diets through mobile food delivery apps. Overall, the study found that people tend to order unhealthy foods via these apps, but there is room for such apps to help promote better eating if they are used to promote healthier food choices. The challenge is the shift of consumer attitude toward the preference of healthy options, although in the convenience-driven context of mobile food delivery services. This study highlights the possibility of impact of mobile health interventions on attitudes but also highlights the challenge overcome of convenience and affordability barriers that often underlie unhealthy eating behavior. Finally, it is concluded that mobile health interventions can considerably affect food consumption attitudes through increasing knowledge, self-efficacy, and engagement. In fact, these interventions address the barriers, like lack of food access and knowledge gaps, but it exploits features like personalisation, social support and persuasive technology in making positive behavioral changes. These interventions, however, are effective to the extent that user engagement, demographic characteristics of the targeted audience, and ability to address both intrinsic and extrinsic barriers to healthy eating are present. Now, future research should continue to explore the long term effects of mobile health interventions on dietary attitudes, especially in underserved populations.

H4: Mobile health interventions (MHIs) have a significant positive effect on adolescents' attitudes toward healthy food consumption.

3 OBJECTIVES OF THE STUDY

1. To examine the impact of marketing strategies on the consumption of high-fat, sugar, and salt (HFSS) packaged foods among adolescents.
2. To assess the influence of advertisement exposure on adolescents' dietary behaviors related to HFSS food products.
3. To evaluate the role of packaging appeal in shaping adolescents' preferences and consumption of HFSS foods.
4. To analyze the effect of mobile health interventions (MHIs) on adolescents' attitudes towards healthy food consumption.

4 RESEARCH METHODOLOGY

The purpose of this study was to examine the effect of marketing, advertisement and packaging on consumption of high fat, sugar and salt (HFSS) packaged foods, as well as the effect of mobile health interventions (MHIs) on teenage attitudes towards consumption of healthy food. A quantitative research design was adopted in order to explicate these relationships in a comprehensive way, and structured survey method and advanced statistical modelling techniques were used for data collection. The study was based on a cross sectional survey based design that is employed for exploring behavioral pattern, attitude and relationships between latent variables like marketing exposure, advertisement, packaging, mobile health interventions and food consumption behavior. Data was collected on various constructs derived from the theoretical framework and measured through observed indicators with the help of a structured questionnaire.

This study was conducted on teenage students enrolled in day schools of Jaipur city, Rajasthan, India and the target population was considered to be these students. The sample included 421 teenage children from four reputed private schools. The purposive sampling was applied by selecting these schools in light of the diversity in terms of their demographic and also accessibility and the willingness to participate in the academic research. The use of purposive sampling is justified as adolescents in day schools settings are most likely to be directly influenced by food advertisements, digital intervention and in store marketing tactics, and since the study needed specific respondents. Purposive sampling also ensures that the participants drawn to the study are of the characteristics necessary to the study, thereby increasing the internal validity of the findings.

A structured questionnaire was used to collect the data which were administered in person within the school premises after obtaining necessary permissions from the school authorities and informed assent from the students and their guardians. Variables measured through Likert scale questionnaire included exposure to marketing, advertisement recall, packaging influence, consumption of HFSS foods and attitudes towards healthy eating promoted through MHIs. The questionnaire was pilot tested on a small group of students not included in the final analysis to insure clarity and age appropriateness, and any modifications necessary to make the questionnaire more readable and comprehendible were made.

It was through statistical software, such as AMOS or SmartPLS, that the collected data were analyzed using Structural Equation Modeling (SEM). The reasons for the use of SEM in this study are related to its ability to examine complex relationships between latent variables simultaneously, taking into account measurement error and testing multiple regression paths in one model.

Table 1. Model information.

Parameter	Details
Estimation Method	ML
Optimization Method	NLMINB
Number of observations	421
Model Constructs	Packaging = PK1+PK2+PK3+PK4+PK5+PK6 Marketing = MK1+MK2+MK3+MK4+MK5 +MK6 Advertisement = AD1+AD2+AD3+AD4+AD5 +AD6 Mobile health interventions (MHIs) = MH1+MH2 +MH3+MH4+MH5+MH6 Consumption of HFSS packaged foods = MHIP1 +MHIP2+MHIP3+MHIP4+MHIP5+MHIP6 Attitude towards consumption of healthy food = MHIK1+MHIK2+MHIK3+MHIK4+MHIK5 +MHIK6
Structural Relationships	Consumption of HFSS packaged foods = Marketing + Advertisement + Packaging Attitude towards consumption of healthy food = Mobile health interventions (MHIs) Key details of the model estimation process and structural relationships

4.1 *Ethical considerations*

Ethical approval was obtained from the appropriate academic body, and necessary permissions were secured from school administrations. Participation was voluntary, and confidentiality of the respondents was ensured throughout the research process. Parental consent and student assent were obtained in accordance with ethical standards for research involving minors.

Parameter estimates with standard errors, confidence intervals, standardized coefficients, Z-values, and significance levels

5 RESULTS

5.1 *Structural equation modelling*

Key details of the model estimation process and its structural relationships are given in Table 1. With a dataset of 421 observations, the optimization technique used was NLMINB (based on ML estimation). The model contains several latent constructs which are measured by a set of the observed indicators.

They are based on constructs of Packaging (PK1 to PK6), Marketing (MK1 to MK6), Advertisement (AD1 to AD6), and Mobile Health Interventions (MHIs) (MH1 to MH6). The study also looks into the Consumption of high fat, sugar, salt (HFSS) packaged foods, assessed by MHIP1 to MHIP6 and Attitude towards the consumption of healthy food, measured through MHIK1 to MHIK6.

The Marketing of HFSS packaged foods and the Advertisement of HFSS food products are shown to be influential in dietary choices through the structural relationship, and it indicates the effect of promotional and branding strategies on dietary choices. Furthermore, Mobile Health Interventions (MHIs) shape Attitude towards the consumption of healthy food, which implies that digital health initiatives have some influence on shaping people's perception and behavior towards healthier food choices. The model gives insight into the interconnections between marketing strategies, consumer behavior and the health related interventions.

The parameter estimates for the relationships of key variables, together with their standard errors (SE), confidence intervals (95%), standardized coefficients (B), Zvalues, and significance levels (P-values) from the relationships are presented in Table 2. The results indicate that there is a very strong and statistically significant positive impact of marketing on consumption of high fat, sugar, and salt (HFSS) packaged foods, with an estimate of 0.883 (SE = 0.1081, B = 0.8188, Z = 8.167, P ¡ 0.001), implying that increased marketing will be associated with higher consumption of HFSS packaged foods. However, there is evidence of a positive and weak effect of advertisement on consumption of HFSS, as indicated by an estimate of 0.384 (SE = 0.1927, B = 0.1552, Z = 1.992, P = 0.046), which is statistically significant but weakly related. On the other hand, consumption of HFSS is not impacted to a large extent by packaging, which is shown by the negative estimate (-0.165), high SE (0.2443) and non-significant P-value (0.499), such that packaging strategies might not be decisive in determining consumption patterns. At the same time, it is found that mobile

Table 2. Parameter estimates.

Dependent Variable P	Predictor	Estimate	SE	Lower 95% CI	Upper 95% CI	B	Z	p-value
Consumption of HFSS	Marketing	0.883	0.1081	0.67104	1.095	0.8188	8.167	< .001
Consumption of HFSS	Advertisement	0.384	0.1927	0.0062	0.761	0.1552	1.992	0.046
Consumption of HFSS	Packaging	-0.165	0.2443	-0.6438	0.314	-0.029	-0.675	0.499
Healthy Food Attitude	Mobile Health Interventions (MHIs)	0.564	0.0656	0.43559	0.693	0.6925	8.601	< .001

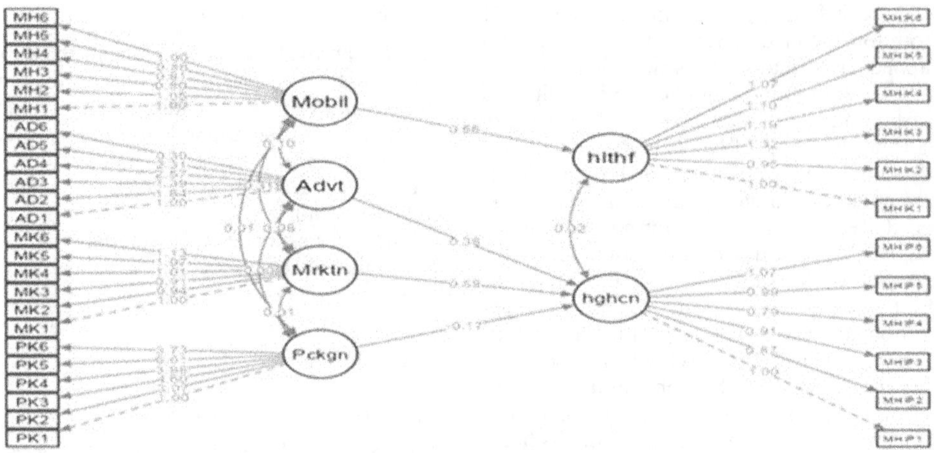

Figure 1. A diagram of the structural equation model network showing relationships between variables.

health interventions (MHIs) have a strong and statistically significant positive effect on attitude towards the consumption of healthier food (0.564, SE = 0.0656, B = 0.6925, Z = 8.601, P ¡ 0.001), indicating that effective MHIs can significantly change consumer's attitude towards healthier dietary choices.

5.1.1 *Marketing and consumption of HFSS packaged foods*
The value of the parameter estimate for marketing in terms of consumption of HFSS packaged foods is 0.883 with a standard error of 0.1081. This estimate is a 95% confidence interval for the true value, which lies between 0.67104 and 1.095. The result of marketing on HFSS food consumption is statistically significant as evidenced by the associated z value of 8.167 and p value of less than 0.001. In other words, marketing has a significant and positive impact on the consumption of HFSS packaged foods and the relationship is highly reliable.

5.1.2 *Advertising and consumption of HFSS packaged foods*
The advertising impact estimate for consumption of HFSS packaged foods is 0.384 with standard error of 0.1927. The range of the confidence interval is 0.00620 to 0.761, in which case the effect of advertising could be anywhere between 0.00620 and 0.761. The z value of 1.992 and p value of 0.046 indicate that this relationship is statistically significant, but it was far less stronger in the effect than marketing. Although advertising has a positive effect on the consumption of HFSS foods, the magnitude is smaller.

5.1.3 *Packaging and consumption of HFSS packaged foods*
The estimate for packaging's effect on HFSS food consumption is -0.165, with a standard error of 0.2443. The confidence interval spans from -0.64381 to 0.314, indicating a negative relationship between packaging and HFSS food consumption, but with a wide range of potential values. The z-value of -0.675 and a p-value of 0.499 indicate that this relationship is not statistically significant, suggesting that packaging does not have a significant effect on the consumption of HFSS packaged foods.

5.1.4 *Mobile media and attitude towards healthy food consumption*
Finally, the parameter estimate for mobile media's influence on the attitude towards healthy food consumption is 0.564, with a standard error of 0.0656. The confidence interval for this estimate is between 0.43559 and 0.693, suggesting that mobile media positively influences attitudes towards healthy eating. The z-value of 8.601 and a pvalue of less than 0.001 indicate that this effect is highly significant, demonstrating that mobile media plays a crucial role in shaping positive attitudes toward healthy food choices.

Figure 1 presents the structural equation model diagram illustrating the complex relationships between the latent constructs in our study

The measurement model results are presented in Table 3, which states the relationship between latent and observed variables. It is a table of estimates, standard errors (SE), 95% confidence intervals, standardized coefficients (B), Z-values and significance levels (p-values).

The reference indicator used for Packaging is PK1 with a fixed estimate of 1. In addition, other observed indicators (PK2 PK6) have estimates ranging from 3.07 to 6.612 with PK5 (B = 0.8557, Z = 2.67, P = 0.008) having the highest factor loading suggesting a strong association.

In MK1, Marketing is the reference and the other indicators (MK2-MK6) have strong loadings (B = 0.5231 to 0.6068) and very significant P-values (¡0.001), indicating a good definition of the construct.

Advertisement: AD1 is the reference indicator, AD2-AD5 have significant relationship (B = 0.3055 to 0.7011, P ¡0.001). However, AD6 weak loading (B = 0.0513, P = 0.37) is not significant and therefore may not be well representing the latent construct. All indicators (MH1-MH6) are highly associated with factor loadings from 0.4323 to 0.6681 and highly significant P values (¡0.001) for Mobile Health Interventions (MHIs). Reference indicator for MHIP1, the indicators MHIP2-MHIP6 are strong and significant loadings (B = 0.6433 to 0.7289, P ¡0.001) and indicate the validity of the construct.

All the indicators (MHIK1-MHIK6) have significant loadings (B = 0.5479 to 0.7549, P ¡0.001) with MHIK3 having the largest factor loading (B = 0.7549, Z = 11.331, P ¡0.001), implying the presence of the latent construct.

In general, the measurement model shows most of the indicators contribute enough to their respective latent variables, with the exception of AD6, which has a weak and non-significant loading.

Table 3 contains the variances of different variables, their standard errors (SE), 95% confidence intervals (Lower and Upper bounds), standardized regression coefficients (B), Z values and p values for statistical significance and relationship between the studied variables. The data contains multiple variables including PK (Packaging), MK (Marketing), AD (Advertisement), MH (Mobile Health Interventions), MHIP (Mobile Health Intervention Practices), MHIK (Mobile Health Intervention Knowledge), and the like and their variance estimates are from 0.01048 to 1.92449. The B values of the relationships vary across the dataset and the highest value is for AD6 (0.997) and most of the estimates are highly significant (p ¡0.001) except for few relationships like Packaging-Marketing

Table 3. Variances and covariances.

Variable 1	Variable 2	Estimate	SE	Lower CI	Upper CI		Z	P
PK1	PK1	0.509	0.035	0.440	0.578	0.98	14.45	¡.001
PK2	PK2	0.257	0.019	0.220	0.295	0.723	13.35	¡.001
PK3	PK3	0.277	0.023	0.232	0.323	0.556	11.91	¡.001
PK4	PK4	0.223	0.018	0.187	0.258	0.585	12.24	¡.001
PK5	PK5	0.167	0.026	0.116	0.219	0.268	6.32	¡.001
PK6	PK6	0.391	0.029	0.334	0.449	0.728	13.38	¡.001
MK1	MK1	0.699	0.050	0.600	0.798	0.706	13.87	¡.001
MK2	MK2	0.555	0.040	0.477	0.634	0.684	13.8	¡.001
MK3	MK3	0.494	0.036	0.423	0.564	0.672	13.76	¡.001
MK4	MK4	0.783	0.056	0.673	0.893	0.726	13.94	¡.001
MK5	MK5	0.599	0.044	0.513	0.685	0.642	13.65	¡.001
MK6	MK6	0.635	0.047	0.544	0.727	0.632	13.6	¡.001
AD1	AD1	1.113	0.078	0.961	1.266	0.953	14.28	¡.001
AD2	AD2	0.390	0.032	0.328	0.453	0.676	12.26	¡.001
AD3	AD3	1.044	0.074	0.898	1.190	0.907	14.04	¡.001
AD4	AD4	0.376	0.038	0.302	0.451	0.508	9.89	¡.001
AD5	AD5	0.414	0.037	0.341	0.487	0.585	11.13	¡.001
AD6	AD6	1.924	0.133	1.664	2.185	0.997	14.5	¡.001
MH1	MH1	0.558	0.040	0.480	0.636	0.647	13.96	¡.001
MH2	MH2	1.344	0.094	1.160	1.528	0.801	14.29	¡.001
MH3	MH3	0.849	0.059	0.732	0.965	0.813	14.31	¡.001
MH4	MH4	0.374	0.027	0.322	0.426	0.65	13.97	¡.001
MH5	MH5	0.361	0.026	0.310	0.412	0.618	13.87	¡.001
MH6	MH6	0.374	0.028	0.320	0.428	0.554	13.6	¡.001
MHIP1	MHIP1	0.537	0.040	0.459	0.616	0.614	13.49	¡.001
MHIP2	MHIP2	0.302	0.023	0.257	0.347	0.539	13.12	¡.001
MHIP3	MHIP3	0.357	0.027	0.304	0.410	0.561	13.24	¡.001
MHIP4	MHIP4	0.297	0.022	0.254	0.341	0.586	13.37	¡.001
MHIP5	MHIP5	0.294	0.023	0.248	0.339	0.469	12.64	¡.001
MHIP6	MHIP6	0.368	0.029	0.312	0.425	0.488	12.79	¡.001
MHIK1	MHIK1	0.376	0.029	0.320	0.433	0.651	13.11	¡.001
MHIK2	MHIK2	0.425	0.032	0.363	0.487	0.7	13.39	¡.001
MHIK3	MHIK3	0.267	0.024	0.219	0.314	0.43	11.03	¡.001
MHIK4	MHIK4	0.409	0.032	0.346	0.472	0.587	12.67	¡.001
MHIK5	MHIK5	0.271	0.022	0.227	0.315	0.525	12.14	¡.001
MHIK6	MHIK6	0.344	0.027	0.291	0.397	0.598	12.76	¡.001
		Construct Variances						
Packaging	0.010		0.008	-0.005	0.026	1	1.34	0.181
Marketing	0.291		0.051	0.192	0.390	1	5.76	¡.001
Advertisement	0.055		0.028	0.0003	0.110	1	1.97	0.049
Mobile Health	0.304		0.047	0.213	0.395	1	6.53	¡.001
HFSS Consumption	0.052		0.013	0.027	0.076	0.152	4.08	¡.001
Healthy Food Attitude	0.105		0.018	0.069	0.141	0.52	5.75	¡.001
		Covariances						
Packaging	Marketing	0.009	0.005	-0.0004	0.019	0.165	1.87	0.062
Packaging	Advertisement	0.004	0.002	-0.0007	0.009	0.164	1.68	0.093
Packaging	Mobile Health	0.011	0.005	0.0005	0.022	0.199	2.06	0.04
Marketing	Advertisement	0.081	0.023	0.036	0.126	0.637	3.51	¡.001
Marketing	Mobile Health	0.309	0.038	0.234	0.384	1.039	8.04	¡.001
Advertisement	Mobile Health	0.098	0.027	0.045	0.150	0.753	3.62	¡.001
HFSS Consumption	Healthy Food Attitude	0.024	0.009	0.007	0.041	0.322	2.75	0.006

(p = 0.062) and Packaging-Advertisement (p = 0.093) that are not statistically significant.

Table 5 presents the intercept values for various variables along with their standard errors (SE), 95% confidence intervals (lower and upper bounds), Z-scores, and p-values, indicating the significance of these estimates. The variables are categorized under different groups such as Packaging (PK), Marketing (MK), Advertisement (AD), Mobile Health Interventions (MH), Mobile Health Intervention Perceptions (MHIP), and Mobile Health Intervention Knowledge (MHIK). The intercept values range from 1.352 (PK2) to 3.454 (AD6), with standard errors varying from 0.029 to 0.068, reflecting the precision of these estimates.

6 DISCUSSION AND CRITICAL CONCLUSION

The aim of the study was to evaluate the effect of mobile health interventions (MHIs) on attitudes towards healthy food consumption for different MHIs including mobile apps, mobile based visual diaries, dietitian support and mobile market programs. The findings showed mobile health interventions can substantially influence the attitudes among individuals on choosing healthier foods highlighting the power of personalization, more of engagement, and more of feedback. The importance of such findings for public health strategies developing healthier eating habits in the population susceptible to them cannot be overemphasized.

Table 4. Intercepts.

Variable	Intercept	SE	Lower 95% CI	Upper 95% CI	Z	P
PK1	1.644	0.035	1.575	1.713	46.808	¡.001
PK2	1.352	0.029	1.295	1.409	46.463	¡.001
PK3	1.553	0.034	1.486	1.621	45.126	¡.001
PK4	1.371	0.030	1.312	1.429	45.588	¡.001
PK5	1.784	0.039	1.708	1.859	46.279	¡.001
PK6	1.610	0.036	1.540	1.680	45.088	¡.001
MK1	2.017	0.048	1.922	2.112	41.581	¡.001
MK2	1.843	0.044	1.757	1.929	41.983	¡.001
MK3	1.784	0.042	1.702	1.866	42.700	¡.001
MK4	2.010	0.051	1.910	2.109	39.706	¡.001
MK5	2.052	0.047	1.960	2.145	43.591	¡.001
MK6	2.135	0.049	2.040	2.231	43.696	¡.001
AD1	2.553	0.053	2.450	2.657	48.462	¡.001
AD2	1.696	0.037	1.623	1.769	45.795	¡.001
AD3	2.603	0.052	2.501	2.706	49.779	¡.001
AD4	1.888	0.042	1.806	1.971	45.026	¡.001
AD5	1.834	0.041	1.753	1.914	44.694	¡.001
AD6	3.454	0.068	3.321	3.586	51.014	¡.001
MH1	2.021	0.045	1.933	2.110	44.678	¡.001
MH2	2.373	0.063	2.249	2.497	37.586	¡.001
MH3	2.105	0.050	2.007	2.202	42.267	¡.001
MH4	1.713	0.037	1.640	1.785	46.326	¡.001
MH5	1.843	0.037	1.770	1.916	49.511	¡.001
MH6	1.867	0.040	1.788	1.946	46.595	¡.001
MHIP1	1.979	0.046	1.889	2.068	43.380	¡.001
MHIP2	1.715	0.036	1.643	1.786	47.024	¡.001
MHIP3	1.772	0.039	1.696	1.848	45.565	¡.001
MHIP4	1.637	0.035	1.569	1.705	47.170	¡.001
MHIP5	1.900	0.039	1.825	1.976	49.260	¡.001
MHIP6	1.895	0.042	1.813	1.978	44.797	¡.001
MHIK1	1.667	0.037	1.595	1.740	45.003	¡.001
MHIK2	1.727	0.038	1.652	1.801	45.484	¡.001
MHIK3	1.729	0.038	1.654	1.804	45.069	¡.001
MHIK4	1.957	0.041	1.878	2.037	48.134	¡.001
MHIK5	1.843	0.035	1.775	1.912	52.617	¡.001
MHIK6	1.841	0.037	1.768	1.913	49.798	¡.001
Packaging	0	0	0	0		
Healthy Food Attitude	0	0	0	0		

Table 5. Intercepts.

Variable P	Intercept	SE	Lower 95% CI	Upper 95% CI	Z
PK1 ¡.001	1.644	0.035	1.575	1.713	46.808
PK2 ¡.001	1.352	0.029	1.295	1.409	46.463
PK3 ¡.001	1.553	0.034	1.486	1.621	45.126
PK4 ¡.001	1.371	0.03	1.312	1.429	45.588
PK5 ¡.001	1.784	0.039	1.708	1.859	46.279
PK6 ¡.001	1.61	0.036	1.54	1.68	45.088
MK1 ¡.001	2.017	0.048	1.922	2.112	41.581
MK2 ¡.001	1.843	0.044	1.757	1.929	41.983
MK3 ¡.001	1.784	0.042	1.702	1.866	42.7
MK4 ¡.001	2.01	0.051	1.91	2.109	39.706
MK5 ¡.001	2.052	0.047	1.96	2.145	43.591
MK6 ¡.001	2.135	0.049	2.04	2.231	43.696
AD1 ¡.001	2.553	0.053	2.45	2.657	48.462
AD2 ¡.001	1.696	0.037	1.623	1.769	45.795

(continued)

Table 5. Continued

Variable P	Intercept	SE	Lower 95% CI	Upper 95% CI	Z
AD3 ¡.001	2.603	0.052	2.501	2.706	49.779
AD4 ¡.001	1.888	0.042	1.806	1.971	45.026
AD5 ¡.001	1.834	0.041	1.753	1.914	44.694
AD6 ¡.001	3.454	0.068	3.321	3.586	51.014
MH1 ¡.001	2.021	0.045	1.933	2.11	44.678
MH2 ¡.001	2.373	0.063	2.249	2.497	37.586
MH3	2.105	0.05	2.007	2.202	42.267

The major conclusion that came from this study is that to achieve the success of mobile health interventions in changing dietary attitudes, user engagement is a key factor. As previous research reiterated time and time again, engagement is critical to health behavior change [8]. Finally, in this study, the participants who had higher engagement with the mobile apps, such as more frequent usage of a mobile based visual diary or dietitian support, had significant improvement in attitudes towards healthy foods, such as fruits and vegetables. This finding is consistent with Kral *et al.* [10] who reported engagement with mobile technology promoted positive dietary change in children with autism spectrum disorder. The results indicate that interactive and personalized attributes of an MHI help users to adapt and sustain positive changes in the consumption of food.

The second critical aspect was that healthy foods were made accessible to people through mobile health programs. For example, attitudes related to food such as increased self-efficacy in preparing healthy meals were associated with mobile markets aimed at food insecure communities. It is consistent with Horning *et al.* [7], who found similar effects in mobile market customers, in which access to healthy foods, whether real or surrogate, had an effect on both behaviors and attitudes. In addition to making these options more accessible, these interventions also gave participants the knowledge and resources to cook healthily, and for those who do not, create healthier meals, covering the largest barriers to healthy eating in those who cannot afford, or have never had nutritious food options.

In addition, introducing persuasive technology, as it has been in interventions for young adolescents, was able to influence attitudes towards healthy eating. As per Kroes and Shahid [11] study, mobile applications used to encourage healthy behaviour, relying on social influence and gamification, produced more positive attitudes toward fruit consumption. The social nature of these technologies and peer interactions was utilised to support healthy food preferences with these persuasive features, which were also part of the present study's mobile health interventions. Moving dietary attitudes was potent psychiatry owing in part to social influence, accompanied by clear attitudinal aims and feedback.

In addition, Choudhury *et al.* [5] used mobile health interventions to promote maternal health and evaluated the effect of mobile health apps on pregnant women's knowledge and attitudes towards nutrition. While there were no ups in behaviors aside from dietary behavior, the interest and willingness to engage with mobile health interventions showed a shift, especially in low resource environments. This mirrors the expansion of the possibility of health knowledge and attitudes towards nutrition improved by mobile health interventions in communities with limited healthcare.

The study also identified the possibility of the use of mobile health for the targeted filling of specific dietary needs for marginalized groups. Combined, they improved the healthiness of these interventions when aimed at the cognitive aspects of healthy eating as well as the practical aspects. For example, in the case of food insecurity, joining food delivery service with enhancing participants' awareness about the value of food through mobile apps produced a powerful intervention model combining food delivery and enhancing awareness for individuals' improved access to nutritious food and change of attitude [13]. These findings support prior studies finding that mobile health combined with community interventions is an effective strategy for treating challenging health and dietary processes [18].

According to the study hypothesis, it can be concluded that mobile health interventions substantially affect attitudes towards the consumption of healthy foods. Particularly, these interventions that provide personal, interactive characteristics and continuous feedback seem to increase individuals' understanding of healthy eating and encourage their healthy dietary behaviors. Based on the study, mobile-based visual diaries, dietitian support, and mobile market programs were found effective interventions to change people's attitudes through increasing their self-efficacy, knowledge, and engagement of healthy food options. As mobile health interventions continue to be part of daily life, mobile health is a promising path for dealing with poor dietary habits, especially in underserved populations. The study stresses the significance of developing mobile health interventions that are engaging, accessible, and aim to address particular barriers to healthy eating to make it more than just knowing the value of healthy food selections but also the means to do it.

7 STUDY IMPLICATIONS

This study's findings have several important implications for public health policy, education, digital intervention design, as well as food industry regulation. The study first brings to light the imperative need for a more rigorous regulation of aggressive marketing, misleading advertising, and manipulative packaging of packaged foods high in fat, sugar, and salt (HFSS) to the extent that they become normalized and promoted to children and adolescents. Commercial strategies have a direct effect on the consumer attitudes and purchasing behavior, which sometimes lead to unhealthy eating patterns. Thus, regulations in terms of how much exposure to HFSS food promotions policymakers can limit through traditional and digital platforms like television, social media, and in-store displays need to be strengthened.

At the same time, the study underscores the promising role of mobile health interventions (MHIs) in fostering positive attitudes towards healthy eating. Personalized, interactive tools such as mobile-based visual diaries, dietitian support, and nutrition education apps showed potential in enhancing user engagement and self-efficacy. Therefore, public health programs should consider integrating MHIs into broader dietary awareness and behavior-change initiatives, especially in underserved communities where access to nutrition education is limited.

Importantly, the combined approach of restricting harmful food marketing while actively promoting evidence-based digital health tools could create a more supportive environment for healthy food choices. Educators, app developers, and health professionals should work collaboratively to ensure interventions are age-appropriate, culturally sensitive, and engaging, while governments should adopt a dual approach that both protects consumers from unhealthy food promotion and empowers them through accessible, technology-driven solutions.

8 THE FUTURE SCOPE

The future scope of this study extends to a comprehensive exploration of both positive and negative influences on food consumption behaviors and attitudes. While mobile health interventions (MHIs) demonstrated potential in improving attitudes toward healthy food choices, there remains significant scope to further investigate how these interventions can be optimized to counteract the pervasive and often harmful effects of aggressive marketing, advertisement, and manipulative packaging strategies promoting high-fat, sugar, and salt (HFSS) foods.

Future studies could explore how MHIs can be designed to actively educate consumers—especially children and adolescents—about deceptive marketing tactics and enhance critical thinking toward food advertising. Additionally, research should examine the comparative and combined influence of digital advertisements, social media marketing, in-store promotions, and visually appealing packaging on food preferences across different age groups and cultural contexts.

There is also a need to evaluate policy-level interventions that regulate HFSS food marketing and packaging, and to assess their interaction with digital health promotion tools like MHIs. Longitudinal and intervention-based studies could further help in understanding the lasting behavioral impacts of repeated exposure to HFSS food advertising versus sustained engagement with health-promoting mobile technologies. Lastly, exploring collaborative strategies where MHIs work alongside school curricula, public awareness campaigns, and community-based programs can offer a holistic approach to reshaping food-related attitudes and curbing the rising consumption of unhealthy packaged foods.

DISCLOSURE STATEMENT

No potential conflict of interest was reported by the authors.

ACKNOWLEDGEMENT(S)

The authors would like to thank all the adolescent participants from the four private schools in Jaipur and their guardians for their cooperation in this research study. We also acknowledge the school administrations for facilitating data collection.

REFERENCES

[1] O. Bera, R. Singh, and S. Bhattacharya, (2023) Food literacy & food labeling laws—a legal analysis of India's food policy, *Journal of Family Medicine and Primary Care*, 12(2) , pp. 606–610.

[2] E. Boyland, (2023) Is it ethical to advertise unhealthy foods to children? *The Proceedings of the Nutrition Society*, pp. 1–15.

[3] E. Boyland and J.L. Harris, (2017) Regulation of food marketing to children: are statutory or industry self-governed systems effective? *Public Health Nutrition*, 20(5) , pp. 761– 764.

[4] G. Buckland, Z. Toumpakari, R. Jago, S. Harding, J. Nobles, J. Horwood, C. Sillero Rejon, W. Hollingworth, S. Cummins, S. Blake, A. Nairn, and F. Vocht, (2024) The quantitative evaluation of the impact of a new outdoor advertising restrictions policy in Bristol: a natural experiment evaluation, *The European Journal of Public Health,* 34(1) , pp. 1–8.

[5] A. Choudhury, Y. Shahsavar, K. Sarkar, M. Choudhury, and A. Nimbarte, (2023) Exploring perceptions and needs of mobile health interventions for nutrition, anemia, and preeclampsia among pregnant women in underprivileged Indian communities: A cross-sectional survey, *Nutrients,* 15(17) , pp. 3699.

[6] A. Gallagher-Squires, A. Isaacs, C. Reynolds, and P.C. Coleman, (2023) Snacking practices from infancy to adolescence: parental perspectives from longitudinal lived experience research in England, *The Proceedings of the Nutrition Society*, pp. 1–9.

[7] M. Horning, B.M. Alver, L. Porter, S. Lenarz-Coy, and N. Kamdar, (2021) Food insecurity, food-related characteristics and behaviors, and fruit and vegetable intake in mobile market customers, *Appetite*, 166 , pp. 105466.

[8] Y. Kato-Lin, V. Abhishek, J. Downs, and R. Padman, (2016). Food for thought: The impact of m-Health enabled interventions on eating behavior, *SSRN*.

[9] S. Kousta, (2020). Reducing sugary drink consumption, *Nature Human Behaviour*, 4(3), pp. 235–235.

[10] T. Kral, L. O'Malley, K.E. Johnson, T. Benvenuti, J. Chittams, R. Quinn, J.G. Thomas, J. Pinto-Martin, S. Levy, and E. Kuschner, (2023) Effects of a mobile health nutrition intervention on dietary intake in children who have autism spectrum disorder, *Frontiers in Pediatrics*, 11 , pp. 1100436.

[11] L. Kroes and S. Shahid, (2013) Empowering young adolescents to choose the healthy lifestyle: A persuasive intervention using mobile phones, in Health and Technology, *Springer*, pp. 117–126.

[12] R. Meiksin, V. Er, C. Thompson, J. Adams, E. Boyland, T. Burgoine, L. Cornelsen, F. de Vocht, M. Egan, A. Lake, K. Lock, O. Mytton, M. White, A. Yau, and S. Cummins, (2021). Restricting the advertising of high fat, salt and sugar foods on the Transport for London estate: Process and implementation study, *Social Science & Medicine*, pp. 114548.

[13] J. Oliveira, L. To, Y. de la Cruz, and G.W. Schneider, (2021) Prompting a fresh start for adults with food insecurity and increased BMI: A case series of four patients in a food prescription program, *Cureus*, 13 .

[14] J. Packer, S. Russell, K. McLaren, G. Siovolgyi, C. Stansfield, R. Viner, and H. Croker, (2022). The impact on dietary outcomes of licensed and brand equity characters in marketing unhealthy foods to children: A systematic review and meta-analysis, *Obesity Reviews*, 23(5) , pp. 1–11.

[15] S. Pombo-Rodrigues, K. Hashem, M. Tan, Z. Davies, F. He, and G. MacGregor, (2020). Nutrition profile of products with cartoon animations on the packaging: A UK cross-sectional survey of foods and drinks, *Nutrients*, 12(3) , pp. 707–720.

[16] C. Richonnet, F. Mosser, E. Favre, M. Robert, F. Martin, and I. Thi´ebaut, (2021) Nutritional quality and degree of processing of children's foods assessment on the French market, *Nutrients,* 14 (1) , pp. 171–179.

[17] M. Tatlow-Golden, C. Boyland, A. Jewell, M. Kettenbach, C. Schwartz, M. Ferrer, A. Lu·ttikhuis, H. Doherty, L. Maher, J. Stead, and A. Adamson, (2015). Tackling food marketing to children in a digital world: trans-disciplinary perspectives, *Public Health*, 138 , pp. 3–6.

[18] X.C. Tham, C. Whitton, F. (2022). Mu·ller-Riemenschneider, and N. Petrunoff, Young adults' use of mobile food delivery apps and the potential impacts on diet during the COVID-19 pandemic: Mixed methods study, *JMIR Formative Research*, 7 , pp. 38959.

Advancement in Engineering and Science – Goyal et al. (Eds)
© 2026 The Author(s), ISBN: 978-1-041-31101-0

Determinants of Teachers' Happiness: A Comprehensive Review

Shalini Singh and Ruchi Goyal
JECRC University, Ramchandrapura, Sitapura Industrial Area Extension, Jaipur, Rajasthan, India

ABSTRACT: Happiness, often synonymous with subjective well-being, is increasingly acknowledged as a vital component of individual welfare, especially amidst the ongoing enhancements in living standards propelled by economic growth. This trend reflects societal inclinations towards prioritizing fulfilment and meaning in life. Despite extensive research on the well-being of college educators and its impact on student outcomes, little attention has been directed towards the happiness of school teachers, who significantly shape students' development over crucial formative years. Understanding teacher happiness is pivotal not only for their own satisfaction but also for its cascading effects on student achievement, societal progress, and national development initiatives. This study aims to explore factors influencing teacher happiness, efficiency, and engagement in private schools, leveraging global research and proposing frameworks for future measurement. While existing literature provides insights into job satisfaction metrics, a comprehensive approach to assessing workplace happiness among educators is essential. By highlighting teacher happiness as integral to educational quality and societal advancement, this research seeks to foster a culture of well-being within schools and facilitating ongoing progress in the field.

Keywords: Employee Well-being, Teacher's Well-being, Job Satisfaction, Teacher's Satisfaction, Workplace Happiness

1 INTRODUCTION

Human life is driven by the pursuit of happiness, characterized by positive emotions influenced by neurotransmitters like dopamine and serotonin. Eudemonia, a Greek concept, encompasses various facets of well-being. Happiness, as defined by Xavier Landes (2015), includes subjective well-being and mood. Happiness is intrinsically linked to work, where individuals seek both financial and non-financial rewards, as highlighted by Saari and Judge (2004). Job satisfaction significantly impacts overall life satisfaction, as noted by Binswanger (2006), emphasizing the importance of happiness in various life aspects. Research by Angner, Hullett, Allison (2011), Jiang, Lu, Sato (2012), and Van Praag, Romanov, Ferrer-i-Carbonell (2010) underscores the association between happiness and subjective well-being. Work plays a crucial role in individuals' lives, providing financial and emotional fulfilment. Saari and Judge (2004) assert a strong link between job satisfaction and overall life satisfaction, emphasizing the broader significance of happiness at work.

In Kosovo's enterprises, theoretical models often don't translate into practical application. Financial incentives, like cash bonuses, are commonly used but may overlook deeper employee needs. Regular communication and frequent rewards are recommended to bridge this gap and reduce turnover. Employees may hesitate to express concerns, highlighting the need for a safe environment where recognition is prioritized. Integrating content and process theories can enhance employee engagement and satisfaction, ultimately reducing turnover and boosting motivation. Engaged employees contribute meaningfully to their workplace, enhancing productivity and organizational outcomes.

Joel's (2010) narrative provides a poignant reflection on his journey into teaching. Starting his career in 2002, he initially faced significant challenges in classroom management despite possessing ample information. His classes were disorderly, leaving him exhausted, frustrated, and feeling disregarded by his students. These struggles, coupled with a sense of isolation and burnout, brought him to the brink of resignation from his school. Thus, happiness of teachers is particularly vital, impacting student outcomes and societal progress. A happy teaching staff fosters student development and school effectiveness, contributing to broader societal goals.

1.1 *Defining the problem*

Despite numerous studies on happiness, limited information exists on the determinants of satisfaction among teachers across all school levels. It remains unclear whether teacher satisfaction differs from that of other professions. Retaining high-quality teachers is crucial for schools worldwide, yet it's a persistent challenge. Existing literature on teacher happiness primarily focuses on various aspects such as workplace happiness, work-life balance, and job satisfaction. However, happiness encompasses a broader spectrum beyond mere job satisfaction or commitment. It's essential for educators, managers, and policymakers to understand the underlying factors contributing to teacher happiness.

This research aims to provide clarity on the determinants of teacher happiness by synthesizing existing global research on happiness, job satisfaction, life satisfaction, work-life balance, and workplace engagement aiming to equip future researches with the necessary insights to measure and enhance teacher happiness, ultimately fostering their growth, development, and well-being.

1.2 *Research methodology*

The research methodology adopted for this study encompasses a systematic approach to understanding the factors contributing to teacher happiness. Initially, an extensive literature review was conducted to identify existing research on teacher happiness, job satisfaction, life satisfaction, work-life balance, workplace engagement, and related topics. Subsequently, a comprehensive research framework was developed based on insights gleaned from the literature review, incorporating various intrinsic and extrinsic factors, work environment conditions, personal attributes, and societal influences. Data collection involved a mixed-methods approach, including surveys, interviews, focus groups, and observations, with a purposive sampling strategy employed to ensure representation across diverse demographics, teaching levels, and geographical locations. Quantitative analysis techniques, such as statistical methods, will be used to identify correlations and patterns among variables, while qualitative analysis, including thematic analysis, will be employed to explore themes and narratives related to teacher happiness. The findings will be validated through triangulation, comparing data from multiple sources and methods, and interpreted within the context of the research framework. Implications for educational policy, practice, and future research will be discussed, along with acknowledgment of study limitations and suggestions for further investigation.

1.3 *Exploring the solution*

Wesarat, Sharif, Majid, and Halim (2014) conducted an extensive review of global research on workplace happiness among teachers, finding that terms like joy, commitment, and fulfilment are often used interchangeably, with various studies measuring different aspects of happiness. This supports the notion that workplace satisfaction encompasses both work and overall life contentment. Workplace satisfaction includes two main components: hedonic, which involves emotional experiences at work, closely linked to work satisfaction, and eudemonic, which focuses on living a meaningful life with a sense of purpose and commitment. While studies in the UK and US primarily focus on job satisfaction among university teachers, research in China, Israel, India, and Pakistan also explores the happiness and job satisfaction of university educators. Studies from various countries such as El Salvador, Mexico, Turkey, the Netherlands, India, Nepal, Iran, Italy, and Jordan investigate different aspects of teacher happiness and job satisfaction, revealing overlapping determinants such as working conditions, pay, management systems, and stress levels. Despite cultural differences, common determinants of happiness among teachers include job satisfaction, positive relationships, and low stress levels. Overall, happiness for teachers encompasses personal fulfilment, positive emotions, and a sense of purpose in their work and lives.

Tables 1, 2 and 3 exhibit a concise framework of the determinants of three between related ideas of bliss at work, work fulfilment and commitment country-wise and the components of educator's work-related joy.

Table 1. Determinants of happiness.

China (Including Taiwan and Hong Kong)	India	Pakistan	Netherlands	Turkey	Latin America (Mexico and El Salvador)
Purposeful, engaged and pleasurable life	Intrinsic factors like things related with confidence, self-realisation both that determine bliss of an instructor from within or inner self	Autonomy	High work demands like time pressure, substantial work overload etc.	The sense of teacher's satisfaction in emotional and cognitive dimensions	Pleasure
Diversity of teachers and human dignity should be completely respected.	Extrinsic factors such as compensation, work environment, health etc.	Environmental mastery	Lack of reciprocity and pupils' misbehaviour	Preponderance of feelings that bring positivity and low frequency of negative feelings in life	Meaning
Free, fair, academic, independent and ecological environment	Work-life issues that are associated with flexibility, adjustment, work-life balance etc.	Positive relationships with other people	Unsupportive colleagues	here the criteria get entirely settled by and for instructors themselves, the process of subjective assessment	Engagement in life
Connection with an incentive system that is flexible.		Purposeful life	Motivation that is self-concordant	Friendship at work	
Objective condition like requirements pertaining to material, safety, spiritual environment, family, self-defence, love, kinship, confidence, regard for other people, want, self-assessment, working circumstances, pay etc.	Job satisfaction	Personal growth		Accept and give support willingly	
Subjective conditions such as perception of one's health, optimistic and pessimistic emotions or moods, confidence in one's future, life evaluation, sense of achievement etc.	Complete sense of harmony in life	Self-acceptance		Be able to do better quality work efficiently	
Job satisfaction	Stress and work pressure			Organised, creative and confident	
Career development				Stress management and self-controlled	
Spirituality					
Relationships with other people					
Pleasant living conditions					
Freedom and/or potential to achieve one's highest occupational ideal					
Self-satisfaction					

Source: author

Table 2. Determinants of engagement.

The Netherlands
Work environment
Job resources
Exchange with supervisor
Opportunities for development
Autonomy at work

Source: author

Table 3. Dimensions of a teacher's occupational happiness.

China	India
Social support	Students' achievement
Teacher–student relationship	Recognition
Work environment	Positive management of work demand
Self-realisation	Support of colleagues' and principal
Income and welfare	-

Source: author

2 SUMMARY PERTAINING EACH COUNTRY

2.1 *India*

In India, studies on instructor satisfaction have often centred on joy, occupation fulfilment, or the balance between serious and fun activities. Rao Vijayalakshmi and Goswami (2018) explored workplace happiness in a private higher education institute in Visakhapatnam. Their study included employees from various fields with a minimum of 3 years' experience. Happiness factors were categorized into intrinsic elements such as confidence and self-fulfilment, extrinsic elements like compensation and workplace environment, and work-life balance issues like flexibility and change.

Age emerged as a significant factor in workplace happiness, especially during the early years of employment. The choice of the teaching profession was largely driven by factors like flexibility, self-realization, and work-life balance rather than ambitious career growth or high pay. Educational institutions can enhance workplace happiness by providing age-appropriate facilities, flexible timings, and financial support.

Mahipalan and Sheena (2018) found significant links between workplace spirituality, gratitude, and subjective happiness among high school teachers. Gratitude was identified as a key mediator influencing workplace satisfaction. Punia and Kamboj (2013) stressed the importance of balancing fun and serious activities for mental well-being and overall life satisfaction among university teachers in India.

Despite the challenges, achieving work-life balance remains crucial for educators' mental and physical well-being. Stressors such as excessive workload, administrative duties, and inadequate support contribute to dissatisfaction. Nigam (2017) highlighted the lack of attention to teacher satisfaction in India compared to global studies. Issues like excessive workload, poor management, and inadequate benefits impact teacher satisfaction significantly.

To improve teacher satisfaction, educational institutions should provide supportive environments, resources for teaching, opportunities for professional development, and address basic personal and professional needs. Efforts to enhance workplace happiness and satisfaction can contribute to a healthier and more productive educational environment in India.

2.2 *China*

Yipeng Tang's (2018) study on rural teachers in China revealed various factors affecting them, notably age, gender, marriage, administrative position, class size, wages, and professional training, with wages being of paramount importance. Chen *et al.* (2006) found that factors like orientation, marital status, and organizational characteristics significantly impacted the balance between serious and fun activities among university teachers in Taiwan.

Previous research on job satisfaction in higher education often focused on students' satisfaction rather than teachers. Hagedorn (1994) highlighted dimensions like salary, interaction with students, support from colleagues, perceived stress, and satisfaction with administration. A model for teacher satisfaction in higher education, proposed by recent studies, includes management systems, organizational vision, benefits, feedback, motivation, and work environment, as teachers play roles in teaching, research, and administration.

Du, Lai, and Lo (2010) identified six job satisfaction factors among professors in Chinese universities, influenced by organizational environment, academic field, performance evaluation, and school management.

Zhongying (2013) emphasized the importance of researching teacher happiness in China, integrating philosophical perspectives like Confucianism, Taoism, and Buddhism. They stressed understanding teachers' happiness from mental, social, and spiritual aspects, proposing customized concepts for teacher well-being.

Zhao (2013) emphasized respecting teachers' dignity and providing fair incentives to maximize their academic potential and job satisfaction. Chen and Duan (2017) developed a happiness index for teachers, considering both objective and subjective factors. Chan (2019) explored three dimensions of happiness among Chinese teachers in Hong Kong, following Martin Seligman's positive psychology theory, aiming to enhance life satisfaction and emotional well-being while managing burnout.

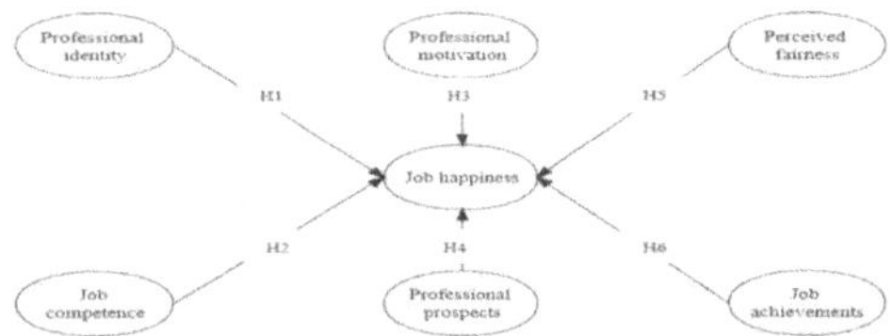

Figure 1. Job happiness relationships model.
Source: https://www.frontiersin.org/files/Articles/1018517/fpsyg-13-1018517-HTML-r2/image_m/fpsyg-13-1018517-g001.jpg

The statement "Job achievements is positively related to teachers' job happiness" suggests that when teachers experience success and accomplishment in their professional roles, they are more likely to feel satisfied and fulfilled in their jobs. This relationship implies that achieving goals, meeting expectations, and experiencing recognition for their work contribute to teachers' overall happiness in their job roles. Based on this hypothetical relationship, the study constructs a theoretical model depicted in Figure 1, illustrating the interconnection between job achievements and teachers' job happiness.

2.3 *Pakistan*

Research in Pakistan has explored teachers' happiness and work fulfillment to enhance their mental well-being and overall satisfaction, aiming to improve academic standards. Akram (2012) compared the psychological well-being of private and public university teachers based on demographic variables like gender, experience, and designation. He assessed mental prosperity across six subscales: autonomy, environmental mastery, purpose in life, positive relations with others, personal growth, and self-acceptance. Female teachers reported higher levels of positive relations and self-acceptance. Unmarried teachers showed more purposeful life and personal growth, while married teachers exhibited more autonomy.

Zafarullah and Pertti (2017) investigated factors affecting teachers' job satisfaction in Sind, Pakistan. They found work fulfillment significantly contributed to teachers' happiness and motivation, aligning with their life and career aspirations. Socio-demographic factors, economic incentives, supportive work environment, and organizational leadership styles influenced job satisfaction. Factors like hierarchical management and leadership styles, lack of growth opportunities, and inadequate support systems led to work dissatisfaction.

Efforts to enhance teacher job satisfaction include adopting a democratic leadership style, enhancing organizational accountability, ensuring job security, fostering communication and positive work relationships, and implementing reward and recognition systems. These initiatives aim to improve teachers' mental well-being and enable them to lead fulfilling professional and personal lives.

2.4 *United Kingdom*

Previous studies in the United Kingdom have predominantly focused on the work satisfaction aspect of teachers' workplace happiness. Hill and Michael (2000) found through the Oxford Happiness Inventory that self-esteem, life regard, mental stability, and life orientation were closely linked to happiness, with introversion and extroversion also playing a role. Jacobs *et al.* (2007) conducted a secondary analysis of data from 13 higher education institutions, identifying factors like physical health, psychological well-being, and organizational commitment as predictors of job satisfaction and performance. They noted the strain on educational institutions to achieve higher grades, funding, and academic credentials, often resulting in elevated levels of stress and lower job satisfaction among teachers compared to non-academic staff.

Similarly, Oshagbemi (1997a) explored job satisfaction among 566 college teachers, highlighting teaching and research-related activities, job stability, and university funding as significant influences. He referenced Herzberg's hygiene-motivation theory and situational occurrences in job satisfaction. Oshagbemi (1997b) categorized teachers into happy, satisfied, and unhappy groups, with the majority falling into the happy and satisfied categories. He proposed strategies to reduce the percentage of unhappy teachers, aiming to enhance overall job satisfaction in higher education.

2.5 *United States of America*

Previous research has highlighted a positive correlation between happiness and various indicators of workplace success. Comm and Mathaisel (2000) surveyed over 600 employees in a private higher education institution in the USA using a service quality model, identifying factors like personnel responsibility, workplace ethics, client-centred management, training and development, and compensation as key determinants of educator satisfaction. Many respondents felt their compensation was inadequate, leading to dissatisfaction and potentially impacting institutional academic quality.

Bozeman and Gaughan (2011) examined faculty job satisfaction, considering individual attributes, institutional work environment, and faculty characteristics. They found that experienced and male teachers tended to be more satisfied, with similarities observed across professions regarding recognition, colleague support, and performance-based incentives. However, career advancement was less significant for faculty compared to other professions.

While both intrinsic and extrinsic factors influence teacher satisfaction, intrinsic factors such as professional passion are often more significant than external factors like pay and benefits. The authors suggest future research explore satisfaction among teachers and other workers while examining the broader relationship between life satisfaction and job satisfaction.

2.6 *Latin America (Mexico and El Salvador)*

Villavicencio-Aguilar *et al.* (2020) conducted a recent study on higher education educators and students in Mexico and El Salvador, noting a lack of relevant research in their context. They developed an "orientation to happiness" scale, focusing on meaning, pleasure, and engagement, akin to previous studies by Chan (2009) and Seligman's positive psychology theories. The authors observed that while higher education institutions prioritize academic achievement and commitment, they often overlook the emotional well-being of their members. Results showed educators reported higher levels of meaning and engagement than students, with joy from leisure activities being the least pronounced. Gender did not significantly affect orientation to satisfaction. While the population of educators and students influenced orientation to happiness, the authors noted other factors within higher education institutions also played a role in shaping satisfaction levels.

2.7 *The Netherlands*

Two studies conducted in the Netherlands shed light on educators' work engagement and happiness. Bakker and Bal (2010) investigated the weekly work engagement of 54 Dutch teachers, finding that both intrinsic and extrinsic factors influenced their commitment. Intrinsic aspects, such as personal growth, and extrinsic factors, like opportunities for advancement, positively correlated with weekly engagement, which in turn related to improved performance. Notably, work engagement in one week predicted resources for the following week, emphasizing the dynamic nature of employees' experiences and their impact on performance.

Tadic *et al.* (2013) explored teachers' happiness across the Netherlands, identifying various factors affecting their well-being. Despite challenges like excessive workload and uncooperative colleagues leading to burnout, some teachers remained content. Positive interactions with responsive students and supportive colleagues contributed to their happiness. The study employed the work demands-resources model and self-determination theory, revealing that an individual's motivation and satisfaction with work demands varied. Notably, aligning job demands with educators' preferences and values positively influenced their happiness.

While both studies offer valuable insights, Tadic *et al.*'s focus on secondary school teachers limits the generalizability of their findings. Nonetheless, their emphasis on understanding the complex interplay between work demands, available resources, and employee well-being underscores the need for further research. By tailoring job demands to individual preferences and interests, organizations can enhance educators' satisfaction and performance. Overall, these studies highlight the importance of considering both intrinsic and extrinsic factors in promoting educators' engagement and happiness at work.

2.8 *Turkey*

Ihtiyaroglu (2018) carried out a research for determining the visionary role of happiness as well as level of by and large life fulfilment among instructors with respect to their study hall the board profiles. The example comprised of educators in training organisations inside the areas of Ankara city, Turkey. The creator saw that the idea of bliss signified to the feeling of a singular educator's fulfilment in both mental as well as profound aspects, greater part of good sentiments and furthermore little recurrence of gloomy sentiments inside their life, alongside a course of emotional evaluation during which the standards are viewed as both by and for the educators. They also said that joy can be evaluated when individual educators were more dynamic in significant exercises, had numerous companions at their working environment, did better quality jobs with high efficiency, gave as well as accepted support willingly, were more self-confident, creative, organised and even made use of effective coping strategies while they were stressed.

3 DISCUSSIONS AND CONCLUSIONS

Various studies across different countries have explored the concept of happiness in the workplace for educators, revealing two main approaches: one focusing on an engaged, meaningful, and pleasurable life, and the other on intrinsic and extrinsic factors related to work-life issues and job satisfaction. While terminology may vary, deeper examination shows common concepts and determinants across studies.

For example, studies in China, Pakistan, Turkey, and the Netherlands identified factors such as a supportive academic environment, opportunities for professional growth, and positive relationships with colleagues as contributors to happiness. Similarly, research in India and China highlighted the significance of work satisfaction in assessing happiness among educators. Zafarullah and Pertti (2017) conducted a comprehensive study on job satisfaction in Pakistan, providing a framework encompassing various determinants mentioned in other studies, including demographics, economic factors, organizational leadership, and opportunities for growth.

Lavy and Bocker (2018) emphasized the importance of meaningful work and relationships in shaping teacher satisfaction, aligning with the broader concept of meaningful life recognized globally. Bakker and Bal (2010) assessed teacher engagement in the Netherlands, highlighting aspects such as autonomy, job resources, and opportunities for development as crucial for job satisfaction. These findings underline the interconnectedness of happiness, job satisfaction, and engagement in the workplace.

Fairbajn Shelley and Gillespe (2022) conducted an international qualitative study comparing the experiences of teacher educators in the United States and India. They found common themes of authenticity, impact, and, uniquely for Indian educators, connection with students, underscoring the importance of personal fulfilment and meaningful interactions in shaping workplace happiness.

In conclusion, understanding the factors contributing to educators‘ happiness is essential for improving overall well-being and performance in schools.

4 FUTURE DIRECTIONS

It's evident that happy educators tend to be more productive, highlighting the importance of understanding and analysing happiness and work efficiency among school teachers. However, there's still much unexplored territory, particularly in terms of happiness in school teachers worldwide and its impact on efficiency. Future research should prioritize longitudinal studies to comprehensively gauge educators' happiness and validate findings over time. While cross-sectional data abound, happiness varies individually and across time, necessitating a more nuanced approach. Longitudinal studies offer a deeper understanding of happiness dynamics, aiding in outcome validation and determinant identification. Such insights are crucial for enhancing educators‘ satisfaction and productivity.

REFERENCES

Akram, M. (2019). Psychological well-being of university teachers in Pakistan. *Journal of Education and Educational Development*, 6(2), 235.

Angner, Hullett, and Allison, (2011); Jiang, Lu, and Sato, (2012) Van Praag Romanov, and Ferrer-i-Carbonell (2010).

Bakker, A.B., and Bal, M.P. (2010). Weekly work engagement and performance: A study among starting teachers. *Journal of Occupational and Organizational Psychology*, 83(1), 189206.

Binswanger, M. (2006). Why does income growth fail to make us happier? Searching for the treadmills behind the paradox of happiness. *The Journal of Socio-Economics,* 35, 366–381. http://dx.doi.org/10.1016 /j.socec.2005.11.040

Bozeman, B., and Gaughan, M. (2011). Job satisfaction among university faculty: Individual, work, and institutional determinants. *The Journal of Higher Education*, 82(2), 154–186.

C D Fisher. (2010). *Happiness at Work.* https://doi.org/10.1111/j.1468-2370.2009.00270.x

Chan, D.W. (2009). *Orientations to happiness and subjective.*

Chen, S.H., Yang, C.C., Shiau, J.Y., and Wang, H.H. (2006). The development of an employee satisfaction model for higher education. *The TQM Magazine.*

Chen, W., and Duan, Y. (2017). Teachers' happiness index based on AHP model of evaluation index system of building and research. *AMSE Journals 2016 Series: Modelling D*, 37(1); 65–76

Comm, C.L. and Mathaisel, D.F.X. (2000). "Assessing employee satisfaction in service firms: an example in high education", *The Journal of Business and Economic Studies,* pp. 43–53, Fairfield, Spring

Comm, C.L., and Mathaisel, D.F. (2003). A case study of the implications of faculty workload and compensation for improving academic quality. *International Journal of Educational Management.*

Driton Sylqa (2020), Motivation of People- Theoretical Models and Practices, *Business Management,* ISSN:2534-8396-Electronic Edition

Du, P., Lai, M., and Lo, L.N. (2010). Analysis of job satisfaction of university professors from nine Chinese universities. *Frontiers of Education in China*, 5(3), 430–449.

Fairbairn, Shelley; Gillespie, Catherine Wilson (2022). Pursuing Happiness and Fulfillment at Work: The Lived Experiences of Teacher Educators in the United States and India, Teacher Education Quarterly. *Spring* 2022, 49(2), 86–105. 20 p.

Hasan Aydin (2012); *Multicultural Education Curriculum Development in Turkey.* doi: 10.5901/mjss.2012.v3n3p277https://images-provider.frontiersin.org/api/ipx/w=410&f=webp/https://www.frontiersin.org/files/Articles/1018517/fpsyg-13-1018517-HTML-r2/image_m/fpsyg-13-1018517-g001.jpg

Ihtiyaroglu, N. (2018). Analysing the Relationship between Happiness, Teachers‘ Level of Satisfaction with Life and Classroom Management Profiles. Universal Journal of Educational Research, 6 (10), 2227-2237

Jacobs, Pamela A., Tytherleigh, Michelle Y., Webb, Christine, Cooper, Cary L. Jacobs, P.A., Tytherleigh, M.Y., Webb, C., and Cooper, C. L. (2007). Predictors of work performance among higher education employees: An examination using the ASSET Model of Stress. International Journal of Stress Management, 14(2), 199–210.

Jacqueline Kin Sang Chan (2009). Assessment for student improvement: understanding Hong Kong teachers' conceptions and practices of assessment, https://doi.org/10.1080/09695940903319737

Jiang, Lu, and Sato, (2012). Identity, Inequality and Happiness: Evidence from Urban China. https://doi.org/10.1016/j.worlddev.2011.11.002

L S Hagedorn (1994). Retirement proximity's role in the prediction of satisfaction in academe. https://doi.org/10.1007/BF02497083

Manju Mahipalan and Sheena (2018). *Workplace Spirituality and Subjective Happiness Among High School Teachers: Gratitude As A Moderator.* https://doi.org/10.1016/j.explore.2018.07.002

Nigam, S. (2017). *Factors Affecting job Satisfaction an Analytical Study of Academician in Selected Private Universities of Central India.*

Oshagbemi, T. (1997a). Job satisfaction and dissatisfaction in higher education. *Education + Training.* 39(9), 354–359.

Oshagbemi, T. (1997b). Job satisfaction profiles of university teachers. *Journal of Managerial Psychology,* 12(1), 2739.

Peter Hills, Michael Argyle (2000). Happiness, introversion-extraversion and happy introverts. PII: S0191-8869(00)00058-1

Punia, V., and Kamboj, M. (2013). Quality of work-life balance among teachers in higher education institutions. *Learning Community*, 4(3), 197–208

Rao, G.V., Vijayalakshmi, D., and Goswami, R. (2018). A study on factors of workplace happiness. *Asian Journal of Management,* 9(1), 251–260.

Ryff, C.D. (1989). Happiness is everything, or is it? Explorations on the meaning of psychological well-being. *Journal of Personality and Social Psychology*, 57(6), 1069.

Saari and Judge (2004). *Employee attitude and job satisfaction,* https://doi.org/10.1002/hrm.20032

So You Want to Teach. June 2010. Web. 21 June 2010. http://www.soyouwanttoteach.com/

Tadic, M., Bakker, A.B., and Oerlemans, W.G.M (2013). Work happiness among teachers: A day reconstruction study on the role of self-concordance. *Journal of School Psychology*, 51(2013), 735–750

Van Praag Romanov, and Ferrer-i-Carbonell (2010). Happiness and financial satisfaction in Israel: Effects of religiosity, ethnicity, and war, https://doi.org/10.1016/j.joep.2010.08.008

Villavicencio-Aguilar, D., Chacón-Andrade, E.R., and DurónRamos, M.F. (2020). Data on orientation to happiness in higher education institutions from Mexico and El Salvador. *Data*, 5(1), 27.

Wesarat, P.O., Sharif, M.Y., Majid, A., and Halim, A. (2014). A conceptual framework of happiness at the workplace. *Asian Social Science*, 11(2), 78–88.

Xavier Landes, (June 2015), *Building Happiness Indicators Some Philosophical and Political Issues.*

Yipeng Tang (2018). What makes rural teachers happy? *An investigation on the subjective well-being (SWB) of Chinese rural teachers.* https://doi.org/10.1016/j.ijedudev.2018.05.001

Zafarullah and Pertti (2017). *Effect of Time Management of the Job Satisfaction and Motivation of Teacher Educators: A Narrative Analysis,* https://erepo.uef.fi/handle/123456789/2594

Zhao, J., and Chen, H. (2013). An exploration of the classified incentives of college teachers based on work happiness. *Psychology Research,* 12, Retrieved from DOI: 10.5503/J. PR.2013.12.012

Zhongying, H.U. (2013). Research and Analysis on the Teachers' Happiness. *Research Journal of Applied Sciences, Engineering and Technology*, 6(10): 1720–172

Author index

For Product Safety Concerns and Information please contact our EU representative GPSR@taylorandfrancis.com
Taylor & Francis Verlag GmbH, Kaufingerstraße 24, 80331 München, Germany

www.ingramcontent.com/pod-product-compliance
Lightning Source LLC
LaVergne TN
LVHW080121011026
849160LV00013B/1153

* 9 7 8 1 0 4 1 3 5 6 0 5 9 *